ICLS

The International Conference of the Learning Sciences

Indiana University 2006

Proceedings of ICLS 2006

Indiana University
Bloomington, Indiana, USA
June 27th – July 1st, 2006

Edited by
Sasha A. Barab
Kenneth E. Hay
Daniel T. Hickey

Support Provided by the Indiana University School of Education, the National Science Foundation and the Indiana University International Travel Program

Published by:
International Society of the Learning Sciences
http://www.isls.org/

Distributed by:
Lawrence Erlbaum Associates
10 Industrial Avenue
Mahwah, NJ 07430-2262
http://www.erlbaum.com/

Printed in the USA

ISBN 0-8058-6174-2 Vols. 1 and 2
ISBN 0-8058-6175-0 CD

Cover & Logo Design by:
Paul Whitener Jr.
Empowered Media, LLC
paul@empoweredmedia.org

Preface

Learning sciences research explores the nature and conditions of learning as it occurs in educational environments, broadly construed. The learning sciences field draws upon multiple theoretical perspectives and research paradigms in order to understand and improve human learning, cognition, and development. Over the last two decades the learning sciences community has developed powerful technological tools, curricular interventions, theories, and methods for understanding and improving teaching and learning as it unfolds in naturalistic contexts.

Learning sciences takes an interdisciplinary approach to the study of learning, cognition, and development in real-world contexts. Learning scientists believe that any investigation of teaching and learning must consider context, cognition, and learning architecture, which we treat as inextricably intertwined. All who are interested in the study of learning in context and the design of learning environments should find the work in these Proceedings to be of interest.

While learning scientists can present rich accounts of learning in complex contexts, convincing policy makers, teachers, and other researchers of the theoretical and practical value of our work; it is not a straightforward process. We must show impact at the local level, while at the same time working to advance claims that have more general value. In other words, we must make clear that the learning sciences make a difference.

Toward this end, the *Seventh International Conference of the Learning Sciences (ICLS 2006)* is explicitly focused on the theme "Making a Difference." Much of the work in these Proceedings demonstrates how our work is making a difference: to students, teachers, schools, and policy makers; to research approaches and methods; to theories and models of learning, instruction, and assessment. Each proposal in these Proceedings was blind reviewed by three independent reviewers to ensure high quality work. We hope that others will find the lessons shared in these pages relevant to their work.

Acknowledgements

Organizing this meeting was a substantial undertaking. Receiving and reviewing proposals, assembling the Proceedings, and organizing the actual conference required many hands. There are many people we owe our sincere thanks in making this year's conference a reality.

We offer special thanks for the tireless hours and work of Melissa Goodnight and Karla Frownfelter in organizing these Proceedings. Similarly, our designer Paul Whitener also made many last-minute changes and developed the artwork. Their hard work has made the editors and the contributors look their best.

We would like to thank members of the Indiana University community for their support, both personnel and monetary. These include IU Learning Sciences Program and Program Head, Dick Lesh; the IU Center for Research Learning and Technology; IU School of Education and Dean Gerardo Gonzalez; IU School of Informatics and Dean Michael Dunn; IU Office of

International Programs; IU Vice President of Research, Michael A. McRobbie; and IU Office of the Chancellor.

Putting on a conference for the first time can be an overwhelming and complex enterprise. Mary Morgan of the IU Conferences office has been an amazing resource and help in juggling all of the demands of a conference co-chair. We would like to extend our sincere thanks for her tireless work, patience and persistence. We would also like to thank IU Learning Sciences Professor Tom Duffy for his initial involvement in organizing the conference.

The National Science Foundation has been a consistent supporter of past and current meetings the ICLS. We would like to once again recognize the foundation and program officers (particularly Elizabeth VanderPutten, Robert Sherwood, and Larry Suter) for their commitment to the field through the significant support of *ICLS 2006*. Special recognition should be mentioned for their support of graduate students and early career scholars. Their forward thinking and support will pay great dividends in the quality of our future.

This is the first ICLS that has had the benefit from a fully formed International Society of the Learning Sciences (ISLS) organization to support and guide the development of the conference. In particular, we would like to thank ISLS members Janet Kolodner, Roy Pea, Claire O' Malley, Nancy Songer, William Sandoval, Chris Hoadley, Danny Edelson, and Cindy Hmelo-Silver for their help and guidance. We would also like to acknowledge the suggestions and help of other ISLS members, particularly our international colleagues, including Paul Kirschner, Sanna Jarvela, Bronwyn Stuckey, and Hans Spada.

We would also like to give a special thanks to the *ICLS 2004* chair, Yasmin Kafai, in helping us plan for the hills and valleys of conference work. Her wisdom in handling the many issues of the *ICLS 2006* has been much appreciated. We hope to do the same for the *ICLS 2008* chairs.

Finally, we would like to recognize the many individuals who reviewed the submitted proposals for all their hard work and the contributors that make the ICLS an exciting conference. We are sure that their creativity and scholarship will make the *ICLS 2006* and these Proceedings a significant contribution to the Learning Sciences community.

Chairs
Sasha A. Barab
Kenneth E. Hay
Daniel T. Hickey

ICLS 2006 CONFERENCE PROGRAM

Conference Co-chairs

Sasha Barab, Indiana University, Bloomington
Kenneth Hay, Indiana University, Bloomington
Daniel Hickey, Indiana University, Bloomington

Conference Steering Committee

ISLS Board Representatives
- Daniel Edelson, Northwestern University
- Cindy Hmelo-Silver, Rutgers University
- Yasmin Kafai, UCLA

International Relations
- Paul Kirschner, Open University of the Netherlands
- Bronwyn Stuckey, Queensland University of Technology

Doctoral Consortium
- Susan Goldman, University of Illinois, Chicago
- Claire O'Malley, University of Nottingham

Jr. Consortium
- Janet Kolodner, Georgia Institute of Technology
- William Sandoval, UCLA

Workshops
- Christopher Hoadley, Pennsylvania State University
- Sanna Jarvela, University of Oulu, Finland

Conference Coordination and Registration
- Mary Morgan, Indiana University Conferences

Student Volunteers
- Joyce Alexander, Indiana University

Web Design
- Paul Whitener, Empowered Media

ICLS 2006 Reviewers

The conference organizers sincerely thank the following individuals who reviewed proposals for the ICLS 2006 conference:

Dor Abrahamson
Faisal Ahmad
Valarie Akerson
Tonya Amankwatia
Chris Amelung
Heejung An
Kate Anderson
Charoula Angeli
Xornam Apedoe
Margret Arnold
Roger Azevedo
Xin Bai
Sasha Barab
Judith Barak
Michael Barnett
Philip Bell
David Bergin
Marina Bers
Madhumita Bhattacharya
Kristen Blair
Paulo Blikstein
Chutima Boonthum
William Brescia
Leah Bricker
Stephen Briner
Sean Brophy
Matthew Brown
Amy Bruckman
Stein Brunvand
Thomas Brush
Roland Bullard
Olin Campbell
Reality Canty
Antonella Carbonaro
Karen Carney
Darla Castelli
Alice Cavallo
Stephanie Cawthon
Hsin-Yi Chang
Elizabeth Charles
Clement Chau
Fei-Ching Chen
Weiqin Chen
Ellina Chernobilsky
Cynthia Carter Ching
Clark Chinn
Doug Clark
Jody Clarke
Tamara Clegg
Allan Collins
Albert Corbett
Jennifer Crawford
Theresa Cullen
Chandima Cumaranatunge
Laura D'Amico
Joshua Danish
Elizabeth Davis
Jason Day
Chris Dede
Donna DeGennaro
Rodrigo del Valle
Vanessa Dennen
Ning Ding
Chaoyan Dong
Corey Drake
Oliver Dreon Jr.
Amy Duffy
Thomas Duffy
Ravit Golan Duncan
Nicholas Duran
Angela Eckhoff
David Eddy Spicer
Daniel Edelson
Eric Ellis
Noel Enyedy
Eva Erdosne Toth
Bernhard Ertl
Howard Everson
Deborah Fields
Barry Fishman
Jim Foley
Paola Forcheri
Andrea Forte
Ina Fourie
Ruth Gannon-Cook
Elhanan Gazit
Xun Ge
Libby Gerard
Janice Gobert
Yuksel Goktas
Ricki Goldman
Susan Goldman
Amelia Gotwals
Jamillah Grant
Ingrid Graves
Jeffrey Greene
Melissa Gresalfi
Phyllis Grummon
Alan Hackbarth
Tony Hall
Bruce Havelock
Kenney Hay
Libby Hemphill
Phillip Herman
Daniel Hickey
Thomas Hills
Cindy Hmelo-Silver
Christopher Hoadley
Douglas Holton
YaHuei Hsu
Roland Hubscher
Jim Hudson
Barbara Hug
Andy Hurford
Yavuz Inal
Adam Ingram-Goble
Ioan Gelu Ionas
Asghar Iran-Nejad
Michael Jacobson
Heisawn Jeong
Kirk Job-Sluder
Aditya Johri
Frankie Jones
Diana Joseph
Yih-Ruey Juang
A. Susan Jurow
Yasmin Kafai
Ugur Kale
Yael Kali
Yanrong Kang
Haijun Kang
Lijie Kang
Victor Kaptelinin
Manu Kapur
Diane Jass Ketelhut
Beaumie Kim
Bosung Kim
Nari Kim
Yanghee Kim
Paul Kirschner
Ben Kirshner
Jayne Klenner-Moore
Melissa Koch
Janet Kolodner
Timothy Koschmann
Beth Kubitskey
Maria Lorna Kunnath
Eun Ju Kwon
Eleni Kyza
James Laffey

Eduardo Lage-Otero
Minna Lakkala
Mary Lamon
Christine Larson
Fai-Kim Lau
Mike Lawson
Victor Lee
JeongMin Lee
Youngmin Lee
Yu-Wei Lee
Mary Leonard
Dalit Levy
Junlei Li
Erin Lightman
Cher Ping Lim
Jung Lim
Guan-Yu Lin
Hsien-Ta Lin
Marcia Linn
Jordan Lippman
Lei Liu
Pei-Ju Liu
Shijuan Liu
Kate Lockwood
Steven Lonn
Loucas Louca
April Luehmann
Kenneth Luterbach
Leilah Lyons
Maria Madiope
Mouna Mana
Rebecca Mancy
Lina Markauskaite
Sandra Martell
Thomas Martens
Fred Martin
Julia Matuga
Philip McCarthy
Michael McCracken
Scott McDonald
Steven McGee
Diane McGrath
Katherine McNeill
Daniel McVeigh
Tom Moher
Gaëlle Molinari
Chrystalla Mouza
Hanni Muukkonen
Mitchell Nathan
Michael Nussbaum
Kevin O'Connor
Claire O'Malley
Maria Opfermann
Chandra Orrill
Jakita Owensby
Ming Fai Pang
Praveen Paritosh
Sanghoon Park
Orit Parnafes
Roy Pea
William Penuel
Hans-Rüdiger Pfister
Corey Pierce
Philip Piety
Niels Pinkwart
Joe Polman
Cassidy Puckett
Sadhana Puntambekar
Chris Quintana
Michael Reigh
Aaron Richmond
Jochen Rick
Ann Rivet
Jenny Robins
Cecil Robinson
Jennifer Robinson
Miky Ronen
Jeremy Roschelle
Michael Rowe
Nikol Rummel
Donna Russell
Nora Sabelli
Troy Sadler
Johann Sarmiento
Tom Satwicz
Leah Savion
Daniel Schwartz
David Shaffer
Patti Shank
Tamara Shanker
Brett Shelton
Miriam Sherin
Wesley Shumar
Bernadette Sibuma
Arnan Sipitakiat
Brian Smith
Hyo-Jeong So
Nancy Songer
Hans Spada
Kurt Squire
Tina Stanford
Haley Steele
Constance Steinkuehler
Reed Stevens
James Stewart
Mike Stieff
Helga Stokes
Jan-Willem Strijbos
Johannes Strobel
Bronwyn Stuckey
Florence Sullivan
Daniel Suthers
Vanessa Svihla
Karen Swan
Elisabeth Sylvan
Ai-Girl Tan
Roger Taylor
Kona Taylor
Stephanie Teasley
YaTing Teng
Timothy Teo
Sharon Tettegah
John Thompson
Heather Toomey-Zimmerman
Stefan Trausan-Matu
Nobuyuki Ueda
Jody Underwood
Leo Ureel II
Phil Vahey
Mark van't Hooft
Wouter van Joolingen
George Veletsianos
Michelle Verges
Geeta Verma
Yusra Visser
Christian Voigt
Joan Walker
Andrew Walker
Feng Wang
Scott Warren
Armin Weinberger
Martin Wessner
Eun Won Whang
Tobin White
Astrid Wichmann
Eric Wiebe
Michelle Williams
Robert Williams
Clyde Winters
Alyssa Wise
Don Wortham
Kenneth Wright
Lisa Yamagata-Lynch
Jude Yew
Susan Yoon
Amir Abbas Zadpoor
Jose Zagal
Raul Zaritsky
BaoHui Zhang
Jianwei Zhang
Meilan Zhang
Steven Zuiker
Laura Zurita
Janet Zydney

Table of Contents

Volume I

Papers

Volume 2

Papers (continued)

Symposia

Papers Continued

The Role-Goal-Activity Framework Revisited: Examining Student Buy-In in a Project-Based Learning Environment

Virginia M. Pitts, Daniel C. Edelson, Northwestern University, 2120 Campus Drive, Evanston, IL 60208
Email: v-pitts@northwestern.edu, d-edelson@northwestern.edu

Abstract: At ICLS 2004 we presented a framework for the study of student participation and engagement in project-based curricula. This framework was specifically designed for the analysis of project-based learning environments in that it explicitly considered the influence of student "buy-in" to an overall scenario on participation and engagement in project-based activities, and identified factors we hypothesized influenced the nature of role- and goal-adoption (including students' scenario-related understandings, attitudes, and beliefs, as well as their perception of the degree of "fit" or alignment between the role and goal and project activities). In this paper, we present the findings of a mixed-methods study we designed, based upon this framework, to examine student role- and goal- adoption in two seventh-grade science classrooms where students participated in the "What Will Survive" life sciences curriculum, and discuss ways in which we plan to revise our framework based on the study results.

Introduction

In project-based curricula, in which students develop content understanding through the pursuit of authentic problems (Blumenfeld et al., 1991), learners are expected to take on a particular goal and role. The goal involves solving a problem (such as predicting temperature on a newly discovered planet, building a playground, or developing a Global Warming recommendation). The role embodies a particular way of interacting, and is sometimes explicit (scientific researcher, urban planner, or Global Warming Advisor) and sometimes implicit (i.e., "inquirer"). An underlying design assumption behind these curricula is that the goal and role will motivate the learning of content, and that learning the content in pursuit of the goal (which serves to "contextualize" instruction) will in turn lead to better content understanding (Blumenfeld et al., 1991, Edelson, 2001, Krajcik, 2001, Rivet, 2000). However, while the goal and role are intended to play a central part in motivating activities, and are in turn one of the reasons project-based learning environments potentially lead to deeper content understanding than do more traditional, non-project-based learning environments, research to date has not explored the extent to which the project role and goal actually motivate student participation in practice. Our current line of research is intended to address that gap, through examining the extent to which students adopt or "buy into" a project role and goal in project-based curricula, and through exploring the individual and contextual influences on such role and goal adoption.

In 2003, we designed a theoretical framework to guide our investigation and analysis of participation and engagement in project-based learning environments. In the following section, we will briefly review the elements of that framework. Then, we will describe a study we designed, based upon that framework, to examine student role- and goal- adoption in two seventh-grade science classrooms where students participated in the "What Will Survive" life sciences curriculum. Finally, we will discuss the implications of these study results for our work going forward, specifically in regards to design of our theoretical framework.

Theoretical Framework

We designed our theoretical framework to represent our "working hypotheses" regarding the factors that influence student "buy-in" to an overall project scenario (that is, their adoption of a project role and goal). In considering the potential influences on such buy-in, this framework focused primarily on students' *understandings* of the role and goal, their *attitudes and beliefs* toward that role and goal, and their *perceptions of the perceived "fit" or alignment* of the role and goal with the activity in which they were engaged. In particular, we hypothesized that:

- Students develop an understanding of the overall scenario (that is, the role they are to play and the goal they are to take on) based on their previous scenario-related knowledge and beliefs *and* the way in which the role and goal are represented in artifacts, teacher talk/interaction, and peer talk/interactions.
- Based on this understanding, students form scenario-related attitudes and beliefs, including the *subjective value* of taking on the role and goal (where subjective value includes intrinsic value, utility value, attainment value, and cost) and their *expectation of success* at that role and goal. "Subjective value" and "expectation of success" come from Eccles' Expectancy-Value Model (Eccles, 1983), which describes factors that determine a student's choices in achievement-related situations.
- The extent to which students adopt or buy-into a particular role and goal is determined by these scenario-related attitudes and beliefs, in conjunction with the extent to which students perceive that the activity they are engaged in "fits" or aligns with the overall role and goal.
- When students are bought in to the overall project scenario (that is, when they have adopted the overall project role and goal), then the scenario contributes to student motivation to participate in the activities and serves to "contextualize" instruction.

Methods

Data collection for this study was completed in Spring 2004, and took place in two 7th-grade science classrooms (of about 20 students each) in a suburban middle school. Students participated in the "What Will Survive" life sciences curriculum, which consisted of two phases:

- In the first phase (which spanned approximately six weeks), students were to play the role of special task force members pursuing the goal of developing a plan to rid the Great Lakes of the sea lamprey. Students were introduced to their role and goal at the beginning of the curriculum, then participated in a series of activities introducing them to concepts required to solve the sea lamprey problem; at the end of this series of activities they were asked to draft a final solution to the sea lamprey problem.
- In the second phase (which spanned approximately three weeks), students played the role of scientists who were pursuing the goal of finding out why, on one of the Galapagos Islands, so many Finches died while others survived during a particular time period in the 1970's. Students conducted their entire investigation using the Galapagos Finches software, which gave them access to actual scientific data on the Finches populations, environmental conditions, etc. for the island they were studying.

According to our theoretical framework, the important elements to consider in examining the ways in which students come to "buy-in" to a project scenario include students' understandings of the role and goal they are being asked to take on (based in part upon the way in which the role and goal are represented "in context"), students' attitudes and beliefs toward that role and goal, and their perceptions of the perceived "fit" of the activity in which they are engaged with the overall goal and role. Therefore, we selected data collection methods that would allow us to gather data on these elements. Methods included:

- In-depth student interviews (conducted with a subset of students at the end of each phase) to gather data on students' understandings of the scenario, their scenario-related attitudes and beliefs, and their perceived "fit" of the activity with the scenario
- Daily mini-surveys (given at the end of most class periods) to gather data on the extent to which students were actively bought in to the overall scenario as they participated in activities, as well as data regarding their attitudes toward the activities
- Classroom observations to gather data on the curriculum "as implemented" (focusing in particular on the ways in which the role and goal were represented "in context").

Findings

In this section we share a subset of the results of the data analysis, focusing primarily on the first phase of the curriculum (or, as we call it throughout the rest of this paper, "the Sea Lamprey phase"). At the end of this section we briefly discuss findings from the second phase of the curriculum ("the Finches phase") as well.

Understanding of the Sea Lamprey Scenario

For the first phase of the project, students were introduced to the project scenario when teachers read them a "made up" letter from the Great Lakes Fishery Commission. When interviewed, all students understood that they were being asked to come up with a plan to rid the Great Lakes of the sea lamprey. However, surprisingly, not all students seemed to realize that the letter was "made up". Of the 12 students interviewed:

- Three students talked as if they were really being asked to help. For example, Leisha, when first asked what she thought about the letter, said, "I was really very excited to help, because we were going to start helping people to find out what was doing this to our fish and to our food."
- Three students indicated it was implausible or unbelievable that they would be asked to help. For example, Michael, when asked what he thought of the letter, said, "I thought it was kind of phony – special task force and we're just kids. How can you be on a special task force? Sounds like something the CIA should do or something."
- Three students indicated that they did not think/care about whether the letter was real or not; rather, they indicated that they thought of the project as "just an assignment" or just something they had to do for school. For example, Diana said of the project, "It's just something we have to do. I don't really care if it's real of not. It's just something that we're going to have to do for science."
- Finally, one student indicated that, though she did not think the letter was real, she chose to pretend that it was. As Kendra explained, "I pretended I was more like a scientist. It seemed like easier to take it on from that point of view."
- Two students gave no indication of their thoughts regarding whether or not the project was real (because we had not initially anticipated students would be confused as to the "reality" of the project, not all students were explicitly asked about this).

These differences in the ways students viewed the overall project are perhaps not surprising, given that neither of the teachers in the study made explicit, clear mention of the fact that this was a "made-up" letter. Certainly it seems that the apparent confusion or misunderstanding on the part of several of the students might have been avoided had the teachers simply been more explicit with the students as to the source of the letter or given the students more guidance as to what to make of it. However, there is something additional we can learn from the fact that some students indicated that they believed they were really working on a project to help real scientists solve the real sea lamprey problem, while other students saw this as just a project for school. This apparent difference in students' interpretations of, or reactions to, what it was they were being asked to participate in seems to indicate that (a) students differ in their view of what is plausible or realistic regarding their role in society and their participation in real world problems, and/or (b) students differ in the extent to which they are willing to "pretend" or "act as if" a made-up scenario is real.

In addition to the separate influences of the desire to pretend that the project is real and the perceived plausibility of the scenario, there may be an interaction between the two. A large "plausibility gap" (that is, a gap between the scenario and what students believe to be plausible or realistic) may inhibit students' ability to take on particular roles or pretend to participate in a particular scenario, whereas a small plausibility gap may make it easier for students to pretend. At the same time, a strong desire to pretend that something is real may, in essence, overcome a large "plausibility gap" such that students basically ignore the "unrealistic" aspects of a problem (paradoxically, for some students, a scenario that is especially unrealistic may for that very reason be especially desirable to take on, in that it allows students to take on a role they might never get a chance to play "in real life"). In fact, it is indeed possible that some or all of the students who talked about the project as if were real were, to some extent, ignoring the "unrealistic" aspects and, in essence, pretending the project was real due to a strong desire that it actually was real.

Scenario-Related Attitudes and Beliefs for the Sea Lamprey Phase

Five of the twelve students interviewed indicated that they cared about the project goal (of solving the sea lamprey problem), and two (of those same five students) indicated that they were excited about the opportunity to play a role different than that they normally play. None of the other seven students interviewed indicated that they found the scenario role or goal itself to be motivating, though several of them indicated that they were initially curious about aspects of the project content (such as how the sea lamprey got into the lake in the first place) or that they thought the project-activities themselves would be fun. It seems, then, that there are multiple ways in which this particular scenario can potentially act as a motivational "hook" for students (we will discuss the extent to which such potential was actually realized later in this paper).

We did find a potential correlation between students' understanding of the scenario, expectation of success at the project scenario, and attitude towards the project scenario, such that it was the students who thought it was real or pretended it was real who thought they could do the project and who cared about the project goal or role. Given our small sample size, this is not a statistically significant finding. However, we have several possible hypotheses to explain such a potential correlation. One hypothesis is that students cared when they believed (or pretended) that their work potentially *mattered* – specifically, when they felt that their work would actually address a condition they were concerned about (seeing one's work matter requires not only that one cares about the problem itself, but requires that one believes one can succeed at doing something about it). Another possible explanation for the pattern we see here is that caring about the problem, in conjunction with expectation of success, influenced the extent to which students approached the project as if it were real. In other words, if students found the problem itself compelling, and believed they could be successful at solving it, they chose to imagine that it really was real (this would assume that even the students who said they thought it was real were, in essence, pretending as well). A similar hypothesis would be that caring about the problem influenced the extent to which students approached the project as if it were real, which in turn influenced expectation of success. We will further investigate these hypotheses in future work.

A Tale of Two Activities - Did Students Buy-In, and Did Buy-In Matter?

Regarding the extent to which students were actively "bought in" to the project scenario while participating in the Sea Lamprey activities, the two activities we discussed in-depth in the interviews were the computer activity (where students worked with a computer simulation of grass, rabbits, and foxes to better understand ecosystem relationships and the effect of adding an invasive species) and the dissecting activity (where students dissected a sea lamprey and a perch in order to learn about how different features of these species allowed them to survive). On both the computer days and the dissecting days, about half of the students said that they at least thought about the overall scenario while participating in the activity. However, with a few possible (and problematic) exceptions, there is no evidence that the students we interviewed were actively "bought in" to the project role and goal; that is, they did not see themselves as special task force members working to solve the sea lamprey problem as they engaged in these project activities (regardless of whether or not they thought the project was real, thought they could solve it, or felt positively toward the overall project scenario).

Not surprisingly, perhaps (given that students were not actively bought in to the role and goal), while students almost unanimously reported being "into" both the computer activity and the dissecting activity, none of their reasons for being into it had anything to do with the project role and goal (rather, they focused on aspects of the activity itself, such as the game-like nature of the computer activity or the fact they got to "cut things open" for the dissecting activity). However, there is evidence that, even when students did not "buy in", the scenario may still have influenced the way students thought about the activities in which they participated. For example, in the computer activity, there is evidence that the scenario may have:

- Provided an opportunity for students to make an analogy between what they were doing in the computer activity and the sea lamprey problem. For example, consider Charla, who explained, "It was just like, as the invasive species got introduced (into the grass-rabbits-foxed ecosystem on the third day of the computer activity), I was like, "Dang! The sea lamprey was an invasive species and they're endangering all the fish, and so, that's what happened with the invasive species on the computers."
- Provided students with the opportunity to apply what they learned in the computer activity to reasoning about the sea lamprey problem. For example, Raemon explained that, in the computer activity, "If you get rid of the prey, then the predators will die out. So like, if you get rid of the animals that the sea lamprey eat, so don't kill 'em, but like, move 'em to somewhere, then the sea lamprey will have nothing to eat and they will die."

While the potential is there for the scenario to influence student thinking, some students may need more scaffolding than others to make connections such as those just described. In examples such as those above, though some students perhaps made the connections between the computer activity and the overall scenario at the time of the activity, others did not make them until the interviews. There were also students who were not able to make this connection even at the time of the interview; as one student put it (in regards to the computer activity), "I really didn't see what that had to do with the sea lamprey. I really didn't get it, 'cause it was on maintaining the foxes and the rabbits."

Looking Across Activities and Across Projects – The Scenario and Motivation

While it seems that for the computer days and the dissecting days the scenario did not play a role in motivating participation and engagement in activities, the story may be different on those days we did not discuss in the interviews (given time constraints, we could not talk about every activity in the interviews, but rather focused on a couple of activities). The days we focused on in the interviews were among the more active/hands-on of all the project activities. Quantitative analysis of the mini-survey data indicates that on days categorized as "non-active", buy-in to the role and goal may have played a bigger part in influencing engagement than on days categorized as "active". We will continue to explore this in future research, as given our small sample size, we cannot be certain that the differences in the influence of buy-in on engagement are due to the "activeness" of the days. However, potential hypotheses to explain this phenomenon include (a) On days when no other source of motivation is "dominant", the scenario may act as a source of motivation for students who are even mildly "bought in", and (b) On very "active" days, sources of motivation that are "local" to the activity (such as the hands-on nature of the task itself) may, in essence, "drown out" or overcome the motivation that comes from the scenario itself.

We also applied our framework to the examination of buy-in in the Finches phase of the curriculum. In that phase, the scenario seems to have played a much more prominent role in motivating activities than it did for the Sea Lamprey phase of the project, for in the Finches phase 7 out of 11 students interviewed indicated that cared about solving, or were interested in, the overall problem scenario, and that they were "into" project in part *because* of their interest in solving the overall problem. At the same time, however, 4 of the 11 students interviewed indicated that they were not into the project activities and did not care about solving the overall problem; rather, they indicated that all they cared about was getting a grade.

Implications of These Findings Regarding the Framework

In sum, our framework proved useful for examining student participation and engagement in this particular implementation. With the framework as our guide, we were able to identify differences in buy-in among students and across activities. We also identified ways in which buy-in to the project scenario (or lack thereof) seemingly influenced student motivation to participate in activities. For this particular curriculum, then, it seems that the overall project scenario does indeed have the potential to influence student participation and engagement.

However, while our findings indicate that the potential exists for the scenario to influence student participation, engagement, and learning, this potential was not fully realized for all students or in all activities. The question now becomes that of "why?" While we cannot answer that question definitively with this particular study, the framework does offer explanations for these differences in buy-in that are consistent with the evidence. In particular, we found instances where it seems that:

- **Understanding of the scenario** influenced scenario-related attitudes and beliefs; these understandings included the plausibility of the scenario (Sea Lamprey phase) and the extent to which the problem had already been solved (Finches phase).
- **Scenario-related attitudes and beliefs** influenced buy-in. This was especially true for the Finches phase, where students who were especially curious about what happened or who wanted to prove to themselves that they could solve the problem were the ones who indicated that they were really working toward coming up with a solution, rather than just doing what they needed to do for the grade.
- **Perceived "fit" or alignment of activity** with the overall scenario influenced buy-in (we see this with the computer activity during the Sea Lamprey phase, where some students did not understand how the activity fit in with the overall scenario).

At the same time, evidence indicates that there are other influences on scenario buy-in that are *not* adequately represented in the original version of our theoretical framework; these include:

- **"Emergent" role and goal** - There is some evidence that role was at times emergent rather than consciously adopted. In particular, during both the dissecting activity (in the Sea Lamprey phase of the project) and the Finches phase of the project, some students indicated that they felt like scientists, even though they were never explicitly asked to play that role. This indicates that students came to see themselves in a particular way *as a result of* their participation (the original framework focused more on how seeing oneself in a particular way *influences* participation). It is plausible that students can come to take on a goal in the same way.

- **Competing goals/roles** – When students do not buy in to a project scenario, it may not always be the case that they do not understand the goal/role, or that they have no desire to take on the goal/role, or that they cannot see what they are doing as "fitting in" with what the goal and role entail. Rather, it may be that other goals/roles were simply more "salient" or "dominant". This may have been the case with students who indicated that they only cared about the grade when they were working on the Finches project, and may also have been the case with some of the students who, during the Sea Lamprey phase of the project, seemed more focused on the immediate goals of the computer and dissecting activities than they did on the overall scenario. For future work, this raises the question of why certain goals and roles might be more "salient" than others for particular students in particular contexts.
- **Influence of nature of participation** on scenario-related understandings, attitudes, and beliefs - While the original framework *did* indicate that one's scenario-related understandings, attitudes and beliefs are influenced by participation in project activities, this relationship was not emphasized, nor were the dynamics of this relationship made explicit. This relationship may require more emphasis in future research on buy-in, for there were several instances where ongoing participation in activity influenced students' scenario-related understandings and attitudes (and, in turn, the extent to which they were "bought in"). This was particularly true during the Finches phase, where some students indicated that the more they learned through participating, the more interested they became, or that the closer they got to figuring out the answer, the more they wanted to find the answer, or that the more they "put into it" over time, the more they cared about seeing their effort "pay off".

We will revise our theoretical framework based on the results of this study, and believe that this framework, as we continue to refine it, will prove useful in guiding future research that will allow us to "design for buy-in".

References

Blumenfeld, P. C., Soloway, E., Marx, R. W., Krajcik, J. S., Guzdial, M., & Palincsar, A. (1991). Motivating project-based learning: Sustaining the doing, supporting the learning. Educational Psychologist, 26(3&4), 369 – 398.

Eccles, Jacquelynne S. (1983). Expectancies, values, and academic behavior. In Janet T. Spence (Ed.), Achievement and achievement motives (75-146). San Francisco, CA: W.H. Freeman and Company.

Edelson, D. C. (2001). Learning-For-Use: A framework for the design of technology-supported inquiry activities. Journal of Research in Science Teaching, 38(3), 355-385.

Krajcik, J. (2001). Learning science content in a project-based environment. In Tinker, R., & Krajcik, J.S. (Eds.), Portable technologies: Science learning in context. Netherlands: Kluwer Publishers.

Rivet, A. Singer, J., Schneider, R., Krajick, J., Marx, R. (2000) The evolution of water: Designing and developing effective curricula. Paper presented at the annual conference of the National Association for Research in Science Teaching, New Orleans, USA

Students' Difficulties in Learning Physics from Dynamic and Interactive Visualizations

Rolf Ploetzner, Stefan Lippitsch, University of Education, Freiburg, Germany
rolf.ploetzner@ph-freiburg.de, stefan.lippitsch@ph-freiburg.de
Matthias Galmbacher, Dieter Heuer, University of Würzburg, Dep. of Physics, Germany
galmbach@physik.uni-wuerzburg.de, heuer@physik.uni-wuerzburg.de

Abstract: In two experimental studies we investigated whether students' difficulties in understanding line graphs in kinematics can be improved by means of dynamic representations. These representations were designed to help students in mentally bridging the gap between motion phenomena and abstract line graphs. In the first study, contrary to our expectations, the employed representations did not only not improve learning - but even impeded it. This finding was underpinned by the second study, in which almost no sign was found of students having internalized the relevant aspects of the dynamic representations. Because similar results have recently been found in other studies, we propose that research on learning with dynamic representations should not only focus on developing guidelines for the external design of representations but also on conceptualising learning strategies which can be taught to students and which help them to successfully process the information presented in the external representations.

Introduction

Physics education aims at helping students to view physics as a consistent system of concepts, principles, models, and techniques related to the physical world. For the past two decades, research on physics education has demonstrated that many students face severe difficulties in learning physics. Various factors may contribute to these difficulties. While some factors are considered to be intrinsic to the students, such as the students' preconceptions about physics, other factors are considered to be intrinsic to the way in which physics is taught.

In teaching physics, educators frequently employ different external representations which make different aspects of a physical situation or a physics concept salient, describe aspects of a physical situation or a physics concept which cannot be described by means of other representations, and complement each other in such a way that more complete representations result. Computers offer the additional opportunity to educators to take advantage of dynamic and interactive external representations to represent physical situations as well as physics concepts that change in time and space.

While the use of different external representations has the potential to improve the learning of physics, it also places various demands on students (for a collection of papers see Ploetzner & Lowe, 2004). For instance, students need to understand how information is encoded in each representation, how each representation is related to the physical world, and how information in one representation can be related to and transformed into information in another representation (e.g., Ainsworth, 1999). Dynamic representations demand students to process continuously changing information (e.g., Lowe, 2003) and if external representations are not only dynamic but also interactive, they require students to carefully prepare, execute, and evaluate their interactions (e.g., de Jong & van Joolingen, 1998).

One notorious problem in physics education is the students' difficulty in understanding line graphs. In this paper we describe two experimental studies. The first study aimed at improving students' comprehension of line graphs in kinematics by means of interactive simulations and dynamic representations. However, in accord with the findings of many other studies on learning with dynamic representations, the students faced severe difficulties in taking advantage of the information encoded in the dynamic representations. The second study aimed at identifying whether students make use of the information encoded in dynamic representations when solving kinematics problems.

Enriching Interactive Simulations in Physics with Iconic Representations

Line graphs such as time-position graphs, time-velocity graphs, and time-acceleration graphs visualize functional relations between time and kinematics concepts. The lower section of Figure 1 shows a time-position (left hand side), a time-velocity (middle), and a time-acceleration graph (right hand side) representing an object's motion.

In physics education, students are expected to acquire (1) the ability to construct a line graph that appropriately represents an object's motion, provided the description of the object's motion is given, and (2) the ability to interpret a line graph, i.e., to formulate an appropriate description of the motion underlying a line graph. In physics textbooks, very often line graphs are "developed" in three steps. In the first step, an object's motion is described by means of a text as well as by means of a picture. In the second step, values of a kinematics concept at various points in time are presented in a table. In the third step, the variable values as well as their interpolation are visualized in a coordinate plane.

Research on physics education has repeatedly demonstrated that very often students have severe difficulties in understanding line graphs (e.g., Berg & Smith, 1994; Scanlon, 1998). These difficulties apply to the construction of line graphs as well as to their interpretation. Even students who successfully construct line graphs in mathematics are often unable to take advantage of their knowledge in physics (e.g., Leinhardt, Zaslavsky & Stein, 1990). In the most frequently observed misinterpretation of line graphs in kinematics, students view line graphs as paths of motion regardless of which kinematics concepts are taken into account by the graphs (e.g., McDermott, Rosenquist & van Zee, 1987). Obviously, many students are hardly able to mentally bridge the gap between observable or simulated motion phenomena on the one hand and abstract line graphs on the other.

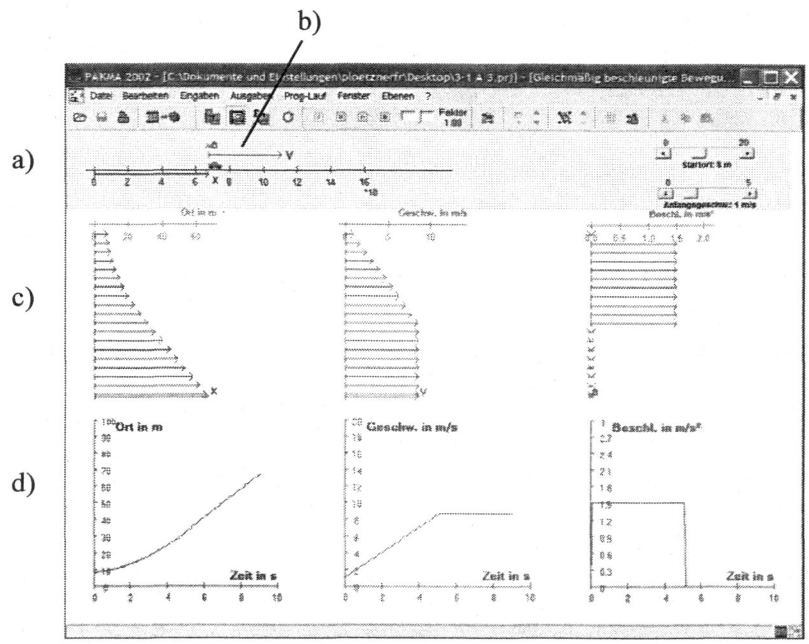

Figure 1. Dynamic representations in PAKMA: (a) simulations of motion phenomena, (b) iconic representations of kinematics concepts, (c) stamp diagrams, and (d) line graphs.

Is it possible to improve students' understanding of how motion phenomena and line graphs are related to each other by means of interactive simulations and dynamic representations? In order to investigate this question, we took advantage of the simulation program PAKMA (Heuer, 2002). Among other phenomena, PAKMA allows for the interactive simulation of motion phenomena. In comparison to textbooks, PAKMA offers the opportunity to visualize how different representations of kinematics concepts dynamically and synchronously change in time.

To help students understand how motion phenomena and line graphs are related to each other, four dynamic representations – exemplified in Figure 1 – are employed in PAKMA: (a) simulations of motion phenomena (abbreviated S), (b) dynamic and iconic representations of kinematics concepts which are superimposed on the simulated motion phenomena (abbreviated DIR), (c) dynamic stamp diagrams (abbreviated STAMPS), and (d) dynamic line graphs. Iconic representations correspond to vector representations of kinematics concepts such as position, velocity, acceleration, and force. Stamp diagrams result from stamping iconic representations in a coordinate plane at defined points in time. Line graphs correspond to the interpolation of the iconic representations' heads in the stamp diagrams. In PAKMA, the simulation can be started and stopped interactively at any time, the simulation can be run continuously or frame by frame, and each representation can be faded in or out interactively.

Study 1

In an experimental study we investigated whether students' understanding of line graphs in kinematics improves depending on the dynamic representations made available to the students. We hypothesized that the availability of iconic representations of kinematics concepts superimposed on simulated motion phenomena (cf. Figure 1a and 1b) would make it easier for students to relate motion phenomena and line graphs (cf. Figure 1d) to each other than the mere availability of simulated motion phenomena and line graphs. We further hypothesized that the additional availability of stamp diagrams (cf. Figure 1c) would help students even more to relate motion phenomena and line graphs to each other.

Method

Design

Three groups were formed, who made use of three different simulation environments. In the first environment (S), various motion phenomena were interactively simulated and line graphs were dynamically displayed. In the second environment (S+DIR), dynamic and iconic representations of kinematics concepts were additionally superimposed on the simulations of the motion phenomena. In the third environment (S+DIR+STAMPS), dynamic stamp diagrams were also displayed.

Participants

Overall, 111 volunteer eleventh graders were randomly assigned to the groups: 39 students to group S, 33 students to group S+DIR, and 39 students to group S+DIR+STAMPS. The students had attended introductory classes on the kinematics concepts of position and velocity. While 54 students were girls, 57 students were boys. Girls and boys were approximately equally distributed across groups.

Learning Material

For each group investigated, the learning material comprised eight physics projects progressing from the two easier concepts position and velocity to the two more difficult concepts acceleration and force (cf. Reif & Allen, 1992). Each concept was addressed by two projects. Every project was made up of a worksheet and a simulation environment. The worksheet aimed at encouraging the students to make use of the corresponding simulation environment in a structured way. A worksheet always started with a text that described a motion phenomenon. Thereafter, various questions had to be answered by the students while making use of the simulation environment. For instance, students were asked to describe how a time-position graph changes in the simulation environment when an object's velocity is interactively altered. The questions were provided with information on how to run the simulation environment. Students were asked to write down their answers to the questions on the worksheet.

Procedure

Initially, the students took a pre-test to determine their knowledge in kinematics as well as their visual-spatial abilities (Raven, 1980). The pre-test addressed the students' knowledge about the kinematics concepts position, velocity, acceleration, and force. It consisted of 14 questions, the answers of which demanded the interpretation of line graphs. Next, the students worked individually on an example physics project in order to learn how to run the simulation environment. This project addressed an object's changing position in such a way that the students were able to focus on running the simulation environment. Thereafter, the students worked individually on the eight physics projects described above. For each student, the learning time was limited to 150 minutes. Finally, the students worked on a kinematics post-test which consisted of 30 questions, the answers of which demanded the interpretation of line graphs, as well as of 12 questions, the answers of which demanded the construction of line graphs.

Results

The students' performances in the pre-test are shown in Table 1. There are no significant differences between the groups. However, on average the students had significantly more success with test items concerning the easier concepts position and velocity than with test items concerning the more difficult concepts acceleration and force ($F = 794.1$, $df = 1{,}110$, $p < .001$).

Table 1. The means (M) and standard deviations (SD) of the relative solution frequencies in the pre-test.

	Simulation environment		
Kinematics concepts	S	S+DIR	S+DIR+STAMPS
Position and velocity	M = 67.9% (SD = 21.2%)	M = 66.3% (SD = 22.2%)	M = 69.2% (SD = 19.0%)
Acceleration and force	M = 26.6% (SD = 22.4%)	M = 26.5% (SD = 23.7%)	M = 31.1% (SD = 22.9%)
Overall	M = 47.3% (SD = 17.9%)	M = 46.4% (SD = 18.8%)	M = 50.2% (SD = 17.5%)

To analyze the students' learning performance, we computed the students' relative learning gain g (cf. Hake, 1998): $g = (\%Correct_{post\text{-}test} - \%Correct_{pre\text{-}test})/(100 - \%Correct_{pre\text{-}test}) \times 100$. By means of a median split, each group of students was divided into two subgroups: a group with low visual-spatial abilities and a group with high visual-spatial abilities. Figure 2 shows the relative learning gains with respect to the different kinematics concepts.

A multivariate analysis of variance did not reveal any significant differences between the groups of students across all kinematics concepts. While a univariate analysis of variance did not reveal significant differences between the groups of students with respect to the concepts position and velocity, it revealed significant differences with respect to the concepts acceleration and force ($F = 4.19$, $df = 2{,}105$, $p < .05$). Concerning the factor "simulation environment", however, these differences are diametrically opposed to our predictions: on average, those students who only had the simulated motion phenomena and the line graphs available received higher learning gains than those students who additionally had iconic representations and stamp diagrams available.

Students with low visual-spatial abilities accomplished significantly smaller learning gains with respect to the concepts acceleration and force than students with high visual-spatial abilities ($F = 4.78$, $df = 1{,}105$, $p < .05$). Although the interaction between the factors "simulation environment" and "visual-spatial ability" is statistically not significant, this is especially true for those students who had the iconic representations available without having the stamp diagrams available: these students performed even better in the pre-test than they did in the post-test.

Study 2

Contrary to all our expectations, dynamic iconic representations and stamp diagrams did not help students to better understand line graphs. With respect to the easier kinematics concepts position and velocity, the availability of these representations made no significant difference. With respect to the more difficult kinematics concepts acceleration and force, the availability of iconic representations and stamp diagrams even hindered learning. Although stamp diagrams partially compensated for the difficulties which were associated with iconic representations, they nevertheless did not improve learning beyond the learning gains which were achieved without iconic representations and stamp diagrams. Although these findings contradict our expectations, they are in accord with the findings of many other studies which demonstrate students' difficulties in learning from and making use of dynamic representations (for an overview see Bétrancourt & Tversky, 2000). In a second study, we aimed at identifying whether students make use of the information encoded in dynamic iconic representations during problem solving.

Method

Design

Two groups were formed who made use of two different simulation environments. While in one environment (S) various motion phenomena were interactively simulated and line graphs were dynamically displayed, in the other environment (S+DIR) dynamic and iconic representations of kinematics concepts were superimposed on the simulations of the motion phenomena.

Participants

Overall, 18 volunteering eleventh graders were randomly assigned to each group. The students had attended introductory classes on the kinematics concepts position and velocity. While 19 students were girls, 17 students were boys. Girls and boys were approximately equally distributed across groups.

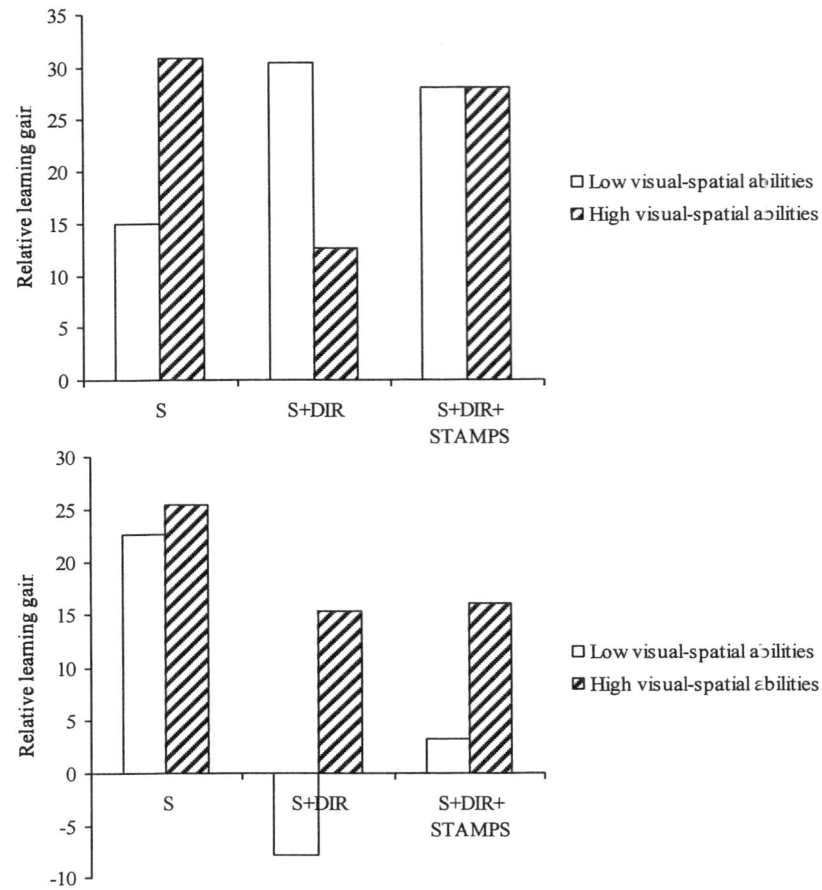

Figure 2. The relative learning gains with respect to the concepts position and velocity (above) and acceleration and force (below).

Learning Material

For each group investigated, the learning material comprised 14 physics projects progressing from the easier concepts to the more difficult concepts. Two projects were on position and time-position graphs, four on velocity and time-velocity graphs, four on acceleration and time-acceleration graphs, and four on force and time-force graphs. Again, every project was made up of a worksheet and a simulation environment which had to be processed by the students.

Procedure

Initially, the students took the same pre-test used in the first study to determine their knowledge in kinematics. Thereafter, the students worked individually on the 14 physics projects described above. For each student, the learning time was limited to 180 minutes. Next, the students worked individually on 6 kinematics problems without having access to the simulation environment. During problem-solving, the students were asked to think aloud (cf. Chi, 1997) and to write down their problem-solving attempts. The students' verbalizations as well as their problem-solving attempts were recorded on the computer. For each student, the problem-solving time was limited to 120 minutes. Before problem-solving took place, the students first watched a video demonstrating the verbalizations of a person solving a puzzle on the computer. Thereafter, the students exercised thinking aloud while solving a variation of the puzzle.

Results

There were no significant differences between groups in the pre-test: the students in both groups gave on average 36% correct answers to the questions. There were also no significant differences between groups in problem solving performance: while the students in group S solved on average 51% of the problems, the students in group S+DIR solved on average 53% of the problems. To assess whether students make use of the information encoded in dynamic iconic representations during problem solving, it was identified how frequently kinematics concepts which change over time were explicitly mentioned in the students' verbalizations and depicted or drawn in their written problem-solving attempts. The frequencies are shown in Table 2. There were no significant differences between groups. In group S+DIR, only two verbalizations and four depictions/drawings of only three students gave rise to the interpretation that these students had developed mental representations which did not only comprise dynamic aspects of kinematics concepts but also iconic aspects.

Table 2. The means (M) and standard deviations (SD) of how frequently the students referred to kinematics concepts that change over time.

	Simulation environment	
Source of information	S	S+DIR
Verbalizations	M = 17.8 (SD = 9.2)	M = 13.7 (SD = 8.4)
Written problem-solving attempts	M = 4.8 (SD = 7.1)	M = 5.8 (SD = 5.9)

Conclusion

In two experimental studies we investigated whether students' understanding of line graphs in kinematics can be improved by means of dynamic iconic representations. These representations were designed to help students in mentally bridging the gap between motion phenomena and abstract line graphs. In the first study, however, the students had severe difficulties in comprehending the information encoded in dynamic iconic representations. This finding was underpinned by the second study, in which almost no sign was found of students having internalized the dynamic and iconic aspects of the employed representations.

It is well possible that learning with the dynamic iconic representations placed too many cognitive demands on the students within too short a period of time. However, because difficulties in learning from dynamic representations have been observed in many recent studies which investigated the acquisition of knowledge in different application domains, it is rather implausible that limited learning time is the only reason for these difficulties. In various studies it has been observed that many students process dynamic representations only superficially (e.g., Lowe, 2003; Ploetzner, Bodemer, & Neudert, in press; Yeo et al., 2004). A growing body of research indicates that the students may have no means at hand to adequately process dynamic representations. The principled design of external representations (e.g., Clark & Mayer, 2003) seems to be only one side of the coin. The other side of the coin seems to consist of the external and internal learning activities which the students actually apply to the external representations. One example in which the design of external representations has been successfully complemented with the design of learning strategies is learning from text. A second example is learning from hypertext.

What makes us assume that students do not need to learn how to learn from dynamic representations? For instance, in order to improve learning from dynamic representations, students possibly need to learn how to identify and analyse relevant components of these representations. Students might also need to learn how to relate the information presented in dynamic representations to other sources of information such as instructional texts. Possibly, in the years to come, we may not only need to develop guidelines for the external design of dynamic representations, but also to conceptualise learning strategies made up of external as well as internal learning activities, which we can teach to students and which help them to successfully process the information presented in the external representations.

References

Ainsworth, S. (1999). The functions of multiple representations. *Computers and Education, 33*, 131-152.

Berg, C. A., & Smith, P. (1994). Assessing students' abilities to construct and interpret line graphs: Disparities between multiple-choice and free-response instruments. *Science Education, 78*, 527-554.

Bétrancourt, M., & Tversky, B. (2000). Effect of computer animation on users' performance: A review. *Le Travail Humain, 63*(4), 311-329.

Chi, M. T. H. (1997). Quantifying qualitative analyses of verbal data: A practical guide. *The Journal of the Learning Sciences, 6*(3), 271-315.

Clark, R. C., & Mayer, R. (2003). *E-learning and the science of instruction*. San Francisco, CA: Pfeiffer.

de Jong, T., & van Joolingen, W. R. (1998). Scientific discovery learning with computer simulations of conceptual domains. *Review of Educational Research, 68*(2), 179-201.

Hake, R. R. (1998). Interactive engagement versus traditional methods: A six-thousand-students-survey of mechanics test data for introductory physics courses. *American Journal of Physics, 66*, 67-74.

Heuer, D. (2002). *PAKMA 2002 – Physik interaktiv simulieren, messen, reproduzieren, modellieren und analysieren* [PAKMA 2002 – Interactive simulation, measurement, reproduction, modelling and analysis in physics; CD-ROM]. Hannover: Schroedel Verlag.

Leinhardt, G., Zaslavsky, O., & Stein, M. K. (1990). Functions, graphs, and graphing: Tasks, learning, and teaching. *Review of Educational Research, 60*, 1-64.

Lowe, R. K. (2003). Animation and learning: Selective processing of information in dynamic graphics. *Learning and Instruction, 13*(2), 157-176.

McDermott, L. C., Rosenquist, M. L., & van Zee, E. H. (1987). Student difficulties in connecting graphs and physics: Examples from kinematics. *American Journal of Physics, 55*, 503-513.

Ploetzner, R., Bodemer, D., & Neudert, S. (in press). Successful and less successful use of dynamic visualisations in instructional texts. In R. K. Lowe & W. Schnotz (Eds.), *Learning with animation - Research and implications for design*. New York, NY: Cambridge University Press.

Ploetzner, R., & Lowe, R. K. (Eds.). (2004). Special issue on dynamic visualisations and learning. *Learning and Instruction, 14*(3), 235-240.

Raven, J. C. (1980). *RAVEN-Matrizen-Test – Advanced progressive matrices*. Weinheim: Beltz Verlag.

Reif, F., & Allen, S. (1992). Cognition for interpreting scientific concepts: A study of acceleration. *Cognition and Instruction, 9*(1), 1-44.

Scanlon, E. (1998). How beginning students use graphs of motion. In M. W. van Someren, P. Reimann, H. P. A. Boshuizen & T. de Jong (Eds.), *Learning with multiple representations* (pp. 67-86). Amsterdam: Pergamon Press.

Yeo, S., Loss, R., Zadnik, M., Harrsion, A., & Treagust, D. (2004). What do students really learn from interactive multimedia? A physics case study. *American Journal of Physics, 72*(10), 1351-1358.

Acknowledgments

The research reported in this paper was supported by the Deutsche Forschungsgemeinschaft (DFG) under contracts HE 2550/3-1 and PL 224/10-1.

True Stories, Storied Truth: Stitching Narrative and Logico-Scientific Discourse Together in an Age of "Spin"

Joseph L. Polman
University of Missouri-St. Louis College of Education
One University Blvd.
Saint Louis, MO 63121
polman@umsl.edu

Abstract: This paper includes a framework for combining narrative and logico-scientific thinking in the consumption and production of stories about the real world, such as journalistic and historical accounts. The framework involves graphical representation, at an intermediate level of abstraction, in "storygrams" showing sequences of actions involving agents, using cultural tools, to serve goals, within contexts of interpreted scenes. The framework also involves four elements of "narrative metacognition", including monitoring of perspectives, precedents, symbolism and narrative frames. Utilizing this framework may help learners better develop their facility at moving back and forth between assessments of "narrative truth" and "logico-scientific truth".

A "true" story, twice told

Consider the following two tellings of the story of the Great Plains of North America, paraphrased from descriptions of historian William Cronon (1992):

> *The Great Plains of North America was a virtual wasteland when the white settlers moved in. Unlike the eastern U.S., the Plains were not easily suited to settlement. Farmers could not simply move in and make the soil consistently productive to farming and building, because the plains were semi-arid and largely treeless. But gradually, the settlers' ingenuity led to successful farming using a combination of irrigation for groundwater and windmills to access aquifers, and successful ranching using barbed wire to contain livestock. This led to rapid expansion, which could not be sustained in natural drought periods like that which led to the "dustbowl" of the 1930s. Government bureaucrats tried to use this tragedy as an excuse to force farmers off the land, but the people stayed, and grew closer to the land, eventually living in harmony with its cycles.*

> *Before the white man came, the Great Plains of North America was a fragile but beautiful ecosystem. But capitalist farmers and settlers did not respect the delicate balance of the land, moving in with their technology and social systems of exploitation. By the 1930s, world capitalism was in decline and crisis, and that crisis manifested itself in massive dust storms on the plains. The former natural wonder of adaptation to the cycles of rain and drought literally blew away on the winds of capitalism's greed.*

These story sketches summarize two accounts of the Dust Bowl by professional historians Paul Bonnifield and Donald Worster, respectively. Utilizing Kenneth Burke's grammar of stories, Cronon (1992) detailed a total of *five* very different accounts of Great Plains settlement published by historians over the years. The interesting thing is, the tellers of these tales seldom disagreed on what "the facts" were—there was a dry landscape with certain things in it, farmers moved in, they struggled at first, they did better after utilizing new technologies, and they had trouble again in the drought of the 1930s. Instead, the historians highlight some events and downplay or just leave out others, and frame their accounts with different descriptions of the scenes on which the action took place, as well as motives by the actors, and outcomes or ends of the tales. Thus, the perspective and agenda of the storyteller makes all the difference in the world (Cronon, 1992; Novick, 1988).

This state of affairs should be familiar to watchers of the media at the turn of the twenty-first century. In the United States, conservatives who criticize "liberal media" like the *New York Times*, and liberals who criticize "conservative media" like Fox News have been lamenting how elusive the truth is amid the spin. When it comes to both past and contemporary events, how is a reader or listener to decide what is true, or at least closer to the truth?

The Problem

The tension described above is the result of the fact that non-fiction or "empirical" stories (e.g., historical and journalistic accounts, Scholes & Kellogg, 1966) relate to two different kinds of thinking or making meaning—narrative and "logico-scientific". Like many journalistic and historical accounts, the empirical stories described above gain their credence from both narrative and logico-scientific coherence. Citizens voting in democratic societies must combine narrative and logico-scientific reasoning when deciding on the believability of candidates' positions. As Bruner (1986, 2002) has pointed out, however, narrative and logico-scientific ways of thinking are not only different but also difficult to combine.

Barton & Levstik (2004), among others, have shown how narrative can lead to oversimplifications in learning history; they thus recommend caution in teachers' use of narrative as a tool for teaching history. But narrative cannot be banished altogether from our discourses. For instance, research has shown how physics professors may ignore their formal knowledge of insulators and choose aluminum foil to keep a soda can cool, because it relates to their narrative memories from childhood (Lewis & Linn, 1994). Relatedly, even well informed U.S. history teachers sometimes promulgate the dominant narrative that all western Native Americans were nomadic, when they know that some tribes were in fact settled farmers (Wills, 1994). In both these cases, educated people are capable of having their logical reasoning "overcome" the compelling—and erroneous—narratives when prompted to use their formal knowledge (Wertsch & Polman, 2001). That tends to be what we do in school: teach students to *erase* their narrative thinking, lest they be fooled. When prompted, students dutifully refer to what the evidence shows or not. But like their teachers, those students are likely to walk through the "everyday" world with narrative "erasing" their logical, critical stance when confronting stories that just sound right.

In both the example of the physics of soda cans and nomadic Native Americans, the light of logico-scientific reasoning reveals falsity in the narrative, but such clarity in determining veracity is not always possible. As Cronon's (1992) analysis referenced above shows, for example, many of the same "facts" can be assembled to tell very different stories—in this case, some of progress, and some of tragedy. But many of these stories cannot be debunked by pointing out flaws in their elements: each part appears logically and scientifically true. Instead, the hearer must decide on a preferred version of environmental history based on overall "narrative truth", which is "judged by its verisimilitude rather than its verifiability" (Bruner, 2003, p. 51). Within political and historical realms, judgments of verisimilitude are too often based solely on what is most comfortable given one's own personal background and biases.

In today's atmosphere of increasingly sophisticated "spin" in political and historical discourse, citizens have a need to stitch together the narrative and logico-scientific. In this paper, I present a set of principles for approaching empirical stories, grounded in the sociocultural approach (e.g., Wertsch, 1998, 2002). I will then briefly describe some practices based on these principles and research on learning.

Towards more sophisticated consumption of true stories

In his analysis of collective remembering of national narratives, James Wertsch (2002) has pointed out that empirical stories serve both a referential and a dialogic function. The referential function of empirical narratives relates to how accurately the story represents the events that actually occurred in the world. The dialogic function of narrative relates to how narratives are told in response to a particular set of circumstances, and for particular purposes; in addition, they are often contested accounts that serve both to describe the events, and position the identities of both creator and the hearer. In order to educate more sophisticated consumers, I propose two main strategies: the development of a representational system for narratives I call "storygrams", and the development of "narrative metacognition."

"Storygrams"

Numerous structural accounts have been developed in narrative theory representing the form and meaning of stories. One of the most extensive was Vladimir Propp's (1968) framework for describing Russian folktales. This framework consists of 7 types of characters or spheres of action, such as the villain, and 31 plot functions, such as "the villain receives information about his victim" and "the villain is defeated." Although it would be possible to adapt a detailed structural account of narratives such as this or others that grow out of the psychological tradition of describing narrative schemas (e.g., Bartlett, 1995), there are reasons to seek out a simpler system for learners to use in representing stories. First, inscriptional forms such as scientific diagrams gain part of their credence through making their content extremely compact and communicable to others (e.g., Latour, 1988). An inscriptional system incorporating a large but limited set of functions and types to choose from, such as an adaptation of Propp's or that developed by Chatman (1978) for film and fiction would be too cumbersome for any but the very committed to utilize well. Second, inscriptional forms at an intermediate level of abstraction have a greater hope of being useful scaffolds for learners that may be taken up as frames for thinking (White, 1993). An example is Bell's (2002) argument maps, which allow learners to describe a scientific argument using a basic set of primitive categories appropriate to the discipline—in the case of science, elements such as "my theory", "evidence for", and "evidence against" (see also Suthers & Hundhausen, 2003).

As a starting point for "storygrams", I have chosen Kenneth Burke's (1979) pentad, which Jerome Bruner (2005) has referred to as the "universal arguments of action". In particular, I propose creating a modified concept mapping system with symbols representing Wertsch's (1998) terms for the five elements of the pentad (see Figure 1), and hypermedia links to details and source text elements.

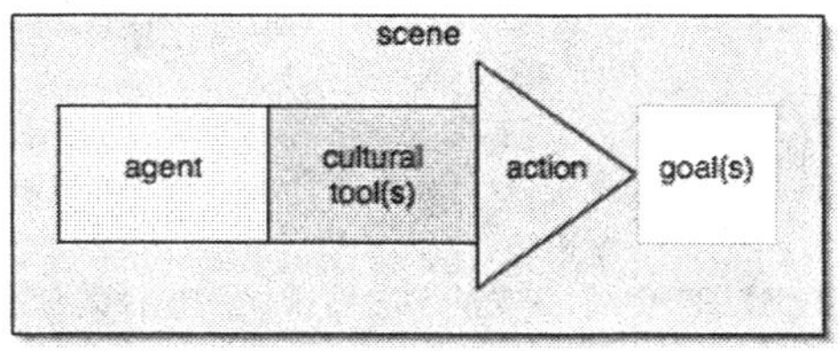

Figure 1: Storygram node with Wertsch's (1998) interpretation of K. Burke's (1979) pentad

The basic unit of the storygram is the action, which according to Burke's analysis always consists of an agent, utilizing cultural tools to take the action, in order to serve a goal or goals, all within the context of some scene. The story is driven forward because of tensions between elements of the pentad, and each major action would be represented on the storygram, with time shown by aligning action nodes from left to right. To make a storygram representing an existing story, a learner would replace the labels of the five elements with descriptors of the scene, agent, cultural tools, action, and goals. The major action sequences that move the story plot forward would be represented, with possibility for further description in notes attached to the base storygram representation, and hyperlinks to source text if desired.

To further clarify, storygrams of the two Dust Bowl in the Great Plains accounts from the beginning of this paper appear in Figures 2 and 3. Figure 2 is a storygram of Paul Bonnifield's narrative, which opened in a scene of a semiarid, treeless, resistant environment. Settlers in this environment could not contain their livestock by building wooden fences as they had done in the lush woodlands of the east, but they adapted by building barbed wire fences. In order to have enough water for their crops, farmers in this environment had to go beyond simple wells, instead building more complex irrigation systems, and using windmills to pump water out of deeper aquifers. Thus, the scene becomes transformed into one of thriving farms within the resistant but changeable environment, and the mood rises. But then conflict arises, when government bureaucrats take advantage of the Dust Bowl droughts to try and force farmers out, with a covert goal of controlling wheat production. The farmers who stayed, however, found ways to re-adapt to this context of government regulation and a changeable environment, coming to thrive and gain more harmony with the land.

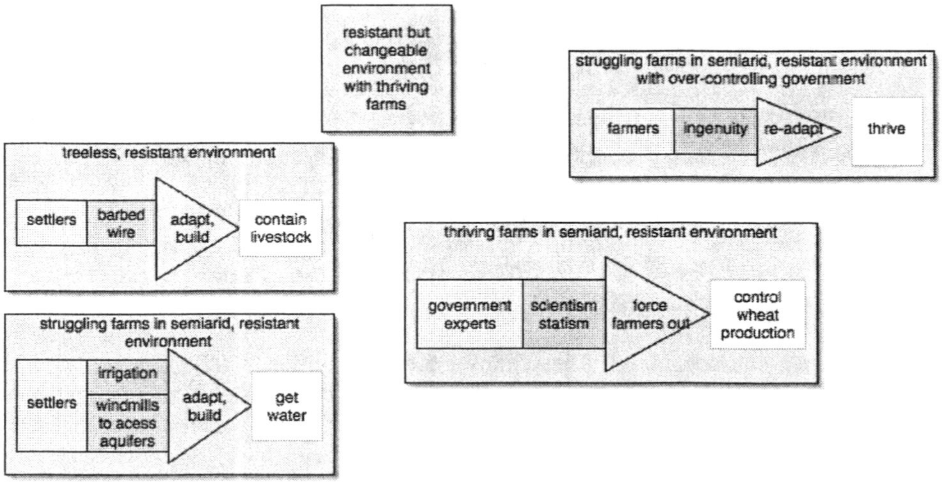

Figure 2: Storygram of Paul Bonnifield's narrative of Great Plains struggle and progress through human adaptation despite government

Donald Worster began with a much different contextual description of the same territory, as depicted in Figure 3. Rather than beginning with merely the physical features of the land, he stressed the decline of world capitalism, within which the unique but delicate ecosystem of the plains existed. As elsewhere, the corrupt capitalist systems exploited the land to expand and grow, using its technology and social systems. Once the ecosystem was knocked out of balance, as exemplified by the droughts, capitalist planners stretched their capabilities in order to prop up their systems of exploitation. Eventually, though, they wasted the landscape, as seen in the Dust Bowl windstorms topsoil blown away.

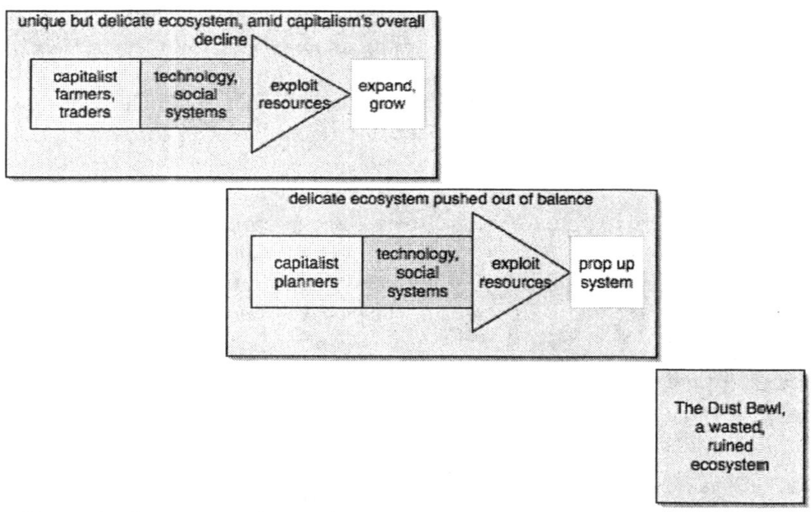

Figure 3: Storygram of Donald Worster's tale of Great Plains declension

As I have conceived of them, Storygrams such as those above could be part of a comprehensive approach to improving the discourse around empirical narratives. Another element of this approach is a focus on developing narrative metacognition.

Narrative metacognition

Educators and researchers have come to recognize metacognition as an important form of thinking across and within disciplines (e.g., Bruer, 1993; White & Frederiksen, 1998). Sophisticated readers use metacognition when they monitor their understandings, while expert problem solvers use metacognition to make predictions on where their work will take them. In order to foster more sophisticated consumption and production of empirical narratives, I propose educating learners to be more effective at some metacognitive practices particularly important to narrative. These include being aware of perspectives, precedents, and symbolism, as well as monitoring the "story frames" within which an account is cast.

In history and social studies education, there is an existing practice of encouraging learners to focus on the perspectives and biases of those who created the artifacts and accounts used as sources, especially in initiatives involving youth in the "doing of history" research utilizing primary sources (e.g., Britt & Aglinskas, 2002; Holt, 1990; Levstik & Barton, 1997).

In addition to this old standby, however, light can be shed on how narrative impacts understanding by considering the "precedents" or existing accounts with which the hearer is familiar, and which the hearer takes as credible. This is similar to law, where previous legal decisions shape the reactions of the courts to new cases which are in effect narratives crafted to link most strongly to case precedents that will provide the most beneficial interpretation—and thus legal decision. As in the law, all tellers of "true tales" appeal to precedents (Bruner, 2002).

In the literature and language arts classrooms of North America, students have long analyzed the symbolism that helps constitute the meaning and message of fictional stories, but such considerations are rarely explored in the context of journalism or history. But compelling metaphors that are inserted either explicitly or implicitly in empirical narrative texts, as well as imagery or music that creates unconscious cues in multimedia artifacts such as documentary films and television shows, are just as important as in fictional worlds. One interesting approach to textual and multimedia accounts of "social worlds" that concern youth has been proposed and explored by Beach and Myers (2002). In their approach, youth attempt to make sense of, critique, and even transform social worlds, in part by better understanding how symbolism operates within those worlds.

Another aspect of narrative metacognition is appreciating how "spin" operates. Although accusing one's political opponents of spin has become commonplace, it is first important to recognize that *all* sides in political arguments utilize spin, and they may utilize it in both honest and deceitful ways. When cast as an accusation against one's opponent, "spin" is usually an allegation of deceit, involving deliberate misinformation, dropping of relevant information, or innuendo. In addition to such practices, it is worth noting that narrators in political and social realms are sometimes not so much trying to *distort* the truth so much as *create* a reality that is possible, but not yet decided. As an example, consider some comments of David Makovsky about the pullout of Israelis from the Gaza Strip in August 2005:

> There could be two narratives that emerge from this disengagement story. One is, it is the revitalization of a center in Israeli politics and Palestinian politics that was decimated with the Intifada ... Basically, both sides acting because they want a better future for their kids, working together to establish a two state solution. If that is the narrative, in my view—and I think it's the correct narrative—[then] this process has a future. If it's going to be that Hamas basically won ... if [this event] will be interpreted as a victory for terror and violence, it will be short-lived. If it is interpreted as the re-emergence of a sane center in both Israeli and Palestinian societies, I think this is a first step towards a very important future.

A refreshing aspect of Makovsky's comments is that he is straightforward about the competing narratives, their basis in fact, and goals each might serve. At the end, he also intimates how the interpretation of one narrative or another not only reflects current reality, but helps to create the future reality. This is an important aspect of any human interpretation.

Finally, I propose "frame monitoring" as an essential aspect of a critical stance toward empirical narratives. George Lakoff (2004) has recently popularized the notion that overarching narrative frames influence political storytelling and message creation. He argues that successful conservative politicians consistently appeal to the notion that citizens need a government which acts as a strict father who lays down inflexible rules and imbues the "family"—the nation's citizenry—with a strong moral order. In contrast, liberal politicians generally frame their account of government as a nurturant parent who teaches the children to pursue personal happiness and care for others. I would argue that these are not the only frames that matter, but critical consumers of supposedly true stories would benefit by attending to how the frame an account is put into often conveniently excludes some "facts", or minimizes them by allowing that although they may be true, they may not be particularly relevant to the main storyline. In addition, the frame chosen for a story includes or emphasizes some apparent "facts", which on closer inspection are revealed as assumptions not supported by evidence but instead a merely coherent storyline.

Learning Environment Design

The above framework, combined with previous cognitive studies of educational practice, could be used as the basis for learning environment design. For instance, a participation structure with narrative metacognition roles (as in Palincsar & Brown's (1984) "Reciprocal Teaching") could be used to externalize the practices of monitoring perspectives, precedents, symbolism, and narrative frames. In such an application of Vygotsky's general genetic law of development, the hope is that the implementation of the roles on the social plane would lead to appropriation by the individual learners. In addition, a computer application for "storygrams" is in prototype (http://www.umsl.edu/~edujpolm/truestories.html) —essentially a specialized concept mapping program that would allow learners to create the narrative diagrams like those in Figures 1-3, with the possibility of embedding hypermedia links to extended notes or commentary on any one element, as well as links to source texts if desired. If groups of learners used this utility to storygram competing empirical narratives, these "cognitive tools" could be used both to support individual understanding, and as props that could drive learning conversations among peers forward. They would thus serve some of the same purposes that "external representations" have been shown to serve in the course of science inquiry, both by children and practicing scientists. As Blumenfeld et al (1991) put it, representational artifacts can become "shared, critiquable externalizations" of knowledge that become useful in learning conversations.

In addition, learners could move from critical consumption such as that described above to production, by involving them in the production of stories about the social or political world. One medium such stories are increasingly utilizing is digital video (e.g., Lambert, 2002). Challenging learners who create public service announcements and short documentaries to take into account the above issues involving the intersection of narrative and logico-scientific thinking could be quite fruitful. This could be encouraged by requiring such projects to adapt the "director's commentary" one sees on commercial DVDs to metacognitive purposes. Specifically, one could interview learners who'd produced media narratives about the decisions made and the motivations for them, or ask learners to write a short paper on this topic. I will be exploring these possibilities for learning environment design over the coming years.

Conclusion

In this paper, I have outlined a framework for understanding the issues involved in narrative representations that are based in empirical reality. I believe exploring the use of this framework, and refining it, may improve democratic participation in discourse about contemporary and historical events. Specifically, learners might be able to improve in both the critical consumption of and production of "true stories." I argue that research on such practices could enable teachers and learners to better develop their facility at moving back and forth between assessments of "narrative truth" and "logico-scientific" truth, so that each way of thinking *informs* the other, rather than *erasing* the other.

References

Bartlett, F. C. (1995). *Remembering: A study in experimental and social psychology*. Cambridge: Cambridge University Press (originally published in 1932).

Barton, K. C., & Levstik, L. S. (2004). *Teaching history for the common good*. Mahwah, NJ: Erlbaum.

Beach, R., & Myers, J. (2001). *Inquiry-based English instruction: Engaging students in life and literature*. New York: Teachers College Press.

Bell, P. (2002). Using argument map representations to make thinking visible for individuals and groups. In T. Koschmann, R. Hall & N. Miyake (Eds.), *CSCL 2: Carrying Forward the Conversation* (pp. 449-485). Mahwah, NJ: Lawrence Erlbaum Associates.

Blumenfeld, P. C., Soloway, E., Marx, R. W., Krajcik, J. S., Guzdial, M., and Palincsar, A. (1991). Motivating project-based learning: Sustaining the doing, supporting the learning. *Educational Psychologist, 26*(3), 369-398.

Britt, M. A., & Aglinskas, C. (2002). Improving students' ability to identify and use source information. *Cognition and Instruction, 20*(4), 485-522.

Bruer, J. (1993). *Schools for thought: A science of learning in the classroom*. Cambridge, MA: MIT.

Bruner, J. (1986). *Actual minds, possible worlds*. Cambridge, MA: Harvard University Press.

Bruner, J. (2002). *Making stories: Law, literature, life*. New York: Farrar, Straus and Giroux.

Bruner, J. (2003). The narrative construction of reality. In M. Mateas & P. Sengers (Eds.) *Narrative intelligence*. Amsterdam/Philadelphia: John Benjamins Publishing.

Bruner, J. (2005). Keynote presentation. First Congress of the International Society of Cultural and Activity Research (ISCAR), Seville, Spain, September, 2005.

Burke, K. (1969). *A grammar of motives*. Berkeley: University of California Press.

Chatman, S. (1978). *Story and discourse: Narrative structure in fiction and film*. Ithaca: Cornell University Press.

Cronon, W. (1992). A place for stories: Nature, history, narrative. *J of American History 78*(4), 1347-76.

Holt, T. (1990). *Thinking historically: Narrative, imagination and understanding*. New York: College Entrance Examination Board.

Lakoff, G. (2004). *Don't think of an elephant!*. Vermont: Chelsea Green.

Lambert, J. (2002). *Digital storytelling: Capturing lives, creating community*. Berkeley: Digital Diner.

Latour, B. (1988). Drawing things together. In M. Lynch & S. Woolgar (Eds.), *Representation in scientific practice*. Cambridge, MA: MIT Press.

Levstik, L., & Barton, K. (1997). *Doing history: Investigating with children in elementary and middle schools*. Mahwah, NJ: Lawrence Erlbaum Associates.

Lewis, E. L., and Linn, M. C. (1994). Heat energy and temperature concepts of adolescents, adults, and experts: Implications for curricular improvements. *Journal of Research in Science Teaching, 31*(6), 657-677.

Novick, P. (1988). *That noble dream: The 'objectivity question' in the American historical profession*. New York: Cambridge University Press.

Palincsar, A. S., & Brown, A. L. (1984). Reciprocal teaching of comprehension-fostering and comprehension monitoring activities. *Cognition and Instruction, 1*, 117-175.

Propp, V. (1968). *Morphology of the folktale*. Austin: University of Texas Press (trans. Laurence Scott).

Scholes, R., and Kellogg, R. (1966) *The nature of narratives*. New York: Oxford University Press.

Suthers, D., and Hundhausen, C. (2003). An empirical study of the effects of representational guidance on collaborative learning. *Journal of the Learning Sciences, 12*(2), 183-219.

Wertsch, J. V. (1998). *Mind as action*. New York: Oxford University Press.

Wertsch, J. V. (2002). *Voices of collective remembering*. Cambridge: Cambridge University Press.

Wertsch, J.V., & Polman, J.L. (2001). The intuitive mind and knowledge about history. In B. Torff & R.J. Sternberg, (Eds.), *Understanding & teaching the intuitive mind* (57-72). Mahwah, NJ: Erlbaum.

White, B. Y. (1993). Intermediate abstractions and causal models: A microworld-based approach to science education. In *Proceedings of the world conference on artificial intelligence in education* (pp. 26-33). Charlottesville, VA: Association for the Advancement of Computing in Education.

White, B., & Frederiksen, J. (1998). Inquiry, modeling, and metacognition: Making science accessible to all students. *Cognition and Instruction, 16*(1), 3-117.

Wills, J. (1994). Popular culture, curriculum, and historical representation: The situation of Native Americans in American history and the perpetuation of stereotypes. *Journal of Narrative and Life History, 4* (4), 277-294.

Learning from Digital Text in Inquiry-Based Science Classes: Lessons Learned in One Program

Sadhana Puntambekar
Department of Educational Psychology, Room 697, Educational Sciences
1025 W. Johnson Street, Madison WI 53706-1796.
Email: puntambekar@education.wisc.edu

Abstract: In this paper, I present a synthesis of the lessons learned from a research program aimed at understanding how students learn from the multiple linked texts in hypertext environments in the context of scientific inquiry. I started with a research agenda intended to systematically understand the importance of several variables that affect learning from hypertext environments. Further, the goal of my research has not only been to understand how students learn from hypertext but also to identify how students use hypertext in the context of inquiry-based science classes. In my research program, I conducted a series a studies to explore these two issues in parallel. My studies have helped identify factors that affect student learning from digital text, moving toward a conceptual model of learning from multiple linked texts. In addition, they have also helped identify successful teacher strategies used to help students learn from hands-on investigations and digital resources.

In the last decade and a half, there has been much discussion about the divide between educational research and practice (Lagemann, 2002) and a need to understand learning in complex real-world contexts (Brown, 1992; Collins, 1992; Cobb, Confrey, DiSessa, Lehrer & Shauble, 2003); DBRC 2003). Design-based research methods in which researchers try to understand the ways in which learning occurred in a particular setting are increasingly being used to understand teaching and learning in classroom settings. Unlike traditional experiments that involve controlling variables, the thrust in design-based research is to characterize the environment in which the intervention is used by developing an understanding of the actors (e.g., teachers, students) and the social structures in a particular setting, in order to develop rich representations of teaching and learning. But challenges of this evolving paradigm have also been recognized, such as the large amounts of qualitative and quantitative data that are collected leading to problems of coordination and analysis, the emergent nature of the questions and issues, (Dede, 2003), and the validity of claims (Shavelson, Phillips, Towne & Feuer, 2003). Shavelson, et al. (2003) have recommended "coupling scientifically warranted knowledge and rich contextual information in some narrative form might lead to increased understanding and use if scientific research in practice" (p. 28). This requires a systematic understanding of learning outcomes as well as the environment in which learning occurs, which has been a goal of my research program in the past five years.

In this paper, I present a synthesis of the lessons learned from a research program aimed at understanding how students learn from the multiple, linked texts presented in a hypertext environment in the context of scientific inquiry. Along with my research group, I started with a research agenda intended to systematically understand the importance of several variables that affect learning from hypertext environments. Further, the goal of my research project, CoMPASS, has not only been to understand how students learn from multiple, digital texts, but also to identify how factors in the classroom context affect student learning. I conducted a series a studies to explore these two issues in parallel.

CoMPASS Project: Motivation and Background

Hands-on activities in which students experience and manipulate scientific phenomena are an integral part of current project- and design-based approaches to science learning (Kafai, 1994; Kolodner et al., 2003; Krajcik, Blumenfeld, Marx, & Soloway, 1991). A concern raised about the focus on hands-on activities is that students can concentrate on the construction activities, and build a working solution by trial and error without understanding the underlying deep science principles and phenomena (Kolodner et al., 2003). Further, as students begin to tackle complex scientific phenomena in higher grades, they increasingly encounter the necessity to utilize other ways to foster scientific reasoning, one of which is the use of text-based resources. But "text is seldom studied in the context of everyday classroom use . . . and there is little attention given to the integration of text with other modes of experiencing and learning science" (Palincsar & Magnusson, 2001, p. 152).

A problem with integrating text in scientific inquiry is the paucity of good science textbooks. Commercially available science textbooks have been criticized for merely imparting facts, emphasizing breadth of coverage over depth, and frequently including "errors, misconceptions, and confusing presentations" (Raloff, 2001). But with the proliferation of technology, electronic texts in the form of hypertext and hypermedia systems (e.g., Azevedo, & Cromley, 2004) as well as digital libraries (e.g., Hoffman, Wu, Krajcik, & Soloway, 2003) are increasingly being used in scientific inquiry. Digital or hypertext documents are nonlinear and flexible, and enable students to follow their own investigation paths. However, the flexibility also poses challenges because students have to make decisions and browse through the space selectively (Bolter, 2001). Successful integration of digital text resources in scientific inquiry requires (a) an understanding of the cognitive processes that students employ while reading from multiple texts in the context of a science classroom; and (b) an understanding of the ways in which electronic resources can be integrated with hands-on science activities. The focus of my research program has been on both these issues.

The CoMPASS project consists of a hypertext system, CoMPASS (Puntambekar, Stylianou & Hübscher, 2003) and curriculum modules based on the pedagogical framework of Learning By Design (Kolodner, et al., 2003). The CoMPASS system is designed with two tightly integrated representations: a textual representation of the content units and a visual representation in a form of concept maps. Each screen in CoMPASS represents a concept such as *mass* or *gravity,* providing both a concept map (left half of the screen) and a textual description (right half of the screen). The maps are dynamically constructed and displayed using the *fisheye* technique (Bedersen & Hollan, 1995)—that is, the focus concept the student has chosen is at the center of the map, with the most closely related concepts displayed in the first ring and the less closely related concepts displayed at the outer ring. The maps in CoMPASS show connections between science phenomena, giving students alternative paths to pursue for any particular activity, so that they can see how different phenomena are related to each other. CoMPASS also supports alternative views of concepts. For example, a student might be interested in learning about the phenomenon of force in the context of objects falling in air. The student can change views at any time to study the same phenomenon (e.g., force) in other contexts, such as linear motion or simple machines.

The CoMPASS software environment is used in conjunction with the curriculum units that we have designed. We have developed a ten-week Simple Machines unit and a Roller Coasters Unit. The "Simple Machines" unit starts by introducing students to the "Can Lift Challenge," in which they are presented with the problem of building a device using simple machines to lift a 16-ounce can of food. In the first couple of days, students brainstorm their initial design ideas and draw plans of their designs. After this, they are introduced to each of the simple machines by way of activities such as using a ramp to raise a heavy object to a certain height. Each activity is designed to enhance students' understanding of science phenomena and revisiting underlying scientific principles. Students go back to the Can Lift designs approximately halfway through the unit and again at the end. Students use CoMPASS throughout the design process. For example, after the initial brainstorming, they refer to the information in CoMPASS to refine their questions. Once they have generated questions they use the system again to find the information and apply it to their designs. They use the software again as they are working on their designs to find out more about the specific topic so that they can revise and optimize their designs and interpret the data that they are collecting.

Summary of Research

In the past five years, I have been working on systematically building an understanding of the variables that affect learning, both how students process texts and factors in the environment that affect learning. In doing so, I have used as the conceptual framework, both theories in comprehension of expository texts as well as lessons recent work in inquiry-based science learning. A range of qualitative and quantitative measures was used, depending on the complexity of the research questions for each study. Some such measures were: (a) a pre-post test with multiple-choice items and an essay question to study change in students' knowledge of Physics; (b) concept-mapping post-test to analyze the richness of students' conceptual understanding; (c) a post-test survey to understand students' use of CoMPASS; and (d) process measures of navigation through CoMPASS, in the form of log files. The navigation data were analyzed using the pathfinder algorithm (Schvaneveldt, 1990) to study the transitions that students make between concepts, relationship to goals, and richness and focus of their navigation patterns.

Four teachers in 40 sixth and eighth grade classrooms by over 800 students have used the CoMPASS materials. While each study examined students' learning outcomes (pre and post test scores and scores on concept mapping tests) in all of the classrooms, I focused on a few questions in each study, incrementally building an understanding of how students learn from digital resources in an inquiry classroom. I conducted studies to understand the role of coherence and metacognition in hypertext, as well as the role of teacher facilitation as students used the CoMPASS materials in the classroom. In the next few sections, I will summarize the key findings.

Learning from multiple texts: Role of structure and coherence

The Construction-Integration model of text learning distinguishes between two levels of understanding – a textbase and a situation model. The textbase can be described as the "the text as it is" (Kintsch, 1998). It reflects the organization of the text as contained in the macro and micro propositions. Text coherence, created by the relatedness and overlap of the propositions that make up a text play a vital role in comprehension. In hypertext systems, a key feature of text structure, global coherence (i.e. coherence between sections), is lost due to the multiple linked texts (nodes). Hypertext environments are different from traditional expository text in two important ways. First, hypertext environments are "multilinear" (Bolter, 2001) in that each text segment can be linked to many others, providing multiple paths to access any node. Second, in traditional text, the organization is embedded in the text itself. In hypertext, however, the organizational information (overviews, outlines, etc) is separate from the text (Dee-Lucas & Larkin, 1995), making it harder to establish global coherence. Learners therefore need to integrate Information from two sources, the text and its organization. In the CoMPASS hypertext system, I have addressed the issue of providing global coherence by using two concept maps that show relations between science concepts. My first set of studies was an attempt to understand how providing maps affect students' navigation and learning. With my graduate students, I conducted studies in sixth and eighth grade classes, that used different versions of the system, one the navigable maps, and the other with an outline in the form of a list, to understand how providing structure affects navigation and learning.

In the eighth grade study, students in two classes (N=36) used the system to learn about 'Forces and Motion' for three days. Students did not use their textbooks for this unit but used CoMPASS as a resource. On each of the days, students used CoMPASS for forty-five minutes. Both classes were taught by the same teacher and followed the same activities. Student understanding was measured with a pre-post test that had multiple choice items and open-ended questions to test students' scientific reasoning. In addition, students drew concept maps at the end of the describing their understanding of the concepts and the relations between them. We found that the version of CoMPASS (map or outline) did not affect students' scores on the multiple-choice portion of the pre and post tests. This showed that as far as the knowledge of factual information as measured by the pre and post tests was concerned, the coherence provided did not affect learning outcomes. However, significant differences between the two groups were found in the open-ended questions in the Physics post test, with the maps group performing significantly than the outline group (ES=.82). Similarly, analysis revealed that while there was no difference in the two groups for the explanations provided for the concepts, there was a significant different in the depth of the science that described connections between concepts (ES=.38). The connections that they made between concepts showed that they had gained a deeper understanding of the relationships between concepts, for example mass and acceleration. Their maps were richer and they also used more formulas.

In the sixth grade study, students used CoMPASS over a seven week period during the simple machines unit. As students engaged in investigations designed for each simple machine (e.g., wedge, pulley, lever), the used CoMPASS to find the information that would help them in their investigations. A total of 80 sixth-grade students from four classes participated in this study. Two of the classes used a maps version of the system and the other two used an outline version. During the 7-week unit, there were a total of 18 sessions in which all the students used CoMPASS, each lasting approximately 20-25 minutes. Similar to the eighth grade study, a multiple choice pre and post physics test and a concept-mapping test were used to measure students' knowledge of physics concepts and principles. We found that there were no differences in the pre and post test scores between the maps and the outline groups. Results suggested that in so far as knowledge of physics principles as measured in the multiple choice pre and post test was concerned, there was no significant difference between the maps-group and the outline-group, indicating that to the extent that knowledge of the factual information represented in science text is concerned, the coherence in the system did not affect learning. However, analysis of students' performance on a concept-mapping test showed that students in the maps-group had a significantly deeper and richer understanding of the science content (ES=.09). Students in the maps-groups seemed to have understood the interconnected nature of the concepts and principles that they were learning across the set of simple machines (Puntambekar & Goldstein, submitted).

These studies suggested that similar to traditional texts, providing coherence plays an important role in learning from hypertext systems. I have described three levels of coherence in CoMPASS – intratextual (within a node), intertextual (between two nodes) and metatextual (among several nodes) (Puntambekar, submitted). The maps provide both intertextual and metatextual coherence by showing the relations between two nodes and by illustrating how a particular node can be placed in relation to several related nodes.

Metacognition in Hypertext: Metanavigation Support

Metacognition, which refers to the knowledge that we have about our own cognitive processes, has been proved to be a significant factor for text understanding. According to Brown and her colleagues (e.g., Brown et al., 1985) important metacognitive differences exist between good and poor readers in the way they process texts. Campione, Brown and Connell (1988), believe that successful learners can reflect on their learning activities, have available powerful strategies for dealing with novel learning situations, and oversee and regulate those strategies efficiently.

In two studies, I examined whether metacognition was a factor that affected student learning from multiple linked texts. The first study (N=74) involved an analysis of students' navigation patterns to group them into clusters, using a k-means clustering technique. Based on this analysis, navigation patterns were grouped into four clusters, enabling us to understand the kinds of support that students needed. This analysis showed that although the maps provided structure, the affordances of the maps were not always obvious to low-knowledge students. Students needed further support to select nodes that were related to (a) the current node and (b) to their goals (Puntambekar & Stylianou, 2005). This formed the basis of the next study that I conducted a study, with one of my doctoral students, in which students' navigation was supported by providing metacognitive prompts for navigation in CoMPASS – metanavigation support (Stylianou, 2003). The metanavigation support enabled students to (i) select concepts based on their goals (ii) make transitions that are coherent, and (iii) understand the nature of the relationships between concepts. Results of the study suggested that providing metanavigation support enabled students to make coherent transitions among the text units. In addition to metanavigation prompts, reading comprehension and prior knowledge significantly predicted students' understanding of science principles and the relationships among them (Stylianou & Puntambekar, 2004).

CoMPASS in Science Classrooms: Understanding the Context

Understanding the elements of a context and addressing research questions relating to the enactment of interventions in varied contexts have been emphasized as important goals for education research (Brown, 1992; Design-Based Research Collective, 2003). Proponents design based methods have advocated the importance of characterizing the situation, understanding the synergistic nature of classroom life (Brown, 1992) and understanding of the classroom as a "learning ecology" (Cobb, et al., 2003) consisting of several interacting components. Very often, this means a systematic analysis of enactments in a setting, in an effort to understand the factors in a local context that may or may not have lead to the success of an intervention. One of the main aspects of such an analysis is studying classroom interactions to develop an understanding of the factors that might contribute to student learning. In our studies, teacher facilitation of class discussions, as well as discussions in student groups were analyzed.

Role of Teacher Facilitation

I have been studying classroom enactments of the COMPASS materials by different teachers (Puntambekar, Stylianou & Goldstein, accepted). Examining how teachers structure the activities in a unit and how they facilitate classroom discussion is important to understand how innovative technology rich curricula work in the context of classroom instruction. In one of our recent studies, we examined students' learning outcomes in classes taught by two teachers. We then analyzed enactments by the two teachers, Mrs. J and Mrs. L, to understand the differences in the learning outcomes. Our quantitative data showed that there were significant differences in the learning outcomes of students in classes taught by the two teachers, with Mrs. J's students significantly outperforming Mrs. J's students in measures of deep understanding. We then analyzed the enactments of the curriculum by the two teachers to understand whether the differences in the enactments might have lead to differences in learning outcomes. We specifically focused on how teacher led discussions can help (a) connect the activities within a curriculum unit and (b) enable deeper conceptual understanding by helping students make connections between science concepts and principles. Analysis of teacher led discussions helped understand (a) the role teacher facilitation played in integrating the software with the design activities and (b) the kinds of facilitation that enabled students to make better connections between their hands-on science exploration and the more abstract activity of finding and making sense of science information.

One of the main differences in the two enactments was that all the different phases of the unit were carried out as an interconnected set of events in Mrs. J's classes, while in Mrs. L's class each activity seemed to be an end in itself. While Mrs. L had all the parts of inquiry, the deep structure that connected all the phases was lacking. Students in Mrs. L's class were on task and completed all of the investigations in the curriculum, Mrs. J's students seemed to have been encouraged to think about the purpose of every activity and how it was connected to the others in the unit. The second major difference was that Mrs. J's strategies during facilitation of whole class discussions were different for the different phases of the unit. In the early part of the unit, Mrs. J focused more on enabling students to ground the current topic in what they already knew about simple machines, while in the later discussions, she asked questions that encouraged students to reason about the science that they were learning, helped make connections between abstract science principles and their concrete hands-on experiences, and connections between concepts. In particular, the two enactments differed in terms of: (a) helping students raise questions that are related to the overall goal of the challenge, (b) helping students see how abstract ideas are related to their experience with physical objects (c) enabling an understanding of how each activity in the unit is connected to the rest of the unit (d) reinforcing the connections between concepts that they are learning and enabling students to understand core principles by reiterating big ideas. While no causal claims can be made based on this study, results of this study have helped me unpack aspects of teacher facilitation that might affect learning, helping with future studies.

Other Studies

I have also conducted other studies, which I cannot discuss in any detail due to space constraints. For example in one study to understand gender differences (Goldstein & Puntambekar, 2004), we analyzed the group conversations during students' work on CoMPASS and their hands-on investigations. The analysis showed that girls might actually be more dominant in a small group setting. Girls generated most of the discussion during both activities in three of the four groups analyzed. The data also indicated that girls generated more novel suggestions than the boys in both activities and that boys asked more questions and generated higher rates of non-goal related talk. In another study, a case study approach was used to examine the relation of metacognitive awareness in reading from traditional expository text and reading from hypertext. Results revealed that there might be a positive relationship between the metacognitive awareness of reading strategies and the navigation behavior while reading from hypertext (Stylianou & Puntambekar, 2003). A study in which high knowledge college students used CoMPASS, I found that the maps were not used by high knowledge students. Interestingly, high knowledge middle school students also did not use the maps, but they missed important information and did not complete their investigation successfully. After each of our implementations, we also worked closely with teachers to get their feedback on the curriculum units, which we have revised over the years.

Lessons Learned and Future Work

Studies conducted in my research program have helped further our understanding of how students learn from digital, multiple texts as well as the classroom factors that facilitate learning. I believe that design based research methods can describe studies within a research program, rather than a single study within a program of research. I have conducted studies in the classroom as well as smaller, more focused studies, and knowledge of how students learn has been accumulated over several studies. A key aspect of my studies has been the use of measures of student outcomes as well as rich narrative descriptions from the classrooms. Each study has helped identify variables that affect student learning. These were then explored further in subsequent studies, and have also provided the groundwork for the next phase of the project. For example, knowledge gained through the studies has helped me move toward formalizing a conceptual model for learning from digital text, describing levels of coherence and understanding the support that students need. In future studies, I will be conducting studies to refine this model to understand the role played by coherence in hypertext systems and its interplay with learner and task variables. With access to digitized content growing rapidly, because of the WWW, the need to understand how students learn from multiple, linked texts is an important line of research. Similarly, my studies have also helped understand factors such as teacher facilitation. Again, in the current phase of the project, I am building on the lessons learned about the role of teacher lead discussions. A study is currently underway to examine how teachers in four different schools implement the CoMPASS intervention. The schools are in different states in varied areas such as inner city, rural and suburban. Each site is different in student population, teacher experience and preparation, and teaching styles and practices. Starting with the strategies identified in this study, we will find evidence for these, or derive new successful strategies that teachers may have used. Multilevel contextual models will be used to include derived variables from the qualitative synthesis of the enactments that may help to explain differential outcomes across conditions.

References

Azevedo, R., & Cromley, J. G. (2004). Does training on self-regulated learning facilitate students' learning with hypermedia? *Journal of Educational Psychology, 96*(3), 523-535.

Bedersen, B. B., & Hollan, J. (1995). *Pad++: A zooming graphical interface for exploring alternate interface physics*. Paper presented at the ACM UIST'94

Bolter, J. D. (2001). *Writing space: Computers, hypertext, and the remediation of print*. Mahwah, NJ: Lawrence Erlbaum Associates.

Brown, A. L. (1992). Design experiments: Theoretical and methodological challenges in creating complex interventions in classroom settings. *Journal of the Learning Sciences, 2*(2), 141-178.

Brown, A. L., Armbruster, B. B., & Baker, L. (1985). The role of metacognition in reading and studying. In J. Orasanu (Ed.), *Reading comprehension: From research to practice*. Hillsdale, NJ: Erlbaum.

Campione, J. C., Brown, A. L., & Connel, M. L. (1988). Metacognition: On the importance of understanding what you are doing. In R. I. Charles & E. A. Silver (Eds.), *Research agenda for mathematics education: The teaching and assessing of mathematical problem solving* (pp. 93-114). Hillsdale, NJ: Erlbaum.

Cobb, P., Confrey, J., diSessa, A., Lehrer, R., & Schauble, L. (2003). Design experiments in educational research. *Educational Researcher, 32*(1).

Collins, A. (1992). Toward a design science of education. In E. Scanlon & T. O'Shea (Eds.), *New directions in educational technology*. New York: Springer-Verlag.

Collins, A. (1999). The changing infrastructure of education research. *Education Research*, 289-298.

Dede, C. (2003). *Future technologies for teaching and learning*. Paper presented at the annual meeting of the Association for the Education of Teachers in Science, Jacksonville, FL.

Dee Lucas, D., & Larkin, J. H. (1995). Learning from electronic texts: Effects of interactive overviews for information access. *Cognition and Instruction, 13*(3), 431-468.

Design-Based Research Collective. (2003). Design-based research: An emerging paradigm for educational inquiry. *Educational Researcher*, 32(1), 5-8.

Goldstein, J., & Puntambekar, S. (Accepted). The brink of change: Gender in technology-rich collaborative learning environments. *Journal of research in science and technology*.

Hoffman, J. L., Wu, H.-K., Krajcik, J. S., & Soloway, E. (2003). The nature of middle school learners' science content understandings with the use of on-line resources. *Journal of Research in Science Teaching, 40*(3), 323-346.

Kafai, Y. B. (1994). *Minds in play: Computer game design as a context for children's learning*. Hillsdale, NJ: Lawrence Erlbaum Associates.

Kintsch, W. (1998). *Comprehension*. Cambridge University Press: Cambridge.

Kolodner, J. L., Crismond, D., Fasse, B., Gray, J., Holbrook, J., & Puntambekar, S. (2003). Putting a student-centered learning by design™ curriculum into practice: Lessons learned. *Journal of the Learning Sciences,* 12(4), 485-547.

Krajcik, J. S., Blumenfeld, P. C., Marx, R. W., & Soloway, E. (1991). A collaborative model for helping middle grade science teachers learn project-based instruction. *The elementary school journal,* 94(5), 483-497.

Lagemann, E. C. (2002, January 24). *Useable knowledge in education: A memorandum for the Spencer foundation board of directors* [Memorandum]. Chicago: Spencer foundation. Retrieved from http://www.spencer.org/publications/useable_knowledge_report_ecl_a.htm.

Palincsar, A. S., & Magnusson, S. J. (2001). The interplay of first-hand and second-hand investigations to model and support the development of scientific knowledge and reasoning. In D. K. S. Carver (Ed.), *Cognition and instruction: Twenty-five years of progress*. Mahwah, NJ: Lawrence Erlbaum Associates.

Puntambekar, S., & Stylianou, A. (2005). Designing navigation support in hypertext systems based on navigation patterns. *Instructional Science*, 33, 5-6.

Puntambekar, S., Stylianou, A., & Goldstein, J., (Accepted). Analyzing classroom discourse for deep conceptual understanding: Lessons learned from two teachers. *Journal of the Learning Sciences*.

Puntambekar, S., Stylianou, A., & Hübscher, R. (2003). Improving navigation and learning in hypertext environments with navigable concept maps. *Human Computer Interaction, 18*(4), 395-426.

Raloff, J. (2001). Errant texts: Why some schools may not want to go by the book. *Science News, 159*(11).

Schvaneveldt, R. W. (1990). *Pathfinder associative networks: Studies in knowledge organization*. Norwood, NJ: Ablex.

Shavelson, R.J., Phillips, D.C., Towne, L., Feuer, M.J. (2003). On the science of education design studies. *Educational Researcher*, 32(1), 25-28.

Stylianou, A. (2003). How do students navigate and learn from nonlinear science texts? Can metanavigation support help? Unpublished doctoral dissertation, University of Connecticut.

Stylianou, A., & Puntambekar, S. (2003). Does metacognitive awareness of reading strategies relate to the way middle school students navigate and learn from hypertext? Paper presented at the annual conference of the Northeast Educational Research Association.

Stylianou, A., & Puntambekar, S. (2004). Supporting Middle School Students Use Nonlinear Science Texts in an Inquiry Classroom. In Y. Kafai, W. A. Sandoval, N. Enyedy, S. A. Nixon, F. Herrera (Eds.), *Embracing diversity on the learning sciences, Proceedings of the sixth international conference of the learning sciences.* pp. 529-536. Mahwah, NJ: Erlbaum.

Acknowledgements

The research described in this paper is supported by an early CAREER grant (#9985158) from the National Science Foundation. Current research is supported by NSF grant #0437660 (IERI) and #0434624 (NSDL).

Estimation as a Catalyst for Numeracy: Micro-Interventions that Increase the Use of Numerical Information in Decision-Making

Luke F. Rinne, Michael A. Ranney
Graduate School of Education, University of California, Berkeley, 4533 Tolman Hall, Berkeley, CA, 94720-1670
Nicholas H. Lurie
College of Management, Georgia Institute of Technology, 800 West Peachtree St. NW, Atlanta, GA, 30308-0520
Email: lrinne@berkeley.edu, ranney@berkeley.edu, lurie@gatech.edu

Abstract: The utilization of available numerical information represents an important aspect of numeracy. Accordingly, we seek to develop decision-making scaffolds that increase the incorporation of numerical information into preferences. Two experiments contrast five techniques for presenting students with numerical information and prompting them to make decisions related to that information. The techniques are based on a method called EPIC (Estimate, Prefer, Incorporate feedback, and Change preference) from the Numerically-Driven Inferencing (NDI) paradigm. Results regarding post-feedback preferences indicate that having students estimate a quantity's value beforehand increases the impact on preferences when the quantity's true value is presented. However, having students state initial preferences does not yield an analogous effect. An attractive explanation for the estimation effect is that estimating diminishes hindsight bias, making information that diverges from expectations more surprising. Variants of the EPIC method may serve as "micro-interventions" that increase the impact of numerical data on preferences.

Introduction

People often fail to fully utilize available numerical information when making decisions (e.g., Bartol, Koehl, & Martin, 1987). The utilization of numerical information may be seen as an aspect of "numeracy," an idea that has been advanced most famously by Paulos (1990) as a parallel in the quantitative realm for what is termed literacy in the verbal realm. Paulos shows how innumeracy often leads to poor decisions by consumers, employees, and citizens. He believes the main cause of innumeracy to be a general lack of mathematical ability, and indeed, in the cases he describes, the best remedy may be to improve people's understanding of mathematical concepts. However, Viswanathan (1993) argues that the notion of numeracy should include not only one's *ability* to use numerical information, but also one's *proclivity* toward using numerical information. That is, he holds that two individuals with comparable mathematical abilities may often differ in the extent to which they use the numbers they have learned to help them make decisions. Viswanathan supported this claim with several studies demonstrating the validity of a measure he developed called "Preference for Numerical Information" (PNI), which is meant to capture individual differences regarding that aspect of numeracy that is not subsumed by mathematical ability.

We embrace Viswanathan's (1993) broader notion of numeracy—according to which the use of numerical information is thought to depend on more than mathematical competence. Consequently, we believe that it may be possible to increase students' use of numerical information in decision-making by means other than improving their mathematics skills. In this paper, we argue that this can be achieved through "micro-interventions" based on methods from the Numerically-Driven Inferencing (NDI) paradigm (e.g., Munnich, Ranney, & Appel, 2004; Munnich, Ranney, Nelson, Garcia de Osuna, & Brazil, 2003; Ranney, Cheng, Garcia de Osuna, & Nelson, 2001). By "micro-interventions," we mean brief activities conducted by teachers in which the presentation of numerical information is preceded and/or followed by particular exercises that scaffold students' decision-making procedures.

Work on preference formation in behavioral decision research supports the promise of a "micro-intervention" approach. Several decision theorists have argued that preferences—which are taken to be what cause individuals to choose in particular ways—should not necessarily be seen as previously-existing, stable features. Rather, in novel situations, preferences are better conceived of as "constructed" in the process of elicitation based on the accessibility of various pieces of information and the ease with which information may be evaluated (Hoeffler & Ariely, 1999; Hsee, 1996; Payne, Bettman, & Johnson, 1992; Slovic, 1995). This contradicts neoclassical economic theory, which assumes that decisions do not depend on the processes through which they are made and that individuals' preferences are simply "revealed" by their decisions (Rabin, 1998). On the constructed preference view, however, prompts for novel decisions do more than simply tap existing preferences; rather, the need to make a novel decision often leads to preferences being formed in the first place. Further, because the prompt itself serves as an additional source of information for the decision-maker, its format may significantly influence the preference that is constructed. This has important consequences, because once preferences in particular domains have been constructed, they may be retained in memory and influence subsequent decisions in the same—or related—domains.

Following the constructed preferences view, it seems likely that when one receives numerical information in a domain with which one has little experience, that information's influence on preferences will be heightened if one is prompted to make a relevant decision right after receiving the information. One will construct a preference in order to reach a decision, and at this stage the numerical information provided will still be highly salient, increasing its incorporation into the preference formation process relative to what would have occurred had much time (e.g., months or years) elapsed between the receipt of information and the first instance in which one was prompted to make a decision for which the information would be relevant. Thus, given that our goal is to increase the impact of numerical information on preferences, it seems clear that our micro-interventions should include prompts for decisions given soon after numerical information is presented. But how else might it be possible to increase the impact of presenting numbers to students? In this study, we investigate whether certain NDI methods—specifically, those that include prompts for estimates and/or initial preferences *before* numerical data are presented—may *further* increase the influence of numerical information. For this purpose, post-feedback decisions, in addition to being part of the intervention, provide a measure of such potential effects.

It will be helpful to review prior research in the NDI paradigm at this point. An initial goal of NDI research was to assess how views on social issues (e.g., abortion or immigration policy) are influenced by relevant pieces of numerical information (e.g., rates of abortion or immigration). To this end, a method called EPIC was developed, which involves prompting people to: 1) **E**stimate the value of a quantity, 2) state a **P**reference related to that quantity, 3) **I**ncorporate feedback in the form of the estimated quantity's true value, and 4) **C**hange their preference (if they wish) in response to this feedback. The EPIC method allows for assessments both of prior beliefs and of the influence of numerical feedback on preferences. Early NDI experiments showed that offering a single, surprising numerical datum can indeed greatly influence preferences, and that changes between initial and final preferences increase with estimate inaccuracy (Garcia de Osuna et al., 2004; Munnich et al., 2003; Ranney et al., 2001).

Recently, Lurie and Ranney (submitted) conducted NDI experiments to study the impact of estimation on preferences and preference change. Preferences elicited using the EPIC method were compared to those obtained using two variants—called PEIC and IC—in which, respectively, the first two steps, **E**stimate and **P**refer, were either reversed in order or left out altogether. (Although no initial preferences were elicited in the IC condition, "C" for "Change preference" is retained for simplicity.) Each group used one of the three procedures—EPIC, PEIC, or IC—throughout, so that the preferences produced by each could be contrasted. In one experiment, estimates and feedback were for the number of mortalities per 100,000 deaths for each of a pair of diseases: either (a) lung cancer and skin cancer, or (b) heart disease and breast cancer (among women only for the latter pair). Preferences were elicited by asking students how they would divide $100 in research funding between prevention efforts for the two diseases in each pair (funds were dedicated to women only for both heart disease and breast cancer). By estimating mortality rates for each disease in a pair, students implicitly estimated the *ratio* of mortalities from one disease to mortalities from the other disease. It was thought that prior beliefs about these ratios would affect preferences for $100 splits, and that in some cases, but not others, these beliefs would deviate considerably from the true values later provided as feedback. The true values—based on Centers for Disease Control and Prevention ("CDC") statistics from 2001—are 8.2:1 and 20.9:1, respectively, for heart disease/breast cancer and lung cancer/skin cancer. While the true ratio for the heart disease/breast cancer pair is 3.2 times higher than the average estimate of 2.6:1, the true ratio for the lung cancer/skin cancer pair is only 1.3 times higher than the average estimate of 15.6:1.

When participants decided on initial allocations before performing any other activities (as in the PEIC condition), they allocated an average of $44.92 for heart disease (vs. breast cancer) and $48.04 for lung cancer (vs. skin cancer). However, when participants estimated mortality rates before stating initial preferences (as in the EPIC condition), average allocations for heart disease were lower—$38.40—while average lung cancer allocations were higher—$57.34. The conclusion was that estimating mortality rates increased the extent to which participants based their decisions on their prior beliefs about mortality ratios, instead of on other reasons (e.g., family members having a disease, concerns about personal responsibility for getting a disease) that would have motivated higher allocations for heart disease and skin cancer. Because estimates of mortality ratios for the lung cancer/skin cancer pair were relatively accurate, EPIC participants' initial preferences (M = $57.34) were closer than PEIC participants' initial preferences (M = \$48.04) to IC participants' preferences (M = \$59.93), which were elicited after simply giving participants the true mortality rate data. Because mortality ratio estimates for the heart disease/breast cancer pair were relatively inaccurate, in this case the effect was reversed; EPIC participants' initial preferences (M = \$38.40) were further away from IC participants' preferences (M = \$55.14) than were PEIC initial preferences (M = \$44.92).

As for final allocations, Lurie and Ranney (submitted) found that in both the EPIC and PEIC conditions, change between initial and final preferences was greater when estimates were inaccurate; the conclusion here was that preference change was driven by how "shocking" the information received was. Interestingly, although differences between groups regarding *post*-feedback allocations were not predicted, such differences emerged nonetheless. Mean post-feedback allocations for the bigger killer in each pair were higher in both the EPIC and PEIC conditions than in the IC condition (lung cancer: $M_{EPIC/PEIC}$ = \$67.54 vs. M_{IC} = \$57.08; heart disease: $M_{EPIC/PEIC}$ = \$64.62 vs. M_{IC} = \$54.68). Because their study was rather tangential to issues of information utilization, Lurie and Ranney did not scrutinize this result. However, such results are critical in the context of our current investigation; it seems that estimating and/or stating initial preferences *before* receiving feedback may have increased the influence of mortality rates *after* students learned the true values. We hypothesized that one of these activities (or perhaps the combination of the two) increased the influence of the actual values on final allocations. This spawned the idea that we might develop instructional techniques involving these activities with the aim of increasing students' incorporation of newly received numerical information into their preferences—beyond what can be achieved by prompting for decisions after information is presented. The present study represents the fruition of this idea.

The remainder of this paper will proceed as follows: First, we present our hypotheses. Second, we present new analyses of data from the aforementioned experiment by Lurie and Ranney (submitted), including some data they collected but did not use—students' written reasons explaining their preferences. Third, we present the results of a new experiment we conducted in order to 1) replicate Lurie and Ranney's results, and 2) tease apart estimation and initial preference effects. The fourth section offers a general discussion, including a proposed explanation of our findings. Finally, we suggest educational implications and directions for future research.

Hypotheses

Hypothesis 1 is that post-feedback allocations to the disease in each pair that kills more people will be significantly higher for EPIC and PEIC students than for IC students. Hypothesis 2 is that such results are due to the increased utilization of numerical information. This can be expressed in terms of two sub-hypotheses, such that support for both would demonstrate support for Hypothesis 2: The first (2a) is that written rationales provided by students in the EPIC and PEIC conditions will cite the mortality rate information provided as explaining their final allocations more frequently than will students in the IC condition. The second sub-hypothesis (2b) is that students who cite mortality rate information as explaining their final allocations will allocate more money to the bigger killer in each pair than will students who do not cite mortality rate information as explaining their allocations. In short, if both of these sub-hypotheses were supported, this would indicate that effects of estimation and/or initial allocation on final allocations are linked to the presence of written rationales that cite the numerical information provided as a reason for the final allocation decision. Hypotheses 1 and 2 are addressed in Experiment 1.

The next three hypotheses correspond to alternative explanations for why post-feedback preferences for the disease in each pair that kills more people might be higher in the EPIC and PEIC conditions than in the IC condition. The first possibility is that (a) there is an independent effect of estimation that increases final allocations, but no similar effect for stating initial preferences. The second possibility is the reverse: (b) there is an independent effect of stating initial preferences that increases final allocations, but no similar effect for estimation. Finally, the third possibility is that (c) increases in final allocations arise due to a joint effect of estimating and stating initial preferences, which means that one or both of the following are true: 1) there are independent, additive, estimation and initial preference effects, both of which increase final allocations, or 2) there is an interaction between estimating and stating initial preferences that increases final allocations. Although these hypotheses do not exhaust all possibilities (e.g., there could be effects of the length of the procedure, the order of estimation and initial preference, etc.), each of these options is mutually exclusive of the others, and each, if manifested, seems unlikely to be confounded with other possible effects. These hypotheses, which will be referred to as the "estimate effect," "initial preference effect," and "joint effect" hypotheses, are addressed in Experiment 2.

Experiment 1

Method

Undergraduates (N = 208) were randomly assigned to one of three groups: EPIC, PEIC, or IC. EPIC participants first estimated the annual number of mortalities, per 100,000 deaths, for each of a pair of diseases, either a) lung cancer and skin cancer, or b) heart disease and breast cancer. After estimating, participants were asked to state how they would prefer that $100 be divided between respective efforts for prevention of the two diseases, and to provide a written reason explaining their preferred allocation. Participants were instructed that estimates for the heart disease/breast cancer pair were to be restricted to the female population, and that all funds allocated for heart disease or breast cancer would be devoted exclusively to prevention among women. Lung cancer and skin cancer prompts were not gender specific. Next, participants received true mortality rates from the CDC for each disease in the pair, also per 100,000 deaths (nb. female deaths for the heart disease/breast cancer pair). After learning the true rates, participants were again asked to divide $100 between respective prevention efforts and to provide a written reason explaining their allocation. This procedure was then repeated for the second disease pair. Both the order in which the pairs were presented and the order of the diseases within each pair were counterbalanced. For PEIC participants, the first two steps of the EPIC procedure were reversed in order, and for IC participants, they were left out altogether. Apart from these changes, the procedures for the PEIC and IC groups were the same as for the EPIC group. The experiment also involved data collection and another manipulation that are not relevant here (see Lurie & Ranney, submitted, for details). There is no indication that these affected the data analyzed in this study.

Written reasons for final preferences were coded to identify instances in which students indicated that mortality rates for either disease in a given pair helped to explain their final allocations. These were coded as "numerical" (NUM), although they may have been attended by reasons of other types as well. Responses of other types were coded "non-numerical" (NON). Cases in which no rationale was given (< 10%) were excluded.

Results

Preferences for $100 splits are given in terms of the disease in each pair that kills more people. EPIC and PEIC students were pooled together to increase statistical power. Planned comparisons assessed Hypothesis 1; final allocations from the pooled group of EPIC and PEIC students were significantly higher than those from the IC group for lung cancer (M_{EPIC} = \$69.72 & M_{PEIC} = \$63.98, vs. M_{IC} = \$57.08), $t(183) = 2.617$, $p < .01$ and heart disease (M_{EPIC} = \$67.93 & M_{PEIC} = \$60.66 vs. M_{IC} = \$54.68), $t(195) = 2.979$, $p < .01$.

To analyze the effect of both estimating and stating initial preferences on the use of numerical reasons for final allocations (Hypothesis 2a), EPIC and PEIC responses were again pooled together and compared to IC responses (see Table 1). Note that because of this pooling, the null hypothesis predicts that within each column, the EPIC/PEIC cell count will be roughly twice the IC cell count. NUM/NON percentages are given only to aid the reader. Chi-Square tests indicate significant positive associations between membership in the EPIC/PEIC group (vs. the IC group) and the use of numerical reasons (vs. non-numerical reasons) for both disease pairs: lung cancer/skin cancer, $\chi^2(1) = 3.96, p < .05$, and heart disease/breast cancer, $\chi^2(1) = 5.67, p < .05$.

Table 1. Counts of Reason-Types for Final Allocations (C)—by Group, Disease Pair, and Rationale Type

	Lung Cancer/Skin Cancer		Heart Disease/Breast Cancer	
	NUM	NON	NUM	NON
EPIC/PEIC	79 (64%)	44 (36%)	85 (71%)	35 (29%)
IC	32 (49%)	33 (51%)	37 (54%)	32 (46%)

But did participants who gave numerical reasons ultimately allocate more money during the final preference phase for research on diseases that kill more people (Hypothesis 2b)? Since different groups gave numerical reasons at different rates, within-group analyses were conducted to control for effects of experimental group that may not have been captured by the mere presence or absence of a particular type of written reason (see Table 2). Within each disease pair/condition, stating a numerical reason was indeed significantly related to allocating more money to the bigger killer (lung cancer: EPIC—M_{NUM} = \$76.86, M_{NON} = \$59.14, $t(70) = 3.979$, $p < .01$, PEIC—M_{NUM} = \$77.76, M_{NON} = \$43.68, $t(46) = 6.684$, $p < .01$, and IC—M_{NUM} = \$69.70, M_{NON} = \$44.06, $t(63) = 4.146$, $p < .01$; heart disease: EPIC—M_{NUM} =\$75.04, M_{NON} = \$49.21, $t(67) = 5.904$, $p < .01$, PEIC—M_{NUM} = \$68.14, M_{NON} = \$50.00, $t(57) = 3.682$, $p < .01$, IC—M_{NUM} = \$68.69, M_{NON} = \$38.91, $t(66) = 6.406$, $p < .01$).

Table 2. Mean Final Allocations (C), by Group, Disease Pair, and Rationale Type

	Lung Cancer (vs. Skin Cancer)		Heart Disease (vs. Breast Cancer)	
	NUM	NON	NUM	NON
EPIC	$76.86	$59.14	$75.04	$49.21
PEIC	$77.76	$43.68	$68.14	$50.00
IC	$69.70	$44.06	$68.69	$38.91

Note that average lung cancer and heart disease final allocations for students giving non-numerical reasons were sometimes strikingly low, particularly considering that these diseases kill many more people than do the diseases they were paired with. Written rationales indicate that lower final preferences for the bigger killer often stem from concerns about tragedy (e.g., breast cancer) or culpability for contracting the disease (e.g., lung cancer).

Discussion

Results from Experiment 1 indicate: 1) the robustness of the effect that estimating and stating initial preferences has on final allocations for the bigger killer in each pair (Hypothesis 1), and 2) that this effect appears to occur due to an increased emphasis on the numerical information provided (Hypothesis 2). However, the results of this experiment offer little help in explaining *why* estimating and stating initial preferences increased students' utilization of the numerical information they received. Because both estimates and initial preferences were elicited in both the EPIC and PEIC conditions, it is unclear whether estimating, stating initial preferences, or some joint effect of doing both produced the differences that were observed. Our next experiment was designed to clarify matters by separating the effects of estimating and stating initial preferences from one another, as well as from potential joint effects. Experiment 2 also served to replicate some of the effects that had been observed to date.

Experiment 2

Method

In order to discriminate among the "estimate effect," "initial preference effect," and "joint effect" hypotheses, we created two new NDI methods, EIC and PIC, which exclude the initial preference and estimation phases, respectively. Thus, we may separate estimation and initial preference effects from one another and from effects of combining the two. Undergraduates (N = 153) were randomly assigned to one of five groups: EPIC, PEIC, EIC, PIC, or IC. Apart from the addition of the EIC and PIC groups, the design, materials, and prompts at each stage (Estimate, Prefer, Incorporate feedback, and Change preference) were the same as in Experiment 1.

Results

If the "estimation effect" hypothesis were true, then one would expect EPIC, PEIC, and EIC students' final allocations for the bigger killer in each pair to be higher than those of PIC and IC students. Alternatively, if the "initial preference effect" hypothesis were true, one would expect EPIC, PEIC, and PIC students' final allocations for the bigger killers to be higher than those of EIC and IC students. Finally, if the "joint effect" hypothesis were true, one would expect EPIC and PEIC students' final allocations for the bigger killer in each pair to be higher than those of EIC, PIC, and IC students. Note that these three alternatives are mutually exclusive.

Generally, this experiment produced significant results that adjudicate among the alternative hypotheses for the heart disease/breast cancer pair, but not for the lung cancer/skin cancer pair. Likely reasons for this are given in the discussion below. Consequently, due to space limitations, only results for the heart disease/breast cancer pair are discussed here. For this pair, however, we see strong evidence for the presence of an estimation effect, and no evidence for other effects (see Table 3 below). Planned comparisons were conducted to test each of the alternative hypotheses. One-tailed tests of the contrasts corresponding to the joint effect and initial preference effect hypotheses were not significant (joint effect: $t(148) = -1.264$, *n.s.*; initial preference effect: $t(148) = -.014$, *n.s.*), while a one-tailed test of the contrast corresponding to the estimation effect hypothesis was significant, $t(148) = -2.378$, $p < .01$.

Table 3. Mean Final Allocations (C) to Heart Disease, by Group

	EPIC	PEIC	EIC	PIC	IC
Mean	$65.48	$63.28	$66.45	$56.17	$56.94

Discussion

The results for the heart disease/breast cancer pair provide strong evidence of an estimation effect, while no evidence was found for either an initial preference effect or a joint effect. Although no significant results were observed for the lung cancer/skin cancer pair, we believe that this may have been due to insufficient statistical power; effect size calculations showed that in Experiment 1, the effect of estimation on final allocations for the lung cancer/skin cancer pair, while still significant, was somewhat smaller than that for the heart disease/breast cancer pair—exacerbating the fact that the number of participants per condition in Experiment 2 was less than half of that in Experiment 1. The effect for the lung cancer/skin cancer pair might be smaller for multiple reasons. First, final allocations for the lung cancer/skin cancer pair appear to have been more variable, perhaps because concerns about responsibility were more influential. Second, as discussed in the next section when we present our explanation for the estimation effect, the size of the effect may well depend on the "surprisingness" of the numerical information presented. Recall that we mentioned earlier that students' estimates for the lung cancer/skin cancer pair were considerably more accurate than their estimates for the heart disease/breast cancer pair. It could be that estimates of the lung cancer/skin cancer mortality ratio were too accurate for an effect to be observed with the sample size used.

General Discussion

This paper's main experimental finding is that estimating the values of quantities before learning their true values increases the influence of the true values on preferences. Why might this be the case? An attractive explanation involves a form of overconfidence called "hindsight bias," which is "the tendency for people with outcome knowledge to believe falsely that they would have predicted the outcome of the event" (Hawkins and Hastie, 1990, p.311). It seems likely that hindsight bias would manifest itself when people are simply given a quantity's value; they will likely tend to believe that, had they estimated the value of the quantity beforehand, their estimate would have been more accurate than would really have been the case. But if one estimates before learning the true value, the potential for hindsight bias becomes greatly diminished or fully eliminated, since one's "cards are on the table," so to speak. This means that, to the extent that estimates of a quantity's value *would, if elicited,* diverge from the quantity's true value, the act of estimating will make the true value of the quantity more surprising.

It seems likely that more surprising information (assuming it is seen as reliable) will have greater influence during preference formation than more mundane information—perhaps for no other reason than that people attend more to surprising information, making it more salient. If inaccurately estimating a quantity's value makes learning the true value more surprising, this may explain why the final allocations of students in groups who estimated mortality rates (EPIC, PEIC, and EIC) were higher than those of students in groups who did not (IC and PIC); students who estimated were more surprised when they learned the true mortality rates, likely causing them to place more weight on mortality ratios. This explanation coheres with and helps account for past NDI findings showing larger differences between estimates and true values to be linked to larger differences between initial and final preferences (Garcia de Osuna et al., 2004; Lurie & Ranney, submitted; Munnich et al., 2003; Ranney et al., 2001).

Educational Implications and Future Directions

If one's goal is to maximize students' utilization of numerical information (although we realize that this may not always be appropriate), then "micro-interventions" based on NDI methods as simple as EIC may offer the best means currently known. One domain in which micro-interventions might be particularly useful is the study of "current events." Students might estimate the values of socially relevant quantities, receive true statistics, and then decide which public policies they think ought to be pursued. Similar applications abound elsewhere, as well.

Although it does not appear that stating initial preferences increases the utilization of numerical information, more research involving NDI methods like EPIC and PEIC is required. First of all, there may be pedagogical, motivation-related, reasons to include initial preferences, such as to increase student engagement. Second, results from pilot experiments show that when people rate NDI procedures in terms of the quality of the decisions they would expect them to yield, procedures that include both estimating and stating initial preferences are generally rated highest. Finally, results from a recent study involving the EPIC method—a study that showed post-feedback preferences to persist several months later—also showed that students' memories of numerical feedback seem to be linked to their memories for how their preferences *changed* in response to feedback (Munnich, Ranney, & Bachman, 2005). In order for such an effect to occur, it may be that students would need to explicitly state initial preferences. Thus, micro-interventions that include prompts for initial preferences may yet prove to be quite useful.

The research presented herein shows that merely providing statistics to students without engaging their expectations—or offering potential applications—is metaphorically like dropping seeds onto unplowed earth. This is reminiscent of science education research on Predict-Observe-Explain activities (White & Gunstone, 1992). In practice, our micro-interventions for increasing the impact of numerical information may be seen as analogous to Ausubel's (1960) "advance organizers" for learning verbal material. Ultimately, we hope that the techniques we suggest will help people incorporate numerical information into their preferences, leading to better decisions.

References

Ausubel, D. P. (1960). The use of advance organizers in the learning and retention of meaningful verbal material. *Journal of Educational Psychology, 51,* 267-272.

Bartol, K., Koehl, D., & Martin, D. (1987). Quantitative versus qualitative information utilization among college business students. *Educational and Psychological Research, 7*(1), 61-74.

Garcia de Osuna, J., Ranney, M., & Nelson, J. (2004). Qualitative and quantitative effects of surprise: (Mis)estimates, rationales, and feedback-induced preference changes while considering abortion. In K. Forbus, D. Gentner, & T. Regier (Eds.). *Proceedings of the Twenty-sixth Annual Conference of the Cognitive Science Society* (pp. 422-427). Mahwah, NJ: Erlbaum.

Hawkins, S. & Hastie, R. (1990). Hindsight: biased judgments of past events after the outcomes are known. *Psychological Bulletin, 107*(3), 311-327.

Hoeffler, S. & Ariely, D. (1999). Constructing stable preferences: A look into dimensions of experience and their impact on preference stability. *Journal of Consumer Psychology, 8*(2), 113-139.

Hsee, C. K. (1996). The evaluability hypothesis: An explanation for preference reversals between joint and separate evaluations of alternatives. *Organizational Behavior and Human Decision Processes, 67*(3), 247-257.

Lurie, N., & Ranney, M. (submitted). *The Effects of Estimates and Base Rates on Preferences and Preference Change: How Thinking About What Is Can Change What One Wants.* University of North Carolina, Chapel Hill, and University of California, Berkeley.

Munnich, E. L., Ranney, M. A., & Appel, D. M. (2004). Numerically-Driven Inferencing in instruction: The relatively broad transfer of estimation skills. In K. Forbus, D. Gentner, & T. Regier (Eds.). *Proceedings of the Twenty-sixth Annual Conference of the Cognitive Science Society* (pp. 987-992). Mahwah, NJ: Erlbaum.

Munnich, E., Ranney, M., & Bachman, M. L. N. (2005). The longevities of policy-shifts and memories due to single feedback numbers. In B.G. Bara, L. Barsalou, & M. Bucciarelli (Eds.) *Proceedings of the Twenty-seventh Annual Conference of the Cognitive Science Society* (pp. 1553-1558). Mahwah, NJ: Erlbaum.

Munnich, E., Ranney, M., Nelson, J., Garcia de Osuna, J., & Brazil, N. (2003). Policy shift through Numerically-Driven Inferencing: An EPIC experiment about when base rates matter. In R. Alterman & D. Kirsh (Eds.), *Proceedings of the Twenty-Fifth Annual Conference of the Cognitive Science Society* (pp. 834-839). Mahwah, NJ: Erlbaum.

Paulos, J. A. (1988). *Innumeracy: Mathematical illiteracy and its consequences.* New York: Hill & Wang.

Payne, J. W., Bettman, J. R., & Johnson, E. J. (1992). Behavioral decision research: A constructive processing perspective. *Annual Review of Psychology, 43,* 87-131.

Rabin, M. (1998). Psychology and economics. *Journal of Economic Literature 36*(1), 11-46.

Ranney, M., Cheng, F., Garcia de Osuna, J., & Nelson, J. (2001, November). *Numerically driven inferencing: A new paradigm for examining judgments, decisions, and policies involving base rates.* Paper presented at the Annual Meeting of the Society for Judgment & Decision-making, Orlando.

Slovic, P. (1995). The construction of preference. *American Psychologist, 50,* 364–371.

Viswanathan, M. (1993). Measurement of individual differences in preference for numerical information. *Journal of Applied Psychology, 78*(5), 741-752.

White, R. T., & Gunstone, R. F. (1992). *Probing Understanding.* Great Britain: Falmer Press.

Acknowledgments

We thank Christine Diehl, Patti Schank, and Geoff Saxe for their help and advice. We also thank Ed Munnich, Sujata Ganpule, Janek Nelson, Michelle Million, Kelvin Chan, Jed Stamas, Sarah Cremer, Sasha Raskin, Myles Crain, Nelson Bradley, Lauren Barth-Cohen, Andrew Galpern, Tammie Chen, Roxanne Garbez, the rest of the UCB Reasoning Group, and the ICBS faculty for their comments and suggestions. Comments and suggestions from three anonymous reviewers were also appreciated. This work was funded by faculty research grants from UCB and the University of North Carolina, Chapel Hill, and various fellowships from UCB and its GSE.

Using Transformative Research To Explore Congruencies Between Science Reform and Urban Schools

Ann E. Rivet, Teachers College Columbia University, 525 W. 120th St., New York, NY 10027, rivet@tc.columbia.edu

Abstract: The Urban Science Education Center at Teachers College, Columbia University is attempting to inform how science reforms are introduced to urban middle school classrooms. In our work we are exploring three levels of congruency necessary in order for new innovations to result in sustained reform in individual school settings. To explore these congruencies we use the framework of transformative research, which is research that while focused on generating new ideas also works to "transform" or improve the teaching and learning of science. This paper describes our collaboration with one public middle school in New York City, using the concepts of congruencies to frame our efforts with the school as we collaboratively developed a project-based school-wide science curriculum plan. Through this process we learned both about ways to consider innovative reforms in relation to this school setting, and more general characteristics of conducting transformative research with urban schools.

Introduction

Many recent science education reform programs have demonstrated success in a variety of educational settings, including urban schools (i.e., Rivet & Krajcik, 2004a; Songer, Lee, & McDonald, 2003). However, little systematic work has been done to explore the process of bringing reform-based science curriculum materials to new learning environments, and to document the ways in which urban teachers enact these materials and adapt them to meet the needs of their differing urban classrooms. These issues are critical for learning how to leverage the best of new science education reforms and bring sustainable change to scale, particularly in urban settings where they are most needed.

The Urban Science Education Center at Teachers College, Columbia University is attempting to change the way science reforms are introduced to urban middle school classrooms. We believe that in order for effective reform to take root, we need to not only capitalize on existing innovative reform programs, approaches and resources for teaching science, but we also need to identify and work with each school's specific goals and needs, while at the same time recognizing and building from the similarities that urban schools share. We describe our approach to research and science education reform through the framework of *transformative research*. Our goals are to learn from the urban classrooms in which we work while also attempting to initiate change and innovation in the school's science program. This is accomplished through developing collaborative partnerships with teachers and the school leadership, and exploring teachers' and students' efforts to think about and engage with science in new ways.

We have partnered with several New York City middle schools to explore these issues in high-poverty neighborhoods such as Harlem, Morningside Heights, and the Bronx. Through our partnerships we are exploring three levels of congruency necessary in order for new innovations to result in sustained reform in individual school settings. First is the congruency between the vision of the innovation and the goals of the teachers and/or school, both in terms of content coverage and pedagogical approach. Second is the congruency between the supports offered in the innovation and the needs and resources of the classroom teachers. Third is the congruency between the contextualization of the innovation with students' experiences and prior knowledge they bring to the learning setting. We believe that the curricular innovation must work at each of these three levels in order for sustained reform to take hold. Achieving congruency at each of these three levels, however, involves an active process of adaptation and development of school ownership with the innovation.

The paper begins with a discussion detailing the three levels of congruency we explored as part of our work with schools to adapt new science innovations, as well as our framework of transformative research which guided our efforts. We then describe in detail our work with the administration, teachers, and students in one of our partner schools, PSW (1) to illustrate how we used the lens transformative research to inform and shape the nature of the reform adaptation process with the school. In our work with PSW we attempt to both identify and work with the school's specific goals and needs, while at the same time recognize and build from the similarities that PSW shares with other urban schools. This process of moving between the specifics of the local setting and the generalities of urban school reform enabled us to reflect upon the congruency of our reform efforts at each of these three levels.

Theoretical Underpinnings

Research describes many of the general challenges facing urban schools in their attempts to reform their science education programs, including overcrowded classrooms, under-prepared teachers, and lack of resources (Goetz, Floden, & O'Day, 1995). However, there is also much variation among individual schools within a given district or urban area. Each school has its own dynamic character and vision for educating its students. These differences arise from the unique personalities that constitute the school culture, including its leadership and administration, teachers, and students, as well as the community and environment in which the school is situated (Tyack & Cuban, 1995). Yet in this era of standardizations and accountability, often all urban schools are painted with the same brush, and assumed that they have the same deficiencies and same needs. This is also true for attempts to reform the teaching and learning of science in urban schools. In order to have the greatest impact and meet as many needs as possible, often reforms address the needs of 'typical' urban schools or try to be as general as possible (Fishman & Krajcik, 2003).

Rather than focus on the adoption of reform-based innovations and the fidelity of program implementation (Cho, 1998; Dede, 2000), designers and researcher are beginning to recognize that innovations must be adapted to fit within the social and instructional contexts into which they are enacted (Fishman et al., 2003), and local conditions likewise adapted to fit the innovation in order for them to succeed in new classroom settings (Ball & Cohen, 1996; McLaughlin, 1990). Similar to the framework for systemic reform described by Blumenfeld and colleagues (2000), we view this mutual adaptation process in terms of three levels of congruency necessary in order for new innovations to result in sustained reform in a particular school setting. The first is congruency between the vision of the innovation and the goals of the teachers and/or school, both in terms of content coverage and pedagogical approach. Second is congruency between the supports offered in the innovation and the needs and resources of classroom teachers. Third is congruency between the contextualization of the innovation with students' experiences and prior knowledge they bring to the learning setting.

Congruency between the vision of the innovation and the goals of the teachers and/or school: Every science education reform program, whether it is a curriculum, a pedagogical approach, or an innovative tool or piece of technology, had its own inherent vision for how science should be experienced by students in order to facilitate learning. Informing this vision is a set of assumptions about both the nature of science and about how people learn. These assumptions are used to define success in both the design and enactment of the innovation. School leaders, including administrators and teachers, also have their own ideas of what it means to teach and learn science and how success is defined in these areas. When there is congruency between the innovation and the school leadership around these ideas, it is easier for the school to adapt the innovation to their setting and a greater likelihood that the reform will be successful (Blumenfeld et al., 2000). However, the vision and underlying assumptions are not always clearly articulated, nor understood by those in the classroom and school settings who are adapting the innovation. Likewise, school administrators and teachers do not always recognize or articulate their own assumptions for learning and teaching science. Unawareness of discrepancies between the innovation and the school leadership in this area can lead to obstacles and roadblocks towards the successful adaptation of new reform programs.

Congruency between the supports offered in the innovation and the needs and resources of the classroom teacher: Urban schools range widely in the resources they have available to support student learning. Likewise, there is also a range of teachers' familiarity and comfort level with the science content, pedagogical support, and use of tools called for in a given innovation. If new innovations are to be successful, they need to provide sufficient support and information in order to allow their programs to be usable by a wide variety of teachers. This is especially true given that new programs often push the boundaries in terms of the types of opportunities students are given to engage in science and the use of new technology tools. The new tools and teaching methods to support these approaches can be demanding, and in some cases overwhelming, to even experienced teachers in the classroom. A direct response to these challenges would be to provide teachers with extensive support, including content and pedagogical resources, samples of variations and adaptations of lessons, models of classroom dialogue, etc. The catch, however, is that providing teachers with sufficient support and resources can quickly become unwieldy. There needs to be a careful balance struck between the providing the necessary information, hints, models, suggestions, and alternatives to help teachers enact the reform, but not too much of this support as to overwhelm them. Too much support can cloud the intent of the intervention itself, and *why* something should be done gets lost in *how* it can get done. However, too little support, whether in the form of materials, tools, or information, can render a reform program useless as well. Therefore congruency is necessary between the teachers' needs and the level of support offered as part of the innovation.

Congruency between the contextualization of the innovation and students' experiences and prior knowledge: Students bring a range of experiences and prior knowledge to science learning settings, including both content and "out-of-school" knowledge of their home, community, and culture. Science innovations attempt to connect to the knowledge and experiences students bring to the classroom through contextualizing aspects of the program, such as driving questions, anchoring events, and real-world application problems (Rivet & Krajcik, 2004b). Research has shown that students develop more integrated understandings of science content and perform better on assessment measures when they make connections between their prior knowledge and experiences and science concepts through the contextualization of the innovation (Rivet, 2004). However, it is a challenge for developers and teachers to identify those contexts which will be both engaging for students as well as provide a useful cognitive framework to support their science learning. Additionally, one group of students may find a context or problem meaningful, while another group may not identify or connect with that same context. Thus it is critical that serious thought be given to the contextualizing features of a new innovation, and how congruent they will be with the prior knowledge and experiences of students in a particular learning setting.

These three levels of congruencies provide a lens through which to view the process of bringing innovative science reforms to new settings, and identify the appropriate types and amount of support needed for the innovation to be successful. In the Urban Science Education Center, we use these three levels of congruencies to frame a transformative research approach to our work with our partner schools.

Transformative Research

The Urban Science Education Center (USEC) is committed to addressing the challenges that face the teaching and learning science in city schools. In doing so, we utilize the lens of transformative research to guide our work. Transformative research is a form of collaborative research that while focused on generating new ideas also works to "transform" or improve the teaching and learning of science, particularly in urban settings. We refer to transformations as occurring in three areas. The first is in transforming *understanding* – our understanding of how schools work, urban students' understandings of the intersections between schooling, science, community and personal interests, and teachers' understandings of their students and their role in school improvement. The second is in transforming *action*, in terms of the direct and immediate application of new understandings to the work we do in schools. The third is in transforming *relationships*, and in particular relationships between colleges of education, urban schools, and communities. As researchers, we bring to schools particular experiences, expertise, and agendas. However, we also recognize the uniqueness of the local contexts in which we work, including the knowledge of the school administrators and teachers, the intricacies of the school culture, and the needs of the community. We need to work together to foster these relationships in order for new understandings and new actions to positively impact teachers and students in these settings.

We view transformative research as a confluence of teacher action research (Briscoe & Wells, 2002; Tillotson, 2000) and design research (Brown, 1992; Design-Based Research Collaborative, 2003; Fishman, Marx, Blumenfeld, Krajcik, & Soloway, 2004), and having many similarities to each of these traditions. Although distinct, action research and design-based research both focus on the intertwining of research and practice. In a similar vein, transformative research attempts to develop both specific and more general understandings of complex classroom environment, as well as transforming practices which occur in those environments through curricular innovation and professional development. Transformative research builds from both of these traditions through a collaborative partnership between researchers and practitioners that is focused on not only learning new information, but also transforming the current situation. As with both action and design research, transformative research is situated at the nexus between research and practice, resulting in findings intended to inform both aspects of the work. We used this approach to frame our work in the USEC with our partner schools. Below we describe an example of such a partnership, and how we utilized transformative research to guide our efforts with the administration, teachers, and students in this urban setting in order to explore the three levels of congruency needed for lasting reform to occur.

Research Setting

PSW is a small public middle school located in the Morningside Heights area of New York City. It was one of the first schools started as part of New York City's small school movement approximately eight years ago. The school has a strong project-based curriculum which integrates technology with humanities and the arts. Classes are intentionally kept small, around 20 students or so, and teams of teachers work together to present multiple subjects at each grade level using a variety of individual and small group instruction strategies (NYC Department of Education, 2005). The student population is diverse, but predominately Hispanic and African American. 70% of students are eligible for the free lunch program. In 2003 the school was labeled with School Under Registration Review (SURR) status by the state due to only 25% proficiency ratings on both the city and state middle school mathematics and reading tests. SURR status required the school to develop a comprehensive improvement plan, which included reorganizing the curriculum and substantially increasing the instructional time given to reading, writing, and mathematics. Consequently, many challenges faced this school as we began to work with the students, teachers, and school administrators through a partnership with the USEC. These challenges included maximizing the limited amount of time allocated to science, providing quality instructional models for science inquiry and project-based curricula, and supporting the teachers' efforts to improve their science instruction, most of whom did not have a science background.

The first step in the transformative research process was to learn about the current science instructional practices and what the teachers and principle wanted to see happen at the school in the future with respect to science instruction. Several sources of data were collected in an ongoing process throughout the school year as conversations progressed between USEC researchers and PSW participants. Detailed fieldnotes of planning meetings between USEC researchers, the principal, AP, and teachers were recorded and artifacts from these meetings (i.e., agendas, curriculum outlines, standards alignment documents) were collected. Classroom observations of science lessons were conducted in conjunction with the related transformative research studies occurring in the school at the same time. Informal interviews were conducted periodically with teachers and school leaders about the process of collaboration and the direction of the curriculum recommendations, during which the interviewer recorded notes both during and after the conversations. These diverse data sources were iteratively reviewed and organized as new information was added. From this data, we described a set of characteristics of PSW which impacted how science was conducted at the school. These characteristics presented us with a unique set of strengths and challenges that would need to be taken into consideration when collaborating with the school to improve its science program. Two key characteristics of PSW are described below.

In terms of current practices, what stood out most about PSW was the intricate way the school had scheduled time for science instruction, in between the demands from the district on the amount of time for literacy and math and the school's focus on project-based work in the humanities. All students took science class for half the year in 6th, 7th, and 8th grades, which alternated with art class the other half of the year. Science and art were taught during the same ninety-minute block twice a week, for a total of three hours of science each week for approximately 20 weeks each year. The science curriculum was also structured in an unusual manner. For science class, the students were further divided into three sections in 6th and 8th grade, and two sections in 7th grade. Rather than one group of students staying with the same science teacher for the whole time, the teachers selected one unit of the curriculum to teach and repeated it two or three times with a new group of students each round. Thus each teacher taught the same unit multiple times during the school year to different groups of students. The history of this schedule was not made clear, however the school had a limited number of teachers and almost all were asked to teach multiple subjects during the day. A 6th grade teacher may teach mathematics, science, reading, and humanities to different groups of students all over the course of a week. Of the five teachers who taught these science classes at PSW, four were certified in literacy or the humanities, with only one as a certified science teacher. Challenges associated with this schedule for science education were many. First there was the limited amount of time allocated for science instruction, much less than in comparable schools. Second, almost all of the science instruction occurred with teachers who were teaching out of field. As a consequence of this, in addition to the lack of an established science curriculum in the school, the administration often let teachers teach topics that they felt most comfortable with and gave a lot of leeway in how science was taught in these classes. However, one benefit of this program was that teachers had three, and in the case of the 7th grade, four opportunities to teach the same unit within one school year. We recognized that this provided an excellent opportunity to study change in practice over multiple iterations of the same unit, and to perform design experiments in collaboration with these teachers.

A second interesting aspect of PSW was the project-based nature of the curriculum. The core of this curriculum was a set of literacy and humanities projects that ran throughout the language arts and social studies curriculum across the three grades. These projects had been developed by teams of teachers several years before and used repeatedly by whoever was teaching that subject at the time. The existence of these projects meant that new teachers entering the school had a base of curriculum materials to work with that was established across teachers and grades, and also led to consistency for the students in both the content and project-based approach to these subject areas. Although project-based approaches were espoused across the school's curriculum, such projects did not exist for literacy, mathematics, or science.

In meetings with researchers, the principal expressed her desire to have a science curriculum in a form that existed outside of individual teachers. In her experience, teachers would leave the school for new positions and take their projects, curricula, and ideas with them, while new teachers would have to re-create their science lessons based on their knowledge and past experiences with very little else to support them. This created a challenge to the consistency of the science instruction which students receive, especially given the high rate of teacher turnover in urban settings. Thus, the principal requested that the curriculum materials that were recommended and adapted to meet the needs of the PSW teachers and students be in a written form that could be passed from teacher to teacher, with records of each teacher's notes and changes from each enactment of the units.

Findings

Building from the information gathered about the characteristics of PSW we worked with teachers and school leaders to formulate a set of recommendations for our partnership, in terms of research areas to purse and changes to be made to address the goal of improving the school's science instruction. Together we decided on two initial steps in this process. The first was to design a school-wide science curriculum plan, which both identified the content that would be taught at each grade and how these content areas aligned with the state's core curriculum for science. The second was to begin to identify existing projects and innovations that could serve as models of project-based science instruction for the teachers, and as a jumping-off point for adaptation and development of the school's own curriculum. In this paper, we situate these efforts in terms of the three levels of congruency described above.

Congruency of Vision

With there already being a project-based focus in other subject areas, we recommended continuing this approach through the PSW science program. Thus the innovations that were selected as models for adaptation by the school included reform-oriented project-based science units and other curriculum resources which had demonstrated previous success in urban settings (Marx et al., 2004). This change resulted in congruency between the vision of the curriculum programs and goals that the school had for teaching and learning science. However, a key challenge was to ensure that the meaning of "project-based" was consistent between the innovation and the school administration and teachers. What we found was that some characteristics of project-based science were common, in particular the focus on a driving question and the development of a final product. However some features were not in agreement. For example, project-based science emphasizes investigations and experiments to address the driving question. The teachers and school leaders viewed investigations differently, and had difficulty conceptualizing the role of experiments in the curriculum. The differences in vision were addressed through multiple conversations and professional development sessions with researchers from the Urban Science Education Center.

Congruency of Teacher Support

In our discussions with teachers at PSW, most expressed willingness, but also discomfort, for teaching science. Since many did not have a science background, they were unclear in how best to engage students with the content or address their questions and curiosities. The highest priorities named by the teachers for the science curriculum included content support, sound curriculum models, and new ideas for pedagogical strategies. However, they also expressed apprehension about letting go of their current practice and taking on new projects. Although they recognized that their science instruction was lacking and that improvements would benefit students in multiple ways, they were concerned both with the time involved in learning how to teach a new unit and with their unfamiliarity with new content in these units. There was also a range of responses from the teachers in the group when it came to this issue. Some were willing to experiment with new approaches, others were willing to follow along with new curriculum units, and others were very reluctant to give up their current practice.

Given this range of responses, we approached achieving congruency between the needs of teachers and the curriculum innovations in two steps. First, to make the most of the unique class schedule at PSW, it was decided that each teacher should be responsible for teaching only one or two units of the curriculum, and for addressing a single broad concept and focus on developing the performance indicators for that concept. This way, each teacher may be able to develop expertise in teaching their unit because they would have multiple opportunities to work with the materials over the course of the year. The second was to begin to identify existing projects and innovations that could serve as models of project-based science instruction for the teachers, and as a jumping-off point for adaptation and development of the school's own curriculum. A challenge in this area was that projects and innovations were often either too advanced or too complicated to be used directly in this setting. Most were structured as 6-10 week units with a minimum of four hours of science instruction each week. Each selected unit needed to be extensively adapted specifically for the school, teachers, and students, both in terms of the background, experiences, and cultures which students engaged with the curriculum, and also adaptations to the structure of the units to fit within the limited instructional time available.

Congruency of Students' Experiences

Initially, the experiences and prior knowledge of students at PSW were taken into account through the use of project-based science programs designed for other urban settings and which had demonstrated success in those areas. These programs were ones in which interest in and engagement with the contextualizing features were used as a way to support students science learning (Rivet, 2004). Some of the contextualizing themes for these innovations could be easily adapted to the PSW setting, such as altering a water quality unit to focus on the Hudson River. Other contextualizing themes were included because they were thought to be of interest more generally to middle school students, such as a focus on diseases. We recognized that each unit needed to be suited to fit each classroom situation and group of students, but that this process would happen gradually as teachers became more comfortable with the programs and adapted them to meet their needs and teaching style. Initial attempts to adapt these contextualizing aspects to PSW classroom settings had mixed results, and appeared to be closely tied with the teacher's interest and enthusiasm in the project. For example, in a study of invasive species students were focused on the introduction of sea lamprey in the Great Lakes. Although this problem is not immediately relevant or connected to New York City youth, the teacher worked diligently to make connections and foster interests in the issue, even dissecting a sea lamprey in class, and consequently the students became very engaged with this problem. On the other hand, another teacher described how she struggled to make a unit about machines interesting to her students, even though there were many machines working on local construction sites near the school.

Conclusions

The new project-based science curriculum units are currently being enacted at PSW. We are actively collecting information about the enactments, their success, and teachers' and students' reactions from working with these materials. The PSW curriculum plan and the adapted curriculum units will be revisited during the upcoming summer with the teachers to consider progress and address additional concerns that were raised after this first enactment of the new plan. Through this process we will address and make concerted efforts to improve the congruency between the new science reform programs and PSW at each of these three levels.

A key characteristic of this effort, which has informed our broader work, has been our developing understanding of the roles taken up by each contributor to this partnership as framed through the lens of transformative research. The role of the researcher expanded beyond the traditional position as data collector and analyzer, and took the form of an advisor, information-gatherer, bringer of new ideas, and facilitator of the partnership for discussions about change. The role of the teacher also expanded in this framework. Rather than being viewed as one who simply implemented an intervention, the teacher was asked to be a risk-taker who was willing to commit to the process, and who needed to recognize and embody the work because the changes had the largest impact on him or her. The administrator's role was found to be particularly important to this process. Their role included supporting and encouraging the process, finding resources, and providing leadership and vision for the broader impact of this work on students and the school more generally, rather than just in individual teachers' classrooms. We have found that it is not simply participation at each of these three levels, but the *quality* of the participation as described by each of these roles, that is critical in order to achieve congruency between the innovation and individual school settings. Without these broader visions and underlying supports, the success of these reform efforts would likely not be possible.

Additionally, this work has begun to identify the characteristics of an urban school science curriculum that need to be considered in order for substantive and lasting reform to take place. Next steps in this process include working with teachers and administrators to adapt and utilize the selected specific innovative curriculum projects in ways that meet the needs of PSW's teachers and students. Through this process, we hope to learn more about utilizing transformative research to frame partnerships with schools to improve the teaching and learning of science in these urban settings.

Endnotes

(1) All people and school names have been changed.

References

Ball, D. L., & Cohen, D. K. (1996). Reform by the book: What is--or might be--the role of curriculum materials in teacher learning and instructional reform? *Educational Researcher, 25*(9), 6-8.

Blumenfeld, P. C., Fishman, B. J., Krajcik, J., Marx, R. W., & Soloway, E. (2000). Creating usable innovations in systemic reform: Scaling up technology-embedded project-based science in urban schools. *Educational Psychologist, 35*(3), 149-164.

Briscoe, C., & Wells, E. (2002). Reforming primary science assessment practices: A case study of one teacher's professional development through action research. *Science Education, 86*, 417-435.

Brown, A. L. (1992). Design experiments: Theoretical and methodological challenges in creating complex interventions in classroom settings. *The Journal of the Learning Sciences, 2*(2), 141-178.

Cho, J. (1998, April). *Rethinking curriculum implementation: Paradigms, models, and teachers' work.* Paper presented at the annual meeting of the American Educational Research Association, San Diego, CA.

Dede, C. (2000). Emerging influences of information technology on school curriculum. *Journal of Curriculum Studies, 32*(2), 281-303.

Design-Based Research Collaborative. (2003). Design-based research: An emerging paradigm for educational inquiry. *Educational Researcher, 32*(1), 5-8.

Fishman, B. J., Hug, B., Honey, M., Light, D., Marx, R. W., & Carrigg, F. (2003, April). *Exploring the portability of reform: One district's approach to adaptation.* Paper presented at the annual meeting of the American Education Research Association, Chicago, IL.

Fishman, B. J., & Krajcik, J. (2003). What does it mean to create sustainable science curriculum innovations? A commentary. *Science Education, 87*(4), 564-573.

Fishman, B. J., Marx, R. W., Blumenfeld, P. C., Krajcik, J. S., & Soloway, E. (2004). Creating a framework for research on systemic technology innovations. *The Journal of the Learning Sciences, 13*(1), 43-76.

Goetz, M. E., Floden, R. E., & O'Day, J. (1995). *Studies of education reform: Systemic reform. Volume I: Findings and conclusions* (Research Rep. No. 35A). Rutgers, NJ: Consortium for Policy Research in Education.

Marx, R. W., Blumenfeld, P. C., Krajcik, J. S., Fishman, B. J., Soloway, E., Geier, R., et al. (2004). Inquiry-based science in the middle grades: Assessment of learning in urban systemic reform. *Journal of Research in Science Teaching, 41*(10).

McLaughlin, M. (1990). The Rand change agent study revisited: Macro perspectives and micro realities. *Educational Researcher, 19*(9), 11-16.

NYC Department of Education. (2005). *MS 250 West Side Colab. M.S.* Retrieved March 21, 2005, from http://www.nycenet.edu/OurSchools/Region10/M250/default.htm?searchType=school

Rivet, A. E. (2004). *Contextualizing instruction: Connecting to urban students' ideas and experiences.* Paper presented at the annual meeting of the National Association of Research in Science Teaching, Vancouver, BC.

Rivet, A. E., & Krajcik, J. S. (2004a). Achieving standards in urban systemic reform: An example of a sixth grade project-based science curriculum. *Journal of Research in Science Teaching, 41*(7), 669-692.

Rivet, A. E., & Krajcik, J. S. (2004b). Contextualizing instruction in project-based science: Activating students' prior knowledge and experiences to support learning. In Y. B. Kafai, W. A. Sandoval, N. Enyedy, A. S. Nixon & F. Herrera (Eds.), *Embracing Diversity in the Learning Sciences: The Proceedings of the Sixth International Conference of the Learning Sciences (ICLS 2004)*. Santa Monica, CA: Lawrence Erlbaum Associates.

Songer, N. B., Lee, H.-S., & McDonald, S. (2003). Research towards an expanded understanding of inquiry science beyond one idealized standard. *Science Education, 87*(4), 490-516.

Tillotson, J. W. (2000). Studying the game: Action research in science education. *The Clearing House, 74*(1), 31-34.

Tyack, D., & Cuban, L. (1995). *Tinkering Toward Utopia: A Century of Public School Reform.* Cambridge, MA: Harvard University Press.

Acknowledgements

This study was funded in part by the Bristol Myers Squibb Foundation. Any opinions expressed are those of the author and do not necessarily reflect the views of Bristol Myers Squibb. Thank to Angela Calabrese Barton and the fellows in the Urban Science Education Center for their support of this work.

Effects of Document Generation and Source Presentation on Historical Understanding and Thinking

Cecil Robinson, Gina Raineri, University of Alabama, Campus Box 870231, Department of Educational Studies, College of Education, Tuscaloosa, AL, 35487-0231
Email: crobinso@bamaed.ua.edu, raine030@bama.ua.edu

Abstract: Students in an Introduction to Lifespan Development course ($N = 108$) participated in an experiment with a 2x2 randomized factorial design that explored the effects of document generation (control, document generation; DGT) and presentation format (single text, multiple documents) on historical understanding and thinking. As predicted, there were no improvements in students' historical understanding in the DGT or presentation format conditions. However, there were main effects for DGT and presentation format on students' depth of processing as measured by the number of added, borrowed and transformed sentences in an argument writing task. There was also a main effect for DGT on students' recall of document source information, an indication of the use of a sourcing heuristic and component of expert historical thinking. Results provide cautionary evidence for educational policy and classroom practice about document-based assessment practices, and the continued advocacy of multiple primary source document use.

A burgeoning number of cognitive studies have explored how students understand and think about historical events (Carretero & Voss, 1994; National Research Council, 2005; Stearns, Seixas & Wineburg, 2001). One prominent line of research is centered on differences between novice and expert historical thinking; that is, the fundamentally different problem-solving heuristics and epistemological frameworks between students and teachers, and historians (c.f., Wineburg, 1991; Yeager & Davis, 1995; Young & Leinhardt, 1998). This research highlights students' and teachers' practices, successes and struggles within the discipline of history, and focuses on instructional approaches that change how students and teachers think about history so that they are more closely aligned with the practices of historians (VanSledright, 2002). A second line of prominent research is focused on understanding historical events. Examples of this research include limitations of textbooks (Beck, McKeown, Sinatra, & Loxterman, 1991; Britton & Gulgoz, 1991), the effects of single and multiple documents (Wiley & Voss, 1999), and the effects of primary and secondary sources (Rouet, Britt, Mason, & Perfetti, 1996). Combined, these lines of research have provided research-supported justification for primary source document (PSD) use within classrooms that 'do history'—that is, classrooms that engage in authentic historical inquiry, and provide instructional practices as a means to foster students' historical thinking and understanding (Levstik & Barton, 1996).

During political times when educational researchers are questioning how to 'make a difference,' this research is affecting classroom practice and national policy. The National Assessment of Educational Progress (NAEP) indicates teachers are using more documents in their history classrooms (Lapp, Grigg & Tay-Lim, 2002). U.S. History standards advocate the use of primary sources (National Center for History in the Schools, 1996). An increasing number of state and national examinations are using document-based questions (DBQs) as assessment items (Grant, 2003). In 2004, federal tax appropriations of \$44 million were allocated for 45 new Teaching American History grants centered on multiple documents to foster historical thinking and understanding (Department of Education, 2004).

Although this research is affecting practice and policy, there are at least two potential concerns related to multiple documents and DBQs that may limit continued adoption of these practices that need to be addressed. The first concern is that increased classroom document use has not translated into gains on achievement test scores in history. Results from the NAEP indicate that 8th and 12th grade students using multiple documents 'every day' scored *lower* than students who encountered multiple documents 'once or twice a week' (Lapp, et al., 2002). Further, there were *no meaningfully significant student performance differences* on the NAEP exam regardless if students were taught exclusively from the text or with multiple documents (Lapp, et al., 2002). These results are corroborated by research indicating that students' historical thinking is fairly resistant to change even when taught by a master teacher using well-chosen PSDs (VanSledright, 2002). These results pose a significant problem given the widespread advocacy of multiple documents, increased document use in the classroom, and allocation of federal monies to further increase document use.

The second concern is the 'authenticity' of DBQs. DBQs present six to eight documents related to a single topic—speeches, graphs, quotations, historian accounts, etc.; ask 'constructed response' questions about the main idea(s) within each document; and ask an essay response that requires students to draw on their background knowledge and from information within the documents. Advocates of DBQs argue making sense of an historical event using documents is consistent with the discipline of history and offers students an engaging way to approach learning history. They also argue that DBQs are examples of authentic large-scale performance assessments. Grant, Gradwell, and Cimbricz (2004) question claims of authenticity by arguing that presenting students with pre-selected (and often uninteresting) questions and documents without the opportunities for revisions is far removed from the work of historians, and demonstrate how these limitations raise pedagogical and assessment issues (Grant et al., 2004). They argue that with few exceptions (c.f., Wigginton, 1978) there are few 'authentic' classroom examples of students 'doing history' and concede that creating truly authentic, disciplinary-based classroom activities and assessments is generally not feasible. As an alternative, Grant et al. suggest that researchers, test-makers, and teachers attempt to create 'more authentic' activities and assessments.

More authentic classroom activities and assessments recognize that authenticity is not tenable, and instead strives to align activities and assessments with authentic historical disciplinary practices as closely as possible given classroom and/or testing constraints. For example, rather than providing students with a fixed question and predetermined set of documents, DBQs could be modified such that students: create their own significant or interesting historical questions, generate a list of potential documents to address a question and select and use documents from a large document set to address a question, to name a few. Each suggestion represents a task that is fairly easy to set up in a classroom or testing setting, and is representative of the types of tasks that historians must complete within their discipline. Although these suggestions appear to be reasonable, they have not been tested. From an instructional standpoint, research is unable to indicate whether each suggestion will significantly influence students' historical understanding and thinking. From an assessment standpoint, research is unable to indicate any of the suggestions can serve as a proxy for historical understanding and thinking.

The purpose of this study is to provide an initial examination into the effects of one of Grant et al.'s (2004) suggestions for more authentic DBQs. Specifically, this study explores whether the generation of a list of documents to address an essay question affects students' historical understanding and thinking. This study also replicates past research about single and multiple document presentation formats on understanding and thinking.

Past historical cognition research has demonstrated how manipulations to instructional tasks and assessments have significant effects on students' historical understanding and thinking. Students demonstrate significantly greater historical understanding when the phrase, "think like a historian" is added to a writing assignment (Wiley & Voss, 1996). Increases in understanding also occur when students are asked to write an argument as opposed to an essay (Wiley & Voss, 1999), a historical event is presented as a controversy (Perfetti, Britt, & Georgi, 1995), and authors' names are included or excluded on a historical text (Paxton, 1997). Beck, McKeown, Sinatra, and Loxterman (1991) demonstrated the significance of modifying the structure of the text—text coherence—on historical understanding. Multiple documents in an on-line environment produced better historical understanding than a single document, but there was no difference between multiple and single documents in paper format (Britt & Aginliskas, 2002; Wiley & Voss, 1999). Students' use of a sourcing heuristic increased when using web-based computer technology was developed to support historical thinking (Rouet, Britt, Mason, & Perfetti, 1996).

Although research has not explored whether the generation of a list of documents—a Document Generation Task (DGT)—will increase students' historical understanding and thinking, past research has demonstrated generation effects in memory tasks and higher-order mathematics problem solving (McNamara & Healy, 1995, 2000). A generation effect is produced when learners are forced to make inferences about an incomplete task. For example, memory recall of word pairs is significantly better when students are presented and asked to memorize the word pair "h_t—cold" in comparison to the word pair "hot—cold." Generating the "o" in "hot" produces semantically encoded information that results in deeper levels of cognitive processing. Deeper processing consistently leads to increases in students' ability to recall information and use previous knowledge to manipulate new knowledge for understanding (Gardiner & Hampton, 1985; Slamecka & Graf, 1978).

Given the findings from past generation effects research, one would predict that incomplete DBQ tasks that require students to generate inferences would increase students' depth of processing. One would also predict that generating a list of documents during a DGT requires more inferences than when presented with an already established set of documents. Further, since the semantically encoded information produced during a DGT is focused on document information, and not the historical content, one would predict increases in the recall of information about the documents used to complete a DGT, but not any increases in the recall of historical content information.

Method

Participants

Students (N=108) enrolled in an Introduction to Lifespan Development class at a public research university in the southeastern U.S participated in the study. Half of the students were male (n = 54) and half were female (n = 54). 68.5% (n = 74) of the students were white, and 26.9% (n = 29) were African-American, and 76% (n = 82) of the students were freshman who had not yet established a college GPA. All students received extra credit for participation in this study.

Materials

A questionnaire was used to gather demographic information and students experiences with history instruction. A one-page summary of facts about events of the Homestead Steel Strike that occurred at the Carnegie Steel Company in Homestead, Pennsylvania in 1892 provided initial background information about the event. The *Document-Based Question* (DBQ) read:

> Although the general facts about the Homestead Steel Strike are known, the cause of the strike is not entirely known. In fact, there is still great debate and controversy among historians about who was ultimately responsible for the Homestead Steel Strike. The purpose of this study is for you to contribute to this debate and argue your opinion of events related to the strike. Your task is to think like a historian and create an argument about the controversy surrounding the Homestead Steel Strike and the extent to which Andrew Carnegie was responsible for breaking up the union. (Adapted from Rouet et al., 1996)

The *Document Generation Task* (DGT) asked students to *generate a list of materials and rationales for using those materials* that they would want to use when creating their argument. Two document sets were used in this study. The *multiple document* set consisted of a textbook excerpt, 2 historian accounts, and 4 PSDs. The *single text* contained the same information, but embedded the historian accounts and PSDs within the textbook excerpt and included transitional clauses between paragraphs (c.f., Britt & Aginlaskas, 2002). The document sets provided students with the data to construct their argument about the Homestead Steel Strike.

A multiple choice and free recall post-test was used to measure students' historical understanding, depth of processing, and historical thinking. Seven true-false questions and six free recall questions provided measures of students' understanding about the events that took place during the Homestead Steel Strike. The six free-recall items asked students to recall three supporting and three opposing arguments from the text(s) about Carnegie's role in breaking up the union. Depth of processing was measured with three situational questions (adapted from McNamara, Kintsch, Songer, & Kintsch 1996; Wiley & Voss, 1999). Each situational question had five responses: one answer item was not found within any of the readings (added), two answer items—one from the textbook and one from a document—were borrowed from the readings (surface processing), and two answer items transformed information from the text (deep processing). Six free recall questions provided measures of students' historical thinking, specifically their ability to recall information about the document sources.

Procedures

Students were randomly assigned to one of four experimental groups within a 2 (Document Generation Task, Control) x 2 (Single Text, Multiple Document) factorial design. All students completed the background questionnaire and were given the one-page summary of facts about the Homestead Steel Strike and the DBQ. A research assistant read the one-page summary and DBQ aloud to ensure that all students were exposed to the background information and the overarching task. Students in the DGT condition completed the DGT, and students in the No DGT condition were given one of the two document sets. Once the students in the DGT condition completed the DGT, they were also given one of the two document sets. After students read through the documents, they composed their argument responses. Once they completed their arguments, they completed the historical understanding and thinking post-test assessments.

Analysis

Historical understanding was analyzed by comparing the number of true-false and free recall questions that students answered correctly on the post-test assessment across experimental conditions. Depth of processing was measured by students' responses on the post-test assessment and by decomposing students' argument responses into sentence-level propositions. The sentence-level propositions were then coded as added, borrowed or transformed (c.f. Wiley & Voss, 1999). Added sentences were sentences with information that was not found in the text. Borrowed sentences represented material that was paraphrased or quoted from the text(s). Borrowed sentences represent a surface level processing of information within the text(s). Transformed sentences were either sentences that combined two or more pieces of information from text(s) in a novel way, or combined information from the text(s) with added information from the student. In both instances, transformed sentences represent deeper levels of processing information and engagement with the text (Wiley & Voss, 1999). Historical thinking was measured by coding sentences in each written argument according to the document source(s) that were used to generate borrowed and transformed sentences, and by comparing the number of correct free-recalled source questions on the post-test measure.

Results

Historical Understanding

A 2x2 ANOVA yielded no main effects or interactions for document generation or presentation format ($p > .05$). This is consistent with our predictions about the DGT using generation effects research, and previous presentation format research and the mixed results from the NAEP.

Table 1. Measures of Historical Understanding

	Document Generation		No Document Generation	
	Single Text	Multiple Texts	Single Text	Multiple Texts
True False	3.4	3.2	3.2	3.1
Arguments	5.1	4.9	4.4	4.7

Depth of Processing

A two-way ANOVA revealed a significant main effect for presentation format on the average added, borrowed, and transformed sentences (ABT average) $F\ (1, 84) = 7.023$, $p = .01$, $d = .54$ (see Figure 1). The effect of presentation format on levels of processing is consistent with past research; multiple documents promote deeper levels of processing than single text accounts. Consistent with past generation effect research, there was a significant main effect for DGT on ABT average $F\ (1, 84) = 6.436$, $p = .01$, $d = .57$. There was no interaction between Document Type and DGT. These results indicate that the DGT promotes additional processing beyond presentation format as the single text, DGT condition produced equivalent results to the multiple text, no DGT condition. This latter finding has implications for cash-strapped classrooms. If teachers do not have access to multiple documents, the inclusion of a DGT task with a single text account can substantially increase levels of processing to levels that are similar to using multiple documents.

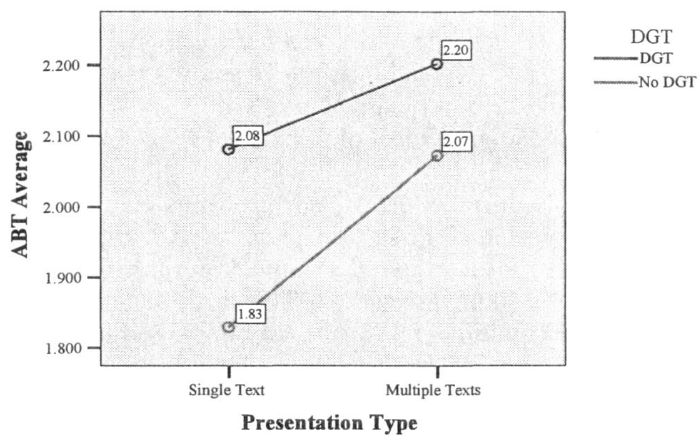

Figure 1. Level of processing by document generation task and presentation format.

Historical Thinking

A 2x2 ANOVA revealed a significant main effect for the DGT on the number of sourcing questions correctly recalled, $F(1, 107) = 4.649$, $p = 0.033$. There was no main effect for presentation format, $F(1, 107) = 0.154$, $p > 0.10$, or interaction between DGT and presentation format $F(1, 107) = 0.674$, $p > 0.10$. These results are consistent with past generation effects research, and indicate that a DGT not only leads to greater depth of processing of information, but that it also leads to greater recall of information of the information being processed. This is further verified by the non-significant increases in historical understanding.

Although there were increases in the amount of source information recalled, analysis of students' written responses indicates that DGT and presentation format did not affect the types of documents used in their argument responses. Across all conditions students used a significantly greater number of secondary documents ($M = 6.97$, $SD = 4.36$) than PSDs ($M = 1.24$, $SD = 1.67$), $t(87) = 12.10$, $p < 0.001$ in their arguments. Post hoc analysis revealed PSDs were used less than historian accounts ($M = 2.97$, $SD = 2.41$) $t(87) = 7.252$, $p < 0.001$ and textbook accounts ($M = 4.00$, $SD = 2.92$) $t(87) = 7.193$, $p < 0.001$. Textbook accounts were used more than historian accounts, $t(87) = 3.117$, $p = 0.002$. These findings are consistent with past research on historical thinking (c.f., Wineburg, 1991; Yeager & Davis, 1995) and support VanSledright's (2002) claim that students are resistant to learning from multiple documents.

Discussion

The purpose of this study was to explore the effects of presentation format and document generation on students' historical thinking and understanding. Results indicate higher student scores for the document generation condition on recall of fact-based information, but these results were not significant. This is consistent with NAEP data and warrant further exploration. If a goal of multiple document use is to increase students' historical understanding and another goal of the field is to continue to make a difference, then researchers will need to better understand the relationship between single and multiple texts and basic historical understanding.

Although there were no significant effects for recall data, there were significant effects for DGT and presentation format on the depth of processing of information within texts. The presentation format results replicate past research (Rouet et al., 1996; Wiley & Voss, 1999) and provide further evidence that suggests that multiple texts foster deeper levels of processing. The results of the DGT on depth of processing add to the historical thinking and understanding literature. These results also provide evidence that expand past generation effects research and the effects on deeper cognitive processing by demonstrating that generation effects are not only present in lower-order cognitive tasks and higher-order math tasks, but also higher-order thinking in history and writing.

From a classroom standpoint, the results of the DGT provide initial validation for Grant et al.'s (2004) argument about the authenticity of DBQs. Namely, that inclusion of 'more authentic' activities will have significant effects on the ways that students approach these tasks. However, the results also highlight the need for a detailed program of research into the differential effects of their suggestions on historical understanding and thinking. For example, the DGT significantly affected students' depth of processing and their ability to recall source information, but did not result in significant changes in students' historical understanding or other aspects of historical thinking beyond recall of source information. Testing the other recommendations of Grant et al. beyond generating documents to include document selection and use, and question generation is a means to develop our understanding of learning from multiple documents and creating classroom environments that are not only modeled on expert disciplinary practices, but also result in the improvement of students' achievement (such as the NAEP).

In an age of accountability and high-stakes testing, any problems with or improvement to assessment items are significant. Document-based questions and PSDs are used on AP Exams, State Exams, and the NAEP assessments, and this study highlights how the addition of a simple task such as document generation creates deeper levels of processing and increased use of a sourcing heuristic. This study also replicated results from the NAEP and other experimental findings; namely that multiple documents may not significantly effect understanding any more than a well-crafted textbook. Although more research is clearly needed, this work adds caution to the wind for advocates arguing that more document be used in the classroom. This work also adds promise for the future of task effects as a means to understand how to create and understand the results of 'more authentic' historical assessments.

References

Beck, I., McKeown, M., Sinatra, G., & Loxterman, J. (1991). Revising social studies text from a text-processing perspective: Evidence of improved comprehensibility. *Reading Research Quarterly, 26*, 251-276.

Britt, M.A. & Aglinskas, C. (2002). Improving students' ability to identify and use source information. *Cognition and Instruction, 20*(4), 485-522.

Britton, B., & Gulgoz, S. (1991). Using Kintsch's computational model to improve instructional texts: Effects of repairing inference calls on recall and cognitive structures. *Journal of Educational Psychology, 83*, 329-404.

Carretero, M., & Voss, J. F. (1994). *Cognitive and instructional processes in history and the social sciences*. Hillsdale, NJ: Lawrence Erlbaum.

Department of Education (2004). *Teaching American History Grant Program: 2004 grant abstracts*. Retrieved November 1, 2004, from http://www.ed.gov/programs/teachinghistory/ 2004tahabstracts/index.html.

Gardiner, J.M. & Hampton, J.A. (1985). Semantic memory and the generation effect: Some tests of the lexical activation hypothesis. *Journal of Experimental Psychology: Learning, Memory, and Cognition, 11*(4), 732-741.

Grant, S. G. (2003). *History lessons: Teaching, learning, and testing in U.S. high school classrooms*. Mahwah, NJ: Lawrence Erlbaum.

Grant, S.G., Gradwell, J.M., & Cimbricz, S.K. (2004). A question of authenticity: The document-based question as an assessment of the students' knowledge of history. *Journal of Curriculum and Supervision, 4*, 309-337.

Kintsch, W. (1998). *Comprehension: A paradigm for cognition*. Cambridge, MA: Cambridge University Press.

Lapp, M.S., Grigg, W.S., & Tay-Lin, B.S.H. (2002). *The nation's report card: U.S. History 2001*. Washington: U.S. Department of Education.

Levstik, L.S., & Barton, K.C. (1997). *Doing history: Investigating with children in elementary and middle schools*. Mahwah, NJ: Lawrence Erlbaum Associates.

McNamara, D.S. & Healy, A.F. (1995). A procedural explanation of the generation effect: The use of an operand retrieval strategy for multiplication and addition problems. *Journal of Memory and Language, 34*, 399-416.

McNamara, D.S. & Healy, A.F. (2002). A procedural explanation of the generation effect for simple and difficult multiplication problems and answers. *Journal of Memory and Language, 43*(4), 652-679.

McNamara, D., Kintsch, E., Songer, N., & Kintsch, W. (1996). Are good texts always better? Interactions of text coherence, background knowledge, and levels of understanding in learning from text. *Cognition and Instruction, 14*, 1-43.

National Center for History in the Schools (1996). *National standards for history: Basic edition*. Retrieved On-line, October 15, 2005 from the National Center for History in the Schools Web site: http://nchs.ucla.edu/standards/toc.html.

National Research Council (2005). *How students learn: History in the classroom*. A targeted report for teachers, M. Donovan and J. Bransford (Eds.), Division of Behavioral and Social Sciences and Education. Washington, DC: The National Academies Press.

Paxton, R.J. (1997). "Someone with Like a Life Wrote It": The Effects of a Visible Author on High School History Students. *Journal of Educational Psychology, 89*(2), 235-250.

Perfetti, C. A., Britt, M. A., & Georgi, M. C. (1995). *Text-based learning and reasoning: Studies in history.* Hillsdale, NJ: Lawrence Erlbaum.

Robinson, C., & Cimbricz, S. (2003, November). *Assessing historical understanding: The document generation task – a glimpse of a 'more authentic' assessment task.* A paper presented at the meeting of the College and University Faculty Assembly, Chicago, IL.

Rouet, J.F., Britt, M.A., Mason, R.A., & Perfetti, C.A. (1996). Using multiple sources of evidence to reason about history. *Journal of Educational Psychology, 88*(3), 478-493.

Slamecka, N.J. & Graf, P. (1978). The generation effect: Delineation of a phenomenon. *Journal of Experimental Psychology: Human Learning and Memory, 4*(6), 592-604.

Stearns, P. N., Seixas, P., Wineburg, S. (2000). *Knowing, teaching & learning history: National and international perspectives.* New York: New York University Press.

VanSledright, B. (2002). In search of America's past: Learning to read history in elementary school. New York: Teacher's College Press.

Wiley, J. & Voss, J.F. (1999). Constructing arguments from multiple sources: Tasks that promote understanding and not just memory for text. *Journal of Educational Psychology, 91*(2), 1-11.

Wiley, J. & Voss, J. (1996). The effects of "playing" historian on learning in history. *Applied Cognitive Psychology, 10,* 63-72.

Wineburg, S.S. (1991). Historical problem solving: a study of the cognitive processes used in the evaluation of documentary and pictorial evidence. *Journal of Educational Psychology, 83*(1), 73-87.

Yeager, E.A., & Davis, O.L., Jr. (1995). Between campus and classroom: Secondary student-teachers' thinking about historical texts. *Journal of Research and Development in Education, 29(1),* 1-8.

Young, K.M., & Leinhardt, G. (1998). Writing from primary documents: A way of knowing in history. *Written Communication, 15(1),* 25-68.

WWW and multicultural democracy: Evaluating U.S. History websites

Cecil Robinson, Douglas McKnight, The University of Alabama, Campus Box 870231, Department of Educational Studies, College of Education, Tuscaloosa, AL, 35487-0231
Email: crobinson@bamaed.ua.edu, dmcknigh@bamaed.ua.edu

Abstract: Claims about the potential of the Internet within social studies and democratic education have been somewhat silent on issues of diversity. To address this problem, this study employed tenets of liberal and multicultural democratic theory, developed an evaluative coding scheme, and examined content of websites that preservice teachers ($N = 20$) selected as resources for U.S. History unit plans. Results indicate selected websites housed a large amount of redundant non-diverse information. Website content was available in local media resources, consisted of textbook accounts, and focused on traditional historical topics; only one of ten websites was diverse. A four-cluster model provides further support for a discussion about the Internet, as currently used and framed, leading to less diversity of ideas and voices within the classroom, anathema to the stated democratic purposes of the social studies.

Although there are an increasing number of claims about the potential of the Internet within social studies and democratic citizenship education (Glenn, 1990; Mason et al., 2000; Whitson & Berson, 2003), social education research has been somewhat silent on issues of diversity and technology (Marri, 2003b; Zambon, 2003). This is problematic because technology, citizenship and diversity have been propelled to the center of the global stage. The Internet brings people, places and events from around the world into our daily lives, and has led to a complex and expanded concept of diversity (Ladson-Billings, 2001) that requires global citizens to interrogate the multiple voices that span class, gender, race and national borders, shape world issues, and provide guidance for one role of the social studies. As stated in the National Council of the Social Studies (NCSS, 2002) standards, "[t]he primary purpose of the social studies is to help young people develop the ability to make informed and reasoned decisions for the public good as citizens of a culturally diverse, democratic society in an interdependent world."

A small number of social education research studies have started to explore the relationships between technology, social education, democracy, and diversity (c.f., Marri, 2003b; Salinas & Robinson, 2002; Zambon, 2003). This paper adds to the literature by presenting liberal and multicultural conceptions of democratic citizenship as a framework to evaluate the content of Internet websites in relation to the NCSS goals on diversity. The present study employed the tenets of liberal and multicultural democratic theory to develop a coding scheme to examine the content of websites that preservice teachers selected for a U.S. History unit plan. The results provided fodder for a discussion of how the Internet, as currently used and framed within social studies and technology research, may lead to less diversity of ideas and voices within the classroom, anathema to the stated purposes of the social studies.

Justification

One of John Dewey's central concerns was "the relationship between the school and the larger life of the community" (1915, p. 20). When this relationship was not congruent, he posited that "certain changes in the methods and materials of the school work" were necessary such that school "might be better adapted to present social needs" (p. 20). These quotes identify the need to adapt both the 'methods' and 'materials' of education to meet social needs. On the surface, it is an obvious statement that educational change can stem from the methods teachers use to guide students' experiences. Less obvious may be the agency attributed to curriculum and materials—particularly media—in creating constraints and affordances that affect whether learning occurs and social needs are met (Dewey, 1958). For Dewey, learning "depends critically on the reflective medium in which activity takes place. … The medium must be capable of instantiating the key elements of a domain of inquiry—broadly construed—in a manner accessible to students" (Schaffer, 2005, p. 14, 15). However, there is a dearth of social studies and technology research focused explicitly on media—most research has centered on methods. Technology research in social studies is typically the 'application' (methods) of technology in social studies classrooms, or the ways teacher educators, teachers and students 'use' technology (c.f., Bolick, Berson, Coutts, & Heinecke, 2003). A similar trend is also present within democratic education research, which focuses on teaching students to use technology to collect, store, analyze and manipulate data as a means to participate in democratic society (Glenn, 1990). Focusing solely on methods reifies technological deterministic impulses that *a priori* assume technology progresses us towards societal and educational ends (McKnight & Robinson, in press). This determinism situates technology and progress as givens and thereby beyond critique. Discussions are not about inherent tensions or limitations of technology, but revolve around lack of access, integration and skills to acquire "more information." Such predilections translate into discussions about the Internet that are not about examination and change, but as an ideal—the amorphous 'potential' of the Internet. This study attempts to resist this potential pitfall by asking the question: What information did preservice teachers select when using the Internet for a U.S. History unit plan? More specifically we ask: "Where did they go? What did they access? Was the information accessed not readily available in other media formats?" Such questions do not assume the inevitability of the Internet as a neutral tool (Bowers, 1988) or necessary societal good (Bromley, 1998). It instead treats the Internet as a historically inscribed cultural artifact that must be examined and interrogated within its social spheres of use (Feenberg, 1995).

Conceptual Framework

"The relationship between the school and the larger life of the community" is measured through "present social needs" (Dewey, 1915, p. 20). Though there are a multitude of claims about the societal justification of social studies in education, perhaps the most common is that social studies is the discipline to develop a democratic citizenry. For Dewey, education and its associated materials and methods were means to political democratic ends, and societal needs were to be evaluated through these political ends. To make claims about the relationship between schooling, its methods and materials and democracy, one must articulate a democratic framework (Dewey's political ends) so that one has a lens to evaluate social needs and educational change. And past technology research has indeed articulated a democratic framework. Consider the following claims by Berson, Lee, and Stuckart (2001) concerning the usefulness of the Internet in social education to create an informed democratic citizen:

> Today, effective citizenship includes a range of computer technology skills.... Citizenship in a democracy implies critical thought, and critical thought requires information. Technology can make more information available to students than ever before. The Internet, in particular, has the ability to dramatically increase the amount of information available to students. (p. 214)

This quote reveals assumptions about relationships between the Internet, democracy and social studies education: citizenship in a democracy requires citizens to reason critically, interpreted as the ability to process large amounts of information; the Internet is a medium that provides access to the information to be processed; and the social studies classroom is a site to practice this skill, assumed essential in a modern democratic state. Each component is useful and has provided a foundation for social studies educators to think about and employ the Internet in their instruction. However, these claims present a narrow account of democracy that creates an incomplete picture of the relationship between democracy, the Internet and social studies. This account disregards—or does not consider necessary—discussion on how diverse information, theoretical perspectives and voices should stem from democratic principles and the ways that the Internet affords and/or constrains these principles. Liberal democratic ideals attempt to avoid this critique by arguing for 'diverse information,' and elaborating on the technology savvy, rational conception that 'more information' enables citizens to engage in democratic deliberation.

> A progressive society counts individual variations as precious since it finds in them the means of its own growth. Hence, a democratic society must, in consistency with its ideal, allow for intellectual freedom and the play of diverse gifts and interests in its educational measures. (Dewey, 1916, p. 305)

Dewey's vision of a progressive democratic society problematizes claims that more information is necessary for democratic citizenry because these claims do not ensure that 'more information' is not 'more of the same information.' To sustain its democratic health, society must seek out variation—differing opinions, ideas and worldviews. This points toward the significance of asking whether information is readily available and replicates the traditional, authoritative narratives that constitute history textbooks, or whether it provides alternative perspectives.

Multicultural Democracy: From Political Diversity to Sociocultural Diversity

Dewey's democratic goals were radical in that he acknowledged the importance of diversity of thought. However, his conception also has the trappings of liberal democratic theory. Dewey only refers to politically diverse thoughts, and was uncomfortably silent about other dimensions of difference such as class, gender and race. This is problematic because in his estimation, educational change is a function of social need and social need is evaluated against democratic ideals. Any democratic ideals that ignore (or discount) issues of diversity will be translated into schooling institutions that do the same. To understand why liberal democracy is silent on issues of socio-economic and cultural diversity, one must look to its central tenets of unity and neutrality. Unity is anchored in the phrase *e pluribus unum* which translates into a process of moving *from many to one* and creates the goal of "transcending difference, conquering and overcoming it" (Parker, 1996, p. 111). Neutrality assumes "all men are created equal" and perpetuates the rugged individualism of "pulling one's self up by the bootstraps." Neutrality creates a path to unity, but requires the explicit elimination of difference and diversity (Marri, 2003a).

Multicultural democracy explicitly acknowledges socio-cultural differences and treats diversity as essential for democracy because it protects liberty and challenges the status quo (Marri, 2003a; Parker, 1996). Within this multicultural frame, *e pluribus unum* is not translated '*from* many, one,' but '*with* many, one' (Parker, 1996). Such translation focuses on *diversity and unity* and allows "larger publics" and "little publics" to coexist. Larger publics are "the normative grid that binds citizens together in a broad political comradeship" (Parker, 1996, p. 118). Little publics are "associations based on religion, ethnicity, language, race, hobbies, labor—interests of all sorts, some of which are incompatible from one group to another" (Parker, p. 118). These publics come together on difficult issues on creative democratic *path*s and are a necessary part of the continuing public discussion, not a means to sustain predetermined democratic *ends* (Dewey, 1916). Parker argues that multicultural democracy "has no end other than the path itself. Ends arise on the path" (1996, p. 114). He goes on to continue, "Viewed as a creative, constructive process, democracy is not already accomplished, in which case citizens today need only to celebrate and protect it, but a trek that citizens in a pluralist society make together" (p. 114). Multicultural democracy enables national discussions to remain open to views that conflict with the "dominant" or "mainstream" common sense perspective, so that democracy does not diminish to the point of irrelevancy. This discussion does not come easy (Gay, 1997), but it is through this struggle of learning to be comfortable being uncomfortable and by "associating and resolving issues with people whose views are different from one's own that democracy is learned" (Marri, 2003a, p. 273).

Acknowledging the importance of diversity within democracy provides grounds for the central questions of multicultural democracy (Parker, 1996). The first question is: Who is and is not participating in democracy? This question ensures that the little publics exist alongside the larger publics. For if one finds that groups are not participating, then one can begin to explore why they are not participating. In this study, we evaluate the Internet within this framework by examining the voices that are present within the websites that preservice teachers accessed for their U.S. History unit plans. The second question is: How wide is the path to participation? This question examines the social structures and paths that affect participation (Marri, 2005). In this study, we address this question by examining two structural paths of the Internet: corporate (website domain names) and disciplinary (types of information, i.e. textbook accounts, primary documents, historian accounts, teaching accounts, etc.). Each reveal paths that constrain and afford different voices within the information accessed.

Method

Participants, Materials and Procedures

20 preservice teachers (PSTs) enrolled in secondary social studies methods at a public university in the southeastern U.S. participated in this study. PSTs were predominantly white (only one African-American), middle to upper-middle class, from the home state of the institution, and there were a balanced number of males and females. All PSTs were juniors or seniors, admitted into the secondary teacher education program, had a minimum cumulative GPA of 3.0, and were blind (including the instructor) to the purpose of this study. During the first two weeks of the course, PSTs participated in six, one-hour technology professional development sessions led by an educational technology faculty member and a graduate assistant. One session was dedicated to web search and evaluation. PSTs learned about search engines, search strings, and the identification of "publication" date, author, and type of domain. Subsequent sessions reviewed these concepts. Early during the semester each PST created a unit plan on any topic of interest in the social studies, and created a "resource database" consisting of 20-25 websites that could be used as teaching, research and/or background resources to support their unit plan (personal communication, Methods Instructor, October 15, 2005).

Analysis

To consistently analyze websites, we limited the possibilities presented with hypertext. If there were links on a web page that PSTs selected, then we analyzed two levels of links. All page links to the initial webpage were analyzed (1st level). If there were any links on 1st level pages, then those additional linked pages were also analyzed

(2nd level). We also assumed that specific website addresses were intentional. If the address accessed a specific area of a larger website, then we analyzed the content within that section, not the content of the larger website.

Website Availability provided a measure of whether the websites selected represented 'more' (i.e., diverse) or 'more of the same' information. Two graduate research assistants, blind to the purpose of this study, independently answered the following for each website: "Do you think the information on this website would be available at a local high school or community library?" They were informed to think of average suburban libraries. Websites that duplicated information easily found through local resources (i.e., www.time.com) were coded as Definitely Available (DA). Websites were coded as Could Be Available (CBA) when availability was not certain, and Not Available (NA) when websites provided access to information that would not be found locally (i.e., www.loc.gov, on-line documents from the Library of Congress). Two training sessions produced moderate inter-rater reliabilities of .78 and .85. There were no discrepancies between DA and NA codes. Discrepancies were resolved conservatively with discrepancies between CBA and NA coded as NA, and CBA and DA coded as CBA.

Website Diversity was coded using the following categories: Traditional History, Race, Class, Gender, and Non-Historical Material. Traditional History was "historical accounts typical of high school history textbooks." The categories Race, Class and Gender were, "historical accounts centered on issues of race, class or gender." If a diverse website was also traditional, then it was coded conservatively as Race, Class or Gender (i.e., Martin Luther King Jr.'s I Have a Dream speech is in high school history textbooks, but was coded as Race). Non-Historical Material focused on teaching methods and lesson plans. Inter-rater reliability was .88 across all categories.

Website Domains provided a measure of the types of websites that were selected. A commercial website domain (.com) generally represents companies or individual's using commercial products (i.e., hotmail.com accounts to create websites). Government (.gov), non-profit (.org), and educational (.edu and .k12) domains also represent different types of organizations and individuals. Each group has different interests and provides different structural paths for Internet use.

Website Disciplinary Information Sources provided a measure of the disciplinary paths of the selected websites. The following information source categories were used: primary sources, textbooks, historian, fictional, teaching, and other. Because websites can contain multiple sources of information, websites were coded according to the proportion of information sources within the site with a 1 representing a document type accounting for some of the website, 2—half of the website, 3—most of the website, and 4—all of the website. The inter-rater reliability for all websites was .93.

Results

PSTs created unit plans and Internet resource databases about the Civil War (6), World War II (4), Civil Rights Movement (3), World War I (3), 1960s, Great Depression, American Revolution and The American Presidency. Combined, the resource databases contained 448 website addresses ($M = 23.4$, $SD = 2.1$). 425 of the 448 website addresses (94.9%) linked to a working website, and formed the data for this study ($N = 425$).

Website Availability

69.4% ($n = 295$) of selected websites were 'definitely available' (DA) within one's community, 19.3% ($n = 82$) were 'could be available' (CBA) and 11.3% ($n = 48$) were 'not available' (NA). There were highly significant differences between the availability of selected websites, χ^2 (2, $N = 425$) = 253.02, $p < .001$, with almost two-thirds of all websites selected representing readily available information within one's local community. To further test website availability, CBA and NA websites were collapsed into a single category, "not and/or could be available" (NCBA). Differences between NCBA ($n = 130$, 30.6%) and DA ($n = 295$, 69.4%) were also significant χ^2 (1, $N = 425$) = 64.06, $p < .001$; even conservative estimates indicate that most of the websites that PSTs selected replicated information available in magazines, on television and history textbooks.

Website Diversity

The majority of websites within PSTs' resource databases focused on traditional topics found in high school history books ($n = 256$, 60.2%). There were a limited number of websites that focused on diverse historical topics. For example, only 8.9% of the websites were focused on issues of race ($n = 38$), 2.5% of the websites were focused on issues of socioeconomic status ($n = 11$), and 0.4% of the websites were focused on issues of gender ($n =$

2). Because of the low number of websites focused on issues of diversity, diverse websites were collapsed into a single category 'different voices' (DV) (n = 51, 11.8%). The remaining websites (n = 118, 27.8%) did not focus on historical topics at all. Rather, these websites focused on lesson plans, or referred to historical texts that were for sale. After collapsing diverse websites into the single category, there were still significantly less websites that focused on different voices than websites that focused on traditional historical accounts and websites that did not even focus on historical topics, χ^2 (2, N = 425) = 154.25, $p < .001$. Indeed, almost 9 of every 10 websites focused on topics that did contain any form of diversity, and 6 of every 10 websites focused on topics that replicated information found in traditional high school history textbooks.

Website Domains

The different types of websites that students selected as part of their research database are presented in Table 1. There were significant differences in the distribution of website origin χ^2 (5, N = 425) = 245.80, $p < .001$. Highly significant post-hoc analyses indicate that commercial websites (.com) were selected more than twice as often as educational (.edu) or organization (.org) websites, χ^2 (2, N = 334) = 67.44, $p < .001$. These results indicate that not only was most information readily available in the local community and focused on traditional historical topics, but that the greatest proportion of information was selected from commercial websites.

Table 1. Distribution of Website Domains

	.edu	.com	.org	.gov	.net	other[a]	Total
# of Websites	79	182	73	33	24	34	425
% of Websites	18.6	42.8	17.2	7.8	5.6	8.0	100.0

[a] Included .k12 and foreign country websites, and search engine results used as resources.

Website Disciplinary Information Sources

Textbook accounts were the most prevalent document type, representing 42.1% of the total content within all websites. Primary sources were the second most prevalent document type (26%). The remaining types of information were as follows: teaching material (17.2%), other material (12.6%), fictional accounts (1.6%) and historian accounts (1.5%). A Friedman Test of the proportions of all information sources indicated highly significant differences χ^2 (5, N = 425) = 508.87, $p < .001$. Post-hoc comparisons using Wilcoxon Signed Ranks Test, and Bonferroni method to control for Type I error, indicate a highly significant greater proportion of textbook accounts than primary source documents (the second highest proportion) T (425) = 4.40, $p < .001$. This result also indicates there were a significantly greater proportion of textbook accounts than any other source type. Indeed, post-hoc comparisons produced significant contrasts across all pairs except Teaching Resource Materials and Other Materials, and Historian and Fictional Accounts. Thus, not only were most websites readily available, focused on traditional historical topics and selected from commercial websites, but the greatest proportion of websites also contained traditional historical content in a textbook-like manner.

Relationships between Availability, Diversity and Disciplinary Sources of Websites

To develop a better understanding of the relationships between the availability, diversity and disciplinary content of these websites, a two-step cluster analysis, using log-likelihood distance measures and Schwartz's Bayesian Criterion, computed the grouping criteria used to identify groups of websites with similar characteristics. A four-cluster model produced the best fit, and accounted for 100% (N = 425) of the total websites. These clusters produced significant distributions across all categories: website availability χ^2 (3, N = 425) = 208.63, p < .000, website diversity χ^2 (3, N = 425) = 323.60, p < .001, and website domains χ^2 (3, N = 425) = 21.89, p < .008.

Cluster 1 can be described as 'Textbook Accounts.' This cluster accounted for 32.7% (n = 139) of the total websites. All websites in this cluster were definitely available, traditional history topics. This cluster contained a significant proportion of text accounts, and significantly excluded primary sources, and historian and fictional accounts. The websites were equally distributed across website domains. Cluster 2 can be described as 'Teaching Resources.' This cluster did not deal with historical content, but was the most prevalent, 36.7% (n = 156). A significant number of websites in this cluster were definitely available (n = 129, 82.7%) and did not contain any history-related information (n = 107, 68.6%). This cluster contained a significant proportion of teaching and other accounts, and significantly excluded primary sources and fictional accounts. The websites were equally distributed across website domains. Cluster 3 can be described as 'Primary Sources,' 20.5% (n = 87). A significant number of websites in this cluster were could be available, and definitely available websites were significantly excluded. Although websites were not readily available, a significant number of websites were focused on traditional historical content (n = 83, 95.4%). This cluster also contained a significant proportion of primary sources and significantly excluded text, teaching and other accounts. Further, unlike the first two clusters, a significant number of websites were from education (.edu) and government (.gov) website domains. Cluster 4 can be described as 'Historian/Fictional Accounts,' 10.1% (n = 43). Websites were evenly distributed between the different levels of availability. Like Clusters 1 and 3, this cluster contained a significant number websites that were focused on traditional history content. This cluster contained a significant proportion of historical and fictional accounts, and significantly excluded all other accounts. The websites were evenly distributed across website domains.

Discussion

Proponents claim that the Internet is a useful tool in social education to create an informed democratic citizen because it provides access to 'more information,' which equals better democratic citizen decision making. In this paper we advanced a rationale for examining the Internet within a multicultural democratic framework that explicitly addressed issues of diversity, rather than a means to access and store more information. Our purpose for this framework is to create a space for Internet research that could lead to greater diversity in democratic citizenship education. This framework concentrates on the curricular content of websites, leading to the question, "When using the Internet, just where do students go to access information and what do they select?"

Results of this study indicate that the Internet might be more accurately described as providing 'more of the same information' when pre-service teachers are not explicitly directed to use the Internet to foreground diverse cultures within American democracy. Only one of ten websites contained information that was not readily available through other local resources, and definitely available websites was a significant grouping criterion for the two most prevalent clusters, Cluster 1—Textbook Accounts and Cluster 2—Teaching Resources; indicating teacher educators should not assume the Internet will inherently provide preservice teachers with access to new information. Only Cluster 3—Primary Sources significantly excluded readily available websites as a cluster-grouping criterion. Given the tendency for the Internet to provide preservice teachers with otherwise available information and Primary Sources as the only cluster that provided otherwise unavailable information, teacher educators may need to explicitly direct preservice teachers to search for primary sources on the Internet if their goal is to provide access to new information. Results also indicate there may be greater success if they are directed to .edu and .gov Internet domains, as websites within the Primary Sources cluster were most often accessed from these domains.

To further justify our description of the Internet as 'more of the same information,' consider that more than half of the websites focused on traditional historical narratives that did not contain any voices of under-represented groups, and over a quarter of the websites contained only teaching resources (that also did not focus on under-represented groups). Only one of every ten websites focused on issues of diversity. Even when students accessed primary sources, Cluster 3, almost all were focused on traditional historical content. Indeed, a cluster-grouping criterion for the Primary Source cluster was the significant *exclusion* of diverse voices. In other words, the website content held little diversity and instead replicated the homogenous approach of textbooks, even when primary sources came into the picture. Simply, the theme is redundancy – the Internet provided more of the same information students have had access to in textbooks and other print, television and video media, shown to be thoroughly lacking in the presentation of diverse voices that speak of different ways of knowing and interpreting the meaning of American history and democracy. This indicates that, from a pedagogical and curricular standpoint, one cannot assume that the Internet will inherently provide access to more diverse information. Just as teacher educators may need to direct preservice teachers to primary sources by searching .edu and .gov domains, teacher educators may also need to be explicit in mandating diversity as a theoretical frame by which to understand what and why preservice teachers must not approach the Internet as a technical, neutral tool.

A potential limitation of this study is the notion that preservice teachers in this study did not intend to use the Internet to support the NCSS goals of developing and maintaining diversity, and that this misuse of the Internet skewed the dataset that informed our analysis. At best, this limitation should necessitate a discussion that revolves around ways to better train preservice teachers to use the Internet. We acknowledge that these preservice teachers were not introduced to the critical, multicultural democratic framework in understanding to what end they were using the Internet, but argue the issue does not lie in their technical use of the Internet. Each preservice teacher had 6 hours of technology training, demonstrated great facility when searching for and evaluating websites, and had no difficulty selecting 20-25 reputable websites for their research database. Rather, we question the Internet as a democratic medium and instead see it as a means to replicate dominant ideologies not by strict governance of websites, but by the ways in which we approach the Internet as unproblematic and neutral. Unless teachers explicitly foreground diversity, students will not do it on their own, as they have been long indoctrinated into the traditional, non-diverse accounts as true and good and hence outside of questioning. As such they will not seek other perspectives on curriculum. If we direct students to use primary sources and historical fiction, our data indicates that they will not largely reproduce the usual information, which meets Dewey's first criteria. But that is only the first step. Students must have a multicultural theoretical framework that addresses race, class and gender perspectives that will direct students away from the largely Eurocentric narrative and toward those voices and perspectives mostly ignored in textbooks except as sideline material. Examining Internet technology in the social studies with a multicultural democratic framework surpasses the technologically savvy concentration because the latter emphasizes the access and manipulation of 'more information' without interrogating whether the information is homogenous, redundant and representative of only one form of thought. In other words, our empirical analyses raise the distinct possibility that providing pre-service teachers with the multicultural democratic evaluative framework to create curriculum could facilitate a pedagogical approach that will actually lead to the increase of diversity in the creation of democratic citizens.

References

Berson, M. J., Lee, J. & Stuckart, D. (2001). Promise and practice of computer technologies in the social studies: A critical analysis. In W. Stanley (Ed.), *Critical issues in social studies research for the 21st century*, pp. 209-230. Greenwich, CT: Information Age Publishing.

Bolick, C. M., Berson, M., Coutts, C., & Heinecke, W. (2003). Technology applications in social studies teacher education: A survey of social studies methods faculty, *Contemporary Issues in Technology and Teacher Education, 3*(3), 300-309.

Bowers, C.A. (1988). *The cultural dimensions of educational computing: Understanding the non-neutrality of technology*. New York: Teachers College Press.

Bromley, H. (1998). Data-driven democracy? In H. Bromley & M. Apple (Eds.), *Education/technology/power: Educational computing as a social practice*, pp. 1-28. Albany: SUNY Press.

Dewey, J. D. (1915). *School and society*. Chicago: University of Chicago Press.

Dewey, J. D. (1916). *Democracy and education*. New York: Macmillan.

Dewey, J. D. (1958). *Art as experience*. New York: Collier Books.

Feenberg, A. (1995). Subversive rationalization: Technology, power and democracy. In A. Feenberg & A. Hannay (Eds.), *Technology and the politics of knowledge*, pp. 3-22. Bloomington, IL: Indiana University Press

Gay, G. (1997). The relationship between multicultural and democratic education. *The Social Studies, 88*(1), 5-11.

Glenn, A.D. (1990). Democracy and technology. *The Social Studies, 81*(5), 215-217.

Marri, A. (2003a). Multicultural Democracy: Toward a better democracy, *Intercultural Education, 14*(3), 263-277.

Marri, A. (2003b). Social studies, race, and the World Wide Web. In G. Ladson-Billings (Ed.), *Critical race theory perspectives on the social studies: The profession, policies, and curriculum* (pp. 247-269). Greenwich, CT: Information Age.

Marri, A. (2005). Building a framework for classroom-based multicultural democratic education: Learning from three skilled teachers, *Teachers College Record, 107*(5), 1036-1059.

Mason, C., Berson, M., Diem, R., Hicks, D., Lee, J., & Dralle, T. (2000). Guidelines for using technology to prepare social studies teachers, *Contemporary Issues in Technology and Teacher Education, 1*(1), 107-116.

McKnight, D., & Robinson, C. (in press). Social education and technological determinism: From technologia to technocracy. *JAAACS: Journal of the American Association for the Advancement of Curriculum Studies.*

Parker, W. C., (1996). "Advanced" ideas about democracy: Toward a pluralist conception of citizen education, *Teachers College Record, 98*(1), 104-125.

Schlesinger, A. (1991). *The disuniting of America*. New York: Norton.

Shaffer, D. W. (under review). Multisubculturalism: Computers and the end of progressive education. Retrieved October 15, 2005 from http://coweb.wcer.wisc.edu/cgi-bin/cv.cgi?REQUEST=show_embed&CAT=New.

Salinas, C., & Robinson, C. (2002). Finding multiple voices through the Internet. *Social Studies and the Young Learner, 14*(3), 31-32.

Whitworth, S., & Berson, M. (2003). Computer technology in the social studies: An examination of the effectiveness literature, *Contemporary Issues in Technology and Teacher Education 2*(4), 472-509.

Zambon, M. (2003). Technology, race consciousness and the oppressor. In G. Ladson-Billings (Ed.), *Critical race theory perspective on social studies: The profession, policies, and curriculum*, (pp.271-290). Greenwich, CT: Information Age Publishing.

Adopt & Adapt: Structuring, Sharing and Reusing Asynchronous Collaborative Pedagogy

Miky Ronen, Dan Kohen-Vacs and Nohar Raz-Fogel
Instructional Systems Department, Holon Institute of Technology, Israel
Email: ronen@hit.ac.il, dan@kohenfamily.net, nohar@hit.ac.il

Abstract: This paper presents a new approach for creating and conducting *structured asynchronous collaborative activities* and incorporating them in the existing instructional setting for all subjects and levels. CeLS is a web-based system designed to create and reuse Activity Structures; runable formats reflecting various collaborative instructional strategies e.g., creating and analyzing a common database, reaching an agreement, peer-product evaluation, contest, creating a group product. The unique feature in CeLS's design is its ability to use learners' products from previous stages and to conduct complex, multi-stage, structured activities. CeLS provides a sample of content-free Activity Structures and a searchable domain of all the activities that were implemented with students. Teachers can explore these examples, adopt them for personal use and adapt their structure and content to suit their specific needs. If none of the existing pre-designed resources seems to suit the needs, they can create new structures using basic building blocks.

Introduction: The Challenge

One of the declared unique advantages of technology for teaching and learning is its potential to support collaborative learning (CL). The first generation of e-learning, and systems designed to facilitate its implementation on a large scale, has regarded learning as an individual process mainly based on content resources. As a result, the corresponding standards developed for Learning Management Systems (LMS) focused on the organization of the resources. Additional tools for conducting free communication with the teacher and between peers (discussion group boards, chats, groupware) were provided, but these elements were not integrated with the other parts of the LMS.

New specifications for Instructional Management Systems based on the concept of "Leaning Design" (IMS-LD) have emerged only recently (Hummel et al., 2004). The IMS-LD engine (CooperCore) and editor (RELOAD) specifies a template that enables creation of synchronized and personalized workflow through a course. New management systems are developed according to these specifications, such as COWS (Peter & Vantroys, 2005) and Gridcole (Bote-Lorenzo et al., 2004). The new specifications support learning scenarios and the management of the activities assigned to students during a course, but they do not yet address the more complex needs of incorporating asynchronous collaborative activities into the instructional process.

Collaborative activities have existed and were successfully implemented by teachers well before the era of e-learning. These activities are not just free group discussions, but instructional strategies that comprise of *well-defined structures*, consisting of *distinct stages* that are *interconnected and based on each other* in various ways. Asynchronous collaboration is nowadays performed using generic tools such as group discussion boards or wikis (Cunningham, 1998). While these generic tools offer effective means for free communication and for collaborative editing (Guzdial et al., 2001), they are not very effective for performing *structured* collaborative activities such as the "scripts" presented by Dillenburg (2002). These needs led scholars to look for other solutions that will support online structured collaborative activities. One way to enhance the effectiveness of CL systems is to reify the scripts in the interface of the learning environment (Dillenburg, 2002). An example of such approach is the C3MS, that uses collaborative portal sites (Schneider, 2004) enabling the teacher to create "pedagogical collaborative scenarios" by combining existing "bricks" such as wikis, forums and interfaces designed for specific purposes.

The limitations of the present specifications for the design of environments that will enable the *execution* of complex CSCL scripts are discussed in the Kaleidoscope report (Hoeksema, 2004). These limitations are related to insufficient support to the modeling of groups, artefacts, dynamic features, complicated control flow and varied forms of social interaction. More specifically, when the different environments used to facilitate the actions involved in a pedagogical scenario are not integrated, it is difficult to follow and to support the flow of information in order to reuse products created in previous phases. Since pedagogical scripts may be endlessly varied, complicated control flow relating actions to participants is crucial, in order to allow flexibility of the instructional design. Some of these issues were addressed by LAMS, a new learning activity management system that enables creation, customization and reuse of collaborative sequences (Dalziel, 2003).

Our goal was to design an *executable* XML-based model that will confront some of these challenges and will provide teachers with a practical tool for creating and conducting complex *structured collaborative activities* in the actual educational setting. Any attempt to design a collaborative learning system is subject to trade-offs (Dimitracopoulou, 2005). Our major concerns were: usability, flexibility, reusability and sharing between teachers. The design was primarily aimed at asynchronous activities that can be performed in large groups (classes). In this paper we shall present the CeLS (Collaborative e-Learning Structures) framework and general structure while focusing on its unique features.

CeLS: Collaborative e-Learning Structures - The Building Blocks

CeLS is a web-based system consisting of a server-side run-time engine and a client side Activity Editor. An additional server module is responsible for administrative aspects. An Activity Structure (AS) may include any number of stages of interaction between a learner and the system. Each stage comprises of any combination of distinct objects of *four different types* (Figure 1):

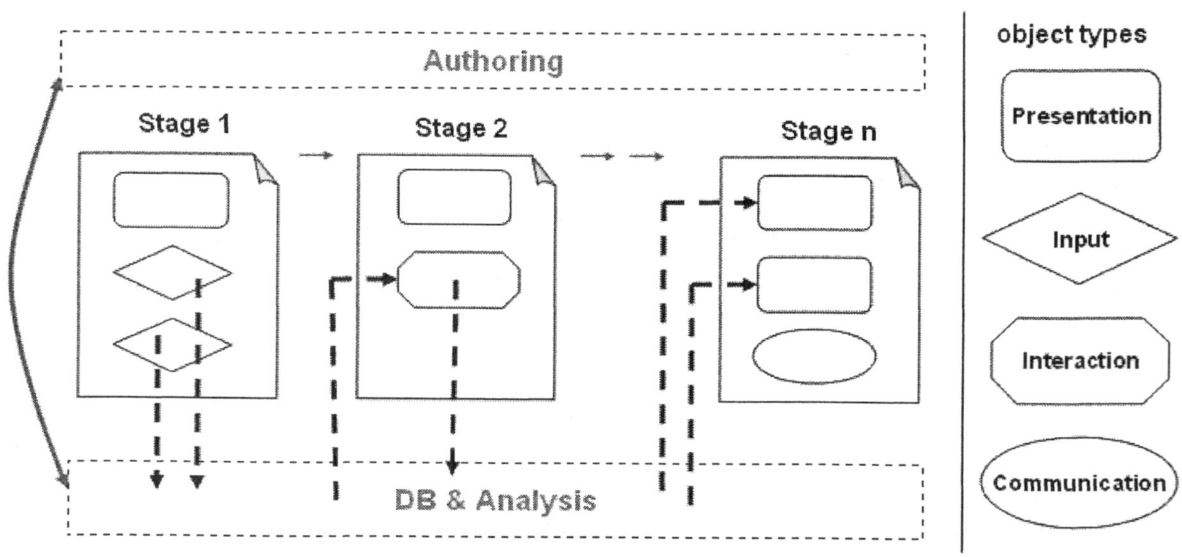

Figure 1: Schematics of an Activity Structure.

- **Presentation** objects are passive elements used to present information of any kind (text, hyperlink, media). This information can be provided by the teacher or consist of learners' *products* from previous stages. A product can be an organized collection of distinct items contributed by different participants (identified or anonymous) or a single item that results from the combined action of a group.
- **Input** objects are interfaces that allow the participant to submit *new data* to the system (text, hyperlinks, media or any kind of attached electronic file or as voting on various scales).
- **Interaction** objects are interfaces that allow participants to *interact with products* created in previous stages, in various ways: by grading, ranking, categorizing and editing or responding to these products via text or graphic manipulations.
- **Communication** objects are interfaces that allow participants to freely communicate with each other or with the teacher.

Each object has properties that can be adjusted by the author. Some properties are generic, for instance, if the completion of an object is mandatory or not, and others are particular to the object or to its type, for instance, maximum or minimum text length or the vocabulary used for a Text Input object.

These basic building blocks are merely technological and do not carry any pedagogical meaning. It is only their *combination* as an Activity Stage and or Activity Structure that creates such meaning.

An activity stage can consist of *any combination* of objects of various types. The functionality is determined by attributing properties related to groups to the stage or to specific objects, so that different participants may encounter different information and perform actions on different data items during the same activity stage. As a result, the process represented by the whole activity is not actually linear, though it may seem linear to each of the participants. A stage may be assigned "start" and "end" times, advance upon completion or according to other conditions defined by the author of the activity.

Groups and Subgroups

The CeLS master group is a class. Groups can be merged to form 'communities' or divided to *families* of subgroups representing subjects assigned to the subgroups or roles played by the subgroups. A family of subgroups has specific properties such as maximum and minimum number of members in a subgroup, number of subgroups, their generic or particular names. An Activity Structure may *use different families of subgroups* in its stages. For instance, in a Jigsaw structure, family A may represent the Projects groups and family B the Experts groups. The first stage of such activity can be performed within subgroups of family A, the second stage is performed within subgroups of family B, the third stage is performed within subgroups of family A using the products of families B, and the last stage is performed in the master group (class) using the products of family A.

The subgroups are only organizational definitions and they *do not have to be populated* (assigned with members) in order to create or to edit an Activity Structure. These organizational definitions are an *integral part* of the Activity Structure and are kept intact when the activity is duplicated for reuse with different learners. Assigning specific students to groups and subgroups can be done just before the actual use of the Activity Structure with students.

Students can be assigned to subgroups in one of three ways: randomly by the system, manually by the teacher, or by self registration within a specified period of time. These options are designed to suit different needs: Automatic population is useful for activities in which participants' identity is not relevant, and self registration suits activities that include face to face work. Manual teacher control is always available and can be applied along with any of the other options.

CeLS Author: Managing Activity Structures

Figure 2 offers a glance at the CeLS authoring capabilities. *My Activities* allows teachers to access their own activities (preview or participate), to manipulate them (edit or duplicate), or to view students' contributions and follow their actions without interfering. Groups and subgroups creation is handled by the *my Groups* options. The definitions of an activity can be edited after the activity has started, enabling the teacher to introduce modifications and adjustments 'on the fly', by adding or changing objects in a stage or adding stages. *Activity Structures* present the teacher with a collection of pre-defined generic structures. These Structures are content-free skeletons and include recommendations for their customization to various needs and settings. The *Sample Activities* option provides a searchable domain of all the activities that were *implemented* with students by the system users, in all institutions, contents and levels. Teachers can view and explore these examples, adopt them for personal use by duplicating them, then adapt their structure and content to their specific needs. If none of the existing resources seems suitable, the teacher can create a *New Structure* using the basic building blocks.

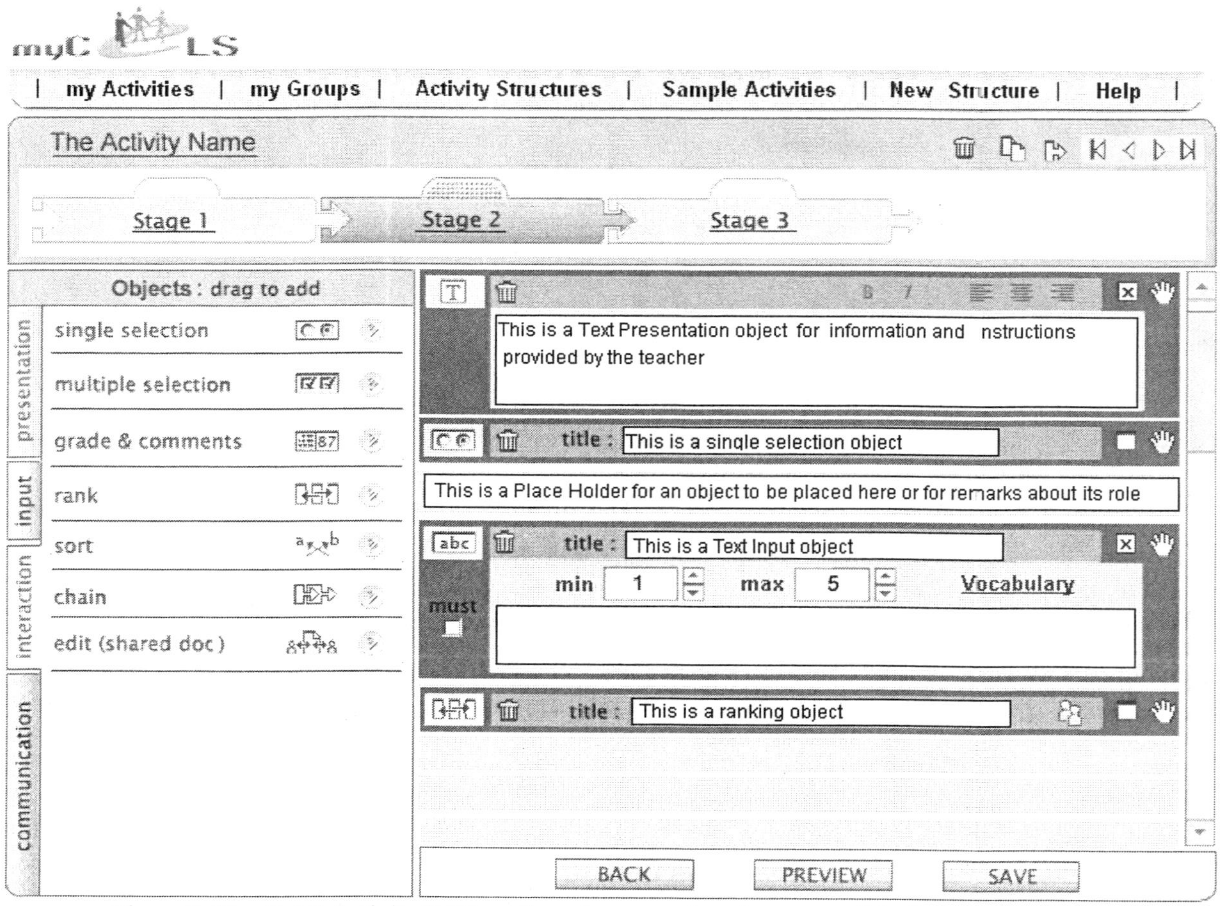

Figure 2: The CeLS Activity Editing. Sample screen showing some of the Interaction objects.

The Student Interface

The student interface is created according to the student's identity, enabling learners to access activities to which they are enrolled. The interface is kept as simple as possible, so that students can focus on the task at hand. The necessary instructions and information are an integral part of the activity stage. Previous peer products are gathered in one place (within Presentation or Interaction objects) in an organized manner, preventing the need to open and scan many messages. Figure 3 shows a sample screen from the second stage of an activity conducted in a photography course (Abrahamov & Ronen, 2005). In the first stage the students were challenged to create photographs with interpretative meaning and submit their products to the system. This stage used a "post before view" approach (Duffy et al., 1998). In the second stage each student was presented with three anonymous peer products out of the 25 items submitted by the class, and was asked to analyze them according to given criteria. In the following stages the analyses of each of the photos were presented, compared and discussed.

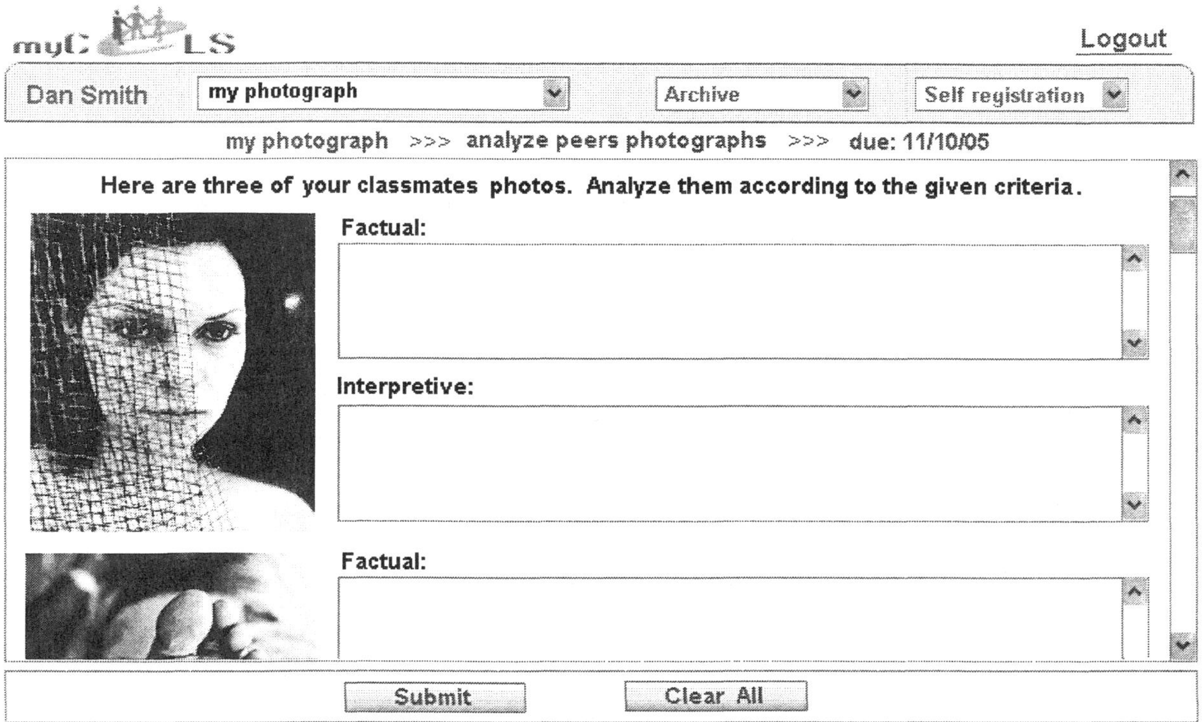

Figure 3: A sample student screen of an activity stage that involves evaluating peers' products.

Sharing and Reusing Activities

CeLS Activity Structures are not pre-programmed entities but are created by a client-side mechanism related to the system metadata. An Activity is tagged by three types of metadata:

- **Descriptive metadata provided by the author**: author identity, activity name, instructional goals and specific remarks and recommendations.
- **Runtime created metadata**: This metadata is *automatically produced* when the Activity Structure is defined or edited, for instance: the number and order of stages and their contents, groups' definitions and their attribution to each of the activities' objects.
- **Informational metadata produced by the system:** This data is extracted from the actual implementation of the activity with students, reflecting its history and evolution: how many times it was used, where and by whom, in which subject matter domain, how many students had participated, and how the structure was changed by users during its "life".

This design facilitates sharing and reusing of Activity Structures. A teacher can search for existing activities according to their content domain, target population, instructional goals, group size, and other characteristics included in the metadata. The teacher can view the activity's history and even contact the authors for personal advice.

First Experiences

CeLS prototype was piloted during 2003-4 in Israel by 25 teachers in 48 courses (1600 students) conducted in 9 universities and colleges, 5 schools and 4 in-service teacher courses. Class size varied between 15 - 64 students. Activities were also tested in a 'community' formed by 5 classes (30 students each) from three different schools. The structured asynchronous activities were used in a variety of subjects including: science, technology, education, medical professions, philosophy, IT and art. The activities tried were variants of AS developed for strategies such as: creating and analyzing a common database, conflict, contest, peer evaluation and peer product evaluation. The length of the activities ranged between 1-8 weeks. In some of the courses the system was used for conducting one activity and in others for up to 10 activities during one semester. Our preliminary findings indicate that overriding motivation for selecting and adapting an AS is the core structure rather than parameters such as age level and content domain. For instance, a structure originally created for elementary school geography was adopted, transformed and used in a university education course.

Challenges of Sharing and Reusing Structured Collaborative Activities

The very flexibility provided by CeLS may become a double-edged sword. A large number of available structures may be confusing or even overwhelming; the limited prototype tested with a small group of teachers revealed more than 100 variants of several basic structures. How can we cope with this challenge, if, as our pilot study suggests, the activity's characteristics that may interest teachers are not necessarily the age group or the subject it is used for, but aspects related to the specific instructional design offered by an activity. Tagging an activity with a particular name is evidently ineffective. Classifying the activities by categories representing major instructional strategies, such as conflict, competition, jigsaw etc., may be a starting point. Such rough classification is not satisfactory for a large collection, since each of these categories can be implemented in different ways with many variants. Furthermore, an AS developed in CeLS may offer any combination of these instructional strategies. The first attempt in this direction was to create different types of sub-categories. An a-priori detailed classification may be useful for anticipated activities but it does not offer a solution for new structures that are developed by users and automatically added to the system database. The classification should be clear and usable to teachers and immediately related to their pragmatic needs. These needs are not necessarily related in the teacher's mind to learning theories or instructional strategies, but may possibly refer to other superficial characteristics. A typical example was a physics teacher looking for activities dealing with visual representations, while this approach eventually led her to find, then effectively adopt and adapt an activity created for an art course. Another challenge lies in following and making sense of the variations of a structure, since even a small detail in the design can make the difference (Kali & Ronen, 2005). One of our challenges is to define an effective method for categorizing the existing activities, as well as the ones that are continuously added, that will allow a teacher to take advantage of peer experience. This effort is based on research currently being conducted with teachers.

Concluding Remarks

We have presented a modest attempt to develop a technological approach and to design a tool that enables teachers to address some of the endlessly varied and complex needs of running structured asynchronous collaborative activities. CeLS is not a comprehensive LMS. It is currently used in conjunction with available LMS (Britannica, Moodle) or as an independent environment. It does not provide solutions for all types of online collaborative activities nor is it meant to replace groupware or collaborative environments designed for learning in specific subject domains. At this point we have not attempted to track or automatically support the individual learning process, though such mechanisms could be added. Rather it is a tool designed to *empower teachers*, enabling and encouraging them to incorporate online collaborative activities into their daily practice by providing them with a flexible tool and many examples that they can *explore*, *adopt* and *adapt*. The first cadre of CeLS's users are teachers, at all levels and subject matter domains, who are already trying to use the available tools for conducting asynchronous structured collaborative activities in their courses. CeLS has enabled them to design and implement activities that were very difficult or impossible to handle before. Judging by the teachers' reactions, we may expect many others to follow.

At this point we neither restricted, nor imposed any specific instructional design. An activity that may seem non-collaborative according to the common definitions of CL (Dillenburg, 1999) may still be pedagogically valid and effective in various ways. Dealing with aspects of students' and teachers' learning, that does or does not occur via the use of CeLS is beyond the scope of this paper. The research that accompanies the system's use will eventually reveal whether and how it affects students' learning and the effectiveness and popularity of the various instructional designs in diverse settings. The most interesting question for us is if, and how, the availability of such facility can contribute to the *professional development of teachers*. The findings will present more directions for improving the design of the next versions and a deeper insight into the potential and challenges of using technology for conducting complex asynchronous structured activities.

References

Abrahamov, S., & Ronen, M. (2005). The double blend: integrating a web-based visual literacy layer into practical photography instruction. *Innovations in Education and Teaching International* (in press).

Bote-Lorenzo, M., Vaquero-Gonzalez, L., Vega-Gorgojo, G., Dimitriadis, Y., Asensio-Perez, J., Gomez-Sanchez, E., & Hernandez-Leo, D. (2004). A tailorable collaborative learning system that combines OGSA grid services and IMS-LD scripting. In *Proc. of the Tenth International Workshop on Groupware: Design, Implementation and Use* (pp. 305-321). Springer-Verlag.

Dalziel, J. (2003). Implementing Learning Design: The Learning Activity Management System (LAMS) In Crisp G., Thiele, D., Scholten, I., Barker, S., & Baron, J. (Eds.) Proceedings of the 20th Annual Conference of the Australasian Society for Computers in Learning (pp. 593-596).

Dillenbourg, P. (1999). What do you mean by collaborative learning? In Dillenburg P. (Ed.) Collaborative-learning: Cognitive and Computational Approaches. (pp.1-19). Oxford: Elsevier.

Dillenbourg, P. (2002). Over-scripting CSCL: The risks of blending collaborative learning with instructional design. In P. A. Kirschner (Ed.), *Three worlds of CSCL: Can we support CSCL?* (pp. 61-91). Heerlen: Open University of the Netherlands.

Dimitracopoulou, A. (2005). Designing Collaborative Learning Systems: Current Trends & Future Research, *CSCL2005 Conference*, May 30-June 4, Taipei, Taiwan.

Duffy, T. M., Dueber, B., Hawley, C. L. (1998). Critical Thinking in a Distributed Environment: A Pedagogical Base for the Design of Conferencing Systems, In: Bonk, C. J. and K. S. King (Eds.), *Electronic Collaborators: Learner-centered Technologies for Literacy, Apprenticeship and Discourse* (p. 73). Mahawah, NJ: LEA associates.

Guzdial, M., Rick, J., & Kehoe, C.(2001) Beyond Adoption to Invention: Teacher-Created Collaborative Activities in Higher Education, *Journal of the Learning Sciences*, *10* (3), 265-279.

Hoeksema, K. (2004). Examples of existing standards to describe CSCL scripts. *Kaleidoscope: concepts and methods for exploring the future of learning with digital technologies*, D23.2.1 (Final).

Hummel, H., Manderveld, J., Tattersall, C., & Koper, R. (2004). Educational modeling language and learning design: new opportunities for instructional reusability and personalized learning. *International Journal on Learning Technology, 1* (1), 111-126.

Kali, Y., & Ronen, M. (2005). Design principles for online peer-evaluation: Fostering objectivity, *CSCL2005 Conference*, May 30-June 4, Taipei, Taiwan.

Peter, Y., & Vantroys, T. (2005). Platform Support for Pedagogical Scenarios. *Educational Technology & Society*, *8*(3), 122-137.

Schneider, D. (2004) Conception and implementation of rich pedagogical scenarios through collaborative portal sites. In Tokoro M. and Steels L., (Eds.), *A Learning Zone of One's Own Sharing Representations and Flow in Collaborative Learning Environments*. Amsterdam : Washington, DC: IOS Press. http://tecfa.unige.ch/proj/seed/catalog/docs/sevilla03-schneider.pdf

Acknowledgements

We would like to thank Liron Shalev for his contribution to the design and the realization of the system and our student Hagai Horowitz for his devoted work. Dr Yael Kali and her team at the Technion and the PhD students Hanna Berger and Osnat Eldar from the Weizmann Institute for their valuable comments, and all the teachers who used the CeLS prototype during its first testing phase.

The CeLS project is partially supported by the Planning and Budgeting Committee (PBC) of the Israeli Council of Higher Education.

Co-Design of Innovations with Teachers: Definition and Dynamics

Jeremy Roschelle, SRI International, 333 Ravenswood Ave, Menlo Park CA 94303, Jeremy.Roschelle@SRI.com
William R. Penuel, Nicole Shechtman, 333 Ravenswood Ave, Menlo Park CA 94303,
William.Penuel@SRI.com, Nicole.Shechtman@SRI.com

Abstract: Researchers in the learning sciences have explored a collaborative approach to developing innovations that fit into real classroom contexts. *Co-design* relies on teachers' ongoing involvement with design of educational innovations. To date, investigators have described the application and results of co-design, but have not defined the process nor explored how it plays out over time. In this paper, we define co-design, suggest seven key process components, and use data from interviews to illustrate how dynamic tensions in the process can unfold over time.

Introduction

We know from studies of educational innovations that teachers' interpretations of their classroom contexts strongly influence the level and nature of adoption (Cohen & Hill, 2001; Talbert & McLaughlin, 2002). Likewise, studies of technology-supported curricula shows that adoption depends on how well teachers' perceive them to "fit" within their goals for students, teaching strategies, and expectations for student learning (Blumenfeld *et al.*, 2000; Means *et al.*, 2001). Researchers in the learning sciences have explored a collaborative approach to developing innovations that "fit" into real classroom contexts. *Co-design* relies on teachers' ongoing involvement with design of educational innovations, which typically involve technology as a critical support for practice. Innovations resulting from co-design processes include a wide range of curriculum materials in school science (Reiser *et al.*, 2000; Shrader *et al.*, 2001) and mathematics (Roschelle *et al.*, 1999). In addition, co-design has been used to develop assessment materials in science (Atkin, 2001; Edelson, 2002) and in reading and mathematics to help teachers improve instruction (Shepard, 1997).

The co-design approach to the problem of "fit" differs from top-down approaches in that the process pays close attention to teachers' everyday work practices. Co-design practitioners pay attention to broad goals for learning and large-scale systems. In contrast to approaches to reform in which teachers are simply expected to follow scripts for teaching, teachers are active participants in co-design and are viewed as professional contributors to reforms.

The co-design approach has close affinities with several other traditions of design. For example, in its attention to teachers' goals for learning, co-design parallels the tradition of *value-sensitive design,* in which successful adoption is assumed to depend on whether designs reflect users' core values and needs (Friedman, 1996). Co-design requires attention to the usability of designs in particular learning contexts, which makes it similar to the focus in *user-centered* (Carr, 1997) and *scenario-based* design processes (Carroll, 1995). In its commitment to the active participation of teachers in the design process, co-design shares many of the same values of *participatory design* (Ehn, 1992; Muller & Kuhn, 1993), a tradition with a rich history in the development of workplace technologies. It also shares assumptions of researchers who have advocated for *learner-centered design* (Soloway *et al.*, 1994), which emphasizes the need to develop tools that can motivate students in a wide variety of contexts. Finally, it shares assumptions with researchers who conduct *design-based research* (Cobb *et al.*, 2003; Design-Based Research Collective, 2003) into the effects of innovations in education.

Co-Design: A Definition

We define co-design to be *a highly-facilitated, team-based process in which teachers, researchers, and developers work together in defined roles to design an educational innovation, realize the design in one or more prototypes, and evaluate each prototype's significance for addressing a concrete educational need.*. Although there are significant roles for teachers as participants in co-design, it is not a fully democratic process. Instead, accountability and ultimate responsibility for quality and decision making rests with the project leaders. In this section, we describe seven characteristic features of co-design as a method.

1. Co-design takes on a concrete, tangible innovation challenge. Like participatory design, co-design begins with a goal of creating a tangible innovation.. At the same time, this aspect of co-design distinguishes it from open-ended, exploratory research on learning innovations in which the goal is to explore a problem-space or theoretical construct.

2. The process begins by taking stock of current practice and classroom contexts. The co-design process begins with field work to understand how potential adopters (teachers and students) perform tasks that are expected to be transformed by the innovation. Ideally, this field work also documents key elements of the context—classroom and student characteristics, community values and perspectives, and local reform initiatives. In this aspect, "taking stock" in co-design has many similarities to rapid ethnographic techniques that are used in the design of workplace technologies (Millen, 2000).

3. Co-design has a flexible target. Flexibility is also important because the input of teacher participants in the design process is likely to alter researchers' conceptions of an educational resource. Co-design differs from traditional waterfall design in this respect; it is related to rapid prototyping methods which gather user input iteratively.

4. Co-design needs a bootstrapping event or process to catalyze the team's work. By "bootstrapping," we refer to a shared experience—such as a design workshop or retreat—that establishes common understanding of the need and requirements for a particular resource to be of help to teachers in the classroom.

5. Co-design is timed to fit the school cycle. Because it involves teachers, the work of design must be timed to fit the school calendar and teachers' work schedules.

6. Strong facilitation with well-defined roles is a hallmark of co-design. Both researchers and software developers actively work to keep everyone involved and excited through what is often perceived by teachers as a long process. Researchers facilitate by helping keep the team focused on educational goals; software developers help the team attend to feasibility and the development process. Teachers help construct the key problems co-design must address, help frame the vision for what is to be created, test the innovation in their classrooms, and provide feedback.

7. There is central accountability for the quality of the products of co-design. Unlike some approaches to participatory design, in which there is formal, shared accountability among workers, designers, and managers for system design, co-design has a central accountability structure for ensuring quality in the co-design of educational innovations. Often, this accountability rests with the Principal Investigator of the grant that funds the effort.

The Dynamics of Co-Design

Co-design often elicits strong emotions among participants. The process of coming to terms with one's role and with the possibilities contained within the scope of a single project often brings alternating feelings of joy and frustration, excitement and boredom. Past research reveals tensions that occur in co-design. We review these briefly below and then illustrate how these tensions played out dynamically over time in one case.

Tensions Revealed in Prior Studies

From studies of participatory design, we can learn about the tensions associated with engaging users in the process. For example, studies have pointed out that end users and designers often have different criteria for success (Blomberg & Henderson, 1990). These differences in goals arise because users and designers occupy different social worlds. Success or failure often turns on whether there is mutual understanding of the unique competencies and contributions of different team members (Bowers & Pycock, 1994).

Educational applications of participatory and co-design ascribe similar importance to developing a common understanding of goals, roles, and contributions of team members (Shrader et al., 2001; Shumar, 2003). At the outset of the project, teachers' notions about curriculum and about goals of projects often differ from developers' notions (Shrader et al., 2001). Overly technical discussions among software developers exacerbate barriers (Bowers & Pycock, 1994). Teachers often see researchers' solutions as too theoretical and not practical enough for real classrooms (Shrader et al., 2001). By contrast, researchers often view teachers' limited content knowledge as a barrier to contributing effectively to design efforts (Brown & Edelson, 1998).

The fact that teachers and researchers who engage in co-design together follow different workplace norms poses a second challenge to the process (Reiser et al., 2000). Through the course of the co-design process, teachers' concerns often focus on usability and on students' capabilities much more than on teaching considerations. By contrast, researchers tend to take a more analytical stance and push teachers to justify goals. Teachers can find such talk unsettling.

Time and productivity pressures are yet another threat to the success of co-design. A principal complaint about co-design is that it is very time intensive. In practice, involving users in design is complicated; it takes time, and users' input is often contradictory (Rheinfrank et al., 1992). Many users find the design process boring (Ehn, 1992). Designers must sift through the contradictory input and are often the only ones with the expertise to implement a new program or software design. Attending to these difficulties is a central problematic of co-design.

Dynamic Pattern Over Time: Trajectory of Co-Design in One Project

In the current study, we sought to investigate teachers' experiences and roles in co-design as they evolved. Appreciating how the dynamics unfold over time can help researchers and teachers understand how the tensions of co-design can be addressed in the context of a project. Further, this knowledge can help participants in the co-design process recognize what kinds of confusions and difficulties are possible and perhaps even appropriate at different phases of a project.

The Project

The project that is the focus of this paper was a research and development effort that explored how handheld computers might support improved classroom assessment in science classrooms at the middle-grades. The design products were three distinct handheld software applications students could use during hands-on activities or other class time to compose questions, review knowledge, or collect data. The design process, facilitated by the researchers and developers, had three phases over the course of the school year that evoked distinct teacher involvement and reactions: (1) collecting requirements, (2) rapid prototyping, and (3) software solidification.

Participants

Teachers of students in grades 4–9 were recruited in a coastal, Southern school district with high ethnic and economic diversity. 10 teachers applied, and all were accepted. Only 7 were able to attend the week-long design conference to kick off the project. The teachers who were selected and who were participants in this study were mostly women ($n = 5$), and were an experienced group (median years teaching = 21). They were mostly White but the classrooms they taught were diverse, with some teaching in classrooms where the majority of students were African American or eligible for free or reduced price lunches.

Sources of Data

The primary source of data was a collection of *interviews*, conducted roughly once per month with all of the team members (including researchers and software developers) throughout the design process by a researcher not involved in the co-design. Interviews took place from September 2002 to May 2003, covering the full course of the design process. The structured protocol asked about the participants' contacts, participants' activities, how the participant saw her or his role on the team, what decisions or progress had been made, what was going well, and what was not going well or was a concern. Teachers' answers to questions (a total of 900 responses) were entered into a database. A team of three investigators made several iterative passes through the data, building categories in the style of grounded theory. Through this process, we came to see how teachers experiences' progressed through three distinct phases of co-design. Providing rich description with a seven-page limit is a challenge; the best we can do is to provide the representative snippets of our data.

The Beginning: "I'm impressed that the team is sticking to it."

In the collecting requirements phase, teachers participated in several intensive interviews about their practices and shared information about the different types of lessons they did, the lab activities their classes did, and the problems they experienced in the classroom. They also provided their opinions about what their needs were and how tools might be able to help. The researchers had the teachers walk through detailed scenarios of how they imagined particular activities playing out in their classrooms.

In this phase, teachers experienced many demands on their time and little that they could directly see or use. Laura, for example, said in September, "I feel like I'm putting a lot of effort into this, but not getting anything in return. I haven't seen any fruits of my labor. I'm not sure they realize how much work is involved for the teachers." An essential dynamic of this phase was around building commitment to a long-term design process that was unfamiliar to teachers. The respect that teachers experienced was core to their continued involvement.

Many teachers felt good about their contributions. One teacher, Sharon, stated, "They're sincerely interested in our opinions on things. We're the teachers. We let them know what works in the classroom, what needs to be tweaked, what a 4th or 5th grader is able to do, and how they handle these things." Edward, in December, stated, "The fact that the researchers could incorporate our ideas into the software is outstanding. Usually in teams like this they don't take laypeople's opinions seriously. They were concerned about our concerns."

Teachers also voiced many concerns and frustrations during this phase. A central concern, which came up month after month for every teacher, was finding time in their already overbooked schedule. As Emily described, "You're 24 hours, 7 days a week working for and with your students. On my weekend, my personal time, that's the only time I get to work on this...It's super demanding to do all our responsibilities and serve on all our committees. It doesn't give us a lot of opportunity to play with technology. As anywhere, everything is due yesterday." The developers and researchers people also noticed that this tension was occurring. Several discussed this in their interviews. One of the developers noted in October,

> I had to clench my teeth...hearing for the 20th time [from a teacher], "It's really simple, if it's a ridiculous answer..." Getting teachers to consider the possibility that it's not quite as straightforward as they think it is, to see that it has more depth to it...I don't think we're trying to be pedantic researchers...if you are going to put it into software, you have to be specific. It's a learning process. We'll get there.

Another researcher reflected, "I'm impressed that the team is sticking to it. The teachers are finding out that they got in for more than they bargained for. But they are still engaged."

The Middle: "We're trying it out in the real world."

As the projects moved forward into rapid prototyping, the teachers' roles shifted. It became more multifaceted: they participated both as designers and practitioners.

As designers, they described their role as "giving feedback," "input on what I see as potential for using the Palm," "tester," and "guinea pig." They were on the front lines trying out prototypes in their classrooms. As Janet described, "We're trying it out in the real world situation to see if what we think will work in theory will actually work in practice." They were observed by the researchers and developers, collected data about the students, and communicated to the team what was going on in their classrooms. They also worked on creating lesson plans to incorporate the tools, offered informed opinions about the software, and worked on more and more refined articulation of their needs. As Emily described, "One of my contributions is that I'm always looking for opportunities and ways to test the program out."

Teachers reported increased engagement during this creative phase. Many were putting substantial effort into finding new ways to integrate the prototypes or actual software into upcoming lessons. Several of the teachers described the excitement of their students with participating in the project. Many also discussed their appreciation of the researchers' openness and ongoing support, as well as their increasing coherence as teams.

Teachers also expressed several concerns and frustrations throughout this phase. Again, time was the most prominent issue. Teachers had difficulty finding the extra time to do all the planning and preparation for the activities.

In parallel with their work as designers, the teachers were also shifting and expanding their teaching practices. Several teachers reported growth over the year in how they were approaching teaching. They reported that the detailed reflection for both the design work and the issues around formative assessment expanded their awareness of their practices and increased their ability to reflect. For example, Emily reported in September, "The process is pretty amazing to us. We are learning so many different ways that our problems can be solved." In February, Emily said,

> The people I'm connecting with are giving me a diversity of opinions to work with about best practices and worst practices. It's catalyzing my growth as a teacher and also myself as a person. It gives me a higher level of satisfaction and enthusiasm. For going into the classroom and teaching with my students, I know that there's something new and better for me to be doing, and a way of doing things more effectively. So it yields a more positive outcome in their learning. If you want to teach, that's everything.

The End: "We're where we wanted to be—even if it was a bit slow"

As rapid prototyping phased into software solidification, the teachers' roles shifted yet again. As Greg put it, "I see my role as somewhat different.... The first year was development, and we're pretty much done with that. Now it's implementing." Teachers could shift their focus toward practice; they spent more time thinking about how to integrate the handhelds into their classrooms.

Furthermore, the teachers found themselves in roles they described as "liaison," "salesperson," and "mentor." Emily and Janet found themselves talking with parents in the community about the project and the use of handhelds. Janet also felt that she was now trying to "sell the benefits of Data Doers to new teachers, especially the new members of the team." Kevin also had begun looking ahead to working with the new teachers next year: "It will be a mentor kind of thing." Sharon also stated, "I'm anxious to see what happens when we add the new people. There are people on our staff who are excited. We'll build the team larger."

In the end, the teachers were pleased with the outcomes of the project, and all expressed satisfaction. Kevin, for example, stated, "I'm very happy about the project; to have had input and really seen come to fruition is really nice. Good stuff." And Greg, who had often expressed frustration over the course of the year, stated, "What's going well is that we got to the point at the end of the year that we wanted...I was frustrated it took so long. But I'm optimistic that we got done what we want to accomplish. We're where we wanted to be—even if it was a bit slow."

Discussion

The key tensions of co-design persist across phases: teachers never have enough time; software developers and teachers never share the same workplace norms; a common language is always a work in progress. Yet, within these tensions, the social dynamic between teachers and researchers evolves over time, particularly with regard to agency and ownership. In the beginning, teachers did not begin with a strong sense of ownership in the project or a clear sense of the roles that they would play. It was not until handheld computers arrived in their classrooms and classroom testing began that teachers began to feel as if the project was at least partly theirs. As teachers came to see how excited their students were about the handheld computers and how pilot versions of the software worked in their classroom, they began to adopt more active roles within the project. By the end of the year, teachers had become strong advocates for the software. They recognized that they would play an important role in introducing and encouraging the use of the software to teachers who would participate in the field trial and the school community.

A key benefit of engaging the teachers in co-design was professional development. The co-design process offered teachers a chance to develop and refine their own ideas about teaching in the framework of exploring how new software works in the context of their classrooms. Two of our teachers reflected on multiple occasions about how they benefited from the opportunity to reflect on their teaching as part of the co-design process. One middle school teacher commented that researchers' perspectives were so different from their own that they gave her a new way to look at her own classroom teaching. She said that their design team meetings included:

> Phenomenal conversations about what improves learning. The team is making me realize that I have always focused on classroom management, not on how the kids are actually learning. This affects my teaching tremendously.

Another elementary teacher observed changes in how her students learned with the software, and these were changes she had not expected. When she introduced her students to software that collects students' questions, she noted:

> I was amazed at the impact of using questions as an assessment tool. When I had the kids ask questions, even on information we had covered and tested before, it really helped me to see the flaws in their understanding. We could then go back and discuss them.

Conclusion

By defining co-design and describing key process steps, we have sought to contribute to refining and spreading this promising method of design. Our account of teachers' experiences in co-design, based upon a systematic database of interview data, suggests the importance of the process steps in managing the tensions that arise as researchers, developers, and teachers work together over an extended period of time. Our case study suggests that managing these tensions led to increased agency on the part of the teachers, increased reflection on their practice, and increased ownership of the resulting design. Technology integration remains an elusive yet important goal. Based upon our experience, the co-design process can play a role in creating a tighter integration of curriculum and technology through the involvement of teachers in the design of innovations that they can meaningfully use in their classrooms.

References

Atkin, J. M. (2001, 2001, April). *How science teachers improve their formative assessment practices.* Paper presented at the Annual Meeting of the American Educational Research Association, Seattle, WA.

Blumenfeld, P., Fishman, B. J., Krajcik, J., Marx, R. W., & Soloway, E. (2000). Creating usable innovations in systemic reform: Scaling up technology-embedded project-based science in urban schools. *Educational Psychologist, 35*(3), 149-164.

Carr, A. A. (1997). User-design in the creation of human learning systems. *Educational Technology Research and Development, 45*(3), 5-22.

Carroll, J. M. (1995). *Scenario-based design.* New York: Wiley.

Cobb, P., Confrey, J., diSessa, A. A., Lehrer, R., & Schauble, L. (2003). Design experiments in educational research. *Educational Researcher, 32*(1), 9-13.

Cohen, D. K., & Hill, H. C. (2001). *Learning policy: When state education reform works.* New Haven, CT: Yale University Press.

Design-Based Research Collective. (2003). Design-based research: An emerging paradigm for educational inquiry. *Educational Researcher, 32*(1), 5-8.

Edelson, D. C. (2002). Design research: What we learn when we engage in design. *The Journal of the Learning Sciences, 11*(1), 105-121.

Ehn, P. (1992). Scandinavian design: On participation and skill. In P. S. Adler & T. A. Winograd (Eds.), *Usability: Turning technologies into tools* (pp. 96-132). New York: Oxford University Press.

Friedman, B. (Ed.). (1996). *Human values and the design of computer technology.* New York: Cambridge University Press.

Means, B., Penuel, W. R., & Padilla, C. (2001). *The connected school: Technology and learning in high school.* San Francisco, CA: Jossey-Bass.

Millen, D. R. (2000). Rapid ethnography: Time deepening strategies for HCI field research. In *Proceedings of the conference on designing interactive systems: Processes, practices, methods, and techniques* (pp. 280-286). New York, NY: ACM Press.

Muller, M. J., & Kuhn, S. (1993). Participatory design. *Communications of the ACM, 36*(6), 24-28.

Reiser, B. J., Spillane, J. P., Steinmuler, F., Sorsa, D., Carney, K., & Kyza, E. (2000). Investigating the mutual adaptation process in teachers' design of technology-infused curricula. In B. Fishman & S. O'Connor-Divelbiss (Eds.), *Fourth international conference of the learning sciences.* (pp. 342-349). Mahwah, NJ: Erlbaum.

Roschelle, J., DiGiano, C., Koutlis, M., Repenning, A., Phillips, J., Jackiw, N., et al. (1999). Developing educational software components. *IEEE Computer, 32*(9), 50-58.

Shepard, L. (1997). *Insights gained from a classroom-based assessment project.* CSE Technical Report 451. Los Angeles, CA: National Center for Research on Evaluation, Standards, and Student Testing.

Shrader, G., Williams, K., Lachance-Whitcomb, J., Finn, L.-E., & Gomez, L. (2001). *Participatory design of science curricula: The case for research for practice.* Paper presented at the Annual Meeting of the American Educational Research Association, Seattle, WA.

Soloway, E., Guzdial, M., & Hay, K. E. (1994). Learner-centered design: The challenge for HCI in the 21st century. *Interactions, 1*(2), 36-47.

Talbert, J. E., & McLaughlin, M. W. (2002). Assessing the school environment: Embedded contexts and bottom-up research strategies. In (pp. 197-227).

Acknowledgements

This material is based in part on work supported by the National Science Foundation (NSF) under Grant Number REC-0126197. Any opinions, findings, conclusions, or recommend-ations expressed in this material are those of the authors and do not necessarily reflect the views of the NSF.

Blurring the Lines: Learning *and* Assessing in Quadrant D
Some Key Lessons from Four Successive Years of Embedded Assessment Design in our Sustainable Earth Project

Ken Rose, Martin Block
Clemente Community Academy, Chicago Public Schools
The Center for Learning Technologies in Urban Schools, School of Education & Social Policy,
Northwestern University, 2115 N Campus Drive, Evanston, IL 60208
Tel: 847-491-7494 Fax: 847-491-8999
Email: rose@northwestern.edu, mblock@clementehs.k12.il.us

Abstract: This design paper describes some of the main characteristics of four successive iterations of an embedded assessment activity used in our annual "Sustainable Earth" project. The details shared here come mainly from a comparative analysis of our last two assessment design cycles, highlighting differences between two common activity structures: a culminating student presentation and a global summit debate. We found that reframing the task and attending to a few specific elements of the teachers' and students' roles both before and during the activity resulted in two significant impacts. First, the debate activity transformed the student learning that took place in terms of its rigor and relevance, making it more characteristic of what we describe as "Quadrant D learning." Second, the debate greatly increased our teachers' ability to assess their students' learning of desired content and skills, making it an even more effective embedded assessment activity than the final presentation alone.

Keywords: curriculum, assessment, instruction

Introduction/Framework

The work reported here is part of a larger research study that closely examines the complex decisions teachers make in the selection and interpretation of learning activities that can make their students' thinking more explicit for both formative and summative assessment. During this broader study, a team of teachers and researchers designed and piloted a series of four consecutive iterations of an embedded assessment activity for a long-term high school environmental science project called "Sustainable Earth." From 2000 to 2003, this project was conducted annually for 3-4 weeks each spring with ninth grade students at a large urban high school in the Midwest.

This particular design paper describes some of the main characteristics of the four successive iterations of the Sustainable Earth project, concentrating on a detailed comparative analysis of the last two assessment cycles, those taking place in the spring of 2002 and spring of 2003. It was in these final two years of implementation that the embedded assessment activity was most extensively changed—from a culminating student presentation about a specific country to a global summit of developed and developing countries. This global summit added a valuable component of structured debate to the final presentation, forcing the students to internalize the project's content, use the synthesis and communication skills they had been taught, and take on multiple perspectives of the countries they represented. Prior research has shown that such a debate, or argumentation, task can be worthwhile in increasing student learning (Snider & Schnurer, 2002; Bell, 1998), as varying perspectives actually strengthen the understanding of the content and its context. We claim here that such debate can be equally valuable as a technique for embedded assessment.

An explicit goal of our design research of novel instruction and assessment strategies has been to increase teachers' awareness and use of more types of formal and informal classroom assessment (Wilson & Sloane, 2000), and to determine how opportunities for such assessment can be improved. Black and Wiliam (1998) define classroom assessment as, "all those activities undertaken by teachers and by their students... that provide information to be used as feedback to modify the teaching and learning activities" in which they are engaged (p. 140). They conducted a survey of about 250 current assessment studies, published during or after 1988, and concluded that significant gains could be achieved by implementing full systems of classroom assessment that incorporate this kind of appropriate formative, as well as summative, function.

The Black and Wiliam review provides clear evidence that classroom assessments by teachers, combined with appropriate feedback to students, can have robust, positive effects on student learning and achievement. Learning gains from systematic attention to classroom assessment were found to be greater than most of those for any other educational intervention. Previous research supports these findings (Crooks, 1988; Fuchs & Fuchs, 1986).

Yet, as strong as those claims may be, classroom assessment practices are currently underdeveloped in most schools, and many unanswered questions remain. Teachers and teacher educators still wonder how to foster its use most effectively to promote student learning. To answer these kinds of questions, the specific design decisions that shape successful classroom assessments need to be examined much more closely in real-world contexts. This study does just that.

There is also a larger issue to be addressed. Researchers have indicated that these more informal classroom assessments are often not even viewed as a significant form of assessment by many teachers, principals, parents, or the general public (Atkin, Black, & Coffey, 2001). Developing it as a valid pedagogical skill is therefore seldom seen as a priority for overburdened classroom or professional development time. This research seeks to change that view.

In this paper, we describe the broader research context and provide a brief overview of the Sustainable Earth project. Then, we share some specific lessons learned from the design decisions we made, based upon our analysis of student learning compared across the last two instances. In general, each successive assessment design provided new constraints and affordances for us to gain insight about our students' understanding, and offered new opportunities for the activity to serve simultaneously as a valuable learning activity as well as an assessment activity. The findings from this ongoing assessment design project suggest specific improvements for our own future instruction as well as important ways to inform our ongoing study of classroom-based embedded assessment.

The design lessons presented here are important because culminating presentations continue to be a very common activity structure for teachers and curriculum designers to use for assessment in project-based learning. However, most final presentations generally lack an adequate amount of rigor and relevance in terms of the academic demands they place on students. In addition, they do not afford opportunities for continued student learning; that is, they are typically not embedded into the instruction, but are instead tacked on at the end of a project as a summative assessment.

We will demonstrate with this example that reframing the task and attending to a few specific elements of the teachers' and students' roles before and during the activity can have at least two significant impacts. It can transform the student learning that takes place in terms of its rigor and relevance, making it more characteristic of what we describe as "Quadrant D learning." It can also greatly increase a teachers' ability to assess what students know and can do, making it a more effective assessment activity.

Method

Research Context

The participants in our larger, ongoing study are part of an urban public high-school-within-a-school project known as the Mathematics-Science-Technology Academy (MSTA). MSTA teachers are collaborating with university researchers in the reiterative design and implementation of computer-supported, collaborative, inquiry-based projects for their students in two Chicago high schools (Kemeny & Kwon, 2002). This study of the assessment design in the Sustainable Earth project was taken from work done in one of those MSTAs each spring, from 2000 through 2003. The school is a medium-sized neighborhood high school, with approximately 800 students and 45 teachers, located in a large urban center in the Midwest.

Two classes of approximately 25 ninth-graders each participated in all four iterations of the project, with a total of 200 students over the course of four years. The freshmen teachers saw each group five times a week, for 45-minute periods, although the periods were sometimes blocked for 90 minutes.

Overview of the Sustainable Earth Project

The Sustainable Earth project grew out of earlier efforts by the Center for Learning Technologies in Urban Schools (LeTUS) and some MSTA teachers at nearby high schools. In the mid-1990s, LeTUS produced a curriculum called Global Warming, which helped middle-school students learn about the effects of the differential heating and cooling of the earth's surface (see http://letus.org/globalwarming.htm for complete details on this curriculum). An MSTA teacher adapted that original curriculum for his ninth graders, adding more population content and deliberately bridging across disciplines to include more social studies. In our subsequent revisions of the curriculum, we added a driving question to kick the inquiry off. We began by posing the following broad problem to the students:

> Exponential human growth and development are threatening Earth's ability to support life. The unsustainability of natural systems and natural cycles is evident, and human development is the cause. Our reliance on nonrenewable sources of energy, our misuse of water and land resources, and our uncontrolled population growth all threaten the natural sustainability of the Earth. Do we control our fate? How can we recreate a more sustainable Earth?

After discussing the driving question, students were divided into groups of 2-4. Each group represented the governing body and heads of state for a particular country from different regions in the world (Mexico, Brazil, China, Japan, India, Germany, Switzerland, Kenya, South Africa, and Sudan). Each country has different needs, different degrees of development, and different problems. However, all countries will be affected if humans continue to disrupt the Earth's natural balances.

During the project the students completed several instructional activities to prepare them for a culminating assessment at the end of the project. They completed a pamphlet and a newsletter to describe different aspects of the country they were assigned. Their research focused upon three major topics: (a) Sources of Energy and Energy Consumption; (b) Water and Land Quality; and (c) Population Growth.

The Sustainable Earth project always had its focus in environmental science, but it involved the participation of the other core subjects—math, social sciences, and English—as well. For example, the math teacher helped the students use linear and exponential equations to project their countries' populations into the year 2050. With these data, they could represent their countries at the summit by making recommendations about the need for laws or programs to control population growth and making decisions about the use of natural or renewable resources over the next 50 years.

In the first three years, our students did oral presentations at the end of their investigation where they provided specific information about their countries. They were given lists of specific data to include in their presentations. This included type of government, demographics, economy/GNP, literacy rate, population growth rate, life expectancy, sources of energy, carbon emissions, and deforestation rates. Students focused on the three main themes of energy, land and water, and population growth in light of each nation's politics, economics, health, education, family life, religion, popular arts, and human rights.

Final Presentations →	Presentations with New Questions →	Presentations with Pen Pal Letters →	Global Summit Debate
2000	2001	2002	2003

Figure 1: Activity Structure Redesign Timeline

Every year, after reflecting on the depth of student learning evident in the project presentations, we decided we needed to do some revisions to the culminating activity (see Figure 1). We were struggling to find a way to get the students to engage with rigorous content and take some ownership over the ill-defined problems being studied. We were trying to find out how much scaffolding they needed—and what kind—in order to successfully see the connections and interrelationships in the issues and nations represented. In the second year, therefore, they were given additional lists of thought-provoking questions to which they should be prepared to respond during their presentations. These questions were very specific, such as: "At the current rate of growth, how large will your population be in 20 years?" or "What is being done in your country to protect natural resources?" In the third year, a new component was added to the final assessment that provided students with a chance to take on more of their country's point of view. We asked that each group write five pen pal letters where they pretended to be a person from the country they were assigned to represent. In these letters, they talked about the homes (building materials, type of structures), education system, transportation, tourist sites, recreation, climate, currency, average income and occupations.

In the fourth year, still frustrated at the lack of deep learning going on, both before and during the presentations, we changed the entire activity structure to that of a global United Nations summit, where students had the opportunity to share and debate their findings with students representing two or three other countries. The summit consisted of students' responding to larger open-ended questions for each of the three major topics. First, each group described its country's current practices. Second, it stated how its country's practices harm its populace and the global community. Third, it developed a plan to effectively solve any environmental threats. Finally, after each group had a chance to speak on all three of the important environmental topics, all countries in the summit had to come to a consensus and agree upon a piece of environmental legislation that will help restore the Earth's sustainability.

There was a rubric used to assess the students' understanding of the issues, but we found that often the activity eventually seemed to be less about the formal assessment of what the students knew and much more about continued learning about the connections and interrelationships between the issues and the countries. Indeed, this summit activity turned out to be a valuable embedded assessment task, and much more of a true learning experience than anything that had come before. We decided to look more closely at the summit activity, to find a way to describe the changes as well as to isolate some of the important design elements that made it a more successful embedded assessment.

Data Collection and Analysis

Our comparative cases are based on primary data collected during each of the project iterations, each spring from 2000 to 2003. We took field notes of classroom observations and our conversations with students. We also videotaped the final assessment activities and collected samples of student work. Finally, we have conducted interviews with participants and one-on-one design meetings between the participants, including the first two authors– a high school classroom teacher and a university researcher involved closely in the project.

One specific tool we found useful for describing the changing academic demands of the task is the Rigor/Relevance Framework (Daggett & Kruse, 1999). This Framework is based on traditional elements of education yet encourages movement to the application of knowledge instead of maintaining an exclusive focus on the acquisition of knowledge. It is based on two concurrent dimensions of higher standards and student achievement (see Figure 2).

First, there is the Knowledge Taxonomy. Located on the vertical axis, it is a continuum based on the six levels of Bloom's Taxonomy, which describes the increasingly complex ways in which we think. It describes the rigor demands of the activity. The low end involves acquiring knowledge and being able to recall or locate that knowledge. The high end labels the more complex ways in which individuals use knowledge, such as taking several pieces of knowledge and combining them in both logical and creative ways. The second continuum is known as the Application Model. Located on the horizontal axis, it is a spectrum of action or relevance. Its five levels describe putting knowledge to use. While the low end is knowledge acquired for its own sake, the high end signifies use of that knowledge to solve complex real-world problems and to create unique projects, designs, and other works for use in real-world situations.

The Rigor/Relevance Framework has four distinct quadrants. Each is labeled with a term that characterizes the learning or student performance at that level. A "Quadrant A" activity could be choosing the right definition for new vocabulary. A "Quadrant B" activity could be comparing a car lease to a car loan. A "Quadrant C" activity could be analyzing symbolism in a poem. A "Quadrant D" activity could be developing guidelines for publishing content on the Internet. This Rigor/Relevance framework provided us a systematic way to analyze curriculum, instruction and assessment across all of the subjects involved in the Sustainable Earth project. We were able to examine the different iterations of the Sustainable Earth assessment task, and characterize them in terms of the academic demands placed on students.

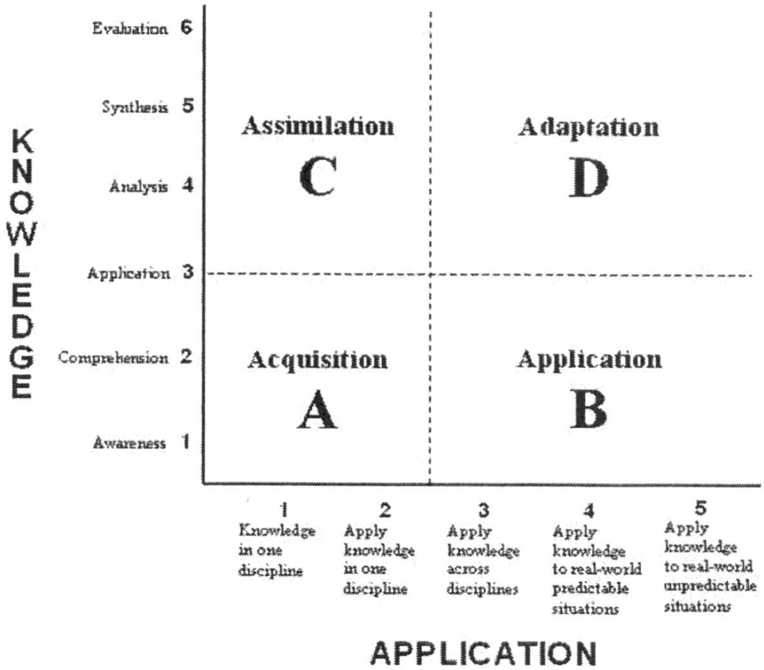

Figure 2: The Rigor/Relevance Framework

While analyzing the assessment activity data in terms of Quadrants A, B, C, and D, we found that we naturally began to attend to some other related dimensions of the project as well. We characterized levels of student ownership of the problem and involvement with the content during the final presentations in 2002 and the global summit debate in 2003. We then described the level of teacher scaffolding of the discussion, the effect of additional opportunities for students to practice beforehand and the changing role of the teachers during the debate. Finally, we looked closely at the effect of taking on the role of the country, or the effect of the students' own perspective.

Results and Discussion/Implications

In reviewing the video clips of the students' final assessments from the last two implementations, one thing stands out clearly. The students who took part in the global summit debate demonstrated a deeper and more contextualized understanding of their country's role in creating a more sustainable earth than the students who made the more formal final oral presentations. The use of the summit debate clearly encouraged more rigorous and relevant learning both before and during the assessment activity. As we looked for a way to describe and explain the differences we saw, we uncovered some rather important design elements.

During the presentations, the students demonstrated learning that we characterized as Quadrant A Learning. They had gathered and stored bits of knowledge and information for their presentations. They were primarily expected to remember or understand this knowledge, but not to use it. The final presentations consisted of lists of facts about each country, memorized and shared with the audience. The presenting students, without exception, followed the order in the guidelines that had been set for them in the task; they had prepared powerpoint slides and often read directly from the slides or from notecards. Questions from audience members, when asked, were surface-level questions like "What is the population of your country?" or "Who is the leader?" In this context, it was the teacher who directed all of the learning, and who had the stake in the learning.

However, during the global summit debates, students clearly demonstrated what we termed Quadrant D Learning. They had the competence to think in complex ways and to apply their knowledge and skills. Even when confronted with perplexing unknowns, they were able to use their extensive knowledge and skills to create solutions that further developed their knowledge. Unlike the final presentations, in which the teachers asked students for specific information so that they could check it off on our rubrics, the summit was much more like an open-ended conversation, grounded in the main issues presented in the project, but broad enough for students to take ownership of the learning.

The move to the debate structure and the transfer of this ownership did not take place automatically. It required a conscious effort on our part to let go. And this was difficult to do. The first few debates we facilitated were in fact very similar to the final presentations, only now the students were seated instead of standing in front of an audience and they were in a different formation with two or three other countries. Not much else was different in those early debates. It seemed very necessary for our teachers to probe for information with questions like "What about when you burn the fossil fuels, what kind of problem does that cause?" We found that, the more the teacher held back with these types of direct questions, though, the more student-to-student discussion took place. After a while, we realized that encouraging students to negotiate and discuss their respective needs provided richer discussions.

The teacher had to play a much more subtle role during the debate than during the presentations. She had to keep reminding the students how they compared with the other nations, modeling the connections between them. This is the most crucial role for the adult in the summit task. In the end, this is what makes it a learning activity as well as an assessment activity. In later debates, we did start to see evidence of students' referring to and building on other students' comments. They responded to what was being said and used information from other groups. Yet this skill had to be modeled deliberately first.

Another less subtle role for the teacher was to remind students to pay attention to what the other country's representatives were saying. The students were encouraged to take notes during the debate, and in subsequent years, were asked to write a formal agreement following the debate. We also added practice sessions so that they could be coached before the summit took place. These sessions were very helpful for the students to gain confidence and flexibility in using their data. We wish we had videotaped them during the practice sessions to compare with the final sessions.

In terms of taking on the role of the country, there were marked differences between the two sets of assessment activities in the number of times the students personalized the content. Those students in the global summit referred to their country's challenges with phrases such as "our population" and "our energy sources." They discussed their solutions with language that showed this perspective; they owned the problems. It was not uncommon to hear them admit: "we have to work on that." However, the students doing formal oral presentations spoke almost completely in the third person. They reported on the current conditions of Germany and China, for example, without taking on the roles or perspectives they were given. They said "Germany should look into alternative fuels" or "China has a policy of..."

As we continue to design and pilot more truly embedded assessments that measure the type of Quadrant D learning we desire, we will strive to keep many of these simple lessons in mind. Above all, we must remember that in order for this kind of assessment to be successful, we must have a real trust in our students; we must believe that they can take ownership of their own learning and demonstrate the deep content understanding and skills we would like to see, as long as we provide them both the freedom and the scaffolding they need to learn.

References

Atkin, J.M., Black, P., & Coffey, J. (Eds.) (2001). *Classroom assessment and the National Science Education Standards*. Washington, DC: Committee on Classroom Assessment and the National Science Education Standards, Center for Education, National Research Council.

Bell, P. (1998). Designing for students' science learning using argumentation and classroom debate. Berkeley, CA, University of California

Black, P., & Wiliam, D. (1998). Inside the black box: Raising standards through classroom assessment. *Phi Delta Kappan, 80*(2), 139-148.

Crooks, T. J. (1988). The impact of classroom evaluation practices on students. R*eview of Educational Research*, *58*(4), 438-481.

Daggett, W., & Kruse, B. (1999). *Taming the educational dinosaur*. Rexford, NY: Leadership Press.

Fuchs, L. S., & Fuchs, D. (1986). Effects of systematic formative evaluation: A meta-analysis. *Exceptional Children*, *53*(3), 199-208.

Kemeny, V., & Kwon, S. (2002). MSTA (Mathematics, Science, and Technology Academy) model of teacher-researcher collaboration. Paper presented at the annual meeting of the American Educational Research Association, New Orleans, LA.

Snider, A.C., & Schnurer, M. (2002). *Many Sides: Debate across the curriculum*. Burlington, VT: IDEA Books.

Wilson, M., & Sloane, K. (2000). From principles to practice: An embedded assessment system. *Applied Measurement in Education, 13*(2): 181-208.

Beyond Essentialist Critiques: The Co-development of Individual and Society within Erik Erikson's Psychosocial Theory of Identity Development

Sage Rose, Cecil Robinson, University of Alabama, Campus Box 870231, Department of Educational Studies, College of Education, Tuscaloosa, AL, 35487-0231
Email: rose021@bama.ua.edu, crobinso@bamaed.ua.edu

Abstract: Erikson's psychosocial theory is often positioned as essentialist, creating the groundwork for criticisms about the resolution of crises as a universal aspect of identity development towards a unified and coherent Self. These critiques represent an oversimplification of Erikson's theory and overlook the centrality of the *co-development of the individual and society* within his theory of identity development. To justify this claim, we examine Erikson's concepts of ego identity (1959, 1968), and demonstrate overlap with Holland, Lachicotte, Skinner, and Cain's 'figured worlds' framework (1998). The purpose of these comparisons is to problematize essentialist critiques of Erikson and create a dialogic space for socio-cultural researchers to consider Erikson's psychosocial theory of identity formation when exploring relationships between identity, agency, power and cultural worlds of practice.

Erikson's psychosocial theory is often positioned within an essentialist framework that conceptualizes identity development as universal across cultures, as an individual and asocial act, and as linearly moving through a series of stages, or identity crises, to create a unified and singular Self. Through such positioning, Erikson's theory is commonly portrayed and criticized for being a rigid, normative, and hierarchical stage-structured approach (Dannefer, 1984; Weiland, 1993, as cited in Kinnvall, 2004). Cultural theorists reject this essentialist position in favor of concepts of identity that are contextually bound (Bourdieu, 1977; Willis, 1977), (re)made through on-going struggles to participate in cultural worlds of practice (Lave & Wenger, 1991; Rogoff, 2003), and manifest through multiple and often conflicting selves that are always forming, never complete (Bakhtin, 1981). Holland, Skinner, Lachicotte and Cain (1998) provide an excellent summary of how the essentialist and cultural stances are often contrasted.

> Cultural studies of the person—including a significant proportion of the anthropological research on (cultural) identity—share an opposition to a general "Western" notion of identity that takes as its prototype a coherent, unified, and originary subject. ... The projects of these newer studies are quite unlike that of Erik Erikson ... with its focus on the tasks any person must successfully accomplish to resolve the psychodynamic dilemmas of maturation and thus establish a coherent identity. ... [N]ewer studies rely upon feminist and later psychodynamic approaches ... which recognize social forces that make such an integrated subject an unlikely occurrence. (p. 7)

These statements highlight the characterization of, and opposition to, Erikson's theory of identity because it is framed within biological and psychological concepts that do not recognize the multiple, conflicting, and irresolvable nature of self-hood, and has little regard toward cultural interactions and associated social power. We argue that such characterization represents an oversimplified account of Erikson's theory, and overlooks the centrality of the *co-development of the individual and society* within his theory of identity development. To justify this claim, we examine differences between Erikson and Freud, his theories about identity development, personality and stages (1959, 1968), and demonstrate conceptual overlap with aspects of Holland, Lachicotte, Skinner and Cain's 'figured worlds' framework (1998).

The overarching purpose of this conceptual examination is to problematize some of the essentialist critiques of Erikson's theory and create a dialogic space such that research may consider Erikson's psychosocial concepts within sociocultural research about identity, agency, and cultural worlds of practice. Such space is important because, as Erikson argues, "We must learn to understand cultural and technological consolidation, for it, ever again, inherits the earth" (1968, p. 33).

Erikson's *Psychosocial* Theory of Identity Development

To understand how the co-development of the individual and society could be central to Erikson's research, one must differentiate Erikson from Freud by historically situating Erikson's work. He worked closely with Sigmund and Anna Freud, used Freudian terms such as id, ego, and superego, and is rightly characterized as a psychoanalytic theorist. Because of the similarities, many have incorrectly considered Erikson's use of terms analogous with Freud's use of the terms, and confused Erikson's *psychosocial theory* with Freud's psychosexual theory. Whereas Freud focused on the primal baseness of human nature, Erikson looked to ways humans could flourish within social and institutional milieus. When Erikson began his American psychological practice in the 1940s, he observed an uncommonly high number of patients who, he believed, were being misdiagnosed with psychosis by Freudian psychoanalysts. As a result, Erikson began to conceptualize his client's struggles in terms of identity conflicts—conflicts that were intimately tied to society. Erikson recognized the changing culture of America, the changing nature of America's identity. Fresh from WWII and in the throes of industrialization, Americans were conflicted with unprecedented economic growth, while their humanity was reduced to labor as a cog in an assembly line (Weber, 1958). Given Erikson's growing conceptualization of the social into his psychoanalytic practice, it was inevitable for him to reformulate Freud's work and emphasize social over biological factors for his theory of epigenetic development (Roazen, 1976). It also explains differences in the use of terms because he felt, "the traditional psychoanalytic method . . . cannot quite grasp identity because it has not developed terms to conceptualize the environment" (Erikson, 1968, p. 24).

Erikson (1968) even explained difficulties of researching identity formation because it was "located *in the core of the individual* and yet also *in the core of his communal culture"* (p. 22, italics original). To address this difficulty and to highlight how individuals and society co-develop, Erikson argued that, "identity formation employs the process of simultaneous reflection . . . by which the individual judges himself . . . [and how] he perceives the way in which others judge him in comparison to themselves." This process is, "luckily, and necessarily, for the most part unconscious except where inner conditions and out circumstances combine to aggravate a painful, or elated, 'identity consciousness'" (p. 22). Identity consciousness is always changing and developing in increasing differentiation and inclusiveness through awareness of others, and there is no separation of:

> Personal growth and communal change, nor can we separate the identity crisis in individual life and contemporary crises in historical development because the two help to define each other and are truly relative to each other. In fact, the whole interplay between the psychological and the social, the developmental and the historical . . . could be conceptualized only as a kind of *psychosocial relativity*. (p. 23)

Erikson's Identity Stages

Identity stages/crises/conflicts are specific forms of identity consciousness that Erikson argues, and critics rightly point out, occur in a developmental sequence; that is, earlier stages must be resolved before later stages can be resolved. Erikson identified the following stages: trust/mistrust (infancy), autonomy/shame and doubt (toddler years), initiative/guilt (preschool years), industry/inferiority (elementary school years), identity/role confusion (adolescence), intimacy/isolation (young adulthood), generativity/stagnation (middle adulthood), integrity/despair (late adulthood). The ways that one resolves these stages govern the epigenisis of one's personality and allows us to "re-emerge from each crisis with an increased sense of inner unity, with an increase of good judgment and an increase in the capacity 'to do well'…" (1968, p. 92-93). This is consistent with Holland et al.'s (1998) claim that his theory revolves around "tasks any person must successfully accomplish to resolve the psychodynamic dilemmas of maturation and thus establish a coherent identity," and sets up their critique that Erikson fails to recognize "social forces that make such an integrated subject an unlikely occurrence" (p. 7). We argue this critique is problematic because Erikson: (1) recognized the social as central to his theory of identity development; (2) viewed the resolution of identity crises as on-going sources of strength and adjustment that enable persons to negotiate social worlds; and (3) did not equate the resolution of identity crises with a unified self.

Social Nature of Identity Crises

Erikson recognizes the social nature of an individual's development. Indeed, the social is consistent with, and is central to, his concepts of psychosocial and cultural relativity. When one revisits the quote in the preceding paragraph by Erikson about the importance of crises in its fuller context, one reads that the individual is able to:

> Re-emerge from each crisis with an increased sense of inner unity, with an increase of good judgment and an increase in the capacity 'to do well' … according to his own standards and to the standards of those who are significant to him. The use of the words 'to do well' of course points up to the whole question of cultural relativity. Those who are significant to a man may think he is doing well when he 'does some good' or … when he learns to conform all around or to rebel significantly; when he is merely free from neurotic symptoms or manages to contain within his vitality all manner of profound conflict. (1968, p. 92)

This quote highlights that at the heart of any increased sense of inner unity is the appropriation of 'doing well.' Further, doing well is contingent on points-of-view and the cultural capital affording those views importance, both of which are inherently social and particular to the cultural context in which one is deemed to do well.

Contested 'Resolutions' of Identity Crises

The term "resolution" is problematic given Erikson's definition of crisis. "Crisis is used here in a developmental sense to connote not a threat of catastrophe, but a turning point, a crucial period of increased vulnerability and heightened potential [for identity formation], and therefore, the ontogenetic source of generational strength and maladjustment" (Erikson, 1968, p. 96). Crises should not be viewed as something to be resolved as a means to some ultimate identity formation, but as critical periods in its on-going development. Therefore, identity is not something that can begin or end through a crisis, period or stage of one's life. Rather, identity is a dynamic change process that is influenced by continuous interactions between person and social systems, and is continuously created, maintained and recreated throughout adulthood.

> For it is through their ideology that social systems enter into the fiber of the next generation and attempt to absorb into their lifeblood the rejuvenate power of youth. Adolescence is thus a vital regenerator in the process of social evolution, for youth can offer its loyalties and energies both to the conservation of that which continues to feel true and to the revolutionary correction of that which has lost its regenerative significance. (1968, p. 134)

Erikson (1959) emphasized that one should not assume that societal norms, and the resulting identity formation, could be grafted onto a genetically asocial individual through the process of disciplines or socialization. Instead, this process occurs through the membership society extends to the individual and the manner the persons resolves the tasks of her epigenetic development while interacting with society. This could be viewed as an interactive (authoritative) parental relationship, which is characterized by enforced rules and the inclusion of individual participation in making the rules. Translated into broader aspects of society this analogy highlights Erikson's stance that without institutional ideologies there can be no identity formation, and without the participation of the individual there can be no institutions.

To support participation in ways that acknowledge both institutional ideologies and individual agency in the process of identity formation, Erikson (1959) argued many cultures create *institutionalized moratoria*—specific social settings/spaces that afford individuals in *psychosocial moratorium* greater agency to explore, experiment with, and develop different roles and identities. Psychosocial moratorium is not synonymous with a specific crisis or stage, but is a period of time during which individuals choose to participate in these less structured social settings in ways that can be different than dictated by institutional ideologies—i.e., cultural norms, practices and values. Combined, institutional and psychosocial moratorium facilitates participation through the freedom to experiment with various roles without expectations of permanent responsibilities and commitments (Côté & Levine, 1988, 2002). This process appears to be consistent with Vygotsky's (1978) theory of play and Bakhtin's (1984) notion of carnival; each concept acknowledges the agentic affordances and opportunities for identity development. And each concept also acknowledges constraints. Consistent with Vygotsky and Bakhtin, Erikson asserts that this period does not have a total lack of structure; it is still dependent upon degrees of conformity to norms and values of adult society. Institutional moratoria that are loosely structured might have liabilities that result in fragile and/or broken identities; for example, WWII and other veterans who struggle within normative, peacetime societies after experiencing ethic and moral institutional and psychosocial moratorium during war (Erikson, 1968).

Erikson observed that these moratoria are most evident during adolescence, and used this observation to explain why adolescence represents a critical period in one's identity development. His observations appear to be similar to the work of Holland and Skinner (1995) that explored the agency and resulting identity formation/self-authoring of Naudada women in Nepal that took place through the songs of the Tij festival. The Tij festival created a type of institutional moratorium on the topics that women were allowed to discuss within the community, and the women entered a psychosocial moratorium as they capitalized on the opportunity to explore different political and gender narratives and roles through the songs they created and performed (Holland & Skinner, 1995).

Identity Crises and a Coherent Self

Erikson did not equate the resolution of identity crises with the creation of a coherent and unified Self. He instead refers to the 'I,' a complex view of sel(ves) that is not unlike the I-self/Me-self distinction of William James (1892) or G.H. Mead (1934). Consider the following comments by Erikson. (1)

> What the "I" reflects on when it sees or contemplates the body, the personality, and the roles to which it is attached for life—not knowing where it was before or will be after—are the various selves which make up our composite Self. There are constant and often shocklike transitions between these selves. (1968, p. 217)

He specifies that different environmental contexts attract reactions from different selves, and attempts to organize our selves are necessary to maintain the 'I.' This is similar to Holland et al.'s, (1998) notion of orchestration—our attempts to make meaning from our multiple voices/selves as we participate within figured worlds. Further, Erikson's illustration of a coherent 'I' and the shock-like transitions between selves appear to be similar to the process of self-authoring. Holland et al. (1998) explain self-authoring as the continuous process of answering and orchestrating multiple voices over time, and through this process how one can develop (although it is by no means a given) a fairly consistent authorial stance, or identity. In accordance with Bakhtin, they also provide caution against any move towards a coherent and unified self by arguing, "Dialogism makes clear that what we call identities remain dependent upon social relations and material contributions. If these relations and material conditions change, they must be 'answered', and old 'answers' about who one is may be undone" (p. 189). In this statement, they provide a reminder that one's identities are never settled. Erikson offers very similar remarks, "Identity is never 'established' as an 'achievement' in the form of a personality armor, or of anything static and unchangeable" (1968, p. 24).

Cultural Theories and Erikson's Psychosocial Theory

If one accepts the arguments that identity formation within Erikson's psychosocial theory is inherently social, on-going, and never completely coherent or unified, then it opens the possibility of a dialogic space for cultural theories and Erikson's psychosocial theory to coexist and potentially inform one another as researchers strive for more complex and informative conceptual frameworks of identity. Holland et al.'s (1998) figured worlds framework provides an example of the ways that such acknowledgement might be mutually informative. Their work is a synthesis of practice theory (Bourdieu, 1977), dialogism (Bakhtin, 1981; Holquist, 1990), and the socio-cultural development of cognitive heuristics (Vygotsky, 1978) as a framework to tease apart and understand the relationship between cultural worlds, power and agency in the formation of identity. However, there are aspects to their framework that are not resolved. For example, they argue that self-authoring is a complex notion of orchestration. They continue to explain that "there is no integrity to self-understanding, but there are degrees of relatedness among the partial selves that respond to sets of our associates, our multiple others" (p. 211-212). Thus, Holland and her colleagues acknowledge that self-authoring (identity formation) happens and provide a basic description. However, they do not provide a theoretical framework about how or why it happens. Instead, they state, "[t]hat is the story [about how self-authoring happens] we will have to leave to another time" (p. 211-212). We believe it is exactly this process that Erikson's psychosocial theory of identity formation addresses. Specifically, Erikson's (1968) theory provides an account of orchestration and identity development such that 'the degrees of relatedness among partial selves' and the process of self-authoring can be conceptualized and understood through the ways that one's ego identity strives to establish a sense of temporal and spatial continuity.

Ego identity is the ego's ability to sustain a sense of continuity in the face of change and is "characterized as the actually attained but forever to-be-revised sense of the reality of the Self within social reality" (Erikson, 1968, p. 211). The ego defines situations and develops constructions of reality while actively managing the Self (Côté & Levine, 2002). The Self is not intended to be a singular orientation, but a compilation of selves that require synthesis/maintenance/orchestration. In particular, Erikson identified four general patterns in which ego identity struggles with issues of coherence. These patterns result over time and are contingent upon how one negotiates experiences of everyday events and critical periods/crises in relation to norms, values and expectations of the cultural worlds in which they participate. The four general patterns are diffusion/confusion, foreclosure, moratorium, and 'more coherent.' (2) Diffusion/confusion is an ego identity lacking coherence and results from the absence of recognizing or orienting one's Self in alignment with or opposition to, social norms and values. As a result, one is not able to take an authorial stance; for example, a high school student to which nothing matters—grades, family, friends, job, and/or life in general. Foreclosure is a coherent ego identity that results from the absence of an identity crisis and is something imposed *on* the individual by society; for example, a Republican who unproblematically and consistently orients/authors one's Self as such because their family and/or community's commitment to Republican ideology. Institutional and psychosocial moratorium, as we have already described above, is striving for ego identity coherence by exploring different authorial stances. An example is a father struggling with and oscillating between their orientation/authorial stance towards his family, career and community. A more coherent ego identity results from the development of a consistent authorial stance from those explored in moratorium. For example, the father who consistently commits to and authors himself as father and family-oriented person, and that this orientation is present in other areas of their lives such as career and community. Note: this is not to argue that an achieved, coherent ego identity results in a unified or unchanging Self. As stated earlier, Erikson fully acknowledges that the "constant shock like transitions between the selves" (as father, community member, male, American, etc.) are ever-present within the Self of an achieved, coherent ego identity (1968, p. 217). Again, one's ego identity is never finished or "static and unchangeable" (p. 24)—through participation in different figured worlds, events and crises can arise that can create moratorium, and can result in a reorientation of one's ego identity.

In short, Erikson's concept of patterns of ego identity provide a means to examine the different ways that persons orchestrate their multiple selves and create (or not), change, and/or maintain, a consistent authorial stance within their figured worlds of practice. Whereas Holland et al.'s figured worlds framework (1998) acknowledge that self-authoring happens, exploring Erikson's psychosocial theory of ego identity provides opportunity to explore how self-authoring happens.

An additional reason to consider the overlap between cultural theories and Erikson's psychosocial theory of identity formation is that past research has attempted to employ Erikson's theory in a way that ego identity could be measured empirically. Thus, not only does such consideration provide fodder for the discussion and conceptualization of identity formation, but it also provides additional research tools for future studies; tools for research that are predicated on almost 50 years of empirical studies. One of the most well known measures of ego identity is the identity status paradigm created by James Marcia (1966). The identity status paradigm consists of a developmental progression through the identity statuses (in developmental order) of: diffused, foreclosed, moratorium and identity achieved, and is loosely based on Erikson's research. Marcia attempted to assess ego identity through semi-structured interviews to identify an individual's specific identity status. Marcia identified two criteria necessary to determine identity statuses: commitment and crisis. Diffusion is the lack of identity crisis/conflict and lack of commitment. Foreclosure requires a commitment, but lacks conflict. Moratorium is when one is in conflict/crisis without commitment. Identity achievement is a commitment a coherent ideological/society stance after experiencing the conflict during moratorium.

Not only can consideration of Erikson's theory provide additional research concepts and tools for cultural researchers conducting identity research, but cultural theories of identity development can also ensure that Erikson's theory is grounded within the social. Though Marcia's work is often considered a direct representation of Erikson's identity theory, it is not without critique. Specifically, critics such as Côté and Levine (1988) argue that Marcia's identity status paradigm oversimplifies Erikson's theory because it relies too heavily on psychological principles and largely ignores the social aspects of ego identity development. Marcia (1976) himself later noted the inconsistency of his identity status paradigm and ego identity development. He stated, "The problem with the statuses is that they have a static quality and identity is never static, not even for the most rigid Foreclosure" (p. 153). Because of this discrepancy, Côté and Levine (1988) consider the paradigm as an inaccurate theoretical representation of Erikson's identity theory and suggest making ego identity status terms more compatible with Erikson by fully integrating the social and historical aspects that make up Erikson's interdisciplinary perspective. We believe that Holland and colleagues' (1998) figured worlds framework can ground the social-historical aspects needed to restructure Marcia's two most stable and static identity statuses (and the two that are most inconsistent with Erikson): identity achievement and foreclosure (1966). Given suggestions of Côté and Levine (1988), we suggest the following changes.

If Identity achievement is viewed as a process of authoring oneself within a figured world, then orchestration, or the attempt to create a coherent "I" in specific social contexts, may serve as an "achieved" portion of identity. This does not mean that the coherent "I" can not be undone, but in that particular context, at that point in history, it has reached an achieved status. Viewing identity achievement as a dynamic process that may change given the social context can maintain a theory that is more compatible to that of Erikson's and Holland et al., and may provide a specific, yet comprehensive explanation of identity that incorporate social, historical, and psychological perspectives.

Marcia's identity foreclosure status has been defined as individuals who rely solely on parental direction in ideology commitment. Erikson (1968), however, described foreclosure as the absence of identity crisis in which moratorium is prematurely ended and is the result of conflict with society. This is similar to Holland et al., (1998) who states, "The 'identities' that concern us are ones that trace our participation, especially our agency, in socially produced, culturally constructed activities - what we call figured worlds" (p. 41). If we move away from Marcia's definition of foreclosure and align it with Erikson's (1968) and build on Holland et al.'s focus on agency, we may conclude that the abrupt ending of moratorium may prevent individuals from self-authoring and limitations may be placed on the ego's sense of agency within that figured world. Such definition provides demonstrates the complementary nature of the two theories, and provides a potentially more nuanced understanding of the development of identity and agency within cultural worlds.

Conclusion

By conceptualizing ego identity development as dependent upon an orchestration of a coherent self within a cultural context, we believe that cultural and psychological researchers can begin to explore the compatibility and overlap of Erikson and Holland et al.'s theories. In particular, we discussed how the ways that ego identity struggles with issues of coherence provides insights into *how* Holland et al.'s concept of self-authoring occurs beyond their claims *that* it occurs. We also discussed ways that Holland et al.'s concept of agency within figured worlds provides insights into the ways that the ego's sense of agency is constrained and afforded during foreclosure and moratorium through participation in society.

We acknowledge that our essay only touches the surface of these constructs, but see it as a starting point for future discussions of other areas of overlap between cultural and psychological theory. For example, a future area of discussion needs to be the relationship of history-in-person and the resolution of crises. Holland et al. discuss how a person embodies their experiences, as history-in-person, and that one's history-in-person is that which interacts with the practices and tools of figured worlds and shape the way one figures themselves into those worlds. Embodied history coming to bear on the present is at the heart of Erikson's theory about the importance of the resolution of crises (i.e., until one is able to historically embody a sense of trust, they will struggle with issues of intimacy later in life). The discussion also needs to be expanded to other theorists. Albert Bandura's social-cognitive theory (1986), which is one of the most thoroughly researched and well-established theories within social psychology, argues that persons who have experienced success or failure in contextually-specific situations will embody that history of success or failure in their self-perceived expectancies, or self-efficacy, about their future ability in similar situations. Indeed, Bandura explicitly theorizes self-efficacy as a contextually-bound theory of agency. Building on Erikson's theory, individuals who have obtained a more coherent sense of ego identity may experience higher levels of self-efficacy (agency) in their abilities to achieve in the future and may have a direct impact on the future success of that person. Tying self-efficacy back to history-in-person, we can identify yet another additional layer. In particular, history-in-person may identify the ways that cultural tools and practices, and issues of power affect one's expectancies and sense of ego coherence, issues that neither psychological theory addresses particularly well.

In this essay we put forth the argument that Erikson's psychosocial theory is generally regarded as an essentialist theory, and is also confused with Freud's psychosexual theory. As a result, his theory is often dismissed by cultural researchers. Our intent of this essay was to demonstrate that these essentialist assumptions are a simplification of Erikson's work and do not acknowledge the centrality of the co-development of the individual and society within his theory. In so doing, we hoped to create a dialogic space that can begin to bridge the gap between cultural, social, historical, and psychological theories for future research to consider a more complex view of identity, agency, power, and cultural practices and tools. Let the conversation begin ...

Endnotes

(1) It is important to note that although consistent, Erikson's use of the "I" is appears to be more comparable to the Me-self rather than the I-self.

(2) We use the term 'more coherent' because Erikson never used the widely acknowledged term 'identity achieved.' Consider the following quote from Erikson (1979):

> I was somewhat shocked by the frequency with which not only the term identity, but also the other syntonic psycho-social qualities ascribed by me to various stages, were widely accepted as *conscious developmental "achievements"*, while certain dystonic states (such as identity confusion) were to be totally "overcome" like symptoms of failure. Thus, my emphasis in each stage on a built-in and lifelong antithesis ("identity" v. "identity confusion") was given a kind of modern Calvinist emphasis. (p. 24, emphasis added, as cited in Côté & Levine, 1988)

References

Bandura, A. (1986). *Social foundations of the thought and action: A social cognitive theory*. Englewood Cliffs, NJ: Prentice Hall.

Bakhtin, M.M. (1981) *The dialogic imagination: Four essays by M.M. Bakhtin*. Ed. M.E. Holquist, trans. Caryl Emerson and Michael Holquist. Austin, TX: University of Texas Press.

Bakhtin, M.M. (1984). *Rabelais and his world*. Trans. Helene Iswolsky. Bloomington: Indiana University Press.

Bourdieu, P. (1977). *Outline of a theory and practice*. Trans. Richard Nice. Cambridge: Cambridge University Press.

Côté, J.E. and Levine, C.G. (1988). A critical examination of the ego identity status paradigm. *Developmental Review*, 8, 147-184.

Côté, J.E. and Levine, C.G. (2002). *Identity formation, agency, and culture: A social psychological synthesis*. Mahwah, NJ: Lawrence Erlbaum Associates.

Erikson, E. (1959). *Identity and the life cycle*. New York: International Universities Press, Inc.

Erikson, E. (1968). *Identity: Youth and crisis*. New York: W.W. Norton and Co., Inc.

Erikson, E. (1979). Report from Vikram: Further perspectives on the life cycle. In S. Kakar (Ed.), *Identity and Adulthood*. Bombay: Oxford Univ. Press.

Holland, D., Skinner, D., Lachicotte, W., & Cain, C. (1998). *Identity and agency in cultural worlds*. Cambridge: Harvard University Press.

Holland, D., & Skinner, D. (1995). Contested ritual, contested femininities: (Re)forming self and society in a Nepali women's festival. *American Ethnologist*, 22, 279-305.

Holquist, M. (1990). *Dialogism: Bakhtin and his world*. New York: Routledge.

Hoover, K. & Eriksen, L.K. (2004). Introduction: the future of identity. In K. Hoover's (Ed.), *The future of identity*. New York: Lexington Books.

James, W. (1892/1985). *Psychology: The briefer course*, G. Allport (Ed.). Notre Dame, IN: University of Notre Dame Press.

Kinnval, C. (2004). Globalization, identity, and the search for chosen traumas. In K. Hoover's (Ed.), *The future of identity*. New York: Lexington Books.

Kroger, J. (2004). Identity in formation. In K. Hoover's (Ed.), *The future of identity*. New York: Lexington Books.

Lave, J. & Wenger, E. (1991). *Situated learning: Legitimate peripheral participation*. Cambridge: Cambridge University Press.

Marcia, J.E. (1966). Development and validation of ego-identity status. *Journal of Personality and Social Psychology*, 3(5), 551-558.

Marcia, J.E. (1976). Identity status six years after: A follow-up study. *Journal of Youth and Adolescence*, 5, 145-160.

Mead, GH (1934). *Mind, self and society*. Chicago: University of Chicago Press.

Roazen, P. (1976). *Erik H. Erikson*. New York: The Free Press.

Rogoff, B. (2003). *The cultural nature of human development*. New York: Oxford University Press.

Vygoskty, L. (1978). *Mind in society: The development of higher psychological processes*. Cambridge, MA: Harvard University Press.

Weber, M. (1958). *The Protestant ethic and the spirit of capitalism*. T. Parsons, trans. New York: Scribner's.

Willis, P. (1977). *Learning to labor: How working class kids get working class jobs*. New York: Columbia University Press.

An analysis of standardized reading ability tests: What do questions actually measure?

Michael Rowe, Yasuhiro Ozuru, & Danielle McNamara, University of Memphis,
202 Psychology Building, Memphis, TN 38152-3230
Email: mprowe@mail.psyc.memphis.edu, y.ozuru@mail.psyc.memphis.edu
d.mcnamara@mail.psyc.memphis.edu

Abstract. This study examined what types of passage and individual item attributes of reading ability tests affect item difficulty. Ninety-six questions from the Gates-MacGinitie Reading Test for 7/9th graders were analyzed in terms of individual item characteristics and passage features that were considered to affect the item's difficulty. Whereas two passage features, word frequency and sentence length, influenced the item difficulty, none of the individual question characteristics were found to affect the item difficulty. Thus, the GMRT may be assessing how difficult a passage readers can comprehend, not how difficult a question readers can answer about a passage. These findings imply that the GMRT may function well when identifying basic reading comprehension skill differences, but not higher level reading skill differences. However, these findings may be the result of the passages in the GMRT having an atypical construction. Specifically, shorter passages tended to be composed of longer sentences.

Introduction

Research on reading comprehension indicates that successful comprehension of text requires the effective execution of a number of sub-processes such as word decoding, lexical access, syntactic processing, and constructing a coherent overall meaning of a text by connecting multiple sentence meanings (Vellutino, 2003). However, in most practical contexts, a student's reading comprehension ability is evaluated in an undifferentiated fashion by standardized tests such as the Gates-MacGinitie reading ability test (GMRT) (Magliano & Millis, 2003). A typical reading comprehension ability test consists of reading a short passage and answering multiple-choice questions based on the passage content. This test format is considered a measure of reading comprehension ability because selecting the correct answer involves reading activities such as understanding the meanings of the passage and the question, and searching for a potential answer in the passage. Indeed, performance on these tests highly correlates with other types of standardized measures of academic ability (e.g., Comprehensive Test of Basic Skills, Preliminary Scholastic Aptitude Test, reading course grades, language course grades; see technical report of Gates-MacGinitie Reading tests, 1989).

Although the benefit of standardized tests is plainly evident, we, along with other researchers (e.g., Embretson, 1994), argue that it is time to move away from an undifferentiated, a-theoretical approach of measuring reading ability. Advances in reading comprehension research have made it possible to analyze item characteristics of reading comprehension test questions in terms of their necessary cognitive processes. A better understanding of the relationship between question item characteristics and the cognitive processes relevant for answering them would facilitate development of more theoretically motivated reading comprehension assessment tools. Such assessment tools would be able to identify specific deficits or problems in readers' comprehension abilities. In sum, reading comprehension ability tests should not only identify who has a comprehension problem, but also diagnose what type of problem they have (Cornoldi, De Beni, & Pazzaglia, 1996).

Analyzing Individual Items of Reading Ability Test

Embretson and Wetzel (1987) examined the item difficulty of several different reading comprehension tests using a number of different coding systems based on the cognitive processing model. According to the cognitive processing model, answering reading comprehension questions involves two stages: 1) encoding a passage, and 2) deciding which answer option to choose. Encoding the passage involves the construction of a coherent representation of the overall meaning of the passage by integrating textbase information and prior knowledge (Kintsch, 1988, 1998). The decision stage involves three components: 1) encoding of the question stem and answer options, 2) mapping and comparing the question and answer options to the passage, and 3) evaluating the truth status of the answer options. According to the cognitive processing model, the processing difficulty of each decision stage component influences item difficulty . Specifically, a question item is expected to be more difficult when: 1) the passage contains more information, 2) the question requests more information,

3) overlap between the question and answer options and the passage content is small, or 4) answer options cannot be explicitly confirmed by the text content.

Based on these hypotheses, Embretson and colleagues (Embretson & Wetzel, 1987; Gorin, Embretson, & Sheehan, 2002) analyzed question items contained in several reading comprehension tests (e.g., Army Services Vocational Aptitude Battery & GRE) and showed that features of the passage and question items were related to item difficulty. More specifically, they found that the propositional density of the passage and the extensiveness of reasoning required to map the question/answer on the passage were two main factors that influenced item difficulty. A similar analysis was performed by Sheehan and Ginther (2001) for reading comprehension questions from a test of English as a Foreign Language. They found that item difficulty was related to the activation value of the information in the passage (e.g., frequency, the location of the target information). Overall, studies have shown that item difficulty of reading comprehension ability tests is related to text and/or individual item features in theoretically meaningful ways. Following this approach, we explored whether the item difficulties of comprehension test items of the GMRT (grade level 7/9; forms K and L) were related to some specific, theoretically important, item characteristics.

Present Study

In this study we followed Embretson and colleague's (e.g., Embretson & Wetzel, 1987) approach, but also included some other theoretically motivated measures. We analyzed the passage difficulty in terms of several text features that are known to affect reading comprehension, including: word frequency, number of words per sentence, adjacent sentence argument-overlap (Britton & Gulgoz, 1991), and the overall propositional density of the text. With respect to word frequency, when a passage contains unfamiliar words, readers often experience difficulty understanding the text, resulting in an increased difficulty of the questions associated with the passage. Processing a longer sentence or a sentence with more propositions places larger demands on working memory (Just & Carpenter, 1992), potentially rendering the passage more difficult to comprehend. Finally, less argument overlap between adjacent sentences places demands on the reader because the reader needs to infer the relations between the sentences to construct a global representation of the text (Britton & Gulgoz, 1991; Kintsch, 1998).

Item characteristics of individual questions are assumed to influence the decision stage in the answering process. To assess these characteristics, we used Embretson's coding scheme, which included: 1) reasoning required to identify the correct answer (Anderson, 1982), 2) confirmability of correct answer, and 3) the number of explicitly falsifiable distractors. In addition, we also included: 1) the degree of inferential processing of the text required to answer a question, and 2) Mosenthal's (1996) coding scheme of abstractness of the requested information, specifically, the level of abstractness in the information requested by the question and target answer. Following Gorin et al. (2002), we expect that more difficult items tend to involve questions requiring more reasoning, more abstract information, or more inferences. We also expect that items tend to be more difficult when the target cannot be directly confirmed and/or distracters cannot be falsified based on the passage content.

Method

Materials

Ninety-six multiple choice questions from the comprehension portion of the GMRT grade level 7/9, forms K and L, were the target of this analysis. The technical report for the GMRT third edition (Gates-MacGinitie Reading Tests Technical Report, 1989) contains item difficulty parameters in terms of the proportion of readers who answered the item correctly. This item difficult score differs from item difficulty parameters based on Item Response Theory used in the Gorin et al. (2002) study. The technical report listed item difficulty for 7th, 8th, and 9th grade children separately for fall and spring semesters. We used item difficulty corresponding to spring 9th grade children for the current analysis. The first two practice questions for each form were excluded from the analysis. Two coders were trained on every coding scheme and rated 15% of total question items from 3 different texts within the GMRT. The two raters agreed at least 80% of the time across all the dimensions of coding. The remainder of the question items and passages were rated by both coders together.

Coding

Ninety-six individual questions and their answer options were coded in terms of their relationship with the target passage in five different ways. The first coding was on abstractness of the information requested by a question using Mosenthal's (1996) scheme. This score addresses the level of abstractness or concreteness of the information requested by the question. Abstractness of the item was classified using a five-point scale. The first classification of questions, *most concrete*, asks for the 'identification of persons, animals, or things.' The *highly concrete* class of questions ask for the 'identification of amounts, times, or attributes.' *Intermediate* questions ask for the 'identification of manner, goal, purpose, alternative, attempt, or condition.' In the *highly abstract* class, the questions ask for the 'identification of cause, effect, reason, or result.' In the *most abstract* class, the questions ask for the 'identification of equivalence, difference, or theme.'

The second coding scheme assessed the degrees of inferential processes necessary to answer questions by examining the degree of overlap between the item (e.g., question and target answer) and the passage. *Text-based* items involved questions and answers that can be found in a single sentence, and the item and passage content were worded the same. *Reworded* items were similar to *text-based* items but items were worded with synonyms to passage content. *Inference* items were those in which the correct answer could not be found directly in the passage. Finally, *integration* items were those that required integration of multiple sentence meanings from a passage to answer.

The third coding system involved the application of Anderson's (1982) rating system used by Embretson and Wetzel (1987). This score addressed the levels of transformation required to match a question item to the passage. There are four levels in this scheme. In the lowest level, *verbatim*, question items use the exact same wording as that used in the passage. The next level is *transformed verbatim question,* in which the same words are used in the question as in the passage, but the sentences are rearranged. In *paraphrased questions,* the question has the same meaning as a sentence in the passage, but different words are used. In *transformed paraphrase questions,* neither the wording nor the phrase order in the question were the same as in the passage.

In addition to the above three schemes that analyze question stem and correct answer together in relation to the passage, we also coded the quality of answer options in two different ways following Embretson and Wetzel (1987). The first score addressed whether the correct answer could be directly confirmed by the passage content. A target answer is *confirmed* if the passage provides explicit textual evidence that the target is the correct answer. However, a target answer is *not confirmed* if the passage has no mention of the target answer. A second score addressed how many of the distractors could be explicitly falsified by the content of the passage. A distractor is *falsifiable* if the passage provides explicit textual evidence that the distractor is incorrect. A distractor is *not falsifiable* if the passage has no mention of the distractor.

Passage features were analyzed using Coh-Metrix (Graesser, McNamara, Louwerse, & Cai, 2004), a computational tool that assesses 238 cohesion and readability measures that are considered to influence comprehension. For the current study, we focused on five measures that are either theoretically or empirically known to influence comprehension difficulty, including: Flesch reading ease, number of propositions, number of words per sentence, word frequency, and adjacent sentence argument overlap. Number of propositions was calculated using the Charniak parser (Charniak, 2000) to count the number of subject level parsings.

Results

Before presenting the results of the detailed analysis on the influence of the individual items and passages on item difficulty, we present the overall, average passage features of the GMRT in Table 1. As indicated, the GMRT is comprised of passages that vary in difficulty from 5th to 12th grade level texts. Also, the data indicate that overall average sentence length is excessive, with the longest sentence having as many as 44 words. These forms of the GMRT had more questions based on narrative (N = 51) passages as opposed to expository (N = 40) passages. The remaining items (N = 5) were based on poetry.

Table 1 Overall passage features used in the GMRT form K and L

	Mean	SD	Min/Max
Flesch Kincaid	7.9	2.40	4.79/12.00
Word per sentence	19.2	8.40	8.40/44.50
Number of words	99.0	22.0	58/130

The results of the main analyses are described in two sections: 1) the effect of the nature of individual questions (question stem and answer options) on item difficulty, and 2) the effect of passage characteristics on item difficulty. Item difficulty is measured in terms of performance (proportion correct) reported in the GMRT manual for the spring 9th grade children. The analysis is split into two sections because passages and question items are affected by different processes. Being able to answer questions about a passage requires more than simply comprehending the passage. That is, information from the passage can be requested in a question item in a number of different ways.

The Nature of Individual Items (Question Stem and Answer Options)

First, we analyzed the item difficulty in terms of the nature of individual question items. As described in the method section, we used three types of coding to identify the nature of requested information by question items: 1) Mosenthanl's (1996) abstractness of the requested information, 2) degree of inference needed about the passage to answer the question item (e.g., text-based, paraphrased, inference, integration of multiple sentences), and 3) how close the wording and the structure of an item (question and correct answer) is to the content of the target passage (adapted from Anderson, 1982). Table 2 indicates the item difficulty parameter as a function of Mosenthal's classification of information abstractness. A one-way ANOVA indicated that there were no significant differences in item difficulty among the five types of requests for information, $F(4, 91) < .1$.

Table 2: Item difficulty as the function of information abstractness

	Most concrete	Highly concrete	Intermediate	Highly abstract	Most abstract
N	9	34	18	23	12
Mean	.65	.66	.72	.66	.65
SD	.12	.16	.15	.16	.17

Table 3 shows item difficulty as the function of the degree of inference necessary to answer questions about a passage, in other words how much the question content is changed from the passage content. A one-way ANOVA indicated that there were no differences in item difficulty among the four types of questions, $F(3, 95) < .1$.

Table 3: Item difficulty as the function of degrees of inference necessary to answer the questions

	Text-based	Re-wording	Inference	Bridging
N	23	26	30	17
Mean	.67	.66	.67	.67
SD	.15	.14	.17	.16

Finally, we examined whether item difficulty was affected by the match between the question stem and the passage content using Anderson's classification scheme. Table 4 indicates item difficulty as a function of Anderson's classification of question transformation. A one-way ANOVA was performed (excluding the verbatim items due to small representation in the sample; $n = 1$). The analysis indicated no difference in item difficulty among the three kinds of items, $F(2, 95) = 1.292$, MSE = .024, $p > .2$.

Table 4: Item difficulty as the function matching between the stem and passage

	Verbatim	Transform Verbatim	Paraphrase	Transform Paraphrase
N	1	13	41	41
Mean	.59	.68	.64	.71
SD	-	.11	.17	.15

Overall item analyses with three different types of coding based on the processing required for answering questions indicated that the nature of the question item is not the primary factor moderating item difficulty in GMRT (7/9th grade) forms K and L.

Following the classification system of Embretson and Wetzel (1987), we analyzed whether confirmability of the target answer and/or falsifiability of distractors based on explicit passage content affected item difficulty. An examination of item difficulty as a function of confirmability of the target answer indicated that there was no difference in item difficulty between items with confirmable target answers (M = .67, SD = .15) and items with target answers that are not confirmable (M = .67, SD = .15), ns. To examine whether the falsifiability of distractors affected item difficulty, we correlated the number of falsifiable distractors (i.e., 0 to 3 answer options) and item difficulty, and found that there was almost no correlation between them ($r = .050$, ns). These results indicated that confirmability and falsifiability of answer options for multiple choice questions do not influence item difficulty in the 7/9th grade GMRT.

The Nature of Passage Characteristics

We correlated item difficulty with several key passage features derived from Coh-Metrix. The correlations are presented in Table 5. The correlations reveal several interesting findings. First, word frequency minimum, a measure representing average lowest frequency word per sentence within each passage, has a significant, positive correlation with item difficulty, indicating that students tend to perform poorly when a question was based on a passage with sentences having more low frequency words overall. In other words, an increase in the percentage of students correctly answering a question can be observed as least frequent words in a passage increase in frequency. When the different types of texts were examined separately, the minimum word frequency was significantly correlated with item difficulty for expository passages ($r = .326$, $p = .43$), but not for narrative texts ($r = .15$, ns.). The average frequency of words for an entire passage was not found to be significant. This finding indicates that the comprehension of a sentence is more closely related to how unfamiliar the least frequent words in a sentence are, as opposed to the overall word frequency level. For example, a sentence containing four frequent words and a single very, unfamiliar word is often more difficult to understand than a sentence containing five moderately frequent words.

Second, a significant, negative correlation between item difficulty and the average number of words per sentence for an entire passage suggested that items based on a passage with long sentences tended to be more difficult. A significant, positive correlation between item difficulty and Flesch reading ease is consistent with these findings because reading ease is calculated based on sentence length and word frequency (i.e., based on word length).

Adjacent argument overlap, an index of local text cohesion, was negatively correlated with item difficulty, suggesting that passages with greater local cohesion tended to be associated with more difficult questions. This finding is contrary to the predicted direction of this correlation, and suggests that a passage with greater co-referential scaffolding between adjacent sentences tends to be more difficult, or at least the questions that target passages with more overlap are more difficult. Finally, contrary to Embretson and Wetzel (1987), number of propositions was found to be positively correlated with items difficulty, suggesting that questions based on a propositionally dense passage tended to be easier in GMRT for 7/9th grade level.

Table 5: Correlation between key passage features and item difficulty parameter

	Item difficulty	Number of propositions	Words per sentence	Reading ease	Word frequency
Number of propositions	.315** p < .01				
Number of words per sentence	-.265** p < .01	-.397** p < .01			
Flesch reading ease	.269** p < .01	.287** p < .01	-.791** p < .01		
Word frequency (min each sentence)	.325** p < .01	.258* p < .05	-.754** p < .01	.738** P < .01	
Adjacent argument overlap	-.216* p < .05	-.116	.598** p < .01	-.628** P < .01	-.480** p < .01

Discussion

This study examined whether question and passage attributes of the GMRT for 7/9th graders affected item difficulty. None of the individual item features were found to be systematically related to item difficulty. There are two possible explanations for this result. Either the coding schemes may be incorrect, or the factors assessed by the coding schemes are not significant predictors for these GMRT item difficulty ratings. The first possibility is unlikely because the items were coded consistently following the instructions provided by the authors who created the coding schemes (e.g., Mosenthal, 1996), and at least two of the coding schemes correlated with each other (Mosenthal & Anderson, $r = .347$, $p <.05$). Thus, the null effect is more likely to be attributable to the presence of other factor(s) that override the influence of individual question features.

Passage attributes appear to override the effect of individual question features in the GMRT. Item difficulty was correlated with minimum word frequency and sentence length in the theoretically predicted direction. A negative correlation was found between item difficulty and minimum word frequency, suggesting that questions targeting passages with more common words are easier to answer. However, this correlation was only found in expository passages suggesting the involvement of different factors in narrative and expository passage comprehension. A negative correlation was also found between item difficulty and sentence length suggesting that it is more difficult to answer questions based on passages composed of longer sentences. These two findings are generally in line with reading comprehension literature (Vellunito, 2003). However, two findings were not in line with the current literature. Item difficulty was correlated with number of propositions and argument overlap of adjacent sentences in a direction opposite of our prediction. Number of propositions was expected to negatively correlate with item difficulty because searching for an answer in a passage with a larger number of propositions is more demanding. Argument overlap of neighboring sentences was expected to positively correlate with item difficulty because larger argument overlap facilitates the construction of a global meaning of a text by providing extra cues to connect sentences. Contrary to these expectations, the results showed a positive correlation between item difficulty and number of propositions and a negative correlation between argument overlap and item difficulty.

The unexpected findings for argument overlap and number of propositions may be due to peculiar features of the passages used in the GMRT. Shorter passages in the GMRT tended to be composed of longer sentences (e.g., a 90-word passage composed of only two sentences). Longer passages were composed of more sentences that were shorter in length. These passage features made longer passages relatively easier to comprehend than shorter passages. Thus, a positive correlation between item difficulty and number of propositions is likely to be a by-product of the presence of numerous propositions in longer passages composed of shorter, easier sentences. Also, a significant positive correlation between argument overlap and the number of words per sentence indicates that longer sentences are more likely to have larger argument overlap because argument overlap in Coh-Metrix is a binary score – if one word overlaps between the sentences, the two sentences are coded as having overlap. Thus, longer sentences increase the chance of having at least one common word between them. Therefore, this negative correlation could also be due to sentence length.

Overall these findings have two important implications with respect to learning science. First, the GMRT primarily assesses reading comprehension ability based on lower level processing proficiency (vocabulary and individual sentence processing) since item difficulty is influenced by passage features, not individual item characteristics (abstractness, inference, etc). In other words, the test primarily differentiates readers' ability based on how difficult a passage one can process. The test appears not to differentiate reading ability based on the higher level reading process of how deeply a reader can process a given text. Since lower level proficiency is mandatory for higher level text comprehension, the GMRT is an effective assessment of reading ability. However, differences in reading ability among readers with sufficient lower level skills to understand difficult passages may not be adequately assessed.

The second implication concerns the limitation and strength of standardized reading ability tests such as the GMRT. The relatively a-theoretical nature of the GMRT is indicated by the small amount of variance of item difficulty explained by theoretically meaningful textual features (i.e., word frequency and sentence length). A multiple regression indicated that word frequency and sentence length together accounted for only 10% of the variance ($R^2 = .11$, $p < .01$), suggesting that a large amount of variance remains unaccounted for by theoretically meaningful attributes of the test. With a more theoretically based assessment the variance associated with known correlates to comprehension ability would be expected to be higher. Thus, deficits found by the assessment for certain readers could be tracked with respect to the overarching factor or factors that are giving them trouble by identifying which question items were missed. However, without such a foundation for an assessment the differentiation and diagnosis of comprehension deficits are at a much grosser level.

One possible reason that this type of standardized assessment is theoretically undifferentiated may arise from its need to assess a wide range of reading abilities associated with a variety of students (i.e., 7th to 9th grade level of students across the U.S.) In this sense, the GMRT may be an appropriate compromise when determining students' general skill level required to understand a variety of text materials. However, this inclusiveness of the assessment tool may undermine the tool's ability to diagnose individual students' specific strengths or problems. Thus, accurate or valid assessment of individual student's ability, in particular the ability of at-risk-students requiring remedies to their comprehension difficulties, needs to be followed up with separate more theory-based assessment tools (e.g., Magliano & Millis, 2003) that can diagnose students' problems in a more differentiated fashion.

References

Anderson, R. C. (1982). How to construct achievement tests to assess comprehension. *Review of Educational Research, 42*, 145-170.

Britton, B. K., & Gulgoz, S. (1991). Using Kintsch's computational model to improve instructional text: effect of repairing inference calls on recall and cognitive structures. *Journal of Educational Psychology, 83*, 329-345.

Charniak, E. (2000). A maximum-entropy-inspired parser. *Proceedings of the North-American Chapter of Association for Computational Linguistics* (pp. 132–139). San Francisco: Morgan Kaufman Publishers.

Cornoldi, C., De Beni, R., & Pazzaglia, F. (1996). Profiles of reading comprehension difficulties: An analysis of single cases. In C. Cornoldi & J. Oakhill (Eds.), *Reading Comprehension Difficulties: Processes and Intervention.* Mahwah, NJ: Lawrence Erlbaum Associates.

Embretson, S. E. (1994). Application of cognitive design systems to test development. In C. R. Reynolds (Ed.), *Cognitive Assessment: A multidisciplinary perspective* (pp 107-135). New York: Plenum Press.

Embretson, S. E., & Wetzel, C. D. (1987). Component latent models for paragraph comprehension. *Applied Psychological Measurement, 11*, 175-193.

Gates-MacGinitie Reading Tests (1989). *Technical report for Gates-MacGinitie Reading Tests Forms K and L.* Chicago, IL: Riverside Publishing.

Gorin, J. S., Embretson, S. E., & Sheehan, K. (2002). *Cognitive and psychometric modeling of text-based reading comprehension GRE-V items.* Paper presented at the 2002 Annual Meeting of the National Council on Measurement in Education: New Orleans, LA.

Graesser, A. C., McNamara, D. S. Louwerse, M., & Cai, Z. (2004). Coh-Metrix: Analysis of text on cohesion and language. *Behavioral Research Methods, Instruments, and Computers, 36,* 193-202.

Just, M. A., & Carpenter, P. A. (1992). A capacity theory of comprehension: Individual differences in working memory. *Psychological Review, 99,* 122-149.

Kintsch, W. (1988). The role of knowledge in discourse comprehension construction-integration model. *Psychological Review, 95*, 163-182.

Kintsch, W. (1998). *Comprehension: A Paradigm for cognition.* Cambridge, MA: Cambridge University Press.

Magliano, J. P., & Millis, K. (2003). Assessing reading skill with a think aloud procedure and latent semantic analysis. *Cognition & Instruction, 21*, 251-283.

Mosenthal, P. (1996). Understanding the strategies of document literacy and their conditions of use. *Journal of Educational Psychology, 88*, 314-332.

Sheehan, K. M., & Ginther, A. (2001). *What do passage-based multiple choice verbal reasoning items really measure? An analysis of the cognitive skills underlying performance on the current TOEFL reading section.* Paper presented at the 2000 Annual Meeting of the National Council of Measurement in Education.

Vellutino, F. R. (2003). Individual differences as sources of variability in reading comprehension in elementary school children. In A. P. Sweet & C. E. Snow (Eds.), *Rethinking reading comprehension* (pp. 51-81). New York: Guilford Press.

Acknowledgements

The research was supported by the Institute for Education Sciences (IES R3056020018-02). Any opinions, findings, and conclusions or recommendations expressed in this material are those of the authors and do not necessarily reflect the views of the IES.

Learning to Collaborate in a Computer-Mediated Setting: Observing a Model Beats Learning from Being Scripted

Nikol Rummel, Hans Spada & Sabine Hauser
University of Freiburg, Department of Psychology, Engelbergerstr. 41, 79085 Freiburg, Germany
<firstname.lastname>@psychologie.uni-freiburg.de

Abstract: In an earlier study we had tested if observing a model collaboration or following a collaboration script could improve students' subsequent collaboration in a computer-mediated setting and promote their knowledge of what makes good collaboration. Both model and script showed positive effects. The current study was designed to further probe the effects of model and script by comparing them to conditions (model-plus, script-plus) in which the learning was further supported by providing elaboration support (instructional prompts and guided self-explanation). 40 dyads were tested, 8 in each of the following conditions: model plus elaboration, model, script plus elaboration, script, control. Observing a model collaboration with elaboration support yielded the best results over all other conditions on several measures of the quality of collaborative process and on outcome variables. Model without elaboration was second best. The results for the script conditions were mixed; on some variables even below those of the control condition.

Introduction

In the face of a growing specialization of knowledge, collaboration of specialists from different disciplines is required in many learning and working contexts. And often these people will be spatially distributed, making it necessary for them to use modern communication technologies to collaborate at the distance. Take the following example: Some symptoms can indicate both a physical as well as a mental diagnosis, making it difficult for an individual psychologist or physician to devise the correct diagnosis and, in consequence, a suitable treatment. Hence, the collaboration of psychologists and physicians is increasingly regarded to be of importance for the well-being of patients. Then, a relevant question is how to encourage and support collaboration among locally distributed medical and psychological practices. In this context video conference systems have been advocated as a particularly suitable solution (Köhler & Trimpop, 2004). Video-mediated communication systems support complex synchronous interactions (Finn, Sellen, & Wilbur, 1997). Participants in different locations can communicate via audio-video connection. In addition, application sharing technologies add the possibility to not only view, but also jointly edit text or visual material.

Ample research has demonstrated that collaboration can be effective for improving problem-solving and learning (Dillenbourg, Baker, Blaye, & O'Malley, 1995, Slavin, 1992). However, this research has also made it clear that not all collaboration is effective, but that the fruitfulness of collaboration depends on characteristics of the interaction (Dillenbourg et al., 1995). Effective collaboration must be learned and requires guidance, instruction, and training (Slavin, 1992). And this is even more so when the challenges of a computer-mediated and interdisciplinary interaction are added to those of collaboration as such (Rummel & Spada, 2005).

Over the past years, numerous research projects in CSCL and CSCW have investigated ways to provide support for computer-mediated collaboration. In this context, our research focuses in particular on pedagogic support measures, i.e. measures that aim at instructing collaborators in ways that enable them to collaborate well and with success subsequently. In a first experimental study (Rummel & Spada, 2005) we tested providing a collaboration model or a collaboration script as instructional methods to promote graduate students ability to collaborate well and with good results in a complex computer-mediated setting and their knowledge of what makes good collaboration. Compared to two control conditions (one with the possibility to learn from prior unsupported practice, and one without any prior learning experiences) both model and script showed positive effects on three levels: (a) the collaborative process (i.e. the way dyads collaborated), (b) the outcomes they obtained, and (c) their individual knowledge about characteristic features of a good collaboration assessed in a posttest. The current study was designed to probe the learning effect of model and script further by supporting elaborative/ meta-cognitive processing of the relevant, instructional elements.

Two Pedagogic Approaches to Instructing Collaboration: Model and Script

One pedagogic approach to instructing people about how to best collaborate, is to provide them with a model of a successful computer-mediated collaboration. The idea behind this approach is that, as they observe the solution steps and the behavior of the model partners, collaborators may learn what aspects to pay attention to during their own future collaboration. Evidence from different strands of research supports this assumption (observational learning: Bandura, 1977; learning from worked out examples: Renkl, 1997; learning from exemplary dialogs: Cox, McKendree, Tobin, Lee, & Mayes, 1999). We refer to the model collaboration as "worked-out collaboration example". This indicates that it was specifically designed to exemplify aspects deemed constitutive of a good collaboration. Such aspects were identified by means of a review of research on collaborative problem-solving and learning (Rummel & Spada, 2005). An "exemplary collaboration" was derived from the literature review and, consequently, a screenplay was written incorporating the relevant theoretical aspects. When writing the screenplay for the current study, we also made use of excerpts of collaboration recordings from our earlier study (Rummel & Spada. 2005). The screenplay was then executed as a dialog by professional actors, and recorded. The recorded model dialog was integrated with text animations illustrating the development of the joint (model) solution. A multimedia presentation resulted, similar to a video, however divided in a number of discrete scenes (i.e. phases of the collaboration). Throughout the scenes, the model presentation illustrated how the model collaborators went about coordinating their collaboration, how they managed their time, and how they made use of their complementary domain knowledge in the problem-solving process. An important feature of our model collaboration was the alternation between individual and collaborative work, which had proven to be a determining factor for a successful collaboration, particularly in the case of complementary expertise of the partners (Rummel & Spada, 2005).

The second pedagogic approach we have taken relates to a well-researched measure to support collaboration: collaboration scripts (face-to-face collaboration: O'Donnell, 1999; computer-mediated settings: Fischer, Mandl, Haake, & Kollar, in press). The main idea of collaboration scripts is to prompt cognitive and social processes by participants that might otherwise not occur, thus enforcing a fruitfully structured interaction, and consequently improving the joint problem-solving and knowledge acquisition. However, collaboration scripts have also been criticized (Dillenbourg, 2002) for dictating interaction in a coercive way. Negative motivational effects may be expected in particular if collaboration is scripted over an extended period of time and over many collaborative sessions (Rummel & Spada, in press). Against this background we have raised the question if the central elements of a collaboration script could be learned from a scripted session. Such sustainable learning effects would make it unnecessary to continue the scripting and risk motivational drawbacks, but collaborators could themselves maintain a fruitful collaboration following the internalized script rules. The results of our first study (Rummel & Spada, 2005) supported our hypothesis that collaboration scripts can trigger learning about collaboration and thus improve subsequent collaboration. Our script was designed to be structurally equivalent to the model collaboration, that is, it instructed participants to engage in the same activities that were demonstrated by the model collaborators. For example, while participants observing the model collaboration would listen to the model collaborators clarifying questions about the patient case at the beginning of their collaboration, participants in the script condition were instructed to do this together with their partner.

Promoting Elaboration during Learning from Model and Script

To summarize: we had established that observing a collaboration model or alternatively following a collaboration script during an initial collaboration can be effective in improving a subsequent unsupported collaboration (Rummel & Spada, 2005). However, there was reason to believe that learning from both model and script could be further improved by providing elaboration support. As Bandura (1977) pointed out, observational learning depends to a great extent on paying attention to the relevant model stimuli, cognitively organizing and rehearsing what has been observed. Also, in research on learning from worked-out examples, self-explanations and instructional explanations have been shown to improve the processing of the examples and, consequently, learning of the demonstrated problem-solving strategies (e.g., Renkl, 2002). For the script side, the cognitive apprenticeship approach (e.g. Collins, Brown, & Newman, 1989) indicates that reflective elaboration of relevant script features might be a promising measure to promote its internalization and acquisition as a standard of subsequent collaboration. In this research, open verbalization and reflection about one's own behavior have proven to be important scaffolding strategies to support the acquisition of complex cognitive skills.

Providing specifically targeted support in order to promote learning from instructional material has been shown to be of great value in a variety of instructional contexts. Of major relevance for the research presented here are findings concerning two means to promote elaboration and learning in particular, and on the way these two should be combined: (1) instructional prompts, and (2) guided self-explanations. *Instructional prompts* are short, attention-guiding explanations provided immediately before or after content is presented. They can be either descriptive, i.e. giving a short summary or paraphrase, or principle-based, i.e. pointing to the core elements or principles underlying the learning contents. Decker (1984) has shown the effectiveness of instructional prompts – he calls them "learning points" – for learning complex social skills, such as conflict management skills, from observing model videos. Renkl (2002) provided evidence for the relevance of instructional prompts in learning from worked-out examples. Secondly, a great number of studies have demonstrated the effectiveness of *self-explanations* in supporting learning (e.g. Chi, Bassok, Lewis, Reimann, & Glaser, 1989). However, it has also become clear that self-explaining activities do not occur naturally, but that they have to be prompted and guided (Renkl, Stark, Gruber, & Mandl, 1998). Recently, collaborative self-explanations have been shown to be a particularly powerful way of supporting learning (Chi & Roy, 2006). In their study, students who collaboratively self-explained while observing recordings of a tutor tutee interaction learned more than individuals. Finally, Renkl and his research group (e.g. Hilbert, Schworm, & Renkl, 2004) demonstrated that for best learning results a transition should be made from providing instructional prompts to prompting self-explanations.

In accordance with the above findings, in the current study we implemented elaboration support for learning from model or script in the following way. *Instructional prompts* directing the learners' attention to the relevant underlying principles were provided preceding each model scene and each script phase. More specifically, participants in the model conditions were advised what they were going to *observe next*, whereas participants in the script conditions were pointed to the relevance of what they were going *do next*. Then, following the model presentation or the scripted collaboration, a *collaborative self-explanation* phase took place in which dyads were encouraged to recapitulate the model collaboration or alternatively their scripted interaction and reflect on what aspects had been important for a successful collaboration.

Method

Collaborative Scenario and Computer-Mediated Setting

Dyads comprised of one medical student and one psychology student were asked to collaborate in a computer-mediated setting and to jointly develop a diagnosis for complicated psychiatric cases. Two patient cases were designed to require medical *and* psychological domain knowledge in order to arrive at the correct diagnosis (i.e. the complementary domain knowledge represented in each dyad). For example, in case 1 the patient suffered from cardiac dysrhythmia, but also showed symptoms of a panic disorder. The contents of the two cases did not overlap so that no transfer of content knowledge was possible from case 1 to case 2. The dyads collaborated via a desktop videoconferencing system including personal text-editors and a shared text-editor.

Experimental Design

The experiment was composed of two phases. During the *learning phase* the experimental variation was implemented. Five conditions were realized: model-plus, model, script-plus, script, control. Participants in the *model-plus* and the *script-plus* condition received additional elaboration support during the learning phase: in addition to the model or the script they were provided with instructional prompts and were guided to engage in self-explaining activities. In the second phase of the experiment, i.e. the *test phase*, dyads in all conditions collaborated without further support. In this phase dependent measures were assessed on three levels: (a) the collaborative process, (b) the outcome of the collaboration, and (c) the individuals' knowledge of important aspects of a good collaboration.

Participants

The sample consisted of 40 dyads in total, specifically 8 dyads in each condition. Dyads were randomly assigned to one of the five conditions. Each dyad was composed of one student of psychology and one medical student. Students were recruited during lectures and seminars; they received a financial compensation for their voluntary participation. All students were at an advanced level of proficiency in their studies.

Procedure

After an initial introduction, all participants received training with the computer-mediated setting. Next the learning phase was administered. Participants in the *model condition* observed worked-out scenes of the collaboration between a psychology student and a medical student on diagnosing case 1. The model collaboration was delivered as a multimedia presentation on the computer screen. Dyads in the *script condition* were guided through their collaboration on case 1 by a collaboration script giving them instructions for their interaction. Each phase of the script was allotted a particular time frame. The script was provided on a second computer screen located next to the one that participants used for their collaboration (i.e., the videoconference and the text editors). The *model-plus* and the *script-plus* conditions were implemented correspondingly. In addition to the instruction provided by observing the model or alternatively working with the script, the participants in these conditions were provided with elaboration support as described above. Dyads in the *control condition* collaborated without further instructional support during both the learning and the test phase. The participants returned one day later for the test phase and the post test. During the test phase, all dyads collaborated on case 2 without further instruction. Finally, each individual filled out the posttest and a questionnaire. During both learning and test phase, the two partners of each dyad were seated in different rooms and collaborated via the desktop videoconference.

Dependent Variables

The *collaborative process* during the test phase was assessed employing a rating scheme that had been developed in the course of the process analyses for the first study (for more details, see Meier, Spada, & Rummel, submitted). It allows to assess collaborative process in an economic fashion from the video recordings and combines a qualitative with a quantitative approach. When looking at the video recording of a dyad's collaboration, process quality was assessed on nine dimensions: sustaining mutual understanding, dialog management, information pooling, reaching consensus, task division, time management, technical coordination, reciprocal interaction, and individual task orientation (assessed for both partners individually). The dyads collaboration was rated for each dimension on a five-point rating scale ranging from 0 (very bad) to 4 (very good).

The *outcome* of the collaboration, that is, the joint diagnosis for case 2, was blind-rated by an expert who had no knowledge of the study's rationale and experimental design. The expert graded the diagnoses of all dyads on a scale from 5 (highest grade) to 1 (lowest grade) with intermediate steps at x.3 and x.7 (this partition is common in the German grading system).

The *posttest* was filled out by each participant individually. It included an open-format question asking participants to describe to colleagues who were going to collaborate on a similar task how they should proceed in order to collaborate successfully. Participants' answers to this question were assessed by applying a checklist; a maximum of 16 points could be achieved.

Finally, each student filled out a *questionnaire* including a translated and adapted version of the Intrinsic Motivation Inventory (IMI; http://www.psych.rochester.edu/SDT/measures/intrins.html) based on the motivation theory by Deci and Ryan (1985), and a number of items to evaluate participants' experiences with the experimental setting. The IMI is composed of six subscales: interest/enjoyment, perceived competence, effort, value/usefulness, felt pressure and tension, and perceived choice. Each subscale consisted of four items, which were rated by participants on a six-point rating scale (ranging from 1 = not at all true to 6 = very true). The reliability of all scales proved to be satisfactory (Cronbach's alpha ranging from $\alpha = 0.75$ to $\alpha = 0.90$).

Results

Table 1 gives an overview of the results that yielded significance ($\alpha = .05$) or showed a clear trend. Compared to the control condition, the model and the script conditions showed positive effects on dyads' collaboration during the test phase. Particularly clear effects were found on process variables concerning the planning and coordination of the collaboration (task division, time management). The dimensions "information pooling" and "technical coordination" revealed the same result pattern, but did not reach statistical significance. On the other hand, the script conditions performed lower than the model conditions, and partly even lower than the control condition, on several variables. Their collaborations were rated lowest on one particular process dimension: individual task orientation (both for the psychology student, P, and the medical student, M). This process dimension aims at shedding light on a motivational aspect, the individual persons' task alignment:

Last but not least the collaborative process will reflect participants' individual motivation and their commitment to their collaborative task…., individual collaborators may employ volitional strategies in order to keep up a high level of expended effort in their contribution toward the joint task, including focusing one's attention on solution relevant information, keeping one's environment free of distractions, or nurturing positive expectations regarding the collaborative outcome (Heckhausen, 1989)." (Meier, Spada, & Rummel, submitted).

The result may thus indicate that dyads in the script conditions experienced motivational problems during their collaboration in the test phase. Interestingly, the self-report of motivation assessed by the IMI did not reveal such effects. We will come back to this result in the discussion. Yet another result points in the same direction: on the questionnaire items asking how useful participants' had found the learning phase (=phase 1) for their collaboration in the test phase (=phase 2) and if they had tried to transfer experiences from the learning phase to the test phase (see bottom of Table 1), script participants gave the lowest ratings. The script conditions also performed lowest on the individual knowledge posttest, and with regard to the quality of their joint diagnosis evaluated by the expert rating (see Table 1). The latter result did, however, not reach statistical significance. A different result pattern was found on the "pressure/tension" subscale of the IMI. Participants in the script conditions expressed they had felt less pressure/tension during their collaboration in the test phase, that is, their second – but first unscripted – collaboration. On the contrary, model condition participants expressed the highest amount of felt pressure/tension during their collaboration in the test phase, which in fact was their first collaboration. Overall, the ratings on this variable were relatively low (max possible was 6). We will discuss this result below. The model-plus condition showed better performances than the model condition on all variables listed in Table 1, with exception of the quality of the joint solution. A similar effect of the elaboration support could not be shown for the script-plus condition.

Table 1. Overview of results

	Model-plus	**Model**	**Script-plus**	**Script**	**Control**		
Collaborative process (N=40)	**M (SD)**	**M (SD)**	**M (SD)**	**M (SD)**	**M (SD)**	**F (p)**	η^2
Information pooling	2.75 (0.71)	2.69 (0.74)	2.25 (0.61)	2.52 (0.72)	1.88 (0.73)	2.09 (.10)	.19
Task division	3.13 (0.56)	2.58 (0.85)	2.13 (1.00)	2.08 (0.87)	1.29 (0.49)	6.04 (<.001)	.41
Time management	3.04 (0.86)	2.25 (0.98)	2.00 (0.84)	1.71 (0.68)	0.83 (0.56)	8.10 (<.001)	.48
Technical coordination	3.33 (0.31)	2.83 (0.69)	2.83 (0.67)	2.83 (0.59)	2.42 (0.58)	2.47 (.06)	.22
Individual task orientation (P)	3.08 (0.24)	2.92 (0.53)	2.38 (0.55)	2.38 (0.60)	2.50 (0.25)	4.08 (.01)	.32
Individual task orientation (M)	2.96 (0.45)	2.88 (0.59)	2.08 (0.79)	2.38 (0.68)	2.54 (0.50)	2.75 (.04)	.24
Collaborative outcome (N=40) Quality of joint diagnosis	3.40 (0.90)	3.96 (0.68)	3.09 (0.99)	2.76 (0.96)	3.26 (0.99)	1.89 (.13)	.18
Individual posttest (N=80) Knowledge about good collaboration	8.63 (1.32)	6.75 (1.97)	6.09 (1.46)	6.09 (1.99)	6.47 (1.42)	6.46 (<.001)	.26
Questionnaire (N=80)							
IMI scale "Felt Pressure/Tension"	3.38 (1.43)	3.15 (1.29)	2.21 (1.00)	1.88 (0.64)	2.44 (1.06)	5.13 (.001)	.22
Items assessing experience with setting							
Phase 1 useful for phase 2	5.38 (0.50)	4.69 (1.25)	4.60 (1.24)	4.00 (1.54)	4.73 (0.96)	2.62 (.04)	.13
Tried to transfer phase1 to phase 2	5.00 (0.63)	3.75 (1.24)	3.20 (1.08)	3.17 (1.27)	4.40 (1.30)	7.39 (<.001)	.30

Discussion

Learning from observing a *model* once again was demonstrated to be a powerful pedagogic approach when trying to promote good collaboration in a computer-mediated setting. Dyads in the model conditions showed good collaborative behaviors and were able to put what they had learned about collaboration into words in the posttest. They also yielded the best results with regard to the quality of the joint solution; however, this result did not become statistically significant. It is noteworthy that the model conditions achieved these results against the background of a highly complex (computer-mediated and interdisciplinary) collaborative setting, and despite having observed only one single model collaboration. In fact, model participants experienced a relatively high amount of pressure compared to the other conditions when trying to put into practice what they had learned during collaboration in the test phase. This is illustrated by the only significant effect found on the Intrinsic Motivation Inventory (IMI): the one for the pressure/tension subscale. The results of the current study have also provided some evidence that elaboration support can further improve learning from a collaboration model.

In contrast, the learning effects that had been demonstrated for the *script* condition in our first study could not be replicated to the same extent. While script condition dyads did show indications of having benefited from their first, scripted interaction in their collaborative behaviors in the test phase, these effects were not reflected in the quality of their joint solution. Nor were participants able to make their tacit knowledge about good collaboration explicit very well in the posttest. So what have they learned during their scripted interaction on case 1? Possibly the concurrent demands of collaborating on the case, following the script instructions, and trying to reflect on the scripting on a meta-level in order to learn, were too high. Then, the additional elaboration support in the script-plus condition obviously could not aid here as it added another layer to the already high demands. The result that students expressed having felt little pressure during their collaboration in the test phase, might thus be an indication of the relief they *experienced* when allowed to collaborate freely in the test phase. On the other hand, dyads' *observable behavior* during their collaboration in the test phase assessed by our process dimension "individual task orientation" indicated that they were less motivated than students in the other conditions. But why did such motivational problems not reveal in the IMI? In fact, the IMI scales did not reveal much at all. Students rated positive subscales high (e.g. interest/enjoyment subscale) and negative subscales low (e.g. pressure/tension) on average. Also, no other IMI subscale but "pressure/tension" revealed any differences across conditions. Self-report scales entail the danger that individuals attempt to present themselves in certain way. The necessity to take into account psychological dynamics such as self-presentation or reactance is also mentioned explicitly by the authors of the IMI (see http://www.psych.rochester.edu/SDT/measures/intrins.html). Then, it might well be that the external rating of a person's motivation as it can be inferred from utterances or actions in the context of a given situation is more objective than the person's self-report.

In sum, the results of the current study are notable given the complexity of the setting and the relatively small number of dyads in each condition. The promising main effect that could be established in both of our studies is that collaboration can be improved through instruction. Whether the learning effects do sustain over time was not tested by our studies hitherto. We think this could be best investigated in a real-world collaboration setting. In conclusion we would like to emphasize that observing a model appears to be a very powerful pedagogic strategy even when instructing complex social skills. This may point a promising direction for research on learning from worked examples. However, a caveat: the time expenditure for developing such models is very high. Secondly we would like to plea for caution when advocating the beneficial effects of collaboration scripts. Collaboration scripts have recently become quite fashionable in CSCL research – and indeed: scripted interactions often lead to better results than unscripted ones. However, so far not many researchers have been concerned with the question of how scripting affects learners' interactions *after* the termination of the scripting. The inconsistent results with regard to learning effects of collaboration scripts that we have found in our two studies clearly call for more research on this question.

References

Bandura, A. (1977). *Social learning theory*. Englewood Cliffs, NJ: Prentice Hall.

Chi, M. T. H., Bassok, M., Lewis, M. W., Reimann, P., & Glaser, R. (1989). Self-explanations: How students study and use examples in learning to solve problems. *Cognitive Science, 13*, 145-182.

Chi, M. T. H. & Roy, M. (2006). Learning from observing tutoring collaboratively: Insights about tutoring effectiveness from vicarious learning. Manuscript submitted for publication.

Collins, A., Brown, J. S., & Newman, S. E. (1989). Cognitive apprenticeship: Teaching the crafts of reading, writing, and mathematics. In L. B. Resnick (Ed.), *Knowing, learning, and instruction* (pp. 453-494). Hillsdale, NJ: Lawrence Erlbaum Associates.

Cox, R., McKendree, J., Tobin, R., Lee, J., & Mayes, T. (1999). Vicarious learning from dialogue and discourse. *Instructional Science, 27*, 431-458.

Deci, E. L., & Ryan, R. M. (1985). Intrinsic motivation and self-determination in human behavior. New York: Plenum.

Decker, P. J. (1980). Effects of symbolic coding and rehearsal in behavior-modeling training. *Journal of Applied Psychology, 65,* 627-634.

Dillenbourg, P. (2002). Over-scripting CSCL: The risks of blending collaborative learning with instructional design. In P. A. Kirschner (Ed.), *Three worlds of CSCL. Can we support CSCL* (pp. 61-91). Heerlen: Open Universiteit Nederland.

Dillenbourg, P., Baker, M., Blaye, A., & O'Malley, C. (1995). The evolution of research on collaborative learning. In P. Reimann & H. Spada (Eds.), *Learning in humans and machines: Towards an interdisciplinary learning science* (pp. 189-211). Oxford: Elsevier/Pergamon.

Finn, K. E., Sellen, A. J., & Wilbur, S. B. E. (1997). *Video-mediated communication.* Mahwah, NJ: Lawrence Erlbaum Associates.

Fischer, F., Mandl, H., Haake, J., & Kollar, I. (Eds.) (in press). Scripting computer-supported communication of knowledge. Cognitive, computational, and educational perspectives. New York: Springer.

Hilbert, T., Schworm, S., & Renkl, A. (2004). Learning from worked-out examples: The transition from instructional explanations to self-explanation prompts. In P. Gerjets, J. Elen, R. Joiner & P. Kirschner (Eds.), *Instructional design for effective and enjoyable computer-supported learning* (pp. 184-192). Tübingen: Knowledge Media Research Center.

Köhler, T., & Trimpop, R. (2004). Sehen und gesehen werden: Teleradiologie mittels Desktop- Videoconferencing. [Seeing and being seen: Tele radiology via desktop videoconferencing]. In W. Bungard, B. Koop & C. Liebig (Eds.), *Proceedings zur 3. Tagung der Fachgruppe Arbeits- und Organisationspsychologie.* München: Rainer Hampp.

Meier, A., Spada, H., & Rummel, N. (submitted). Evaluating collaboration: A rating scheme for assessing the quality of collaborative process. Manuscript submitted for publication.

O'Donnell, A. M. (1999). Structuring dyadic interaction through scripted cooperation. In A. M. O'Donnell & A. King (Eds.), *Cognitive perspectives on peer learning* (pp. 179-196). Mahwah, NJ: Lawrence Erlbaum Associates.

Renkl, A. (1997). Learning from worked-out examples: A study on individual differences. Cognitive Science, 21, 1-29.

Renkl, A. (2002). Learning from worked-out examples: Instructional explanations supplement self-explanations. *Learning & Instruction, 12*, 529-556.

Renkl, A., Stark, R., Gruber, H., & Mandl, H. (1998). Learning from worked-out examples: The effects of example variability and elicited self-explanations. *Contemporary Educational Psychology, 23,* 90-108.

Rummel, N., & Spada, H. (2005). Learning to collaborate: An instructional approach to promoting collaborative problem-solving in computer-mediated settings. *Journal of the Learning Sciences, 14(2)*, 201-241.

Rummel, N. & Spada, H. (in press). Can people learn computer-mediated collaboration by following a script? In F. Fischer, H. Mandl, J. Haake & I. Kollar, *Scripting computer-supported communication of knowledge. Cognitive, computational, and educational perspectives.* New York, Springer.

Slavin, R. E. (1992). When and why does cooperative learning increase achievement? Theoretical and empirical perspectives. In R. Hertz-Lazarowitz & N. Miller (Eds.), *Interaction in cooperative groups: The theoretical anatomy of group learning* (pp. 145-173). New York: Cambridge University Press.

Acknowledgements

The present research was supported by the Deutsche Forschungsgemeinschaft (DFG; [German Science Foundation]) with project grants Sp 251/16-2 and 16-3. We would like to thank our student research assistants Dejana Diziol, Jana Groß Ophoff, Cindy Günzler and Friederike Renner for their help in the material development, data collection and data analysis. Furthermore, we would like to acknowledge Anne Meier, who has made a substantial contribution to this project: the rating scheme for the collaborative process analysis was largely developed as part of her thesis work.

It's Okay to be Wrong: Recognizing Mechanistic Reasoning During Student Inquiry

Rosemary S. Russ, Paul Hutchison, University of Maryland, Toll Physics Building, College Park, MD 20742
Email: rsruss@physics.umd.edu, hooch@wam.umd.edu

Abstract: Recent reforms in science education place emphasis on engaging students in inquiry similar to that of research scientists. In their attempt to assess this goal, many educators and researchers evaluate student inquiry based on how well their conceptual understanding aligns with canonical knowledge. Such assessments fail to recognize other more valuable aspects of inquiry. We assert that mechanistic reasoning, shown by the history and philosophy of science literatures to be vital in the construction of scientific knowledge, is a more appropriate dimension along which to measure the quality of inquiry. We present a coding scheme designed to identify this reasoning and use it to analyze a discussion among second grade students about why juice boxes collapse when you suck on their straws. Assessing their mechanistic reasoning in this way reveals a value and sophistication that is obscured by current measures of conceptual correctness.

Introduction

The concept of 'inquiry' is central in the primary documents of the current science education reform movement *(The National Science Education Standards* (National Research Council, 1996) and *Science for All Americans* (American Association for the Advancement of Science, 1993)). In them, inquiry is viewed as both the normal activity of scientists and what reformers want students to do in science classrooms.

Given its prominence in science reform, educators and researchers quite reasonably want to assess the quality of students' inquiry. However, much of the research evaluates student inquiry based upon tests of conceptual understanding (e.g. Lee and Songer, 2003; Marx et al, 2004). We find such assessments problematic because they fail to recognize aspects of inquiry that are ultimately more valuable than correctness. One such aspect, mechanistic reasoning, is shown by the history and philosophy of science literatures to be vital in the construction of scientific knowledge. We believe students doing inquiry should engage in mechanistic reasoning. In this work we use a framework for identifying mechanistic reasoning to reveal valuable aspects of student inquiry overlooked by much current research.

The following explanation given by a first grade student for why seeds will not grow in sand provides a rich example of the type of mechanistic reasoning we consider valuable.

> **Teacher:** And so that seed in the sand?
> **Elisabeth:** Is just left alone without the s- the water that helps it grow in soil. Because the soil is like hard and the water is like, pssshhh, blocked. Like with all those sticks and stuff- it's real hard so the water won't get through. But in sand since usually sand will be blown away not sticks into the sand- it's easy that it's not blocked so it just goes—shhhhhhwweeee. (Motions with both hands water flowing down.)

Elisabeth reasons (mechanistically) that since water falls straight through sand, the seed is left alone and cannot get the water it needs to grow. It would be inappropriate to disregard Elisabeth's inquiry merely because her final conclusion about seed growth is wrong. The nature of her sophisticated thinking still warrants attention that the framework we present here is intended to provide.

This example demonstrates that assessing students based on how well their conceptual understanding aligns with canonical concepts may misrepresent their inquiry. As above, it might give an impoverished view of good inquiry that arrives at incorrect conclusions. Alternatively, it might judge inquiry highly in instances when the students provided correct answers they do not understand. Such judgments assume (perhaps tacitly) that if students do inquiry well they'll get the right answer. However, the history of science is full of examples where eminent scientists arrived at conclusions later judged incorrect (Darden, 1998). Good scientific inquiry does not guarantee true knowledge - either historically or in the classroom.

The use of mechanisms to construct new knowledge about the physical world provided the foundation for the Scientific Revolution (Westfall, 1986). Prior to that time, natural phenomena were explained by appealing to occult powers that mediated matter, itself possessing both life and perception. With the rise of modern science as we know it today, scientists like Descartes, Galileo, and Newton began grounding their explanations in mechanisms involving inert matter in motion. Their use of mechanistic explanations as a means of understanding and describing natural phenomena allowed for significant advances in scientific knowledge. Even today, searching for and articulating mechanisms for natural phenomenon is central to science (Machamer, Darden, and Craven, 2000; Glennan, 2000; Thagard, 1998).

Given the role of mechanistic reasoning in modern science, we argue assessments of student inquiry must be attentive to it. Here, we use a coding scheme based in the mechanism literature from the philosophy of science to assess the quality of a discussion among a group of second grade students and their teacher about why the sides of a juice box move inward when they suck on the straw. For our purpose mechanism is defined as "entities and activities organized such that they are productive of regular changes from start or set-up to finish or termination conditions." (Machamer et al., 2000). In what follows we describe the coding scheme, its foundation, and how it was used to analyze the student discussion.

Characterizing Mechanistic Reasoning: A Coding Scheme

We briefly review Machamer et al.'s (2000) mechanism framework and provide descriptions of the coding scheme based on it we use to recognize mechanistic reasoning. This coding scheme is appropriate in settings where students are describing their reasoning. To date it has been used to code both student discussions (Russ et al., in preparation) and written work. Below we provide code examples from the discussion highlighted in the introduction – first graders discussing seed growth in sand.

Describing Target Phenomenon

Scientists may either begin with knowledge of the phenomenon and then inquire into the mechanism that produces it; or they may describe phenomena as predictions based on their prior knowledge of entities and activities. The phenomena scientists identify are stable, regular and reliably produced because the mechanisms that underlie them "work always or for the most part in the same way under the same conditions." (Machamer et. al, 2000) Given that formulating mechanistic accounts in science requires clear description of the phenomena, we look for moments when students state/demonstrate the particular phenomenon or result they are trying to explain. Such comments are coded as "Describing Target Phenomenon." For example, a student saying "I think that seeds will not grow in sand." describes the target phenomenon he hopes to explain.

Set-up Conditions

Scientists' goal "in establishing and displaying mechanism is to show how one stage produces the next, and so on." (Machamer, 2004) Set-up conditions are descriptions of the organizations (spatial and temporal) among entities and activities that begin the regular changes of the mechanism that produce the phenomenon. This aspect of Machamer et al.'s (2000) framework lends itself readily to a coding scheme - we can identify utterances in a transcript when students identify particular enabling conditions of the environment that must be met at the beginning in order for the mechanism to run. Such comments are coded as "Set-Up Conditions." For example, a student saying "But if you have [the seed in] a cup, it could just be like protected." is suggesting a set of starting conditions to use in their explanations.

Identifying Entities

Scientists recognize that one component of mechanistic descriptions are entities - the things (or objects) that play roles in producing the phenomenon. Physicists may consider electrons (entity) pushing on one another while biologists may talk about restriction enzymes (entity) cutting DNA. Since it is important for students to articulate objects that affect the outcome of the phenomenon, we code such comments as "Identifying Entities" even if the entity has been previously identified. For example, a student says "[I]f you put a seed in the sand it won't grow because there's no food for the plant" recognizes the necessary entity of food.

Identifying Activities

Along with knowing the entities in a mechanism, scientists also need to know the relevant activities. Activities are the components of mechanisms that produce change – they are types of causes. Most generally, activities are "the various doings in which these entities engage." (Craver and Darden, 2001) Given that activities are a major component of mechanisms, students who articulate the actions and interactions that occur among the entities are coded as "Identifying Activities." We use this code whenever students describe the things that entities "do" that cause changes in the surrounding entities, even if it has been previously identified. For example, a student saying "[T]he sand... sucks *UP* the water, like keeps it to itself, like takes the water away from the seed." identifies the sand can suck up water and keep it away from the seed.

Identifying Properties of Entities

Isolating the relevant properties of the entities is a vital part of scientific discovery. Often, scientists pare down the number of variables they need to consider by neglecting surface features of entities that do not affect the mechanism. When coding for "Identifying Properties of Entities," we look for students who articulate general properties of entities that are necessary for this particular mechanism to run. For example, a student describes the properties of sand and soil by saying, "When I pick up sand it easily kind of goes through my fingers really fast but when I do with soil it really does not do that."

Identifying Organization of Entities

In science, there are many phenomenon for which the mere presence of the necessary entities is insufficient for the mechanism to run. Rather, in order for a specific mechanism to take place, "Entities often must be appropriately located, structured, and oriented." (Machamer et al., 2000) When students identify where entities are located spatially and how they are organized, we code their comments as "Identifying Organization of Entities." For example, a student saying "Because if the water is going through... the water is going near the bottom and if it's going near the bottom, it's not near the seed it's by the top." identifies an important spatial organization between the water and the seed.

Chaining: Backward or Forward

A general reasoning strategy that aids the discovery and articulation of mechanisms involves using knowledge about the causal structure of the world to make claims about what must have happened previously to bring about the current state of things (backward) or what will happen next given that certain entities or activities are present now (forward). We code both types of reasoning as "Chaining" and use the following criteria to help us understand it as forward or backward.

By knowing the general properties of entities involved, much to be said about the activities that must have produced them. Similarly, "characteristic features of an activity may provide clues as to the entities that engaged in it." (Darden and Craver, 2002) Such comments answer the questions "What activities could have given rise to entities with these properties?" or "What entities were necessary in order for this activity to have occurred?" As with backward chaining, the general properties of entities can also speak to the activities in which they can engage, and the occurrence of an activity can indicate the entities it might produce. These comments answer the question "What activities could these entities with these properties be expected to engage in?" or "If this activity occurred, what would I changes would I expect in the surrounding entities and their properties?" For example, a student (forward) chains when he says "I think [the seed] would grow because, because the water goes through [the sand], and if if the water goes through [the seed] might receive some water."

Hierarchy of Codes

The codes above are sequentially arranged based both on our intuitions about scientific sophistication and on the conjecture that information gained by the lower level reasoning is needed in higher level reasoning. Describing phenomenon (with varying detail) including starting conditions is a basic skill of scientific inquiry, and thus these codes fall first in the hierarchy. After initially considering the physical situation, students can speculate about which entities or activities may play a role in the mechanism. When the entities have been identified, their relevant properties and organization can be explored. Finally, backward and forward chaining involve using information about the components already established to construct a step-by-step story for the mechanism runs. These final two codes seem (both intuitively and experientially) to be the most difficult and sophisticated.

Additional support for this arrangement comes from Metz's (1991) work on student explanations of sets of gears. She identifies three developmental phases of explanation that coincide with our hierarchy of mechanistic reasoning - "(a) function of the object as explanation, (b) connections as explanation, (c) mechanistic explanation."

In associating causality with the function of an object, the youngest students are identifying entities in the mechanism. By attending to connections, students are considering properties and organization of entities. Finally, what Metz calls the mechanistic phase of the oldest children is equivalent to our identification of activities and subsequent forward and backward chaining. Given that Metz observed 3-year-olds constructing connections explanations that were nascent versions of mechanistic reasoning, it is not unreasonable that we would find instances of the mechanism codes described above in school science discussions.

Context for Analysis

We apply the mechanism framework to a discussion between seven second graders and a science teaching specialist about why juice boxes collapse when you suck on the straw. These students met occasionally with this teacher throughout the year for enrichment sessions. Since he did not have to cover the standard county curriculum in this context, the teacher was free to choose topics based on what he thought would engage the students. This topic was chosen because the teacher speculated the students would have productive intuitions about it based in their experience.

Inter-rater Reliability

Both authors coded each student line on a transcript of the class discussion. In cases where a speaking student was interrupted by the teacher or another student we coded each line separately, but considered the student's adjacent lines when interpreting the meaning. This is particularly relevant when students use indexical words like "this" or "that". Codes are not mutually exclusive, so one line of transcript can have multiple codes. It is also possible for a line to receive no codes.

We evaluated inter-rater reliability in two ways. First, we checked for agreement among the 'codability' of lines. That is, do the researchers agree about which lines are examples of mechanistic reasoning and which are not. We obtained high inter-rater reliability, 93%, which indicates the coding scheme is very reliable at recognizing statements that are relevant to mechanistic reasoning. Second, for each mutually coded line we checked whether the highest codes agreed so as to assess how reliable the coding scheme is for identifying the most sophisticated aspect of each comment. This measure is important given that we are making claims about the overall sophistication of student reasoning. Our inter-rater reliability on this measure was 74% before discussion and 97% after. Our discussion revealed that low initial agreement did not result from difficulties with the coding scheme itself, but rather from differing interpretations of student meaning that were resolved with discussion. Interpretation discrepancies arose from the ambiguity inherent in second graders' language and our decisions about whether or not to interpret some statements based on adjacent comments.

Student Mechanistic Explanations

During the discussion the students presented three possible explanations for the phenomenon - only one of which is correct when judged against the physics canon. Below we provide an account of two of the explanations, one right and one wrong, including excerpts from the student discussion. We then use these particular examples of dialog to show how the coding scheme was implemented and what work the mechanism framework can do in terms of revealing valuable aspects of student reasoning.

Incorrect Explanation: A Push From the Inside the Juice Box

Three of the students focused on the role of the air and/or juice inside the juice box. In one form of this 'inside pusher' model, one student suggested the juice inside the box pushes out on all the sides of the box. Another student suggested that the air inside the juice box actively blows out or pushes against the sides of the box, holding the box in its "normal" shape. Thus whenever juice or air is removed from the box, there is no longer anything pushing from the inside to hold the box out, so the sides cave in. Some students articulated that the amount the sides of the box cave in is related to the amount of air left inside the box. While some of these students merely did not mention the air outside, others explicitly asserted that air outside the box is irrelevant to the box caving in.

For example, Erin explained her reasoning by discussing the role of the air inside the juice box.

Erin: I think because since you sucked out the air, it's like, it caves in because there's not any air so it has no, nothing's pushing it in from the inside to make it like [?flat] -
Teacher: Like this?
Erin: - like its normal shape. Yeah.
Teacher: Nothing's inside there so -
Erin: There's not much, not as much is inside so it's, it, there's not mu, as much pushing out so it caves in.
Teacher: Oh. So you mean right now there's air in there pushing out to make it the box shape.
Erin: I think so.
Teacher: And then what happens when I suck? What's -
Erin: You take some of the air out so -
Teacher: - and so why should the sides. (Side comment to another student.) Why should the sides then cave in? I mean, is there anything pushing –
Erin: No –
Teacher: - the outside in?
Erin: - there's nothing pushing.
Teacher: There's nothing pushing.
Erin: So when –
Teacher: Nothing pushing where, on the inside or the outside?
Erin: Inside.

Should we discount Erin's explanation of the phenomenon solely because her inquiry lacks conceptual understanding of air pressure? Certainly not! How do we account for its value? Although Erin's answer is incomplete (she explicitly rejects the idea of the air outside pushing on the box), her reasoning is mechanistic. She begins by identifying the starting conditions – the sides of the box are in their "normal shape." She then describes a relevant entity – the air inside the box – that pushes out (activity) on the sides holding the box in its starting conditions. Erin forward chains and claims that when the air that was pushing out on the box from the inside is removed, the box collapses. The inferences she makes in her forward chaining are all plausible based on her everyday experiences (for example with balloons). It is her ability to forward chain from activities to entity properties using her intuitions that makes her model valuable even though it is incorrect.

Correct Explanation: An Imbalance of Pushes from Inside and Out

Only one student in the class gives a correct explanation for why the juice box caves in – noting that both the air inside and outside the box contribute. He states a 'tug-of-war' model - air inside actively pushes to hold the sides out while the air outside pushes in. When air from the inside is removed, the amount of air (and thus the push) on the inside and outside are no longer equal, so the box collapses.

Hunter: Um. What I was thinking was when it's empty there's air inside -
Teacher: Okay.
Hunter: - and if you suck up, and there's like air pushing on the sides. And there's air pushing on the inside, there's air pushing on the sides to keep them out. And outside, um there's air pushing on the outside. [?And it -]
Teacher: Pushing. So the air outside is pushing which way?
Hunter: Um it's, um the sides in.
Teacher: Pushing the sides in. And then -
Hunter: And then [??when we took] some of the air out it won't be equal so, um, the sides start to [?cave/get] in.
Teacher: Equal. That sounds like a math term. What do you mean by that?
Hunter: Um.
Teacher: What's not equal?
Hunter: They both um, the amount of air is the same.
Teacher: By the amount the same you mean on the inside and on the outside?
Hunter: Yeah.

Should we say that Hunter is doing good inquiry solely because he gets the correct answer? Again we say "No!" He does give a correct explanation, but even more importantly he gives a mechanistic explanation. Hunter begins by giving the starting conditions and entities that are important to his explanation of the phenomenon - the juice box begins filled with air. He also identifies where that air is located – inside the box - and what activities air engages in – pushing. In a similar way he describes another relevant entity, its location, and its activity – the air outside pushes the box in. Hunter then forward chains, laying out a causal sequence of events that follow from one another based on the entities, activities, and properties he has asserted – sucking on the straw removes air from inside the box, which causes an imbalance of the in and out pushes. Since the inward push is now greater the box caves in. It is this forward chaining that marks Hunter's explanation as highly mechanistic. To assess his response based solely on his conceptual understanding misses the sophistication of his reasoning.

Discussion: The Quality of Mechanistic Inquiry

These two excerpts demonstrate how we use the mechanism coding scheme to assess student inquiry rather than assessing with conceptual standards. Particularly notable is that our assessment of these two explanations identifies similar sophistication in the reasoning used, despite the fact that judged against canonical knowledge one is wrong and the other is correct.

In the discussion students rarely engage in discourse at the lowest levels of the coding scheme – describing target phenomenon and articulating starting conditions. One reason we don't observe the lowest levels is that the students have already established the "What" of the question and quickly move onto the "How." We observe that for them it is insufficient to just make observations; they must also consider what causes the phenomenon. This in itself is quite sophisticated. It is likely that the teacher's role in soliciting these types of explanations is significant. While not the focus of this paper it is an important dimension that should be explored in future work.

Even more importantly, during moments of especially sophisticated inquiry students use the highest level of mechanistic reasoning - forward and backward chaining. They move beyond naming relevant components and use their physical intuitions about what kinds of things can happen to construct plausible explanations. We believe this strategy of using ideas about the entities and activities in one step of the mechanism to reason about another step is the hallmark of quality mechanistic inquiry. It is the students' use of forward and backward chaining to construct their explanations that leads us to assess their inquiry so highly.

We suspect that higher level mechanistic reasoning like that used by these students is the kind of thinking that contributes to the progress of science. Forward and backward chaining allows scientists (and students) to assess hypotheses by pursuing the implications of an idea to a place where they can be empirically tested. Similarly, it helps students trace and evaluate the individual steps of rival hypotheses to identify inappropriate conclusions and ultimately decide among them. Finally, its reliance on physical intuition encourages students to search for explanations that are plausible when judged against their knowledge from everyday experience.

In this work, we assert that evaluating students based on conceptual understanding gives an impoverished view of their scientific inquiry. We present mechanistic reasoning as another dimension along which to measure the quality of inquiry. Assessing mechanistic reasoning allows us to observe student sophistication in areas that the history and philosophy of science have shown to be valuable for understanding science, even more valuable than immediately obtaining a correct answer.

References

American Association for the Advancement of Science (1989). *Science for All Americans*. New York, NY: Oxford University Press.

Craver, C., & Darden, L. (2001). Discovering mechanisms in neurobiology. In P. Machamer, R. Grush, & P. McLaughlin (Eds.), *Theory and Method in the Neurosciences* (pp. 112 – 137). Pittsburg, PA: University of Pittsburg Press.

Darden, L. (1998). *The Nature of Scientific Inquiry*. Retrieved Oct. 31, 2005 from http://www.philosophy.umd.edu/Faculty/LDarden/sciinq/index.html

Darden, L., & Craver, C. (2002). Strategies in the interfield discovery of the mechanism of protein synthesis. *Studies in History and Philosophy of Biological And Biomedical Sciences,* 33, 1-28.

Glennan, S. (2000). Rethinking mechanistic explanation. *Philosophy and Science*, 69, S342-S353.
Lee, H. & Songer, N. (2003). Making authentic science accessible to students. *International Journal of Science Education*, 25(8), 923-948.
Machamer, P. (2004). Activities and causation: The metaphysics and epistemology of mechanisms. *International Studies in the Philosophy of Science,* 18(1), 27-39.
Machamer, P., Darden, D., & Craver, C. (2000). Thinking about mechanisms. *Philosophy of Science,* 67, 1-25.
Marx, R., Blumenfeld, P., Krajcik, J., Fishman, B., Soloway, E., Geier, R.,et al. (2004). Inquiry-based science in the middle grades: Assessment of learning in urban systemic reform. *Journal of Research in Science Teaching*, 41(10), 1063-1080.
Metz, Kathleen E. (1991). Development of explanation: Incremental and fundamental change in children's physics knowledge. *Journal of Research in Science Teaching*, 28(9), 785 – 797.
National Research Council. (1996) *National Science Education Standards.* Washington DC: National Academy Press.
Russ, R., Scherr, R., and Hammer, D. (in preparation). Tracking mechanistic reasoning in first graders' discussion of motion.
Thagard, P. (1998). Explaining disease: Correlations, causes, and mechanisms. *Minds and Machines*, 8, 61-78.
Westfall, Richard S. (1986). *The Construction of Modern Science: Mechanisms and Mechanics.* New York, NY: Cambridge University Press.

Acknowledgements

We gratefully acknowledge the support of the National Science Foundation under grants ESI-9986842 and REC-440113.

Inquiry into Mediated Action: The Implementation of an Innovative Online Problem-Based Unit into K-12 Classrooms

Donna Russell, Ph.D., University of Missouri-Kansas City, russelldl@umkc.edu

Abstract: The purpose of this study was to understand how teachers implement an innovation cluster that included an online workspace and a framework for a problem-based learning environment. The researcher focused on three progressive research issues during data structuring: 1) What factors in a teacher's school environments influence the implementation of an innovation cluster? 2) How does a teacher's participation in collaborative professional development influence the implementation of an innovation cluster? 3) How does a teacher's belief about learning and technology influence the implementation of an innovation cluster? Using Activity Theory for apriori structuring of the data set and these three progressive issues for invivo analysis, the researcher found that the teachers implemented the innovation cluster in relation to their ability to identify and overcome contradictions in their work activity.

Theoretical Background

The theoretical grounding for this study was sociocultural theory of human interaction and development (Vygotsky, 1978; Bruner, 1990) with an emphasis on understanding the processes of mediated activity (Wertsch, 1998). The researcher used Activity Theory, (Engeström, Miettinen, & Punamaki, 1999; Il'enkov, 1977) in order to design a systems-based framework for understanding the implementation processes in context and over time. Activity Theory defines the elements of human interactions systemically and allowed the researcher to design analytical procedures that developed systemic and contextual relationships among the dataset (Barab, Hay & Yamagata-Lynch, 2001; Schoenfeld, 1999). Using a systems-based methodology, the researcher studied the interactions of the constituents of the system that produce behavior (Aronson, 2003) and developed explanations that link the components as a "consilience of inductions" (Wilson, 1998, pg. 98). The compelling purpose of systems analysis then is to recognize the organizing relationships between entities in the system from which emerge the unique properties of the systems (Banathy, 1991). This form of analysis provides contextually relevant responses to complex social systems by making the interactions in the system explicit so both practical and theoretical conclusions can be developed. The overarching premise for this analysis was that the nature of human development is socially embedded and fundamentally activity oriented resulting in an outcome. (Cole & Engeström, 1993).

Using Activity Theory (AT) to define the constituent components, nodes, of the work activity of the teachers, the researcher then used N*UDIST software to structure the nodes of the AT model (e.g., motive, goal, subject, mediation, object, community, rules, division of labor, outcome) and integrated the theoretical constructs from related fields (e.g., professional development, innovation, collaboration) into operational categories of interactions in the work activity of the teachers. When external elements, such as new mediational tools, become part of a teacher's work activity system, internal contradictions, or tensions, result between two nodes of the activity system. The researcher identified the contradictions in the work activity, structured around the three progressive issues, then focused on defining the turning points resulting from these contradictions as behaviors changing the implementation of the unit and finally evaluated the resulting behaviors as a type of reformulation of the teachers' objects, the implementation of the unit with the potential outcome, motive, of developing advanced problem-solving abilities in their students.

Methods

This study connects two interrelated educational innovations, an advanced online learning technology and an instructional design template for a design problem-based unit, as mediational tools (Wertsch, 1988). The progressive questions in this study define the relationship among aspects of the implementation of this innovation cluster including defining the characteristics of innovative educational technologies (Rogers, 1995; Hall, Wallace, & Dossett, 1973; Wilson, Sherry, Dobrovolny, Batty, & Ryder, 2001) and the characteristics of the collaborative implementation of a constructivist-based learning environment (Jonassen, 2000; Savery & Duffy, 1996; Lave & Wenger, 1991; Schank, 1994; Salomon, 1993).The data collection process used interpretive research practices (Fraenkel & Wallen, 1996) to capture the dynamics and complexity of the educational settings. The data collected from the teachers included initial and follow-up interviews, transcripts from a phone conference and seven chatroom conferences, messages posted on discussion boards, reflective questionnaires related to their design of the unit and the principles of constructivist learning, an online journal, and the documents the teachers produce related to the unit and technology.

The researcher studied four eMINTS teachers who work with students in 4th and 5th grades in four different cities throughout Missouri who were voluntarily implementing a collaborative online problem-based unit during the final quarter of the 2001-2002 school year. Enhancing Missouri's Instructional Networked Teaching Strategies (eMINTS) is a program developed by Missouri's Department of Elementary and Secondary Education (DESE). It establishes classroom computer labs in order to illustrate the use of technology in classroom instruction and develop models of inquiry-based instruction. These four eMINTS teachers were invited to participate in a pilot project at MOREnet (Missouri Research and Education Network) called the Pioneers Program that involved learning about a new online tool, Shadow netWorkspace™ (SNS) and collaboratively developing and implementing a problem-based unit that incorporates constructivist-based learning methods and takes advantage of the many affordances of SNS. Because of their involvement in the eMINTs program, the Pioneers teachers had the same prior amount of technology training, 3 years, and the same quantity of technology in place in their classrooms. Table 1 below identifies the classroom settings.

Table 1: Setting of the study

	Grade	Community	Students	Technology Access
Linda	4th	suburban	12 boys and 10 girls, all Caucasian	As a part of their participation in the eMINTS program, each teacher has 12-14 Pentium3 LCD computers, a teacher workstation, laptop, a Smartboard and projector, a scanner, a color printer, and a digital camera.
Helen	4th	rural	12 boys and 12 girls, all Caucasian	
Janice	5th	urban	7 boys and 10 girls, all Black or African-American	
Carolyn	4th	mid-size city	9 boys, 10 girls; 11 Caucasian, 8 Black or African-American	

Findings

Secondary contradictions were identified within each individual teacher's activity setting. These contextual contradictions defined the progressive issue, what factors in individual teacher's school environments influenced the implementation of an innovation cluster? The researcher designed an AT teacher model for each teacher to show secondary contradictions. An example of a teacher's post-unit AT model is shown as Figure 2 below. Contradictions unresolved are shown as solid broken lines in AT Model. Resolved contradictions are shown as dashed broken lines. The top of the triangle represents the new tools (SNS and problem-based unit) inserted into the work activity of each teacher. In this study there were two new tools the problem-based unit design template and SNS. The middle of the triangle shows the subject (teacher) on the left with an arrow connecting over the course of the unit the subject to the object. In this study the object was the implementation of the unit using SNS. The outcome of the object is the ultimate potential for the unit. The teachers described their potential outcome as the development advanced problem-solving abilities in their students with the awareness of multiple perspectives. The bottom of the triangle depicts the contextual issues, the aspects of her local environment that impact her ability to meet her goals. These categories include rules, the rules in her school or district, community, others in her local context that can aid or hurt her ability to reach her goal such as her principal and division of labor, those people necessary for her to reach her goal such as technology support personnel. The factors I identified for each node were assigned after initial interviews with the teachers. A post-unit AT Model for Linda is shown below as Figure 2. All the teachers encountered multiple unresolved contradictions in their classrooms as they implemented their units. Linda had two unresolved tool-based contradictions, one related to subject, her beliefs about problem-based learning, and the other to object, the unit itself. She overall narrowed her object by ending the online dialogs with the other classes. She stated that the synchronous chats were "chaotic". Helen had two context to object contradictions, one that was division of labor, she did not communicate with her technology support person, and the other community-based, she shortened her unit to stay with the online teachers and could not complete the unit as a result.. Overall she disintegrated her object by not completing the unit. Janice had a rule to object, departmentalization issue, and tool to object contradiction, issues with SNS. Despite these context-related issues she overall expanded her object as result of her collaborative efforts. Carol had two subject-related contradictions, one related to her concepts of a tool, the unit which she thought was too difficult for her students, and one related to a rule, her class within a class structure. She overall expanded her object by completing all the unit activities in conjunction with the other teachers despite her belief that the unit was too difficult and her students were not learning useful knowledge.

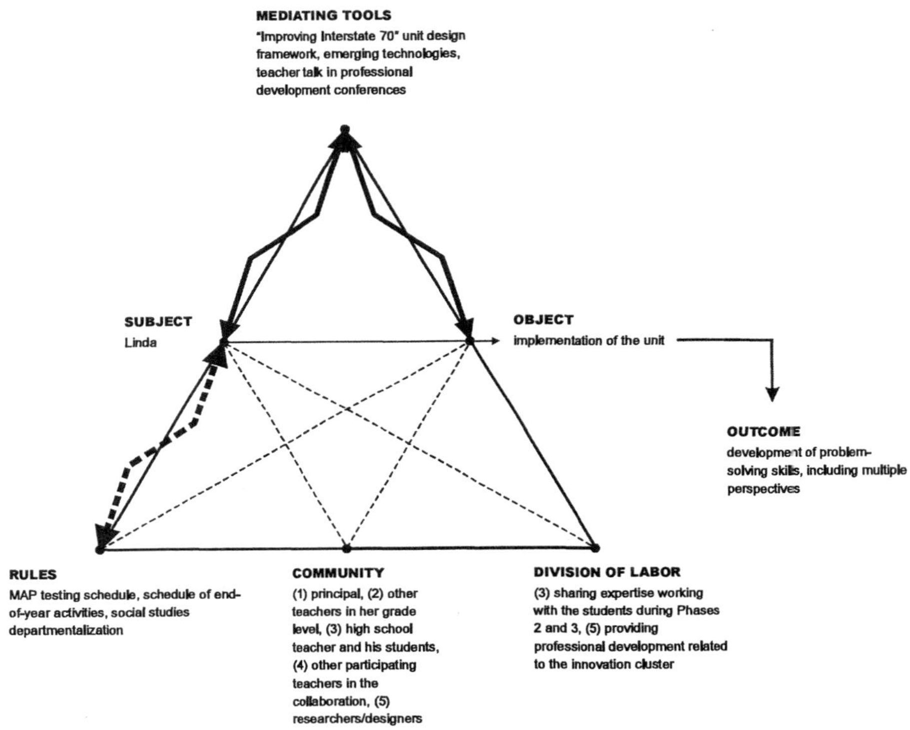

Figure 1. AT Model of Linda's Work Activity System

A tertiary contradiction occurs between interacting activity systems. This type of contradiction occurred when the teachers collaborated to define a common object. The researcher coded the teachers' online dialogs to define the dialogic turning points as text instances when the teachers redefined their object and changed an aspect of their implementation of the unit in their classrooms (Kärkkäinen, 1999). This type of contradiction defined the second progressive issue, how does the individual teacher's participation in collaborative professional development influence the implementation of an innovation cluster? Three of the teachers reformulated their object because of these online collaborative processes. Janice shortened her schedule as a result of collaboration dialogs despite her own concerns about the schedule and she was unable to complete the unit as a result. Both Janice and Carol were able to widen their objects, adding activities and evaluations, as a result of the online collaboration process. Linda made no changes in her implementation as a result of the online chat dialogs.

A primary contradiction defines the relationship between motive and outcome. A primary contradiction is as negative tension between the concepts underlying the implementation of the object, in this study the motive was defined as development of advanced learning abilities in the students, and the ultimate result that the agent hopes to achieve, outcome. This type of contradiction defined the progressive issue, how do individual teacher's beliefs about learning and technology influence the implementation of an innovation cluster? The researcher identified relationships between the pre and post levels in outcome in order to evaluate their relationship to the overall development of their object. The researcher coded these as hierarchical levels of the teacher's philosophy of learning using Bereiter's Scheme of Knowledge to identify changes in her learning goals for her students (Bereiter, 2001) as each teacher stated them pre and post unit. These overall transformative processes developed into contradictions in the development of two of the units. Linda narrowed her object, stopping the chats among her students and the other students, because of her belief that the learning processes augmented by the online technologies, the development of multiple perspectives during problem-solving, were not beneficial to her students. She stated in her post-unit interview that she did not want to develop problem-based learning processes in her students but instead prepare them for the standardized test. Janice, the urban teacher, widened her object from her pre-unit motive as a result of identifying and overcoming her primary belief contradiction that her students were unable to develop advanced learning processes as a result of their interactions in the problem-based unit. She credited the online professional development program with her ability to fully implement the unit and develop advanced problem-solving abilities in her urban students. Carol did not resolve contradictions between her ideas of her students' capabilities and the problem-based unit. She felt the unit was too complex for her students and a "waste of time." Helen did not have any pre-unit contradictions about the learning unit and the online technology.

The researcher designed the Transformation Model, figure 2 below, to depict the identified contradictions across the cases as they occurred during the study. Each of the teacher's final AT model is shown in the center of the circle. The collaboration process is shown as a broadening and narrowing line outside the circle. It enlarges if the teacher resolves a contradiction and narrows if she does not. The progressive AT Models of the teachers are shown outside the circle as Pre-Unit, Phases 1, 2, and 3. Turning points, changes in teacher activities in their classrooms, are identified as a TP in the line going through the AT models for each teacher. Using this transformation model the researcher found that all the teachers were unable to resolve contradictions during a difficult collaborative phase of the unit when all their students were online in synchronous chatrooms. Additionally the two teacher who described themselves as collaborative in the pre-unit interview did not resolve any contradictions as a result of the online dialogs and either narrowed or disintegrated their object. The two teachers who described themselves as not collaborative in the pre-unit interview both expanded their object as a result of the online interactions. Linda and Helen were coded as givers of information in their online dialogs with Janice and Carol coded as asking questions which they subsequently used to develop new processes in their classrooms.

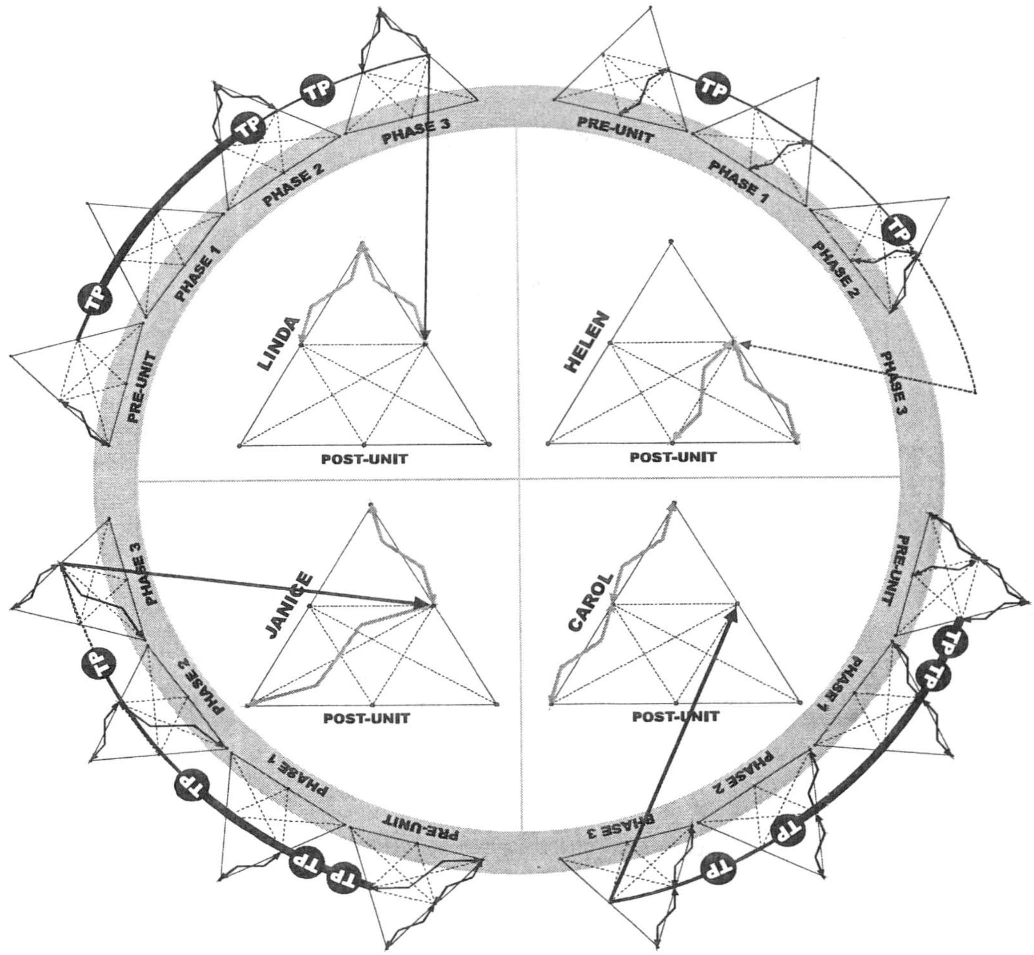

Figure 2. Transformation Model

Conclusions

In response to the first progressive issue, local context, teachers who are implementing innovation should develop communication support structures in their local community that allow them to resolve the eventual contradictions in their local activity setting. Anticipatory problem-solving and design processes are beneficial constructs for reform-based professional development models for innovative educators. In response to the second issue, collaboration processes, the researcher found that teachers implementing innovation who are working in local contexts with little collaboration experiences can benefit by collaboration outside their local environment with other innovative teachers implementing similar units. However, teachers who are already working at a high level of innovation in collaborative and supportive local contexts may not benefit, or can even reduce the effectiveness of their reform units, as a result of collaboration with other teachers below their level of innovation (Russell, 2004). Collaborative processes should be designed to fit the varied levels of previous and current collaboration and innovation of the participating teachers. In response to the third issue, beliefs about learning, teachers implementing units designed to develop advanced learning processes in their students can have primary contradictions between their beliefs about learning and the processes required for practical implementation of the mediational tools that they bring into their classroom in order to meet these learning goals for their students.

Teachers who are designing and implementing constructivist-based learning environments need a reflective proactive form of communication as part of their professional development in order to "clarify concepts, ideas, and alternative courses of action" (Korthagen, 1993, p. 318). Teachers who design and implement innovation into their classrooms must be ready to adapt their instruction to meet the demands of a "complex and multifaceted endeavor" (Blumenfeld, Soloway, Marx, Krajcik, Guzdial, & Palincsar, 1991, p.390). Elbaz (1991) illustrated that teachers' knowledge is non-linear, holistic, imbued with personal meaning and largely tacit. Clark (1979) found that teachers' actions seem to be governed by rules and routines, with decision-making in a studied, deliberate sense taking a minor role in their interactive thinking. These studies demonstrate that creating a reflective professional development program for innovative educators can help teachers identify their tacit knowledge and understand the types of innovative pedagogical knowledge that can aid them in developing new pedagogical and philosophical concepts in order to implement innovative learning environments. A professional development model for innovative educators should help teachers be both problem-solvers and proactive collaborators and communicators. In order to develop innovation effectively, teachers need to be supported by varied processes and forums of interactions with other teachers or mentors working on similar innovations. Innovative teachers need the challenge and support gained through productive social interactions in order to clarify what they believe and gain the courage to pursue their beliefs (Zeichner & Liston, 1996) in order to be effective innovators.

References

Aronson, Daniel. (2003). *Targeted Innovation: Using systems thinking to increase the benefits of innovation efforts*. R & D Innovator. (6.2).

Banathy, B. (1991). *Systems design of education: A journey to create the future*. Englewood Cliffs, N.J: Educational Technology Publications.

Barab, S. A., Hay, K. E., Yamagata-Lynch, L. C. (2001). Constructing networks of activity: An in-situ research methodology. *The Journal of the Learning Sciences, 10*(1&2), 63-112.

Bereiter, C. (2002). *Education and mind in the knowledge age*. New Jersey. Lawrence Erlbaum Associates.

Blumenfeld, P.C., Soloway, E., Marx, R., Krajcik, J.S., Gzdial, M., & Palincsar, A. (1991). Motivating project-based learning: Sustaining the doing, supporting the learning. *Educational Psychologist, 26,* 369-398.

Bruner, J. (1990). *Acts of meaning*. Cambridge, MA: Harvard University Press.

Clark, C.M., & Yinger, R. J. (1979). Teachers' thinking. In P.L. Peterson & H.J. Walberg (Eds.), *Research on teaching: Concepts, findings, and implications* (pp. 231-263). Berkeley, CA: McCutchan.

Cole, M., & Engeström, Y. (1993). A cultural-historical approach to distributed cognition. In G. Salomon (Ed.), *Distributed cognition: Psychological and educational considerations*. Cambridge, MA: Cambridge University Press.

Elbaz, F. (1991). Reserarch on teachers' knowledge: The evolution of a discourse. *Journal of Curriculum Studies,* 23(1), 1-19.

Engeström, Y. (1987). *Learning by expanding: An activity-theoretical approach to developmental research*. Helsinki: Orienta-Konsultit.

Engeström, Y., Miettinen, R., & Punamaki, R. (Eds.). (1999). *Perspectives on activity theory*. Cambridge, U.K.: Cambridge University Press.

Fraenkel, J.R., & Wallen, N.E. (1996). *How to design and evaluate research in education*. NY: McGraw-Hill, Inc.

Hall, G.E., Wallace, R.C., & Dossett, W.A. (1973). *A developmental conceptualization of the adoption process within educational institutions,* Austin, TX: Research and Development Center for Teacher Education, The University of Texas.

Il'enkov, E. V. (1977). Dialectical logic: Essays in its history and theory. Moscow: Progress.

Jonassen, D. H. (2000). Toward a design theory of problem solving. *Educational Technology Research and Development, 48*(4), 63-85.

Kärkkäinen, M. (1999). *A longitudinal study of planning and implementing curriculum units in elementary school teacher teams.* Retrieved March 3, 2002, from University of Helsinki, eThesis: Electronic Publications at University of Helsinki: http://ethesis.helsinki.fi/english.html.

Korthagen, F. (1993). Two modes of reflection. *Teacher and Teacher Education, 9(*3), 317-326.

Lave, J., & Wenger, E. (1991). *Situated learning: Legitimate peripheral participation.* Cambridge, UK: Cambridge University Press.

Rogers, E. M. (1995). *Diffusion of innovations* (4th ed.). NY: The Free Press.

Russell, Donna. (2004). Paradigm Shift: A Case Study of Innovation in an Educational Setting. *International Journal of Instructional Technology & Distance Learning*. December 2004. Volume 1

Number 12. ISSN 1550-690

Salomon, G. (1993). No distribution without individuals' cognition: A dynamic interactional view. In G. Salomon (Ed.), *Distributed cognitions: Psychological and educational considerations*. NY: Cambridge University Press.

Savery, J. R., & Duffy, T. M. (1996). Problem based learning: An instructional model and its constructivist framework. *Educational Technology, 35*(5), 31-38.

Schank, R. C. (1994). Goal-based scenarios. In R. C. S. a. E. Langer (Ed.), *Beliefs, reasoning, and decision making: Psycho-logic in honor of Bob Abelson*. Hillsdale, NJ: Lawrence Erlbaum Associates.

Schoenfeld,A.(1999).Looking towards the 21st Century: Challenges of educational theory and practice. *Educational Researcher, 28(7)*, 4-14.

Schön, D. A. (1987). *Educating the reflective practitioner.* San Francisco: Jossey-Bass.

Vygotsky, L.S. (1978). Mind in Society: The development of higher psychological processes. Cambridge, MA: Harvard University Press.

Wertsch, J. (1998). *Mind as action.* NY: Oxford University Press.

Wilson, B. (Ed.). (1996). *Constructivist learning environments: Case studies in instructional design*. New Jersey: Educational Technology Publications.

Wilson, B., Sherry, L., Dobrovolny, J., Batty, M., & Ryder, M. (2001). Adoption of learning technologies in schools and universities. In H.H. Adelsberger, B. Collis, & J.M. Pawlowski (Eds.), *Handbook of Information Technologies for Education & Training*. New York: Springer-Verlag.

Wilson, Edward O. (1998). *Consilience: The unity of knowledge*. New York. Alfred A. Knopf.

Zeichner, K. & Liston, D. (1996). Reflective teaching: An introduction. New Jersey: Lawrence Erlbaum Associates, Inc.

Assessment of Argument in Science Education: A Critical Review of the Literature

Victor D. Sampson, Douglas B. Clark, Arizona State University
College of Education, Division of Curriculum and Instruction, 203 Payne Hall, Tempe, AZ 85287-0911, USA
Email: victor.sampson@asu.edu, douglas.b.clark@asu.edu

Abstract: Theoretical and empirical research on argumentation in science education has intensified over the last two decades. This article reviews and synthesizes analytical methods used to assess and characterize the nature of rhetorical arguments generated by students as part of this research. This synthesis of the current state of argumentation analysis in science education research provides a comprehensive framework for future research on rhetorical argumentation.

Introduction

Research on argumentation in science education has expanded and intensified considerably over the last decade. In this article, we examine the various analytical methods that have been developed to assess rhetorical argumentation within the context of science education. Our overall goals involve (a) illustrating the logic and assumptions that have pervaded research in this field, (b) summarizing the constraints and affordances of these different approaches, and (c) making recommendations for new directions.

Methods to Assess Argument Quality

Many initial efforts to evaluate students' discursive practices in science have focused on the ways in which students develop arguments or how the arguments generated by students compare to arguments developed by scientists. According to Passmore and Stewart (2002), "Scientific inquiry is fundamentally about reducing the world to order; those reductions take the form of explanations" (p. 188). In order to accomplish this task, scientists make observations, identify patterns in data, then develop and test explanations for those patterns. In constructing an argument, scientists attempt to establish the acceptability of the explanations that they have developed. Studies of scientists doing science indicate that this goal is accomplished by coordinating supportive or contradictory evidence with a particular explanatory or descriptive claim for an observed phenomenon (Kuhn, 1970; Latour, 1987). However, in order to be persuasive, this process must be carried out in way that is consistent with the epistemological criteria used by the larger scientific community for 'what counts' as valid and warranted scientific knowledge. Examples of important epistemological criteria in science include (a) the need to provide evidentiary backing or rationales for knowledge claims and proposing tests of claims (Hogan & Maglienti, 2001), (b) the need for coherence between theoretical frameworks and observations of phenomena (Passmore & Stewart, 2002), (c) establishing the credibility of evidence (Driver et al., 2000), (d) parsimony (Sandoval & Reiser, 2004), and (e) the importance of basing arguments on reasoning that is logically valid (Zeidler, 1997). Thus, in order to generate a scientific argument, an individual must learn the kinds of claims scientists make, how they advance them; what kinds of evidence is needed to warrant an argument, and how that evidence can be gathered and interpreted given community standards.

How do students, who are not members of the scientific community, generate arguments? What type of reasoning do students use when they construct arguments and how is it different than scientists? Are students able to assimilate the desired practices of argumentation as a result of classroom instruction? To answer these types of questions, researchers must develop tools to evaluate the quality of the arguments generated by students. Our review of the literature indicates that a diversity of approaches for analyzing rhetorical argumentation exists across studies. Substantial variation is observed, for instance, in the perspectives on argument quality, the questions addressed, the analytical methods adopted, and the specific units of analysis chosen. A critical analysis of these different approaches can provide valuable information about the benefits and limitations of the different analytical methods and assumptions that underlie this field of research.

Toulmin's framework: Examining the structural aspects of arguments

Historically, science education researchers have been heavily influenced by Toulmin's perspectives on argumentation. In *The Uses of Argument* (1958), Toulmin made a distinction between the idealized notions of the logical-formal arguments as they are used in mathematics and how arguments are used in linguistic contexts. Toulmin's argument framework suggests that the statements that make up an argument have different functions that can be classified into one of six categories: claims, data, warrants, backings, qualifiers, and rebuttals. According to this framework, a claim is the assertion that an individual makes and data are the facts that a person explicitly appeals to as a foundation for their claim. Warrants are used by individuals to justify why data is relevant to the claim. The strength of the warrant is indicated by including a modal qualifier. The backings of an argument are the comments that are used to establish the general conditions that strengthen the acceptability of the warrants so that the connection between the data and the claims will not be scrutinized. Finally, a rebuttal indicates the "circumstances in which the general authority of the warrant would have to be set aside" (p. 101). Toulmin describes the process of constructing a scientific argument primarily as a process of using evidence, warrants and backings to convince others of the validity of a specific claim. From this perspective the strength of an argument is based on the presence or absence of these different structural components. Stronger arguments contain more of these different components than weaker arguments.

Analyses of arguments constructed by students using Toulmin's argument framework have primarily examined how students provide warrants for claims, when they do so, and on what basis (e.g., Jimenez-Aleixandre, Rodrigues, & Duschl, 2000; Kelly, Druker, & Chen, 1998; Osborne, Erduran, & Simon, 2004). These studies have provided a great deal of information about the form of student talk or writing in various setting but have provided little information about how well students engage in argument construction in terms of content quality or normativity. As a result, analytic methods that examine argument quality solely from a structural perspective provide little or no information about how (or if) students' conceptual ideas about the subject matter influence how they coordinate theory with evidence as they construct an argument in support of a particular viewpoint.

Another constraint of Toulmin's argument framework is the fact that it provides little information about *field-dependent* features. According to Toulmin's framework, claims, warrants, data, and backings are *field-invariant* features of an argument that can be used to study the structure of an argument regardless of context. However, what counts as an appropriate claim, warrant, backing, or datum are *field-dependent* features of an argument (Toulmin, 1958). Unfortunately, because the majority of the research using Toulmin's argument framework has focused on the field-invariant features of an argument, we know very little about the how well arguments constructed by students adhere to the criteria shared by the scientific community for judging quality. For example, do students incorporate evidence that is valid and reliable as part of their argument? Do students attempt to coordinate their claim with all available data or just the data that supports their particular viewpoint? Answers to these types of questions can provide valuable insights into students' reasoning. However, since these criteria for constructing a scientific argument are grounded in certain logical and epistemological commitments specific to science (Hogan & Maglienti, 2001; Sandoval, 2003), different analytical methods are needed to explore these field-dependent features of an argument.

Zohar and Nemet's framework: Examining the structure and content of arguments

Zohar and Nemet (2002) modified Toulmin's argumentation framework based on the work of Means and Voss (1996) to evaluate the quality of written arguments generated by students based on structure and content. Zohar and Nemet define an argument as consisting "of either assertions or conclusions and their justifications; or of reasons or supports" (p. 38). Therefore, strong arguments have multiple justifications to support a conclusion that incorporate relevant, specific, and accurate scientific concepts and facts. Weak arguments consist of individual non-relevant justifications. Conclusions that do not include some type of justification are not considered arguments. Zohar and Nemet also collapsed Toulmin's data, warrants and backings into a single category to sidestep many of the reliability and validity issues associated with Toulmin's framework (see Kelly et al., 1998 for examples). Justifications are analyzed to determine if they include (a) no consideration of scientific knowledge, (b) inaccurate scientific knowledge, (c) non-specific scientific knowledge (we need to do more tests before we can reach a conclusion), or (d) correct scientific knowledge.

While Zohar and Nemet's framework offers several affordances, the framework involves some limitations as well. The accuracy of the claim itself is not evaluated in this analytical framework. As a result, this framework works better when used to analyze arguments generated in the context of socio-scientific issues (such as family planning based on genetic testing) rather than in the context of scientific debates. In response to socioscientific dilemmas that Zohar and Nemet studied, valid opposing claims can be made from multiple perspectives. However, when arguments are scientific, claims are explanatory conclusions or descriptive frameworks. The accuracy of these revel student's understanding of scientific content and how well they were able to coordinate claims with evidence. Another constraint of this analytical framework is that it does not analyze how well students were able to coordinate claims with all available evidence. Cognitive studies of students' experimentation across scientific and quasi-scientific domains reveal that most students have a great deal of difficulty coordinating data with causal ideas or hypotheses (Zeidler, 1997). Students often fail to see patterns emerging across experiments and often ignore anomalous data or distort it to match their personal beliefs (Zeidler, 1997). As a result, students may be able to construct elaborate arguments consisting of several relevant justifications that include accurate scientific knowledge, but their claim can be inaccurate because they did not attempt to coordinate their claim with all available evidence. This is a significant constraint to this method, especially because justifications for scientific claims are often based on interpretations of data gathered across multiple experiments.

Kelly and Takao's framework: Examining the epistemic status of propositions

Kelly and Takao (2002; Takao & Kelly, 2003) developed a method to analyze longer and more complex written arguments by examining term papers produced by students enrolled in an oceanography course. The term paper required students to support an abstract theoretical conclusion based on multiple data representations. The arguments generated by these students often contained multiple propositions in order to support their particular explanatory conclusion. Kelly and Takao's analytic framework focuses on the relative epistemic status of these propositions and how these propositions are linked together by the author to form a persuasive argument. In order to develop this framework, Kelly and Takao relied heavily on rhetorical studies of science writing (e.g., Bazerman, 1988; Latour, 1987). To analyze an extended rhetorical argument using this framework, propositions are identified and then sorted based on epistemic level. These epistemic levels are defined by discipline-specific constructs and reflect a general distinction between lower level descriptions of data and epistemologically higher level appeals to theories within the particular domain. Once classified, Kelly and Takao determine how these propositions are linked together and use this information to produce a graphical representation of an argument that shows how students coordinate propositions in their writing.

One limitation of the framework involves the lack of appraisal of how sensible the links between propositions are or even if the propositions are scientifically accurate. Without this type of evaluation, it is difficult to determine if the author understands the theories they apply or how well the data supports the conclusion. Kelly and Takao pointed out this limitation in their own analysis. In fact, Kelly and Takao found several discrepancies between how they rated arguments and how the instructor of the oceanography course rated them. This variation could be attributed to the accuracy of the propositions and the appropriateness of how they were linked or it could be the result of a lack of sufficient evidentiary support for the students' conclusions (which are all field-dependant features an argument). Kelly and Takao's work once again illustrates the importance of evaluating the quality of arguments based on the standards developed within the discipline rather than solely relying on field-invariant structures (Toulmin, 1958).

Despite these limitations, Kelly and Takao's framework shows promise as an analytical tool. The examination of the epistemic status of the knowledge claims provides a way to characterize the types of propositions students use to support their conclusions and the extent to which individuals adhere to genre conventions of the scientific community. The development of this framework also highlights the importance of considering the nature of the task and the rhetorical aspects of argument construction when choosing or developing an analytical method to assess argument quality. For example, Kelly et al. (1998) found that students tend to rely on a series of relatively short arguments consisting of only a single claim as they attempt to persuade a lab partner of the accuracy of their ideas. In this type of task, Toulmin's framework works relatively well because arguments tend to be simple and the rhetorical aspects of the discourse are straightforward. On the other hand, the nature of the arguments found in the oceanography midterm papers examined by Kelly and Takao were much more complex. In these papers, students needed to formulate a line of evidence based on multiple data representations, which required students to reference specific data, identify specific geological features, and then explain how these features related to their abstract theoretical conclusions. Using Toulmin's or Zohar and Nemet's framework to analyze these arguments would have neglected important aspects of the rhetorical nature of these complex scientific arguments, such as the importance of moving rhetorically from specific grounded claims to more generalized statements or the importance of embedding claims within a larger argument (Bazerman, 1988; Latour, 1987). Taken as a whole, this research indicates that the nature of the academic task will influence the type of argument developed by an individual and consequently the analytical methods needed to assess it.

Sandoval's framework: Examining the conceptual and epistemic quality of arguments

Sandoval (2003; Sandoval & Millwood, 2005) has developed an alternative framework for judging the quality of scientific arguments generated by students. Rather than examining arguments based on the field-invariant structural components of arguments, his coding scheme attempts to assess how well students generate arguments based on field-dependent criteria. Specifically, Sandoval's coding scheme assesses two dimensions of scientific arguments. First, conceptual quality measures how well the individual has (a) articulated causal claims within a specific theoretical framework, and (b) warranted these claims using available data. Second, epistemological quality measures how well the individual has (a) cited sufficient data in warranting a claim, (b) written a coherent causal explanation for a given phenomenon (see Sandoval, 2003) and (c) incorporated appropriate rhetorical references when referring to data (see Sandoval & Millwood, 2005). This analytical framework is particularly useful for two reasons. First, it determines if students can generate an argument that explains a particular observed phenomenon using a specific theory, such as natural selection. Second, it provides information about the epistemological criteria students use when generating arguments as an end product of their own inquiry and how these criteria align with the criteria used within particular scientific domains.

Sandoval's coding scheme suggests that constructing high-quality arguments requires (a) a conceptual understanding of relevant scientific theories and their application to a specific problem as well as (b) an epistemic understanding of the criteria for high-quality arguments. Sandoval argues for the importance of the latter component because the manner in which students incorporate and refer to data in their writing reflects their implicit epistemological commitments about the nature and role of data in the generation and evaluation of scientific knowledge. For example, in Sandoval and Millwood's (2005) analysis indicates that students are able to apply their understanding of natural selection to generate an argument that is consistent with the major tenets of natural selection. However, the overall pattern of warrant and evidence citation suggests that although students understand the importance of linking evidence and claims, students tend to rely on a single piece of data when supporting a particular claim. As a result, students often do not include a comparison of data from multiple sources when warranting a claim even when such comparisons are needed. Sandoval's (2003) work also indicates that students often interpret data incorrectly even though they can articulate a specific explanation in terms of a guiding theory. Taken together, this analytical framework highlights the importance of examining scientific arguments in terms of field-dependent criteria.

Lawson's framework: Examining the hypothetico-deductive validity of arguments

Lawson (2003) argues that science educators should focus their efforts on helping students learn how to generate the type of arguments that are used and valued by scientists rather than focusing on a more general account of argument structure. From his perspective, the goal of developing an argument in science is to "determine which of two or more proposed alternative explanations (claims) for a puzzling observation is correct and which of the alternatives are incorrect" (p. 1389, emphasis in original). This process requires the generation of an argument that consists of not only a tentative explanation that may be correct but also includes how this explanation was tested based on the generation of specific predictions and the analysis of evidence. Lawson describes this type of argument as a hypothetico-predictive argument. According to Lawson, this type of argument, which evaluates the validity of alternative explanations based on hypothetico-deductive reasoning, is much more convincing than arguments that rely on evidence, warrants, and backings to convince others of the validity of a claim because it can provide evidence for one explanation and at the same time provide evidence against another.

The process of constructing a hypothetico-predictive argument begins with an observation that provokes a casual question and the generation of one or more tentative explanations. Once generated, these explanations must be tested in order to establish their validity. To test the validity of an explanation, one must begin by assuming that the explanation is correct. Next, one must imagine a test that, together with the explanation, should produce one or more specific observable results. The words, "if/and/then" are used to link the explanation and the imagined test to the prediction. Once a test is planned and conducted, the observed results constitute evidence. This evidence is then compared with the prediction. This match or mismatch of evidence and prediction can then be used to draw a conclusion regarding the validity of the explanation. Lawson indicates that the overall quality of this type of argument should be evaluated based on its deductive validity rather than the presence and strength of warrants, which he contends, is the same criterion used by scientists to assess the quality of arguments generated by the scientific community.

Synthesis, conclusions, and recommendations for improving the analytical methods used to study rhetorical arguments in science education

As previously mentioned, scientific arguments are grounded in certain logical and epistemological commitments that are valued by the scientific community. Epistemological commitments refer to the philosophical assumptions and beliefs about the nature and limits of knowledge and its acquisition (Kitchener, 1983). These shared commitments make science different from other ways of knowing (Hogan & Maglienti, 2001; Sandoval,

2003). Consequently, several science educators have argued that students need to learn how the scientific community uses arguments in order to construct knowledge and the criteria for what counts as a good argument in science (e.g., Driver, Asoko, Leach, Mortimer, & Scott, 1994; e.g., Sandoval & Reiser, 2004). Unfortunately, as we have outlined in this article, the majority of the analytical methods that have been developed to assess and characterize the nature of the rhetorical arguments generated by students in science classrooms have provided very little information about how the rhetorical arguments generated by students reflect these criteria.

Although there is no single answer to the question of what constitutes a good argument in science, an operational definition for quality scientific argumentation would facilitate research and curricular development. As Osborne and colleagues (2003) suggest, using a generic framework to characterize argumentation across different science content areas and contexts can help students achieve a *basic understanding* of the processes and practices of science because there are several criteria that transcend specific disciplines and make science unique from other ways of knowing. For example, all scientists rely on evidence in order to justify ideas or knowledge claims because sooner or later the validity of scientific claims is settled by referring to observations of phenomena (Driver et. al., 2000). As Driver and colleagues (1994) suggest, scientific argumentation "is characterized by the explicit formulation of theories than can then be communicated and inspected in light of evidence" (p. 8). Once individuals develop this basic understanding, individuals can then learn the discipline specific practices and norms for creating and supporting knowledge claims within a particular domain. Nevertheless, developing a consensual view of quality argumentation from a scientific perspective requires linking research and theoretical perspectives on argument from various fields including, educational research, socio-cultural studies, literacy studies, history of science, and philosophy of science. Calls for such a link have been made before, yet little has been done. We therefore outline five criteria for examining the quality of scientific arguments that we view as essential *as a first step towards this goal.*

Criteria 1: Examine the nature and quality of the knowledge claim

In scientific arguments, claims are explanatory conclusions or descriptive frameworks rather than definitions or personal opinions. Scientists do not simply form context-specific conclusions or describe their observed results; they work to develop generalizable explanations for why something happens or descriptions of how something happens. Unfortunately, few students see science as a process of creating and testing frameworks and theories; instead science is seen as a steady accumulation of facts about the world. For example, Driver et al. (1996) found that students tend to describe scientific claims as "observations about the world" instead of descriptive frameworks and explanations that can be tested empirically. Similarly, Carey et al. (1989) found that students do not distinguish between experimental findings and the ideas that experiments are designed to test. Research also suggests that students rarely provide causal mechanisms for an observation based on an interpretation of data unless they are explicitly told to do so or they are scaffolded in a way that requires them to do so (Sandoval & Reiser, 2004). Taken together, this research suggests that students must learn more about the kinds of claims scientists make and how they advance them. Analytic methods should therefore focus on the type of claims students make as a result of their inquiry and whether or not the claims answer the research questions that guide their inquiries. Finally, assessments should also make judgments concerning the conceptual quality of these claims. The accuracy of a student's claim from a scientific perspective can revel a great deal about how a student understands content and how well the student is able to coordinate claims with available evidence.

Criteria 2: Examine how (or if) the claim is justified

Several studies have shown that although students are able to generate claims to explain data when asked to do so, students usually do not justify their claims unless they are challenged (Jimenez-Aleixandre et al., 2000; Kelly et al., 1998). When warrants are included as part of an argument, many people tend to rely too heavily on unsubstantiated explanations to justify their claims (Kuhn, 1993) or simply use plausible explanations as a way to replace evidence that is lacking or missing (Brem & Rips, 2000). In science, empirical evidence is an important consideration for evaluating the validity of scientific claims (Jimenez-Aleizandre, Rodriguez, & Duschl, 2000), therefore students must learn to not only provide empirical evidence in support of their ideas but also learn what kinds of evidence is needed to warrant an argument and how that evidence can be appropriately interpreted given community standards. Analytic methods should not only focus on whether or not students are justifying their claims but also on how individuals attempt to accomplish this task. In addition, assessments should also make judgments concerning the types of reasons and evidence that are used to support a particular claim. Do students rely on an appeal to authority figure in order to justify their ideas? Do they understand the difference between correlation and causation? Do students rely on empirical data or personal experiences as evidence? The types of reasons and evidence used by students and how they use them can tell us a great deal about what they consider good explanations or warranted knowledge.

Criteria 3: Examine if a claim accounts for all available evidence

A central activity of a scientist is to construct arguments determining which of the various conjectures about a puzzling phenomenon are most convincing in light of all available evidence and to obtain additional evidence when the available evidence is insufficient or lacking (Lawson, 2003). Unfortunately, a great deal of research suggests that students often fail to attend to important patterns in data and tend to preferentially consider a single piece of evidence rather than a set (Driver et al., 1996). Research also suggests that students often select, ignore, or distort evidence (Zeidler, 1997) especially when it threatens strongly held ideas. As a result, students are often able to generate arguments that consist of an inaccurate claim that is supported by empirical evidence because students tend to rely on a single piece of evidence while ignoring other data (Clark & Sampson, 2005). These findings indicate that analytical methods should also include a judgment of how well an individual is able to coordinate their claim with all available evidence.

Criteria 4: Examine how (or if) the argument attempts to discount alternatives

Students need to understand that scientific theories and conclusions are human constructs. As it often happens in science, more than one claim may be an acceptable explanation for the same phenomenon. Arguments are the preferential tool for resolving controversies in science, but when scientists have to make choices, evidence is never totally determinate, nor are arguments overwhelmingly convincing. More than one alternative is not just possible but often also plausible. As a result, students should learn to challenge alternative explanations for the same phenomenon by addressing weaknesses in other possible explanations or frameworks as a part of their argument. Unfortunately, research suggests that students are poor at presenting arguments 'for and against' or examining different points of view on the same issue (Driver et al., 2000). Analytical methods should therefore evaluate an individual's ability to "postulate possible interpretations and then examine the arguments for each in the light of the evidence that is available to them" (Driver et al., 2000, p. 299). Although it is not always possible to exclude all but one explanation in science, students should be able to assess the acceptability or usefulness of alternative explanations using criteria such as: (a) the ability of the claim to account for all observations relating to the phenomenon, (b) its usefulness in predicting the behavior of the phenomenon, and (c) the consistency of the claim with the other accepted knowledge about how the world works (Driver et al., 2000; Passmore & Stewart, 2002).

Criteria 5: Examine how epistemological references are used to coordinate claims and evidence

As students engage in the construction of arguments they must do more than simply justify their ideas with evidence, they must also learn to justify that the evidence was appropriately gathered and interpreted given community standards. Therefore when constructing an argument that can be used to persuade, the ability to justify a claim by including a discussion concerning, for example, the validity of an experimental design or the interpretation of data is extremely valuable. Unfortunately, current research suggests that students' understanding of the epistemological commitments of science, especially an understanding of what counts as warranted scientific knowledge and what methods can satisfactorily generate such knowledge is poor (Sandoval & Millwood, 2005). Students frequently indicate that the results of an experiment are enough to prove ideas right or wrong without ever questioning the methods used in the experiment or how the data was analyzed (Carey et al., 1989). Working to help students address the validity and reliability of their evidence, as well as the presence of other confirming or disconfirming evidence, will be important if students are to generate productive scientific arguments.

In conclusion, a key question we should ask about any analytic framework of rhetorical argumentation concerns what the framework can tell us about the quality of the arguments generated by students when they are asked to explain or describe a complex phenomenon. Structural analyses of arguments have made explicit the difficulties students encounter in marshaling evidence, drawing on their conceptual understanding of the topic, and composing arguments in support of a scientific knowledge claim. The epistemic demands of argument construction, however, engage the criteria to which knowledge claims are held within a community of practice. Although it is important to help students learn to construct elaborate arguments in order to facilitate the development of their thinking and informal reasoning skills across contexts (Osborne et al., 2004), we must also recognize the significance of enabling learners to engage in argumentation in a way that reflects the standards used to construct and evaluate arguments by the scientific community. Ultimately, this analysis strongly suggests the need for further development and improvement of the tools used to study argument in science education. The five criteria for the assessment of rhetorical arguments outlined in this article are a first step towards this goal.

References

Bazerman, C. (1988). *Shaping written knowledge: The genre and activity of the experimental article in science.* Madison, WI: University of Wisconsin Press.

Brem, S. K., & Rips, L. J. (2000). Explanation and evidence in informal argument. *Cognitive Science, 24*(4), 573-604.

Carey, S., Evans, R., Honda, M., Jay, E., & Unger, C. (1989). 'An experiment is when you try it and see if it works': A study of grade 7 students' understanding of the construction of scientific knowledge. *International Journal of Science Education, 11*(Special Issue), 514-529.

Clark, D. B., & Sampson, V. (2005). *Analyzing the quality of argumentation supported by personally-seeded discussions.* Paper presented at the Computer Supported Collaborative Learning Conference, Taipei, Taiwan.

Driver, R., Asoko, H., Leach, J., Mortimer, E., & Scott, P. (1994). Constructing scientific knowledge in the classroom. *Educational Researcher, 23*, 5-12.

Driver, R., Leach, J., Millar, R., & Scott, P. (1996). *Young people's images of science.* Philadelphia: Open University Press.

Driver, R., Newton, P., & Osborne, J. (2000). Establishing the norms of scientific argumentation in classrooms. *Science Education, 84*(3), 287-313.

Hogan, K., & Maglienti, M. (2001). Comparing the epistemological underpinnings of students' and scientists' reasoning about conclusions. *Journal of Research in Science Teaching, 38*(6), 663-687.

Jimenez-Aleixandre, M., Rodrigues, M., & Duschl, R. A. (2000). 'Doing the lesson' or 'doing science': Argument in high school genetics. *Science Education, 84*(6), 757-792.

Kelly, G. J., Druker, S., & Chen, C. (1998). Students' reasoning about electricity: combining performance assessments with argumentation analysis. *International Journal of Science Education, 20*(7), 849-871.

Kelly, G. J., & Takao, A. (2002). Epistemic levels in argument: an analysis of university oceanography students' use of evidence in writing. *Science Education, 86*(3), 314-342.

Kitchener, K. S. (1983). Cognition, metacognition, and epistemic cognition: A three-level model of cognitive processing. *Human Development, 26*, 222-232.

Kuhn, D. (1993). Science as argument: Implications for teaching and learning scientific thinking. *Science Education, 77*(3), 319-337.

Kuhn, T., S. (1970). *The structure of scientific revolutions* (2nd ed.). Chicago: University of Chicago Press.

Latour, B. (1987). *Science in action: How to follow scientists and engineers through society.* Cambridge: Harvard University Press.

Lawson, A. (2003). The nature and development of hypothetico-predictive argumentation with implications for science teaching. *International Journal of Science Education, 25*(11), 1387-1408.

Means, L. M., & Voss, J. F. (1996). Who reasons well? Two studies of informal reasoning among children of different grade, ability, and knowledge levels. *Cognition and Instruction, 14*(2), 139-178.

Osborne, J., Erduran, S., & Simon, S. (2004). Enhancing the quality of argumentation in science classrooms. *Journal of Research in Science Teaching, 41*(10), 994-1020.

Passmore, C., & Stewart, J. (2002). A modeling approach to teaching evolutionary biology in high schools. *Journal of Research in Science Teaching, 39*(3), 185-204.

Sandoval, W. A. (2003). Conceptual and epistemic aspects of students' scientific explanations. *Journal of the Learning Sciences, 12*(1), 5-51.

Sandoval, W. A., & Millwood, K. (2005). The quality of students' use of evidence in written scientific explanations. *Cognition and Instruction.*

Sandoval, W. A., & Reiser, B. J. (2004). Explanation driven inquiry: Integrating conceptual and epistemic scaffolds for scientific inquiry. *Science Education, 88*(3), 345-372.

Takao, A. Y., & Kelly, G. J. (2003). Assessment of evidence in university students' scientific writing. *Science & Education, 12*(4), 341-363.

Toulmin, S. (1958). *The uses of argument.* Cambridge: Cambridge University Press.

Zeidler, D., L. (1997). The central role of fallacious thinking in science education. *Science Education, 81*, 483-496.

Zohar, A., & Nemet, F. (2002). Fostering students' knowledge and argumentation skills through dilemmas in human genetics. *Journal of Research in Science Teaching, 39*(1), 35-62.

Teaching Students to Evaluate Source Reliability during Internet Research Tasks

Christopher A. Sanchez, Jennifer Wiley, Susan R. Goldman, University of Illinois at Chicago, Department of Psychology, 1007 W. Harrison St. (M/C 285), Chicago, IL 60614
Email: csanch4@uic.edu, jwiley@uic.edu, sgoldman@uic.edu

Abstract: Despite the overwhelming use of the Internet as an educational/informational resource, research has found that learners are woefully in need of guidance on how to use this resource effectively, and subsequently identify reliable sources of information from unreliable. This study seeks to address this issue through the SEEK training program, which encourages learners to evaluate the source and quality of the information, and also how well it resonates with their existing prior knowledge. Learners were either trained or not trained using the SEEK program when they completed an initial Internet research task. Learners were then asked to complete a second Internet research task in another domain without any additional guidance several days later. Results indicate that learners who had received the SEEK training not only were better able to identify relevant from irrelevant sources, but also showed both higher overall levels of learning, and also greater learning gains.

Introduction

Internet research and inquiry tasks are a popular assignment in today's classrooms. A majority of both secondary school students and undergraduates report using the internet as the sole source for their class assignments, even when projects are not specifically assigned as an internet-based research task. Fewer and fewer visit the library and use actual books. Even published sources (journal articles) are being accessed in electronic form more and more. (Jones, 2002)

In previous studies investigating how students learn from internet research tasks on science topics, we have found that successful learning is directly related to the ability to discriminate between reliable and unreliable sources and the selection of reliable reading material for a high percentage of the research time (Wiley, Goldman & Graesser, 2002; Wiley, Goldman, Graesser, Sanchez & Ash, in preparation) Thus, the ability to recognize reliable sources seems to be a critical skill for effective learning from online research tasks. At the same time, even the best learners in our earlier studies seemed to have a fragile understanding of what reliability is. Very few could verbalize it or use it to justify their evaluations of reliability.

Based on these results, it was clear that students needed instruction in evaluating the reliability of information that they found on the Internet. Work by Brem, Russell & Weems (2001) has shown that in general students are fairly uncritical of the arguments they read on web pages.

Similar conclusions have been noted by other researchers. For example, Britt, Perfetti, Van Dyke, & Gabrys (2000) have noted the lack of use of source information and evaluation when students write reports in history from multiple sources in history. To address this they developed the Sourcer's Apprentice program to improve student sourcing skills in that domain. Slotta and Linn (2000) also incorporated web page evaluations as a part of WISE (a web-based inquiry learning environment). Based on our current findings, it seems this element of the inquiry environment may have been critical.

Using an analysis of the behaviors we observed in more and less successful learners in our studies, as well as information from the research cited above on student sourcing and evaluation skills, we identified 4 key areas in which students needed support: considering the source of the information, considering the evidence that was presented, thinking about how the evidence fit into an explanation of the phenomena, and evaluating the information with respect to prior knowledge. To address these needs, we developed an educational unit in which students were taught to consider the Source, Evidence, Explanation, and evaluate the information given in terms of their prior Knowledge (SEEK). This unit represents a set of activities designed to help learners adopt a critical stance while doing research online and with multiple sources by encouraging (1) thinking about the reliability of Sources, (2) evaluating the Evidence and Explanations provided, and (3) relating new information to prior Knowledge. Thus, this training encourages learners to not only consider information about the source itself, but also the nature of the information that is presented by each source and how well this information coincides with relevant prior knowledge. The SEEK unit is based to some extent on the Sourcer's Apprentice program developed by Britt, Perfetti, Van Dyke, & Gabrys (2000).

The present studies was run to test the effectiveness of the SEEK training unit on learning from internet research tasks. SEEK training was given through a series of static web pages in a separate training session before the target learning task. The topic of the training task was to determine whether the Atkins Diet was safe. The topic of the transfer task was to determine the causes of Mt St Helens' eruption from the output of a Google search. Importantly, no SEEK training was given during this second task. The effects of the SEEK training were assessed on performance on the volcano task, by comparing groups who received training with a no-training control.

Importantly, although the SEEK training is similar in a number of respects to interventions used in earlier studies, this study is the first to look at how training students to evaluate the reliability and usefulness of information they read on web pages can affect the learning of new subject matter from internet research tasks.

Methods

Participants and Design

60 undergraduates ($N = 60$) from the University of Illinois at Chicago participated in this study. 30 were given SEEK training and 30 were not. Both groups were matched for prior knowledge of volcanoes, based on a volcano concepts pretest given at the start of the first session.

Materials and General Procedure

In part one of this study, all students performed an internet research task on the Atkins Diet. The search task consisted of a list of six sites that had been returned from a Google search on the subject. The participants' goal was to identify which of the 6 possible sources should be used if someone was interested in determining whether the diet is harmful or not. The six sites in this search task (in order of intended reliability) were: 1) The Journal of the American Medical Association (specifically a published article reporting a controlled randomized trial), 2) BusinessWeek.com (specifically an article describing the JAMA study), 3) atkinsdietalert.org, a not-for-profit organization of (vegetarian) physicians providing information for laypeople with questions and concerns about high-protein diets, 4) WeightWatchers.com (specifically a page on "the truth about carbs"), 5) Atkins.com and 6) a testimonial on the effectiveness of the Atkins diet from a personal homepage.

After reading all 6 of the sites, participants were required to rank the sites in order of reliability from 1-6 and justify their rankings of each site (i.e., explain why they had ranked a certain site where they did). Students in the SEEK training condition were given explicit guidance in their evaluations both before and after their reliability rankings (detailed below). The control condition was not given any additional information. This first portion of the study took no longer than an hour.

The SEEK training consisted of 3 distinct parts: an initial instruction page, a worksheet to complete while reading, and finally comparison of learner ratings to expert ratings. The initial instruction page (presented before the actual sources) identified several important considerations that learners should keep in mind before evaluating/reading the sites, such as: who the author is, how reliable the site is, and how well the site actually explained the information. Similarly, the worksheet (used during the actual search task) prompted participants to identify other relevant information about the author (i.e., motivation), and also whether or not the information was consistent with other reliable sources and based on scientific evidence. The worksheet accomplished this by requiring learners to answer such questions as: "Is the person who is providing the information someone who is knowledgeable?"; "Is the information based on scientific evidence?"; and "Does the explanation fit together with your prior scientific knowledge or with information from other reliable sites?". Finally, after completing their reliability ratings, SEEK participants were then asked to compare and contrast their ratings with those of 10 hypothetical 'experts', with an emphasis on identifying how their ratings differed from the experts and why.

In contrast, the control condition did not receive any kind of instruction on the initial search page, and were only allowed to take notes, and not given the worksheet while reading. Additionally, they did not compare their ratings to those of experts.

All participants returned several days later for the second part of the experiment, in which they were given a similar search page about volcanic eruptions. Just as in the first portion of the experiment, participants were presented with the output of a Google search, and were given the goal of developing an argument about what caused the eruption of Mt. St. Helens. Importantly, neither group received any instruction in this second part of this study. The volcano search output page contained 3 reliable sources, 3 unreliable sources, and 1 reliable but ambiguous source. The reliable sources were taken from the United States Geological Survey, NASA, and PBS. The unreliable sites were pages written by a business consultant who was selling his predictions of volcanic eruptions, an inventor who had developed an non-oil based engine (who claimed that oil drilling caused earthquakes and bad weather), and an astrology site giving the star chart for Mt. St. Helens at the time of the eruption. The ambiguous page was a commercial educational site on volcanoes, volcanolive.com, which contained reliable information (i.e., information that fits with the correct causal model provided by the USGS, NASA and PBS sites), but had a .com URL. Participants were given an hour to complete reading all 7 of the sources.

After the hour for research was up, students had about a half hour to write their essays. After essay writing, all students completed volcano concepts posttests. Then participants were asked to rate the 7 sites in order of their reliability, and to provide written justification for each of these rankings.

Results

Performance on the Atkins Diet Task Reliability Rankings

All students, regardless of condition, ranked the JAMA site as the most reliable and the Business Week site as the second most reliable. Both groups ranked the personal testimony site as least reliable. Thus, all students seemed to have some basic ability to recognize reliability. However, the average rankings of the reliable and unreliable sources were more _extreme_ for the SEEK training group. On average, the SEEK group ranked the reliable sources around 2.5 and unreliable around 4.4, while the average reliable source ranking for the control group was 3.1, and for unreliable, 3.9. These between-group differences in rankings were significant, $t(31) = 2.13$, $p < .04$. Thus, the SEEK training produced a significant advantage in discriminating reliable from unreliable information.

Effects of SEEK Instruction on the Transfer Task

Students in the training condition received SEEK instruction only during the Atkins Diet internet research task. During the volcano task, neither group received any instruction. Thus, the volcano internet research task served as a test of whether the SEEK skills taught on the Atkins Diet task would transfer and support better learning during the second internet research task.

Reliability Ratings

The average reliability ranking of the 3 reliable pages for the volcano task was lower (2.21 vs. 2.59) and the unreliable pages higher (5.8 vs. 5.38) for the training group versus the control group. These results are presented in Figure 1. The difference between the reliable and unreliable rankings (which can be seen as the ability to discriminate between reliable and unreliable information) was significantly larger for the training group, $t(58)= 2.93$, $p < .01$.

Further, in their justifications for these rankings, the training group was more likely to refer to the evidence provided in the web sites and the source of the information, $t(58) = 2.00$, $p < .05$, whereas the justifications of the control group were more likely to refer to whether or not the page specifically contained information on Mt. St. Helens, whether or not they believed the page, and whether or not they liked the style of the page, $t(58) = 2.57$, $p < .01$. The control group was also significantly more likely to make vague/uncodeable justifications for their rankings, $t(58) = 2.29$, $p < .03$. Thus, the ratings of the SEEK group were more likely to be based in evaluation of the content, rather than based on the surface appearance of the site.

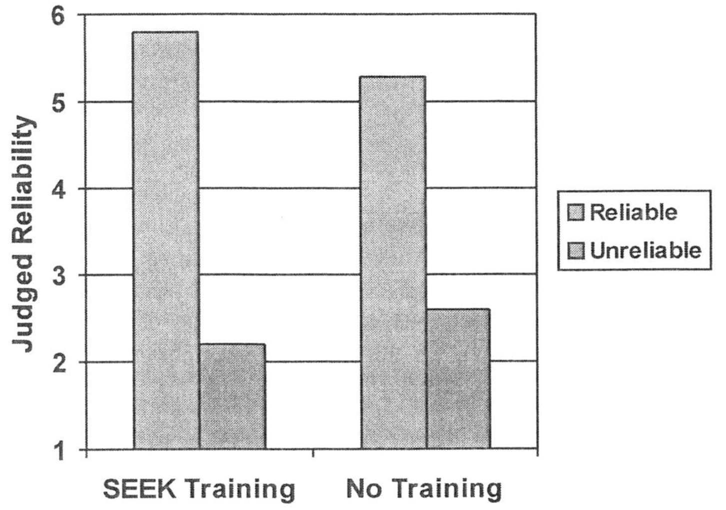

Figure 1. Reliability Ratings on Transfer Task.

Essay Results

Participants that received the SEEK training included significantly more correct causal concepts in their essays ($M = 6.8$) than the control group ($M = 5.6$, $t(58) = 2.02$, $p < .05$). Additionally, those that had received the SEEK training also included *fewer* misconceptions in their essays ($M = .23$) than the control group ($M = .67$, $t(58) = 2.13$, $p < .04$). Thus, in terms of the essay responses, those participants that had received the SEEK training not only included more correct causal information in their essays, but also *less* incorrect information, which can be taken as evidence of a more appropriate overall mental model. These results are presented in Figure 2.

Volcano Pre-Posttest Gains

Participants who received SEEK training on the Atkins Diet task showed greater learning gains on the volcano concepts task than did the control group ($t(58) = 2.04$, $p < .05$). The SEEK training group showed an average improvement of 2.4 correct volcano concepts from pre to post-test, while the control group only gained an average of .77 concepts. These learning gains are also visible in Figure 2.

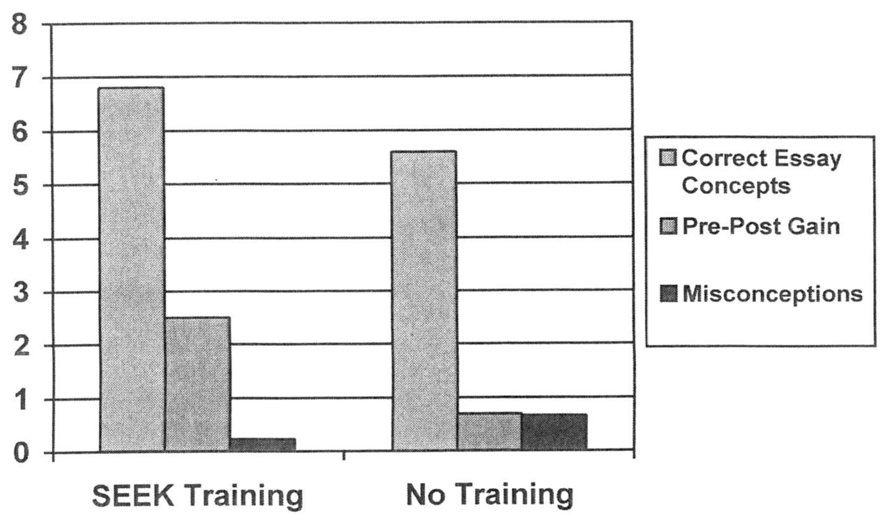

Figure 2. Learning Measures on Transfer Task.

Discussion and Conclusions

Learners that received the SEEK unit were not only able to learn to use critical evaluation skills during training (e.g., the Atkins diet task), but were also able to transfer these same inquiry based skills to another task (e.g., learning about the eruption of Mt. St. Helens). The critical skills taught in the SEEK unit allowed learners to better identify relevant from irrelevant information within an internet research task. This ability was evidenced by the larger difference between the ratings of reliable and unreliable sources, compared to the ratings of untrained students.

Similarly, the effectiveness of encouraging participants to take this critical stance was also evident on how well they learned from the volcano internet research task. Participants who had received the SEEK training not only included more correct causal concepts in an open-ended essay response, but also demonstrated a significant gain in knowledge over their initial levels of understanding. Additionally, the SEEK training also assisted in preventing irrelevant knowledge from intruding on conceptual understanding of the information, as evidenced by fewer misconceptions contained in the essay responses.

In conclusion, these results demonstrate the effectiveness of our SEEK educational unit on learning during internet research tasks. By encouraging a critical stance within learners using the SEEK unit, learners were not only able to better identify relevant sources of information, but also able to form a better understanding of the topic. These results are important for research in the learning sciences in the sense that it provides the first attempt at evaluating and encouraging appropriate strategies that are useful in developing understanding from internet research search tasks. Also, these empirical results, from a randomized, controlled study, suggest that the training unit itself is an important contribution. Thus, this project has provided a practical and effective tool for teachers to use before they permit students to do internet research projects.

Despite the mass of worthwhile information contained on the internet, the information returned from keyword searches are often fraught with irrelevant, misleading information. Encouraging potential learners to actively evaluate the motivations of authors who create this information, the nature of the information returned, and also how this information relates to their prior knowledge, should enable learners to better 'sift' through the overwhelming amount of information (both relevant and not) to get to facts that they actually need. Our SEEK training was designed to help learners do exactly this, and the above results demonstrate that the SEEK training does accomplish exactly what it was designed for.

References

Brem, S. K., Russell, J., & Weems, L. (2001). Science on the web: Student Evaluations of scientific arguments. *Discourse Processes, 32* (2-3), 191-213.

Britt, M.A., Perfetti, C.A., Van Dyke, J., & Gabrys, G. (2000). The Sourcer's Apprentice: A Tool for Document-Supported History Instruction. In P. Stearns (Ed.), *Knowing, Teaching and Learning History: National and International Perspectives*. New York: NYU Press.

Jones, S. (2002). *The Internet Goes to College. How Students are Living in the Future with Today's Technology.* Washington, DC: Pew Internet and American Life Project.

Slotta, J. D., & Linn, M. C. (2000). The Knowledge Integration Environment: Helping Students use the Internet Effectively. In M. J. Jacobson& R. B. Kozma (Eds.), *Innovations in science and mathematics education: Advanced Designs for Technologies of Learning.* Mahwah, NJ: Lawrence Erlbaum Associates.

Wiley, J., Goldman, S. R., & Graesser, A. (2002) Promoting Critical Inquiry from Web Sources. In W. G. Gray and C.D. Schunn (Eds.),*Proceedings of the 24th Annual Conference of the Cognitive Science Society (pp. 23).* Mahwah, NJ: Erlbaum.

Wiley, J., Goldman, S. R., Graesser, A., Sanchez. C. A., & Ash I. K. (in preparation) How readers learn science from web pages.

Acknowledgements

This project was funded by a grant from the National Science Foundation to Jennifer Wiley, Susan Goldman and Art Graesser (REC 0126265 Understanding in Science). All opinions expressed herein are those of the authors are do not necessarily reflect the funding organization.

Collaborative learning with animated pictures: The role of verbalizations

Mirweis Sangin, Gaëlle Molinari, Pierre Dillenbourg,
Ecole Polytechnique Fédérale de Lausanne (EPFL), School of Computer and Communication Sciences CRAFT,
EPFL-CRAFT CE 1 631 Station 1 CH-1015 Lausanne Switzerland,
{mirweis.sangin, gaelle.molinari, pierre.dillenbourg}@epfl.ch
Cyril Rebetez, Mireille Bétrancourt,
University of Geneva TECFA, Acacias 54 CH-1227 Carouge Switzerland,
{cyril.rebetez, mireille.betrancourt}@tecfa.unig.ch

Abstract: The present study examines the benefits of instructional animations in a collaborative learning situation. We investigated the interactions that occur during collaborative learning from different materials: animated versus static pictures, both with or without persistency of information. The animation factor had no effect on the types of interactions but the persistency of information led to fewer content-focused interactions. We also analyzed the impact of these interactions on learning performances: Two types of interactions (content-focused and social relations and coordination management) mediate some of the effects of the permanence factor on learning performances.

Introduction

The present study is aimed at deepening some findings from a larger investigation of the benefits of multimedia instructions in two different settings: individual and collaborative learning. We used two complementary theoretical frameworks, cognitive research on multimedia learning (e.g., Mayer, 2001; Schnotz & Lowe, 2003) and sociocultural studies of collaborative learning (e.g., Baker, 2002; Dillenbourg, 1999). The latter were further explored to highlight the mediating functions of the peers' interaction on learning effects.

Learning with animation

Animated pictures are used in multimedia environments to represent the dynamic aspects of complex subject matters in an explicit way (Lowe, 2004). According to Schnotz and Rasch (in press), animations have two different positive functions in learning. First, they enable learners to perform more cognitive processing (*enabling function*) by providing them with additional information that cannot be displayed by static pictures (e.g., the temporal relationships of entities within a system). Second, they help learners to build a dynamic mental representation (*facilitating function*) by giving them an external support for simulating the behavior of the system depicted.

Although there is some evidence that animations have positive effects on the understanding of dynamic situations (e.g., Mayer & Anderson, 1992), research failed to establish systematic benefits of using animated graphics instead versus static ones (e.g., Bétrancourt & Tversky, 2000). In some cases, animations may even prejudice learning (Lowe, 2004). Lowe (2004) suggested two different types of problems to explain these negative results, i.e., *overwhelming* and *underwhelming*. First, given the limited capacity of working memory, learners may not be able to meet the additional processing demands associated with animations. When learning from dynamic visualization, they have to select relevant elements (for the purpose of the task) from a larger amount of information provided by multiple frames (rather than by the single frame of a static picture) in a very limited time. They have also to keep in memory and integrate information distributed either spatially across the display area or temporally through the different frames of the animation. In other words, the overwhelming effect appears when some aspects of animation (e.g., the overflow of information, their transient aspect) impose a cognitive load that leads learners to reduce their cognitive resources available for learning (see also Sweller, 1999). In contrast, underwhelming may arise when dynamic presentations induce in learners either an illusory feeling of understanding or an investment withdrawal (usually caused by the complexity of the animations). In consequence, these learners do not process information at a deep enough level to ensure learning. This type of problem may occur when learners do not have adequate prior knowledge on the domain to be learned: To avoid cognitive overload, they may focus their attention on some partial aspects of the animation. Moreover, Schnotz and Rasch (in press) showed that the facilitating function of animations can be harmful for experts who do not need external support for cognitive manipulations.

Collaborative learning with animation

Over the past decades, research on collaborative learning has been predominantly carried out within what has been termed the "interactions paradigm" (Dillenbourg, Baker, Blaye, & O'Malley, 1996). They therefore mean that "*The question 'under which conditions is collaborative learning efficient?' is splited into two (hopefully simpler) sub-questions: Which interactions occur under which conditions and what effects do these interactions have*" (Dillenbourg et al., 1996). Researchers focused on "constructive" interactions such as conflict resolution, explanation or mutual regulation, and identified them as potential vehicles of conceptual learning. Indeed, they have in common that they lead students to verbalize knowledge (that would remain otherwise tacit) necessary for building a shared representation of the task.

According to Roschelle (1992) or Crook (1998), collaborating students may benefit from external representations such as pictures or animations, because they can play the role of referential anchors that may resource the construction of a shared understanding. Schnotz, Böckheler and Grzondziel (1999) also argued that computer-based learning environments with animations would be well appropriate for collaborative learning because they could enhance the possibilities for interaction and exploration. In order to test this hypothesis, they carried out an empirical study in which they compared learning from animated versus static pictures in a collaborative situation. Contrary to their previous study on individual learning with the same materials, learning with animations resulted in lower performances with two different tasks. The authors interpreted these negative results in terms of cognitive load (Sweller, 1999). The animations would impose a heavy extraneous cognitive load that would be increased with the social interaction load needed to manage interaction with the peer.

Goal and research questions

This paper reports a study conducted to investigate the effectiveness of animated and static pictures under the conditions of individual and collaborative learning (Rebetez, Sangin, Bétrancourt, & Dillenbourg, 2005; Sangin, Rebetez, Dillenbourg, & Bétrancourt, 2005). Our first results provided evidence that animated pictures result in higher retention and inference performances compared to static pictures. Moreover, contrary to Schnotz et al. (1999), the positive effect of animations on inference performance was higher in collaborative situations than with individual situations. Our results also indicated that, in the individual condition, learners benefit from snapshots of previous steps of animations (permanently presented on the screen). In contrast, this "persistency of information" (or permanence tool) led to lower scores in the collaborative condition. According to Sangin et al. (2005), two possible explanations for this negative (and also counter-intuitive) result could be assessed. First, a *split-interaction effect* could occur due to the addition of cognitive load associated with the interaction with the computer interface on one hand, and with the interaction between peers on the other hand. The second explanation could be some sort of *socio-cognitive underwhelming* effect: The permanence of information could lead the learners being insufficiently engaged in the construction of a shared understanding.

The analysis presented here focuses on the collaborative learning settings. It is conducted according to the "interactions paradigm", and dissociates 3 types of questions (see Figure 1):
A) What is the effect of learning conditions ("animation" and "permanence" factors) on intermediate variables (types of interaction)?
B) What is the relationship between categories of interaction and learning outcomes, i.e., the effects these interactions may have on retention and inference performances?
C) How the intermediate variables (types of interactions) mediate the relationship between learning conditions and learning effects?

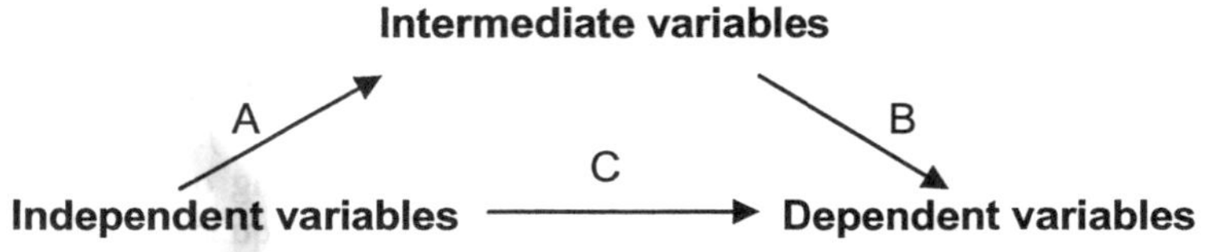

Figure 1. The interactions paradigm (Dillenbourg et al., 1996)

Method

Participants and design

Participants were 80 French-speaking students from the Swiss Federal Institute of Technology (Lausanne) and the University of Geneva. We used a factorial 2 x 2 between-subjects design with the first factor being the mode of presentation (static slides vs. animations) and the second factor being the permanence of information ("with-permanence" vs. "without-permanence") according to whether permanent snapshots of the previous sequences were presented or not. In each group, there were 20 participants who worked in dyads. Moreover, all participants reported low prior knowledge in the 2 learning topics (Venus transit and tectonic plates) through an individual pre-test questionnaire (5 multiple-choice questions per topic).

Material and instruments:

Instructional material. The material consisted of 2 successive multimedia instructions (images accompanied by audio narration), the first one designed to explain the phenomenon of the Venus transit (astronomy), and the second one the phenomenon of the tectonic plates (geology). Two versions of each multimedia instruction were constructed. The first version was composed of 12 animated sequences ("animations" version), the second of 12 static pictures ("slides" version). In the static version, each slide corresponded to the most significant picture taken from the corresponding animation. In addition, the static and animated pictures had the same size (800 x 600 pixels), and were laid out on the top-right part of the interface. In the "with-permanence" conditions, 24 grayed labels (12 in the "Venus transit" phase, 12 in the "tectonic plates" phase) (320 x 200 pixels) were provided on the left side of the screen (see Figure 2). After either a slide (slides/with-permanence condition) or an animated sequence (animations/with-permanence condition) was shown, a new label became colored and gave access to a static snapshot. Participants could see a bigger version of the snapshot by moving the mouse over the corresponding label (640 x 480 pixels). The snapshots in the slides condition were the same as those in the animations condition, and thus represented the critical steps of each studied phenomenon. Finally, there were no snapshots in the "without-permanence" conditions (slides/without permanence condition; animations/without-permanence condition).

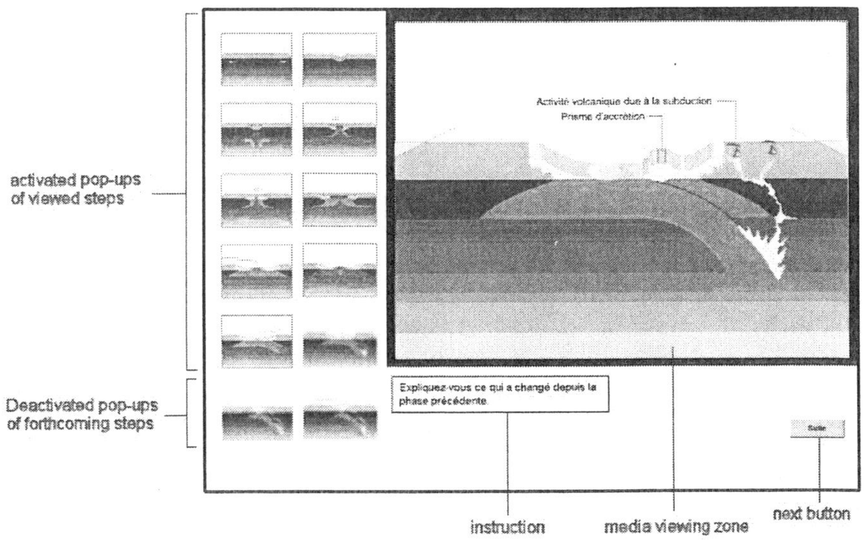

Figure 2. Interface screen-shot of the "with-permanence" condition after the ninth sequence

Learning tests: The testing procedure followed the conventional paradigm used to evaluate the mental model constructed during multimedia learning (Mayer et al., 1992). After the presentation of each multimedia instruction (Venus transit and tectonic plates), all participants were provided with an individual post-test consisting of 2 types of multiple-choice questions (presented in either a graphical or a textual format): 9 retention questions and 7 inference questions. The retention questions measured what participants can remember about each topic; their answers were explicitly quoted either in the images or in the audio narration. The inference questions tested a deeper understanding of each described phenomenon. Indeed, they involved inferring information from the learnt dynamic mental model. Finally, the retention and inference questions were presented in random order.

Apparatus: All instructional materials and (pre- and post-test) questionnaires were computer-based (Authorware software). Responses to multiple-choice questions were recorded by the computer. In addition, the verbal interactions of the 10 dyads were audio and video recorded.

Procedure and scoring

Procedure: The experimental session consisted of two phases – the "Venus transit" phase followed by the "tectonic plates" phase – of 3 parts each: (a) pre-test questionnaire (b) learning phase, (c) post-test questionnaire. Moreover, each learning phase was composed of 2 sub-parts. In the first sub-part, participants were asked to individually study a media-based introduction designed to provide them with prior knowledge necessary to understand the upcoming instructional material. In this introduction, 2 or 3 illustrated paragraphs were presented describing some general concepts on the solar system topic (e.g. movement of planets, transit phenomena) or on the tectonic plates topic (e.g. various layers, movements). In the second sub-part, one pair member had to leave his/her working station, and to join his/her peer to explore together the multimedia presentation. Between each slide or each animation, the instruction – "explain what has changed since the last part" – appeared on the screen; it aimed to encourage peers to interact with each other and to synthesize together the lastly presented information.

Interaction coding system: All videotaped interactions were transcribed verbatim. Turn-taking was used as criteria for the audio corpus segmentation. For purposes of statistical analysis, we decided to use a simple but relevant coding system to analyze the interactions. The coding system was inspired by the RAINBOW method (Baker, Quignard, Lund, Molinari, & Séjourné, 2005) and modified on the basis of our own research interests. The set of categories we used is based on three main distinctions: (a) between interaction that is "inside" the collaborative activity or "outside" (off-task activity) of it, (b) within "inside" activity, between interaction that is "content-focused" or "not content-focused" (social relation, interaction management, task management), and (c) within the "content-focused" interaction, between "information seeking" and "information providing". In addition, the last category was divided into 3 sub-categories corresponding to 3 levels of elaboration (see Table 1). A unique and mutually exclusive category code was associated to each corpus segment and was systematically counted for each participant (two researchers analyzed the interactions; inter-coder reliability was good: Kappa = .81, $p < .0001$).

Table 1. Mutually exclusive codes for the between peers' interaction corpus.

	category	code	description
Content-focus categories	elaborated	A	Elaborated segments based on the pedagogical content plus information not provided by the material (learners' prior knowledge, inferences, deductions etc.; high level elaboration)
		B	Summarizing segments based on all past multimedia sequences. (medium level elaboration)
		C	Summarizing segments containing information based only on the latest multimedia sequence (low level elaboration)
	Information seeking	D	Segments composed of any questioning and information requests
Non-content-focus categories	Interaction-management	E	Segments concerned with interaction management activities
	Task-management	F	Segments related to task management and interface manipulation activities

Results

According to the interactions paradigm, we present the results in 3 steps, respectively represented as A, B and C on Figure 1.

A) How factors determine group interactions?

To explore the influence of the main factors on the intermediate interaction variables, we performed a set of one-way ANOVA tests. The factors are "presentation mode" (slides/animations) and "permanence" (with-permanence/without-permanence). The verbal interactions are either 'content-focus' (categories A, B, C, D in Table 1) or non-content-focused (categories E & F). Since interaction time was not controlled, frequencies (number of interactions divided by the total time) are used for all the following analyses (instead of raw data). We found no significant effect of the "presentation mode" factor on verbal interactions, but an effect of the "permanence" factor: The "content-focused" interactions are more frequent in the "without-permanence" condition ($M = 1.43$) than in the "with-permanence" condition ($M = 1.07$), ($F(1, 75) = 10.95$, $p < .01$).This difference does not appear for "non content-focused" interactions ($F(1, 75) =.46$, $p > .1$).

B) Intermediate and performance variables' relations

In order to test the relations between the interaction intermediate variables and the performance variables, regression analyses were conducted with the intermediate variables as predictors of the retention and inference scores. Concerning the relation between the retention scores and frequency of the "content-focused" interactions, the regression analysis showed a positive significant relation ($\beta = 0.331$, $p < .01$). A positive significant relation was also found between the "content-focused" intermediate variable and the inference scores ($\beta = 0.250$, $p < .03$). The more the peers provide content-focused utterances, the better their scores seem to be; both on retention and inference items. The regression analyses revealed no significant relation between the frequency of "non-content-focused" interactions and neither the retention scores ($\beta = 0.163$, $p > .1$) nor with the inference scores ($\beta = 0.078$, $p > .5$).

To deepen our understanding of the relations between the interaction variables and the learning scores, a regression analysis was conducted with each functional verbalization categories (namely A, B, C, D, E and F categories; see Table 1) as predictors and peers' learning performance scores as dependent variables. The predictors explained more than 49% of the peers' retention scores ($R2 = 0.49$, $p < .01$). Two of the 6 predictors reached the significant level: the A category ($\beta = 0.25$, $p < .02$) and the E category ($\beta = 0.27$, $p < .01$). When we used the inference scores as a dependant variable, the same model explained more than 51% of the peers' inference scores ($R2=0.51$; $p < .01$). As for the retention scores, the same 2 categories reached the significant level, namely the A category ($\beta = 0.261$, $p < .02$) and the E category ($\beta = 0.260$, $p < .02$). Hence the 2 best predictors for the retention and inference scores are high elaborated information providing segments of the peers' verbalizations (category A) and the segments concerned with interaction management (category E).

C) Mediation of the performance scores by the intermediate variables

Interaction variables were examined as variables potentially mediating the effect of the permanence factor on the inference scores, i.e., the measure on which the performance of the "without-permanence" conditions' peers was higher than the "with-permanence" conditions' peers (Sangin, Rebetez, Dillenbourg, & Bétrancourt, 2005). Four steps were taken to assess mediating effects using regression methods as suggested by Baron and Kenny (1986). The first step is met when variations in the level of the independent variables significantly account for the variation in the level of the presumed mediating variable (see Figure 1, path A.). The second step is verified when the variation of presumed mediating variable significantly account for the variation in the dependent variable (see Figure 1, path B.).

Regression analyses were performed to verify these 2 first steps by taking our interaction categories as potential mediators, the permanence factor (coded -1 for "without-permanence" and +1 for "with-permanence") as an independent variable and the inference scores as a dependent variable. Two of our variables reached the significant level on the 2 steps. The regression test confirmed that the "content-focused" variable was significantly and negatively related to the "permanence" independent variable ($\beta = -0.357$, $p = .002$), and significantly and positively related to the "inference score" dependent variable ($\beta = 0.250$, $p = .03$). The dialogue category E (interaction management) was also significantly and negatively related to the permanence independent variable ($\beta = -0.293$, $p = .01$), and significantly and positively related to the inference dependent variable ($\beta = 0.298$, $p = .009$). The third step was to verify the relation between the independent and the dependent variables (see Figure 1, path C.) which was marginally significantly negative ($\beta = -0.210$, $p = .069$). This step is the same for our 2 mediating variables.

According to Baron and Kenny (1986), in the last step, we entered both the independent variable (permanence) and the mediator variable ("content focused" and Category E) at the same time as predictors for the dependant variable (inference scores). Concerning the "content-focused" mediating variable, this last regression showed that permanence was no longer a significant predictor (β = -0.138; p = 0.26) whereas the "content-focused" variable was still marginally a significant predictor (β = -0.210, p = .069). Thus, it can be concluded that the frequency of "content-focused" interactions mediates some of the permanence factor's effect on the peers' inference scores. Concerning the E category (interaction management), this last step showed that permanence was also no longer a significant predictor (β = -0.134; p = .252) whereas the E category was still a significant predictor (β = 0.259, p = .002). Thus, it can be suggested that E variable did also mediate some of the effects of the permanence factor on the learners' inference scores.

Discussion

Our previous research had suggested benefits of animated pictures for collaborative learning on both retention and inference performances (Rebetez et al., 2005; Sangin et al., 2005). A second factor was also used in this previous research which offered a permanence tool providing snapshots of the movie critical steps as a memory and grounding support. Surprisingly, the results indicate a negative effect of the permanence tool on collaborative learning. Indeed, peers who were not provided with this permanence tool performed better. Two possible explanations were provided to account for this negative effect, i.e., split-interaction effect and the socio-cognitive underwhelming effect. Do the new results enable us to choose between these explanations?

The interaction analyses suggest that only content-focused interactions are related with peers learning performances. Indeed, the results suggest positive and significant relation between the amount of "content-focused" verbalizations and the retention and inference scores whereas no significant relations occurred between "non-content-focused" verbalizations and the learners' performances. The results are consistent with those found by Webb (1991): Elaborated explanations are positively correlated with explainers' performances. Nonetheless, verbalizations about interaction management are also positively correlated to subjects' performances. A possible explanation of this second effect is that argumentation and negotiation of the collaboration process, even when students do not talk about the content to be learned, are still beneficial for learning (Dillenbourg, 1999).

Regarding our main factors, results suggest no effect of the animation factor on the social interactions. Peers do not verbalize more or less when provided with static pictures versus animated pictures. Regarding the fact that content-focused verbalizations are positively related to learners' performances, no evidence of a potential mediating effect of the verbal interactions on the benefits of animated pictures on learning performances could be provided. Conversely, concerning the permanence factor, the results showed that the permanence of information reduces learners' amount of "content-focused" verbalizations. Moreover, the results support a (partly-) mediating effect of the frequency of interactions on the detrimental effect of the permanence tool on inference scores. This decrease of interaction frequency induced by the permanence of information supports our socio-cognitive underwhelming hypothesis: Offering a permanence tool which primarily aimed to facilitate the grounding processes by stabilizing referential objects occurs to be detrimental to collaborative learning processes because it decreases the learners' verbalizations and interaction management processes.

In this paper, we focused on data concerning the relations between the subjects' verbal productions and their learning scores. Actually, a deeper analysis of our results requires to dissociate the role of the explainer and the explainee, and to treat separately the effects at the individual or the pair level through multilevel analyses.

References

Baker, M. J. (2002). Argumentative interactions, discursive operations and learning to model in science. In P. Brna, M. Baker, K. Stenning, & A. Tiberghien (Eds.), *The Role of Communication in Learning to Model* (pp. 303-324). Mahwah, NJ: Lawrence Erlbaum Associates.

Baker, M. J., Quignard, M., Lund, K., Molinari, G., & Séjourné, A. (2005). *The elaboration of argumentative knowledge in multi-representational computer-mediated debates.* Manuscript submitted for publication.

Baron, R. M., & Kenny, D. A. (1986). The moderator-mediator variable distinction in social psychological research: Conceptual, strategic, and statistical considerations. *Journal of Personality and Social Psychology*, *51*, 1173-1182.

Bétrancourt, M. & Tversky, B. (2000). Effect of computer animation on users' performances: A review. *Le travail Humain*, *63*(4), 311-330.

Crook, C. (1998). Children as Computer Users: The Case of Collaborative Learning. *Computers Education, 30*(3/4), 237-247.

Dillenbourg, P. (1999). What do you mean by collaborative learning? In P. Dillenbourg (Ed.), *Collaborative learning: Cognitive and Computational Approaches* (pp. 1-19). Oxford: Elsevier.

Dillenbourg, P., Baker, M., Blaye, A., & O'Malley, C. (1996) The evolution of research on collaborative learning. In E. Spada & P. Reiman (Eds.), *Learning in Humans and Machine: Towards an interdisciplinary learning science* (pp. 189-211). Oxford: Elsevier.

Lowe, R. K. (2004). Animation and learning: Value for money? In R. Atkinson, C. McBeath, D. Jonas-Dwyer, & R. Phillips (Eds.), *Beyond the comfort zone: Proceedings of the 21st ASCILITE Conference* (pp. 558-561). Perth, 5-8 December.

Mayer, R. E. (2001). *Multimedia Learning*. Cambridge: Cambridge University Press.

Mayer, R. E., & Anderson, R. B. (1992). The instructive animation: Helping students build connections between words and pictures in multimedia learning. *Journal of Educational Psychology, 84*(4), 444-452.

Rebetez, C., Sangin, M., Bétrancourt, M., & Dillenbourg, P. (2005). *Learning from animations is enabled by collaboration*. Manuscript in preparation.

Roschelle, J. (1992). Learning by collaborating: Convergent conceptual change. *The Journal of the Learning Sciences, 2*, 235-276.

Sangin, M., Rebetez, C., Dillenbourg, P., & Bétrancourt, M. (2005). *Collaborative learning with animated pictures: From the persistency of information to the split-interaction effect*. Manuscript in preparation.

Schnotz, W., Böckheler, J., & Grzondziel, H. (1999). Individual and co-operative learning with animated pictures. *European journal of psychology of education, 14*(2), 245-265.

Schnotz, W., & Lowe, R. K. (2003). External and internal representations in multimedia learning. *Learning and Instruction, 13*(2), 117-254.

Schnotz, W, & Rasch, T. (in press). Enabling, facilitating, and inhibiting of animation in multimedia learning: Why reduction of cognitive load can have negative results on learning. To appear in *Educational Technology Research and Development*.

Sweller, J. (1999). *Instructional design in technological areas*. Camberwell, Australia: ACER Press.

Webb, N. M. (1991) Task related verbal interaction and mathematics learning in small groups. *Journal for Research in Mathematics Education, 22*(5), 366-389.

Acknowledgments

We gratefully acknowledge the contribution of Patrick Jermann, Florence Colomb, Shuja Parvez and Jean-Baptiste Haué. This research was funded by the Swiss National Science Foundation (grant #11-68102.02).

Supporting Science Teacher Thinking Through Curriculum Materials

Rebecca Schneider, University of Toledo, Toledo, OH, 43606, Rebecca.Schneider@UToledo.edu

Abstract: Teachers need high quality materials to support their work with students and promote teacher learning from classrooms beyond what would normally be the case. Such teacher educative materials would be designed to explicitly enhance teacher thinking in relationship to students and science in classroom contexts. Designing materials specifically for teacher learning, however, is an intriguing yet largely untested idea. In this study, one 7th grade teacher used five inquiry science units with varying amounts and types of educative features over a two year period. Written pre and post lesson teacher reflections, informal interviews, and daily classroom videotape were collected. Analysis focused on aspects of inquiry teaching that are challenging for teachers to learn and illustrate pedagogical content knowledge. Comparisons overtime and between lessons with different types and amounts of educative support in the materials were made. Analysis identified characteristics of materials that guide teacher thinking and support inquiry science teaching.

Introduction

Teaching excellence can have a substantial impact on student learning (Darling-Hammond, 1999). To ensure excellence, however, teachers need high quality materials to support their work with students and promote teacher learning from classrooms beyond what would normally be the case (Cohen *et al.*, 2002; Putnam & Borko, 2000). To address the concerns of reformers in science, teachers need continuing support to develop skill in guiding student inquiry (e.g. designing investigations and developing explanations), supporting collaboration, and incorporating learning technologies in ways that engage all students in actively constructing deep understanding of important science concepts (NRC, 1996). One promising new idea is to include explicit support for teachers to learn about teaching within curriculum materials making them educative for teachers (Davis & Krajcik, 2005; Schneider *et al.*, 2002). Such educative materials would be designed to explicitly enhance teacher thinking in relationship to students and science in classroom contexts. What is needed, however, are specific design ideas based on classroom research to guide developers in creating teacher educative materials. The goal of this study was to identify characteristics of materials intended for teacher use that guide teacher thinking in ways that encourage excellence in science teaching.

Theoretical Framework

Designing materials to be educative for teachers is a relatively new idea. The idea is to develop materials to explicitly support teacher learning, beyond what would normally be the case, through their use in classrooms. This vision, however, is dependant upon development of specific ideas for design of materials to meet teachers' needs for learning and enactment support. Many possible approaches have not yet been fully explored, however, research on teaching and teacher learning can guide our thinking and research on this innovative approach to supporting teachers in reform-oriented teaching.

Reform-oriented Science Teaching

Reformers interested in improving teaching are encouraging teachers to utilize student-centered instructional practices. In science, inquiry learning environments are recommended to engage students in seeking answers to questions, experiencing phenomena, sharing ideas, and developing explanations of science embedded in the everyday world (NRC, 1996). Student inquiry is characterized by opportunities for students to find solutions to real problems by asking and refining questions, designing and conducting investigations, gathering and analyzing information and data, making interpretations, drawing conclusions, and reporting findings (Minstrell & Van Zee, 2000). To guide students in their inquiry efforts teachers need to press students to explain, justify, critique, and revise their ideas as they examine their experiences with phenomena. To support meaningful discussions teachers need to help students participate in dialogues that require listening, questioning, and responding among peers and teachers. To create inquiry learning environments in their classrooms, science teachers will need to develop expertise in guiding student inquiry, supporting collaboration, and incorporating learning technologies in ways that address goals for student learning.

Classroom-based Experiences

Research suggests that some of the most powerful and motivating learning opportunities for teachers are grounded in classroom experiences (Putnam & Borko, 2000). One example that supports this claim comes from a study of reform initiatives in California. Only those professional development opportunities that focused on curriculum and students resulted in improved student scores (Corcoran, 1995). Providing access to classrooms, however, is not sufficient to guarantee teachers will develop appropriate knowledge and skills. Teachers need guided opportunities to think about and reflect on students' thinking (Putnam & Borko, 2000; Wilson & Berne, 1999). Moreover, teachers need experiences that are consistent with current ideas about how students learn science. We have evidence to suggest that reform materials with detailed lesson descriptions can help teachers enact inquiry (Schneider *et al.*, 2005). To be educative, however, materials need to engage teachers in thinking about teaching as they offer teachers experiences with students that are consistent with current standards for teaching science.

Pedagogical Content Knowledge

One useful construct to guide our thinking about teacher learning in and out of classrooms is pedagogical content knowledge (PCK). PCK is an amalgamation of content, pedagogy, and context knowledge described as knowledge unique to teaching (Shulman, 1986). For science teachers PCK includes knowledge of science specific strategies, various ways to represent content, and students' thinking about science ideas (Magnusson *et al.*, 1999). Although more evidence is needed we have some evidence to suggest that teachers need to understand science from a pedagogical perspective (i.e. PCK) in order to make the most impact on student learning (Nathan & Petrosino, 2003; Wayne & Youngs, 2003; Wilson et al., 2001). Efforts guided by PCK have been very successful in promoting teacher leaning. For example, Daehler and Shinohara (2001) are creating modules that guide teachers first in exploring a specific concept in depth as a student, then in considering how students think and learning about these ideas. Materials for teachers focused on developing PCK would encourage teachers to think intellectually about teaching and prepare teachers to think about their students and learn from classroom situations.

Educative Design Ideas

Materials designed intentionally to be educative for teachers would have specific features to address teachers' learning needs. Straightforward strategies address teacher knowledge directly through descriptive overviews or written notes to the teacher to explain content and pedagogy as well as specific strategies, representations, and students' ideas. There is evidence that teachers pay attention to features which target PCK specifically such as explanations of how a specific strategy or representation supports student thinking or information on student ideas such as probable prior knowledge, likely responses, appropriate level of understanding, and which concepts are challenging for students (Schneider & Krajcik, 2002). Based on the idea that teachers think about teaching in cases or stories some developers use descriptive scenarios to illustrate how a lesson might be enacted in the classroom, albeit with mixed results (Collopy, 1999). There also is evidence that teachers can learn by observing students as they participate in lessons that make evident student thinking and that materials can highlight these instances as opportunities for teacher learning (Remillard, 2000).

Guided by ideas from research on teaching and teacher learning, ideas about educative design (Davis & Krajcik, 2005), and by my research with educative materials in classrooms (Schneider et al., 2002; Schneider & Krajcik, 2002; Schneider et al., 2005), I propose that educative materials could:

(a) *engage teachers in planning and teaching* by describing and explaining specific strategies and representations to address specific science ideas, predicting student responses, describing links to ideas and events in future lessons, clearly indicating when text is for teachers' learning or to be read to students, and explaining how to use the materials for planning and their own learning;

(b) *develop teachers' pedagogical content knowledge* by suggesting activities that make student thinking visible to teachers, focusing teachers' attention on students' thinking, providing help to interpret students' responses, and offering suggestions for how to guide student thinking; and

(c) *match teachers' learning needs* by considering teachers' prior knowledge and skill, offering consistent educative support embedded in lessons, providing scenarios and questions in the voice of the teacher, and repeating use of specific strategies and supports for students across lessons.

Purpose of the study

Designing materials specifically for teacher learning is an intriguing yet largely untested idea. Research tells us that pedagogical content knowledge (PCK) of accomplished teachers enables them to guide and develop students' thinking. Research does not tell us, however, what features of materials are most helpful in developing teachers' PCK. The purpose of this study is to explore how reform-based science materials can help teachers develop skill in inquiry teaching. Specifically, three questions guided the research: 1) *What does classroom teaching look like when teachers use reform-oriented materials with supports for teacher learning?*, 2) *What do teachers learn about inquiry teaching when using reform-oriented materials with supports for teacher learning?*, and 3) *What types of educative features are most helpful in supporting inquiry teaching and teacher learning?* In this exploratory study, one teacher used five inquiry science units in her 7th grade classroom over two years. The development guidelines for these units did include educative features for teachers. However, these ideas were included in varying degrees for each unit. Variation in inquiry teaching and PCK across these units can help identify the types of educative supports that are most helpful. In order to design educative materials we need a better understanding of the specific supports teachers need while enacting inquiry in their classrooms. Understanding how teachers use educative materials and how these materials influence teaching will enable developers to create materials teachers can use to enact inquiry in ways appropriate for their students' learning needs.

Methods

This study was conducted in a midsized, urban middle school. Students in this school were predominantly white (92%) with 25% of student classified as economically disadvantaged. Pass rates on the statewide achievement test in science were 66%. Ms. Shirley was certified as an elementary teacher with a focus on science and had 5 years teaching experience, all in science. Ms. Shirley enacted five inquiry-based science units with all 5 of her 7th grade science classes over a two year period. She had previously participated in inquiry science professional development not associated with this project. In addition, she attended a ten day summer institute for teachers new to these units between year one and year two. Ms. Shirley was interested in hands-on activities and was comfortable trying new teaching ideas in her classroom but had not taught an extended inquiry unit prior to participating in this study.

Each unit was designed to engage students in science by seeking a solution to an overall question or problem. Materials for teachers included lesson descriptions and varying levels and types of educative support. Ms. Shirley enacted two, eight-week inquiry science units in year one and three units in year two (Table 1). One of the units from year one was repeated in year two. Weekly written pre and post lesson teacher reflections, monthly informal interviews, and daily classroom videotape were collected.

Table 1. Inquiry science units.

Unit 1: year 1*	Unit 2: year 1	Unit 3: year 2	Unit 4: year 2	Unit 5: year 2*
Life science 8 weeks on communicable disease; Investigate where bacteria are found	*Physical science* 8 weeks on force and motion; Investigate velocity with motion sensors	*Life science* 4 weeks on adaptation, observe, explanation; Investigate animal behavior	*Physical science* 8 weeks on global temperature; Investigate factors influencing temperature	*Life science* 8 weeks on communicable disease; Investigate where bacteria are found

*Unit 1 and unit 5 were the same unit. This unit was updated between enactments.

The written materials for lessons intended to orient teachers to the lesson, guide teachers through the lesson and transition teachers to the next lesson were characterized for how they: (a) engaged teachers in planning and teaching, (b) developed teachers' pedagogical content knowledge, and (c) matched teachers' learning needs. Guided by the specific features listed above each lesson was rated for the extent and depth of support in each category (Table 2).

Analysis was focused on aspects of inquiry teaching that are challenging for teachers to learn and require PCK. Specifically, I looked for and coded (a) opportunities for students to ask and refine questions, gather and analyze data and information, make interpretations, draw conclusions, and report findings; (b) guidance for students to explain, justify, critique, and revise ideas; and (c) support for students to listening, questioning, and responding during discussion among peers and teachers. Comparisons of teacher PCK overtime and between lessons with different types and amounts of educative support in the materials were made. Also, the types of lessons that appeared to be most helpful for teacher learning were identified.

Table 2. Type of teacher educative support characteristic of each unit.

Unit	Engage in plan and teach	Develop PCK	Match teacher learning need
1	Describe active & thought task Responses not listed Few links Some teacher text highlighted	Activities use student ideas Challenging ideas explained Some learning goals up front Suggested discussion question	Few teacher prior ideas addressed Sporadic educative support Some questions teacher voice Strategies vary
2	Explain active & thought tasks Response to questions & tasks Links ideas, events throughout Teacher text highlighted	Activities revise student ideas St. thinking for phenomena, responses, explanations Learning goals throughout How and why to guide attention, discuss, collaborate	Some teacher prior ideas addressed Consistent educative support Questions and scenarios in teacher voice throughout Repeated strategies
3	Describe active & thought task Some responses to tasks Links to future lessons Some teacher text highlighted	Activities build on student ideas Challenging ideas, responses explained, check student ideas Learning goals throughout How to guide attention, collab.	Short lessons, familiar project Consistent educative support Questions in teacher voice Repeated strategies
4	Directions for active tasks Response to questions listed Links in orient section Teacher text content only	Activities elicit student ideas Student misconceptions listed Learning goals up front How to correct responses; many content questions	Long and technical lessons Consistent content support Little text in teacher voice Strategies vary
5	Explain active & thought tasks Responses preferred listed for questions Link to future lessons up front Some teacher text highlighted	Activities use student ideas Some challenging ideas explained Learning goals throughout How to guide attention and ideas, discussion questions	Few teacher prior ideas addressed Consistent educative support Questions in teacher voice Strategies vary

Findings

Inquiry teaching. Ms. Shirley's initial enactments were consistent with the nature of enactments by teachers who purposefully used materials to guide their teaching (Schneider et al., 2005). In year one, Ms. Shirley gave students ample opportunities to explore phenomena, work with peers in groups, and to create artifacts. She also struggled with guiding student thinking during small group work and focusing students on explaining and revising their ideas during whole class discussion. She did, however, ask for students' ideas. Over time, Ms. Shirley improved her ability to guide thoughtful discussions, particularly when materials provided questions and described possible discussion scenarios. Support for thinking in small group work continued to be relatively weak. In year two, Ms. Shirley continued to provide students with ample opportunities but she also began to provide students with more structure to guide their work. She described more phases for investigations, defined the tasks for small group work, and focused students on their own ideas during discussions. She continued, however, to struggle with how to guide students' thinking toward accurate ideas while building from their own ideas, particularly in small groups.

Teacher learning. Ms. Shirley's ideas about inquiry developed over the two year period (Table 3). Initially she attempted to fit the new lessons into her previous teaching framework. In year two she began to think about teaching within a framework consistent with the intent of the materials. Midway through year two she began to question components of the lesson with this new framework. For example, she wondered why the unit did not focus students on the bigger question of the unit more often. As Ms. Shirley gained experience with these inquiry units she demonstrated a need for more detailed or finer grained support. For example, in unit one she needed questions she could use in discussions and to have the basic strategies described. By unit five she was focusing on specific details of strategies. Her attention to students' thinking also developed over time. In year one, she was concerned about what she might say that would impart misconceptions. In year two, she moved from noticing students' experiences, then students' ideas, to finally making plans to support their developing ideas.

Table 3. Summary description of teacher thinking for each unit based on self report and observation.

Unit	Ability to plan and teach	Level of PCK	Teacher learning need
1	Difficult to interpret materials Uses previous teaching framework, strategies Long term planning is hard	Did not know how students would respond or what would happen Focus on actions, fun Excitement evidence of learn	Prior idea: students do not read Needed explicit guidance for tasks; specific questions and strategies to use with students
2	Usually able to interpret materials Trying new strategies Worries about time in lessons	Did not want add misconceptions Noticed students prior experience Surprised students could do tasks Struggle evidence of boredom	Prior idea: students should not struggle with tasks or ideas; Relied on teacher voice text
3	Able to interpret materials Begin to use new framework Time not an issue	Understood goal, intent of task Considers student thinking States students learn faster w inquiry	Prior idea: too much time on a topic is boring for students Needed more specific guidance for investigation
4	Difficult to interpret materials Questioned recommend tasks Unable to plan long term	Noticed student misconception States goals of student groups Added appropriate context	Prior idea: st. have difficulty working in groups, writing Needed strategies to support student conversation or collab.
5	Usually able to interpret materials Begin to plan for process, link ideas, refining new strategies Plan time for lesson, long term	Noticed students needed guidance in group work; goals, decisions for student thinking Surprised at students' interest in reading	Prior idea: students need excitement Needed fewer questions/topics to focus on per lesson; finer grained support for strategies

Educative features. In the materials, scenarios and questions that were intended to be read aloud to students not only illustrated what inquiry might sound like but also scaffolded Ms. Shirley's initial efforts with discussions to introduce and wrap up lessons. Ms. Shirley struggled with predicting time, initially for lessons but particularly with long range planning. Her ability to plan time improved over time and specifically when the materials had shorter more focused lessons. When materials were explicit on how components of a lesson contributed to the overall goals, enactments were more thoughtful. Student activities that did not have a physical product, such as discussion to develop a plan or make a decision, seemed to help Ms. Shirley focus on student ideas over completing tasks. She continued to need specific questions and explicit learning goals for tasks such as discussions.

Discussion

The findings in this study indicate that teachers do use materials to guide their teaching; however, to support their efforts it is necessary to be quite descriptive and focused. When the materials did not describe specific goals, how events would play out, or how students would respond, Ms. Shirley had difficulty guiding her students. Lessons with multiple goals and tasks also were difficult to understand. Findings also demonstrate that teachers, like their students, are not blank slates. As learners, they have ideas from prior professional development, textbooks, and experiences with students. Ms. Shirley often relied on her prior ideas about teaching and students even though those experiences may or may not have been consistent with inquiry. For example, Ms Shirley's idea that students will not read was based on experiences with textbooks. Guiding students in developing science process ideas such as designing an investigation appears to be particularly difficult. Also, teachers new to extended inquiry, like novice teachers, have trouble judging time (Putnam & Borko, 2000). It is particularly difficult to make long range plans that support activities weeks in advance. When Ms. Shirley began to use a new framework for thinking about teaching she was better able to interpret materials and make plans for her students.

This study provides evidence that materials can help teachers learn and enact inquiry. Ms. Shirley's practice improved over time, but specifically when materials provided particular supports. For example, when the materials provided detailed descriptions of student misconceptions partnered with tasks that highlighted these ideas within their own students, Ms. Shirley noticed that her students had misconceptions. This also illustrates how materials can support teachers in learning about teaching by studying their students and their practice. Consistent with the construct of PCK, it appears to be necessary to for teachers to integrate ideas about teaching science with an understanding of their own students (Magnusson et al., 1999). This highlights the importance of selecting tasks that make students' thinking visible to teachers (Remillard, 2000). In addition, as learners teachers will need student tasks that will address their own prior ideas. For example, the literature tells us that many teachers believe students need only to be active in order to learn (Meyer, 1997). Ms. Shirley relied on activity – fun and excitement – as evidence of learning. Materials could actively address teachers' prior ideas. In this case, a focus on how to determine their students' ideas before and after lessons would be appropriate.

To engage teachers in planning and teaching developers must be quite explicit in describing lessons – how to enact specific strategies, guide discussions, or illustrate phenomena – but also, *why* they should attend to specific aspects of tasks and *how* they can support student learning. This includes consistently describing the specific and long range learning goals of each task. Developers also need to better predict student responses and describe outcomes. To develop teachers' PCK developers need to focus teachers' attention on student thinking, particularly their own students' thinking. Student activities that clearly focus on cognitive products can be included to help teachers learn how to guide students' thinking as well as doing in inquiry. To match teachers' learning needs developers need to reconsider the variety and amount of activities they ask teachers to enact. Challenges seen suggest developers should consider smaller but key initial steps such as questions or tasks that elicit students' ideas and encourage students to consider others' ideas. Lesson that help teachers learn inquiry would benefit students also. For example, lessons with one clear goal, focused questions, and support for how to discuss this idea would help teachers and students focus on student thinking. Finally, when scenarios intended illustrate how a lesson might play out are also designed to be read aloud with students they appear to match teachers' natural inclination to read such scenarios to their students (Collopy, 1999).

Writing materials to be educative for teachers will not be easy, but neither is learning and teaching inquiry. If designers do not paint a picture of inquiry through their lesson descriptions, teachers will not see it. Teachers, quite understandably, will use their prior knowledge of teaching to makes sense of lessons. Moreover, it will be important, yet challenging, to leave room for teachers to participate in planning and teaching in thoughtful ways. This will require developers to plan for teachers' learning in addition to students' learning. Designers need to focus not on what teachers need to know to get it right, but rather, what teachers need to learn to take an active role in enacting inquiry with their students.

Conclusion

The importance of this study lies in its ability to inform efforts to create innovations that teachers can use to learn and enact new practices. Through a better understanding of how inquiry teaching develops over time, what teachers learn, and how materials can help, we can begin to develop effective resources to support teachers' work with students. Wonderful materials for students are becoming available but if teachers cannot use them as intended they will not have the impact on student learning hoped for. Teachers are encouraged to use inquiry teaching methods but are rarely given explicit support to guide them in how or why to guide their students in investigating questions, working collaboratively, or engaging in thoughtful discussions. Although researchers can work closely with small numbers of teachers to support their efforts this is not possible on a large scale. Reform materials will need to incorporate explicit supports for teachers' learning. Designers need to carefully consider teachers' thinking and learning needs, as well as students', as they develop innovations to impact student learning.

References

Cohen, D. K., Raudenbush, S. W., & Ball, D. L. (2002). Resources, instruction, and research. In R. Boruch, F. Mosteller & P. Janeway (Eds.), *Evidence matters: Randomized trials in education research* (pp. 80-119). Washington D. C.: Brookings.

Collopy, R. (1999). *Teachers use of and learning from curriculum materials.* Unpublished doctoral dissertation, University of Michigan, Ann Arbor.

Corcoran, T. B. (1995). *Helping teachers teach well: Transforming professional development.* Philadelphia, PA: Consortium for Policy Research in Education.

Daehler, K. R., & Shinohara, M. (2001). A complete circuit is a complete circle: Exploring the potential of case materials and methods to develop teachers' content knowledge and pedagogical content knowledge of science. *Research in Science Education, 31*, 267-288.

Darling-Hammond, L. (1999). *Teacher quality and student achievement: A review of state policy evidence*: Center for the study of teaching and policy, University of Washington.

Davis, E. A., & Krajcik, J. S. (2005). Designing educative curriculum materials to promote teacher learning. *Educational Researcher, 34*(3), 3-14.

Magnusson, S., Krajcik, J. S., & Borko, H. (1999). Nature, sources and development of pedagogical content knowledge for science teaching. In J. Gess-Newsome & N. G. Lederman (Eds.), *Examining pedagogical content knowledge* (pp. 95-132). Netherlands: Kluwer Publishers.

Meyer, K. M. (1997). *Catalysts and impediments to change in science teachers' beliefs and practices.* Unpublished doctoral dissertation, University of Michigan, Ann Arbor.

Minstrell, J., & Van Zee, E. H. (2000). *Inquiry into inquiry learning and teaching in science.* Washington D.C.: American Association for the Advancement of Science Press.

Nathan, M. J., & Petrosino, A. (2003). Expert blind spot among perservice teachers. *American Educational Research Journal, 40*(4), 905-928.

National Research Council. (1996). *National science education standards*. Washington DC: NAP.

Putnam, R. T., & Borko, H. (2000). What do new views of knowledge and thinking have to say about research on teacher learning? *Educational Researcher, 29*(1), 4-15.

Remillard, J. T. (2000). Can curriculum materials support teachers' learning? Two fourth-grade teachers' use of a new mathematics text. *The Elementary School Journal, 100*(4), 331-350.

Schneider, R. M., Blumenfeld, P., & Krajcik, J. (2002). Designing materials to support teachers in reform. In P. Bell, R. Stevens & T. Satwicz (Eds.), *Keeping learning complex: Proceedings of the fifth international conference of the learning sciences (ICLS)* (pp. 398-405). Mahwah, NJ: Erlbaum.

Schneider, R. M., & Krajcik, J. (2002). Supporting science teacher learning: The role of educative curriculum materials. *Journal of Science Teacher Education, 13*(2), 167-217.

Schneider, R. M., Krajcik, J., & Blumenfeld, P. (2005). Enacting reform-based science materials. *Journal of Research in Science Teaching, 42*(3), 283-312.

Wayne, A. J., & Youngs, P. (2003). Teacher characteristics and student achievement gains: A review. *Review of Educational Research, 73*(1), 89-122.

Wilson, S. M., & Berne, J. (1999). Teacher learning and the acquisition of professional knowledge. *Review of Research in Education, 24*, 173-209.

Wilson, S. M., Floden, R. E., & Ferrini-Mundy, J. (2001). *Teacher preparation research: Current knowledge, gaps, and recommendations* (No. R-01-3): University of Washington.

Acknowledgements

This study was funded in part by the National Science Foundation as part of the Middle school science curriculum materials, grant 0137807. Any opinions, findings, and conclusions or recommendations expressed in this material are those of the author and do not necessarily reflect the views of NSF.

Effects of Innovation versus Efficiency Tasks on Recall and Transfer in Individual and Collaborative Learning Contexts

David A. Sears, Stanford University, 485 Lasuen Mall, Stanford, CA 94305-3096
dasears2006@gmail.com

Abstract: Two experiments tested the effects of a framework for promoting productive collaboration and transfer. The framework uses the dimensions of innovation and efficiency to characterize learning tasks according to the types of knowledge they should promote. Innovation tasks involve the construction of novel solutions to unfamiliar problems while efficiency tasks feature repeated application of optimal solutions. The former are intended to help students appreciate key features of an expert solution while the latter aim to increase speed and accuracy. The overarching hypothesis was that having an opportunity to innovate would promote productive collaboration and learning more than efficiently copying and studying correct answers. The first experiment, involving third graders, found benefits of innovation for individual learning. The second, with university students working collaboratively, found effects of innovation on interaction.

Traditional instructional activities often emphasize efficient drill-and-practice methods to the neglect of greater exploration and guided discovery. Procedural mastery and the ability to apply one's knowledge with speed and accuracy are important benefits of efficient approaches to instruction (Anderson, Conrad, & Corbett, 1989; Klahr & Nigam, 2005; Tennyson, Park, & Christensen, 1985). However, without opportunities for broader exploration, deeper understanding arising from opportunities to integrate new concepts with prior knowledge and from chances to notice invariant features of a problem may be lacking (Schroth, 1995; Schwartz & Martin, 2004; Vollmeyer, Burns, & Holyoak, 1996). For these reasons, Schwartz, Bransford, and Sears (2005) recently suggested that a combination of innovation-oriented and efficiency-oriented activities might promote optimal learning. This proposal describes two tests of this claim—one in an individual context, the other in a collaborative context. The hope is that the innovation-efficiency framework may characterize optimal learning and instruction methods both for individuals and groups.

While the innovation and efficiency dimensions are still being empirically tested to determine their key features, a basic characterization is possible. Innovation tasks involve the use of prior knowledge to construct novel solutions to unfamiliar problems. Instructionally, these activities should help students understand the contexts and key features of a problem. Efficiency tasks, by contrast, involve repeatedly applying optimal solutions. They should promote speed and accuracy.

Evidence for the importance of these dimensions to optimal learning came from recent work by Schwartz and colleagues. Schwartz and Bransford (1998) and Schwartz and Martin (2004) divided students into three conditions: one in which they attempted an innovation activity and then an efficiency activity, a second involving only innovation activities, and a third involving only efficiency activities. The innovation plus efficiency condition did significantly better than the other two, particularly on measures involving transfer. Thus, Schwartz and colleagues provided evidence for the notion that innovation followed by efficiency promotes learning more than either method alone. Both of these studies involved high school or college students doing a math or a graphing task. These studies preceded the recent explication of the innovation-efficiency framework and contributed to its formulation. The first experiment described below attempted to extend this work to other domains and populations by utilizing a reading and concept-mapping task with third graders. In addition, this study explicitly tested the innovation-efficiency framework for its effects on individual learning. The hypothesis was that the innovation condition, which had an opportunity for greater exploration and knowledge construction before receiving expert feedback, would show more learning than the efficiency condition.

Going beyond individual learning, the second experiment tested the hypothesis that an activity with opportunities for innovation would yield more knowledge-sharing and productive collaboration than one emphasizing efficiency. Why might we expect these dimensions to have different effects on collaborative learning? First, informal observations from an innovative statistics task suggested that students were very engaged in generating, discussing, and testing potential solutions (Schwartz & Martin, 2004). Second, other tasks showing benefits of collaboration have features in common with innovative tasks (e.g. Laughlin, Zander, Knievel, & Tan, 2003; Schwartz, 1995; Steiner, 1972). In each case, participants could build upon and revise each other's insights to progress toward more effective solutions. Finally, previous research has indicated that efficiency tasks such as list-learning and copying, have negative effects or no benefits under collaboration conditions (Andersson & Rönnberg, 1995; Phelps & Damon, 1989; Rummel & Spada, 2005; Steiner, 1972). For these reasons, the innovation and efficiency dimensions may offer a useful framework for characterizing productive collaborative tasks.

If successful, such a framework could be beneficial to practitioners because teachers have found current scaffolds of collaboration difficult to implement in their classrooms (Antil, Jenkins, Wayne, & Vadasy, 1998). Current approaches have tended to rely on social structures, such as motivational interventions (Johnson & Johnson, 1999; Slavin, 1996), scripts and roles (Coleman, 1998; King, 1999; O'Donnell, 1999), and training (Gillies & Ashman, 1998; Rummel & Spada, 2005) to achieve positive (and often impressive) outcomes. The current approach attempts to support behaviors associated with productive collaborative outcomes, such as explanations (Webb, 1983), joint-attention and building dialogue (Barron, 2003), and metacognition (King, 1999), via the intrinsic demands of the task. In this way, the second study builds upon insights expressed by such distinct and notable scholars as Cohen (1994) and Steiner (1972) to understand how different tasks may support or undermine collaborative learning. This is a topic that has been relatively understudied and, in addition to its practical implications, could prove informative to theory. If the innovation-efficiency framework characterizes tasks that naturally afford productive collaborations, then we can deepen our understanding of the specific collaborative behaviors that support learning, a widely recognized goal for the field (Azmitia, 1996; Olivera & Straus, 2004; Slavin, 1996).

Study 1 Overview

This study examined the hypothesis that an innovative activity would yield greater learning and transfer than an efficiency activity even with equal time on task. The study involved third-graders making a concept map about energy transfer and computers. Concept mapping software known as Betty's Brain assisted this process. Betty's Brain is a teachable agent, so called because students teach it concepts and causal relationships in order to learn (Biswas, Schwartz, Bransford, & TAGV, 2001). Students can ask Betty questions about the relationship between concepts in their map as they make it, and Betty can respond by tracing through the causal-links in the map to state how they affect each other. In this process, students can reflect on what they have taught Betty and on their own understanding. Betty also can give students feedback on what percentage of their map is correct, allowing them to check if they are on the right path.

Over the two days of the experimental intervention, participants read two passages on energy transfer and computers. Each day, after reading the passage, participants in the Innovation condition used the text to create links between the disconnected concepts provided in their Betty map. Participants in the Efficiency condition were given a list of all the pair-wise links so they could copy both the concepts and the links into their Betty map. Figure 1 shows an expert version of the complete map. One notable feature of this map is that each concept (except one—Computer Power) had a technical name and a common object associated with it, such as Mechanical Energy (Dancing) and Chemical Energy (Brain).

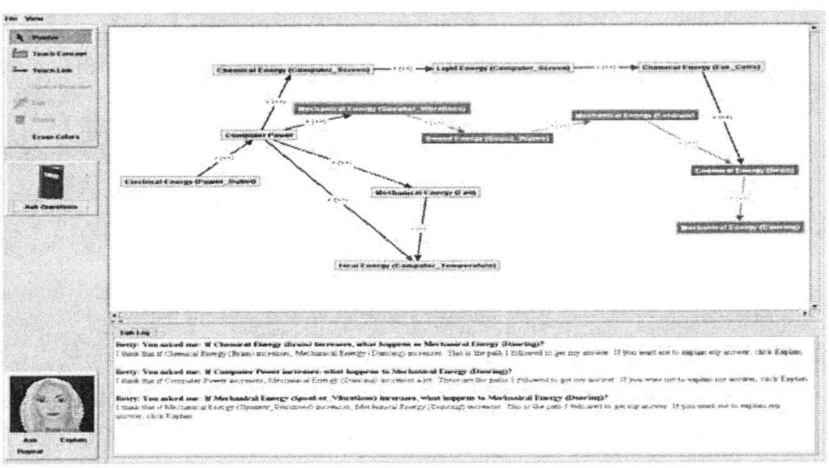

Figure 1. The Complete Concept Map with Day2 Concepts Highlighted.

Methods

Participants—Thirty-four third-graders from a suburban parochial school were randomly assigned to one of two conditions, Innovation versus Efficiency. One student was absent from the Efficiency condition at posttest, so a total of 33 participants completed the study.

Procedure and Design—Table 1 outlines the study procedures and materials. It shows the activities that all participants did, regardless of condition. For the intervention days, the experimenter started by reading that day's passage aloud to the participants as they read along silently. Then the participants made their maps; each working at their own computer. Because some participants did not create a perfect Day1 map, a correct concept map from Day1 was provided to every participant on Day2, so that they could build upon it with the new links and concepts they received that day. As on Day1, this map included the Day2 nodes in it for the Innovation participants, and it was their job to use the text to determine how to link them together and to the original Day1 map. Efficiency Dyads received a list of all the new pair-wise links and had to copy them into the Day1 map along with the new concepts. To restate, the difference between conditions was that the Innovation participants had the opportunity to search and find the appropriate links between concepts from the text before checking Betty's Brain for feedback while the Efficiency participants were given the answers on a sheet of paper to copy into their map and study if time permitted. Both conditions utilized the full class periods to create their maps.

Table 1: Study Procedures and Materials.

	Training Day	*Intervention Day1*	*Intervention Day2*
Location: Computer Lab	Betty Software Demonstration and Practice. Topic: Roller-coasters Time: 30 min.	Map-making with Betty Software. Passage: "Energy Transfer and the Computer" Map: 8 Concepts, 8 Links Time: 50 min.	Continued Map-making with Betty Software. Passage: "Computers and Sound" Map: 4 New Concepts, 5 New Links Time: 30 min. Delay: 30-40 min.
Location: Regular Classroom	Concept Map Demonstration. Topic: Scab formation Time: 30 min.		Posttest: 13-item short-answer quiz. Map re-drawing task. Time: 30 min.

Performance on the Betty map-making task served as an initial learning check. The posttest consisted of a quiz and map re-drawing task. The 13-item short-answer quiz included three questions from Day1 materials, six from Day2, and four transfer questions. The Day1 and Day2 questions were fact-recall questions such as, "What vibrates in our ear that causes us to hear sound?" Three of the transfer questions required explanations that were meant to reflect participants' understanding of the passage and whole concept map. One question stated, "Imagine an amazing invention was recently created—frictionless motors and wires! How would this affect your computer? Would any part of the computer become less important?" The fourth transfer question consisted of three parts, each requiring participants to state how different concepts in a new map affected each other. It is important to note that these were not questions designed to measure spontaneous transfer (e.g. Gick & Holyoak, 1983); rather, they were designed to measure participants' ability to apply their previous learning in new contexts or to solve novel problems (e.g. Schwartz & Bransford, 1998).

The map re-drawing task required participants to draw the complete concept map on paper from memory. The maps were scored as the percentage of all the possible relationships that could be traced in the expert map that their map could answer correctly. The visual layout of participants' redrawn maps had no relevance to the scoring procedure.

Results

As shown in Figure 2, no significant differences were found between conditions on any of the map measures. Participants scored similarly on their Betty maps, suggesting that neither group started with an advantage due to better initial performance on the learning activity. In addition, both conditions did poorly at re-drawing their maps from memory.

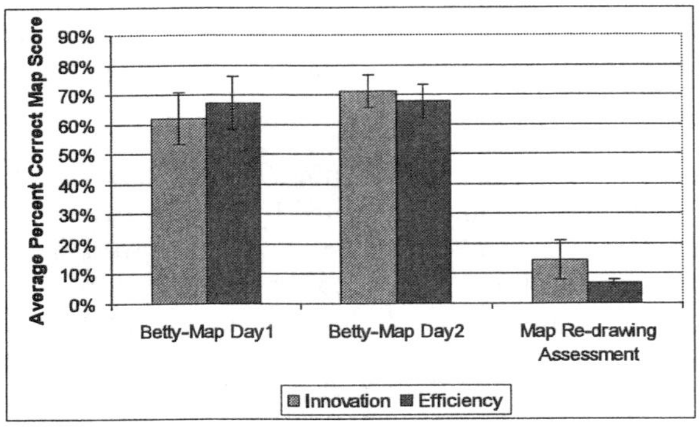

Figure 2: Average Map Scores by Condition (±SEM).

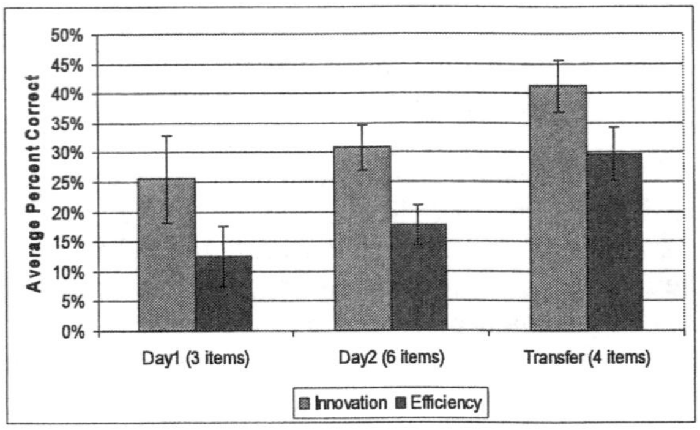

Figure 3: Average Quiz Scores by Condition (±SEM).

Unlike the map measures, the 13-item quiz revealed a number of differences between the conditions, as shown in Figure 3. To score the quiz, eight of the questions were given one point if correct and zero if wrong. Four of the remaining questions had multiple parts, each of which received one point if correct and zero if wrong. The remaining question and one other sub-question, both from the transfer questions, were too difficult for the participants, so answers that were relevant to the topic, though not necessarily correct, were given credit. (If these items were removed, the analyses would show similar results, though the difference by condition on the transfer questions would be less significant $t(31) = 1.3$, $p < .10$ (one-tailed)). If every question was answered perfectly, it would be possible to score 24 points on the quiz, three points on Day1 questions, 13 on Day2 questions, and eight on transfer questions.

The Innovation condition scored significantly higher on the quiz than the Efficiency condition ($t(31) = 2.8$, $p = .009$). A multivariate analysis of variance (MANOVA) using the three questions types (Day1, Day2, Transfer) as the dependent measures revealed that Innovation scored significantly higher for Day2 questions ($MS = 0.139$, $F(1,31) = 6.6, p = .015$), and marginally higher for Transfer questions ($MS = .109$, $F(1,31) = 3.3$, $p = .079$).

Conclusion

As expected, the Innovation condition showed greater learning and transfer than the Efficiency condition while performing similarly on map-recall. The greatest differences were on Day2 and transfer questions. The lack of a significant difference on Day1 questions may be due to students in the Innovation condition trying to use the Betty feedback feature to construct their maps in guess-and-check fashion on Day1 rather than relying on the passage. Clearly, this was not the desired form of "innovation." On Day2, students were restricted to seeking Betty feedback twice, and observationally, they searched the text more that day.

Some may suggest that the Innovation participants were bound to show better performance on the quiz given that they read the text more than the Efficiency participants. This may be true, but I suspect the approach to the reading was equally important. Specifically, Innovation participants had an opportunity, via greater exploration, to connect their prior knowledge to the new concepts and relationships they read about. Some evidence for this comes from their map re-drawings where they showed a tendency to recall the common terms more than the technical ones (29 common terms recalled versus 12 technical) whereas Efficiency participants were more equal (23 versus 19). In other words, Innovation participants often put the map into terms they understood.

Study 2 Overview

Study 1 examined effects of activities with an emphasis on innovation versus efficiency on learning outcomes. Study 2 investigated effects in a collaborative context. This study tested the hypothesis that a task with opportunities for innovation would cause more productive collaborative interactions and greater learning than a task focused primarily on efficiency. Dyads read a one-page passage about cholesterol. They also worked with the "Betty's Brain" concept mapping teachable agent (Biswas, Schwartz, Bransford, & TAGV, 2001). Participants taught Betty based on the cholesterol passage (e.g., "Exercise *decreases* LDL").

When creating their concept maps, dyads in the innovation condition had to determine the links between 16 concepts in the passage. Dyads in the efficiency condition received a list of all 23 pair-wise links. They used these links to make a completely connected map.

Methods

Participants—Thirty-eight participants, mostly undergraduates, were paired and randomly assigned to one of two conditions. Ten dyads were assigned to the Innovation condition and nine to the Efficiency condition.

Procedure and Design— Table 2 summarizes the study design, including periods of work done together versus alone. The unusual component of this design is that students took two tests: one immediately after creating their initial map, and one after they had a chance to learn a second time by reviewing an expert map and the passage. This second test permitted an estimate of how well students were prepared to learn. The map-making phase was 20 minutes for both conditions, and the map-revision time depended on how long it took for participants to revise their Betty map until it matched the provided expert map (usually two to five minutes). Dyads were videotaped while collaborating. Scoring of participants' re-drawn maps followed the same method as in Study 1. Quizzes were scored as percent correct based on the number of correct items out of 12 possible.

Table 2: Design of Study 2.

<table>
<tr><th>Step</th><th>Context</th><th>Innovation</th><th>Efficiency</th></tr>
<tr><td>1</td><td>Alone</td><td colspan="2">Read Passage on Cholesterol</td></tr>
<tr><td>2</td><td>Together</td><td>Generate Map Links</td><td>Make Map from List of Links</td></tr>
<tr><td>3</td><td>Together</td><td colspan="2">Get corrective feedback on 3 possible links. Have Betty trace through map and study it if time.</td></tr>
<tr><td>4</td><td>Alone</td><td colspan="2">Test-1: Redraw the Map and Answer 12 Multiple-choice Questions</td></tr>
<tr><td>5</td><td>Together</td><td colspan="2">See an Expert Map and Revise Until Match</td></tr>
<tr><td>6</td><td>Alone</td><td colspan="2">Re-read Cholesterol Passage</td></tr>
<tr><td>7</td><td>Alone</td><td colspan="2">Test-2: Redraw the Map and Answer 12 new Multiple-choice Q's</td></tr>
</table>

Results

Learning outcomes are presented first, followed by analyses of interactions, then associations between the two. A marginally significant difference in gain-over-time from Test-1 to Test-2 was found in favor of the Innovation condition (*Wilks' lambda* = .90, $F(1, 32) = 3.4$, $p < .10$). Neither condition significantly outperformed the other on either test.

Regarding group process, observations suggested that Efficiency dyads handed off answers from list-reader to link-maker. Innovation dyads, by contrast, often co-constructed their answers. Transcript analyses add rigor and further insight to these observations, but first, a description of their setup. The transcript included turn-by-turn conversation. It also included which link was created on which turn. Because the map re-drawing assessment involved the same links that participants created in their maps, it was possible to connect turn-by-turn conversation around a link to learning and memory of *that specific link*. To my knowledge, this is the only study to use such a fine-grained coupling of interaction-process and learning-outcome in its analyses, and it yielded some interesting results. For example, this arrangement allowed a comparison of memory for links that were explained at some point in dyads' discourse versus links that were not explained. (Explained links were recalled significantly more; however, this effect was driven primarily by the Efficiency condition.)

As expected, Innovation dyads took significantly more turns per link they created in their Betty maps than Efficiency dyads ($t(16) = 2.9$, $p = .01$). Efficiency dyads averaged less than three turns per link (2.9 ±0.2). Innovation dyads averaged over four turns per link (4.5 ±0.5). At the micro-level, no significant correlation was found between turns-taken on a link and successful recall of that link for either condition (*r's* between ±0.06). In other words, it was not the quantity of discussion around a link that determined dyads' recall of it.

At the macro-level, greater discussion may have contributed to greater knowledge sharing, as measured by similarity of partners' Map1 re-drawings. Map1 similarity was determined by summing the number of correct, wrong, and missing links held in common by both partners in a dyad. As one might expect, Innovation dyads showed greater Map1 similarity than Efficiency dyads, though only marginally ($t(17) = 1.3$, $p < .10$ (one-tailed)). Across conditions, Map1 similarity was a strong predictor of gains on Map2 (partial correlations after removing Map1 association with Map2: $r's = 0.80$ and 0.72, $p's < .05$ for Innovation and Efficiency, respectively). In other words, greater knowledge sharing was associated with greater learning after revision. (It is worth noting that statistical analyses of dyads reduce sample size by half; therefore, although some of these effects are only marginally significant, they still merit consideration).

Conclusion and Discussion

The innovation and efficiency task structures were moderately successful at producing different interaction patterns that appeared to have consequences for learning. As expected, Innovation dyads showed greater discussion during map-making than Efficiency dyads. Efficiency dyads showed little discussion, averaging just 2.9 turns per link. In other words, a typical interaction would involve one partner stating the link and the other copying it into the map. Not surprisingly, then, Innovation dyads appeared to share knowledge marginally better, and this was associated with greater learning-gains following feedback. The failure of the Innovation condition to significantly outperform Efficiency after feedback is likely due to Innovation dyads generating errors in their initial Betty maps (8.0 ± 1.9 versus 0.3 ± 0.3 for Efficiency).

Two aspects of this study's design merit comment. First, the tight coupling of interaction processes around a link with memory for that link demonstrated a unique and powerful tool that could help us achieve the widely recognized goal of connecting social processes to learning outcomes (Azmitia, 1996; Olivera & Strauss, 2004; Slavin, 1996). Second, by assessing learning after innovation and again after revision, otherwise hidden differences between conditions were found. This opportunity to revise was a feature of tasks yielding successful collaborations. Thus, cycles of innovation and revision may be an important feature of productive collaborative tasks.

To summarize, the first study found benefits of innovation for learning on a transfer measure while the second found effects on interaction that may have supported learning after feedback. It is possible that the collaborative study would have also found differences in learning favoring the innovation condition if a transfer measure was used, but this remains an empirical question. Taken together, these studies provide preliminary support for Schwartz et al.'s (2005) claim that opportunities for innovation before more efficiency-oriented instruction can put students on a trajectory toward adaptive expertise (Hatano & Inagaki, 1986). In addition, they provide initial evidence that the innovation and efficiency framework may provide a useful characterization of tasks for promoting collaboration—an aspect of collaborative learning that has been relatively understudied and could have significant benefits for practitioners.

References

Anderson, J., Conrad, F., & Corbett, A. (1989). Skill acquisition and the LISP tutor. Cognitive Science, 13, 467-505.

Andersson, J., and Rönnberg, J. (1995). Recall suffers from collaboration: Joint recall effects of friendship and task complexity. Applied Cognitive Psychology, 9, 199-211.

Antil, L., Jenkins, J., Wayne, S., and Vadasy, P. (1998). Cooperative learning: Prevalence, conceptualizations, and the relation between research and practice. American Educational Research Journal, 35, 419-454.

Azmitia, M. (1996). Peer interactive minds: Developmental, theoretical, and methodological issues. In P.B. Baltes & U. M. Staudinger (Eds.), Interactive minds: Life-span perspectives on the social foundation of cognition. Cambridge: Cambridge University Press.

Barron, B. (2003). When smart groups fail. The Journal of the Learning Sciences, 12, 307-359.

Biswas, G., Schwartz, D., Bransford, J., & the Teachable Agents Group at Vanderbilt (2001). Technology support for complex problem solving: From SAD environemtns to AI. In K. Forbus & P. Feltovich (Eds.), Smart machines in education: The coming revolution in educational technology.

Cohen, E.G. (1994). Restructuring the classroom: Conditions for productive small groups. Review of Educational Research, 64, 1-35.

Coleman, E. (1998). Using explanatory knowledge during collaborative problem solving in science. The Journal of the Learning Sciences, 7, 387-427.

Gick, M.L., & Holyoak, K.J. (1983). Schema induction and analogical transfer. Cognitive Psychology, 15, 1-38.

Hatano, G., & Inagaki, K. (1986). Two courses of expertise. In H. Stevenson, H. Azuma, & K. Hakuta (Eds.), Child development and education in Japan (pp. 262-272). New York, NY: Freeman.

Johnson, D. and Johnson, R. (1999). Making cooperative learning work. Theory into Practice, 38, 67-73.
King, A. (1999). Discourse Patterns for Mediating Peer Learning. In A. O'Donnell and A. King (Eds.), Cognitive perspectives on peer learning (pp. 87-115). Mahwah, New Jersey: Lawrence Erlbaum Associates, Inc.
Klahr, D., & Nigam, M. (2004). The equivalence of learning paths in early science instruction. Psychological Science, 15, 661-667.
Laughlin, P., Zander, M., Knievel, E., & Tan, T. (2003). Groups perform better than the best individuals on letters-to-numbers problems: Informative equations and effective strategies. Journal of Personality and Social Psychology, 85, 684-694.
O'Donnell, A. (1999). Structuring dyadic interaction through scripted cooperation. In A. O'Donnell and A. King (Eds.), Cognitive perspectives on peer learning (pp. 179-196). Mahwah, New Jersey: Lawrence Erlbaum Associates, Inc.
Olivera, F., and Straus, S. (2004). Group-to-individual transfer of learning: Cognitive and social factors. Small Group Research, 35, 440-465.
Phelps, E., and Damon, W. (1989). Problem solving with equals: Peer collaboration as a context for learning mathematics and spatial concepts. Journal of Educational Psychology, 81, 639-646.
Rummel, N., and Spada, H. (2005). Learning to collaborate: An instructional approach to promoting collaborative problem solving in computer-mediated settings. Journal of the Learning Sciences, 14, 201-241.
Schroth, M. (1995). Variable delay of feedback procedures and subsequent concept formation transfer. Journal of General Psychology, 122, 393-399.
Schwartz, D. (1995). The emergence of abstract representations in dyad problem solving. Journal of the Learning Sciences, 4, 321-354.
Schwartz, D.L. & Bransford, J.D. (1998). A time for telling. Cognition and Instruction, 16, 475-522.
Schwartz, D., Bransford, J. & Sears, D. (2005). Efficiency and innovation in transfer. In J. Mestre (Ed.), Transfer of learning from a modern multidisciplinary perspective. CT: Information Age Publishing.
Schwartz, D., & Martin, T. (2004). Inventing to prepare for learning: The hidden efficiency of original student production in statistics instruction. Cognition & Instruction, 22, 129-184.
Slavin, R. (1996). Research for the future: Research on cooperative learning and achievement: What we know, what we need to know. Contemporary Educational Psychology, 21, 43-69.
Steiner, I. (1972). Group process and productivity. New York: Academic Press.
Tennyson, R., Park, O., & Christensen, D. (1985). Adaptive control of learning time and content sequence in concept learning using computer-based instruction. Journal of Educational Psychology, 77, 481-491.
Webb, N. (1983). Predicting Learning from student interaction: Defining the interaction variables. Educational Psychologist, 18, 33-41.
Vollmeyer, R., Burns, B., & Holyoak, K. (1996). The impact of goal specificity on strategy use and the acquisition of problem structure. Cognitive Science, 20, 75-100.

Acknowledgments

This material is based upon work supported by a Spencer RTG pre-dissertation grant and the National Science Foundation under Grants No. SLC-0354453 and REC-0196238. Any opinions, findings, and conclusions or recommendations expressed in this material are those of the author and do not necessarily reflect the views of the National Science or Spencer Foundations. I would like to thank Dr. Daniel Schwartz for his helpful insights and suggestions.

The Pasteurization of Education

David Williamson Shaffer, Kurt D. Squire, University of Wisconsin, 1025 W. Johnson St., Madison, WI 53706
Email: dws@education.wisc.edu, kdsquire@education.wisc.edu

Abstract: Stokes (1997) has argued that research projects can be described by their contributions to theoretical understanding and the solution of practical problems. Building on this model, scholars have suggested that the learning sciences should focus "use-inspired basic research." With this move has come a focus on projects with the potential to create systemic change rather than naturalistic studies of learning in context and design research to develop innovative interventions. We argue that this is based on a misreading history, and is counter-productive for learning science research. To make this case, we use Latour's (1983) study of Pasteur to suggest an alternative model for research-based transformation of education. By way of illustration, we use a brief example of a research project to ground a discussion of the broader implications of this alternative conceptualization of the process of learning sciences research.

Introduction

For decades educational technologists have struggled with the problem of how to transform school systems to meet the needs of post-industrial, knowledge-based economy and society. In recent years, reformers have looked to Donald Stokes' *Pasteur's Quadrant* (1997) as a framework for reorganizing research on educational technology in order to create more lasting impacts on the practice of education.

Stokes argues that research can be described by its contribution to theoretical understanding and contribution to the solution of practical problems. His model maps the landscape of inquiry into four "quadrants":

1. Bors' Quadrant of pure basic research: lots of theory but little practical application;
2. Edison's Quadrant of pure applied research: lots of practical application but little theoretical contribution;
3. Pasteur's Quadrant of use-inspired basic research: contributions to theory and practical applications;
4. and the ignominious, unnamed quadrant of research for its own sake: little contribution to anything at all.

Perhaps in response to those who suggest with thinly-veiled contempt that all of contemporary education research is in the unnamed, useless fourth quadrant, scholars in recent years have argued that studies should focus more on Pasteur's Quadrant of "use-inspired basic research" (Sabelli & Dede, 2001). With this move has come an emphasis on projects driven by "use-inspired" questions with the potential to create systemic changes, and a reliance on randomized controlled trials as the preeminent method of investigation—and a consequent devaluation of naturalistic studies of learning in context and design research developing innovative educational interventions, as well as the methods of inquiry that support them.

We argue that this current predilection is both counter-productive and based on a misreading of the processes through which scientific investigation addresses practical problems. To make this case, we look more closely at the operationalization of Stokes' *quadrant model* in the field of education, suggesting that its short-term focus on systemic change is based on a misunderstanding of history. Based on Latour's (1983) study of Pasteur, we then suggest an alternative *lever model* that emphasizes the transformation of educational practices through technological innovation. We argue that the renewed focus on use inspired research in education, while important, has placed undue emphasis on tinkering around the edges of existing educational systems without seriously reconsidering the fundamental values or organizing structures behind schooling. In short, it has led to a privileging of research programs that work within the current constraints of schooling rather than those that have the potential to change it.

Inhabiting Pasteur's Quadrant

Over the past decade, Pasteur's Quadrant has been taken up as a rallying cry for the reform of educational research, particularly among researchers in the learning sciences working on developing innovative learning technologies (Sabelli & Dede, 2001). Stokes, who was a political scientist before his death in 1997, argued that policy makers have long held an oversimplified view of science. Too many people in the public and in policy making communities, he suggested, believe that innovation is simply the result of doing "basic" research, generating results, and then applying them outside the laboratory. In practice, Stokes pointed out, the distinction between "basic" and "applied" science is messy: each overlaps and informs the other. Writing for policy makers, Stokes argued that rather than exclusively funding "basic" research, the government (particularly the National Science Foundation) should also fund research projects driven by pragmatic questions, such as those faced by educators and educational technologists. He describes Pasteur's work as a prototype for this kind of use-driven research, and the National Institutes of Health as a grant-giving agency that exemplifies this commitment to solving problems while furthering fundamental understandings (Sabelli & Dede, 2001; Stokes, 1997).

Building on Stokes' argument, some scholars have suggested that "use-inspired" research—research in Pasteur's Quadrant—might rescue the "awful" reputation of educational research by simultaneously creating successful interventions and developing fundamental understandings about educational practice (Kaestle, 1997). Sabelli and Dede (2001), for example, argue that "now that the causes underlying educational dysfunctions are better understood, practitioners and policy makers are asking researchers to focus on applied larger studies that improve practice in a sustainable, affordable, and scaleable manner" (p. 12). In suggesting this application of the concept of Pasteur's Quadrant, educational researchers have often interpreted "use-driven research" as meaning *research that addresses the everyday questions of teachers and principals in typical—or more often, "problem"—schools*. Sabelli and Dede explain: use-driven problems are problems "stemming from issues in curriculum, pedagogy, assessment, professional development, etc" (p. 4).

In this model, in other words, researchers should focus on what Sabelli and Dede call *scholarship of practice*: questions that speak to practitioners' concerns—"curriculum, pedagogy, assessment, professional development, etc"—with an eye toward improving extant practices. One can only assume that conference sessions such as "Evidence-based motivation-related outcomes of mathematics improvement interventions: Collaborative adventures in Pasteur's quadrant" (a collection of papers at the 2005 American Educational Research Association annual meeting reporting on projects in the National Science Foundation Math and Science Partnership Program) would be part of such a scholarship of practice—asking use-inspired questions about programs or policies that work within the existing grammar of schooling (Tyack & Tobin, 1994).

The goal of such work is interventions that can be disseminated beyond specific research contexts. Fishman et al (2001), for example, describe the current conundrum facing educational researchers as one of developing innovations that "scale". The problem with technological innovations, from this perspective, is that design experiments that show what might be accomplished with new learning technologies too often die off when they are taken out of the original research context and integrated into school settings. As Fishman et al (2001) suggest:

> This form of research has been and will continue to be essential to developing both new technologies and refined understanding of the learning process. But it is insufficient for ensuring that the lessons learned about how to foster increased student learning find a foothold in everyday practice in classrooms that do not enjoy the same focused attention and support. The result is that the most valuable uses of technology are not achieving meaningful *scale*, and more importantly, are not becoming a part of the everyday or *systemic* practices of schools or school reform. [Emphasis in the original.]

The metaphor of "scaling up" is core to this approach, which focuses on creating interventions that can be deployed beyond the context in which they are developed. The *quadrant model*, as interpreted by these researchers, is thus to answer use-inspired questions by developing scaleable, sustainable interventions that operate with the current assumptions and under the current conditions of schooling. And, of course, the way to evaluate such interventions, from this point of view, is with randomized controlled experiments which provide policy makers the data they need to decide which programs work best. As Feuer, Towne, and Shavelson (2002) explain: randomized, controlled experiments are "still the single best methodological route to ferreting out systematic relations between actions and outcomes" (p. 8)—and thus for deciding what interventions are worth bringing to scale and what programs are scaling successfully.

Inhabiting L'Ecole Normale Supérieure

Unfortunately, this view of educational reform as "scaling up research in Pasteur's Quadrant through randomized, controlled experiments" is problematic, both practically and metaphorically, because it is based on a misreading of the processes of change and innovation. While Stokes accurately described Pasteur's interest in basic research that addresses applied problems, his presentation of Pasteur's work—and thus the image on which the quadrant model is built—did not describe the *mechanisms* by which Pasteur connected the two. A more careful analysis of how Pasteur's "basic" research methods were "applied" to real-world problems suggests that the metaphor of "scaling up" is not the only (and perhaps not the best) way to conceptualize technological innovation in education.

In his studies of the history of science, for example, Latour (1983) recounts in some detail the process by which Pasteur isolated the anthrax bacillus in his laboratory at L'Ecole Normale Supérieure and developed a vaccine for the disease that was endemic to French farms in the late 19th Century. Anthrax had already been the subject of much study, of course, but outbreaks did not appear to follow any regular pattern. Veterinarians had concluded that local conditions played a large role in determining when and where anthrax appeared, and were suspicious that the disease could be linked to any single organism.

Pasteur's approach to the challenge of anthrax was to take his laboratory apparatus into the field—to start working with the natural conditions in which the problem occurred, trying to isolate as precisely as possible the conditions under which outbreaks occurred. Pasteur's team systematically studied the natural history of the disease, and the life cycle of the organism they hypothesized as its cause.

Once a prospective organism was identified based on this naturalistic inquiry, Pasteur and his team returned to L'Ecole Normale Supérieure to grow the bacillus in culture. Under controlled conditions they were able to demonstrate that the organism was a critical agent in the spread of the disease. By designing systems for breeding the bacillus under a range of conditions, Pasteur was able to attenuate and strengthen strains of the organism, mimicking the variation observed in the disease in its natural setting. More important, by creating attenuated strains of the bacillus, Pasteur was able to produce, in his laboratory, the first ever artificial vaccine: a vaccination for anthrax. As Latour suggests, Pasteur was able to "do inside his laboratory what everyone tries to do outside but, where everyone fails because the scale is too large, Pasteur succeeds because he works on a small scale" (p. 149).

Having developed a vaccination in his laboratory, Pasteur moved to a field trial at Pouilly le Fort. But moving the vaccine back into the applied setting did not mean adapting the vaccine for use in the more complex and less controlled setting of French agriculture. Rather, it meant extending the practices of Pasteur's laboratory into the field. The conditions of the trial at Pouilly le Fort were carefully negotiated so as to recreate in a farm setting the conditions of Pasteur's laboratory that were essential to the success of the vaccination. The success of the field trial appeared "miraculous" to the public because Pasteur was able to show that all the vaccinated animals survived and all the unvaccinated animals contracted the disease and died. But as Latour is quick to point out, the trial was really a "staged" experiment, repeating results Latour had already achieved in his laboratory, and the "dissemination" of the vaccine was not so much a process of scaling up as it was a transformation of farming practices to mimic the conditions of Pasteur's research. As Latour explains, Pasteur's achievement was that "on the condition that you respect a limited set of laboratory practices—disinfection, cleanliness, conservation, inoculation gesture, timing and recording—you can extend to every French farm a laboratory product made at Pasteur's lab" (p. 152).

Latour describes Pasteur's method as a series of "translations" between farm and laboratory: the initial naturalistic inquiry that isolates the bacillus for study in the laboratory; the subsequent designed strains of the bacillus and controlled "outbreaks" within the laboratory setting; the transformation of pathogen into vaccine; the recreation of the conditions of the laboratory in the field at Pouilly le Fort; and finally the reorganization of French agriculture to accommodate the scientific practices that make inoculation effective.

In 1881, when Pasteur developed the first artificial vaccine, it was possible for a single scientist to undertake this process of naturalistic inquiry, laboratory research, and transformation of practice. But as problems—and the social and technological systems in which they arise—become more complex, progress comes rather from researchers working at various stages in this process, with each research program gaining leverage on the problems it tackles by building on the work of those focusing on other stages: naturalistic investigations provide the basis for laboratory research, which in turn provide models for the transformation of practice. Pasteur's own practice was, as Latour suggests, not merely "use-inspired basic research"; it was a series of levers by which problems and contexts were more deeply understood, tools and techniques were developed, and systems and practices were reorganized in light of the resulting process of inquiry.

We thus argue that this *lever model* of Pasteur's work is a more appropriate "translation" of Pasteur's methods to education research than the quadrant model described above. The lever model suggests that we need to support systematic naturalistic inquiries into the mechanisms by which learning takes place, in both exemplary and problematic situations. We need to support systematic experimental and design research into understanding these mechanisms more deeply and developing "ideal" practices and contexts which show how students can learn effectively. And we need to reconceptualize the process of "dissemination" as one of "transformation," in which practices developed in controlled settings become images that drive the reorganization of schooling in fundamental ways.

In the next section we describe an example of this process, showing how the lever model implies a different and powerful way of thinking about both education research and educational reform.

The lever model in action

One hundred and twenty three years after Pasteur used the new science of microbiology to defeat anthrax at Pouilly le Fort, ten middle schools students in Madison, Wisconsin were writing about cutting-edge research to cure Alzheimer's disease using stem cells. These students were participating in ***Science.Net***, a role-playing game in which they became science journalists, reporting on scientific developments and discoveries and their impact for an online science newsmagazine.

As in a real newsroom, these cub reporters attended news meetings where they pitched stories for the health and medicine, technology, and environment sections of the magazine. Working with desk editors for each section, the cub reporters interviewed sources, submitted stories for copyediting, and copyedited each other's work. To produce finished stories they learned to write leads and headlines, to use the neutral journalistic "voice of the newspaper," to source their stories using AP style, to include art and captions, to format their work for distribution on the web, and to prioritize copy on the section front. In a three week summer outreach program at the University of Wisconsin-Madison, these students collectively reported and produced some 50 news articles about science and technology.

Along the way, not surprisingly, students who play a game like ***Science.Net*** learn a lot about journalism. In a shorter pilot version of the study in which we interviewed students before and after the role-playing game, students use of journalism terms went up by 188% (mean before=3.5, after=10, $p<.01$), and more than twice as many students (9/12 compared to 4/12) said they thought journalism is about informing the public. For example, before playing the game one student said: "A journalist is someone who would write because they want to but they get paid to do it, so [journalists] bring stories that they're interested in and write something about it." After the game, the same student said: "To be a journalist [is] to inform people about current events by writing them."

Also not surprisingly, these students learned a lot about science. To be sure, they learned scientific facts and theories related to their stories, whether about nanotechnology ("Small Technology Goes to War"), ecology ("Study: Phosphorus Threatens Mendota"), or information technology ("Can games really help children?"). Perhaps more significant, writing about science and learning about science in the context of science journalism—and thus in the context of informing the public about events that impact their lives—helped expand these students' understanding of what science is and why it matters. Before playing the game one student said:

> I think science is... things that include electricity or the human body or... I just, like, do science... I don't really think about what science is.

After role-playing as a science journalist, the same student explained:

> I think science can be a lot of different things. Science can be technology, environment, health and medicine. Football fields can be considered science. Someone had to like help like make things up, inventing things. How to grow the grass... Like how long the yards are going to be... I didn't know science could be health and medicine. Things like environment... before I just thought they were what they were... [but I think about them differently after] picking the articles and finding stories about them and writing about them.

Overall, as shown in Figure 1, students came to describe science less in terms of school subjects and topics ("electricity or the human body") and more in terms of the impact of science on society. (The changes in both categories of the graph are significant with $p<0.05$.)

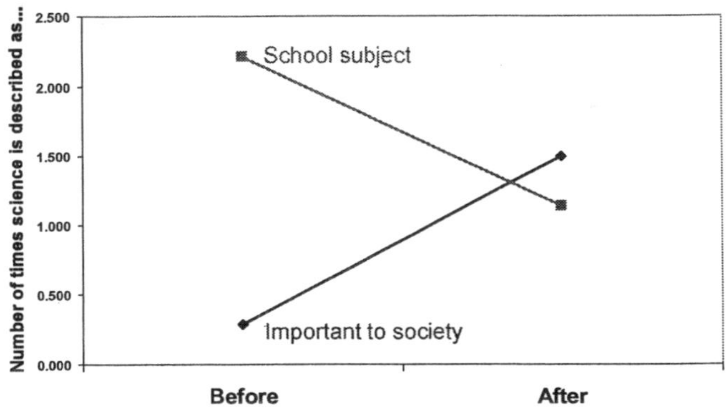

Figure 1. Change in students' description of science before and after role playing as science journalists. Points represent the mean number of times students refer to science as a school subject or topic and as something important to society. Both changes are statistically significant with $p<0.05$.

Our research on ***Science.Net*** suggests that what makes this role-playing game effective is that students are participating in an authentic recreation of the practices of journalists—or, more precisely, a recreation of the professional practicum through which journalists are trained (Shaffer, 2004). That is, students are learning about science by learning to work as—and thus think like—reporters. A role-playing game like ***Science.Net*** is thus based on the practices by which journalists are trained, and creating ***Science.Net*** meant conducting careful ethnographic observations of journalists in training—naturalistic study of the context in which reporters learn to think like journalists.

Elsewhere we have described this kind of game based on the practices of real-world professionals as an *epistemic game* (Shaffer, 2005, in press; Shaffer, Squire, Halverson, & Gee, in press). We raise the example here to ask: Where does an intervention such as this fit in our understanding of technology-based educational reform? Is this better conceived as a point in (or out) of Pasteur's Quadrant, or as an example of Pasteur's Lever?

Quadrant v Lever

Is ***Science.Net*** in Pasteur's Quadrant as interpreted by educational researchers? It certainly addresses a real, persistent, and continuing educational problem: getting students deeply engaged in scientific issues, and in this sense might qualify as "use-inspired research" similar to Pasteur's laboratory study of the anthrax bacillus. However, ***Science.Net*** is not focused on scientific thinking in the context of schools as currently constituted. Indeed, we deliberately work *outside* of school settings because the structures of school—mandated curricula and assessments, 50-minute periods, permissions for field trips, and large class sizes—make it difficult to simulate the conditions of journalistic practice. ***Science.Net*** is not driven by issues of "curriculum, pedagogy, assessment, professional development, etc." as currently constituted within our schools; rather, it is a deliberate attempt to reconsider such issues in light of the affordances of new technologies. As such, it is not a *scholarship of practice* as described by Sabelli and Dede (2001) but quite deliberately *scholarship of the possible*.

On the other hand, ***Science.Net*** is an excellent example of the lever model applied to education. In ***Science.Net***, naturalistic study of a context in which learning takes place is the basis for a design experiment in a controlled setting. Methods from the naturalistic study are refined through successive iterations under "laboratory" conditions until an effective curricular model is developed. ***Science.Net*** is surely not yet as refined as Pasteur's final anthrax vaccine—and whether it will ever be is an open empirical question. However, the basic processes are similar: studying a real world context, simulating its essential elements within a laboratory setting, and developing a potentially powerful intervention through design and experimental research.

The reason that it matters whether we think of ***Science.Net*** as a good example of Pasteur's Lever or a poor exemplar of research in Pasteur's Quadrant is that each of these models has a different implication for the question: What next?

In the quadrant model, Science.Net would need to "scale up"—to be implemented in a large number of classrooms and compared to traditional instruction in randomized controlled trials. To make that possible, it would have to be re-adapted to the existing conditions of practice—rescaled to the class sizes, periods, content, and assessments of middle school science instruction. We haven't done those experiments, but even without empirical data, it is easy to see that reworking an intervention based on the authentic simulation of real world practices to fit the existing structures of school would be about as likely to succeed as handing Pasteur's vaccine to a 19th Century farmer and asking him to inject it into his cows without changing anything else about the organization of his farm.

But, of course, that is precisely *not* what Pasteur did. Latour's point is that successful implementation of the vaccination Pasteur developed at L'Ecole Normale Supérieure meant adapting the conditions of practice to recreate the features of the laboratory essential to the success of the intervention. The *quadrant model* for educational research argue that design experiments under laboratory conditions are not useful because they "are not becoming part of the everyday or systemic practices of schools or school reform" (Fishman et al., 2001). But the point of the *lever model* is that the role of such experiments is not to adapt to existing practices but rather to provide guidelines for the transformation of practice. Following the lever model, the pathway would be to develop more and larger contexts that can accommodate Science.Net and other epistemic games of its kind—thus providing an engine for improving schools in fundamental ways rather than tinkering within the constraints of what is clearly a complex and very stable system.

Conclusion

We argue, then, that the Stokes' concept of Pasteur's Quadrant may not be the most productive metaphor for thinking about educational reform in the context of new technologies. A more careful reading of the practices by which Pasteur used the new technologies of microbiology and experimental science to transform 19th Century animal husbandry suggests that educational research needs to abandon the notion that successful "scaling up" in the rough-and-tumble world of extant schools is the only meaningful test of an intervention. There is, of course, a place for research that directly addresses the needs of practitioners. But not all research can or should be conceived in that way, particularly research with and about new technologies, which have the potential to transform practice in more radical ways.

Rather, we should conceive of the role of research on educational technology as also being about finding ways to reorganize schools in more fundamental ways. To this end, we suggest adopting the concept of Pasteur's Lever. In the lever model, naturalistic study of extant contexts provides the foundation for design-based laboratory research. This design research leads to new and powerful interventions that serve as models for large-scale transformation of schooling. That is, we suggest that rather than focusing on "scaling up" an intervention by adapting it more broadly to the conditions of practice, we emphasize "scaling up" the transformation of schools by adapting them more broadly to the conditions under which meaningful learning takes place. We suggest that in an age of technologies that have the power to expand the limits of our pedagogical imagination, we provide conceptual space for research that looks broadly at the possible future rather than narrowly at the here-and-now—scholarship that focuses deliberately on the ideal rather than doggedly on the practical.

References

Feuer, M. J., Towne, L., & Shavelson, R. J. (2002). Scientific culture and educational research. *Educational Researcher, 31*(8), 4-14.

Fishman, B., Soloway, E., Krajcik, J., Marx, R., & Blumenfeld, P. (2001). *Creating Scalable and Systemic Technology Innovations for Urban Education.* Paper presented at the American Educational Research Association Annual Meeting, Seattle, WA.

Kaestle, C. (1997). Improving the awful reputation of educational research. *Educational Researcher, 26*(7), 26-28.

Latour, B. (1983). Give me a Laboratory and I will Raise the World. In M. Mulkay (Ed.), *Science observed: Perspectives on the social study of science* (pp. 141-170). London: Sage.

Sabelli, N., & Dede, C. (2001). *Integrating educational research practice: Reconceptualizing goals and policies: How to make what works, work for us?* Retrieved July 17, 2005, from http://www.virtual.gmu.edu/ss_research/cdpapers/policy.pdf

Shaffer, D. W. (2004). Pedagogical praxis: The professions as models for post-industrial education. *Teachers College Record, 106*(7), 1401-1421.

Shaffer, D. W. (2005). Epistemic Games. *Innovate, 1*(6).

Shaffer, D. W. (in press). Epistemic games. *Computer Education.*
Shaffer, D. W., Squire, K. D., Halverson, R., & Gee, J. P. (in press). Video games and the future of learning. *Phi Delta Kappan*.
Stokes, D. E. (1997). *Pasteur's quadrant: Basic science and technological innovation*. Washington, D.C.: Brookings Institution Press.
Tyack, D., & Tobin, W. (1994). The Grammar of schooling: why has it been so hard to change? *American Educational Research Journal, 31*(3), 453-479.

Tools and Task Structures in Modeling Balance Beam

Ji Shen, Department of Physics, Washington University in St. Louis,
One Brookings Drive, St. Louis, MO 63130, Email: jishen@wustl.edu

Abstract: In the study I investigated the role of tools and task structures for science teachers of K-8 on the topic of balance in a professional development course. The findings show that the teachers tended to generate an additive rule, which is limited and contextualized, of balance condition, and failed to incorporate the more general multiplicative rule when thinking about balance. The study also shows that the teachers had difficulty in grasping a mathematical formula of balance condition. The learning outcome was partly a natural result of the materials the teachers used and the tasks they carried out. I conclude that learning tools and instructional tasks provide opportunities for understanding science content, but the understanding is confined to the tools and tasks employed.

Introduction

While much research has been devoted to the area of how learners think or manipulate materials under certain context, how learning materials contribute to learning processes and how learners appropriate energy in minds-on or hands-on, less attention has been paid to examining the structure of learning tools and the characteristics of learning tasks and their consequences in learning. Educators often advocate for providing a rich set of activities with hands-on materials, and are aware these activities will not necessarily lead to conceptual growth (Carter, Westbrook, & Thompkins, 1999; Lazarowitz & Tamir, 1994). But the mechanism of the constraints of such activities and the nuances of the advantages are not carefully investigated.

In the paper I will investigate the structure and characteristics of tools (hands-on materials or mathematical objects) and task structures (sequence and contents of tasks) and how they influence the learning processes for science teachers of K-8 in a professional development program at Washington University. On the one hand, I will focus on the conceptual growth of the teachers, especially two teachers, on the topic of balance based on assessments and class conversations; on the other hand, I will examine step by step the linkage between the teachers' conceptual progression and their manipulation with the balance beams.

Theoretical Framework

Vygotsky (1978) extended the notion of mediation of tools to signs (language in particular), which are an embodiment of the historical development of human society. He (1978) discussed the interaction between humankind and environment (natural and social) and its consequence in intellectual development. The main arguments focused on the genetic priority of language over thought in children's early intellectual development, which was a counter argument of Piaget (1970)'s genetic epistemology. Categorizing both in mediated activity, Vygotsky (1978, chap.4) distinguished signs from tools: tools are used to influence or change the external environment—there are consequences in psychological development though—while signs are used to control one's psychological behavior. In addition, signs are inherently societal, since they bear the purpose of human communication.

The distinction of sings from physical tools is important for theoretical discussion, but not the focus of the paper. I name both types of mediation—physical tools and abstract signs—tools. By definition, any object that is used with certain purpose is a tool. In hands-on activities, the tools include concrete materials; in minds-on processes, the tools include mathematical symbols and other abstract forms of representations. Tools are used to mediate higher level psychological functions. Any mediated learning is liberated through and confined by the tools that are utilized.

Another theoretical line in science education following Vygotsky's work is the Activity Theory (Engestrom, 1987, , 1999). The relationships among subjects, instruments, rules, community, division of labor and objects (activities) are depicted in the activity theory (Engestrom, 1999). A fundamental commitment of Activity Theory is that learning is essentially a social process. The internalization of mediating tools and signs is a vehicle to communicate with one's social community and natural environment. A problem is that internalization being realized, how creation and externalization can take place (Engestrom, 1999).

While acknowledging a broader social aspect of the learning activities (e.g., social interactions such as discourse among learners and instructors), in this paper I will put my primary focus only on the role of tools and task structures, which are elements of activities, in teachers' conceptual development of balance. I will examine how the task structures, proposed by instructors and symbolized social input, were internalized by the teachers. Also I will examine in the process of fulfilling the social expectations, how variations were carried on by the teachers.

Methodology and Research Context

Context

The data of the paper was extracted from a course for science teachers of K-8 on force and motion. The course is one of many courses which are a part of a continuing education certificate program in elementary science education and of a more extensive program leading to a master's degree in elementary science education. The course was 15 weeks long for 2.5 hours per week. Sixteen teachers were enrolled in the course (3 male and 13 female; 3 African-Americans, 1 Asian-American and 12 Caucasians). The average age of the teachers was 42.1 yrs (Std=12.4). The average years of teaching experience was 13.1 yrs (Std=12.1). There were three instructors, Jack, Pat, and Ann for the course who had been co-taught for about ten years. Pat was a professor at the department of physics, Jack was an experienced teacher and Ann was a science coordinator for a school district. As a team, the instructors believe there are two important aspects in learning science. (1) Learners are expected to understand the meaning of the operational definitions of scientific words. Therefore external physical reality is the key to inter-subjective understandings. (2) To bridge the understanding of complicated situations, learners build upon what they have experienced or can understand. In this, learning is a process of self-construction. The instructors carefully selected hands-on activities, aligned modules with the National Science Education Standards (National Research Council, 1996) and the state standards, implement research-based assessments, and emphasized the storyline of the physics content (Shen, Gibbons, Wiegers, & McMahon, 2005).

Data Collection and Analysis

The study used multiple sources of data. (1) With the consent of the teachers, I videotaped and took field-notes for each class. (2) During the course, pre- and post-assessments and three formative assessments were administered (only the first formative assessment was related to this paper). A coding system for the teachers was used to ensure that the results of the tests did not affect the final grades of the teachers and to protect the anonymity during the class discussion on the results of the tests. (3) Each teacher was required to write a journal every week, and all the teachers' journals were photocopied at the beginning of the class every week.

The study primarily focused on two teachers, Cindy and Kathy, since they were articulate and the focus of the camera. Their actions and conversations were recorded, which helped me understand how they made progress in understanding the concept of balance. Also, the results of formative assessment were analyzed, which reflected the common understanding of the whole class. The results of the class showed that Cindy and Kathy's understanding was not rare.

An appropriate unit of analysis is critically important and closely related to one's theory. For examples, Piaget chose schema, Vygotsky chose word meaning, and Wertsch chose mediated action (Wertsch, 1991). The unit of analysis of this study is a concept. A concept is not necessarily individualistic. It might be across individuals. Since I only focused on the concept of balance, all the data were extracted if they were related to the topic. This topic of balance spanned the first few weeks of the course. The videotapes on the topic of balance were all transcribed. The journals that were related to balance were compiled together.

Data and Findings

In the activity of balance beam, I will show (1) the progress of the teachers' understanding about the beam-balance, (2) the role of tool in learning, and (3) the role of task in learning.

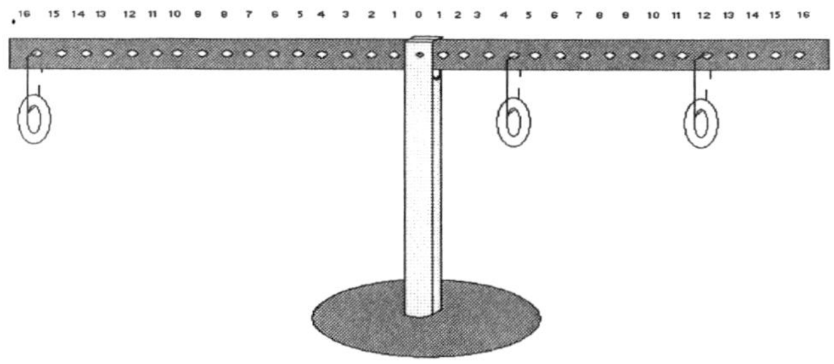

Figure 1. The beam balance used in the course.

Each set of the equipment included a pegboard beam with holes punched on it with equal distance (see Figure 1), a wooden base and support, screws that can mount them together, several washers, some paper clips. The purpose of the activity of the beam balance is for the teachers to be able to (1) balance a pegboard beam without trail-and-error, and (2) achieve the objective understanding: *the lever would balance if the product of mass and its horizontal distance to fulcrum was the same on both sides* (the *multiplicative rule*).

Step 1: One washer on one side, two washers on the other.

At first, Jack, one instructor, demonstrated how he balanced the beam with one washer on the left side at the 16th hole and two washers on the right side at the 5th and 11th hole, respectively. Then with the left side untouched, the teachers were asked to find as many re-arrangements for the right hand side that would balance. The first round of data is 2,14; 3,13; 2,15; etc., and the data were recorded in a table on the blackboard by the instructors. The teachers recognized the pattern of the data quickly: the sum of the positions (or the numbers of holes) of the two washers on the right side equals the position of the washer on the left side—the additive rule. The general rule was a natural result of the task designed, for the pattern was easily discerned and the data table well presented.

One observation was that some teachers did not abstract the variables, distance, but merely counting the number of holes. For example Nicole summarized, "what was on the right, mathematically, equaled the left." It is a strong signal that teachers like Nicole did not explicitly model the variable of distance. Nicole merely referred to the invariant quantity as mathematical number. Some other teachers referred to the general rule as counting holes (see the section *formative assessment*).

Step 2: Two washers on one side, three washers on the other.

The new challenge was to put two washers on the left at the 8th hole, then take three washers on the right side to balance the beam. The intension was that the teachers were able to induce the multiplicative rule. For example, if one puts two washers at the 5th hole and one washers at the 6th hole on the right side, it would balance the two washers on the left. And the equation would write as $Left : 2 \times 8 = 2 \times 5 + 6 : Right$

However, Cindy and Kathy's approach illustrated that many teachers still employed the additive rule. They balanced the beam by the combination of 2, 4 and 10 and 3, 5, and 7, and 4, 5, and 6. Cindy immediately noticed that they had the recent two combinations with a sum of 15 and the first combination with a sum of 16. Cindy suggested Kathy to redo the first trial to see if 15 would be a better choice—being consistent with the last two trials. They tried out the combination of 2, 4 and 9, as Kathy calculated. It worked: Kathy claimed that the beam worked with 16 for the left side and 15 for the right side. As a conclusion, Kathy summarized "On this [left] side, our distance, we have the 16 holes, in order to make it balance, we can only go about a distance of 15 holes on this [right] side."

In the first step, some teacher did not model the variable of distance (and the results of the formative assessment will show that it was a common case). Their conception is based on the concrete experience of counting holes. I do not think it is that trivial. Distance can be measured in various ways: counting holes with equal intervals, using meter sticks, using one's feet. Each provides an instantiation of the concept of distance, but none of them can fully capture the concept of distance. When experiencing the measurements of certain variables, the learner should explicitly associate the measurement with the variable. In the second step, Cindy and Cathy did model the variable of distance, but none of them paid attention to the mass of the washer. This was the case for the majority. I will argue later that this result was embedded in the equipment setup. It was also the result of the design of the task order. Since in the first step the teachers had already come up with the additive rule, in later steps they merely tried to apply the additive rule they generated to new situations. The additive rule worked with most teachers (some variation with Kathy and Cindy).

Another interesting point was that Cindy and Kathy found in their equipment that the balance worked in an odd way: the sum of the holes for the right side should be one less than that for the left side (henceforth the one-less rule). This finding was due to the beam-balance they were using. According to their conversation later, Cindy and Kathy knew that the balance was supposed to have equal sums for both sides. It was evident that their choice to stick with the one-less rule was because they were seeking the rule for their own balance equipment, not balance scales in general. A general pattern for them only meant a rule induced from the specific activity they did.

Step 3: Three washers on one side.

The first two tasks were posed by the instructors. Now Cindy and Kathy wondered if this rule worked when they put three washers on the left side at 8—a new task posed by themselves. Cindy predicted that they needed *four* washers at holes that added up to 15 to balance since in their last trials they had *three* washers at holes that added up to 15 on the right side. This reasoning was based on the two configurations they had done as shown in the Table 1. The prediction was sound: on the left side, the number of washers that was set increased from one, two to three; on the right side, the number of washers increased from two, three to four and the sum of holes was kept as 15. But Cindy did not notice the sum of holes on the left side had changed. This was because she did not do the calculation in their previous trials—Kathy did—and therefore she did not pay much attention to it.

Table 1. Cindy's prediction for the right side based on step 1 and 2.

Step	Left Side		Right Side	
	# of Washers	Sum of holes	# of Washers	Sum of holes
1- data	1 (at 16)	16	2	15
2- data	2 (at 8, 8)	16	3	15
3- Prediction	3 (Kathy: at 8, 8, 8) 3 (Cindy: not clear)	-	4	15

Kathy was aware that the sum of the holes on left side had changed. She reminded Cindy that if they added one more washer, the sum of holes on the left side was going to be 24. Cindy agreed and predicted immediately that on the right side the sum should be 23, according to the one-less rule they produced previously.

The negotiation of the task was not over yet. Cindy was unhappy about Kathy's plan of hanging three washers on the left side at the 8th hole. She noticed that Jack first hung one washer on 16, then two washers on 8. The position was in half while the sum was still 16. So the impression was in the next step they ought to use (1) the 4th hole (position in half) with (2) a number of washers that gave the sum of 16 (sum in constant) (see Table 2). Kathy did not agree that they should keep the sum as constant. She reasoned that the number of washers should increase one on each time, hence the current step should use three washers. Unfortunately, it was not possible for them to "do three into 16." That is, if sticking with Cindy's condition that the sum should be kept as 16, Kathy got 16/3 as the position of the hole. This was not an integer, hence not applicable to the equipment as given—the holes were already punched—unless they were not using the holes to hang washers. Cindy gave in and agreed to carry out Kathy's original plan, hanging three washers at the 8th hole.

Table 2. Proposed task for next step based on step 1 and 2.

Step	Left Side		
	# of Washers	Position of hole	Sum of holes
1	1	16	16
2	2	8	16
3 (Kathy's)	3	16/3	16
3 (Cindy's)	4	4	16

Having reached an agreement about hanging three washers at the 8th hole on the left side as the next step, Cindy and Kathy first tried the configuration 15, 5, and 4 (sum=24) on the right side and it was balanced. Cindy moved the washer from 15 to 14, it was still balanced. Inspired by this move, they tried a combination of 12, 6, and 5 (sum=23). Again, this confirmed what they found in the previous step that the sum on the right side should be one less than the sum on the left side.

In the three steps, we see how the equipments brought benefits (learn the rule that regulates the beam balance) as well as constraints. In particular, they influenced the generalizations and subsequent models in the following way. (1) When Kathy wanted to do three washers with a sum of 16, she found it not possible (unless they just hung it on the beam, not at any holes). This was because the holes on the beam were already punched, which limited the choices of the positions of the washers. (2) The one-less rule they induced was highly affected by their balance beam. Because of the limited precision of the balance, one was not able to discern the variance of a one-hole movement. (3) The additive rule was induced mostly because of the unit mass they were using, which in effect made weight an invisible variable functioning in units of one.

Also, we see that the task structures naturally shaped the learning outcome. In the first step, the task was fairly easy and the teachers generated the additive rule quickly. In the following steps, the teachers just applied what they had found out. Since Cindy and Kathy had an amendment of their first rule (right side has to be one less) because of the tool they employed, in the last step, they tried to test the revised additive rule. The expected multiplicative rule was not generated. Though the instructors hoped that the setup of the second step would elicit the multiplicative rule, the previous step had blueprinted the outcome.

Step 4: Summarizing.

Nonetheless, Kathy introduced multiplication in her summarization. But Cindy reminded Kathy the additive rule was the more basic rule for them according to the activity. Here they argued:

> Kathy: Hole *times* washer
> Cindy: It's the number of the washers *times*
> Kathy: The hole they're in, *times* the hole that they're in.
> Cindy: No, it's *not times* the hole they're in, cuz that only works at, the *total*, (Kathy: It's the *total*) the *total* of the holes they're in,
> Kathy: The *total* of holes on right, on left,
> Cindy: It's the *total* of the holes, yeah washers are in,
> Kathy: Equals *total*, equals, is
> Cindy: Is *total* going to be one more,
> Kathy: Yes, that's going to be one more, the *total* on the left

The use of the term of "times" was shifted to "total" after Cindy pointed out that the additive rule was more generally applicable. The multiplicative rule was only needed in the situations where more than one washer was hung on the same hole. The general rule, the multiplicative rule, was a "special" case for them.

The additive rule arises naturally from the equipment used. The activity employs washers (with the same size and mass) as standard units of weight, hence in the formula of the general rule for the beam balance the mass of the washers can be cancelled out as shown below.[7]

$$left: m_1 \times d_1 + m_2 \times d_2 + ... = right: m_1 \times d_1 + m_2 \times d_2 + ...$$

$$\text{since } left: m_1 = m_2 = ... = m = right: m_1 = m_2 = ...$$

$$\Rightarrow left: d_1 + d_2 + ... = right: d_1 + d_2 + ...$$

Therefore, in this activity the multiplicative rule is equivalent to the additive rule. But the additive rule was more straightforward. Especially, after the first step when the additive rule was induced, the teachers held on it and applied it for different configurations.

Formative Assessment

The first question of formative assessment 1 (two weeks later) asked "what is your general rule?" All the teachers who stated their general rules mentioned the word "equal"—they understood there was an invariant involved. Table 3 summarizes the teachers' responses to the second part in question one.

Table 3. Teachers' responses to formative assessment 1.

The variable whose sum should be equal	Number of teachers
Number (of holes)	5
Distance (from fulcrum)	4
Weight	1
Mass and distance	2
N/A	4

No one indicated that the conserved variable was the sum of the product of each mass and its distance. Therefore, the objective understanding of the unit was not reached for the class.

Discussions

Achievement notwithstanding, the objective understanding, *the lever would balance if the product of mass and its horizontal distance to fulcrum was the same on both sides* (the *multiplicative rule*), has not been reached by most teachers. In the following discussion, I will explain why this is the case by two types of barriers.

Internal Barrier

There are two types of barriers in the activity: internal and external with respect to the activity. The internal barriers have the tendency to prevent any individual from succeeding; it is inherently embedded in the activity. The external barriers are generated by the learners; it is outside of the activity. In real learning processes, these two types of barriers often occur concurrently and are hard to distinguish.

The internal problem has two parts. The first part arises from the equipment used in a task. The activity employs washers as standard units of weight, hence in the formula of the general rule for the beam balance the mass of the washers can be factored out as shown in the section *Step 4: Summarizing*. Therefore, in this activity the multiplicative rule is mathematically equivalent to the additive rule. In fact, some teachers thought the additive rule was more general than the multiplicative rule because they did not model the variable of mass. The second part of the internal barrier is the task structure. In fact, when the instructors posed the second task (step 2), they asked the teachers to set two washers on one side and to hang three washers on the other to balance the beam. If the two washers were hang on a position that the sum of the positions of the two washers could be divided exactly by 3, say, the 6th hole (sum=12) instead of the 8th hole (sum=16), then the teachers would be able to hang three washers on the other side in one hole, say the 4th hole. This amendment could allow the teachers to induce a rule closer to the multiplicative one because they could summarize the data in a form as: 2(weight) x 6(position) = 3 (weight) x 4 (position).

External Barrier

The external barrier is external to the task but closely related to the learners. Again there are two parts in the external barrier. The first aspect lies in the way the learners manipulate the objects. This is of course closely connected with the mental states of the learners and with the internal barriers of the activity. But even with the right thoughts and appropriate equipment, there are still problems of manipulation. Mostly, these are just mal-manipulation and somewhat accidental. For example, errors in mathematical calculation, not full implementation of a plan, etc.

The other aspect of the external problem lies in representation. For the multiplicative rule, if one uses sentences, it is really laborious to remember. Additionally, there is a problem of unpacking an abstract representation. In the beam balance activity, one instructor, Pat, also provided a compact formula, $\sum_{i}^{left} m_i \cdot d_i = \sum_{j}^{right} m_j \cdot d_j$ without explaining the formula in detail. When applying the formula, some teachers calculated incorrectly: instead of calculating the products for each mass and then adding them together finally, they added all the masses together and added all the distance together and then multiplied the two sums. The result of the calculation contradicted their experimental data and the teachers were confused. In brief, the teachers have difficulties in unpacking the compacted formula.

In summary, the internal barriers include the materials and the structure of activities; the external barriers include the way subjects carry out the activity and the way the subjects represent (or read the representation) their knowledge.

Conclusion

In the paper, I examined the progress and difficulties of the teachers of K-8 in manipulating beam-balance and understanding the concept of balance in a force and motion course. The following problems were found in the balance activity. (1) Because of the hands-on experience with the balance activity, teachers' general rules rely heavily on the contextualized situation—counting holes. The variable of distance is not modeled. For some teachers, the referent of their general rule was referred to the particular balance scale they used. A general referent was not in consideration. (2) Due to the setup of the activity (equipment and task), teachers' general rules are bonded with the additive rule instead of the more general multiplicative rule. The variable of weight is not modeled. (3) Teachers have not mastered a compact mathematical formula. The succinct mathematical model is not mastered. I argue that these difficulties will keep arising if the role of the tools is not carefully investigated.

At a more general level, I have shown the ways of which the tools and tasks used in the balance activity provided both advantages and constraints. I propose that the learning tools, hands-on materials or minds-on equations, and the instructional tasks can either assist or constrain learning. That is, hands-on experience provides the concrete grasp of the concepts developed, but the objects of the hands-on experience might limit the learning with the concreteness. High level representation liberates learners from concrete and contextualized situations when they conduct abstract thinking, but the unfamiliarity with the objects of the higher level representation might prevent leaner from understanding the basic meaning.

The intention of the paper is not to provoke the reader to think ways to fix the instruction in this particular case—change the task structure, use different tools. I believe there must be better ways to do the instruction. My concern is more about learning in general. Since the advantages and constraints are inherently bonded with the tools and task structures, each time when one introduces new ways to fix an unsuccessful instruction, one introduces new constraints. Therefore, I suggest that in any science inquiry activities, the properties of learning tools and the structure of tasks be examined carefully. We should not assume that learners have acquired the necessary skills of using learning tools, nor shall we assume that learning tasks that we designed lead to the objective understandings automatically. I believe that a high level of awareness of the structure of tasks and characteristics of tools will free learners from the inherent limitations of the activities.

Reference

Carter, G., Westbrook, S. L., & Thompkins, C. D. (1999). Examining Science Tools as Mediators of Students' Learning about Circuits. *Journal of Research in Science Teaching, 36*(1), 89-105.

Engestrom, Y. (1987). *Learning by expanding: An activity theoretical approach to developmental research.* Helsinki, Finland: Orienta-Konsultit Oy.

Engestrom, Y. (1999). Activity theory and individual and social transformation. In Y. Engestrom, R. Miettinen & R.-l. Punamaki (Eds.), *Perspectives on Activity Theory* (pp. 19-38). New York: Cambridge University Press.

Lazarowitz, R., & Tamir, P. (1994). Research on using laboratory instruction in science. In D. Gabel (Ed.), *Handbook of research on science teaching and learning* (pp. 94-130). New York: Macmillan.

National Research Council. (1996). *National Science Education Standards.* Washington, DC: National Academy Press.

Piaget, J. (1970). *Genetic epistemology.* New York: Columbia University Press.

Shen, J., Gibbons, P. C., Wiegers, J. F., & McMahon, A. (2005). *A Framework of a professional development program for K-8 science teachers.* Paper presented at the National Association for Research in Science Teaching Dallas, TX.

Vygotsky, L. S. (1978). *Mind in Society: The development of higher mental processes* (A. Kozulin, Trans.). Cambridge, MA: Harvard University Press.

Wertsch, J. V. (1991). *Voices of the mind: a sociocultural approach to mediated action* (Paperback ed.). Cambridge, MA: Harvard University Press.

Acknowledgements

This material is based upon work supported by the National Science Foundation under Award No. ESI-0227619. Any opinions, findings, and conclusions or recommendations expressed in this publication are those of the author and do not necessarily reflect the views of the National Science Foundation.

Effects of Handheld Games on Students Learning in Mathematics

Namsoo Shin, University of Michigan
School of Education 4031SEB, 610 E. University, Ann Arbor, MI 48109-1259, namsoo@umich.edu
Cathleen Norris, University of North Texas,
Department of Technology and Cognition, PO Box 311335, Denton, TX 76203, norris@unt.edu
Elliot Soloway, University of Michigan
Dept of EECS, College of Engineering, 2200 Bonisteel, 3106 ERB, Ann Arbor, MI 48109, soloway@umich.edu

The main purpose of this study was to investigate the effects of handheld gaming on student learning in mathematics. During the four-month instructional period, 50 2nd grade students from three classes used a handheld *Skills Arena* software program or paper-based flash cards under various conditions depending on their teacher's preference. Overall results proved that the handheld game activity in the classroom was beneficial to students in learning mathematics, especially for low-ability students, regardless of gender and ethnic background. In a non–experimental, correlational analysis, the results reveal that handheld game scores and attitude toward mathematics correlated significantly to students' scores on a mathematic test. In the results of a quasi-experimental control-group design with Repeated Measures, handheld gaming students outperformed students who did not use a handheld game on a mathematic test. Additionally, handheld low-level students outperformed those who did not use a handheld game on the same test.

Handheld devices in K-12 education have a great potential to improve teaching and learning. The essential value of a handheld learning environment is that every student has immediate access to a learning tool in a small and mobile package (Norris & Soloway, 2003). The high mobility of handheld devices enables students to be lifelong–learners with no limit of time and place (Crawford, Vahey, Lewis, & Toyama, 2002; Norris & Soloway, 2003). Educational programs have been developed to attain maximum benefits from handheld devices in learning activities such as game–based instructional programs. Games have been incorporated in the classroom for learning and understanding complex subjects. A game is a set of rule-guided, goal-directed activities that have no real-world consequences (Crookall, Oxford, & Saunders, 1987; Dempsey, Haynes, Lucassen, & Casey, 2002). Essential features in a game environment are authentic fantasy contexts, rules/goals, and challenges (Gredler, 1996; Thornton & Cleveland, 1990). Game research proved that the game features enhance dynamic cognitive processes for meaningful learning (Garris, Ahlers, & Driskell, 2002; Pillay, Brownlee, & Wilss, 1999; Rieber, Smith, & Noah, 1998; Rosas et al., 2002). The literature review of games and handheld devices has shown that there would be promising benefits to student learning in handheld gaming environments. The results of handheld game studies proved that games on handheld devices are easy to use and allow learners to focus on activities because of the small size of the handheld (Zurita, Nussbaum, & Sánchez, 1999). However, there are very few studies about the use of handheld games in classroom settings. Empirical evidence regarding educational handheld games in classrooms is insufficient to support favorable effects of handheld games on learning (Dempsey et al., 2002). Hence, comprehensive empirical studies are needed to support the idea that handheld gaming can potentially have a substantial impact on teaching and learning.

The primary purpose of this study is two fold. First is to explore what aspects of learners' characteristics influence student learning in a handheld gaming environment. Second is to investigate whether educational handheld games could promote student learning. The specific research questions of this study were:

- What aspects of learners' characteristics (attitude toward mathematics, attitude toward a handheld game, handheld gaming performance, gender and ethnicity) influence student learning in a handheld gaming environment?
- What is the impact of handheld games in the classroom on student learning, especially for female and low–ability students?

Methodology

Participants

The participants of this study were 50 2nd grade students attending an elementary school near a large city in the Midwest. The students were primarily upper middle class and Caucasian. The 50 participants were from three classes and included 28 male and 22 female students. The three classes had 21, 20 and 9 students, respectively. The ethnic composition of the participants was 31 Caucasians, eight Asians, six African Americans, four others and one Hispanic. We lost one female student because she transferred to another school.

Materials

An educational game program entitled *Skills Arena* was used in this study. The program was designed to teach students about basic arithmetic skills (such as addition and subtraction). The games were designed using a handheld GameBoy™. In *Skills Arena* students can create their own character with their name for playing the game. They are able to choose their game type and level based on their ability and learning goals. The game has several options for speed level, game type and arithmetic task. Six speed levels, from the easiest to the most difficult, are presented in the form of cartoon characters. The game types are mental, extension and place games. The mental game is the easiest, dealing only with single digit numbers such as "___ + 3 = 10". The extension game is the moderately difficult level game. For instance, "300 + 400 = _____, or 260 - 50 = ______". The place game is the highest level using multiple digit numbers such as "245 + 563 = ______, or 437 – 36 = ____." Each game has three options for arithmetic tasks which are addition, subtraction, and mixed addition and subtraction. The arithmetic problems in the *Skills Arena* are composed of one, two, three, and four digit numbers. Students have to solve the problems before the questions fade out on the GameBoy™ screen. As the students answer a question, they receive immediate feedback as to whether they have correctly or incorrectly answered the question. The game displays a performance summary immediately after each game finishes. The summary shows the total number of problems solved, and the number of correctly solved problems in each game. It also tells the total number of solved problems and correctly solved problems in the games they have played over time (see Figure 1).

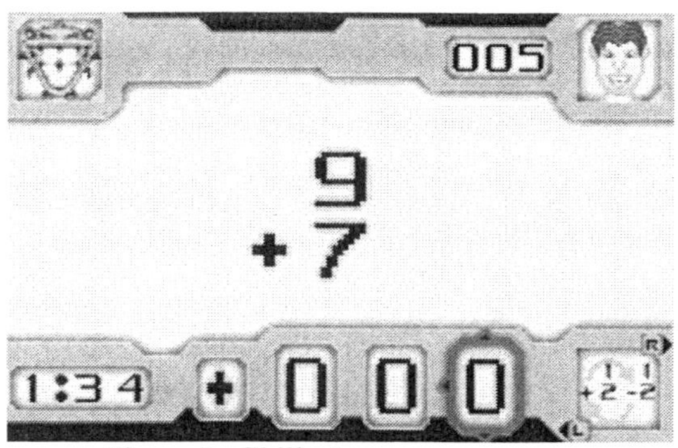

Figure 1. Skills Arena game screen

Treatment

Handheld Game Group

The handheld game group (HG) was composed of the 20 participants in class two. Students used a GameBoy™ and the *Skills Arena* software program. For the first ten days of the *Skills Arena* handheld gaming, the students played the game for 15 minutes, five times per a week. After that, they worked on the *Skills Arena* activities for 15 minutes, three times per a week during the five-week instruction. After five-weeks of game activities, the students played the game for 15 minutes, twice per week for 13 weeks. They were kept from playing the game except for the period of handheld gaming activities.

Card Game Group

The card game group (CG) consisted of the 21 students in class one. Students used flash fact cards for practicing basic arithmetic skills during a five-week instructional period. The flash fact card is a triangle shape that has three numbers, one on each angle, and either an addition or subtraction sign in the middle of the card. Individual students have their own cards. A pair of students was teamed up. One student held a card by hiding one of the three numbers, and asked the other student what number was hidden on the card. The other student in the pair answered the question using the two remaining numbers and the arithmetic sign on the card. They repeated the procedure with all the cards that a questioner had and then they switched their roles once the questioner was finished with the cards.

They exercised addition and subtraction flash card activities for 15 minutes, three times per a week. After five weeks of flash card activities, the students used a GameBoy™ and the *Skills Arena* software program for the remaining 13 weeks of the semester. The first ten days with *Skills Arena,* the class two activities were the same as those of the HG. After that, they played the game for 15 minutes, three or four times per a week. Further, the students were also allowed to play the game anytime they finished their other class assignments.

Delayed Handheld Game Group

The delayed handheld game group (DG) consisted of the 9 students from class three. Class three joined this study ten weeks later after conducting a pre-test. Students used a GameBoy™ and the *Skills Arena* software program for eight weeks. The directions for the handheld game activity were the same as those of the CG.

Measures

Mathematic Scores and Handheld Game Scores

A 70 item instrument was developed to assess mathematics skills. The test items were directly aligned with the second grade mathematics curriculum standards of the participating school. The test had two sections. Part I consisted of 50 questions with 25 addition items and 25 subtraction items to measure basic arithmetic skills. Part II of the test had 20 questions including 10 addition and 10 subtraction items to assess advanced arithmetic skills. Face validity for this instrument was verified by the teachers at the participating school. The students took Part I of the test in 15 minutes and Part II in 5 minutes. We administered this test before starting any gaming, after 5-weeks and after 13-weeks of game activities.

The *Skills Arena* game maintains a record of the total number of solved problems and the total number of correctly solved problems in the games students have played over time. Hence, the students' game scores could be extracted from the summary page of the *Skills Arena* game when the mathematics test was administered. The students' game score is the number of correctly solved programs in the *Skills Arena* game.

Attitude Toward Mathematics and Attitude Toward Handheld Games

The subjects' attitude toward mathematics was measured using the Attitude Toward Math Survey. This survey, developed by Pearce, Lungren, & Wince, was designed focusing on closely balanced representations of positive and negative statements with respect to young students' attitudes toward mathematics (Pearce, Lungren, & Wince, 1998). The teachers presented 23 statements orally to students. The students responded by marking yes or no to the statements on their answer sheet. Finally, an 8-item debriefing questionnaire was developed to capture qualitative data regarding participants' attitude toward elements of the game such as the interface of the program, the usefulness of the feedback for learning math, the sounds and colors of the game, the likeability of the game, their attitude toward handheld games and additional comments. The items were a combination of "Yes or No" and open-ended questions. The participant teachers checked the readability of the items for second grade students. A researcher conducted an individual interview with all the students in order to get participant responses on each item.

Procedures

The study was conducted for a four–month period during the spring semester of 2005. The pretest was done under the supervision of teachers and two investigators before the handheld gaming instruction was given. Two investigators conducted a one-hour training session for teachers and students before the handheld game use began. Most students had previous experience playing games on the GameBoy™. Students were able to play the game with the basic guidelines we provided.

During the five weeks of mathematics classes, all the students in the Handheld Game group (HG) used a GameBoy™ and the *Skills Arena* software program. In the Card Game group (CG), the students worked on addition and subtraction activities using the flash cards for the same number of hours as the HG students. After five–weeks of instruction, the teachers and the investigators administered the posttest. After the posttest, all students in these two groups used a GameBoy™ and the Skills *Arena* software program for 13 weeks following their teachers' directions. After 10 weeks and conducting a pre-test, the delayed handheld group (DG) used a GameBoy™ and the *Skills Arena* software program for eight weeks. The teachers and the investigators administered the final test in the three classes after the four-month handheld game instruction intervention. Finally, the teachers administered the survey of students' attitudes toward mathematics.

During the implementation stage of the handheld game, a researcher and an assistant researcher conducted a classroom observation for the HG and CG classes twice a week. During the five-week instruction, the main purpose of the classroom observation was to ensure that the *Skills Arena* game was implemented in the handheld game group as intended. For the flash card game group, the observation was to guarantee that students' arithmetic skill practice hours would be the same as the handheld game group. During the 13-week instruction, the classroom observation was conducted to confirm that the handheld game students played the game constantly in an appropriate way, and the *Skills Arena* game was precisely implemented in the flash card group.

Research Design and Data Analysis

This paper includes two research designs and data analyses to investigate the impact of handheld games on learning. The results of two data analyses can support each other to validate the analysis and provide concrete evidence to conclude the effects of handheld games on student learning. In Research Design One, 50 students from three groups (HG, CG and DG) were used for data analysis. This was a non-experimental, correlational analysis of the predictors of students' performance in mathematics. Multiple regression was used to test the relationship between mathematics scores and the predictor variables including attitude toward the handheld game, attitude toward mathematics, ethnicity, gender and performance with a handheld game (number of correctly solved problems).

In Research Design Two, 37 students from the two groups (HG and CG) were used for conducting data analysis. Three male students were excluded from the analysis because they did not take the pre–test. During the five-week instruction, the study provided information regarding the performance differences between the Handheld and Non-Handheld game groups. In the 13–week handheld gaming instruction, the results showed differences on student learning based on the playing time of the handheld game. This was a quasi-experimental control-group design with Repeated Measures. The data analysis for student performance was carried out as a Repeated Measures with two groups (Card game and Handheld game) as a between factor, and Time of Measurements (pretest, posttest and final test) as a within factor. Dependent variables were scores of the mathematics tests.

The Repeated Measures was employed to analyze gender differences as well. The analysis for low–level student performance was conducted using a Repeated Measures with only low–level students from both of the groups. The students were divided into low- and high-level groups based on their pretest scores. The low-level group consists of the students who had scores lower than 42 on the pretest. The sample size of each low–level group ($n = 10$ from HG and $n = 11$ from CG) was relatively small. Assumptions for the statistical measures were checked by the significant Levene's test for equality of variances among the groups. The data of the low–level samples met the assumptions. The statistical analysis was interpreted to examine the effects of the handheld game on the low–level students. Additional information is provided by the effect sizes obtained from the differences of two groups. Significance values given are *** ($p < .001$), ** ($p < .01$), and * ($p < .05$).

Multiple Regression Results

To understand how students in the three groups performed on the mathematic test, descriptive analysis of each group were conducted (see Table 1). In order to detect multicollinearity among the independent variables, we computed Pearson correlation coefficients for the entire sample. There was no potential of multicollinearity among variables. In the first step of the analysis, all the predictor variables, including attitude toward mathematics, attitude toward handheld games, scores of handheld gaming, gender and ethnicity were entered into the model simultaneously. Only two variables, handheld game scores, $ß = .42$, $t = 3.61$, $p = .001$, and attitude toward mathematics, $ß = .39$, $t = 3.30$, $p = .002$, emerged as significant predictors of mathematics test scores. In the second step of the analysis, to reduce the error term associated with the inclusion of nonsignificant predictors in regression models, we included only the significant predictors from the first regression analysis. In this step, attitude toward mathematics, along with handheld game scores, was a significant predictor of mathematics test scores. Handheld game scores $ß = .48$, $t = 4.32$, $p < .000$, and attitude toward mathematics, $ß = .40$, $t = 3.52$, $p < .001$, accounted for 45% ($p < .000$) of the variance in mathematics test scores. Overall, students who had higher attitudes toward mathematics and handheld game scores were more likely to achieve high scores on the mathematics test. Attitude toward the handheld game, gender and ethnicity were not significant predictors of mathematics test scores. The regression results from the first and second step analyses are summarized in Table 2.

Table 1. Mean scores among three tests by treatment.

Group		Pre test *M* [%]	*(SD)*	Post test *M* [%]	*(SD)*	Final test *M* [%]	*(SD)*
Card (n = 20)							
Math total (70)		37.05 [53]	(15.58)	39.95 [57]	(17.00)	47.60 [68]	(16.92)
	Basic (50)	34.80 [70]	(13.40)	34.85 [70]	(14.31)	39.30 [79]	(11.48)
	Advanced (20)	2.25 [11]	(2.65)	5.05 [25]	(3.86)	8.30 [42]	(6.05)
Game score	Total[1]	--	--	--	--	3560.00	(2850.39)
	Correct[2]	--	--	--	--	2371.03	(1677.05)
Ability	Low (n=11)	25.36 [36]	(10.85)	28.81 [41]	(15.23)	37.00 [53]	(15.92)
	High (n=9)	51.33 [73]	(3.50)	53.44 [77]	(4.61)	60.56 [87]	(4.42)
Gender	Male (n=12)	44.67 [64]	(12.38)	45.67 [65]	(13.49)	54.25 [78]	(11.46)
	Female (n=8)	25.63 [38]	(13.02)	31.38 [45]	(19.01)	37.63 [54]	(19.52)
Handheld (n = 17)							
Math total (70)		37.06 [53]	(14.31)	44.71 [64]	(12.62)	45.53 [65]	(15.22)
	Basic (50)	35.12 [70]	(12.32)	40.18 [80]	(9.75)	40.06 [80]	(11.57)
	Advanced (20)	1.94 [10]	(2.59)	4.53 [23]	(3.59)	5.47 [27]	(5.21)
Game score	Total	--	--	917	(414.82)	3369.59	(1403.14)
	Correct	--	--	770	(423.83)	2790.82	(1408.22)
Ability	Low (n=10)	27.00 [38]	(9.32)	38.50 [55]	(12.76)	38.80 [55]	(16.22)
	High (n=7)	51.43 [74]	(2.51)	53.57 [77]	(4.93)	55.14 [79]	(6.31)
Gender	Male (n=9)	39.22 [56]	(14.88)	43.33 [63]	(13.73)	44.67 [64]	(17.05)
	Female (n=8)	34.63 [48]	(14.22)	46.25 [65]	(11.97)	46.50 [66]	(13.97)
Delayed (n = 9)							
Math total (70)						46.78 [67]	(15.86)
	Basic (50)					41.33 [83]	(12.10)
	Advanced (20)					5.44 [27]	(5.05)
Game score	Total	--	--			4910.89	(2263.57)
	Correct	--	--			3286.33	(1806.89)
Gender	Male (n=4)					55 [79]	(6.06)
	Female (n=5)					40.20 [57]	(18.81)

Note. 1. The total solved problems of the game. 2. The correct answers in the solved problem of the game.

Table 2. First and second steps of simultaneous regression analysis for variables predicting mathematics scores.

Variable (N = 50)	B	SEB	ß	t	p
Game scores	3.88	0.00	0.42	3.61	.001
Math attitude	1.11	0.34	0.39	3.30	.002
Gender	-5.87	3.55	-0.19	-1.65	.106
Game attitude	2.24	4.16	0.06	0.54	.592
Ethnicity	-2.54	1.42	0.00	-0.02	.986
Constant	13.17	24.47		0.54	.593
First step regression analysis. $R^2 = .48$ ($p < .000$)					
Game scores	4.52	0.00	0.48	4.32	.000
Math attitude	1.12	0.32	0.40	3.52	.001
Constant	15.04	6.04		2.49	.016
Second step regression analysis. $R^2 = .45$ ($p < .000$)					

Violations of any assumptions of multiple regression analysis were checked in the overall plot and normal probability plot of residuals. Overall results of the residual graphs indicated that the samples of this study met the assumptions of multiple regression analysis and the multiple regression technique can be used to analyze the data of the mathematics test. Finally, we used the technique of cross-validation to determine whether the prediction equation has a chance of being successful when it is used with a new group of individuals. The results confirmed that the prediction equation of the mathematics scores works for students other than those who were used to develop the equation.

Repeated Measures Results

The results of the Repeated Measures show a significant Time of Measurement X Group effect $F\ (2, 34) = 5.61$, $p = .008$ in the total math scores. It indicated that a statistically significant difference in the mathematics scores' changes over time in the two groups (HG and CG). In the five-week instruction with the handheld game only for the handheld game group, the handheld game group (HG) outperformed the card game group (CG) from the aspect of improving scores. The HG and CG groups had similar scores on the pretest at the beginning of the instruction. The HG group scored higher than those of the CG group on the posttest. The HG students gained 11% (M = 7.65, SD = 7.84) from the pretest to the posttest. In the case of the CG group, students increased only 5% (M = 2.90, SD = 6.46) on the tests. The effect size of the total gain difference between the two groups was .61. In the next 13-week instruction period with the handheld game for the both groups, the CG group outperformed the HG group on gain scores. The CG students increased 11% (M = 7.65, SD = 6.15) from the posttest to the final test. The HG students increased only 1% (M = 0.82, SD = 6.54) on the tests. The effect size of gain difference between the two groups was 1.04 (see Figure 2).

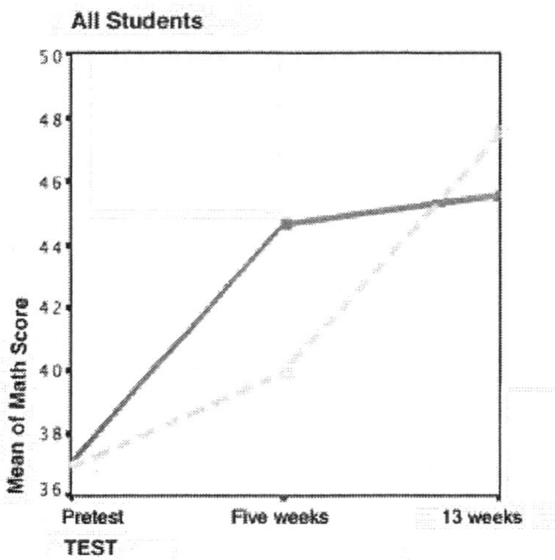

Figure 2. Overall students on math score.

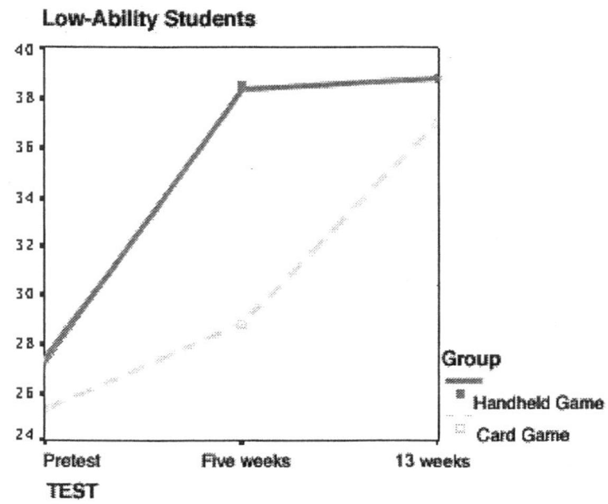

Figure 3. Low-ability students on math score.

The results of repeated measures with only low-level students revealed that there was a significant Time of Measurement X Group effect, F (2, 18) = 4.04, p = .036, indicating a statistically significant difference in the mathematics scores' changes over time in the two groups as well. The HG low-level students using the handheld game gained 16% (M = 11.50, SD = 7.12) from the pretest to the posttest. In case of CG group, students increased only 5% (M = 3.45, SD = 8.34) on the tests. The effect size of total gain difference between the two groups was .97. In the next 13-week instruction period with the handheld game for the both groups, the CG low-level students outperformed those of the HG group on gain scores. The CG low-level students increased 12% (M = 8.18, SD = 7.64) from the posttest to the final test. The HG low-level students increased almost 0% (M = 0.30, SD = 7.32) on the tests. The effect size of gain difference between the two groups was 1.03 (see Figure 3). However, there was no significant result with respect to gender difference on the test.

Discussion and Implications

The main purpose of this study was to investigate the effects of handheld gaming on student learning in mathematics. Based on the results of this study, it can be concluded that the handheld game activity in the classroom is beneficial to the students, especially low-ability students, in learning mathematics regardless of gender and ethnicity. It is consistent with previous research on handheld technology and games that indicates they could be an effective tool for facilitating student learning (Cordova & Leper, 1996; Knezek, 1997; McFarlane, Sparowhawk, & Heald, 2002; Rosas et al., 2002). Additionally, the results of analyses reveal that the students' scores on the mathematics test were not different based on ethnicity and gender. The gender difference was expected with the hypothesis that the handheld game would be more favorable to female students because the game's nature was not aggressive. However, the t-test results of the attitude scores revealed that there was no significant attitude difference toward the handheld game between 21 male and 16 female students. Therefore, a general conclusion that the handheld game would equally influence student learning without bias of gender and ethnic differences could be drawn.

There are several key findings from this study. First, on gain scores on the mathematic test, the students who used the handheld-based arithmetic game outperformed those who did not use it. Second, students who played the handheld game more than four times per a week outperformed those who used the game only twice a week. Also, on gain scores on the same mathematics test, low-ability students who had used the handheld game outperformed those low-ability students who had not used it. Lastly, the cumulative number of problems solved correctly as indicated by the handheld game scores and the students' attitude toward mathematics significantly correlated to the students' scores on the mathematics final test. Overall results prove that the handheld gaming environment impacts positively on students' learning in mathematics, especially for low-ability groups. Nonetheless, this study sample size was relatively small for conducting statistical analyses, especially gender and ability-level analyses. The small sample size might skew the result. Hence, more extensive study with a larger sample size would be required to generalize the results of this study about the effects of a handheld gaming environment on student learning in mathematics.

References

Cordova, D., & Leper, M. (1996). Intrinsic motivation and the process of learning: Beneficial effects of contextualization, personalization, and choice. *Journal of Educational Psychology, 88*, 715-730.

Crawford, V., Vahey, P., Lewis, A., & Toyama, Y. (2002). *Palm Education Pioneer Program – March 2002 Evaluation Report.*

Crookall, D., Oxford, R., & Saunders, D. (1987). Towards a reconceptualization of simulation: From representation to reality. *Simulation/Games for Learning, 17*, 147-171.

Dempsey, J., Haynes, L., Lucassen, B., & Casey, M. (2002). Forty simple computer games and what they could mean to educators. *Simulation & Gaming, 33*(2), 157-168.

Garris, R., Ahlers, R., & Driskell, J. (2002). Games, motivation, and learning: A research and practice model. *Simulation & Gaming, 33*(4), 441-467.

Gredler, M. (1996). Educational games and simulations: A technology in search of a (research) paradigm. In D. H. J. (Ed.) (Ed.), *Handbook of research on educational communications and technology* (pp. 521-540). New York: Macmillan.

Knezek, G. (1997). *Computers in education worldwide: Impact on students and teachers*, from http:// www.tcet.unt.edu/research/worldwd.htm

McFarlane, A., Sparowhawk, A., & Heald, Y. (2002). *Report on the educational use of games: An exploration by TEEM of the contribution which games can make to the education process*, from http:;//reservoir.cent.jui.es/canals/octeto/es/440

Norris, C., & Soloway, E. (2003). Handhelds impact K-12: The technology perspective. *Leadership, 3*, 55-70.

Pearce, K., Lungren, M., & Wince, A. (1998). *The effects of curriculum practices on first graders' attitudes, activity preference, and achievements in Mathematics*, 2005, from www.findarticles.com/p/articles/mi_qa3673/is_199810/ai_n8825517

Pillay, H., Brownlee, J., & Wilss, L. (1999). Cognition and recreational computer games: Implications for educational technology. *Journal of Research on Computing in Education, 32*(1), 203-216.

Rieber, L., Smith, L., & Noah, D. (1998). The value of serious play. *Educational Technology, 38*(6), 29-37.

Rosas, R., Nussbaum, M., Cumsille, P., Marianov, V., Correa, M., Flores, P., et al. (2002). Beyond Nintendo: design and assessment of educational video games for first and second grade students. *Computers & Education, 40*, 71-94.

Thornton, G., & Cleveland, J. (1990). Developing managerial talent through simulation. *American Psychologist, 45*, 190-199.

Zurita, G., Nussbaum, M., & Sánchez, J. (1999). *Usabilidad de Juegos Educativos*. Paper presented at the Taller Internacional de Software Educativo. TISE'99, Santiago de Chile.

Acknowledgments

The authors thank to the two teachers, Anne Proctor and Donna Ramsey who gave us valuable feedback and continuous support to collect high quality data from their classes.

Self-concept and self-efficacy in mathematics: Relation with mathematics motivation and achievement

Einar M. Skaalvik, Sidsel Skaalvik
Norwegian University of Science and Technology, 7491 Trondheim, Norway
Email: einar.skaalvik@svt.ntnu.no, sidsel.skaalvik@svt.ntnu.no

Abstract: In two longitudinal studies we examined if mathematics self-perception (self-concept and self-efficacy) predicted subsequent achievement over and above the prediction that could be made by prior achievement. We also tested if the impact of self-perception on subsequent achievement could be explained by students' goal orientation, interest, or self-esteem. Participants were 246 middle school students and 484 high school students in study 1 and 2, respectively. Achievements were indicated by final grades in two successive school years, whereas self-perceptions, interest and goal orientation were measured at the beginning of the second school year. Data were analyzed by means of structural equation modelling. The analyses showed that students' self-perceptions strongly predicted subsequent achievement over and above the prediction that could be made from prior achievement. However, there was no evidence that the effect of self-perception on subsequent achievement was mediated through students' interest, goal orientation, or their self-esteem.

In research on self-perception there is overwhelming evidence of a moderate to strong positive relation between achievement in a particular domain (for instance mathematics) and both self-concept (e.g., Marsh & Yeung, 1997; Skaalvik & Skaalvik, 2004) and self-efficacy (e.g., Pajares, 1996; Skaalvik & Skaalvik, 2004; Zimmerman & Bandura, 1994) in the same domain. Still, there is no agreement about the causal relations between achievement and self-perception (self-perception is here used to refer to both self-concept and self-efficacy).

In the self-concept literature there has been an ongoing debate about the causal relations between academic achievement and academic self-concept (see Byrne, 1996). Several authors have pointed out that causal predominance remains yet an unresolved issue (Byrne, 1996), and that it will be difficult to prove conclusively a causal direction in the relations (Wigfield, Eccles, & Pintrich, 1996). The self-efficacy literature has been less concerned with the causal ordering of self-efficacy and achievement.

Despite the long going debate there are few empirical studies examining causal relations between academic achievement and self-concept. Most of the studies of these constructs have used cross-sectional designs, making them unsuited as a basis for suggesting causal interpretations. Some recent studies have addressed methodological problems by means of more sophisticated designs (e.g., Guay, Marsh, & Boivin, 2003; Marsh, 1990a; Marsh & Yeung, 1997; Skaalvik and Hagtvet,1990). Some of these studies give support to a skill development model in early elementary school years, indicating that during elementary school years mathematics self-concept is mainly a consequence of achievement, but that it does not significantly affect later achievement (Skaalvik & Hagtvet, 1990). However, recent studies indicate that in high school achievement is affected by self-concept and that by this time there may be reciprocal causal relations between the constructs (Marsh, 1990a; Marsh & Yeung, 1997).

Like the self-concept research there are few empirical studies examining causal relations between academic achievement and self-efficacy. Most of the studies of these constructs show correlations between the variables. A number of cross sectional studies analyze models letting self-efficacy predict achievement. These studies demonstrate positive relations between these constructs, but do not provide evidence of causal ordering (e.g., Pajares, 1996).

Despite the ongoing debate about causal predominance there is a general agreement that self-perceptions are formed through experience in the environment. More concretely, there is substantial evidence that prior academic achievement affects subsequent academic self-perceptions. The critical question is, therefore, if academic self-perception affects subsequent achievement (e.g., Guay, Marsh, & Boivin, 2003).

During the last decade much research on motivation has focused on students' goal orientation. Goal orientation researchers typically differentiate between task-orientation (or learning goals) and ego orientation (or performance goals) (Elliott & Church, 1997). Several studies have shown task orientation to be positively related to academic self-concept (Middleton & Midgley, 1997; Skaalvik & Skaalvik, 2005). Studies of relations between performance orientation and academic self-concept are, however, less conclusive (see Skaalvik & Skaalvik, 2005). Research evidence also shows that task orientation is linked to a number of adaptive learning behaviors, for instance interest, seeking challenge, help seeking behavior, and deep processing of course material (e.g., Harackiewicz, Barron, Carter, Lehto, & Elliot, 1997; Skaalvik, 1997). We should therefore expect task orientation to be positively related to academic achievement.

Interest may be conceptualized as a component of intrinsic motivation. Previous research has revealed a strong relation between self-concept and interest (Skaalvik, 1997; Skaalvik & Skaalvik, 2004). For instance, Skaalvik and Skaalvik (2004) found a correlation of .80 between mathematics self-concept and a 7-item measure of interest in working with and liking to work with mathematics. Interest has also been found to predict deep level learning strategies (Schiefele & Krapp, 1996). Thus, we might also expect that self-perception may affect subsequent achievement through increased interest in the topic.

Historically, research on self-concept has focused on a general, overall, or global construct, often labeled "self-esteem" (see Marsh, 1990a). A problem with this nomothetic or unidimensional model of self-concept was that is was given a variety of definitions. The lack of a clear definition led to the construction of very different instruments for measuring a global self-concept, often labeled self-esteem. One approach was summing self-descriptions in very different areas, for instance academic, social, physical, and moral (e.g., Coopersmith, 1981). A problem with these measures is that they overlook the fact that the impact of particular self-evaluations on global self-esteem is dependent on how important each aspect is to the individual (Rosenberg, 1979). Another problem is that in such measures the meaning of self-esteem changes depending on the particular areas that researchers include in their instruments (Snow, Corno, & Jackson, 1996). Other researchers argue that self-esteem should be measured separate from area specific self-concepts. These researchers have therefore attempted to measure self-esteem by using items that do not refer to particular areas or contexts (e.g., Rosenberg, 1965, Marsh, 1990b). Implicit in these instruments is that self-esteem is defined as general self-acceptance, self-regard, or valuing of oneself. It therefore refers to more generalized affective responses to oneself (Rosenberg, 1979; Wigfield & Karpathian, 1991).

In the 1980s and 1990s self-concept researchers have emphasized the multidimensionality of self-concept (Byrne & Shavelson, 1986; Marsh, Byrne & Shavelson, 1988). The focus on the multidimensionality of self-concept in contemporary research has led to a lack of attention towards general self-esteem in educational research. Some researchers explicitly state that self-esteem may not be a particularly useful construct (e.g., Bandura, 1981; Marsh, 1993). For instance, Bandura (1981) contends that global measures of self-concept detracts from their power to explain behavior. Our interest in self-concept, however, should not be limited to the prediction of observable behavior. Research indicate that self-esteem is predictive of students' goal orientation (Skaalvik, 1997; Skaalvik, Valås, and Sletta, 1994).

Purpose of the studies

One purpose of the present studies was to examine if mathematics self-perception predicted subsequent achievement over and above the prediction that could be made by prior achievement. An additional purpose was to test if the impact of self-perception on subsequent achievement could be explained by goal orientation, interest, or self-esteem.

Method

Design

We designed two longitudinal studies, each with data collection a three points of time. Grades in mathematics were collected at time 1 and 3, at the end of two successive school years. Time 1 was in grade 9 and 10, respectively. Self-concept, self-efficacy, intrinsic motivation, goal orientation, and self-esteem were measured at time 2, which was in October in the second year.

In Norway 10th grade is the last year in middle school. Thus one important difference between the two studies is that the participants in study 1 attended middle school at all three points of time (9th and 10th grade) whereas the participants in study 2 attended middle school at time 1 and high school at time 2 and 3. The samples in the two studies will be referred to as the *middle school sample* (study 1) and *the high school sample* (study 2)

We tested both simple and extended models. The simple models are presented in figure 1. The students were given one final grade in mathematics at the end of each school year. Thus, in the models grades are represented by observed variables. Self-perception is in the models a latent variable indicated by self-concept and self-efficacy. This solution was based on previous research showing that at the domain level of specificity, self-concept and self-efficacy beliefs may not be separable (e.g., Pajares, 1996; Skaalvik & Bong, 2003; Skaalvik & Rankin, 1996).

Measures

Self-concept in mathematics was in both study 1 and 2 defined as the general feeling of doing well or poorly in mathematics in school, and measured by a modified six-item version of the mathematics subscale of the Self-description Questionnaire II (Marsh, 1990b). Math self-concept was measured without reference to any particular context. Examples of items are: "I always do well in Mathematics" and "Mathematics is easy for me." Response categories were: false, mostly false, sometimes false/sometimes true, mostly true, and true and responses to each item were scored 1 to 5 with 5 indicating the highest self-concept. Cronbach's alphas were .91 and .95 for the scales used in study 1 and 2, respectively.

Mathematics self-efficacy at the domain level of specificity was in both studies measured by a five-item scale adapted from Zimmerman and Bandura (1994) asking the students to indicate on a 10-point scale how certain they were that they would get a grade better than 1, better than 2 etc. in mathematics (grades in Norwegian schools are given on a scale from 1 to 6 with 6 as the best grade). Cronbach's alphas were .88 and .95 in study 1 and 2, respectively.

Intrinsic motivation was only measured in study 1. It vas specified as interest in working with mathematics and was measured by a four-item interest scale representing a short version of the Skaalvik and Rankin (1995) Intrinsic Motivation Scale. Examples of items are: "I like mathematics" and "Working with mathematics is fun". Response categories were: false, mostly false, sometimes false/sometimes true, mostly true, and true and responses to each item was scored 1 to 5 with 5 indicating the highest motivation.Cronbach's alpha for the scale was .93.

Self-esteem was only measured in study 2. It was measured by a modified eight-item Norwegian version of the self-esteem subscale in the Self-description Questionnaire II. Examples of items are: "I have a lot to be proud of", "I like myself the way I am", and "I wish I were a different person". Cronbach's alpha was .88.

Two dimensions of *goal orientation* were measured in study 1 (task orientation and performance-approach orientation). In study 2 one additional dimension was added (performance-avoidance orientation). Each dimension was measured by a four-item scale presented elsewhere (see Skaalvik, 1997). Examples of items are: "In math classes it is important for me to learn something new" (task orientation), "I always try to do better than other students in mathematics" (performance-approach orientation), and "When I am in math classes it is important for me to avoid looking stupid" (performance-avoidance orientation). Response categories were: false, mostly false, sometimes false/sometimes true, mostly true, and true and responses to each item were scored 1 to 5. Cronbach's alphas for task orientation were .70 and .74 in study 1 and 2, respectively. Alphas for performance-approach orientation were .86 and .87 and Alpha for performance-avoidance orientation in study 2 was .85.

Analysis

We used structural equation modelling (SEM) by means of the AMOS program (version 5) to assess the adequacy of the theoretical models and to examine direct and indirect relations between the variables.

Results

Simple models

We first tested simple models including grades at time 1 and 3 and self-perception at time 2 (see Figure 1). The models had very good fit to the data both in the middle school sample (χ^2 (1) = 2.34, χ^2/df = 2.34, *CFI* = .99, *IFI* = .99, *TLI* = .99, and *RMSEA* < .01) and in the high school sample (χ^2 (1) = .236, χ^2/df = .236, *CFI* = .99, *IFI* = .99, *TLI* = .98, and *RMSEA* = .05). These results clearly demonstrated the adequacy of using measures of math self-concept and self-efficacy measured at the domain level as indicators a latent math self-perception variable.

In the middle school sample the correlation between grades at time 1 and 3 was .81. In comparison, the SEM analysis showed that the direct effect (standardized regression weight) of grades at time 1 on subsequent grades was .47, whereas the indirect effect through self-perception was .33. Thus, the results strongly indicate that the stability of grades from time 1 to time 3 partly was mediated through students' math self-perception.

In the high school sample the correlation between grades at time 1 and 3 was .65 whereas the SEM analysis showed no significant direct effect of grades at time 1 on subsequent grades (regression weight = .08, p = .06). However, a strong indirect effect (.57) was revealed. Thus, in the high school sample the results indicate that the stability of grades from time 1 to time 3 almost entirely was mediated through students' math self-perception.

Extended models

The extended models (Figure 2 and 3) had acceptable fit to the data: χ^2 (26) = 44.73, χ^2/df = 1.72, *CFI* = .99, *IFI* = .99, *TLI* = .98, and *RMSEA* = .05 for the middle school sample and χ^2 (42) = 128.14, χ^2/df = 3.05, *CFI* = .97, *IFI* = .97, *TLI* = .95, and *RMSEA* = .06 for the high school sample. These models revealed that the effect of the self-concept/self-efficacy latent trait on subsequent achievement was not mediated through intrinsic motivation, self-esteem, or goal orientation.

In the middle school sample both task orientation, performance-approach orientation, and intrinsic motivation was strongly predicted by self-perception. Still, these constructs did not predict subsequent achievement. In the high school sample task orientation, performance-approach orientation, and self-esteem was predicted by self-perception, but did not predict subsequent achievement. Also, in the high school sample self-esteem positively predicted task orientation and negatively predicted performance-avoidance orientation.

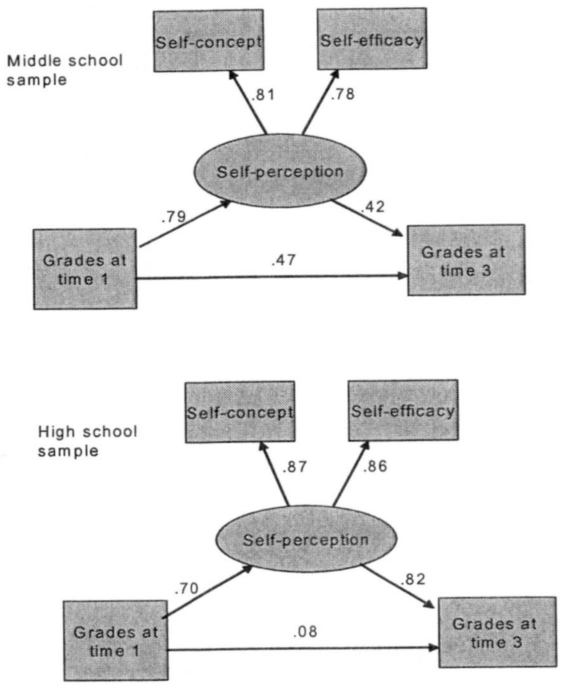

Figure1. Simple models of relations between grades at time 1 and 3 and self-perception at time 2.

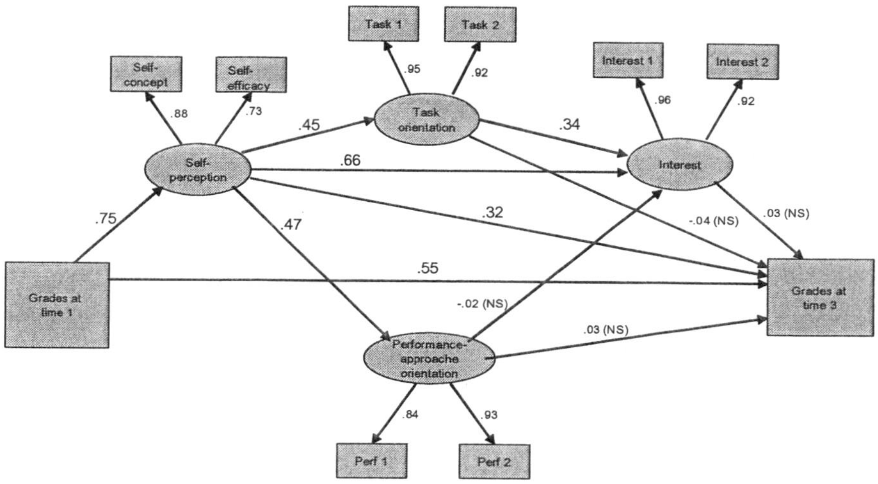

Figure 2. Extended model for the middle school sample

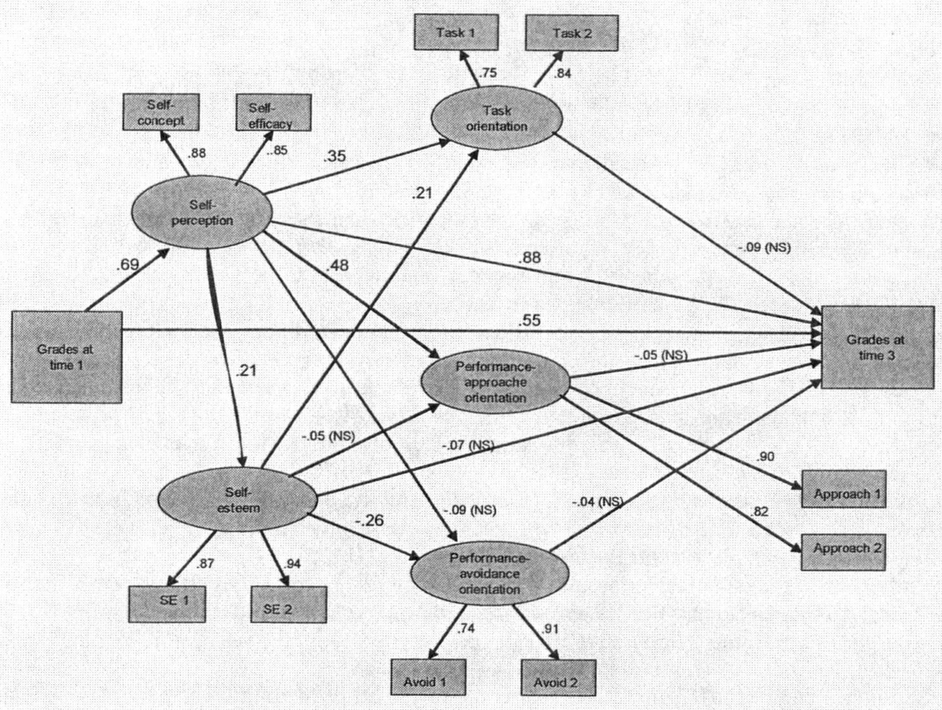

Figure 3. Extended model for the high school sample

Conclusion

The results of both studies strongly indicate that self-concept and self-efficacy are important mediators of academic achievement. In other words, the studies strongly support the notion that students' self-perceptions are important prerequisites for learning and achievement. In particular, after the transmission from middle school to high school we found a very strong effect of the self-concept/self-efficacy latent trait on subsequent achievement. A possible conclusion that should be tested in future research is therefore that self-perception is particularly important in new situations or contexts.

An important question is through which processes students' self-perceptions affects subsequent achievement. In the studies reported we were not able to show that the effect of self-perception on subsequent achievement was mediated through students' interest in mathematics, which is one component of intrinsic motivation, through students' goal orientation, or their self-esteem. Still, the impact of self-perceptions must be mediated through some psychological processes or study behaviour. Gaining better understanding of these processes is very important both from a theoretical and a practical point of view. Future studies should look at emotional variables like anxiety, but also motivational variables in terms of behaviour, for instance effort, endurance, and self-regulated learning strategies.

The study support previous research showing that students' goal orientation is related to self-concept and self-efficacy as well as to general self-esteem. Domain specific self-concept and self-efficacy are positively related to task orientation and to performance-approach orientation whereas self-esteem relates positively to task orientation, but negatively to performance-avoidance orientation. Thus, even if self-esteem does not predict observable behaviour, more attention should be paid to this construct in educational research

References

Bandura, A. (1981). Self-referent thought: A developmental analysis of self-efficacy. In J. H.

Bandura, A. (1997). *Self-efficacy: The exercise of control.* New York: Freeman.

Byrne, B.M. (1996). Measuring self-concept across the life span. Issues and instrumentation. Washington, DC: American Psychological Association.

Byrne, B. M. & Shavelson, R. J. (1986). On the structure of adolescent self-concept. *Journal of Educational Psychology, 78*, 474-481.

Coopersmith, S. (1981). *Self-Esteem Inventories*. Palo Alto, California: Consulting Psychologists Press.

Elliot, A. J., & Church, M. A. (1997). A hierarchical model of approach and avoidance achievement motivation. *Journal of Personality and Social Psychology, 72*, 218-232.

Guay, F., Marsh, H. W., & Boivin, M. (2003). Academic self-concept and academic achievement: Developmental perspectives and their causal ordering. *Journal of Educational Psychology, 95*, 124-136.

Harackiewicz, J. M., Barron, K. E., Carter, S. M., Lehto, A. T., & Elliot, A. J. (1997). Predictors and concequences of achievement goals in the college classroom; maintaining interest and making the grade. *Journal of Personality and Social Psychology, 73,* 1284-1295.

Marsh, H. W. (1990a). The causal ordering of academic self-concept and academic achievement: A multiwave, longitudinal path analysis. *Journal of Educational Psychology, 82*, 646-656.

Marsh, H.W. (1990b). *SDQ II. Manual & Research Monograph*. New York: The Psychological Corporation, Harcourt Brace Jovanovich, Inc.

Marsh, H. W. (1993). Academic self-concept: Theory, measurement, and research. In J. Suls (Ed.), *Psychological perspectives on the self*, Vol. 4, (pp. 59-98). Hillsdale NJ: Erlbaum.

Marsh, H. W., Byrne, B. M., & Shavelson, R. J. (1988). A multifaceted academic self-concept: Its hierarchical structure and its relation to academic achievement. *Journal of Educational Psychology, 80*, 366-380.

Marsh, H. W., & Yeung, A. S. (1997). Causal effects of academic self-concept on academic achievement: Structural equation models of longitudinal data. *Journal of Educational Psychology, 89*, 41-54.

Middleton, M. J., & Midgley, C. (1997). Avoiding the demonstration of lack of ability: An under-explored aspect of goal theory. *Journal of Educational Psychology, 89,* 710-718.

Pajares, F. (1996). Self-efficacy beliefs in academic settings. *Review of Educational Research, 66*, 543-578.

Rosenberg, M. (1965). *Society and Adolescent Self-Image*. New York: Princeton University Press.

Rosenberg, M. (1979). *Conceiving the self.* New York: Basic Books, Inc.

Schiefele, U. (1990). The influence of topic interest, prior knowledge, and cognitive capabilities on text comprehension. In J. M. Pieters, K. Breuer, & P. R. J. Simons (Eds.), *Learning environments* (pp. 323-338). Berlin: Springer.

Schiefele, U., & Krapp, A. (1996). Topic interest and free recall of expository text. *Learning and Individual Differences, 8*, 141-160.

Skaalvik, E. M. (1997). Self-enhancing and self-defeating ego-orientation: Relations with task and avoidance orientation, achievement, self-perceptions, and anxiety. *Journal of Educational Psychology, 89*, 71-81.

Skaalvik, E. M. & Bong, M. (2003). Academic self-concept and self-efficacy: How different are they really? *Educational Psychology Review, 15*, 1-40.

Skaalvik, E. M., & Hagtvet, K. A. (1990). Academic achievement and self-concept: An analysis of causal predominance in a developmental perspective. *Journal of Personality and Social Psychology, 58*, 292-307.

Skaalvik, E. M. & Rankin, R. J. (1995). A test of the Internal/External Frame of Reference Model at different levels of math and verbal self-perception. *American Educational Research Journal, 32*, 161-184.
Skaalvik, E. M. & Rankin, R. J. (1996, April). *Self-concept and self-efficacy: Conceptual analysis*. Paper presented at the Annual Meeting of the American Educational Research Association in New York.
Skaalvik, E. M., & Skaalvik, S. (2004). Self-concept and self-efficacy: A test of the Internal/External Frame of Reference model and predictions of subsequent motivation and achievement. *Psychological Reports*, *95*, 1187-1202.
Skaalvik, S., & Skaalvik, E. M. (2005). Self-concept, motivational orientation, and help-seeking behavior in mathematics: A study of adults returning to high school. *Social Psychology of Education*, *8*, 285-302.
Skaalvik, E. M., Valås, H. & Sletta, O. (1994). Task involvement and ego involvement: relations with academic achievement, academic self-concept and self-esteem. *Scandinavian Journal of Educational Research*, *38*, 231-243.
Snow, R. E., Corno, L., & Jackson III, D. (1996). Individual differences in affective and conative functions. In D. C. Berliner & R. C. Calfee (Eds.), *Handbook of educational psychology* (pp. 243-330). New York: Prentice Hall International.
Wigfield, A., Eccles, J. S., & Pintrich, P. R. (1996). Development between the ages of 11 and 25. In D.C. Berliner & R.C. Calfee (Eds.), Handbook of educational psychology (pp. 148-185). New York, Prentice Hall International.
Wigfield, A. & Karpathian, M. (1991). Who am in and what can I do? Children's self-concepts and motivation in academic situations. *Educational Psychologist*, *26*, 233-262.
Zimmerman, B. J., & Bandura, A. (1994). Impact of self-regulatory influences on writing course attainment. *American Educational Research Journal*, *31*, 845-862.

Shared Referencing of Mathematical Objects in Online Chat

Gerry Stahl[1,2], Alan Zemel[1], Johann Sarmiento[1,2], Murat Cakir[2],
Stephen Weimar[1], Martin Wessner[1,3] & Martin Mühlpfordt[3]
Virtual Math Teams Project, a collaboration of:
[1]Math Forum @ Drexel, www.mathforum.org
[2]College of Information Science & Technology, Drexel University, Philadelphia, USA
[3]Fraunhofer IPSI, Darmstadt, Germany
Gerry.Stahl@drexel.edu

Abstract. We conceptualize referencing as a primary means of establishing intersubjective meaning and, therefore, as an important consideration in supporting collaborative learning. What we call group cognition is a discourse-centered analysis of the interactional basis of collaborative knowledge building, establishing common ground and co-constructing shared meaning. This epistemological perspective has methodological, technological and pedagogical implications. It directs empirical analysis toward the manifold forms of referencing that constitute small-group communication. Studies of how students actually make sense of, adapt and adopt referential affordances in computational media are used to inform the design of educational software environments. In particular, we are developing an online service for groups of people to discuss mathematical themes. This paper looks at how a group of students used methods of referencing to co-construct geometric objects in a chat room with graphical referencing tools.

Epistemology of Referencing

Referencing is a primary means for humans to establish joint attention and to make shared meaning. Vygotsky, in a particularly rich passage, described the interactional origin of pointing as an example of how gestures become meaningful artifacts for individual minds through social interaction:

> A good example of this process may be found in the development of pointing. Initially [e.g., for an infant], this gesture is nothing more than an unsuccessful attempt to grasp something, a movement aimed at a certain object which designates forthcoming activity.... When the mother comes to the child's aid and realizes this movement indicates something, the situation changes fundamentally. Pointing becomes a gesture for others. The child's unsuccessful attempt engenders a reaction not from the object he seeks but from another person. Consequently, *the primary meaning* of that unsuccessful grasping movement *is established by others....* The grasping movement changes to the act of pointing. As a result of this change, the movement itself is then physically simplified, and what results is the form of pointing that we may call a true gesture. (Vygotsky, 1930/1978, p. 56, italics added)

The pointing gesture is perhaps the most basic form of deictic referencing. In its origin where the infant begins to be socialized into a shared world, the meaning of the gesture emerges interactionally as the participants orient to the same object and recognize that they are doing so jointly. In grasping, the infant's being-in-the-world is intentionally directed at the object; it is a being-at-the-object (Husserl, 1929/1960). When the mother joins the infant by transforming this grasp into a joint engagement with the object, the intentionality of the infant's grasp becomes intersubjective intentionality, constituting the infant and child as being-there-together-at-the-object (Heidegger, 1927/1996, §26). This fundamental act of collaborative existence simultaneously comes to be symbolized for them by the pointing gesture, which is practiced, repeated and abstracted by them together over time. The mother and infant become a small group, caring for shared objects by being-in-the-world-together and understanding as collaborative practice the symbolic meaning of the physical gesture as a referencing artifact.

As researchers, we can see new referencing gestures being created within interactions among collaborating people, particularly when their interaction is taking place via a new medium that they must learn how to use. In the analysis below, a chat posting—"What is the area of this shape?"—constitutes the participants in the chat as a group by designating them as the intended collective recipient and as the expected respondent to the question (Lerner, 1993).

The group is the intended agent who will work out the mathematics of the proposal to compute the area. Simultaneously, by referencing a mathematical object ("this shape"), the posting constitutes the group as a being-there-together-at-the-object. We shall see that both these aspects of being a group may necessitate considerable interactional work by the participants. Before the elicited answer about area can be given in response to the question, the group has to negotiate what it as a group takes the object to be. Also, it may require a number of actions for group participants to co-construct the shared object and their being-there-together-at-the-object. In attempting to do this, they constitute themselves as a group and they may also establish referential gestures or terms that take on a shared meaning of intending the new math object. The interactional work of the group involves making use of the resources of the environment that mediates their interaction. This is particularly noticeable in online interaction. Vygotsky's infant and mother could use fingers, gaze, touch, voice. Online participants are restricted to exchanging textual postings and to using features of the mediating software (Garcia & Jacobs, 1999; Stahl, 2005b).

As designers of online education, we are interested in understanding how students collaboratively create new communicative gestures or interactional methods, including ways of referencing objects for joint consideration. More generally, an interactional understanding of referencing and meaning making leads to a theory of group cognition—rather than individual cognition based on mental representations—as a basis for studying collaborative learning (Stahl, 2006).

Technology for Referencing in a Chat Environment

In our design-based research at the Virtual Math Teams project (Stahl, 2005a), we started by conducting chats in a variety of commercially available environments: AOL Instant Messenger, Babylon, Blackboard, WebCT. Based on these early investigations, we concluded that we needed to add a shared whiteboard for drawing geometric figures and for persistently displaying notes. We also found a need to minimize "chat confusion" by supporting explicit referencing of response threads (Cakir *et al.*, 2005; Fuks, Pimentel, & de Lucena, 2006). We decided to try ConcertChat, a research chat environment with special referencing tools (Mühlpfordt & Wessner, 2005). By collaborating with the software developers, our educational researchers have been able to successively try out versions of the environment with groups of students and to gradually modify the environment in response to what we find by analyzing the chat logs.

ConcertChat provides a variety of referencing supports for math chats:

A shared whiteboard allows chat participants to create drawings. As new objects appear in the drawing, an implicit form of referencing occurs. Participants typically refer with a deictic term in their textual chat to a new addition to the drawing, whose recent appearance for the group makes it salient.

When someone types a new chat message, they can select and point to a rectangular area in the whiteboard. When that message appears in the chat as the last posting or as a selected posting, a bold line appears connecting the text to the area of the drawing (see figure 1).

Similarly, a chat message can point to one or more earlier textual postings. ConcertChat includes a threaded view of the chat postings that, based on the explicit references between postings, displays them like a typical threaded discussion with responses indented under the posting that they reference.

Of course, one can also make all the usual verbal references: using deictic terms (*that*, *it*, *his*, *then*); quoting part of an earlier posting; or citing the author of a previous posting.

In May 2005, we conducted a series of chats using ConcertChat. We formed five virtual math teams, each containing about four middle-school students selected by volunteer teachers at different schools across the USA. The teams engaged in online math discussions for four hour-long sessions over a two-week period. They were given a brief description of a non-traditional geometry environment: a grid-world where one could only move along the lines of a grid (Krause, 1986). The students were encouraged to come up with their own questions about the grid-world, such as questions about shortest paths between points A and B in this world.

The chats were facilitated by a member of our research project team. The facilitator welcomed students to the chat, pointed them toward the task, briefly demonstrated the graphical referencing tool and then kept generally quiet until it was time to end the session. We are now analyzing the resultant chat logs in order to draw design implications for a full-scale online math discussion service.

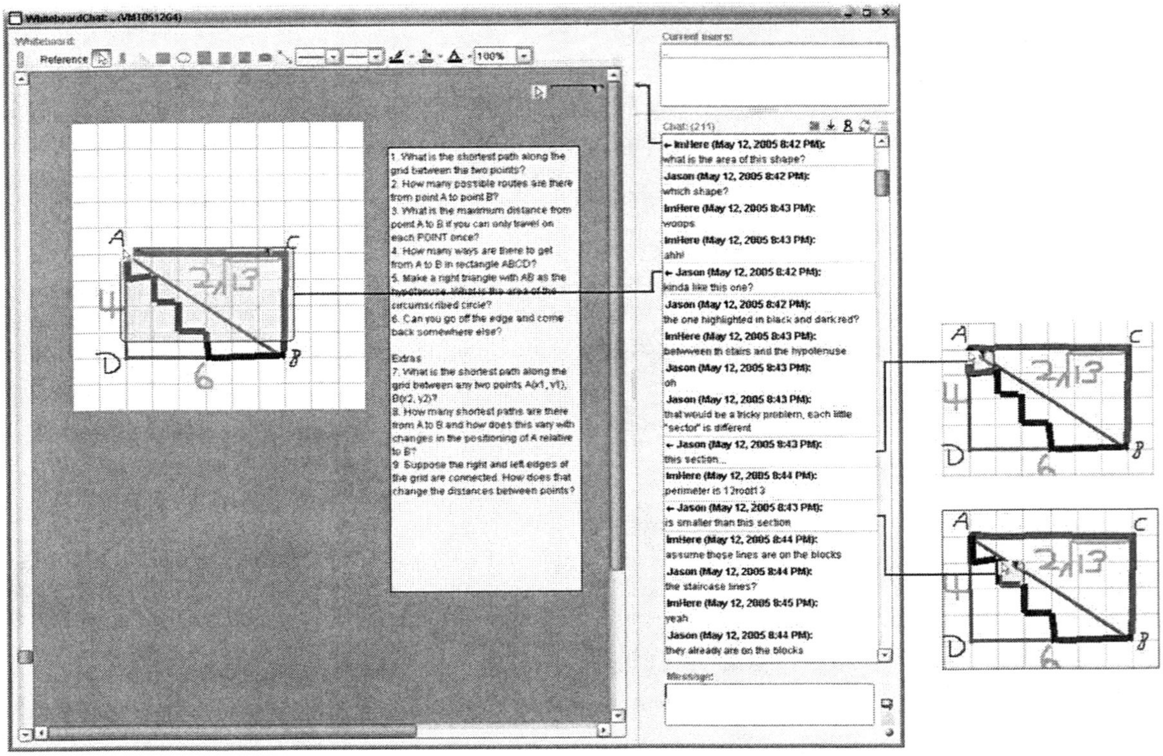

Figure 1. Screen view of ConcertChat with referencing. The image has been modified to show graphical references from chat lines 1, 5, 10 and 12 to the whiteboard. Only the reference from a single selected chat line would actually appear at any given time.

An Analysis of a Case of Referencing

The chat log excerpt visible in figure 1 is reproduced in figure 2 (with line numbers added for referencing in this paper). In this interactional sequence, two students discuss parts of a drawing that has already been constructed in the shared whiteboard. The students had created the drawing as part of discussions about shortest paths between points A and B in a grid-world. In particular, a red triangle, ABD, was drawn with sides of length 4, 6 and 2√13. A thick black staircase line was drawn as a path on the grid from A to B. In this excerpt, the students propose a math problem involving this drawing.

The message in line 1 of the chat (see figure 2) proposes a mathematical question for the group to consider: "What is the area of this shape?" This is accompanied by a graphical reference to the whiteboard. The reference does not indicate a specific area—apparently ImH did not completely succeed in using this new referencing tool. Line 2 raises the question, "Which shape?" pointing out the incompleteness of the previous message's reference. The proposal in line 1 calls for a response, such as an attempt to answer the question. However, the question was incompletely formed because its reference was unclear so it received a call for clarification as its immediate response. Lines 3 and 4 display a recognition and agreement of the incomplete and problematic character of the referencing.

Lines 5 and 6 offer a repair of line 1's problem. First, line 5 roughs in the area that may have been intended by the incomplete reference. It includes a complete graphical reference that points to a rectangular area that includes most of the upper area of rectangle ACBD in the drawing. The graphical referencing tool only allows the selection of rectangular areas, so line 5 cannot precisely specify a more complicated shape. The text in line 5 ("kinda like this one?") not only acknowledges the approximate nature of its own referencing, but also acknowledges that it may not be a proper repair of line 1 and accordingly requests confirmation from the author of line 1. At the same time, the *like* reflects that this act of referencing is providing a model of what line 1 could have done. Peer instruction in the use of the software is taking place among the students as they share their growing understanding of the new chat environment. Line 5 is accompanied by line 6, which provides a textual reference or specification for the same area that line 5 pointed to: the one highlighted in black (the staircase line) and dark red (lines AC and CB). The inexact nature of the graphical reference required that it be supplemented by this more precise textual reference. Note how the sequence of indexical attempts in lines 1, 2, 5 and 6 successively focuses shared attention on a more and more well-defined geometric object. This is an interactive achievement of the group (the interaction between ImH and Jas, observed by others and situated among the math objects co-constructed by all).

Lines 5 and 6 were presented as questions calling for confirmation by ImH. Clarification follows in line 7 from ImH: "between the stairs and the hypotenuse." Line 8's "Oh" signals mutual understanding of the evolving reference and the establishment of an agreed upon boundary object (Star, 1989) for carrying on the mathematical investigation incompletely proposed in line 1 (Clark & Brennan, 1991). Now that a complete reference has been co-constructed to a math object that is well enough specified for the practical purposes of carrying on the chat, Jas launches into the problem solving by raising an issue that must first be dealt with. Line 9 says that calculating the area now under consideration is tricky. The tricky part is that the area includes certain little "sectors" whose shapes and areas are non-standard. Line 9 textually references "each little 'sector'." *Little* refers to sub-parts of the target area. *Each* indicates that there are several such sub-parts and *sector*, put in scare quotes, is proposed as a name/description of these hard-to-refer-to sub-parts.

Clarification of the reference to sectors is continued by lines 10 and 12. These lines compare two sectors, demonstrating that they are different by showing that one is smaller than the other. Lines 10 and 12 reference two different sectors, both with the same textual, deictic description: *this section*. It is possible to use the identical description twice here because the text is accompanied by graphical references that distinguish the two sectors. Line 10 points to the small grid square inside of rectangle ACBD in the upper left-hand corner adjacent to point A. Line 12 points to the next grid down the hypotenuse (see figure 1). Because of the roughness of the graphical reference tool, lines 10 and 12 can only indicate the squares of the grid, not the precise odd-shaped sectors that are of concern to the group discourse. On the other hand, the textual clause, *this section* has been given the meaning of the odd-shaped sub-areas of the area "between the stairs and the hypotenuse," although it cannot differentiate easily among the different sections. The carefully constructed combination of graphical and textual referencing accomplished in lines 10 and 12 was needed to reference the precise geometric objects. The combination of the two textual lines, with their two contrasting graphical references, joined into one split sentence was necessary to contrast the two sectors and to make visible the tricky circumstance. In this way, the discourse succeeded in constituting the complicated geometric sectors despite the limitations of the tool and of textual description by themselves.

Line 13 responds to the tricky issue by treating it as a non-essential consequence of inaccurate drawing. By proposing that the group "assume those lines are on the blocks," this posting treats the difference among the sectors as due to the inaccuracy of the drawing of the thick black staircase line in not precisely following the grid lines.

1	ImH:	what is the area of this shape? [REF TO WB]
2	Jas:	which shape?
3	ImH:	woops
4	ImH:	ahh!
5	Jas:	kinda like this one? [REF TO WB]
6	Jas:	the one highlighted in black and dark red?
7	ImH:	between th stairs and the hypotenuse
8	Jas:	oh
9	Jas:	that would be a tricky problem, each little "sector" is different
10	Jas:	this section [REF TO WB]]
11	ImH:	perimeter is 12root3

Physical drawings are necessarily rough approximations to idealized mathematical objects in geometry. Lines drawn with a mouse on a computer screen tend to be particularly rough representations. The implication of line 13 is that the tricky issue is due to the inaccurate appearance of the lines, but that the faults of the physical drawing do not carry mathematical weight and can be stipulated away. But line 14 questions this move. It first makes sure that line 13's reference to *those lines* was a reference to *the staircase lines* that form part of the perimeter of the target area and of its different-sized sectors. When line 15 confirms that line 13 indeed referenced the staircase lines, line 16 responds that "they already are on the blocks"—in other words, the tricky situation was not due to inaccuracies in the drawing but the staircase lines were indeed already *taken as* following the grid for all practical purposes. The problem was still seen to be a tricky one once the mathematical object was clearly referenced and specified.

We see here that referencing can be a complex process in online mathematical discourse. In a face-to-face setting, the participants could have pointed to details of the drawing, could have gesturally described shapes, could have traced outlines or shaded in areas either graphically or through gestures with ease. Conversationally, they could have interrupted each other to reach faster mutual orientation and understanding. Online, the interaction is more tightly constrained by the affordances and more burdensome due to the restricted nature of the software environment. On the other hand, we have seen that middle-school students who are new to the graphical tools of ConcertChat, as well as to online collaborative mathematics, can call upon familiar resources of textual language, drawing, pointing and school mathematics to construct interaction methods that are seen to be amazingly sophisticated, efficient, creative and effective when analyzed in some detail.

Methods of Making Referential Sense

We have here only been able to look at some of what took place in a single effort to reference a mathematical object (see Mühlpfordt & Wessner, 2005, for other usages of the referencing functionality). In the series of chats that this effort was taken from, we observed groups of students engaging in a variety of other referencing methods within ConcertChat. Common methods included:

Graphical references to previous messages were sometimes used to make salient a message from relatively far back in the chat. Without the graphical referencing functionality, this would require a lengthy textual explanation justifying change of topic and quoting or describing the previous message.

Some students used graphical references to previous messages to specify a recipient for their new posting. If a student wanted to address a question to a particular student rather than to the group as a whole, he or she would accompany the question with a graphical reference to a recent posting by that student. (This was a use of graphical referencing not at all foreseen by the software designers.)

It is common in chat for someone to spread a single contribution over two or more postings (e.g., lines 10 and 12). In conversation, people often retain their turn at talk by indicating that they are not finished in many ways, such as saying "ummm." In generic chat systems, people often end the first part of their contribution with an ellipsis (…) to indicate that they will continue in a next posting. In ConcertChat, students sometimes graphically referenced their first posting while typing their second. Then the two parts would still be tied together even if someone else's posting (like line 11) appeared in the meantime.

Similarly, students graphically referenced their own previous posting when repairing a mistake made in it. The reference indicates that the new posting is to replace the flawed one.

In chat, where the flow of topics is not as constrained as in conversation, it is possible for multiple threads of discussion to be interwoven. For instance, line 11 starts to discuss perimeter while area is still being discussed. Graphical references are used to tie together contributions to the same thread. For instance, line 12 might have referenced line 10 graphically.

The graphical referencing tool is treated as one of many available referencing resources. Deictic terms are frequently used—sometimes in conjunction with graphical referencing (e.g., line 5).

In chat, as in conversation, sequential proximity is a primary connection. By default, a posting is a response to the preceding posting. Chat confusion arises because sequentiality is unpredictable in chat; people generally respond to the most recent posting, but by the time their response is posted other postings may intervene. Interestingly, the recentness of drawings may function as a similar default reference. Students frequently refer to a line that was just added to the whiteboard as *that line* without creating a graphical reference to it.

Of course, purely textual references are also widely used to point to postings, people, groups, drawings, abstractions and math objects.

The many forms of referencing in chat tie together the verbal and graphical contributions of individual participants into a tightly woven network of shared meaning. Each posting is connected in multiple ways—explicit and implicit—to the flow of the shared chat (Stahl, 2005a). The connections are highly directional, granting a strong temporality to the chat experience (hard to fully appreciate from the log). The being-there-together in a chat is temporally structured as a world of future possible activities with shared meaningful objects. The possibilities for collaborative action are made available by the social, pedagogical, technical and discourse context (world, situation, activity structure, network of relevant significance) (Heidegger, 1927/1996, §18). While the shared context is opened up, enacted and made salient by the group in its chat, aspects of the context appear as designed, established or institutionalized in advance. They confront the participants as a world filled with meanings, priorities, resources and possibilities for action. It is a situation whose features, meanings and co-inhabitants are initially largely unknown. Students who enter this world must choose to either become engaged or be silent and log out.

Pedagogy of Referencing Math Objects

In the investigation reported here, we tried to encourage relatively open-ended explorations of mathematical inquiry by online teams of math students. We presented them with a non-traditional form of geometry in which notions like distance, area or shortest-path have to be renegotiated. While trains of inquiry can go in many directions, in a collaborative effort each step of the path may be clarified and shared. New math objects emerge and develop out of the discourse, including geometric figures and terminology. In this study, the analysis of a snippet of this process in a concrete empirical case has suggested the centrality of joint referencing to collaboration. This may serve as an additional clarification of what is meant by defining collaboration as "a continued attempt to construct and maintain a shared conception of a problem .... an emergent, socially-negotiated set of knowledge elements that constitute a Joint Problem Space" (Roschelle & Teasley, 1995, p. 70). The persistent whiteboard serves as a "group external memory" that plays a useful role in grounding shared understanding at the meso level of CSCL problem solving (Dillenbourg & Traum, 2006, p. 122f), in contrast to Clark & Brennan's (1991) linguistic micro level. The intertwining uses of the dual workspaces of whiteboard and chat mirror the intertwining of problem solving and communication that is characteristic of collaborative learning (Barron, 2003, p. 310).

Widespread conceptions of math learning as the memorization of "math facts" or the mastery of formulaic algorithmic solutions are oriented to the routine application of arithmetic rather than to the creative process that inspires mathematicians. The history of mathematics as a branch of scientific inquiry and knowledge building is a systematic unfolding of new domains through the shared construction of new math objects, like complex numbers, fractals, curved spaces. To share these boundary objects (Star, 1989), mathematicians have had to define new vocabularies, procedures and representations for referencing objects that do not exist as such in the physical world.

People who do not understand mathematical references can scarcely be expected to share the wonder and excitement that mathematicians feel who can "see" (Goodwin & Goodwin, 1994) what is being referenced. It is likely that much of the general population simply does not share the understanding of what is referenced in most mathematical proofs and discussions. Since our goal is to increase mathematical appreciation and participation through opportunities for online math discourse, we are keen to understand shared referencing and to support it in our environments.

References

Barron, B. (2003). When smart groups fail. *Journal of the Learning Sciences (JLS), 12* (3), 307-359.

Cakir, M., Xhafa, F., Zhou, N., & Stahl, G. (2005). *Thread-based analysis of patterns of collaborative interaction in chat.* Paper presented at the international conference on AI in Education (AI-Ed 2005), Amsterdam, Netherlands. Retrieved from http://www.cis.drexel.edu/faculty/gerry/pub/aied2005.pdf.

Clark, H., & Brennan, S. (1991). Grounding in communication. In L. Resnick, J. Levine & S. Teasley (Eds.), *Perspectives on socially-shared cognition* (pp. 127-149). Washington, DC: APA.

Dillenbourg, P., & Traum, D. (2006). Sharing solutions: Persistence and grounding in multimodal collaborative problem solving. *Journal of the Learning Sciences, 15* (1), 121-151.

Fuks, H., Pimentel, M., & de Lucena, C. J. P. (2006). R-u-typing-2-me? Evolving a chat tool to increase understanding in learning activities. *International Journal of Computer-Supported Collaborative Learning (ijCSCL), 1* (1). Retrieved from http://ijCSCL.org.

Garcia, A., & Jacobs, J. B. (1999). The eyes of the beholder: Understanding the turn-taking system in quasi-synchronous computer-mediated communication. *Research on Language and Social Interaction, 34* (4), 337-367.

Goodwin, C., & Goodwin, M. H. (1994). Professional vision. *American Anthropologist, 96* (3), 606-633.

Heidegger, M. (1927/1996). *Being and time: A translation of Sein und Zeit* (J. Stambaugh, Trans.). Albany, NY: SUNY Press.

Husserl, E. (1929/1960). *Cartesian meditations: An introduction to phenomenology* (D. Cairns, Trans.). The Hague, Netherlands: Martinus Nijhoff.

Krause, E. (1986). Taxicab geometry: An adventure in non-Euclidean geometry. New York, NY: Dover.

Lerner, G. (1993). Collectivities in action: Establishing the relevance of conjoined participation in conversation. *Text, 13* (2), 213-245.

Mühlpfordt, M., & Wessner, M. (2005). *Explicit referencing in chat supports collaborative learning.* Paper presented at the international conference on Computer Support for Collaborative Learning (CSCL 2005), Taipei, Taiwan.

Roschelle, J., & Teasley, S. (1995). The construction of shared knowledge in collaborative problem solving. In C. O'Malley (Ed.), *Computer-supported collaborative learning* (pp. 69-197). Berlin, Germany: Springer Verlag.

Stahl, G. (2005a). *Group cognition in chat: Methods of interaction / methodologies of analysis.* Paper presented at the Kaleidoscope CSCL SIG Workshop on Analysis of Interaction and Learning (NAIL 2005), Gothenburg, Sweden. Retrieved from http://www.cis.drexel.edu/faculty/gerry/pub/nail2005.pdf & http://www.cis.drexel.edu/faculty/gerry/pub/nail2005ppt.pdf.

Stahl, G. (2005b). *Sustaining online collaborative problem solving with math proposals [winner of best paper award].* Paper presented at the International Conference on Computers and Education (ICCE 2005), Singapore, Singapore. Proceedings pp. 436-443. Retrieved from http://www.cis.drexel.edu/faculty/gerry/pub/icce2005.pdf & http://www.cis.drexel.edu/faculty/gerry/pub/icce2005ppt.pdf.

Stahl, G. (2006). *Group cognition: Computer support for building collaborative knowledge*. Cambridge, MA: MIT Press. Retrieved from http://www.cis.drexel.edu/faculty/gerry/mit/.

Star, S. L. (1989). The structure of ill-structured solutions: Boundary objects and heterogeneous distributed problem solving. In L. Gasser & M. N. Huhns (Eds.), *Distributed artificial intelligence* (pp. 37-54). San Mateo, CA: Morgan Kaufmann.

Vygotsky, L. (1930/1978). *Mind in society*. Cambridge, MA: Harvard University Press.

Acknowledgments

The Virtual Math Teams Project is a collaborative effort at Drexel University. The Principal Investigators are Gerry Stahl, Stephen Weimar and Wesley Shumar. A number of Math Forum staff work on the project, especially Stephen Weimar, Annie Fetter and Ian Underwood. The graduate research assistants are Murat Cakir, Johann Sarmiento, Ramon Toledo and Nan Zhou. Alan Zemel is a post-doc. The following visiting researchers have spent 3 to 6 months on the project: Jan-Willem Strijbos (Netherlands), Fatos Xhafa (Spain), Stefan Trausan-Matu (Romania), Martin Wessner (Germany), Elizabeth Charles (Canada). The ConcertChat software was developed at the Fraunhofer Institute IPSI in Darmstadt, Germany, by Martin Wessner, Martin Mühlpfordt and colleagues. The VMT project is supported by grants from the NSDL, IERI and SoL programs of the US National Science Foundation. The perspectives expressed in this paper are those of the authors, not necessarily NSF or others.

Fostering Scientific Habits of Mind in the Context of Online Play

Constance Steinkuehler & Marjee Chmiel
University of Wisconsin-Madison, 225 North Mills Street, Madison WI 53706
steinkuehler@wisc.edu, muchmiel@wisc.edu

Abstract: In today's increasingly "flat" world of globalization, the need for a scientifically literate citizenry has only grown more urgent; yet, by some measures, we have done a poor job at fostering the right *scientific habits of mind* in schools. Recent research on informal games-based learning indicates that such technologies/communities may be one viable alternative – not to teachers and classrooms but to textbooks and science labs. In this paper, we provide empirical evidence substantiating previous claims about the potential of games for learning and offer specific *design heuristics* that might inform their future production and use. Using codes based on AAAS benchmarks and Chinn and Malhotra's (2002) framework for evaluating inquiry tasks, we examine the scientific habits of mind that characterize online discussion forums of the MMOG *World of Warcraft* and the features of the game – both as designed object and emergent culture – that appear to foster them.

Scientific Literacy: More than Stones

In 1905, at a gathering of the world's greatest minds in the physical sciences, Henri Poincare reflected on the rapid progress of scientific inquiry and the means through which the scientific community at the turn of the 20th century and beyond would refine our understanding of the world. In his historical address, Poincare warned against the seduction of reducing science to a domain of seeming facts, stating, "Science is built up of facts, as a house is built of stones; but an accumulation of facts is no more science than a heap of stones is a house" (1905/2001, p.141). One hundred years later, his admonition against the framing of science as a "rhetoric of conclusion" (Schwab, 1962, p.24) still holds, with science scholars and educators from Dewey on repeatedly warning us against the teaching of science as only content rather than process. In Dewey's own words, "the future of our civilization depends upon the widening spread and deepening hold of the *scientific habit of mind* [italics added]... the problem of problems in our education is therefore to discover how to mature and make effective this scientific habit" (1910, p.127).

In today's increasingly "flat" world (Friedman, 2005) of massive globalization and technological interconnectivity, the need for a scientifically literate citizenry in the United States has only grown more urgent; yet, by some measures, it seems we have done a poor job at fostering the right habits of mind in our schools. Currently only one in five Americans are scientifically literate (Miller, 2004) despite mandatory instruction. In a recent study of contemporary classroom practice, Chinn and Malhotra (2002) found that standard "inquiry" activities not only failed to engender scientific habits of mind but in fact actually fostered epistemological beliefs directly *antithetical* to them. Recent assessment of high school laboratory activities by the National Research Council (Singer, Hilton, & Schweingruber, 2005) reach similar conclusions: science labs, long heralded as *the* site for engaging students in science practice, fail. Meanwhile, as our national quandary over how to teach scientific theory of human origins demonstrates (Chmiel & Owens, 2005), the misconception of science as "built up of facts" rather than intellectual practices only compounds, leaving the public increasingly hostile to the scientific enterprise itself (Elsner, 2005). Perhaps as Gates (2005) argued in his National Education Summit address, American schools have become obsolete: "Training the workforce of tomorrow with the high schools of today is like trying to teach kids about today's computers on a 50-year-old mainframe. It's the wrong tool for the times" (¶12).

Leveraging Online Play

But, if our educational system is not the right "tool for the times," what is? Despite dismissals as "torpid" and inviting "inert reception" (Solomon, 2004) in some mainstream press, videogame technologies may be one viable alternative – not to teachers and classrooms but rather to textbooks and science labs. Recent studies indicate that the intellectual activities that constitute successful gameplay are nontrivial, including the construction of identities (Gee, 2003; Steinkuehler, in press), collaborative problem-solving (Squire, 2005; Steinkuehler, 2006; cf. Nasir, 2005), literacy practices that exceed our national standards (Steinkuehler, 2005b), systemic thinking (Squire, 2003), and, as one might expect, computer literacy (AAUW, 2000; Squire & Steinkuehler, 2005). Games, however, are more than just the sum of their intellectual practices (as important as those may be); they are, in fact, *simulated worlds*:

> The first step towards understanding how video games can (and we argue, will) transform education is changing the widely shared perspective that games are "mere entertainment." More than a multi-billion dollar industry, more than a compelling toy for both children and adults, more than a route to computer literacy, video games are important because they let people participate in new worlds. (Shaffer, Squire, Halverson, & Gee, 2005)

As simulations, games allow "just plain folk" (Lave, 1988) to build situated understandings of important phenomena (physical laws, for example) that are instantiated in those worlds amid a culture of intellectual practice that render those phenomena culturally meaningful (Steinkuehler, 2006). Their potentials for learning have not gone unnoticed, and the last two years have witnessed a marked rise in interest across various academies in leveraging game technologies toward educational ends: the Woodrow Wilson Foundation's Serious Games Initiative, the Games, Learning and Society program at the University of Wisconsin-Madison, the Education Arcade project at MIT, the Games for Social Change Movement, and Stanford University's Media X "Gaming To Learn" Workshop, to name a few.

One genre of videogame in particular offers distinctive promise in terms of fostering scientific habits of mind: *massively multiplayer online games*. Massively multiplayer online games (MMOGs) are 2- or 3-D graphical, simulated worlds played online that allow individuals to interact, through their digital characters or "avatars" not only with the designed environment in which activities take place but also with other individuals' avatars as well. Previous ethnography of such online worlds demonstrates their function as naturally occurring learning environments (Steinkuehler, 2004, 2005a), yet the forms of scientific argumentation, model-based reasoning, and theory-evidence coordination that arise in the context of MMOG play warrant further investigation. In MMOGs, individuals collaborate to solve complex problems within the virtual world, such as figuring out what combination of skills, proficiencies, and equipment are necessary to conquer an in-game boss monster. As part of developing efficient and effective solutions, players are customarily expected to research various game strategies and tactics by consulting on- and offline manuals, databases, and discussions and by using such knowledge as the basis for in-game action. Thus, as part of standard gameplay (particularly beyond the beginning levels), individuals share their own hypotheses about what strategies work by proposing models for solutions, justifying their "theories" with evidence (such as tabulated mathematical results aggregated across multiple trials), and debating the merits of conflicting hypotheses – not as aimless contentious discussion (although there is a bit of that as well) but rather as part and parcel of the *collective intelligence* (Levy, 1999) amassed through patterned participatory consumption (Jenkins, 1992), the hallmark of interactive "entertainment" media such as games.

Innovative NSF projects such as Harvard University's *River City* (e.g., Dede, Ketelhut, & Ruess, 2003) and Indiana University-Bloomington's *Quest Atlantis* (e.g., Barab, Arcici, & Jackson, 2005) have begun to tackle the complexities of designing MMOGs for science learning, offering proof of concept of the argument presented above. Yet, as Lave and Wenger (1991) note, understanding informal contexts for learning is crucial if we are to forward educational theory and practice beyond the contexts we ourselves contrive. Therefore, in order to forward our understanding of the forms of scientific reasoning that emerge as a natural part of gameplay in informal MMOGs and the design features that appear to foster them, this paper presents an examination of an online forum discussion of the "off the shelf" MMOG *World of Warcraft*. In this investigation, we analyze a threaded discussion in which participants attempt to work out a best-fit solution to one of the MMOG's in-game mechanics: the "druid talent build." Using codes based on the AAAS benchmarks for scientific literacy (AAAS, 1993) and Chinn and Malhotra's (2002) theoretical framework for evaluating inquiry tasks, we highlight the scientific habits of mind displayed within the discussion and the features of the game – both as designed object and emergent culture – that appear to foster them. Our goal here is to move beyond arguments about the *potentials* of MMOGs for learning by ferreting out which *specific* scientific literacy practices emerge within such game-related online communities (and which do not) and then, based on those findings, take a first step toward developing *MMOG design heuristics* that might inform and enable future instructional design.

Data Collection & Research Methods

Context of the Research & Data Corpus

The context for this investigation is *World of Warcraft*, a successful MMOG released in November 2004 and currently boasting the single largest share of the market in North America and well over four million subscribers globally. The game is set in a fantasy world in which players of various classes (eight total) wander the environment hunting, gathering, questing, battling, and crafting in order to strengthen or "level" their character in various ways.

The data analyzed for this particular study consist of a threaded discussion that took place mid-October of 2005 on the "druid forum" of the official *World of Warcraft* website. Although there are a number of relevant online forums to be found, the official website alone features 24 separate forums totaling well over 40,000 separate, active threads; therefore, we chose to limit our data corpus by selecting a discussion thread that (a) was contained within one of the character class-related forums (rather than, say, the general discussion forum which includes off-topic socializing), (b) related to specific in-game problem-solving (here, druid talent builds, discussed below), (c) began with a question (given the forms of reasoning under investigation), and (d) had a high number of "unique account views" (i.e., was read by a large number of individual players). The discussion thread selected for analysis, comprised of 75 individual posts by 31 individuals, was entitled "Imp Mark of the Wild" and the content of the first post consists of a single, simple question: "Why is it nearly every template I see skips this ability?" A bit of context is necessary, however, in order to make sense of this initial query.

In *World of Warcraft*, players individualize their avatar by allocating talent points, earned through time spent hunting in game, across the various tiers within their class-specific "talent tree" (see Figure 1). "Imp [Improved] Mark of the Wild" refers to one talent that one class of players, *druids*, can choose to invest in. These refinements, represented as selections within the talent trees, are commonly manifested as statistical improvements of some form or another to one's current abilities. For example, by investing five talent in the "Improved Mark of the Wild" branch on the skill tree rather than another, a druid can get a 35% increase in the effect of their armor-enhancing buff spell named "Mark of the Wild," thereby improving her function in some collaborative problem-solving situations and decreasing her capability in others. Such choices impact one's contributions to in-game collaborative problem-solving; therefore, a great deal of communal value placed on making wise choices when developing one's particular "talent build." Players convene in online discussion forums to discuss and debate the merits of different builds, at times even refusing to play with others who have made choices that go against the communal wisdom developed therein. Thus, *World of Warcraft* participants have good reason to pay close attention to forum discussions as they represent the collective work of many toward developing best-fit solutions for specific groups, and it is not unusual to have discussion threads that receive 300,000+ unique account views. In the forum thread analyzed herein, a non-druid player asks why a skill improvement called "Improved Mark of the Wild," is left out of many recently fan-posted druid talent templates or "builds." In response, community members offer various competing theories, arguments, and evidence for what constitutes the most efficacious use of the limited resource of talent points.

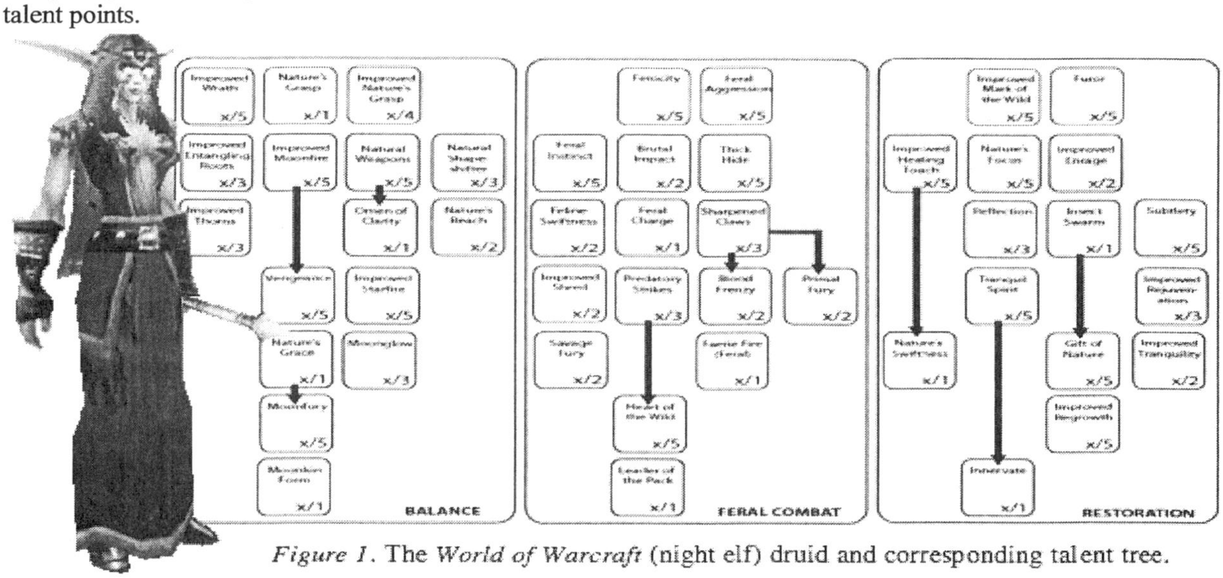

Figure 1. The *World of Warcraft* (night elf) druid and corresponding talent tree.

Method of Analysis

In order to assess the *scientific habits of mind* that characterize (or fail to characterize) the data corpus examined here, we developed a set of codes based in combination on a subset of the AAAS benchmarks for scientific literacy (AAAS, 1993) and Chinn and Malhotra's (2002) theoretical framework for evaluating inquiry tasks. Both reports have been quite influential in science education, with the former serving as the basis of the National Research Council's (1996) Science Standards and many state science standards for K-12 education in the United States. The codes were selected from these sources based on a combination of a priori assumptions about the forms of scientific reasoning such spaces ought to generate (e.g. understanding systems and feedback among components of a system) and previous games related literature (Gee, 2003; Squire, 2003, 2005; Steinkuehler, 2004, 2005a, 2005b). Our goal was to focus on scientific reasoning as "the building of houses" rather than the "collection of stones" per the vision of science practice articulated by Poincare (1905/2001) and science education forwarded by Dewey (1910) and Schwab (1962); therefore, important aspects to scientific understanding that are specific to *content knowledge* rather than practice per se (e.g. an understanding of natural forces), are notably absent. However, given the focus of our interests (scientific practices rather than content) and the nature of the phenomenon under investigation (a simulated world that makes no claims of correspondence with the natural one), we felt such omission was justified. Figure 2 below includes the full list of 21 codes; Table 1 presents a subset (given space constraints) of their definitions. Both authors, each of whom had over a year of participant observer experience within the game, coded a subset of roughly 12% of the data corpus to establish interrater reliability (92%); one author then coded the remainder of the data corpus.

Table 1. A subset of the analytic codes used to assess scientific habits of mind.

Scientific Discursive Practices
• **Build on Others' Ideas.** Restate or summarize others accurately what others have said, ask for clarification or elaboration, and express alternative positions (AAAS, 1993)
• **Multiple Forms of Argument.** Employ multiple forms of argument, not only simple deductive reasoning (Chinn & Malhotra, 2002)
Model-Based Reasoning
• **Systems Analysis.** Understanding systems analysis, specifying its boundaries and subsystems, indicating its relation to other systems, and identifying its inputs and outputs (AAAS, 1993)
• **Mathematical Models as Insight.** Understanding mathematical modeling as finding a mathematical relationship that behaves in the same ways as the objects/processes under investigation and that such models may or may not give insight into how those objects/processes work (AAAS, 1993)
Understanding Theory & Evidence
• **Pragmatic Understanding of Theory.** Understanding that, no matter how well a theory fits observations, a new theory might fit them as well or better and that the ongoing process of testing, revising, and occasionally discarding theories leads to better but not to absolute truth (AAAS, 1993)
• **Theory-Data Coordination.** Coordinating one's theoretical model with multiple sets of complex, sometimes partially conflicting data (Chinn & Malhotra, 2002)

Findings

The results from this analysis are presented in Figure 2, which shows the percentage of posts that exhibit each scientific habits of mind for which we coded. Here, we see the saturation of key characteristics of scientific reasoning skills across the set of 75 posts that comprise the selected threaded discussion. Several interesting patterns emerge from this analysis.

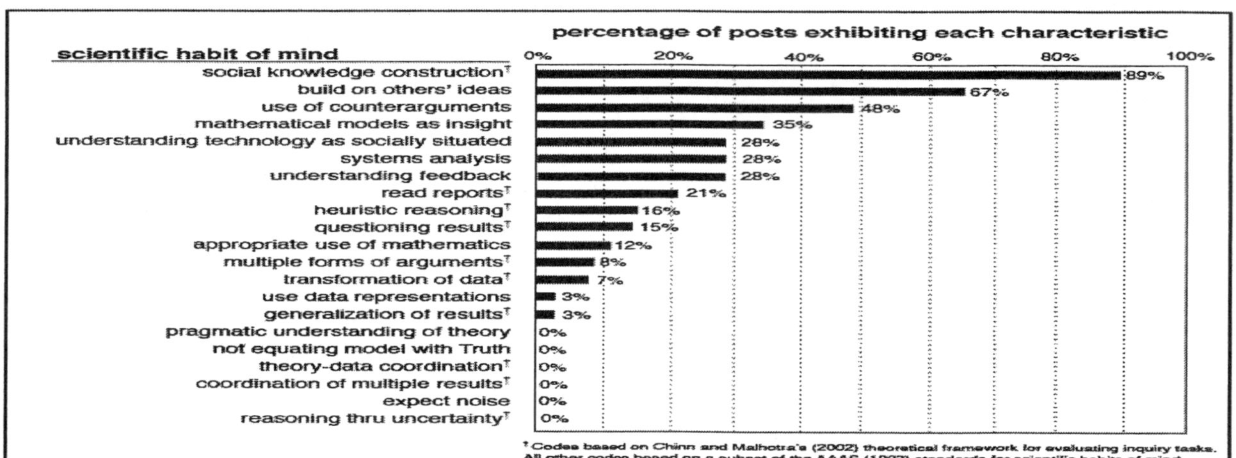

Figure 2. Proportion of posts within the data corpus that exhibit each scientific habit of mind under examination.

Scientific Discursive Practices

First, *scientific discursive practices* such as collaborative knowledge construction, building on the ideas of others, and the use of counterarguments are the most prevalent scientific habit of mind exhibited by posts within the discussion. That *World of Warcraft* players engage in mindful discussion and debate should come as no surprise given the "collectively intelligent" (Levy, 1999) nature of such communities; however, it is interesting that forms of *scientific* argumentation are prevalent within this informal context given previous findings that indicate that such practices do not come naturally and are difficult to foster (Kuhn, 1991; Osborne, Erduran, & Simon, 2004). In these data, is not unusual for participants to explicitly reference the reports of others, question one another's results, and leverage mathematical data as evidence for one's thesis. The following post illustrates:

> I see this over and over again in threads and I think it is myopic. Playing the percentages alone is narrow and limited thinking... Repeat after me, an increase is an increase... would you rather have 285 or 385, 12 or 16, 20 or 27? ...like everything else in this amazingly complex game, there are trade-offs and often times things are situational. Furor [alternative to Improved Mark of the Wild], as a couple of the other posters point out, is solo-buffing whereas MoTW [Mark of the Wild] is group-buffing. [post #59]

Model-Based Reasoning

Second, forms of *model-based reasoning* such as understanding systems, feedback mechanisms among their components, and the usefulness of describing such relationships mathematically are also regularly displayed by discussion participants (close to one third of all posts), although to a lesser extent than the scientific discursive processes discussed above. Given the design of character improvements within the game (i.e. the druid talent tree), participants are faced with the challenge of finding the best-fit solution to a problem of limited resources (talent points) for distribution across multiple variables, each with their own mathematical relationship to underlying avatar characteristics (e.g., hit points, mana points, regeneration speed). Thus, within the fantasy context of orcs and druids, heals and buffs, participants sometimes find themselves engaged in explicit analyses of complex systems. Consider, for example, the following post in which a participant compares various potential states of the druid talent tree in order to claim the superiority of one final template or build over another:

> ...To get what I want to get in Balance [first subsystem of the druid talent tree] while still majoring in Feral [second subsystem] (31/32pts), I can only afford 5 points for Restoration [third subsystem]. Considering the rest of my build (Feral), I'm far better off getting instant rage/ energy on shift [benefits of "Furor, an alternative to "Mark of the Wild"] than I am blowing those points on IMoTW [Improved Mark of the Wild]. Keep in mind, IMoTW [Improved Mark of the Wild] only increases MoTW's [Mark of the Wild's] effect by 35%, it is not an overall 35% buff. At L60 [level 60] that translates to +100 armor, +4 attributes and +7 to resists over the unimproved L60 [level 60] MoTW [Mark of the Wild]. While every little bit helps, for those precious 5 points, Furor [alternative to Improved Mark of the Wild] helps a lot more... [post #3]

Notice, however, that two key scientific habits of mind related to model-based reasoning are entirely absent within the data corpus examined here: (1) awareness that, even in simple systems, it may not always be possible to accurately predict the result of changing some part or connection ("expect noise"), and (2) realizing that even a close match between a model's predictions and one's observations does not necessarily mean that the model is the only "true" model or one that would work ("not equating model with 'Truth'"). Both habits of mind are crucial to understanding the appropriate function and use of models in science, yet neither emerges throughout the discussion. One explanation may be that model-based reasoning in the context of synthetic worlds takes on the characteristics of *reverse engineering*, operating under the assumption that there *is* a single correct algorithm underlying phenomena and it is only a matter of finding it (discussed below).

Understanding Theory & Evidence

Finally, scientific habits of mind related to understanding the function and relationship of *theory and evidence* are noticeably rare among posts within the discussion. Although participants do, on occasion (roughly one tenth of all posts), engage in heuristic rather than simple algorithmic reasoning and transform their observations into alternative data formats, other related scientific habits of mind are nearly or completely absent. In only three percent of the posts do individuals tackle the potential generalizability of their solutions and we find no evidence of individuals coordinating their theories with multiple sets of data, reason through uncertainty in their arguments, or displaying a pragmatic understanding of theory (defined above). If we treat the entire *discussion group* as our unit of analysis (aggregating across all 31 individuals), these features actually emerge as participants collectively engage in comparing various data-warranted claims; however, it remains an open question as to whether *individual participants* might be ascribed such habits of mind rather than the group as a whole. If so, it may be that the disputative nature of online forum discussions (a product of the fact that agreements are rarely posted, Hine, 2000) simply discourages expressions of uncertainty, noise or doubt.

Design Implications

Again, our goal has been not only to provide empirical evidence to substantiate claims of the potential of MMOGs as sites for studying science learning but also to offer a beginning set of heuristics that might inform the future design of intentional learning environments. Analysis of the scientific habits of mind that characterize the data corpus examined here reveal patterns in the forms of scientific argumentation, model-based reasoning, and theory-evidence coordination that arise in the context of online discussion of MMOG play. These patterns point to certain characteristics of MMOGs, both as designed objects and emergent cultures, that seem to *afford* the emergence of some scientific habits of mind and *constrain* others, characteristics of off-the-shelf MMOGs that may be of interest to designers of online mediated environments specifically for science education. Given the preliminary nature of this data analysis, however, these design recommendations are still tentative, yet we argue they might productively serve as a worthwhile starting point for future design experiments of virtual worlds.

MMOGs are designed experiences ostensibly analogous to any well-crafted piece of instruction, yet they are also fully realized simulated worlds exhibiting emergent, unpredictable properties. Unlike the simple one or two variable experiments characteristic of science classrooms (Chinn, & Malhotra, 2002), MMOGs (1) offer *multivariate problems of real complexity and of genuine social import* to those solving them. Based on these data, we would argue that model-based reasoning can be fostered by giving groups complex systems to collaboratively understand whose outputs are consequential for each individual. (2) *Problem-solvers are therefore stakeholders* in that efficient and effective solutions become the basis for future action, both their own and that of their peers. For example, in the environment studied here, the outputs of the system actually change the very nature of one's virtual body or avatar; therefore, individuals have a vested interest in finding and sharing potential solutions. Moreover, while science classrooms often focus on questions that can be answered with Google, MMOGs capture a more authentic sense of inquiry into (3) *problems whose solutions are generally unknown and require distributed teams of people doing simultaneous, partially overlapping, partly conflicting lines of research* – much like science out "in the wild." Thus, the forms of inquiry such virtual worlds afford are authentic even though synthetic. Scientific discursive practices emerge when participants are given the chance to solve such problems in contexts where there is (3) *individual opportunity to make a genuine contribution to the collective intelligence* (Levy, 1999) of their community. In such contexts, solutions developed by one person are referenced, debated, and built upon by other participants. The resulting forms of argumentation and model-based reasoning set an impressive standard for scientific thinking to which our designed learning environments (e.g. *River City*, *Quest Atlantis*) typically aspire. However, model-based reasoning in the context of synthetic worlds also appears to take on the characteristics of reverse engineering, with participants operating under the assumption that there is indeed a single correct algorithm underlying phenomena and it is only a matter of finding it. Such conditions are bound to be true of any game-based learning environment since the worlds contained therein are simulations based on algorithms, their interaction, and some added dose of random noise. Therefore, virtual worlds designed specifically for science learning might do well to include "what if" comparisons between the simulated world and the natural world it (partially) models. Activities which (4) *prompt learners to reason through, on a meta-level, the function and role of simulations* within a given domain of study might mitigate the propensity toward essentialized notions of theory and its relationship to evidence.

References

AAUW. (2000). *Tech-savvy: Educating girls in the new computer age*. Washington DC: American Association of University Women Educational Foundation.

AAAS. (1993). *Benchmarks for science literacy*. New York: Oxford University Press.

Barab, S., Arcici, A., & Jackson, C. (2005). Eat your vegetables and do your homework: A design-based investigation of enjoyment and meaning in learning. *Educational Technology, 45*(1), 15-21.

Chinn, C. A. & Malhotra, B. (2002). Epistemologically authentic inquiry in schools: A theoretical framework for evaluating inquiry tasks. *Science Education, 86*(2) 175-218.

Chmiel, M.U. & Owens, T. J. (2005). *Anti-evolution literature and its hidden pedagogical value: confronting the 'creationism' dilemma*. Presented at the Eighth International History, Philosophy, Sociology & Science Teaching Conference Leeds, UK, July 15-18.

Dede, C., Ketelhut, D. & Ruess, K. (2003). Motivation, usability, and learning outcomes in a prototype museum-based multiuser virtual environment. In P. Bell, R. Stevens, & T. Satwicz, (Eds.), *Proceedings of the Fifth ICLS.* Mahwah, NJ: Erlbaum.

Dewey, J. (1910). Science as subject matter and as method, *Science, 31*(787), 121-127.

Elsner, A. (2005, October 28). Is US becoming hostile to science? *CNN.com*. Retrieved October 31, 2005 from http://www.cnn.com/2005/TECH/science/10/28/science.debate.reut

Friedman, T. L. (2005). *The world is flat*. New York: Farrar, Straus, and Giroux.

Gates, B. (2005, February 26). *National Education Summit on High Schools*. Retrieved October 31, 2005 from http://www.gatesfoundation.org/MediaCenter/Speeches/BillgSpeeches/BGSpeechNGA-050226.htm

Gee, J. P. (2003). *What video games have to teach us about learning and literacy*. New York: Palgrave.

Hine, C. (2000). *Virtual ethnography*. London: Sage.

Jenkins, H., III. (1992). *Textual poachers: Television fans & participatory culture*. Routledge: New York.

Kuhn, D. (1991). *The skills of argument*. Cambridge, UK: Cambridge University Press.

Lave, J. (1988). *Cognition in practice*. Cambridge UK: Cambridge University Press.

Lave, J. & Wenger, E. (1991). *Situated learning*. Cambridge: Cambridge University Press.

Levy, P. (1999). *Collective intelligence*. (Robert Bononno, trans.). Cambridge MA: Perseus Books.

Miller, J. D. (2004). Public understanding of, and attitudes toward, scientific research: What we know and what we need to know. Public *Understanding of Science, 13*(3), 273-294.

Nasir, N. S. (2005). Individual cognitive structuring and the sociocultural context: Strategy shifts in the game of dominoes. *The Journal of the Learning Sciences, 14*(1), 5-34.

National Research Council. (1996). *National Science Education Standards*. Washington DC: National Academy Press.

Osborne, J., Erduren, S., & Simon, S. (2004). Enhancing the quality of argumentation in school science. *Journal of Research in Science Teaching, 41*(10), 994-1020.

Poincare, H. (2001). Science and hypothesis. In S. J. Gould (Ed), *The value of science: Essential writings of Henri Poincare*, (pp. 7-180). New York: The Modern Library. (Original work published 1905).

Schwab, J. J. (1962). *The teaching of science as enquiry*. Cambridge MA: Harvard University Press.

Shaffer, D. W., Squire, K.D., Halverson, R., & Gee, J.P. (2005). Video games and the future of learning. *Phi Delta Kappan, 87*(2), 105-111.

Singer, S. R., Hilton, M., & Schweingruber, H. A. (2005) *America's lab report: Investigations in high school science*. Washington DC: The National Academy Press.

Solomon, A. (2004, July 10). The closing of the American book. *The New York Times*, p. A17.

Squire, K. (2003). *Replaying history: Learning world history through playing Civilization III*. Unpublished dissertation. Bloomington IN: Indiana University, Bloomington.

Squire, K.D. (2005). Educating the fighter. *On the Horizon 13*(2), 75-88.

Squire, K. D. & Steinkuehler, C. A. (2005). *Gaming and the significance for information literacy learning*. Presented at the ALA Midwinter Conference, Boston, January 14.

Steinkuehler, C. A. (2004). Learning in massively multiplayer online games. In Y. B. Kafai, W. A. Sandoval, N. Enyedy, A. S. Nixon, & F. Herrera (Eds.), *Proceedings of the Sixth ICLS* (pp. 521–528). Mahwah, NJ: Erlbaum.

Steinkuehler, C.A. (2005a). *Cognition and learning in massively multiplayer online games: A critical approach*. Unpublished dissertation. Madison WI: University of Wisconsin-Madison.

Steinkuehler, C. A. (2005b). *The literacy of massively multiplayer online gaming versus national standards*. Presented at the Annual Meeting of AERA, Montreal Canada, April 11–15.

Steinkuehler, C. A. (2006). Why game (culture) studies now? *Games and Culture, 1*(1), 1-6.

Steinkuehler, C. A. (in press). MMOGaming as participation in a Discourse. *Mind, Culture, & Activity*.

Increasing Representational Fluency with Visualization Tools

Mike Stieff, Michelle McCombs, University of California-Davis, One Shields Avenue, Davis, CA 95616
mstieff@ucdavis.edu, mrmccombs@ucdavis.edu

Abstract: The present article reports on the use of one visualization tool, Connected Chemistry, to increase chemistry student's representational fluency, or use of accepted chemical representations and reasoning from submicroscopic perspectives. The tool was embedded in a unit on the particulate nature of matter and implemented in three high school classrooms. Analysis of learning via pre-post test measures revealed a significant increase in representational fluency among all Connected Chemistry students compared to students learning from more traditional lecture-and-text method; however, comparable improvements in declarative knowledge were not evident.

Visualization Tools for Teaching Science

Increasingly, visualization tools show promise for improving learning and achievement in science. Such tools are varied in structure and function and include a range of technologies that provide animations of physical objects (e.g., Wu, Krajcik, & Soloway, 2001), models of scientific data (e.g., Wu et al., 2001), and simulators of dynamic systems (e.g., Wilensky, 1999). An equally diverse array of theoretical frameworks motivates the design and use of visualization tools in the classroom. For example, some tools illustrate imperceptible phenomena (Stieff & Wilensky, 2003), others model authentic scientific investigations (Reiser *et al.*, 2001), and still others allow students to manipulate scientific data (Edelson, Gordin, & Pea, 1999). Concerted efforts to validate the use of these tools have revealed their potential both in research settings and in genuine classrooms. Here, we report on the development of one visualization tool, Connected Chemistry, and its potential to support learning in high school chemistry.

Connected Chemistry utilizes a suite of molecular-level simulations of chemical phenomena (e.g., http://education.ucdavis.edu/~stieff/Assets/DiscoveringMatter/DiscoveringMatter.html). Designed in the NetLogo modeling environment (Wilensky, 1999), Connected Chemistry offers students direct access to the submicroscopic objects and phenomena under study in chemistry. As such, Connected Chemistry simulations teach chemistry from the perspective of emergent phenomena (Wilensky, 2001). That is, the simulations emphasize how the submicroscopic interactions between molecular objects result in macroscopic concepts and symbolic representations learned in the classroom. Students can manipulate various parameters of Connected Chemistry simulations to make predictions based on their understanding and then compare their observations with their predictions. By facilitating the iterative process of observe-predict-test, Connected Chemistry offers students with the opportunity to engage in the same processes of inquiry that define scientific practice (NRC, 1996).

Previously, several studies have reported on four particular benefits of Connected Chemistry for improving student learning in chemistry (Levy & Wilensky, 2004; Stieff & Wilensky, 2003). First, Connected Chemistry simulations help students clarify and strengthen their conceptual understanding of fundamental chemistry concepts. Second, with Connected Chemistry students can simulate macroscopic laboratory experiments to isolate fundamental factors that describe a concept. Third, Connected Chemistry offers simultaneous presentations of the submicroscopic, macroscopic, and symbolic representations used in chemistry to better connect molecular interactions, concepts, and chemical representations for students. Finally, Connected Chemistry supports a greater sense of ownership of scientific knowledge by providing students with learning opportunities outside of textbooks.

The results from these previous investigations suggest that similar affordances of Connected Chemistry may be realized when embedded in a classroom curriculum. Typical high school chemistry curricula do not provide students with direct access to the molecular world. Instead, students must rely on two-dimensional diagrams or verbal representations, which creates a considerable barrier to learning about the dynamic interactions of atoms and molecules (Gilbert, 2005). Connected Chemistry offers one avenue to address this barrier by (1) supporting reasoning about dynamic interactions at the submicroscopic level and (2) illustrating the use of accepted chemical representations. Taken together, these skills comprise a students' *representational fluency* in chemistry, which is necessary for students' to reason about fundamental chemistry objects and concepts using canonical symbolic representations.

Improving Representational Fluency with Connected Chemistry

Presently, we have explored students' development of representational fluency while learning about the particulate nature of matter. To that end, we have embedded a Connected Chemistry simulation in a guided inquiry activity, *Discovering Matter!*, and implemented the activity in three high schools. *Discovering Matter!* was developed by a work circle of researchers, chemists, and high school teachers. Work circles combine the expertise of teachers and educational researchers through all stages of curriculum development and assessment. The approach has been particularly effective in the development and sustained implementation of several computer-based science curricula (e.g., Reiser *et al.*, 2000).

Structure of The *Discovering Matter!* Activity

Discovering Matter! includes three modules that students can complete in three 40-minute sessions. In the *Laboratory Module*, students perform a standard laboratory experiment. Here, students explore and observe macroscopic chemical phenomena commonly observed in the laboratory. To improve the flexibility of the activity, Connected Chemistry does not mandate experiments, but suggests options to provide teachers several choices based on their needs and resources. In the *Simulation Module*, pairs of students explore a Connected Chemistry simulation to understand the nature of the submicroscopic interactions responsible for macroscopic observations. Here, each pair completes a guided inquiry exploration of the simulation in which they make predictions and draw representations of submicroscopic objects and interactions. In the *Discussion Module*, the teacher and students link the submicroscopic and macroscopic levels. Here, the teacher guides students to reflect on their observations from the laboratory and simulation to understand how important concepts emerge from molecular interactions.

In *Discovering Matter!* students use a Connected Chemistry simulation in concert with a laboratory experiment on physical and chemical change to learn about the particulate nature of matter. This topic is typically covered early in instruction and forms the foundation of modern chemistry. In the activity, students classify elements, compounds, and mixtures according to the composition and behavior of submicroscopic particles. Students have significant difficulty understanding this fundamental concept as the relationship between particle behavior and macroscopic observations is not directly apparent (Johnstone, 1993). Indeed, students as well as chemistry student teachers are often unable to accurately define the concept or illustrate it with accepted chemical representations (Calik & Ayas, 2005).

Context of the Present Study

The work circle implemented and assessed *Discovering Matter!* in three classrooms at different schools with largely different populations. Edgewater High (Mr. Drake), located in a low-SES urban community, serves a primarily Hispanic and White student body and has a statewide rank in the 4th decile. Shadylane (Mr. Thorp) High, located in a middle-class urban community, serves a primarily Asian and Hispanic student body and ranks in the 7th decile. Finally, Lakeview High (Mrs. Kraft), located in an affluent suburban community, serves a primarily White student body and ranks in the top decile (10th). The workcircle conducts development and assessment activities with these sites deliberately to develop a self-contained curriculum that meets the needs of diverse populations and schools.

For the present study, differences in the implementation of Connected Chemistry (CC) occurred at each site. Mr. Drake and Mrs. Kraft both began with a lecture to introduce the use of simulations and followed with the simulation and discussion modules. Neither Mr. Drake's nor Mrs. Kraft's classrooms completed a laboratory module. At Shadylane, students first performed a laboratory experiment on chemical and physical changes. Mr. Thorp then introduced the simulation via lecture and his students completed the simulation module. Throughout the discussion module Mr. Thorp used macroscopic demonstrations to help the students connect their observations of the simulations with those of the laboratory. Each teacher also taught a lesson on the particulate nature of matter to a comparison class (NoTool) using lecture-and-text methods. All classes received five days of instruction on the topic.

Assessing Representations Fluency via Connected Chemistry

Learning outcomes were assessed via pre- and post-test measures. All students completed the pre-test one day before and the post-test three days after instruction. The 10-item measure included a variety of items that asked students to define relevant terms, classify different types of matter, and draw particle-level representations. Given space constraints, the present analysis addresses the overall test score and two items (7 and 10) that required the generation of chemical representations. Each item is summarized here and detailed analyzed below. Figures 1 and 2 illustrates examples of Items 7 and 10, respectively.

Item 7. Draw a submicroscopic picture of a heterogeneous mixture. Explain your drawing in words.

Item 7 assessed (1) knowledge of mixtures and (2) submicroscopic representation of mixtures. Briefly, correct responses included the definition of a heterogeneous mixture (i.e., a non-uniform mixture of two or more substances) and a representation of particles constituting a heterogeneous mixture.

Item 10. Water can exist as both steam and ice. Draw a submicroscopic picture of liquid water, steam, and ice. Explain, in words, each of your drawings.

Item 10 assessed (1) knowledge of particle motion in the states of matter and (2) submicroscopic representation of the states. Correct responses stated that water molecules in ice vibrate in close proximity, in liquid water they slide past one another in close proximity, and in steam they move with high velocity and large distances between particles. Correct representations illustrated these relationships *and* indicated that water molecules maintained the same chemical composition regardless of state.

Two work circle members assessed the measures using a 30-point scale. Comparison of the independent scores yielded 98% agreement on 3700 items. Disagreements were resolved uniformly by discussion. After initial scoring, Items 7 and 10 each received two additional binary scores according to whether the given answer contained (1) an accepted chemical representation and (2) a submicroscopic drawing. Item 7 also received (1) a binary score according to whether the representation was *heterogeneous* and (2) a binary score according to whether the definition was a *heterogeneous*.

Results & Discussion

The present analysis addresses overall performance and improvement in representational fluency via use of submicroscopic reasoning and accepted chemical representations.

Overall Learning Gains

Table 1 summarizes the total scores for each classroom. Using post-test score as a final outcome measure, the dataset was analyzed via a 2 (curriculum) x 3 (teacher) ANCOVA with pre-test score as the covariate. Controlling for pre-test score, the analysis revealed a main-effect of curriculum, $F(1,175) = 17.64$, $p < 0.001$). Across schools CC students scored slightly higher ($M = .62$, $SD = .14$) than NoTool students ($M = .60$, $SD = .17$). The analysis indicated a main-effect of teacher, $F(2,175) = 4.08$, $p = .018$; in addition, an interaction between curriculum and teacher was observed, $F(2,175) = 4.51$, $p = .012$. For each teacher, analysis of post-test scores via ANCOVA revealed the nature of the detected interaction. No significant differences were observed between the CC and NoTool students at Lakeview, $F(1,63) = 0.60$, $p = .44$. Significant differences were observed at Edgewater High, $F(1,49) = 7.24$, $p = .01$, and Shadylane, $F(1,61) = 10.8$, $p = .002$.

Table 1. Mean scores on pre-post test measures for each school and curriculum

	Lecture-and-Text		Connected Chemistry	
School	Pre-Test (n)	Post-Test (n)	Pre-Test (n)	Post-Test (n)
Lakeview	0.39 ± 0.17 (34)	0.64 ± 0.15 (32)	0.27 ± 0.14 (34)	0.59 ± 0.12 (35)
Edgewater	0.50 ± 0.16 (27)	0.54 ± 0.20 (27)	0.41 ± 0.16 (25)	0.54 ± 0.11 (26)
ShadyLane	0.45 ± 0.19 (31)	0.60 ± 0.16 (30)	0.44 ± 0.18 (35)	0.70 ± 0.14 (34)

Note. Mean scores are indicated for each class ± 1*SD*.

Further inspection of Table 1 clarifies the impact of Connected Chemistry on achievement. Across schools, Connected Chemistry yielded a negligible gain (0.13). At individual sites, however, gains were varied: no gain was observed at Lakeview, a small gain (.25) was observed at Edgewater, and a moderate gain (.62) was observed at

Shadylane. Note that the analysis controls for prior knowledge and indicates that despite equivalent post-test scores at Edgewater, CC students gained more learning with the simulations than NoTool students did from their texts. Field observations of the implementation suggest causal mechanisms for these site-specific outcomes. Of the three schools, Shadylane students alone completed a simulation, discussion, *and* laboratory module. Moreover, Mr. Thorp conducted macroscopic demonstrations of several reactions simulated in Connected Chemistry for whole-class discussion. Conversely, NoTool students at Lakeview completed a modeling activity (Remington, 1980) and a drawing activity to practice using chemical representations. Our preliminary conclusion is that the additional activities at Shadylane and Lakeview, and the lack of a laboratory module at Edgewater, may explain the site-specific differences between classrooms.

Although the gains as measured by total score for the three sites was negligible, the gross analysis does not adequately address representational fluency. Rather, a detailed inspection of student inscriptions is needed to clarify the use of submicroscopic reasoning with accepted chemical representations.

Reasoning with submicroscopic representations

A detailed inspection of student responses on Items 7 and 10 reveals significant differences in the use of submicroscopic reasoning, as evidenced by the number of submicroscopic representations used (Table 2). Analysis via logistic regression revealed that CC students were more likely to draw submicroscopic phenomena in answer to test items than NoTool students. On Item 7, 89% of CC students drew submicroscopic representations compared to 76% of NoTool students, $\chi^2(1, N = 177) = 5.09, p = .02$. On Item 10, 98% of CC students drew representations at the sub-microscopic level compared to 87% of NoTool students, $\chi^2(1, N = 184) = 9.24, p = .02$.

Table 2. Total students using submicroscopic representations on Item 7 and Item 10

	Item 7		Item 10	
Curriculum	Submicroscopic	Other	Submicroscopic	Other
Lecture-and-text	65	20	77	12
Connected Chemistry	82	10	93	2

Figure 1 illustrates sample answers taken from a CC and a NoTool student for Item 7, which asks students to define a heterogeneous mixture and draw a submicroscopic example. In the example, both students provided accurate definitions, and both drew acceptable representations of heterogeneous mixtures; however, their two answers reflect reasoning at different levels of perspective. To illustrate a heterogeneous mixture, the NoTool student drew a macroscopic picture of a basket of apples and plums and the CC student drew a submicroscopic picture of copper atoms and water molecules.

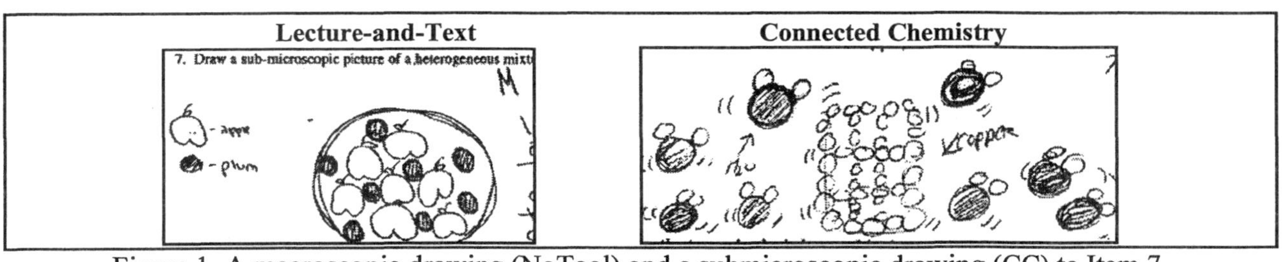

Figure 1. A macroscopic drawing (NoTool) and a submicroscopic drawing (CC) to Item 7.

The macroscopic example is a common example seen in chemistry texts. While the drawing indicates that the basket contains noticeably different objects throughout, it does not communicate the level of detail in the submicroscopic drawing of the CC student. The CC student has accurately represented the nature of a heterogeneous mixture. Her drawing illustrates two types of particles in different phases: the copper atoms remain vibrating together immersed in the flowing water molecules. Although the NoTool student provided an accurate definition and common drawing, when viewed from the system-level, he has actually represented a homogenous mixture: the two fruits are uniformly distributed throughout the basket. As such, it is not apparent that the NoTool students possesses the more accurate understanding of heterogeneous mixtures communicated by the CC student.

Illustrating phenomena with accepted chemical representations

Further inspection of the representations used on Items 7 and 10 reveals that CC students were more likely to use accepted chemical representations of submicroscopic objects, as in Table 3. On Item 7, 66% of CC students used an accepted chemical representation compared to 27.5% of NoTool students, $\chi^2(1, N = 159) = 24.63, p < .001$. Likewise on Item 10, 93.7% of CC students used accepted chemical representations compared to 60.7% in NoTool classrooms, $\chi^2(1, N = 101) = 32.70, p < .001$.

Table 3. Student use of acceptable chemical representations on Item 7 and Item 10

	Item 7		Question 10	
Curriculum	Generic	Chemical	Generic	Chemical
Lecture-and-Text	50	19	35	51
Connected Chemistry	30	60	6	89

Figure 2 illustrates examples of the different quality of representations used by CC and NoTool students on Item 10, which requires an illustration of how water molecule behavior changes among states. As in the example above, both students have provided acceptable representations that indicate the particle-level differences in each state. The NoTool student has used generic circles to represent water molecules; however, the CC student has used the correct space-filling models that highlight each atom in the molecule. Such examples were common among CC students, and likely reflect their increased exposure to such representations in the simulations.

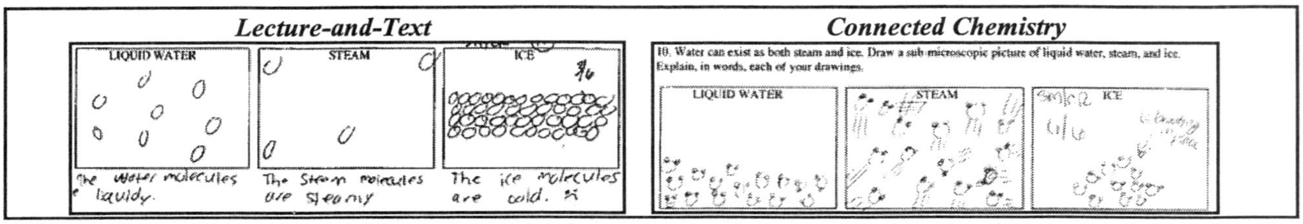

Figure 2. Sample representations on Item 10 from students in lecture-and-text and Connected Chemistry.

A closer look at Figure 2 illustrates a more striking difference between the students: The CC student has correctly illustrated the motion of the particles that result in macroscopic observations. In the figure, the CC student has used small lines and text to indicate the differences in molecular motion in steam and ice relative to liquid water. Conversely, the NoTool student has illustrated the relative differences of particle distance in each state, but has not referenced molecular motion, which fundamentally determines state. Moreover, the NoTool student's description of each panel refers to macroscopic level reasoning. For example, the student states that "The steam molecules are *steamy*", thus attributing macroscopic characteristics to the submicroscopic objects. Such confusions were common among NoTool students, and suggest that they did not understand the information embedded in acceptable chemical representations as accurately as CC students.

Acquisition and Application of Declarative Knowledge

Although significant increases in the use of submicroscopic reasoning and accepted chemical representations were evident, it was not apparent that CC students made significant gains in declarative knowledge after completing *Discovering Matter!*. Analysis of the accuracy of definitions and representations to reflect heterogeneous mixtures on Item 7 clarifies the issue. Table 4 summarizes the raw number of students who used accurate heterogeneous definitions and representations. Analysis via logistic regression revealed no significant differences between the percentage of NoTool (41%) and CC (33%) students who provided a heterogeneous definition, $\chi^2(1, N = 194) = 1.69, p = .19$. Likewise, no significant differences were found between the percentage of NoTool (46%) and CC (37%) students who drew a heterogeneous representation, $\chi^2(1, N = 184) = 1.61, p = .20$.

Table 4. Student use of heterogeneous definitions and representations on Item 7.

	Definition		Representation	
Curriculum	Other	Heterogeneous	Other	Heterogeneous
Lecture-and-text	56	40	48	41
Connected Chemistry	66	32	60	35

Together with the above analyses, this last finding indicates that CC students increased their use of accepted chemical representations at the submicroscopic level, but they may not have significantly improved their fundamental knowledge of chemistry. For example, CC students were more likely to draw space-filling diagrams on Item 7; however, those diagrams often represented homogenous mixtures, single molecules, and pure substances. Such responses were equally likely in NoTool classrooms, where students responded incorrectly with abstract symbols or macroscopic diagrams. In sum, both groups acquired only a minimum understanding of the nature of heterogeneous mixtures, or general concept of the particulate nature of matter, as reflected in the low grand mean (.60) on total post-test score.

General Discussion

An inability to relate symbolic and imagistic representations to fundamental domain concepts is a primary difficulty in chemistry that may underlie many misconceptions and problem solving errors (Johnstone, 1993; Gilbert, 2005). The above analyses indicate that Connected Chemistry activities may address this challenge by improving representational fluency. That is, the activities improve learning by supporting students' reasoning with accepted submicroscopic chemical representations. As seen in the present study, teachers that combine laboratory, discussion, and simulation activities achieve the greatest gains with Connected Chemistry. The illustrated examples also suggest that Connected Chemistry can help students resolve "levels confusion" (Wilensky & Resnick, 1999) in chemistry. Namely, Connected Chemistry helps students to relate events on the submicroscopic level to observations on the macroscopic level without misattributing properties across levels. Levels confusion has been implicated as a source of difficulty in other science domains, and its impact in chemistry is now being explored.

The present work also suggests the limitation of visualization tools. Our analysis suggests that representational fluency did increase among Connected Chemistry students; however, declarative knowledge did not. This finding may be expected given that the *Discovering Matter!* activity provided a disproportionate amount of time on visual representations compared to terminology: Each teacher used less than 10 minutes to discuss the term "heterogeneous", and students were given no supporting materials outside of the classroom activity. Consequently, Connected Chemistry students may simply have not realized which type of mixture was defined by the term. The equally poor performance of the lecture-and-text students underscores the need for further curriculum development efforts, likely supported by visualization tools, to improve learning in chemistry. Building on these findings, we are continuing to optimize Connected Chemistry activities for use in diverse settings and to further explore the potential of visualization tools for increasing representational fluency and understanding in chemistry.

Reference List

Calik, M., & Ayas, A. (2005). A comparison of level of understanding of eight-grade students and science student teachers related to selected chemistry concepts. *Journal of Research in Science Teaching*, *42*(6), 638-667.

Edelson, D. C., Gordin, D. N., & Pea, R. D. (1999). Addressing the challenges of inquiry-based learning through technology and curriculum design. *Journal of the Learning Sciences*, *8*(3/4), 391-450.

Gilbert, J. K. (2005). Visualization: A metacognitive skill in science and science education. In J. K. Gilbert (Ed.), *Visualization in science education* (pp. 1-27). Dordrecht: Springer.

Johnstone, A. H. (1993). The development of chemistry teaching. *Journal of Chemical Education*, *70*(9), 701-705.

Levy, S. T., & Wilensky, U. (2004, April). Connected chemistry - a study of secondary students using agent-based models to learn chemistry. In U. Wilensky, & S. Papert (Eds.), Networking and complexifying the science classroom: Students simulating and making sense of complex systems using the Hubnet networked architecture. *Symposium conducted at the annual meeting of the American Educational Research Association*, San Diego, CA.

National Research Council [NRC]. (1996). *National science education standards*. Washington, D.C.: National Academy Press.

Reiser, B. J., Spillane, J. P., Steinmuller, F., Sorsa, D., Carney, K., & Kyza, E. (2000). Investigating the mutual adaptation process in teachers' design of technology-infused curricula. In B. Fishman, & S. O'Connor-Divelbiss (Eds.), *Proceedings of the fourth international conference of the learning sciences* (pp. 342-349). Mahwah, NJ: Erlbaum.

Reiser, B. J., Tabak, I., Sandoval, W. A., Smith, B., Steinmuller, F., & Leone, T. J. (2001). Bguile: Strategic and conceptual scaffolds for scientific inquiry in biology classrooms. In S. M. Carver, & D. Klahr (Eds.), *Cognition and instruction: Twenty-five years of progress* (pp. 263-305). Mahwah, NJ: Erlbaum.

Remington, L. D. (1980). Teaching the nuts and bolts of chemistry. *Science Teacher*, *47*(9), 35-37.

Stieff, M., & Wilensky, U. (2003). Connected chemistry - incorporating interactive simulations into the chemistry classroom. J*ournal of Science Education and Technology*, *12*(3), 285-302.

Wilensky, U. (1999). *Netlogo* (Version 3.0) [Computer Program]. Evanston, IL: Center for Connected Learning and Computer Based Modeling, Northwestern University.

Wilensky, U. (2001). Modeling nature's emergent patterns with multi-agent languages. P*aper presented at the EuroLogo 2001*, Linz, Austria.

Wilensky, U., & Resnick, M. (1999). Thinking in levels: A dynamic systems perspective to making sense of the world. J*ournal of Science Education and Technology*, *8*(1), 3-18.

Wu, H.-k., Krajcik, J. S., & Soloway, E. (2001). Promoting conceptual understanding of chemical representations: Students' use of a visualization tool in the classroom. *Journal of Research in Science Teaching*, *38*(7), 821-842.

The Ideal Science Student and Problem Solving

Florence R. Sullivan , University of Massachusetts, Amherst, 14 Furcolo Hall, 813 N. Pleasant St., Amherst, MA 01003, fsullivan@educ.umass.edu
Xiaodong Lin , Teachers College, Columbia University, 322C Thompson Hall, 525 W. 120th St., New York, NY 10027, xlin@tc.edu

Abstract: We examined the nature of students' social mental models of the ideal science student, whether or not these models vary with student ethnicity, and the relationship of these models to problem solving strategies used, and problem solving ability in a robotics challenge. Participants were twenty-six, academically advanced, eleven and twelve year olds. Two social mental models were identified, a traits-based model and a robust model. While models do not appear to vary with ethnicity, a significant association was found between model group and strategy usage (p = .032). In addition, the robust group achieved higher scores on their final solution than the traits-based group (p = .03). The robust group made excellent use of the tools in the environment to solve the problem. The traits-based group did not. The robust group evidenced an environmental view of learning. The traits-based group displayed a mental representations view of learning.

Problem solving has been identified as an important aspect of student learning in science and technology and in the development of scientific literacy (National Research Council, 1996). Social factors, such as student beliefs about what it means to be an ideal student and their implicit theories of personality appear to influence student academic activity, problem solving approaches, and achievement (Dweck & Leggett, 1988; Hogan, 1998; Lunenberg & Vollman, 1999). However, these social factors have not been a focus of science education research (Patrick & Yoon, 2004). Indeed, many investigations of student problem-solving in science focus on either cognitive factors (e.g., Chang, C.Y., 2002; Dhillon, 1998; Reid, N. 2002;), or on students' science epistemological beliefs (e.g., Hammer, 1995; Lin & Chiu, 2004). Consequently, we know little about the specific relationship of social factors to student problem solving activity and achievement in science. The purpose of this study is to address this lack of knowledge by examining the relationship of middle school students' social mental models of the ideal science student to their problem solving activity and achievement in a robotics environment.

Social Mental Models

A social mental model is defined as an individual's understanding of the functioning of society and societal entities. For most children in the developed world, school is the dominant societal entity in their lives. Students' social mental models of school are developed by participation in school (Hatano & Wertsch, 2001), and they appear to be influenced, in part, by teachers (McRobbie & Tobin, 1996), other students (Cashmore & Goodnow, 1985), the classroom environment (Ames & Archer, 1988), the school environment (Buchanan-Barrow & Barrett, 1996), and parents (Smith, 1982). Students create a social mental model of the school as a dynamic system that includes not only individuals, but also rules, roles and distributions of power and authority that govern the relationships of the individuals in the school system (Buchanan-Barrow & Barrett, 1998). Researchers have investigated student social mental models from two perspectives, the ideal student construct and implicit theories of personality research.

The Ideal Student

What is meant by the term "ideal student?" According to Durkheim (1972/1922), "...every society sets up a certain ideal of man" (p. 203); he argues that members of the society come to share this ideal, to a certain degree, through the mechanism of schooling. Durkheim (1972/1922) argues that one of the purposes of education is to instill in the members of a society the ideals of that society. Further, he reasons that the values of varying societal groupings will affect the ideals held by members of these groups. Therefore, while a general societal ideal exists, variations in the ideal develop as a function of specific positional differences in societal groupings.

Ideal student research has been limited and it has primarily focused on identifying variations in social mental models of the ideal student (Cashmore & Goodnow, 1985; Lin & Schwartz, 2003; Ten Dam, 1995). As Durkheim (/19721922) predicted, the "ideal" is not defined singularly or even similarly by individuals residing in the same society. Indeed, researchers have found that student social mental models of the ideal student appear to differ based on age, country of origin, gender, and school type (Cashmore & Goodnow, 1985; Lin & Schwartz,

2003; Lunenberg & Volman, 1999; Ten Dam, 1995). Lunenberg and Volman (1999) also investigated the relationship of students' social mental model to their classroom activity. The researchers found that students who viewed the ideal student as a passive receiver of knowledge from the teacher, behaved in just this fashion in class.

Given the small number of existing studies, it is not possible to draw strong conclusions about the variation in and effect of student social mental models of the ideal student on learning activities. However, there is evidence that models vary based on societal positioning and that social mental models may be aligned with subsequent learning activities. Therefore, we hypothesize that students with varying societal positioning will have varying social mental models of the ideal science student and these variations in models will be associated with variations in learning activities.

Implicit Theories of Personality

The second perspective from which students' social mental models have been investigated is through their implicit theories of personality. Implicit theories of personality are naïve theories that each of us develop as a result of everyday lived experience; we use these theories to explain the behavior of self and other (Bennet, 1993; Moscovici, 1981). A students' social mental model of the ideal student may be considered a specific instance of their implicit theory of personality (Dweck & Leggett, 1988). In other words, the ideal student construct is related to the notion of an implicit theory of personality inasmuch as it represents the student's model, shaped by everyday societal experience, of a specific personage and the behavior governing attributes this personage will possess.

Dweck & Leggett (1988) present a research based social-cognitive model of motivation and personality that is offered as an approach to understanding the relationship of students' implicit theories and motivation to problem solving and achievement. The model posits students' implicit beliefs about the nature of intelligence as related to their subsequent learning goal orientation, problem solving strategy use, and achievement in the classroom. In this model, Dweck & Leggett (1988) have defined two beliefs that students might hold: the belief that intelligence is a fixed trait (entity theorists), and the belief that intelligence can be increased through effort (incremental theorists). Researchers have investigated Dweck and Leggett's model and it has garnered empirical support (Ablard, 2002; Leonardi and Gialamas, 2002). For instance, Stipek & Gralinski (1996) found that students who endorse entity beliefs are more likely to adopt performance goals and to use "superficial learning strategies that undermine their achievement" (p. 404), than their incrementalist counterparts.

Domain Specificity

Dweck & Leggett (1988) reasoned that their model might be useful in understanding behavior in domains other than intelligence. Subsequent research has produced mixed results regarding the cross-domain generality of beliefs (Bempechat, London, & Dweck 1991; and Stipek & Gralinski, 1996). For instance, Bempechat, et al., (1991) report that fourth and fifth graders held different beliefs in the different domains of intelligence, sociability, physical skills, and physical appearance. For example, an individual may hold an entity view about intelligence but an incremental view about sociability. Meanwhile, Stipek and Gralinski (1996) found that elementary school students in their study did not hold differentiated beliefs about the nature of intelligence in regards to the academic domains of math and social studies. Based on these studies, it remains unclear as to whether or not students' implicit theories about intelligence vary by domain.

Much research regarding students' beliefs about intelligence has been conducted using forced choice questionnaires. There are two problems with this approach. First, when using forced choice questionnaires the student-generated viewpoint is left out (Quihuis, Bempechat, Jimenez & Boulay, 2002). Second, forced choice questionnaires present hypothetical situations that a student might face. Presenting decontextualized, hypothetical situations to students may not indicate their actual beliefs or reveal the actual actions they would undertake when confronted with a real problem-solving activity (Schunk, 1995). There is a need for more field-based research into students' beliefs and behaviors that focus on actual problem-solving activity, not self-reports of what one might do in a given situation. Additionally, this research should occur in a more diverse learning environment as much of the present data has been collected from white, middle class students (Quihuis, et al., 2002).

The research undertaken in this study addresses these issues by investigating the domain specificity of student social mental models of the ideal science student using an open-ended questionnaire. Furthermore, it examines the relationship of these social mental models to problem-solving activity and achievement in a more ethnically diverse, authentic robotics problem-solving environment. This study advances our understanding of the relationship of social factors to problem solving in science.

Methods

Three over-arching research questions are investigated in this study: 1) what are student social mental models of the ideal science student? 2) Is there a relationship between varying social mental models and student ethnicity? And 3) How are students' social mental models of the ideal science student related to student problem solving and achievement in the robotics environment?

The data for this study was collected at one of the Center for Talented Youth's summer camp programs. The students in the study are considered academically advanced based on their scores on standardized tests. Participants attended either of two three-week long, intensive summer robotics sessions. Twenty-six eleven and twelve year-old students participated, 22 boys and four girls. Fourteen of the participants were white (12 boys and two girls), nine were Asian American (eight boys and one girl), and three were bi-cultural students (two white and Middle Eastern – one boy and one girl), and (one white and Native American boy). Socio-economic status was not available; however, the camp was expensive and none of the students were receiving scholarship assistance.

The research design was correlational and observational. Students completed two questionnaires on the first day of class, a demographic survey and the Ideal Science Student survey. This survey asked students to write five qualities the ideal science student would have. In the last week of both sessions, each student individually engaged in a robotics problem-solving activity that was videotaped. Students were instructed to think-aloud during the problem solving session. The robotics challenge was as follows: The robot must follow a black line on the track provided. When it bumps into an object, it will back up six inches, make a complete 360-degree turn and stop.

Robotics, in this study, refers to the RCX microprocessor created at MIT, the Robolab software program created at Tufts University, and the Lego Mindstorms kit. The use of specific tools is an important aspect of problem solving in robotics. In this study, the students had available in the task environment a paper track (with a ruler inscribed on it), the microprocessor, input sensors, various structural resources (i.e. different sized wheels, different Lego pieces, etc.) and the Robolab program itself.

Results

Social Mental Models

Quantitative content analysis (Chi, 1997) was used to analyze the responses on the ideal science student survey. Two graduate students were trained on the use of the codes with the data and interrater reliability was achieved at $k = .86$. All coding disagreements were resolved through discussion. Four categories of response were identified: 1) learning strategies and performance; 2) classroom order and discipline; 3) motivation, interest and effort; and 4) personal traits. Learning strategies and performance refers to responses that focus on external and outcome oriented academic aspects of classroom behavior. Classroom order and discipline refers to responses that focus on external, non-academic, orderly student behavior in the classroom. Motivation, interest, and effort refer to responses related to student internal motivation and interest in science, and their external effort in the science classroom. Personal traits refer to internal personality traits that a student may possess.

Two primary social mental models of the ideal student emerged from the analysis of the category responses, a traits-based social mental model group with responses falling primarily in the traits category and a group with a richer social mental model whose conception of the ideal science student included not only personal traits, but also motivational, behavioral, and learning strategy and performance aspects. Students with this fuller and richer view of the ideal science student are termed the robust social mental model group. The traits and robust categories are similar to those reported by Bempechat et al., (1991). They found that students categorized as entity theorists were likely to use trait terms as evidence to support their attributional judgments, and fifth grade students categorized as incremental theorists were likely to use action or process terms as evidence to support their attributional judgments of behavior. Therefore, our categorization aligns with the findings of previous researchers.

We systematized the classification of the students into one of these two groups by developing a metric that could be applied to each case. The metric developed for determining classification in the traits-based social mental model group is as follows: 1) the majority of responses to the ideal science student survey (at least 60%) must be categorized as a personal trait response; and 2) all responses must fit into just two categories overall, the personal traits category and one other category. Using these criteria, ten students were classified as having a traits-based model. The metric developed for classifying students as having a robust social mental model of the ideal science student is as follows: the responses are categorized in at least three of the four response categories. Therefore, none of the categories receive a majority of responses. Fourteen students were classified as having a robust social mental model. Using these metrics, two students of the 26 students fit into neither classification. Both of these students were male; one is Asian American, the other white. Of these two students, one had primarily motivation, interest and effort responses, and the other student had mostly classroom order and discipline based responses. These two students were dropped from further analysis.

Social Mental Models and Ethnicity

Of the 24 students who remained in the study, eight of the students are of Asian American descent, 13 of the students are white, and three of the students have bi-cultural backgrounds (two are middle-eastern and white and one is Native American and white). Chi square analysis of student ethnicity and social mental model group membership revealed no association, x^2 (2, n =24) = 2.479, p = .290.

Social Mental Models and Problem Solving

Descriptive written logs of student activity during problem solving were created through multiple viewing of the videotapes. The unit of analysis was shift in activity (Jordan & Henderson, 1995). A shift in activity refers to an attentional shift from one element or task in the challenge to another element or task. The transcripts were analyzed to identify the problem solving strategies students used to solve the challenge. Five domain specific strategies and four domain general strategies were derived from the viewing of the videotapes.

Domain specific strategies are ones that derive from the domain itself. As previously mentioned, robotics is a tool-intensive activity. Therefore, most of the domain specific strategies deployed in a robotics environment regard use of the available tools. The strategies thus identified were: 1) measure with ruler on map; 2) take light readings with the light sensor; 3) simulate the movement of the robot; 4) use the Robolab context-sensitive help; and 5) make structural adjustments with Lego pieces. Four of these five strategies are self-explanatory. Simulate the movement of the robot refers to the observed student activity of reading the challenge, picking up the RCX and affixing a light sensor, manually moving the RCX over the black line on the paper track, and reasoning aloud about the factors involved in programming the robot to follow the black line. Domain general strategies are those that may be used in any domain. Such strategies used by students in this study were: 1) guess and check; 2) sub-goal analysis; 3) ask questions; and 4) take notes. These nine strategies were used to code each student log. A graduate student was trained on the use of the codes; interrater reliability was established at k = .94. All disagreements were resolved through discussion. The ratio of domain specific to domain general strategies used by each student was calculated and used to designate students as using primarily domain specific or domain general strategies.

A chi square test of independence was conducted to examine the association of social mental model group and strategy type primarily used. A significant association was found, x^2 (1, n=24) = 4.608, p = .032. Students with a robust social mental model are more likely to use domain specific strategies than students with a traits-based social mental model.

Students' scores on their final problem solutions serve as a measure of problem solving ability. These final solutions were scored using a conceptual rubric. The computer science concepts inherent in the problem were input/process/output, procedural flow, and iteration. Possible scores ranged from zero to seven points. Points were allocated based on judgment of difficulty and complexity of each concept as embodied in the challenge. For example, the line following task engaged the input/process/output concept and was considered to have a high level of difficulty and complexity because students had to take into account a number of factors to solve it correctly, including how many light sensors to use, where to place the light sensors, and the variations in light reflection due to sensor placement and/or temporal fluctuations in the quality of light in the room. Content validity of the rubric was achieved when two Robolab experts independently reviewed the rubric and agreed that it accurately reflected the difficulty and complexity of each concept as embodied in the challenge. Students' final problem solution scores were tabulated using the conceptual rubric. A one-way ANOVA (see Table 1) was conducted to test the significance of differences in the group mean scores.

Table 1. Solution Score by Social Mental Model Group ANOVA

Source	SS	df	MS	F	p
Between Groups	18.31	1	18.31	5.367	.030
Within Groups	75.03	22	3.41		
Total		23			

The test was significant, $F = 5.367$, $p = .030$, the effect size was $\eta^2 = .196$, and the observed power was .601. Students with a robust social mental model obtained significantly higher solution scores ($M = 3.07$, $SD = 2.06$) than the traits-based students ($M = 1.30$, $SD = 1.49$).

Discussion

The results of the study indicate that while students have varying social mental models of the ideal science student, these models do not vary based on ethnicity. However, variations in social mental models are associated with variations in problem solving activity. These differences may be attributed to students' use of the distributed intelligence inscribed in the tools found in the task environment (Pea, 1991). The traits group relied largely on their mental representations to solve the robotics problem; they did not take advantage of the affordances for solving the problem offered by the tools as evidenced by their strategy usage. Students in the robust group made excellent use of the provided tools and, by extension, the distributed intelligence in the tools themselves. This is exhibited by the robust groups greater use of domain specific strategies to solve the problem.

To what may we attribute the relationship of a specific social mental model to the decision to use or not use the distributed intelligence in the task environment to help solve the problem? We conjecture that students' social mental model of the ideal science student may be related to their beliefs about learning and cognition. Greeno (1991) distinguishes two views of learning and cognition, a mental representations view and an environmental view. The former view relies on internal representations to reason about problems. The latter view relies not only on internal representations, but also on physical and social resources in the environment to reason about problems. It is possible that the traits group has a mental representations view of learning and cognition, hence they relied on their internal representations and well-known domain general strategies to reason about the robotics challenge. Whereas, the robust group may have an environmental view of learning and cognition that relies not only on mental representations and known strategies, but also employs the domain specific strategies made possible by the available tools in the task environment to reason about and solve the problem. In this study, the students with an environmental view displayed greater problem-solving ability. These students, by virtue of their tool use, continued to construct their knowledge of robotics as they solved the challenge. The learning space of these students was expanded by their active engagement with the resources available to them.

Implications and Conclusions

This study has important implications for educational policy and classroom teaching. These results suggest that standardized assessments that rely on mental representations may be an inadequate form of assessment. Students who utilize the affordances of physical and social resources to solve problems may be at a disadvantage when such resources are not available to them. In essence, students may be capable of much more than what these tests are able to discern. Therefore, expanding methods of assessment beyond tests of mental representations will provide a better picture of both what students have already learned and what they are capable of learning. Regarding classroom teaching, If a teacher has a social mental model of the ideal science student that is traits-based, and a mental representations view of learning and cognition, this teacher may not provide a classroom environment that includes the physical and social learning resources utilized by environmental learners. This type of classroom may put these learners at a distinct disadvantage. Indeed, Thomas, Pederson, and Finson (2001) find teachers' beliefs about themselves as science teachers influence the type of classroom environment they create. Furthermore, the use of tools in science is an important element of developing scientific understanding (Roth, 2001). The NRC (1996) emphasizes tool use as an important aspect of scientific literacy.

This study offers thought provoking results to those interested in social factors related to student problem solving in science. It is presented as a first foray into the thicket of such factors and their relationship to learning. The generalizability of these findings are limited due to the small number of participants, and the lack of academic and socio-economic diversity of the participants. Therefore, future research should address these issues.

References

Ablard, K.E. (2002). Achievement goals and implicit theories of intelligence among academically talented students. *Journal for the Education of the Gifted*, 25(3), 215-232.

Ames, C., & Archer, J. (1988). Achievement goals in the classroom: Sudents' learning strategies and motivation processes. *Journal of Educational Psychology*, 80(3), 260-267.

Bempechat, J., London, P., & Dweck, C.S. (1991). Children's conceptions of ability in major domains: An interview and experimental study. *Child Study Journal*, 21(1), 11-35.

Bennett, M. (1993). Introduction. In Mark Bennett (Ed.) *The development of social cognition.* New York: The Guilford Press.

Buchanan-Barrow, E., & Barrett, M. (1998). Individual differences in children's understanding of the school. *Social Development*, 7(2), 250-268.

Buchanan-Barrow, E., & Barrett, M. (1996). Primary school children's understanding of the school. *British Journal of Educational Psychology*, 66, 33-46.

Cashmore, J.A., & Goodnow, J.J. (1985). Agreement between generations: A two-process approach. *Child Development*, 56, 493-501.

Chang, C.Y., (2002). An exploratory study on students' problem-solving ability in earth science. *International Journal of Science Education*. 24(5), 441-451.

Chi, M.T.H., (1997). Quantifying qualitative analyses of verbal data: A practical guide. *Journal of the Learning Sciences*, 6(3), pp. 271-315.

Dhillon, A.S. (1998). Individual differences within problem-solving strategies used in physics. *Science Education*, 82, 379-405.

Durkheim, E. (1972). *Education and society.* (A. Giddens, Trans.). Cambridge: Cambridge University Press. (Original work published 1922).

Dweck, C.S., & Leggett, E.L. (1988). A social-cognitive approach to motivation and personality. *Psychological Review*, 95(2), 256-273.

Greeno, J. (1991). Number sense as situated knowing in a conceptual domain. *Journal of Research in Mathematics Education,* 22(3), 170-218.

Hammer, D. (1995). Epistemological considerations in teaching introductory physics. *Science Education*, 79(4) 393-413.

Hatano, G. & Wertsch, J.V. (2001). Sociocultural approaches of cognitive development: The constitutions of culture in mind. *Human Development*, 44(2/3), 77-83.

Hogan, K., (1998). Relating students' personal frameworks for science learning to their cognition in collaborative contexts. *Science Education*, 83(1), 1-32.

Jordan, B., & Henderson, A., (1995). Interaction analysis: Foundations and practice. *Journal of the Learning Sciences*. 4(1), 39-103.

Leonardi, A., & Gialamas, V. (2002). Implicit theories, goal orientations, and perceived competence: Impact on students' achievement behavior. *Psychology in the Schools*, 39(3), 279-291.

Lin, H.S., & Chiu, H.L., (2004). Student understanding of the nature of science and their problem-solving strategies. *International Journal of Science Education*, 26(1), 101-112.

Lin, X.D., & Schwartz, D.L. (2003). Reflections at the crossroads of culture. *Mind, Activity and Culture*, 10(1), 9-26.

Lunenberg, M.L., & Volman, M. (1999). Active learning: views and actions of students and teachers in basic education. *Teaching and Teacher Education*, 15, 431-445.

McRobbie, C., & Tobin, K. (1995). Restraints to reform: The congruence of teacher and student actions in a chemistry classroom. *Journal of Research in Science Teaching*, 32(4) 373-385.

Moscovici, S. (1981). On social representations. In Forgas, J.P., (Ed). *Social cognition: Perspectives on everyday understanding*, (pp. 181-209). London: Academic Press.

National Research Council, 1996. The national science standards. Retrieved April 5, 2005 from the World Wide Web: http://www.nap.edu/readingroom/books/nses.

Patrick, H. & Yoon, C., (2004). Early adolescents' motivation during science investigation. *Journal of Educational Research*, 97(6), 319-328.

Pea, R.D., (1991). Practices of distributed intelligence and designs for education. In Gavriel Salomon (Ed.), *Distributed cognitions: Psychological and educational considerations* (pp. 56-67) Cambridge: Cambridge University Press.

Quihuis, G., Bempechat, J., Jimenez, N.V., & Boulay, B.A. (2002). Implicit theories of intelligence across academic domains: A study of meaning making in adolescents of Mexican descent, *New Directions for Child and Adolescent Development*, 96, 87-99.

Reid, N., (2002). Open-ended problem solving in school chemistry: a preliminary investigation. *International Journal of Science Education*, 24(12), 1313-1332.

Roth, W.M., (2001). Learning science through technological design. *Journal of Research in Science Teaching*, 38(7), 768-790.

Schunk, D.H. (1995). Implicit theories and achievement behavior. *Psychological Inquiry*, 6(4) 311-314.

Smith, T. E. (1982). The case for parental transmission of educational goals: The importance of accurate offspring perception. *Journal of Marriage and the Family*, 44, 661-664.

Stipek, D., & Gralinski, J.H. (1996). Children's beliefs about intelligence and school performance. *Journal of Educational Psychology*, 88(3), 397-407.

Ten Dam, G.T.M. (1995). Drop out from adult education: social environment, school culture and perceptions. *International Journal of Lifelong Education*, 14(1), 51-63.

Thomas, J.A., Pedersen, J.E. & Finson, K., (2001). Validating the draw-a-science-teacher-test checklist (DASST-C): Exploring mental models and teacher beliefs. *Journal of Science Teacher Education*, 12(3), 295-310.

Congruence and Tension among Activity Systems in a Tripartite Partnership for Systemic Reform

Daniel D. Suthers, Joyce Yukawa and Violet H. Harada, Department of Information and Computer Sciences, University of Hawai`i at Manoa, 1680 East West Road, Honolulu, HI 96822, U.S.A.
suthers@hawaii.edu, yukawa@hawaii.edu, vharada@hawaii.edu

Abstract: Systemic reform often involves partnerships between multiple communities of practice (CoP). In order to understand the strengths and challenges of a partnership, it is necessary to examine the objectives and practices of the constituent communities and the forces that shape these practices. This paper presents an activity theory analysis of relationships between three CoPs in a systemic reform effort, Hawai`i Networked Learning Communities. Essential tensions between the activity systems of the CoPs are analyzed to understand key issues encountered in the implementation, particularly with respect to the role of technology in mediating systemic reform.

Introduction

Systemic reform—the effort to effect sustainable changes in the functioning of a school system that lead to improved student achievement (Fullan, 2001; Harris, 2005)—is typically undertaken as a partnership among multiple communities of practice (Huffman & Hipp, 2003, Schlager et al., 2004). For example, the systemic reform initiative that is the topic of this paper, Hawai`i Networked Learning Communities (HNLC), is a partnership between a state school-system and university researchers. Partners bring not only different strengths to the collaboration but also enact distinct practices under different reward systems and sets of constraints (Hildreth & Kimble, 2004). In order to understand the strengths and challenges of a partnership, it is necessary to examine the objectives and practices of the constituent communities and the forces that shape these practices. Such reflections on a reform process should be an ongoing affair, conducted not only at the outset during the planning process but also during implementation as experience provides an empirical basis for further reflection and identification of problems motivates its urgency.

This paper is the product of ongoing reflection within the HNLC initiative, which is in the fourth year of its implementation. Several theoretical frameworks are being employed. In this paper we report on our use of Activity Theory (Cole & Engeström, 1993; Engeström, 2001) to identify congruences and tensions between the partner communities that help us understand key issues encountered in the implementation of HNLC, particularly with respect to the role of technology in mediating systemic reform (Suthers et al., 2004). This analysis is augmented with the concept of *dualities* from Communities of Practice theory (Wenger, 1998). We write from our point of view as the university partner, and have grounded our claims about the activity systems of other partner communities in qualitative data including surveys of teacher cohorts, focus groups, interviews and other communications, meeting notes, and documents resulting from our joint effort such as strategic plans and reports. As explained below, we view our partnership as a tripartite one between school system staff, teachers, and university researchers. This paper will focus on how activity theory and dualities helped us conceptualize observed tensions that involve the activity systems of all three of these communities.

Background

Hawai`i Networked Learning Communities

Hawai`i Networked Learning Communities (HNLC) is a Rural Systemic Initiative funded by the National Science Foundation. Its goal is to empower educators to prepare students in economically disadvantaged rural schools for life and careers in today's complex and technological world by enabling them to attain high standards in science, mathematics, and technology. The initiative involves a partnership between the Department of Information and Computer Sciences (ICS) at the University of Hawai`i (UH) and the Advanced Technologies Research Branch (ATRB) of the Hawai`i Department of Education (HDOE). The HDOE is the only statewide school district in the United States. Approximately 40 K-12 schools have participated in HNLC, having joined the initiative in four successive cohorts starting in 2002.

Alongside our other roles as project leaders and facilitators, the UH team provides technology support for the systemic reform effort (Suthers, et al., 2004). Our intent is to support the change process itself, especially as manifest in teacher professional development and the collaborative reflection of practitioners. While ATRB focuses on application of technologies in the classroom as vehicles of instruction or the object of study, we offer information technologies in the form of an interactive web site (hnlc.org) to support collaboration and share resources across institutional and geographic boundaries between isolated rural schools in our island state. This "virtual community center" is designed to support the needs of special purpose groups that are embedded in a statewide virtual community of educators. This nested community approach is intended to capitalize on the advantages of larger groups such as resource sharing and potentials for new interpersonal relationships (Resnick, 2002) while also meeting local needs and enabling negotiability of purpose (Wenger, 1998). Community support includes a membership directory, a database of educational resources particularly relevant to Hawai`i educators, and a community forum for news and announcements. Smaller groups are supported by workspaces that collect together wiki pages, file sharing, and document-centered discussion tools.

The concept of communities of practice (Wenger, 1998) has been central to our initiative. However, the subject of systemic reform—the state school system—is not a unitary community of practice. In HNLC we soon found that the most salient distinction (expressed by participants as well as substantiated by our own observations) is between "the state" and "the schools." "The state" is the statewide administrative system in Honolulu, of which ATRB constitutes one branch. "The schools" are the teachers, principals and other support personnel who work together within schools geographically distributed across the islands. Our systemic reform effort includes a third community of practice, university researchers, forming a tripartite relationship. Although ideally all participants will function as one community (Barab, Schatz & Scheckler, 2004), the current reality is that multiple communities of practice are involved. The functioning of the entity formed of these three communities of practice is influenced by the orientation of each community's practice, its resources, and its constraints; so conceptual tools are needed to understand each partner community in relation to the others.

Theoretical Foundations

Activity theory provides a useful framework within which to understand the primary focus of each community, the resources with which a community replicates its practices, and the influences and tensions generated by the context within which its members work. Originating in Vygotsky's (1978) recognition that cultural artifacts mediate human action, the second generation of activity theory provided conceptual tools to understand cultural-historical resources for and constraints on collective action (Cole & Engeström, 1993; Engeström, 2001). The activity of any subject is directed towards an object in order to achieve some outcome. Object-directed activity may be accomplished directly, or may be mediated by tools, including language and other representational tools as well as physical devices, and by participation in a community, which is organized by rules and division of labor. Mediation is a key concept and can be applied analytically between any three elements of the activity system. For example, the subject's relationship to a community is mediated by rules that enable or constrain the ability to enact his or her role. Problems and the potential for change can be understood in terms of contradictions or tensions within and between elements of the activity system. More recently, a "third generation" of activity theory considers networks of interacting activity systems (Engeström, 2001), the approach taken in this paper.

Like Barab et al. (2004), we find that multiple analytic models are needed. Activity theory provides a structural model within which tensions are to be identified, but additional guidance is needed to analyze these tensions. Our analysis incorporates the dualities of Wenger's (1998) communities of practice (CoP) model. A duality is not a binary variable, nor even a spectrum along which a system has some value. Both elements of the duality are always present and interact both problematically and productively. Wenger (1998) identifies four dimensions that address "the fundamental issues of meaning, time, space, and power," namely: (1) participation and reification, (2) the designed and the emergent, (3) the local and the global, and (4) identification and negotiability. While Wenger uses the concept of dualities to examine the forces that create and sustain CoPs, we apply this concept to understand forces between as well as within communities.

Three Communities, Three Activity Systems

This section outlines an activity-theoretic characterization of the three major participants in our systemic reform effort. The activity systems are illustrated in Figure 1, along with relationships between them and "emergent activity systems" to be discussed later.

Teachers act as members of a school community. Students are the object of their activity and student learning the outcome (lower right, Figure 1). The artifacts that mediate teachers' student-oriented activity include curricular resources such as unit and lesson plans, instructional media, and technologies. According to our survey and focus group data, tensions within the teachers' activity system that affect the systemic initiative include resource limitations of all types—curricular and technological resources, technical knowledge, experience with collaborative technologies, and time for professional development activities (constrained by the need to hire substitute teachers). During the course of our project, the state content and performance standards were revised twice, creating added challenges for teachers endeavoring to organize their curriculum plans by the standards. The threat of No Child Left Behind sanctions can result in de-prioritization of all activities—including implementation of the place-based inquiry learning advocated by HNLC—other than preparation for standardized tests.

Our systemic reform effort is a collaboration with the Advanced Technologies Research Branch of the state-level Department of Education. ATRB team members who are tasked with HNLC responsibilities direct their activity towards teachers as their object and change in practice as the intended outcome (upper right, Figure 1). ATRB seeks the implementation of assessment-driven, standards-based curricula through activities that engage student interest and participation, in particular, place-based inquiry learning leveraging the environmental, economic, and cultural context and concerns of students. ATRB team members seek to achieve this outcome through professional development (PD). The "mediating artifacts" include plans for PD sessions and the incorporation of available PD materials. Tensions within this activity system affect success at reform efforts. Revisions to the content and performance standards created ambiguity over which version to use in professional development activities before the new version was officially adopted. Budgetary and political pressures result in operational directives that change priorities and constraints (e.g., limiting travel for school visits) or mandate new foci and methods (e.g., curriculum mapping or creating learning communities).

The University of Hawai`i (UH) team, the other systemic reform initiative partner, consists of members of the Laboratory for Interactive Learning Technologies in the Department of Information and Computer Sciences (ICS). The university team's activity system as a research team and associated tensions and constraints are familiar to many readers of this paper (left side, Figure 1) As an actor in the systemic reform effort, the UH team has as its object both the teachers (lower left, Figure 1) and the ATRB team members (upper left, Figure 1). Desired outcomes in both cases are changes in practice, and the primary mediating artifact considered in this paper is the use of hnlc.org to support collaboration and community. With teachers as the object, the UH team shares some of the outcome objectives with ATRB, but additionally has an emphasis on communities of practice. Tensions within this activity system include the competing priorities of project implementation and the need to examine the technological mediation of communities and collaboration, directed towards research findings and publications as outcomes.

Relationships Among Activity Systems

A systemic reform effort involving partners from three distinct communities of practice cannot be fully understood by considering those communities individually. More complex relationships—pair wise and tripartite in this case—must be considered to understand challenges and potential for change (Engeström, 2001). A multi-system analysis is particularly important in systemic reform where one partner introduces tools that are intended to mediate the activity of the other two, as in the present case.

When the members of one community are oriented towards members of another community as their object, we might expect that a new activity system that reflects the relationships between the communities will emerge. The mediational triangles of these *emergent activity systems* are illustrated in

Figure 1, placed between the communities from which they are to be formed and framed in ellipses. For example, the ATRB team's activity system oriented towards teachers is intended to engage teachers in a new system (right ellipse, Figure 1) in which their curricular resources are the objects and professional development is the mediating tool. Similarly, the UH team activity system oriented towards teachers seeks to engage teachers in a new system (lower ellipse, Figure 1) in which they are oriented towards their curricular resources as the object mediated by a community of practitioners using hnlc.org; and UH oriented towards ATRB similarly seeks to engage ATRB staff in facilitating community of reflective practitioners supported by hnlc.org (upper ellipse, Figure 1). In this section we identify both congruences (structural similarities) and tensions between both the primary and emergent activity systems in our partnership.

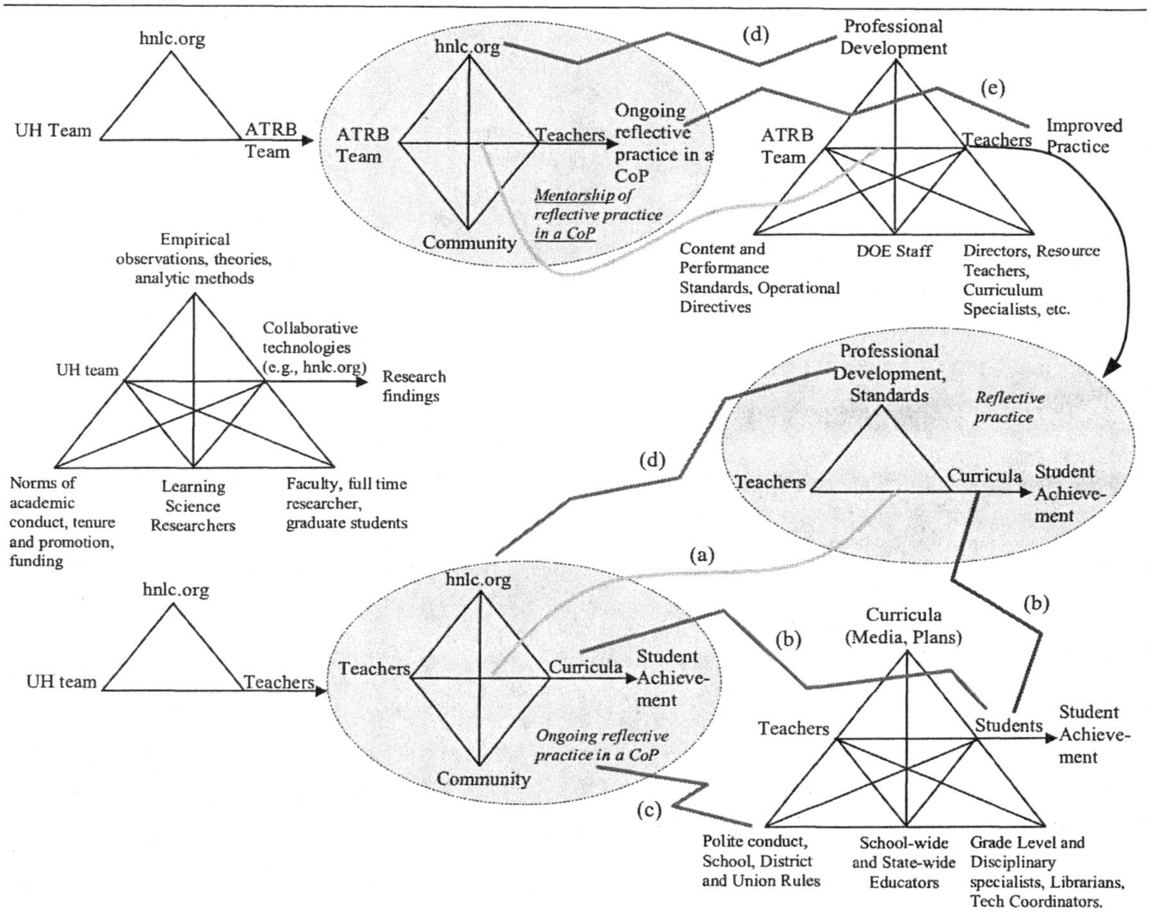

Figure 1. Relationships between three primary activity systems.

(a) Congruence of teacher orientation towards curricula between emergent activity systems fostered by both ATRB's and UH's orientation towards teachers.
(b) Participation/reification tension between teachers' orientation towards students and the orientation towards curricula in the emergent activity systems sought by ATRB and UH.
(c) Cultural and local/global tensions between teachers' norms of noncritical conduct and reflection in a community of practice sought by UH orientation towards teachers.
(d) Mismatch in mediating artifacts emphasized in emergent activity systems sought by ATRB and UH.
(e) Emergent activity system sought by UH places greater emphasis on ATRB's role as mentors of teachers' ongoing reflective practice in a CoP.

Congruence in Reflective Practice

Both the ATRB and UH teams want to help teachers become *reflective practitioners* (Schön, 1983; York-Barr et al., 2001), reflecting on their instructional resources and unit and lesson plans and how they are implemented in the classroom towards the objective of improving student achievement. This common goal is congruent in the emergent activity systems that both ATRB and UH teams seek to create in their orientations towards teachers (curved lines, Figure 1(a)). Teachers' mediating artifacts (curricula) become the objects of inquiry in the activity system of the reflective practitioner.

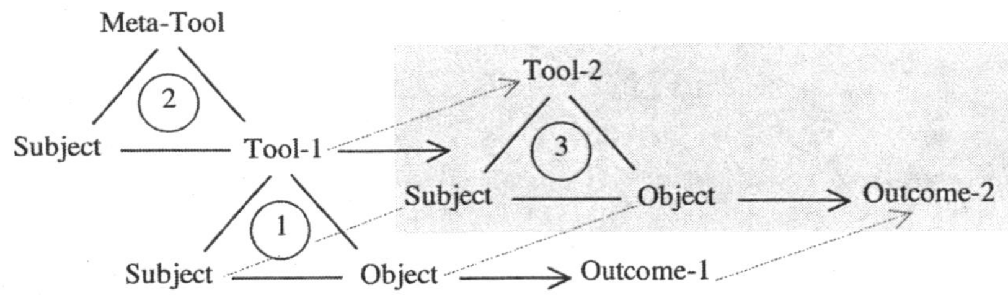

Figure 2. In reflective practice, the tools for the current practice (1) become the object of reflection (2) leading to a revised practice (3).

A schema for reflective practice is shown in Figure 2. Practitioners are engaged in a primary practice indicated by the lower activity system (1). For example, teachers are the Subject, students the Object, and curricular resources and plans are the Tool (Tool-1 at time 1). In the reflection process, the mediating tools of this activity system (Tool-1) become the objects of deliberation, criticism, innovation, and revision (2). Other aspects of the primary practice, such as rules and division of labor, may also be considered and revised; this is omitted from the present paper for simplicity. A meta-tool is employed as the tool by which reflective consideration of the primary tool is accomplished. For example, the meta-tool can be theory, professional development materials and activities, and/or discourse within a community. Tool-1 of the primary activity system is deliberately revised into a new one, Tool-2, in order to improve outcomes. As a result, the primary activity system is transformed into a new activity system using Tool-2 with different (hopefully improved) outcomes (3). The process repeats with this transformed activity system: in an ongoing process of expansive learning (Engeström 2001), reflective practitioners must simultaneously maintain a reflective activity (2) in order to continuously transform practice in the primary activity (1 ⇒ 3).

Tensions Between Activity Systems

Some tensions may be noted between the emergent activity system (reflective practice) and teachers' primary activity system. In order to engage in the professional development activity, teachers must reify their curriculum planning so that it can become an object of inquiry in itself. This reification can be difficult for those who practice a more spontaneous approach to instruction (jagged lines, Figure 1(b)). For teachers who are not accustomed to critically examining their own practice, the focus on teacher performance (in addition to student performance) is a paradigm shift. In the community version of reflective practice, teachers are asked to share their reified tools with other teachers for co-reflection, which can be threatening in a culture where teachers seldom critique each other (Figure 1(c)). This is one among several factors accounting for the lack of peer commentary on teachers' units in hnlc.org. A local/global tension also complicates the exercise: will the plans teachers developed to fit their situation make sense in other schools and classrooms? This duality also has a top-down manifestation: does the statewide set of standards and other criteria and practices promoted by the professional development program make sense in every teacher's classroom?

We noted that there is congruence between the ATRB and UH teams' intended emergent activity systems for teachers. However, there is also a difference: ATRB focuses on its professional development activities while UH focuses on technology-mediated community in hnlc.org (Figure 1(d)). The need to integrate hnlc.org with ATRB's PD planning has been an ongoing issue in the project. The same tension is evident in a comparison of the UH-oriented-to-ATRB emergent activity system and ATRB's primary activity system. These tensions between planned professional development and practitioner discourse reflect both designed/emergent and identification/negotiability dualities. In inviting ATRB staff to use hnlc.org, we are attempting to implement a model that equates professional development with ongoing facilitation and mentorship of the reflective practice of members of a community of practice. Although the object of activity in the emergent activity system remains the same (i.e., teachers), we are asking ATRB staff to use a different mediating artifact, the online tools for collaboration and community support, and to orient their activity towards the outcome of an ongoing community of practice (Figure 1(e)).

The use of technology (hnlc.org) in itself is not a challenge for members of an Advanced Technology Research Branch. Difficulties we have encountered are better explained by our assumption of identification with (1) a community of practice model of professional development, and (2) the need to mentor teachers to support such a model. Further negotiation towards consensus on these outcomes is needed, and will impact the role of technology as mediator. In addition to ATRB's orientation toward helping teachers use technology for student learning, technology becomes a mediator for teacher learning. It should be noted that ATRB promotes both reflective practice and learning communities. The issue is what these terms mean to different people, whether the concepts are integrated as reflective practice *in a community of practice*, and the consequent implications for the role of technology. We are presently working with ATRB to negotiate a shared conception of professional development and better integrate our offerings.

Structural Issues in Mediation

Like any school system, the HDOE is a hierarchical system in which system administrators and staff produce reifications of "best practices" for replication—desired practices to be adopted by teacher practitioners. Yet, change in practice is not imposed from outside (Osterman & Kottkamp, 1993). Teachers and HDOE staff need to negotiate a shared object (Engeström, 2001): the practices that are promoted by professional development. In an attempt to support HDOE's efforts towards best practices with a technological artifact, the UH team inadvertently became an intermediary in (and a barrier to) this conversation. The technological artifact is the "unit plan template," a web-based form for describing a unit plan. HDOE professional development staff wanted to guide teachers through an assessment-driven backwards-mapping approach to unit planning (Wiggins & McTighe, 2001), and requested that the unit plan template enforce this process. According to this model, teachers should first identify the content and performance standards to be addressed and then identify the assessment instruments to be used to measure outcomes, before indicating student activities and the materials needed to support these activities. This scripted approach to unit authoring is the opposite of many innovative teachers' approach of identifying an engaging activity first and designing a unit around this activity. While this designed/emergent tension is a significant issue, the greatest problem lies in a failure of negotiability. The web-based unit template was controlled by the UH team, and therefore served to place us in a mediating role between HDOE staff and teachers. HDOE staff requested revisions in the template's structure, while teachers who were using the template expressed frustration with its inflexibility and noted incompatibilities with formats being used in their local school. When the UH team tried to respond to one community, the other sometimes disagreed with the changes. Our role as designers of the artifact intended to mediate between the systemic reform agenda and teachers' practice placed us in the role of mediator of conversations about tensions between this agenda and teachers' practice, conversations that should have taken place directly between HDOE staff and teachers. We realize in retrospect that a better choice would be to provide tools for reification that are accessible to both HDOE staff and teachers, and associate these tools with support for conversation about the reifications. Then teachers and professional development staff could negotiate directly over the timing and content of reifications such as the unit plan template.

Conclusions

Most if not all systemic reform efforts are a partnership between multiple communities. Ideally, they would function as one community, but reality demands that reform leaders examine their practices to find congruences and potential tensions between partners. Activity theory, augmented with concepts of dualities in communities of practice, provided us with tools for this analysis. This approach was applied to understand a tripartite partnership in a systemic reform effort involving staff in a statewide school district, school-based teachers, and us as university researchers. Examination of the corresponding activity systems and the emergent activity systems sought by these partnerships identified congruence in objectives of reflective practice, along with tensions in the role of technology to support this reflection, individual versus community (collaborative) reflection, and a risk unique to tripartite relationships: that one partner might become intermediate to negotiations that should take place directly between the other two. We are using this information in engaging partners in re-examining goals and strategies. The paper also illustrates a theoretical point: communities of practice are activity systems, and communities and their activity systems are nested. Therefore, concepts developed for analysis of *internal* tensions of communities and their activity systems can also be applied to understanding relationships *between* communities and their activity systems: intra- and inter- are two views on the same relations.

References

Barab, S. A., Schatz, S., Scheckler, R. (2004). Using Activity Theory to conceptualize online community and using online community to conceptualize Activity Theory. *Mind, Culture, & Activity, 11*(1), 25-47.

Cole, M. & Engeström, Y. (1993). A cultural-historical approach to distributed cognition. In G. Salomon (Ed.) *Distributed Cognitions: Psychological and Educational Considerations.* Cambridge: Cambridge University Press, pp. 1-46.

Engeström, Y. (2001) Expansive learning at work: Toward an activity theoretical reconceptualization. *Journal of Education and Work 14*(1): 133-156.

Fullan, M. (2001). *The New Meaning of Educational Change.* New York: Teachers College Press.

Harris, E. (2005). *Key Strategies to Improve Schools: How to Apply Them Contextually.* Lanham, MD: Scarecrow Press.

Hildreth, P. & Kimble, C. (2004). *Knowledge Networks: Innovation Through Communities of Practice.* Hershey, PA: Idea Group Publications.

Huffman, J. & Hipp, K. (2003). *Reculturing Schools as Professional Learning Communities.* Lanham, MD: Scarecrow Press.

Osterman, K.F. & Kottkamp, R.B. (1993). *Reflective Practice for Educators: Improving Schooling through Professional Development.* Newbury Park, CA: Sage.

Resnick, P. (2002). Beyond Bowling Together: SocioTechnical Capital. In J. Carroll (Ed.) *HCI in the New Millenium.* (pp. 647-672.) New York: Adddison-Wesley.

Schlager, M.S. & Fusco, J. (2004). Teacher professional develoment: Are we putting the cart before the horse? In S. Barab, R. Kling, & J. Gray (Eds.), *Designing Virtual Communities in the Service of Learning.* Cambridge: Cambridge University Press.

Schön, D.A. (1983). *The Reflective Practitioner.* New York: Basic Books.

Suthers, D., Harada, V., Doane, W., Yukawa, J., Harris, B. & Lid, V. (2004). Technology-Supported Systemic Reform: An Initial Evaluation and Reassessment. *Proceedings of the Sixth International Conference of the Learning Sciences*, Santa Monica, CA - June 22-26, 2004. pp. 537-544.

Vygotsky, L. S. (1978). *Mind in Society: The Development of Higher Psychological Processes.* Cambridge, MA: Harvard University Press. (Originally published in 1930.)

Wenger, E. (1998). *Communities of Practice: Learning, Meaning, and Identity.* Cambridge: Cambridge University Press.

Wiggens, G. & McTighe, J. (2001). Understanding by Design. Upper Saddle River, NJ: Prentice Hall.

York-Barr, J. et al. 2001. *Reflective Practice to Improve Schools.* Thousand Oaks, CA: Corwin.

Acknowledgments

We are grateful to the numerous individuals who have contributed towards HNLC, including Vicki Kajioka (HNLC co-PI and ATRB director), Claudia Atta and Pat Donohue (former HNLC project directors), and the other members of the ATRB and UH teams for their hard work during the period reported in this paper: Sam Joseph, Viil Lid, Paulo Maurin, Heidi Salvador, Kyle Shodai, Joshua Wingstrom, and Ryan Yoshioka. This work was supported by the National Science Foundation under Cooperative Agreement No. 0100393. Any opinions, findings, and conclusions or recommendations expressed in this paper are those of the authors and do not necessarily reflect the views of the National Science Foundation, the HDOE, or UH.

Berta's Tower: Developing conceptual physics understanding one exploratoid at a time

Gina Navoa Svarovsky, David Williamson Shaffer
University of Wisconsin, 1025 W. Johnson St., Madison, WI 53706
Email: mnsvarovsky@wisc.edu, dws@education.wisc.edu

Abstract: In this paper we describe a study that investigates whether—and how—authentic recreations of engineering practices can help students develop conceptual understanding of physics. We focus on the design-build-test cycle used by professional engineers in simulation-based rapid modeling. In this experiment, middle school students worked for 10 hours to solve engineering design challenges using SodaConstructor—a Java-based microworld—as a simulation environment. As a result of the experiment, students learned about center of mass. Our data further suggest that in the process of simulation-based modeling, rapid iterations of the design-build-test cycle progressively linked students' interest in the design activities and understanding of the concept of center of mass. We suggest that these rapid iterations of the design-build-test cycle functioned as *exploratoids*: short fragments of exploratory action in a microworld that cumulatively develop interest in and understanding of important scientific concepts.

Petroski (2003) argues that young people are "born engineers" because of their natural tendencies to explore, build, and create. Previous studies have shown that engineering design activities can be a fruitful context for students to develop important science skills and understandings through the pursuit of personally meaningful projects (Kolodner, Crismond, Gray, Holbrook, & Puntambekar, 1998). Much of the extant design-based curricula for pre-college students focuses on students solving engineering problems with physical materials. The resulting tangible products can be a motivating factor (Sadler, Coyle, & Schwartz, 2000), but working with physical materials also be limiting—and thus also limit the insights gained.

Practicing engineers face similar concerns over funding, safety, and time, particularly when dealing with new problems. In such situations, engineers often use computer simulations in the early stages of the design process. Simulations are less expensive, faster, and safer, so engineers can evaluate several design ideas before committing to a prototype. That is, simulations help engineers understand a problem by increasing the iterativity of the *design-build-test (DBT) cycle*: the process by which engineers incrementally plan, construct, evaluate, and redesign elements of an emerging design (Elger, Beyerlein, & Budwig, 2000). Engineering design is characterized by shorter and more frequent DBT cycles when problems are difficult or complex (Dym & Little, 2000).

The problem that professional engineers face when solving novel problems is similar to the problem faced by students dealing with an engineering challenge for the first time. The theory of *pedagogical praxis* (Shaffer, 2004b) suggests authentic recreations of professional practices can provide a useful framework for designing technology-based learning environments. Building on this theory, we hypothesize that solving engineering design challenges using a computer simulation may help middle school students understand key concepts in physics. Our goal in the preliminary study we present here is to examine whether this hypothesis is correct, and if so, to explore the cognitive processes at work in such a learning environment.

Theoretical Framework

Engineering design

The engineering design process has been well studied and documented in engineering literature (see, for example: Bucciarelli, 1994; Vincenti, 1990). Here, we concentrate on a particular aspect of engineering design: the *design-build-test* (DBT) cycle (Elger et al., 2000), which is an iterative process through which engineers develop and evaluate design alternatives. In each iteration of the cycle, engineers *design* a solution to the problem at hand, *build* a prototype of the proposed design, and then *test* the prototype to determine its potential effectiveness. As engineers start to work on a new problem with unfamiliar parameters, the DBT cycle is one of the ways in which they come to understand the physical systems with which they are working (Dym & Little, 2000). In this paper, we examine whether and how younger students can use a similar process to develop scientific understanding.

Professional engineers often use simulations to develop their understanding about the physical systems with which they are working—and as a testing ground for their initial design ideas. Simulations are computational systems that model the natural world (Edwards, 1995). By providing a virtual representation of a physical system, simulations allow users to engage in inquiry that is otherwise impractical or even impossible. For example, civil engineers test the effects of strong winds on a skyscraper design by creating a simulation to observe the amount of wind shear the structure can withstand (Dym & Little, 2000). Through the use of such tools, engineers reduce the cost in time and materials of each iteration of the DBT cycle. Thus they can increase the number of design iterations—and as a result, their potential understanding of the problem at hand.

Microworlds

Simulations are a form of computational *microworld*, which Hoyles, Noss, and Adamson (2002) define as "environments where people can explore and learn from what they receive back from the computer in return for their exploration". Previous studies (see, for example: Resnick, 1997; Wilensky, 2001) have shown open-ended projects using such tools can be a rich and motivating way for students to develop mathematical and scientific understanding. In this study, we focus on two key factors associated with student learning with microworlds: *autoexpressivity*, a property of the tool, and *expressivity*, an affordance users experience when interacting with the tool.

Autoexpressivity. Microworlds possess an embedded set of relationships from a particular domain, thereby allowing users to investigate these relationships within a virtual setting (Noss & Hoyles, 1996) by repeatedly articulating ideas in the microworld and then interpreting the microworld's response. Students explore the relationships within a domain by testing out their ideas in the microworld and then observing the resulting feedback. A key feature of microworlds is that the feedback provided by the simulation depends on the way in which a student has used the relationships and concepts from the domain being modeled (Papert, 1980). Microworlds are therefore *autoexpressive* (Noss & Hoyles, 1996), meaning the behavior of the tool reflects the extent to which the student can represent the underlying domain principles with the grammar of the tool. As students test and revise their projects in the microworld, they also test and revise their understanding of the embedded domain.

Expressivity. Generally speaking, microworlds make it easy for students to create, manipulate, and test prototypes with few constraints on their design imagination. Not all of their design ideas will work, but they are free to explore the design space and incorporate personal design choices into their work. When microworlds are used in open-ended activities, they allow students to develop understanding through *expressive* projects: that is, projects that allow students to explore their own individualized design decisions, to create solutions that are inventive, unique, and personalized. This freedom to explore can be both meaningful and motivating for students, affording them a sense of control and personal investment in their inquiry (Noss & Hoyles, 1996; Papert, 1980; Shaffer, 1997).

Islands of Expertise

Here we will explore what happens when students conduct rapid iterations of the engineering DBT cycle to solve expressive problems using an autoexpressive tool. We propose to explain this process using the theory of *islands of expertise* (Crowley & Jacobs, 2002), topics "in which children happen to become interested and in which they develop relatively deep and rich knowledge" (p. 333). In other words, islands of expertise are forms of scientific understand that are inextricably linked to personal interest. Islands of expertise develop through small, seemingly insignificant—yet collectively transformative—conversations between parent and child: short fragments of explanatory talk where the parent provides information to the child on a topic of interest which they refer to as *explanatoids*. As the child comes to understand more about the topic from each interaction, he or she becomes more interested in the topic—leading to further conversations and deeper understanding. These individually unremarkable interactions cumulatively provide a motivating and powerful connection between interest and understanding (Shaffer, 2004a).

Berta's Tower

In this study, we examine whether and how middle school students can learn about concepts in physics through design activities by following the engineering practice of rapid prototyping using simulations. We hypothesize that just as engineers understand a novel problem through repeated iterations of the DBT cycle, students will develop understanding of the center of mass through repeated, short cycles of design and testing in a computer simulation environment. Moreover, we propose to extend the theory of islands of expertise (Crowley & Jacobs, 2002) beyond parent-child interactions and apply it to the context of students working with microworlds. In exploring mechanisms by which students learn through rapid prototyping in a simulation environment, we hypothesize that the short explorations students carry out in microworlds function in a manner similar to explanatoids, cumulatively forging a powerful linkage between interest and understanding of scientific ideas.

Method

The Berta's Tower Project conducted two workshops for 12 middle school students in the spring of 2003. Each workshop consisted of 10 hours of instruction over 2 days. Students were recruited with the help of school administrators and teachers from middle schools in an urban Midwestern city. The students came from a variety of socio-economic backgrounds. There were ten males and two females; five participants were students of color. The first workshop consisted of 7th graders; the second workshop consisted of 6th graders.

Description of tool

The participants in this study used the SodaConstructor microworld (http://www.sodaplay.com), a Java-based spring-mass modeling system that allows users to create structures in a virtual design space and test them against gravity. SodaConstructor provide users with three design elements: fixed point masses (displayed as a small square on the screen), free point masses (displayed as a small circle), and springs (displayed as lines). Students utilized two modes of the tool. In CONSTRUCT mode, students built their structures, placing springs and free masses into the design space by selecting from a drop-down menu and clicking in the design space to position the selected object. Students tested their constructions by switching to SIMULATE mode, which would subject their structures to the force of gravity. Students moved back and forth between CONSTRUCT and SIMULATE modes, saving their work in their personal SodaConstructor accounts prior to testing.

Workshop activities

Students solved a series of engineering design problems created by the researchers and civil engineering undergraduates on SodaConstructor, such as "build a multi-story structure". These design problems were meant to help students learn about the design-build-test cycle from engineering as they iteratively piloted their design ideas, and about center of mass as they discovered design choices that would make their structures stand in SIMULATE mode. Students worked individually to produce designs to address each challenge. Midway through each problem, students discussed their progress within their design team. Students then refined and redesigned their structures. At the end of each challenge, students chose their "best design" to display on their computer for a 10-minute virtual poster session. At the conclusion of the viewing session, students and workshop leaders came together for a whole group discussion focusing on the designs and on the important concepts introduced by the challenge.

Data Collection

Students were given clinical pre- and post-interviews (Denzin & Lincoln, 1998) where they were asked to define the center of mass, identify the location of the center of mass for a series of pictures, and answer two conceptual physics textbook problems. Students were asked to justify or explain their answers. In the post-interview, students were also asked to comment their experiences using SodaConstructor and in the workshop. Student activities and interactions during the workshop itself were captured on video by a member of the research team. The video data were not systematically collected; therefore, no quantitative analysis was done on the excerpts. However, the data were useful in providing specific examples of the events or processes identified in the post-interviews.

Data analysis

Pre- and post-interviews from the workshops were transcribed and analyzed within a grounded theory framework (Strauss & Corbin, 1998). Ten emergent categories were used for coding student responses: correct center of mass references, incorrect center of mass references, scientific answer justification, intuitive answer justification, testing, iteration, expressivity, autoexpressivity, positive comments about SodaConstructor, and negative comments about SodaConstructor.

Results

We present the results from Berta's Tower in two parts: the outcome data, which examines student gains in conceptual physics understanding, and the process data, which explores the mechanism involved in this learning environment.

Outcome data

References to Center of Mass. Students' correct references to center of mass increased from pre- to post-interview (paired t-test, mean difference +11.5 in correct references, $p<0.01$). For example, when asked for their definition of the center of mass, one student responded in the pre-interview:

> "Maybe where it's like the strongest ...?"

However, during the post interview, the same student said:

> "Center of mass is like not the middle, but the point where weight is divided evenly. The weight is distributed on both sides...Center of mass is like where most weight is equal. Kind of like the place where you put your finger and balance something on it without falling. Pretty much where all the weight is equaled out and you can balance... it doesn't have to be in the middle. It depends I guess on what the object looks like. The shape of it... where there's more weight."

Conceptual physics textbook problems. The students gave more scientific justifications of their answers to textbook problems (paired t-test, mean difference +5, $p<0.01$) and less intuitive justifications (paired t-test, mean difference -2, $p<0.01$) from pre- to post-interview. For example, one problem said: "A man balances on his two hands with his feet in the air. Then he lifts his right hand off the floor and stands on the left one alone. How must his body shift if he is to keep from falling?" During the pre-interview, one student answered:

> "I don't know what to say. He just picks up his hand and maybe leans over...? I'm not sure why, that's just what I think – he will fall over to this side."

In the post interview, the same student said:

> "This goes like that *(draws the shifting figure)*...he'd have to shift over to the left side to make sure that his center of mass is over his arm and hand and lines up. He'd fall over if he didn't do any shifting because the center of mass would still be over here - I think he would fall over. I think he would have to even out [his weight] by moving to the left side."

In other words, during the Berta's Tower workshops, students developed their understanding of center of mass, a fundamental concept in physics, and were able to use more scientifically-based reasoning when defending their answers to textbook physics problems.

Process data

We next present a brief video case study as a window into the means by which two students developed their understanding of center of mass through designing spring mass structural models using SodaConstructor during the workshop. The case study presents four excerpts from the work of a design team of two sixth grade boys, Carl and Rick.

Excerpt one: Expressivity and interest. Carl and Rick were working at their own computers on the second design challenge, which asked them to "build a multi-story structure"—that is, a structure consisting of several shapes stacked on top of each other. Rick wanted to build a three-story building, and his first design is shown in Figure 1a. Figures 1b and 1c show what happened when he simulated his design.

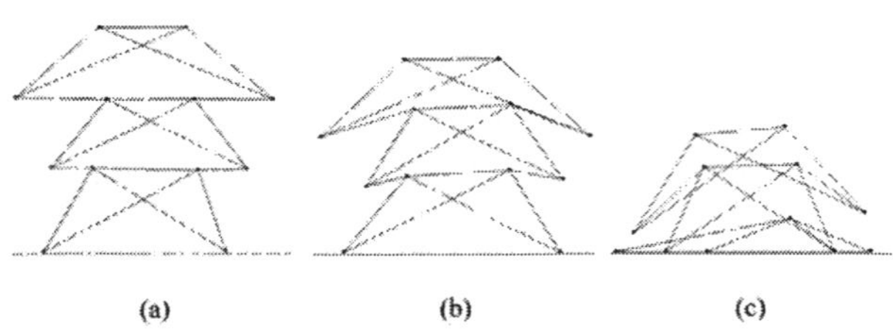

Figure 1. Rick's first attempt at solving a design challenge: 1a is in CONSTRUCT mode, 1b is the result of switching to SIMULATE mode and activating gravity, and the final equilibrium state is seen in 1c.

Rick then reloaded his saved design (Figure 2a) in order to modify it. The conversation between Rick and Carl that ensued illustrates both the highly iterative nature of the design-build-test cycle and the high level of enthusiasm students had for their design work.

Rick: *(while building)* This is cool... I want to do this all the time...I could do this all day.

Carl: *(looking at Rick's screen, see Figure 3a below)* This [design] is amazingly better. Tell me when you simulate it.

Rick: Alright.

Carl. Oh, that's not going to work.
Rob: It might not work because I made the top triangle to big
Carl: Simulate it!
Rick: I have to save it first -
Carl: *(louder)* Simulate it!
Rick: *(describing the results, see Figures 3b and 3c)* Woo it works!

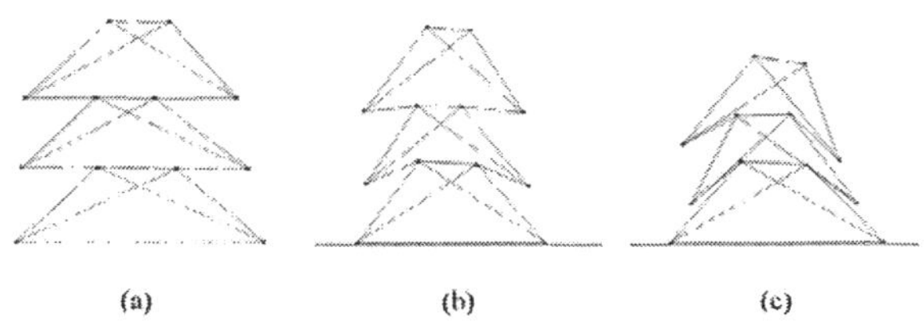

Figure 2. Rick's second attempt to solve the design challenge. Once again, 2a shows his design in CONSTRUCT mode, 2b is when he first SIMULATEs, and 2c is the final equilibrium position.

As a comparison of Figures 1 and 2 shows, Rick decided to modify each of the stories, making them more uniform, which included narrowing the top story and widening the base of the bottom story. This second design did not collapse as much as the first, and Carl noted the second iteration "stood up more" than the previous one, which pleased Rick. However, Rick wanted to minimize the "droop" of his three-story structure. In a final iteration of the DBT cycle, he added members along the side of the structure, again saved it in CONSTRUCT mode, and then simulated it with success.

Excerpt two: Autoexpressivity and understanding. During this part of the workshop, Rick and Carl were working on a design challenge in which they had to build a base for an irregular shaped object. In the design work that followed, Carl came to understand the critical relationship between the center of mass of an object and its base in determining stability.

Carl: (referring to Figure 3a) This won't work.
Rick: Try it!
Carl: (pause) Ok, I'll try it, oh wait, I should save it first.. I still don't think this will work... let's try it (simulates design and it falls over, Figure 3b)...Grrr... Oh, I know what to do!

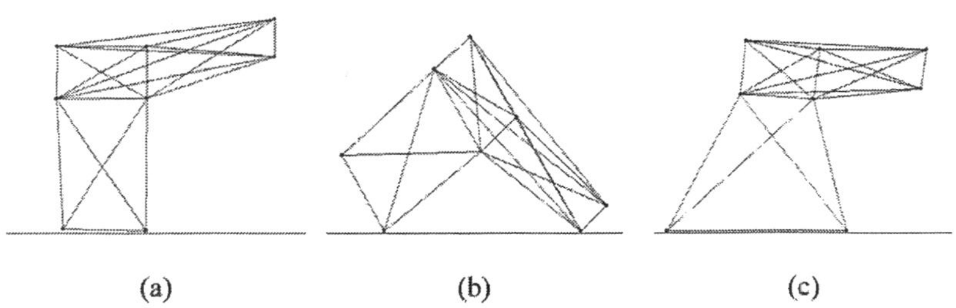

Figure 3. Two iterations of Carl' design cycle. 3a shows his first design in CONSTRUCT mode, and 3b is the result in SIMULATION mode. 3c shows his revised design in SIMULATE mode. There were no changes in 3c from CONSTRUCT to SIMULATE mode because the structure was stable.

In Carl's first design the base was too narrow to support the top half of the structure. After observing the design fall, he recognized he needed to widen the span base in order to include the center of mass within its horizontal boundaries and thus prevent tipping.

Excerpt three: Expressivity, autoexpressivity, and iteration. The last video excerpt comes near the end of the workshop. The students' final design challenge on SodaConstructor was to create a cantilever with both the widest span and the narrowest base possible. Rick decided he wanted to build his cantilever on a tall foundation, extending to the left and to the right. He began by building a wide slab supported at the center by narrow base (see Figure 4a).

Rick simulated this design and it fell over to the right. He reloaded it and modified it by rebuilding the cantilever, adding more members and connecting each mass in the slab to at least four other masses. After he simulated this design (see Figure 4b), which stood for a few seconds before slowly falling over to the right, he said:

> "With the extra supports it actually works; it bends over a little bit more than before...But I think it fell because the center of mass is a little more on this side when I was making it... yeah, now it's further out."

Rick continued to modify his design by reloading saved iterations of his work and making incremental changes: adding more members to the slab, reconstructing the base, adding a second story, adding vertical supports to the slab (see Figures 4c and 4d). Once he had a stable design that did not easily collapse or tip over, Rick began to lengthen the cantilever arms to increase the span-to-base ratio. Before his last iteration, he said:

> "You know it doesn't look like it goes out very far... I don't know, I have to figure it out... Oh! I know what I can do!"

In his last iteration (see figure 4e), he added weight to the back half of his cantilever in order to shift the center of mass to the left. At the end of the design challenge—and a total of 19 versions of his design—Rick was able to build a structure with a span-to-base ratio of 6:1.

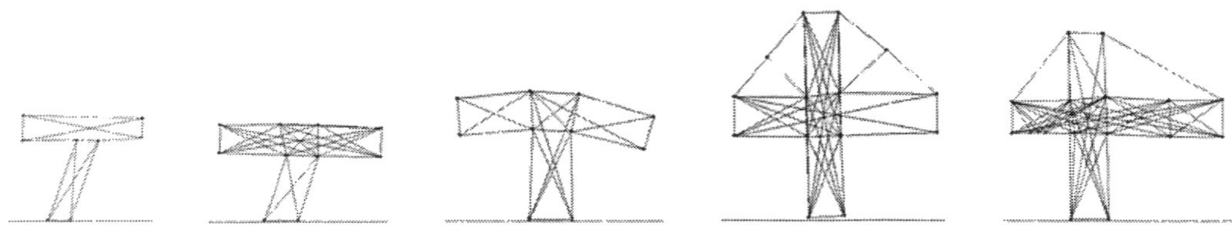

(a) (b) (c) (d) (e)

Figure 4. Iterations of Rick's cantilever design work for the final design problem.

What we see in this excerpt from Rick's design work is that Rick's initial design decision to have a cantilever supported in the middle and extending in both directions was preserved through 19 design-build test cycles. At the same time, the autoexpressive feedback from SodaConstructor helped Rick develop the understanding of center of mass and its relationship to the design of cantilevered structures that he needed to implement that design decision as a response to an engineering challenge. In other words, the highly-iterative process of rapid prototyping in an autoexpressive computational microworld made it possible for Rick to incrementally develop scientific understanding in the context of an expressive and personally-motivating project. We have shown elsewhere (Svarovsky & Shaffer, in press) that these ideas of autoexpressivity, iteration, expressivity, and the linkages between them were common across the experiences of the majority of the participants in Berta's Tower.

Discussion

Our data suggest that the middle school students in the Berta's Tower project developed understanding of center of mass through virtual engineering design challenges using a computer simulation. Moreover, these results suggest that this learning took place through rapid iterations of the DBT cycle as students solved expressive design challenges in an autoexpressive microworld. In the discussion that follows, we argue that this process can be usefully characterized by the concept of *exploratoids*.

Exploratoids

Students went through multiple iterations of the DBT cycle for each design challenge, frequently and rapidly testing small ideas in the simulation in a manner similar to the rapid prototyping that marks the early stages of engineering design. As a result, they gained small and yet meaningful insights about physics from SodaConstructor's graphical feedback—that is, from the autoexpressive properties of the tool. These insights accrued over time the students reloaded previously saved designs and refined them for their next design idea. Their motivation to continue refining their images in this intensive process came from the way in which the tool and activities allowed them to build designs that reflected their personal interests—that is, from the expressiveness of the endeavor. The students built their understanding of center of mass and their interest in using SodaConstructor cumulatively and incrementally through expressive activity in an autoexpressive tool.

As we described above, Crowley and Jacobs (2002) argue that young children often develop scientific understanding through explanatoids: short fragments of explanatory talk between a child and parent that accumulate over time into a stable base of interest in and understanding of a topic. We propose extending this idea to explain how students develop scientific understanding through expressive activities in an autoexpressive microworld. Just as conversations between parent and child function as explanatoids that create a motivating connection between interest and understanding, iterations of the DBT cycle function as *exploratoids*: short fragments of exploratory action between a student and microworld that over time accumulate to build interest and understanding.

The concept of exploratoid is a useful construct for understanding the experiences of students in the Berta's Tower workshops—and more broadly, for understanding how solving expressive design challenges in an autoexpressive microworld develops interest and understanding. In particular, it shows how and why the engineering practice of simulation-based rapid modeling may be a useful model for the design of learning environments where students learn scientific concepts through simulation-based design activity.

References

Bucciarelli, L. L. (1994). *Designing engineers*. Cambridge, MA: MIT Press.

Crowley, K., & Jacobs, M. (2002). Building islands of expertise in everyday family activity. In K. Crowley (Ed.), *Learning conversations in museums*. (pp. 333-356): Lawrence Erlbaum Associates, Publishers.

Denzin, N. K., & Lincoln, Y. (Eds.). (1998). *Collecting and interpreting qualitative materials*. Thousand Oaks, CA: SAGE Publications.

Dym, C. L., & Little, P. (2000). *Engineering design : a project-based introduction*. New York: John Wiley.

Edwards, L. D. (1995). Microworlds as representations. In R. Noss (Ed.), *Computers and exploratory learning* (Vol. 146, pp. 127-154). Berlin: Springer-Verlag.

Elger, D. F., Beyerlein, S. W., & Budwig, R. S. (2000). *Using design, build, and test projects to teach engineering*. Paper presented at the 30th Annual Frontiers in Education Conference -Building on a Century of Progress in Engineering Education, Oct 18-Oct 21 2000, Kansas, MO, USA.

Hoyles, C., Noss, R., & Adamson, R. (2002). Rethinking the microworld idea. *Journal of Educational Computing Research, 27*(1&2), 29-53.

Kolodner, J. L., Crismond, D., Gray, J. T., Holbrook, J., & Puntambekar, S. (1998). *Learning by Design from theory to practice*. Paper presented at the International Conference of the Learning Sciences, Atlanta, GA.

Noss, R., & Hoyles, C. (1996). *Windows on mathematical meanings: Learning cultures and computers* (Vol. 17). Dordrecht: Kluwer Academic Publishers.

Papert, S. (1980). *Mindstorms: Children, computers, and powerful ideas* (2nd ed.). New York, NY: Basic Books.

Petroski, H. (2003). Early education. *American Scientist, 91*(May-June), 206-209.

Resnick, M. (1997). Learning through computational modeling. *Computers in the Schools, 14*(1 -2), 143-152.

Sadler, P., Coyle, H., & Schwartz, M. (2000). Engineering competitions in the middle school classroom: Key elements in developing effective design challenges. *The Journal of the Learning Sciences, 9*(3), 299-327.

Shaffer, D. W. (1997). *Design, collaboration, and computation: The design studio as a model for computer-supported collaboration in mathematics*. Paper presented at the Computer Support for Collaborative Learning '97, Toronto, Ontario.

Shaffer, D. W. (2004a). *Epistemic frames and islands of expertise: Learning from infusion experiences*. Paper presented at the International Conference of the Learning Sciences (ICLS), Santa Monica, CA.

Shaffer, D. W. (2004b). Pedagogical praxis: The professions as models for post-industrial education. *Teachers College Record, 106*(7).

Strauss, A., & Corbin, J. (1998). *Basics of qualitative research* (second ed.). Thousand Oaks, CA: Sage Publications, Inc.

Svarovsky, G. N., & Shaffer, D. W. (in press). SodaConstructing knowledge through exploratoids. *Journal of Research in Science Teaching*.

Vincenti, W. G. (1990). *What engineers know and how they know it : analytical studies from aeronautical history*. Baltimore: Johns Hopkins University Press.

Wilensky, U. (2001). *Modeling nature's emergent patterns with multi-agent languages*. Paper presented at the EuroLogo, Linz, Austria.

Who Knows Whom in a Virtual Learning Network? Applying Social Network Analysis to Communities of Learners at the Computer Clubhouse

Elisabeth Sylvan, MIT Media Laboratory, 20 Ames Street Cambridge MA 02139, sylvan@media.mit.edu

Abstract: Social network analysis can be used to describe influence, group dynamics and collaboration in learning networks. The current analysis focuses on a distributed community of learners' email communication and represents the first step in understanding the community's social dynamics. It focuses upon the online intranet presence of the Computer Clubhouse, a network of after-school computer learning centers. The paper presents network analysis and graphs that highlight characteristics of the relationships between the youth, such as strength of their ties, gender, and location of emailing dyads. Implications for future network analysis of learning communities are discussed.

Introduction

Social network analysis (SNA) can be used to describe influence, group dynamics and collaboration in learning networks. In other fields it has provided great insight on a range of social issues such as who gets hired for different positions in businesses (Erickson 2001), where power resides in organizations (Lin 2001), and how ideas flow through individuals and across communities (Valente 1996). The current analysis focuses on a distributed community of learners' email communication and represents the first step in understanding the community's social dynamics.

A social network is the social structure of people or organizations. Social network analysis (SNA) evaluates the structure of groups of people using statistical methods. Individual people are represented as nodes and connections between individuals as lines or edges. An edge could represent different intensities or types of relationships such whether a person knows another at all, how well they know each other, or whether one person likes or dislikes another. The general shape of the network can be described numerically or graphically, specifying who is connected to whom, how strong the connections are ("tie strength"), and who contacts others via intermediaries (Degenne & Forsé 1999).

This study describes the characteristics of the learners, the use of an online resource, and the email exchanges between members of the group. The email exchanges are analyzed in a network analysis that describes who emailed whom and how email connections are different throughout the network. These findings lay the groundwork for more extensive use of SNA techniques with this community and suggests the ways in which it can be useful in the learning more generally.

The study focuses upon the online presence of the *Computer Clubhouse*, a network of after-school computer learning centers where young people from under-served communities work with adult mentors to explore their own ideas (Computer Clubhouse web site n.d). The Computer Clubhouse network is composed of 107 centers supporting a total of about 20,000 youth members. Sixty-nine percent are in the United States. Thirty-eight percent are located in 21 other countries or political regions: Ireland, Northern Ireland, the Netherlands, Denmark, Germany, Israel, the Palestinian Territories, Jordan, South Africa, India, Taiwan, the Philippines, Australia, New Zealand, Mexico, Costa Rica, Panama, Columbia, and Brazil. A central overarching organization coordinates activities, goals, and information across the network, but within the network structure, each learning center functions independently and is run by its own Clubhouse Coordinator. Different clubhouses may have very different cultures in which youth engage in different activities such as using Photoshop filters to make portraits of themselves, creating 3D worlds using 3D Studio MAX and creating their own games using GameMaker.

A challenge in a distributed learning environment such as this one is coordinating the flow of information and encouraging interactions across locations. To address this need, the *Computer Clubhouse* has its own intranet called the *Village* (see Figure 1). Through the *Village* members of the community have the unusual opportunity to discuss who they are and what interests them, and to share their ideas and projects with youth around the world (Computer Clubhouse Village web site n.d).

Figure 1. The Computer Clubhouse Village

The *Village* is used to disseminate programmatic information, coordinate events, share the youth's creation and suggest activities and ideas to inspire new projects. It has five main sections: *Projects*, *People and Clubhouses*, *Software Studio* (an area that lists all the software available at the clubhouses, along with help and online software), *Talk* (which has discussion groups and email), and *Topic Tree* (information on various Clubhouse issues such as sustainability, tutorials, digital photography, web design, and gender equity.). From their homepages, members can post photo albums, galleries and describe who they are. With the Village, youth can get involved with new projects and interact with others outside their clubhouse in ways unimaginable without it.

Who Uses the Village

As of October of 2005, the *Computer Clubhouse Village* has over 3000 users. Eighty-two percent of Village users are youth members, while the remainder are adult coordinators, mentors, and other staff. An equal number of male and female members use the *Village* (1213 male and 1214 female). The mean age of the youth is 15.28 (see Figure 2.)

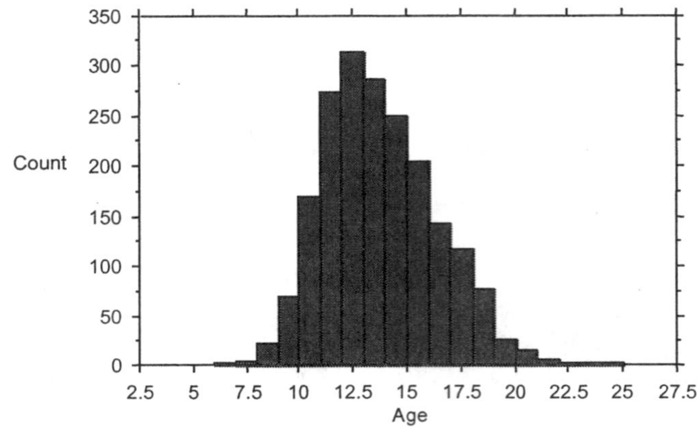

Figure 2. Count of Age of Members of the Clubhouse

Though youth from many countries use the *Village*, sixty-nine percent of the users are from the United States. Beyond that, five percent are from Columbia and the Philippines respectively, four percent from Mexico and Northern Ireland, respectively, and the remaining are from Australia, Brazil, China, Costa Rica, Denmark, India, Ireland, Israel, Jordan, the Netherlands, New Zealand, the Palestinian Territories, Panama, South Africa, and Taiwan. Seventy-nine percent of the youth describe their primary language as English, 13 percent Spanish, 3 percent Filipino and the remaining 4 percent all other languages including Chinese, Danish, Dutch, German, Hebrew, Hindi, Kannada, Portuguese, and Russian. Currently most of the Village content is in English though menu bars are available in many languages and some content is in Spanish.

How the Users are Connected Via Email

Of the 2427 registered youth users of the Village, 712 sent email between August 21 2005 and Sept 15 2005 when the current data was collected. These emails were between 1854 distinct pairs of users. Thirty-seven percent of these pairs were single emails that the receiver did not respond to. For these emails, it is possible that many members use the Village to reach out to others, perhaps outside of their usual circle, and do not get a response. Sixty-three percent of the emails were two emails within the pair. Two pairs of youth emailed each other 93 and 277 times respectively. These pairs may be using email more like instant messages.

In Figure 3, the graph on the left shows the entire social network of 712 youth with no adults including in any of the following analyses. Lines between members indicate that they exchanged emails. The width of the line indicates the number of emails sent between the two individuals. The relationships between the different shapes roughly indicate which members are more closely tied to others. From this graph we see two subgroups, one large cluster at the bottom left side and one smaller cluster near the top. We can see there are many members on the peripheries as well. Many of these peripheral members have tie strengths of 1: that is only one email was sent between the pairs. There are several explanations for these peripherals. First the senders could be "spamming" people. Second they could be social isolates. Third they could be more central to the network but not enough data has been collected. In the future, collecting more data and analyzing the directions of the emails will help to clarify this issue.

The graph on the right side of Figure 3 is identical to that on the left except it shows only ties with at least 3 emails sent between each pair. Comparing the stronger ties on the left with all ties on the right, one can see better where stronger ties exist. These ties are in the more central part of graph. There seems to be several members spanning the two cohesive groups with many relationships, some with strong and some weak ties. The members that bridge two distinct groups may be instrumental in spreading ideas through the different subgroups. (Granovetter 1973). The characteristics of these members and their groupings are presented next.

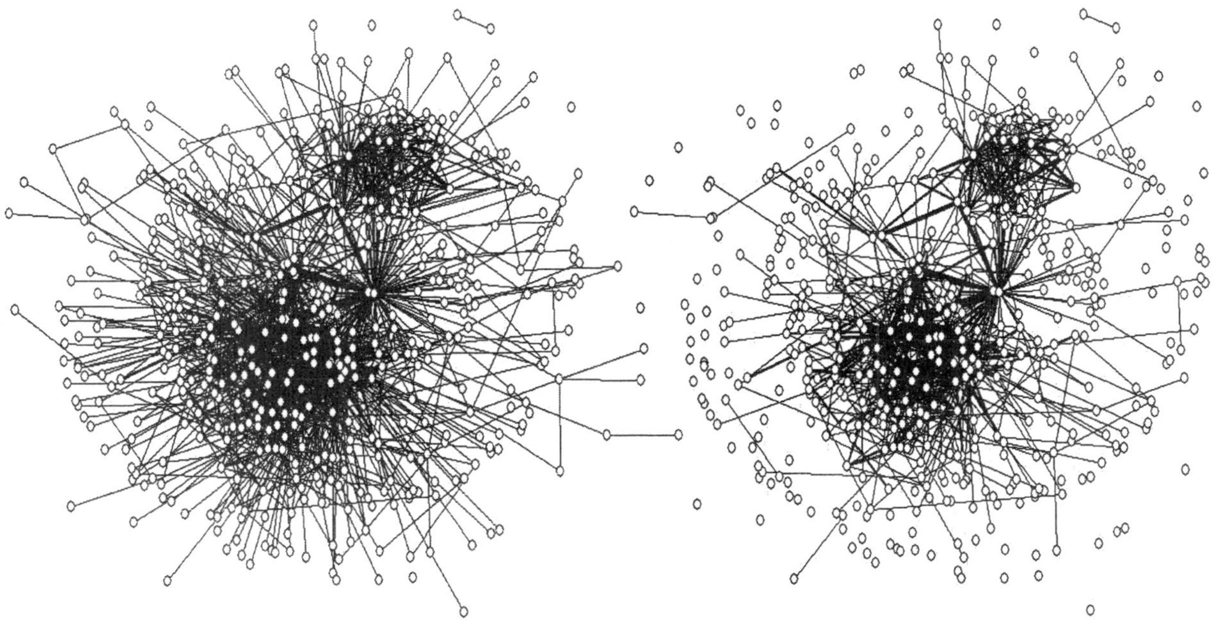

Figure 3. All Tie Strengths versus Strong Ties Only

Figure 4 is the same basic graph as those in Figure 3 except a *gray line* between two shapes demonstrates that emails were exchanged between two youth *in the same clubhouse* whereas a *black line* indicates they are *at different clubhouses*. Many ties, including strong ones, were made between members in different clubhouse, including the ones connecting the two subgroups. From this graph it seems the Village is succeeding in its goal to connect youth with others outside their neighborhood clubhouse.

What about connections made within clubhouses? The graph reveals that many of the weaker ties on the extreme perimeters of the network are connections within clubhouses. This result is hard to interpret. It is possible that these members simply emailed others who don't use Village. Connections were also made within clubhouses on the perimeters of the two subgroups whereas the center is composed of connections across clubhouses. These ties may be instrumental in getting information through the network (Granovetter 1973). The next graph addresses the same concept of regions, but considers countries instead of clubhouses.

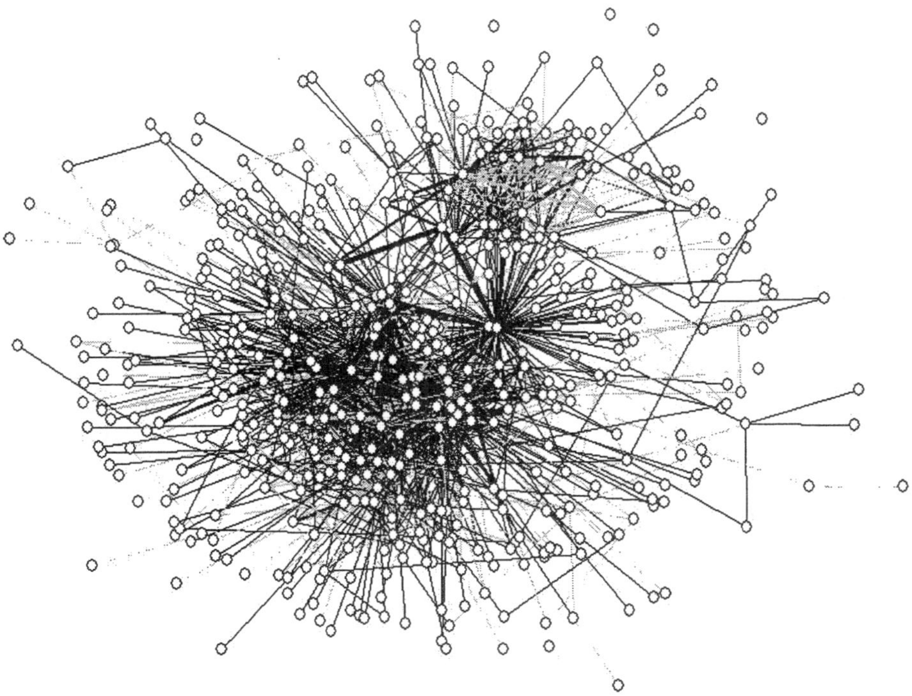

Figure 4. Emails Between Members from Different and the Same Clubhouses

Grey lines in Figure 5 demonstrate a connection within clubhouses, whereas black lines represent emails exchanged between countries. The shape of the nodes represents the country of the individual. The large subgroup that we noticed in previous graphs is primarily composed of triangles, representing the United States. The other large subgroup is composed of double triangles, representing the Philippines. As one would expect, there are far fewer connections between countries than there are between clubhouses. Still a few connections are scattered throughout. In particular, members communicate between the US and the Philippines. Since the network staff does not report any particular activities, this finding is unexpected. It will be interesting to see if this pattern continues over time and whether additional connections develop between these countries and others.

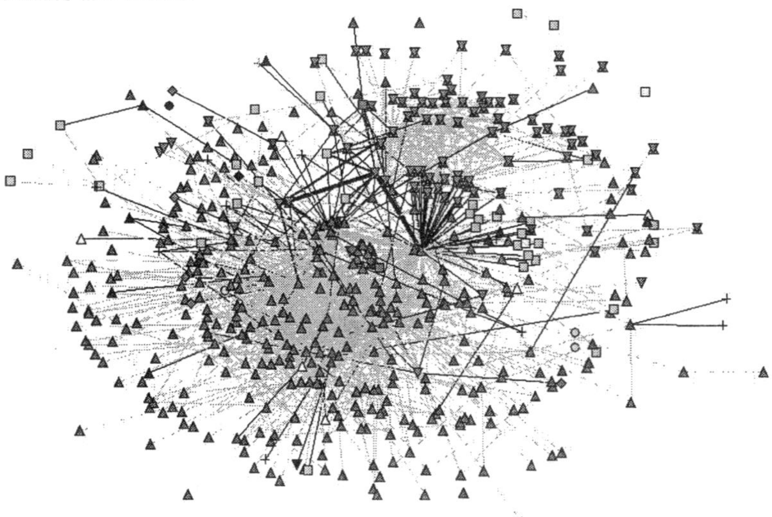

Figure 5. Emails between Members in Different Countries

Figure 6 shows the gender of email communicators. Every square represents one girl and every triangle represents one boy. A gray line between two shapes demonstrates that emails were exchanged between two youth of the same gender, whereas a black line indicates a connection across genders. From the graph we can see that communication between different genders is far more common than same gender. Perhaps we are observing flirting? We also see that girls email more than boys and appear more centrally located than boys. The bridges between the two main subgroups are girls from the US emailing with boys from the Philippines.

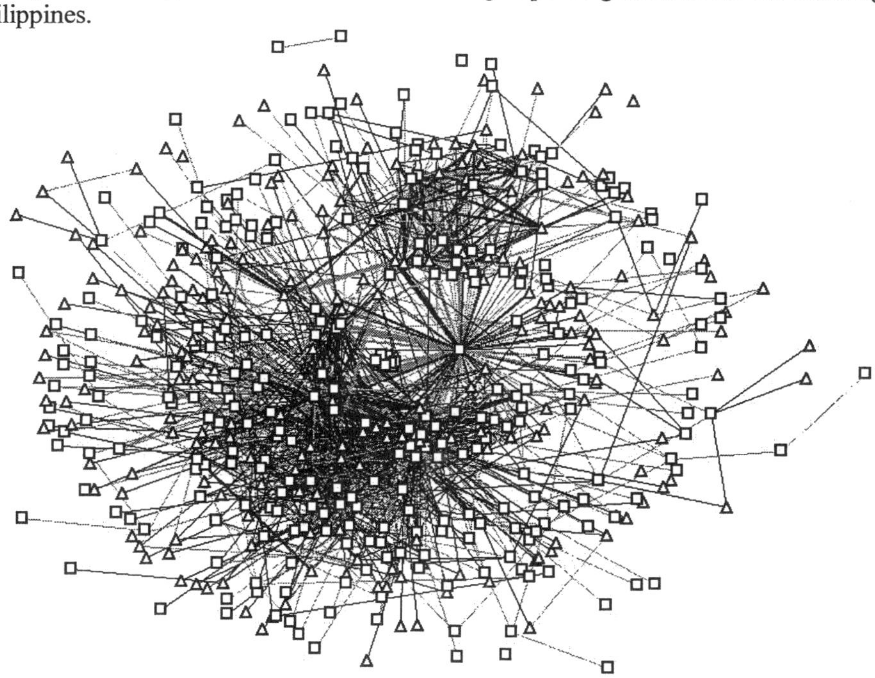

Figure 6. Social Network and Gender

From these series of network graphs we have a picture of what happens with email on the village. Two subgroups emerged primarily representing members from the US and the Philippines, respectively. A few members connect these two groups while an encouraging amount of communication occurs between clubhouses and even countries. It is likely that the youth are emailing with others they have never met in person. It is exciting that some pairs email intensively and interesting that girls seem to email more but cross gender communication is far more common than within gender.

Future Work

Understanding the ways groups of learners interact with one another is tricky. Researchers interested must unpack a complexity of individuals' processes and development, and the multiple social interactions that influence them. SNA is an exciting tool for learning science researchers interested in group dynamics, group influences, and the social aspects of learning. It provides methodologies for addressing how learners in a community interact with each other, gain knowledge from, and influence each other's learning.

This exploratory analysis of who is connecting with whom on the Computer Clubhouse Village is a first step in understanding how networks of learners function. Viewing the graphs and exploring the statistics provides an understanding of overall communication trends across the network. A few analyses will improve the understanding of members' communication:

- *Changes over time*: This includes what changes, what remains the same, and what precipitates change (such as school vacations or special Clubhouse events).
- *Direction of email:* How much do members send versus receive email and what does this say about their contribution to and gain from the network?

- *Cohesion*: How well connected is the network overall and how connected are particular groups? Do regions, gender or ages characterize cohesive subgroups?
- *Email Content*: Ask members what they discuss including projects, personal preferences, differences between their worlds, and whether they flirting.

Once the nature of the relationships are better understood, the next step will be to explore project-related data. SNA allows researchers to understand how ideas move through a network through a process called diffusion of innovation. "Diffusion is the process by which an innovation is communicated through certain channels over time among members of a social system." (Rogers 1983 quoting Beal & Bohlen 1955). Analysis of the flow of innovation might help researchers understand how ideas are adopted in learning communities, how network structure influences who adopts, and the factors that influence widespread adoption. In the case of the Village, this includes who posts projects, who looks at them, who creates their own version of a project, and who adopts project ideas into a new space. Are the youth who email a lot considered active social participants within their clubhouses? How much are active emailers considered active project creators? What role do they have in the transference of project ideas? This type of work would be profoundly exciting for those who are interested in how groups of learners influence one another.

Conclusions

This paper considers the structure of the *Computer Clubhouse* social network by looking at email: who emails whom and how much members email people outside their clubhouse. These analyses help to describe the nature of a community of distributed learners. The author argues that these types of analyses are only a first step in applying SNA to learning communities and as this work progresses, it may uncover insights into how ideas move through a network of learners and how learners influence each other.

References

Computer Clubhouse website. (n.d.). http://www.computerclubhouse.org

Computer Clubhouse Village website. (n.d.). http://village.computerclubhouse.org

Degenne, A and Forsé M (1999). Introducing Social Networks. *Sage Publication,* Thousand Oaks, CA.

Erickson, B. (2001). *Good Networks and Good Jobs: The Value of Social Capital to Employers and Employees*. Lin, et al (eds.), Social Capital: Theory and Research. *Aldine de Gruyter*, New York.

Granovetter M (1973). The Strength of Weak Ties. *American Journal of Sociology*, 78 (May): 1360-1380.

Lin, (2001). Building a Network Theory of Social Capital. Lin, et al (eds.), Social Capital: Theory and Research. *Aldine de Gruyter*, New York.

Rogers. E (1995) The Diffusion of Innovations, 4th Edition. *The Free Press*, New York.

Valente T (1996) Social network thresholds in the diffusion of innovations. *Social Networks*, *18*: 69-89.

Acknowledgments

The author thanks Mitch Resnick, Ingeborg Endter, Chris Garrity, Mikhail Rutman, Liz Doherty, and the Computer Clubhouse Network staff for their support of this project.

Enhancing Learning of Expository Science Texts in a Remedial Reading Classroom via iSTART

Roger S. Taylor, Tenaha O'Reilly, Grant P. Sinclair, Danielle S. McNamara
Institute for Intelligent Systems, The University of Memphis, Department of Psychology

Abstract: Scientific literacy is a critical skill that requires the ability to deeply comprehend challenging scientific concepts. This research investigated the effectiveness of extended classroom practice with an automated reading strategy training program (iSTART) that is designed to enhance the comprehension of expository science text. Twelve 9th grade students, enrolled in a high school remedial reading program, were trained with the iSTART program. They were compared to a control group of twelve other 9th grade students, who were comparable in reading ability but who did not receive such training. There were no significant pretest-posttest differences between the groups on comprehension questions that could be answered from a single sentence within a passage. However, the iSTART training group performed significantly better than those in the control group on bridging inference questions, which require the generation of inferences between two or more sentences within a passage.

Introduction

The impact of science literacy on our economy and society in general is significant, and has been widely documented (e.g. AAAS, 1993; NRC, 1996). The recent report by the National Academy of Sciences (NAS, 2005) describes how American leadership in the areas of science and technology has been eroded, and lays out the serious economic problems that will result if this trend is not reversed. The committee rated as "most urgent" the key recommendation to "Increase America's talent pool by vastly improving K-12 mathematics and science education" (p. 4-2).

A primary mode of science instruction involves the reading of expository science texts. Given that the intended purpose of such texts is the introduction of new and unfamiliar concepts, it is not surprising that many students have difficulty reading such materials (Bowden, 1999; Snow, 2002). This problem is exacerbated because students do not typically use good reading strategies (Cox, 1997; Garner, 1990). Therefore, one promising approach is to improve students' ability to comprehend and learn from science texts through training in the use of more effective reading strategies. Empirical studies have demonstrated that interventions targeting the enhancement of reading strategies have been successful in improving reading comprehension (e.g. Pressley et al., 1992; Rosenshine & Meister, 1994; Rosenshine, Meister, & Chapman, 1996).

Recently, attention has been given to a reading intervention called Self-Explanation (Chi, De Leeuw, Chiu, & LaVancher, 1994). Self-explanation is a process in which a learner attempts to construct a more coherent mental representation of a poorly understood phenomenon, such as those in science texts. Previous research demonstrated impressive learning gains for students when they were prompted to self-explain (e.g., Chi et al., 1994). McNamara and colleagues have built upon this research by providing learners with scaffolded training in metacognitive reading strategies (McNamara, 2004; McNamara, Levinstein, & Boonthum, 2004). In the training program, called self-explanation reading training (SERT), students learned to use six metacognitive reading strategies: comprehension monitoring, paraphrasing, prediction, logic and common sense, elaboration, and bridging inferences. Overall, the results of SERT training indicate that it results in improved comprehension, particularly for low-knowledge readers (McNamara, 2004; O'Reilly, Best, & McNamara, 2004).

Interactive Strategy Training for Active Reading and Thinking: iSTART

While previous SERT results have been encouraging, there are two limitations. First, the high cost of human tutors makes widespread adoption of the program extremely difficult, particularly in economically distressed areas. Second, the structure of the SERT program does not allow for dynamic instruction that is tailored to the specific needs of the learner. Consequently, McNamara and colleagues developed an automatized version of SERT training called iSTART (Interactive Strategy Training for Active Reading and Thinking, see McNamara et al., 2004). Training with iSTART occurs in three phases and takes approximately 2 1/2 hours. The delivery of information and feedback provided to the students is accomplished using animated pedagogical agents. The content of the feedback is determined based on the quality of the students' self-explanations, as assessed via a set of algorithms (for details, see McNamara et al., 2004).

The first phase of training is strategy *Introduction*. This phase includes definitions and examples of self-explanation and five reading strategies (i.e., comprehension monitoring, paraphrasing, prediction, bridging inferences, and elaboration). After each strategy is presented, students are asked to answer four multiple-choice questions and are then provided with immediate feedback by the program. The second phase of training is strategy *Demonstration*. In this phase, pedagogical agents model the use of the reading strategies while self-explaining a science text. Students are asked to identify the strategies used by the pedagogical agent during self-explanation, and again are provided with immediate feedback. The third phase of training is strategy *Practice*. In this phase, students read two short science passages and are asked to apply the newly learned strategies while typing self-explanations of the sentences in the texts. As they proceed through the text, several algorithms are employed to evaluate the quality (e.g., self-explanation length and the number and type of content words) of the generated self-explanations (McNamara et al., 2004). Based upon this analysis, scaffolded feedback is provided. For instance, a student providing an "impoverished" self-explanation that does not go beyond the content of the text's sentence is prompted by the agent to provide more information.

The iSTART system is adaptive and responsive to the user by providing feedback that is appropriate for specific level of the student. Investigations have revealed that using iSTART improves comprehension as compared to normal reading controls (O'Reilly, Sinclair, & McNamara, 2004a). Furthermore, research has shown the benefits of self-explanation training for low-knowledge readers, less-skilled readers, and for readers with little or no prior knowledge of reading strategies (Magliano et al., 2005; McNamara, 2004; McNamara, O'Reilly, Best, & Ozuru, in press; O'Reilly, Sinclair, & McNamara, 2004b). However, to date, there has been no study examining how self-explanation training affects the comprehension of less skilled readers over an *extended* period of post-training self-explanation practice.

Current Study

In the current study, we investigated the impact of iSTART in an ecologically valid, but highly challenging situation. That is to say, the administration at a local high school approached our research team for some assistance in helping with a remedial reading program. The administration had identified the 50 students exhibiting the lowest scores on an eighth grade reading comprehension proficiency exam, and offered them the opportunity to participate in a remedial reading class to enhance their reading comprehension skills. Twenty-five students were offered the class in the fall semester. Fifteen students accepted the offer.

Our goal was to integrate iSTART into the remedial reading class. At the beginning of the academic year we designed a curriculum that included iSTART training, followed by three weeks of extended practice using the iSTART reading strategies. We compared the iSTART-trained students to regular students on several comprehension measures at various points throughout the training/extended practice period to assess any beneficial effects of the iSTART training.

It is again emphasized that this study has high ecological validity because the intervention (i.e. pre-testing, iSTART training and extended practice, post-testing) was conducted by high-school teachers in their regular classes. In addition, all the texts used during the extended practice sessions were taken directly from the students' textbooks.

Method

Participants

The initial sample consisted of 93 9th grade students from a suburban Tennessee high school who were enrolled in a 9th grade life science course. Fifteen of these students, identified by the school as having reading comprehension difficulties based on an 8th grade reading exam, were enrolled in a special reading class designed to improve their reading comprehension. Three of the 15 reading class students did not complete the pretest reading ability measure and were, therefore, not included in these analyses. The remaining twelve students served as the *iSTART* group. Twelve students from the life science class were found who matched the iSTART students based on their pretest scores on a standardized measure of reading ability. This matched group of 12 students from the life science class served as the *control* group.

Materials

Standardized Reading Ability. Reading ability was measured by the Gates-MacGinitie reading skill test for grades 7/9 (form K at pretest, form L at posttest). The Gates-MacGinitie is a 48 item, four-alternative, multiple-choice measure of reading skill designed to assess comprehension on several short text passages.

Prior Science Knowledge. Prior science knowledge was measured with a 20–item, four-alternative, multiple-choice test to assess students' science knowledge. The test covered several areas including biology, chemistry, earth science, research methods and mathematics. Questions were selected from high school science texts collected from several states (i.e., Colorado, Georgia, Kentucky, Tennessee, Virginia).

Pretest Passage Comprehension. The pretest passage was a 333 word passage on earthquakes which described the definition and causes of various types of earthquakes. The 25 sentence passage had a Flesch Reading Ease of 61.46 and a Flesch-Kincaid Grade Level of 8.0. An accompanying set of eight open-ended questions were developed for the passage. The answers to four of the questions could be found within a single sentence of the passage, and are referred to as *text-based* questions. The answers to the remaining four questions required the reader to combine information contained in two or more sentences of the passage, and are referred to as *bridging inference* questions. An example of a text-based question was "What is a subduction boundary?" while an example of a bridging inference question was "Describe how earthquakes occur according to the elastic-rebound theory."

Posttest Passage Comprehension. The posttest passage was a 284 word passage on red blood cells which described the structure and function of red blood cells in the human body. The 21 sentence passage had a Flesch Reading Ease of 59.06 and a Flesch-Kincaid Grade Level of 8.4. Eight open-ended questions (four text-based and four bridging inference questions), similar to those in the pretest, were developed based on the content of the posttest passage. An example of a text-based question was "How does sickle-cell disease get its name?" while an example of a bridging inference question was "Explain why blood plasma is a poor carrier of oxygen?"

Procedure

Prior to the experiment, the remedial reading class teacher attended a two day workshop that covered general principles of learning, memory, and reading comprehension, as well as a detailed lecture on iSTART and how to utilize it in the classroom.

The experiment consisted of four phases: pretest, training, extended practice, and posttest. The pretest and posttest phases were identical for both the iSTART and control conditions, while the iSTART training and extended practice were performed only by students in the iSTART condition.

During the pretest, students in the iSTART and control group were administered the pretest measures in the following order and time frame: prior science knowledge (10 minutes), Gates-MacGinitie reading measure (Form K, 15 minutes), and the passage on earthquakes along with the set of comprehension questions (15 minutes).

During the training, students in the iSTART group progressed through the three sections of the iSTART program over the course of three class periods on three consecutive days. Beginning the following week, participants in the iSTART condition entered the extended strategy practice phase. This phase took place over the course of three consecutive weeks. Each week the students self-explained two texts that were taken directly from the textbooks used in their regular courses. On day one, the students used the computer portion of iSTART practice to self-explain text one, with feedback being provided by the pedagogical agent in the same manner as during the practice phase of iSTART training. On the following day (day two), the teacher led the class in a self-explanation task of text 1, and provided feedback on performance. On day three, students used the practice section of iSTART to self-explain text 2, while on the following day (day four) the teacher led the practice for text 2. The time spent on practice each week on the two texts was approximately three hours, one and a half hours of iSTART practice and one and a half hours of teacher-guided practice. On the fifth day of the week, students were given quizzes on the material that had been covered during that week. The quizzes were also administered to the control subjects, who had studied the material in the classroom in the manner normally used by the life science teacher.

During the posttest, students in the iSTART and control groups were administered the posttest measures in the following order and time frame: Gates-MacGinitie reading measure (Form L, 15 minutes), and the passage on red blood cells along with the set of comprehension questions (15 minutes).

Results

Pretest Equivalence: Reading Comprehension and Prior Science Knowledge

The twelve students in the iSTART condition were matched with twelve students in the control condition based on the number of correct responses and the number of questions attempted on the standardized measure of reading comprehension (Gates-MacGinitie pretest scores). T-tests revealed no significant difference in pretest reading scores between the iSTART condition ($M = 9.75$, $SD = 4.29$) and the control condition ($M = 9.92$, $SD = 4.36$), $t(22) = 0.09$, $p = .93$ (2-tailed), and no significant difference in pretest prior science knowledge scores between the iSTART condition ($M = 0.35$, $SD = 0.09$) and the control condition ($M = 0.39$, $SD = 0.10$), $t(22) = 0.97$, $p = .34$ (2-tailed).

Text-Based Questions

Performance on the text-based questions was assessed by scoring the number of correct answers to the text-based questions as a proportion of the total number of text-based questions ($n = 4$). A mixed-model ANOVA was performed on the between-subjects factor of condition (iSTART, control) and the repeated-measures factor of time (pretest reading comprehension, posttest reading comprehension). Due to problems with the high-school computer network, the data for six students' pretest reading comprehension scores was incomplete. These observations were replaced with means based on the total sample[1]. There was a significant increase in performance over time, $F(1, 22) = 10.6$, $p = .004$. There was no significant effect of condition, $F(1, 22) = 1.08$, $p = .311$. The interaction of time and condition was not significant, $F(1,22) = 0.038$, $p = .847$.

Bridging Inference Questions

Performance on the bridging inference questions was assessed by scoring the number of correct answers to the bridging inference questions as a proportion of the total number of bridging inference questions ($n = 4$). A mixed-model ANOVA was performed on the between-subjects factor of condition (iSTART, control) and the repeated-measures factor of time (pretest reading comprehension, posttest reading comprehension). As noted earlier, missing data for six students' pretest reading comprehension scores for the pretest text were replaced with means based on the total sample[2]. There was significant improvement in performance over time, $F(1, 22) = 58.15$, $p = .000$. There was a significant effect of condition, $F(1, 22) = 7.68$, $p = .011$. Most importantly, the interaction of time and condition was significant, $F(1,22) = 7.65$, $p = .011$ (see Figure 1), and indicated that the students in the iSTART condition exhibited a greater increase in performance from pretest ($M = 2.00$, $SD = 2.09$) to posttest ($M = 35.42$, $SD = 14.92$) than that of the students in the control condition from pretest ($M = 2.08$, $SD = 7.22$) to posttest ($M = 17.71$, $SD = 14.56$). Additionally, the difference between the iSTART condition and the control condition at posttest was significant, $t(22) = 2.94$, $p = .004$.

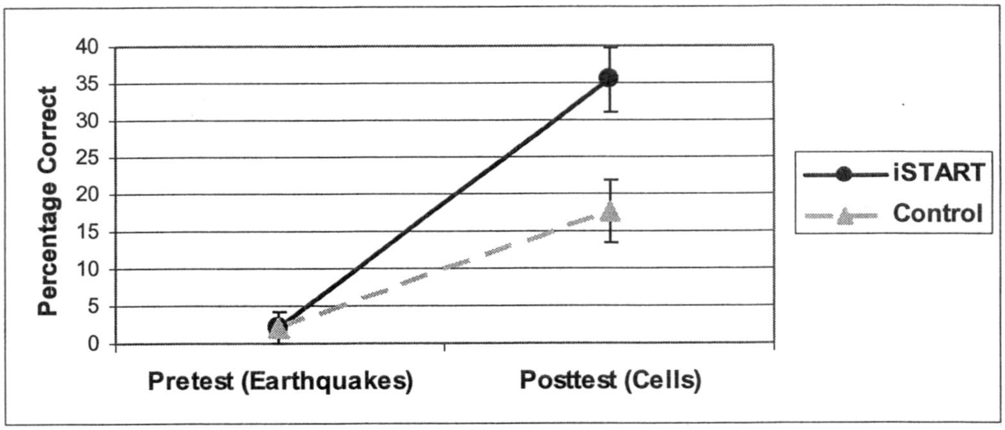

Figure 1. Percentage of correct bridging inference questions between conditions.

Discussion

The aim of this study was to examine the potential enhancement of student learning from expository science texts with extended classroom practice using the iSTART system. The key finding from this work was that this type of instructional intervention did in fact result in significantly greater performance on comprehension questions that required students to make inferences between different parts of a science text passage. This finding is especially important because this improved performance occurred on a more challenging aspect of comprehension.

During the course of the pretest phase, it was discovered that the school's computer system was not as reliable as had been believed, resulting in some data loss during that phase of the experiment. As a result of that discovery, the iSTART system has been reconfigured so that data collection can be managed independently of a school's computer network. Thus, this classroom experience helped us to identify a weakness in the software which, because we were able to address the problem, improves the viability of the iSTART program in school settings.

It should be noted that the passage for pretest comprehension assessment was on the physical science topic "earthquakes," while the passage for posttest assessment was on the biological science topic "red blood cells." A possible explanation for the higher overall scores on the posttest questions (red blood cells) is that the students in the study were enrolled in a life science class (a pre-biology course). Therefore, it is possible that the students were more familiar with the posttest materials. Nonetheless, it is clear that the iSTART trained students exhibited greater ability at answering the bridging inference questions after the training and practice phases of the experiment.

One of the main strengths of this study was its high ecological validity. Upon receiving a request to integrate the iSTART system into a local public high-school's remedial reading program, we were able to provide the teacher with the ability to conduct the training and practice in a normal classroom setting using texts from the student's textbooks. In the past, iSTART, and its feedback algorithms that are implemented during the practice phase, only included two training texts. This study indicated that iSTART practice can be readily extended to other texts.

A second encouraging factor is that, even with a limited number of students in a single remedial reading class, it is clear that the iSTART training had a significant facilitative impact on reading comprehension ability. While computer problems at pretest resulted in partial data loss, it is still clear that in comparison to the control group, the iSTART group performed significantly better on the posttest comprehension questions. Moreover, this result emerged on the more challenging bridging inference questions. In other words, the iSTART training helped these students, identified as needing remediation by the school system, to more deeply understand difficult expository science texts. We are currently performing more fine-grained analyses, including the hand-coding of the self-explanations, to more precisely determine the mechanism via which the training can enhance learning.

Previous research has suggested that iSTART training is effective because it improves the quality of students' elaborations (McNamara, O'Reilly, Best, and Ozuru, in press) and encourages students to use their general knowledge to construct deeper representations of the text (McNamara, 2004). The current results make sense with respect to these previous findings given that the more challenging bridging inference questions often require the use of elaborations and general knowledge.

With growing recognition of the national importance of science literacy, the ability to meaningfully read and learn from expository science texts is a critical educational issue. The results presented here demonstrate the value of using a powerful educational tool such as the iSTART instructional system.

Endnotes

(1) The results were the same when the missing values were replaced with the matched students' scores.
(2) The results were the same when the missing values were replaced with the matched students' scores.

References

American Association for the Advancement of Science (AAAS), Project 2061. (1993). Benchmarks for science literacy. New York: Oxford University Press.

Bowen, B. A. (1999). Four puzzles in adult literacy: Reflections on the national adult literacy survey. *Journal of Adolescent & Adult Literacy, 42*, 314–323.

Chi, M. T. H., De Leeuw, N., Chiu, M., & LaVancher, C. (1994). Eliciting self-explanations improves understanding. *Cognitive Science, 18*, 439-477.

Cox, B. D. (1997). The rediscovery of the active learner in adaptive contexts: A developmental-historical analysis of transfer of training. *Educational Psychologist, 32*, 41-55.

Garner, R. (1990). When children and adults do not use learning strategies: Toward a theory of settings. *Review of Educational Psychology, 60*, 517-529.

Magliano, J. P., Todaro, S., Millis, K. K. Wiemer-Hastings, K., Kim, H. J., & McNamara, D. S. (2005). Changes in reading strategies as a function of reading training: A comparison of live and computerized training. *Journal of Educational Computing Research*, *32*, 185-208.

McNamara, D. S. (2004). SERT: Self-Explanation Reading Training. *Discourse Processes, 38*, 1-30.

McNamara, D. S., Levinstein, I. B., & Boonthum, C. (2004). iSTART: Interactive strategy training for active reading and thinking. *Behavior Research Methods, Instruments, & Computers, 36*, 222-233.

McNamara, D. S., O'Reilly, T., Best, R., & Ozuru, Y. (in press). Improving adolescent students' reading comprehension with iSTART. *Journal of Educational Computing Research.*

National Academies of Sciences (NAS). (2005). *Rising above the gathering storm: Energizing and employing America for a brighter economic future*. Washington, DC: National Academy Press.

National Research Council (NRC). (1996). *National science education standards*. Washington, DC: National Academy Press.

O'Reilly, T., Best, R., & McNamara, D.S. (2004). Self-Explanation Reading Training: Effects for low-knowledge readers. In K. Forbus, D. Gentner, T. & Regier (Eds.*), Proceedings of the 26th Annual Meeting of the Cognitive Science Society* (pp. 1053-1058). Mahwah, NJ: Erlbaum.

O'Reilly, T.P., Sinclair, G.P., & McNamara, D.S. (2004a). Reading strategy training: Automated versus live. In K. Forbus, D. Gentner, T. & Regier (Eds.), *Proceedings of the 26th Annual Meeting of the Cognitive Science Society* (pp. 1059-1064). Mahwah, NJ: Erlbaum

O'Reilly, T.P., Sinclair, G.P., & McNamara, D.S. (2004b). iSTART: A web-based reading strategy intervention that improves students' science comprehension. In Kinshuk, D. G. Sampson, & P. Isaías (Eds.), *Proceedings of the IADIS International Conference Cognition and Exploratory Learning in Digital Age: CELDA 2004* (pp. 173-180). Lisbon, Portugal: IADIS Press.

Pressley, M., Wood, E., Woloshyn, V. E., Martin, V., King, A., & Menke, D. (1992). Encouraging mindful use of prior knowledge: Attempting to construct explanatory answers facilitates learning. *Educational Psychologist, 27*, 91-109.

Rosenshine, B., & Meister, C. (1994). Reciprocal teaching: A review of the research. *Review of Educational Research, 64*, 479-530.

Rosenshine, B., Meister, C., & Chapman, S. (1996). Teaching students to generate questions: A review of the intervention studies. *Review of Educational Research, 66*, 181-221.

Snow, C. (2002). *Reading for understanding: Toward an R & D program in reading comprehension*. Santa Monica, CA: RAND.

Multimodal Interaction in Children's Programming with Tangible Artefacts

Jakob Tholander and Ylva Fernaeus
Department of Computer and Systems Sciences, Stockholm University
Forum 100, 164 40 Kista, Sweden
jakobth@dsv.su.se, ylva@dsv.su.se

Abstract: In this paper we will investigate and document some of the practices that a group of children use to form an activity of creating a screen-based interactive play world using a tangible programming system. A specific focus is on the resources that the children use to create and maintain a sense of shared understanding of what they are building. We emphasise the embodied aspects of interaction in the activity and how physical resources and bodily action must be viewed as intrinsically intertwined with the children's process of argumentation and articulation.

Introduction

A trend in the design of tools for children's programming is to specifically address co-located and collaborative activity through the use of tangible artefacts. New technologies of this kind also requires renewed studies of the interaction that users of these tools engage in. However, studies of children's activities with new programming tools have usually not had the explicit purposes of analysing properties of the social interaction involved in the activity, but have instead aimed at exploring how computer programming may or may not support the development of abstract "thinking skills" and learning of scientific and mathematical concepts (e.g. Resnick, 2003, Noss and Hoyles, 1996, diSessa, 2000). In CSCL (Ivarsson, 2001, Stahl, 2002, Roschelle, 1992) and CSCW (Heath and Luff, 2000, Button and Dourish, 1996) there are lines of research that focus on discourse and social interaction in the use of technology. The results of such studies are used for understanding collaborative activities with new technologies, while also providing input to new and refined designs. Moreover, recent studies of classroom interactions have emphasised the complexity of the social interaction that young students engage in (Wortham, 2001, Ford, 1999). Ford for instance, emphasised the sophisticated communicative competence involved in such activity, which must be taken into account when analysing collaborative activity.

We take an analytical perspective grounded in the tradition of interaction and conversation analysis (Jordan and Henderson, 1995, Pomeranz and Fehr, 1997), with a focus on how social interaction is *practically* achieved in relation to an overall activity. An important starting point from this perspective as proposed for instance by Koschmann, T., Zemel, A., & Stahl, G. (in press) is that making *a priori* assumptions of the purpose of an educational, or any other activity becomes problematic. Instead, an analytical commitment is that the objective of an activity should be considered a *participants' concern* that must be investigated through close analysis of what the participants are actually doing. This includes investigating the role played by talk and all other social action, such as bodily conduct and use of physical artefacts that may carry meaning for the participants (Koschmann and LeBaron, 2002). A vivid example is provided in Goodwin's (2000) study of girls' social interaction when playing hopscotch, where the grid drawn on the ground provides a structure to the activity, allowing the girls to use gesture and phrases like 'this' and 'that' to refer to different squares in the grid.

This perspective has been introduced in some studies of children's programming activities, showing how the activity of programming must be understood through the embeddedness of external resources and context (Fernaeus and Tholander, 2005; Ivarsson, 2001). To conceptualise the character of children's programming with visual and tangible representations the notion of *embodied programming* has been proposed (Tholander and Fernaeus, 2004). This emphasises how visual and tangible representational artefacts turns programming into a bodily and social activity rather than something that is primarily characterised through individual and internal "thinking". In this paper these notions are further explored through closely investigating how a group of 10-year-old children interact in and through a tangible programming space, designed specifically to let children create their own dynamic systems in collaborative settings (Fernaeus & Tholander, 2005).

Setup of study

The activity accounted for here consisted of three two-hour sessions, resulting in the children building an interactive play-world that they named Desert City. The materials that the children used were physical resources for decorating the space on the floor, as well as tangible objects for programming a virtual space displayed on a large screen display (see Figure 1 and 2). The activity included discussing and deciding what to construct, as well as to create a physical world on the floor and to implement it as a system to run on the screen. All the sessions were recorded on video.

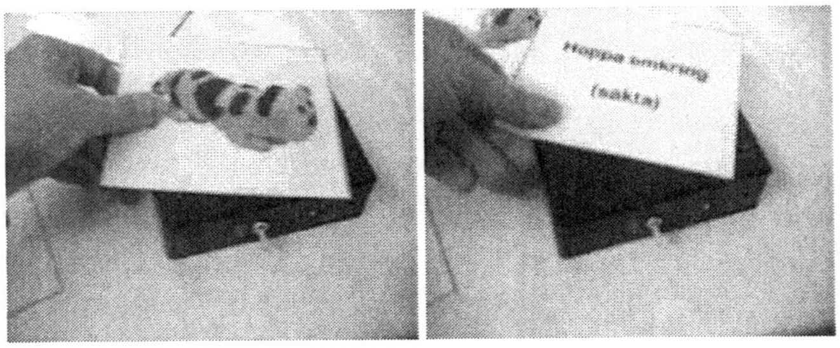

Figure 1 Programming cards: Picture (left) and behaviour (right) are placed on creator bocks on top of the mat

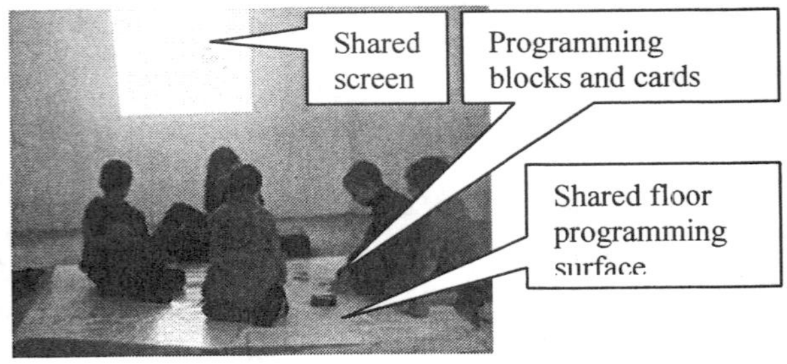

Figure 2: The children working in the programming space

When initially looking at the data, it appears to present a rather disorderly activity of a group of children interacting and playing with the resources without any obvious common goal or specific ways of coordinating their work. However, the way that the children presented their work to friends and family at a public event after the workshop suggests that there was a strong feeling of common ownership within the group around what they had achieved together. This was also reflected in the actual product that the children produced. Figure 3 shows the screen display of the final system as it looked like when being programmed. All the characters and objects in the system have been assigned a colour by the children (displayed as a surrounding square). This assignment of colours follows an elaborate system of rules that the children developed collectively, and which they also appear to have maintained throughout the activity. "Good" characters and objects have been assigned the colour "green", evil ones have been given the colour "red", and "blue" was used for things considered as "food" in their fantasy world. Black was the colour used for walls. The coloured squares on top of the characters represent different behaviours for movements and collisions.

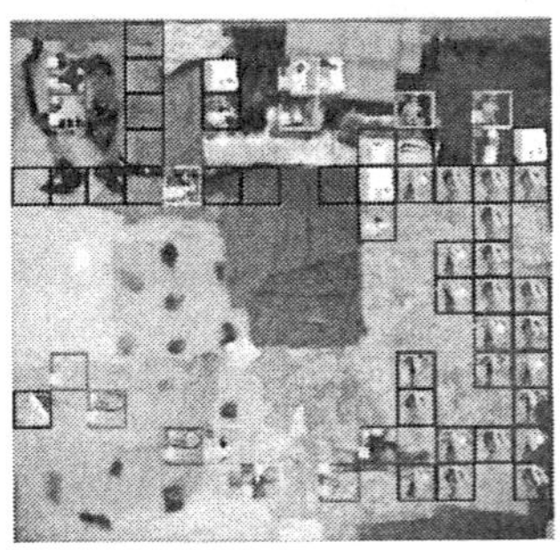

Figure 3. Screen-shot of the "desert city" when in programming mode.

This suggests that one cannot understand this situation as a group of children playing in a disorderly fashion. Instead, we must assume that the children do have ways of coordinating their work even if these are not immediately available to us on a surface level of observation. Our analytical goal is therefore to develop an understanding of how the children go about organising themselves and how the participants in the group create, sustain and shift focus as the activity develops. This includes identifying the role that the designed resources play in the process of collaboratively conducting the activity.

Analysis

The data presented here consists of three short subsequent fragments of an episode where the children are programming one of the characters in their computer play world. Prior to this activity the children have spent one hour playing with the system to learn how it works, and another hour deciding what to build with the system. In these earlier sessions the children had decided to build a "desert city" and created a number of clay figures to populate this city. At the beginning of the current session, the children have been given new programming cards with pictures of their own clay figures, and also some fabric and other materials used for building a background world for their desert city. The children have just started to actually program their world, and much of the negotiations concerns how to use the available resources for actually implementing the ideas discussed in earlier sessions. We found this episode interesting since it involves a substantial amount of negotiations that became of importance in the activities that followed, and also since it illustrates several important aspects of how the tangible resources are used to create, maintain, and shift focus of attention in these interactions.

The interlinking of verbal and physical action

In the first excerpt, the children are in the process of programming the first object that they have added to the screen, a picture of a baby Bedouin. When the excerpt starts Sebbe is holding one of the readers, and moves it upon the surface of the mat while his gaze is directed towards the projection on the wall (see illustration). The other children in the group also have their attention directed towards the screen surface, where a green square indicates the position of the reader on the mat. It should be noted that there are more readers available on the mat surface, but at this point all the children are focusing on the one currently controlled by Sebbe.

1.	Sebbe:	(positions reader on mat, looks at the screen. The focus point on the screen is at the baby Bedouin)
2.	Ivan:	*so*
3.	Ivan:	*and move it also*
4.	Sebbe:	(takes "jump around"-card, drops it on reader) *like that* (feedback from system)
5.	Niki:	*It can be blue*

Excerpt 1

The excerpt starts with Sebbe positioning the reader on the mat, while looking at the wall projection. Immediately after the screen indicates that the reader is positioned on the picture of the baby character, Ivan concludes by saying "*so*" and also proposes a next action "*and move it also*". Sebbe continues by placing a card on the reader, with the effect that the "move" behaviour becomes added to the picture on the screen. Sebbe completes this action and concurrently says "*like that*" presumably to indicate that the programming action is completed. The completion of the sequence through "*like that*" is taken up by Niki saying that "*it can be blue*" which works to suggest a new course of action, to add a colour property to the object.

The formulation of Ivan's utterance "*so and move it also*" is interesting considering that a literal construal of its meaning in this particular situation does not immediately correspond to the meaning that the participating children seem to ascribe to it. It could be taken as that Ivan is suggesting that an object, either on the screen or on the floor, should be moved to another position. The utterance "*So and move it also*" is also typical example of how children often produce verbal responses to physical actions and manipulations of tools. However, based on Sebbe's subsequent action it seems that he is not interpreting Ivan's utterance as a suggestion to move an object on the floor. But by viewing Ivan's utterance in the light of Sebbe's subsequent action, i.e. placing a behaviour card on top of the reader, Sebbe seems to be taking the utterance as a suggestion or an *instruction* for placing the "jump around" card on the reader, thereby adding the behaviour to the screen object on which the reader is placed. Ivan's utterance "*so and move it also*" is thereby a response to Sebbe's action of positioning the reader on the mat at the location of the object that they are about to program. Hence, making sense of what Ivan is saying in this situation requires that we interpret it in relation to Sebbe's gaze towards the projection while simultaneously physically positioning the reader on the mat. It then appears to be the object on the screen that should be made to move (through adding a behaviour), not the artefact that Sebbe holds in his hand.

What we would like to point out is how Ivan's statement does not make much sense if only considered through its relation to the surrounding talk. Instead, physical action and manipulation of artefacts of different kinds must also be considered as *conversational turns* of equal relevance as verbal action for the meaning making activity. This means that the meaning of verbal actions in this setting must be understood as constructed through its relation to talk and physical actions produced by the other participants, the configurations of the physical resources, the feedback provided by the software on the computer, and how these different forms of representations are made available to all the participants taking part in the activity.

Programming together

In the next excerpt, which begins immediately after the end of the transcript above, the children discuss what "colour"-property that they should assign to the picture that they are programming. The logical property of colour could be added to any picture on the screen, as a way of being able to specify interaction between specific objects.

5	Niki:	*it can be blue* (puts hand on the "blue" card on the floor)
6	Sebbe:	(puts hand on the same card as Niki)
7	Niki:	*no no it can be=*
8	Sebbe:	*=green* (looks at Niki's face)
9	Carl:	*green is the oth- other*
10	Sebbe:	*yeah green* (picks up "green" card, next to the "blue" card)
11	Sebbe:	[(moves card towards reader, looks at Carl)
12	Carl:	[*and the green are friendly*
13	Niki:	[*yeah it can (.) it is green*
14	Sebbe:	*e- the red are the evil* (points,and holds card in other hand)
16	All:	*yeah*
17	Sebbe:	(places card on the reader)
18	Ivan:	*Yeah*

Excerpt 2

In this excerpt, we would like to emphasise how programming in this setting is largely a collaborative activity to which all five children are contributing. We will also draw attention to the embodied nature of the negotiations and discussion. The excerpt starts with a short negotiation regarding what colour-property that they should assign to the baby Bedouin. This results in the agreement to give it the colour "green" (turn 5-12).

Note for instance how the group of children has arranged themselves to participate in the activity. The physical resources being spread on the floor surface allows the children to physically position themselves to face one another and at the same time keep their focus directed towards the set of physical resources collected on the surface between them. Consider for instance how Sebbe, who in this sequence is most active in the actual manipulation of the programming the tools, is facing away from the screen display (see Figures in Excerpts 1 and 2). To check what is happening on the screen requires that he turns away from the rest of the group. Such an action thereby becomes an embodied way of signalling a temporary shift of attention: away from the group and towards the screen display. Thereby the physical distribution of the tools and the physical positioning of the children in the group provide additional options for indicating to others what one is doing at a particular moment, through bodily as well as verbal action. In a more conventional PC-setting such shifts of attention becomes more subtle, requiring more work e.g. through pointing and verbal explanations, in order to create a shared focus throughout the activity.

The role of bodily action for the joint construction of meaning is particularly evident in Niki's utterance in turn 5, "*it can be blue*", while she simultaneously puts her hand on a card. In other instances throughout the activity the names of colours were a cause of confusion in the group, since having a colour can refer to an object's natural colour as well as a programmed property of an object. However, through Niki's pointing towards a programming card she provides a contextual framing that indicates that it is the programming property "blue" that she is referring to here, which also appears to be how this is interpreted by the other children. The physical action thereby serves to demarcate the range of potential meanings that the spoken utterance could otherwise have.

Another example of the social character of the negotiation is how Niki at line 7, and without any prior spoken conversation appears to change her mind regarding the colours. Just as Sebbe is about to pick up the "blue"-card, which she initially had suggested to use, she suddenly appears to hesitate, saying: "*no no it can be*", holding her hand on the card and through this action obstructing Sebbe from actually taking the card. Since the children are still in the process of programming the first object to be added on the screen, it would at this point in the programming process not matter which colour property to be added to the baby-character. However, for the process of jointly creating a fantasy world, it could be important that everyone agrees with the decisions made at this moment. Through saying "*no no it can be*" – leaving her statement open instead of suggesting another colour, Niki opens up for further negotiation in the group, making it possible for everyone to become part in making this important decision (turns 8-17). After this point it appears as Sebbe, and also the other children in the group, starts addressing Niki's hesitation by proposing alternative colours to add to the object on the screen.

Similarly Sebbe, who during this sequence seems to hold the responsibility of adding cards on the reader, repeatedly acts to make the rest of the group involved in this aspect of the activity. Just as Sebbe is about to place the "green"-card on the reader (line 14), he moves back, rises slightly and points with his index finger saying "*and the red are the evil*". In doing this, he signals to the group a possible consequence of this action: if the baby should be "green", then a feasible effect could be that the "evil" ones (e.g. the "Dracula"-character) should have the colour property "red". Note how Sebbe's talk is expressed along with very specific bodily action: lifting his gaze from the reader and the cards to instead face the group, and temporarily moving the card away from the reader. Through these actions, Sebbe provides a space for anyone who would like to object to his idea to do so, while also indicating that there should be joint understanding of the suggested programming action.

Talking trough the cards

The next excerpt illustrates how the talk is becoming closely intertwined with bodily actions conducted with the programming cards. When the transcript begins, Sebbe is just about to place the "green"-card on the reader (turn 15). In parallel to this, Niki turns around to locate a behaviour card lying behind her on the floor. In the following turns, the children discuss whether they should add a behaviour to the baby Bedouin, one that would make it "eat" other pictures in the world that they build.

15. Sebbe: *(places card on the reader)*
16. Niki: *(turns around, locates and picks up the "eat blue" card on the floor)*

17. Niki: Yeah it eats blue *(shows a card)*

18. Ivan: No it should not eat anything *(takes card from Niki)*
19. Sebbe: No it doesn't eat anything *(looks at Niki)*

20. Ivan: The baby shouldn't eat anything *(holds card towards Niki)*
21. Niki: It bites:: grr:

Excerpt 3

At turn 17, Niki holds forward a card (the card reading "eat blue") and says "*Yeah and it eats blue*". As a direct response to this proposal, Ivan takes the card from Niki's hand saying "*No, it shouldn't eat anything*" (turn 18 and picture). At this very moment, Sebbe has turned his focus back from the screen display, and immediately agrees with Ivan "`No it doesn't eat anything`". Ivan holds the card towards Niki, and says once again "`the baby shouldn't eat anything`". As a response to this, Niki suggests "`it bites`", upon which she and some of the other children bursts into a short laughter.

What we would like to point out in this excerpt is how even though the children are quite explicit in their talk, physical action with the cards is a very significant part of the negotiation. The talk being closely intertwined with bodily actions conducted with the programming cards shapes the relevant meaning of words like "eating" and "blue" to referring to being about eating and having a colour as properties one can ascribe to objects being programmed. Note for instance how the card that Niki initially puts forward is moved between the children, and thereby becomes a means of *representing arguments* in the negotiation and also "transporting" these between one another. Ivan saying "`no it shouldn't eat anything`" could here be interpreted as a way of updating Sebbe of an aspect of the negotiation by giving account for an action that Sebbe was not able to be a part of (as he was facing away from the group when Niki was holding up a card). Thus the ability to physically act with the resources does not only make the meaning of the spoken words more explicit by offloading some of the argumentation, that would otherwise have to be articulated verbally, into the physical resources themselves. This means that the card may function as external *"memories"* of the current status of the discussion, while also being the means used for actually completing what gets agreed upon. The spoken conversation has the function of explaining the actions performed with the physical resources, so that these can be understood and shared in the group. An important aspect of this is that the card is not just any physical object, it is also the actual resource that the children use to actually completing the result of the negotiation. Acting with the cards therefore became closely interweaved with children's talk, negotiation and decision-making throughout the whole programming process. To talk in this situation is a way of "doing" programming just as much as placing the cards on the readers is. And also the other way around, the programming cards are resources for "negotiation" and discussion, just as much as spoken language.

That it was Niki who suggested the baby to have the behaviour "`eat blue`", was possibly also an effect of that the card was located right beside her. It had for instance been less likely for Carl, who was sitting at the other side of the mat and much further away for that specific card, to come up with the same suggestion. The cards therefore work as structuring resources for suggesting new ideas, not only as resources for making existing ideas more explicit. Hence, we see how bodily action and use of artefacts plays a key role for the children in creating a shared focus around the programming actions that they need to agree upon to build their system.

Discussion

The notion of embodied programming have previously been used to emphasise how programming with physical and tangible representations becomes an activity where bodily actions play a significant role in the meaning-making processes of building systems. This analysis has intended to further elaborate this idea.

The interaction between the children did to a large extent concern deciding upon and defining the "conceptual content" of the objects and the relations between objects to be programmed. One could expect that deciding upon a conceptual content of assigning properties and defining relations within a group of five children would require substantial verbal elaborations in order to be settled. This was partly the case also for this group, but just as importantly, the children extensively relied upon and made use of bodily action and manipulations of interface elements in achieving their communicative and collaborative objectives. Actions like glancing at the wall projection, holding up a card, handing over a card to someone, all significantly shaped the interaction around and coordinated their work with the programming space.

What would appear at first to be resources primarily for implementing a system on the screen, turned out to play a central role in coordinating and sharing the activity in the social context where the ideas are developed and negotiated. The artefacts were used not only as tools for creating the system but also for developing a shared understanding of what to build. These results are in line with work in CSCW (e.g. Heath and Luff, 2000) and studies of social interaction (e.g. Goodwin, 2000), but have rarely been introduced in studies of children's programming. By closely considering participants' non-verbal actions we could see how these actively shaped and contributed to the ongoing conversation, and not just as complimentary to verbal action. Therefore the meaning that the children create cannot be understood from their talk only, but requires that we include bodily actions and use of physical resources as conversational *turns* in the interaction.

We have seen how the relation between negotiating ideas and to actually implement them on the computer becomes more interweaved in settings like these than would be possible in a more conventional programming setting where all resources are located on the computer screen. When children collaborate in PC-settings, they do not have the ability to make use of the programming resources in their social interaction to the same extent as we have seen here. A possible effect of this is that negations regarding the actual manipulations of programming resources become less prominent if the resources take physical form, and also changing the nature and the role of the verbal actions in argumentation and negotiation.

In traditional PC-settings controlling the mouse and keyboard often becomes a source of negotiation and control of power. In the setting studied here, the technology is distributed over a fairly large number of tangible artefacts. Thereby, it becomes difficult to take individual control of the technology since this would require one person to hold on to all the available cards and the readers at the same time. This potentially requires more effort to be put into coordinating the actions performed with these different resources in the group. Note how the children throughout the sequence never fall into discussions of whom to control a specific device or how actually a command should be practically realised, aspects which are normally under constant negotiation when children collaborate in PC-settings. Programming in this setting seems to become more of an issue of agreeing in the group about what to build rather than working out how to actually implement it.

An extensive part of the interaction in this sequence is expressed in the form of physical action with external resources and an analytical understanding of the activity of programming in this setting has required careful consideration these actions. By looking at the product that the children finally end up with, only a limited portion of the meaning that they have ascribed to it in the process of building it is manifested. Therefore we find it problematic to attempt to separate social interaction from the practical implementation of the system. Neither is more important than the other, instead both involve equally necessary and important aspects of the situation. This means that in order to meaningfully analyse collaborative programming activities it could be a mistake to degrade the role of social interaction, since it is such a central part what the activity is about for the participant. Therefore we find it limiting to see only the representation of a particular idea as the core of the activity. The final product must instead be understood within a larger context of the children's creative work, and by investigating these issues we hope to contribute to further understanding of the educational value of programming activities like these.

References

Button, G. and Dourish, P. (1996), Technomethodology: Paradoxes and Possibilities. Proceedings of CHI 1996.

diSessa, A. (2000) *Changing Minds: Computers, Learning, and Literacy,* MIT Press.

Fernaeus, Y. and Tholander, J. (2005), "Looking At the Computer but Doing It on Land": Children's Interactions in a Tangible Programming Space. in (McEwan, T., Gulliksen, J. and Benyon, D (eds.x) *HCI 2005 - The Bigger Picture*, Springer.

Ford, C. (1999) Collaborative construction of task activity: Coordinating multiple resources in a high school physics lab. *Research on Language and Social Interaction,* **32,** 369-408.

Goodwin, C. (2000) Action and Embodiment Within Situated Human Interaction. *Journal of Pragmatics* **32**, 1489-522.

Heath, C. and Luff, P. (2000) *Technology in Action,* Cambridge University Press.

Ivarsson, J. (2001), Illusory Intersubjectivity: Pointing, talking and learning in computer-supported environments. Presented at the 9th European conference for research on learning and instruction. Fribourg, Switzerland.

Jordan, B. and Henderson, A. (1995) Interaction Analysis: Foundations and Practise. *The Journal of the Learning Science, 4,* 39-103.

Koschmann, T. and LeBaron, C. (2002) Learner Articulation as Interactional Achievment: Studying the Conversation of Gesture. *Cognition and Instruction,* **20,** 249-282.

Koschmann, T., Zemel, A., & Stahl, G. (in press). The video analyst's manifesto (or the implications of Garfinkel's policies for studying practice within design-based research). In R. Goldman, B. Barron, S. Derry & R. Pea (Eds.), *Video research in the learning sciences*. Mahwah, NJ: Lawrence Erlbaum Ass.

Noss, R. and Hoyles, C. (1996) *Windows on Mathamatical Meanings. Learning Cultures and Computers,* Kluwer Academic Press.

Pomeranz, A. and Fehr, B. J. (1997) In *Discourse as Social Interaction.*, Vol. 2 (Ed, Dijk, T. v.) Sage, London.

Resnick, M. (2003) Thinking Like a Tree (and other forms of ecological thinking) *International Journal of Computers for Mathematical Learning,* **8,** 43-62.

Roshelle, J (1992). Learning by collaboration: Convergent conceptual change. *Journal of the Learning Sciences, 2,* 235-276.

Stahl, G. (2002), Understanding Educational Computational Artifacts Across Community Boundaries. Proceedings of ISCRAT 2002. Amsterdam, NL.

Tholander, J. and Fernaeus, Y. (2004), Embodied Programming. Children's interaction with visual and tangible representations. SIG-CSCL. Lausanne, Switzerland.

Wortham, S. (2001) Interactionally situated cognition: a classroom example *Cognitive Science: A Multidisciplinary Journal,* **25,** 37-66.

The Expert Novice

Bobbie Turniansky, Dina Friling, Kaye College of Education, Beer Sheva, Israel
bobbie@erez.org.il, friling@macam.ac.il

Abstract: The central proposal of this paper is that the novice experience is critical to the learning process of groups as well as individuals. How do "experts" become "novices" and move in directions that require them to put aside their theories of action? How does a group of experts collectively accomplish that? From our experiences as members of the ACE teacher educator team, and the research we have done on the team over the past three years, we propose that not only is the novice state of mind essential for professional development, change, and creativity, it also enables the teacher educator to empathize with students' experiences of being novices. We propose a new way of looking at the term "professional development" which suggests that "novice" is not the opposite of "expert". These two states are not different sides of the same continuum - they can exist simultaneously.

The Concept of Novice Within the Community

Often, making a difference involves making a change and transformational change means learning. This paper will briefly examine the development of a community of learners, a team of teacher educators, and the importance of the concept of "novice" within that community. The central proposals of this paper are that the novice experience is *critical to the learning processes* of the group as well as the individuals and that the novice state of mind *fosters the conditions that enable change* in those two spheres. As opposed to the traditional way of looking at professional development as a linear progression from novice to expert, we propose that these are not different sides of the same continuum - that "novice" is not the opposite of "expert". These are two states of mind and ways of being that can exist simultaneously.

The authors of this paper are members of the ACE team and the data on team processes were gathered through participant observation and content analysis of semi-structured interviews with all team members, meeting protocols, email exchanges and informal conversations over the past three years.

Where it all Started

The ACE staff is a group of experienced teacher educators working together to develop and implement an experimental program of teacher education within the Kaye College of Education in Israel. The long-range goal of the program is to bring about a transformation in teacher education and a resulting change in the state educational system.

Over the past four years the program has moved from an idea to a reality and the program staff has transformed itself from a collection of individuals to a "group" and eventually, a "team – "a small number of people with complementary skills who are committed to a common purpose, performance goals, and approach for which they hold themselves mutually accountable", (Katzenbach & Smith, 1993, p. 45). This process was accompanied by differences of opinion, trial and error, fights over territory and status and the necessity of learning to cope with a high level of ambiguity. It was also accompanied by feelings of achievement and satisfaction, group cohesiveness and support, and a clear program and team identity.

One of the central features of the program that resulted from this multi-faceted experience is *practical wisdom*. This approach sees knowledge as emerging through experience but experience in and of itself is not enough. That experience must also be researched and learned in order to be understood. Since learning is the main topic that concerns the team, developing its own practical wisdom, researching and understanding its own experiences, is a natural part of the group process.

The Past as Prologue

No group starts out as an empty shell just waiting to be filled. When talking about a community of learners, it is important to realize that each individual comes into the group with the outcomes of past individual learning. Whether people come together to form a group or someone joins an existing group, each member of these groups comes with a past – with an inheritance that becomes a "dowry". From this point on, a process of mutual interaction begins. Each person, who they are and what they bring with them, interacts with the group as a unit and with the individuals within it. There is a web of interaction and influence and although it cannot usually be determined exactly what influences what or who influences who and to what degree, the one certainty is that there are mutual influences. Therefore, it is important to understand who comprises the team and what the members of the team bring with them.

This year's team of 10 is a heterogeneous group whose diversity finds expression on a variety of dimensions. The team can collectively be described as women and men with an age range of about 15 years, married and single, with children and without, grandparents and the parents of school-age children. They were brought up in Israel, America, Romania and Egypt and are Jewish, Moslem and Druze with mother tongues of Hebrew, Arabic, English, Romanian and French. They live in big cities, suburbs, rural areas and kibbutz spread out geographically over an area of 185 kilometers. They have formal education in philosophy, educational counseling, biology, literature, psychology and education and have taught in higher educational settings, kindergarten, primary and secondary schools and have been school principals.

Each individual has numerous theories of action (Argyris & Schon, 1978), theories, learned or developed, that tell them what to do to achieve a specific outcome in a specific situation. As experienced teacher educators and as experts in their specific fields, ACE team members have theories of action that have served them well. One proof that their theories of action are successful is that they were selected to join the ACE program on the basis of past performance. But on the other hand, one of the missions of the program is to develop something new – a different way of helping students prepare themselves for the teaching profession in hopes of educating teachers who will make a difference.

In many cases of change, there is a gap between knowledge and practice; between vision and reality. Often, resistance to change is responsible for much of that gap. What helped this team overcome some of the obstacles of change? How do "experts" move in directions that require them to put their theories of action on the side? How does a group of experts do that as a collective? What are the cognitive and affective aspects of the process? These are questions that will be briefly considered in this paper.

Professional Development and the Novice State of Mind

Most views of professional development assume that novices will develop expertise based on the experiences in their work setting (Daley, 1999). Many definitions of professional development view it as linear improvement as professionals progress in their career. Sometimes this viewpoint is clearly expressed and sometimes it is implied. The professional starts out at point A and progresses to point B and beyond. Often it is conceptualized as "keeping current". For example, the Commission on Applied and Clinical Sociology (undated) defines professional development as "a process of learning and keeping up-to-date in one's area of expertise". Fullan (1991) looks specifically at the professional development of teachers and takes a much broader view by including "the sum total of formal and informal learning experiences throughout one's career from pre-service teacher education to retirement" (p. 326).

In light of the ACE team experience, we would like to endorse looking at the term "professional development" in a way similar to more recent perspectives on teacher professional development (Villegas-Reimers, 2003). This approach to professional development is characterized by a focus on a series of related events based in a constructivistic pedagogy that emphasizes the active learner rather than one-time workshops or lectures using on a transmission-based model in which the learner is passive. Professional development is a collaborative process of culture building and not mere skill training (Cochran-Smith and Lytle, 2001) and therefore it must be linked to a realistic context and work to develop staff member communities of learning and inquiry.

We propose that if this view is accepted, the most effective way to further professional development is to adopt the novice state of mind and act in accordance with it.

Ruthi and Ariela - Two Views of "Novice"

Ruthi, an ACE team member from its inception, talked about the juxtaposition of expertise and learning, in her interview. The experience of "being in two worlds" became apparent to her when this "expert" teacher, with long-term experience in both secondary and higher-education, had to face the task of teaching others to teach.

> "I think that on one side it's because I'm new. I never supervised student teachers in the field before, and I don't have all the most basic knowledge or expertise. Right, I'm a teacher and I've been a teacher for many years and that's a type of expertise also but I feel much more comfortable in this part because there is nothing that I feel I built inside myself that is stable and solid and that has proved itself and that I want to insist on. I'm more open. I accept a lot of things and it's become clear that I learned a lot of things that I thought I already knew. But with time, I discovered that I didn't know them well enough. I'm still pretty much in the learning stage about different aspects of supervising including all kinds of paradoxes and uncertainties and things are very, very open."

On the surface, this quote from Ruthi seems to present a paradox. The lack of knowledge she expresses here tells us that she is a novice. However, admitting doubt or a lack of knowledge requires a basic confidence in her own abilities, a state not typical of novices (Daley, 1999).

Ruthi tells us that when she has a solid, proven theory of action she is likely to insist on its correctness and its implementation. But when it comes to field supervision, she has no theory as yet. She admits she is a novice and therefore is open to learning. Only because of her expertise can Ruthi identify what she knows and does not know and isolate a specific area in which her novice state is acknowledged. However, Ruthi is not a novice in the traditional sense of the word. She is an expert and she is aware of her expertise and this awareness is the tool that allows her to admit her inexperience.

The novice experience can also be conceptualized as a state of mind not connected to a specific perceived lack. After a routine staff meeting in which the concept of "novice" was briefly mentioned, Ariela talked about the co-existence of expert and novice and its implications for her in an email exchange with other staff members.

> "One of my strongest experiences in starting to act in a new field is a feeling of dissonance, cognitive and professional, that is created as a result of the tension between my professional repertoire and experience that I bring with me and the desire to put it on the side in order to permit newness, listening to others and a real dialogue aimed at creating something new. When trying to do this I rely on Freire's argument that in order to have a real dialogue, you have to feel that the other person has something worth learning and if I know so much, it will be hard to teach me. On the other hand, I discovered that for me, the cost of doing this is heavy because shedding my cloak of professional knowledge and experience sometimes leaves me feeling naked, I have nothing. I'm left with the question of "what's my part in this new dialogue?"
>
> But in the end, I don't really remove my cloak of professional knowledge. It changes along with me in this process of renewed dialogue. In this way, when I put it across by shoulders again, both of us are already in a new place. In short, I don't take off my uniform, leave the field and return to the place I knew before. Rather I continue in the field that I was in, alone and with others, and redefine it: different, improved, new and known together."

In this quote, Ariela is basically giving us a description of professional development as a process of transformation. Through reflective dialogue, her understandings and knowledge are constantly changing although her basic professional identity remains the same. As Don Schon said, "Our systems need to maintain their identity, and their ability to support the self-identity of those who belong to them, but they must at the same time be capable of transforming themselves" (Schon 1973, p. 57). Although he was talking about organizational systems, his views of the process and necessity of transformation can be applied to individuals as well. How can this process of change and identity maintenance be nurtured and sustained? What does it mean to change and not change at the same time?

Each team member came into the ACE program with a "double dose" of expertise. Each individual was formally educated in a specific subject matter and each is also an experienced teacher educator. But as Ariela's quote shows, openness to learning with and from others is possible only if our own expertise is not allowed to take center stage. We have to become "*zipped experts*", meaning the expertise is moved to the background although it is always available to be called into action, or *unzipped*, when needed. The essence of individual expertise doesn't shrink; only the volume that it takes up in day-to-day working. The aspect of being an expert in a specific field of knowledge is preserved but the aspect of expert as conferring overall status is rejected. The specific subject matter expertise retains a lot of its flavor but the teacher education expertise becomes open to change. Having individual expertise is what gives confidence, a faith in oneself that allows one to "zip it up" and at the same time to admit vulnerability and be willing to take risks in a changing, uncertain and complex environment. Individually and collectively, team members can say "I don't know", "I'm not sure", or "Let's try it and see what happens". They are not really novices in the true sense of the word - they might better be called "expert novices" or having "the novice state of mind" and they are willing to act accordingly.

From this perspective, it seems that these two states of being - novice and expert - are not different sides of the same continuum - they can exist simultaneously.

Easier Said Than Done

Even when the team culture encourages, supports and even subtly requires its members to adopt the novice state of mind, there is no guarantee they will do so. What is obvious and taken for granted by some members may be unnoticed or unappreciated by others.

The novice state of mind is an essential part of becoming a full member of the ACE team and all that implies. The limited scope of this paper does not permit an explanation of what it means to be a member of the team, but suffice it to say that it is a very intensive, high involvement experience. Although the ideal situation would be otherwise, the team is not a single unit. That reality was expressed in the interviews when veteran members of the team were referred to by terms such as "the inner circle" and "the nuclear team".

The veteran team members, those who joined the program during the first 2 years, went through a personal and collective novice stage. The process was a natural one, inherent in the process of developing something new - a new program aimed at changing the perceptions of teaching and learning in the educational system. The staff realized that going in a new direction meant being willing to put their old perceptions and ways of doing things on the side. In addition, change always entails frustration and ambiguity and being part of a group of novices legitimates that feeling. But even at that starting point, not all of the original staff members opened themselves to that experience. They stayed within the confines of their expertise and the result was turnover of some staff members during the first year and at its end.

Towards the end of the second year, as a result of reflection on the team's ways of working and being, "novice" became one of the team's central values and took on a life of its own. Being a novice was no longer viewed as just part of a developmental process that occurred and then ended. "Being a novice" became a state that was actively encouraged and in its ideal form, non-ending.

After that initial two-year period, new members who joined the team did not go through the same experience and there are several possible explanations why they did not. One possibility is that newcomers entering an established group with a strong group identity may believe they have to prove themselves and may not feel they have the luxury of putting their knowledge aside and opening themselves up totally to the new experience. From this point of view, it may be unreasonable to expect that newcomers will allow themselves to show their uncertainty. Their actions may also have been a display of "respect". Perhaps they did not feel comfortable raising the questions and doubts of the novice because they perceived themselves as entering something already formed, something other people had put a lot of time and effort into, something that had been carefully thought out. From the other side, perhaps the veteran members did not encourage questions and doubts as fully as they should have because of an unconscious desire to protect what they had worked on so long and so hard.

Individual confidence is not enough to allow the novice state of mind to emerge. Other conditions are necessary and the basic one is trust - trust in others that the outcomes of openness and of exposed vulnerability will be used in positive ways and not as ammunition. If newcomers do not have basic trust in the rest of the group they will not allow themselves to join the novice experience. Whatever the reasons, the outcome was that the newer members were socialized into an existing situation rather than taking an active part in developing that situation. The end result was that they stayed within their expertise and therefore, for the moment at least, on the periphery of the team.

Professional Development as integral to Organizational Learning

Learning, change and development are terms used in both individual and organizational spheres. The processes in these two spheres are not identical but they support each other. Previously the question of simultaneously changing and maintaining identity was raised and it was proposed that this is what occurs when the novice and the expert co-exist. Perhaps some answers about facilitating that process can be found in the way the ACE team views learning, knowledge and expertise. Once again, Ruthi provides a cogent perspective on the effect that ACE had on her approach to knowledge and learning.

> "There's a different type of thinking here. In my first year I was very confused and I felt I wasn't working. It took me a long time until I started to see how things were done and that's exactly what I think parallels to a certain extent the difference between the perception that says that your knowledge is your personal knowledge. You acquire it or create it, build it, whatever. But it's yours. It's personally yours. You control it. There's a difference between that approach and the creation of group knowledge that doesn't turn into the exclusive possession of one person. In this sense it's a completely new experience, completely new. It took me a long time to understand what's going on, to understand that it's okay – I don't have to be the sole possessor of this knowledge and it doesn't have to stay only with me. It's out there and everyone needs to use it. That is, all of us together own the knowledge."

This quote illustrates how the approach to knowledge, to expertise, to learning within ACE differs from the approach that many academics are used to. As much as possible, members each place their individual dowry into the collective pot and everyone else is free to, and expected to, use it. But use refers to something more than passive use. Using knowledge, becoming part of the collective ownership of knowledge, implies changing that knowledge, adding to it, making it personal. Although it may seem like a contradiction in terms, making learning and knowledge "personal" also exists on the group level. In other words, individual learning is diffused among the whole team and becomes both individually owned by each team member and collectively owned by the group. The person who is most open to the process of learning is the one who has adopted the novice state of mind.

On the individual level, professionals are expected to continually learn and obviously, professional development means learning. In addition, just as there is professional development on the individual level, there is professional development on the group level and this collective process is a crucial element in organizational learning. But the question is "what are we learning"? We can learn how to do what we do in a better way – that is, we can "improve" what we are doing. This type of learning, what Argyris and Schön (1978) refer to as single-loop learning, does not raise the question of whether what we are learning to do better is the thing we should be doing at all. Single-loop learning is instrumental, adaptive learning that changes strategies of action or assumptions underlying those strategies in ways that leave the values of a theory of action unchanged. Although we may keep improving, we can easily fall into what Levitt & March (1988) term a "competency trap" – continuing to do what we are doing because it works although there may be something much better that we could be doing.. In much the same way, Tucker et al, (2002) argue that organizational learning can be prevented by problem-solving behaviors that focus solely on remedying or overcoming immediate obstacles in part because short-term success diminishes motivation to remove underlying causes of problems.

On the other hand, the learning process can be one in which everything we have done in the past is open to examination and re-evaluation. Double-loop learning (Argyis & Schön, 1978) is anticipative and generative learning that occurs when underlying norms, policies, and objectives are examined and modified if they need to be. The basic assumptions concerning the connections between actions and outcomes are re-evaluated.

The learning organization has to deal with various paradoxes including the tensions inherent in having to slow down in order to speed up (action versus reflection), and the use of conflict and confrontation to enable collaboration (Laiken, 2001). Organizations tend to be conflict-adverse (Laiken, 1994 in Laiken, 2001) but in the learning organization, problems and differences of opinion are viewed as opportunities for learning. Mistakes can be admitted because the culture is one of problem solving and not one of assigning blame.

What is the role of the novice state of mind in this process? Individuals in the novice state of mind view questions as a necessity, see everything as requiring explanation, regard nothing as sacred and know that the possibility of making a mistake is always lurking in the background. Novices in this situation are allowed to make mistakes, something real novices fear (Daley, 1999). In short, the novice state of mind fosters the conditions conducive to double-loop learning.

The Importance of the Novice State of Mind

The present state in which not all of the staff members are fully integrated into the team is not the ideal situation to be in. Each year there are some changes in membership, consequently, there are always newcomers. Therefore it is important to ask how the team can improve their processes: What can the team do to let "newcomers" voice their opinions, their doubts, their expectations and desires? How can the team enable/encourage newcomers to experience the situation of being a "novice" as the veteran team members did? How can the image of what it means to be a "novice" be made into a positive, crucial position that newcomers will not shy away from?

There are no easy answers to these questions and they have formed the basis of several discussions over the past two years. The first step towards changing the situation has been taken - the issue has been acknowledged. The next step is still to be built and it forms a central focus of the team's learning.

ACE focuses on helping its students learn to "read the situations" they are in. This approach is based on the idea that educational situations are complex situations composed of actors, settings, institutions, behaviors, thoughts, emotions, and so on in addition to the interactions between these elements. Therefore, it is usually ineffective to just pick a solution out of a learned repertoire and implement it "as is" in a given situation. Reading a situation involves asking oneself what is known and what needs to be learned about it, what I already know about being in this situation and what I have to approach with fresh eyes - that is, to be a novice. In the beginning this is easy because the students are novices in the truest sense of the word. But ACE would like them to see the value in becoming experts while retaining the novice spirit in the future also. By this we mean "reading the situation" by integrating the expert who is self confident enough to approach the "unknown" situation with the fresh eyes of the novice who faces each situation as new. The field is always novel in some way therefore learning the experience is always necessary and that means always retaining the novice experience in some sense in spite of the temptation to rest on expertise alone.

Looking at these two foci, the novice state of mind the team hopes their students will develop and retain long after they leave the program and what goes on within the team itself, it can be seen that both cases refer to the same thing - learning. The novice state of mind is what allows the learning process to continue - both on the individual and on the group level. It allows for true dialogue based on the premise that there is always room for what I can learn from others and with others.

The novice state of mind, trust, sharing, individual and group learning - all these are critical components of true professional development and enablers of the double-loop learning necessary for real change to occur.

References

Argyris, C. & Schön, D. (1978) *Organizational Learning: A theory of action perspective*. MA: Addison-Wesley.

Cochran-Smith, M. & Lytle, S. (2001). Beyond certainty: Taking an inquiry stance on practice. In A. Lieberman & L. Miller (eds.). *Teachers Caught in the Action: Professional development that matters.* New York: Teachers College Press.

Commission on Applied and Clinical Sociology (undated). Glossary. Retrieved March. 5, 2006 from http://www.sociologycommission.org/docs/GLOSSARY-%205-16-03.htm.

Daley, B. (1999). Novice to expert: An exploration of how professionals learn. *Adult Education Quarterly. 49*, 133-147.

Fullan, M., with Steigelbauer, S. (1991). *The New Meaning of Educational Change* (2nd ed.). New York: Teachers College Press.

Katzenbach, J. & Smith, D. (1993). *The Wisdom of Teams*. Cambridge, MA: Harvard University Press.

Laiken, M. (2001). Models of organizational learning: paradoxes and best practices in the post industrial workplace. NALL Working Paper #25. Toronto, Canada: The Research Network on New Approaches to Lifelong

Learning, Ontario Institute for Studies in Education of the University of Toronto. Retrieved March. 5, 2006 from http://edu.oise.utoronto.ca/depts/sese/csew/nall/res/25MarilynLaiken.pdf.

Laiken, M. (1994). Conflict in teams: Problem or opportunity? *Lectures in Health Promotion Series No. 4.* Toronto, Canada: Centre for Health Promotion, University of Toronto.

Levitt, B. & March, J. (1988). Organizational learning. *American Review of Sociology*, *14*, 319-340.

Schön, D. A. (1973) *Beyond the Stable State. Public and private learning in a changing society.* Harmondsworth: Penguin.

Tucker, A., Edmondson, A. & Spear, S. (2002). When problem solving prevents organizational learning. *Journal of Organizational Change Management*, *15*, 122-137.

Villegas-Reimers, E. (2003). *Teacher Professional Development: An international review of the literature.* Paris: UNESCO - International Institute for Educational Planning.

Does an Interface with Less Assistance Provoke More Thoughtful Behavior?

Christof van Nimwegen, Herre van Oostendorp, Utrecht University, Padualaan 14, 3584CH Utrecht, The Netherlands
christof@cs.uu.nl, herre@cs.uu.nl
Daniel Burgos, Rob Koper, Open University of the Netherlands, Valkenburgerweg 177, 6401DL, Heerlen, The Netherlands
daniel.burgos@ou.nl, rob.koper@ou.nl

Abstract: This paper investigates effects of interface style and cognitive style on problem solving performance. It is often assumed that performance improves when information is *externalized* onto the interface. Although relieving working memory this may discourage planning, understanding and knowledge acquisition. When information is *not externalized,* it must be *internalized,* stored in the user's memory, requiring more planning and thinking, perhaps leading to better performance and knowledge. Another variable influencing behavior is the cognitive style of users. We included "Need for Cognition" (NFC), the tendency to engage in cognitive tasks. We investigated the effects of interface style and NFC using planning tasks. The internalization interface led to more planful behavior and smarter solutions, but NFC had no effect. Understanding reactions to interface information is crucial in designing software aimed at education and learning. To facilitate active learning and provoke better performance, designers should take care in giving users (too) much assistance.

Introduction

Computers are indispensable in many working environments and multimedia are nowadays omnipresent in education, training and cultural institutions such as museums or science parks. A recurring issue in software design guidelines to assure some degree of usability is minimizing "user memory load", referred to as computational offloading (Scaife & Rogers, 1996). The working memory of a user has to be relieved so that a maximum of cognitive resources can be devoted to the task. *Externalization* of information, providing information on the interface to structure and guide problem-solving, often is thought to be a means by which user memory load can be minimized. The need to plan is reduced and externalization can limit the possibilities in a given situation, thus reducing the problem space (Zhang & Norman, 1994). A way to implement some degree of externalization is to make parts of the interface context-sensitive, e.g. by hiding or disabling inapplicable functions. The user is "taken by the hand" by limiting choices and providing feedback (Van Oostendorp & de Mul, 1999; De Mul & Van Oostendorp, 1996). This is related (but not equivalent) to the concept of scaffolding (Soloway, Guzdial & Hay, 1994), adopted in research on technological supports for learning. It refers to interface support to assist learners in mindfully participating in work that would otherwise be too complex. The difference is that scaffolding is meant to provide structure and guidance during learning a *new* task that a user cannot do alone. However, externalization as we use it here (and others), is *not* meant to specifically motivate mindful participation, but is rather supposed to free up cognitive resources to eventually smoothen task execution. Examples where externalization of information is applied are software installation wizards or grayed-out menu-items that don't permit using them thus offering a context-sensitive interface with only "possible" actions. For example, in Word you cannot select "paste" from the menu when nothing is copied first. "Paste" shown in gray color indicates its presence *and* its (temporary, situation dependent) unavailability. It informs users about the applicability of operators and makes remembering this unnecessary. Zhang and Norman (1994) found that relieving working memory by externalizing information could be useful for cognitive tasks: the more is externalized, the easier it is to solve the problem. But one could also argue that externalization may have negative consequences for task performance and knowledge acquisition. There is research in the context of externalization and feedback depicting current states of objects and changes of objects. For a discussion in the light of cognitive load theory (CLT) (Sweller, 1994) concerning the effects of different external visualizations on the acquisition of problem solving skill, see Scheiter, Gerjets and Catrambone (2006). They showed that use of certain animations (meant to explain) led to a substantial increase in learning time and a decrease in performance. The animations used to visualize solution procedures were more harmful than helpful for conveying problem-solving skills. They state that these visualizations may reduce learner activity and induce a passive style of processing. This could prevent learners from performing effortful cognitive processes required for understanding.

There is a general notion that learning is more effective when people experiment and discover for themselves and exploratory learning as a whole has been a subject of research in many domains. Carroll (1990) for example, already more than a decade ago propagated minimalism in design and instructions. When the design of a system is "incomplete" on purpose, users must explore the system actively, make guesses and learn from mistakes. Kerr and Payne (1994) pondered why active learning *with* the target system would be more effective than with reading instructions. Is it because the user is free to set his own goals, or to use their own words, "*is it that the learner has to attempt to solve problems himself, actively choosing or inferring the next command, rather than merely reading and applying potted solutions?*". In their experiment different types of training for MS Excel were compared, using active (problem-solving) and passive (tutorial-like, prompted interaction) learning contexts. They found that in training versions where users had to actively perform problem-solving, already during training users had a clear learning advantage. One can imagine situations in which performing skills in the long term is more important than performing well immediately after training. Charney and Reder (1986) found that a condition that provided added difficulty for learners (problem-solving) resulted in poorer initial performance than other conditions (e.g. "guided practice"), but to better delayed performance. An explanation could be that the more difficult condition perhaps instigates a deeper level of cognitive processing which eventually results in more effective learning.

What will be the influence of externalization on learning? Perhaps knowledge gained using an externalization-based interface is more volatile and difficult to transfer to other situations. This is undesirable when learning or gaining insight *itself* is the aim or when making errors is costly. Payne, Howes and Reader (2001) state that when information is externalized on the screen, users are reluctant to store relevant information in memory and are more inclined to use the external representation. O'Hara and Payne (1998, 1999) showed that dependence on exploration-support may indeed have a negative effect. Having to internalize information on the other hand may lead to more planning, better task performance and more knowledge acquisition. They distinguished between plan-based and display-based problem solving. In plan-based problem solving one uses detailed problem strategies from long-term memory. Display-based problem solving makes little use of acquired knowledge but relies on interface information. Plan-based activity leads to shorter solution routes, because steps are planned, and no unnecessary steps are taken, while a display-based strategy involves more steps because of more searching. Plan-based behavior was provoked by varying the operator cost in the interface of a puzzle, which existed in a low-cost interface and a high-cost interface. The latter imposed a longer lockout time (system response time) on subjects than the low-cost interface after an action, which made the system harder to use. The high-cost interface induced a plan-based approach which led to better performance, and the task knowledge acquired was more easily transferred to problems within the same domain. From a CLT point of view (Sweller, 1994), provoking plan based behavior is comparable with increasing "*germane load*". It refers to the degree of effort involved in processing and construction schemas, and is associated with motivation and interest. In CLT, *extraneous* load should be minimized. Extraneous load takes up valuable working memory resources away from the task and could be compared with effects of "externalization".

The design of problem-solving environments should *not discourage* planning. Strong reliance on the visual display may result in less transfer of skills and less planning. Externalizing information may not be beneficial when the goal is to achieve better, transferable task performance and knowledge. Besides better transfer to other situations, one could imagine that possessing better internal knowledge-elements, leads to better performance when one has worked with the application some longer time ago. Van Nimwegen, van Oostendorp and Tabachneck-Schijf (2004) studied this using an abstract version of the "Missionaries and Cannibals" puzzle. They investigated effects of internalization vs. externalization on task performance, knowledge, and transfer to a different problem in the same domain. The puzzle, called Balls & Boxes existed in two interface styles: externalization and internalization. Externalization was realized by graying out inapplicable (momentarily unavailable) buttons needed to perform certain operations. In the internalization condition this support was absent. To their surprise, not ever and not on any measure did externalization subjects perform better. Moreover, internalization subjects had better *knowledge* afterwards, and 8 months later the internalization subjects *still* had better knowledge and now also better performance. In addition these subjects performed better at transferring acquired rule-knowledge to a different but similar task. In a follow up study Van Nimwegen et al. (2005) investigated whether possible *differences in attitude* to problem solving were of influence. Besides interface style it was tried to influence task conception or attitude by giving instructions encouraging plan-based behavior in one group and encouraging display-based behavior in the other group. They used specific instructions to change the affective state of a user. It could be either a low-planning instruction ("solve as fast as possible, mistakes are not a problem") or a high-planning instruction ("solve as economically as possible, it will pay off"). Again internalization subjects performed better and had better knowledge. The instructions had no effect on externalization subjects: there was no difference in behavior between subjects that received high-planning vs. low-planning instructions. Upon being confronted with the externalization interface, subjects ignored or even forgot the planning instruction altogether. However, instructions *did* have effect on *internalization* subjects. With a low-planning instruction, they made twice as many illegal moves and more unnecessary moves, as compared to those with high-planning instruction.

The Current Research Problem

A drawback from the tasks used in the experiments above is that findings may not be relevant in realistic tasks. We argue that in problem-solving situations where people need to learn the underlying rules of a system, or make as little mistakes as possible, the use of a plan-based approach is preferred. If a using plan-based approach is preferred, as can be the case in learning situations, we should find out how people can be persuaded into using that approach. We will again investigate our assumptions, but now with a more realistic, more life-like task.

Interface Style

We will investigate the influence of interface style on performance on a problem-solving task. We define the externalization of the underlying rules as visualizing the result of *applying a set of constraints* onto the interface. Externalization shows which actions are allowed, comparable to grayed out menu items in for example Word, where it is shown that the current situation does not permit a function to be used because the constraints are not met.

Cognitive Style

We included subjects' differences in attitude to problem solving, because it could have an influence on behavior and performance. We used "need for cognition" (NFC), a psychological construct that measures the tendency of individuals to engage in and enjoy effortful cognitive tasks (Cacioppo, Petty & Kao, 1984). Both persons high and low on NFC need to make sense of their world, but tend to do this in different ways. A person with a high NFC loves to seek, reflect on and reason about information, whereas someone on the other end of the continuum only thinks as hard as (s)he has to and is inclined to rely on others. Crystal and Kalyanaraman (2005) demonstrated that NFC can influence perceived system usability and responses, or as they put it: "*If, in a particular HCI context, individuals high in NFC exhibit significantly different behavior than individuals low in NFC, usability could likely be improved by providing interfaces optimized for each group.*" Also other literature on adaptation and learning systems emphasizes the importance of adapting the external representation to the emotional state of learners (Kort, Reilly and Picard, 2001), or proposes adapting to various constant and volatile user characteristics (Brusilovsky, 2001). In this context, this could perhaps mean that a person with a high NFC in the externalization condition might still exercise a high amount of planning, as opposed to a low NFC subject, who is reluctant to plan.

Hypotheses

H1: Internalization leads to a more plan-based strategy and better performance than externalization. Externalization, providing assistance, tempts users not to form plans, but to rely on the interface. The internalized condition lacks this guidance and encourages planning. This planning involves spending effort on activities such as studying relevant elements of the situation, and construction and application of strategies based on elements retrieved from memory. We expect that requiring internalization will lead to better task performance and knowledge.

H2: High NFC leads to a more plan-based strategy than low NFC. People with high NFC have high intrinsic motivation to think and engage in cognitive tasks, will show more plan-based behavior. Consequently, we expect the subjects with a high NFC to have better task performance and knowledge.

Method

DESIGN AND SUBJECTS

The experiment had a 2X2 design with two independent variables: interface style (internalization or externalization) and cognitive style (low or high NFC, based on median). 43 university students (aged 19 to 32 years) participated, and received a five € reward. The experiment took an hour at most.

Material

NFC questionnaire

We used a Dutch translation of the 18-item NFC scale (Cacioppo, Petty & Kao, 1984). Subjects rated each statement (e.g. "Learning new ways to think doesn't excite me very much") on a Likert-scale ranging from one to seven. A score of one meant 'strongly disagree' and a score of seven meant 'strongly agree'. We averaged the scores on the 18 items, and split the groups on the basis of the median in "low-NFC" and "high-NFC" groups.

The Conference Planner Application

A software application called "Conference Planner" was developed by The Open University of The Netherlands and funded by the European UNFOLD Project. It simulated the planning of speakers for a conference, and consists of different components. The first one is the dynamic interface that shows every set of demands for a conference and allows the user to solve the problem based on drag & drop movements. The second one is the core of the application, the set of rules and related algorithms. Here the permitted actions and subsequent consequences are defined. The third one is the set of tasks with all the scenarios (there were 5 different scheduling situations). The conference speakers (each with different demands) had to be scheduled in one of three rooms (each with its own facilities and availability). The tasks are not difficult, but a certain approach is necessary to solve the situation in an economic manner. Without planning, the scheduling will not be optimal and extra (superfluous) moves are necessary. An adequate strategy is to look for speakers with many constraints and schedule them first. It can also be effective to first identify slots that are hard to fill and then assign speakers to those. Less smart would be to start from the top and work your way down, because at some point remaining speakers cannot be placed anymore and speakers have to be moved around. The latter strategy and also approaches such as "trial and error" do not involve much planning. The list of speakers with their constraints was shown on the left. The task was to place all the speakers on the timetable. The difference between externalization and internalization was implemented by showing, in the externalization condition where speakers can be placed (see Figure 1). When clicking on a speaker, the "legal" time slots (satisfying the constraints and being available) turned green. It however does *not* show the *best* slot, only legal ones. To move a speaker from left to right an icon in front of the speaker's name had to be "picked up" and "dragged" to its destination with the mouse. Some timeslots where always unavailable, indicated with light-gray. Empty available timeslots were white, and those occupied by a speaker would display the name of a speaker in it.

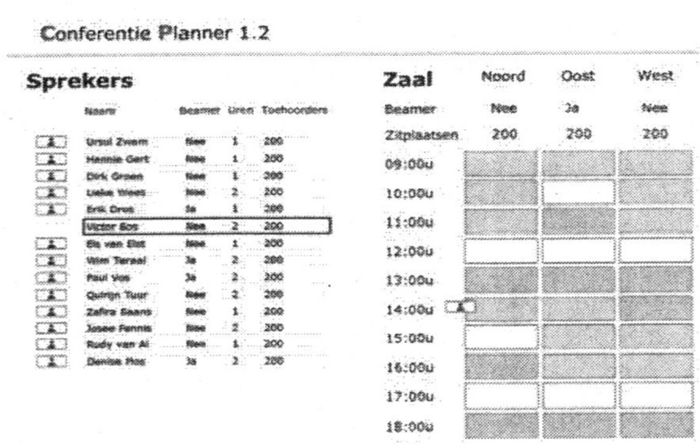

Figure 1. The externalization condition

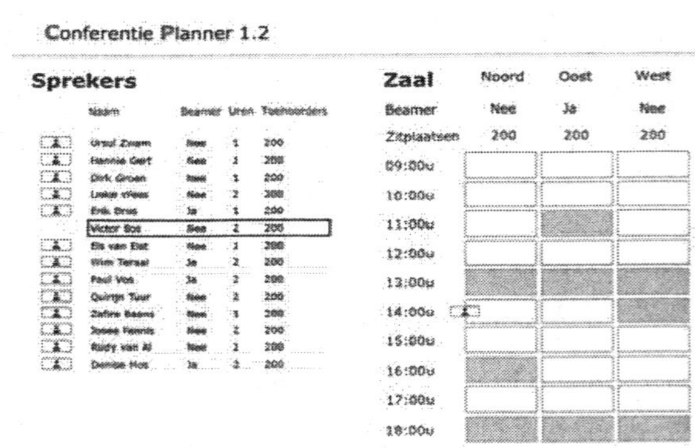

Figure 2. The internalization condition

In the internalization condition this feedback was absent (see Figure 2) and the legality of moves had to be inferred. A solution where each speaker was scheduled always existed. There were 5 tasks, with varying constraints:

- Amount of hours they will speak (1 or 2, in Dutch: uren)
- Whether a beamer* is needed (yes/no, in Dutch: ja/nee) (*Dutch/German pseudo-anglicism meaning "projector")
- Number of expected listeners (in Dutch: toehoorders)

Our quantitative measures can be divided in time-based measures (durations of actions) and move-based measures (solution paths). All the sessions were captured, and for each of the 5 tasks we analyzed whether or not subjects started solving the problem with the best strategy (first moving the speakers with the most stringent constraints).

Post-experimental questionnaire

After the 5 tasks subjects completed a questionnaire assessing knowledge of the problem. We assessed *declarative knowledge* and *procedural knowledge*. Mostly the questions explicitly asked for explanations ("why?"), besides "yes" or "no". A picture of a situation accompanied most of the questions.

- *Declarative knowledge*: Essay questions about situations that were either legal or illegal given the constraints. It had to be decided whether or not situations could occur, and why (or why not).
- *Procedural knowledge:* Essay questions concerning solution procedures. Parts of situations were given and the questions were formulated as "how would you do this?" and "is this a smart move?"

Procedure

The experiment was conducted in the Usability Lab of the Center for Content and Knowledge Engineering, Utrecht University. It started with the NFC questionnaire, followed by a textual introduction and a small video-clip showing how the application and its controls worked. After this, subjects started to work on the 5 problem solving tasks. Finally the electronic post-experimental questionnaire had to be completed.

Results

We analyzed the results using ANOVA ($p < 0.05$). All subjects eventually solved the 5 tasks correctly (see Table 1). The minimum and maximum average score on the NFC-scale were 2.39 and 6.50. The mean score was 4.89 (SD 0.83), with the median at 5.06. There were no interaction effects.

Time and moves

Table 1: Time (sec) and moves for each condition

	Internalization				Externalization			
Average for the 5 tasks	Low NFC		High NFC		Low NFC		High NFC	
	Mean	SD	Mean	SD	Mean	SD	Mean	SD
Total time needed	155.2	33.4	124.3	28.7	136.2	33.9	129.5	34.4
Time before first move	21.6	2.1	16.0	2.1	14.3	2.2	14.5	2.1
Time between moves	5.3	1.7	4.3	1.0	4.2	1.4	3.7	1.1
Superfluous moves	2.9	2.8	2.1	2.3	4.1	2.1	4.4	3.9
Correction moves	1.1	0.3	1.0	0.3	1.8	0.4	1.6	0.3
Reconsidered moves	0.5	0.5	0.4	0.5	1.7	0.5	2.4	0.5

Total time: time needed to complete a task

There were no significant main effects of interaction style or cognitive style on the average total time for the tasks. However, we did find the tendency that low-NFC subjects tended to need more time, $F(1,39)=3.58$, $p=0.07$, (M=146, SD=34 vs. M=127, SD=31). There was no effect of cognitive style.

Time before first move: time between facing/studying the problem and placing the first speaker

There was a significant main effect of interface style on the time before the first move in each of the 5 tasks, $F(1,39)=4.34$, $p<0.05$. Internalization subjects took more time than externalization subjects, M=18.9, SD=1.5 vs. M=14.4, SD=1.6. There was no significant effect of cognitive style.

Time between moves: time between placing one speaker and starting to place the next

There was a main effect of interface style on the average time *between* moves, $F(1,39)=4.82$, $p<0.05$. Internalization subjects took more time between moves than externalization subjects, M=4.8, SD=1.4 vs. M=3.9, SD=1.3. There was no significant effect of cognitive style.

Superfluous moves: all unnecessary moves (attempted, actually done, reconsidered etc.)

There was a significant main effect of interface style on the amount of superfluous moves, $F(1,39)=4.17$, $p<0.05$. Internalization subjects made fewer superfluous moves than externalization subjects, M= 2.46, SD=0.61 vs. M=4.27, SD=0.63. For cognitive style, there was no significant effect.

Correction moves: all legal moves that were actually done, minus the ideal amount of moves

The effect of interface style on the number of correction moves was nearly significant, $F(1,39)=3.80$, $p=0.06$. Externalization subjects made more correction moves than internalization subjects, M=1.70, SD 0.25 vs. M=1.1, SD=0.24. There was no significant effect of cognitive style.

Reconsidered moves: moves that were started, but reconsidered and put back during dragging

The effect of interface style on the number of reconsidered moves was significant too, $F(1,39)=9.59$, $p<0.01$. Internalization subjects reconsidered their moves less often than externalization subjects, M=0.46, SD=0.36 vs. M=2.05, SD=0.37. There was no significant effect of cognitive style.

Strategy analysis

Subjects who were required to internalize showed a tendency to use the 'most constraints first' strategy more often than subjects in the externalization condition, but it was just a tendency ($F(1,39)=3.21$, $p=0.08$). Internalization subjects used that strategy 2.4 times (SD=1.76) out of 5 (tasks) whereas externalization used it 1.5 times out of 5 (SD=1.5). There were no effects of cognitive style.

Knowledge

The effect of interface style on answers to *declarative knowledge* questions, was practically significant at $F(1,38)=3.73$, $p=0.06$. Internalization subjects answered more of those questions correctly than externalization subjects (M=8.0, SD=0.2 vs. M=7.7, SD=0.7). The scores on *procedural knowledge* showed no differences for interface style. No effects of cognitive style were found.

Conclusion and Discussion

Our first hypothesis stating that internalization leads to more planning and better performance is supported. Internalization resulted in longer thinking times before starting to work on the problem and to more time between moves. It indicates that when information has to be internalized, more contemplation is provoked and users ponder longer before acting. With the move-based measures the issue was not so much "can they solve it?" but "how smart or economical do they solve it?". Internalization subjects solved the problems with fewer superfluous moves, thus with greater economy. These moves included self-correcting moves after being stuck, illegal moves and reconsidered moves (changing your mind *while* making the move). We infer that this stems from better planning, confirming O'Hara and Payne (1998) who found that a plan-based approach resulted in fewer moves than a display-based approach, and that "backtracking" (undo a move and return to the previous situation) occurs more during display-based behavior. Our results suggest that internalization provokes more "thinking before acting" than externalization. Regarding the strategy that subjects chose to use, a qualitative analysis of the results also indicated a more plan-based approach by internalization subjects. They filled the timetable by first scheduling speakers with the most constraints more often. This strategy suggests planning, because people think about whom they are going to schedule before starting with the task. It will be interesting to examine *strategy choice* more deeply in the future. Declarative knowledge was tested afterwards by giving subjects questions in which they had to judge situations where rules (sometimes) were violated. The effect of interface style on declarative knowledge was almost significant; internalization subjects gave more correct answers. Perhaps the fact that they planned more in the previous tasks caused a training effect that made them more accurate. The procedural knowledge questions focused on insight on solving the problem. Here, interface style had no influence, perhaps not surprising, since the problems were not so difficult and all subjects solved them eventually. This confirms earlier findings of Van Nimwegen et al. (2004, 2005): a positive effect of internalization on declarative knowledge, and not on procedural knowledge. The second hypothesis was rejected. Pre-existing attitudes towards problem solving along the dimensions of NFC had no effect on performance or knowledge. Only interface style predicted problem solving behavior.

To sum up conclusions, not at any measure, externalization resulted in better performance. Once more we found positive effects of *internalization* on problem-solving behavior: it led to more plan-based behavior, smarter solution paths and better declarative knowledge. Externalization led to a more display-based approach resulting in less economic solutions and shallower thinking. It is worthwhile to reflect on *what* was externalized and visualized. The interface showed legal actions, the outcome of the *application* of the rules, a common feature in a broad range of software applications. We showed that this had undesirable effects. One has to be careful with providing interface cues that give away too much and must design in such a manner that the way users think and act is optimally supported. Designers could consider making interactions "less assisted" to persuade users into specific behavior. This issue is beyond plain usability issues and focuses on more meta cognitive aspects of interface-induced behavior such as planfulness and user engagement. Also Guttormsen Schar, Schluep, Schierz and Krueger (2000) recognize the importance of other interface design standards than *only* those suggested by common usability guidelines. They stated that "*the user-interface can play a major role in the success of learning by supporting or inhibiting certain strategies*". They do not recommend less user-friendly interaction design, but propose to extend usability guidelines with extra cognitive factors, because usability (including user satisfaction) should not be optimized at the cost of learning performance. It is a challenge to understand how people react to interface information (based on cognitive findings). Our work contributes to building bridges between cognitive science, human computer interaction and educational practices and can be valuable in the development of applications in the realms of education, multimedia learning or game based learning. Tweaking a small part of the interface had impact on behavior, but externalization and internalization were not extremes on a continuum. It refers to the *amount* of externalization. In the future it will be interesting to *adaptively varying* the level of externalization, depending on performance (Brusilovsky, 2001).

References

Brusilovsky, P. (2001). Adaptive hypermedia. *User Modeling and User-Adapted Interaction, 11*, 87-110.

Cacioppo, J.T., Petty, R.E. & Kao, C.E. (1984), The efficient assessment of need for cognition. *Journal of Personality Assessment, 48*, 306-307.

Carroll, J.M. (1990). The Nurnberg Funnel: Designing Minimalist Instruction for Practical Computer Skill. Cambridge, MA: MIT Press.

Charney, D.H., & Reder, L.M. (1986). Designing interactive tutorials for computer users. *Human-Computer Interaction, 2*, 297-317.

Crystal, A. & Kalyanaraman, S. (2005), Personality variables and information processing on the web: Methodological issues and empirical evidence. *Paper presented at the International Communication Association Annual Meeting*, New York, NY.

De Mul, S. & Van Oostendorp, H. (1996). Learning user interfaces by exploration. *Acta Psychologica, 91,* 325-344.

European UNFOLD Project: http://www.unfold-project.net

Guttormsen Schär, S., Schluep, S., Schierz, C. & Krueger, H. (2000). Interaction for computer-aided learning. *Interactive Multimedia Electronic Journal of Computer-Enhanced Learning, 2*(1).

Kerr, M.P. & Payne, S.J. (1994). Learning to use a spreadsheet by doing and watching. *Interacting with Computers, 6*, 3–22.

Kort, B., Reilly, R. & Picard, R. (2001). External representation of learning process and domain knowledge: Affective state as a determinate of its structure and function. *Paper presented at the 10th International Conference on Artificial Intelligence in Education.* San Antonio, TX.

O'Hara, K.P. & Payne, S.J. (1998). The effects of operator implementation cost on planfulness of problem solving and learning. *Cognitive Psychology, 35*(1), 34-70.

O'Hara, K.P. & Payne, S.J. (1999). Planning and the user interface: The effects of lockout time and error recovery cost. *International Journal of Human-Computer Studies, 50*(1), 41-59.

Payne S.J., Howes, A. & Reader, W.R. (2001). Adaptively distributing cognition: A decision-making perspective on human-computer interaction. *Behaviour & Information Technology, 20*(5), 339-346.

Scaife, M. & Rogers, Y. (1996). External cognition: How do graphical representations work? *International Journal of Human-Computer Studies, 45*(2), 185-213.

Scheiter, K., Gerjets, P. & Catrambone, R. (2006). Making the abstract concrete: Visualizing mathematical solution procedures. *Computers in Human Behavior, 22* (1), 9-25.

Soloway, E., Guzdial, M., & Hay, K. E. (1994). Learner-centered design: the challenge for HCI in the 21st century. *Interactions, 1*(2), 36-48.

Sweller, J. (1994). Cognitive load theory, learning difficulty and instructional design. *Learning and Instruction, 4*, 295–312.

Van Nimwegen, C., Van Oostendorp, H. & Tabachneck-Schijf, H.J.M. (2004). The over-assisting interface: The role of support in knowledge acquisition. In *Proceedings of HCI2004: Design for Life* (pp. 133-136). Bristol, UK: Research Press International.

Van Nimwegen, C., Van Oostendorp, H. & Tabachneck-Schijf, H.J.M. (2005). The role of interface style in planning during problem solving. In *Proceedings of The 27th Annual Cognitive Science Conference* (pp. 2771-2776). Mahwah, NJ: Lawrence Erlbaum.

Van Oostendorp, H. & De Mul, S. (1999). Learning by exploration: Thinking aloud while exploring an information system. *Instructional Science, 27*, 269-284.

Zhang, J., & Norman, D. A. (1994). Representations in distributed cognitive tasks. *Cognitive Science, 18*, 87-122.

Acknowledgments

We thank Hermina Schijf (Utrecht University) for her involvement and assistance during this research project.

Is Neuroscience a Learning Science?

Sashank Varma, Daniel L. Schwartz, Stanford University
450 Serra Mall, Building 160, Stanford, CA 94305-2055
sashank@stanford.edu, danls@stanford.edu
Bruce McCandliss, Sackler Institute for Developmental Psychobiology
Weill Medical College of Cornell University, 1300 York Avenue, Box 140, New York, NY 10021
bdm2001@med.cornell.edu

Abstract: Should education and neuroscience be connected? We review eight arguments against and eight arguments for connecting the two disciplines. We conclude that ultimately, whether education and neuroscience have anything to offer one another is an empirical question – one that is worth engaging.

Introduction

In an early appraisal of the prospects for connecting education and neuroscience, Bruer (1997) pronounced it "a bridge too far." This was particularly noteworthy because at the time, Bruer was director of the McDonnell Foundation and was actively funding research in both disciplines. Even though it was in his best interests to find connections between them, he found few. Eight years have passed since Bruer's cautionary evaluation. In the interim, the maturation of functional Magnetic Resonance Imaging (fMRI) has brought an exponential increase in the data on the neural bases of cognition, including those complex forms most relevant to education, such as language comprehension and mathematical reasoning. The time has come once again to ask whether education and neuroscience should be connected.

This question is addressed in two complementary sections. The first offers eight reasons against bridging between education and neuroscience. The second section counters these with eight reasons for bridging between the two disciplines. To preview our conclusions, we believe that reasoning against and reasoning for will only get us so far, and that it is an empirical question whether combining education and neuroscience will yield important empirical, theoretical, and practical advancements. Furthermore, we believe this is an experiment worth undertaking, and that its success will depend critically on educational researchers and neuroscientists collaborating across disciplinary boundaries.

Reasons Against Connecting Education and Neuroscience

A number of reasons against connecting education and neuroscience have appeared in the literature and have been shared with us in conversations with colleagues. The issues are real, although space constraints prohibit us from drawing all implications and listing supporting examples here.

Scientific: The Differences Between Brain and Behavioral Data

(1) ***Neuroscience data will never have anything to offer education.*** Even if the mind is in the brain, and therefore cognition is the product of neural computation, this does not mean that the particular neural locations of cognitive competencies are relevant for educational researchers, whose goal is to foster these competencies in children (Mayer, 1998, p. 394). For example, does it matter to curricula for teaching sentence structure whether syntax is localized in left Inferior Frontal Gyrus (IFG), the hippocampus, or striate cortex? Does this inform the pedagogy in any way? And of course, the mind as we find it in the classroom is *not* just in the brain. Behavior is profoundly shaped by context. Neuroscience methods, however, demand highly constrained and artificial contexts. For example, in fMRI experiments, participants lie inside a large and noisy cylindrical magnet and, in the vast majority of cognitive paradigms, are shown projected screen images and only permitted to press a button, which they must do for hundreds of trials to generate signals that rise statistically above the noise. In contrast, when collecting behavioral data in educational settings, context becomes the most important variable because it is what can be manipulated to change large-scale behaviors.

Philosophical: The Differences in Vocabularies and their Reduction

(2) ***The vocabularies of education and neuroscience are incommensurable.*** Education and neuroscience are different disciplines, and have evolved vocabularies appropriate for the different phenomena they study. The vocabulary of education belongs to social science and includes *mental* terms like meaning and understanding. The vocabulary of neuroscience belongs to biological science and includes *material* terms like hemodynamic response and neural pathway. It is possible that these vocabularies are fundamentally incommensurable because one is about mind and one is about body. The Cartesian dualism will preclude any dialogue between the disciplines (Byrnes & Fox, 1998, p. 299). Moreover, even if the vocabulary of education could be reduced (i.e., translated) to that of neuroscience, there would be no value in substituting neuroscience terms for proven educational terms (Byrnes & Fox, 1998, p. 299). For example, consider a child having difficulty mastering the indirect object construction. Nothing is gained by calling this "syntactic deficit" a "left IFG deficit" instead.

(3) *Even if education can be reduced to neuroscience, reductionism is a disservice to those we educate.* The significant parameters of education occur at the level of classroom dynamics, and these cannot be adequately reduced to brain function. The norms that regulate classroom interaction, for example, cannot be described as patterns of activations. Moreover, even if we could reduce the whole of education to neuroscience, this would not help pedagogy (just as reducing education to physics – translating educational theories into the language of fermions and bosons – would not help either). In fact, given the cumbersome nature of the lower-level terminology, the more likely consequence would be negative. We would lose sight of the lives we educate, because the reduction would force us to consider educationally-irrelevant details such as the statistics of neural spike trains.

Pragmatic: The Timeline of Research Developments

(4) *We don't know enough about how the brain works at the current time to inform any educational topics.* The study of how the brain performs the complex forms of cognition of greatest relevance to education is still in its infancy. We do not yet know enough about the neural localization of language comprehension, mathematical problem solving, or scientific reasoning to inform reading, mathematics, or science education (Bruer, 1997, p. 4). Cognitive neuroimaging is, after all, a relatively recent development. The number of neuroimaging studies of cognition has exploded over the past fifteen years. It still remains for cognitive neuroscientists to make sense of these data and to deliver theories of brain function at a level of abstraction appropriate for educational behaviors and changes.

Historical: Dissemination of Findings

(5) *Too often in the past, neuroscience findings have become <u>neuromyths</u>.* Several times in the recent past, neuroscience findings have been inappropriately extrapolated into educational advice of dubious value (Goswami, 2004, p. 11). For example, based on animal studies of synaptogenesis, critical periods, and environmental enrichment, claims have been made regarding the "neuroscientifically appropriate" sequencing of instruction for young children (Bruer, 1997). One still hears educational researchers speaking of the left and right hemispheres as if they are distinct organs with nothing in common. Educational researchers become frustrated when neuroscientists fail to derive from their laboratory research clear lessons that can be straightforwardly transferred to the classroom. Conversely, neuroscientists become frustrated when the precision and scope of their work are ignored in over-zealous educational applications, however well-intentioned. The general lesson appears to be that neuroscience findings must be unduly stretched, distorted, and over-simplified to make contact with educational topics.

Institutional: Requirements for Training Teachers

(6) *We cannot expect teachers to master neuroscience.* Teachers are already asked to master multiple disciplines during their training: education, cognitive and developmental psychology, content domains, cultural analysis, etc. They do not have the additional time to learn enough about brain function to make sense of the neuroscience literature. Brain anatomy alone requires weeks (if not months) of sustained study. For example, different papers refer to the same brain tissue as Broca's area, left IFG, pars triangularis, Brodmann area 45, and voxel (–44, 3, 29) in Talairach space. Teachers-in-training do not have the time to master these multiple and redundant brain geographies, let alone the details of the networks of brain areas that implement different cognitive competencies.

Financial: The Cost of Research

(7) *It is too expensive to conduct neuroimaging studies in education.* The research funding available for educational research is fixed (or perhaps even shrinking). It costs hundreds of dollars per hour to run participants in neuroimaging experiments versus a few dollars per hour to run them in behavioral classroom experiments. A cost-benefit analysis does not support spending two orders of magnitude more money on neuroscience studies, and thereby reducing educational studies in proportion.

Disciplinary: Ownership of the Research Agenda

(8) ***If education cedes control to neuroscience, it will never get it back.*** In the "decade of the brain" just ended, neuroscience exploded. The first casualty was cognitive psychology, which went from (a) a standalone discipline known for exquisite behavioral demonstrations and decompositions of human competencies to (b) an arm of neuroscience – so-called cognitive neuroscience. Debates in cognitive psychology increasingly turn on neuroimaging data, with behavioral data given short-shrift. A generation of cognitive psychologists has been rendered second-class citizens in their own discipline. Educational researchers will face a similar fate if neuroscience is allowed to enter.

Reasons for Connecting Education and Neuroscience

The eight reasons against connecting education and neuroscience, though compelling, do not constitute an ironclad case. Here, we present eight corresponding reasons for connecting the two disciplines.

Scientific: The Differences Between Brain and Behavioral Data

(1) ***Neuroscience data can be used to generate new educational hypotheses.*** Neuroscience data can be used to generate novel educational theories (Byrnes & Fox, 1998, p. 337). They are often counter-intuitive, and reveal different "joints" in cognition than are visible at the behavioral level. For example, neuroimaging studies find that the multiplication of one-digit numbers (4x2=?) activates brain areas where one would expect the "mental multiplication table" to be stored (i.e., angular and supramarginal gyrus). Surprisingly, subtraction exhibits a different pattern of activation, even though subtraction facts are also well-known. Specifically, the subtraction of one-digit numbers (4-2=?) activates areas known to perform visuospatial processing (i.e., intra-parietal sulcus and superior parietal lobule). One interpretation of this difference is that one-digit multiplication problems are solved by verbally retrieving the relevant arithmetic facts whereas single-digit subtraction problems are solved by constructing and scanning a "mental number line" (Dehaene, Piazza, Pinel, & Cohen, 2003). This *dissociation* at the brain level is invisible at the behavioral level, and demands new conceptions of multiplication and subtraction. One new hypothesis is that subtraction of natural numbers differs from multiplication in that it is open, not closed, and therefore requires use of a mental number line to check whether the result crosses zero into the range of negative numbers (2-4=?), whereas multiplication does not. In this way, counter-intuitive neuroscience results can force us to carve phenomena at different joints (e.g., whether a mathematical operation is open or closed) than we would expect based on the behavioral theories of education.

Although the contexts and behaviors permitted within fMRI experiments are restricted, it is still possible to examine the effects of context and complex behaviors. For example, participants can be separated into two conditions where they complete a month of lessons on a mathematical topic. In the 'memorization' condition, people can memorize the solutions to problems. In the 'hands-on' condition, people can work with physical manipulatives to learn the solutions to the problems. Participants in both conditions can learn to ceiling, so they are able to complete a set of 50 problems from memory. They can then be scanned during a posttest that includes two types of problems – those they memorized and new problems they have not studied. The patterns of brain activation should be different for the two conditions on the problems they have memorized, even though all participants should be able to solve these problems perfectly. Participants in the memorization condition should show activation in verbal (i.e., temporo-parietal) areas whereas participants in the hands-on condition should show activation in motor (i.e., fronto-parietal) areas. Moreover, when solving new problems, participants in the memorization condition should show diffuse activation and perform poorly, whereas those in the hands-on condition should recruit the same motor areas to successfully solve the problems. This would be true, even though their only overt behavior in the impoverished context of the scanner would be pressing a button to indicate their answers.

Philosophical: The Differences in Vocabularies and their Reduction

(2) ***Neuroscience may help resolve incommensurabilities in vocabulary.*** As neuroscience theories appear that address those cognitive competencies of greatest interest to education, there is every reason to believe that some will make contact with educational theories of how to teach those competencies (Byrnes & Fox, 1998, pp. 300, 329, 337). If one is skeptical of this claim, it is important to realize that pointing exclusively to the incommensurables between education and neuroscience is to ignore incommensurables within education itself. For example, within education, different methods are used to study the cognitive, motivational, and emotional dimensions of performance, and the results of such studies are published in different journals. By contrast, neuroscience provides a common biological vocabulary for describing cognitive, motivational, and emotional phenomena. In fact, the overlapping and intertwined networks of brain areas associated with these phenomena are a burgeoning area of research (as evidenced by journals such as *Cognitive, Affective, & Behavioral Neuroscience*). For this reason, neuroscience has the potential to overcome some of the incommensurabilities within education.

Educational researchers use constructs like 'conceptual knowledge', 'understanding', 'hands-on learning', 'constructivist activities', 'exploration', and 'inquiry' in ways that are not always consistent with one another. Neuroscience allows us to go beyond the vagueness of constructs and to also organize results in a place-based manner. A current push in some cognitive neuroscience journals is to require authors to provide a table of the brain coordinates that showed activation during a task. This permits other researchers to identify common patterns of activation across different studies, tasks and constructs. In other words, rather than anchoring findings to ambiguous labels, they are anchored to precise locations. Another important development in cognitive neuroscience is the use of meta-analyses based on these tables. For example, the preceding finding that subtraction and multiplication activate different areas was found by analyzing the data from many different studies that varied on a number of dimensions (e.g., presentation mode), but that reported their results in a place-based manner (i.e., by brain coordinates).

(3) *Reductionism in not bad if it is not eliminative reductionism.* Eliminative materialism is the doctrine that neuroscience explanations should not just anchor, but replace educational explanations (Byrnes & Fox, 1998, p. 300). Except in large paradigm shifts, eliminative reductionism has not been the natural course of events. For example, neuroscience has embraced the terminology and findings of information processing *and* behaviorism. Biology provides a nice example of maintaining levels of analysis within a reductionist paradigm. Biology attempts to make a corridor of explanation from cellular processes to ecosystems. The explanations at each level are consistent with one another, but they cannot *a priori* predict one level from the other. Similarly, reduction from education to neuroscience does not presuppose elimination.

At the same time, it is naïve to believe that all educational phenomena, such as the norms of classroom discussion, will be addressable by neuroscience in the near future. In connecting the disciplines, we need to select cross-over regions carefully. One general principle is that when neuroscience has reduced a complex cognitive ability to a set of component processes and mapped each process to a distinct brain area, then remediation programs for the ability can be developed that strengthen each component process in turn. An example of this principle is given in the next section.

Pragmatic: The Timeline of Research Developments

(4) *There are already signs of success.* A number of educational topics have already been informed, or are in the process of being informed, by neuroscience data. The canonical example comes from reading (Byrnes & Fox, 1998, p. 322; Goswami, 2004, 7-8). Neuroscience identified the brain areas associated with reading disability, mapped them to the processing of sounds corresponding to letters, and was poised to investigate the role of experience in modifying activity in these areas. At this point, education provided tried-and-true (though perhaps theoretically limited) methods for remediating phonological difficulties in kids. This partnership between neuroscience and education has informed our understanding of normal reading development, reading disability, and why some interventions are effective for some individuals, and is expanding in interesting ways, such as new investigations that leverage these insights to investigate the early roots of dyslexia in infants (McCandliss & Wolmetz, 2004). Another example comes from mathematics education, where neuroscience research is informing the design of diagnostic tests and remedial programs for dyscalculia, i.e., problems in reasoning mathematically (Landerl, Bevan, & Butterworth, 2004). On the horizon is guidance for the teaching of second languages from the neuroscience data on bilingual language comprehension (Petitto & Dunbar, 2004, pp. 2-10). And if education is defined broadly enough to include the special populations that are increasingly being mainstreamed into regular classrooms, then it will surely be informed by the rapidly expanding neuroscience literature on ADHD and Asperger's syndrome (Petitto & Dunbar, 2004, p. 1).

Historical: Dissemination of Findings

(5) *Although neuroscience findings cannot be safely extrapolated to make contact with educational topics, they can be interpolated.* Although neuroscience findings have been inappropriately applied to educational topics in the past (Bruer, 1997, pp. 4-5), this does not have to be the case in the future (Geake & Cooper, 2003, p. 13). The lesson here is not that neuroscience has no implications for education, but rather that useful implications are more likely to be drawn when neuroscience data are interpolated, not extrapolated. To continue the example of the previous section, it was not until neuroscience had painstakingly documented the brain areas responsible for the letter-sound mapping that a bridge could be built to educational research on dyslexia. As our understanding of the neural bases of other forms of complex cognition grows, so will the likelihood that this understanding will make contact with educational topics in a way that results in new pedagogy.

Institutional: Requirements for Training Teachers

(6) ***Properly abstracted findings from neuroscience might be easier for teachers than current models.*** The fact that teachers and the public at large readily embrace neuroscience theories suggests they might be more comfortable models with which to reason about cognition. The alternative we favor is that people are especially facile with spatial models of phenomena. Educational theories are abstract, typically taking the form of linguistic assertions. As a result, it is difficult to imagine how their components interact over time. Neuroscience theories, by comparison, make heavy use of spatial models – visual depictions of brain areas, the pathways that connect them, and their engagement during task performance. These models might be a powerful way for would-be-teachers to organize their understanding of cognition – which is typically presented piecemeal on a domain-by-domain basis – into a coherent whole. The challenge for teacher training, then, is to exploit the affordances of the spatial models of neuroscience to distill the literature in a way that is comprehensible to interested novices.

Although neuroscience is a complex subject, there are several ways to make it tractable for teachers-in-training. One is to focus on those aspects of brain function – learning and memory – most relevant for education, which is concerned with the acquisition, organization, and application of knowledge (Geake & Cooper, 2003, p. 14; Goswami, 2004, p. 1). Another strategy is for education to adopt the same stance towards neuroscience as medicine does toward biological science. We do not expect doctors to conduct research in biological science, but we do expect them to make sense of its literature. Analogously, the goal should not be to turn teachers into neuroscientists, but rather to prepare them to be intelligent consumers of reviews of the neuroscience literature.

Financial: The Cost of Research

(7) ***Educationally-relevant neuroscience will bring more money into educational research.*** That neuroimaging experiments are more expensive than behavioral experiments on a participant-by-participant basis is a problem only if we assume that educational funding is fixed. There are two reasons why this assumption is likely to be incorrect. The first is that, generally speaking, scientific grant proposals that promise social applications are ranked more highly than those that do not. In particular, neuroscience grant proposals are more likely to be funded if their results are relevant for education (Geake & Cooper, 2003, p. 17). Therefore, if educational researchers partner with neuroscientists on projects of mutual interest, these projects can be supported by neuroscience funding without cannibalizing educational funding. The second reason is that if education and neuroscience prove to be a fecund combination, this will attract new funding for all educational research. If the 1990s was the decade of the brain, then perhaps the 2010s will be the decade of the educable brain.

Disciplinary: Ownership of the Research Agenda

(8) ***Ask not what neuroscience can do for education, but what education can do for neuroscience.*** A common assumption in discussions about the relation between education and neuroscience is that influence runs in only one direction: neuroscience can inform education, but education has nothing to offer neuroscience. This assumption is incorrect. Education is well-positioned to make important contributions to neuroscience (McCandliss, Kalchman, & Bryant, 2003). Early neuroimaging studies targeted low-level forms of cognition, such as visual search. Current neuroimaging studies are targeting higher-level forms of cognition, such as language comprehension and mathematical reasoning. What phenomena will the next generation of neuroimaging studies target? One place to look is education (Byrnes & Fox, 1998, p. 333; Mayer, 1998, p. 395). Educational researchers have documented and analyzed the acquisition of complex forms of cognition. These analyses can contribute to the framing of the next questions for neuroscience to address. For example, neuroscientists are currently documenting the neural bases of mathematical competencies such as enumeration, magnitude comparison, estimation, arithmetic, and place-value. They are poised to connect with math educators, who have been researching these topics for many decades. Math educators have invented representations and designed activities and instructional sequences to foster their development. They have documented the misconceptions and errors that arise and developed appropriate

remediation strategies. Over the next few years, we expect these two research communities to cross-pollinate and the result to be a better understanding of the development of mathematical competence during the early elementary grades (and its derailment in dyscalculia).

Conclusion

We conclude with three observations that have been useful to us in thinking about research at the border between education and neuroscience.

Domains, not Disciplines

There exists a natural tension between disciplines that must be resolved for interdisciplinary research is to occur. One way to do this is to stop focusing on the different disciplines from which we come and start focusing on the common domains which we are interested in studying. If one's goal is to conduct research within math education, for example, then it is natural to defend one's discipline against incursions by neuroscientists and other outsiders. However, if one's goal is instead to understand the nature of mathematical reasoning, then many disciplines potentially offer insights: the history of mathematics, the development of mathematical cognition, the mathematical abilities of other species, neuroimaging studies of normal young adults, neuropsychological studies of patients with brain lesions – and of course the math education literature. When we define ourselves by the domains we study, then other disciplines become useful sources of information.

Collaboration, not Competition

Educational researchers and neuroscientists do not have to view themselves as competitors for the same knowledge. It is more fruitful for them to view themselves as collaborators (McCandliss et al., 2003). This is particularly true in light of the first observation: that educational researchers and neuroscientists should focus on common domains rather than disciplinary differences. Such collaborations can potentially leverage the strengths of each discipline's methods and theoretical frameworks.

An Empirical Matter, not a Logical Matter

Ultimately, the relation between education and neuroscience is an empirical matter (Mayer, 1998). Logical arguments that neuroscience should be ignored and counter-arguments that it should be embraced are moot in the long run. The question is whether the collaborative research of educational researchers and neuroscientists on domains of mutual interest yields interesting new insights. We believe this question is worth engaging.

References

Bruer, J. T. (1997). Education and the brain: A bridge too far. *Educational Researcher*, *26*, 4-16.

Byrnes, J. P., & Fox, N. A. (1998). The educational relevance of research in cognitive neuroscience. *Educational Psychology Review*, *10*, 297-342.

Dehaene, S., Piazza, M., Pinel, P., & Cohen, L. (2003). Three parietal circuits for number processing. *Cognitive Neuropsychology*, *20*, 487-506.

Geake, J., & Cooper, P. (2003). Cognitive neuroscience: Implications for education? *Westminster Studies in Education*, *26*, 7-20.

Goswami, U. (2004). Neuroscience and education. *British Journal of Educational Psychology*, *74*, 1-14.

Landerl, K., Bevan, A., & Butterworth, B. (2004). Developmental dyscalculia and basic numerical capacities: A study of 8–9-year-old students. *Cognition*, *93*, 99-125.

Mayer, R. E. (1998). Does the brain have a place in educational psychology? *Educational Psychology Review*, *10*, 389-396.

McCandliss, B. D., & Wolmetz, M. (2004). Developmental psychobiology of reading disability. In B. J. Casey (Ed.), *Developmental psychobiology of reading*. Washington, D. C.: American Psychiatric Publishing.

McCandliss, B. D., Kalchman, M., & Bryant, P. (2003). Design experiments and laboratory approaches to learning: Steps toward collaborative exchange. *Educational Researcher*, *32*, 14-16.

Petitto, L.-A., Dunbar, K. (2004). *New findings from educational neuroscience on bilingual brains, scientific brains, and the educated mind.* Paper presented at the Conference on Building Usable Knowledge in Mind, Brain, & Education, Cambridge, MA.

Pugh, K. R., Mencl, W. E., Jenner, A. R., Katz, L., Frost, S. J., Lee, J. R., Shaywitz, S. E., & Shaywitz, B. A. Neurobiological studies of reading and reading disability. *Journal of Communication Disorders*, *34*, 479-492.

Acknowledgments

We thank Minna Hannula, Robb Lindgren, Janet Go, Jammie Chang, John Bransford, John Geake, Paul Howard-Jones, Sue Pickering, and Usha Goswami for comments on these ideas. This material is based upon work supported by the National Science Foundation under Grants No. REC 0337715 and SLC-0354453. Any opinions, findings, and conclusions or recommendations expressed in this material are those of the authors and do not necessarily reflect the views of the National Science Foundation.

Design-based science learning: Important challenges and how technology can make a difference

Swaroop S. Vattam, Janet L. Kolodner
Georgia Institute of Technology, 801 Atlantic Drive, Atlanta, GA 30332-0280
Email: svattam@cc.gatech.edu, jlk@cc.gatech.edu

Abstract: The affordances of design activity for science learning are well-recognized. However, the implementation of design-based science learning in classrooms presents a number of significant challenges. We have been exploring some of these challenges in our design-based approach to science learning called Learning by Design (LBD). In this article, we describe two significant challenges we faced in implementing our LBD approach and present two strategies that we have implemented in our software, SIMCARS, to address them. We also present the results of a pilot study which suggest that when SIMCARS was integrated into one of LBD's science units, it helped the participants of our study to overcome the identified challenges of learning effectively from design activity.

Design-based science learning (DBSL) (Fortus et al., 2004; Kafai, 1996; Kolodner et al., 2003; Penner et al., 1998) continues to receive significant attention in educational circles because of the widely recognized affordances of design activity for learning. But there is also an ongoing discussion about the various challenges involved in implementing a DBSL approach in classrooms (Hmelo et al., 2000; Kafai, 1996; Kolodner et al., 2003; Penner et al., 1998; Schauble et al., 1995). We add to this ongoing discussion by focusing on two challenges that we have found in implementing our DBSL approach, Learning by Design (LBD) (Kolodner et al., 2003). First, we have to meet learners' need for explicit support for constructing scientific understanding from their design experiences. Second, we have to find ways to suitably complement the real world design environment, compensating for situations where the real world prevents learners from having the right kind of design experiences to be able to emphasize principled understanding due to time, material or environmental constraints. In this paper, we discuss these two educational challenges associated with DBSL and a technological solution involving our educational software package called SIMCARS. Addressing the first challenge, SIMCARS incorporates an explanation tool that scaffolds students to explain the design phenomena that they experience in "scientific" terms, enhancing their abilities of connecting observed physical phenomena to the underlying science content. In order to address the second challenge, we have included in SIMCARS a simulation-based design environment. SIMCARS' virtual design environment complements learners' real world design environment by including more possibilities for design than in the real world and by allowing investigation under conditions which cannot be easily made to exist in the real world. We will also discuss a study which shows that when we had learners use SIMCARS in the context of one of LBD's units, SIMCARS helped some students to connect their design experiences to the science content, enhancing their scientific understanding in the context of designing. It also showed potential to overcome many of the limitations of the real world design environment that were preventing the learners from learning effectively from a DBSL approach.

Connecting design experiences to scientific understanding

One of the important challenges for DBSL is fostering scientific understanding in the context of design activity. Schauble et al. (1995) reported that the nature of design activity can often shift students' focus to creating outcomes rather than constructing understanding. We have grappled with this issue in our LBD approach. To address the challenge of helping learners construct scientific understanding from their design experiences, we previously introduced the *Rules of Thumb (RT)* activity into the LBD approach (Ryan & Kolodner, 2004). In this activity, a class converges upon a set of student-generated *rules of thumb* to guide their future designing based on an analysis of their past designs and design experiences. These rules are used by teachers to scaffold students as they connect their design decisions to the science governing the designed artifact. We have studied the implementation of the RT activity in one of our LBD units called *Vehicles in Motion (VIM)* - a physical science unit where students build, experiment with, and redesign model cars and their propulsion systems to learn about forces and motion. Our studies show that in cases where the RT practice was done well, students consistently use science to explain and justify design decisions and solutions, articulate science concepts and principles in a more "scientific" manner, and demonstrate better ability to use content knowledge in new situations.

But our studies also found that the success of the RT activity in bridging design and science depends on a number of factors that are beyond the curricular set up. Success depends on how well the teacher orchestrates the elements of the RT protocol and on the quality of rules that emerge, which in turn depends on the scaffolding that the teacher provides for students as they are generating these rules. Success also depends on how fluent teachers are with the science content. With fluency, they can better help students diagnose their "troubled" designs from a science perspective. With this in mind we began to ask the question "can we devise a technological innovation that shares some of the burden of bridging design and science?"

Our proposed solution to this educational challenge is an explanation construction tool. DBSL approach often requires students to iterate over their designs, making structural changes to their artifact each time, and seeing how close that takes them towards achieving the goals of the design challenge being addressed. The explanation tool will be used whenever learners are investigating the structural changes to their design. This tool will scaffold explanation of the accompanying behavioral changes in their designs using the science content they learn in the curriculum unit. This has two advantages. (1) It brings goal-orientedness to their use of science because scientific explanation is situated in the context of changes they are investigating; (2) by linking structural changes to behavioral changes, we provide specific scaffolding to bridging design and science. SBF theory (Goel & Chandrasekaran, 1989) says that modeling the behavior of a system requires one to consider the underlying causal mechanisms – if a system can be viewed as a *Function⇒Structure* mapping, then it is the *Behavior* that explains how a particular structure achieves a particular function via its internal causal mechanisms. Representing behavior requires one to take into account the organizing natural phenomena and the science that goes with it.

Complementing real world design environment

The second challenge for DBSL deals with engaging learners in a wide enough variety of design experiences to be able to gain deeper understanding and with the issue of the extent to which students can realistically have all the experiences with concepts they need in the environment of the classroom. Each variation in a design only paints part of the science picture. To uncover the big picture of science concepts through design experiences, one has to explore many variations of the application of those concepts. In the real world, exploration of the design space is limited by time, material, and environmental constraints. Because there is only limited time and materials in classrooms to cover any specific topic, the speed with which learners construct their designs and the extent of variations that they can investigate effects the number of experiences they will have revisiting science and refining their understanding. For instance, in VIM learners may have to design and test many variations of model cars having different kinds of wheels with varying thickness and weight to understand that the net force involves a tradeoff between mass and surface area of the wheels. Although exploring a wide variety of designs and incrementally improving them are important from a learning perspective, the time and material constraints in the real world environment can sometimes prevent the students from carrying out such extensive explorations.

The real world is also confusingly complex. Sometimes it is difficult to highlight the important phenomena of a domain clearly and independently. Doing so may require downplaying complexities. For instance, studies show that students have difficulty with the concept of momentum even though it is a regular feature of the real world and they routinely take momentum into account in their everyday experiences (e.g., playing soccer, sailing) (White, 1984). This is because most real world situations do not satisfy Newton's second law in simple ways. The real world is complex with the constant presence of friction and gravity, which may even cause the real world to behave in ways counter to what the law says. The real world design environment can not only overconstrain but also overwhelm students with irrelevant complexities. It is difficult to have complete control over one's experiment in the real world in terms of repeatability and frequency of the occurrence of events. Unavoidable complexities, coupled with students' novice construction capabilities can lead to the inability of learners to collect fully consistent and precise data.

Our proposed solution to this challenge explores the use of a simulation-based virtual design environment to complement the real world design environment. Both design environments have unique affordances and limitations. Working within a combination of both real world and virtual design environments can maximize investigative potential. Our software, SIMCARS, was specifically designed for the VIM unit. Some of the features of its virtual design environment include allowing students to isolate and examine factors affecting their model car designs resistant to isolation in the real world, conduct tests in an idealized world that is less prone to complicating external factors, have more options to explore and experiment with (in terms of both the raw materials for design and the target environments for deploying the designed artifacts), and do so in a time-efficient way.

SIMCARS: System description and design rationale

The two main components of SIMCARS are a simulation-based virtual design environment where the students can quickly design and test virtual models cars, and an explanation construction tool that scaffolds construction of scientific explanations in the context of designing.

The virtual design environment

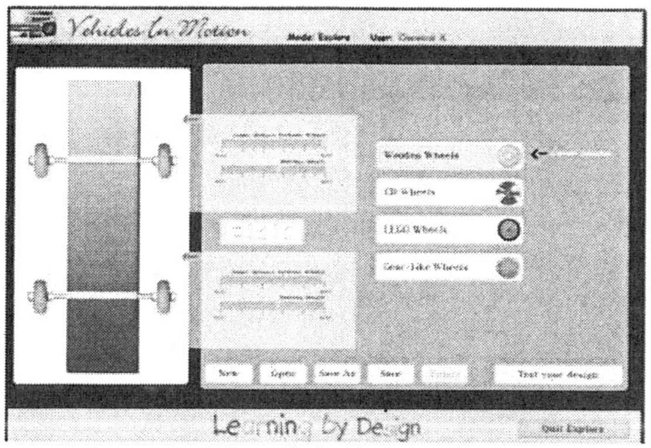

Figure 1. Virtual design environment

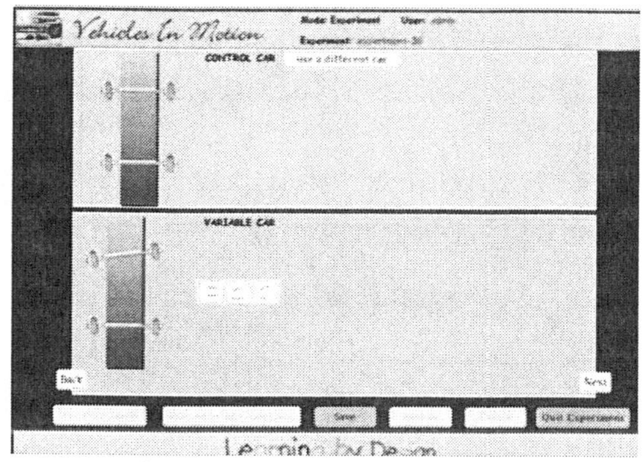

Figure 2. Experimental setup

A learner can interact with SIMCARS' design environment in two operational modes, the *Explore* mode and the *Experiment* mode. These two modes respectively support the two types of activities that occur in LBD classrooms, "messing about" and "experiment" activities (Kolodner et al., 2003). In order to understand SIMCARS' Explore mode, we have to understand the nature of *messing about* in classrooms – specifically, when and why it happens and what sort of support is needed there. "Messing about" is an exploration activity, geared towards helping learners become familiar with the design space. In this activity, learners come up with potential design possibilities by trial and error. Testing possible designs generate design-related issues and science-related questions that can then be investigated in greater detail. In a typical classroom session, students can explore at most three or four design variations. Designing in SIMCARS' environment affords quicker and more expansive messing about, leaving more time for detailed investigation. As shown in figure 1, learners can quickly configure a car by clicking on the various parts of the car and adjusting their parametric values. Learners can also compare two or more designs and make quick and informed decisions with the help of useful visualizations.

Compared to messing about, experimentation is more structured and hypothesis-driven. Here, once a question is identified to be investigated, being able to quickly experiment and get reliable answers is desirable. But neither is completely achieved in classrooms because construction takes time, and the world is complex and noisy. Interaction with SIMCARS in the Experiment mode takes the user sequentially through steps involved in designing and running an experiment: (1) capturing the question being investigated, (2) setting up an experiment by configuring a control design and a test design, and (3) running the experiment and getting feedback on the outcome of the experiment. Figure 2 shows a snapshot of Experiment mode. It depicts that particular step in the experiment where the students specify control and test designs.

The explanation construction tool

We determined that experiments provide a good context for learners to engage in explanation activity because this is a key activity where they systematically investigate the effects of structural changes in their designs. We also decided that the explanation tool would be best launched in the Experiment mode between step 2 (after setting up the control and test designs) and step 3 (before seeing the outcome of the experiment). Upon launching, it prompts students as they make predictions about the outcome of their experiment. For instance, they would predict that "the control car will go farther than the test car." Then there would be an option for them to explain their prediction. If they choose to explain, the explanation tool scaffolds them in generating an explanation using the concepts and principles they learn in VIM. Once they are done with their prediction and explanation, they are ready to see the actual outcome of the experiment accompanied by a feedback on their explanation. They can run the explanation tool again here to explain unexpected results. Scaffolding for explanation takes the form of partially filled templates. Each template captures a portion of the causal model of phenomena underlying the outcome of the experiment. Providing the right explanation is reduced to completing the template, as shown in figure 3. Further scaffolding is provided by making the unfilled blanks in the template a multiple choice selection.

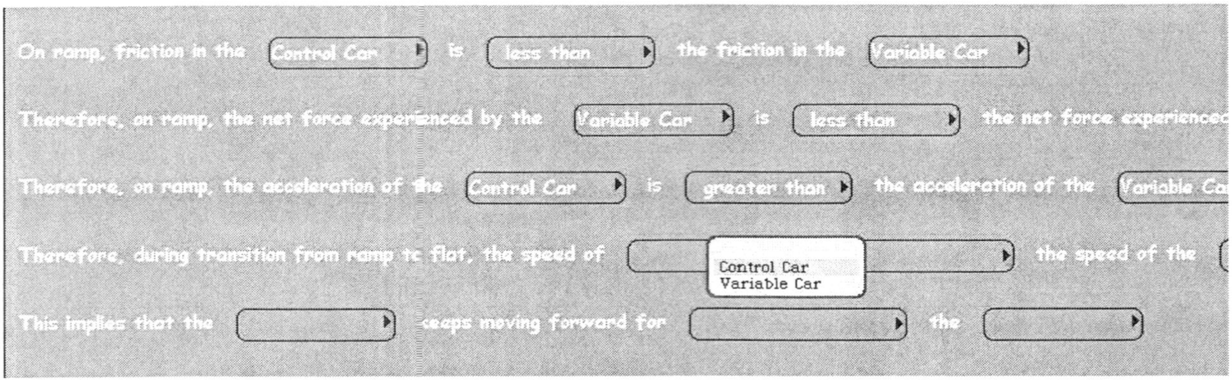

Figure 3. A sample template from the explanation tool

Evaluation and findings

How well does SIMCARS help learners generate good explanations? If so, how does it contribute to the bridging of the design-science gulf among learners and contribute towards enhancing scientific understanding? How does working with the simulations contribute to the learning experiences of students? These are some of the questions we set out to answer in our pilot study.

Our pilot study was conducted in the context of an after-school program involving 16 students who were in 6th grade. We implemented a short version of the VIM curriculum, making sure the adapted version retained the "flavor" of the original unit. There were two learning segments in this unit. In the first segment, students focused on the Coaster car challenge to learn about forces, friction and gravity. A coaster car is a simple car pulled down a ramp and across the floor by gravitational forces. In the second segment, students focused on the Balloon car (coaster car plus a balloon propulsion system) challenge to learn about combination of forces. We made suitable modifications to the unit to integrate SIMCARS into the curriculum. Learners built a physical car as a first pass of the messing about activity. They then explored design variations in SIMCARS' design environment in Explore mode. Experiments were done entirely in SIMCARS. They ran experiments to gather evidence and create and justify design rules of thumb. Our study was qualitative in nature. Since the researchers were also the instructors for the unit, our data came in the form of video recordings of the sessions and field notes written "in retrospect" immediately after each session.

Transformed science talk: effects of bridging

During initial stages of the unit, consistent with the first challenge mentioned above, we noted from classroom discussions that some students were indeed "lost" in the world of design and did not relate their design activities to the science concepts underlying their designs. Their designs were more informed by trial and error than by their conceptual understanding. We also noted that some students were equally "lost" in the world of abstract concepts and did not apply their conceptual understanding to their designing. Even though such students' "science talk" was above the ordinary, their designs suffered from the same problems that were seen in those of other students. But as the sessions progressed, discussions in the class became more sophisticated. In sessions following SIMCARS activity, we found that the discussion was not only maturing but also that students' science talk paralleled the explanations elicited from them using SIMCARS explanation tool. The following is an illustration of how a particular student's science talk changed over the course of the unit.

During the initial stages of the unit, in response to instructor's question about why one choice of axle-wheel arrangement (axle is fixed and the wheels spin around the axle) was better than the other (wheels and the axle spin as a single unit within a straw acting as a bearing), the student replied:

Student: ... because with the wheels spinning instead of the axle [it] will create more friction, because spinning of the wheel will [create] friction with the axle. Then the car slows down.

A little later in the unit after SIMCARS was deployed and used, in response to instructor's question regarding a particular design choice to keep the bearing's length shorter, the following conversation with the same student ensued:

Student: *... they rub against the nut, against the wheel, which is bad, cause the rubbing causes the friction.*
Instructor: *We'll know what happens then, right?*
Student: *the car won't go very far*
Instructor: *why?*
Student: *well, if the friction is more, the car has less force pushing it on the ramp compared to a less friction car, causing less speed up. So, when the car comes off the ramp it carries less speed with it.*
Instructor: *So less speed means*
Student: *less speed means less travel, car doesn't go that far.*

Our analysis showed that the reasons and explanations offered by at least some students incorporated appropriate scientific vocabulary after they used the explanation tool. This was in accordance with our prediction about the effects that "bridging" design and science would bring about.

More exploration, more gain

It is not possible for us to accurately estimate how many designs every group explored using SIMCARS. However, we closely followed one group's messing about activity. That group explored approximately twelve different variations of designs in less than one after-school session, compared to three or four when working with physical models. A more extensive exploration of the design space helped at least some students in their discovery of variables affecting the performance of their vehicles. For example, early in the Balloon car challenge, students constructed and tested their first physical versions of their cars. In the classroom discussion that followed, we asked them to identify the variables that affected their vehicle designs. They were able to identify only two variables - the number of balloons on the engine and the number of straws forming the nozzle of the balloon engine - both easily perceivable. The actual number was at least four. They had left out the length of the straws (nozzle) and the number of layers of balloons. The SIMCARS exploration activity followed. In the discussion that followed, students identified all the four variables.

While we expected more exploration in SIMCARS' design environment and better science learning from it, we discovered two more advantages of quick and easy exploration made possible by SIMCARS. The first advantage relates to motivation. Early in our study, we observed that some groups or individuals were not motivated enough to bring their (on paper) design ideas to fruition. The realization of conceptual design ideas in the real world involves the intermediate step of construction, which can take significant time. Some students were reluctant to invest their time in construction of variations of what they had already constructed before; instead, they wanted to "move on" to designing other types of vehicles. While their designs often looked good on paper, they were not well-realized through robust construction. As a result, the performance of their vehicles suffered – not due to bad conceptual design but due to bad construction, the chief reason being lack of students' motivation to pay sufficient time and attention to construction. These problems did not arise when designing in the SIMCARS environment. Learners could easily put together their designs by the click of a few buttons in the virtual world, test them immediately, and receive feedback. SIMCARS provided an alternate medium for some students to complement their real world design-based learning. The second advantage relates to confidence. We also observed that some students were "construction phobic." These students were inherently reluctant to build things with their own hands. While they chose not to participate in construction directly, their overall participation and contribution to the conceptual design was valuable to their groups. In SIMCARS, students did not have to worry about construction woes. Therefore it seemed to level the playing field for such "construction phobic" individuals or groups. In fact we noticed this in our data. We found that the designs of all the individuals, whether construction phobic or not, converged onto a best design in the SIMCARS environment. All the students figured out the right combination of parametric values for their virtual designs, and in the end, all of them were able to build the best car possible.

But not all of our results were as positive as we would have liked. Our analysis indicated that not all students derived full learning benefits from the explanation activity. Concepts related to nonobservable vector quantities like velocity and its relation to quantities like gravity and friction remained confusing for some students. More analysis is required to determine the reasons behind this observation and their implications for the explanation tool in particular, and LBD in general.

Discussion

Our results suggest that integration of SIMCARS into a DBSL unit like VIM will have a positive impact. The benefits of using the virtual design environment - reducing the time and effort involved in realizing designs and testing them, expanding the possibilities for designing, removing some of the hard constraints present in the real world, reducing the irrelevant complexities and highlighting the phenomenon of interest – not only helped our participants meet some of the challenges of learning from design activity, but also allowed us to implement our DBSL unit in a meaningful way in the short amount of time that was available to us (The actual VIM unit runs for 30 days, and we had only 15 days). The advantages of SIMCARS' design environment could be misread as implying that designing real artifacts in the real world can be avoided. This is contrary to our opinion. Designing and conducting experiments on real artifacts have significant value for learning. (1) Producing tangible artifacts is sometimes more motivating and promotes a deeper sense of having actually "made" something; (2) interaction with tangible artifacts is more embodied and natural. They provide more manipulability, thus being more open to subtle and creative variations. We do not recommend a replacement of physical designs. We suggest, instead, that simulations offer important complementary benefits.

When one looks at the literature on the use of computer simulations for learning, the general conclusion is that there is no clear outcome favoring the use of simulations to promote learning without providing the appropriate scaffolding (De Jong, T., & Van Joolingen, W. R., 1998). Varying degrees of learning outcomes can be effected through the use of simulations by combining them with other forms of instructional support, ranging from simple support for planning and monitoring of exploration to more elaborate support for structuring discovery learning processes (De Jong, T., & Van Joolingen, W. R., 1998) and, in some cases, even providing support for learners to construct their own models that run the simulations (Jackson et al., 1996). Our research effort is related to these, but does not exactly fit into the same category. In the category of the cited cases, simulation and modeling are the primary conduits for change and central to the learning process. In our case, however, learning process is centered around designing artifacts, and the role of simulations is to expand the design environment to compensate for some of the limitations of the real world; take away the simulations and there is still our DBSL process. But we have tried to incorporate a number of useful principles suggested by research on educational simulations (e.g., ThinkerTools (White, 1984)) in designing our simulation environment (e.g., representing the phenomena of the domain clearly, eliminating the irrelevant complexities from the simulated world, encouraging better ways of representing and thinking about the domain).

SIMCARS' explanation tool is comparable to many research efforts that employ technology for enhancing learners' conceptual understanding by engaging them in model-building (e.g., Model-It (Jackson et al., 1996)). But there is a key difference. Instead of modeling the system in its entirety, the explanation tool allows learners to capture only the local changes they make to the system and their scientific understanding of the effects that follow. We claim that this form of local modeling is more appropriate for the DBSL approach because our context is such - learners are always making incremental changes to their artifacts in pursuit of their design goals. Local modeling is more connected to their ongoing activity. Therefore the explanation tool has more potential to be seamlessly integrated into DBSL approaches than more traditional model-building tools.

References

De Jong, T., & Van Joolingen, W. R. (1998). Scientific discovery learning with computer simulations of conceptual domains. *Review of Educational Research*, 68, 179-201.

Fortus, D., Dershimer. C. R., Krajcik, J. S., & Marx, R. W. (2004). Design-Based Science and Student Learning. *Journal of Research in Science Teaching*, 41(10), 1081-1110.

Goel, A., & Chandrasekaran, B. (1989). Functional representation of designs and redesign problem solving. In *Proceedings of the Eleventh International Joint Conference on Artificial Intelligence* (pp. 1388–1394). Los Altos, CA: Morgan Kaufmann.

Hmelo, C. E., Holton, D. L., & Kolodner, J. L. (2000) Designing to Learn about Complex Systems. *Journal of Learning Sciences*, 9(3), 247-298.

Jackson, S. L., Stratford, S. J., Krajcik, J., & Soloway, E. (1996). A learner-centered tool for students building models. *Communications of the ACM*, 39(4), 48-49.

Kafai, Y. (1996). Learning design by making games: Children's development of design strategies in the creation of a complex computational artifact. In Y. Kafai &M. Resnick (Ed.), *Constructionism in practice: Designing, thinking, and learning in a digital world* (pp. 71–96). Mahwah, NJ: Lawrence Erlbaum Associates, Inc.

Kolodner, J. L., Camp, P. J., Crismond, D., Fasse, B., Gray, J., Holbrook, J., Puntambekar, S., & Ryan, M. (2003). Problem-Based Learning Meets Case-Based Reasoning in the Middle-School Science Classroom: Putting Learning by Design™ Into Practice. *Journal of the Learning Sciences*. 12(4), 495-547.

Penner, D. E., Lehrer, R., & Schauble, L. (1998). From physical models to biomechanics: A design-based modeling approach. *Journal of the Learning Sciences*. 7(3&4), 429–449.

Ryan, M. T. & Kolodner, J. L. (2004). Using 'Rules of Thumb' Practices to Enhance Conceptual Understanding and Scientific Reasoning in Project-Based Inquiry Classrooms. *Proceedings of the International Conference of the Learning Sciences*, (pp. 449-456). Los Angeles, CA: Lawrence Erlbaum Associates, Inc

Sandoval, W. A. (2003). Conceptual and Epistemic Aspects of Students' Scientific Explanations. *Journal of the Learning Sciences*, 12(1), 5-51.

Schauble, L., Glaser, R., Duschl, R. A., Schulze, S., & John, J. (1995). Students' understanding of the objectives and procedures of experimentation in the science classroom. *Journal of the Learning Sciences*, 4, 131-166

White, B. Y. (1984). Designing computer games to help physics students understanding Newton's laws of motion. *Cognition and Instruction*, 1, 69-108.

Contrasting cases: What we can learn from students' perceptions of "good" design

Joan M. T. Walker, Long Island University, School of Education, 720 Northern Boulevard, Brookville, NY 11458, joan.walker@liu.edu
Paul H. King, Department of Biomedical Engineering, Vanderbilt University, Nashville, TN 37325, paul.h.king@vanderbilt.edu

Abstract: Set in the context of an engineering design course, this study used contrasting cases to examine undergraduates' (1) ability to discriminate poor and excellent examples of student design projects, and (2) students' justifications for their ratings. At the beginning of the yearlong course, only 76% of students correctly identified the better project. Toward the end of the course, the majority of students correctly identified the superior example; however, many failed to note serious flaws in the poor example. Analyses of student justifications showed that most students used superficial reasons (e.g., readability) initially and deeper structural reasons (e.g., process) on the post-test. Results are discussed in terms of expert-novice differences, and how educators can support students' ability to notice salient problem features.

Introduction

Expertise is the goal of education in any domain. However, educators struggle with how best to teach for expertise (e.g., Bransford, Brown & Cocking, 1999; Hatano & Oura, 2003; Lajoie, 2003). Research in recent decades has advanced our understanding of expertise and points to interesting avenues for designing instruction that supports its development. Among the most striking findings to emerge is evidence that novices and experts view the world very differently. For instance, when asked to organize several physics problems, experts grouped them according to their deeper principles (e.g., conservation of energy) whereas novices arrayed them according to their surface features (e.g., involved inclined planes; Chi, Glaser & Farr, 1988). In other work expert teachers, advanced beginners and novice teachers were asked to state what they noticed when observing a teacher engaged in classroom instruction (Sabers, Berliner & Cushing, 1991). Experts were far more likely to offer evaluative comments and interpretations of what they observed and to make suggestions for improvements. By contrast, novices and advanced beginners were only able to offer descriptions of what they saw, much like a sports announcer offering play-by-play during a basketball game.

Differences between experts and beginners are consistent with theoretical and philosophical arguments that the world is invariant; it is only our perceptions that change (Gibson & Gibson, 1955). Further, this phenomenon supports the idea that learning can be measured as changes in perception (Lave & Wenger, 1998). However, assessments that tap into this phenomenon are rarely included in classroom instruction. One recently developed technique that may help students develop the critical thinking skills that are a hallmark of expertise is contrasting cases, which involves using carefully arranged contrasts to underscore conceptual differences (Barron, Schwartz, Vye, Moore, Petrosino, Zech & Bransford, 1998; Bransford & Schwartz, 1999).

From the perspective of cognitive psychology, the ability to discriminate features of a problem is developed through experiences that provide opportunities to notice important contrasts and similarities among problems (Bransford, Franks, Vye & Sherwood, 1989). For instance, Broudy (1977) has argued that in addition to "knowing that" and "knowing how" (i.e., replicative and applicative knowledge, respectively) people "know with." Knowing with means that an individual "thinks, perceives and judges with everything he has studied…, even though he cannot recall these things on demand" (p. 12). This suggests that novices fail to differentiate problem features because, relative to experts, they have experienced fewer opportunities to notice what is similar and different or relevant and irrelevant across problems they encounter. Thus, it is logical to assume that educators can support the development of critical thinking skills by creating opportunities for students to reflect on the underlying structural features of problems and the quality of solutions that address them.

This study used contrasting cases to reveal differences in how experts and novices view the practice of engineering design. This work is important because a common task for many engineers is the analysis of an existing design with an eye toward its improvement. Given its importance in the profession of engineering, design is a required course for seniors in the majority of engineering programs in the US. However, design instruction and research often focuses on students' ability to generate a design solution rather than critique the merits of existing ones. For instance, a major requirement in most design courses is the completion of a senior design project and research in design education often focuses on students' responses to problem-solving scenarios and their conceptions of the design process (Atman & Turns, 2001; Cross, 2001; Newstetter & McCracken, 2001; Walker, Cordray, Brophy & King, in press; Walker, Cordray, King & Fries, 2005). Promoting analytical skills in the field of design is important because if engineers are responsible for critiquing and improving existing designs then they must be trained to notice important design features. You cannot fix what you do not see.

Specifically, excellent and poor examples of design were drawn from the archives of former student design projects collected at a major university's engineering program. Students' perceptions of the projects' quality were then compared to the evaluations of experts. The study had several goals. The first goal was to understand what students valued as attributes of good design and their ability to differentiate between two designs of very different quality. It was also intended to help students focus attention on concepts of design quality and to understand the requirements by which their own design projects would be judged. Finally, the study was designed to offer engineering educators an alternative and 'user-friendly' form of student assessment.

The study posed four research questions: (1) can students correctly identify the better of two design projects, (2) are students' quantitative ratings similar to the ratings of experts, (3) how do students justify their ratings, and (4) do students' perceptions of the projects' quality become more expert-like over time? It was expected that at the beginning of a yearlong course, many students would fail to correctly identify the better project, and that this would stem, in part, from basing their judgments on surface features (e.g., meeting content requirements and presentation style) rather than deeper structural features such as the underlying engineering process and emergent product. In the second semester, after students had experienced the challenge of developing their own senior design project, the number of students who correctly identified the better project was expected to increase. Students' perceptions were expected to become more expert-like with increased references to engineering content as a basis for judging the quality of a design.

Methods

Participants included three experts (senior biomedical engineering faculty) and 42 seniors enrolled in an undergraduate engineering design course at a private university in the mid-South of the United States. Experts evaluated the projects in the spring of 2003 and 2004 at the conclusion of the design course. Projects could earn a maximum of 100 points. Criteria for judging the projects included four categories: *Efficiency*, which includes the project's engineering goals (20 points), and demonstrated ability to design system, component or process (25 points); *Innovation,* which includes the project's creativity (20 points) and consideration of alternatives (20 points); *Clarity* of communication and persuasiveness (10 points), and *Ethics* (e.g., issues of exclusion, 5 points).

The contrasting cases were selected on the basis of the experts' ratings. One project explored a technique for imaging the heart and had been rated as "excellent" ($M = 92.00$, $SD = 6.55$; range = 86-99). The other project sought to improve devices designed to assist newborns' breathing and was rated "below average" ($M = 65.66$, $SD = 16.19$; range = 47-76). Descriptive statistics for each project by category are presented in Table 1. Strengths of the excellent example included the level of challenge, creativity when setbacks were encountered, and the development of a working prototype. Weakness of this project included the fact that the paper describing the project's development was "annoyingly redundant at times" and contained technical jargon without explanation of those terms. Strengths of the below average paper included a thorough literature review, and clear writing and formatting. Weaknesses of this project were considerable and included the fact that no quantitative analyses were performed, and that the authors "drew intuitive and appealing conclusions, which did not require any engineering." In short, the excellent project demonstrated engineering and research skills, whereas the below average project demonstrated excellent research but no follow-through in engineering. Although the number of expert ratings is small, there was clear consensus among this group's evaluations. Specifically, they were expected to provide sufficient contrasts in quality and a basis for evaluating whether students valued 'function over form.'

Students rated the projects at two time points during a yearlong course analogous to the experience of student teaching for teacher education majors. The first time point was in the fall semester when students attended a traditional lecture-driven course focused on design principles and knowledge. The second time point was in the spring when students spent a full semester in direct field experience, working as a team under the guidance of an advisor, to develop a design project. Students were e-mailed instructions to download papers describing the two former student projects from the course web page. After reading each paper students evaluated it with the same scoring rubric used by faculty; however, students were not informed of the faculty evaluations prior to completing the task. In addition to assigning numeric ratings, students were asked to explain their evaluations. When both papers had been graded, students were asked to explicitly compare the two papers, decide which one was better and explain why.

Analyses and Results

Seventy-six percent of students correctly identified the best project. Variability in student ratings was considerable. Descriptive statistics for student ratings for each project by category are summarized in Table 1.

Table 1. Descriptive statistics for student and expert ratings by project and by category at pre-test

		Below average project			Excellent project			
Category		Mean	SD	*Range*	Mean	SD	*Range*	*t(43)*
Efficiency	Student	34.47	5.52	*22-44*	40.40	3.95	*32-45*	
	Expert	28.00	4.35	*23-31*	41.33	3.51	*38-45*	*1.90+*
Innovation	Student	31.88	5.09	*18-40*	34.05	4.04	*21-40*	
	Expert	25.67	11.01	*13-33*	36.67	2.88	*35-40*	*2.12**
Clarity	Student	7.53	1.53	*3-10*	8.27	1.51	*3-10*	
	Expert	7.00	1.00	*6-8*	9.00	1.00	*8-10*	*1.08, ns*
Ethics	Student	4.68	0.67	*2-5*	4.36	.83	*2-5*	
	Expert	5.00	0.00	*5-5*	5.00	0.00	*5-5*	*.54, ns*
Total	Student	78.57	10.51	*49-97*	86.62	9.02	*63-100*	
	Expert	65.67	16.20	*47-76*	92.00	6.56	*86-99*	*2.23**

+ = p < .06, * = p < .05

Second, we compared students' quantitative ratings to those of experts. Comparison of the groups' average ratings showed that students and experts had similar perceptions of the excellent project but that students rated the poor project much higher than experts. Experts' total ratings of the two projects differed by an average of 25 points, whereas students' ratings differed by less than 10 points. Ratings differed most for the categories of Efficiency and Innovation. The two groups had similar perceptions of the projects' Clarity and Ethics

Preliminary analyses of students' justifications for their ratings suggested that those who correctly identified the excellent project found the task relatively straightforward (e.g., *"Comparing these two papers is like night and day;" "This exercise points out that it is imperative to use math and engineering principles to help prove your design;"* and *"The second paper simply tests a design that has already been made"*). By contrast, students who chose the below average project appeared unaware of its flaws or judged the project on the basis of form rather than content (e.g., *"It was ... easier to read;" "good overall readability; the [other] paper was boring and seemed to keep going and going"*). This led to the development of a coding scheme with four categories. The first two categories, meets content requirements (e.g., "contained everything it was supposed to") and readability (e.g., "easy to read, understand"), represent a *Surface* approach to evaluation. The second two categories, product (e.g., "generated a working prototype") and process (e.g., "tested and revised their idea") indicate attention to engineering content or a *Deep* approach to evaluation. Almost all of the students (92%) used surface reasons to justify their ratings, whereas 71% used Deep reasons. Wilcoxon signed rank tests showed the distribution of these related variables to be significantly different ($z = 3.00$, $p < .01$).

Following this assignment, the course instructor revealed the faculty ratings to students and held an in-class discussion of the observed differences between student and faculty evaluations. Students also received extensive feedback from teaching assistants about their performance. This feedback focused on the fact that while many students could identify the strong points of the excellent project, they were less successful in identifying the poor project's weaknesses. The instructor emphasized how this would be problematic when students faced the task of troubleshooting an existing design. Teaching assistants provided students with a list of this project's problems and urged students to "consider this list seriously, because your understanding of this assignment can make or break your final project." Students were told that they would complete a similar assignment again in the spring semester.

Post-test: Procedures, Analyses and Results

Participants and procedures were identical to the pre-test; however, the contrasting cases changed. Experts had rated one project, a new approach to a dosage inhaler device, as excellent ($M = 92.67$, $SD = 4.93$; range = 87-96); the other project explored alternative approaches to the design of a cardiac catheter and was rated as "average" ($M = 72.33$, $SD = 5.85$; range = 68-79); both projects were chosen because they shared many of the strengths and weaknesses identified in the pre-test exemplars. For instance, the average project had a strong literature review but failed to generate a prototype, drawings or specifications. Descriptive statistics for student and expert ratings for each project by category are summarized in Table 2.

Table 2. Descriptive statistics for student and expert ratings by project and by category at post-test

		Average project			Excellent project			
Category		Mean	SD	*Range*	Mean	SD	*Range*	*t (43)*
Efficiency	Student	32.17	6.88	*9-20*	40.97	3.07	*12-41*	
	Expert	32.67	.57	*32-33*	41.33	2.88	*38-43*	*.03, ns*
Innovation	Student	30.05	5.45	*13-40*	35.17	2.85	*26-40*	
	Expert	27.00	6.24	*22-34*	37.66	1.52	*36-39*	*1.49, ns*
Clarity	Student	6.43	1.71	*3-10*	8.31	1.54	*3-10*	
	Expert	8.00	1.00	*7-9*	8.67	1.15	*8-10*	*1.01, ns*
Ethics	Student	3.83	1.43	*0-5*	5.00	.00	*0*	
	Expert	4.66	.58	*4-5*	5.00	0.00	*5-5*	*.17, ns*
Total	Student	72.10	12.43	*40-90*	86.62	9.02	*63-100*	
	Expert	72.33	5.85	*68-79*	92.67	4.93	*87-96*	*.42, ns*

Analyses were identical to the pre-test. On the post-test 94% of students correctly identified the better project; the variability of student ratings remained considerable. Similar to the pre-test, students rated the excellent example higher on all dimensions with the exception of ethics, which was at ceiling. Unlike the pre-test, students and experts saw the same degree of difference in the two projects' quality (see t-test results in Table 3). Wilcoxon signed rank tests for students' reasons used on pre- and post-tests showed no change in use of surface reasons ($z = 1.00$, $p < .31$; pre-test $N = 39$; post-test $N = 37$) and increased use of deep reasons ($z = 1.73$, $p < 05$; pre-test $N = 30$, post-test $N = 36$).

Discussion

Grounded in evidence that experts and beginners view the world differently, this study used contrasting cases to learn about the development of students' abilities to notice important conceptual features of engineering design. Results suggest that advanced beginners can often recognize the better of two design solutions; however, they do not always recognize the serious flaws and limitations of poor design work. Specifically, these students appeared to mistake good research for good design. They did not recognize that merely exploring and describing alternatives was essentially a failure to design. Moreover, students' reasons for evaluating the quality of a design is not necessarily related to its deeper structural features such as engineering content or the quality of the underlying design process. These findings are consistent with arguments that novices and beginners sometimes engage in critical thinking without explicit attention to the bases for their judgments (Broudy, 1977).

Students demonstrated enhanced critical thinking skills on a similar task at the end of their design experience. Improvements on the post-test included an increased ability to recognize the better project, greater alignment with experts' quantitative evaluations, and increased use of deep reasons for choosing the better project. This improvement occurred despite the fact that the contrast between the post-test materials was less stark than the contrast between the pre-test materials. We believe that students' improved performance on the post-test is due to their immersion in the field and the opportunity to take on the duties and identity of a designer. Through engaging in the practice of design students gain insight into the myriad of conditions and details associated with the design process. This experience helps them to notice the design decisions of others. In the context of these students' educational experiences, it appear that moving from an abstract understanding of design developed during a lecture-based course to a more intimate knowledge of the practice of design helped students 'see with new eyes' and supported their ability to discriminate the quality of two design projects.

An outstanding question is how students' design knowledge might become further differentiated with instructional support. Addressing this question, we are currently conducting several studies using contrasting cases as an intervention. First, we are currently replicating this study. Second, we have developed and used an additional contrasting cases task, which asks students to choose the better of two proposals addressing the same problem (rather than choosing the better of two solutions addressing different design issues, which is the task described here). Preliminary analyses of these data show that students perform much better on this task at pre-test, suggesting that an optimal scaffolding of students' critical thinking skills would initially demand near comparisons followed by comparisons across an increasingly wider range of problems. This task is also important because it offers a window into how students rate the work of designers who are not their peers. For instance, students might have hesitated to be critical of the projects used here because they knew they were the work of former design students. We are also increasing the size of our expert sample, and assessing the generalizability of this work by exporting the measures described here to other engineering programs.

In sum, by drawing from the products created in their own classrooms engineering educators can develop authentic, meaningful assessments for students that acknowledge the legacy of former design students while promoting the development of their current students' critical thinking skills and differentiated knowledge of design.

References

Atman, C. J. & Turns, J. (2001). Studying engineering design learning: Four verbal protocol studies. In C. Eastman, M. McCracken & W. Newstetter (Eds.) *Design knowing and learning: Cognition in design education,* pp. 37-62. New York: Elsevier.

Barron, B., Schwartz, D. L., Vye, N. J., Moore, A., Petrosino, A., Zech, L., & Bransford, J. D. (1998).Doing with understanding: lessons from research on problem- and project-based learning. *Journal of the Learning Sciences, 7,* 271-311.

Bransford, J.D., & Schwartz, D. L. (1999). Rethinking transfer: A simple proposal with multiple implications. In A. Iran-Nejad and P. D. Pearson (Eds.) *Review of Research in Education, 24,* 61-100. Washington, DC: American Educational Research Association.

Bransford, J. D., Franks, J. J., Vye, N. J., & Sherwood, R. D. (1989). New approaches to instruction: Because wisdom can't be told. In S. Vosniadou & A. Ortony (Eds). *Similarity and analogical reasoning* (pp. 470-497). New York, NY: Cambridge University Press.

Bransford, J. D., Brown, A. L., & Cocking, R. R. (1999) *How people learn: Brain, mind, experience, and school.* Washington, DC: National Academy Press.

Broudy, H. S. (1977). Types of knowledge and purposes of education. In R. C. Anderson, R. J. Spiro, & W. E. Montague (Eds.). *Schooling and the acquisition of knowledge* (pp. 1-17). Hillsdale, NJ: Erlbaum.

Chi, M. T. H., Glaser, R., & Farr, M. J. (1988). *The nature of expertise.* Hillsdale, NJ: Erlbaum.

Cross, N. (2001). Design cognition: Results from protocol and other empirical studies of design activity. *Design knowing and learning: Cognition in design education,* pp. 79-103. New York: Elsevier.

Gibson, J. J., & Gibson, E. J. (1955). Perceptual learning: Differentiation or enrichment? *Psychological Review, 62,* 32-41.

Hatano, G., & Oura, Y. (2003). Commentary: Reconceptualizing school learning using insight from expertise research. *Educational Researcher, 32*(8), 26-29.

Kuhn, D., & Udell, W. (2001). The path to wisdom. *Educational Psychologist, 36(4),* 262-264.

Lajoie, S. P. (2003). Transitions and Trajectories for Studies of Expertise. *Educational Researcher, 32*(8), 21-25.

Lave, J., & Wenger, E. (1991). *Situated learning: Legitimate peripheral practice.* New York: Cambridge University Press.

Newstetter, W. C. & McCracken, W. M. (2001). Novice conceptions of design: Implications for the design of learning environments. In C. Eastman, M. McCracken & W. Newstetter (Eds.) *Design knowing and learning: Cognition in design education,* pp. 63-78. New York: Elsevier.

Sabers, D. S., Cushing, K. S., & Berliner, D. C. (1991). Differences among teachers in a task characterized by simultaneity, multidimensionality, and immediacy. *American Educational Research Journal, 28*(1), 63-88.

Sternberg, R. J. (2001). Why Schools Should Teach for Wisdom: The Balance Theory of Wisdom in Educational Settings, *Educational Psychologist, 36,* 227-245.

Walker, J. M. T., Cordray, D. S., Brophy, S. P., & King, P. H. (in press). Design scenarios as a measure of adaptive expertise in design. *International Journal of Engineering Education.*

Walker, J. M. T., Cordray, D. S., King, P. H., & Fries, R. C. (2005). Novice and expert definitions of biodesign: Developmental differences with implications for educators. *International Journal of Engineering Education,* 21, 467-479.

Acknowledgements

This work was supported by the Engineering Research Centers Program of the National Science Foundation (Award #EEC9876363).

The Effect of Multiple-Perspective Thinking on Problem Solving

Yan Wang, Enis Dogan, Xiaodong Lin, Teachers College, Columbia University,
525 west120th street, Box 8, New York, NY, 10027
Email: yw2009@columbia.edu, ed346@columbia.edu, xlin@tc.edu

Abstract: The purpose of this study was to explore the relationship between people's multiple-perspective (MP) thinking ability and their problem solving performance (defining problems and generating solutions). The reasons why people seek other perspectives were also investigated. The results showed that the number of perspectives used in defining problems was significantly correlated with the number of solutions generated later. Subjects with higher MP thinking scores were able to define problems from more perspectives and generate more solutions. Native English speakers wanted to hear other perspectives more because they wanted to confirm their thinking, while non-native English speakers wanted other perspectives more because they wanted to understand the scenarios better. The main implication is that there may be a culture difference in people's MP thinking ability and perception of multiple perspectives, and it might be possible to train people on their MP thinking to improve their problem solving performance.

Introduction

The purpose of this study was to explore the relationship between people's multiple-perspective (MP) thinking ability and their problem solving performance. The reasons why people seek other perspectives were also investigated.

Wicklund (1999) defined "multiple perspectives" as a certain social phenomenon: people can recognize that an event may be viewed, defined or perceived in more than one manner, through several social focal points. Learning from multiple perspectives is not a new idea. Researchers have been experimenting with this idea in different fields. For instance, Case Technologies to Enhance Literacy Learning (CTELL) incorporated different perspectives (from different experts) to help pre-service teachers understand best practices of early literacy education (Schrader et al., 2003). Schwartz et al (1999) used MP approach to help preservice teachers design and learn about inquiry-based instruction in Star.Legacy program. Especially, learning from multiple perspectives is considered to be helpful for students in mastering skills in ill-structured problem solving and decision making (Spiro, Feltovich, Jacobson, & Coulson, 1992). According to Cognitive Flexibility Theory, acquiring knowledge through multiple perspectives and use of cases would increase learners' cognitive flexibility (which could be reflected by MP thinking), and thus facilitate knowledge transfer (Jacobson & Spiro, 1995). However, before designing MP learning environment, the relationship between MP thinking and problem solving performance should be investigated. Research has been carried out on the relationship between multiple-perspective thinking and problem solving thinking of well-defined problems (Russo, 2004; Gorenflo & Crano, 1998), but few of these research explored how multiple-perspective thinking affect people's performance in solving ill-defined problems. In addition, the reasons that drive people to seek other people's perspectives were seldom explored. To address these issues, the following questions were investigated in this study:

1. Are people with higher multiple-perspective thinking ability able to view a problem from more perspectives? Are they able to generate more solutions?

2. What are the reasons people seek other people's perspectives? Do people with different multiple-perspective thinking ability have different reasons? Do people with different problem solving performance have different reasons?

Theoretical Framework

D'Zurilla and Goldfried (1971) defined five-stage in problem solving: (1) Problem Orientation; (2) Problem Definition and Formulation; (3) Generation of Alternatives; (4) Decision-Making; and (5) Solution Implementation and Verification. Ill-structured problems are usually defined as problems which present one or more of the problem elements (Shin, Jonassen, & McGee, 2003) and possess multiple solutions, solution paths, or no solutions at all (Kitchner, 1983). Many of the complex problems faced by teachers are ill-defined or ill-structured because these problems are situated in and emergent from a specific content (Jonassen, 1997) and lacking solutions that are indisputably correct (Kagan, 1993). Because of these reasons, being flexible in the second stage of the problem solving process – problem definition – is especially critical in solving ill-structured problems.

Theories on creative problem solving suggest the advantage of being able to think from multiple perspectives. Guilford (1984) stated that the ability to generate a large number of alternatives can increase the number of options one has in problem solving. He also argued that the most obvious aspects of creative thinking appear to depend on the ability to do divergent-productive thinking and to effect transfer of information. Therefore flexibility and divergent thinking are pointed out as important components in creative thinking and in the context of problem solving (Guilford, 1975; Runco, 1991).

Carr and Borkowski (1987) further theorized that being able to think from different perspectives is a basic foundational element of metacognition and it enhances the development and execution of cognitive processes. Multiple perspectives serve as a basis for strategic analyzing, discriminating, synthesizing and integrating information in complex decision making. According to Flavell (1979, 1987), metacognition consists of both active monitoring and regulation of cognitive processes. Metacognitive experiences involve the use of metacognitive strategies or metacognitive regulation (Brown, 1987). Therefore it can be argued that, because people with high multiple-perspective ability are able to view a problem from more aspects, they would be more inclined to reflect and evaluate their ideas and decide which one is more effective or relevant. As a result, these people can be expected to have a better understanding of the problem and better chance of generating more and differentiated solutions.

Methods

A group of 84 graduate students volunteered to participate in the study. The majority of these subjects was first and second year students in education related programs. Participants were first asked to complete a MP ability survey adopted from Multiple Perspectives Inventory created by Gorenflo and Crano (1998). The survey consisted of 20 self-descriptive statements and participants were asked to rate the extent to which they agreed or disagreed with each statement on a 7 points Likert-scale. After they completed this section, subjects were presented with two case scenarios describing common problems a typical school teacher would face. One case was about a teacher's frustration over low performance of a student and the other was about a student's loss of interest in studying. There were two questions for each case. The first question asked participants to define (articulate) the problems/ issues within the case and the second question asked for suggestions of possible solutions regarding these issues. The last section of the study contained seven questions investing subjects' interest in hearing about other participants' perspectives and the reasons they might want to know others' perspectives. At the end of the experiment, participants were informed about the purpose of the study.

Data Sources

Among 84 students who volunteered to participate in the study, 7 of them did not finish all sections of the study, so their partial answers were excluded from the analysis. As a result, final sample consisted of 77 subjects with no missing data.

Seven of the 20 statements in the MP ability survey are reverse-worded items. Ratings on these items were reversed coded and added to the rest of the rating scores in order to obtain a composite MP thinking score.

Coding schemes were developed for each open-ended problem solving questions after first round of draft coding. Each coding scheme consisted of categories of issues (problem definition section) or suggestions (solution generation section). Each category represented a perspective which can be used to interpret or address the scenario. For instance, in one scenario, there was a kindergarten student who couldn't answer his teacher's question about alphabetic letters and the teacher became frustrated. The categories of problems/issues ranged from social-cultural perspective (this child is from a poor family) to instructional design perspective (the teacher's strategy for assessing students' understanding is inadequate). The details regarding these perspective categories will be discussed in the results section.

After the draft was finalized, each entry was coded by two independent raters for what categories of issues/suggestions and how many categories it contained based on these coding schemes. The inter-rater reliability was .917 for problem definition scores and .916 for problem solution scores. Discussions between raters resolved all the differences among their ratings. The number of problem definitions generated by the subjects tapping on distinct categories was added to obtain a 'Problem Definition Score' (PDS). The number of problem solutions falling into different solution categories was added to obtain participants' 'Problem Solution Score' (PSS). For problem definition section, the association among problem definition categories was also investigated.

The participants were asked whether they would like to hear other people's perspectives about the cases and rate to what extent they agreed with the six reasons why they would like to do so. These six reasons fell into two broad categories: improving their understanding of the problems (Reason 1) or confirming their suggestions to the problems embedded in the scenarios (Reason 2). The subjects' ratings on two categories of reasons were then converted to 'Reason Preference Score' (RPS1 and RPS2) by means of adding their ratings on each reason. The difference between RPS1 and RPS2 was then computed by means of subtracting RPS2 from RPS1 to obtain 'Reason Difference Score' (RDS). Therefore higher RDS indicated that the subject wanted other perspectives because they wanted to understand the case scenarios better more than they wanted to confirm their thoughts. Because the study was administrated in English, participants were also asked whether they were native speakers of English so that the effect of language could be taken into consideration in the analysis.

As a result five different variables were measured: Problem Definition Score' (PDS), Problem Solution Score (PSS), MP ability score, Reason Difference Score (RDS) and Language. The relationships among these variables were investigated through a series of regression and correlation analyses.

Results and Conclusions

Alpha coefficients for the 20 items in MP ability survey, the three Reason 1 and the three Reason 2 questions were .852, .903 and .850 respectively.

Independent sample t test results showed that there was a significant difference in MP ability score ($t = 3.139$, $p = .002$) and number of ideas in defining problem ($t = 2.458$, $p = .016$) and generating solutions ($t = 3.017$, $p = .003$) between native English speaking students and non-native English speaking students. Native speakers of English scored higher on all of these variables.

Results indicated that the number of perspectives used in problem definition (PDS) was significantly correlated with the number of solutions generated (PSS) ($r = .627$, $p = .001$). On the other hand, the regression analyses showed MP ability score was a significant predictor of PDS even after controlling for Language ($t= 1.99$, $p=.05$) (see Table 1). MP ability score was also a significant predictor of PSS ($t =2.00$, $p=.049$) after controlling for Language again (see Table 2). The interaction between language (English) and MP ability didn't have significant effect on either defining problems ($t = .49$, $p = .62$) or generating solutions ($t = .38$, $p = .71$).

RDS was not significantly correlated with the MP ability score, PDS, or PSS. Independent T test showed that non-native speakers of English scored significantly higher than native speakers on RDS ($t = 3.17$, $p = .002$) indicating that non-native speakers rated Reason 1 (improving their understanding of the cases) higher than Reason 2 (confirming their thoughts about the cases) as to why they wanted to hear other perspectives.

Table 1: Summary of Regression Analysis for Variables Predicting Problem Defining (N = 77)

Variable	B	SE B	β
Multiple-perspective Ability	.027	.014	.229*
English	.641	.381	.193

Note. $R^2= .116$, $F_{2,74} = 4.875$, $p = .010$
* $p < .05$

Table 2: Summary of Regression Analysis for Variables Predicting Solution Generating (N = 77)

Variable	B	SE B	β
Multiple-perspective Ability	.025	.013	.225*
English	.831	.358	.261*

Note. $R^2 = .154$, $F_{2,74} = 6.746$, $p = .002$
* $p < .05$

A close look at the relationship between categories subjects used to define the problems/issues in two scenarios also revealed interesting results. For the first scenario (a kindergarten teacher and her student from different social and cultural background), six categories of perspectives emerged from subjects' answers to the problem definition question. They include perspectives on social-cultural influences (this child is from a poor family), special education (the child may have learning disability, such as speech impediment), inadequate prior learning experience (the child could lag behind his peers in his earlier education), cognitive misconception (the child has wrong concepts about English alphabets), improper instructional design (the teacher's strategy for assessing students' understanding is inadequate) and teacher personality (the teacher is not patient and encouraging enough). Hierarchical Cluster Analysis of these categories produced the following pattern (see Figure 1).

Figure 1. Hierarchical Cluster Analysis of problem definition categories (case 1)

As seen in Figure 1, the perspective of social-cultural influences and the perspective of inadequate prior learning are clustered together. Special education perspective is close to cognitive misconception perspective. The implication is that subjects who raised social-cultural perspective also tended to think the child's possible inadequate prior education could be the reason why he couldn't answer the teacher's question.

For the second scenario regarding a Chinese student losing interest in his course work, seven categories of perspectives emerged in defining the issues. They include perspectives on expectation (the student has wrong expectation), cultural difference (difference between Asian and American schools), adjustment management (he needs adjustment skills), environmental issues (the college doesn't have a friendly learning environment), relationship difficulties (he has problem developing connections), self-concept problems (his self-esteem, perception), academic experience/performance (inadequate contribution in class; courses too hard or too easy for him). Hierarchical Cluster Analysis of these categories resulted in the following production for the second case (see Figure 2).

Figure 2. Hierarchical Cluster Analysis of problem definition categories (case 2)

As seen in Figure 2, adjustment management perspective was clustered together with self-concept perspective. Environmental factor joined them later. This means subjects who suggested adjustment problems of the Chinese student (in case 2) also tended to raise the perspective that the student might have improper self-concepts.

Environmental factors seemed to be considered relevant to the above two issues. The perspective of relationship factor and the perspective of the students' academic performance seemed to be clustered together too.

Discussion

This study explored how multiple-perspective thinking ability affected ill-structured problem-solving performance. It is found that although native English speaking students had better performance in problem solving than non-native English speaking students, subjects with higher multiple-perspective thinking ability defined the case scenarios from more perspectives and generated more solutions after controlling for language. The results also showed that native English speaking subjects wanted to hear other perspectives mostly because they wanted to confirm their thoughts, and non-native English speaking subjects wanted to know other perspectives mostly because they wanted to improve their understanding of the cases. This may indicate a cultural difference in multiple perspective thinking.

The study also has several limitations. First, subjects' teaching experience was not measured in this study. Teaching experience is a variable which could contribute to how well subjects perform in solving the ill-structured problems. Next, the measurement of subjects' problem solving ability can be improved. Probably in addition to analyzing the subjects' final answers to the questions, their cognitive process during the problem-solving task need to be recorded to provide further enlightenment to the relationship between multiple-perspective thinking and ill-structured problem solving. Moreover, the reason why native English speaking subjects had better performance in problem solving than non-native English speaking subjects need to be further examined.

Today, Internet and other multimedia technology have made exposure to multiple perspectives not just possible and but also unavoidable. How to live harmoniously with opinions and perspectives that are different or even conflicting to our own becomes more and more important. Also, in dealing with complex problems or situations, people may need to hold their assumptions and avoid jumping into conclusions. Enhancing people's multiple-perspective thinking could be one of the solutions to the above situations. Before designing any training projects to improve multiple-perspective thinking ability, it is crucial to understand how MP thinking affects people's performance in problem solving. This study revealed the connection between multiple-perspective thinking and ill-structured problem-solving performance. It provides the basis for future study on how to design programs to improve performance in ill-structured problem solving by learning from multiple perspectives. It is essential to investigate what kind of preparation people need in order to enhance their multiple perspective thinking ability. Whether people of different cultural backgrounds, cross-culture experience or personalities would react differently to training programs are also worthy of further exploration.

References

Brown, A. L. (1987). Metacognition, executive Control, self-regulation, and other more mysterious mechanisms. In F. E. Weinert & R. H. KLuwe (Eds.), *Metacognition, motivation, and understanding* (pp. 65-116). Hillsdale, New Jersey: Lawrence Erlbaum Associates.

Carr, M., & Borkowski, J. G. (1987). Metamemory in gifted children. Gifted Child Quarterly, 31, 40-44.

D'Zurilla TJ, Goldfried MR: Problemsolving and behavior modification. J Abnorm Psychol 78:107–126, 1971

Flavell, J. H. (1979). Metacognition and cognitive monitoring: A new area of cognitive-developmental inquiry. American Psychologist, 34(10), 906-911.

Flavell, J. H. (1987). Speculations about the nature and development of metacognition. In Weinert, F. E., & Kluwe, R. H. (Eds.) Metacognition, motivation, and understanding. Hillsdale, NJ: Lawrence Erlbaum Associates.

Gorenflo D.W. & Crano, W.D. (1998). The Multiple Perspectives Inventory: A Measure of Perspective-taking. *Swiss Journal of Psychology*. 57(3), 163-177.

Guilford, J. P. (1975). Varieties of creative giftedness, their measurement and development. Gifted Child Quarterly, 19, 107-121.

Guilford, J. P. (1984). Varieties of divergent-production abilities or functions. Journal of Creative Behavior, 18, 1-10.

Jacobson, M. J., & Spiro, R. J. (1995). Hypertext Learning Evironments, Cognitive Flexibility, and the Transfer of Conplex Knowledge: an Empirical Investigation. *Journal of Educational Computing Research, 12*(4), 301-333.

Jonassen, D. H. (1997). Instructional design models for well-structured and illstructured problem solving learning outcomes. Educational Technology, Research & Development, 45(1), 65-94.

Kagan, D. (1993). Contexts for the use of classroom cases. *American Educational Research Journal*, 30(4), 703-723.
Kitchner, K. S. (1983). Cognition, metacognition, and epistemic cognition: A three level model of cognitive processing. *Human Development*, 26, 222-232.
Runco, M. A. (1991). Divergent thinking. Norwood, NJ: Ablex
Russo, C. (2004). A Comparative Study of Creativity and Cognitive Problem-Solving Strategies of High-IQ and Average Students. *Gifted Child Quarterly*, 48(3), 179-190
Schrader, P. G., Leu, D. J., Jr., Kinzer, C. K., Ataya, R., Teale, W. H., Labbo, L. D., et al. (2003). Using Internet Delivered Video Cases, To Support Pre-Service Teachers' Understanding of Effective Early Literacy Instruction: An Exploratory Study. *Instructional Science, 31*(4-5), 317-340.
Shin, N., Jonassen, D. H., & McGee, S. (2003). Predictors of well-structured and ill-structured problem solving in an astronomy simulation. *Journal of Research in Science Teaching*, 40(1), 6-33.
Spiro, R. J., Feltovich, P. J., Jacobson, M. J., & Coulson, R. L. (1992). Cognitive flexibility, constructivism, and hypertext: Random access instruction for advanced knowledge acquisition in ill-structured domains. In T. M. Duffy & D. H. Jonassen (Eds.), *Constructivism and the technology of instruction: A conversation* (pp. 57-76). Hillsdale, NJ: Lawerence Erlbaum Associates.
Spiro, R. J., & Jehng, J. C. (1990). Cognitive flexibility and hypertext: Theory and technology for the nonlinear and multidimensional traversal of complex subject matter. In D. Nix & R. Spiro (Eds.), *Cognition, education, and multimedia: Exploring ideas in high technology* (pp. 163-205). Hillsdale, NJ: Lawrence Erlbaum Associates.
Wicklund, R. A. (1999) Multiple perspectives in person perception and theorizing. Theory & Psychology. 9(5), 668-678.

Acknowledgments

A special thanks from the first author goes to, Prof John Black at Teachers College, Columbia University, who provided constant feedback and support during the design and the implementation of this study.

Designing an Online Service for a Math Community

Martin Wessner[1,3], Wesley Shumar[1], Gerry Stahl[1,2], Johann Sarmiento[1,2], Martin Mühlpfordt[3], Stephen Weimar[1]
Virtual Math Teams Project, a collaboration of:
[1]Math Forum @ Drexel, Philadelphia, USA
[2]College of Information Science & Technology, Drexel University, Philadelphia, USA
[3]Fraunhofer IPSI, Darmstadt, Germany
martin.wessner@ipsi.fraunhofer.de

Abstract. In the Virtual Math Teams project an online service for groups of people to discuss and collaboratively solve mathematical problems is being developed. The paper takes a qualitative approach to looking at the design-based research process of developing the platform for a synchronous math problem solving environment. We sketch the transition from early experiments with commercially available tools to a series of studies conducted with a research tool finally to the design of a platform which provides the technical basis to a scalable public service. For this design we had to take into account requirements from students, tutors, the service provider as well as researchers from various disciplines. We discuss some design decisions which lead to a platform which addresses the diverse requirements of the various stakeholders. The paper underscores the value of a design-based research process and a self-reflexive process as we develop insights about online math problem solving.

Enabling and Supporting an Online Math Community

So much math done by students is done at the individual level. Even when students work on math problems together they are often doing the work individually. The goal of the Virtual Math Teams (VMT) project is to provide an online service, as part of The Math Forum's regular suite of interactive math education services, that would allow students the opportunity to work together collaboratively in a synchronous environment in order to talk about math and solve math problems. The idea of the VMT project is to bring together students, teachers, designers and researchers all in a collaborative way to help design, develop, test, and use an online collaborative math chat service.

The ultimate goal of the VMT project is to create a self-sustaining system that would allow individuals to join a chat, become part of a well-working group, and make progress together toward increasing their math knowledge and problem solving skills. But this ultimate goal raises several important challenges. First, are there specific dynamics of a good online group. There is some conflicting literature regarding the work of collaborative groups that is unclear about whether similar ability groups work best together or if mixed ability groups work best (Ireson and Hallam, 2001). Also, should there be specific roles in the group of online problem solves and should those roles be arbitrarily pre-assigned to students or should the system pick people with different characteristics to assign them to a group together. Perhaps the most challenging issue is how to support a group as they attempt to make progress in problem solving and what to do if the group gets stuck at some point in their problem solving activities.

Theoretical Considerations

The VMT project has taken a design-based research perspective (Stahl et al., 2006, The Design-Based Research Collective, 2003; Hoadley 2002). As Stahl et al. (2006) describe, the project involves the iterative development of the online synchronous math chat service. That iterative design process involves a number of collaborators: research team, students, and math teachers. Here we will discuss the role of the research team a bit and talk more about the students and the teachers later in the paper. The research team is collaborative group of researchers from a number of different fields and math educators who meet weekly to develop and discuss the evolution of the online synchronous math chat system. The research team has done everything from collaboratively designing services to working on the analysis of data from a number of different perspectives. The research group also includes a number of off-campus collaborators who follow the research progress of the team and some of whom become on-site visiting researchers for periods of time.

For the purposes of this paper we are taking a more ethnographic perspective to talk about the overall design development process in the research team. Barab et al (2004:254) define critical design ethnography as "…a process that sits at the intersection of participatory action research, critical ethnography, and socially responsive instructional design." From their perspective their goal was to effect social change through a process of being immersed in a community and at the same time providing for that community educational design work that was developed in collaboration with the community. Porpora (1999) has suggested that action research is the highest stage of service learning because it is a form of educational opportunity where students learn from real life service opportunities in living communities, a truly inquiry and experience based process. Reason (2004:270) makes some similar points reflecting Barab et al. (2004). He suggests that action research is at the intersection of "knowledge in practice" and "participation and democracy". Barab et al. are describing a kind of parallel process to both Porpora and Reason where the immersion of the design team in the life of the community enriches the work of both groups.

The VMT is not a critical design ethnography project. However it shares several features of that work and involves an ethnographic component to the self-reflection that the research group engages in. The work in the VMT is a highly collaborative and reflective process. The research team works through all design issues and research issues together as they think about what effects changes in the chat environments are having on student participants. They also think about the nature of the math problems and which problems are best suited to collaborative online work as well as the nature of the mathematical conversations the students are having in the chats. The research team also has engaged in problem solving themselves in the chats as they attempt to get a feel for the experience of the participants in math chats. Finally the research team has involved students in the process encouraging them to tell us about what worked in the chats and what they would like to see changed in future versions of the chats. Recently we have also begun to work with a group of teachers on the project as well.

The current paper attempts to take an ethnographic perspective in that it is a large overview of the development of the chat environment and it critically reflects on the progress that we have made so far and the challenges we face. As such the data for the current paper comes from the notes that we have taken on our own process as we have in part become the subjects of our own analysis.

First Phase: Experimenting with Diverse Tools

In our design-based research at the Virtual Math Teams project (Stahl *et al.*, 2005), we started by conducting chats in a variety of commercially available environments: AOL Instant Messenger (AOL IM), Babylon, Blackboard, WebCT. Most of the early work concentrated on the use of AOL Instant Messenger for a set of math chats that we called PoW-wows after the Math Forum's Problem of the Week (PoW) on which the chats were based. The choice of AOL IM was a simple one, it was a piece of technology that most students had on their computers and could be used to self organize math chats very quickly. Further in our informal conversations with students they liked AOL IM very much and saw it as a "cool" medium in which to construct the math chats. Finally AOL IM is a very basic piece of synchronous chat technology and so it was a good place to start from in order to see what other features we might need to enhance math chats.

The early experience with the PoW-wows was very interesting. There were many interesting things that we began to see about the math chats themselves and several researchers on the project undertook an effort to code the chat data to look for patterns of interaction in the conversation. The chats were also analyzed from a conversation analysis perspective (Stahl 2005a; 2005b; Stahl et al., 2006; Zemel, Xhafa, F, Cakir, 2005; Zemel, Xhafa, & Stahl, 2005).

But beyond the content based research that was taking place in the project there were a number of critical design issues that began to clearly emerge from the chat process. An interesting feature of chat is that it is a medium that moves very quickly. People often do not write whole sentences and ideas flow very rapidly. This is especially true if there are more than two people in a chat. It has become very clear that one thing that was needed was a place where a group could save some ideas that they developed through the chat. They needed a place to store established ideas and a way to organize those established ideas and math facts.

It was also the case that students often missed ideas that others in the group articulated. This is a funny kind of "shunning" that goes on in online chats. On the one hand it may be that an idea is articulated by a member of the group and the rest of the group does not see the idea. On the other hand the idea may fall outside of the main flow of the conversation and because the conversation is moving so fast people do not take the opportunity to respond to the person who's posts fall outside of the main focus of the conversation. Another related process that goes on is that sometimes in these chats two or more conversations would occur in parallel at the same time. This meant that participants needed to let the others know which conversation thread s/he was posting a response to.

Due to the complexity of the problem or time restrictions of participants in many cases the problem solving involves several chat sessions. In later sessions groups would like to review the conversation they had in previous sessions. Thus, they could easily identify the state of the problem solving in their group. This would be especially helpful when group membership changes between sessions as it was the case in our experiments due to coordination problems or drop outs. It would also allow late-comers or participants who missed one session to catch up with the other group members quickly. To support changing membership and multi-session processes a persistent storage of the chat conversation is needed by the students.

Finally it became clear that with many of the math problems the student were doing it was helpful to have a shared graphical representation of the problem and the problem solving. When they did the problem solving together in AOL IM they often drew on a sheet of paper and talked about their drawing on IM. They also began to upload drawings to the Math Forum site so they could share drawings with each other while they talked about the problem.

All of this interaction made it clear that there were some very specific features that such a math chat needs. First it was clear that students need a space where they could put ideas. They need a text box where the questions they wanted to address could be listed, or the ideas they had could be listed or formulas used could be listed etc. Related to this kind of listing function, it became very clear that it would be useful for students to have a place where they could draw or place drawings in order to facilitate the problem solving process. In addition, they need a persistent storage of chat logs to allow late-comers or new group members to fully participate in the group and to provide bridges between different problem solving sessions. Finally the students needed a "referencing" function where they could point to posts in the chat or place in the drawing and bring other participants attention to specific places. These four functions, listing, drawing, storage and referencing became the core of the next phase of a specific chat development.

There were some additional problem solving issues that the team is continuing to think about even as the design of phase two was going ahead. One thing we found in the problems is that there were two dominant modes of discourse in the problem solving. We've labeled these modes expository and exploratory (Stahl et al, 2006). In the expository mode one or more participants are explaining how to do the problem to the others in the group. The others may or may not know how to do the problem solving that the explainer is talking about at that point. In the exploratory mode, all participants are exploring together how to solve the problem and that exploration may or may not be successful. These patterns of interaction have raised the question of whether groups should be mixed or same ability, and then how those groups ought to be scaffolded if they need scaffolding. The research team is continuing to think about these issues as they involve some teachers in the project and plan deeper, more context based explorations of how the kids are thinking about the problem solving.

Second Phase: Using ConcertChat Rooms

The VMT project decided to use ConcertChat, a research chat environment with a shared whiteboard, persistent storage and special referencing tools (Mühlpfordt & Wessner, 2005). In collaboration between the software developers and the educational researchers several versions of the environment have been tried out by the researchers as well as with groups of students. In response to the analysis of the chat logs as well as other information gathered from the moderators, service providers, and the students the environment was gradually modified.

To address the above mentioned four requirements (listing, drawing, storage and referencing) ConcertChat provides a variety of features supporting math chats (see figure 1 for a screen view):

- Listing and drawing: A shared whiteboard allows chat participants to list ideas, formulas etc. and to create drawings using circles, squares, lines, free-forms, text-boxes etc. In addition, participants can place pictures on the whiteboard taken from a gallery, the file system or from any part of the screen using the screenshot feature.

- Storage: All chat messages, editing activities on the whiteboard and all systems messages (e.g. about joining or leaving participants) are stored persistently in the chat environment. Late-comers or new group members can load all previous messages from the room's history. This also allows asynchronous participation in the problem solving process.

- Referencing (1): When someone types a new chat message, they can select and point to a rectangular area or an object on the whiteboard. When that message appears in the chat as the latest posting or as a selected posting, a bold line appears connecting the text to the area of the drawing (see figure 1).
- Referencing (2) Similarly, a chat message can point to one or more earlier textual postings or parts of postings to indicate for example a response to a previous posting. ConcertChat also includes a threaded view of the chat postings that, based on the explicit references between postings, displays them like a typical threaded discussion with responses indented under the posting that they reference.

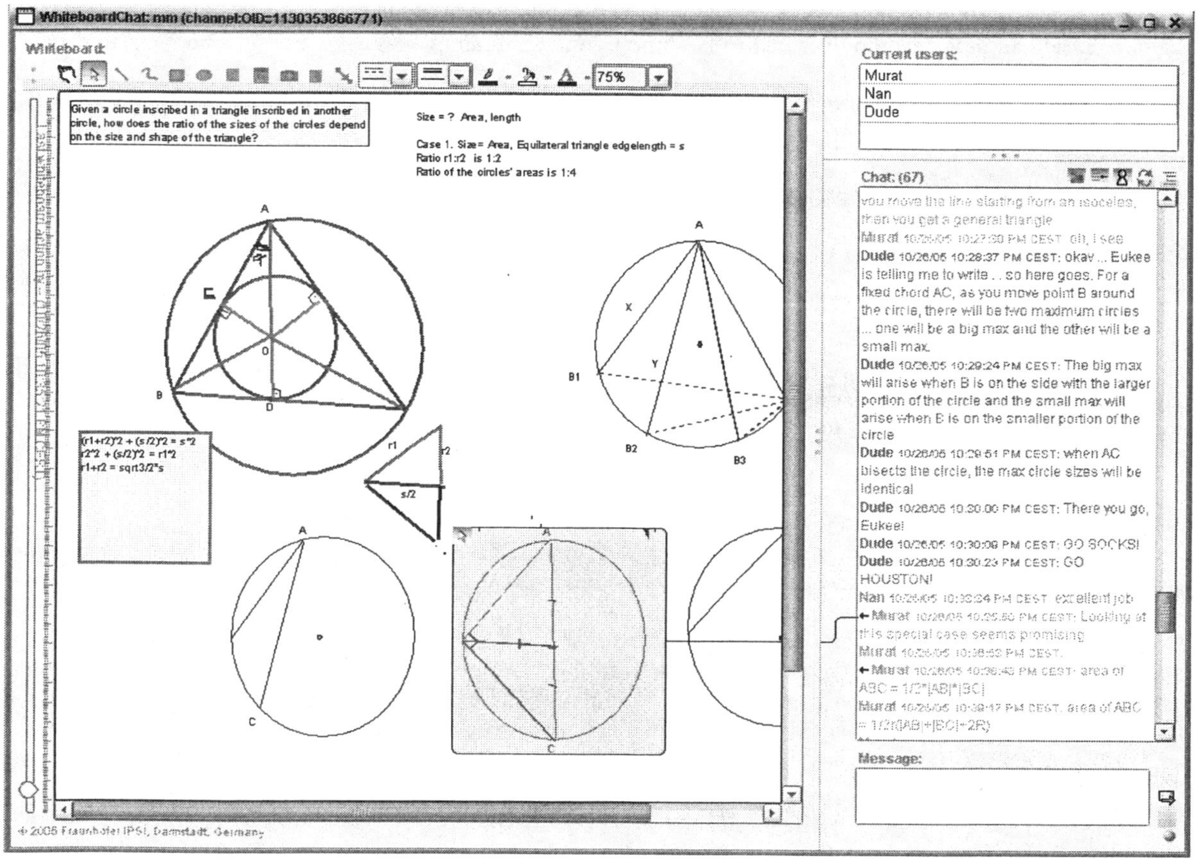

Figure 1. Screen view of a ConcertChat room. One of the messages provides a graphical reference to an area on the whiteboard. The whiteboard also contains textboxes to present the problem and to list ideas and formulas.

In May 2005, a series of chats using ConcertChat have been conducted. Five virtual math teams were formed, each containing about four middle-school students selected by volunteer teachers at different schools across the USA. The teams engaged in online math discussions for four hour-long sessions over a two-week period. They were given a brief description of a non-traditional geometry environment: a grid-world where one could only move along the lines of a grid (Krause, 1986). The students were encouraged to come up with their own questions about the grid-world, such as questions about shortest paths between points A and B in this world.

Technically, the students received a URL for each session where they accessed their group's chat room. From the administrator's point of view a web page provided a list of all available chat rooms and the functionality to create new rooms.

The chats were facilitated by a member of our research project team. The facilitator welcomed students to the chat, pointed them toward the task, briefly demonstrated the use of the system focusing on the graphical referencing tool and then kept generally quiet until it was time to end the session.

The new functionality, the shared whiteboard and the graphical referencing functionality were accepted by the students. However, the degree of usage varied between different groups. Reasons include the lack of an exhaustive manual as well as some usability issues as we learned from the chat logs (some usability issues were mentioned and discussed by the students during the sessions) as well as from our own experiments with the tool.

The instructional design for the experiments with the students included gathering ideas in the individual groups in the first session. In the second session students were asked to reflect on all ideas gathered by all groups and to select those ideas they want to work on. This required some preparation on the side of the moderators in order to collect and prepare the groups' results. Also the initial assignment of students to groups, the distribution of the problem and the handling of drop-outs had to be done by the facilitators. In general, it became clear that an ideal environment should not only provide support for (multiple) chat rooms but also provide support the formation of groups and help to bridge different groups and sessions to allow (self-) organization, awareness of other groups and their problem solving activities and results.

As mentioned above, the ultimate goal of the VMT project is to provide a self-sustaining system which offers a maximum of flexibility to engage in joint math problem solving. For this additional issues have to be taken into account. One critical issue is to support the communication between the groups and a tutor. This includes submitting a solution, requesting feedback on the problem solving process or asking for help if a problem occurs. Another issue is how to communicate the "state" of a chat room to other groups and individuals. This includes questions like: Am I allowed to join that room? Does this group need additional group members? Is the problem already solved? Do they plan to continue this problem solving? From the legal point of view there must be a way to handle rude or even illegal behavior in chat rooms. As a default all activities are stored in the chat history including pictures posted to the whiteboard etc. Questions of ownership, of personal accountability arise (not only) from this legal perspective.

From Multiple Rooms to a Math Community

As a third phase we are currently extending the ConcertChat environment to address the above mentioned issues. As a new component of the system a "Lobby" has been designed and implemented which provides the starting point for all problem solving activities in the math community. Here, students find a list of problems they can work on and all chat rooms they can enter to jointly work on a given or self-defined problem. They also can create new rooms either for new groups or to work with the same group on a new problem. A chat in the lobby supports communication between all students, across groups as well as self-organized group formation. Students can explore all other rooms including rooms where they already have participated and rooms of other groups as long as these are not restricted. This allows communication and collaboration between groups and exchange of ideas, material and group results. For each room a number of fields exists which communicate the state of the room. All online and offline members, the owner, the related problem and other information such as room name or planned session times can be seen for each room. In addition, it is clear from the system's room organization which rooms can be accessed by whom. See figure 2 for a screen view of the Lobby.

With respect to the rooms different types of rooms have been designed in order to meet the different kinds of problems and groups. This ranges from rooms where the problem and the participants are assigned by a facilitator in advance, rooms with a given problem but open to self-organizing groups to rooms which can be used by all students to work on arbitrary problems. Thus both self-forming of groups and tutor-formed groups can be supported. Inside each room the room topic and problem description is available as well as communication facilities which allow the group and the tutor to communicate not only via chat but also asynchronously via email.

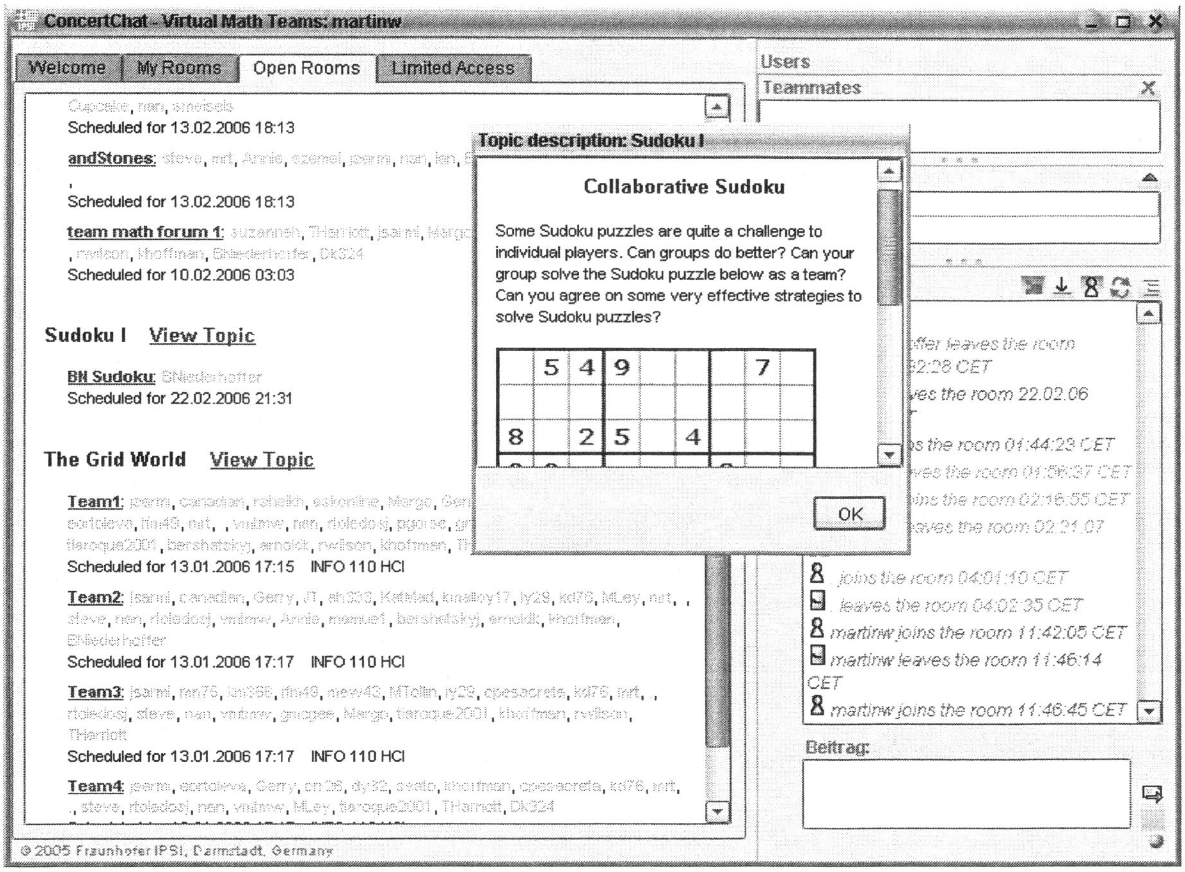

Figure 2. Screen view of the ConcertChat Lobby. On the left side the rooms are organized by access rights (see tabs "Welcome", "My Rooms", "Open Rooms", "Limited Access") and topics (listing of rooms in each tab). For each room additional information on participants and their online-status, scheduling etc. is displayed. The small window presents the view of one topic, here: a collaborative Sudoku.

Conclusions and Outlook

In the process of designing and using the Concert Chat environment we have made many important realizations about math problem solving and math problem solving online. Math is a subject that is challenging for many students. Using chat takes advantage of a medium that is very popular with kids and one where it is possible to lose oneself a bit in the interaction process. These are potentially good things for the math student. But chat can also be so dissipating that one may not only lose oneself but lose sight of where one is in the problem solving process. And so to that end we have attempted to outfit a chat environment with many of the tools one will need to engage in successful collaborative math problem solving. This includes listing, drawing, storage and referencing to improve the math collaboration in a group as well as various organizational aids to facilitate group formation, access rights and community building.

Further we have begun to work toward a whole community of online problem solvers and problem solving activities. Our experiments with different kinds of math problems have shown us that perhaps some problems need a more structured group in order to fruitfully get through the problem. While other math problems can casually be explored by groups that come together just to talk about a little math. And finally for those groups that want to develop continuity over time they can do so. ConcertChat will provide an environment where individuals might find very different kinds of groups and different kinds of problems. This evolution is very in keeping with the tradition of The Math Forum where different kinds of learners can find the level of support they need in order to improve their ability to engage in fruitful mathematical conversation and become deeper mathematical thinkers.

References

Barab, S., Thomas, M. K., Dodge, T., Squire, K., Newell, M. (2004). Critical design ethnography: Designing for change. *Anthropology and Education Quarterly* 35(2)254-268.

Design-Based Research Collective (2003). Design-based research: An emerging paradigm for educational inquiry. *Educational Researcher* 32(1)5-8.

Hoadley, C. P. (2002). Creating context: Design-based research in creating and understanding CSCL. In G. Stahl (Ed.), *Computer support for collaborative learning: Foundations for a CSCL community* (pp. 453-462). Proceedings of the Conference on Computer Support for Collaborative Learning (CSCL) 2002, Boulder, USA. Hillsdale, NJ: Lawrence Erlbaum.

Ireson, J. & Hallam, S. (2001). *Ability grouping in education.* London: Sage Publications.

Krause, E. (1986). *Taxicab geometry: An adventure in non-euclidean geometry.* New York, NY: Dover.

Mühlpfordt, M., & Wessner, M. (2005). Explicit referencing in chat supports collaborative learning. In T. Koschmann, D. Suthers, & T. -W. Chan (Eds.), *Computer Supported Collaborative Learning 2005: The Next 10 Years.* Proceedings of the Conference on Computer Support for Collaborative Learning (CSCL) 2005, Taipei, Taiwan. Mahwah, NJ: Lawrence Erlbaum.

Pimentel, M., Fuks, H., & Lucena, C. (2005). *Mediated chat development process: Avoiding chat confusion on educational debates.* In T. Koschmann, D. Suthers, & T. -W. Chan (Eds.), *Computer Supported Collaborative Learning 2005: The Next 10 Years.* Proceedings of the Conference on Computer Support for Collaborative Learning (CSCL) 2005, Taipei, Taiwan. Mahwah, NJ: Lawrence Erlbaum.

Porpora, D. V. (1999). Action Research: The Highest Stage of Service Learning? In Ostrow, J., Hesser, G. and Enos, S. (Eds), *Cultivating the Sociological Imagination: Concepts and Models for Service Learning in Sociology.* Washington, DC: American Association of Higher Education in association with the American Sociological Association.

Reason, P. (2004). Critical Design Ethnography as Action Research. *Anthropology and Education Quarterly* 35(2)269-276.

Stahl, G. (2005a). *Sustaining online collaborative problem solving with math proposals.* Paper presented at the International Conference on Computers and Education (ICCE 2005), Singapore, Singapore.

Stahl, G. (2005b). *Group cognition in chat: Methods of interaction / methodologies of analysis.* Paper presented at the Kaleidoscope CSCL SIG Workshop on Analysis of Interaction and Learning (NAIL 2005), Gothenburg, Sweden.

Stahl, G., Weimar, S., Fetter, A., & Sarmiento, J. (2005). *Virtual Math Teams: Studying and supporting online collaborative problem-solving.* Paper presented at the Annual Meeting of the National Council of Teachers of Mathematics (NCTM 2005), Anaheim, CA.

Stahl, G. (2006). *Group cognition: Computer support for building collaborative knowledge.* Cambridge, MA: MIT Press. Retrieved from http://www.cis.drexel.edu/faculty/gerry/mit/.

Zemel, A., Xhafa, F., & Cakir, M. (2005). *What's in the mix? Combining coding and conversation analysis to investigate chat-based problem-solving.* Paper presented at the 11th Biennial Conference of the European Association for Research on Learning and Instruction (EARLI 2005), Nicosia, Cyprus.

Zemel, A., Xhafa, F., & Stahl, G. (2005). *Analyzing the organization of collaborative math problem-solving in online chats using statistics and conversation analysis.* Paper presented at the CRIWG International Workshop on Groupware, Racife, Brazil

Acknowledgments

The Virtual Math Teams Project is a collaborative effort at Drexel University. The Principal Investigators are Gerry Stahl, Stephen Weimar and Wesley Shumar. A number of Math Forum staff work on the project, especially Stephen Weimar, Annie Fetter and Ian Underwood. The graduate research assistants are Murat Cakir, Johann Sarmiento, Ramon Toledo and Nan Zhou. Alan Zemel is a post-doc. The following visiting researchers have spent 3 to 6 months on the project: Jan-Willem Strijbos (Netherlands), Fatos Xhafa (Spain), Stefan Trausan-Matu (Romania), Martin Wessner (Germany), Elizabeth Charles (Canada). The ConcertChat software was developed at the Fraunhofer Institute IPSI in Darmstadt, Germany, by Martin Mühlpfordt, Martin Wessner and colleagues. The VMT project is supported by grants from the NSDL, IERI and SoL programs of the US National Science Foundation. The perspectives in this paper are those of the authors, not necessarily NSF or others.

Communication through the Artefact by Means of Synchronous Co-construction

Astrid Wichmann, Markus Kuhn, Ulrich Hoppe
Collide Group, Institute for Computer Science and Interactive Systems,
University of Duisburg-Essen, Forsthausweg 2, 47057 Duisburg, Germany
{Wichmann, Kuhn, Hoppe}@collide.info

Abstract: This paper examines the collaborative features of a tool environment called Cool Modes. Cool Modes provides different modelling environments allowing learners to co-construct representations of domain-specific models. These systems range from curriculum topics such as stochastic to subjects with a non-standard character such as astronomy. In the current study we focus upon the Stochastic palette and the Moon palette, which both provide visual languages to support modelling activities specifically in the subject matter area of mathematics. These visual languages are embedded in the Cool Modes Framework providing tools for annotating and enriching the co-constructive modelling process. Both palettes have been tested and adapted for learning scenarios taking place in formal and informal learning environments. In this paper we report the findings from observational material collected from 3 classes in Germany using Cool Modes. The observation concentrates upon assessing the effectiveness of supporting co-constructive modelling activities in a synchronous learning setting.

Introduction

According to the socio-cognitive perspective learners construct knowledge by actively engaging in collaborative activities such as formulating arguments and sharing ideas. We aim to support the socio-cognitive argument/hypothesis that learning is grounded in participating in an activity. The social aspects that enable students to create knowledge are triggered through using computational artefacts to stimulate collaborative knowledge exchange by communication through the artefact (Dix, Finaly, Abowd & Beale, 1997). In order to support students to not only participate, but actively engage in the knowledge construction process, we develop learning environments that allow collaborative manipulation of scientific artefacts. In face-to-face settings, allowing learners to frame the learning activity using "computational objects to think with" can facilitate this collaborative knowledge construction process (Hoppe, 2004). Inspired by Jonassen's (2000) notion of mindtools we develop learning scenarios to establish a reciprocal environment that engages students to co-construct representational objects.

Collaboration

Communication through an artefact is characteristic of co-construction in shared workspace environments, in which the artefact-based communication complements natural language-based exchange (Hoppe, 2005). From a design point of view, the emphasis is on increasing awareness of collaborators' actions, whereby the artefact is treated as the mediation device. A peer-to-peer group can manipulate representational objects establishing control and feedback and thus communicate through the learning object. Both can observe each other's actions. This communication is necessary to improve and re-adjust the decision making process that is represented by the artefact. While this feedthrough communication is important for both asynchronous and synchronous learning settings, it is also the direct communication within and across groups that can be facilitated when co-constructing models. Observing the direct communication in synchronous classroom and informal lab settings is critical when evaluating the learning process. Different dynamics of communication can be noticed during a modelling session: Question asking (often to the instructor), peer-to-peer discussions and knowledge exchange on a group level (across peer groups). The communications differ in content depending on the problems that occur. In a computer-supported environment the communication that concerns the functionality of the learning environment is a thread that can be observed, in addition to task-related and further non-task-specific communication. This tool-related information is necessary. Conversely this can take up limited cognitive recourses that could be otherwise used for the task when constructing a scientific model.

During the scenarios that have been analysed here, students conducted scientific experiments by constructing models using an inquiry approach (de Jong & Joolingen, 1998). During this study we focus on the direct communication within and across groups using observation as an instrument of assessment. The feedthrough communications were assessed using log files containing time stamps indicating the evolvement of models created by students. The learning objects are stored and retrieved in a Learning Object Repository called LOR (Pinkwart, 2005). This software logging method was used as a complementary evaluation method for observation.

Learning Environment

The learning environment CoolModes (Pinkwart, 2003) is a framework for various visual languages with domain specific semantics that support modelling activities. Representations with different semantics (e.g. Petri Nets, System Dynamics, Concept Maps) can serve as either operational or conceptual models, which can be enhanced through annotating these models using visual languages to support argumentations and scientific inquiry. The Cool Modes framework allows the learner to mix different modelling languages including annotation tools in the same workspace. Discrete palettes indicate the domain to what the modelling activities are related to.

The Stochastic palette (Kuhn, Hoppe, Lingnau & Wichmann, 2005) for example is related to probabilistic experimentation activities. It is an open modelling environment where students are required to solve the task of probabilistic problems such as the "Birthday Problem". The task is not only to adjust parameters, but also in constructing a model to select and combine elements of the visual language "stochastic experiments" in collaboration with peers, to represent as well as run and analyse an experiment within the field of stochastics (see Figure 1).

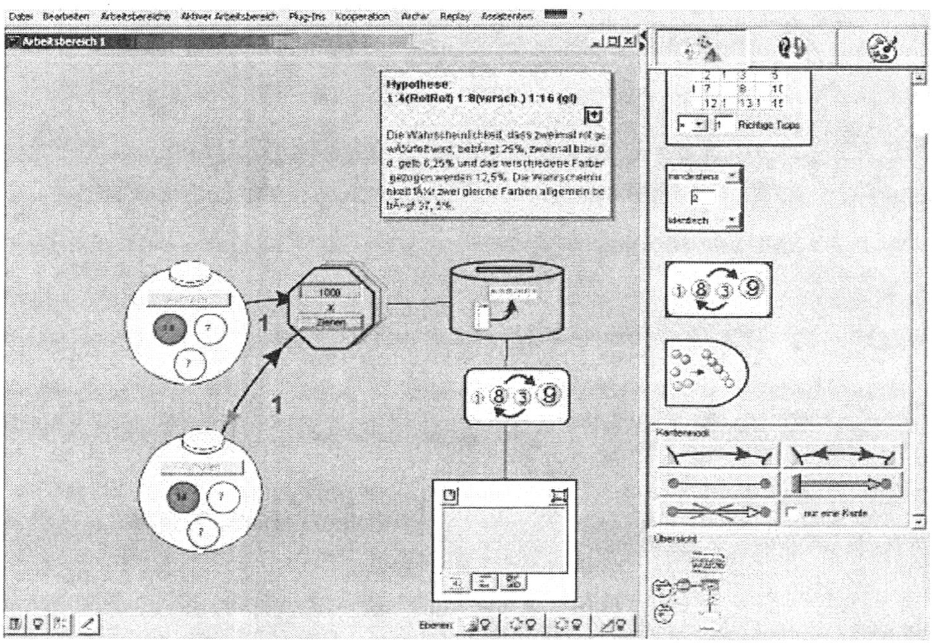

Figure 1. Model of a stochastic experiment with hypothesis note

The Modelling activities in Cool Modes are the results of selecting and linking elements of a visual language that includes random generators, simulation controller and displays. Every element has its own meaning and semantics, which are represented by its visual appearance. Appropriate elements can be linked according to the dataflow. These elements are generated as a subset from the model of a probabilistic experiment. The control element repeats the simulated experiment. A "collector" allows storing the experiment results, displayed as either a list or diagram. Another palette, the Moon palette (Hoeksema, Jansen & Hoppe, 2004) allows learners to load and measure distances on the moon using modelling and calculation tools. Students can make astronomical observations by taking photos using small telescopes or utilizing available pictures that can be displayed in the Cool Modes workspace (see Figure 2). Students calculate the height of lunar craters by determining the radius of the crater and calculating the shadow length using the intercept theorems.

To be able to measure lunar heights learners can model calculation trees to visualize mathematical operations. Collaborative features such as a voting activity and visualization of arguments accompany the modelling activities. These framing activities can be attached in the same workspace as the modelling activities taking place using either the voting palette or the discussion palette. Even though the extra-curricular character of Astronomy has a non-standard aspect to it, the modelling activity itself requires students to work with standard mathematical topics; namely Sentence of Three, and Theorems of Similar Triangles.

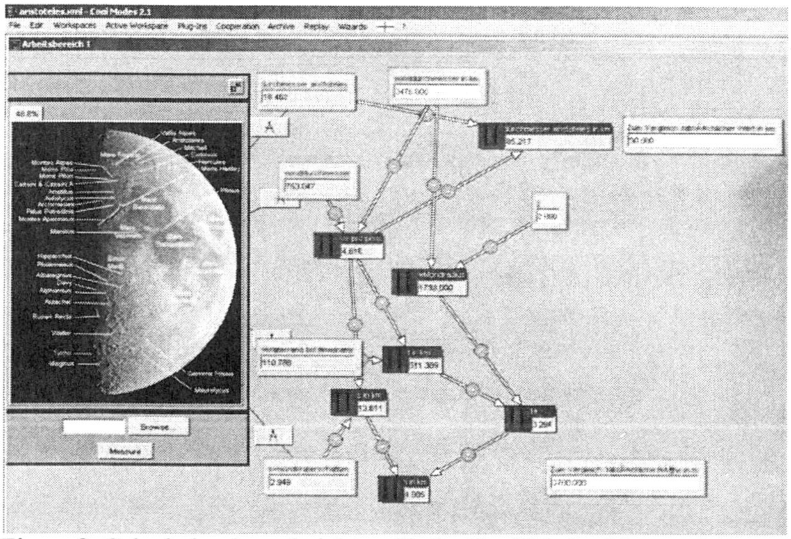

Figure 2. Calculating lunar heights with the Cool Modes Moon palette

The feature in both palettes described above uses multi-modal representations. Self-generated hypotheses are to be represented within the capabilities of the Cool Modes environment. The students have a set of model representations available that can help to make useful decisions within the choice of collaboratively constructing an appropriate model that leads to solving a problem. During the Cool Modes modelling activities a feature for collaboration support is available through a communication server called "MatchMaker". Through MatchMaker learners can share objects in a joint real-time session. Shared representations can be individually annotated by coupling workspaces.

Besides the synchronous object sharing capabilities, Cool Modes comes with an interface to a Learning Object Repository (LOR) that allows for the index, storage and retrieval of specific learning objects for immediate or later re-use. The uploading mechanism includes semantic indexing that autonomously stores contextual information of the artefacts to facilitate the students' active learning, rather than spending time on indexing artefacts themselves.

Focus of Study

The study was carried out as part of the final evaluation of the EU funded project COLDEX (IST-2001-32327). The activities were integrated in the rich context of remote and face-to-face scenarios developed to support scientific experimentation activities in formal as well as informal learning settings. The face-to-face settings for this study allowed us to intensively observe the collaborative behaviour of students engaging in scientific activities such as constructing models, measuring distances and interpreting simulation data. The focus of the study was on the technological development whereby the basis was in assessing to what extent students were really supported by the environment to engage in effective collaboration. Based on the work by Grudin (1988) we decided to conduct field evaluation to be able to assess social-psychological and anthropological effects of the environment appropriately. More specifically we were interested in the effectiveness of the learning scenarios adapted to run in both formal and informal learning settings. The focus of observation was the level of interaction that took place during the scenario. One goal of the COLDEX scenarios was to allow technology immersion by supporting scientific practice (Reiser, Tabak, Sandoval, Smith, Steinmuller & Leone, 2001) through co-constructing knowledge using features of the tool environment CoolModes.

Method

Study Setting

The evaluation study with 3 classes took place in two computer labs and one outside of the formal school environment. The participants consisted of complete school classes, while the teachers were responsible for delivering both the theory and the student activities. Two researchers assisted with the technology. Only one palette of CoolModes was assessed at a time. The palette "Stochastic" was tested with two classes. The palette "Moon" was used by one class. All three classes were participating for the duration of 1 day in a computer lab at university. In all cases the teacher introduced the students to the topic of Stochastic in previous lessons.

Participants

The students were 9th grade and from German high schools. All three classes had no prior experience of using the Cool Modes environment. Scientific Inquiry skills such as hypothesis building and collecting data were introduced as elementary methods in science classes. Autonomous student activities as well as teacher-centred instruction were part of all lessons. The theoretical introductions to subject matter and the short introduction to Cool Modes tended to be more teacher-centred. During the Cool Modes activities students were working on one table of 4-8 people to allow different modes of collaboration (e.g. peer-to-peer, small group, whole group). Two students shared a single computer.

Data Source

Participant observation techniques were chosen to observe the students' mode of interaction. A category system was developed to specifically capture interaction patterns in connection toward whether the type of instruction encouraged using the learning technology or not. The assessment of teaching / instruction styles in conjunction with technology integration seems necessary because in synchronous learning settings the teaching methods can affect the level of technology integration (Painter, 2001). The category system developed for that observation was translated into a rating scale that identified four discrete levels (1 = low, 4 = high) of interaction. The focus of observation was the students' interactions and teaching styles. The categories regarding students' interactions (see Table 1) aims at helping to assess the level and type of collaboration (e.g. peer-to-peer collaboration vs. collaboration across groups vs. knowledge sharing), support of arguments (visualising arguments, using discussion threads etc.) and type of communicated content. To further analyse the quality of communicated content, we distinguished between tool-related communication and task-related communication. Tool-related communication included content that was related to the functionality of the Cool Modes software. Task-related content refers to communication regarding the task itself, e.g. constructing a model in Cool Modes. The coded instructional styles concentrate upon the overall teaching method (learner-centred vs. teacher-centred) and level of teacher involvement in student activities. During the course of observation a list of program related bugs and interface problems that students encountered were generated. Additional material to observation: Additionally to the interaction and annotations, student artefacts were used for convergent validation and pictures were taken throughout the instructional learning unit.

Table 1: Excerpt of 4 (out of 12) Interaction Patterns for Coding

1) *Types of Collaboration*	No **one-to-one** peer collaboration	Little **one-to-one** peer collaboration
2) *Types of Collaboration*	No Collaboration **within** one group	Little collaboration **within** one group
3) *Types of Collaboration*	No collaboration **among** groups	Little collaboration **among** groups
4) *Types of argumentation*	**Requests** no information from other groups or only when prompted	**Requests** little information from other groups

Every Observer was briefed about the observation material and methodology to attain the highest level of standardization across each test. The observational material that consisted of rating scales was explained beforehand

and the appropriate method of recording observations was introduced. Since the rating scales that were developed for this observation are considered complex, a legend (including schemes) was attached to the rating scales and openly discussed with each observer. Every item of the scale was explained, and its specific meaning agreed upon in order to achieve a high comparability of the observed data. Observation of *all* students who are involved in an activity was considered to be too resource intensive, therefore we decided upon an appropriate sampling method. According to Baber (2005) taking the sociological approach by seeking to collect data from a smaller sample group, but over a comparatively longer duration of time, can control extraneous variables and better reflect real practice in real environments. Four experienced evaluators were selected as observers, choosing one or two peer-to-peer groups to observe them throughout one learning unit. In total 11 groups were observed. The students were informed beforehand that an observation would take place. Permission was gained from the students via the appropriate method of informed consent. The samples for observation were selected depending on their activeness in the activity. This decision of disregarding generalisability was made in favour of capturing rich descriptive results.

Analysis and Results

After the observation took place, the observers shared and discussed their observational material. This consisted of the annotated scales as well as rich descriptions of content and activity that the students were working with during the observation. The different material was discussed to ensure equality of initial conditions and context of activities. The reviewed results of the scales were aggregated. This was done for every unit. The aggregated results of every unit were then compared with other units.

In summary, three units were observed. The unit Stochastic took place twice, with different classes and teachers; the unit Moon took place once. Categories were determined depending on type of instruction and content. We compared the level of collaboration and interaction within the following sessions that are applicable throughout the classes: Introduction to the theory/ task, Introduction to the environment Cool Modes, Cool Modes Practice Session I, II and III, and LOR (Learning Object Repository) session. During the LOR session, students uploaded and retrieved their artefacts to the LOR via an interface in Cool Modes.

A comparison between theory-related instruction and Cool Modes related instruction mode showed expected differences in the level of student interaction. We observed that theory-related session engaged students to a smaller extent in collaborative activities across groups than within peer groups. It was observed that little communication took place during theory-related instruction. During the Cool Modes session, more communication took place. Here, students actively exchanged information. Furthermore, it was observed that learners shared ideas across group members and requested information related to the tool as well as task-related question. Besides comparing different modes of instruction, we compared the change of collaborative behaviour during one mode of instruction over a period of time. It could be observed that quality and intensity of collaboration changed during one Cool Modes session. In Cool Modes Session I, students collaborated only in small group settings (peer-to-peer) within peer settings. Little or no collaboration was observed across groups and therefore little knowledge exchange took place in the whole class. In Cool Modes Session II, and III group structures softened and students exchanged information across peer-groups. In particular the quality of information exchange increased and the learning objects built included more annotations such as formulating hypotheses etc. First, we observed more one-directional communication in the sense that students requested small pieces of information. After working with the Cool Modes environment for a while, sharing of ideas and small discussions could be observed. In Cool Modes Session III, students exchanged ideas freely across groups, exchanging problems about the functionality and sharing experiences of choosing appropriate objects to construct a model. While the collaboration across groups and level of knowledge exchange increased over the day when working with Cool Modes, the peer-to-peer group collaboration maintained a strong performance from the first until the third Cool Modes session.

Students discussed content-related issues (task-related) and issues regarding the functionality of Cool Modes (tool-related). Tool-related communication included for example how to resize tables in the Cool Modes workspace, how to save files, where to find other palettes, how to scale nodes and how to open a file. This type of communication was addressed using the term tool-related. Task-related content on the other hand, addressed communication about subject matter, such as discussions about a given task, problems with understanding instruction. Comparing the results of both, theory-related and Cool Modes-related, instruction mode, we observed more task-related discussions within the Cool Modes sequence than in the theory-related sequence. Tool-related content was only applicable in the Cool Modes Sequence and was therefore only observed there. In a second step, we analysed the change of communication during Cool Modes sequences over the course of the whole lesson. In the beginning of the Cool Modes session, we observed some task-related communication and much tool-related communication.

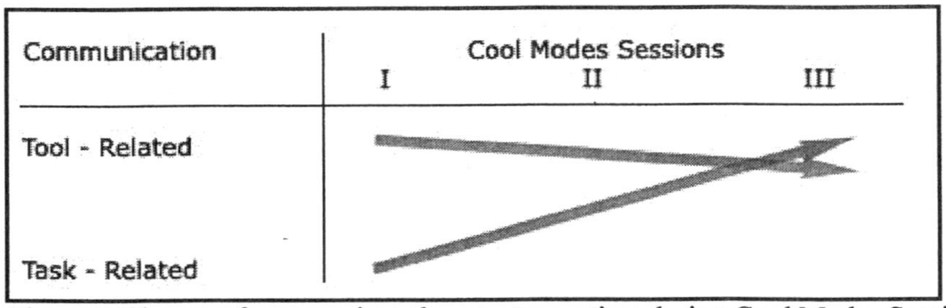

Figure 3. Change of communicated content over time during Cool Modes Session

Towards the end of the Cool Modes activities students discussed more task-related content, even though tool-related communication only slightly decreased (see Figure 3). Students created operational models in all three Cool Modes sessions. Only in the second Cool Modes session and especially in the last session students annotated these models by adding explanations and hypotheses. Also then students autonomously tried out other palettes and integrated them in the existing workspace. During the LOR session tool-related communication prevailed. The interface for uploading artefacts includes section where artefacts can be described by the authors. Especially then, students discussed in peer groups how to distinguish between the models that have been created. However most communication took place between the students and the teacher about how to use the LOR interface properly.

Conclusions

We conducted observations over two different scenarios of the EU project COLDEX to gain insights into the way the Cool Modes software supports interactive behaviour with an emphasis on observing collaboration between students within and across group behaviours. Our results indicate that both, the scenarios of Stochastics and Moon within the Cool Modes learning environment engaged students in rich collaborative behaviour. During theory-based discussions that took place without involving Cool Modes, students collaborated very little. This was expected due to the teacher-centred nature of instruction during the theory session. The Cool Modes sessions allowed for an enhanced opportunity to interact with peers and to discuss problems as and when they arose. It appeared that the more the students became familiarised with the software and the more they were able to open up to other groups in order to share ideas within the class community the more they engaged with the task itself.

When looking at the content that was communicated in discussions, it became apparent that the learners initial reactions to the Cool Modes software was that the students' primary focus was centred on the functionality rather than on the subject matter itself. Furthermore, it appeared that in the beginning, students expelled the majority of their cognitive resources to cope with the software. After getting accustomed to the software we observed a change of behaviour towards more task-related discussions, and thus the software tool became transparent, allowing for the learner to allocate a greater cognitive load to the actual subject matter. Students spent more time with for example discussing and rethinking hypotheses.

Collaboration has been assessed on a behavioural level using observational data. Log-data was used to support this observed data on a more formalised level. Results showed that the Cool Modes software enabled students to engage in different types of collaboration. Students worked on models and rule-sets within peer groups as well as across groups. Cool Modes seemed to support and enhance collaboration, especially after students overcame the basic task of familiarising with the software. We observed that in the initial phase of working with Cool Modes, students used their cognitive resources to collaboratively explore the tools while neglecting the task (e.g. building a model) itself. After this initial phase, students constructed models using the Cool Modes software while actively discussing and planning the learning process. Students did not only exchange ideas with their peer group but also with the whole class in its entirety, within both informal and formal settings.

Discussion

It is a commonly accepted and discussed phenomenon (Kalyuga, Chandler & Sweller, 1998) that when students perform a new complex task, more cognitive resources are needed and a higher cognitive load is associated with it.

The fact that we found that students allocated more cognitive effort towards the task at the end of the learning sequence could suggest that the students became more and more experts in using the software and therefore the cognitive load reduced. This is in line with Van Merriënboer et al. (Van Merriënboer, Kirschner & Kester, 2003) who describe that learners at a certain level of expertise can perform routines without investing extra mental effort. Future design efforts should have the goal to speed up this process of turning complex processes related to functionality into automated schemata and thus allowing the learner to concentrate on the task and the subject matter content related to it. Cognitive load theorists distinguish between extraneous cognitive load and intrinsic cognitive load. It is the extraneous cognitive load that we can affect by developing an environment that reduces unnecessary working load.

References:

Baber, C. (2005). Evaluation in Human Computer Interaction. *Evaluation of Human Work: A Practical Ergonomics Methodology*, 3rd Edition. London: Taylor and Francis

Dix, A. J., Finaly, J. E., Abowd, G. D., & Beale, R. (1997). *Human-computer interaction*. 2nd ed. Upper Saddle River, NJ: Prentice Hall.

Grudin, J. (1988), *Why CSCW Applications Fail: Problems in the Design and Evaluation of Organizational Interfaces,* in Proceedings of ACM CSCW'88 Conference on Computer-Supported Cooperative Work, Perspectives on Evaluation, pp. 85-93.

Hoeksema, K., Jansen, M., Hoppe H. U (2004). *Interactive Processing of Astronomical Observations in a Cooperative Modelling Environment.* In: Kinshuk, Chee-Kit Looi, Erkki Sutinen e.a. (eds). *Proceedings of the 4th EEEE International Conference on Advanced Learning Technologies, ICALT 2004*, Joensuu, Finland, pp. 888-889

Hoppe, H. U., Pinkwart, N., Oelinger, M., Zeini, S., Verdejo, F., Barros, B., & Mayorga, J. I. (2005). *Building Bridges within Learning Communities through Ontologies and "Thematic Objects"*. In Proceedings of the International Conference on Computer Supported Collaborative Learning. Mahwah (NJ), Lawrence Erlbaum Associates, pp. 211-220.

Hoppe, H.U. (2004). Collaborative mind tools. In Tokoro, M. & Steels, L. (Eds.): *The Future of Learning*. Amsterdam: IOS Press.

Jonassen, D.H. (2000). *Computers as Mindtools for Schools: Engaging Critical Thinking*. Columbus, OH: Prentice-Hall.

Jong, T., de & Joolingen, W.R. van (1998). Discovery learning with computer simulations of conceptual domains. *Review of Educational Research*, *68*, 179 – 201

Kalyuga, S., Chandler, P. and Sweller, J. (1998). Levels of expertise and instructional design. *Human Factors*, 40(1), 1-17.

Kuhn, M., Hoppe H. U., Lingnau A., Wichmann (2005): Computational Modelling and Simulation Fostering New Approaches in Learning Probability. *Innovations in Education and Training International Journal (IETI)*

Painter, S. (2001). Issues in the observation and evaluation of technology integration in K-12 classrooms. *Journal of Computing in Teacher Education*, 21-25.

Pinkwart, N. (2003). *A Plug-In Architecture for Graph Based Collaborative Modeling Systems*. In U. Hoppe, F. Verdejo & J. Kay (eds.): Shaping the Future of Learning through Intelligent Technologies. Proceedings of the 11th Conference on Artificial Intelligence in Education, pp. 535-536. Amsterdam, IOS Press.

Pinkwart, N., Malzahn, N., Westheide, D., & Hoppe, H. U. (2005). *Community Support Based on Thematic Objects and Similarity Search.* In L. Aroyo & D. Dicheva (Eds.), Workshop proceedings of the 12th International Conference on Adaptive Hypermedia (p. 57-60). Amsterdam (The Netherlands), University of Amsterdam.

Project COLDEX (Collaborative Learning and Distributed Experimentation). Download from http://www.coldex.info

Reiser, B.J., Tabak, I., Sandoval, W.A., Smith,B. K., Steinmuller, F., & Leone, A.J. (2001). BGuILE: Strategic and conceptual scaffolds for scientific inquiry in biology classrooms in Carver, S.M. & Klahr, D. (Eds.), *Cognition and Instruction: Twenty-five Years of Progress*: 263-305. Mahwah, NJ: Erlbaum.

Van Merriënboer, J. J. G., Kirschner, P. A., & Kester, L. (2003). Taking the load of a learners' mind: Instructional design for complex learning. *Educational Psychologist*, 38(1), 5-13.

An Initial Characterization of Engagement in Informal Social Learning Around MIT OCW

David Wiley, Shelley Henson, Utah State University, Center for Open and Sustainable Learning
david.wiley@usu.edu

Abstract: Open Learning Support is a social software system integrated with MIT OpenCourseWare that allows users to find each other in order to ask and answer each other's questions. This paper presents a snapshot of activity within the system eighteen months after launch, utilizing descriptive statistics, social network analysis, and discourse analysis to characterize learner engagement. Future directions for the software based on this analysis are discussed.

Study Context: MIT OCW and Open Learning Support

In September of 2002 MIT launched a website in support of an ambitious OpenCourseWare (OCW) initiative to make the course materials used in all of its approximately 2000 courses available online in an open access format. The new website contained lecture notes, syllabi, and other materials for thirty-two courses taught at MIT, ready to be downloaded, used, and reused in a variety of ways in support of teaching and learning.

MIT sees the OCW initiative in many lights, and frequently highlights the connection between OCW and MIT's mission to "advance education and serve the world" (Potts, 2005). Some critics, however, have argued that freely sharing educational content will not have the desired educational and service impact. And indeed, MIT OCW staff readily admit that the offering does not include some of the pieces necessary for an effective learning experience, such as the opportunities to exchange views, ask questions, and receive feedback afforded by social interaction with faculty and peers.

In 2003, we established a relationship with MIT OCW and entered into an agreement to provide a social software "wrap around" for the MIT OCW courses. Based on research in informal learning interactions around open access resources carried out under an NSF CAREER award, and with financial support from the William and Flora Hewlett Foundation, we designed a system called "Open Learning Support" (OLS; http://mit.ols.usu.edu/).

Because there is no guarantee of faculty involvement and no financial support for moderators of any kind through MIT OCW, the design of the OLS system would have to support self-organization by its users. The site users would have to ask and answer all the questions; they would have to help each other find the particularly useful messages within the system; they would have to police the spam and pornography out of the system. From previous analyses of successful online social systems (e.g., Slashdot circa 2001) using self-organization as an analytical lens (Wiley and Edwards, 2002) we knew two things: the first key to enabling the emergence of intelligent behavior is sustaining a sufficient number of interactions among a sufficient number of users (Bonabeau, Dorigo, and Theraulaz, 1999), and the second key is preparing an interaction space that affords the right kinds of interactions.

Two philosophies guided the initial design of the system. We take the minimalist perspective of Antoine-Marie-Roger de Saint-Exupery: "Perfection in design is achieved not when you have nothing more to add, but when you have nothing more to take away." Second, and perhaps more importantly, we view our work from the perspective of "research as design" as explicated by Kelly, in which we attempt to work with "the results of active innovation and intervention" to "address, simultaneously and iteratively, the scientific processes of discovery, exploration, confirmation, and dissemination" (Kelly, 2003, p. 3). We hoped that, through the integration of OLS into the MIT OCW web site, learners would find each other and provide informal, social support to one another in their learning and use of the MIT OCW materials.

As launched, OLS has four primary features. First, OLS is an asynchronous, threaded discussion environment, including the "new post" and "reply" functionality common in such systems. Second, OLS contains a "kudos" features that enables users to identify high quality contributions and say thank you to each other. This is implemented as text appended to the bottom left of each message reading, "Did you find this helpful?" followed by a hyperlinked word "Yes." Third, OLS contains a "fire alarm" feature by which users can flag messages that violate the terms of service such as unsolicited email or spam. This is implemented as text appended to the bottom right of each message reading, "Report an inappropriate message" with the word "Report" hyperlinked. This takes users to another screen in which they describe the reason they believe the message to be in violation of the terms of use. This message is then sent to a system administrator who, if need be, can delete the post and send the offending user an email warning. Finally, OLS includes a very basic reputation management system. Users can thank one another for a useful post by giving "Kudos." A high number of Kudos for a user would indicate that several others felt that user's messages had been useful. The number of kudos awarded to a post are shown in the kudos solicitation message as follows: "X other people found this message helpful. Did you?" followed by a hyperlinked word "Yes." Figure 1 shows these features in the context of a typical thread.

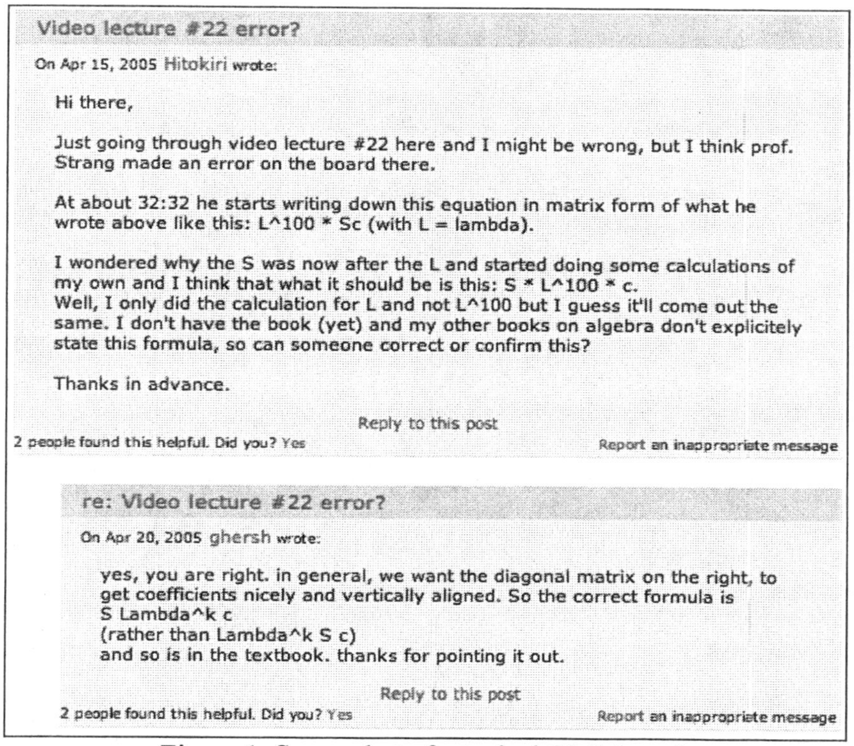
Video lecture #22 error?

On Apr 15, 2005 Hitokiri wrote:

Hi there,

Just going through video lecture #22 here and I might be wrong, but I think prof. Strang made an error on the board there.

At about 32:32 he starts writing down this equation in matrix form of what he wrote above like this: L^100 * Sc (with L = lambda).

I wondered why the S was now after the L and started doing some calculations of my own and I think that what it should be is this: S * L^100 * c.
Well, I only did the calculation for L and not L^100 but I guess it'll come out the same. I don't have the book (yet) and my other books on algebra don't explicitely state this formula, so can someone correct or confirm this?

Thanks in advance.

Reply to this post

2 people found this helpful. Did you? Yes

Report an inappropriate message

re: Video lecture #22 error?

On Apr 20, 2005 ghersh wrote:

yes, you are right. in general, we want the diagonal matrix on the right, to get coefficients nicely and vertically aligned. So the correct formula is
S Lambda^k c
(rather than Lambda^k S c)
and so is in the textbook. thanks for pointing it out.

Reply to this post

2 people found this helpful. Did you? Yes

Report an inappropriate message

Figure 1. Screenshot of a typical OLS thread.

Methodology and Findings

In characterizing the structure of the informal, social interactions within OLS, we have relied upon several methodologies. These include basic descriptive statistics with regard to the messages themselves, social network analysis of the structure of the communications and relationships among OLS users, and discourse analysis, always paying special attention to the way in which individuals use the special features of the site that facilitate self-organization.

Descriptive Statistics

The OLS system and its integration with MIT OCW launched in mid-2004, approximately eighteen months prior to this analysis. Forums are now available for 424 (or just over one third of) the MIT OCW courses. Of these 424 forums, only 56 of these have any messages posted within them, and 22 of those 56 forums contain only one post. All told, 2120 people have registered to use OLS and have posted 504 messages. The top ten countries of origin for OLS users are the US, India, China, Canada, Taiwan, Pakistan, the UK, Greece, Brazil, and Korea. The most active forum has been that attached to the Linear Algebra course, one of MIT OCW's most popular courses (due largely to its inclusion of video lectures). 145 of the total 504 messages were posted in the Linear Algebra forum.

Social Network Analysis

Social network analysis reveals a young community: 243 actors in the network (meaning only about 1 in 10 site registrants have posted), network density of .04%, and reciprocity levels of 14%. As density is defined as the sum of the existing links divided by the number of possible linkages, we are unsurprised to see a lower density number given the large number of actors in the network, and the portioned nature of the site as very few users post in multiple forums. Figure 2 is a visualization of the social network, in which nodes represent OLS users with at least one connection in the social network. Nodes (circles) represent people and edges (arrows) represent messages sent from one person to another; nodes are scaled relative to the number of connections between them and other nodes.

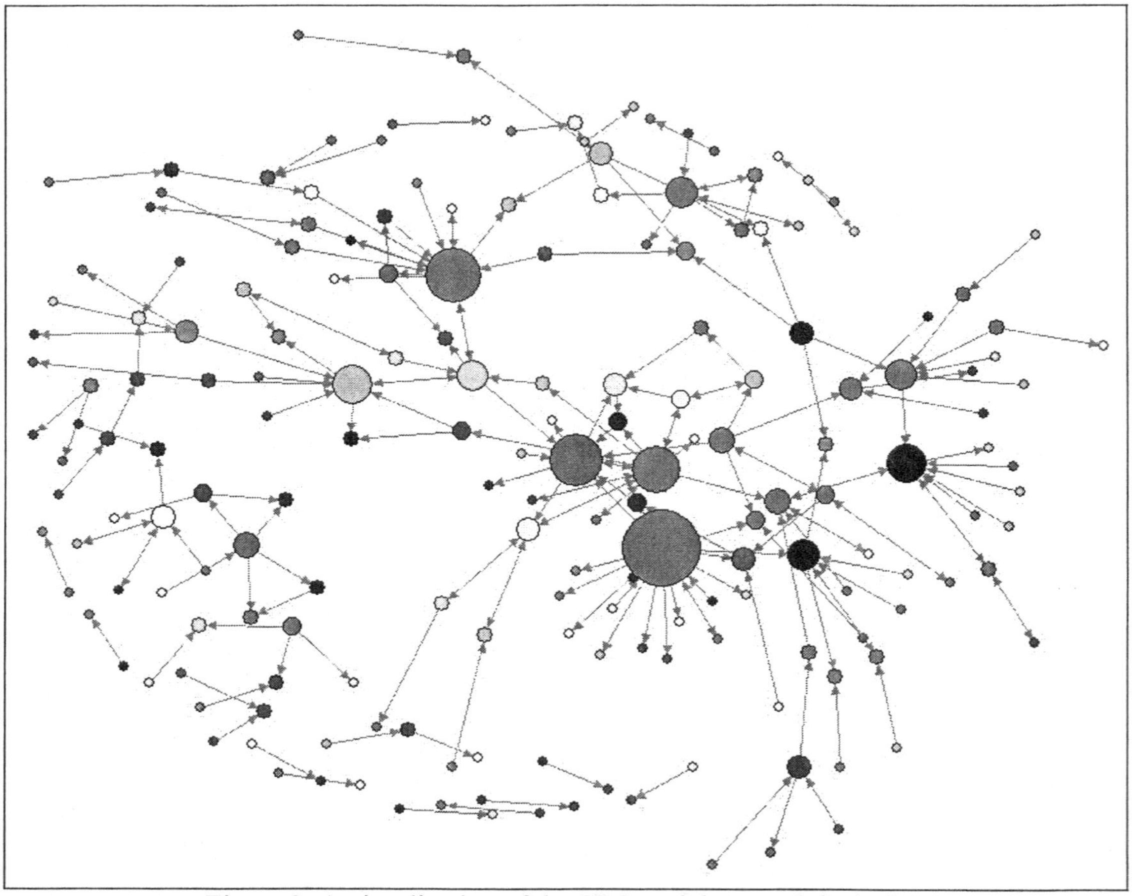

Figure 2. A visualization of the OLS social network including all users connected to at least one other user.

Discourse Analysis

Analysis of exchanges like those in Figures 1, 2, and 3 indicate that the system is to some degree serving its intended purpose – helping users of MIT OCW find each other to ask and answer questions. The topics of discussion vary from content-related questions (see Figure 1 on page 2), to technical questions (see Figure 3), to more cultural questions (see Figure 4). The use of emoticons, as demonstrated in Figure 2, points to the emergence of friendlier, more social interaction between users, another indicator of community health.

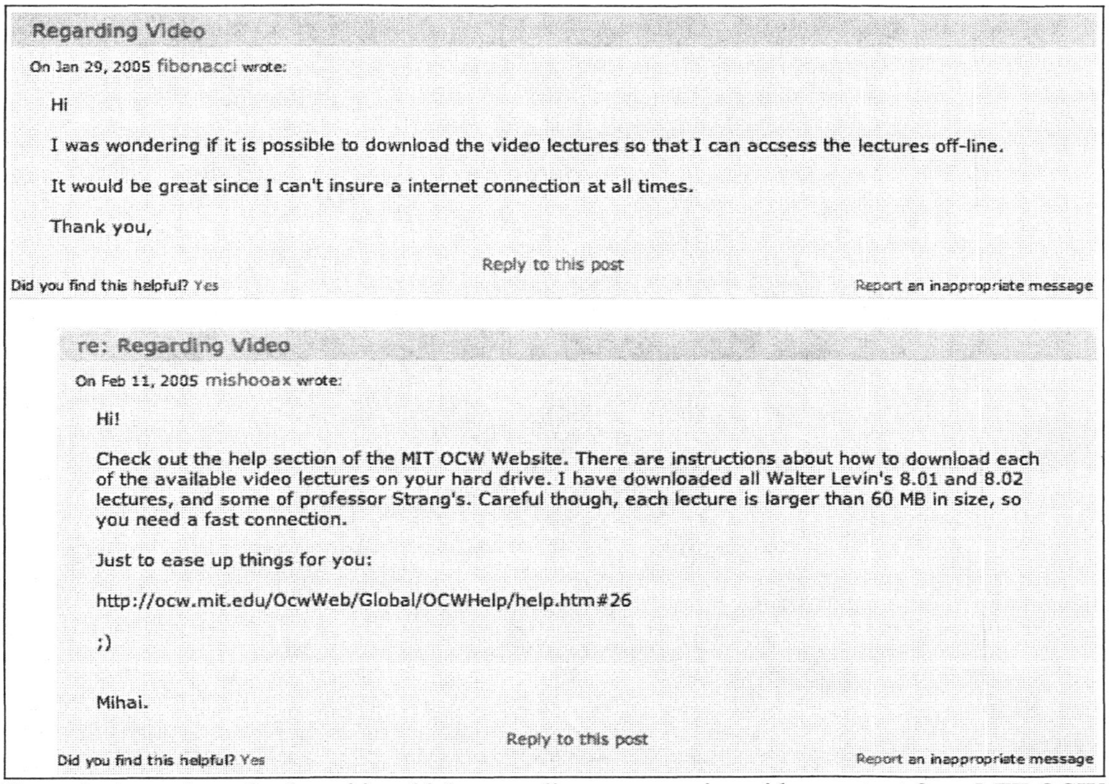
Regarding Video

On Jan 29, 2005 fibonacci wrote:

Hi

I was wondering if it is possible to download the video lectures so that I can accsess the lectures off-line.

It would be great since I can't insure a internet connection at all times.

Thank you,

Reply to this post

Did you find this helpful? Yes

Report an inappropriate message

re: Regarding Video

On Feb 11, 2005 mishooax wrote:

Hi!

Check out the help section of the MIT OCW Website. There are instructions about how to download each of the available video lectures on your hard drive. I have downloaded all Walter Levin's 8.01 and 8.02 lectures, and some of professor Strang's. Careful though, each lecture is larger than 60 MB in size, so you need a fast connection.

Just to ease up things for you:

http://ocw.mit.edu/OcwWeb/Global/OCWHelp/help.htm#26

;)

Mihai.

Reply to this post

Did you find this helpful? Yes

Report an inappropriate message

Figure 3. A portion of a thread in which users discuss accessing video content from MIT OCW.

Use of Special Features

We hypothesized that providing the opportunity for users to give each other kudos would encourage users to make more posts and make more useful posts. This hypothesis has proven difficult to test without engaging users in conversation directly. However, a few pieces of evidence suggest that kudos are being awarded in a thoughtful way. First, if kudos were awarded randomly across all messages, then the correlation between the number of posts made by a user and the number of kudos they had received would be 1.0. In the current data, this correlation is only .603. This indicates that kudos were not awarded randomly. Adding strength to the argument that kudos are awarded thoughtfully as opposed to randomly is our finding that the overwhelming majority of kudos have been awarded to "answer" posts, indicating that individuals value the support provided by their peers.

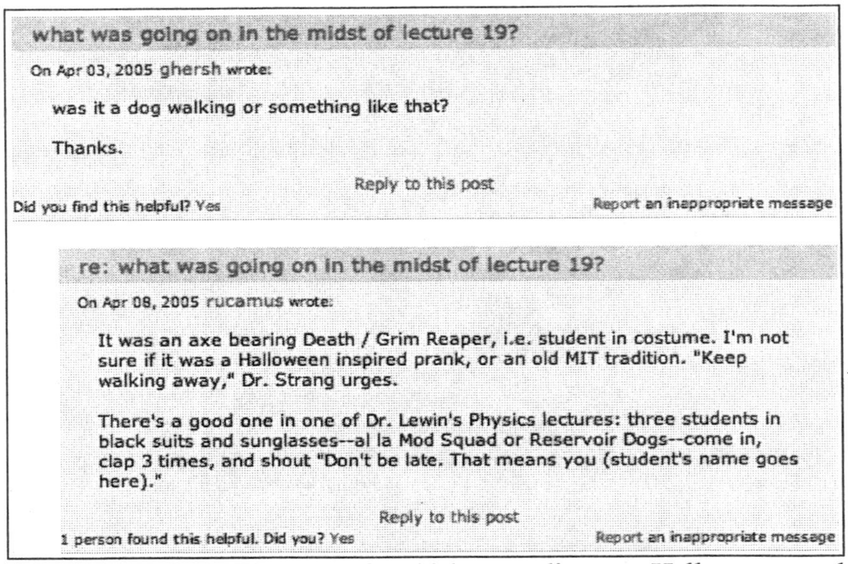

Figure 4. A portion of a thread in which users discuss a Halloween prank occurring within a video lecture from MIT OCW.

Preece (2001) provided several metrics for judging the degree to which a person is engaged in an online community. To her suggested metric of *number of posts* made by a person, we add *number of kudos* received, *degree* of the individual in the social network, and *usefulness*, a metric we calculate by dividing the number of kudos received by the total number of messages posted. Though all these measures are clearly related, examining the users with the top ten ratings in each category is instructive. As shown in Table 1, ordering of users in Posts and Degree are closely correlated, and these are somewhat related to Kudos. Usefulness is less correlated with any of these three measures. In fact, there is no cross over at all between users who posted the most and users who scored highly on the usefulness measure.

Table 1. Top ten OLS users ranked by number of Posts made, number of Kudos received, Degree in the social network, and Usefulness (Kudos / Posts)

Posts	**Degree**	**Kudos**	**Usefulness**
michael	david	lerman	bart_
david	michael	Frodo	lerman
tristanreid	tristanreid	michael	antreality
agenor	mishooax	mishooax	Gaborphy
govsocgrad89	agenor	tristanreid	Martin
sean_mcilroy	sean_mcilroy	david	milind
KP123	lerman	antreality	villate
zuyaoteoh	Ionas	agenor	bchadek
mishooax	zuyaoteoh	bart_	brent
Ionas	Frodo	bchadek	Frodo
Vikranth	Vikranth	brent	senya72

Also of interest is how the kudos measure appears to be central to all 4 categories, with the most users in its top ten list who also appear in other categories. Users who received the most Kudos were also more likely to cross over and score highly on the measures of degree, posts, and usefulness.

Finally, the Fire Alarm mechanism as worked as intended, allowing users to flag inappropriate content (mostly spam). The Fire Alarm has been pulled on fewer than ten users.

Conclusion and Future Directions

OLS is a relatively young community struggling to grow into its potential. Analyses at the eighteen-month point indicate that growth in registrations and activity is slow but steady. For the community to achieve its potential – for site users to be able to more successfully self-organize to support one another – the system must facilitate interactions between many more people until the participation passes a tipping point.

Because the rate at which users will discover OLS through MIT OCW is unlikely to grow dramatically in the near future, the system must change in order to connect more of the people who are arriving at the site to each other. The system is currently being redesigned to facilitate these interactions by aggregating forums at higher, topical levels (so that learners coming from Linear Algebra and Calculus courses at MIT OCW end up in a common Mathematics forum). We are also exploring the possibility of combining forums currently integrated with other open access content repositories (e.g., OLS is also used by Rice's Connexions initiative), so that users from multiple origins arrive at the same discussion destination.

Finally, as a result of this analysis we are able to identify community leadership from a variety of perspectives (as measured by the metrics in Table 1). We will work with willing individuals from this group to expand reputation management features in OLS in order to provide meaningful incentives to greater participation by existing users.

References

Bonabeau, E., Dorigo, M., & Theraulaz, G. (1999). *Swarm intelligence: From natural to artificial systems*. Oxford University Press: New York, NY.

Kelly, A. (2003). Research as Design. *Educational Researcher*, *32*(1), 3-4.

Potts, J. P. (2005). MIT OCW Quick Fact Sheet. Retrieved November 11, 2005 from http://ocw.mit.edu/NR/rdonlyres/E44B238B-5108-4E9D-BA14-83CF4C227BF9/0/QuickFactSheet.pdf

Preece, J. (2001) Sociability and usability: Twenty years of chatting online. *Behavior and Information Technology Journal*, *20*(5), 347-356.

Wiley, D. A. & Edwards, E. K. (2002). Online self-organizing social systems: The decentralized future of online learning. *Quarterly Review of Distance Education, 3*(1), 33-46.

Using Cognitive Ethnography to Study Instruction

Robert F. Williams, Lawrence University, Appleton, WI 54912-0599, robert.f.williams@lawrence.edu

Abstract: Advances in digital media support a form of inquiry called cognitive ethnography. Cognitive ethnography employs traditional ethnographic methods to build knowledge of a community of practice and then applies this knowledge to the micro-level analysis of specific episodes of activity. The principal aim of cognitive ethnography is to reveal how cognitive activities are accomplished in real-world settings. Cognitive ethnography is a particularly apt method for studying instruction in both formal and informal settings. This paper discusses the practicalities of doing cognitive ethnographic research, including such issues as deciding what to record, selecting data for analysis, re-representing data, and analyzing data. Illustrative examples are provided from a recent cognitive ethnographic study of time-telling instruction.

Introduction

New technologies create new forms of inquiry. While ethnographic research has always relied on fieldnotes, the questions that could be asked and answered changed with the advent of tape recording, photography, and film. Today, new forms of digital media open new avenues of inquiry into human cultural activity. One promising new avenue is cognitive ethnography, an event-focused method for investigating how cognitive activities are accomplished in real-world settings. This chapter introduces cognitive ethnography and its application to the study of instruction, highlighting the issues involved in using the method while providing examples from a recent study of time-telling instruction.

Cognitive ethnography

Cognitive ethnography is rooted in traditional ethnography but differs from it in a fundamental way. Whereas traditional ethnography is concerned with the meanings that members of a cultural group create, cognitive ethnography is concerned with *how* members create those meanings. Traditional ethnographers might interview group members about kinship terms in an effort to delineate how they understand kinship relations and the effect this understanding has on the organization and functioning of their society. Cognitive ethnographers would be more likely to record and analyze episodes of activity in which kinship relations determine important outcomes such as control of valuable resources, seeking to understand how cultural models of kinship relations are brought to bear in processes of group decision-making. While traditional ethnography identifies the material and conceptual resources that make up group members' life worlds, cognitive ethnography examines how those resources are employed in cultural activity. Traditional ethnography gives us insight into the ways of thinking that define cultural groups, illuminating the vast range and diversity of human experience along with the commonalities that make us all human. Cognitive ethnography looks at process: at the moment-to-moment development of activity and its relation to sociocultural (often institutional) processes unfolding on different time scales. Traditional ethnography describes knowledge; cognitive ethnography describes how knowledge is constructed and used.

The contrast between cognitive ethnography and traditional ethnography should not imply a divorce of one from the other. A successful cognitive ethnography develops out of traditional ethnography, using the time-honored methods of participant observation, interviewing, artifact analysis, and the like to build the knowledge base through which specific episodes of activity can be interpreted and analyzed. How can we examine how material and conceptual resources are brought to bear in activity without knowing what material and conceptual resources are available? How can we reveal the meanings that participants construct without being familiar with the participants, their relations, and their prior history of interaction? Traditional ethnography informs cognitive ethnography; cognitive ethnography extends ethnographic research in the direction of process-level analyses.

As a method of inquiry, cognitive ethnography has several key roles to play in cognitive science (Hutchins, 2003). Its aim is to reveal how cognitive processes unfold in real-world settings—the very phenomena we are most interested in explaining. Cognitive ethnography can lend ecological validity to experimental studies by determining which questions are relevant and by developing more realistic, culturally appropriate tasks to use in laboratory investigations. Cognitive ethnography can also inform simulation studies by providing detailed descriptions of the phenomena we wish to simulate. In other words, cognitive ethnography is an important tool in the cognitive scientist's toolkit, and when used in conjunction with other tools, it can boost our confidence in the relevance and validity of our findings.

Studying instruction

Because cognitive ethnography is a tool for studying situated activity, it is particularly apt for investigating the nature of instruction in real-world contexts, whether formal or informal. Instruction is a form of social interaction that distinguishes the human species. Through instruction, we are able to perpetuate the cultural practices (literacy, numeracy, and skilled performance in myriad domains) that maintain the cognitive sophistication of our societies across generations. Instruction may be formal, occurring in institutions specifically set up for that purpose (schools, colleges, training centers) or it may be informal, emerging during episodes of everyday discourse in many different settings (at work, during recreation, at home). Instruction may occur within activities that are highly structured or relatively unstructured; it commonly appears in structured activity where more-experienced participants guide the participation of those less-experienced. Instruction may be carefully planned (even rehearsed) or wholly spontaneous, but it is always, like other forms of discourse, improvised moment-to-moment in the unfolding of activity. How instruction develops from moment to moment, how it makes use of various material and conceptual resources, and how the micro-scale phenomena of instruction relate to cognitive, social, and cultural processes on broader timescales are exactly the sorts of questions that can be addressed by cognitive ethnographic research using digital video and analysis tools.

A recent cognitive ethnography of time-telling instruction (Williams, 2004) will help to highlight important methodological issues related to this kind of research. Here the researcher was concerned with questions in cognitive science related to the use of cognitive artifacts and the forms of cultural activity that perpetuate artifact-bound practices across generations. The study focused in particular on clock-reading and instruction in time-telling. Data for the study were collected during mathematics lessons in four classrooms (one 1st-grade, two 2nd-grade, and one 3rd-grade) in two elementary schools (an inner-city church school with a mixed student population and a mostly-white private school in an affluent community). The researcher brought to the study several forms of pertinent expertise: first, expertise in time-telling (as a competent adult member of society); second, knowledge of schools and teaching (as a licensed and experienced schoolteacher); and third, knowledge of relevant scientific theories and methods (as a member of the cognitive science research community). While these forms of expertise were essential background for the study, they were not sufficient for a successful cognitive ethnography. What was also needed was expertise about the particular community of practice in which the activities being studied took place. The researcher used traditional ethnographic methods—observation, participation, interviewing, collecting artifacts, etc., over a period of many months—to construct the knowledge base needed to analyze specific episodes of activity. Within this ethnographic research process, decisions were made about which events to capture in digital videorecordings. In this study, recordings were made only of lessons where time-telling was a focus of instruction. Because such instruction occurred somewhat rarely and sporadically throughout the school year, the researcher had to maintain close contact with the community in order to avoid missing the key events that were the target of the study.

Deciding what to record

Why not simply record everything to ensure full coverage and to amass a library of video data for future studies? Given sufficient resources, such a strategy might be appealing, but in practice, it tends to be both impractical and undesirable. Aside from the (admittedly declining) expense of such blanket recording, recording everything can be a poor strategy for several reasons. It rapidly produces unwieldy amounts of data, making it harder for the researcher to locate relevant episodes and to isolate the phenomena of interest. Just as importantly, it turns the ethnographic project into a documentary project, focusing effort on recording while diminishing the other forms of ethnographic participation needed to interpret the video data: finding a role within the community (albeit a peripheral one), forming relationships, gaining experience as a participant, interacting closely with other participants, building knowledge of the community and the relations among members, building knowledge of the activity, and so on. This concern can be ameliorated by having multiple researchers so that one is free to participate while the other records, but this also escalates the expenses of the study. If the study is concerned with phenomena that are low-frequency and unpredictable, then a broad use of recording would be warranted, but for most studies, blanket recording conveys the impression that the researcher lacks focus (i.e., does not have clearly defined research questions), and, indeed, the researcher can begin to lose focus as many different phenomena are recorded and reflected upon. Finally, and perhaps most importantly, it seems unlikely that such blanket video would really be of much use for other studies. When recording activity for a cognitive ethnography, the researcher makes key decisions—often moment-to-moment—about where to place the camera, where to point it, what to include in the frame, which participants to focus on, when to zoom in for close-ups of details and when to pull back for wide shots that capture the broader context of activity, where to direct the microphone to capture talk or other sounds, and so on. These decisions depend directly upon the questions the researcher is trying to answer, and they produce a video record with a point of view and focus that is unlikely to capture what would be needed for a research study with different questions. In addition, a subsequent investigator would lack both experience in the community of practice and context derived from being present when and where the video was made. Lacking experience and context, the investigator would be forced to "read into" the video in order to construct a coherent account of events. Such "reading in" draws from whatever the investigator has in mind—the residua of past experiences, secondhand accounts, and depictions in the media; biases from preconceived notions; anticipations of what will be found; and so on—resulting in a default interpretation of events that is likely to be slightly or even wholly inaccurate. The problem is either not being able to interpret the video or over-interpreting the video through some largely imagined context.

This is not to say that video-recordings made for one study can never be used for another, or that it would be impossible to amass a library of video data for use in multiple studies. In fact, new innovations in technology—see, e.g., the discussion of DIVER (Pea *et al.*, this volume)—make it possible to use an omnidirectional camera to make general recordings of activity in a setting such as a classroom) and then to use "guided noticing" software to craft videoclips relevant to particular research projects, in effect postponing the videographer's moment-to-moment decisions until sometime after the event. A library of general classroom recordings could, for example, be used to investigate various questions about teacher or student behavior, although here, too, problems can arise due to the lack of context, limiting the types of questions that can be asked and answered. For most cognitive ethnographic studies, the most practical course of action is to make judicious use of recordings that focus on the phenomena of interest, walking the line between the twin dangers of failing to capture key phenomena and drowning in largely irrelevant data.

Returning to the study of time-telling instruction: because the researcher was concerned with how the teacher's talk and actions guide the mappings of concepts onto the clock face and help the students construct time readings, the decision was made to record time-telling lessons with the camera placed behind the students and focused on the teacher, in essence capturing the students' point of view (while also minimizing the distracting presence of the camera). The shots were framed to include relevant aspects of the setting, including sufficient background to provide a sense of place as well as the specific objects the teacher handled and referred to during the lesson. The camera was zoomed in just enough so that the teacher's actions and inscriptions could be seen clearly while still retaining some students (those nearest the teacher) in the shot, providing samples of student participation in the activity. Because students were seen mostly from behind, this setup also helped to preserve their anonymity. During recording, the camera direction and/or zoom were adjusted slightly to ensure that relevant items and participants were retained in the shot. Only when it seemed unavoidably necessary would the camera direction or zoom be changed more drastically, such as when a participant moved to another part of the room or made an inscription too small to be otherwise captured. Panning away from the main subject (in this case, the teacher) or zooming in on a detail (such as a student's writing) both increase the likelihood that some important action will fail to be captured in the video. Once the instructional portion of the lesson was finished and the students were set to work on their own (completing worksheets at their desks), the camera was switched off and the researcher began circulating in the room, observing students, questioning them about their work, and making fieldnotes that would later be used to warrant claims about the video data. This was part of the ethnographic component needed to inform and support analyses of the instructional episodes.

Selecting video data for analysis

For the sake of illustration, let's consider a single lesson in a 1st-grade class. The teacher had recently had the students practice dividing a circle into halves and then into fourths. In the recorded lesson, she introduced quarter-hours on the clock, preparing the students to read times as "quarter past" (the goal of the current lesson) and "quarter till" (the goal of the next lesson). The teacher had the students sit on a rug in front of her in order to receive instruction and then return to their seats to complete exercises in their workbooks. The instructional portion lasted about nine minutes and was recorded on digital video. The recorded portion of the lesson was later segmented into parts as shown in Table 1.

Table 1. Segments of instructional portion of time-telling lesson on reading "quarter past."

Activity	Focus	Duration (min:sec)
Presentation	Reviewing dividing a circle into halves and fourths on felt board	0:34
Presentation	Equating one fourth to one quarter by analogy to money	0:30
Presentation	Dividing the clock face into quarters	0:33
Presentation	Reading a time as "quarter past"	0:41
Group practice	Reading *a quarter past eight* with prompting	0:15
Group practice	Reading *a quarter past ten* and *a quarter past three*	0:15
Presentation	Counting on the clock face to read the time as "_ fifteen"	0:26
Group practice	Reading *five fifteen* and *a quarter past five*	0:17
Group practice	Reading *a quarter past seven* and *seven fifteen*	0:13
Individual practice	Reading *eight fifteen* and *a quarter past eight*	0:29
Individual practice	Reading *a quarter past two* and *two fifteen*	0:28
Presentation	Writing two fifteen as '2:15'	0:14
Individual practice	Reading *a quarter past four* and *four fifteen*; writing *4:15*	0:46
Individual practice	Reading *six fifteen* and *a quarter past six*; writing *6:15*	1:23
Individual practice	Reading *ten fifteen* and *a quarter past ten*; writing *10:15*	1:52

After segmenting the video, the next step in the process of cognitive ethnography is to select particular segments for detailed analysis. Here the guiding principle is to choose segments that exhibit the phenomena of interest, i.e., those pertinent to the research questions being investigated. Direct instruction from the teacher occurred mainly during the presentation portions of the lesson but also sporadically during group and individual practice when students needed additional prompting or made errors. Because the researcher was interested in how instruction guides mapping of conceptual elements onto the clock face, two especially relevant segments from presentation portions of the lesson were selected as the initial focus of analysis: 'dividing the clock face into quarters' and 'counting on the clock face to read the time as "__ fifteen."'

Re-representing video data

Once segments are selected, they need to be re-represented in a way that supports analysis. With video data, this re-representation is normally some form of transcription. Speech is conventionally transcribed as written text with or without annotations for pauses, emphasis, and the like. Transcribing gestures and other actions remains problematic. Gesture researchers often code gestures for such things as type, handshape, location, and motion. For the study of time-telling instruction, the researcher cared most about the relation of talk, gesture, and object-manipulation to one another, including how gestures coupled with objects the teacher was manipulating. For this reason, simply coding gestures in this way would have been insufficient. Instead, the researcher elected to use a multimodal transcript format inspired by Goodwin (see, e.g., 2003) in which talk was transcribed in conventional conversation analysis format with indications of emphasis, volume, vowel lengthening, pause length, and so on, and actions were represented via annotated still images from the video. Annotations of gestures were done in red, while annotations of object manipulations were done in blue. Each annotated image was linked to a box around the speech that co-occurred with that gesture or action. A sample transcript (much reduced and reproduced in grayscale) appears in Figure 1.

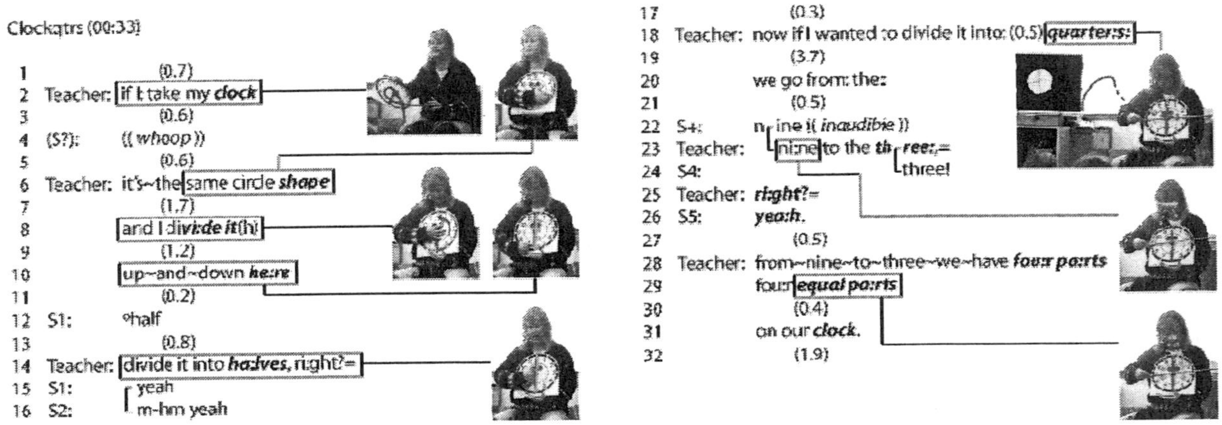

Figure 1. Transcript of the 'dividing the clock face into quarters' segment.

This multimodal transcript format has the advantages of depicting visual aspects of the discourse in visual form and clearly showing how actions were embedded in the material setting. The format has the disadvantage of leaving gestures uncoded, making it difficult to do classificatory or quantitative analyses. These multimodal transcripts are also difficult to construct, presenting issues of image choice (which image—beginning, middle, or end—best captures the gesture or action), annotation (how best to indicate form and motion, especially if these change during the gesture or action), and layout (how to fit the images and speech together on the transcript). Because of the many choices involved, multimodal transcripts typically need to be constructed by the primary researcher rather than delegated to research assistants. Fortunately, the challenging process of transcription leads to insights that inform and enrich the analyses. A more ideal form of transcript (and one that seems feasible given the state of the art in multimedia documents and web pages) would be a multimodal transcript like that shown here but with each image linked both to a videoclip showing the full gesture or action and to metadata that code the gesture by type and components, supporting other forms of gesture analysis.

Analyzing data

Looking at the transcript in Figure 1, several aspects of the instructional discourse are immediately apparent. The teacher does nearly all of the talking. She also structures both the timing and content of student talk, thus retaining control over the sequence of activity and the forms of student participation. Student talk indicates agreement or understanding or fills in pieces of information when cued by the teacher. This information may come from recall of material from previous lessons or from recognition of some state of events displayed by the teacher along with recall of an associated label. The teacher talk also follows a regular pattern: a series of single well-formed clauses or phrases ending with emphasis on a word or phrase of conceptual importance (*clock*, *shape*, *divide it*, *here*, *halves*, *quarters*, etc.) followed by a pause of a half-second or more. The effect is one of introducing one piece of information at a time and pausing while that information is processed. Here we see that although the teacher appears to control the discourse, the discourse is constrained by the students' abilities to take in and make sense of new information (i.e., by their working memory and processing capacities and present states of knowledge). The content of the discourse is shaped both by the teacher's immediate goals and by the group's shared history. A recent lesson on dividing circles, for example, becomes a resource for introducing division of the clock face. Shared history creates intersubjective awareness of states of knowledge and expectations about likely responses to particular utterances or actions; a researcher lacking domain expertise and experience as a participant-observer would be crippled in this respect.

The transcript in Figure 1 could be the basis for various analyses. Because of the structure of teacher talk (introducing one conceptual element at a time) and a research focus on how instruction guides conceptualization, the researcher elected to proceed line by line through the transcript, diagramming how each teacher utterance, gesture, or action contributed to the construction of meaning in the discourse. Such an analysis requires a conceptual framework for analyzing meaning construction. For this, the researcher drew upon the field of cognitive semantics, chiefly conceptual integration theory (Fauconnier & Turner, 2002), an account of how meaning is constructed in networks of mental spaces, and the theoretical construct of material anchors for conceptual blends (Hutchins 2005), an account of how the world is used to anchor mental spaces during reasoning or problem-solving—in essence, an account of the functioning of various cognitive artifacts. There is not sufficient space here to review the details of these theories; for a full account, the reader is referred to the sources cited above.

Proceeding as described, the researcher began with the statement "If I take my clock" (line 2), which the teacher utters while picking up a clock face facsimile with geared hands but no mechanism for keeping time, and worked line by line to "on our clock" (line 31), the utterance that completes construction of the Clock Quarters conceptual blend. For each line of teacher talk or action, the researcher followed the conventional format of conceptual integration analyses by diagramming the mental space inputs, cross-space mappings, and resulting blended space (typically an interpretation of the clock face with particular elements as the locus of attention). The complete diagrams can be found in chapter 5 of Williams (2004); a single example will provide a flavor of the analysis. The diagram associated with line 6 of the transcript ("It's the same circle shape") is shown in Figure 2.

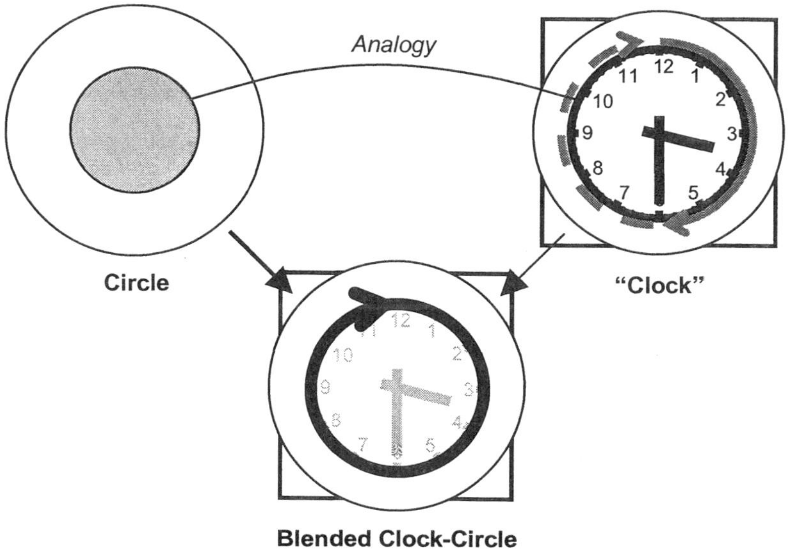

Figure 2. Conceptual integration diagram for line 6: "it's~the same circle ***shape***."

In the diagram, circles represent mental spaces and a box behind a circle shows that the mental space is anchored by structure in the world (typically by the object the students are looking at). In line 6, the word "circle" activates conceptual knowledge represented by the mental space in the upper left of the figure. "Shape" profiles a property of the clock face, represented by the mental space in the upper right anchored by the object the teacher is holding. The word "same" sets up an analogical relation (a cross-space mapping) between the conceptual circle and the clock face. The tracing gesture that coincides with "same circle shape" serves both indexical and iconic functions (see Goodwin, 2003, for discussion of this aspect of traces). Indexically, the trace highlights a portion of material structure, in this case, the clock band. Iconically, the path of the trace outlines a conceptual entity, the circle. The net effect is to superimpose the conceptual circle over its material counterpart. In the parlance of conceptual integration theory, the utterance and trace map a conceptual element onto a material anchor—in other words, they associate a conceptual entity with a material structure that will anchor it in the ensuing discourse. The resulting blended space is shown at the bottom of the figure; here the clock-circle is in profile (i.e., is the current locus of attention). In the remainder of this segment, other conceptual elements—vertical and horizontal dividing lines—are similarly mapped onto material anchors: the vertical clock hands (in a notably unclocklike configuration) and a pointing stick placed horizontally across the clock face. Again, speech profiles the conceptual element being mapped while a co-timed trace maps the conceptual element to its material anchor. In one instance (lines 20-23), the trace is executed by the eyes shifting gaze along the pointing stick from one location to another. By the end of the segment (line 31), the teacher has manipulated objects to prepare anchors for conceptual elements and used speech and co-timed gestures to map elements onto anchors, ultimately producing an anchored blended space in which the students perceive the clock face as divided into canonical clock-quarters. This blended space provides the basis for a new way to read times: as "quarter past" or "quarter till." These time readings can be constructed by reasoning within the blended space and from the blend to its associated inputs. The clock face anchors the conceptual entities during this reasoning process, maintaining the set of conceptual relations used to generate a time reading. Indeed, this stabilizing function was a critical part of Hutchins' (2005) argument that cognitive artifacts anchor conceptual blends; what the current analysis shows is how such anchored blends get constructed in instructional discourse, making it possible for new generations to use the artifact successfully and thus keeping important cultural practices like time-telling alive.

Returning to Figure 2, we can note another important function of the gesture. Although the circle could have been traced in either direction from any starting position on the clock band (such as the location nearest the teacher's right hand), the trace started at the top of the clock face, proceeded in a clockwise direction at steady speed (continuing for a full second after the utterance), and ended when the tracing finger reached the top of the clock again. In addition to outlining a circle, the gesture also defines a path of motion that is important to time-telling: the path of the minute hand through one clock hour. In terms of cognitive semantics, the gesture imposes image-schematic structure—namely, a source-path-goal image schema—that is relevant to the current activity and that is not profiled in the accompanying speech. In other portions of the same lesson and the next day's lesson on "quarter till" (analyzed in Williams, 2004), gestures are often seen to add path information to the conceptualization.

The analysis of this excerpt would have been impoverished without knowledge gained from participant-observation, such as knowing that students had recently learned to divide a circle into halves by drawing a line down the middle and then into fourths by drawing another line across the circle from left to right—exactly the way the teacher superimposed the conceptual dividing lines on the clock face. Yet another crucial source of constraint and insight during analysis comes from juxtaposing analyses of different segments of data, looking for common patterns or contradictions. Discoveries made in one analysis often lead to re-evaluation of previous analyses. Commonalities across analyses increase both the coherence of the account and the confidence that the patterns observed in the current data are likely to generalize to instances of similar phenomena in other data. In this way, we move increasingly from descriptive to explanatory accounts.

Conclusion

As we have seen, advances in digital media have opened the way to cognitive ethnographic studies of instruction, offering new insights into the nature and function of instructional discourse. Cognitive ethnography is not for the faint-hearted, however. Because it is a tool for studying cognitive activity in real-world settings, the outcomes of a study can never be cleanly predicted. Issues of access, privacy protections, observer effects, and equipment failure loom large. Methods need to be adapted on the fly as new phenomena reveal themselves, and new forms of representation and analysis need to be developed to make sense of the data. Undertaking a cognitive ethnographic study requires an act of faith: that the phenomena of interest will appear in the data, that they will be captured in a way that supports analysis, that the findings will merit the considerable effort involved, and that we will be surprised in ways we cannot anticipate. If we believe that the phenomena we investigate are actually there in the world and that they permeate human activity, then we can be confident that once the initial shock is over—that of looking at our data and not seeing anything at all—if we persevere, new discoveries await us. That anticipation of discovery sustains us as we watch the same videos again and again, waiting for the scales to fall from our eyes and the long-invisible processes to reveal themselves.

References

Fauconnier, G., & Turner, M. (2002). *The way we think: Conceptual blending and the mind's hidden complexities*. New York: Basic Books.

Goodwin, C. (2003). Pointing as situated practice. In S. Kita (Ed.), *Pointing: Where language, culture, and cognition meet* (pp. 217-242). Mahwah, NJ: Lawrence Erlbaum Associates.

Hutchins, E. (2003). Cognitive ethnography. Plenary address at the 25th annual meeting of the Cognitive Science Society.

Hutchins, E. (2005). Material anchors for conceptual blends. *Journal of Pragmatics, 37*(10), 1555-1577.

Williams, R. F. (2004). *Making meaning from a clock: Material artifacts and conceptual blending in time-telling instruction*. Ph.D. dissertation, Department of Cognitive Science, University of California, San Diego.

Acknowledgments

The author is indebted to Ed Hutchins for seminal ideas related to this work. The research discussed in this chapter was supported in part by a dissertation fellowship from the Spencer Foundation.

Ways of Working:
A Three-tiered Interpretive Model for Video Research

Donald W. Wortham , Sharon J. Derry, Department of Educational Psychology, University of Wisconsin-Madison
1025 W. Johnson St., Madison WI 53706
Email: dwortham@gmail.com, derry@education.wisc.edu

Abstract: In this "ways of working" paper, we describe a three-tier interpretive model for analyzing video data of social interaction. Since members of a research team often work from different theoretical perspectives, individual members' analyses of "what happened and why" are not always congruent. The model and process described here require making explicit methodological (and technological) links between layers of interpretation. Individual group members benefit because the connections between their analyses and data can be effectively warranted; the larger group benefits because the location of interpretive differences is more precisely exposed.

Introduction

The method described in this paper may point to the solution of a problem that confronts much current research on social interaction, especially research that captures this interaction using rich media. Conceptually, a consumer of video research should be able to trace a path from data highlighted by analysis, down through any interim representations (such as transcripts), to the raw data. This capacity to trace a path from highest level of analysis down to raw data would allow the consumer to better understand both nomothetic generalizations and ideographic particulars of the social interaction being studied. In practice, these connections are almost always absent, and our field's current reliance on print media for publication passively discourages these connections. The situation is exacerbated when video research investigates subjects' taken meanings (emics) rather than structural features of social interaction (etics). Since researchers regardless of methodology agree that an important goal of social science is the uncovering of subjective meaning (c.f., Angelillo, Rogoff & Chavajay, in press; Nystrand, Wu, Gamoran, Zeiser, and Long, 2003), this opacity regarding the connections between data and analysis is worrisome.

In our own lab, we have been confronted by these same problems, since a variety of theoretical perspectives are represented among our group's members. Working from a particular theoretical viewpoint, one of us will "see" something in data and construct an analysis based on this apperception. To build a case for this perspectival viewpoint, and more importantly to help others see what they might otherwise not, we have begun to explore a number of interrelated practices. First, we have put forth a model of interpretation, and come to basic agreement about what can be known (and what cannot) from each of the three layers in our model. Second, we make explicit linkages between our analyses and the various forms of data we study. These linkages are both conceptual and technical, so that we can now trace an interpretive path from highest layer of analysis, down through interpretive representations such as transcripts, to our raw video data. Since we believe that these efforts, while still provisional and in an early stage of development, may be instructive for other researchers working with video, we connect our discussion to a broader discourse within the learning-science community about the establishment of standards for video research (e.g., Derry, in press).

The Three-Layer Interpretation Model

Let us begin with a very simple visual analogy: our Three-Layer Interpretation Model is like a three-ring toddler's toy. The toy consists of a wooden base, a spindle, and three rings of decreasing size. Our model consists of a base (the event stream…especially social interaction captured in rich media), and three interpretive levels: a large layer (raw data), a medium layer (observed events), and a small layer (analytic statements). Each of these layers has certain epistemological and technical constraints, and results in specific work products.

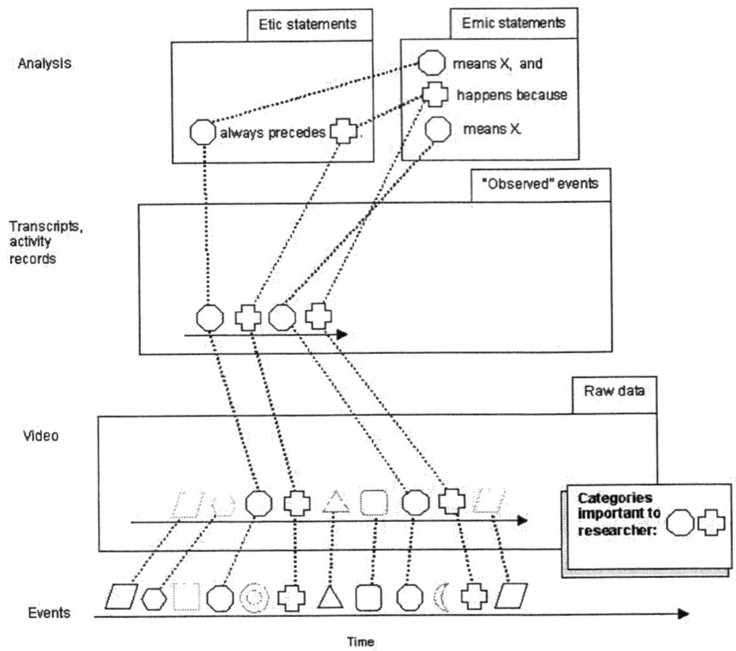

Figure 1. Three-layer interpretive model.

The toddler's toy differs from our model in two important ways: first, rather than being discrete from the layers, the spindle in our model is instead a contiguous set of relations among the layers. Secondly, the top ring is of two parts, corresponding to two different goals for research. In the sections below, we describe our model in brief, working from the bottom up.

The Base: Event Matrix

The toddler's toy has a base, a ground. The base referred to in our three-level model corresponds to an "event matrix" that appears to particular observers as event streams. Since, ontologically, the event matrix exists whether or not we as observers make any inferences about it, the event stream itself is not *per se* part of our inference model.

An event matrix is comprised of the multiple causal chains that transpire in a particular location: in a classroom, or in the vacuum of space, or inside a paramecium. Event streams are available to sensory experience, but in practice unknowable in their entirety. The actions of teachers and students, the movements of planets and stars, or the functions of the paramecium's organelles are indeed occurring, but the full scope of this activity is never available to us as observers. Nonetheless, our research efforts are directed toward investigating aspects of this event matrix and making warrantable statements about it. The belief that we can succeed in this effort is grounded in the notion that video analysis is a social meaning-making process, with an aim towards achieving intersubjectivity among researchers, irrespective of their differences. For certain phenomena, we expect intersubjectivity to be high enough so that at least some kinds of statements about what is happening in the event matrix can be made with a high degree of confidence (often *etic* statements, discussed later). For other sorts of statements, we assume that intersubjectivity will be lower (most often *emic* statements, also discussed later). In fact, the point of the method outlined here is precisely to identify where and why intersubjectivity is low, so that our group's understanding is stretched or even changed through alternative interpretations of events.

Layer 1: Raw Data Layer

The first *interpretive* layer of our model is the "raw data" layer, which most often takes the form of digital video recordings of social interaction. This pseudo-tangibility of digital video is a fantastic asset. We can move digital video around, share it, take it apart, observe discontinguous segments contiguously, and so forth, yet it is also has the properties of being fixed and permanent, unlike our recollections about what happened, which are subject to both degradation and importations of meaning. This "captured" aspect of videotaped social interaction allows us to later make public what was transitive and ephemeral in the event stream.

Even though we can regard the material stuff of the raw data layer to be a high-fidelity, fixed accounting of social interaction, it must be regarded as limited in two important ways. First, the raw data layer is itself interpretive, and not an exact rendering of social interaction; something is always left out. When we videotape a classroom, we capture only certain aspects of social interaction. We further acknowledge that interactions off-screen, and cognitions "in the head" of participants have an impact on the very things we are filming. The upshot is that raw data always has a point of view, and furthermore that our point of view is never privileged, and is always imperfect.

Sometimes this is obvious, as when one participant's movement occludes our camera-eye view of a second participant. But there are more subtle ways in which we leave things out. When our cameras focus on one part of an interacting whole, we miss out-of-view interactions that may dynamically change the very interactions that are our focus. Our situation is no different from other scientists who observe phenomena *in situ*: when astronomers monitor the position of stars in our expanding universe, they focus on a small sector of the sky, all the while knowing that the movements of other heavenly bodies are both "out of the picture" and affecting the movements of those objects "within the picture." For us, this means we must always regard our statements about *what is happening* in our video...the descriptions that become our "observed data layer," discussed at length below...as tentative, and as circumscribed by the fact that we simply have not captured everything that was happening. This is necessarily the case even if levels of intersubjectivity are high regarding what is occurring in the event stream.

This recognition allows researchers to carry out a set of research actions that are fair game with respect to the raw data layer. These include selecting, rejecting, expanding, and focusing raw data. These actions are very close to their common-sense meanings: *selecting* raw data is the action of noticing something interesting and setting it aside for purposes of further analysis; *rejecting* means eliminating raw data from further consideration (most often because the video has been spoiled in some way, or records "dead time"); *expanding* means bringing multiple data sources together to understand a particular sequence of events, such as multiple video views, stills of particularly interesting actions or artifacts, and written artifacts; *focusing* means limiting our field of vision on the raw data to particular aspects of the social interaction (or other behavior) occurring on screen.

Before leaving this discussion, we must note that issues at the raw data layer span both the epistemological and the technological: certain technical processes can positively affect epistemological problems. If what Jordan and Henderson (1995) say is true...that "video recordings replace the bias of the researcher with the bias of the machine," then making improvements to mechanical aspects of video capture is likely to lessen this unintentional but still real bias. For instance, the knowledge that our raw data cannot capture everything nonetheless inspires us to capture in our raw data as much of the event matrix as is practically possible. Our model is in essence a trickle-up model, so information excluded from raw data is likewise excluded from all subsequent interpretation. Like many other research labs in the learning sciences, ours has, over time, developed strategies and techniques to mitigate some of practical concerns related to videography. For instance, we know through experience that we get more complete renderings of the event matrix when we use multiple cameras. However, our focus in this paper is not the mechanics of raw data capture, nor the placement of recording devices, nor the storing of digital information, nor even the techniques for making links between the raw data layer and other layers of interpretation. Rather, our goal here is to share our model and outline the processes we are exploring, so we will say little more about purely technical considerations, even while acknowledging their importance.

Layer 2: Observed Events Layer

The focus of this section is the second data layer of our three-tier model, what we call the observed events layer. This layer depends upon the existence of raw data, and the previously-mentioned allowable operations performed on it...selecting, rejecting, expanding, or focusing.

The end-product of this layer is a document that re-renders what we as observers "see" in a selected segment of raw data. As the graphic in Figure 1 above shows, not all aspects of the raw data trace are included in the observed events layer. The point is not that aspects are excluded, but that researchers can, with high degrees of intersubjectivity, agree about the nature of *what is included.* This requires that we have a shared "observed event syntax." The key to developing an observed event syntax is to come to agreement about the level of description. In practical terms, this may not be as difficult as it sounds; research suggests that humans recognize a "basic" level of events, similar to Roschian perception of basic-level categorizations of objects (Zacks and Tversky, 2001). When building a record of observed events, the focus is on what early ecological psychologists (e.g., Barker and Wright, 1954) considered *molar* actions, those "observable by the naked eye," which conform to basic-level events. We refer to this basic unit of description as the *action*. An action is an observable event that conforms to a subject-mediator-object syntax where the subject is an individual. According to this perspective, "Caroline watered Pot One with a pipette" and "Robert held the sample up to the Munsell chart" are actions.

Our research group typically studies inquiry-learning environments, where multiple subjects interact with each other, with various representations, and with physical objects in the environment. Our model handles this complexity by employing focal-subject observation techniques borrowed from ethology (Lehner, 1996; Lorenz, 1981). When using this method, we "track" each participant in a selected segment, and describe (using short, direct statements) what the participant is doing and saying. These observations are recorded in a contiguous row of cells in a matrix. Once one subject has been observed and his or her actions recorded, a second subject is taken up, until all interacting participants have been followed over the course of the segment.

After all participants have been observed and their actions (including speech acts) recorded, individual records are aligned according to time codes and intersecting actions, the entire record is reviewed against the raw video data to ensure that all observable actions have been noted, and sequence indicators are assigned to each subject's action. This way, the record of social interaction can be followed as if it were a typical one-channel, vertical transcript, even though it is multi-channel and horizontal. Once complete, the resulting product is not unlike a digital animation score, where characters occupy particular horizontal "channels" and the entire sequence can be followed by reading left-to-right, and within a particular column according to a sequence indicator in each cell. Ideally, each segment is directly linked back to raw video, so that researchers can continually check to make sure that this re-rendering of activity captures the common-sense, "observable to the naked eye" view of the reality captured on video. This linkage is part of the "spindle" (discussed more fully below) that connects each layer in our interpretive model. The record in Figure 2 below is an example of one of these products (from the first author's dissertation):

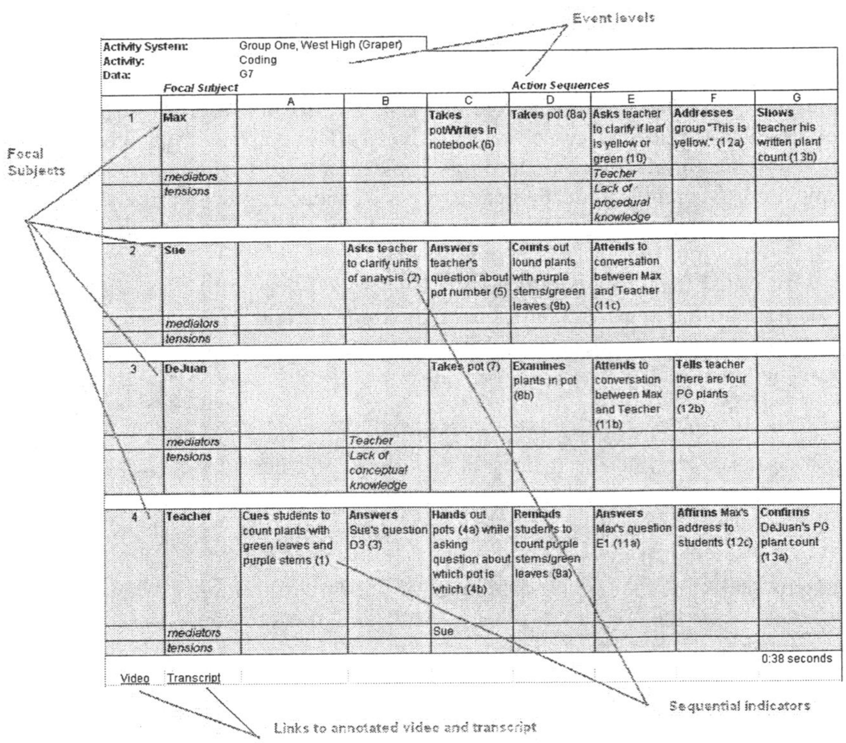

Figure 2. Observed-events record from an inquiry-science classroom

As a practical matter, we should note that the building of observed-event records depends critically on the capacity of digital video to be slowed down, stopped, and re-played, and on the observers' patience. The capacity to "see" what each individual in a social group is doing, and to describe it so that it is intersubjectively available, are critically dependent upon having a syntax of description that specifies the level of observation, being able to slow things down, and having the wherewithal to go over and over short segments of raw data.

Layer 3: Analysis Layer

A product like the record of interaction shown in Figure 2 above serves up working data for the top tier of our three-layer interpretation model. The uppermost interpretive layer is where analytic (if probabilistically hedged) statements are made regarding *what* has happened in the event stream...as it boils up through raw data and into observed events; and *why* or *how* these events have transpired.

Here's an example of how this works in practice. One of our ongoing research projects (the first author's dissertation work) involves studying how students in inquiry science classrooms develop the ways of working of scientists. Borrowing ideas from Charles Goodwin (1994), we are viewing video of students and teachers conducting heredity experiments to see if and where they "create" data by coding aspects of the plants that they are experimentally manipulating. This interpretive process occurs in several steps. To begin, we work with raw data to look for instances of the category of interest, in this case students' creating data by coding. Once these segments are selected (one of the allowable research maneuvers at the raw data level), we can review the raw video data, focus on participants and their actions, and build an observed-events record (Figure 2). This record allows us to probe the sequences, and ask questions such as, "Who is participating?" "What is the pattern of interactions in the segment of interest? We find that questions about "what" and "who" can be answered in a reasonably straightforward manner, if we follow the observed-events syntax discussed above.

Of course we must ask how and why questions as well: "How did the students know what 'mattered' in terms of coding?" "Why did Max ask the question about leaf color that he did?" In accordance with our working model, we explicitly distinguish between questions of the first sort and questions of the second, calling them *etic* and *emic* respectively. This acknowledges epistemological differences in the sorts of statements that we can make from our data. Since this distinction is crucial to our model, we review it in some detail.

More than fifty years ago, Kenneth Pike introduced the terms *etic* and *emic* to social science (Pike, 1954). Pike, a linguist, suggested that the distinction between phon*etics* (physiological patterns resulting in sounds) and phon*emics* (the meanings that humans assign to speech behavior) could be profitably applied to the study of human behavior beyond language. Pike recognized that with *phonetics*, language could be studied and understood at arm's length from the people that speak it. One need not understand what a speaker is saying to distinguish performative aspects of speech, such as differences between an aspirated [p] phonetic and a non-aspirated [b] sound, nor distributional aspects (that, for instance, pathologies such as velopharyngeal fricative speech often co-occur with cleft palate). Pike saw the study of *phonemics* as different, requiring the observer to access the meaning system of the speaker. Pike's critical test for phonemic difference was to determine if exchanging one phoneme in a string changed the meaning for the speaker (Pike, 1954). For instance, substituting *r* for *l* as the first sound in the string //ip changes the meaning of the string (/r/ip versus /l/ip).

Extrapolating from this, Pike's use of the terms etic and emic in social and behavioral research refers to making a distinction between analysis of a behavior stream from a perspective *other than that of the actor* (etic) and a rendering of the same behavior *from the perspective of the actor* (emic). For instance, to describe an action as "the subject used an overhand motion with an inward turn of the wrist to propel a solid sphere toward its target" is to employ an *etic* (if ungainly) description. Etic statements make minimal (if any) reference to a particular cultural meaning system; in principle, they can be understood by anyone with basic communicative competence (c.f. Habermas, 1981). To make the distinction clear, we can experiment with the statement concerning the sphere and its target. If we reformulate it to say "the pitcher threw a slider, it missed the strike zone," we are making an *emic* statement that is only meaningful if one participates in the language of baseball. This is made particularly salient if we change the sentence, so it reads "the pitcher threw a slider at the batter's *head.*" For those knowledgeable about the game, throwing a pitch at a batter's head has a very different meaning than merely failing to deliver a strike...it is seen as an aggressive act.

One of the reasons for making the etic/emic distinction is that it forces us to acknowledge that we are adopting a specific perspectival frame when we make emic statements in an analysis. Leander's (2002) excellent study of "silencing" in classrooms provides a useful example. In this work, Leander investigates four special categories of social interaction in classrooms: students can be active participants, they can be "silent," they can "silent and being silenced," or finally they can be "speaking while being silenced." While the first of two of these categories can be readily observed by anyone with basic communicative competence, the latter two require that the observer participate in the meaning system developed by Leander in his article, and presumably shared by his subjects. These are therefore emic descriptors. By no means does this make them invalid; quite the opposite. To our way of thinking, social science progresses to the degree that new understandings...such as what it means to be "silenced"...develop and diffuse through the community of researchers.

The Spindle

We now come to the discussion of our three-level interpretive model's spindle: the relations that connect statements at one level with statements at another, like the central spindle of a toddler's toy. The spindle in our model is a conceptual entity that becomes manifest as links between various data documents and our raw digital video. By allowing researchers to traverse these connections, the spindle ultimately grounds interpretation in raw data. This proves particularly valuable when team members' interpretations are novel, or develop out of a theoretical perspective not shared by the group. In a sense, the spindle helps research teams like ours to keep track of "fissures of interpretation."

At the very onset of this paper, we stated that interpretability gaps caused by weak links or even holes between what individuals "see" and what others in a group see are a central problem for research teams. To resolve this problem, we have been experimenting with ways to ensure that theoretical concepts and categories...when applied through analysis...are traceable to actions in transcripts (at the observed events level), and one tier down, to the video of the raw data corpus. We surmised that when connections among levels of interpretation are explicit and direct, they can be followed more easily by others who may not share a particular theoretical perspective, or who are simply less familiar with video data projects (peripheral participants in research, such as practitioners and even scholars-in-training). These connections constitute our spindle.

Other researchers seem to be moving in similar directions; Leander's (2002) study on "silencing" again provides a useful example. In his own musical score-style transcripts (which bear structural resemblance to our own example shown in Figure 2 above), Leander embeds codes derived from his theory of social silencing directly into his transcript. This is invaluable for the reader, since it allows us to "see" exactly *where* Leander "sees" the action of silencing occurring in the classrooms he studies. To embody the three-tier model we discuss here, all that remains is for the author to directly connect this annotated transcript *up* to his analysis, and *down* to the raw video data he captured in the classrooms. Of course, neither of these steps is technically possible in the medium of paper-based print, so we can hardly blame Leander for not making these connections. Indeed, our working model begs many questions about the adequacy of current academic norms for conducting and reporting video research in the learning sciences.

The Problem that the Three-Layer Model Solves

Let us sum up. We believe that the three-layer model and the processes that follow from it hold potential for solving a key problem for research groups: by explicitly naming layers of the model, by concretizing interpretive processes, and by demanding that interpretations must "link down" to raw data, the model can illuminate opaque connections among categories and codes used in research, empirical data, and analysis. In practice, this helps to effectively channel subjectivity—or better, creativity—so that any private or closely-held meanings have a fighting chance of becoming intersubjectivity held. The model and process require making technical (in addition to methodological) links among layers of interpretation: video researchers need methods for explicitly showing connections among analytic statements, records of observed events, and raw data. Using off-the-shelf data-handling tools, we are exploring these practices in our work. To date, they have proven useful for us. As we share them with the larger community, we ask if...perhaps...we should all consider making these connections explicit.

References

Angellio, C. & Rogoff, B. (in press). Examining shared endeavors by abstracting video coding schemes with fidelity to cases. In R. Goldman, R., Pea, B. Barron, & S. Derry (Eds.), *Video Research in the Learning Sciences.* Mahwah, NJ: Erlbaum.

Barker, R.G. & Wright, H.F. (1954). *Midwest and its children.* Evanston, IL: Row Peterson.

Derry, S. J. (in press). Video research in classroom and teacher learning: Searching for standards in a complex terrain. In R. Segall, R. Pea, B. Barron, & S. J. Derry (Eds.), *Video Research in the Learning Sciences.* Mahwah, NJ: Erlbaum.

Goodwin, C.A. (1994). Professional vision. *American Anthropologist* 96(3), 606-633.

Habermas, J. (1981). *The Theory of Communicative Action: Reason and Rationality of Society, Vol. 1.* Boston: Beacon.

Jordan, B. and Henderson, A. (1995). "Interaction analysis: Foundations and practice." *The Journal of the Learning Sciences, 4*(1): 39-103.

Leander, K.M. (2002). Silencing in classroom interaction: Producing and relating social spaces. *Discourse Processes 34*(2), 193-235.

Lehner, P. (1996). *Handbook of Ethological Methods (2nd edition).* Cambridge: Cambridge University Press.

Lorenz, K. (1981). *The Foundations of Ethology.* New York: Springer-Verlag.

Nystrand, M., Wu, L.L., Zeiser, S., and Long, D.A. (2003). Questions in time: Investigating the structure and dynamics of unfolding classroom discourse. *Discourse Processes 35*(2), 135-198.

Pike, Kenneth L. (1954). *Language in relation to a unified theory of the structure of human behavior.* Glendale, Calif., Summer Institute of Linguistics.

Zacks, J. M., & Tversky, B. (2001). Event structure in perception and conception. *Psychological Bulletin, 12*, 3-21.

The Role of the Backchannel in Collaborative Learning Environments

Sarita Yardi, UC Berkeley School of Information, 102 South Hall, Berkeley, CA 94720, yardi@sims.berkeley.edu

Abstract: Students at UC Berkeley's School of Information have participated in a persistent, online "backchannel" chatroom during class since the Fall of 2004. This paper describes the affordances offered by this technology for enhanced peer-to-peer and teacher-student interactions in a collaborative learning environment.

Introduction

Over the past year, leaders in education, academia, and mainstream media have discussed the role of the backchannel in presentations, conferences, and the classroom. Internet Relay Chat (IRC) is an online, synchronous chat environment that enables groups of people to collaborate and chat from any physical location in the world (Harris, 1995; Dewes, Wichmann, & Feldmann, 2003). The definition of the term backchannel varies with context and usage. To some it suggests an intangible, clandestine community. To others, it suggests an empowering toolkit for participation, collaboration, and interaction. The central function of the backchannel is its use as a secondary or background complement to an existing frontchannel, which may consist of a professor, teacher, speaker, or lecturer. It offers a unique communication medium, a novel toolkit through which students can create, identify, and filter new modes of learning.

The recent surge in interest has generated a number of conference-based case studies that attempt to study the implications of backchannel chats. Participants in these conferences expressed a wide range of opinions about the usefulness of the backchannel in context of the frontchannel discussion. A number of educators have similarly considered the effects of unrestricted wireless access in the classroom, some of whom have attempted to incorporate these technologies into their lectures and lesson plans (Anderson, Anderson, VanDeGrift, Wolfman, & Yasuhura, 2003; Campbell & Pargas, 2003; Franklin & Hammond, 2001; Karabenick, 2003; Ratt, Shapiro, Truong, & Griswold, 2003; Hembrooke & Gay, 2003, VanDeGrift, Wolfman, Yasuhara, & Anderson, 2002). However, little research has been conducted on how chatrooms affect learning experiences and environments. Chatrooms could transform how students learn, course content, learning behaviors and practices, and interactions between students and teachers, fundamentally changing the ways in which teachers and students create and disseminate ideas, knowledge and understanding.

This paper presents a study of a real backchannel community in a natural academic setting, located at the University of California at Berkeley's School of Information (iSchool)[1]. It will first describe the physical and virtual community. It will then analyze the characteristics of the chatroom and users' interactions and behavior. Finally, it will suggest hypotheses and implications for the role of the chat in educational communities. What sort of new virtual communities does it enable? What types of interactions occur in this backchannel and how do they contribute to the academic learning community? How does this communication medium change techniques for information and knowledge sharing? Is there a compelling story to be told or is it simply noise – wasted bandwidth that distracts participants from the face to face environment they are in? In light of the increasing role of technology and computer-mediated communication as ubiquitous tools in our everyday lives, there is a need for a better understanding of how these tools can be incorporated into the classroom environment to facilitate enhanced teaching and learning.

This study analyzes the iSchool IRC chat logs from October 2004 to October 2005. The logs contain over 200,000 user entries, with an average of over 400 user postings per day. Software visualization tools are use to plot chat statistics over time in order to highlight trends in adoption and usage within the classroom. In Figure 1, user count is plotted versus the first six weeks of the Spring 2005 academic semester, showing a general increase in user participation. This suggests that students become more engaged in the chatroom community over time. Figure 2 shows total user entries by user. The curve shows a power log trend in behavior, indicating that a few users participate most often. Educators will need to facilitate and construct a classroom environment that enables equal access and participation.

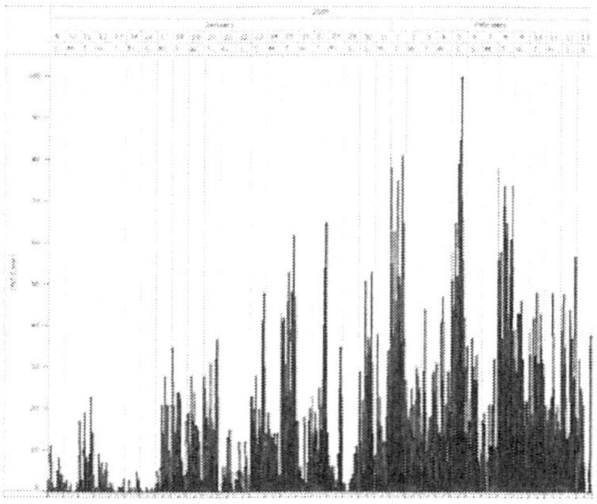

Figure 2. Number of Chat Entries Over First Six Weeks of Spring 2005 Academic Semester

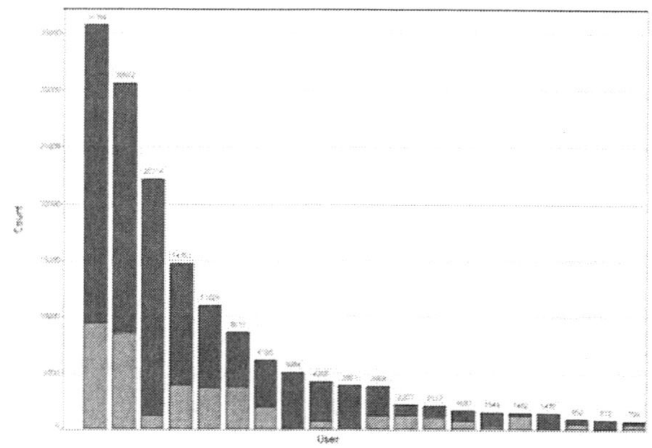

Figure 1. Total Chat Entries By User Between Oct 2004 and Oct 2005

Implications for Education

The use of technology in education and learning has been discussed at length by educators, instructional designers, and technologists (Haythornthwaite & Kazmer, 2004; Scardamalia & Bereiter, 1994; Hoadley & Kilner, 2005; Barab et al., 2004). The field of Computer Supported Collaborative Learning (CSCL) describes how scaffolding can support students' learning through a number of different methods, including situated learning (Lave & Wenger, 1991), peer-to-peer learning, and constructivist learning (Vygotsky, 1978; Bruner, 1996). These theories are based on the same underlying assumptions that individuals are active agents who are purposefully seeking and constructing knowledge within a meaningful context. The collaborative affordances offered by IRC chat suggest that learning can be enhanced through interactions between participants in the chatroom. A primary function of CSCL software is to promote reflection and inquiry, which the chatroom enables through unrestricted participation and a minimally rule-based environment that encourages intentional knowledge creation and sharing. The following sections highlight the salient factors in developing an effective tool for learning and theorize how an IRC chatroom might be incorporated successfully into an education environment. Hoadley (2004) states that "if we find out how people learn in natural situations, we can create educational environments more conducive to learning." The goal of this case study is to provide useful guidelines for future implementations of chatrooms in the classroom.

Situated Learning and Communities of Practice

Situated learning describes learning as a function of the activity, context and culture in which it occurs (Lave & Wenger, 1991). This contrasts with many classroom learning environments that are abstract and out of context, in which a teacher may structure a lesson plan based on an activity which is not personally relevant or meaningful to the students. Social interaction is a critical component of situated learning. Learners become involved in a "community of practice" that embodies certain beliefs and behaviors to be acquired. As the beginner or newcomer moves from the periphery of this community to its center, he becomes more active and engaged within the culture and assumes the role of expert, a process described as "legitimate peripheral participation" (Lave & Wenger, 1991). Brown, Collins, & Duguid (1989) describe the need for a new epistemology for learning that emphasizes collaborative social construction of knowledge over rote memorization of facts and concepts. There exists an immense potential and opportunity for incorporation of this backchannel into the classroom to enhance situated learning. The social cohesiveness among students increases in proportion to their levels of communication and interaction within the group. iSchool students affirm that one source of great value in their iSchool education arise in their interactions with other students. In this light, incorporating the backchannel into the iSchool community augments and enhances a student's ability to actively and intently learn from his peers in a positive manner (Rogoff, Paradise, Arauz, Correa-Chavez, & Angelillo, 2003). The section below elaborates on ways in which this peer-to-peer learning can occur.

Peer-to-Peer Learning

Peer-to-peer learning in the backchannel describes a type of collaborative learning in which students share knowledge through self-motivated participation and engagement. Mercer and Fisher (1997) describe three kinds of peer-group discussions: disputational, commutative, and exploratory, and argue that exploratory discussion has the highest educational value. Successful exploratory peer-to-peer discussions are characterized by brainstorming, challenges, hypotheses testing, consensus, and decision-making. For example:

Jan 25 10:48:10 <Student1> so whats non-repudiation?
Jan 25 10:48:21 <Student1> tracing back to source?
Jan 25 10:48:39 <Student2> it means not being able to deny your own messages

Failed exploratory peer-to-peer discussions may occur when ideas are accepted unchallenged or because continuous disputation leads to a breakdown of communication within the group. Exploratory peer-discussions rarely broke down in this manner in the iSchool community. As a graduate student community, the learning context of the iSchool is different than that of K-12 or undergraduate classrooms. Failed peer discussions might occur far more frequently in younger learning environments where students are more susceptible to competition or immature group behaviors. In these environments, it would be important to have rules to minimize breakdowns in group communication. These might include guidelines that describe the information, assumptions, tasks, and evaluative criteria for constructive collaborative group work. This could be implemented through the presence of a teacher or teaching assistant within the chatroom or a post-mortem review of the chat logs on a regular basis in which the dynamics of the group could be studied and improved for future classes.

Constructivist Learning

Much of the potential success of peer-to-peer learning in a chatroom is rooted in the theory of constructivist learning. According to this theory, learning is an active process in which learners construct new ideas or concepts based upon their current and past knowledge. The learner selects and transforms information, constructs hypotheses, and makes decisions, relying on a cognitive structure to do so (Bruner, 1966). Classes in which students participate in discussions encourage them to go beyond merely plugging numbers into formulas or memorizing terms (National Research Council, 1997). Educational researchers argue that students learn best when given the opportunity to learn skills and theories in the context in which they are used, then construct their interpretations of a subject and communicate those understandings to others (Brown et al., 1989). Students are creating their own knowledge by having the freedom to direct the backchannel discussion in ways that are relevant, contextual, and instructional for their own learning purposes. The ways in which students use chatrooms emulates their culture of learning, communicating, and interacting. Peer-to-peer interactions support flexible, learner-centered designs in which learning is active and organic rather than static.

Multi-Tasking and Cognitive Overload

Many opponents to the backchannel highlight its potential for distraction (Schwartz, 2003). Although students have always been subject to distractions during class, in a modern wireless-enabled physical space, the possibilities for distractions increase (Phalen, 2003). Some have suggested the term "continuous partial attention" to describe a student's cognitive ability to pay attention to the teacher's presentation when simultaneously engaged in the backchannel. Others, somewhat cynically, suggest that "continuous partial inattention" is a more appropriate description (McCarthy & boyd, 2005). Regardless of how well intentioned a student may be, a backchannel is going to elicit reactions and engagement from the students that will be asynchronous and off-topic to the teacher's lecture. The following example took place in an iSchool class:

Oct 25 18:42:31 <Student1> Wait, what did she say? Something about ADD. I wasn't paying attention. Oooh, a birdy...

Students may be distracted in the classroom and find themselves processing information at increasingly superficial levels while they attempt to juggle tasks and transfer attention across multiple domains simultaneously (Hembrooke & Gay, 2003; Hembrooke & Gay, 2002). Multi-tasking has emerged at the forefront of discussions related to both childrens' and adults' uses of technology (Ransford, 2005; Rideout & Foegr, 2005; Hafter, 2001). Educators need to determine if and how the tendency towards multi-tasking can be taken advantage of through the use of technology in the classroom rather than being given up on as an entirely negative outcome of wireless technologies. Some studies have indicated that learners can effectively multi-task in the classroom (Kennedy et al., 2005; Kaplan-Leiserson, 2003). At the iSchool, multi-tasking sometimes provided more insightful backchannel discussions through the posting of links and reflective comments. For example:

Jan 31 11:25:29 <Student1> did he conclude the difference between copyright->employer and patent->employee?
Jan 31 11:25:33 <Student1> or did I just miss it?
Jan 31 11:30:17 <Student2> http://www.uscourts.gov/courtlinks/

Other times, it simply provided distractions that were off-topic to the professor's lecture. For example:

Feb 03 17:31:28 < Student1> yeah. I had a roommate who went running with friends and ran like 10 miles. He came home and was eating jam directly out of the jar. It was funny.
Feb 03 17:32:01 < Student1> I never saw anyone adult eat jam directly before.

Feb 03 17:32:17 < Student2> i eat pb straight from the jar sometimes

Can synchronous classroom activities be designed around conceptually related tasks to encourage deeper processing and greater learning of classroom content? Can the connectivity and real-time discussion facilitated by chat and the multi-tasking capabilities of students contribute to new learning opportunities in the classroom?

Emerging Guidelines and Hypotheses

As technology becomes an increasingly ubiquitous component of everyday life, educators will be left with little choice but to find a way to incorporate technology into the classroom. Computer and technology use and behavior is dynamic and evolving with the changing demands of the users and disciplines in which they occur. Ethnicity, gender, experience, and personality are all variables that factor into technology use. This paper is not an attempt to prescribe blanket statements or predictions about how technology can be used in the classroom. Rather, it is an effort to offer a set of hypotheses which educators, academics, industry leaders, and researchers can use to guide their own future research. A thorough understanding of the characteristics and implications of how this chatroom fits into the classroom structure will enable educators to design a better framework for learning.

Implementations of the backchannel will and should vary across different contexts and domains

This analysis of the backchannel is unique to the iSchool graduate community. However, implementations of the backchannel could exist across a number of domains, including K-12, undergraduate classes, graduate programs, law schools, business meetings, conferences, and online learning or eLearning environments. Schools, in particular, need to incorporate the notion of communities of practice in combination with contemporary learning theories to become more intentional and systematic for improving learning and education. For example, the ways in which a backchannel could be used in a 5th grade classroom will differ significantly from its use in a law class. Teachers may need to implement a more controlled and disciplined environment in younger grades whereas law professors could assume that a Socratic teaching method will effectively command their students' full attention.

Teaching styles should take advantage of the social and educational affordances the backchannel offers

Technology by itself cannot improve instruction (Hestenes, Wells, & Swackhamer, 1992). However, technology can enhance the effectiveness of a good instructional design (Hoadley & Enyedy, 1999). Many teachers will be more likely to adopt chatroom technology in their classrooms if they are first provided support and instruction on how to use the technology (Cuban, 1993). Teachers may need to teach in shorter cycles to hold students' attention. They should adjust their curriculum and teaching styles to provide different and improved environments for scaffolding than the standard lecture format. A tighter integration of the backchannel may require their lectures to be more permeable and the right level of focus and formality will need to be determined. Students should be enabled to continually build upon their own knowledge and use the backchannel to share and enhance their learning process (Bruner, 1966). For example:

Jan 23 16:17:30 <Student1> if anyone wants a free stats package thats about 10x more powerful than the most expensive version of SPSS, http://www.r-project.org/. I'm going to be learning that, so we can pool resources.

Jan 23 16:18:27 <Student2> i'm in Student1

Jan 23 16:18:31 <Student3> it looks powerful, Student1, & on [professor's] list. but unsure of ease of learning - user manual, support community?

A better understanding of the socially constructed dynamics around the technology is essential to improving its use in the classroom (DeGennaro, 2005). One option is to use two publicly-projected chatrooms: one for comments, one for questions. In the latter chatroom, students could post questions for the teacher. A second option is to use a chatroom robot to monitor a channel and provide basic information as well as perform a heuristic analysis of events for post-analysis. For example, entering the command "@define constructionism" would automatically return a definition from nerdbox. Nerdbox, the iSchool robot, can be programmed to take a variety of different types of commands. A third option is to display the backchannel on the screen in front of the classroom so that students would be less inclined to contribute off-topic postings and would instead focus on the academic discussion. Similarly, a teaching assistant could participate in the backchannel and help facilitate interactions by guiding the discussion and providing scaffolding for the learners.

Chatrooms should enable teacher self-assessment

Presenters want to be able to obtain feedback (Anderson et al., 2003; DiMicco, Lakshmipathy, & Fiore, 2002). For example, Classroom Presenter supports the ability for a student to send a question or comment to the professor as well as the location on the PowerPoint slide to which it relates (Anderson et al., 2003). Teachers should be able to analyze the chat logs of a particular lecture and self-assess their own effectiveness. Did students understand their lecture? Were students engaged in the material? Did they feel comfortable asking questions either in the classroom or in the backchannel? Were all students participating equally in the backchannel? For example:

Oct 19 10:51:08 <Student1> Did [lecturer] ever show us the dataset and its format?
Oct 19 10:51:30 <Student2> I don't think he did
Oct 19 10:52:17 <Student3> but you can find it in [source]
Oct 19 10:52:47 <Student2> Actually, I think this is the link
Oct 19 10:52:48 <Student2> [URL to java source code]

Researchers at MIT's Media Lab have designed a number of tools to visualize chat conversations with the goal of evoking intuitive understandings of the nature of the discussion (Mutton, 2004; Donath, 2002). These visualization tools could be used to reveal the structure of the students' discussions, and understanding of the material.

A backchannel should encourage social interactions and community building

In the same way that the physical classroom environment, as well as corporate environments, business meetings, and conferences, all encourage moderate levels of informal chat and humor, the backchannel should also permit the same dynamics. Students' desire to participate in the backchannel is increased if they have a sense of community within the channel, which is most easily built through social interactions and shared experiences. Within the iSchool community, the sense of shared context is easily increased through the daily personal interactions that users experience in their face-to-face environment. By chatting informally in the classroom hallways, during lunch, or in outside social settings, users establish a sense of trust that is transferred to their interactions in the online environment. The more shared context participants have, the easier it is for them to negotiate their sense of interpersonal trust and reputation and therefore facilitate discussion and conversation online. A fostered community of learners will result in greater levels of metacognition, reflection, discourse, deep content knowledge, distributed expertise, instruction, and assessment (Brown & Campione, 1996). For example:

Jan 19 13:28:35 <Student1> how is social constructivism different from geist?
Jan 19 13:28:48 <Student1> is it?
Jan 19 13:29:26 <Student2> seems more inter-cultural than intra-cultural

A backchannel etiquette will need to be developed

Is a socially acceptable intellectual dialogue better than no engagement at all? How about if the dialogue includes an occasional off-topic or rude comment? For example:

Jan 19 13:27:32 <Student1> i think we should have a goal this semester
Jan 19 13:27:53 <Student2> to get [student3] a girlfriend?

Wireless technologies change how people interact with one another and etiquettes will need to evolve around these technologies. However, it will be difficult to construct a one size fits all set of rules. Rather, etiquette will be contextual and evolving, based on environment, users, and needs (White, 2005; Cox, 2005).

Future Work

We are currently developing a visualization tool[2] of a standalone chat client as part of our iSchool Master's Final Project. This visualization will be developed and tested in iSchool classes throughout the Spring of 2005. We hope to complete a prototype of this tool, which will serve as a proof of concept of the possibilities in providing such a tool to teachers and professors in academic environments. The eroding distinction between the cultures surrounding education, work, play, and technology poses new methodological challenges within the learning environment. What are learners' rights with regards to wireless use in the classroom? Designing for new educational environments using these technologies requires the use of iterative and reflective design methods to explore what works, what is important, and how it enhances learning. This nascent subject offers a rich opportunity for growth and exploration.

Endnotes

(1) Since the original paper submission, the school changed it's name from the School of Information Management & Systems (SIMS) to the Information School (iSchool)
(2) This tool is under ongoing development at http://dream.sims.berkeley.edu/groups/classchat/chatviz/ and the group website is located at http://dream.sims.berkeley.edu/groups/classchat/

References

Anderson, R. J., Anderson, R., VanDeGriff, T., Wolfman, S. A., & Yasuhara, K. (2003). Classroom presentation from the tablet PC. In Proceedings of the 8th Annual Conference on Innovation and Technology in Computer Science Education (Thessaloniki, Greece, June 30-July 2, 2003), ACM Press, 238.

Barab, S., Kling, R., Gray, J. H., Pea, R., Brown, J. S., & Heath, C. (2004). *Designing for Virtual Communities in the Service of Learning*. Cambridge University Press.

Brown, J., Collins, A., & Duguid, P. (1989) Situated Cognition and the Culture of Learning. *Educational Researcher, 18*(1), 18-42.

Brown, A.L., & Campione, J.C. (1996). Psychological theory and the design of innovative learning environments: On procedures, principles, and systems. In L. Schauble & R. Glaser (Eds.), *Innovations in learning: New environments for education* (pp. 289-325). Mahwah, NJ: Erlbaum.

Bruner, J. (1966). *Toward a Theory of Instruction.* Cambridge, MA: Harvard University Press.

Bruner, J. (1996). *The Culture of Education.* Cambridge, MA: Harvard University Press.

Campbell, A. & Pargas R. (2003). Laptops in the Classroom. Proceeding of the 2003 ACM SIGCSE Technical Symposium, February 19-23, 2003.

Cox, A. (2005). *Where are your wireless manners?* Retrieved October 18, 2005 from http://www.cnn.com/2005/TECH/10/17/wireless.manners/index.html

Cuban, L. (1988). *Teachers & machines: The classroom use of technology since 1920.* NY: Teachers College Press.

Cuban, L. (1993). Computers meet classroom: classroom wins. *Teachers College Record, 95*(2), 185-210.

DeGennaro, D. (2005). Should We Ban Instant Messaging in School? *Learning and Leading with Technology, 32*(7).

Dewes, C., Wichmann, A., & Feldmann, A. (2003). An analysis of Internet chat systems. In Proceedings of the 3rd ACM SIGCOMM Conference on Internet Measurement (Miami Beach, FL, October 27 - 29, 2003), ACM Press, 51-64.

DiMicco, J.M., Lakshmipathy, V., & Fiore, A.T. Conductive Chat: Instant Messaging With a Skin Conductivity Channel. Poster Presentation, Conference on Computer Supported Cooperative Work (New Orleans, LA, November, 2002).

Donath, J. (2002). A semantic approach to visualizing online conversations. *Communications of the ACM, 45*(4), 45–49.

Franklin, D. & Hammond, K. (2001). The Intelligent Classroom: Providing competent assistance. In Proceedings of Autonomous Agents (Montreal, Canada, May, 2001), ACM Press, 161–168.

Gay, G., & Hembrooke, Helen. (2002). Collaboration in Wireless Learning Networks. In Proceedings of the 3rd Hawaii International Conference on System Sciences (Waikoloa, Hawaii, Jan., 2002).

Golub, E. 2005. On audience activities during presentations. *The Journal of Computing Sciences in Colleges. 20*(3), 38-46.

Hafter, K. (2001, April 12). Teenage Overload, or Digital Dexterity? *The New York Times.*

Harris, S. (1995). *IRC Survival Guide: Talk to the World with Internet Relay Chat.* Addison-Wesley Longman Publishing Co.

Haythornthwaite, C., & Kazmer, M. M. (Eds.) (2001). *Learning, culture and community in online education: Research and practice.* New York: Peter Lang Publishers.

Hembrooke, H. & Gay, G. (2003). The Laptop and the Lecture: The Effects of Multitasking in Learning Environments. *Journal of Computing in Higher Education, 15*(1).

Hestenes, D., Wells, M., & Swackhamer, G. (1992). Force concept inventory. *The Physics Teacher, 30*, 141-158.

Hoadley, C. (2004) Learning and design: Why the learning sciences and instructional systems need each other. *Educational Technology, 44*(3), 6-12.

Hoadley, C. M. & Kilner, P. G. (2005). Using technology to transform communities of practice into knowledge-building communities. *SIGGROUP Bull. 25*(1), 31-40.

Hoadley, C & Enyedy, N., (1999). Between information and communication: Middle spaces in computer media for learning. In C.Hoadley and J. Roschelle (Eds.), *Proceedings of the Third International Conference on Computer Support for Collaborative Learning* (pp 242-251).

Kaplan-Leiserson, E. (2003, December 15). We-Learning: Social Software and E-Learning. *Learning Circuits, American Society for Training and Development.* Retrieved October 29, 2005 from http://www.learningcircuits.org/2003/dec2003/kaplan.htm.

Karabenick, S. A. Seeking Help in Large College Classes: A person-centered approach. *In Contemporary Educational Psychology*, 28, 2003. Academic Press, pp. 37–58.

Kennedy, T., Golub, E., Stroope, B., Kee, K., Powell, A., & Zehnder, S. (2005, October). *Wireless Communication in the Classroom: A "Back Channel" to the Learning Process?* Paper presented at Internet Research 6.0: Internet Generations, Chicago, IL, United States of America.

Kirschner, Strijbos, Kreijns, & Beers. (2004). Designing Electronic Collaborative Learning Environments. *Educational Technology Research and Development, 52*(3), 47–66.

Lave, J., & Wenger, E. (1991). *Situated Learning: Legitimate Peripheral Participation*. Cambridge, England: Cambridge University Press.

McCarthy, J. F., boyd, d., Churchill, E. F., Griswold, W. G., Lawley, E., & Zaner, M. (2004). Digital backchannels in shared physical spaces: attention, intention and contention. In Proceedings of the 2004 ACM Conference on Computer Supported Cooperative Work (Chicago, Illinois, November 06 - 10, 2004). ACM Press, New York, NY, 550-553.

McCarthy, J. F. & boyd, d. m. (2005). Digital backchannels in shared physical spaces: experiences at an academic conference. In CHI '05 Extended Abstracts on Human Factors in Computing Systems (Portland, OR, April 02 - 07, 2005). ACM Press, New York, NY, 1641-1644.

Mercer, N., & Fisher, E. (1997). The importance of talk. In P. Wegerif & P. Scrimshaw (Eds.), *Computers and talk in the primary classroom* (pp. 13-21). Clevedon, UK: Multilingual Matters.

Mutton, P. 2004. (2004). Inferring and Visualizing Social Networks on Internet Relay Chat. In Proceedings of the Eighth International Conference on Information Visualization (Washington, DC, July 14-16, 2004), IEEE Computer Society, pp 35-43.

National Research Council. (1997). *Science teaching reconsidered: A handbook.* Washington, DC: National Academy Press.

Phalen, K. (2003). Taking a Minus and Making it a Plus. *Info. Technology & Communication. 7*(1).

Ransford, M. (2005, September 23). Average person spends more time using media than anything else. *Ball State University NewsCenter.*

Ratto, M., Shapiro, R. B., Truong, T. M., & Griswold,W. G. (2003). The activeclass project: Experiments in encouraging classroom participation. In Computer Support for Collaborative Learning 2003.

Rideout, V., Donald R., & Foegr, U. (2005). *Generation M: Media in the Lives of 8-18 Year Olds*. Menlo Park, CA: The Henry J. Kaiser Family Foundation.

Rogoff, B., Paradise, R., Mejía Arauz, R., Correa-Chávez, M., & Angelillo, C. (2003). Firsthand learning by intent participation. *Annual Review of Psychology, 54*.

Scardamalia, M., & Bereiter, C. (1994). Computer support for knowledge-building communities. *The Journal of the Learning Sciences, 3*(3), 265-283.

Schwartz, J. (2003). Professor Vie with Web for Class's Attention. *The New York Times,* January 2.

Soloway, E., Grant,W., Tinker,R., Roschelle, J., Mills, M., Resnick, M., Berg, R., & Eisenberg, M. (1999). Science in the Palm of Their Hands. *Communications of the ACM, 42*(8), 21-26.

VanDeGrift, T., Wolfman, S. A., Yasuhara, K., & Anderson, R. J. (2002). Promoting interaction in large classes with a computer-mediated feedback system. Univ. of Wash., Comp. Sci. & Engineering.

Vygotsky, L. S. (1978). *Mind in society: The development of higher psychological processes*. (M. Cole, V. John-Steiner, S. Scribner, & E. Souberman, Eds. And Trans.). Cambridge, MA: Harvard University Press.

White, J. (2005, October 17). *Wireless technology changing work and play*. Retrieved October 26, 2005 from http://www.cnn.com/2005/TECH/10/17/wireless.overview/index.html

A Learning Journey in Problem-based Learning

Jennifer Yeo, Seng Chee Tan, Yew-Jin Lee
National Institute of Education, Nanyang Technological University, Singapore
Email: acjyeo@nie.edu.sg, sctan@nie.edu.sg, yjlee@nie.edu.sg

Abstract: This ethnographic case study describes what happened when a high school biology teacher in Singapore adopted problem-based learning (PBL). Using activity theory, we compare her instructional unit with a reference PBL model derived from the literature. We found disparities in the motives driving these two activity systems, which we attribute to differences between the lived-realities of practitioners and academics. As the researchers collaborate with practitioners through joint reflective practices, our goal is to work towards an equilibrium point whereby PBL could be implemented meaningfully and realistically in an Asian society that has long placed a premium on academic achievement.

Introduction

Most educational theorists now promote "learning in context" (Driscoll, 2000), "activity in context" (Duffy & Cunningham, 1996) or "authentic activities" (Brown, Collin & Duguid, 1989) to engender more meaningful forms of learning. Problem-based learning (PBL) is one such example whereby students work in groups to solve "real world" problems. Popularized during the 1960s, it tries to engage students with ambiguities that prevail in everyday situations, integrating learning across subjects/disciplines through the active construction of knowledge (Barrows & Tamblyn, 1980). Its focus on content knowledge and metacognitive skills made it a popular choice with school practitioners for its promised transfer to real life applications rather than acquisition of inert knowledge.

This paper discusses an ongoing design research in which researchers and teachers work collaboratively on a PBL curriculum. The ethnographic study was conducted in the context of an Asian society (Singapore) where national examinations are highly valued as they are often regarded as the determinants for future educational and career prospects. Driven by this goal, an efficiency model towards learning is usually adopted by teachers and students to achieve the instructional objectives as defined in the national curriculum. Thus far, this strategy has yielded favorable results in international tests, especially in the areas of mathematics and science (Gonzales et. al., 2004). However, the call for a shift to developing critical inquiry by the local Ministry of Education has seen schools attempting alternative learning approaches such as PBL. In part, this move was triggered by the growing realization that innovation and creativity are the key to plugging into the knowledge-based economy. Changing to more progressive forms of instruction requires not only systemic changes to the learning environment but also challenges prevailing beliefs and values inside and outside of school. In the process of change, teachers and students often straddle between the theory-practice divide, which is perhaps a necessary journey towards their end goals.

Through the lens of cultural-historical activity theory, we sought to reveal disparities and contradictions that existed between one school-based PBL learning unit and that described in literature. For example, when PBL was implemented in these schools undergoing change, how did it change the socio-material resources? Would some of these conflicts between the newly introduced practices and old philosophies of learning be so entrenched as never to effect expansive learning? The many contradictions that arose thus serve as useful nodes where we can engage practitioners in critical reflection of their practices and develop their learning trajectory. Similarly, it caused us to reflect and evaluate our original purposes for the research; was it transformatory, exploitative or hegemonic? Were we mindful of the lived realities in school? The ultimate goal is to reach an equilibrium point between theory and everyday school practices so that PBL can be meaningfully and realistically implemented in a society which long placed a premium on academic achievement. In the following sections, we present the methodology, our interpretation of the PBL activity system as derived from the literature, and then contrast it with the PBL classroom in our case study in order to uncover the numerous tensions that Singaporean teachers currently face. We conclude with some suggestions for facilitating the learning journey in PBL.

Methodology

The fieldsite was a public high school that adopted PBL in an attempt to achieve an integrated approach for teaching science. This school launched an Integrated Program, which aimed to engage students in deep learning through problem solving in contrast to the traditional approach whereby science was separated into its main disciplines. Our ethnographic case study focused on a group of four students in a class of 23 high ability and mixed gender students in Miss Chen's (a pseudonym) ninth grade foundation science classroom. In our sample, the students worked on a problem involving the protein structure of hair and went through six lessons, each of about one and a half hours duration, to solve the problem.

We adopted a design research approach to the design of the learning environment. Data from each phase of the design research provided important information for us to work with the teachers in the design of the next phase of the research cycle. It also informed us on the necessary interventions that had to be introduced into the cycle. In this study, we looked at the implementation of the PBL approach in the classroom described above. The activity or discourses of the students were captured on video, transcribed, and then analyzed using cultural-historical activity theory. The components of the activities of both the actual enacted classroom and the theoretical one were compared and contradictions were identified.

The Activity System of Problem-based Learning Environments

Problem-based Learning is a learning approach that was originally developed for medical education (Barrows, 1986). With the goal of developing both students' problem solving strategies and disciplinary knowledge bases and skills, it is a robust, constructivist process, shaped and directed primarily by the students themselves. Since the inception of the PBL model for medical education, it has been adapted for different levels of students for different disciplines (see Gallagher et. al., 1995; Guzdial et. al., 1997; Maxwell et. al., 2001). However, all PBL models share key features such as learning initiated with a problem, exclusive use of ill-defined problems, and collaborative learning among the students with the teacher as metacognitive coach (Savery & Duffy, 1995). It embraces both liberal education and operational curricula, with opportunities for students to construct and refine meaning for themselves as they generate and test their hypotheses while solving real world problems.

In general, PBL follows a process in which groups of four or five students, presented with an ill-structured authentic problem, work collaboratively to generate hypothesis, identify relevant facts and learning issues, investigate hypothesis and gather information, analyze results or information, and present and analyze information. This new level of understanding gives rise to the next cycle of the PBL process until a suitable solution is found (Savery & Duffy, 1995). Through this iterative process, students learn to deal with the complexity that comes with authentic problems, and construct and refine scientific meaning inherent in the artifacts. The process of PBL resembles the inquiry process that scientists use for knowledge creation. Furthermore, the potential for deep understanding of domain-specific concepts and problem solving skills make it a popular choice to break out from traditional methods of instruction.

Problem-based learning, characterized by its language, tools, explicit roles, procedures and regulations, and implicit behaviors and rules, are well reflected within the framework of activity theory. Studying how the tools, rules and roles mediate the activities between the subject, object and community provides a better understanding of the forms of human activity such as cognition taking place in the PBL environment. Figure 1 below illustrates the use of activity theory to describe the activity system of problem-based learning, based on our interpretation of the typical descriptions in literature. We can refer to this as the reference PBL activity system.

The activity of PBL is driven by the motive of acquiring problem-solving strategies, content knowledge and skills. The focus of attention (object) of a group of learners (subject) is the given problem space, attempting to find a solution (outcome) to the problem. Content knowledge is regarded as a mediating tool for the learners in making sense of the problem and refining their hypothesis. Other mediating artifacts can include resources such as information resources (tools), ways of interacting (rules) such as collaboration and negotiation. Everyone in the community, which could be made up of groups of students, teacher and even an expert in the field, is a co-constructor in the learning activity.

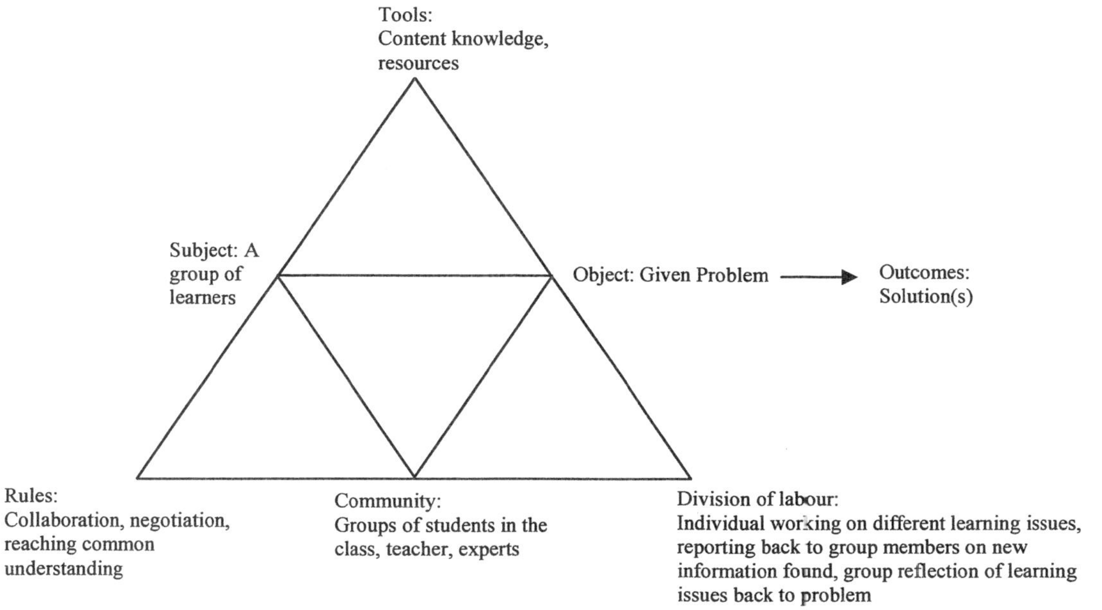

Figure 1. The activity system of the reference PBL environment

Findings and Discussions

In this section, we describe how PBL was implemented in Miss Chen's classroom, in terms of participants' goals, actions and mediating tools. Contrasting that with the typical PBL activity system as discussed above, we analyzed the contradictions and interpreted it in the context of a larger school and society-wide activity system.

The Activity System of Miss Chen's Instructional Unit

The lesson started with an authentic problem presented by the teacher about a teenager who was seeking help for his badly damaged hair, together with the task and assessment criteria to the class. The task was to find a scientifically sound solution for the teenager. In groups of four or five, students spent around five hours of curriculum time over three days to explore the problem, search information about the protein structure, investigate their hypotheses and find a solution to the problem. They were given guiding questions to scaffold their search for protein structure. Given that PBL was completely new to this group of students, and seemingly to allay the fear of the students, the teacher gave the assurance, "Don't worry, I'll do damage control later". This sentence perhaps encapsulates the numerous tensions that Miss Chen experienced as she taught this biology unit using PBL. At a macro level nonetheless, the stages of the instructional process resembled that of a typical PBL in Figure 1.

We then observed what the students did after the problem initiation stage. With the learning issues identified for them in the form of guiding questions, students focused their attention on searching for answers to these questions. They split the task among the group members, trawled the internet for answers, and compiled information by copying and pasting. These actions were carried out with little discussion among themselves as each of them was working on different sub-questions. The data found was then reported back to the teacher when she sat down with the group of students for a discussion in the next lesson. The intellectual discussion was tightly directed by Miss Chen as she called upon each of them to report what they had found. There were some further discussions directed to problem solving among the students until the content knowledge deemed important by the teacher was touched on.

In one instance, one of the group members, Eric, was trying to explain what could cause protein to be denatured (Transcript 1). As he was explaining, the rest of the group members were trying to reach a common understanding as they added information to make the explanation clearer or questioned him in areas which they were doubtful. The interaction was a dialogic one, whereby students negotiated and co-constructed understanding. The voice of the teacher was seldom heard, other than to question misconceptions.

Transcript 1

Eric	It is also said that there are several factors that lead to protein being denatured, which include high temperature and extreme pH values.
Sandra (another student)	Extreme pH values mean that if the sea is too salty, you can't go in?
Eric	Erm, what, what?
Miss Chen	pH and salt?
Eric	It's, I mean, it's true that sometimes in shampoo -
Sandra	Your shampoo consists of acid and alkali?
May	Ya, sometimes they put in citric acid.
Eric	You know, okay, I -
Miss Chen	Don't believe advertisement.
Eric	Okay, this is extra information. You know, when you shower, you know why there's conditioner and shampoo? There are two different reasons, right? Shampoo is acidic lah. So when you wash your hair, everything, right? What happens is the hair, right, that layer layer thing you know, will come up and fray and your hair becomes very rough, right? Maybe guys hair is different.
Sandra	What layer layer thing?
Eric	You know your hair, right? Can I see that picture? Hair has scales, right?
Students	Scales?
Eric	Scales like these, right?

However, the dynamics of this kind of discussion stopped later when the "crux" of the problem was discussed. In Transcript 2, we see Miss Chen playing a very active role in the discussion, acknowledging, expanding and clarifying concepts, and emphasizing the key points of the protein structure as Sandra presented the four structures of protein.

Transcript 2

Sandra	At different levels. And basically, the first one is the primary structure, the second one secondary structure, the third one tertiary structure, the fourth one quaternary structure.
Miss Chen	Okay. Tell me about the primary structure.
Sandra	The primary structure
Miss Chen	**This one ah, time out. This one must know ah.**
Eric	Okay.
Sandra	This is a picture of the protein structure.
Miss Chen	Okay.
Sandra	And it is made up of amino acids.
Miss Chen	Okay. Amino acids.
Sandra	And is made of a chain of peptide bonds. So if I'm not wrong, these are the peptide bonds, is it? (pointing to the picture on the tablet screen)
Miss Chen	Ya. They just show bonds by lines lah. Essentially, your amino acids like that right? (pointing to a simplified version of the protein structure on the screen which she had drawn). Primary structure focuses on the fact that there are amino acids connected to each other by peptide bonds. **Do you know the structure of amino acids? (pause) Okay, you need to know.**

As the reporting back phase went on, the teacher continued to emphasize and stress the importance of the information that they needed to know [in bold] (as stipulated in the official syllabus) as she expanded and summarized the important points. The students were seen to be taking notes as the teacher ensured that they understood the content. After the session, the students organized their notes, clarified understanding with each other, making sure that they had not left out essential information about the protein structure. During the discussion of the protein structure, there were few other instances of sharing of understanding or co-construction among the students.

It is evident from the description that in working towards a solution and presentation, students adopted an efficiency "divide and conquer" model to completing the given task. The presentation turned out to be information giving to the classmates who seem to anticipate that the teacher would do "damage control" at the end of all the presentation. Figure 2 shows the activity system of the enacted PBL classroom.

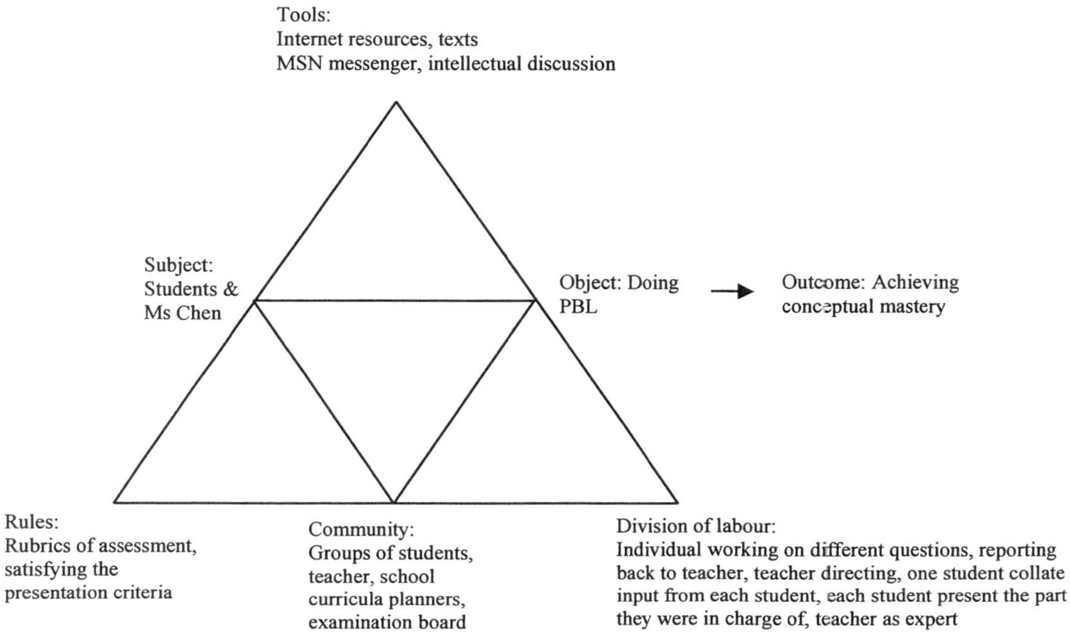

Figure 2. The PBL activity system in Miss Chen's classroom

Contradictions Between the Activity Systems

When we compared the observed activity system in the classroom with a typical PBL activity system, several tensions or contradictions became apparent (in italics) (Table 1).

Table 1. Comparison of activity systems

	The reference PBL activity system	**The observed PBL classroom**
Subject	A group of 4 – 5 students	A group of 4 students and teacher
Object → outcome	*Object: Solving problems* *Outcome: Solution(s) to the problem*	*Object: Doing PBL* *Outcome: Achieve content mastery*
Tools	Resources (cognitive tools, collaborative tools, information resources), content knowledge	Information resources (internet and texts), MSN messenger, intellectual discussion
Rules	*Iterative cycle of hypothesis generation, information gathering as resources to solve problem, investigation and reflection through collaboration, multiple solution*	*Rubrics of assessment*
Community	*Groups of students in the class, teacher, experts*	*Groups of students, teacher, school curricula planners, examination board, societal expectations*
Division of Labour	Group search for *problem space* (applying prior knowledge to the problem, identify learning issues, hypothesis generation), negotiating common understanding of information found, reflection, and investigation. Individual working on different learning issues, reporting back to group and	Individual student worked on different questions and reported back to teacher. The teacher also does her part of the work to achieve *conceptual mastery* by connecting the information found by each student, and expanding and clarifying important concepts. The information compiled by individual student

	self reflection. Teacher acts as the metacognitive coach.	was then compiled together into a presentation slide.

From the above comparison, the main contradiction lies with the motive driving the two activity systems. Every activity is driven by a motive; what distinguishes one activity from another is the object, which gives direction to the activity (Leont'ev, 1978). All actions are hence in relation to this driving "force". In Miss Chen's PBL unit, acquiring and mastering content knowledge seemed to be the primary object whereas ideally in PBL, the problem is the primary focus, with the content knowledge being a mediating tool in problem solving. This is a perfect instance that demonstrates the "strange reversal of object and instrument" in school learning (Engestrom, 1987, p. 74) due to the historical isolation of school from other societal activities. As a result, the primary motive in schools is primarily to learn well and succeed in examinations, rather than to seek far transfer to real life applications.

The object of the activity in Miss Chen's biology PBL class thus (largely) aligned towards content knowledge mastery, as she emphasized the importance of getting the content knowledge "right" by stressing to the students that protein structure is the "crux" of the whole lesson (and through other discursive turns not reflected here). Co-constructing this activity is the group of students whose interaction changed when they immediately sensed the importance of knowing the protein structure (the content knowledge) from teacher talk/actions. They took down notes as the teacher explained the protein structure to them, making clarification when in doubt. Metacognitive skills, problem solving skills and collaborative skills now took secondary importance that stands in contrast to the more interactive discussion when less high-stakes content was taught in other lessons. An efficiency model was adopted in completion of the biology task by splitting up the work and then compiling each person's contribution into a presentation. This inadvertently short-circuited the iterative problem-solving process of hypothesis testing and investigation, which would lead to deep understanding of content knowledge as students applied and reflected on their new understandings. This resulted in low levels of collaboration and reflection as students often worked individually on their assigned parts of the presentation as we observed.

The primary contradiction here can alternatively be attributed to the tension between the exchange value and use value of the object—examination grades (Lave & Wenger, 1991, p. 112). Problem solving skills and metacognition are useful and essential skills in dealing with everyday problems but may not be so crucial in getting by in high-stakes examinations which test mainly recall and procedural knowledge. In other words, Miss Chen's PBL classroom activity is embedded within a larger activity system that values good grades in examinations. Although teacher and students worked through the PBL stages, they were very much constrained by the latter, and seemingly more entrenched activity system. What Miss Chen did was to balance, as well as she could, the ideals of "real/authentic" education using PBL versus the demands of a schooling system slowly undergoing change. Underneath the observable activity system that resembles the PBL approach to science learning lay the "invisible" activity system that ultimately drove the action of *all* the participants—teacher and students alike.

Concluding Remarks

What really counts as true PBL? This paper presents tensions between researchers' and practitioners' perspectives of PBL in a traditional yet academically high-achieving Asian society in Singapore. In the spirit of design research, we do not profess that our interpretation of PBL is superior. What contradictions and expectations Miss Chen faced on a daily basis was not what the researchers encountered as part of their everyday work practices. Rather, what is exhibited as PBL on the ground entails the on-going, contextual interpretations and negotiations of meaning within the team (researchers, students and teachers). Thus, these contradictions should not be taken negatively. Although an activity system is a virtual disturbance producing machine, the contradictions can provide impetus for change, innovation and expansive learning. It is thus crucial for the researchers and practitioners to work collaboratively to find a balance between theory and practice, between the ideal and do-able. One approach we currently adopt is to engage the teachers in professional development programs such as reflection and design experiment so that there is both vertical and horizontal increase in expertise. The ultimate goals and trajectory of learning in PBL have to be negotiated so that there is a balance in theory (academic) and everyday (practitioner) practices—what we term the elusive equilibrium point.

References

Barrows, H.S. & Tamblyn R.M. (1980) *Problem-based learning: An approach to medical education*. New York: Springer Publishing Company

Barrows, H. S. (1986). A taxonomy of problem based learning methods. *Medical Education, 20*, 481-86.

Brown, J.S., Collins, A & Duguid, P (1989). Situated cognition and the culture of learning. *Educational Researcher, 18(1),* 32-41.

Driscoll, M. P. (2000). *Psychology of learning for instruction*. Needham Heights, MA: Allyn & Bacon.

Duffy, T. M. & Cunningham, D. J. (1996). Constructivism: Implications for the design and delivery of instruction. In D. H. Jonassen (Ed.), *Handbook of research on educational communications and technology*. New York: Scholastic.

Engeström, Y. (1987). *Learning by expanding: An activity-theoretical approach to developmental research.* Helsinki: Orienta-Konsultit.

Gallagher, S. (1995). Implementing problem based learning in science classrooms. *School Sciences and Mathematics, 95 (3)*, 136-146.

Gonzales, P., Guzman, J. C., Partelow, L., Pahlke, E., Jocelyn, L., Kastberg, D., & Williams, T. (2004). *Highlights from the Trends in International Mathematics and Science Study (TIMSS)2003.* (NCES 2005-005). U.S. Department of Education, National Centre for Education Statistics. Washington, DC: U.S. Government Printing Office.

Guzdial, M., Hmelo, C., Hubscher, R., Newstetter, W., Puntambekar, S., Shabo, A., Turns, J., & Kolodner, J. (1997). Integrating and guiding collaboration: Lessons learned in computer supported collaboration learning research at Georgia Tech. *Proceedings of Computer-Support for Collaborative Learning (CSCL '97),* Toronto, Ontario, 91-100.

Lave, J., & Wenger, E. (1991). *Situated learning: Legitimate peripheral participation*. New York: Cambridge University Press.

Leont'ev, A.N. (1978). *Activity, consciousness, and personality.* Englewood Cliffs, NJ: Prentice-Hall.

Maxwell, N., Bellisimo Y. & Mergendoller, J. (2001). Problem-based learning: Modifying the medical school model for teaching high school economics. *The Social Studies*, 92 (2), 73-78.

Savery, J. R. and Duffy, T. M. (1995). Problem based learning: An instructional model and its constructivist framework. *Educational Technology, 35 (5),* 31-37.

Acknowledgements

This on-going research is funded by the Learning Sciences Lab, Singapore. (Project code: LSL 1/04 TSC)

Feedback and Adaptation Within a Complex Systems Approach to Designing for Scalable and Sustainable Professional Development

Susan A. Yoon, Graduate School of Education, University of Pennsylvania, 3700 Walnut Street, Philadelphia, PA 19104, Tel: 215-746-2526, Fax: 215-898-4399, Email: yoonsa@gse.upenn.edu
Eric Klopfer, Teacher Education Program, Massachusetts Institute of Technology, 77 Massachusetts Avenue, Cambridge, Massachusetts 02139, Tel: 617-253-2025, Email: Klopfer@mit.edu

Abstract: This paper reports on the efficacy of a professional development framework premised on four complex systems design principles of which two are detailed here—feedback and adaptation. The framework is applied to the design and delivery of the first two years of a three-year study aimed at improving teacher and student understanding of computational modeling tools. We demonstrate that structuring a professional development program around these principles facilitates the development of important strategies such as the identification of salient system variables, effectively distributing expertise, and constructing curricular adaptations. We discuss two meta-level themes that may account for the success of the principles: attending to structure vs. agency and setting short-term vs. long-term goals. Each illustrates the tension existing between competing variables that need to be considered to effectively program for professional development around educational technology with the goal of sustaining and scaling innovations in real world complex educational systems.

Purpose

The complexity of implementing educational change has been a recent focus of many educational leaders interested in understanding how curricular and pedagogical reform efforts can have a scalable, enduring impact in educational systems. In his *Change Forces* series, Fullan (cf. 2003) uses complex systems theory as an organizing framework to reveal core concepts such as non-linearity, unpredictability and multi-level agency that are important issues to contend with in real-world educational systems. In reference to scale, Elmore (1996) writes about the difficulties experienced by nested clusters of innovation when trying to move from local to global contexts. Coburn (2003) reinforces the notion of complexity stating that problems of scale stem from the inability of research to address the inherent multidimensionality between and within classrooms, schools and districts. Cuban et al., (2002) likewise remark that changes of deeply entrenched systemic organizational and operational factors must take place in order to move beyond simple fleeting modifications to practice. Collectively, there is ample evidence to suggest that a complex systems approach for the design and implementation of an educational improvement program is a prudent undertaking. This paper reports on the results of a research study in which complex systems processes are used to organize, harness and evaluate professional development activities around educational technology. Described in greater detail below, the proposed complex systems approach is applied to a comprehensive large-scale NSF-funded project under the program title *Information Technology Experiences for Students and Teachers* (ITEST). The specific purpose of this paper is to reveal outcomes of two design principles in the complex systems approach—*feedback* and *adaptation*—in the first two years of a three-year project implementation.

Theoretical Framework

Examples of complex systems run from relatively micro levels of cellular organization to more macro levels of companies, cities and ecosystems. Despite variation in physical components or agents, complex systems can be generally defined as existing when any given number of interconnected elements, parts or individuals, communicate in non-linear ways. The patterns of interactions form a collective network of relationships that exhibit emergent properties that are not observable at subsystem levels. When perturbations occur, the network self-organizes in, often unpredictable ways where new properties can emerge. The manner in which complex systems communicate, respond to perturbations and self-organize is understood by studying the dynamical processes through which they evolve over time. Acquiring information from their environment, complex systems identify regularities in that information and use this to modify behavior in the real world (Gell-Mann, 1994). In this way, they are said to be *adaptive*. To understand how a system's adaptive attributes emerge, a necessary process to consider is *feedback*, i.e., how systems handle information acquired from the environment. Such complex system processes have already been used to inform research with the goal of *designing* structures and strategies to improve the success of organizations outside of education (cf. Senge, 2000).

Methods

The Program

The ITEST project entitled *New Mexico Adventures in Modeling (AIM)*, consisted of activities structured around two modeling tools called *StarLogo* (Colella & Klopfer, 2000)—a desktop computer application that allows users to interact with agent-based complex systems simulations and Participatory Simulations (Klopfer et al., 2005)—handheld computer simulations. Previous research efforts were channeled into creating stable modeling tools and developing accompanying curriculum materials (Colella et al., 2001). The focus of the present study was to understand how the modeling tools and curriculum materials could be applied in formal school settings.

Professional Development Framework

Using four design principles (of which the first two are reported here), feedback, adaptation, network capital and self-organization, a professional development framework was constructed to inform the scope and sequence of professional development activities that included: 1) A 10-day 60 hour intensive summer teacher workshop; 2) Bi-monthly whole group face-to-face meetings; 3) Access to local expert facilitators; and 4) Communication of a shared on-line bulletin board. How the concepts of feedback and adaptation were applied is described below.

Feedback

The design principle of feedback was used to gather important information about how the professional development community was operating at every stage of the project. Continuous and multiple data collection techniques such as pre/during/post-workshop surveys, video and audio-taped workshop discussions, assessment of online community, participant interviews, focus group discussions, timelines, curriculum plans and researcher field notes, were used to evaluate the success of the program at specific instances in time. This information was used as starting points for the redesign of program activities to influence the alignment of system variables with program learning goals so that outcomes were mutually beneficial to participants and the program.

Adaptation

The second design principle in the complex systems framework was adaptation. In attending to environmental and individual conditions garnered from feedback activities, the program sought to respond to context-dependent factors that influenced individual teaching experiences, and curricular and system-wide purposes. Through continuous modifications to program structures and goals, professional development strategies evolved toward meeting the needs of multiple constituencies.

Participants

47 middle and high school teacher participants were recruited from school districts in a mixed urban-rural area in the southwestern part of the U.S. Teachers were recruited to participate in either the 2003-2004 (Cohort 1) or 2004-2005 (Cohort 2) academic school years. Teaching subjects included Mathematics, Earth Science, Biology, General Science Social Science, Computers and English. Computer programming skills and complex systems understanding ranged from expert to novice. Of the 47 teachers recruited, 43% were female and 57% were male, half had a masters degree or higher, 45% taught less than 6 years, 19% taught between 6-10 years and 36% taught more than 10 years. The instructional team consisted of three local facilitators and three research investigators.

Data Sources and Data Analyses

The extensive list of data sources used in the study is outlined in the section on *Feedback*. The intent of the multiple data source collection was to capture as many of the implementation details as possible. The methodology was qualitative in nature (Lincoln & Guba, 2000) with the assumption that categories and themes would emerge from the data. Codes, categories and themes for the data set were, for the most part, negotiated amongst the investigator team (Strauss & Corbin, 1998). An external rater was used to obtain inter-rater reliability (90%) for the topology of affordances and barriers to implementation presented in Table 1. A categorization manual for the topology was constructed using the categories of structure, function and behavior described in Hmelo (2000). The variables were further divided into micro, meso, and macro level variables that reflect the organization of

Table 1. Topology of Affordances and Barriers to Implementation

Levels	Structure	Function	Behavior
Micro	• individual teaching time constraints	• a teacher's ability to integrate AIM activities with the standard curriculum • number of years of experience a teacher has • a teacher's experience in previous careers e.g., being a computer programmer • a teacher having ready-made curriculum materials to implement AIM activities • a teacher's skill in using information technology • the subject domain of a teacher and grade level applicability • a teacher's classroom management skills • a teacher's programming knowledge/skills	• a teacher's self-efficacy beliefs • a teacher's preferred teaching style, e.g., student-centered vs. teacher-centered • a teacher's level of innovativeness • a teacher's complex systems understanding • a teacher's epistemological beliefs about teaching • a teacher's risk-taking threshold • a teacher's comfort level using technology
Meso	• lack of classroom space to house computers within the school • organization of the school day within the school • centralized control of computer lab, i.e., one person with the key • location of computers in the school, e.g., computer in a lab vs. computers in each classroom • AIM facilitator accessibility, e.g., how facilitator's have been organized or allocated • one vs. several teachers implementing AIM activities in a school • inadequate computer hardware in a school • disorganization at the school level	• a school's demographics, e.g., economically challenged, high ESL • administrator's support within a school • quality of AIM instructor facilitation, e.g., behavior, energy level, enthusiasm • face-to-face AIM community support and collaboration • on-line AIM community support and collaboration • intensive summer workshop to learn how to implement AIM activities • on-going post-summer workshop support • one or no technology support staff available	• teacher envy in a school, e.g., innovators vs. status quo • a school's or departments commitment to or disposition toward other curricular/instructional programs • school culture, e.g., beliefs or philosophies that encourage innovation
Macro	• other district-wide edicts or agendas • insufficient technology funding at the district level • district level disorganization • standardized testing • No Child Left Behind legislation	• AIM program connections to outside educational programs such as the New Mexico Adventures in Super Computing Challenge and Los Alamos National Labs	• motivation to choose high paying PD workshops because of low teacher's salaries in the state • a districts commitment to or disposition toward other curricular/instructional programs

educational systems. The micro, meso and macro level categorization has been used in a range of different domains to characterize complex system organization (cf. Liljenstrom & Svedin, 2005). In this study, micro level variables encompassed individual teachers and their classrooms; meso level variables encompassed multiple teachers within the school or within the *New Mexico Adventures in Modeling* project; and macro level variables encompassed multiple schools, district-wide activities and beyond.

Results

This section is organized by evidence and/or outcomes under each of the design principles that illustrate or reveal the evolving nature and success of the professional development activities undertaken in the project.

Feedback

Table 1 shows a topology of affordances and barriers to implementation constructed from the structure, function, behavior—micro, meso, macro taxonomy. The topology was used to support several program activities.

Identifying a Propensity Toward Change Hierarchy

Surveying the topology of variables allowed the project team to identify which variables were the most difficult, comparatively, within which to facilitate change. Structural variables presented the greatest challenge. For example, the location of computers within a school appeared to be a ubiquitous concern for our participants, many of whom complained about having to waste valuable teaching time tracking down the computer lab manager, reorganizing schedules to accommodate available space, and moving classes between rooms that were often located in different halls or even different buildings. These structural variables were ones that the project team had little control over. The pattern of difficulty also appeared to increase, not surprisingly, moving from micro to macro levels, e.g., from the individual to the school-wide district. Behavioral variables were the next most difficult to work with, however, many of these variables showed small increments of growth as participation in program activities increased over time. For example, teacher's risk-taking thresholds and comfort levels in working with both the desktop and handheld computer simulations improved with successive iterations of classroom implementations. Frequent availability of facilitators and willingness to provide technical, pedagogical and moral support was found to be a key change mechanism. Thus, in terms of behavioral variables, the role of some members of the project team was one of edification, a kind of support or resource that was continuously available as changes in self-efficacy beliefs, for example, emerged. However, similar to structural variables, the locus of control generally existed just outside the purview of the project team. Likewise, the level of difficulty in effecting change generally increased as the size of the system increased. Functional variables were by far the easiest ones to facilitate in terms of working toward improving implementation conditions. Apart from two variables, i.e., number of years of experience a teacher has and a teacher's experience in previous careers, the project team had some level of control over all other variables that enabled relatively immediate action. For example, teacher's indicated that they would be more inclined to use StarLogo activities in the classroom if they had ready-made curriculum materials available to them. Therefore, compiling and constructing subject-specific models and curricula became a focal aspect of our professional development workshops where previously, skill in programming and the development of complex systems theoretical understanding took the greatest priorities.

Distributing Expertise

Understanding specific implementation needs enabled us to select from the available bank of expertise and assign activities to the most appropriate project members. For example, due to his previous career experience as a manager for various web-based games and simulations projects one of our lead facilitators assumed the responsibility for the design and construction of the web-based models library. Another facilitator, with 40 years of teaching experience, had worked in various leadership capacities including district-wide technology coordinator, and had an implicit understanding of teacher self-efficacy issues in science and technology classes. She had also developed a vast and intricate educational network in which she could draw on the expertise of former colleagues and make valuable connections between people. She visited several of our struggling teachers to lend moral support and in two cases, through her network of connections, secured extra computers in classrooms that had insufficient hardware to run StarLogo models. Through her work with after school programs in the local school district, another of our lead facilitators became well connected with the various middle and high school administrators in the district. Furthermore, because her own children were attending district area schools, she knew exactly when special events were being held, when schools were closed and when teachers would be tied up with other professional commitments. All of this information was very useful in planning, for example, when our key informational open houses would be held to showcase the program to schools and administrators.

Adaptation

Adaptations made to key professional development components in the project included the categories of recruitment, partnerships & networks, administration, workshops, facilitation structure, curriculum development and communication tools. Three components are discussed in detail below that show the evolution of adaptive professional development strategies.

Workshops

Three major goals underpin the program framework: working with teachers to develop and integrate Adventures in Modeling curriculum in their specific content areas; facilitating a shift toward understanding phenomena from a complex systems perspective; and teaching computational skills to construct, manage and interpret models or simulations. Although all three serve important roles, arguably the most critical of these is the ability to use AIM curricula in the classroom. However, what we found from participant feedback was that learning the StarLogo programming language was the first barrier to entry in terms of teacher self-efficacy beliefs, comfort levels and risk-taking thresholds. For a majority of our participants who were novice programmers, this perception became a deterrent for using AIM activities with their students. Consequently, a good portion of workshop instructional time during the first year focused on helping teachers improve programming skills. Yet despite this effort, teachers continued to struggle with this dimension. Obviously some changes needed to be made. According to discussions with facilitators and long-time StarLogo users, there was underrepresented potential and value in exploring uses of existing models. It was revealed that more experienced StarLogo teachers often began with working code and simply made minor modifications to suit the purpose of the particular concept being illustrated. In order to follow this curricular route, however, teachers needed to have a solid understanding of the complex system they wanted to model. The focus of the second summer and follow-up workshops thus shifted to address the latter two of the three major goals. Not coincidentally, the percentage of teachers who incorporated StarLogo activities within the first term of the school year increased from 41% with Cohort 1 to 65% with Cohort 2.

Facilitation Structure

Initially the program began with three instructional facilitators (tier 1) who had differing levels of responsibilities, time commitments and flexibility in their workday that constrained or enabled participation in the project. The inner-city science teacher for example, could not leave his school during the day to facilitate in another teacher's classroom. After school time was also tied up with detentions and/or staff meetings focused on school improvement. The facilitator with the greatest flexibility in her schedule was the after school program coordinator. She indeed had an enormous impact helping teachers work with their students on AIM activities, however, she was only one person and there were many more teachers who could have benefited from the assistance. To address this issue, the program moved toward a more decentralized facilitation model during the second year of the project in which four Cohort 1 participants became mentors in their own schools as tier 2 facilitators. The hope was that this would alleviate some of the time constraints previously experienced by tier 1 facilitators and that small communities would emerge around a nucleus of like-minded teachers. After some time, we found that, although there was a strong desire to create local community structures, the notion of decentralized facilitation still could not overcome the day-to-day teaching issues such as difficulties in finding common times to meet across different subjects and grade teams. In the Winter '04 and Spring '05 terms, the facilitation structure became a combination model of within school decentralized facilitation accompanied by two centralized non-teaching facilitators who shared classroom visitation and facilitation duties across program schools. This structure appeared to suit the greatest number of participant needs allowing for more informal collaboration between tier 2 facilitators and the teachers in their schools and more formal classroom assistance conducted by tier 1 facilitators.

Curriculum Development

Changes made in the curriculum development component are perhaps the most illustrative of how the program continuously adapted to emergent professional development foci. Four curriculum tools were developed over the course of the two-year implementation, each reflecting participant needs at the time of development. As previously discussed, it was determined after the first summer workshop that a major barrier to program efficacy was teachers' understanding of StarLogo programming and model construction. In order to assist teachers, one tier 1 facilitator created a comprehensive modeling tutorial and provided pedagogical strategies that would help teachers use the tutorial with their own students. A models library (http://education.mit.edu/starlogo/library) became the next curriculum piece to be developed as participant needs and program foci shifted to curriculum integration. A multi-media case of exemplary StarLogo use in the classroom (http://education.mit.edu/aim-cases/index.php) was also constructed as teachers voiced their concerns about not being able to observe how AIM activities would work in real classroom settings. And finally, the curriculum binder was constructed with ready-to-use sample units parsed into subject content areas and grade levels. It was expected that participants would continue to add lessons to the binder and maintain it for their own purposes. Although the curriculum binder may seem to be a trivial addition, it represented movement toward a more autonomous, self-organized point within the professional development continuum where teachers were poised to take more ownership of their own learning. After each curriculum tool was introduced, participants showed overwhelming interest and used them to more or less degrees in their curricula.

Discussion and Educational Implications

Reiser et al. (2000) have written about the importance of attending to mutual adaptation of research goals and local contexts in order to support educational reform efforts. Fishman et al. (2004) present a list of key issues to explore when dealing with technology innovations and the capacities of the educational contexts the technologies are intended for. By highlighting the mechanisms of feedback and adaptation we have offered practical insights for professional development efforts in a number of different ways. When looking across the evidence, two meta-level themes can also be hypothesized to account for the success of the framework. Also rooted in a complex systems explanation, these themes: structure vs. agency and short-term vs. long-term goals, have promising implications for professional development and educational reform. The tension between structure and agency is an essential characteristic of real world complex systems. As Watts (2003) notes, "It is through our surrounding structure that we order and make sense of the world. Yet too much structure, too strong a hold of the past on the future, can…be a bad thing, leading to stagnation and isolation" (p. 100). Ensuring a balance between structure and agency appeared to be a critical enabling component of our professional development framework. Structure can be interpreted in at least two ways, i.e., the structure of professional development activities and the educational structure as outlined in the topology of implementation variables (Table 1). Similarly, multiple levels of agency existed in the program, i.e., individual participant personal and professional agency, facilitator/researcher agency, a collective group agency as educators in our distinct community or educators within the more global educational system. Understanding the context within which we operated through feedback—the physical barriers such as centralized computers, broader educationally imposed barriers such as NCLB and the like, then applying this information to promote adaptation, facilitated a constant development and exchange between structural (e.g., construction of curricular tools) and agency-related (self-efficacy beliefs) variables.

Lemke (2001) presents a model for understanding multi-scale complex systems that is premised on interpreting processes and activities that occur within and between different levels of organization. He suggests that how we come to understand the meaning of something is often contingent on the accumulation and transfer of information, acquired through short-term events, that may be distant from each other in space and time. Thus, we must be cognizant of the notion that change can happen over shorter and longer periods of time. He also states, "To analyze human social activity, development and learning across multiple time scales, we must be as willing to look at biography and history as at situations and moments, as methodologically and theoretically prepared to study institutions and communities as to study students and classrooms" (p. 25). In Table 1, we presented a topology of implementation variables that include biographical and historical information (e.g., previous career experiences) as well as contextual or environmental information that potentially impacts the success of the program. These implementation variables have also been analyzed to take account of the multiple levels of systems we work with. But perhaps the greatest use of the topology that we have found has been as a tool for setting short-term and long-term program goals as well as for understanding short-term and long-term participant goals. Identifying hierarchies of change and determining which variables were the most feasible to address at different times, provided the project team with a manageable structure from which to proceed toward positive project development.

Conclusions

The purpose of this paper was to demonstrate the efficacy of a professional development framework informed by two complex systems design principles of feedback and adaptation. We have shown that structuring a professional development program around these principles facilitates the development of important strategies and processes for program organizers such as the identification of salient system variables, effectively distributing expertise, and adaptation of essential professional development resources and activities. We hypothesize two meta-level themes that may account for success. Each illustrates the tension that exists between competing variables that need to be considered in order to work effectively in real world complex educational systems. We believe that knowledge gleaned from this study contributes to our understanding of how the complex systems mechanisms of feedback and adaptation can have potentially powerful impacts on scalable and sustainable professional development and educational reform.

References

Coburn, C. (2003). Rethinking scale: Moving beyond numbers to deep and lasting change. *Educational Researcher, 32*(6), 3-12.

Colella, V. & Klopfer, E. (2000). Seeding change: Bringing modeling to science teachers and their students. *The Bulletin of The Santa Fe Institute*, 15(2).

Colella, V., Klopfer, E. & Resnick, M. (2001). *Adventures in Modeling*. New York: Teachers College Press.

Cuban, L., Kirkpatrick, H. & Peck, C. (2002). High access and low use of technologies in high school classrooms: Explaining an apparent paradox. *American Educational Research Journal, 38*(4), 813-834.

Elmore, R. (1996). Getting to scale with good educational practice. *Harvard Educational Review, 66*(1), 1-26.

Fishman, B., Marx, R., Blumenfeld, P., Krajcik, J. & Soloway, E. (2004). Creating a framework for research on systemic technology innovations. *Journal of the Learning Sciences, 13*(1), 43-76.

Fullan, M. (2003). *Changes Forces: With a Vengeance*. London: RoutledgeFalmer.

Gell-Mann, M. (1994). *The Quark and the Jaguar*. New York: W. H. Freeman and Company.

Hmelo, C., Holton, D. & Kolodner, J. (2000). Designing to learn about complex systems. *Journal of the Learning Sciences, 9*(3), 247-298.

Klopfer, E. Yoon, S., Perry, J. (2005). Using palm technology in Participatory Simulations of complex systems: A new take on ubiquitous and accessible mobile computing. *Journal of Science Education and Technology, 14*(3), 285-298.

Lemke, J. (2001). The long and the short of it: Comments on multiple timescale studies of human activity. *Journal of the Learning Sciences*, 10(1&2), 17-26.

Liljenstrom, H. & Svedin, U. (2005). *Micro Meso Macro: Addressing Complex Systems Coupling*. London: World Scientific Publishing Co., Inc.

Lincoln, Y. S. & Guba, E. G. (2000). Paradigmatic controversies, contradictions, and emerging confluences. In, N. K. Densin & Y. S. Lincoln, (Eds.), *Handbook of Qualitative Research*. Thousand Oaks, CA: Sage.

Reiser, B.J., Spillane, J. P. & Steinmuller, F., Sorsa, D., Carney, K., & Kyza, E. (2000). Investigating the mutual adaptation process in teachers' design of technology-infused curricula. In B. Fishman & S. O'Conner-Divelbiss (Eds.), *Fourth International Conference of the Learning Sciences* (pp. 342-349). Mahwah, NJ: Erlbaum.

Senge, P., Cambron-McCabe, N., Lucas, T., Smith, B., Dutton, J. & Kleiner, A. (2000). *Schools that Learn*. New York: Doubleday.

Strauss, A. L. & Corbin, J. M. (1998). *Basics of Qualitative Research: Techniques and Procedures for Developing Grounded Theory* (2nd edition). Newbury Park, CA: Sage.

Acknowledgements

We would like to gratefully acknowledge Judy Perry for her assistance on the data analysis portion of this paper. This research was supported by a National Science Foundation ITEST Grant (Award # 0322573).

Comparing Instructional Methods for Teaching Technology in Education to Preservice Teachers Using Logistic Regression

Dongping Zheng, Michael Young, University of Connecticut, Neag School of Education, Department of Educational Psychology, University of Connecticut, 249 Glenbrook Road U-2064, Storrs, CT 06269
Email: dongping.zheng@uconn.edu, myoung@uconn.edu

Abstract: This analysis was completed in the context of an ongoing design project for a junior level course (Technology in Education) in the teacher preparation program in a large New England public university. We implemented a design during Fall 2003 comparing two types of instruction: problem–based learner-centered learning cycles (PBLC) and didactic direct instruction (DI), both of which reflected our previous research findings concerning best instructional practices. Analysis using Logistic Regression identified a model that differentiated the PBLC and DI approaches in areas of preservice teachers' perceived knowledge of technology integration and technology competencies, and revealed that preservice teachers who reported more favorable computer use and more knowledge of e-portfolio development were more likely to be in the PBLC approach.

Introduction

Means & Coleman (2000) have demonstrated that not only can the wise use of educational technology improve student achievement but it can also improve students' self-concept and motivation. In contrast, according to a report by the National Center for Education Statistics (Smerdon et al., 2000), only approximately 33 percent of teachers reported feeling very well prepared to integrate educational technology into classroom instruction. In 2001, the U.S. Department of Education initiated the Preparing Tomorrow's Teachers to Use Technology (PT3) program with the goal of ensuring that new teachers enter the classroom prepared to effectively use the computers that await them. However, "technology integration is complex and teachers with little classroom experience typically have no context in which to apply what they may learn in university computer courses" (Sayvenye et al., 2003).

Technology in Education, a one-credit course, required for students who enter in their junior year into the teacher preparation program of a large New England public university, was the context for an ongoing design experiment. Constraints, such as being only one-credit, and presenting to students without classroom teaching experiences, provided us a challenging context in which to realize the course goals. The course aimed to develop students' awareness of a broad range of educational technologies and to have students consider potential technology integration into their future K-12 classrooms. Our goal in this study was to identify best research-based instructional practices related specifically to developing preservice teachers' understanding and willingness to integrate educational technology into their future teaching. Not only did we seek to find out how to effectively teach preservice teachers about educational technology by using instructional design theories, but we also hoped to contribute to the field our views regarding what preservice teachers should learn to enable them to educate children in the "new literacies" for the 21st century (Collins, 1996; Leu & Kinzer, 2000; Reigeluth, 1999; Leu et al. 2004).

Theoretical Framework

The comparative course approach (Problem-based Learning Cycles vs. Didactic Instruction) was based upon application of instructional-design theories. "An instructional-design theory is a theory that offers explicit guidance on how to better help people learn and develop. The kinds of learning and development may include cognitive, emotional, social, physical and spiritual" (Reigeluth, 1999, p. 5). Reigeluth (1999) further described the characteristics of instructional-design theory as "design oriented, they describe[describing] methods of instruction and the situations in which those methods should be used, the methods can be broken into simpler component methods, and the methods are probabilistic" (p. 7). The simpler component methods are referred to as component (mini) methods by Reigeluth. They are probabilistic, rather than deterministic, which means that providing abundant examples of concepts will not ensure that the goals for the students will be attained, but will increase the probability that they will be attained. Reigeluth stated that even though the component (mini) methods are "highly interrelated and usually highly situational in their effects on attaining the desired outcomes, an instructional-design theory is easier to apply if it describes methods on a relatively detailed level" (p. 11).

Problem-Based Learning Cycles

Learning cycles were adapted as an approach to problem-based learning in teacher technology integration because they were deemed to have a broad foundation in cognitive science (Schwartz et al., 1999). One of the purposes of using learning cycles was to contextualize preservice teachers' thinking about learning and instructional design (Schwartz et al., 1999) and to move them away from implementing technology for technology's sake. Preservice teachers in their first year of education courses have only their own experiences as students to draw on and have not yet been in the role of teacher in the classroom. Learning cycles are typically organized around two or three successive challenges that present hypothetical realistic situations. The order of the components for the learning cycles is not prescriptive. It is flexibly adaptable to learners' and teachers' needs (Schwartz et al., 1999). As shown in Figure 1, Schwarz et al. (1999) proposed that learning cycles include seven components: look ahead and reflect back, the initial challenge (beginning of the first inquiry cycle), generate ideas (about issues and answers), multiple perspectives, research and revise (to help students to explore a challenge), test your mettle (formative assessment), go public (progressive deepening, general reflections and decisions), and assessment. These basic components of instruction have since been adapted to several different contexts (Bransford, Vye, Bateman, Brophy, & Roselli, 2004; Vanderbilt, 2003). The adaptation of this design for preservice teacher technology preparation is described below.

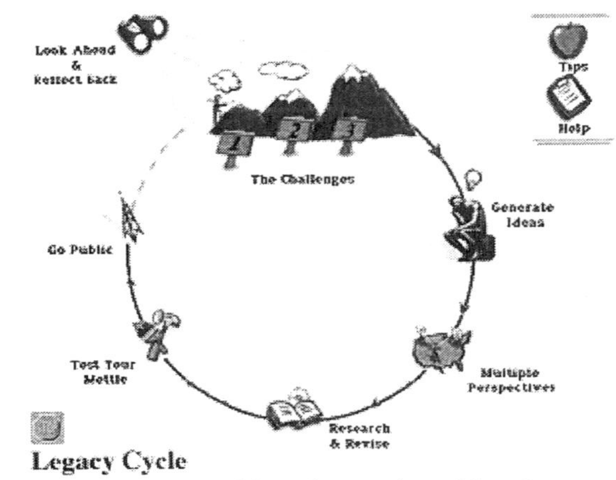

Figure 1. Main screen and learning cycles of Star Legacy

Didactic Instruction

Gagné's instructional theory has three major components: taxonomy of learning outcomes; conditions of learning (Gagné, 1977); and nine events of instruction (Gagné, Briggs, & Wagner, 1992). A central notion in Gagné's theory is that different kinds of learning outcomes (intellectual skills, cognitive strategies, verbal information, attitudes and motor skills) have different internal and external conditions that support them (Gagné et al., 1992). The external conditions are parameters that the teacher or instructional designer controls during instruction. The internal conditions are skills and capabilities that each learner brings to the instructional setting. Information-processing theory provided the basis for Gagné to propose an instruction model incorporating nine major events. Gagné et al. (1992) suggested that the Nine Events of Instruction are always relevant, even though they will vary with the type of learning outcome being achieved, and with the specific content of the learning. The nine external instructional events are gaining attention, telling learners the learning objective, stimulating recall of prior learning, presenting the stimulus, providing learning guidance, eliciting performance, providing feedback, assessing performance, enhancing retention and transfer to other contexts. This approach provided the basis for our direct instruction condition.

Research Design

Context

Technology in Education is a required course taken each Fall semester by approximately 130 juniors starting their first year of a 5-year integrated bachelors/master's teacher preparation program. The course was taught in eleven sections of approximately 12 students per section, each taught by a graduate teaching assistant or professor. A faculty professor oversaw the organization, design, implementation, and teaching of the course. Each lab section met 1.25 hours per week for 12 weeks. For our 2003 implementation, there was one faculty instructor and four TAs on staff. The faculty instructor taught 3 sessions, and each TA taught 2 sessions. In Fall 2003, participants took the course implementing one of three instructional pedagogies, varying on the course section based on normal registration (no random assignment): PBLC, DI, or Hybrid 2002 Design (HD, as a comparison condition). Each instructor was assigned to and used only one of the pedagogies except for the faculty member. Instructor assignment was self selected (see Table 1). All instructors taught in treatment conditions that they never taught before, except for the faculty instructor who taught one of the HD conditions. The pre-exposure effect in PBLC and DI conditions was thus minimized. For the simplicity of comparison and providing parsimonious interpretation, in this paper, we focus on PBLC versus DI in relation to student technology competencies and integration. In our method, each instructional pedagogy was taught by two instructors, which allowed us to somewhat gain some evidence concerning instructor versus pedagogy (i.e., whether superior student performance is due solely to the selected pedagogy and materials of one approach or due to superior instructor ability, or an interaction of the two).

Table 1. Instructor Assignment

PBLC	DI	HD
Faculty instructor and TA1 each taught 2 sessions	TA2 and TA3 each taught 2 sessions	Faculty instructor taught 1 session, TA4 taught 2 sessions

Problem-Based Learning Cycles

The PBLC format organized the course into five cycles, implemented in WebCT campus edition (a course management tool) each starting with a challenge or problem (Delisle, 1997) (see http://www.education2.uconn.edu/EPSY240/learningsciences06/PBLC.htm): 1) assistive technology used for special and regular education students; 2) the Web as a data and communication tool, including a view of "new literacies" involved in online reading comprehension; 3) technologies such as Lego robotics, online games and simulations that support problem-based and project-based learning; 4) video and multimedia technologies including digital stills and movies, cable TV and live web broadcasts; and 5) online forums for teacher professional development through e-portfolios, threaded discussions, synchronous chats, and video. The PBLC design was adapted from Schwartz et al. (1999), to our local needs (see Figure 2). This PBLC design featured five major steps: 1) Present the cycle's challenge; 2) Brainstorm and develop initial solutions; 3) Consult experts and resources that consider the problem from multiple points of view; 4) Assess the solution against objective criteria and dyad partners; and lastly, 5) Publish it to WebCT as a peer effort. By repeatedly revisiting an issue at deeper levels and from differing perspectives, it was hoped students would gain deeper and more elaborated understanding.

Preservice teachers who were in PBLC treatment sections were assigned to dyads and started each learning cycle individually with Your Challenge, Completed Initial Thoughts individually and then worked through the cycle collaboratively starting with Perspectives and Resources. The challenges were case-based, anchored in realistic but fictitious contexts (CTGV, 1990, 1992). Having students experience many narratives and approaches was intended to lead to students toward creating richer case-based experiences and better case-based reasoning (Jonassen & Hernandez-Surrano, 2002; Kolodner & Guzdial, 2000). Such activity may foster generative learning (Wittrock, 1989), elicit prior knowledge (Gagné, 1977), avoid "inert" knowledge (Whitehead, 1929), and make learners' thinking explicit when putting their thoughts in the private discussion forum (Lin & Lehman, 1999). As part of the Perspectives and Resources stage of some cycles, dyads had to explore hands-on Treasure Hunt (TH) activities, again in dyads. Each TH activity consisted of instructions that gave context, directions for operating various technology and reflection questions. This design provided naive learners with multiple representations in the spirit of designing for cognitive flexibility (Spiro, Feltovich, Jacobson, & Coulson, 1991) and allowed peers to anchor their thinking and reflection in a realistic (if not real) context, which fostered knowledge in depth, and nurtured a respect for a diversity of opinion through peer collaboration. Dyads tested their understanding of the case through reflections and had opportunity to achieve mutual understandings through social construction of knowledge (Lave & Wenger, 1991). Students then posted their later thoughts in public on WebCT and social construction of knowledge expanded from dyads to the whole class as students commented on one another's solutions to the challenge. From this we expected students in the PBLC sections would likely have deeper understanding of educational technologies and thus be aware of technology skills and applications in depth, compared to those receiving direct instruction.

Didactic Instruction

Didactic or Direct Instruction is the most well-established way to meet educational goals, especially in situations where high stakes objective tests are the sole measure of student achievement *(Stebbins et al., 1977)*. For example, see http://www.jefflindsay.com/EducData.shtml. In contrast to the "learning cycles" approach, the sections that were taught using the objectivist didactic instruction followed the idea of "teaching by telling" (see http://www.education2.uconn.edu/EPSY240/learningsciences06/DI.htm). In this mode of instruction based on the work of Siegfried Engelmann, the teacher tells the students about a specific subject and delivers whole-class recitation questioning for recall. The students' task is primarily defined as remembering exactly what the teacher taught and to reproduce that information later, usually on an objective multiple choice test. In this type of lesson plan, the focus is on recall of information, not deep understanding or transfer. The five areas of technology integration concepts used in the PBLC sections were in this approach delivered in a lecture-like format (that could include the use of PowerPoint presentations, overheads, videos, and worksheets.). These lessons included expository learning, demonstration, and drill-and-practice. This is a very efficient form of instruction and fits within the limited amount of time available in the lab, which, as a one-credit class, meets for only 75 minutes one day per week for 10 weeks. Threaded discussions on WebCT campus edition were also used for facilitating lectures in the form of teacher–centered questions and answers, as opposed to the social collaborative student-centered use of discussion in the PBLC approach. The lessons were highly organized, planned and scripted and usually contained the following components:

- Link of lesson plan to subject curriculum course of study or state standard
- Materials needed
- Interesting opening of teacher and student activities
- Instructional teacher and student activities with clear focus and visual aids
- Closing teacher and student activities that provide summary
- Clear assessment tools to measure acquisition of facts and information

In designing these lessons, we attempted to adhere to Gagne's Nine Events of Instruction. The focus on the lesson was the delivery of information in a clear straightforward manner without the benefit of hands-on explorations, higher-order questioning, and with limited need for collaboration with peers. Because didactic instruction was teacher centered and student-teacher interactions were direct and short in order to fulfill the pre-defined objectives or recitation, we expected students would likely become aware of a broader range of educational technologies and thus be aware of technology skills and applications in breadth, rather than in depth compared to the PBLC sessions.

Data Source

A Likert-type scale (from 1 strongly disagree to 5 strongly agree) pre-post online survey measured student attitudes, self-reported technology competencies, comfort with technology, and preference for collaborative learning regarding projects involving educational technology (Zheng, Young & Sulzen & 2003). One-hundred-thirty-eight participants filled out the pre-survey and 122 participants filled out the post-survey. After matching pre and post data entries and filtering based on signed informed consent forms, 101 complete data sets were analyzed, a combination of 78 in both PBLC and DI conditions.

Results

An Independent Samples T-test conducted on the pre-data revealed no mean differences between the PBLC and DI groups. Independent-samples T-tests were conducted on selected variables (see Table 2) according to the aforementioned theoretical premises to detect statistical differences across the levels of the dependent variable, Instructional Group (PBLC vs. DI). Except for the Support Learning variable, Homogeneity of Variance of other variables was confirmed. Please refer to the online survey (Zheng, Young & Sulzen & 2003) for item stems.

Table 2. Result of Independent Samples T-Test (n=78)

	T	*df*	*P*
WebTech	.667	76	.507
EPortfolio	-4.319	76	.000

Paperless	-2.003	76	.049
Computer Use	-2.998	76	.004
Support Learning	-1.998	76	.049

The goals of the analysis were to predict the Instructional Group in order to determine a model that differentiated the PBLC and DI approaches in the posttest variables, in the areas of students' perceived knowledge of technology integration and technology competencies; and to rank the relative importance of the variables. Through an examination of the correlations among variables, multicollinearity was not severe. The tolerances for all variables (range from .604 to .883) were larger than .25 and the values for VIF were less than 4. The likelihood ratio test results showed that the five-variable-model fit best, $\chi 2$ = 28.87 df= 5, at p = .000 level, G = 28.87 (D_0 = 106.628, D_{m1} = 83.815, D_{m2} = 77.762). When WebTech was added to the model, it reduced deviance to 77.762. Therefore $R^2_L = 1 - D_{m2} / D_0 = 1 - 77.762 / 106.628 = .27$, indicating 27% of true proportion of reduction in deviance. The five-variable-model better differentiated the PBLC and DI approaches, in that it helped us detect in what degree and in what areas PBLC and DI approaches had stronger impact on students' perceived knowledge of technology integration and technology competencies. Hosmer & Lemeshow goodness of fit test (C- hat = 9.951, df = 8, p = .295) showed that there was a good consistency between observed and predicted probabilities.

Table 3. Variables in the Equation

	B	S.E. (B)	Wald's	Sig.	Exp(B)/OR	95.0% C.I. for EXP(B)	
						Lower	Upper
WebTech	-1.222	.532	5.279	.022	.295	.104	.836
EPortfoio	1.463	.439	11.088	.001	4.321	1.826	10.225
Paperless	-.121	.362	.112	.738	.886	.436	1.801
Computer Use	.689	.325	4.482	.034	1.991	1.052	3.767
Support Learning	.404	.464	.759	.384	1.498	.604	3.716
Constant	-3.727	2.322	2.577	.108	.024		

Results shown in Table 3 indicate that Computer Use (*Wald's* = 4.48, p = .034), EPortfolio (*Wald's* = 11.088, p =.001), and WebTech (*Wald's* = 5.279, p =.022), were the most salient variables in distinguishing between the PBLC approach and DI in the five-variable model. Computer Use, (1.99-1)* 100=99 %, can be interpreted as one unit of increase in computer assignment increases the odds of being in the PBLC group by 99%., EPortfolio, (4.321-1)*100 =332.1% can be interpreted as one unit of increase in EPortfolio increases the odds of being in the PBLC group by 332.1%. WebTech, (.295-1) *100 = -70.5 %, can be interpreted as one unit of increase of Web technology use decreases the odds of being in the PBLC group by 71%. The WebTech variable should be interpreted with caution since Independent samples T-test showed no statistical differences between PBLC and DI groups. Adjusting for base rate, classification error was reduced by 48% (τ_p=.48) using the five-variable model. 72.5 % of the DI and 75.7% of the PBLC were correctly predicted.

Discussion

By using the current dataset measuring preservice teachers' technology competencies, professional development, comfort with technology, and preference for collaboration regarding educational technology projects, a model to predict group preservice teachers' membership in either PBLC or a DI condition was identified through logistic regression. Students' comfort with giving their students an assignment requiring extensive *Computer Use* and students' ability to create an *EPortfolio* were the most salient variables predicting group membership. Positive slope (B) of these two variables indicated that those students who rated themselves high on these two variables tend to belong to the PBLC group. The Odds Ratio (OR) was about 2.0 for the Computer Use variable, indicating preservice teachers reporting more higher comfort giving assignments with computer use were about twice as likely to be in PBLC groups. The OR was 4.3 for the EPortfolio variable, indicating preservice teachers reporting higher EPortfolio creation skills were 4.3 times more likely to be in PBLC groups. The School of Education adopted the TaskStream™ online portfolio system for supporting EPortfolio development. EPortfolios were products developed as a result of Professional Development Learning Cycles. One way to explain why students in the PBLC condition reported much more favorable portfolio creation is that Learning Cycles might progressively promote students' understanding of their development of teaching and technological skills in a realistic setting. Students put more effort into developing their EPortfolios, and thus they rated their knowledge of EPortfolios much higher. This result informed the design team's subsequent decision-making for the following year. Given both the teacher training program's and the university's efforts to EPortfolio assessment, the finding of this study helped us in making design decisions on how best to teach EPortfolio development. Computer Use was an indicator of transfer, suggesting the PBLC group was more comfortable using what they learned in the course. In the PBLC approach, students extensively used online discussion tools and problem-based prompts for guided exploration and discussion of educational technology. Using online threaded discussions in the learning cycle format afforded future teachers direct experience with the educational value of communication technology and hence, their comfort with using computers for their own teaching may have increased. Teacher effects remain a possible limitation of the study. Even though efforts were made to maximize treatment fidelity, including informal training at TA meetings, uniform lesson plans within each treatment, and class observations, latent constructs such as teacher personality and student's interactions with teachers were not subject to experimental control. As with any design research, without replication, our evidence should be considered with caution.

Educational Importance of the Study

The importance of identifying research-based instruction in teaching educational technology to preservice teachers can be evidenced at both local and national levels. The preservice teachers in this five-year highly-competitive teacher education program are educated to be leaders with the ability to envision future needs of the work force. Research has shown that wise use of technology allows people to solve problems effectively and shorten the gaps of communication among cultures (Ge & Land, 2003; Schlager, Fusco, & Schank, 2002; Uribe, Klein, & Sullivan, 2003). Although research such as *Project Followthrough* has shown (Stebbins et al., 1977) that direct instruction is the most effective approach in three areas: skills (reading, language, spelling, and math), cognitive skills, and affective behavior, the development of 21st Century literacies and transfer from courses that occur before student teaching to eventual teaching behaviors may require more. As Reigeluth (1999) stated employers now want people who will take initiatives to solve problems and who will bring diversity, especially diverse perspectives, to the workplace. Our finding that PBLC experiences may be the best instructional practice to educate preservice teachers to embrace technology in their future teaching profession is critical to young learners in the 21st century. Furthermore, the design research technique and logistic regression may also prove useful to other teacher preparation programs that have similar circumstances and constraints in terms of how to teach educational technology.

References

Barab, S. A., Eun-Ok, B., Schatz, S., Scheckler, R., Moore, J., & Job-Sluder, K. (2002). *Illuminating the braids of change in a web- supported community: A design -experiment by any other name*, from http://inkido.indiana.edu/research/onlinemanu/papers/designilf5print.pdf

Baumgartner, E., Bell, P., Brophy, S., Hoadley, C., Hsi, S., Joseph, D., et al. (2002). *The Design-Based Research: an emerging paradigm for educational inquiry*. Unpublished manuscript.

Bransford, J. D., Vye, N., Bateman, H., Brophy, S., & Roselli, R. J. (2004). Vanderbilt's AMIGO project: Knowledge of how people learn to enter cyberspace. In T. M. Duffy & J. R. Kirkley (Eds.), *Learner-centered theory and practice in distance education, cases from higher education* (pp. 209-234). Mahwah: Lawrence Erlbaum Associates.

Brown, A. L. (1992). Design experiments: Theoretical and methodological challenges in creating complex interventions in classroom settings. *The Journal of the Learning Sciences, 2*(2), 141-178.

Coiro, J., Sulzen, J., Zheng, D., & Zhang, H. (2002). *Instructional design proposal for technology in education: EPSY240.* Storrs, CT.: University of Connecticut.

Collins, A. (1992). Toward a design science of education. In E. Scanlon & T. O'Shea (Eds.), *New directions in educational technology* (pp. 15-22). New York: Springer-Verlag.

Collins, A. (1996). Design issues for learning environments. In S. Vosniadou, E. De Corte, R. Glaser & H. Mandl (Eds.), *International perspectives on the psychological foundations of technology-based learning environments* (pp. 347-361). Hillsdale: Lawrence Erlbaum Association.

Delisle, R. (1997). *How to Use Problem-Based Learning in the Classroom.* Washington, DC: Association for Supervision of Curriculum Developers.

Gagné, R. M. (1977). *The Conditions of Learning* (3th ed.). New York: Holt, Rinehart & Winston.

Gagné, R. M., Briggs, L. J., & Wagner, W. W. (1992). *Principles of Instructional Design* (4th Ed.). Fort Worth: HBJ College Publishers.
Ge, X., & Land, S. M. (2003). Scaffolding students' problem-solving processes in an ill-structured task using question prompts and peer interactions. *Educational Technology Research and Development, 51*(1), 21-38.
Lave, J., & Wenger, E. (1991). *Situated learning*. New York: Cambridge University Press.
Leu, D. J., & Kinzer, C. K. (2000). The convergence of literacy for information and communication. *Reading Research Quarterly, 35*(1), 108-127.
Leu, D. J., C. K. Kinzer, et al. (2004). Toward a theory of new literacies emerging from the internet and other information and communication technologies. In R. B. Ruddell and N. Unrau (Eds.), *Theoretical models and processes of reading* (5th ed.) (pp.1568-1611). International Reading Association.
Lin, X., & Lehman, J. D. (1999). Supporting learning variable control in a computer-based biology environment: effects of prompting college students to reflect on their own thinking. *Journal of Research in Science Teaching, 36*(7), 837-858.
Means, B., & Coleman, E. (2000). Technology supports for student participation in science investigations. In M. J. Jacobson & R. B. Kozma (Eds.), *Innovations in Science and Mathematics Education* (pp. 287-319). Mahwah: Erlbaum.
Reigeluth, C. M. (1999). What is instructional-design theory and how is it changing? In C. M. Reigeluth (Ed.), *Instructional-design theories and models: a new paradigm of instructional theory* (Vol. II, pp. 5-29). Mahwah: Lawrence Erlbaum Associates.
Robinson, L., Zheng, D., Sulzen, J., & Young, M. F. (2002). *Course syllabus for technology in education.* Retrieved February 25, 2006, from http://sp.uconn.edu/~myoung/EPSY240web/syllabus.htm.
Sayvenye, W., Brush, T., Middleton, J., Julian, M., Horn, P. J., Oksuz, C., et al. (2003). *Developing and evaluating online teacher videocases for learning technology integration.* Paper presented at the American Educational Research association, Chicago, Illinois.
Schlager, M. S., Fusco, J., & Schank, P. (2002). *Evolution of an on-line education community of practice*. Retrieved February 25, 2006, from http://www.tappedin.sri.com/info/papers.html.
Schwartz, D., Lin, X., Brophy, S., & Bransford, J. D. (1999). Toward the development of flexibly adaptive instructional designs. In C. M. Reigeluth (Ed.), *Instructional-design theories and models: a new paradigm of instructional theory* (Vol. II, pp. 183-213). Mahwah, NJ: Lawrence Erlbaum Associates.
Smerdon, B., Cronen, S., Lanahan, L., Anderson, J., Lannotti, N., & Angeles, J. (2000). *Teachers' Tools for the 21st Century: a report on teachers' use of technology*. Washington, DC: U.S. Department of Education.
Spiro, R. J., Feltovich, P. J., Jacobson, M. J., & Coulson, R. L. (1991). Cognitive flexibility, constructivism, and hypertext: Random access instruction for advanced knowledge acquisition in ill-structured domains. *Educational Technology, 5*(31), 24-33.
Stebbins, L. B., St. Pierre, R. G., Proper, E. C., Anderson, R. B., & Cerva, T. R. (1977). *Education as experimentation: A planned variation model.* Cambridge, MA: Abt Associates.
Sulzen, J., Robinson, L., Zheng, D., & Young, M. F. (2002). *The University of Connecticut's Technology in Education Course for Preservice Teachers.* Paper presented at the Northeastern Educational Research Association, Kerhonkson, NY.
Vanderbilt, T. P. G. a. (2003). Three AMIGOs: Using "anchored modular inquiry" to help prepare future teacher. *Educational Technology Research and Development, 51*(1), 105-123.
Whitehead, A. N. (1929). *The aims of education*. New York: MacMillan.
Wilson, B. G. (1995). *Situated instructional design: Blurring the distinctions between theory and practice, design and implementation, curriculum and instruction.* Paper presented at the National Convention of the Association for Educational Communications and Technology, Washington D.C.
Zheng, D., Young, M. F. & Sulzen, J. (2003). *EPSY240: Technology survey.* Retrieved February 25, 2006, from *http://www.education2.uconn.edu/EPSY240/presurvey.cfm and http://www.education2.uconn.edu/EPSY240/EPSY240_survey/postsurvey.cfm*

Acknowledgements

Thanks to Dr. Ann O'Connell for her statistics expertise and feedback. Thanks to Dr. Robert Hannafin for his support and valuable input.

Flow Blocks as a Conceptual Bridge Between Understanding the Structure and Behavior of a Complex Causal System

Oren Zuckerman, MIT Media Lab, 20 Ames Street, Cambridge, MA 02139 orenz@media.mit.edu
Tina Grotzer, Project Zero, Harvard Graduate School of Education, 124 Mount Auburn Street, Cambridge, MA 02138 Tina_Grotzer@pz.harvard.edu
Kelly Leahy, Harvard Graduate School of Education, Appian Way, Cambridge, MA 02138, kellyleahy75@gmail.com

ABSTRACT: Complexity exists in the world all around us. While it has garnered the focus of scientists in forms such as quantum mechanics and chaos theory, complexity also exists in the every day world. For instance, in order to understand the transmission of a common cold, one needs to understand probabilistic causation, branching causal patterns, and distributed agency. In this paper we argue that students need opportunities to learn the causal concepts related to complexity and we review research in support of this assertion. We introduce a set of materials called "Flow Blocks" that are designed to give children the opportunity to explore complex causal relationships and their analogical relationships to real world systems. We go on to share exploratory research that we conducted using Flow Blocks and to discuss what the finding suggest for learning about the nature of complexity.

Introduction: Learning About Complexity And Systems Concepts

Research shows that very young children hold fragile developing concepts related to forms of complex causality and yet, the science education literature repeatedly shows that students of all ages tend to make simplifying default assumptions about the nature of causality that undermine learning (Grotzer, 2003). The problematic nature of these assumptions is particularly evident in concepts that have obvious systems-thinking aspects, such as ecosystems relationships or the spread of disease, but can also be problematic for learning "everyday science concepts" (Grotzer, 2004).

Hmelo, Holton, and Kolodner (2000) introduced the Structure-Behavior-Function framework (SBF) in the context of complex systems. Borrowed from systems approaches to artificial intelligence (Goel & Chandrasekran, 1989), it draws distinctions between structures, functions, and behaviors of systems and the connections between them to illuminate types of reasoning about systems. According to Hmelo and colleagues (2000), *structure* refers to the actual physical structures of a system, such as the lungs and alveoli, *function* refers to the purpose of the system or subsystem, so the transport of oxygen throughout the body, and behavior refers to the *dynamic* mechanisms and processes that enable the structures to carry out their function. Hmelo and colleagues (2003) found that students were more likely to perceive the structural aspects of a system and to miss the behavioral or functional aspects.

Building on this earlier work, we hypothesize that particular kinds of learning scaffolds may help children bridge between the different SBF layers, specifically the structural and the behavioral layer. Our assumption is that people's tendency to focus on the structural layer is rooted in children's early learning of causal models. Children learn about causality from interaction with the physical world around them, acquiring knowledge through the senses. Since the senses perceive the physical, visible world, children naturally develop a good understanding of simple causal models, models that can explain children's interaction with the physical world. For example, playing with physical objects such as blocks or stones help children learn about direct cause-and-effect: one pushes the block, and the block moves. Andersson (1986) referred to this as the experiential gestalt of causation (EGC) and argued that students extend the primitive notion, learned in infancy, of an agent that physically affects an object to a sense of "the nearer, the greater the effect" to difficulties in learning various science concepts. Water, sand, and other natural materials help children refine these understandings. But the same interactions create an over-emphasis on direct, short-term, visible cause-and-effect relationships. The natural world is full of more complex cause-and-effect relationships, such as the water cycle and photosynthesis. But the processes underlying these causal relationships are invisible to the human senses. Therefore, people's intuitive reasoning is about the visible and the physical, rather than the invisible interacting processes.

Flow Blocks: New Type of Educational Technology

In exploring the question "How might scaffolding impact children's ability to grasp different levels within a system?" we introduced Flow Blocks, a learning technology designed at the MIT Media Lab (Zuckerman, Arida, and Resnick, 2005). Flow Blocks are a set of physical blocks, each with embedded computation, that snap together using magnetic connectors. Children connect the blocks in different arrangement, and then send a light signal through the blocks, creating a visible chain reaction of 'moving lights'. Just like LEGO® bricks, that help children experience how different arrangements can result in different physical structures (a house, car, train, or person), Flow Blocks help children experience how different arrangements can result in different causal structures (a linear chain reaction, circular chain reaction, reinforcing chain reaction, or probabilistic causation).

We reasoned that Flow Blocks might bridge children's intuitive reasoning about the structural layer to the more advanced reasoning about the behavioral layer. The design of Flow Blocks makes the behavioral layer visible (the moving lights), along with the structural layer (the physical blocks), so children can acquire new causal-models and develop a new intuition in a gradual process, at their own pace, in the same way that an infant learns about direct cause-and-effect through play with physical objects. In part, whether or not children are able to learn about systems using Flow Blocks depends upon their ability to see them analogically—as more than just a set of blocks, but as a structural and/or behavioral analogy to how systems in the world work. In order to draw an analogy, one must be able to see a relationship between whole systems of connected relations and to match them—to find structural alignment (Gentner, 1983).

Methodology

Design. In order to consider how scaffolding impacted students' ability to grasp the structural, behavioral, and analogical aspects of complex systems concepts, we conducted an exploratory study focused on children's ability to make the transition between physical or structural components of a system to behavioral or processes within a system. We did not focus on how children responded to functional aspects of a system as in the earlier research (Hmelo et al., 2003).

Participants. Fourth and fifth grade students (n = 18) from an elementary school in Cambridge, MA with an ethnically and socio-economically diverse population participated in the study. The students received no formal exposure to systems-thinking or complex causality concepts. Eight fifth graders, with even representation from each gender, and ten fourth graders, with a higher representation of girls (eight girls and two boys) comprised the interviewees. Classroom teachers selected the students for participation. Teachers were asked to select students who were average achievers from those who had returned parental permission slips.

Procedure. Each student participated in one 50-60 minute session exploring Flow Blocks with one other student of the same age and gender, and an interviewer who is a graduate student at MIT. The students were paired with another student to encourage communication between them and offer a window into their thinking with minimal researcher probing. Each session was videotaped for later analysis.

The interview technique proceeded from little researcher support (highly open-ended) to increasingly scaffolded questioning. The interview was comprised of three sections as follows. In the first part of the session, the students were given a basic introduction to the blocks. The researcher told them what each block did in a technical sense and demonstrated how to connect the blocks. The students were given a limited set of blocks to start with, and new blocks were added in parallel with the students' progress. The interviewer handed the blocks to the students and said, "Let's see what you can do with the blocks." The interviewer was careful not to use terms such as "build" that would imply one type of focus (structural, for example) over others (behavioral or functional, for example). After a few minutes, the interviewer added, "Try to explore different configurations. Let me know when you are done exploring this set and ready to move on." When students said they were ready to move on, the researcher added two more blocks. The additional blocks enabled the completion of a closed shape (see Figure 1.).

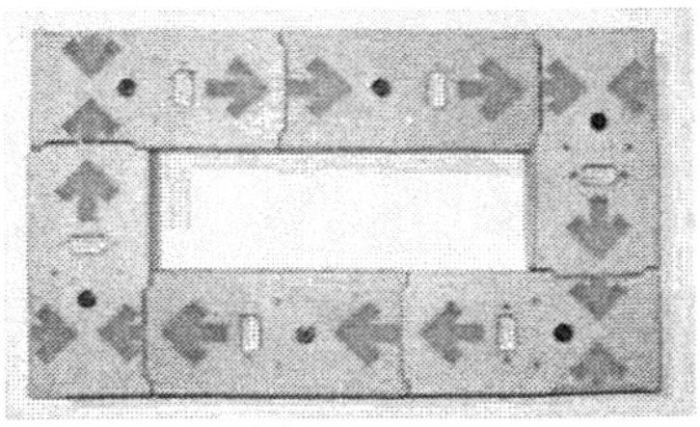

Figure 1.
"Rectangle" Loop

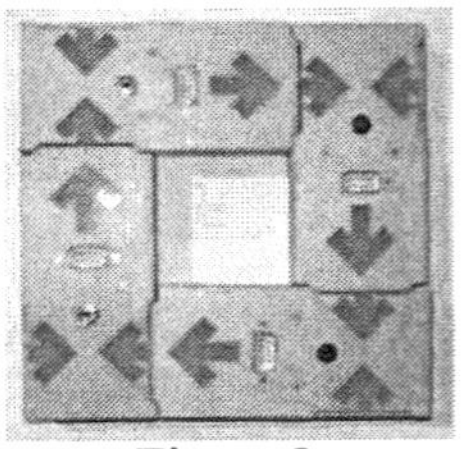

Figure 2.
"Square" Loop

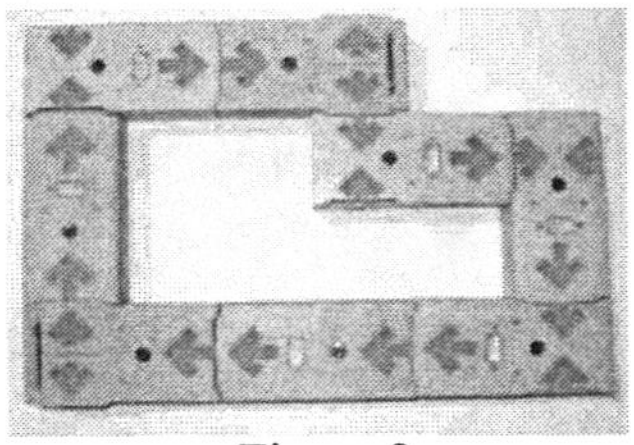

Figure 3.
"Non-Symmetric" Loop

The limitation in the blocks' design is intended to guide the students toward cyclic structures and the investigation of the behavior of circular causality. The researcher used simple, non-leading probes such as "Can you tell me about what you are doing?" or "Can you tell me about what you made?"

In the second part of the interview, the interviewer added two blue blocks, to enable the creation of more complex configuration, and said to the students, "Let's see what you can do with this set of blocks." After 10 minutes, if the students had not created the non-symmetric loop, the researcher presented a picture of one (see Figure 3), and said, "Another student made this and called it a 'circle', is this 'circle' similar or different than the previous ones you formed?" If the students only mentioned similarities, the interviewer probed for differences and vice versa.

Next, the interviewer introduced a set of analogies for the circular pattern in a given order for each set of students to see how well they could map the particular analogy. The analogies were asked in an order that started with simpler causal concepts becoming increasingly complex. For each one, the researcher asked: "Is this example similar or different to what is going on with the blocks"? The analogies were: (1) Dominoes falling over. (2) Toy train going around a track. (3) Bicycle chain. (4) Gerbil running on a wheel. (5) Water cycle. The first analogy, dominoes falling over, involves causality that is linear, sequential, and discrete. It is a type of chain reaction where there is causality local to each interaction point. The second analogy, a toy train going around a track, involves cyclic, sequential causality, where causality is local to each interaction point. The third analogy, the bicycle chain, involves cyclic simultaneous causality that is both local to the point where it is pedaled and distributed across the chain. The fourth analogy, the gerbil running on a wheel, is also cyclic simultaneous causality that is both local to the point where the gerbil is running. The final analogy, the water cycle, involves cyclic causality that is sequential in the specific example but simultaneous in a global sense, with local causality driving the pattern. We were interested in whether students would be able to map the relationship between the components of the blocks to the components of each example and what aspects of the causal relationship they picked up on.

Coding and Analysis. The videotaped sessions were transcribed, and coders worked from the transcriptions and the videotape. They were coded independently by two researchers for statements that indicated a focus on structure and on behavior of a system. The researchers coded for statements that suggested whether students were focusing on structural, behavioral, or analogical relationships and/or features of the blocks. Examples of behaviors and comments with a structural focus include:

- ...building a physical structure where the lights don't work.
- ...paying more attention to the notch in the block than the arrows.
- ...building complex loops without testing them in terms of the light.
- ...making bigger loops (but not additional loops for different behaviors).
- ..."I can use it to make the letter "T."

Examples of behaviors and comments with a behavioral focus include:

- ...talking about the behavior of the light. "It goes round and round."
- ...referring to the square shape as a circle or a loop (which emphasizes the behavior of the light over the physical geometric shape.
- ...explicit distinctions between its geometry ("it is in the shape of a square") and its behavior ("but it goes around in a circle.")
- ..."they are passing light to each other."

Examples of behaviors and comments with an analogical focus include:

- …"it is kind of like a merry-go-round."
- …"it works like a spinner board."

The researchers also noted whether students mapped the relationship between the components of the blocks to the components of each analogy example and which aspects of causality students picked up on in their comments about the analogies.

One researcher coded 100% of the protocols. A second researcher coded a randomly selected 25% of the protocols. The scoring system was refined until initial agreement of at least 85% was reached. A second round of scoring was conducted with clarifications to the scoring rules resulting in agreement of 93%. Remaining cases were discussed until there was 100% agreement.

Findings And Discussion

Most students began by forming configurations with the blocks. Their comments suggested a clear focus on the physical, structural aspects of the blocks. In the following excerpts from the interviews transcripts, the letter 'I' represents the interviewer.

K: You could build a city.
T: Yeah. With the longest….the sens….
K: A giant road.
T: San Francis… Oh man, I can't say this.
K: What?
T: San Francisco Bridge or something.
I: San Francisco?
T: Yeah, bridge.
K: Oh, the San Francisco bridge.
I: The Golden Gate.
T: Bridge.
K: Yeah, the red one?
T: And that's the way to go.

I: What are you trying to make?
K: A square.
T: It looks kinda like a snake.
I: Like a snake?
T: A sneaky snake.
I: Ok.
T: And that's the head.
I: Ok. It looks like a snake.
T: And those are the eyes and that's the nose.
I: Ok.
T: And that's the mark on it.

Interestingly, all of the student pairs did start with linear patterns. It was interesting that even though one team of girls wanted to make a circle right away, the physical creation of it was tricky for them.

As the students gained more 'play time' with the Flow Blocks, more students started to differentiate between the physical configuration and the behavior of the blocks. There was clear evidence that the students distinguish between the physical structure of the blocks and the patterns of the light. They were quite articulate about the difference between geometrical shapes and patterns of behavior. Some of the students also show a clear focus on the relationship between pattern and behavior. There were great terms here for distinguishing pattern from physical structure ("repeatedly", "circulating" "self-contained").

I: Ok. And what do you think about this shape? What would you call this one?
C: Um, a square.

I: A square?
A: A circle.
I: Circle?
C: Square or circle.
A: Well, for this it would be like a circle because…
C: Yeah, um, geometrically it's like a square.
A: A square.
C: But if, like, we're using circuits and stuff you would refer to it as a circle.
A: It depends on what kind of shape, because this is, like, a rectangle, and you couldn't make a circle out of it, so it would be a circle sort of.
I: So what's circle about it? Is it like, geometrically it's a square, right?
C: Yeah.
I: So, but circle is still a good name for it?
C: Yeah, well if you're only, if you're able to talk about, like, um, how you, I don't know how to explain it exactly. Say you wanna talk about how you're using, um, like, circuits and batteries, you would, um….I, like… Ok, so this would be, you would say it's a circle if you're only talking about using a circuit or a battery or something, but… if you're, like, if you want, if you wanna talk about, like, geometrically what shape it is you would say it was a square.
I: Ok. So if you talk about the circuit it's a circle and if you talk about the geometrical shape it's a square?
C: Yeah.
I: What do you think A?
A: I think it would be a circle, sort of, because you can't really make a circle out of this shape. Geometry, like… it would be considered a square.
I: Um hmm.
A: But it's really it would be sorta like a circle, for this matter.
I: For this matter it's a circle?
A: Yeah.
I: Why?
A: Because it travels like that. And so, like, a circle kind of pattern.
I: Pattern? What do you mean when you say pattern?
A: Well, I mean, like, if you draw a circle it would sorta seem like you were drawing this.

K: I'm trying to make it go, make it so it can go around in a circle either way, but I could just change this completely.
S: […inaudible…]
I: Go around in a circle, you said?
K: Yeah.
S: Yeah, go around in a circle either way.
I: What do you mean, circle?
S: Well, a square actually, I think.
K: Yeah. Well, like, so it keeps going on and on and on.
S: Like we had before, but she wants it to go on so if it's…so if it goes this way it'll go around. It won't go around okay?
K: Yeah.
S: But if it goes this way it'll go around.
I: You know that when I play with people with this, some kids say circle and some kids say square. What do you think it is?
K: Well, the shape is a square or a rectangle.
S: Yeah but technically it's going around in a circle.
K: But like, a circle you think it, like, keeps going around and around forever.
S: Yeah, so…
I: So what word do you think is better to use, or what is the difference between using them?
S: Well, a square has corners and is actually going around
K: The actual shape is this.
I: Um hmm.
K: Is a square, but, um, the concept of what you wanna do is different.

S: Than what it actually is.
I: So the circle is more of the concept?
K: Yeah.
I: Like if the rectangle is a shape, so what is a circle?
S: A circle is a shape, but it's going around in a pattern that much like a circle.

Some of the students had already studied a unit on electrical circuits. Those students had a hard time seeing beyond that and were most likely to focus on the underlying mechanism of what made the blocks light, than on the actual behavior of the lights themselves. This mechanistic approach seemed to make it hard for students to use the blocks as an analogy to new situations and likewise transfer information from the blocks.

Once students began to focus on the behavior of the lights, they seldom reverted back to discussing physical structure except in contrast with behavior or in discussing the mechanics of sticking the blocks together. The point of transition for most students was the point at which they constructed a loop and the pattern in the blocks departed from a domino causality to a cyclic sequential pattern. It took students a varying amount of time to get to this point, with some of the teams making a number of configurations (all flat on the table) as with building blocks before switching to a focus on the behavioral aspects of the blocks. But once students made this switch, they pretty quickly started to explore various possibilities for creating loops.

Interestingly, there was little spontaneous generation of analogy, but students were able to analyze the analogies given with some success by noting aspects of the underlying causal forms, and were able to generate analogies when prompted. For instance, the following examples reveal some ability to map the components of the domino and cyclic relationships:

K: And, um, the light is, um… the light is like the, the… well the arrow is like the thing that hits it and the light makes it fall cause the next one…
M: Like the arrow is the domino and the light is the domino that started it.
K: That's hitting it.
M: So it keeps going. So it's like they're pushing the other one down so that if it's like in a line, if you push that one down… um, it will hit that one. So that's kind of like what the light is doing. Except it's the same thing.

--
K: So it's like the train is going on the track.
M: And the green one is probably the, uh, the tracks that curve.
K: ….the light is the train that goes round and round on the tracks.
M: And the blocks are the tracks.
K: There's no end for it…. It would just keep on going round and round cause this is there and there's arrows there.

It is possible that students focused first on observing the behavioral aspects of the blocks and would only begin to make spontaneous analogies later given sufficient time to explore the behavioral aspects. An interesting extension to this study would be to give the blocks to students to play with for extended periods of time and videotape their actions to see if they move through different phases in how they play with them (beyond what was noted here with the move from physical structure to behavioral aspects). With the educational scaffolding built into the block design, the students were able to move beyond the structural level and focus on behavioral aspects of the causality within the system. This is promising given earlier research that suggests that students have difficulty moving beyond the structural features of a system. For example, using an aquarium as an ecosystem, Hmelo-Silver, Pfeffer, and Malhotra (2003) found that children and novices assumed that the role of plants in an aquarium is decorative only, that the plants are there to please the viewer--exemplifying how novices focus on the physical, visible parts of a system, or the structural level. People with greater expertise in the subject matter (such as teachers, aquarium enthusiastic, or academic experts) were able to separate between the structure and behavior levels, reasoning about the role of the plant in the aquarium and its interaction with other components.

An important extension of this work would be to consider whether the blocks could be used as scaffolds for deeper understanding of systems such as an aquarium or other ecosystems studied in school. So while the design of the blocks did help students notice behavioral aspects of the blocks themselves, the broader question of their ability to function analogically remains to be explored in greater depth and with more complex analogies and subject matter.

References

Andersson, B. (1986). The experiential gestalt of causation: A common core to pupils' preconceptions in science. *European Journal of Science Education, 8*(2), 155-171.

Gentner, D. (1983). Structure-mapping: A theoretical framework for analogy. *Cognitive Science 7*, 155 – 170.

Goel, A. & Chandrasekran, B. (1989). Functional representation of designs and redesign problem-solving. In Proceedings of the Eleventh International Joint Conference on Artificial Intelligence (pp. 1388-1394). Los Altos, CA Morgan Kaufmann.

Grotzer, T.A. (2003). Learning to understand the forms of causality implicit in scientific explanations. *Studies in Science Education, 39,* 1-74.

Grotzer, T.A. (2004). Putting science within reach: Addressing patterns of thinking that limit science learning. Principal Leadership, October, 2004.

Hmelo, C.E., Holton, D.L., Kolodner, J.L. (2000). Designing to learn about complex systems. The Journal of the Learning Sciences 9(3) 247-298.

Hmelo-Silver, C.E., Pfeffer, M.G., & Malhotra, B.A. (2003, April). *Fish swim and rocks sit: Understanding structures, behaviors, and functions in a complex system.* Paper presented at the American Educational Research Association Annual Meeting, Chicago, IL.

Zuckerman, O., Arida, S., & Resnick, M. (2005). Extending tangible interfaces for education: Digital Montessori–inspired initiatives. In the proceedings of CHI 2005, Portland, Oregon.

Posters

Showing Evidence; Analysis of students' arguments in a range of settings

Issam Abi-El-Mona, Barbara Hug, University of Illinois, Champaign, IL
Email: abielmon@uiuc.edu; bhug@uiuc.edu

Abstract: The purpose of this study is to investigate evidence-based arguments generated through the use of a web based tool, *Showing Evidence.* Six of 40 sample classrooms during 2004-2005 were purposefully sampled from the tool's database. Analysis focused on identifying the physical and argumentation schematic structures of possible evidence based explanations using Toulmin (1958) and Walton (1996) frameworks. Findings demonstrate student's ability to depict proper data for claims yet inability in structuring overall explanations.

Introduction

Recent reforms in science education are encouraging the practice of constructing *evidence based* explanations in science classrooms through scientific inquiry (National Research Council, 1996; Kuhn & Reiser, 2005). These explanations form the basis of arguments student construct to show their understanding of science concepts. The practice of argumentation is an essential feature in education.

Statement of the Problem

Students have difficulty in creating logical and reasoned arguments. These difficulties are compounded by the fact that the meaning of explanations are largely determined by the socio-interactive discourse that occurs within various contexts (e.g. Anderson, Chinn, Chang Waggoner & Yi, 1997). Many types of explanations generated from various levels of cognitive reasoning exist (Nagel, 1961). These issues have led the drive towards developing methodical tools for supporting both teachers and students as they engage in argumentation skills (Osborne, Erduran & Simon, 2004). One example is the Intel designed *Showing Evidence* software. In creating an explanation, students collect evidence, evaluate the evidence, and then make visible the connections between the evidence and the scientific concepts being investigated. This then needs to be communicated to the community (Kuhn & Reiser, 2005; NRC, 1996). These features are supported in the *Showing Evidence* tool. The goal of this study is to investigate how students used the supports present in the tool to construct evidence based explanations. Specifically, it is the feature of using evidence in argumentation that this study investigates. This study identifies both argumentation and explanation as both a process and product that students and teachers engage in during instruction (Kuhn & Reiser, 2005). Argumentation often includes the use of individual explanations generated by students to provide support to the larger issue. Argumentation is not only a reasoned causal account of how or why something occurred but also the use of evidence within a social context. Argumentation in the context of this study is seen as both a social and cognitive process. Argumentation is viewed as a scientific based activity whereby valid arguments and explanations are those that clearly demonstrate the relationship between evidence and claims and thus are designated as evidence based arguments. The research questions are: What types of explanations or arguments are generated across different grade levels? How are these explanations or arguments different or similar?

Method

Six of 40 sample classrooms during 2004-2005 were purposefully sampled from the database by selecting for science-based issues. Of the samples, random samples of 10 artifacts were taken per class. All targeted science based debate topics with subject matter ranging from health sciences, physics, biotechnology, genetics, geology and mathematics. Data included students' written claim to a given question, written evidence, explanation and conclusion. Analysis involved identifying features and forms of existing arguments. Analysis was based on a rubric adapted from Toulmin (1958) and Walton (1996).

Findings

Initial findings demonstrated students were able to develop multiple explanations but not all explanations were linked to a fully developed argument. In looking at the components of the explanations, a number of interesting findings suggest the tool is helping students develop explanations but additional support might be needed. We have seen: (1) In all samples evidence relies largely on authoritarian sources (e.g. science text, internet based science topics, science professional journals). However there is a distinction between upper and lower grade levels as to what represents an authoritarian source. For example, the majority (27.4%) of high school samples used data sources taken from science professional journals whereas the majority of middle and elementary levels depended on public news media (41%). (2) Supporting evidence for explanations included redundancy for most samples (i.e. groups tended to use the same sources) but this was exceptionally higher in middle and elementary levels (10%); In addition, high school students supporting evidence emphasized specific scientifically topic relevant data (60%) whereas middle and elementary emphasized individual beliefs/ interpretations of data (70%). (3) For all samples, evidence represents scientifically grounded facts yet explanations rarely show clear connections between the evidence presented and claim noted. Student groups tended to list highly relevant data and yet they do not seem to be able to: (a) relate data sources to each other and (b) use them to relate to the claim(s). (4) Structures of explanations are largely in the form of claims for all samples with predominance demonstrated in middle and elementary levels (30% high school; 86.4% middle and elementary levels). Rarely found were complete arguments where claims, warrants and data were clearly connected. Justifications, when present, rely heavily on repeating supporting evidence and rarely consider counter claims to their original claims. Middle and elementary school samples (1.4%) demonstrate the proper choice of counterclaims yet no clear justification as to HOW they are used to strengthen the overall explanation is given. (5) Argumentation schemes were largely arguments from example (81%) for high school levels. This means high school levels rationalize explanations of data used by providing examples related to previous scientific content learned. Middle and elementary levels largely use arguments from sign (46%). Such samples used a general observed event from personal experience.

Implications

Implications on improving the tool are suggested: providing options for uploading other sources of data, inserting additional dialogue boxes promoting users to construct a sentence that demonstrates HOW data relate to claim, providing tests credibility of chosen data, prompts challenging explanation validity, and changing explanation prompts to scaffold students in writing specific- topic content related (in this case science evidence based) explanations.

References

Anderson, R., Chinn, C., Chang, J., Waggoner, M. & Yi, H. (1997). On the logical integrity of children's arguments. *Cognition and Instruction, 15*(2), 135-167.

Kuhn, L. & Resier, B. (2005, April). *Students constructing and defending evidence based scientific explanations.* Paper presented at the annual meeting of the National Association for Research in Science Teaching, Dallas, TX.

Nagel, E. (1961). *The structure of science.* London: Routledge and Kegan Paul.

National Research Council (1996*). National science education standards*. Washington, DC: National Research Council.

Osborne, J., Erduran, S., & Simon, S. (2004). Enhancing the quality of argumentation in school science. *Journal of Research in Science Teaching, 41*(10), 994-1020.

Toulmin, S. (1958). *The uses of argument*. Cambridge, UK: Cambridge University Press.

Walton, D. (1996). *Argumentation schemes for presumptive reasoning.* Mahwah, NJ: Lawrence Erlbaum and Associates.

'Hybrid Modeling': Advanced Scientific Investigations Linking Computer Models and Real-World Sensing (an interactive poster)

Paulo Blikstein and Uri Wilensky, Center for Connected Learning and Computer-Based Modeling
School of Education and Social Policy, Northwestern University - 2120 Campus Drive, Evanston, IL – 60208
Email: paulo@northwestern.edu, uri@northwestern.edu

Abstract: 'Hybrid modeling' is an innovative technological platform that enables students to link multi-agent models ("in" the computer) and electronic sensors ("outside") in real time. The platform is designed for learners to validate, refine, and debug their computer models using real-world data. Also, the technology broadens the types of scientific explorations possible in classrooms. Pilot studies suggest a real-to-virtual reciprocity that catalyzes further inquiry toward deeper understanding.

What do we obtain from "going out to the world" as a learning resource? Multiple aspects of such learning experiences have been explored by different schools of thought in education. John Dewey (1916) was one of the first to emphasize the importance of connecting school learning and real-world experiences. Critical pedagogy and situated-learning advocates argue that departing from the learner's out-of-school context is crucial to foster emancipating and motivating learning (Freire, 1974; Lave & Wenger, 1991). Constructionist educators (Papert, 1991) posit that building personally-meaningful public artifacts is central to promote sustainable and deep learner engagement. However, does the world afford the necessary information and opportunities for students to learn the 'official' school content? For instance, are acid-base reactions amenable for student inquiry? School laboratories, as we explain, do not always provide the necessary solutions.

While concurring with claims about the relevance of the learner's context, background, and concrete experiences for education design, we acknowledge that the current tools for scientific exploration available for students limit the domains and complexity of their real-world investigations. Thus, we submit that the disconnect between what one could potentially learn in a situated environment and the more traditional school content may be due to the lack of appropriate tools to 'dissect' reality to the appropriate level of analysis. Even if, by definition, Physics, Chemistry, and Biology are 'out-there' in the world, most phenomena are invisible to human vision and time scale. Many patterns in nature are too long, too fast, too small, or too large for learners to extract and understand the underlying structures. Canonical examples are weather behavior, chemical reactions, housing and traffic patterns, particle physics, and population ecology. Conventional school laboratories are not well equipped to support students in developing hypothesis about the information they gather. For example, a student studying a chemical reaction might discern the components and even hypothesize as to the relations between these components; however, the investigation cannot go much further. Needed are tools that provide continuity between observation and model-building, furnishing the 'missing link' between data-gathering and the construction of theories using computational representations. That is, to make the study of these phenomena accessible to all students, we need new technological tools that foreground and unveil the deep structures. This poster will focus on *'hybrid modeling,'* a framework for 'trans-media' scientific exploration and modeling which merges two types of educational technologies commonly used (separately) in schools. The first kind is robotics and sensing (Martin, 2000; Resnick, 2000) that uses computer-controlled electronic sensors and actuators to enable a wide range of experimental activities in the real world. The second technology is multi-agent modeling-and-simulation environments, such as NetLogo (Wilensky, 1999), where learners model complex natural phenomena by embedding very simple behaviors into elementary computational agents (Wilensky & Resnick, 1995). We have linked the two technologies – the "real" and the "virtual" so as both to broaden the possibilities of *situated investigations* and ground computer modeling with real-world validation.

Typically, students build a *computer model* of a particular scientific phenomenon, such as heat transfer (see Figure 1) or gas laws (see Figure 2), and a *physical device* equipped with electronic sensors. The models are then linked in real time through a low-cost, easily programmable analog-to-digital interface - the *GoGo Board* (Sipitakiat, Blikstein, & Cavallo, 2004). Students are able to run their computer model in tandem with the physical apparatus, comparing their outcomes, and debugging their model until it matches adequately the real-world data. We built various proof-of-concept systems for 'hybrid' explorations in heat transfer, gas laws, acid-based and oscillating reactions, and Materials Science. Our main goal, however, is to create a technological infrastructure to enable students to build their own systems.

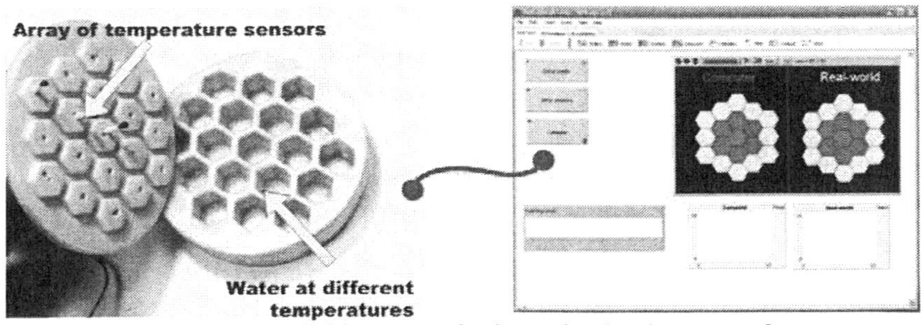

Figure 1. A 'hybrid' system for investigating heat transfer.

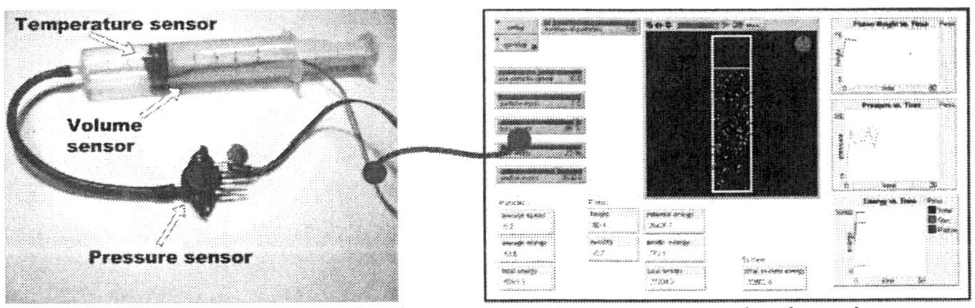

Figure 2. A 'hybrid' system for investigating pressure, temperature, and volume in a gas container.

In a pilot study, we compared artifacts generated by undergraduate and graduate students under two distinct conditions. In the first condition, students created multi-agent models *with no* sensors or robotics. In the second situation, another group of students built 'hybrid' models *with* sensors. All students built their models as an assignment in an 'Educational Design' course. Our data include students' artifacts, field notes and transcriptions of interviews. Preliminary results suggest that students attended to phenomenal factors which they would otherwise have overlooked, such as energy loss, reversibility, and measuring error. In turn, students "complexified" their computer models so as to include these factors. This interactive poster will exhibit the platform in action, present student artifacts, and summarize our findings and conclusions.

References

Dewey, J. (1916). *Democracy and Education: And Introduction to the Philosophy of Education*. New York: Macmillan.

Freire, P. (1974). *Pedagogy of the oppressed*. New York,: Seabury Press.

Lave, J., & Wenger, E. (1991). *Situated Learning: Legitimate peripheral participation*. Cambridge, England: Cambridge University Press.

Martin, F., Mikhak, B., Resnick, M., Silverman, B., Berg, R. (2000). To Mindstorms and Beyond: Evolution of a construction kit for magical machines. In A. Druin (Ed.), *Robots for Kids: Exploring New Technologies for Learning Experiences*. San Francisco: Morgan Kaufman / Academic Press.

Papert, S. (1991). Situating Constructionism. In S. Papert & I. Harel (Eds.), *Constructionism*. Cambridge, MA: MIT Press.

Resnick, M., Berg, R., Eisenberg, M. (2000). Beyond black boxes: Bringing transparency and aesthetics back to scientific investigation. *Journal of the Learning Sciences, 9*(1), 7-30.

Sipitakiat, A., Blikstein, P., & Cavallo, D. P. (2004). *GoGo Board: Augmenting Programmable Bricks for Economically Challenged Audiences*. Paper presented at the International Conference of the Learning Sciences, Los Angeles, USA.

Wilensky, U. (1999). NetLogo. Evanston, IL: Center for Connected Learning and Computer-Based Modeling. http://ccl.northwestern.edu/netlogo.

Wilensky, U., & Resnick, M. (1995). New Thinking for New Sciences: Constructionist Approaches for Exploring Complexity. *Presented at the annual conference of the American Educational Research Association.*

College Students' Understandings of Pressurized Air Movement: Do Isomorphic Questions Elicit Isomorphic Answers?

Jason L. G. Braasch & Susan R. Goldman
Center for the Study of Learning, Instruction, and Teacher Development
University of Illinois at Chicago, 1007 West Harrison Street, Chicago, IL 60607
Email: jbraasch@uic.edu, sgoldman@uic.edu

Abstract: College undergraduates' explanations of pressurized air movement for two everyday situations were examined. Responses were categorized into one of five categories on two isomorphic, everyday events (tire pressure, balloons). The two items elicited similar kinds of explanations in the group as a whole, and in individual students. However, the majority of responses were at the least sophisticated levels of explanation. Consistently held simple models may be particularly resistant to instruction aimed at moving thinking forward.

Introduction and Rationale

Students' difficulties understanding pressurized air movement often stem from their use of intuitive understandings of the world (Basca & Grotzer, 2001). These may be adequate for day-to-day events but may be "at odds" with the accepted scientific conceptions (Hunt & Minstrell, 1994). For example, children intuit pressurized air movement as unidirectional and linear, a conception that often impedes instruction designed to convey the more scientifically accurate relational causality (Engel Clough & Driver, 1985). The degree to which intuitive understandings of pressurized air movement are susceptible to instruction may depend on the coherence and completeness of the intuitive models. That is, if individuals provide different explanations for air movement in different everyday situations (e.g., a deflating balloon and a deflating tire), it may be that the underlying model is weak or that there are multiple models. If, on the other hand, individuals are consistent in the way they explain air movement across different everyday situations, the underlying model may be more firmly established, coherent, and thus more resistant to instruction attempting to change the model. To date, there is limited empirical information that speaks to the coherence of individuals' understanding(s) of pressurized air flow across different everyday situations. This poster reports the kinds of explanations undergraduates provide for two everyday pressurized air movement situations and describes the scientific characteristics and consistency of the explanations across the two situations.

Methodology

College students (n= 99) were given an open-ended inventory consisting of 10 prompts designed to elicit student conceptions of everyday events. Three concepts (pressurized air movement, condensation, and evaporation) had 2 isomorphic items each; the pressure-related items were: *When you press a gauge on a tire why does air come out?* and *When you untie or poke a hole in a balloon, why does air come out?* Four filler questions were also included. The coding system was a modified version of Basca & Grotzer's (2001) five-category system. Changes reflected fewer intermediate level responses and more complex levels as compared to 8th – grade category. The five categories shown in Table 1 were used to score the undergraduates' responses. Inter-rater reliability for 20% of the data was 92.5%.

Table 1. Coding Categories, Example Responses, and Percentage of Students per Category for each Item

Coding Category	Examples of Responses	Tire	Balloon
1. Simple causal mechanisms	The opening is there and the air just bounces out.	51	55
2. Air pressure as an entity	Air comes out because pressure is pushing it out.	21	21
3. Vague reference to pressure and/or pressure differences	Air comes out because there is higher pressure inside the tire/balloon.	12	7
4. Explicit reference to pressure differential	There is a difference in pressure causing air to move from the inside to the outside of the tire/balloon.	4	5
5. Explicit reference to pressure differential and pressure equalization as an end state.	The difference between the high pressure inside and lower pressure outside causes air to flow out. Air stops when the pressures on the inside and outside are equal.	12	12

Results and Discussion

The first analysis concerns the range of responses provided by the undergraduates across the two situations. As Table 1 suggests, the two situations (tire and balloon) elicited similar kinds of explanations when considering the distributions of responses for the group as a whole. The majority of explanations were simple causal mechanisms for each of the situations. Only 12% of the students provided the most sophisticated explanation involving pressure differential and equalization. The similarity in responding was confirmed by a significant Spearman rank-order correlation, ($r_s = .97$, $p < .001$). To examine if individual students responded consistently to the two situations, we looked at whether responses were categorized in the same or in different coding categories. College students' responses were significantly more likely to be coded in the same category (Matchers = 72%) across the two situations than in different categories (Mismatchers = 27%), $Z = 4.12$, $p < .001$. The majority of categorical matches (almost 60%) involved simple causal mechanisms (see table 2). Only 15% of the matchers responded with the full relational model. Among those who gave responses in different categories, the most inconsistencies were found in the less sophisticated categories.

Table 2. Percentile/Number of Individuals Categorized as Matchers or Mismatchers by Coding Categories

Coding Category	Matchers (n = 72)		Mismatchers (n = 27)	
	%[a]	# of Ind.	%[b]	# of Ind.
1. Simple causal mechanisms	58	42	30	8
2. Air pressure as an entity	16	12	33	9
3. Vague reference to pressure and/or pressure differences	7	5	26	7
4. Explicit reference to pressure differential	3	2	7	2
5. Explicit reference to pressure differential + equalization	15	11	4	1

[a] Percentages in this column are computed with a base of 72 matchers.
[b] Percentages in this column are computed on a base of 27 mismatchers.

The results indicate that, overall, undergraduates are more consistent than inconsistent in their explanations of everyday situations that manifest the same underlying concept. Moreover, it is encouraging that individuals who responded with good conceptual understanding (level 5) tended to do so for both situations. On the other hand, and somewhat troubling, is the finding that the majority of responding – consistent and inconsistent - was at the less sophisticated levels of understanding. And at those levels, the overwhelming majority were consistent in their responses across the two situations. From an instructional viewpoint, it may be difficult to move these individuals to more sophisticated understandings because their consistency suggests that they hold a coherent, simple model. Events that appear to scientists to represent discrepancies may be assimilated to the same simple causal model instead of stimulating an examination of the model. Turning to those who were inconsistent, the results indicate that they also tended to provide less sophisticated explanations. However, inconsistency may be a positive sign because it suggests instability in the underlying representation of the concept, perhaps making these individuals more open to examining their understanding of pressurized air movement. Finally, an important instructional implication of these results is to remind us that the "same" instructional strategy may lead to quite different results depending on the conceptions that students hold prior to instruction. The research reported here points to an important dimension of prior knowledge analyses: Not only is the model students hold important but the consistency with which is it applied to everyday situations is also important, especially for the design of learning experiences.

References

Basca, B. & Grotzer, T.A. (2001). Focusing on the Nature of Causality in a Unit on Pressure: How does it Affect Student Understanding? Paper presented at the annual meeting of the American Educational Research Association. Seattle, WA. April 10-14, 2001.

Engel Clough, & Driver, R. (1985). What do children understand about pressure in fluids? *Research in Science and Technological Education*, *3*(2), 133-144.

Hunt, E. and Minstrell, J. (1994). A collaborative classroom for teaching conceptual physics. In K. McGilly (Ed.), *Classroom lessons: Integrating cognitive theory and classroom practice*(pp. 51-74). Cambridge: MIT Press.

Metalanguage among Families in a Marine Science Museum

Carol B. Brandt, Doris Ash
University of California Santa Cruz, Department of Education
1156 High Street, Santa Cruz, CA 95060
Email: carolb@ucsc.edu, dash5@ucsc.edu

Abstract: Metalanguage, talking about talk or talk about text, is a heightened awareness of language, and how language functions in a socio-cultural setting. Using video and audio data from 20 Spanish-speaking families in a marine science center in north-central California, we describe our system for identifying metalanguage in dialogue as families visit the science museum. Our goal is to understand ways in which metalinguistic practice contributes to meaning making around biological concepts.

Introduction

In our research with bilingual families in science museums, we are interested in how parents and children move from everyday language and appropriate scientific language. As these family members talk about talk, or talk about text, they are engaged in metalanguage (Coupland & Jaworski, 2004). O'Connor and Michaels (1996) have also referred to this practice as "revoicing" and a strategy to establish mutual understanding in dialogue. We describe our system for identifying metalanguage in bilingual dialogue, the coding scheme that we applied to our data, and look at how metalinguistic practice contributes to, or detracts from, meaning-making about biological concepts. Our research questions are: What metalinguistic features can we identify in dialogue among families as they use a marine science museum? How do exhibit texts appear in metalanguage? And similarly, are dialogues about science taken up metalinguistically?

Research Methods

Our analysis is centered on a large, naturalistic data set of 20 Spanish-speaking families in a marine science center in north-central California. Each visit consists of at least two children and one parent, plus a bilingual mediator who translates English signage and answers questions. We rely on a socio-cultural theoretical framework rooted in dialogue and in activity (Engestrom, 198l; Wells, 1999). Meaning is built over time by successive dialogic episodes that can be discontinuous in time (Ash, 2004). Using video data, observation, interviews, stimulated recall methods (Gass and Mackey, 2000). Our research follows families as they make sense of science dialogically.

Examples of our coding scheme

Our identification of metalanguage follows a systemic-functional approach (Halliday & Hassan, 1985). We coded dialogue by indicating: the person who was the Speaker, the person who was the Respondent, the type of Metalanguage (see below), Gestural References (e.g. pointing), and the Object of the metalinguistic reference (text or dialogue). Types of Metalanguage include (metalinguistic markers in italics):

A. Claiming authority (A1), transferring authority to another speaker (A2), or hedging (A3)
Son: (Flipping through photographs and referring to sea lions) Look, come, let's see, look, here are the other types, look. I thought, I didn't think that they had hair, then *my mom says* that they do have hair. Look, there it is, there are others, look at the other types of seals there are. (B Family visit 1, line 1422)

B. Intertextuality – bringing other sources of information into the conversation
Son: The whale like.... *I have read in a book that* when it goes to sleep it goes up to the edge of the sea.... (indicating with his hand hear the surface of the water). (B Family stimulated recall, line 500)

C. Clarifying information – rephrasing or repeating what another person has said
Bilingual Mediator: *So, when you said that*, that it had...that it looked like a shark but it could be that it has the shape of a shark....
Dad: Ah, hah, it has, it has.... because it's not, it's not, it's not the same. To me this one is.... not, not, I don't know how, how, how to explain to you, but to me it's not a fish. (B Family visit 2, lines 324-328)

D. Conversation continuity – usually involves repeating the other speakers words
Daughter: [Speaking about whales] I don't know. I just like that sound they make.
Mediator: Oh, *you like the sound they make.* Okay. Okay.
Oh, *you like the sound they make.* Okay. Okay. [Turns to Mother] What did you think, Senora, when your daughter was talking to you about ----- Did it surprise you that she knew so much [about whales]? (J Family visit 1 stimulated recall, lines 48-50)

Results: The Qualities of Metadiscourse

Preliminary observations from our research show that even with the translation by a bilingual mediator and their English-speaking children, families rarely re-voice or reference exhibit text. Metadiscourse is most often shared between the mediator and parents recount their museum visit in the stimulated recall session, and less metalanguage occurs between parents and children, or among all participants on the science museum floor. In these results we compare the occurrence of metalanguage relative to the dialogue across the entire visit at the museum.

Conclusions and Significance

Our study is one of the first times metalanguage has been applied to naturalistic studies of dialogue in science museums. Metalanguage is valuable for understanding how authority is constructed among speakers and is one way that parents tentatively incorporate more "scientific" terms into their lexicon. In our research we found that by rephrasing or using "clarifying" phrases through metalanguage, helps to negotiate the meaning of science content. The opportunity to practice using science terms and concepts has metalinguistic features, especially as one adopts new terminology and the set of values that are attached to science. In museums docents can use metalinguistic skills to more effectively scaffold learning for diverse audiences.

References

Ash, D. (2004). Reflective scientific sense-making dialogue in two languages: The science in the dialogue and the dialogue in the science. *Science Education, 88,* 855-884.

Coupland, N., & Jaworski, A. (2004). Sociological perspectives on metalanguage: Reflexivity, evaluation, and ideology. In Jaworski, A., Coupland, N., & Galasinski, D. (Eds.), *Metalanguage: Social and ideological perspectives*, pp. 15-51. Berlin: Mouton de Gruyter.

Engeström, Y. (1999). Activity theory and individual and social transformation. In, Y. Engestrom, R. Miettinen, & R. Punamaki (Eds.), pp. 19-38. *Perspectives on activity theory.* Cambridge, UK: Cambridge University Press.

Gass, S. M., & Mackay, A. (2000). *Stimulated recall methodology in second language research*. Mahway, NJ: Lawrence Erlbaum.

Halliday, M.A.K., & Hasan, R. (1985). *Language, context, and text: aspects of language in a social-semiotic perspective.* Oxford: Oxford University Press.

O'Connor, M., & Michaels, S. (1996). Shifting participant frameworks: Orchestrating thinking practices in group discussions. In D. Hicks (Ed.), *Discourse, learning, and schooling* (pp. 63-103). New York, NY: Cambridge University Press.

Wells, G. (1999). *Dialogic inquiry: Towards a sociocultural practice and theory of education*. New York: Cambridge University Press.

East Austin Stories Exchange: Facilitating 'Empathy' for Differing Perspectives

Damien Brockmann, MA, Todd C. Reimer, PhD, University of Texas, Austin, TX
missirabah@yahoo.com, t-reimer@mail.utexas.edu

Abstract: The East Austin Stories Exchange is a web-based platform where junior high and high school students can share personal films about their community and empathize with the perspectives presented in other students' films. The goal of the project is to foster students' ability to incorporate perspectives different than one's own into a developing worldview. This poster presentation will present our needs assessment, design solutions, and demonstrate the *Exchange*'s functionality.

Introduction

The *East Austin Stories Exchange* is a design experiment that aims to use a web-based community to facilitate the development of 'empathy' in junior high and high school students for perspectives and worldviews different than their own. The *Exchange* is an extension of *East Austin Stories*, a 3-year old project in the Radio, Television & Film Department at the University of Texas that enables students to learn about their community through the production of personal documentaries, specifically focusing on the stories of people and places in East Austin.

Needs Assessment

The purpose of the *East Austin Stories* project is to prompt students to explore their community by uncovering stories, cultural perspectives, and personal histories. While participating in the production of a film may lead to a deeper understanding of the film's subject matter, the project team's experience over the past three years indicates it is insufficient to help students gain empathy for perspectives presented in other students' work.

Empathy is the imaginative intellectual and emotional participation in another's experience. An individual must extend beyond their personal view, and be able to experience other perspectives as if it were his or her own (Bennett, 1998). The affective nature of film affords it the potential to invoke a sense of 'sympathy' in a viewing audience, by prompting them to imagine what it is like to be someone else. However, these emotions are frequently disconnected from cross-cultural contexts. East Austin is a diverse community of Latino, African American and immigrant families; while socio-economically diverse, the community consists of many middle to lower income households. Currently there is no mechanism in the East Austin Stories project to enable students to make the necessary connections between the films they produce and the diverse perspectives they represent. These connections are essential in order to foster a greater sense of empathy for the various perspectives presented.

There are several obstacles to experiencing empathy that we seek to address in this project. Students are often unaware of their own cultural bias or perspective and often make the mistake of believing that everyone shares a common perspective. Additionally, empathy is a complex phenomenon of intellectual and emotional awareness that often requires a certain quality of serendipity and randomness (Duane and Hill, 1996). The existing design of East Austin Stories currently lacks any consideration for these obstacles. In addition, the current design lacks a wider social context where those tacit assumptions can be discussed, challenged, and explicated (Wells, 2000).

Design Solution

The *East Austin Stories Exchange* extends the objective of the current project by providing a web-based platform where students can incorporate their work into the context of the multiple perspectives presented through the work of other students. Prior to exploring connections between student films, a teacher facilitates a discussion of the different perspectives presented in the documentaries in order to help students acknowledge that each film, including their own, presents a unique, independent, and subjective worldview. Once the students are grounded in this concept, they can utilize the *Exchange* to explore the films of others.

Our design solution is to create a complimentary website to the existing course allowing students to index scenes within their films by theme and cross-reference them with other films that deal with similar topics. They are encouraged to explore the films serendipitously, using the hyperlinked tags to jump from scene to scene in different movies (which are related by their connected themes). The indexed buttons embedded in the videos allow students to view the videos out of chronological sequence, in a manner that allows their imaginations to wander freely through the content of the videos. It is hoped that this vicarious experience will lead students to extend their boundaries between themselves and the external world (Eisenberg and Strayer 1987), and students will experience the video segments as if they were an internal construct of their own minds (Bennett, 1998).

Through this method of exploration and discovery, students are able to uncover themes and connections among the movies that may not have been apparent otherwise. Students are encouraged to use their explorations to engage topics of interest, research them and submit these themes into the *Exchange* website for discussion. The resulting social interaction prompts students to acknowledge bits of information and viewpoints other than their own, and frequently leads to a cognitive conflict that triggers disequilibrium and drives intellectual development (von Glaserfeld, 1987).

Conclusion & Next Steps

Upon completing the production of the *Exchange*, we would like to expand the use of the project to teachers in other subject areas— particularly in Language Arts and Social Sciences. We will be conducting user-tests of The *East Austin Stories Exchange* to provide our overall design with formative feedback, as well as indications for future design work and research.

References

Bennett, M. (1998). Overcoming the Golden Rule: Sympathy and Empathy. *Basic Concepts of Intercultural Communication*, M.J. Bennett, ed., 191-214.

Duan, C. & Hill (1996). The Current State of Empathy Research. *Journal of Counseling Psychology*, 43(3), 261-274.

Eisenberg, N. and Strayer, J. 1(987). Critical issues in the study of empathy. *Empathy and its Development*, N. Eisenberg & J. Strayer, eds., 3-16.

von Glaserfeld, E. (1987). Learning as a constructive activity. In *Problems of representation in teaching and learning math* (pp. 3-17). Hillsdale, NJ.

Wells, G. (2000). Dialogic inquiry in education: Building on the legacy of Vygotsky. In C. D. Lee & P. Smagorinsky (Eds.), *Vygotskian perspectives on literacy research: Constructing meaning through collaborative inquiry* (pp. 19-30). Cambridge, UK: Cambridge University Press.

Winn, W. (2003). Everyday Cognition and Situated Learning. *Handbook of Research for Educational Communications and Technology*, David Jonassaen, ed., 79- 112.

The Effects of Base Ratio and Conceptual Structure on Accuracy in Multiplicative Situations

Reality S. Canty & Susan R. Goldman
Institute for Mathematics and Science Education
Center for the Study of Learning, Instruction, and Teacher Development
University of Illinois at Chicago, 1007 West Harrison Street, Chicago, IL 60607
Email: rcanty1@uic.edu, sgoldman@uic.edu

Abstract: We examined the effects of base ratio and conceptual structure on accuracy in multiplicative situations. Forty-eight 3rd and 5th graders solved 36 problems that varied in base ratio and conceptual structure. ANOVA results indicated that conceptual structure made a greater impact on accuracy than did the size of the base ratio. The effect of structural constraint on accuracy supports the call for deeper conceptual instruction and learning in mathematics education.

Introduction

Research on children's arithmetic understanding has concentrated on addition, rather than multiplication. Three common constructs of the investigations in both additive and multiplicative research are strategy (Sherin & Fuson, 2005), problem size, and problem structure (Vergnaud, 1983). Historically, these constructs have been studied independently of one another. This paper reports on one part of a larger effort to build a more integrated understanding of relationships among strategy, problem size, problem structure, and tool use. We examine the link between the effects of base ratio and conceptual structure on 3rd and 5th graders' accuracy in multiplicative situations.

Method

Third-grade (n=24) and fifth-grade (n=24) public school students in a large urban district were individually asked six sets of six questions. Accuracy (accurate/inaccurate) was measured as a function of grade, base ratio, and conceptual structure. Base ratio was systematically varied across the six sets, with each set using different ratios, specifically, 1:6, 1:5, 1:4, 1:2, 1:3, and 1:9. The six questions in each set tapped four conceptual structures based on Vergnaud's (1983) theory of conceptual fields (see Figure 1). The first three questions were consistent with structure *a* but varied in number magnitude (i.e., 5, 8/9, and 10). The other three questions mapped on to structures *b*, *c*, and *d*, respectively. The six questions were presented in a fixed order hypothesized to reflect increasing question difficulty.

M_1	M_2		M_3	M_2		M_1	M_2	M_3		M_1	M_2
1	a		1	a		c	a	1		1	a
n	?		n	?		?	b	n		?	n
(a)			(b)			(c)				(d)	

Figure 1. Conceptual structures for the six question types in the structured interview.

For each set, students first answered three simple proportion problems (Q1-Q3) followed by another simple proportion problem in which the dimensions changed (Q4), which in turn was succeeded by a concatenation of two simple proportions problem (esp., quotitive division). The structural variance of these five questions, coupled with the invariant question order lead to the following predicted order of accuracy:

$$Q1 \approx Q2 \approx Q3 > Q4 > Q5 \qquad (1)$$

Because Q1 and Q3 had number magnitudes of 5 and 10, we wanted to evaluate the relationship between these two questions. Additionally, a sixth question, Q6, was asked to examine the children's use of pragmatic knowledge to solve simple quotitive division problems that involved a remainder.

Results

Grade x Base Ratio

Figure 2a illustrates mean accuracy as a function of grade and base ratio. Employing a 2 (grade) x 6 (base ratio) mixed model ANOVA, with grade (3, 5) as the between-groups variable and base ratio (1:6, 1:5, 1:4, 1:2, 1:3, 1:9) as the within-groups variable, we found main effects for grade (F (1, 46) = 4.46, p = .04, η_p^2 = .09) and base ratio (F (5, 230) = 2.50, p = .03, η_p^2 = .05) on accuracy. The interaction was not significant. *Post hoc* comparisons of base ratio means using the Fisher-Hayter procedure indicated that despite a main effect for ratio, no significant difference was detected between the largest (1:6; $M = 4.25$, $SD = 1.64$) and (1:9; $M = 3.73$, $SD = 1.85$) smallest group means.

Grade x Question

Mean accuracy as a function of grade and question is presented in Figure 2b. A 2 (grade) x 6 (structure) mixed design ANOVA was performed on accuracy with grade (3, 5) as the between-groups factor and conceptual structure of the questions (Q1, Q2, Q3, Q4, Q5, Q6) as the within-groups factor. Not surprisingly, the analysis showed a main effect for grade ($F\ (1, 46) = 4.37, p = .04, \eta_p^2 = .09$) and also question ($F\ (5, 230) = 61.66, p < .001, \eta_p^2 = .57$) and no grade x question interaction.

Figure 2b shows that simple proportion questions (Q1-Q3) were about equal in accuracy, Q4 was more difficult, and Q5 and Q6, the two quotitive division questions, were least accurate. A planned comparison using customized contrast coefficients aligned with the prediction in Equation 1 showed general trend agreement, $F_{fit}\ (4, 184) = 100.90, p < .001, \eta_p^2 = 25$. This finding was validated by a confirmatory test of model-to-data fit, ($F_{failure}\ (1, 138) = 1.50$, *ns*), indicating that nothing other than structure contributed to the differences in the means. An additional planned comparison revealed a significant mean difference between Q1 ($M = 5.50$, $SD = 1.09$) and Q3 ($M = 4.96$, $SD = 1.66$) on accuracy, $F\ (1, 46) = 8.78, p < .01, \eta_p^2 = .16$. The results show that the conceptual structure of the question tempered solution accuracy: Those involving quotitive division (Q5 & Q6) were more difficult than simple proportion questions (Q1-Q3). Simple proportion problems were more difficult when the dimensions changed (Q4).

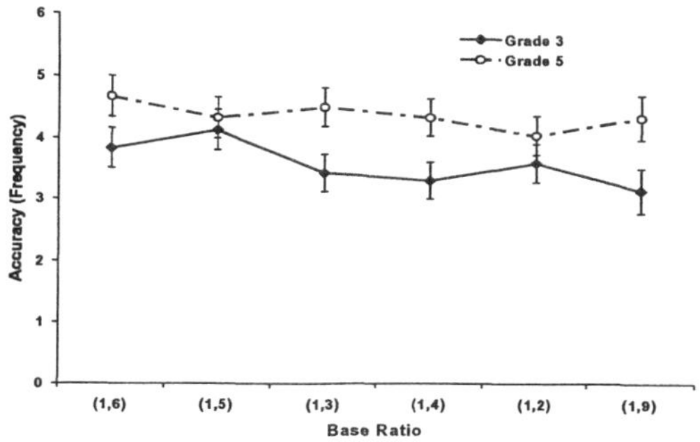

(a)

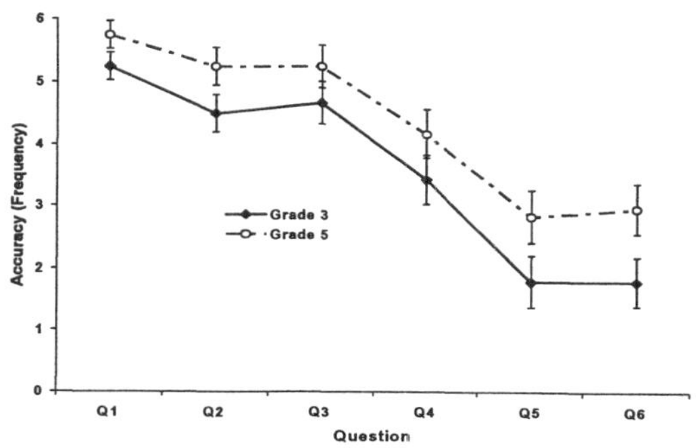

(b)

Figure 2. Accuracy as a function of base ratio (a) and question (b).

Discussion

This study's findings support NCTM's (2000) recommendation for deeper conceptual learning and instruction of mathematics concepts. Our data do not support the notion that small problems are solved more accurately than large problems. Actually, our results showing no differences due to base ratio suggest that the dimensional and relational structure of multiplicative concepts impose greater constraints on response accuracy than problem size does for 3rd and 5th grade students. This is substantiated by differences in the effect sizes of the tested models and the finding that difference in mean accuracy between Q1 and Q3 were not large enough to invalidate the test of the model to the data even though that difference was a function of number magnitude (i.e., 5 vs. 10). Finally, the accuracy means of the division questions were nearly identical, [Q5 ($M = 2.31$, $SD = 2.10$) and Q6 ($M = 2.38$, $SD = 2.04$)]. This finding counters the idea that division-with-remainder is more difficult than simple division. Future research will evaluate the relation between conceptual structure and students' strategies, reasoning, students' tool (graph, table) use in learning, and teachers' use of tools in ininstruction.

References

National Council of Teachers of Mathematics. (2000). Principles and standards for school mathematics. Reston, VA: NCTM.

Sherin, B., & Fuson, K. (2005). Multiplication strategies and the appropriation of computational resources. *Journal Journal for Research in Mathematics Education*, 36, 347 – 395.

Vergnaud, G. (1983). Multiplicative structures. In R. Lesh & M. Landau (Eds.), *Acquisition of mathematics concepts and processes,* pp. 127 – 174. New York: Academic Press.

Facilitating Inquiry using Technology and Teams in Exercise Physiology: The FITT Project

Darla M. Castelli, Ellen M. Evans, & Mark M. Misic
University of Illinois at Urbana-Champaign

Abstract: The link between physical inactivity and disease has become a major public health priority. The aim of this project was to reform Exercise Physiology laboratory instruction through curriculum mapping and the implementation of inquiry-based modules. Use of a quasi-experimental design, content knowledge, interviews, modules, and a questionnaire provided evidence of student performance. There was a significant knowledge difference between groups and increased comfort with the majority of course content resulting from inquiry-based versus traditional instruction.

The FITT Project:

In the last decade, due to the link with many lifestyle related diseases, physical inactivity has become a major public health priority. On a national level, a growing number of professional organizations are promoting physical activity for all ages (NASPE, 2004; USDHHS, 2000). Many Kinesiology majors will be asked to apply their knowledge in pragmatic settings targeting special populations (e.g., children, older adults, etc.) and yet the undergraduate curriculum remains traditional in its structure and enactment. Additionally, barriers such as lack of impact of traditional instruction on student learning (Rio, Collins, & DiCarlo, 2002) and a deficiency of teacher assistant pedagogical knowledge (DePauw, 2003), often plague exercise physiology courses. The pedagogical method of inquiry combined with the use of on-line modules promotes critical thinking, facilitates learning through an increased depth of knowledge, and integrates content beyond the classroom in authentic contexts.

Purpose

The purpose of this project was to reform core undergraduate Exercise Physiology laboratory courses through curriculum mapping and the implementation of inquiry-based teaching strategies. During the first year, using instructor and student feedback data, the instructors and researchers realigned course content through curriculum mapping strategies. Key concepts across the curriculum were chunked and progressively sequenced. Also created were six online learning modules containing probing questions, brief quizzes on reading materials, additional resources on the lab topic, description of specific laboratory procedures, video of lab procedures, and data analysis strategies. The modules were completed prior to a lab session in order to hold students accountable for creating their own hypotheses regarding the experimental outcomes and to facilitate discussion of the probing questions during the lab experience. Following group discussion, the participants took on the specific responsibilities related to the experiment. This differed from traditional lab instruction where no outside class time was used in preparation for lab sessions and data collection, and resulting discussions were teacher centered.

Method

After obtaining informed consent, 189 students (males = 91) in 6 lab sections, were randomly categorized as traditional instruction or FITT project inquiry-based instruction based on laboratory section. Different intact laboratory sections of the exercise physiology course were utilized, but all participants received the same course lectures. Within their laboratory sections, the participants completed a pre and post content knowledge test (maximal score = 100 pts) and questionnaire to identify their level of comfort with course content and specific lab techniques (e.g., taking blood pressure, administering graded exercise testing). The quasi-experimental design allowed the researchers to capture the complexity of the interactions through focus group interviews, field notes, and images (e.g., digital video and still) during the laboratory instruction. Quantitative data were analyzed using a 2 x 2 ANOVA (time x lab group), while constant comparison (Lincoln & Guba, 1985) and inductive reasoning were used to reduce and analyze the qualitative data. Codes and frequency counts of student responses were used to develop patterns and themes.

Results

At baseline, there was no significant difference between groups in content knowledge ($M_{traditional} = 48.14 \pm 13.78$, $M_{inquiry} = 50.56 \pm 12.64$; $p = .65$). Both the traditional and inquiry-based learning groups increased their content knowledge; however, the inquiry group had a greater change in content knowledge score than the traditional group (65.90 ± 10.97 vs. 54.43 ± 14.87; $p < .01$). Comfort with lab techniques increased, however, questionnaire data revealed no significant difference between groups regarding comfort with laboratory techniques ($p = .36$). Analysis of the qualitative data resulted in the identification of three themes: (a) authentic engagement, (b) teacher assistant capacity, and (c) accessibility issues. Many participants were more comfortable with the laboratories because they had completed the initial steps of the module prior to the scheduled lab session. The field notes and videotapes revealed an important difference between groups in lesson enactment. Student engagement was more evident in the inquiry-based lessons, as traditional lessons contained an average of 30 minutes of teacher-led explanation. During inquiry lessons, this time was utilized more effectively by developing hypotheses and discussing related findings in the literature. The second theme, teacher assistant capacity, suggests that the level of implementation of these techniques was dependent upon the teacher assistant as well as the make up of the lab group. Though the teacher assistants were provided the same materials and training, some embraced their new role as facilitator while others just "tried" the strategies. The final theme was accessibility issues. Despite the best efforts of the researchers and instructors to provide equal opportunity for all participants to access the on-line modules, there was some frustration related to the modules. Participants using antiquated technology struggled to retrieve the modules from their homes, thus university resources served as their only access point.

Conclusions

Findings suggest that this initial attempt at transforming the Exercise Physiology laboratory learning experiences has been effective. Students in the inquiry-based learning group spent more time engaged with the content and interpreting their results compared to the traditional group that spent more time learning how to use the equipment. It has been recommended that the modules be expanded to include simulations, a scientific database that contains data from classic experiments across the lifespan (not just the college-age students who conduct the experiment on a peer), and a culminating project as an outgrowth of module completion. Despite positive signs of inquiry-based learning effectiveness, progress has been hampered by technological glitches, specifically with regard to streaming video over the Internet.

References

DePauw, K.P. (2003). Changing faculty roles and responsibilities: Expanding the skill set of faculty perspective- from a graduate dean. *Quest, 55*(1), 18-25.

Lincoln, Y., & Guba, E. (1985). *Naturalistic Inquiry*. Beverly Hills: Sage Publications.

Rao, S.P., Collins, H.L., DiCarlo, S.E. (2002). Collaborative testing enhances student learning. *Advances in Physiology Education*, *26*(1), 37-41.

National Association for Sport and Physical Education [NASPE]. (2004). *Physical Activity for Children: A Statement of Guidelines for Children Ages 5-12.* (2nd ed.). Reston, VA: NASPE Publications.

U.S. Department of Health and Human Services [USDHHS]. (2000). *Healthy people 2010: Understanding and improving health.* Washington: USDHHS. Retrieved from http://www.healthypeople.gov/Document/tableofcontents.htm#under on May 5, 2003.

Active Citizenship through Technology: Collaboration, Connection, and Civic Participation

Clement Chau, Ashima Mathur, Marina Bers
Tufts University, 105 College Ave., Medford, MA 02155
Email: clement.chau@tufts.edu, ashima.mathur@tufts.edu, marina.bers@tufts.edu

Abstract: This poster presents results from a workshop, Active Citizenship through Technology, with eighteen college freshmen. Participants collaboratively designed a virtual college campus by researching information online, interviewing faculty and administrators, using graphics programs, and designing a campus with our software Zora. Zora, an Identity Construction Environment, was purposefully created to encourage participants to explore issues of identity, decision-making, and personal values. Results showed that participants engaged in meaningful deliberation about issues related to college life.

Introduction

Different types of online tools have been incorporated in education settings of all levels to promote collaboration and meta-cognitive thinking. As Koschmann (1996) has described, new educational technologies created in the CSCL paradigm have been successful in bridging instruction and participation, knowledge and enacted practices, and process and outcome. Thus, it seems that educational technologies, especially CSCL-orientated computer softwares, have been beneficial additions to the classroom curriculum. However, there is a growing concern, especially in educational policies, for the increasing lack of classroom and civic participation in today's youth, possibly because of the greater immersion into the world of computer-mediated communication (CMC) technologies.

The purpose of this study is to investigate and demonstrate the extent to which a well designed curriculum and CSCL technology, namely Zora, could indeed encourage collaborative learning and promote civic discussion and participation. Reported in this poster is a description and results of a workshop (titled Active Citizenship through Technology) conducted on incoming first-year students at a university. The university has reported a growing concern for a lack of campus engagement among the undergraduate population, thus warranting the need for innovative and meaningful ways to develop a civically active student body.

The Zora Identity Construction Environment

Zora was developed and piloted by Bers (2001) as a type of virtual Identity Construction Environment (ICE). Based on Papert's (1980) *constructionism*, the concept of ICE asserts that open-ended virtual constructionist environments afford youth the space for testing, experimenting, and developing their decisions and personal values. Zora, which gives users a blank world at the start along with specifically designed graphical tools, allows its users to build a virtual city out of interactive objects and personal biographies. As a goal, Zora sets a stage for youth to interact and develop their sense of civic identity, moral, and attitudes, and thus leading to meaningful decision-making and contributive actions. Furthermore, the city metaphor in Zora encourages youth to work collaboratively, thus requiring them to deliberate and make community decisions. As shown by recent research (Dahlberg, 2001; Papacharissi, 2002), civic deliberation is one of the most important ways through which networked computer technologies can be used to encourage and develop civic identities and engagement.

Workshop: Active Citizenship through Technologies

Given the concern for civic engagement among college students, a three-day workshop was created to examine the utility of Zora as an innovative means to promote engagement in school activities and social connections among students. Eighteen entering first year students volunteered to participate in this workshop. The primary goal of the workshop was to develop an interactive curriculum with Zora that could promote collaboration and encourage students to think about campus issues that could positively and negatively influence their college lives. We hoped that by thinking and deliberating about issues related to college life, students would learn to see the impact of these concerns and would begin to realize how they could contribute to their new college environment.

Methods and Data Collection

Workshop activities were designed to accommodate the overarching learning objective. First, students learned how to manipulate the functions in the Zora environment to create their virtual campus. This required participants to research other campus' resources and designs, to learn to use graphic design programs, to find resources via the Internet, to interview faculty and administrators, and to implement their own designs using various computation tools on Zora. Participants were encouraged to rely on each other for help instead of asking trained peer leaders for direct answers. Then, students were encouraged to design their own campus collaboratively, thus requiring them to deliberate among themselves the pros and cons of various campus designs, and to discuss how different designs might reflect different values that were cherished by their ideal campus. The design of the campus extended beyond architectural design to encompass the rules, laws, rituals, and decisions about campus life.

The Zora environment readily provided a log of all online activities that happened throughout the workshop. Log files from the workshop were read and coded by the coordinator/teacher of the workshop and by an outside evaluator, who took no part in the actual teaching and activities of the Zora workshop, for cross-validation.

Results

By the end of the workshop, participants were able to create a successful virtual model of a university campus. After many discussion and deliberations, every member agreed upon the final model. Results showed that participants were also able to immerse themselves in deliberations to discuss civic values as related to their campus. For example, admission policy was an important topic to the participants. As can be seen in this brief excerpt from the logs, participants deliberated and came to a decision for their virtual school policy on admission.

A: Anyone have strong feelings about the admission process?
B: I think that peer review will be a better way at processing people. Maybe on a sub-personal level
C: To what degree?
D: What do you mean by peer review?
A: Would peer review take the place of an essay?
B: Like interviews
E: More like having admitted students read applications and give their feedback; the common applications with a supplemental essay

Conclusion

This study demonstrated that an open-ended virtual environment developed under the ICE model could indeed be useful in encouraging peer collaboration and civic deliberation. Simply by engaging in the curriculum and building a virtual campus in the Zora program, participants were thinking about campus life, their role as students, and factors to be wary of as they began their college careers. ICE environments such as Zora have the potential to impact youth's civic life. Given the right tool and right curriculum, teachers and practitioners can turn the computer, once a solitarily tool, to a computer-supported collaborative learning environment that promotes collaboration, civic deliberation, and civic mindedness.

Reference

Bers, M. (2001). Identity construction environments: Developing personal and moral values through the design of a virtual city. *The Journal of the Learning Sciences, 10*(4), 365-415.

Dahlberg, L. (2001). Computer-mediated communication and the public sphere: A critical analysis. *Journal of Computer-Mediated Communication, 7*(1).

Koschmann, T. (1996). Paradigm shifts and instructional technology: An introduction. In T. Koschmann (Ed.), *CSCL: Theory and practice of an emerging paradigm* (pp. 1-24). NJ: Lawrence Erlbaum.

Papacharissi, Z. (2002). The virtual sphere: The Internet as a public sphere. *New Media and Society, 4*(1), 9-27.

Papert, S. (1980). *Mindstorm: Children, Computers and Powerful Ideas.* New York: Basic Books.

Positive Technological Development: A systems approach to understanding youth development and educational technology

Clement Chau, Marina Bers
Tufts University, 105 College Ave., Medford, MA 02155
Email: clement.chau@tufts.edu, marina.bers@tufts.edu

Abstract: Youth development is multifaceted. While educational researchers have paid attention to one or few of these foci, it is imperative to understand how our technologies influence the various facets of youth development. We developed the *Positive Technological Development* research model to detail the overall impact of a technology on youth. We present a study describing how the *PTD* model illustrates the impact of an educational technology, while illuminating design areas that need to be revised.

Introduction

It is well acknowledged that computer technologies can be used to support youth's cognitive, social, and personal developmental concerns. For example, researchers have shown the potential of Lego Logo programming in facilitating young children's development of problem solving, hypothesis testing, and abstract thinking skills (Rogers & Portsmore, 2004). Other researchers have demonstrated successful use of computer technologies in promoting youth's confidence, motivation, and sense of efficacy (Dede & Ketelhut, 2003), in bringing together entertainment and learning to promote motivation and interests (Barab, Thomas, Dodge, Carteaux, & Tuzun, 2005), and in encouraging collaboration and meta-cognitive thinking (Bers, New, & Boudreau, 2004). Taken together, these and many other research studies have shown that computer technologies can function as more than just a cognitive manipulative; computer technologies have the potential to affect many facets of youth's development.

Although the field of research in the learning sciences acknowledges the multifaceted nature of learning with technologies, policy makers and practitioners often fail to see these connections. We suggest that this may be partly because research reports in the field of technologies and learning sciences have largely been one-dimensional; that is, individually, researchers have focused on just one of the many youth developmental concerns.

Positive Technological Development

Guided by a research model from applied development sciences termed *Positive Youth Development* (Lerner et al., 2005), which is a systems approach to youth development, we developed the *Positive Technological Development* theoretical model that details the multi-faceted nature of youth development and educational technologies. The *Positive Technological Development* model looks at six variables that have been deemed important development concerns in the youth development literature (Scales et al., 2000). These six variables are Competence, Confidence, Connection, Caring, Character, and Contribution. Given the growing concern for bridging the gap between learning, educational technologies, and youth development, it is imperative that researchers who hope to promote positive development in children and adolescents pay attention to these developmental concerns (see Figure 1).

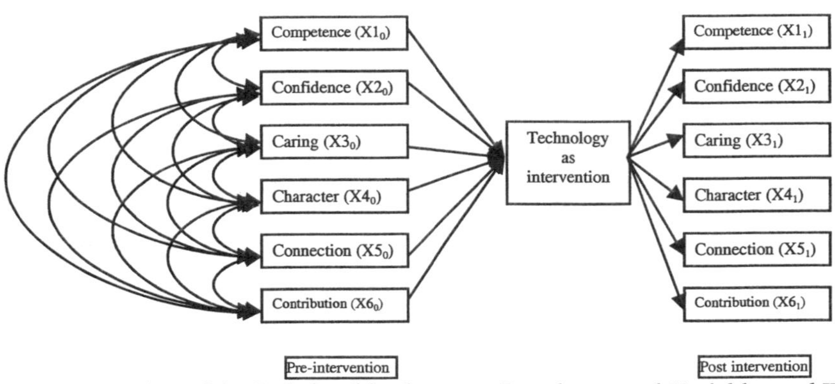

Figure 1. An Illustration of the Relationships between Developmental Variables and Technology.

In order to understand these developmental variables in the context of technology and learning, we have also developed the *Positive Technological Development Questionnaire*, which assesses these six variables in detail. This poster presents our *Positive Technological Development* model and describes a research study as a case study that exemplifies how this model and this questionnaire apply to research in the context of technology and learning sciences.

Case study: Lego robotics workshop

Thirty-seven children in the first and second grades participated in this research study with their parents. The workshop was designed to teach participants basic Lego robotics building and programming skills using the RoboLab© software. Both parent and child participants received instructions on Lego robots building and programming. Each parent-child pair worked on their own project throughout the workshop. Children participants completed the *Positive Technological Development* questionnaire before and after the workshop. Differences in scores related to the six variables were interpreted as changes due to the workshop. Table 1 summarizes the results of the questionnaire with t-tests for significance.

Table 1. Differences in scores in *PTD*'s six C variables before and after the workshop.

Developmental Variable	Difference (std. dev)	*t*	Developmental Variable	Difference (std. dev)	*t*
Competence	1.19 (.69)	10.38**	Connection	-0.35 (1.00)	-2.11*
Confidence	0.43 (.42)	5.01**	Caring	0.11 (1.14)	.58
Character	0.05 (1.64)	.19	Contribution	-0.19 (0.81)	-1.42

Note. *$p < .05$. **$p < .01$.

As table 1 illustrates, participants indeed increased their perceptions of competence and confidence in technological abilities. However, connection, which indexed participants' perception of the extent to which technology influenced their social connections with peers, decreased after the workshop. This could be because participants worked in pairs with their parents and the workshop curriculum did not encourage children to work with other peers. The *PTD* analysis model successfully demonstrated that, although the goal to teach participants skills in working with Lego robotics was reached, the workshop might have resulted in participants feeling less connected to peers when using the technology. Thus, the curriculum may need to be revised to address this important issue.

Conclusions and Implications

Our case study illustrated the importance of looking at the many facets of youth development when we develop technologies as a learning tool for young people. While it is important to set priorities as to which aspect of youth development (cognitive, social, or personal) our technologies may have the greatest impact, it is imperative to also examine how our technologies may influence other aspects of development. The *Positive Technological Development* theoretical model and questionnaire are tools designed to help researchers get a sense of how their technology may influence the various developmental concerns in youth. Using this model and questionnaire can guide researchers in their continuing effort to revise and develop their technologies and curricula.

References

Barab, S., Thomas, M., Dodge, T., Carteaux, R., and Tuzun, H. (2005). Making learning fun: Quest Atlantis, a game without guns. *Educational Technology Research and Development, 53*(1), 86-107.

Bers, M., New, R., and Boudreau, L. (2004). Teaching and learning when no one is expert: Children and parents explore technology. *Early Childhood Research & Practice, 6*(2), n.p.

Dede, C., and Ketelhut, D. (2003). *Designing for motivation and usability in a museum-based multi-user virtual environment*, from http://muve.gse.harvard.edu/muvees2003/documents/AELppr.pdf

Lerner, R. M., Lerner, J. V., Almerigi, J., Theokas, C., Phelps, E., Getsdottir, S., et al. (2005). Positive youth development, participation in community youth development programs, and community contributions of fifth-grade adolescents: Finding from the first wave of the 4-H study of positive youth development. *Journal of Early Adolescence, 25*(1), 17-71.

Rogers, C., and Portsmore, M. (2004). Bringing engineers to elementary school. *Journal of STEM education, 53*(3-4), 17-28.

Scales, P. C. B., P.L., Leffert, N., Blyth, D.A. (2000). Contribution of Developmental Assets to the Prediction of Thriving Among Adolescents. *Applied Developmental Science, 4*(1), 27-46.

PD3: A Handheld Observation Tool to Support Instructional Leadership

Mark Chung, William R. Penuel, SRI International, 333 Ravenswood Avenue, Menlo Park, CA 94025
Email: mark.chung@sri.com, william.penuel@sri.com

Abstract: We designed and developed a handheld classroom walkthrough to support data-based decision making about professional development and school improvement planning. We used methods of participatory design to maximize the usability and value of our technology to policymakers, school leaders, and teachers, who had different and conflicting goals and concerns. We describe design decisions that met their constraints and led to a tool with potential for wide adoption, and impact at the local level.

Introduction

An enduring goal of school reform has been to prepare principals to be better instructional leaders in the school (Andrews & Soder, 1987; Bossert, Dwyer, Rowan, & Lee, 1982; Hallinger, Bickman, & Davis, 1996; Spillane, Halverson, & Diamond, 2001). Although scholars and reform advocates differ in their definition of what constitutes instructional leadership, there is agreement that it involves principals taking a more active role in guiding the improvement of instruction in the school. To guide instruction, principals need to know what is happening in classrooms, and one model that has gotten increasing attention among state, district, and local school leaders is a "classroom walkthrough," first brought to the research community's attention by Elmore's (1997) examination of leadership in New York's District 2.

A classroom walkthrough is a brief visit by a principal designed to give an instructional leader a snapshot of what is happening in a teacher's classroom. The focus of the walkthrough can be on teacher's instructional practice, the content they are teaching, or on student engagement. Principals can use the data to determine whether teachers may need immediate coaching to improve instruction (as in the District 2 model), to inform professional development and school improvement planning, or as part of a collective data-based decision making process at the school.

In 2004, the Miami Museum of Science (MMOS) contracted our research team to design a handheld tool and Web site to support principals in conducting walkthroughs focused on mathematics and science instruction. MMOS had observed that few principals felt comfortable making judgments about their teachers' mathematics and science instruction and believed a handheld tool that could prompt principals what to look for when making a visit to a classroom could help them and that data from the tool could also be used to inform professional development decision-making at the school level. Using methods of participatory design (Schuler & Tamioka, 1993), we sought to maximize the value of our technology to policymakers and school leaders by involving them in design. As part of our project, MMOS staff, district administrators, and school leaders and teachers contributed to scenario development, requirements analysis, interaction design, and user testing. In this poster, we illustrate some of the design decisions we had to make along the way and explain why the contributions of stakeholders were so critical in framing the SRI team's discussion of those decisions and in ensuring that the technology could yield valid data about teachers' instructional practices.

Design Decisions We Faced

Developing a Common Understanding of Goals

Our stakeholders – state policymakers, district staff, principal trainers, and former teachers – had different and conflicting goals and concerns. State policymakers were interested in a tool that would become part of a principal's toolkit for becoming better instructional leaders. Principals were eager to have a decision support tool and wanted to give feedback on visits to teachers. Teachers wanted assurances of privacy - that the data could not be linked back to them - and were concerned about accurate representation of their teaching. We worked with the stakeholders to develop a set of personas, or fictitious users to inform our design process, and scenarios of usage involving the personas. To address the privacy issue, we initially proposed not collecting teacher IDs, but ultimately put this decision in the tool for maximum flexibility across schools and districts.

Observing Content: Who Can Be a User?

We felt that being able to matrix instructional strategies with the content taught was important for selecting among subject-specific professional development opportunities. However, there was disagreement among the stakeholders as to whether principals would be able to identify the topic of a lesson reliably. District content specialists had little confidence in the ability of non-subject matter experts to discriminate between benchmarks. They maintained that content experts should observe content and principals should observe instruction. This would create a validity problem for the matrix approach. Principals countered that they have scope and sequence documents to know what to expect each week. Another option for them is to ask the teacher; if visits were scheduled in advance, the principal could ask the teacher what topic was to be covered – but this would not work in unannounced visits. We decided to allow the principals to select the high-level strand as an alternative to selecting a benchmark, since we had consensus that a principal would be able to determine the strand with sufficient accuracy.

Selecting Displays of Data

We presented a focus group of retired principals with a task that asked them to decide on teacher professional development opportunities given a variety of data displays we were considering including in the tool. The participants wanted the display to be simple and easy to use with no memorization, and said that the time they could spend using the application was extremely limited. They wanted the tool to indicate deficiencies in professional development and indicate a course of action. Given the low number of visits anticipated, it was unrealistic to expect the tool to do an analysis, and prescriptive use of the tool was beyond our scope of work. Instead, we addressed the desire for simplicity and a minimal number of visits required by repositioning the tool as part of a larger data collection process for school improvement and limiting the number of representations to two: box plots and scatter plots.

Discussion

We argue that our project illustrates an important general theoretical principle that should guide learning sciences research if it is to have impact at the local level: stakeholders' own goals, expected uses of designs, and constraints on their time must all be considered when developing tools intended to have a positive impact on the educational system. Future research using this tool could investigate its direct effects on principal leadership practice and its indirect effects on classroom instruction and, more distally, student learning.

References

Andrews, R. L., & Soder, R. (1987). Principal leadership and student achievement. *Educational Leadership, 44*(6), 9-11.

Bossert, S., Dwyer, D., Rowan, B., & Lee, G. (1982). The instructional management role of the principal. *Educational Administration Quarterly, 18*(3), 34-64.

Elmore, R. F. (1997). *Investing in teacher learning: Staff development and instructional improvement in Community School District #2.* NY: National Commission on Teaching and America's Future.

Hallinger, P., Bickman, L., & Davis, K. (1996). School context, principal leadership and student achievement. *Elementary School Journal, 96*(5), 498-518.

Schuler, D., & Tamioka, A. (Eds.). (1993). *Participatory design: Principles and practices.* Hillsdale, NJ: Lawrence Erlbaum Associates.

Spillane, J. P., Halverson, R. R., & Diamond, J. B. (2001). Investigating school leadership practice: A distributed perspective. *Educational Researcher, 30*(3), 23-27.

Socio-technical Factors of Practice Transmission in an Online Creative Tool Community

Eric Cook, Stephanie D. Teasley, Mark Ackerman
School of Information North, University of Michigan
1075 Beal Avenue, Ann Arbor, MI 48109-2112
Email: [ericcook, steasley, ackerm]@umich.edu

Abstract: Digital artists using modular visual production environments can now create highly customized creative tools such as virtual musical instruments, as well as readily sharing and reusing such tools. Aspects of this process both impede and support practice learning. This poster describes an ongoing case study analyzing the socio-technical factors influencing development and transmission of practice and informal learning within one example community, the users of Native Instrument's Reaktor™ software.

Background

Over the last decade, the domain of digital art and music has seen a growing popularity of highly customizable visual production environments such as MAX/MSP, Reaktor, Synthedit and PD. Drawing on visual and functional metaphors taken from circuit diagrams, programming flowcharts and physical modular analog audio synthesis, users in these environments can create virtual musical instruments, performance interfaces and audio/video composition tools by drawing connections between small functional units (such as oscillators, filters, audio samplers, etc). These systems allow a high degree of tool customization, expandability and flexibility. They also support tool-sharing and reuse, as completed "instruments" (sometimes called "ensembles" or "patches," depending on the choice of host environment), which may be distributed to other artists using the same program.

The communities of practice (CoP) literature (Wenger, 1998; Lave & Wenger, 1991) is useful in framing the informal learning and practice development within the user communities surrounding these production environments. The application of the CoP perspective is further extended by social theories of creativity (Moran & John-Steiner, 2003; Mitchell et al, 2003; Csikszentmihalyi, 1996) as well as by descriptions of the social dynamics of practice in both folk and professional "art worlds" (Becker, 1984). Even though the numbers of users is in the tens of thousands, much of the interaction between users of these modular production systems is instantiated online. Therefore, the primary context for practice development and transmission in these communities is virtual and technologically mediated.

There are several questions motivating the research presented here. How is creative practice transmitted and learned by members of these online communities? How is practice developed in this setting, both collectively and individually? The highly customizable nature of these production environments should increase the tension between individual and collective practice. At the same time, the affordance of easy dissemination and reuse of others' work online allows shared instruments to act as learning objects, a form of reified practice for the rest of the community to examine. This work seeks to investigate the socio-technical factors influencing this complex dynamic in this informal learning context.

Site and Participants

This poster describes an ongoing case study analyzing the development and transmission of practice within one such online community of practice, the Native Instruments Reaktor™ user community. Reaktor, a commercial visual programming language environment, allows users to take software representations of similar low-level components or "modules," and connect them together into larger functional units called "ensembles." These ensembles can be thought of as complete programs for sound generation, and can be used like musical instruments for recording or performing. Any user who creates his/her own ensembles may share these with any other user. One of the primary modes of sharing ensembles is via the "User Library," an online collection of over 2050 ensembles (as of November 2005) accessed via the "Community" section of the Native Instruments website. This archive is accessible to all registered users of Reaktor, and is comprised entirely of user-made ensembles that were contributed freely over the past five years. Norms of practice and community behavior are learned and transmitted in two primary locations on the Native Instruments website: in the User Library (via attributed comments, anonymous voting, and contributed ensembles) and in the User Forum (via a threaded discussion board), located at: http://www.nativeinstruments.com/forum_us/ and http://www.native-instruments.com/index.php?id=userlibrary_us, respectively.)

Research Methods and Data

This research is designed as an observational study utilizing a mixed-methods approach. Specifically, qualitative assessment of behavior and textual communications will be combined with statistical analysis of activity and contribution within both the Reaktor User Library and User Forum. For the initial phase of data collection, 232 megabytes of html pages were retrieved from the User Library in July 1st 2005. These pages represent the 1994 ensembles visible from the entry pages of the Library at the time and an additional 991 "hidden" ensembles, which encompass earlier versions of some ensembles (these are publicly accessible but non-linked pages). Aggregate activity visible on these pages includes 1,457,193 total items downloaded from the library, 50,656 anonymous scoring votes, and 8436 distinct comments. Examining individual user activity reveals 503 ensemble contributors, 263 of which were repeat contributors and 1441 comment contributors, 616 of which were repeat comment contributors. The next phase of data collection will focus on the User Forum, which contained 7,233 threads comprised of 50,937 individual posts as of October 31, 2005.

Discussion

This poster will present and discuss the current findings of this study, highlighting differing notions of legitimate participation and authentic practice within subgroups of the community. In addition, comparison of these data to data generated by studies of learning in other virtual communities will be addressed, paying particular attention to unique characteristics of practice transmission by new media artists.

References

Becker, H. S. (1984). *Art Worlds*. University of California Press, Berkeley.

Csikszentmihalyi, M. (1996). *Creativity: Flow and the Psychology of Discovery and Invention*. HarperCollins.

Lave, J. & Wenger, E. (1991). *Situated Learning: Legitimate Peripheral Participation*. Cambridge University Press, Cambridge, UK.

Mitchell, W. J., et al (eds.). (2003). Beyond Productivity: Information Technology, Innovation and Creativity. National Academies Press, Washington DC.

Moran, S. & John-Steiner, V. (2003). Creativity in the Making: Vygotsky's Contemporary Contribution to the Dialectic of Creativity & Development. In . R. K. Sawyer (ed.). *Creativity and Development*. Oxford University Press. 61–90.

Wenger, E. (1998). *Communities of Practice: Learning, Meaning, and Identity*. Cambridge University Press, Cambridge, UK.

The Role of Technology in Preservice Teachers' Images of Their Future Classroom

Theresa A. Cullen, Indiana University, tacullen@indiana.edu

Abstract: Participant drawings, descriptive essays, surveys, and interviews were used to assess how 160 beginning preservice teachers envisioned technology in future classrooms. Results were analyzed with the constant comparative method (Glaser & Strauss, 1967) and trait coding (Haney, Russel, & Bebell, 2004). Data demonstrated persistence of teacher-centered technology uses and inconsistencies between espoused views and participant drawings. Results could be used to design interventions for transfer through a better understanding of beginning beliefs of preservice teachers.

Introduction

Preservice teachers lack the context of teaching experiences by which to frame their experiences and make meaning of technology models and experiences. Past research has shown that preservice teachers often don't easily incorporate student-centered technology teaching strategies into their repertoire. For example Willis and Sujo de Montes (2002) found that preservice teachers often replicate teacher-centered technology uses. A study by Wang (2002) demonstrated that when preservice teachers observed expert teachers using technology, they did not view teacher-centered methods differently than student-centered methods. When these preservice teachers taught classes, they more often chose teacher-centered uses of technology based on their memories of being taught themselves. In classroom placements, preservice teachers have a tendency to use technology for their planning and administrative tasks, but often are not comfortable enough to implement student-centered technology activities (Dexter & Riedel, 2003). These preservice teachers are viewing technology differently than their inservice counterparts, these studies have documented how their actions differ, but little research has been done to document how preservice teachers think about technology's role in their classrooms. Understanding how these future teachers think about technology in their envisioned classrooms is vital to designing instruction and interventions to make technology a more integral part of how they plan to teach.

The purpose of this study was to look at the relationship between preservice teachers ideas about teaching and technology integration and how they envision their future classroom. This study investigated the following two research questions: What role do preservice teachers envision technology having in their future classrooms and teaching? and What is the relationship between student's beliefs about teaching and learning and their vision of future technology use?

Methodology

Elementary education students were asked to participate in a drawing task. Participants were nine classes of twenty-five students enrolled in their first methods block, during which they were engaged in science, mathematics and technology methods instruction. Each group of students was asked to draw their future classroom, without monetary limitation, designing the space and requesting materials so that they would promote student learning and good teaching practices. All participants were asked to write a short essay explaining their design to a community member and complete a short survey to share demographic information and their ideas about teaching and learning. Students also participated in a class debrief focused on learning environments for science based on the National Science Education Standards.

Data Analysis and Follow Up Interviews

The drawings were analyzed using trait coding to focus scoring on target aspects (technology representations and classroom arrangement) while allowing for incorporation of emerging themes (Haney, Russell, & Bebell, 2004) and eight students were asked to participate in follow-up interviews to explain their drawings and their ideas about teaching and learning. Students were purposely sampled in order to represent the diversity of responses.

The constant comparative method was used to identify emergent themes from the essays, survey responses, debrief transcripts and interview transcripts (Glaser & Strauss, 1967; Bogdan & Biklen, 1998). Characteristics present in the drawings, essays and survey results about teaching and technology beliefs were summarized to understand the general attitudes of the class and to facilitate selecting diverse participants for interviews. The drawings, essays, surveys, and interviews triangulated student responses adding reliability to the findings along with member checks for validity and the use of multiple coders for inter rater reliability (Bogdan& Biklin, 1998).

Results and Discussion

Results show that when students draw their future classrooms, technology is not one of the main components they focus on, instead most classrooms focused on language arts. In fact, even after being prompted in an interview, one participant said, "I can see what you are going for, but really I don't think technology is necessary for me to be a good teacher." Additionally, students drew technology in very teacher-centered ways. The majority of students drew 6 to 10 computers placed in the periphery of the classroom. When asked in group debriefs about this, students stated, "That is all we have ever seen in a classroom." Other students would describe good teaching as being student centered, but many of these preservice teachers would design classroom learning spaces where desks were in rows or in a U shaped, with the teacher's desk as the focus of all activity. For example, the student drawing in figure 1 was accompanied by a characterization of a good teacher as "someone who is focused on the needs of the student." Some students did design collaborative learning environments such as Figure 2 where the future class was designed with collaborative pods of desk with laptops arranged around a group discussion area.

Drawings provide a special opportunity to explore students' conceptions of technology in the classroom. Student beliefs are not always consistent with their interview or written responses and a drawing can be quick way to illicit beliefs and emotions (Hancock & Gallard, 2004; Weber & Mitchell, 1996). Students had persistent teacher centered beliefs upon entering a teacher education program, these beliefs need to be discussed and addressed in order to promote reformed based teaching practices. Students did not see technology as a tool to assist students in everyday learning activities and collaborative learning designs utilizing technology were not prevalent.

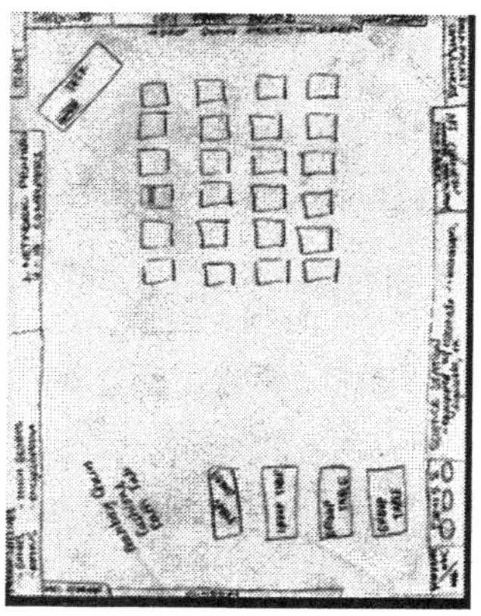

Figure 1: Traditional Design

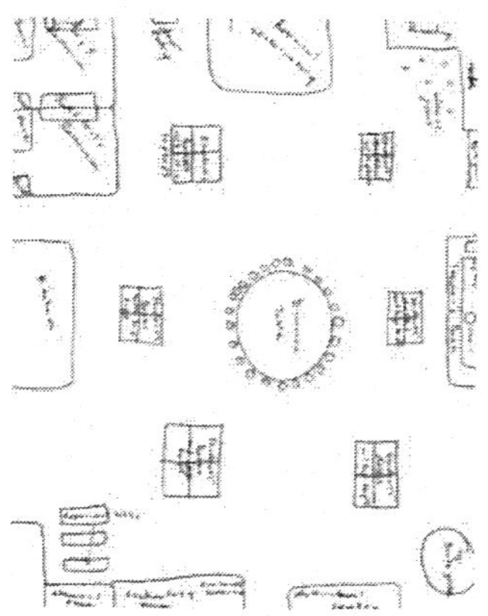

Figure 2: Collaborative Design

Significance of the Study

Since drawings help participants to discuss persistent ideas and reflect on how they impact their teaching, this activity could be useful in encouraging reflective practice in preservice teachers. By better understanding of beginning beliefs, interventions can be planned that focus on transfer, where activities can be designed to bridge from preservice beliefs to ideas that are more consistent with successful professional practice (Perkins & Soloman, 1988). The question persists, are the drawings artifacts of persistent teacher centered beliefs or a lack of student-centered or collaborative models and experiences? How can learning experiences be designed to encourage preservice teachers to overcome persistent images and develop new paradigms of environments for student learning that plan to use technology to cognitively assist students and make the use of computer assisted learning environments (Scardamalia & Bereiter, 1991) as a part of daily classroom practice. Also, the origin of these images (past learning, field experiences, etc.) may provide insight as to the reasons for why teachers do not plan for technology in their future classrooms.

References

Due to limited space – complete references available at:
http://portfolio.iu.edu/tacullen/CullenICLSProceedings.pdf

Professional Development, Cognitive Tools, and Thinking Skills

Katherine McMillan Culp, Lauren B. Goldenberg, and Dara Wexler
Education Development Center's Center for Children and Technology, New York, NY
Email: kculp@edc.org, lgoldenberg@edc.org, dwexler@edc.org

Abstract: This poster shares findings from an on-going, formative evaluation of a professional development workshop for K-12 teachers that is designed to engage teachers in creating classroom projects that use cognitive tools to foster higher-order thinking and 21st century skills across the disciplines. Findings show teachers used the tools to "make students' thinking visible," help students compare ideas, and to stimulate group discussions; the remaining challenge is to explicitly target students' higher order thinking skills.

Introduction

This poster presents findings from a formative evaluation of a program that provides guidance for educators on how to use web-based, cognitive software programs that engage students in higher-order thinking (Beyer, 2001), and 21st century skills (Partnership for 21st Century Skills, 2003). Specifically, the Intel Workshop on Teaching Thinking with Technology presents three tools that help students visualize and represent their thinking: (1) *Seeing Reason* focuses on cause and effect relationships through the construction of causal maps; (2) *Visual Ranking* focuses on prioritizing information, exploring perspectives, and building consensus through ranking items in a list; and (3) *Showing Evidence* focuses on generating claims and evidence to support or refute arguments by using an interactive visual organizer. This poster provides findings related to the research question: How do participants who have gone through the training make use of the Workshop resources? Specifically, to what extent is participants' classroom follow-up (such as using the online thinking tools with students) consistent with the instructional practices and learning goals the resources are intended to support?

Theoretical Framework

With the distinction between *social scaffolding* and *technological scaffolding,* Pea (2004) points to the relationship between student learning and technology. A Workshop participant, then, needs to envision, understand, and enact the simultaneous management of a particular instructional context (a classroom focused on project-based learning, at least for a particular time period) and a particular set of interactions with the technology (effective use of the online thinking tools). The professional development literature (Garet, Porter, Desimone, Birman & Yoon, 2001; Kennedy, 1999) suggests that in order to have an impact on student learning the concrete ideas and materials teachers take back to the classroom with them need to embody both the instructional ideas (in the case of this project, facilitating a project-based approach to learning) and the ideas about student learning (the higher-order thinking skills the online thinking tools are intended to scaffold) that are communicated in the Workshop.

Research Methods and Data Sources

The research design for the larger study from which this poster is drawn included a range of data collection strategies: online surveys, interviews, classroom observations, email correspondences, document analyses of curricular materials, observations at trainings and curricular planning meetings, and an analysis of unit plans generated at the professional development training. Both qualitative and quantitative analysis methods were employed.

Findings

This poster presents two of the study's major findings.

Finding #1: Participants primarily employed the tools to enhance their curriculum in two ways: making student thinking more visible and stimulating group discussion. They were unlikely to focus specifically on engaging and building students' higher-order thinking skills. Both trainers and participants expressed a particular interest in the idea of "making student thinking visible." In addition, in the unit plans analyzed, one or more tools were chosen to make "students' thinking visible" to themselves or to their peers. However, project descriptions and procedures suggested that teachers anticipated using the tools would organically lead students to communicate with one another in meaningful small and large group discussions. Teachers did not include in their unit plan documentation questioning strategies to prompt student discussions nor any focus or goals for the discussions, but instead, noted that students' use of the tools will lead to sharing and communicating about similarities and differences among students' representations of their thinking. Additionally, few unit plans focused explicitly on building students' "information and communication skills," which would indicate an intention to address the quality or strength of students' use and articulation of the information involved in the project. Only seven of the thirty unit plans identified developing students' information and communication skills.

Finding #2: The tools are consistently used to support documentation of students' thinking, comparison of results, and discussion of ideas. They are not typically used to support sustained collection of evidence, rigorous evaluation of evidence, or drawing conclusions about the validity or strength of hypotheses or conclusions. Classroom observations, a review of unit plans, and responses to the Follow-Up Survey all indicated that teachers use the online thinking tools in a project-based context, although the scope and depth of projects varied widely. Projects and activities typically provided significant structure for students, guiding them step-by-step through a process but inviting them to construct unique responses to the driving prompt or question. Both observed classes and sample unit plans suggest that while teachers often include the collection and presentation of evidence as a part of a project that involves the tools, this portion of the activity is not typically emphasized. For example, in observed classrooms teachers did not spend a significant amount of time discussing the process of selecting or evaluating evidence to include in the tool space, and in none of the observed classes or the sample unit plans was the collection of evidence tied to any larger inquiry process beyond populating the student space within a given tool. Teachers instead placed their emphasis on the idea that students should construct and present a perspective or a belief, and then share their representation and compare it with others.

Conclusions and Implications

Most teachers responded positively to the Workshop experience and the tools, and thought these tools had the potential to foster positive classroom practices such as student collaborative work, research, and discussion among students. Moreover, most participants are successfully creating unit plans that link the use of the tools to their current classroom practice and that are broadly project-based in their structure. However, not all teachers developed projects that were aligned with the learning concepts the tools were designed to address. Creating projects that brought together tool use, higher-order thinking skills, project-based learning approaches and facilitated student learning around these concepts proved challenging for teachers. The distinction between *social scaffolding* and *technological scaffolding* (Pea, 2004) points clearly toward the critical qualities of effective instruction and effective use of technology in the classroom. In each case, resources need to be designed and deployed to support students by extending their reach — by bringing their cognitive skills and ability to ask and answer questions into broader, deeper, and more complex territory than they could navigate on their own. From a professional development perspective, this means that teachers need to develop both instructional skills as well as an understanding of how to deploy specific features of technology effectively to support students' emergent learning. If teachers are able to use the tools effectively in a project-based context, students will have the opportunity to build up a deeper understanding of the conceptual material and cognitive skills the tools are intended to support, and, by extension, to understand new aspects of academic content.

References

Beyer, B. K. (2001). Putting It All Together to Improve Student Thinking. In A. L. Costa (Ed.), *Developing Minds: A Resource Book for Teaching Thinking*. Alexandria, VA: Association for Supervision and Curriculum Development.

Garet, M.S., Porter, A.C., Desimone, L., Birman, B.F. & Yoon, K.S. (2001). What makes professional development effective? Results from a national sample of teachers. *American Educational Research Journal 38*(4): 915-945.

Kennedy, M. (1999). *Form and Substance in Mathematics and Science Professional Development* (NISE Brief 3(2). Madison, WI, National Center for Improving Science Education: National Institute for Science Education.

Partnership for 21st Century Skills Report (2003). *Learning for the 21st Century: A Report and MILE Guide for 21st Century Skills*. Retrieved April 18, 2005, from http://www.21stcenturyskills.org.

Pea, R.D. (2004). Commentary: The social and technological dimensions of scaffolding and related theoretical concepts for learning, education and human activity. *The Journal of the Learning Sciences, 13*(3), 423-451.

Acknowledgments

This paper is based on work supported by the Intel Foundation. Any opinions, findings and conclusions expressed in this material are those of the authors and do not necessarily reflect the positions or policies of the Intel Corporation.

The Role of People Knowledge in Learning Narrative and Domain Content

Joan Davis, Tiffany Lee, Nancy Vye, John Bransford, University of Washington
Email: joand@u.washington.edu, tlee13@u.washington.edu, nancyvye@u.washington.edu, bransj@u.washington.edu
Daniel L. Schwartz, Stanford University, daniel.schwartz@stanford.edu

Abstract: We argue that the addition of people knowledge to curricula has the potential—still largely unrecognized—to improve classroom learning. We describe the results of two studies on people knowledge and learning. Study 1 indicates that narrative information organized around familiar, as contrasted with unfamiliar, people is better remembered and judged to be more interesting and concrete by learners. Study 2 focuses on people knowledge and learning and transfer of pedagogical content knowledge.

Rationale and Background

People's exceptional memory for other people suggests that *knowledge organized around people* may have a special status, much like spatial organization and script-based organization have special mnemonic effects. We use the term "people knowledge" to refer to this phenomenon. The ubiquity of people knowledge may have a unique neural basis; alternatively, it may be a type of knowledge where many forces conspire to make it special (e.g., people are one of the primary sources of early learning, people are motivating, people are discrete but change locations and appear in different contexts). The basis of people knowledge and whether it can be dissociated from other forms of learning are important questions to explore (Lin & Bransford, 2005; Hong & Lin, 2005). One reason it is important is that instruction does not take advantage of people knowledge to help students learn. Most knowledge presentations are person-neutral (e.g., a textbook voice), and this may reflect a missed educational opportunity.

This poster describes the results of two preliminary investigations of people knowledge on learning. Our studies are different from some approaches to instruction that tie a particular theory to a person: for example, "Newton created thermodynamics." While we think this approach can be valuable, people knowledge is probably most useful when there is some meaningful connection between the theory (or action) and the person, such that one can imagine why the person has a particular theory (or actions). Studies of effective elaboration provide support for this view (e.g., Stein, Morris & Bransford, 1978).

Study 1: The Effects of People Knowledge on Interest and Memory for Narrative

Study 1 was designed to investigate the degree to which learning can be enhanced by organizing information around familiar, rather than unfamiliar, people. Twenty-six graduate students participated in the study. They read a five-person conversation in which each person was marked only by their names (e.g., Len, James, Jenny, etc.). Then the participants rated the comprehensibility of the conversation. Next, the participants were randomly assigned to two groups: Unfamiliar People and Familiar People. The Unfamiliar People group read the same conversation a second time and rated it for changes in interest and concreteness. The Familiar People group was reminded of five people whom they all "knew" (characters from a short movie they had seen 2 weeks prior for a different, unrelated purpose) and then were asked to read the same conversation a second time—with one difference: the initial names (e.g., Len, James, etc.) had been replaced with names of the familiar people (i.e., characters from the movie). The Familiar Knowledge group also rated the conversation for changes in interest and concreteness.

The results indicate that participants in both groups rated the first conversation as equally comprehensible (mean rating of 2.6 and 2.8 on a 4-point scale for the Unfamiliar People and Familiar People groups, respectively). However, participants in the Familiar People group rated the second conversation as significantly more interesting ($t(24) = 4.960$, $p=.000$) and more concrete ($t(23) = 7.064$, $p=.000$) than students in the Unfamiliar People group. The Familiar People students also recalled significantly more of the main ideas of the conversation ($t(24) = 2.087$, $p=.000$) than the Unfamiliar People students.

Study 2: An Investigation of People Knowledge on Learning Pedagogical Content Knowledge

Study 1 revealed that information organized around familiar people is better remembered and judged to be more interesting and concrete by learners. Study 2 extends this work by focusing on the question: How does instructional material organized around people improve learning of pedagogical content knowledge?

In Study 2, 48 undergraduates learn about mathematics pedagogy using one of two types of instructional documents: expository text (Expository) and a teacher's journal (People Knowledge). Participants in the Expository group read text on the development of young children's whole number sense (i.e., counting and quantity). The text defines various principles (e.g., cardinality, one-to-one correspondence) and presents examples that illustrate each principle. Participants in the People Knowledge group read a teacher's journal that tracks the mathematical development of three fictional students and contains some information about each student's background (e.g., SES, home life, etc.) and personality (e.g., shy, energetic, etc.). Where the expository text presents general examples to illustrate children's understanding of the mathematics principles, the teacher's journal defines and describes these principles in the context of the individual students. It is important to note that the introductory sections of the teacher's journal and the expository document were identical.

Dependent measures include 1) interest, imagery, and comprehensibility ratings occurring at four time points in each document, 2) recall of the mathematics principles described in the documents, and 3) transfer of these principles to a teaching situation. In the transfer task, participants read a transcript of a first grade mathematics class and made judgments about students' understanding of counting and quantity. Our hypothesis is that participants who read the teacher's journal containing "people knowledge" will be more interested in and better able to remember the content because they would be able to draw inferences and elaborate based on their knowledge of the people involved.

Participants in the People Knowledge group rated the teacher's journal significantly higher for comprehensibility ($F_{1,46}$= 10.638, p=.002), interest ($F_{1,46}$ = 18.032, p=.000), and imagery ($F_{1,46}$ = 32.647, p = 0.000) than participants in the Expository group. Ratings were made on a 4-point scale (see Table 1). Interactions were significant for interest ($F_{3,138}$ = 3.721, p=.013) and imagery ($F_{3,138}$ = 2.820, p=0.041) but not for comprehension. A multiple comparison procedure revealed that comprehension, interest, and imagery ratings for the introductory section (rating made at time point 1) of both documents were not significant. Since the introductory section was verbatim for both documents, it follows that there should be no difference in ratings.

Table 1: Means for Expository/People Knowledge main effect

	Expository	People Knowledge
Comprehension Ratings	2.85	3.37
Interest Ratings	2.06	2.74
Imagery Ratings	2.54	3.36

Data from the recall and transfer tasks are currently being analyzed. Results of this analysis will indicate whether the differences in ratings reflect how well participants learn and transfer pedagogical content knowledge.

References

Hong, H., & Lin, X. (2005). Effect of people knowledge on science learning. Paper presented at the meeting of the American Educational Research Association, Montreal, Canada.

Lin, X. D., & Bransford, J. (2005). People knowledge: A useful ingredient for bridging cultural differences between teachers and students. Paper presented at the meeting of the American Educational Research Association, Montreal, Canada.

Stein, B.S., Morris, C.D., & Bransford, J.D. (1978). Constraints on effective elaboration. *Journal of Verbal Learning and Verbal Behavior, 17*, 704-714.

Fostering Generative Reasoning about Complex Phenomena in Genetics

Ravit Golan Duncan, Rutgers University, Graduate School of Education 10 Seminary Place New Brunswick NJ 08901, rgduncan@rci.rutgers.edu

Abstract: The notion of systems is an important idea in science and science education. Genetic phenomena, in particular the mechanisms that link genes to their observable effects, are examples of complicated multileveled systems that students find difficult to understand. Developing generative understanding of the mechanisms underlying genetic phenomena is a critical aspect of scientific literacy in this domain. Here, I describe the design and evaluation of a high school genetics unit aimed at fostering such understandings.

Introduction

The notion of systems is an important and pervading idea in both science and science education (AAAS, 1989). Genetic phenomena and the mechanisms that link genes (genotype) to their observable effects (phenotype), such as eye color or the symptoms of a genetic disorder, are examples of complicated multileveled systems that students find difficult to understand (Horwitz, 1996; Marbach-Ad, 2001; Venville & Treagust, 1998). Understanding the mechanisms involved in genetic phenomena is critical for scientific literacy and the ability to make informed decisions about personal and public issues concerning genetics (Lewis & Wood-Robinson, 2000). Moreover, such understandings need to be generative in nature to allow students to reason about novel and unfamiliar genetic phenomena they may encounter in the future. Fostering the development of generative thinking in genetics entails an understanding of what sorts of knowledge are critical for such reasoning. In earlier work I presented a cognitive model of reasoning in genetics that highlighted essential knowledge forms that undergraduate students employed to successfully reason about genetic phenomena in both novel and familiar contexts. This cognitive model informed the design of a high school curricular unit aimed at fostering generative understandings in genetics. In this poster I discuss the key elements of the instructional design and findings from the implementation of the curriculum in a high school biology classroom.

The Instructional Design

Scientific literacy in genetics involves understanding how the genetic information brings about observable features (phenotype) such as our physical traits, symptoms of genetic disorders, etc. In this regard it is crucially important that students understand that there is an extensive causal chain linking genes to their phenotypical effects and that genes do not directly specify the features as we see them. That is, genes do not directly determine the color of the eye rather they determine the properties of entities whose interactions result in eye color. This is a subtle but critical understanding since it foregrounds the underlying causal mechanism. In my prior work I identified several conceptual understandings that were particularly powerful for reasoning about the genetic causal mechanisms: 1) the understandings that genes directly specify only the structure of proteins, 2) the understanding that proteins are thus central entities in the causal mechanisms of genetic phenomena, 3) knowledge of important and common roles proteins play in those mechanisms, and 4) the understanding that explanations in genetics entail accounting for the complete mechanism (across all biological organization levels) linking genotype and phenotype. Our design team, composed of four biology high school teachers and myself, adopted the four key understandings described above as the learning objectives for the unit.

We employed several design strategies to scaffold student learning of these ideas. In order to help students develop an understanding of the central role and multiple functions that proteins have in genetic phenomena we focused the unit on a detailed investigation of the biological mechanisms underlying a single genetic disorder - Familiar Hypercholesterolemia (FH). In their investigations students compare data from eight cases of patients with FH and four cases of healthy individuals, to uncover the underlying causes of the disorder. Students begin the exploration at the organism level examining the observable effects (symptoms) of the FH gene and through a cyclical process of sequentially delving into lower organization levels (organs, tissues, cells, and proteins) they uncover the complete biophysical mechanism. The major feature of this approach is that it emphasizes mechanisms and much of the time is devoted to exploring the role of proteins in those mechanisms. At this stage students do not discuss how the genetic information is mapped onto the physical mechanism, rather the focus is on the mechanism itself. To help students understand that the genetic information only specifies the structure of proteins we introduce genes only after students have uncovered the cellular and molecular mechanisms involved in FH. Once most of the underlying causal mechanism has been accounted for the only role left for genes is to specify the structure of proteins; thus motivating the need for information only at the protein level. In this part of the unit students explore the way in which the genetic code determines the structure of proteins, and how changes to that code (mutations) alter the structure and resulting function of proteins. To reinforce students understanding of the nature of explanations in genetics we ask them to create a comprehensive account of the biological basis of FH as the consequential task for the FH investigation. Students write a letter to an assigned case patient explaining the underlying causes of the disorder by providing an account of the mechanisms at each organization level (gene, protein, cell, tissue, organ/organism). This task emphasizes the nature of explanations in the domain and builds on students' experiences in the preceding activities. Again, the focus is on mechanism, the role of proteins, and the mapping between the genetic information and the physical causal mechanism. To further facilitate generalization and application of the knowledge students acquired, the final set of activities in the unit entails compiling information about the biological mechanisms involved in three additional genetic disorders (the information is provided in a set of readings) and creating a complete and coherent account of the biological basis for those disorders. This unit was implemented in an honors 8th and regular 9th grade biology classroom in a Chicago public high school. In the following sections I briefly describe some of the key findings from that study.

Methods

To determine students' understanding of the target concepts identified in the curriculum, as well as students' ability to reason generatively about problems and phenomena in genetics, I conducted qualitative and quantitative analyses of several data sources: pre and post written assessments (n=100); pre and post clinical interviews (n=11), video of classroom instruction, and artifacts of student work (the consequential task). Interviews and written assessments were administered prior to and following the instruction period (5 weeks). Interview tasks focused on eliciting students understandings of the mechanisms underlying genetic phenomena, whereas, the written assessments focused mainly on their understandings of entities and relationships. Artifact analysis ascertained the completeness and connectedness of students' accounts of the causal mechanism of FH.

Results and Discussion

Overall my findings suggest that the curriculum was successful in supporting students' learning of the target objectives. As a result of instruction students developed more sophisticated understandings of genetic phenomena and the underlying mechanisms and were able to reason generatively about novel phenomena and generate plausible and domain-appropriate explanations. Specifically, analysis of the written assessments showed that 68% of students' responses post instruction indicted an understanding that genes code for proteins (versus 1% pre instruction). Moreover, after instruction the majority (64%) of the students were cognizant of the central role proteins play in genetic phenomena and were able to identify proteins as a key link between genes and their effects (4% pre instruction). Analysis of students' explanations of the biological basis of FH showed that the majority (68%) of students' explanations accounted for all five organization levels (genes, proteins, cells, tissues, organ/organism). These explanations not only referred to the different organization levels, but most of them also connected the levels by inferring the causal relationships between them- i.e. how changes at one level (mutation in the gene) would affect subsequent levels (change to a protein and subsequently the cell, etc). That it, most of students' explanations (78%) made 6 or more connections (out of a possible 8) between levels, creating a complete and coherent account of the underlying causal mechanism.

References

American Association for the Advancement of Science (1989). *Science for all Americans*, New York: Oxford University Press.

Horwitz, P. (1996). Teaching science at multiple space time scales. *Communications of the ACM*, 39(8), 100-102.

Lewis, J., &Wood-Robinson, C. (2000). Genes, chromosomes, cell division and inheritance -- do students see any relationship? *International Journal of Science Education*, 22, 177 - 195.

Marbach-Ad, G. (2001). Attempting to Break the Code in Student Comprehension of Genetic Concepts. *Journal of Biological Education*, 35(4), 183-189.

Venville, G. J., & Treagust, D. F. (1998). Exploring conceptual change in genetics using a multidimensional interpretive framework. *Journal of Research in Science Teaching*, 35 (9), 1031-105.

Mobile Devices to be applied as supporting tools in Research Methods Class for Undergraduate Students

Eteokleous Mikleia, P.A. College, P.O.BOX 40763, 6307-Larnaca, Cyprus
Email:nikleia@cytanet.com.cy

Abstract: Mobile devices are becoming part of the educational environment. In this case, mobile devices role as supporting tools is under investigation. Specifically, undergraduate college students appear to have time-management and organization problems regarding designing, and constructing the research process and developing their research reports. Hypothesis is made that if a SMS alert system remind students for deadlines and other organizational issues related to the research process, the time management and organization problems will be addressed.

Introduction to the Problem

Mobile technology integration has already started. Mobile devices are everywhere, and mobile learning (m-learning) has emerged to support the learning and teaching process. Mobile tools immerse in the learning environment as tools, some being purely assistive and supportive in nature and others are becoming increasingly intelligent. M-learning is defined as e-learning that uses wireless transmission and mobile devices such as such as PDAs (Personal Digital Assistants), mobile phones, laptops and tablet PCs. In other words, m-learning is simply learning that takes place with the help of mobile devices (Attewell, 2005; Dawabi, et al. 2004; Trifonova, & Ronchetti, 2005). In P.A. College (private college in Cyprus) undergraduate students attend two Research classes in subsequent semesters. The main aim of the overall course is to provide students with knowledge and skills as well as with an understanding and application of the research process and steps in constructing and carrying out a formal research report. Through these two modules, students are expected to take an exam, to develop and submit a research proposal, the various chapters of their dissertation in specific deadlines, submit a research study, and finally take an oral exam. Each academic year, while fourth-year students attend the Dissertation modules, confusion and anxiety exist. The above happens most probably because it is their first experience in developing and conducting research and it is less structured than a regular class. Due to the above, it has been noticed that students appear to have time-management and organization problems. It is revealed to have difficulty in organizing their research reports based on the guidelines given (organization problems) and in managing time, and putting in schedule the research process within the time limits given by the college (time-management problems). They consistently forget deadlines and have questions on numerous structural and organizational issues related to their dissertation. For example, the format/structure of the research proposal/report, what to study for their midterm, what to emphasize for the oral exam, the contents of each chapter, how to reference books, articles, internet sites etc.

Purpose – Methodology

The current study investigates the role of mobile devices as supporting tools in Research Methods Class for undergraduate students studying for a degree in Business Administration. The study makes the hypothesis that by sending students pre-programmed messages regarding deadlines, paper format structure and guidelines; time management and organization problems are addressed. An SMS-based alert and reminder system was tested on 30 students from P.A. College. During the two month experimental period, pre-programmed messages sent to students' mobile phones: 1) as reminders for deadlines (midterm, research proposal first and final draft, literature review first and final draft and midterm date) and 2) as answers to students' requests on format and structure guidelines (research proposal and literature review structure, chapters and concepts included in the midterm, and reference secondary sources). At the conclusion of the 2-month experimental period, the analysis (a) tested the effectiveness of this innovative method and (b) evaluated the potential of introducing mobile technologies to support students in the teaching and learning process. This piece of research applies a case study design. Qualitative data was collected through in-depth interviews gathered from a pull of 30 college students. An interview protocol with semi-structured, open-ended questions was used to collect formal reactions and objective as well as to discuss their attitudes, experience with the SMS time assistant, and possible future expectations from system upgrades.

Data Analysis and Major Outcomes

To begin with, students were asked to comment on their experience regarding the mobile use as a supporting tool in the teaching and learning process. The majority of them reported that they enjoyed the use of mobile device for educational purposes. A student that appeared to be very excited after the experiment reported that "...this is perfect idea and a very interesting concept to be applied". Another one suggested that "...it widens the opportunities for mobile devices, since they can be used to support learning". Overall, positive reactions were recorded by the students which they mentioned that they really liked the SMS alert system. Specifically, more than half of the participants concluded that it was really helpful since it helped them to keep track with the deadlines and managed to submit their assignments on time. One said "I cannot believe it!! I was getting SMSs on what my research proposal should include. It is really great!!". Eleven students pointed out that they liked getting messages reminding them regarding deadlines as well as giving them guidelines. "It is a smart method to engage students in learning as well as enhance their performance since mobiles are currently used by almost all of the college students....", a student concluded. "I was really enjoying it when I was getting messages on how to reference secondary sources. It is a process that I hate doing from the first year of my undergraduate studies. I was using the mobile phone, as soon as I had a question on how to reference for example an internet site and the answer was there for me in zero time". The majority of the students mentioned that as result, when they had meetings with their supervisors they did not spend time on organizational problems and time scheduling rather than they focused on the content of their dissertation. This was really important since they emphasized more on getting effective and corrective feedback on the content which it was significantly improved in comparison to other years. Finally, they reported that they were feeling less confused and stressed regarding the dissertation process. To conclude, the effectiveness of this method evaluated based on the following parameters: the fact that students managed to meet the deadlines and submit the required materials on time, the fact that they had more time to spend with their supervisors on getting feedback on the content of their dissertation and not on time scheduling and organizational issues and last but not least the fact that the anxiety and stress level was reduced.

Only six students appeared to be skeptical regarding this approach. They mentioned that they do not feel that mobile devices are appropriate for educational and teaching purposes. One of them said that as supporting tools it might be possible to be used in education but not for any other reason, for example directly in the teaching and learning process. One of them said "...I was getting frustrated when I was getting a SMS on when I have to submit my research proposal. In some causes the messages made me become even more stressed ". Three of them said that they send SMS to the server to give them guidelines on what to study for the midterm and they found it really difficult to understand what to read. Two of them pointed out that it might be more effective to use PDAs to do this experiment. A student concluded that the major problem regarding mobile phones is that not much information can be given through a SMS.

Given the overall positive feedback from students, it appears that there is a great potential of introducing mobile technologies to support students in the teaching and learning process. Learning through mobile devices seems to be promising. Given the positive reactions and encouraging results from the study a more sophisticated system applying mobile devices is its way to be developed to function as a tool for students that directly and indirectly influence the teaching and learning process. Further, more experiments will be designed to examine the effectiveness and potential of mobile devices to be directly used in the teaching and learning process and not only as a supporting tool. Studies of this kind are still rare, since this field is relatively new. It provides the foundation for further development and expansion of mobile devices integration in higher educational systems.

References

Attewell, J., 2005. Mobile learning: reaching hard-to-reach learners and bridging the digital device. *In*: G. Chiazzese, M. Allegra, A. Chifari, S. Ottaviano, ed. *Methods and Technologies for Leaning*. Southampton: WIT Press, 361-365.

Creswell, J. W (2002). Research design: Qualitative, quantitative and mixed methods approaches (2nd ed.). Thousand Oaks, CA: Sage.

Dawabi, et al. 2004. Using mobile devices for the classroom of the future. *In:* J. Attewell, C. Savill-Smith, ed. *Learning with mobile devices, research and development.*UK: Learning and Skills Development Agency, 55-60.

Trifonova, A. & Ronchetti, M. 2005. Prepare for a bilingualism exam with a PDA in your hands. *In*: G. Chiazzese, M. Allegra, A. Chifari, S. Ottaviano, ed. *Methods and Technologies for Leaning*. Southampton: WIT Press, 343-347.

Identities and Astronomy Camp: How individual campers make meaning of science experiences

Deborah A. Fields, University of California, Los Angeles, Moore Hall Box 951521, University of California, Los Angeles, CA 90095-1521
stareyes@gmail.com

Abstract: This study uses the concept of affinity space to analyze youth participation in a summer science camp, examining how students took on virtual identities as astronomers, merged them with their real identities, and, to varying degrees, adopted projective identities of themselves as scientists. Analyzing camper interviews, I investigate the degree to which Astronomy Camp is an affinity space and present individual cases of ways campers make meaning of their research experiences by creating different identities.

Gee (2004) argues that *affinity spaces* (physical or virtual designed spaces tied by a shared interest or endeavor) allow for a particular interplay of personal identities: virtual, real, and projective. Although his illustration of this potentially transformative interplay of identities is grounded in video or computer games, he argues that it would be much more powerful if learners create virtual and projective identities that can be carried into the real world rather than a virtual gaming world, for instance taking on the virtual identity of a scientist in a classroom or other space, merging it with a real-world identity, and creating a projective identity of a certain type of scientist that will have a history and future. Researching affinity spaces with the potential for real-world projective identities and the ways that learners create and merge identities within them can illuminate ways to encourage a student to "know that he or she has the *capacity*, at some level, to take on the virtual identity as a real-world identity" (Gee, p.114). This study uses Gee's concept of affinity space to analyze youth participation in a summer science camp, to examine how students took on virtual identities as astronomers, merged them with their real identities, and, to varying degrees, adopted projective identities of themselves as scientists.

Background

The Advanced Astronomy Camp is an eight-day summer camp directed by a professional research astronomer where youth ages 14-18 create research questions, develop proposals, investigate their questions in groups with professional instrumentation and telescopes, flesh out theories for how their data relates to current published research, and present their findings to the entire camp. The camp purposefully links itself to professional astronomy and astronomers through its view of youth as 'guest astronomers', its access to astronomers and students in various stages of becoming astronomers (e.g. graduate and undergraduate student counselors), tools of astronomers, and an intensive research process. The camp has been operating for over fifteen years and has a high reputation among attending youth, their teachers, and their parents. The camp's strong reputation and its emphasis on immersing youth in research posed a distinctive opportunity to consider what aspects of this informal science learning environment interest and motivate the youth who attend and how youth create identities at camp that can change the way they imagine their futures.

Method

Ten of thirty-three campers, four of eight counselors, and the director of the Advanced Astronomy Camp in the summer of 2002 were interviewed. In addition to the interviews, the researcher observed and took field notes for the entire Advanced Astronomy Camp. Campers were chosen through a form of random sampling that accounted for three different variables in order to include a range of participants representative of the population of the camp that summer: age, gender, and previous Astronomy Camp experience. This allowed for a breadth of opinion and experience of the youth. The camp was equally distributed in gender and high school grade level; just over one-third of campers had attended an Astronomy Camp in the past. In semi-structured interviews, campers were asked questions regarding three themes anticipated to be relevant to their experiences: affective aspects (confidence, community, personal interactions), science knowledge (science, math, critical thought), and ways of being in the world (careers, higher education, what scientists do). Based on grounded theory, an initial two-step open coding process (Charmaz, 2000) was used to analyze the interviews, generating common themes among all campers or counselors interviewed. Using the interviews, I look for ways that camper descriptions of Astronomy Camp align or do not align with Gee's (2004) theory of affinity spaces. Within this context, I individually analyze each interview to understand how campers brought their previous knowledge, experiences, and identity to bear on their interpretation of what they found most important about the camp and any ways that they created projective identities for the future.

Findings

The findings of this analysis are illustrated here through the case of one individual, although the full poster will present the full set of cases. Consider Pam (pseudonym), in the summer before her senior year in high school and having attended Astronomy Camp before. Pam specifically expressed a virtual identity as an astronomer: "You know, it's like being a real astronomer." The following two quotes from her interview illustrate the rich ways that her real-world identity and virtual identity interplayed to help her create a projective identity as a researcher and astronomer.

> There's so many challenges that you gotta break through, there's so many unknowns you know, and you, you learn that and you learn how really hard it is, and we're constantly discovering new things, that we've, we discover them, but we don't know what they are, and that's just, that's great ... so it's really kind of changed my perspective on a lot of stuff. Um, and just made me want to learn a lot more, like more physics. Like I didn't understand a lot of things last year, so I went back and took like two years of AP Physics in one, you know, and just like, the camp did that for me.

> Well, I think it's really going to suck for me for the first few years of college because I'm gonna be taking these classes, and knowing, that I've been up here...I've already done this and this and I actually did it on a telescope ... I think that's gonna be really hard for me, um, and so I'm definitely gonna go and seek out a lot more research opportunities

In these quotes, Pam expresses a view of science as difficult to do and changing with new discoveries. In fact, she speaks of scientists as "we" not they, positioning herself as a scientist through her research experiences at camp. Her Astronomy Camp experience in a previous summer helped her realize that there was a lot of physics that she needed to know in order to understand more astronomy, so she engaged in an ambitious year of physics classes. In addition, she has discovered that research of the type they did at camp where they made up their own questions and had access to professional equipment like 40" and 60" telescopes is not necessarily a part of the college experience. Pam has created for herself a projective identity of a persevering future astronomer who will pursue appropriate knowledge and research opportunities to get herself through the loopholes of becoming an astronomer.

The full poster will demonstrate the ways in which Astronomy Camp is an affinity space and the different ways that campers create an identity within it. Through individual cases, it will illustrate different campers' ways of making meaning of their virtual identities at Astronomy Camp as they interplay with their real-world identities in their home situations and some campers' creation of projective identities as either professional or amateur scientists and even Mars astronauts. This analysis provides an opportunity to explore characteristics of a real-world affinity space and the ways that youth can interact in it to create new identities for themselves.

References

Charmaz, K. (2000). Grounded theory: Objectivist and constructivist methods. In N. K. Denzin & Y. S. Lincoln (Eds.), *Handbook of Qualitative Research* (pp. 509-535). Thousand Oaks, CA: Sage Publications.

Gee, J. P. (2004). *Situated language and learning: A critique of traditional schooling*. New York, NY: Routledge.

Give Learners Questions to Answer While Watching Animated Examples

Brian D. Gane & Richard Catrambone, Georgia Institute of Technology, 654 Cherry St., Atlanta, GA 30332
bgane@gatech.edu, rc7@prism.gatech.edu

Abstract: Participants (N = 93) watched animated examples of a computer algorithm. Participants had either a small set of examples (6) to watch or a larger set of examples (21) from which they could choose which examples to watch. Additionally, participants either watched the animations before answering questions or had questions to answer while watching animations. Participants scored highest when they had questions with the animations; giving these participants a choice amongst multiple examples also reduced learning time.

Although computer scientists have developed many animation systems to demonstrate the operation of algorithms, empirical evaluations of the pedagogical effectiveness of these animations have yielded mixed results (Hundhausen, Stasko, & Douglas, 2002). These inconsistent results might be because the majority of the animation systems have not utilized findings from research on learning. The goal of this study is to utilize two educational concepts, *learning scenario* and *learner involvement*, to investigate how the presentation of the animations can be altered in order to improve learning.

Most algorithm animations studies have used a *study scenario*, in which learners watch algorithm animations for a set period of time, rather than a *homework scenario*, in which learners answer questions while they view animations (Hundhausen et al., 2002; Kehoe, Stasko, & Taylor, 2001). Of the 24 algorithm animation studies reviewed by Hundhausen et al. (2002), only two used a homework scenario. A study scenario might hinder learning because novices have difficulty determining which aspects of an animation to focus on (Lawless & Brown, 1997; Stasko, Domingue, Brown, & Price, 1998). In a homework scenario, however, questions can act as guides, allowing students to focus on the critical parts of the animations.

Learner involvement in example creation might encourage learners to develop and test inferences about the algorithm (Hansen, Narayanan, & Schrimpsher, 2000). Giving learners the ability to input values into the algorithm can increase students' interest and motivation (Stasko et al., 1998). Complete control of inputs is problematic, however. First, novices have difficulty recognizing what input data will demonstrate interesting results (Stasko et al., 1998). Second, complete control requires learners to decide what behavior they want to see and the inputs to demonstrate that behavior; this mental workload could hinder their ability to understand the algorithm (Lawless & Brown, 1997; Sweller, 1999). Therefore, we gave learners some freedom to choose examples, while eliminating the need to create the examples from scratch. To do this, we used multiple animations that demonstrate the same concept, but with different data. We hypothesized learners would gain understanding of the algorithm if, before selecting an animation, they reasoned about which example would provide the information they needed to learn.

Method

Ninety-three participants were recruited from the Georgia Institute of Technology and were compensated with course credit. We used a 2 x 2 between-subject design to cross learning scenario (homework or study) with learner involvement (high or low). Participants were given questions to answer as they viewed the animations (homework) or after they finished viewing the animations (study). Participants could choose which animations to view and the order (high involvement), or they viewed a predetermined set of animations (low involvement). Participants were randomly assigned to conditions.

Twenty-one animations demonstrated how algorithms manipulated a binomial heap data structure. Nine of the animations demonstrated INSERT, EXTRACT-MIN, and UNION operations. The remaining animations illustrated low-level details about binomial heaps (e.g., number of nodes in a binomial tree). Narrated explanations of the animations were simultaneously presented via headphones. The 21 animations consisted of six classes of examples. Each class had either three or six animations that demonstrated key concepts and illustrated variations due to differences in the data contained in the binomial heap. For instance, depending on the existing heap, the INSERT operation will invoke a recombination of none, some, or all of its trees. Therefore, for the class of INSERT examples, one example showed a binomial heap with no trees recombined, one showed some trees recombined, and one showed all trees recombined. Participants in the high involvement condition could choose any combination of the three INSERT examples to watch; participants in the low involvement condition could not choose which animation to watch (i.e., only one was available to watch). For each example class we selected the animation that we considered the most informative, and we made it available to participants in the low involvement condition.

On the interface, animations were grouped by example class, yielding six groupings; each animation had a short title that summarized the animation. In the low involvement condition, only one animation from each example class was available (i.e., a total of six animations available); participants were able to watch each animation as many times as they liked but could not return to previous examples. In contrast, learners in the high involvement condition could choose any animation in any order (i.e., a total of 21 animations available). Because there was not enough time to watch all 21 animations, participants in the high involvement condition had to choose a subset of animations.

Participants in the study condition were given 35 minutes to watch the animations. The software then shut down and they had 15 minutes to complete Posttest1. Participants in the homework condition had 50 minutes to watch the animations and answer the Posttest1 questions; they were allowed to divide their time however they wished. After completing Posttest1 all participants had 20 minutes to finish Posttest2. The posttests included procedural, conceptual, near transfer, and far transfer questions. Posttest1 contained 14 questions and Posttest2 contained 19 questions.

Results

Viewing behavior and test performance were analyzed. Our measure of viewing time is the time elapsed between starting the first animation and stopping the last animation. This measure might overestimate the viewing time for those in the homework condition because they could answer questions while the animations were running. Given this caveat, there was a significant interaction between learning scenario and learner involvement on viewing time, $F(1, 89) = 5.98$, $MSE = 41.39$, $p = .02$. Post-hoc contrasts were conducted to examine the simple effects of learner involvement; although the following comparisons are not significant they remain informative. In the study scenario, the low involvement condition yielded a shorter study period ($M = 26.63$ min, $SD = 5.11$ min) than the high involvement condition ($M = 29.96$ min, $SD = 4.52$ min), $F(1, 89) = 3.15$, $p = .08$. In the homework scenario, the low involvement condition yielded a longer study period ($M = 33.75$ min, $SD = 6.86$ min), than the high involvement condition ($M = 30.56$ min, $SD = 8.54$ min), $F(1, 89) = 2.84$, $p = .10$.

Homework scenario participants scored higher on Posttest1 ($M = 11.09$, $SD = 1.96$) than study scenario participants ($M = 10.09$, $SD = 1.99$), $F(1, 89) = 5.90$, $MSE = 3.94$, $p = .02$. There was not a significant effect of learner involvement nor a significant interaction. A post-hoc contrast examined whether learner involvement affected scores in the homework scenario; there was not a reliable difference between the low involvement condition ($M = 10.78$, $SD = 2.35$) and the high involvement condition ($M = 11.39$, $SD = 1.47$), $F(1, 89) = 1.08$, $p = .30$. For Posttest2, there was not a significant effect of learning scenario or learner involvement, nor was there an interaction.

Discussion

The homework scenario increased participants' performance on Posttest1. When a small, predetermined set of animations was used, the homework scenario increased study time while improving performance. Furthermore, the homework scenario, when paired with the high involvement condition, resulted in a lower study time and a higher Postest1 score. Therefore, providing learners with questions, and the choice between multiple examples that can answer those questions, appears to be an efficient method for teaching with animations. This combination of questions with multiple examples reduced study time without lowering posttest performance.

References

Hansen, S. R., Narayanan, N. H., & Schrimpsher, D. (2000). Helping learners visualize and comprehend algorithms. *Interactive Multimedia Electronic Journal of Computer-Enhanced Learning*, 1.

Hundhausen, C. D., Douglas, S. A., & Stasko, J. T. (2002). A meta-study of algorithm visualization effectiveness. *Journal of Visual Languages and Computing*, 13, 259-290.

Kehoe, C., Stasko, J. T., Taylor, A. (2001). Rethinking the evaluation of algorithm animations as learning aids: An observational study. *International Journal of Human-Computer Studies,* 54, 265-284.

Lawless, K. A. & Brown, S. W. (1997). Multimedia learning environments: Issues of learner control and navigation. *Instructional Science*, 25, 117-131.

Stasko, J.T., Domingue, J., Brown, M.H., Price, B.A. (eds.). (1998). *Software Visualization: Programming as a Multimedia Experience*. Cambridge: MIT Press.

Sweller, J. (1999). *Instructional design in technical areas*. Melbourne, Australia: ACER Press.

Semiotics: Mediation Tools That Can Fill ELearning Gaps

Ruth Gannon Cook, Ed.D., DePaul University School for New Learning

Abstract: ELearning is particularly susceptible to the transference of print documents to the web which often only provides text and information tidbits to students. But researchers in the learning sciences are finding dramatic improvements in student knowledge acquisition in web-based courses that include semiotic tools. The knowledge gaps that can exist between what students know and need to learn can be filled through the use of semiotic mediation tools. The research of this study looks at why these tools can provide an important bridge between the sociocultural knowledge already existent in students and instructional content and discusses lessons learned in the compilation of the research for this study.

Introduction

While critics of semiotics as a separate and unique field of study often purport that symbols, narratives, and text are, de facto, parts of every document and web page, the truth is that many of these critics are not aware of the impact these semiotic representations have on knowledge acquisition. ELearning is particularly susceptible to the vagaries of many instructors who simply transfer their textbook documents to the Web. In these types of information vehicle transformations and transitions, often important aspects of knowledge transference are omitted from those transmissions. Knowledge gaps can exist that go undetected and, unless identified, could leave students emerging without retaining the desired learning materials. What happens is that the students read the new content information presented in this textbook-online transference, but fail to integrate it into their consciousness.

So, what are the gaps between what the students are presented and what the students absorb and integrate? This was the question I asked to conduct research on "knowledge gaps" in eLearning. Do gaps exist between new web-based information and what the learners read and absorb? What are the findings in the research literature in the field of eLearning that address eLearning and the success of elearning on student acquisition of knowledge? I researched this topic and also the field of Semiotics and conducted four action research studies, three at a southwestern public university, and one at a Midwestern private university, to see if there was a difference between retention in web-based studies created as text-transfer Internet courses and in courses that were designed to use semiotic tools as mediation devices with students' existing knowledge.

This roundtable discussion will present the findings of these four studies and compare the findings of those studies with seminal research in the fields of eLearning and Semiotics. The seminal research studies include studies of student achievement in higher education and in professional training environments to see which factors have had the greatest success in learner knowledge acquisition and retention. It will use both archival data from cross-disciplinary studies and the action research studies conducted by the researcher over the last three years, from 2002-2005 (September). While the findings of this study may not generalizable, the findings suggest further research should be conducted into the incorporation of semiotic tools into the design of web-based eLearning to mediate new information with students' current knowledge. Further research could also look at the potential benefits of conscious inclusion of semiotic tools into instructional designs of eLearning to reduce any knowledge gaps in student learning."

Review of Literature

Research over the last several years has taken a broad look at what factors influence learning in students, particularly higher or continuing education students using technology in their coursework (Cole, 1985; Davidov, 1985; DelRio & Alvarez, 1995; Gee, 1990; Greene, 1997; Lee, 1985; Olsen, 1995; Popkewitz, 1998 Warner, 1997). But research in the arena of commerce has found some interesting data on what influences learning that may shed new light on the importance of semiotics (Zaltman, 1997), and even more interesting is the research conducted over thirty years ago that pointed to semiotic elements that influenced language and learning.

Often in the creation of a new medium of knowledge communication, such as the Internet, old successful methods of communication are by-passed (McLuhan, 1968, 1976). The history of the human race is based not only on the achievements of individual minds but on the recognized forms of representation available to the ancestors that enabled them to make their ideas and feelings public through culture forms (p.349).

Literacy includes the forms of representation that convey anthropological, historical, artistic, and inherently recognizable meaning on multiple levels of cognition. Current iconic representations and metaphors used in technology are rapidly taking on grass-roots recognition among peoples of many cultures and languages. So, to assure this new evolving "technoculture" is thoroughly integrated into on-line courseware design, the "old" knowledge must converge with the new (Gannon-Cook, 1998; Gannon-Cook, Crawford, 2006).

Semiotics can provide technology with imprints, familiar symbols, metaphors and narratives that can mediate with the mind to facilitate learning (Wertsch, 1985). Without finding a way to sift through the overwhelming amount of raw information on-line, it might be difficult to assess how learners best utilize all of this information, particularly learners from diverse cultures, socio-economic backgrounds, and learning styles. Tools that mediate between this technoculture and human consciousness could provide a safety zone where new blueprints could be drawn for both. Symbols and metaphors can render the process of relevance-making possible and could be particularly useful in mediating with a rapidly developing global culture that functions at warp speeds and creates virtual tourists and gypsies, not citizens (Freiberg & Driscoll, 1995; Gannon-Cook, 1998; Salomon, 1997).

Summary

This study has presented the concept that semiotic tools can facilitate the scaffolding of new knowledge on primal knowledge through tool mediation and reinforce learning in online courses. More research in this area could prove invaluable in the contribution to the body of knowledge on web-based learning. Students who may not be comfortable with online courses may feel differently if there were alternative online models that offered embedded semiotic symbols, metaphors, and narratives that enlist prior sociocultural knowledge of the learners. With the planned inclusion of semiotics n eLearning courses, there could be a broader range of students who can navigate and complete online courses.

References

Cole, M. (1985). The zone of proximal development: Where culture and cognition create each other. In J.W. Wertsch (Ed.), *Culture, communication and cognition*. Cambridge, England: Cambridge University Press.

Danesi, M. (1993). *Vico, metaphor, and the origin of language*. Bloomington: Indiana University Press.

Dant, T. (1991). *Knowledge, ideology and discourse: A sociological perspective*. London: Routledge.

Davydov, V. and Radzikhovskii, L. (1985). Vygotsky's theory and the activity-oriented approach in psychology. In J. W. Wertsch (Ed.), *Culture, communication and cognition*. Cambridge, England: Cambridge University Press.

Del Rio,P. & Alvarez, A. (1995). Changing architectures of mind and agency. In J. Wertsch (Ed.) *Sociocultural studies of mind*. Cambridge, England: Cambridge University Press.

Gallini, J., Seaman, M., & Terry, S. (1995). Metaphors and learning new text. *Journal of Reading Behavior*, 27(2), 187-191.

Gee, J. (1990). *Social linguistics and literacies: Ideology in discourses*. London: The Falmer Press.

Gannon-Cook, Ruth (1998). Semiotics in Technology, Learning and Culture. *Bulletin of Science, Technology & Society*, 18(3), 174-179.

Gannon-Cook, Ruth, Crawford, Caroline (2006). What Can Cave Walls Teach Us? (A. Edmundson, Ed.). *Globalized E-Learning Cultural Challenges*. Minneapolis, MN: eWorld Learning.

Messy Learning Environments: Busy Hands and Less Engaged Minds

Christina M. Gardner, Tamara L. Clegg, Oriana J. Williams, Janet L. Kolodner
Georgia Institute of Technology
85 5th Street, Atlanta, GA 30332
tlclegg, cmgardne, oriana, jlk @cc.gatech.edu

Abstract: In an environment where learners are engrossed in highly interactive and fun hands-on activities, how do we get their minds as engaged as their hands? We have found that busy hands help sustain learners' motivation and interest but can distract their minds from doing the necessary reflection on their actions. This paper and the accompanying poster describe conditions and affordances of media and prompts that focus and encourage distracted learners reflection.

Introduction

Sixteen 5th grade learners scramble around the makeshift kitchen locating ingredients, reading off instructions, measuring, and mixing up wonderful baked creations. Flour dusts tabletops and everything else in its path, and hands are sticky with corn syrup. In this messy informal learning environment, children are engaged in hands-on cooking and science exploration. To learn from these activities, they need to step back from time to time to reflect on their actions and record observations for later reflection. Through the Kitchen Science Investigators (KSI) project, we are looking at how to facilitate science learning in such messy environments. One of the emergent goals of this design study is to understand the affordances of media that will not take the fun out of these interactive activities while promoting reflection-in-action and the note taking needed for later reflection-on-action (Schon, 1987). This type of media is needed because it is hard for young learners to disengage themselves from fun activities to record their experiences, but waiting until an activity is over to record experiences can result in too much being forgotten for productive learning. We found this to be especially true in an after-school study of 5th grade learners' engaged in cooking activities, to learn the science behind cooking. Where there was often contention for learners' attention between the physical activity of cooking and the cognitive activity of reflecting, usually resulting in learners focusing their attention on the cooking. Analysis of learners' responses generated by prompts for reflection through use of different media, revealed affordances and conditions of use of the media that were successful in getting learners to reflect and others that were inhibitors. This paper and accompanying poster focuses on getting the learners to make observations to facilitate reflection-in-action which is a necessary condition for subsequent reflection-on-action.

The Learning Environment and Description of Media

We studied sixteen 5th grade learners during an after-school science-cooking club we created in a suburban private middle school. The learners participated in ten 90 minute weekly sessions where they engaged in cooking and science experiment activities with the goal of learning the science behind the roles of various leaveners in brownies, cookies, pizza, and cake. During the first five weeks, their recipes, instructions for experiments, plans for altering and remaking recipes, and all observations were made using paper-and-pencil media. They were introduced to using all of their five senses for making observations using a *Five Senses Chart* on 8 ½ x 11 sheets of computer paper. Each of the column headers on the chart featured a human sense and each of the row headers was a short summary of the major activity of a recipe or experiment step and its number. Learners used these charts to record observations while they were cooking or experimenting for one session. They then began using large 2 ½ x 3 ½ feet posters posted on a wall near-by their workspaces to make observations. At first, each poster represented a step with the *same short step summary* as described in the five senses charts. Then as learners became more comfortable with making observations and began making alterations to the recipes, we changed the labels to the step number and then to just their group names. During the 6th week, we introduced software that learners used while cooking that displayed the recipe and strategically placed textboxes for jotting down observations. We used the software for the remaining four weeks of the program. During the entire ten weeks, we encouraged learners to use cameras to take pictures while preparing their baked goods as experience memory joggers. Learners worked in four groups of four using the different media to make observations.

The *short step summary* we used as prompts for learners to make observations are analogous to "stop and think prompts" and/or "generic prompts" used in Davis (2003). Davis found that generic prompts help middle school learners to reflect (e.g. state what they are thinking) more broadly, allowing them to think about many different ideas. She also found that learners who used the opportunities provided by the prompts to identify where their knowledge needed improvement had reflection that was more productive for learning. Both Schon (1987) and Davis (2003) agree that learning requires reflection and cite a number of others that demonstrate this to be true as well. We couple Davis's use of prompts "to get learners to reflect on many ideas" with Schon's idea of "reflection-in-action" and Davis's "opportunities for learners to identify their weaknesses" as activities that are associated with Schon's "reflection-on-action" (Schon, 1987).

Our use of generic prompts to promote reflection-in action extends Davis's work on placement of generic prompts within activities. We analyzed the learners' responses to the various prompts (i.e. prompts with different levels of descriptiveness) against one another for each day, each type of prompt, and each media using the prompt (within and across groups) and coded the responses based on descriptiveness of articulation. Use of video data and field notes were used to triangulate these findings. We didn't explicitly set out to explore the affordances of different media, our initial research goal involved characterizing the learning environment without computer technology and then characterizing and measuring the introduction and impact of technology on the learning environment. As such the fading descriptiveness of generic prompts was a byproduct of quick prototyping. The impetus for analysis of prompts based on the media was an emergent trend found in the learners' responses.

Findings and Discussion of Findings

Affordances and conditions of media use for success in getting learners to reflection-in-action include: (1) Making media visible enough that its presence reminds learners to reflect (e.g. media is hanging on a very visible wall that learners can't miss); (2) Prompts that tell them when reflection is useful (e.g. after you have added an ingredient or after each step); (3) Use of media for reflection when the cognitive load of the interactive activity has plateaued (e.g. when the initial overwhelming excitement of "we're cooking" wears off); and (4) Fading the specificity of when to reflect as learners become better at remembering to make observations (e.g. they are making them more frequently and the descriptiveness in increasing). Affordances and conditions for learner success in reflection-on-action: (1) Ease of indexing and locating observations, and (2) Fun and contextualized activities that illustrate the importance of good observations for science learning. The presence of these features in a given medium and learning environment made for more descriptive observations. Inhibitors to reflection-in-action: (1) not seeing others explicitly making reflections and the lack of presence of each groups reflections (e.g. media that allows learners to make reflections at their own workstations without being visible to others); (2) reflection that requires finer levels of granularity while learners are engaged in highly interactive activities; and (3) bad interfaces for making observations that leads to loss of observations.

Overall, regardless of the media for observation, the more engaged learners were in the activity, the less interested they were in doing the kinds of reflection that lead to learning. We are still searching for the right level of engagement in the cooking that won't sacrifice the fun, sustaining the motivation and interest that is necessary for implementing science learning interventions. However, these findings show that getting to reflection-in-action is a function of learners remembering to reflect, followed by knowing when to reflect, and finally having the flexibility to reflect in ways that are meaningful to them. It is hard to get learners that are cognitively overloaded with the physical part of the interactive activity to stop and think. Thus, patience and waiting on the part of the researcher and teacher for the grand novelty of the highly interactive physical activity to fade and/or making the appropriate adjustment in the activity design is needed before abandoning a prompt intervention. It is also equally important to physically situate the media in the learning environment so that its persistent presence is a reminder to reflect. In this way, when they have learned to manage the cognitive load of the physical activity then they can start attending to the reflection part of the activity and see other people doing it as well. The second important affordance of a medium is to tell learners when to reflect, skillfully reducing this scaffold to allow learners to record their observations at times *they* think are valuable, as they are more willing to invest time in describing them.

References

Schön, D. A. (1987). Teaching artistry through reflection-in-action. In Educating the Reflective Practitioner. San Francisco, CA: Jossey-Bass Publishers.

Davis, E. A. (2003). Prompting Middle School Science Students for Productive Reflection: Generic and Directed Prompts. Journal of the Learning Sciences, Vol. 12, No. 1, p 91-142.

Help-Seeking Behavior and Learning with Hypermedia

Pragati Godbole-Chaudhuri, Fielding I. Winters, Roger Azevedo, Neil Hofman, Dept. of Human Development, 3304 Benjamin Bldg.,University of Maryland, College Park, MD 20742
pgodbole@umd.edu, fwinters@umd.edu, razevedo@umd.edu, neil_hofman@yahoo.com

Abstract: The help-seeking behavior of 67 learners (29 low and 38 high conceptual-gain) using a hypermedia environment to learn about the circulatory system was investigated in a naturalistic tutoring condition. Results showed that participants who demonstrated greater conceptual gain (from pretest to posttest) asked significantly greater number of *cognitive* questions relating to the content of the material than *context* questions pertaining to the environment. The study has implications for understanding the role of help-seeking behavior during learning with hypermedia and the design of hypermedia tools to facilitate help-seeking behavior.

Help-Seeking Behavior

The ability to identify need for assistance and then obtain help from appropriate sources has been identified by many as a key behavior for coping with difficulties encountered during learning (Newman, 2002; Pintrich, 2000). Academic help-seeking requires the learner to be monitoring progress toward the learning goals. If the learner faces difficulty, she/he must become aware of a need for assistance, identify an appropriate source for help, and subsequently communicate this need effectively to obtain the appropriate response from the source of help. Help-seeking is thus an adaptive behavior that forms an essential part of the arsenal of a learner's self-regulatory skills. Further, help-seeking behavior serves as the link that ensures that the external regulation provided by a teacher, peer or some other externally regulating agent (Azevedo, Cromley, Winters, Moos & Greene, 2005) is in tune with the internal regulation performed by the learner.

Although, a significant body of work so far has underscored the importance of help-seeking as a learning strategy, help-seeking has been relatively less studied with interactive and hypermedia environments (Aleven, Stahl, Schworm, 2003; Graesser & Person, 1994). It has been even less studied for ill-structured tasks, such as learning about challenging domain-specific topics. Furthermore, most studies have been self-report studies that fail to capture actual instances of help-seeking and the social-interactional aspect of help seeking behavior.

The present study evaluated help-seeking behavior of learners in a naturalistic tutoring condition while learning about a challenging science topic (the circulatory system) from a hypermedia environment. Our study examined the difference in types of help seeking behavior between learners who gain in conceptual understanding and those who do not. The study has important implications in understanding the role of help-seeking behavior during learning with hypermedia and in informing the design of hypermedia tools for learning.

Method

Our participants were 67 students from an urban, mid-Atlantic middle school, high school and University and constitute a subset of participants (57%) from a larger study. Twenty-six 7th grade students (mean age = 12.1 years) and 18 high school students (mean age = 14.7 years) received community service credit and 23 University students (mean age = 21.1 years) received extra credit for a course for participating in the study. These participants were chosen as a subset of the larger sample because all were classified as starting with low conceptual understanding, based on pretest mental model, and making little conceptual gain (Low group), or making high conceptual gain (High group), based on post-test mental models of the circulatory system.

Students spent 20 minutes completing a pretest (from Azevedo et al., 2005), including an essay for assessing students' mental models of the circulatory system. An introduction to using the hypermedia environment was then given; showing the contents and features, including multiple representations of information, of three articles most relevant articles for learning about the circulatory system.

Participants had 40 minutes for the learning task and had access to the instructions and the global learning goal ("*Make sure you learn about the different parts and their purpose, how they work both individually and together, and how they support the human body*") during the period. All participants worked with the same human tutor who facilitated their self-regulated learning by prompting students to activate their prior knowledge, plan their time and effort, monitor their progress towards goals and to use several strategies such as summarizing, coordinating informational sources, hypothesizing and drawing. The students were able to engage in help-seeking during the learning task but the tutor did not provide knowledge extraneous to the information in the hypermedia environment. After the learning task, a 20 minute posttest, identical to the pretest, was administered to all participants.

Data Analysis & Results

The coding and scoring of the pretest and posttest mental models and the segmentation of the participants' verbalizations during the tutoring session was identical to that of Azevedo and colleagues (2004). For this study, students' scores on their pretest and posttest mental models were used to categorize them into groups based on how much they learned during the session. A more fine-grained analysis of students' help-seeking behavior based on the coded transcription was conducted by the first author, and each instance was coded into one of two types: *cognitive* or *contextual help-seeking behavior*. *Cognitive help-seeking behavior* included requests by students for help in understanding the content of the hypermedia articles, clarification of an idea, delimiting the task, and confirmation of understanding (e.g. "*Aren't like arteries thicker than veins?*").While *contextual help-seeking behavior* included requests by students for help in navigating the hypermedia environment, clarification of task and tutor's role, and instructions (e.g. "*I can take notes you said, right?*").

We categorized students based on the type of help-seeking they engaged in most during the tutoring session. We conducted 3X2 chi-square analyses to determine whether the different conceptual understanding groups differed on their majority type of help-seeking behaviors. The chi-square was significant (χ^2 [2, N = 67] = 7.47, $p <$ .05) and revealed that 30% of students in the low conceptual-gain group engaged in more *context help-seeking* than *cognitive help-seeking*, compared to only 5% of students in the high conceptual-gain group. Eighty-three percent of high students engaged in more *cognitive help-seeking* than *context help-seeking*, compared to 56% of students in the low group. Four students in both groups engaged in equal numbers of *cognitive* and *context help-seeking*. These results demonstrate that higher percentage of students in the high group engaged in significantly more *cognitive* than *context help-seeking* than their low conceptual-gain counterparts, who engaged in more *context* than *cognitive help seeking* compared to students in the high group.

Discussion

Our results demonstrate that in a naturalistic human tutoring condition students engage in help-seeking behavior. However, not all help-seeking behavior is alike. This study demonstrates differences between the kind of help solicited by learners who show large gains in understanding versus help solicited by learners who do show low or no gains in understanding. It is possible that since students who do not show large gains in understanding after a learning session engage in more questions regarding superficial details of the learning task that these learners are unable to formulate appropriate questions that will help them draw closer to their learning goals. While this is an initial study on the topic of help-seeking while learning with hypermedia, it is expected that with further research into the correlates of help-seeking behavior can yield a deeper insight on the role of the behavior in mediating self- and external regulated learning. Future research also needs to focus on ways of facilitating help-seeking behavior in those who need help most while learning with hypermedia.

References

Aleven, V., Stahl, E., & Schworm, S. (2003). Help seeking and help design in interactive learning environments. *Review of Educational Research, 73*(3), 277-320.

Azevedo, R., Cromley, J.G., Winters, F.I., Moos, D.C. & Greene, J.A. (2005). Adaptive human scaffolding facilitates adolescents' self-regulated learning with hypermedia. *Instructional Science (Special Issue on Scaffolding Self-Regulated Learning and Metacogntion: Implications for the Design of Computer-Based Scaffolds), 33*, 381-412.

Graesser, A.C. & Person, N.K. (1994). Question asking during tutoring. *American Educational Research Journal, 31*(1), 104-137.

Newman, R. S. (2002).What do I need to do to succeed…When I don't understand what I'm doing?:Developmental influences on students' adaptive help seeking. In A. Wigfield, & J. Eccles (Eds.), *Development of achievement motivation* (pp.285-306). San Diego, CA: Academic Press

Pintrich, P. (2000). The role of goal orientation in self-regulated learning. In M. Boekaerts, P. R. Pintrich & Z.Moshe (Eds.) *Handbook of self-regulation* (pp. 451-502). San Diego, CA: Academic Press.

Learning as Perspective Taking: Conceptual Alignment in the Classroom

James G. Greeno, University of Pittsburgh, LRDC, jimgrno@pitt.edu
Brian MacWhinney, Carnegie-Mellon University, Dept. of Psychology, macw@mac.com

Abstract: This poster presents an extension of the psycholinguistic theory of perspective taking to the analysis of reasoning and problem solving in discursive interaction. This extension amends and generalizes schema theory. We present illustrations of perspectival alignments achieved when constructing causal explanations or solving problems, including ways that perspectives shifted during the interactions. We hypothesize that successful learning arises in classrooms when students realign their perspectives with new models.

Following Rommetveit (1987), Tomasello (1999), Fauconnier (2000), and others, we hold that conveying perspectives is a fundamental function of language. Like earlier proposition-based theories of understanding (e.g., Kintsch, 1998), perspective theory assumes that understanding a sentence corresponds to cognizing an information structure with entities, properties, and relations. However, perspective theory adds an assumption that meaning structures have a point of view. The viewer may be enmeshed in the perspective (enactive/projective) or the viewer may be viewing from outside, representing and operating on the entities in the perspective (depictive/descriptive). When the viewer cognizes the scene from outside, her or his perspective includes foregrounding and a focus of attention. At the level of single sentences, perspective theory analyses can account for psycholinguistic phenomena such as constraints on anaphoric reference, garden-pathing, structural ambiguity, and the relative processing difficulty for embedded relative clauses (MacWhinney, 2005).

We have extended perspective theory to analyze episodes of interaction in which participants generate understanding of systems they interact with or of problems they are assigned to solve. Our empirical material includes videotaped episodes of teacher-student or student-student interaction in a mathematics classroom, parent-child or staff-visitor interaction in a science museum, and a discussion by a group of secondary-school science teachers. In some episodes participants achieve impressive mutual understanding, in spite of initial discrepancies between their perspectives. We show how these new understandings can be expressed constituents of perspectival constructions that emerged in interaction. We interpret these cases of successful communication as collaborative generation of perspectival constructions and we offer a model of that process, which includes effortful constructive listening. In other episodes one of the participants gives a monologue that represents a perspectival construction and the other participant(s) give little or no evidence of adopting that perspective. One of our goals is to develop and evaluate hypotheses about social practices that support the arduous activities of achieving mutual understanding through alignment of perspectival constructions.

We propose specific amendments to standard schema theory to represent the effects of perspective taking. As in standard theory, we annotate constructions in terms of embedded propositional trees. At the top of these trees are propositions that express the goals of participants as active agents. For example, they may involve enactive statements such as "I turn the crank" or assignment statements such as "I treat the distance between the perimeters of two rectangles as a variable." Embedded under these high-level enactive statements are subtrees of statements that represent the mechanical operations of equations, derivations, and known causal relations. These embedded trees also involve tracing of perspective through the embedded devices. Shifts in perspectival constructions arise primarily from attentional shifts on the higher levels, since the embedded device constructions are usually fully solidified.

We propose that the dynamics of perspectival constructions can explain how learners shift from vague patterns of understanding to clearer causal models. For some of the episodes we have analyzed, it is implausible to hypothesize a previously known pattern that accounts for the understanding that the participants achieve. In these cases, we hypothesize that processes of exploratory construction of perspectival understanding can account for what is accomplished. These processes include use of schemata for constituents of understanding and constraint satisfaction for combining those constituents into a coherent overall perspectival construction. We also propose that hypotheses of constructive constraint satisfaction for generating perspectival understandings are consistent with hypotheses about reasoning by analogy and with mental models and with classical Gestalt concepts of recentering and other quasi-perceptual processes.

We have begun to develop a taxonomy of perspectival constructions, related to cognitive functions of activities in which they occur. The episodes we have analyzed thus far are of two kinds: constructing causal explanations and solving problems—we expect to find others, such as resolving differences, in future work.

The form of our representations of perspectival constructions (to be illustrated in our poster) is a set of interconnected labeled tree structures that correspond both to a sentential form and to a component of activity (when the perspective is enactive) or a component of the situation (when the perspective is depictive). Location of an element as the sentential subject corresponds to its being the primary focus when the component of that tree is in the foreground. A shift of perspective usually changes the foregrounded component with one of the other elements promoted to the subject position (i.e., it becomes the main focus of attention).

Our analyses of causal explanations include shifts between focus on performing an operation to focus on a causal consequence of the operation, and shifts from a system function (such as physically connecting two systems components) to an enablement. We account for construction of perspectival understandings by hypothesizing knowledge of schemata that include domain-specific requirements of causal systems. The information that we represent in these analyses includes potential answers to many "why" questions, which would be appropriate in different contexts, reminiscent of previous extensive analyses of question answering.

The problem-solving episodes we have analyzed, which come from mathematics classrooms, include actions of writing components of symbolic representations and performing calculations. Constituents of perspectival understanding include recognizing the kinds of components of representations that are constructed (variables, expressions, equations) and semantic relations between the symbols and quantities they refer to. Differences between initial perspectival understandings of different participants provide accounts of difficulty in their communication.

Our perspectival approach provides a convenient way to represent differences of agency between different activities in problem solving. Specifically, we distinguish what Pickering (1995) called conceptual agency and disciplinary agency. We hypothesize conceptual agency when the problem solver chooses to represent some aspect of the problem by identifying a variable or forming an expression or an equation, and we hypothesize disciplinary agency when the problem solver carries out a calculation or solves an already-formed equation.

References

Fauconnier, G. (1985). Mental spaces. Cambridge, MA: MIT Press

Kintsch, W. (1998). Comprehension: a paradigm for cognition. New York: Cambridge University Press

MacWhinney, B. (2005). The emergence of grammar from perspective taking. In D. Pecher & R. Zwann (Eds.), The Grounding of Cognition (pp. 198-223). Cambridge, England: Cambridge University Press.

Pickering, A. (1995). The mangle of practice. Chicago: University of Chicago Press.

Rommetveit, R. (1987). Meaning, context, and control. Inquiry, 30, 77-99.

Tomasello, M. (1999). The cultural origins of human cognition. Cambridge, MA: Harvard Universit

Acknowledgments

This work was supported by a grant from the Spencer Foundation.

Nurses' Informal Argument: Learning to Justify the Claim and Reach Agreement

Debra Hagler, Sarah Brem, Arizona State University, Tempe, Arizona
Debra.Hagler@asu.edu, Sarah.Brem@asu.edu

Abstract: Nurses convince their peers of the need for ongoing action and monitoring during change-of-shift discourse about patient health issues. Twenty pairs of critical-care nurses participated in a qualitative study of authentic everyday argument at the bedside. The process of providing and evaluating evidence for claims and justifying decisions during nursing shift report included pragmatic and structural aspects of persuasive argument in the context of a high-stress, high-stakes, time-pressured environment.

Background

Change of shift report (CSR) is a form of informal argumentative dialogue (Zarefsky, 1995) in which nurses justify recent clinical decisions they have made under conditions of uncertainty. The CSR is an event of intense communication and social cognition with an expectation of accountability for decisions and actions. Nursing CSR, as a form of socially situated cognition, illustrates the potential benefits that come with cooperative practice (Wertsch, 1991). Elaboration of evidence through nursing dialogue helps explain the underlying assumptions and may lead to better collaboration in care. Nursing CSRs are an opportunity to identify how nurses use a sociopolitical approach to cognition in their important everyday work.

The interactive setting of nursing CSR is an authentic environment for study of communication, informal argument, social cognition, and epistemological development. The context for bedside nursing decisions, typical of other naturalistic decision-making settings, includes such elements as high stakes, conflicting data, disparate goals, competing values, time pressure, and team dynamics (Zsambok & Klein, 1997). Furthermore, the decision-making process includes not only gathering data and making a choice, but also communication and justification of that choice (Kuhn, 1991). Learning to tell the story of the patient and the related nursing decisions well requires knowledge of who has expert information, what evidence is relevant, what underlying assumptions and values connect evidence to claims, and how to persuade others to follow a particular course of action.

Participants and Methods

Twenty pairs of registered nurses from 4 critical care units in 3 hospitals volunteered to participate. The nurse participants averaged 10.6 years working in nursing, 7.9 years working in critical care, and 3.7 years of experience working in the current unit. Participants' experience ranged from three months to 29 years in nursing. While some nurses had worked in the same hospital facility and same critical care unit for their entire careers, others had worked in as many as 20 different hospitals on traveling contracts. Ten identified themselves as having a bachelor's degree in nursing, while the remaining nurses reported diplomas, associate degrees, or did not report educational status.

The 28 patients included in CSRs had complex and serious health alterations including multiple injuries, body system failure, dependence on life-support technologies and interventions, or recovery from open-heart surgery. Some were alert; others were unconscious or sedated. Most were physiologically unstable, requiring continuous electronic monitoring and direct observation through the hall window even during the CSR.

Each pair of nurses was audio recorded and observed during CSR in the hallway outside the patient's room. The offgoing nurse was interviewed privately after CSR, while the oncoming nurse completed a brief written survey before meeting the patient. Semistructured interviews and surveys included discussion of communication strategies, epistemological factors, nursing expertise, and argument in the CSR. Data collection and analysis followed federal guidelines (USA) for the protection of human subjects and the confidentiality of health information. Observation field notes, audio recorded shift reports and interviews, and written surveys were transcribed and qualitatively analyzed using Atlas TI 5.0 and Inspiration 7.5 to organize open coding via a line-by-line analysis, axial coding and hierarchical coding. Transcripts were reviewed throughout the data collection process to identify areas of focus for subsequent participants and to narrow the field of study. Data coding within themes reached interrater agreement levels of 85% for goals, 90-94% for time perspective, and 90-93% for types of argument claims. Identified themes and relationships were further validated through member checks by critical care nurses.

Findings and Implications

Nurses' goals for CSR included giving an accurate account of the shift, creating an understanding of the patient for the oncoming nurse, or fostering psychological comfort and confidence in the oncoming nurse. Offgoing nurses' goals for shift report targeted their own behavior, that of the oncoming nurse, or both. When offgoing nurses described goals focused only on their own performance, oncoming nurses consistently reported problems with the information and organization of the reports they received.

Nurses predominately focused on the shift that was ending in their CSR. Across all reports, the relative number of CSR words coded as current items was 63%, past items was 22%, and future items was 14. Nurses receiving the CSR stated that they were more likely to believe the evidence that the offgoing nurse observed directly, rather than more distant historical events.

High information flow was a challenging aspect of the discourse. Word counts of a verbal CSR ranged 586-4435 words, with a mean count of 1955 words. The longest reports produced 17 double-spaced transcript pages. In nearly every case, the CSR was interrupted multiple times to answer a sounding alarm, a patient's call, a phone call, or to dodge other staff moving equipment in the hall. Background noise levels were generally high, but waxed and waned throughout the conversations as CSRs took place simultaneously at several hallway locations in front of the critical care unit patient rooms.

Nurses described the CSR as a process of reaching agreement about the patient status through questioning, responding, and continued discussion until both nurses were satisfied. All twenty oncoming nurses believed they shared the same view of the patient with the offgoing nurse after receiving report; 18 of the 20 offgoing nurses thought that agreement had been reached.

Argument structures were examined by clustering data related to individual patient issues, then classifying data within each issue of concern using definitions of types of evidence, warrants, and claims. Data coding across 28 patients and 197 claims reached 90-93% inter-rater agreement for types of argument claims made in the CSR. Argument claims ranged from recommendations for very specific and detailed interventions (27%) to more general suggestions that some unspecified intervention (10%) or some type of monitoring (63%) at an unspecified time. Warrants serving to connect evidence with argument claims were often implied rather than stated outright, which could be an efficient process for nurses with shared knowledge and assumptions. Evidence provided in CSR ranged from reproducible numerical data to behavioral descriptions and appeals to authority. Oncoming nurses clearly expressed that they found numerical data and first-person accounts of assessments or events more credible than other types of evidence.

Nursing CSR reflects both the structural aspects of formal argument with components of evidence, warrants, and claims, and the pragmatic aspects of informal argument with components of interpersonal, social, and environmental/contextual cues. Rather than merely reporting information during CSR, nurses use informal argument to convince their peers of the need for ongoing actions and monitoring. The process of providing and evaluating evidence during CSR is an under-appreciated opportunity for social learning and epistemological development in the nursing workforce.

References

Kuhn, D. (1991). *The skills of argument.* Cambridge: Cambridge University Press.

Wertsch, J. (1991). *Voices of the mind: A sociocultural approach to mediated action.* Cambridge, MA: Harvard University Press.

Zarefsky, D. A. (1995). Argumentation in the tradition of speech communication studies. In F. H. van Eemeren, R. Grootendorst, J. A. Blair & C. A. Willard (Eds.), *Perspectives and approaches: Proceedings of the Third International Conference on Argumentation* (Vol. 1, pp. 32-52). Amsterdam.

Zsambok, C. E., & Klein, G. (1997). *Naturalistic decision making.* Mahwaw: Lawrence Erlbaum Associates.

Design principles for the Knowledge-Practices Laboratory (KP-Lab) project

Hakkarainen, Kai, Muukkonen, Hanni, Department of Psychology, P.O. Box 9, SF-00014 University of Helsinki, Finland, Email: kai.hakkarainen@helsinki.fi, hanni.muukkonen@helsinki.fi
Markkanen Hannu, EVTEK University of Applied Sciences, Vanha maantie 6, FIN-02650 Espoo, Finland, Email: hannu.markkanen@evtek.fi, and the KP-Lab Research and Development Community

Abstract: The poster introduces the design principles for the Knowledge-Practices Laboratory (KP-Lab) project. KP-Lab is based on technological, theoretical, pedagogical, and social innovations aimed at facilitating innovative practices of working with knowledge, "knowledge practices", in education and workplaces. In order to be truly productive, collaborative technologies cannot fully be specified beforehand but need to co-evolve with social practices and be further modifiable according to the users' emerging needs and practices.

Introduction

Future challenges of European society require policy makers, educators, researchers, technology developers and teachers to devise ways to prepare learners to engage in intensive work focused on deliberate knowledge advancement (Bereiter, 2000; Hakkarainen, Palonen, Paavola, & Lehtinen, 2004). Knowledge work requires managing complex knowledge through dynamically evolving forms of collaborative teamwork and sustained knowledge sharing. Innovation and knowledge creation activities are becoming commonplace and the most important sources of new material and intellectual wealth. In terms of the educational practices, a challenge for the knowledge society is that students, teachers, professionals, designers, and researchers take part not only in knowledge acquisition or social participation processes, but also knowledge creation focusing around shared objects of activity. The *Knowledge-Practice Laboratory* (KP-Lab) project will focus on creating the KP-Lab learning system aimed at facilitating innovative practices of working with knowledge ("knowledge practices") in education and workplaces. The system is considered in a number of its real-life instantiations whose data provide feedback for its continuing refinement. KP-Lab is a five-year (2006-2010) integrated project concerning the Technology-Enhanced Learning (Information Society Technologies) program of the European Community. University of Helsinki and EVTEK University of Applied Sciences coordinate the project, involving 22 organizations from 14 European countries. The design principles shaping the KP-Lab project are as follows: Principle 1. Organizing activity around collaborative advancement of knowledge artefacts; Principle 2. "Symmetric knowledge advancement" (Scardamalia, 2002) around authentic problems; Principle 3. Deliberate transformation of knowledge practices; Principle 4. Co-evolution of tools, social practices, and agents. These design principles will be implemented throughout the project in order to generate four types of innovation.

Theoretical innovation

As a theoretical innovation, the KP-Lab represents an approach to human cognition which assists going beyond acquisition (monological, within mind approach) and participation (dialogical, interactive approach) metaphors of learning to consider also knowledge-creation processes, and related tools and practices critical for answering the challenges of the emerging innovation society. According to the knowledge-creation approach, cognition is seen to develop through collaborative work in systematically developing shared, conceptual or material artefacts, such as concepts, plans, products, or social practices (Paavola, Lipponen, & Hakkarainen, 2004, Paavola & Hakkarainen, 2005). These kinds of processes are considered to be "trialogical" in nature in terms of the participants activities mediated through jointly developed knowledge artefacts. This kind of approach has deep historical roots, but their analysis and more importantly their assessment are in the infancy stage. The KP-Lab project will develop and explicate the theoretical foundations of the knowledge-creation ("trialogical") approach. In addition it will develop and test concrete models and tools for trialogical knowledge practices in various contexts (higher education, polytechnics, working life, secondary-level education).

Pedagogical innovation

Innovative knowledge practices will be facilitated across multiple domains of knowledge by organizing a series of technology-mediated KP-Lab courses in which students solve complex problems for real customers (i.e., enterprises, research communities or public organizations) and pursue field training in professional communities. This pedagogy requires teachers to function more like managers of knowledge-intensive companies than simple distributors of knowledge. Student teams supported by tools of ubiquitous computing are asked to engage in either concrete or virtual knowledge-creating activities that involve breaking boundaries of their educational institutions and building novel connections with professional communities and corresponding knowledge practices. These efforts will create new student-expert partnerships as well as novel networks of polytechnics, universities, and professional communities in terms of shared efforts of advancing knowledge practices throughout Europe.

Social innovation

KP-Lab's design principles emerge from two decades of educational and socio-cognitive research concerning technology-enhanced learning. These investigations indicate that technology-enhanced learning transforms educational practices only through transformed social practices. In order to deal with this challenge, KP-Lab puts reflective social practices around shared knowledge artefacts into the core of technology-enhanced learning. Toward that end, it provides the participants tools for reflecting on, making visible, and transforming their knowledge practices. The challenge is to design technical tools and solutions that encourage the users to engage in thinking and collective reflection, so as to promote organizational intelligence and deliberate transformation of knowledge practices within the social matrix of knowledge creation. An essential aspect of KP-Lab will be to design virtual change-laboratory tools based on "change-laboratory" (Engeström, Virkkunen, Helle, Pihlaja, & Poikela, 1996) interventions that will allow participants, whether they are students, teachers, or professionals, to master, together, the challenges of the current activity and to work deliberately for innovative redesign of their collective activities. Participants of KP-Lab, whether they are students of higher education or professionals, will be engaged to jointly reflect on and make visible their knowledge practices in order to set these up as objects of deliberate change and improvement.

Technological innovation

KP-Lab will be a modular, flexible and extensible system consisting of a cluster of inter-operable applications (i.e., shared collaborative spaces, semantic web knowledge services, communication platform, ubiquitous user agents, inter-institutional access) which organize participants' collaborative activity around shared knowledge artefacts. Ubiquitous user agents provide end-users with inter-institutional access to KP-Lab services such as shared collaborative working spaces, semantic web knowledge repository, and real-time multimedia communication for individuals and groups. The KP-Lab system will be designed according to openness, modularity, and compatibility with the Semantic Web technology. The KP-Lab intends to research and develop a generic middleware supporting flexible knowledge management services for learning applications. It will be made available as an open-source software also for end-user applications beyond the present project. In order to be truly productive, collaborative technologies cannot fully be specified beforehand but need to *co-evolve* with social practices and be further modifiable according to the users' emerging needs and practical innovations. Consequently, the KP-Lab is intended to be a "laboratory" in terms of providing a testbed for developing transformative knowledge practices for educational institutions and workplaces. The project will be carried out through several stages that involve iterative technology development and empirical testing and piloting of KP-Labs technologies and practices. A special effort will be invested to identify and analyze reciprocal individual and social transformations taking place across sustained trialogical efforts of knowledge advancement undertaken in KP-Labs.

References

Bereiter, C. (2002). *Education and Mind in the Knowledge Age*. Hillsdale, NJ: Erlbaum.

Engeström, Y., Virkkunen, J., Helle, M., Pihlaja, J., & Poikela, R. (1996). The change laboratory as a tool for transforming work. *Life Long Learning in Europe, 2*, 10-17.

Hakkarainen, K., Palonen, T., Paavola, S., & Lehtinen, E. (2004). *Communities of networked expertise: Professional and educational perspectives*. Amsterdam: Elsevier.

Paavola, S., Lipponen, L., & Hakkarainen, K. (2004). Models of Innovative Knowledge Communities and Three Metaphors of Learning. *Review of Educational Research 74*(4), 557-576.

Paavola, S., & Hakkarainen, K. (2005). The knowledge creation metaphor – An emergent epistemological approach to learning. *Science & Education, 14*, 537-557.

Scardamalia, M. (2002). Collective cognitive responsibility for the advancement of knowledge. In B. Smith (Ed.), *Liberal Education in a Knowledge Society* (pp. 67-98). Chicago: Open Court.

Enhancing children's learning in museums: A Design-Based Research Approach

Tony Hall, Learning Sciences Research Institute, University of Nottingham, UK, tony.hall@nottingham.ac.uk
Liam Bannon, Luigina Ciolfi, Paul Gallagher, Kieran Ferris, Interaction Design Centre, University of Limerick, Ireland,
Email: liam.bannon@ul.ie, luigina.ciolfi@ul.ie, paul.gallagher@ul.ie, kieran.ferris@ul.ie
Ruth Mulhern, The Hunt Museum, Limerick, Ireland, ruth@huntmuseum.com
Nora Hickey, Lewis Glucksman Gallery, University College Cork, Ireland, nora.hickey@ucc.ie

Abstract: This paper reports research, conducted in collaboration with the Hunt Museum, Limerick, Ireland, which explored the design and deployment of novel ubiquitous computing to augment children's learning in museums. The paper summarises a Design-Based Research process. The poster will display the final results of the research. The authors have presented the initial and interim findings at the previous two ICLS conferences (e.g. Hall et al, 2004).

The Design-Based Research Process in the Hunt Museum

The aim of the research described here was to make a difference in the way children experience artefacts and museums. Thus, it was of paramount importance that the design process was sensitive to the museum's many important stakeholders. Previous research (Rogers & Edwards, 2002) had identified lack of consultation with educational and curatorial stakeholders as a major barrier impeding the design of successful exhibitions in museums. Furthermore, it was decided to adopt a Design-Based Research (DBR) approach because there is a commitment within DBR both to improve design practice and also to enhance scientific understanding of how design affects learning (Barab & Squire, 2004) In all, the Hunt Museum DBR process encompassed six main design activities or consultations:

1. Technical experimentation (six probes, where the interactive capabilities of a number of innovative computer technologies (e.g. RFID, WebCam tracking) were tested, both in lab settings and in the Hunt Museum);
2. Consultation of children's history and museum education policy (as outlined in the Irish Primary School History Curriculum and the ICOM (International Council of Museums) charter);
3. Design, development and evaluation of a large-scale interactive museum exhibition, *Exploring Digital History* at Nottingham Castle and Museum, which preceded and significantly informed the development work for the exhibition in the Hunt Museum;
4. Observational studies (of schoolchildren's interactions in two interactive museum workshops, a simulated archaeology dig and time machine);
5. Consultation of museum and Hunt family experts (docents (the museum's specialist guides), curators, museum education officers, Hunt family biographer);
6. Scan and evaluation of physical/spatial constraints of the museum.

As is characteristic of most Design-Based Research, the design process was closely informed by an orienting theoretical perspective. The conceptual or theoretical framework for the Hunt Museum comprised eight major design concerns or themes: (1) materiality; (2) narrativity; (3) sociality; (4) activity; (5) multi-modality; (6) engagement; (7) computer as augmentation tool; and (8) pedagogical activity.

The Design Product: *Re-Tracing the Past*

The space limitations of a conference poster proposal constrain the depth of the discussion of the analytic data, particularly as over sixty hours of video data, (in addition to other data collection activities and instruments such as questionnaires, interviews and pre- and post-visit school visits), were collected and analysed. Overall, the evaluation of the exhibition revealed that *Re-Tracing the Past* had a positive impact in terms of the eight design themes: materiality, narrativity, etcetera. For detailed discussion of data pertaining to each theme, the authors refer the reader to more comprehensive accounts of the research (Hall & Bannon, 2005) on which this paper is based. The images below show children interacting with various features of the highly innovative and successful interactive exhibition. The final design in the museum was a replica study room and adjoining mysterious room, which contained interactive fittings. The design of the exhibition in the Hunt Museum embodied the theoretical frame described previously, and children's experience of *Re-Tracing the Past* was a highly positive one.

	Rachel (girl with red hair at the bottom of the picture) explores sonic properties of the Dodecahedron at the Virtual Touch Machine.
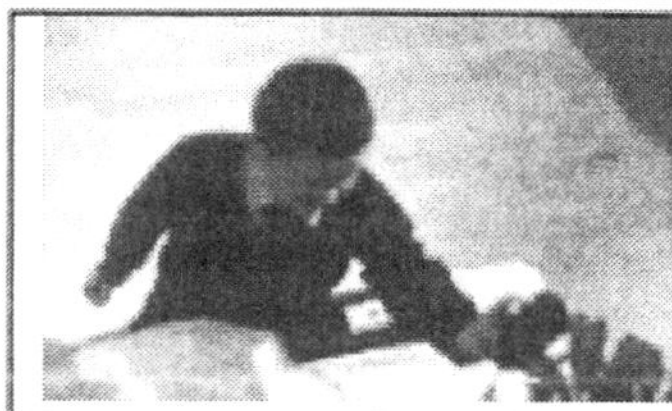	Tim turns the handheld for the Virtual Touch Machine to see the decorative designs on the Oxford Disc.
	Michael is impressed when he sees one of the animations about the Oxford Disc at the interactive Trunk.
	Martina and Nicole tactually explore the replica Stone Ball.

Figure 1. Snapshots of children's interactions in *Re-Tracing the Past*.

References

Barab, S., & Squire, K. (2004). Design–Based Research: Putting a Stake in the Ground. In Kolodner, J., Barab, S., Eisenberg, M. (Eds.) *The Journal of the Learning Sciences*, *13*(1), 1-14.

Hall, T., & Bannon, L. (2005). Co-operative design of children's interaction in museums: A case study in the Hunt Museum. *CoDesign: International Journal of CoCreation in Design and the Arts*, *1*(3), 187-218.

Hall, T., Ciolfi, L., Ferris, K., Bannon, L., Gallagher, P., Hickey, N., Hedman, A., & Tobiasson, H. (2004). Tools for Open Interpretation: using novel computing to support multiple perspectives in children's historical understanding. *ICLS2004: The Sixth International Conference of the Learning Sciences*, June 22-26, 2004, Santa Monica, California.

Rogers, R., & Edwards, S. (2002). The Big Sink: a report on the key factors for designing, building, equipping, using and managing creative spaces in galleries, museums and schools. *Group for Education in Museums (GEM) News*. No. 86. Summer 2002, 8-9.

Cognitive Effects of Chess Instruction on Students At Risk for Academic Failure

Saahoon Hong, William Bart M, University of Minnesota, Department of Educational Psychology, 204 Burton Hall, 178 Pillsbury Dr. SE, Minneapolis, MN 55455
Email: hong0083@umn.edu, bartx001@umn.edu

Abstract: This study examined the cognitive effects of chess instruction on thirty-eight students at risk for academic failure. The analysis found no significant differences between the cognitive changes registered by the treatment group and the control group. However, for the chess group, participant chess rating was significantly correlated with TONI-3 scores. The findings indicated that student acquisition of high chess ratings contributes to the improvement of cognitive skills rather than student mere exposure to chess.

Introduction

Chess playing provides numerous opportunities for players to practice higher order cognitive skills. It involves comprehension of chess positions, analysis of moves and their sequences, and evaluation of positions resulting from certain moves (Bart, 2004; Gobet & Simon, 1996). Higher order cognitive skills play a major role in enabling students to better establish and attain goals, identify potential response alternatives in the decision-making process, and achieve self-regulated learning (Wehmeyer, Palmer, Agran, Mithaug, & Martin, 2000). These skills are considered to be transferable skills (Ericsson & Staszewski, 1989; Ericsson & Kintsch, 1995; Gobet & Simon, 1996)

Although little research has been conducted to identify the effect of chess, chess instruction shows that it produces significant effects on student performance in both cognitive and academic tasks. Horgan's (1987) study was the first study in providing a model for chess instruction, emphasizing teaching of principles, frequent feedback, and specific chess drills. Research on chess instruction demonstrates that children who play chess improve analytical reasoning, problem solving skills, and even academic achievement (Chrisiaen & Verholfstadt, 1978; Frank & D'Hondt, 1979; Smith & Cage, 2000), while studies on the relation between visuospatial ability and chess skill showed mixed results (Waters, Gobet, & Leyden, 2002).

But can chess instruction have salutary cognitive effects with other types of students such as students at risk or students with disabilities? Storey (2000) suggested that chess instruction could also benefit children with disabilities, even though only anecdotal evidence is available for the effect of chess play on students with disabilities (Remsen, 1998; Russo, 1997; Wojcio, 1995). Thus, this study will examine this issue as it concerns various kinds of students who are at risk for academic failure. A relation between chess skill and higher order cognitive skills will be investigated to support a model that chess instruction benefits students at risk.

Methods

Participants

Thirty-eight students, ages 8 to 12, from three elementary schools participated. These schools are located in Seoul, Korea. Of these students, all students enrolled in an after school program for students at risk. Among them, six students received special education services at a resource room setting, too. Students at risk were identified according to criteria developed by the Korean Ministry of Education.

They possessed poor math, reading, and writing skills. Approximately 2-3% of students per school fell into this category. They have significant deficits in more than one area among the domains of reading, writing, and math. Playing chess was new to most of the students. Although one student stated that he sometimes played chess with his brother and his knowledge of basic chess rules was shallow.

Procedures

The study began with administration of the two pretests after the consent forms were returned. A researcher and a research assistant administered tests in the first week of this study. At the beginning and end of the chess intervention, Test of Nonverbal Intelligence, Third Edition, (TONI-3) and Raven's Progressive Matrices (RPM) were given to the students.

The participants were randomly assigned to an experimental (18) or a control group (20). The experimental group received a 90-minute chess lesson once per week and the control group students attended regular school activities after class.

A chess intervention was divided into 12 separate lessons over a 3-month period. Each lesson consisted of three segments: reviewing, lecturing, and chess playing. A chess instructor provided a set of quizzes after each lecture. The last six lessons were implemented in a computer lab by using chess software.

Results

The results of this study indicate no cognitive effect of chess instruction. In the analysis of two cognitive tests, the experimental group performance on the test was not different from the control group performance.

For internal analysis of the experimental group, the partial correlation of the TONI-3 Posttest scores and the Chess Ratings with the TONI-3 Pretest score being held constant was .520, $p < .05$. However, the effect size for the experimental group was small ($d = 0.29$) on TONI-3.

Discussion

Although there are a few limitations, the results of this study demonstrate that young novice chess players at risk for academic failure can benefit from chess instruction through improving their chess skills. They require more time for chess instruction than a twelve-session chess instruction period. One year or more of chess instruction is suggested for strong salutary cognitive effects on the students at risk.

In addition, chess instruction should focus on student acquisition of higher chess skill ratings rather than mere exposure to chess. If the chess instruction focused on improvements in student chess skill ratings through practicing higher order cognitive skills, then the chess instruction might well engender salutary cognitive effects. For the development of chess instruction, individual differences and unique needs should be taken consideration.

Thus, we recommend that the cognitive effects of chess performance on students at risk for academic failure continue to be studied. The heretofore-mentioned methods for improving chess instruction could be incorporated into such an inquiry. Chess instruction specially configured may prove to be very efficacious in producing salutary cognitive effects among students at risk for academic failure in the USA, and elsewhere in the world.

References

Bart, W. (2004, May). *Cognitive enhancement: An approach to the development of intelligence.* Poster session presented at the annual meeting of the American Psychological Society, Chicago, Illinois.

Christiaen, J., & Verholfstadt, D. C. (1978). Chess and cognitive development. *Nederlandse Tydschrift voor de Psychologie en haar Grensbebieden, 36*, 561-582.

Ericsson, K. A., & Kintsch, W. (1995). Long-term working memory, *Psychological Review, 102*, 211-245.

Ericsson, K. A. & Staszewski, J. (1989). Skilled memory and expertise: Mechanisms of exceptional performance. In D. Klahr and K. Kotovsky (Eds.), *Complex Information Processing: The Impact of Herbert A. Simon.* Hillsdale, N.J.: Erlbaum.

Frank, A., & D'Hondt, W. (1979). Aptitudes and learning chess in Zaire. *Psychopathologie Africane, 15,* 81-98.

Gobet, F., & Simon, H. A. (1996). The roles of recognition processes and look-ahead search in time-constrained expert problem solving: Evidence from grandmaster-level chess. *Psychological Science, 7*, 52-55.

Horgan, D. D. (1987). Chess as a way to teach thinking. *Teaching, Thinking and Problem Solving, 9*, 4-11.

Pelts, R., & Alburt, L. (1992). *Comprehensive chess course volume 1 (4th edition).* New York, NY: Chess Information and Research Center.

Remsen, D. (1998). Churchill school for learning disabilities wins three trophies at nationals. *Chess Life, 53,* 622

Russo, A. (1997). Chess versus drugs: When chess is more than a game. *Chess Life, 52*, 7.

Smith, J. P., & Cage, B. N. (2000). The effects of chess instruction on the mathematics achievement of Southern, rural, Black secondary students. *Research in the Schools, 7,* 19-26.

Storey, K. (2000). Teaching beginning chess skills to students with disabilities. *Preventing School Failure, 44*, 2, 45-49.

Waters, A. J., Gobet, F., & Leyden, G. (2002). Visuospatial abilities of chess players. *British Journal of Psychology, 93*, 557-565.

Wehmeyer, M. L., Palmer, S. B., Agran, M., Mithaug, D. E., & Martin, J. (2000). Teaching students to become causal agents in their lives: The self-determining learning model of instruction. *Exceptional Children, 66*, 439-453.

Wojcio, M. (1995). Chess is very special. *Chess Life, 50,* 767.

Automated Social Network Analysis as a Tool for Evaluating Sociability

Kirk Job-Sluder, Indiana University, 639 North Maple St., Bloomington, IN 47404, csluder@indiana.edu

Abstract: Although the tools for mediating Internet-based learning communities have exploded in the last few years, our theoretical understanding of how to evaluate attempts to build online communities has lagged behind (Carroll, 2001). We used automated tools to build social network maps of an educational children's multi-user virtual environment using two modes of CMC. Internal "E-mail" was most frequently used within groups. Short "telegram" messages were frequently used within groups but also provided between-group interaction.

Purpose and Theoretical Background

The growth of the Internet has inspired a large number of projects investigating its potential as a medium for collaborative learning environments. One central argument for the construction of Internet-based learning environments is Internet messaging allows learning to take place without constraints of shared location and time (Hara, Bonk, & Angeli, 2000). This opens the possibility for "anytime anywhere" instruction and professional development. Sociability, the quality of a technical system to enable collaboration between participants, has joined usability as a design criterion.

The larger project from which this study comes is an online educational environment for late-elementary children. Participating engage in instructional content through a 3D Multi-User Virtual Environment and a fictional game-like context. Participating students and teachers are located at sites in the United States, Australia, China, Singapore, Sweden, Turkey and Denmark. One question of concern to this project is to what degree do participants use the available communications tools to interact with participants from other classrooms and other countries. Hampton and Wellman (2003) propose that CMC-based networks interact with and build upon traditional "face to face" networks. If so, the networks constructed using CMC should show a large number of messages sent within local classroom groups. The other hypothetical extreme would involve participants actively seeking out new contacts, resulting in minimal within-group messaging.

Methods

Social Network Analysis (SNA) is another diverse set of methods for examining the relations between individuals and groups (Wasserman & Faust, 1994). A relation can be any form of social interaction including knowing the other person by name, communication, or shared membership within a group. Hampton and Wellman (2003) examined Internet interactions, name recognition and residence visits. While Paolillo (2001) examined responses in chat interactions. SNA provides powerful methods for quantifying the size, shape and scope of a given network.

This paper is based on data from two weeks of activity during May 2005 within the MUVE, examining two modes of communication. Telegrams are short private messages sent from one sender to a single recipient and are persistent until read. The data sample included 1,071 "telegram" messages sent by 77 participants. Mail messages are long private message sent from one sender to multiple recipients and are persistent until deleted. The data sample included 253 messages sent by 82 participants.

Sender and recipient information was automatically extracted from the message headers and used to build social network analysis matrices. Relations were aggregated by classroom membership. The sna package for R (Butts, 2005) was used to create visual maps of this data (see figure 1 below.) In addition, all of the data was read for case characterization, and structural discourse analysis statistics (Herring, 2004) performed to describe the message samples.

Results

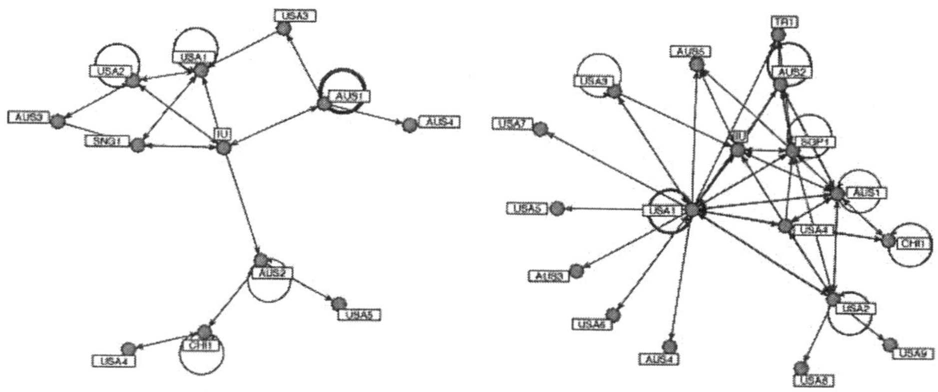

Figure 1. Network maps for mail (left) and telegrams (right). Messages sent within groups are displayed as closed loops. Thickness of lines indicates number of messages.

For internal email, most of the messages were sent within groups, and a handful of messages sent between groups. However, the telegram messages were more frequently used between groups. In addition, classrooms that received direct support from the project researchers and staff were more central within the social networks than classrooms not receiving direct support. Although this paper focused on relationships between classrooms, more sophisticated analysis is possible.

References

Butts, C. (2005). *S Routines for Social Network Analysis in the R environment.* Retrieved November 15, 2005 from http://erzuli.ss.uci.edu/R.stuff/

Carroll, J. M. (2001). Community computing as human-computer interaction. *Behavior & Information Technology*, 20(5), 307-314.

Hampton, K., & Wellman, B. (2003). Neighboring in Netville how the Internet supports community and social capital in a wired suburb. *City & Community*, 2(4), 277-311.

Hara, N., Bonk, C. J., & Angeli, C. (2000). Content analysis of on-line discussion in an applied instructional technology course. *Instructional Science*, 28(2), 115-152.

Herring, S. C. (2004). Computer-mediated discourse analysis: An approach to researching on-line behavior. In S. A. Barab, R. Kling, & J. H. Gray (Eds.), *Designing for virtual communities in the service of learning* (pp. 338-376). New York: Cambridge University Press.

Paolillo, J. C. (2001). Language variation on Internet Relay Chat: A social network approach. *Journal of Sociolinguistics*, 5(2), 180-215.

Walmsley, D. J. (2000). Community, place and cyberspace. Australian Geographer, 31(1), 5-19. Wasserman, S., & Faust, K. (1994). *Social network analysis: Methods and applications.* New York: Cambridge University Press.

Acknowledgements

This research was supported in part by a CAREER Grant from the National Science Foundation, REC-9980081 and by the National Science Foundation Grant #0092831. Other members of the QA research team including Andrew Brown, Sasha A. Barab, and Bronwyn Stuckey provided valuable assistance in collecting data for this project.

Seeds of a Computer Culture: An Archival Analysis of Programming Artifacts from a Community Technology Center

Yasmin B. Kafai, Kylie A. Peppler, Mabel Alavez, & Omar Ruvalcaba
University of California, Los Angeles 2331 Moore Hall Los Angeles, CA 90095
kafai@gseis.ucla.edu, peppler@gmail.com, m_1080@yahoo.com, indigo@ucla.edu

Abstract: We examined the genre and complexity of computer programs created by members of a community technology center. We collected 240 projects during a six-month period. The program genres reflected animations, games, and graphics in about equal numbers. While the number of computer programs decreased over time, the number of advanced programs remained constant suggesting that members either abandoned programs or paired up with more experienced programmers and continued to develop more complex programs.

About 25 years ago, Seymour Papert (1980) described the necessity of creating computer cultures rather than isolated experiences to learn with and about technology. He defined a computer culture as a place promoting access to technology fluency — in contrast to computer literacy — and by emphasizing technology production and personal expression as essential catalysts for learning. As the history of school classrooms has shown the creation of such cultures has proven to be a challenging enterprise, in particular what concerns programming activities. Even in informal learning environments such as community technology centers dedicated to technology fluency, computer programming has rarely become part of design activities.

Our research was situated in a Los Angeles community technology center (CTC) visited by a predominantly Latino/a and African-American youth ages 8-18. The center, where children and youth are considered "members" (as opposed to students) of a learning community, encourages them to devise multi-media, multi-application activities that are founded upon their personal interests (Resnick, Rusk, & Cooke, 1998). We introduced Scratch, a new programming environment oriented towards media production (Resnick, Kafai & Maeda, 2003). In Scratch, programmers do not need to write program code; rather they select and manipulate blocks to create scripts that control objects or characters on the screen. These blocks also facilitate manipulation of existing media such as imported graphics from the Internet or creation of videos, animations, and music. For this poster we will focus on the programming projects created by CTC members over the course of the six months. We considered these projects to be potential seeds, or indicators, of a computer culture that would tell us about members' interest in programming and their development of programming skills.

Methods

A member of the research team collected, on a regular basis, all of the Scratch projects stored on the central server by doing a file search for files with .scratch extensions. By collecting projects on a weekly basis we were able to track the number of projects and possible progress of individual projects, gathering multiple copies of a single project that had been reworked over a longer period of time. For the analysis, we took screenshots of program graphics and code and entered them into a spreadsheet along with short descriptions of content and functionality. In addition, we noted the name, gender, and age of programmer (if known) and possible collaboration with a mentor. Programs were coded into four categories based on project type (animation, game, story, graphics, and other) and classified into three levels of programming complexity: *exploratory* with no programming and only graphics, *basic* with simple programming scripts and of short length, and *advanced* with programming structures such as looping, conditionals, and random.

Findings

Over the course of six months, we collected 240 programming projects created by members of the CTC, some designed alone others with mentors. We found that 44% of these projects fell into the category animations with and without user manipulation, followed by 23% of graphics projects, and 15% of game projects focusing on fighting, sports and adventure; 14% or 34 projects escaped a clear categorization because they did not provide enough detail. In terms of program complexity, 30% or 72 projects were considered exploratory, 59% of the projects fell into the basic category, followed by 11% advanced projects. A longitudinal analysis revealed that over the time period of six months the total number of program projects decreased (see Figure 1a) while the number of advanced projects remained constant (see Figure 1b).

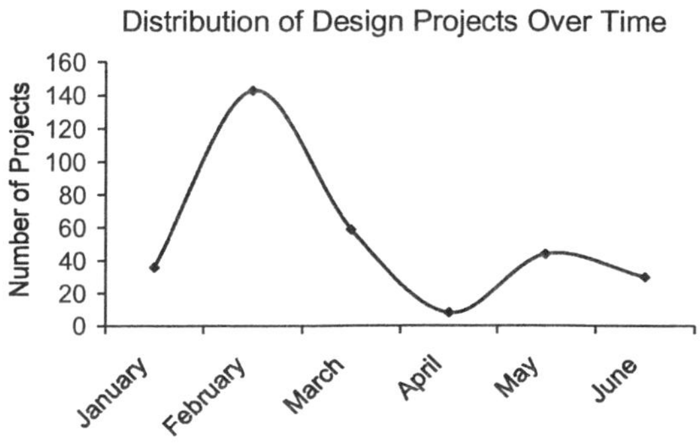

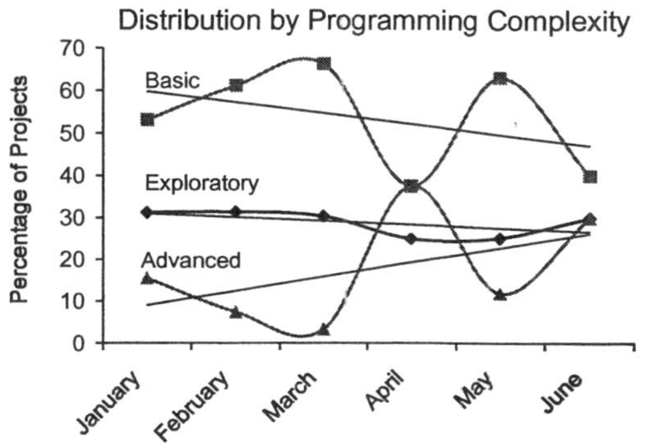

Figures 1a and 1b. The left graph illustrates the distribution of designed projects from the start of introducing Scratch (in January) with reaching a peak in February and a slow down in the second quarter from April to June. The right describes the distribution of projects in terms of programming complexity with the lines capturing general trends.

Discussion

We realize that this archival analysis of programming artifacts provides us only with a partial access to a computer culture for multiple reasons: to begin with, our archive while extensive did not capture all Scratch program designed but only those saved. The archive does not tell us what motivated CTC members to create their programs, what they value in their designs, and how they compare them to their other design projects. We also could not address the equally important social and local influences at work that contributed to the design of the programs. Notwithstanding these limitations, the large number of Scratch programs provides a compelling example that members were active in creating numerous programs over an extended period of time and that even without explicit curricular goals, grades or instruction. More importantly, the complexity of programs created remained constant while the total number of program projects decreased over time suggesting at least several explanations: members who generated exploratory programs dropped out of the CTC, members decided to team up with more experienced members or mentors to work on programs, or members developed their exploratory and basic programs into more complex projects. Our next steps will be to construct case studies for a select number of Scratch programs and to collect information from field notes about the design process and context and to conduct interviews with members about their projects and about programming in general.

References

Papert, S. (1980). *Mindstorms.* New York: Basic Books.

Resnick, M., Kafai, Y. B., & Maeda, J. (2003). *A Networked, Media-Rich Programming Environment to Enhance Technological Fluency at After-School Centers in Economically-Disadvantaged Communities.* Proposal (funded) to the National Science Foundation: Arlington, VA.

Resnick, M., Rusk, N., and Cooke, S. (1998). Computer Clubhouse: Technological fluency in the inner city. In D. Schoen, B. Sanyal, and W. Mitchell (eds.), *High Technology and Low-Income Communities.* Cambridge, MA: MIT Press.

Acknowledgments

We would like to thank Shiv Desai and Grace Chiu for their participation in research activities. The work reported in this poster is conducted in collaboration with Mitchel Resnick's research group at the MIT Media Lab and supported by a grant of the National Science Foundation (NSF-0325828). The views expressed are those of the authors and do not necessarily represent the views of the supporting funding agency or the University of California, Los Angeles.

A Model for Video-based Virtual Field Experience

Ugur Kale, Jung Won Hur, Theano Yerasimou, Thomas Brush, Indiana University
Email: ukale@indiana.edu, jwhur@indiana.edu, tyerasimou@indiana.edu, tbursh@indiana.edu

Abstract: The purpose of this project is to introduce a model of using video-based virtual field experiences for pre-service teachers mainly in social studies. Although video-based virtual fields become more practical for pre-service teachers to observe various teaching situations, the use of such video-based classroom cases may be limited to provide meaningful experiences. This paper presents four key affordances of a model that may alleviate such limitations.

Theoretical Background

In order to integrate effective teaching strategies into their teaching, pre-service teachers need to observe diverse classroom teachings, interact with in-service teachers and students, and receive targeted feedback on their initial attempts at teaching related activities in field-based experiences. However, difficulties in finding appropriate placements, coupled with the number of students who need to be placed, make field-based experiences less feasible (Allen, 2003; Wilson & Floden, 2003). Providing online video case classroom vignettes may be an effective and efficient way to help pre-service teachers gain rich field experiences. There are existing examples of video-based databases that focus on classroom activities in different subject matters (Bitter et al., 2004; Schrader et al., 2003; Stirling et al., 2004; Teale et al., 2002). Observing such video-based cases, pre-service teachers are not only exposed to a variety of teaching and learning situations but also have a chance to observe and analyze them in detail as they have flexible control over viewing the videos. However, the linearity of such video clips can limit pre-service teachers' attention on the classroom activities. Pre-service teachers are less likely to grab the important aspects in the activities as they can easily attend to trivial and individual segments in the clips (Dolk et al., 2002). Pre-service teachers, without guidance or activities that direct them to particular aspects of video cases, can only gain very little knowledge. Also, without opportunities to critically reflect on and discuss the teaching and learning situations pre-service teachers cannot gain meaningful observations from these video cases.

A Virtual Experience Laboratory

Aforementioned problems with the use of video-based classroom cases led us to seek for a model, which may help pre-service teachers gain more meaningful virtual field experiences. The model discussed in this paper has been recently implemented in a program of virtual field experiences for pre-service history teachers-PIH - LVFE (Persistent Issues in History Laboratory for Virtual Field Experience). The PIH – LVFE is an online database that provides video cases of authentic classroom practices. It also includes multimedia teaching resources and tools to enable social studies teacher educators to assist pre-service teachers with problem-based historical inquiry. Effectively utilizing these resources and video cases, teacher educators introduce and promote the development of teaching skills needed to effectively implement problem based historical inquiry strategies in secondary classrooms.

Affordances of the Model for Using Video-based Cases

Followings are the key affordances of the model that are likely to enable pre-service teachers to have more meaningful virtual field experiences.

Observe:

Pre-service teachers observe video-based classroom cases in order to be familiar with pedagogical issues that arise in real classroom settings. However, providing only linear classroom vignettes to be observed cannot benefit pre-service teachers who need to make sense of the classroom applications from a professional teacher's perspective. In the model, however, pre-service teachers listen to the classroom teacher as she reflects on what is going on in the classroom and explains the important issues and problems faced during classroom implementation. In the PHI-LVFE program, pre-service teachers observe not only classroom videos but also additional clips of pre- and post- classroom interviews of in-service teachers regarding their experiences.

Read:

Pre-service teachers should read and be able to focus on particular aspects of a video-based classroom that will likely make their observation more meaningful. Teacher educators involved in the PHI-LVFE program are provided with an annotation tool that enables them to link additional information (e.g., comments about the video) to a specific video segment so that pre-service teachers focus on the specific aspects of the video cases.

Discuss:

Sharing and discussing video-based classroom cases can enhance pre-service teachers' observations. Listening to a teacher's thoughts on a classroom case, pre-service teachers can gain multiple interpretations and thus be aware of their incomplete observation of the case (Dolk, 2002). PHI-LVFE allows pre-service teachers to communicate with one another through an online forum and an online journal. They can discuss their observations and reflect on them by creating message threads in the online forum.

Participate:

In order to gain meaningful field experiences, pre-service teachers should be able to get involved in pedagogical activities focusing on teaching issues observed in the video classroom cases. PIH-LVFE provides teacher educators with a tool to develop such activities. The activity development tool enables teacher educators to combine many video-based cases and segments along with their discussion questions that pre-service teachers can be assigned to work on.

Summary

This paper aims to introduce a model with its affordances that may overcome the main obstacles observed in pre-service teachers' video-based virtual field experiences. While the model has been recently applied in a pre-service teacher virtual field program, its effectiveness in providing meaningful experiences will be investigated as more student teachers use the program.

References

Allen, M. (2003). Eight questions of teacher preparation. What does the research say? Eric Document Reproduction Service # ED479051.

Dolk, M., den Hertog, J., & Gravemeijer, K. (2002). Using Multimedia Cases for Educating the Primary School Mathematics Teacher Educator: A Design Study. *International Journal of Educational Research, 37*(2), 161-178.

Schrader, P., Leu, Jr., D., Kinzer, C., Ataya, R., Teale, W., Labbo, L., & Cammack, D. (2003). Using Internet delivered videocases to support pre-service teachers' understanding of effective early literacy instruction: An exploratory study. *Instructional Science*, 31, 317-340.

Stirling, D., Williams, M, & Padgett, H. (2004, March). Investigating the effectiveness of video case use in teacher education. Paper presented at *the annual meeting of the Society for Information Technology and Teacher Education*, Atlanta, GA.

Teale, W., Leu, Jr., D., Labbo, L., & Kinzer, C. (2002). Exploring literacy on the Internet. *The Reading Teacher*, 55(7), 654-659.

Wilson, S. M. & Floden, R. E. (2003). Creating effective teachers: Concise answers to hard questions. An addendum to the report "Teacher Preparation Research: Current Knowledge, Gaps, and Recommendations." Eric Document Reproduction Service # ED476366.

Visualizing Discussion by the Use of the Conversation Chain Model

Sabina Karkin, Elizabeth S. Charles, Janet L. Kolodner
Interactive & Intelligent Computing, Georgia Institute of Technology, 801 Atlantic Drive, Atlanta, GA 30332-0280
Email: gtg741a@mail.gatech.edu, echarles@cc.gatech.edu, jlk@cc.gatech.edu

Abstract: Identifying how students acquire an understanding of a particular subject in a classroom involves studying verbal interaction. In middle school science classrooms, we can analyze this interaction through videos and transcripts; however, it is still difficult to track and measure the development of students' scientific reasoning skills without visualizing this change. The *conversation chain model* offers this visualization by illustrating questions and responses elicited during poster sessions, portraying their interpretation and quality of the discussion.

Sense-making discussions are a large part of science classrooms as they allow students to articulate to their peers their experimental results and what they learned and concurrently allow peers to engage in question-asking aimed towards understanding the experiment. Studying students' understanding of science concepts and tracking this development in this type of environment requires keeping track of who is eliciting and participating in discussion, what types of questions are raised, and what types of responses are given. These occurrences can be identified through analysis of video and transcript data. We wanted to use that data to study ways students come to understand the meaning of questions raised during discussion and their evolving abilities to respond to them (Charles, Karkin, Kramer, Kolodner, 2006), and also how this shapes the overall discourse. We needed a visual representation of the interaction to allow us to map this out. The visual representation allows us to see the degree of each individual student's participation overtime, quality of presentations, degree of teacher involvement, and the changing quality of discourse. The *conversation chain model* we developed affords this.

We are studying discourse situated in an inquiry-based approach to science learning *Learning by Design* (LBD; e.g., Kolodner, Camp, Crismond, Fasse, Gray, Holbrook, Puntembakar, Ryan, 2003). Included in LBD's practices is a public activity called a poster session in which student groups present their individual procedure and results and discuss their implications. As in a cognitive apprenticeship (Collins, Brown & Newman, 1989), early on the teacher models the kinds of questions students might ask of each other. Gradually, the students take on question-asking roles. They seem to get better at asking good questions, understanding the questions of others, providing meaningful responses, and participating in clarification and sense-making dialogs. The particular teacher we were observing used what we called cueing questions. We saw kids appropriate her questions and we wanted to track this, specifically the participatory and cultural resources of the poster session activity (the role of the teacher versus the roles of the students) and the types of interactions that occurred (student-student and student-teacher). Figure 1 below shows an example.

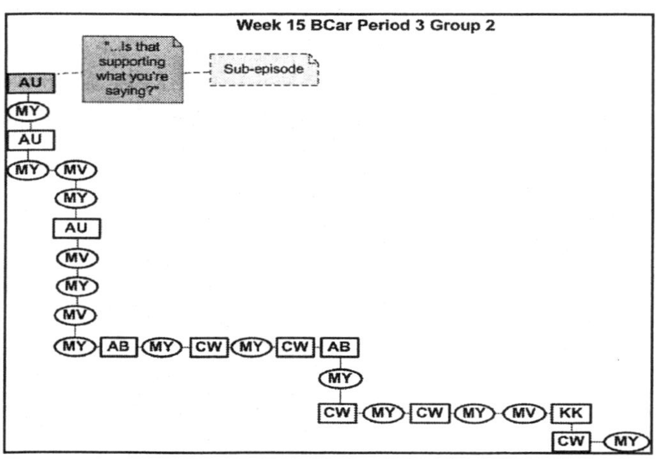

Figure 1. Conversation chain model illustrating discourse.

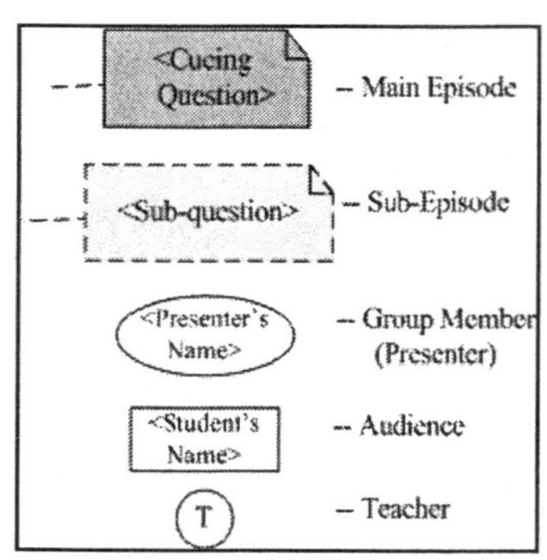

Figure 2. Components of the model.

The full set of components of the conversation chain model include main episodes composed of cueing questions (e.g., What is your recommendation?) and sub-episodes with sub-questions related to the main question but incomplete by themselves (such as a simple "Why"). Comments made by presenters, audience, and teacher are each denoted by a different shape (see Figure 2) where each piece represents a turn in the discourse. Responses are represented by vertical or horizontal chains, depending on whether the next utterance is normal turn-taking without elaboration (noted vertically) or adding/expanding/constructing shared meaning (noted horizontally). A vertical chain signifies a more unproductive discussion, as students do not build on each other's comments and do not have a shared goal. A horizontal chain, on the contrary, denotes a richer and more productive discussion that involves students' elaborating on each other's comments as they try to achieve a mutual goal by participating in grounding (Clark & Brennan, 1991). Thus, the longer the horizontal chain, the greater the sophistication of the discourse.

Data represented vertically include shut-down responses that do not allow for further elaboration; clarification questions that allow only for limited responses; and directive comments made towards a particular student regarding his/her current state. Data represented horizontally include responses that rephrase what was said for confirmation; agreeing responses that encourage others to make additional comments or continue; responses that elaborate on previous comments, providing further explanation/reasoning; conclusions drawn from previous comments; statements that repair perceived miscommunications in the conversation (Schegloff, 1991); and questions challenging previous statements by asking "Why?" and "How do you know?"

The example in Figure 1 describes an episode from week 15, period 3, group 2 where students engage in a discussion about evidence support. MC has just asked "What is your rule of thumb?" A rule of thumb is a principle that specifies the conditions under which some behavior might happen. We have seen that students begin by understanding this question as requesting for factual and procedural information and later understand it as requesting for scientific explanations that generalize their findings. In this sub-episode, AU (a student) asks "Is that supporting what you're saying?" The conversation first develops vertically, with AU, MY, and MV voicing confusion and providing clarification (MY, MV: "Which one?") and negative comments (MY: "Excuse me, I did this work"). It evolves into a horizontal chain after MY questions the significance of the argument, which is over an insignificant variance of mere millimeters in the reading of velocity. AB elaborates on MY's comment and provides an explanation for it, which results in elaboration of hypotheses by others. The conversation becomes vertical again for a short time at the point where MY voices confusion ("Which one?") and again becomes horizontal when they continue to build on each others' comments (MV: "It probably should be because it pushes it up." KK: "It's going up. He just tells it what it does."). Note that this discussion includes no teacher involvement, which implies that the students are able to elicit and maintain a meaningful and productive discussion by themselves.

The conversation chain model provides a way to visualize the classroom progress as a whole and study the parts that create that whole. The approach allowed us to make comparisons between classes across different periods, helping us identify question-asking and answering practices of students (Charles, Karkin, Kramer, Kolodner, 2006).

References

Charles, E. S., Karkin, S., Kramer, C., & Kolodner, J. L. (2006). From mechanical to meaningful classroom questions. Paper to be presented at the *7th International Conference of the Learning Sciences*: Bloomington, IN.

Clark, H.H. & Brennan, S.E. (1991). Grounding in communication. In L.B. Resnick & S.D. Teasley (Eds.), *Perspectives on Socially Shared Cognition*, (pp.127-149).

Collins, A., Brown, J. S., & Newman, S. E. (1989). Cognitive apprenticeship: Teaching the crafts of reading, writing, and mathematics. In L. B. Resnick (Ed.), *Knowing, learning, and instruction: Essays in honor of Robert Glaser* (pp. 453–494). Hillsdale, NJ: Lawrence Erlbaum Associates, Inc.

Kolodner, J.L., Camp, P.J., Crismond, D., Fasse, B.B., Gray, J., Holbrook, J., Puntambekar, S. & Ryan, M. (2003). Problem-Based Learning Meets Case-Based Reasoning in the Middle-School Science Classroom: Putting Learning by Design into Practice. *Journal of the Learning Sciences,* 12(4), 495-547.

Schegloff, E. (1991). Conversation analysis and socially shared cognition. In L.B. Resnick & S.D. Teasley (Eds.), *Perspectives on Socially Shared Cognition*, (pp.150-171).

Acknowledgments

This research is funded by the National Science Foundation. Great thanks to all LBD members.

Individual Differences in Sense of Classroom Community

Fengfeng Ke, Pennsylvania State University, 314 Keller Building, University Park, PA 16802
Email: lilyke@psu.edu

Abstract. The paper proposed reports a causal-comparative study that were conducted to examine whether the sense of community development differs by students' characteristics in both traditional and online course setting. Subjects comprise 171 undergraduate students enrolled in a major American university. Specifically, the researchers investigate whether students' learning preference, gender, and peer-acquaintance level influence their sense of community after controlling for initial differences, and whether their sense of community correlates with course grades.

Introduction

The value of social bonds in the learning process has been widely acknowledged in the education field (e.g. Vygotsky, 1978; Lave & Wenger, 1991). As an endorsement of this observation, building sense of community within classrooms has become a widely-accepted practice (Palloff & Pratt, 1999). Sense of community, as defined by McMillan and Chavis (1986), refers to "a feeling that members have of belonging, a feeling that members matter to one another and to the group, and a shared faith that members' needs will be met through their commitment to be together" (p. 8). Drawing on this definition, Rovai (2002) have specified four components of a classroom community as *spirit*, *trust*, *interaction*, and *learning*.

For the past decades, quite a few empirical studies have indicated that in a classroom setting, stronger sense of community promotes both the socialization and learning outcomes of students, such as persistence in courses, cooperation among members, perceived cognitive learning, and learning motivation (Bruffee, 1993; Dede, 1996; Moore & Brooks, 2001; Rovai, 2002).

However, few empirical studies reported on variables that influence students' sense of community. Rovai (2001) did report that in a virtual classroom female sense of community was significantly higher than that of males, but his finding was extracted from a small group of participants (18 in the total). Regis (1988) found that the likelihood of acquaintances predicted the sense of community at a face-to-face setting. His study, however, was more descriptive than experimental. Graff (2003) concluded that in a blended learning environment, students with intuitive cognitive style reported a lower sense of community than students with an intermediate or analytic style. Then, he suggested a replication of his study using more individual differences dimensions.

Research Purpose and Methods

The research was intended to verify previous researchers' supposition on the relationship between individual difference and sense of community, by doing empirical studies in both face-to-face and online course setting. Specifically, this causal-comparative study was conducted to investigate whether the sense of community differs by students' learning style, gender, and peer-acquaintance level, after controlling for initial differences. The study also sought to indicate if sense of community would predict students' course grades.

Participants

Participants comprised 171 undergraduate students (111 males and 60 females, with a mean age of 20.7) in a major university. 74 of them enrolled in a teamwork-oriented face-to-face course offered by the business school. The other 97 participants were engineering-majored undergraduate students who attended an ANGEL-based online science course that was balanced between teamwork and individual project.

Instruments

Classroom Community Scale (Rovai, 2002) is an instrument to assess students' sense of community and the extent of community development. The CCS contains 20 five-point Likert-scaled items, ten items each for the subscales of *connectedness* and *learning*. It has a theoretical maximum score of 100, with higher scores reflecting a stronger sense of community. Rovai (2002) reports the internal consistency of the total scale as .93 and a high degree of face validity. A 16-item Likert-scaled solitary/social learning style survey was constructed by the researchers based on a well-established LSO Learning Styles Inventory (Advanogy.com, 2003). It has a theoretical maximum score of 80, with higher score indicating a more social learning style and lower score indicating a more solitary style. A solitary-styled learner is more private, introspective, and independent; a social-styled learner, on the contrary, typically prefers learning in groups or classes (Ke, 2004). A panel of experts consisting of two university professors in educational psychology has vetted the content validity of the test questions. A pilot study of the survey was carried out toward a blend of 140 graduate and undergraduate students at the previous academic semester, indicating a KR-20 reliability of .76. A short survey was also developed to collect students' demographic data, including gender, race, and year in college. In the survey, participants were asked to self-report their acquaintances with their teammates in a three-point scale.

Procedure

Students' demographic data, which include gender and peer-acquaintance level, were collected at the beginning week of academic semester. Then, measured by Classroom Community Scale (CCS), data of students' sense of community was collected at the second week and the concluding week of the semester.

Findings

A 2 x 2 x 3 MANCOVA (with pre-measurement of CCS as covariate) was conducted to examine if students' learner preference, gender, and peer-acquaintance level would influence their scores at the CCS and each of its subscales. A correlation analysis then was used to measure the strength and direction of relationship between sense of community and course grades.

No main effects of learning style, gender, or acquaintance level were observed for the overall CCS scale. But a significant interaction effect was found between learning style and gender ($F = 4.893$, $p = .032$). A Bonferroni test of post-hoc comparisons indicated that females with a solitary learning style ($M = 65.9$) reported a lower sense of community than all the other groups ($p < .01$), while females with a social learning style ($M = 76.6$) reported the highest sense of community ($p < .01$). Additionally, a significant effect of learning style was noted for the *connectedness* subscale ($F = 4.109$, $p = .021$). A Bonferroni test showed that students with a solitary learning style reported a significantly lower sense of connectedness than students with a social learning style (Msol = 32.5, Msoc = 37.4, $p = .014$). No effects of learning style were noted for the *learning* subscale. No effects of gender or acquaintance level were observed for both of the two subscales. Because students' course grades are non-parametric (A, B, C, D, or F), Spearman's Rho correlation coefficient was computed to determine bivariate correlation between CCS scale score and course grade. The correlation was positive (.49) and statistically significant at the .01 level (two-tailed).

References

Bruffee, K. A. (1993). Collaborative learning: Higher education, interdependence, and the authority of knowledge. Baltimore: John Hopkins University Press.

Dede, C. (1996). The evolution of distance education: Emerging technologies and distributed learning. *American Journal of Distance Education, 10*(2), 4-36.

Graff, M. (2003). Individual differences in sense of classroom community in a blended learning environment. *Journal of Educational Media, 28*(2-3), 203-210.

Lave, J. & Wenger, E. (1991). *Situated learning: Legitimate peripheral participation.* Cambridge: Cambridge University Press

McMillan, D. W. & Chavis, D. M. (1986). Sense of community: A definition and theory. *American Journal of Community Psychology, 14*(1), 6-23.

Moore, A., and Brooks, R. (2001). Learning communities and community development: Describing the process. *International Journal of Adult and Vocational Learning.*

Palloff, R. & Pratt, K. (1999). *Building learning communities in cyberspace: Effective strategies for the online classroom.* San Francisco: Jossey-Bass.

Regis, H. A. (1988). Communication and the sense of community among the members of an immigrant group. *Journal of Cross-Cultural Psychology, 19*(3), 329-340.

Rovai, A. P. (2001). Building classroom community at a distance: A case study. *Educational Technology Research and Development, 49*(4), 33-48.

Rovai, A. P. (2002). Development of an instrument to measure classroom community. *Internet and Higher Education, 5*, 197-211.

Vygotsky, L. S. (1978). *Mind in society.* Cambridge, MA: Harvard University Press.

Assessing Conceptual Change in an Anchored, Case-Based Environment

Charles K. Kinzer, Teachers College, Columbia University, New York, NY, U.S.A., kinzer@tc.columbia.edu
Manu Kapur, National Institute of Education, Singapore, Manu_Kapur@hotmail.com
Dana W. Cammack, Montclair State University, Montclair, NJ, U.S.A., cammackd@mail.montclair.edu
Sarah Lohnes, Teachers College, Columbia University, New York, NY, U.S.A., scl2103@columbia.edu

Abstract: We (1) present an argument that anchored, case-based instruction, delivered interactively over the WWW has benefits for the conceptual development of preservice teachers, and (2) argue that a commonly-used measure can be modified to provide sophisticated insights into conceptual change. These goals are met by providing evidence from a two-group, large-scale experimental study of preservice teachers using multimedia, anchored cases in their preservice literacy methods courses.

Teachers deal with complex issues in classroom instruction, and anchored, case-based methods provide a way for learners to engage this complexity while developing their content knowledge in context (e.g., Kinzer et al., in press; Merseth, 1991). The CTELL (Case-Based Technologies for Literacy Learning) project (Kinzer et al., in press; Shrader et al., 2003) provides a vehicle where the complexity of classroom environments is presented in an anchored case-analysis format through an unstructured, multimedia interactive environment. Embedded in the CTELL cases are 12 principles of effective reading instruction that are grounded in the research literature (these have been described elsewhere, e.g., Shrader et al., 2003). From a research perspective, and the subject of this presentation, the issues become: How can conceptual change be measured?, and How does conceptual change differ across groups of learners instructed with and without the CTELL cases? To measure conceptual change, we draw heavily on Beyerbach (1988; see also Artiles & McClafferty, 1998). We agree that concept webs provide insight into how learners restructure their knowledge (in our case, their knowledge of the principles of effective reading instruction) in ways that make them central to their conceptual understanding.

Method

N = 365 preservice teachers in literacy methods classes were administered a concept web assessment at the beginning (pre) and the end (post) of the semester (n = 199 experimental, using CTELL cases; n = 166 control, traditional instruction through lectures, field experiences and readings). After a discussion and three sample concept webs were provided, they were asked to draw a central node labeled "effective reading/literacy instruction," and were given ten minutes to draw a concept web around that node. To investigate the effect of CTELL cases, conceptual change was operationalized through changes in the concept maps of students pre-and post-instruction. Treating the concept map as the data unit, the two commonly-used measures for conceptual change were the *degree of differentiation* (total number of discrete nodes) and the *degree of hierarchical organization* (maximum number of subordinate levels) (Beyerbach, 1988). In this proposal, we refer to the former as *intensity* and the latter as *depth*. Beyerbach (1988) argued that change in intensity and depth correspond to conceptual change. More formally, counting the central node as level 0, if there were n_1 nodes at level 1, n_2 nodes at level 2, and so on, up to n_l nodes at level l, then intensity, $I = n_1 + n_2 + \ldots + n_l$ and depth, $D = l$.

Treating gain in intensity and depth as the two dependent variables, a MANOVA did not reveal any significant difference between the control and experimental groups ($F = 1.275$, $p = .281$). Univariate analysis also did not reveal any differences on gains in intensity ($F = .469$, $p = .494$) or on depth ($F = 1.235$, $p = .267$). Thus, using these commonly-used measures of intensity and depth leads one to conclude that there was no significant difference in the conceptual change of students who were taught with vs. without CTELL cases. However, a limitation of this analysis is that it considers intensity and depth as separate measures of conceptual change. We argue that a more powerful measure of conceptual change would be one that combines the differentiation and hierarchical organization characteristics of a concept web. Insofar as we are aware, these measures do not exist. Applying the mathematical principle of rearrangements, two adjusted measures were developed.

The intensity of a node was adjusted for its hierarchy (Morine-Dershimer, 1993). For a node that occurs l levels away from the central node (the center node being level $l = 0$), its hierarchical leverage is $1/l$, i.e., the further it is away from the center node, the lower its leverage. Thus, by multiplying the number of nodes at a particular level with their hierarchical leverage, we obtained an adjusted measure of intensity, $I^1 = \frac{n_1}{1} + \frac{n_2}{2} + ... + \frac{n_l}{l}$. Gain/loss on this measure better captures an overall movement up or down a concept map's hierarchy, providing evidence for cognitive reorganization (Jones & Vesilind, 1996). To get a more accurate measure of hierarchical organization, the depth of a concept web was normalized by its un-adjusted intensity to give adjusted depth, $D^1 = \frac{l}{n_1 + n_2 + ... + n_l}$. It is easy to see that a given number of nodes distributed over fewer levels imply lower depth in the concept web whereas the same number of nodes distributed over many levels implies greater depth in the concept web.

When the previous statistical analysis was repeated with the adjusted measures of intensity and depth, results suggested a significant multivariate difference between the control and experimental groups ($F = 6.799$, $p = .001$). Univariate analysis revealed that experimental groups ($M = 2.31$, $SD = 4.39$) had significantly ($F = 6.540$, $p = .011$) greater adjusted intensities than control groups ($M = 1.08$, $SD = 4.79$). Furthermore, experimental groups ($M = -.043$, $SD = .11$) had significantly ($F = 11.696$, $p = .001$) lower depth in their concept maps than the control groups ($M = -.0063$, $SD = .09$). These results—using both unadjusted and adjusted measures—provided *confirmatory* evidence for an exploratory analysis (not reported here due to space constraints) of experimental data from the previous year ($n = 166$ control, $n = 201$ experimental). Thus, using these measures of intensity and depth in place of the more commonly-used measures noted above, one can find differences in conceptual changes that would not have been discovered.

Discussion and Implications

The results indicate that preservice teachers became more aware of the centrality of the literacy principles; thus the CTELL cases prove a potential vehicle to broaden their understanding. While there were no differences in the number of discrete nodes, nodes were closer, in terms of ordination, to the central node in the concept webs of experimental groups. This provides evidence of cognitive reorganization in terms of movement up the hierarchy of the concept map. Because there was also no difference in the maximum number of sub-ordinate levels, this implies that the upward movement was accompanied with a spreading across the levels. Our results using the reconceptualized measures to analyze concept webs imply that CTELL cases are effective in providing an understanding of the centrality of concepts related to the principles of effective reading instruction.

References

Artiles, A. J., & McClafferty, K. (1998). Learning to teach culturally diverse learners: Charting change in preservice teachers' thinking about effective teaching. *Elementary School Journal, 98*, 189-218.

Beyerbach, B. A. (1988). Developing a technical vocabulary on teacher planning: Preservice teachers concept maps. *Teaching and Teacher Education, 4*, 339-347.

Kinzer, C., Cammack, D., Labbo, L., Teale, W., & Sanny, R. (in press). The need to (re)conceptualize pre-service literacy teacher development. In M. McKenna, L. Labbo, R. Keiffer, & D. Reinking, D. (Eds.), *International handbook of literacy and technology* (Vol. 2). Mahwah, NJ: Erlbaum.

Merseth, K. K., (1991). The early history of case-based instruction: Insights for teacher education today. *Journal of Teacher Education, 42*(4), 243-249.

Morine-Dershimer, G. (1993). Tracing conceptual change in preservice teachers. *Teaching and Teacher Education, 9*, 15-26.

Schrader, P. G., Leu, D. J., Kinzer, C. K., Ataya, R., Labbo, L. D., Teale, W. H., & Cammack, D. W. (2003). Using Internet delivered video cases, to support pre-service teachers' understanding of effective early literacy instruction: *An exploratory study. Instructional Science, 31*, 317–340.

Acknowledgement

This material is based upon work supported by the National Science Foundation under Grant No. 0089221. Any opinions, findings, and conclusions or recommendations expressed in this material are those of the authors and do not necessarily reflect the views of the National Science Foundation.

Systematic formation of reading comprehension in visually impaired children

Kosonen Kari, Hakkarainen, Kai, Department of Psychology, P.O. Box 9, SF-00014 University of Helsinki,
Email: kari.kosonen@hotmail.com, kai.hakkarainen@helsinki.fi

Abstract: The focus on the present work-in-progress was to develop and test intervention method for facilitation of reading comprehension by blind teenagers. The study relied Vygotsky's theory of internalization, and specifically on Piotr Gal'perin's theory of stepwise formation of mental actions. The participants were helped to generate what Gal'perin called the 'orienting basis' (abstract representation) through providing them with a external physical model to structure the their comprehension activities. Theory and methods are described and results of the first case study provided.

Introduction

The present investigation focuses on developing and testing an interventional method for facilitating reading with understanding by visually impaired (blind) children. The study, in the cultural-historical (Vygotski 1983; Engeström, 1987) tradition, considers mental actions and psychic representations as derivatives of external actions. Piotr Gal'perin's theory further proposed the *stepwise formation of mental actions* and has previously been applied to children's reading queue readiness and the development of their phonetic awareness. The primary element of his learning theory is the so-called the "*orienting basis*" (Haenen, 1996). In Gal'perin's theory the orienting basis refers to an evolving generalized representation of problem situation and the adaptive forms of activity related to it. It guides the scaffolding of a learner's activity in the process of acquiring new knowledge and skills. It may have a pre-set form, but it will be modified and elaborated in the course of the formation process. The orienting basis initially depends on an external model and signs, through which the text's relevant content, elements and relations can be understood. This kind of external tool that represents the most important dimensions in the text supports the conscious processing of corresponding coherence relations (see Groesser, McNamara, & Louwerse, 2003). Broadly, we sought to develop and test Galperin's theory of stepwise formation of mental actions in supporting intervention for reading comprehension amongst visually-impaired children. Specifically we aimed to develop the orienting basis (generalized representation) through providing a corresponding, external physical model with marking tools. The orienting basis cannot, however, be created mechanically; it needs to be tailored to the needs of each specific child. Although the purpose is to create a method of clinical intervention that can be generalized, it must be approached through a number of case-studies, during which necessary tools and their appropriate time phasing are sought. The study addressed the following questions: a) how does the external model function in reading with understanding; b) how does the model become gradually internalized (from externally and orally supported to internally represented model); c) how does the orienting basis generalize from one to another subject domain; and d) how does the participant develop his or her agency in relation to the orienting basis (expressions of ownership, identity formation; elaboration and further transformation of the orienting basis).

Participants and method

The participants of the study are 5 blind teenagers (17-18 years old) who are struggling to cope with the increased information load of their high school studies. The participants were prematurely born in the 22-24th week. The price of saving these children's life in an oxygen chamber was losing their eye sight permanently. Because, as neonates, these persons had underdeveloped brains, they are likely to have various kinds of minor or moderate learning difficulties. The study is being carried out as an individual intervention with each participant of the study. The intervention focuses on each participant's competencies concerning reading with understanding as well as structuring of knowledge that the participant has found from the Internet or produced by him- or herself. The intervention includes 10-20 pre-structured individual meetings in 1-2 week intervals. The orienting basis that supports reading with understanding is a kind metamodel (abstract representation) that helps visually-impaired children to capture the deeper meaning connections in the text (see Figure 1a). The physical model provided to participants is a clock face because it has special significance in a blind person's orientation. The physical model of the clockface, presented in Figure 1b, involves paper clips that allow the participant to add notes written in Braille to the surface of the model. During the clinical meetings we systematically use the physical model to help to structure the information obtained (often short articles from regular newspapers); it helps to generate questions regarding the information search, and supports analysis from various textual sources. Information search is followed by generation of written synthesis with the help of the orienting basis. This type of work may be connected with topics selected by the participants. The objective of the activity is also to create a presentation or study report of this school work. During the clinical meetings, the intervenor and participant will practice the use of the orienting basis regarding a particular topic. In this way, the intervention aims at supporting the development of participant's analysis, thinking and self-regulation. All meetings will be videotaped.

Result analyses and expected results

A case report will be constructed concerning each participant. On the basis of the video material, it will contain an analysis of the interaction between the intervenor and the participants. A special emphasis will be on examining specific expressions and non-verbal aspects of interaction as well as the use of the external scaffolding model. The model of reflective processes involved in reading with understanding will be used to classify the content of the interactive episodes. Independent co-raters who are not familiar with the study will be used to examine reliability of classifying the material. The analysis will focus on testing how to the models serves its purpose as collected data concerning form of reflection involved in learning and regarding its object.

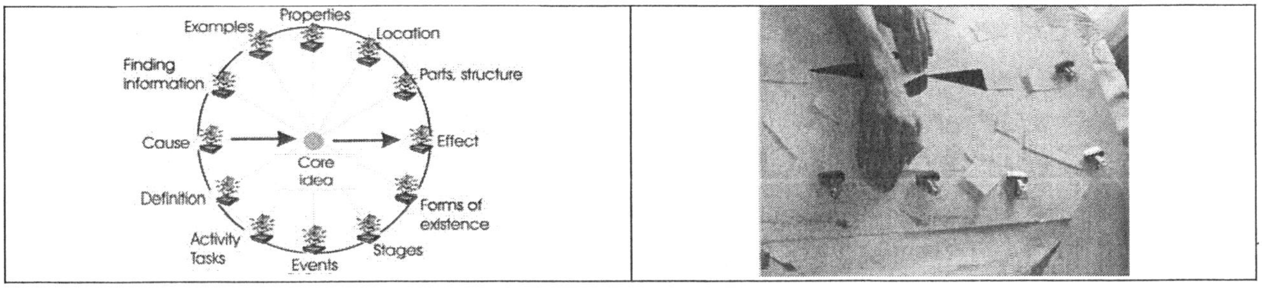

Figure 1. An abstract description of the orienting basis used in the study (in the left).
A blind subject utilizes a actual version of the orienting basis written in Braille (in the right)

Intervention with 2 participants has been going on for 12 months. The results are promising: the participants have begun to a) internalize the orienting basis, b) become increasingly skillful in applying it for learning from various types of text, and c) improve their school achievement. Case description of one participant will be provided. She spontaneously characterized appropriation of the orienting basis as acquiring "novel tools of thinking". In the first part of the investigation the orienting basis (a kind of abstract representation), as manifest in the physical model, was developed and tested. A visually-impaired child cannot, however, picture this type of representation in the same way visually as a normal child. For this reason numerous signifying relations were developed and represented in Braille diagrams (for example causality, time continuums), through which a visually-impaired child can picture the meaning relations in a text. At first they were learned by recognizing and naming through Braille, but later they were internalized so that no external support was necessary. Overall, our evidence is that the Galperinian methodology provides an interesting, theoretically sound and practically relevant foundation for this anti-Cartesian theory of learning.

References

Galperin, P. (1959) Razvitije issledovanij po formirovaniju umstvennyh dejstvij. Teoksessa Psihogitsheskaja nauka v SSSR. Moskva: Izdatelstvo APN RSFSR. (441-469)

Galperin, P. (1965) Osnovnyje rezultati issledovanij po probleme "formirovanije ymstvennyh dejstvij i ponjatij". Moskva. MGU Filosofskij fakultet, otdelenije psihologii.

Galperin, P. (1978) Poetapnoje formirovanije kak metod psihologitsheskogo issledovanija. Teoksessa Galperin.P., Zaporozhets, A., Karpova, S. Aktualnyje problemi vozrastnoi psihologii. Moskva Izdatelstvo Moskovskogo universiteta.

Haenen, J. (1996) Piotr Gal'perin: Psychologist in Vygotsky's Footsteps. New York, NJ: Nova Science.

Groesser, A., McNamara, D. & Louwerse, M. (2003). What do readers need to learn in order to process coherence relations in narrative and expository text. In A.-P. Sweet & C.E. Snow (Eds.). Rethinking reading comprehension (pp. 82-98). New York, NJ: Guilford.

Vygotski, L. (1983) Istorija razvitija vyshih psihitseskih funktsij. Moskva Pedagogika.

Enhancing Mathematical Discourse in Elementary Classrooms

Mitzi Lewison, Ingrid Graves, Lenny Sanchez, Indiana University, 201 North Rose Ave., School of Education, Bloomington, IN 47405-1006
Email: lewison@indiana.edu, igraves@indiana.edu, olsanche@indiana.edu

Abstract: Using conversational formative routines among students, this study focuses on the discursive practices found in two fifth-grade mathematics classrooms. The analysis considers student identity work situated in meaningful engagement in knowledge practices. Particular attention is paid to how students become proficient in speaking the language of mathematical communities and the relationship this has on their identity within the group.

Introduction

Accountability-oriented reforms present new challenges for elementary mathematics instruction. The passage of the *No Child Left Behind* (NCLB) act requires increasing percentages of students to score at or above proficient benchmarks each year on criterion-referenced achievement tests. Additionally, elementary mathematics lessons are composed of instructional methodology based on I-R-E, Initiate, Respond and Evaluate (Mehan, 1979); with limited time devoted to mathematical discourse involving students in meaningful peer discourse, supportive reasoning, engagement, and revision of thinking intended to enhance metacognitive awareness. Herrenkohl and Guerra (1998) propose that "engagement can be viewed in terms of discourse practices that extend beyond the behavior of individual students and involve both social and cognitive activity" (439).

Additionally, Barnwell, Leung, Morgan and Street (2005) argue the need to view mathematical language abilities as socially embedded in linguistic practices within the classroom. Gee (2003) points out that much of the knowledge in academic domains (i.e. mathematics) involves going beyond everyday vernacular and is manifested in the non-vernacular specialist language of the discipline. As such, students need to be mentored into the discourse of practice in order to become fluent in mathematical reasoning and usage of mathematical concepts. In this investigation, we use student talk as a window into their experiences, competing perspectives, and abilities to linguistically engage in sophisticated mathematical concepts. We document the social practices and discursive models that illuminate the divide between vernacular and scientific linguistic practices in mathematics. In short, "discursive acquisition is the lynchpin of schooling. . . It is learning to walk, talk, write, and think. . . like a mathematician" (Gallas, 2000).

This presentation describes the first year of a three year study funded by the National Science Foundation (NSF) (Hickey, Mewborn & Lewison, 2005) building upon an underlying multi-level/multi-type model for alignment of instruction, assessment and testing (Hickey & Zuiker, 2005) also funded by NSF. Using informal math assessments, to enhance and inform teachers' instructional practices, this study continues the investigation into linguistic practices of elementary students as they engage in small group mathematics discussions.

Method

This paper focuses on two fifth grade classrooms, each at different schools in the Midwest. The first school serves a working-class neighborhood with 54% of its students eligible for free and reduced lunch. The second school is situated within a middle-class community with 16% of its students eligible for free and reduced lunch. Both classrooms use the *Everyday Mathematics* program (University of Chicago, 2003) for math instruction. Five times during the semester, students individually complete three open-ended Math Investigations. These items were carefully selected from the *Balanced Assessment in Mathematics* (McGraw-Hill, 2005) and relate closely to what has been taught in the classroom. In small groups, students discuss how they solved the problems and explain their rationale. Once each semester the students watch two animated video clips, which show a group of students discussing one of the problems the students in the classroom have just discussed. The students observe and discuss the differences between vernacular talk and academic mathematical discourse by the video coaches. The whole class then discusses how they would rate each video coach discussion and then identify the characteristics of mathematical discourse that were embedded in the more academic video clip. Using a rubric, the students go back to their small groups and informally assess their own math conversations and score themselves as compared to the ratings they assigned the video coaches. At this point, field notes and videotapes of the small group discussions are analyzed using grounded theory and discourse analysis to assess classroom implementation, students' participation and growth in mathematical discourse.

Outcomes and Implications

This study explicates the distance between students' understandings of mathematical concepts using everyday language and their ability to engage in authentic, fluent, mathematical discourse. By enacting and embedding student-led mathematical discourse as a regular part of teachers' instruction, we are able to show how to fine-tune individual understandings, build collective participation in mathematical communities, and increase student achievement. Students and teachers often require explicit coaching on the methods in which to engage in a particular discourse community, in this case that of mathematics. Our findings extend those of Southerland, Kittleson, Settlage and Lanier (2005) who state, "the exercise of power within group-exchanges guided not only group discussions but also the learning of the individual in those groups and the power of a persuasive speaker, a power that comes not from empirical grounding but from a learner's need to have ideas explicitly evaluated and explained."

Through discourse analysis of small group student interaction, we were allowed to examine how students take on multiple and varied identities through the uses of informal *Math Investigations* and video coaches. Osborne, Erduran and Simon (2005) make a strong argument for "engaging students in argumentation and its evaluation" and additionally submit that argumentation "offers a means of transcending the dogmatic, uncritical, and unquestioning nature of so much of the traditional fare offered in classrooms" (p. 1017). This study demonstrates the power of teaching students to question, argue, and evaluate their own mathematical solutions.

References

Barnwell, R., Leung, C., Morgan, C., & Street, B. (2005). Applied linguistics and mathematics education: More than words and numbers. *Language and Education, 19(2),* 142-147.

Gallas, K. (2000). Story time as a magical act open only to the initiated: What some children don't know about power and may not find out. *Trend & Issues in Elementary Language Arts,* Graham, B. 87-101.

Gee, J. (2003). Opportunity to learn: A language-based perspective on assessment. *Assessment in Education, 10(1),* 27-4.

Herrenkohl, L. & Guerra, M.(1998). Participant structures, scientific discourse, and student engagement in fourth grade. *Cognition and Instruction, 16(4),* 43 1-473.

Hickey, D., Mewborn, D., & Lewison, M. (2005, July). *Multi-level assessment for enhancing mathematical discourse, curriculum, and achievement in diverse elementary school classrooms.* Grant from the US National Science Foundation's Research on Learning Environments (ROLE) program to Indiana University.

Hickey, D. T., & Zuiker, S. J. (2005). Engaged participation: A sociocultural model of motivation with implications for assessment. *Educational Assessment, 10(3),* 277-305.

McGraw-Hill. (2005). *Balanced Assessments in Mathematics* [Website of CTB McGraw-Hill]. Retrieved, Mar 1, 2006, from http://www.ctb.com/products/product_detail.jsp?FOLDER%3C%3Efolder_id=1408474395217571&bmUID=1121286347770

Mehan, H. (1979). *Learning lessons: social organization in the classroom.* Cambridge, MA: Harvard University Press.

Osborne, J., Erduran, S., & Simon, S. (2004). Enhancing the quality of argumentation in school science. *Journal of Research in Science Teaching.* 41(10). 994-1020.

Southerland, S., Kittleson, J., Settlage, J., & Lanier, K. *(2005).* Individual and group meaning-making in an urban third grade classroom: Red fog, cold cans, and seeping vapor. *Journal of Research in Science Teaching,* 42(9), 1032-1061.

University of Chicago School Mathematics Project. (2003). *Every Day Mathematics Center.* [Homepage of the University of Chicago School Mathematics Project]. Retrieved, October 31, 2005, from http://everydaymath.uchicago.edu

Lessons Learned From Using an Asynchronous Online Discussion Board to Facilitate Scientific Thinking in a Large Cognitive Psychology Lecture Class

Jordan Lippman, James Pellegrino, Renee Koziol, Emily Whitehair, University of Illinois at Chicago, Psychology Department (M/C 285), 1007 W. Harrison St., Chicago, IL 60657,
Email: lippmanj@hotmail.com, pellegjw@uic.edu, reneek2217@yahoo.com, Patchie6@aol.com

Abstract: Students' responses to scientific reasoning questions posted on an online discussion board were coded for completeness, coherence, accuracy, use of evidence, reasoning, and comprehensibility. Early performance was low for every dimension. By the end of the term, ratings of coherence and completeness increased but use of evidence decreased, and other dimensions stayed the same. Implications regarding the types of feedback students need to improve their understanding and use of scientific argumentation are discussed.

Introduction

As part of an ongoing instructional redesign effort, driven by theories of how people learn and the design of powerful learning environments (National Research Council, 2000), different constellations of course components have been implemented in a large lecture course on Cognition. Components were implemented and then modified, added, or removed based on student performance and reactions to an extended end-of-term evaluation. Thus, our approach to instructional design and assessment resembles the description of design research provided by Collins, Joseph, and Bielaczyc (2004).

One component was an asynchronous online discussion board (DB) designed to create smaller discourse communities (of roughly seven students) within the large lecture class. We wanted students to think deeply and make public their reasoning about course content, and especially the relationship between theory and evidence, as a means of formative evaluation of student learning and thinking (National Research Council, 2001). For each of seven questions spread over the term, students had to post initial responses before seeing those of their peers. Students were instructed to spend about 30 minutes writing a paragraph or two and to use (and reference) any sources they wished (e.g., the textbook and/or class PowerPoint slides). Once everyone had responded, each student chose a peer's initial post and provided constructive feedback. Throughout the term and in each of the questions, students were instructed to use empirical evidence to support the theoretical claims in their responses. Our objective was to help students improve their thinking and writing through multiple forms of feedback including assignment of grades to each post, graded peer feedback for each post, anonymous posting of best responses for the entire class to view, and emails from the teaching assistant about common misconceptions and mistakes in generating responses.

Method

The DB was implemented in an upper-level Introduction to Cognition lecture course at a large, urban, Midwestern University during the Spring 2004 semester. Students' initial responses to two questions – one from the beginning and one from the end of the term – were analyzed. The first question asked students to take a position (and support it with evidence) on whether knowledge is represented in the mind using multiple or a single representational system. The late semester question asked students to argue (using evidence as support) whether learning would always be best if a text is highly coherent or if incoherent texts could also facilitate learning.

The authors worked as a team to develop a coding scheme that captured the quality and variability in students' responses. The final coding scheme had six dimensions, which were all applied to each post on a scale of 0 (incorrect/incomplete) to 4 (scientific/excellent). The six dimensions were: *completeness* (answered all, some, or none of the parts of the question), *coherence* (quality of writing, structure, logical flow of ideas, brevity), *accuracy* (correctness of descriptions of theories and terms), use of *evidence* (amount, relevance, and/or quality of empirical or other type of less-scientific data used), *reasoning* (effectiveness of use of disconfirmatory, confirmatory, or less-scientific logic to present and connect evidence to their position), and *comprehensibility* (global assessment of level of understanding and integration of concepts and/or materials from class and text). Details of the coding scheme dimensions and definitions of the rating scale are available upon request. The initial posts of seventy-two students

(78% of the class) who responded to both questions (and who provided informed consent) were independently coded by two undergraduate raters who then reached agreement on ratings of each dimension.

Results

Qualitative descriptions of the modal response on the first question for each dimension illustrate the typical student's performance at the beginning of the term which turned out to be weak on multiple dimensions as expected. *Completeness* (mode = 2) - some aspects of the question were missing or left implicit. *Coherence* (mode = 2) - satisfactory writing quality: somewhat structured and coherent, but the flow of ideas is not highly logical. *Accuracy* (mode = 2) - fairly accurate: erroneous descriptions/use of some terms and/or minor conceptual contradictions. *Evidence* (mode = 0) - mostly anecdotal or irrelevant empirical evidence (if any) used. *Reasoning* (mode = 2) - failed to tie components of the answer together and/or ineffective/fallacious (i.e. study x *proved* theory y) reasoning. *Comprehensibility* (mode = 1) - response indicated faulty understanding, and/or no integration of concepts from class and text.

The Stuart-Maxwell test – a nonparametric statistic for matched-samples – was used to assess equivalence (i.e. nonsignificant results) of ratings on the early versus late semester questions. These analyses revealed nonsignificant changes for *accuracy, reasoning*, and *comprehension* but significant changes for *completeness*, *coherence*, and *evidence*. Students' responses were more likely to have higher *completeness* (mode = 4) and *coherence* (mode = 3) ratings, but lower ratings of their use of *evidence* (mode = 0) on the second question. Thus, despite some improvement over time, the quality of the students' responses remained weak in terms of scientific reasoning. Interestingly, using Spearman's rho (a nonparametric correlation), no performance dimension was significantly correlated with the TA's grading on the first question. For the second question, all of the dimensions except evidence were significantly and moderately correlated with TA evaluations; reasoning had the strongest correlation. This is likely due to the TA's leniency in grading the first question.

Conclusions and Implications for Instruction

At the beginning of the term, students had difficulty writing clear and concise arguments for a theoretical position and effectively using evidence to support their position. The DB activities and the various types of associated feedback appear to have helped them learn to write more coherent and complete answers by the end of the term. However, the objectives of helping students learn to more effectively use evidence and reason scientifically were not met. We think that the feedback provided was not explicit enough in these areas and that peer feedback may have focused on issues related to style (e.g., completeness and coherence). It may not be possible to use peer-feedback to accomplish our original learning goals if it is not mediated by a knowledgeable instructor. Additionally, students may need explicit feedback, guided by a rubric such as that derived for subsequent data coding. In the future we will be using a rubric to guide student writing and TA grading of responses. Finally, it may be difficult to achieve these learning aims in a truly low-stakes, formative manner without turning the activities into high-stakes assessments; when we subsequently made the DB voluntary rather than obligatory, it was rarely used at all despite students' perceptions of its potential learning value.

References

Collins, A., Joseph, D., & Bielaczyc, K. (2004). Design Research: Theoretical and Methodological Issues. *The Journal of the Learning Sciences, 13(1)*, p. 15-42.

National Research Council. (2000) *How People Learn: Brain, Mind, Experience, and School: Expanded Edition.* Bransford, J. D., Brown, A. L., Cocking, R. R., Donovan, S., & Pellegrino, J. W. (Eds.) Washington, D.C.: National Academy Press.

National Research Council (2001). *Knowing What Students Know: The Science and Design of Educational Assessment.* Pellegrino, J. W., Chudowsky, N., & Glaser, R. (Eds.). Washington, DC: National Academy Press.

Misconceptions in Natural Selection: Conceptual Change Through Time in Biology Classrooms

Christine Manzey, Kevin Pugh, Kristin Kelly, Victoria Stewart
University of Toledo, 2801 Bancroft Street, Toledo, Ohio 43606
Email: christine.manzey@utoledo.edu, kevin.pugh@utoledo.edu, kristin.kelly@utoledo.edu

Abstract: Our findings concurs with previous studies that high school biology students hold misconceptions explaining and applying key concepts in natural selection. We explored specific misconceptions prior to instruction, immediately following instruction, and five weeks later. We found qualitatively distinct categories of conceptual understanding suggesting levels in the development of conceptual understanding and tracked changes over time. We found classroom practices can impact conceptual change, with students possessing initial misconceptions often developing hybrid understandings.

Theoretical Framework

In the last few decades, the topic of conceptual change has received considerable attention (e.g., Posner, Strike, Hewson, & Gertzog, 1982). We now know that students' existing beliefs have a significant affect on their learning and that instruction needs to address these existing beliefs to be effective (Hewson, Beeth, Thorley, 1998). Considerable research has investigated students' existing beliefs in regard to core science concepts. Natural selection is one of the core concepts in biology that students have traditionally failed to grasp and have instead hung on to their existing beliefs. Clough and Wood-Robinson (1985) found misconceptions centering around natural selection when they interviewed 12, 14, and 16 year olds. They contended that even young children have "well established theories to explain inheritance" which all too frequently include the inheritance of acquired characteristics and confusions about the term *variation*. Brumby (1984) studied the misconceptions that medical students had about natural selection as they applied "intuitive Lamarckian" thought to a series of questions posing adaptive scenarios. Even the most able science student confidently proclaimed organisms "need" to adapt to changing environments and then pass these acquired changes to their offspring. These studies are valuable in that they identify specific misconceptions related to natural selection and illustrate the persistence of these misconceptions. However, the process of conceptual development over time remains unclear and researchers have yet to define levels of conceptual understanding. This information is important to understanding the conceptual change process and addressing practical issues such as assessment and individual student growth over time. The purpose of this study was to define qualitatively distinct levels of conceptual understanding of natural selection and track conceptual change from pre-instruction to post-instruction to five weeks after instruction.

Methods

167 students (33% male, 66% female) enrolled in high school Biology courses during the spring of 2005 participated in the study. A learning assessment targeting two common misconceptions was administered prior to instruction on adaptation and natural selection (Pre), on the exam immediately following instruction (Post), and five weeks after instruction (Follow-up). The first misconception targeted was the belief that change in a species is the result of *individuals* changing (often intentionally) to fit the needs of their environment, rather than adaptation being the result of natural selection acting on a population (individual change misconception). A sample question (modified from Engel Clough &Wood-Robinson, 1985) involved pale and dark caterpillars in a forest being found on pale and dark tree trunks. The students were asked to explain how this came about and predict what would happen if the dark tree trunks began to change. The second misconception targeted was the belief that acquired characteristics can be passed on to offspring (acquired traits misconception). A sample question (modified from Brumby, 1984) involved a married couple (who were not particularly talented naturally as runners) who trained hard to become good runners. The students were first asked whether or not the children would automatically be good runners and then asked to make a prediction about children in this family after several generations of training. Categories representing distinct levels of conceptual understanding were develop through a qualitative analysis. All responses were then coded into these categories by two independent raters. Inter-rater reliability was .91 for items targeting the individual change misconception and .88 for items targeting the acquired traits misconception.

Findings

Due to the limited space, here we describe the findings for the items targeting the individual change misconception (results for items targeting the acquired traits are similar and will be presented in the poster). Five categories emerged for these responses: (1) clear misconceptions (e.g., "The sun in the desert turned the lizards' skin brown"), (2) misconceptions with scientific language (e.g., "They adapted to their environment. ...If the dark trees became light then the caterpillars would become light too"), (3) misconceptions competing with correct understanding (e.g., "The caterpillars learned to blend in with their environment...The dark caterpillars would probably die off [if the dark tree became light] because they wouldn't be able to survive that environment"), (4) correct but lacking explanation (e.g., "The caterpillars adapted to the tree...If the color of the tree changed the dark caterpillars would be vulnerable to predators and die off"), and (5) correct understanding (e.g., "The caterpillars that lived on the dark trees survived longer if they blended in with their surroundings so they were dark like the trees....The light ones didn't survive as long because they didn't blend in, so their light-colored genes weren't passed on, but the dark-colored genes were"). Categories 2 and 3 represent a hybridized understanding. That is, the students adopt some of the scientific language (e.g., adapt, evolve) or recognize that when the environment changes, unfit species will die off or become less dominant. However, they still hold onto a belief that individual organisms change in response to the environment. A large percentage of students possessed clear misconceptions or hybridized conceptions prior to instruction (see Figure 1). Students showed conceptual growth over time, however, many students still held onto their misconceptions. Only about 20% were able to fully articulate an understanding of natural selection after instruction. Detailed analysis of change over time reveals that students possessing a clear misconception prior to instruction could achieve a correct understanding, however the majority maintained the same level of understanding or developed a hybridized understanding. See poster for further details.

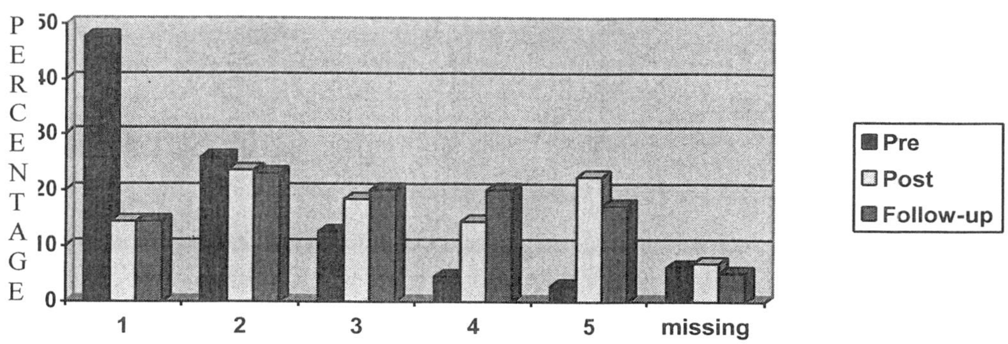

Figure 1. Comparison of students' understanding of natural selection at the Pre, Post, and Follow-up

Conclusions and Implications

Our results concur with previous studies indicating that high school biology students arrive to class with deeply held misconceptions about the mechanism of change in natural selection and acquired characteristics. Our study indicates (a) that conceptions of natural selection can be represented by qualitatively distinct levels and (b) many students incorporate correct understanding of a concept into their faulty framework and construct a *hybrid* understanding resulting in misapplications of fundamental principles. These results provide Biology teachers with a framework for evaluating their students' conceptual level and understanding the process of conceptual change.

References

Brumby, M. N. (1984). Misconceptions about the concept of natural selection by medical biology students. *Science Education, 68*(4), 493-503.

Engel Clough, E. & Wood-Robinson, C. (1985). How secondary students interpret instances of biological adaptation. *Journal of biological education, 19*(2), 125-130.

Hewson, P. W., Beeth, M. E. & Thorley, N. R. (1998). Teaching for conceptual change. In B. J. K. G. Tobin (Ed.), *International handbook of science education, part one* (pp. 199-218). London: Kluwer Academic Publishers.

Posner, G. J., Strike, K. A., Hewson, P. W., & Gertzog, W. A. (1982). Accommodation of a scientific conception: Toward a theory of conceptual change. *Science Education, 66*, 211-27.

Slides, Sushi, and Sixth-Graders: A Case Study of Elementary Student Art-Based Learning in a Museum Setting

Sandra Toro Martell, University of Wisconsin-Milwaukee, UWM-School of Education, P.O. Box 413, Milwaukee, WI 53201-0413, smartell@uwm.edu

Abstract: This poster presents findings from an ethnographic study about elementary students' art-based learning in accordance with students' personal, physical, and sociocultural contexts of learning (Falk and Dierking, 2000). Findings include that while art activities integrated learning about Japanese art history and aesthetics and engaging in artistic production by creating sushi and watercolors, as a community of practice, (Hapgood and Palincsar, 2002,) the group engaged in traditional classroom-based behavior and conversational structures (Cazden, 1988; Phillips, 1972).

Theoretical Framework

Visitors often go to museums as part of informal or formal groups, including families and school groups. Group members' behavior and talk is "jointly negotiated, appropriated, and deployed," and conversations and activities reflect this (Rowe, 2002, p.22). My research questions for this study were: How do students build knowledge or make meaning together as demonstrated by their conversations and behavior during group activities?; How does the museum teacher act as a mediator of learning?; and What does art-based learning look like?

K-12 school groups' personal, sociocultural, and physical contexts of learning (Falk & Dierking, 2000) may look quite different from those of adult groups, families, and parents and children. There is less diversity in terms of age and prior knowledge in school groups, but possibly more due to ethno-race, and socio-economic status. However, learning still includes cognitive or conceptual change as well as "social interaction, cultural norms, and a range of tools and methods" (Griffin, 2004, p. 60). For both families and school groups, motivation or purpose, choice, and ownership enable learning while, for students and teachers, there is more of a perceived relationship between what is learned at the museum and what is learned at school (Griffin, 2004). Learning art for members of a school group involves more than acquiring and mastering the skills needed to make a painting or a sculpture. Approaches like discipline-based art education, developed and introduced by the Getty Center for Education in the Arts (Alexander & Day, 1991) involve understanding that art has four main components or "discipline perspectives" (Alabama Institute for Education in the Arts, 2005, no page,) including art criticism, aesthetics, art history, and art production.

Data Sources and Methods

The Pacific Northwest museum where I conducted my study provides hands-on learning experiences that link science, art, and technology in a natural setting. The research participants attended an urban K-6 public school in the Puget Sound region in Washington. Students worked in groups of eight or nine students with a "field guide instructor."

A multi-sited ethnographic approach was used in order to "trace relationships that stretch out across time and space" (Eisenhart, 2001, p.22) by searching for connections, parallels and contrasts across different museum sites such as the exhibition hall, a pond, and a marsh. I accompanied the students from one site to another at the museum while videorecording their experiences in order to describe in rich detail the activities they engaged in and the kinds of conversations they had as a group in relation to their personal, physical, and sociocultural contexts. I looked at the content of the group's talk and their behavior in relation to the idea a "community of practice" in the museum (Hapgood and Palincsar, 2002). A community of practice in a museum, like other environments, approaches and engages in investigations in particular ways, with shared conventions, for example, about proper behavior or values. My unit of analysis was the "conversational episode" (Fienberg & Leinhardt, 2002), "that could be seen as having a natural start and end in that [it is] focused on a coherent topic" (p.176). A sample of conversational episodes was selected randomly, described, and analyzed in relation to a broader narrative about the art activities. I described the conversational episodes in terms of what is going on or what is being talked about; where the group and/or individuals are and what the site looks like; what the group and/or individuals are doing and talking about and I analyze group discussions in terms of amount and kind of talk.

Conclusion

Art activities included four disciplines of art, a strong orientation, and interaction with authentic objects. Students learned about aspects of Japanese *art history* and *aesthetics*, including the use of different kinds of space and perspective as compared to Western art and that how one arranges one's sushi contributes to the overall appreciation and beauty of the display. Students also engaged in *art criticism* by learning and talking about the formal qualities of sushi compositions and displays, including how certain foods must be used because of their color. Finally, students engaged in *art production* by creating sushi rolls and painting watercolors. Students listened and watched passively while adults talked and provided knowledge. (During a slide talk, students did not talk). During sushi making, the artist and the instructor dominated conversations with students or else spoke amongst themselves. But, the artist did engage students in the process of making the sushi, by walking students through each of the steps. The instructor gave information and asked questions to assess knowledge. Unlike the artist, he did not demonstrate how to use the watercolors or how the students should compose their pictures. In sum, as a community of practice, the group followed a traditional classroom conversational structure, the initiation-response-evaluation (IRE) model where the teacher makes a comment or poses a question, students respond and then the teacher evaluates the response (Cazden, 1988; Lemke, 1990). However, the students do more than listen and respond as they engaged in artistic production by making their own sushi and watercolors. The artist demonstrated what to do and helped students learn to use utensils, assemble food, and arrange sushi. Students worked quietly and intently, appearing to enjoy both making the sushi and painting the watercolor pictures. (In general, the higher socio-economic status (SES) girls spoke the most).

Significance

This study raises important questions about how learning in a museum may actually look like learning in a traditional classroom for a school group on a field trip. Further research on school group learning can pursue how IRE models of teacher/student interaction work differently than parent/child interaction models (Ash, 2004; Crowley & Jacobs, 2002) described in research about learning among family groups, particularly for diverse students. With thousands of students visiting museums every school year, it behooves school teachers and administrators as well as researchers and parents to try to understand more about what children actually experience in museums in order to better assess the impact of different approaches to teaching on student learning in museums.

References

Alabama Institute for Education in the Arts (2005). Comprehensive Disciplined-Based Arts Education: What is comprehensive disciplined-based arts education? (n.p.). Retrieved May, 1, 2005 from http://www.artseducation.org/dbae.html

Alexander, K. & Day, M. (Eds.) (1991). Discipline-Based Art Education: A Curriculum Sampler. Los Angeles: The J. Paul Getty Trust.

Ash, D. (2004). Reflective scientific sense-making dialogue in two languages: The science in the dialogue and the dialogue in the science. *Science Education*, 88, 855-884.

Cazden, C. B. (1988). *Classroom Discourse.* Portsmouth, NH: Heinemann.

Crowley, K. & Jacobs, M. (2002). Islands of expertise and the development of family scientific literacy. In G.Leinhardt, K. Crowley, & K. Knutson (Eds.) Learning conversations in museums. Mahwah, NJ: Lawrence Erlbaum Associates.

Eisenhart, M. (2001). Educational ethnography past, present and future: Ideas to think with. Educational Researcher, 30(*8*), 16–27.

Falk, J. H., Dierking, L. D. (2000). *Learning from museums: Visitor experiences and the making of meaning.* Walnut Creek, CA: Altamira Press.

Feinberg, J., Leinhardt, G. (2002). Looking through the glass: Reflections of identity in conversations at a history museum. In Leinhardt, G., Crowley, K., Knutson, K., (Eds.)

Griffin, J. (2004). Research on students and museums: Looking more closely at the students in school groups. *Science Education* 88 (*Suppl. 1*), S59-S70.

Hapgood, S. E., Palincsar, A. S. (2002). Fostering an investigatory stance: Using text to mediate inquiry with museum objects. In Paris, S. G. (Ed.) *Perspectives on Object-Centered Learning in Museums*. Mahwah, NJ: Lawrence Erlbaum Associates, Inc., 171-189.

Lemke, J. (1990). *Talking Science: Language, Learning, and Values.* Norwood, NJ: Ablex.

Rowe, S. (2002). The role of objects in active, distributed meaning-making. In Paris, S. G. (Ed.) *Perspectives on Object-Centered Learning in Museums*. Mahwah, NJ: Lawrence Erlbaum Associates, Inc., 37-54.

A Comparison of Students' Conceptions about the Nature of Argumentation in School and Professional Science

Kelli A. Millwood, UCLA, Moore Hall 2027, P.O. Box 951521, Los Angeles CA 90095-1521
millwood@ucla.edu

Abstract: This paper explores the relationship between students' conceptions about warranting claims in science class and their beliefs about how professional scientists warrant claims. An interview was used to measure beliefs about school science, and a questionnaire was used to measure beliefs about professional science. The difference of these expressed ideas in the two contexts have implications for understanding students' personal epistemologies of science as well as the coherence of students' epistemological beliefs.

Most students leave high school with overly simplistic ideas about the nature of scientific knowledge and how such knowledge is produced (Driver, Leach, Millar, & Scott, 1996). Research on epistemological beliefs in general has been criticized for conflating beliefs about the nature of knowledge with beliefs about how best to learn (Hofer & Pintrich, 1997), while research on students' beliefs about the nature of science (NOS) has been critiqued for making unwarranted assumptions about the coherence of presumed philosophical positions held by students . Recent research shows the inconsistency of students' epistemological ideas about science across varying contexts (Leach, Millar, Ryder, & Séré, 2000; Sandoval & Morrison, 2003). This raises the question of just what "science" students are thinking of when asked to consider the epistemological nature of science: professional science, the science that scientists do, or school science, the science that students do in school? In this study I will explore this question by narrowing in on one aspect of science, argumentation, and analyze students beliefs about argumentation in school science and how this relates to students beliefs about professional scientists argumentation. I chose the specific practice of *warranting claims* (justifying a scientific claim with evidence) during argumentation because this is one of the main ways scientific knowledge is created. Therefore, focusing a study on warranting scientific claims is really focusing on one of the foundations of science: warranting scientific claims to produce scientific knowledge.

Methods

Thirty-three students from one 7th grade science classroom participated in this study. The students in this study attend a public urban middle school located in a middle-income area of a large metropolitan city. All of the students participated in a plant inquiry module, *Sensing the Environment*, that was developed by UCLA's Center for Embedded Networked Sensing (CENS) as part of an ongoing effort to help science students engage in complex reasoning about real-world data. Students in this study used one network of sensors to pursue the ecological question, "Why do plants look different?".

Before students began the module they completed a 10 item open-ended questionnaire, Positions of Scientific Epistemology (POSE), to measure students' beliefs about the nature of professional science. This questionnaire is a version of Views of the Nature of Science (VNOS) developed by Lederman and his colleagues (2002), modified by the developers to simplify the language for middle school students. At the culmination of the module each student wrote an essay about why plants look different. To measure students' beliefs about their own warranting claims practices, students were interviewed about their essay. Interview questions focused on the claims students made in their essay and their warrants for these claims.

Data Analysis

To develop a fine-grained understanding of students' beliefs about warrant claims, as well as their beliefs about how professional scientists warrant claims, a categorizing analytic strategy was applied. With this strategy interview and POSE responses were categorized to determine the frequency with which students express various thematic ideas. Different themes and associated codes emerged from the interview data and POSE data. The one theme that emerged from the interview data was students' beliefs about warranting claims; four warrant types that emerged: authority based, data based, fact based, and causal based. Two themes emerged from POSE data these were students beliefs about (1)how scientists know things (2)what scientists use evidence for (3)why scientists disagree.

Findings and Implications

Most students (64%) relied on data based warrants when they described the reason why they believed their claim. When students were asked to explain why they believed the claim they made they generally described the empirical evidence that they examined and explained how they interpreted it to supported their claim. The majority of the students' (77%) said that scientists know things because of some specific type of evidence, such as fossils or bones. Forty-nine percent of the students said that they thought scientists use evidence to prove something, find something out (24%), or get the right answer (12%). Students said they thought scientists disagreed because they have different opinions (28%), looked at different evidence (7%), lacked evidence (10%), one scientist was wrong (10%), or because scientists will never know the truth (8%). Thirty-three percent of the students could not provide an explanation for why scientists disagree.

Students were able to distinguish between the claims they made in their essay and the evidence used to support their claims. Students also recognized that they needed to interpret the evidence to make a claim. However, students expressed beliefs about how scientists warrant claims are very different then their expressed beliefs about how they warrant claims in school science. Students did not distinguish between scientists' claims and the evidence used to support their claims. None of the students mentioned anything about scientists interpreting their data; instead their expressed beliefs were about data being the final result. Most of the students were unable to provide a reason for why scientists disagree. Students may not have known why scientists disagree because possibly they do not think that scientists disagree since they do not think that evidence is interpreted. If a student thinks there is no room for interpreting evidence, and evidence is the proof, then why would scientists disagree?

The implications of these findings support the view that students do not have coherent epistemological frameworks across different contexts. Students are relying on a different set of beliefs about their own warranting claims practice, than their beliefs about scientists warranting claims practices. Mainly, students expressed beliefs on POSE are similar to what has been found in other studies (i.e., students have naïve ideas about scientists work) and their responses to the interview and their expressed beliefs during the Sensing the Environment activity show that students ideas about their own warranting claims practice are not naïve. Students express that in their own work a claim is different from evidence, and evidence needs to be interpreted to make a claim. However, students do not articulate the distinction between scientists' claims and evidence, and do not mention that scientists interpret evidence to make claims. More research needs to be conducted to understand how students' beliefs about warranting claims influence their practice of warranting claims. Since students have informed beliefs about their own warranting claims practice, how does this influence their efforts to warrant claims during inquiry?

References

Driver, R., Leach, J., Millar, R., & Scott, P. (1996). *Young people's images of science*. Buckingham, UK: Open University Press.

Hofer, B. K., & Pintrich, P. R. (1997). The development of epistemological theories: beliefs about knowledge and knowing and their relation to learning. *Review of Educational Research, 67*(1), 88-140.

Leach, J., Millar, R., Ryder, J., & Séré, M.-G. (2000). Epistemological understanding in science learning: the consistency of representations across contexts. *Learning and Instruction, 10*, 497-527.

Lederman, N. G., Abd-El-Khalick, F., Bell, R. L., & Schwartz, R. S. (2002). Views of nature of science questionnaire: Toward valid and meaningful assessment of learners' conceptions of nature of science. *Journal of Research in Science Teaching, 39*(6), 497-521.

Sandoval, W. A., & Morrison, K. (2003). High school students' ideas about theories and theory change after a biological inquiry unit. *Journal of Research in Science Teaching, 40*(4), 369-392.

Playshop as Space for Emergent Learning

Yoshiro Miyata, Chukyo University, Toyota, Japan, miyata@sist.chukyo-u.ac.jp
Nobuyuki Ueda, Doshisha Women's College of Liberal Arts, Kyoto, Japan, nueda@doshisha.ac.jp

Abstract: We propose a framework for learning as an emergent process where everyone involved experiences mutual transformation. We have organized many playshops for emergent learning in which people can re-invent their own view of themselves, re-design their own learning environment, and discover new potentials in themselves and the environments. Based on a three-phase model of trans-cultural collaboration, we discuss and outline how such emergent learning process can be facilitated and sustained.

Emergent Learning in Playshops

We need a new vision for learning in order to capture learning that goes beyond "acquisition of predefined knowledge and skills" and beyond existing cultures in our increasingly globalized society. We have designed and organized many "Playshops" as "space for playful learning" based on a set of concepts centered around "playful spirit", which means to try to create new meanings by realizing full potentials of people and objects in any situation. (Mudpie Unlimited, 1999, 2001) In a playshop, we view learning as emergent: rather than making explicit goals of learning as in traditional instructional approach, we try to let a situation emerge where everyone involved experiences mutual transformation.

In this presentation, we try to illustrate our framework based on playshops we have organized from 2000 to 2004 on themes ranging from music, cross-cultural collaboration, to artworks, with participants ranging from primary school to university students. Based on analyses of these examples (Miyata et al., 2003, 2004 for detailed discussion) we discuss the kind of learning, the processes that supported learning, and what we have learned from these playshops.

As Table 1 summarizes, we can understand our playshops as going through three basic phases. The columns describe: the kind of activities we design (A); the roles the participants tend to assume (B); the kind of interactions that tend to occur (C); the focus of the participants' awareness (D); and the ways they tend to view themselves and other people (E).

Table 1. Summary of our framework for playshop

Phases	(A) Activity	(B) Role	(C) Interaction	(D)Awareness	(E) View
Begin	**Getting into the mood** Feel familiar	**Participant** Passive One-way	**Communicating** One-to-one	**Individual** Awareness of individual characteristics	**Disembodied** Individuals as separate entities
Continue	**Expressing** Make and share	**Facilitator** Help each other	**Supporting** Help others to communicate	**Group** Awareness of relationships	**Embodied** Individuals as situated, contextualized
Discover	**Reflecting** Discover, taste	**Designer** Redesign relations	**Meta-Supporting** Help others to support others.	**Whole** Awareness of community	**Reflective** Individuals as meaning makers

Below, we discuss those aspects that are especially relevant to emergent learning.

(E) View: From Disembodied to Embodied/Reflective View of the Self:

We found in each playshop that many participants experienced some kind of transformation of the way they view music, expression, foreign countries, people, or themselves. The transformations can be characterized as shifting from "disembodied view", in which one views oneself as separate from other people and objects, to "embodied or relational/emergent view" in which one views oneself as realizing one's potential by relating to other people and objects.

(C) Interaction: Supporting Each Other's Learning: In online communication in a cross-cultural collaboration, involving several high schools and universities from Taiwan and Japan, we found that the shift to more embodied and reflective view was associated with changes in the nature of interaction. (Miyata et al. 2005) Through the four months collaboration, increasing number of "support expressions" were observed, which tried to facilitate communication between other, often less experienced, members. Moreover, "meta-support expressions" increased, which tried to support "support expressions", in both experienced and less experienced members.

(B) Role: Learner as Designer: The participants of the playshop not only participated in the activities provided, but also often found their own goals and roles, involved other people, and tried to design environments in which to create something meaningful. The participants of learning environments turned themselves into designers of learning environments. By actively collaborating with others to create meaning, they are motivated to create learning environment for others, which in turn becomes their own learning environment.

Toward a Sustainable Learning Community: Moreover, the act of designing learning environment seems to propagate to new generations, resulting in a sustainable learning community. It is only when the environment we create motivates the people to re-create their own environments, that such an environment would become autonomous and sustainable. Such an environment involves not only the physical space or software, but also the relationships with the other people and the outside community as critically important factors.

Reinventing people's personal theories of the self: Dweck and her associates (2000) report that whether children(people) view intelligence as an expandable competence, or as fixed entity, structure many aspects of people's achievement and affect regarding learning, especially the goals they try to achieve: trying "to become smarter" vs. to "look smart". While Dweck's study has focused on personally-oriented theories of the self, analyses of our playshops suggest that it can be extended into socially-oriented theories. We believe that playshop is a space and opportunity for people to redesign their view of the self, so that they can re-design the relations with other people and objects in their own daily environment thereby re-discovering their potentials.

Learning Art: In this sense, emergent learning is an artistic process to awaken the potential for learning, by viewing one's own environment from new perspectives to discover the boundless potentials hidden there, and create new meanings by making best use of the potentials. In our current project "Learning Art", we explicitly treat participating children as workshop designers for younger children. Also, in this project, we view learning as a dynamic, artistic process, which tries to involve the communities surrounding the workshop so that people can appreciate and evaluate the learning that happens in the workshop.

References

Dweck, C.S.(2000). *Self-Theories,* Taylor & Francis.

Mudpie Unlimited (1999). *Playful Pieces,* Child Research Net

Mudpie Unlimited (2001). Connections and Emergence, *Workshop in the 18th meeting of the Japanese Cognitive Science Society.*

Miyata, Y. & Yamaguchi, T. (2003). For Embodied Self View – In Multi-Cultural Collaboration、*Proceedings of the 4th International Conference on Cognitive Science*, p431-436

Miyata, Y., Shinohara, H., Sakakibara, K. & Tsuruoka, A. (2004). Learning and support structure in a long-term multi-cultural collaboration, *Proceedings of the 21st Meeting of the Japanese Cognitive Science Society*, p374-375

Miyata, Y., Ueda, N. & Weintraub, H. (2005). Learning Support in Multi-Cultural Collaboration, *Proceedings of EdMedia 2005*, Montreal

Acknowledgements

We would like to thank CAMP, Child Research Net, and MEXT for supporting this research.

Metaskills of Collaborative Inquiry in Higher Education

Hanni Muukkonen, Minna Lakkala, University of Helsinki, Dept. of Psychology, Finland
hanni.muukkonen@helsinki.fi, minna.lakkala@helsinki.fi

Abstract: Even if learners' expertise is bound to a specific field of inquiry, there are generalizable skills and competencies that provide intellectual resources for managing new problem-solving situations. Higher-level skills that emerge through sustained efforts of advancing knowledge may be called *metaskills*, their development being an appropriate long-term goal for higher education. Considering these goals, the individual, collective and knowledge-creation aspects of regulation of inquiry were examined within a university course.

Collective aspects of regulation of learning

There is proposed shift to extend the cognitive (individualistic) and social (participatory) approaches on learning towards the inclusion of a knowledge-creation approach (Hakkarainen, Palonen, Paavola, & Lehtinen, 2004). The knowledge-creation approach addresses the question how people develop new artefacts and products or ways of working collaboratively over longer periods. Importantly, it concentrates on the interaction through these common objects (or artefacts) of activity, not just between people, or within individual minds.

The term metaskills is used to describe metalevel monitoring and regulation of academic inquiry. For Hakkarainen et al. (2004) it refers to higher-level skills that emerge through sustained efforts of advancing knowledge. A way to facilitate the knowledge creation process is to provide a learning community a heuristic model for engagement in inquiry, as in the model of progressive inquiry (Muukkonen, Lakkala, & Hakkarainen, 2005).

The present research explores collaborative inquiry in university education by examining the collective aspects of regulation of learning, which are conceived to involve the exercise of metaskills. Prior research on metacognition takes into consideration the individual actor's metalevel processes or working with a peer, but not the collective metalevel work toward and through shared knowledge objects. Thus, the units of analysis of personal epistemology and metacognition have remained firmly located in the individuals' processes. In recent research on social metacognition, the skills required in interactions with peers have been proposed as a distinct dimension of metacognition and co-regulation of learning (Jost, Kruglanski, & Nelson, 1998; Salomon & Perkins, 1998; Salonen, Vauras, & Efklides, 2005). There is a need for a more contextualized examination of metacognitive processes (Hofer, 2004). Thus we seek to expand from individual or peer regulation of learning towards a collective artifact-mediated and contextualized process, where participants monitor and co-regulate the collective process and the advancement of objects of inquiry besides exercising individual self-regulation.

Methods and results

A course was designed to engage undergraduate students in inquiry practices for eleven weeks, following the progressive inquiry framework. During face-to-face meetings, three tutors used systematic methods to facilitate development of the group's research questions and plans for a collective final report. We carried out a content analysis of the database discourse within the Future Learning Environment (FLE3; http://fle3.uiah.fi/) and of students' self-reflections provided at the end of the course.

To examine regulation of collaborative inquiry, we employed a framework that consisted of three encompassing levels: (1) monitoring and regulating individual process, (2) monitoring and regulating collective process, and (3) monitoring and regulating efforts in knowledge building (Scardamalia, 2002) and advancement of shared objects. We devoted the least attention to individual monitoring since it has been extensively investigated. The second level, the social interaction level, is addressed by group dynamics research or process management studies within learning communities. The third level, we hypothesized, would presuppose individuals' exercising self-regulatory skills, and require their commitment to work on shared objects and intentionally build on each other's ideas.

An analysis of the database discourse suggested that students' were aiming at question-driven inquiry. However, differences were found on how the collaboration succeeded in advancing collective understanding and knowledge-creation versus simply joining separate participants' work under a common heading in the final report. One of the three groups, distinctively, had lengthy exchanges about how they should proceed both in content and process. Further, in this group each member at least once rewrote their report instead of merely providing a section, which we consider evidence for a particular emphasis on a shared object of inquiry.

For the self-reflections, categories emerged which differentiated between individual and collective commitment, as well as between individual and collective knowledge building. To illustrate the two latter categories, a student reflecting on her own effort wrote, "At first there was a high threshold for me to start writing my thoughts on the computer, because I had the feeling that my thoughts were not in a ready form". In contrast, a student reflecting on the collective knowledge building wrote, "In the final stages, we experienced moments that we discussed the topic of our work with new concepts and were throwing ideas in the air. We explained unclear points to each other. I feel I learned a great deal from the other students in my group."

In sum, only a subset of students gave particular emphasis to collective knowledge building, and those who succeeded in such collective advancement had, in their self-reflections, also devoted most reflection to the collective process. The data provided evidence for that the students most advanced in their studies, had, on average, addressed more often challenges of collective commitment and engagement in collective knowledge building. The students less successful in collective knowledge building were, however, active in explaining how --through their participation or receiving appropriate guidance-- their collective inquiry could have made more progress, suggesting that they were considering the challenges of novel inquiry practices introduced by the course.

Conclusions

As the course setting involved three tutors, it is not an example of an average setting for higher education. However, the three levels for modeling metaskills helped to explicate qualitative differences in the three student groups' collective processes and students' self-reflections. Engaging in truly collective inquiry --i.e., using collective metaskills-- was a process only partially achieved in the groups. Such inquiry, however, may simply be too challenging an endeavor for such a tight timeframe with unfamiliar people. In boarder terms the course did, nevertheless, expose participants to practices of developing artefacts collaboratively, which provided an educational experience on knowledge creation practices.

To conclude, metaskills of collaborative inquiry are proposed to address commitment to collective, artifact-mediated, and prolonged inquiry efforts, which are not reducible to individual productions. However, understanding the characteristics of collective object-oriented inquiry and translating them to pedagogical practices call for further theoretical and empirical research activities.

References

Hakkarainen, K., Palonen, T., Paavola, S., & Lehtinen, E. (2004). *Communities of networked expertise: Professional and educational perspectives*. Amsterdam, The Netherlands: Elsevier.

Hofer, B. K. (2004). Epistemological Understanding as a Metacognitive Process: Thinking Aloud During Online Searching. *Educational Psychologist, 39*(1), 43-55.

Jost, J.T., Kruglanski, A.W., & Nelson, T.O. (1998). Social metacognition: An expansionist review. *Personality and Social Psychology Review, 2*, 137-154.

Muukkonen, H., Lakkala, M., & Hakkarainen, K. (2005). Technology-mediation and tutoring: how do they shape progressive inquiry discourse? *The Journal of the Learning Sciences, 14*(4), 527-565.

Salomon, G., & Perkins, D. N. (1998). Individual and social aspects of learning. *Review of Research of Education, 23*, 1-24.

Salonen, P., Vauras, M., & Efklides, A. (2005). Social interaction – What can it tell us about metacognition and coregulation of learning? *European Psychologist, 10*, 199-208.

Scardamalia, M. (2002). Collective cognitive responsibility for the advancement of knowledge. In B. Smith (Ed.), Liberal education in a knowledge society (pp. 67-98). Chicago, IL: Open Court.

Acknowledgements

The work of the first author has been supported in part by a grant (2005) from the Finnish Work Environment Fund.

Tupelo Enacted: How Teachers Shape Learning Opportunities in Middle Grades Mathematics

Chandra Hawley Orrill, University of Georgia, corrill@uga.edu
Holly Garrett Anthony, Tennessee Technical University, hanthony@tntech.edu
Andrew Izsák, University of Georgia, izsak@uga.edu
Ernise Singleton, University of Georgia, esinglet@uga.edu

Abstract: Building from the triangle of interactions outlined by Cohen and Ball, this study considers the implications of enactment for student learning opportunities in three classrooms. Data included classroom videotapes and teacher interviews that allowed the researchers to understand the implications of three different enactments of the same open-middle mathematics problem. . The findings highlight implications of different implementations for the mathematical concepts that students had opportunities to learn in each classroom.

Background

Research in education and psychology has demonstrated that adults and children often understand shared experiences in very different ways, but much less is known about how teachers and their students understand shared lessons or how classroom learning occurs as teachers' and students' understandings interact over sequences of lessons. In this poster we adopt Cohen and Ball's (1999) framework of interactions that describes classroom instruction as a function of interactions among teachers, students, and content as mediated in curricular materials. To explore this framework, we consider how a single open-middle problem from the *Connected Mathematics Program* (CMP; Lappan, Fey, Fitzgerald, Friel, & Phillips, 2002) called the Tupelo Township problem was enacted in three teachers' classrooms. As with Simon and Tzur (1999), we account for teachers' practices by explaining them from the perspectives of the researchers. Our initial research interest was to understand how students' learning opportunities were shaped by the teachers' enactment of the problem.

Methodology

Data for this report were collected across one to four days of instruction in each of three sixth-grade classrooms. These data included all days of instruction for the task, which provided a map of a town that was unequally divided among various landowners and asked students to consider what fraction of the land each landowner held. Students had to partition the parcels of land further in order to answer this question. From our perspective, these problems involve adding and multiplying fractions but do not require formal computation procedures.

We used two cameras to videotape each lesson: one camera followed the teacher and one focused on student and teacher writing. Later the same day, we combined the video and audio using an audiovisual mixer to create a *restored* view (Hall, 2000) that captured much of what each teacher and her students said and were looking at during the lesson. We then videotaped interviews with students from each class and asked them to explain their reasoning as they solved the problem and to comment on video segments of the lesson that we played back for them. Finally, we videotaped teacher interviews in which we used video segments of their lessons and their students' interviews to engage the teachers' reflections on their teaching strategies, goals, and student thinking. We analyzed the videos using fine-grained analysis of talk, hand gestures, and drawings. These data were drawn from a larger body of data that included these kinds of data for an entire unit of instruction lasting 6-10 weeks in each classroom.

We analyzed data in three stages. First, during data collection we identified segments of classroom and student interview video to include in our interview efforts. Second, we conducted a retrospective analysis using a version of the constant comparative method described by Cobb and Whitenack (1996) for conducting longitudinal analyses of classroom video recordings. We analyzed interview transcripts for links among teacher's instructional actions, students' classroom activity, students' responses and subsequent activity during the interviews, and the teacher's reactions and reflections on all of the above. Third, we focused the analysis in three key areas based on the initial findings from the first passes through the data. These three areas were: teacher response to student difficulties (what happens when kids make suggestions that are different from what the teacher had in mind?); the intermediate goals set by the teacher as part of this experience; and the skills and processes stressed in each classroom. In an effort to understand how students were making sense of these data, we also looked for evidence of connections among mathematical ideas.

Findings

The Tupelo Township investigation allows for multiple approaches for reaching the solution, is exploratory in nature, and is cognitively complex. Each of the teachers in this study made adaptations—with the intent of simplifying their students' work, narrowing the mathematical scope of the problem, or managing the class. Ms. Reese interpreted the investigation as a stepping-stone in a path to more important concepts—operations with fractions—and accordingly set the pace for her students, providing intermediate goals and structure for accomplishing the goal of the lesson. She anticipated student difficulties and organized the lesson to prevent confusion and to limit time spent on what she thought were non-constructive solution strategies. Ms. Moseley remained open to the possibility that her students could, in individual groups, reason their way through the investigation. As a result, she provided little upfront structure but offered immediate and specific feedback to groups. Her main task was to keep students focused on a single section of the map and on finding fractional portions of land—she was not concerned with acreage. Unlike Ms. Reese and Ms. Moseley, the third teacher, Ms. Archer, did not fully anticipate the challenges embedded in the investigation, and she therefore initially let the problem remain open to students' interpretations only to guide all of the students to do it her way as they progressed through the activity. Ms. Archer's students pursued many dead-ends that were met with guidance to "extend the lines" and led to Ms. Archer announcing hints to prevent the rest of the class pursuing the same erroneous paths.

In our analysis, we found important differences between classrooms (e.g., how one teacher set a series of intermediate goals that limited the open-ended possibilities of the problem, while another left the problem completely open to student interpretation) and explored the mathematical implications of those differences (e.g., one teacher told struggling students to focus on what they already knew and another told similar students to begin by extending the lines). In so doing, we tie our results back to the interaction triangle (Cohen & Ball, 1999) noting the nuances embedded in the triangle that have not been previously explicated and articulated. By looking at these three cases closely, we begin to understand how teachers make sense of open-ended problems, student understanding, and their roles as teachers. We also make strides toward a better articulation of the factors impacting teachers' instructional decisions when teaching with open-ended problems.

References

Cobb, P., & Whitenack, J. W. (1996). A method for conducting longitudinal analyses of classroom videorecordings and transcripts. *Educational Studies in Mathematics*, *30*(3), 213–228.

Cohen, D. K., & Ball, D. L. (1999). *Instruction, capacity, and improvement* (No. CPRE–RR–43). Philadelphia, PA: Consortium for Policy Research in Education.

Hall, R. (2000). Videorecording as theory. In A. E. Kelly & R. A. Lesh (Eds.), *Handbook of research design in mathematics and science education* (pp. 647–664). Mahwah, NJ: Erlbaum.

Lappan, G., Fey, J. T., Fitzgerald, W., Friel, S. N., & Phillips, E. D. (2002). *Connected mathematics series*. Glenview, IL: Prentice Hall.

Simon, M, & Tzur, R. (1999). Explicating the teacher's perspective from the researchers' perspectives: Generating accounts of mathematics teachers' practice. *Journal for Research in Mathematics Education, 30*(3), 252-264.

Acknowledgements

This research was funded by the National Science Foundation under Grant No. REC–0231879. The research findings and opinions described here are those of the authors and do not necessarily reflect the views of NSF. The authors wish to thank members of the CoSTAR team for their efforts in the data collection efforts. The authors also extend their gratitude to the three sixth-grade teachers and their students for allowing us to learn about fractions with them.

Music By Ear: An interactive system to teach *old-time fiddle*

Matthew Osment, Dr. Todd Reimer, The University of Texas at Austin, 715-A Brownlee Circle, Austin, TX 78703
mattosment@gmail.com, todd_reimer@mail.utexas.edu

Abstract: Our learning module is a virtual, interactive training environment designed to guide learners through the stages of learning to play the *old-time fiddle*. Students are placed in mastery oriented learning situations that reflect informal, historical settings where students learn music as part of a community. In our design, students benefit from *just-in-time* interactions while developing their identity within a community of practice. This presentation highlights our needs assessment, design solutions, and our system's functionality.

Introduction

The historical method of learning *old-time fiddle* music is intended to develop a mastery orientation and avoids the competitive drawbacks of performance-oriented art forms (Dweck & Leggett, 1988). Our design solution models this traditional, informal learning environment of old-time fiddle music and delivers it via a virtual, interactive tutoring system. Our design places the student at the center of activity by immersing him or her in a variety of playing environments that reflect ways children have historically learned to play instruments as part of an informal learning community (Resnick, 1987).

Needs Assessment

Performance anxiety has been found to be a deterrent to student development and understanding (Dweck & Leggett, 1988; Blumenfeld & Marx, 1997). If a student's only exposure to music comes from professional recordings and well-rehearsed live performances, he or she will not be likely to understand the months and years of development that precede an expert's musical performance. This lack of exposure to the realities of learning to play a musical instrument, coupled with the inherent self-expressive nature of music, potentially creates a large degree of performance anxiety upon the novice.

In today's public school structure, it is difficult for a student to receive instruction that is geared to his or her individual skill level (Kliebard, 1986). This lack of specificity leads to student frustration or boredom when the learning materials are too advanced or when the subject matter is too easy. For optimal progression, the challenge to the student must dynamically meet his or her abilities (Csikszentmihalyi, 1975, 1990). As the student's skills develop, the learning materials must also become more complex. To optimize learning, students must have choices based on interests and degree of difficulty (Deci & Ryan, 1985, 1992). Interest has been found to play a key role in whether or not students are motivated to learn and participate in class activities (Renninger, 2000).

Our Design Solution

Our design specifically addresses performance anxiety, one of the greatest obstacles to learning to play a musical instrument, in four ways. First our system places the learner in a virtual community of practice in which a mastery orientation is fostered by encouraging continued musical development in common social playing situations. Students experience the successes as well as the struggles of other musicians within their community of practice. As students learn to identify themselves with like-peers on the pathway towards full community participation, self-efficacy grows due to an evolving perception awareness of developing music potential. Unlike traditional situations where students have limited access to experts and near-peers with whom to compare themselves, our system offers clear possibilities for growth to peripheral participants.

Second, working alone can prevent a student from gaining necessary access to experts and a wider culture of music. Our design solution allows students to work independently, while at the same time maintain access to expert guidance and virtual playing situations with groups of musicians. Our instructional system anticipates a student's mistakes so that these mistakes can be addressed at the moment of disequilibrium. This *just-in-time* learning allows students to make mistakes *necessary* in order to develop, prompting students towards proficiency without creating the drawbacks of performance anxiety.

Third, our design mirrors old-time fiddle communities by scaffolding the learner through each stage of development by placing him or her in a progression of playing situations from novice through advanced. This progression of levels allows the student to reinforce the skills he or she has acquired while still introducing new challenges. By providing access to a range of legitimate and full participatory situations, our design is intended to lessen frustration and prevent boredom.

Finally, our instructional system gives students a wide variety of choices to accommodate individual areas of interest. Students may choose from a variety of playing styles as well as levels of difficulty. Expert-recommended regimes can directly address specific needs historically encountered by novice players. Students may participate in relaxed playing situations, work intensively on skills, or accompany a virtual ensemble.

Next Steps

This instructional tutor seeks to replicate a cultural way of learning to play music that is quickly disappearing. By using an interactive, virtual learning system, we will be able to study the effectiveness of the traditional ear training methods used by *old-time* musicians. Through user-testing and iterative design, we shall introduce our system into public schools to examine how students instructed in this method contribute to their wider music communities within their schools. We are also interested in exploring how this learning environment could be applied to other instruments and genres of music.

References

Blumenfeld, P., & Marx, R. (1997). Motivation and cognition. In H. J. Walberg & G. D. Haertel (Eds.), *Psychology and educational practice* (pp. 79-106). Berkeley, CA: McCutchan Publishing Corp.

Csikszentmihalyi, M. (1990). *Flow: The psychology of optimal experience*. New York, NY: HarperCollins Publishing.

Deci, E., & Ryan, R. (1985). *Intrinsic motivation and self-determination in human behavior.* New York, NY: Plenum Press.

Deci, E. L., & Ryan, R. M. (1992). The initiation and regulation of intrinsically motivated learning and achievement. In D. H. Schunk & J. L. Meece (Eds.), *Student perceptions in the classroom* (pp. 9-37). Hillsdale, NJ: Lawrence Erlbaum Associates.

Dweck, C. S., & Leggett, E. L. (1988). A social-cognitive approach to motivation and personality. *Psychological Review, 95*, 256-273.

Ginsburg, H. P., & Opper, S. (1988). Learning, development, and education. In *Piaget's theory of intellectual development* (pp. 208-256). Englewood Cliffs, NJ: Prentice Hall.

Lave, J. and E. Wenger (1991). *Situated learning: Legitimate peripheral participation.* Cambridge, MA, Cambridge University Press.

Renninger, K. A. (2000). How might the development of individual interest contribute to the conceptualization of intrinsic motivation. In *Intrinsic motivation: Controversies and new directions.*

Resnick, L. B. (1987). Learning in school and out. *Educational Researcher, 16*, 13-20.

Schank, R. (1990). *Tell me a story.* Evanston, IL: Northwestern University Press.

von Glaserfeld, E. (1987). Learning as a constructive activity. In *Problems of representation in teaching and learning math* (pp. 3-17). Hillsdale, NJ.

Creative Codings: Investigating Cultural, Personal, and Epistemological Connections in Media Arts Programming

Kylie A. Peppler and Yasmin B. Kafai
University of California, Los Angeles 2331 Moore Hall Los Angeles, CA 90095
Email: kpeppler@ucla.edu, kafai@gseis.ucla.edu

Abstract: The focus of this poster is to turn our attention to the arts as an understudied area in the learning sciences and examine how studying the learning of arts and programming can open new avenues of research. Results from a case study analysis suggest that appropriation builds on multiple connections: cultural connections such as referencing popular iconography, personal connections such as including family pictures, and larger epistemological connections to larger bodies of knowledge.

Introduction

Learning science researchers have paid little attention to the field of arts education as the more prominent focus has been on science, math and to a lesser degree, social studies and language arts. Among a number of reasons that can explain this absence of interest is the lack of new technologies in the arts education curriculum. Recently, the Arts Education Partnership (AEP) issued a call for research to further investigate 'New Technologies and Arts Learning,' noting that "[n]ew technologies…are changing the nature of arts education" (AEP, 2004). The intersection of arts and technology (called "media art" here) is a relatively new avenue of research that has implications for both the arts and computer sciences, and more generally, the learning sciences. The focus of this poster is to turn our attention to the understudied area of the arts and examine how the learning of arts and programming can open new avenues of research.

A design studio found at a community technology center in South Central Los Angeles presents an interesting opportunity to explore the ways in which youth culture are already making use of new media as tools for expression, particularly capitalizing on software that promote computer programming. The studio and its design software were created with a constructionist theory of learning in mind, which poses that people learn best when they are active participants in design activities and share their design with others (Papert, 1980). The findings outlined here build on one of the main concepts of constructionism, *appropriation*, which posits that learners construct knowledge by making it their own. Resnick (1996) points to two constructional-design principles, which allow the creator to appropriate knowledge through the making of (1) personal connections (i.e., connections to outside interests, past experiences, or prior knowledge) and (2) through epistemological connections (i.e., the ability to connect to important domains of knowledge). We add a third component to this analysis, (3) cultural connections (i.e., connections to larger cultural context). The results suggest that youth leverage previous knowledge in the design process, appropriating the design software through personal, cultural, and epistemological connections to their work.

Methods

Over the past year, we have documented design activities that incorporate computer programming at a design studio with predominantly Latino/a and African-American youth ages 8-18 through extensive ethnographic field note taking (Creswell, 2003). Young artists created a variety media arts projects such as animated stories, Videogame art, and interactive or playable art using pop culture images and sounds. Using a comparative case study approach, the artist in this study was selected from over 30 other case study participants based on the prototypical nature of her work and her persistent interest over a period of multiple weeks in using computer programming for expression. Field notes were open and axial-coded for themes derived from the theoretical framing.

Findings

For this analysis, we draw from an example of a "dance video" called "k2b," created by a thirteen-year-old female software designer, who modeled the piece after a Gwen Stefani music video. When the viewer presses a start button, music begins to play, characters dance on the screen, and the background changes between several different images. At the start of the project, the first-time designer had an existing interest in pop music and chose to use "Hollaback Girl" as the basis for her music video. As a result, she chose images and music that reflected her perception of pop culture and music videos. The use of a shared cultural context (i.e., the pop music video) resonated with other members of the design studio. During the design process, members would gather behind the designer to watch the "k2b" video, being drawn in by the music. In addition to her interpretation of the well-known music video, the designer made additional personal connections to the piece such as choosing to insert both a picture of herself and her younger brother as two of the dancers in her music video.

Undoubtedly, when designers create media art they are connecting to many different bodies of knowledge, here we focus on connections to the traditional arts and computer programming. The aesthetics of the images played an important role in the design process. In the search for "k2b" images, it was less important to her to insert an image of herself, as it was to find one that fitted her perception of how a music video should appear, underscoring the importance of understanding and emulating contemporary art and pop culture aesthetics in media art production. Additional connections to traditional arts include the designer's attention to the choreographing the dancers. "k2b" required precise timing and unique dance moves of each of the characters. During these design moments, programming took a back seat to design considerations of when characters should enter and exit the stage and how each of the dancers should move—roles that seldom assumed by youth in the traditional arts. The designer also made connections to computer science. This is exemplified by the designer's use of programming concepts like looping constructs, conditionals, and assembling programs out of base components — concepts that are even new for novice computer science majors. In addition, she was able to repurpose code in a meaningful way and accomplish artistic design goals for the piece by taking pieces of code and creatively recombining them for new characters.

Discussion

This case study illuminates how programming within an arts context is very different from context of math and science. Programming in this context is less about code and more about personal expression. While case studies of work in the design studio give us only a partial understanding of the larger design culture, they do provide us with an understanding of how individuals are able to repurpose the design environment for personal expression. The advantages of this work are at least threefold: (1) Media arts have implications for broadening the participation and applications of traditional programming courses in K-12 which tended to focus on mathematics and science; (2) Media arts are an essential component to artistic expression in a digital era—a tool that has an arguably increasing importance for youth and society at large; and (3) these projects emphasize graphic, music and video — media that have been found to be at the core of technology interests for youth and thus could provide new opportunities to encourage and broaden participation of youth from under-represented groups to become designers and inventors with new technologies.

References

AEP (2004). *The Arts and Education: New Opportunities for Research*. Washington, DC: Arts Education Partnership (AEP).

Creswell, J. W. (2003). *Research Design: Qualitative, Quantitative, and Mixed Methods*. Thousand Oaks, CA: Sage Publications, Inc.

Papert, S. (1980). *Mindstorms: Children, Computers, and Powerful Ideas*. New York: Basic Books.

Resnick, M., Bruckman, A., & Martin, F. (1996). Pianos Not Stereos: Creating Computational Construction Kits. *Interactions, 3*(6).

Sefton-Green, J., & Buckingham, D. (1998). Digital Visions: Children's 'Creative' Uses of Multimedia Technologies. In J. Sefton-Green (Ed.), *Digital Diversions: Youth Culture in the Age of Multimedia* (pp. 62-83). London: UCL Press.

Acknowledgments

The work reported in this poster is conducted in collaboration with Mitchel Resnick's research group at the MIT Media Lab and supported by a grant of the National Science Foundation (NSF-0325828). The views expressed are those of the authors and do not necessarily represent the views of the supporting funding agency or the University of California, Los Angeles.

Learning Communities and Laptops: A Design Experiment

Todd C. Reimer, Felicia Rader, The University of Texas, Austin, Texas
Department of Curriculum & Instruction, 1 University Station Stop D6500 Austin, Texas 78712
Email: t-reimer@mail.utexas.edu, frader@mail.utexas.edu

Abstract: In order to create a technologically fluent community of learners, one College of Education implemented a Laptop Initiative for pre-service teachers. The laptop requirement was a design experiment created to form a community of practice within the College of Education, centered around ubiquitous computing and situating technology use into the classroom practice. The experiences of a cohort of foreign language pre-service teachers are highlighted as an example of this situated community of practice.

Introduction

This poster focuses on a "design experiment" (Brown, 1992; Collins, 1992; Collins, Joseph, and Bielaczyc, 2004) in the form of a laptop initiative for pre-service educators set forth by a College of Education at a major research institution in the American Southwest.

Needs Assessment

The laptop requirement came about for primarily two reasons within the College of Education: (1) the administration recognized the need to prepare future teachers to meet state technology competencies, (2) they perceived a disconnect between the existing computing tools course and using technology as an integrated part of one's teaching practice. Research indicates pre-service teachers are not being prepared adequately to integrate technology in their teaching. A 1995 study by the Office of Technology Assessment and a national survey conducted by Morsund and Bielefeldt (1999) reported the stand-alone courses offered in the majority of university teacher preparation programs were not as effective as integrated approaches to technology training. Both studies indicated pre-service teacher programs were not training future teachers adequately due to the types of courses offered, the lack of faculty modeling and use, and lack of use in field experiences. By the fall of 2003 there were 13.6 million computers in schools, creating a ratio of 1 computer for every 4 students (Cattagni, 2001). Despite the availability of computers, emerging research indicates technology is being systemically underutilized (Tyack & Cuban, 1995; Cuban, Kirkpatrick, & Peck, 2001). These authors consistently found that teachers use technologies to enhance regular instruction, but rarely use technology to transform their teaching. Instead, these authors report teachers made infrequent and limited use of computers and typically used computers to maintain and reinforce current classroom practices.

Design Solution: The Laptop Initiative

The Laptop Initiative was created to form a community of practice within the College of Education, centered around ubiquitous computing and situating technology use into the classroom practice (Lave & Wenger, 1991; Rogoff, 1994). Every student enrolled in the pre-service program was required to purchase a laptop. The entire education building was made wireless, allowing students and faculty to use their laptops anywhere in the building or surrounding areas. The college's technology center was re-organized so students and faculty would be supported "just in time" via a student help-desk. A support-center was created for faculty, providing instructional staff to model and support ways technology can be incorporated into one's teaching practice. Additionally, other resources such as access to online tutorials for individualized learning and peripheral equipment were secured so students could utilize their laptops as part of their pre-service teaching requirement. The computing tools course was phased out and each faculty within the college became responsible for integrating technology into their curricula. By providing both students and faculty with equal access to technology and support, the administration wants each pre-service cohort to form a learning community (Brown & Campione, 1996; Bielaczyc & Collins, 1999), sharing their collective struggles and successes integrating technology into their classroom practice. The Laptop Initiative is based largely on a pedagogical model of learning via enculturation, or legitimate peripheral participation (Lave & Wenger, 1991), with faculty and pre-service teachers experimenting with ways to integrate technology both at the university and out in the schools.

Findings and Discussion

The data reported in this poster was collected as part of a year-long qualitative study during the end of the second and beginning of the third year of the Laptop Initiative. The study focused on a cohort of pre-service foreign language teachers and their computer experiences in the field during student teaching. In order to document the entire design experiment, from development through implementation, administrators and faculty were interviewed and observed throughout this time. The findings are preliminary due to on-going efforts to analyze this large data set and triangulate developing assertions with study participants.

Of the pre-service foreign language teachers participating in the study, the portability of the laptop was most often mentioned as a positive feature of the college's initiative. During student teaching, they reported using their laptops for researching lesson ideas, investigating cultural information, and creating lesson plans. There were two other uses of the laptop frequently reported during student teaching: (1) computer-based activities for their students utilizing the Internet for research, and (2) in-class grammar presentations using the laptop. The ways in which the pre-service teachers used their laptops have been reflective of the models observed from university courses and faculty modeling. However, many of the pre-service teachers report never taking their laptop to school. Repeatedly, the pre-service teachers commented that knowing how to use the computer does not equal knowing how to use the computer to teach. In the field, the pre-service teachers felt restricted in their student teaching because of either a lack of school computer resources, or due to working with teachers who did not use computers in their practice. More significantly, many participants report not being adequately prepared in their content area to integrate technology in ways appropriate for the subject. In conclusion, the ways that pre-service teachers report using technology at the university may be beginning to transform their practice; however, how this developing expertise is being transferred to their field experiences is inconclusive.

Next Steps

At this stage of analysis, this study indicates simply requiring each student to purchase a laptop and providing institutional support does not ensure technology usage will be situated in the field outside of the college. If pre-service teachers are to become technologically fluent in their teaching practice, their experiences with technology must go beyond the community of practice established within the walls of the college. In particular, more research needs to be conducted in how technology is being integrated into pre-service teachers subject matter classes, outside of the College of Education at the university level. Additionally, the design experiment needs to be revised to include providing support for schools and teachers supporting the pre-service teachers in the field as part of their student teaching.

References

Brown, A., & Campione, J. (1996). Psychological theory and the design of innovative learning environments. In L. Schauble & R. Glaser (Eds.), *Innovations in Learning: New environments for education* (pp. 289-325). Mahwah, NJ: Lawrence Erlbaum Associates.

Cattagni, A., & Farris Westat, E. (2001). *Internet Access in U.S. Public Schools and Classrooms: 1994-2000*. U.S. Department of Education Office of Educational Research and Improvement.

Collins, A., Joseph, D., & Bielaczyc, K. (2004). Design Research: Theoretical Issues and Methodological Issues. *The Journal of the Learning Sciences, 13*(1), 15-42.

Cuban, L., Kirkpatrick, H., & Peck, C. (2001). High access and low use of technologies in high school classrooms: Explaining an apparent paradox. *American Educational Research Journal, 38*(4), 813-834.

Cuban, L., & Tyack, D. (1995). *Tinkering Toward Utopia*. Cambridge: Harvard University Press.

Lave, J., & Wenger, E. (1991). *Situated Learning: Legitimate peripheral participation.* Cambridge, MA: Cambridge University Press.

Moursund, D., & Bielefeldt, T. (1999). *Will New Teachers be Prepared to Teach in a Digital Age? A National Survey on Information Technology in Teacher Education*: Milken Exchange on Education Technology.

Rogoff, B. (1994). Developing understanding of the idea of communities of learners. *Mind, Culture, and Activity, 1*(4), 209-229.

Teachers and Technology: Making the Connection. (No. OTA-EHR-616)(1995). Washington D.C.: U.S. Congress, Office of Technology Assessment.

A Comprehension Tool for Mathematics?: The Math Forum@Drexel's Online Mentoring Guide

K. Ann Renninger, Lillian S. Ray, Ilana Luft, Erica L. Newton,
Swarthmore College, 500 College Ave., Swarthmore, PA, 19081
Email: krennin1@swarthmore.edu, lsray1@gmail.com, ilanaluft@yahoo.com, erical1813@gmail.com

Abstract: Two studies of the Math Forum's Online Mentoring Guide (OMG) address whether and how online comprehension tools might support mathematics learning. In Study 1, the culture of the preservice teachers' (PTs') mathematics classroom and their work with the OMG and its impact on their developing comprehension of mathematics and mentoring is described. In Study 2, the impact of content-informed scaffolding of PTs' work with the OMG is investigated.

Introduction

Nason and Woodruff (2004) recently suggested that computer supported collaborative learning environments have been unsuccessful in their support of mathematics learning because they do not include rich problems and tools that support the development of comprehension. Given the identified ability of the online environment to both engage and provide a source of direct dissemination of reform practices to teachers (Renninger & Shumar, 2004), the potential to develop online comprehension tools for mathematics seems likely. The open question is of what such tools need to consist. In order to explore this question, two studies of preservice teachers' (PTs') work with the Math Forum's *Online Mentoring Guide* (OMG, mathforum.org), a research and development project, were undertaken. The studies focus on elementary and middle school PTs' use of the OMG and both their mathematical content knowledge and their ability to scaffold solutions to nonroutine challenge problems online. In particular, three questions are addressed: (a) Can PTs who have weak mathematics skills assess strengths and weaknesses of pupil submissions and use this information to mentor effectively? (b) Given some weakness in mathematics, are PTs' abilities to mentor mediated by their level of interest for mathematics or their stance toward problem solving? (c) And, what would an online mentoring guide need to provide in order to support PTs to develop their mathematics abilities and be an effective collaborative mathematics comprehension tool?

Background on the OMG

The OMG is an asynchronous collaborative tool for supporting PTs to learn how to provide online scaffolding to elementary pupils working with nonroutine challenge problems, as a way to help PTs to learn how to scaffold their future students. Lessons in the OMG each include a 4-phase process of doing, reflecting/discussing, interacting with an experienced mentor, and synthesizing the experience of the previous three phases. After completing the lessons in the OMG, PTs are assigned elementary student submissions (threads) to the Math Forum's Fundamental Problem of the Week (FunPoW) to scaffold. PTs draft a response to the solution, which is read over by an approver who either sends it back to the PT with feedback about the needed revisions or sends it on to the elementary student. All data from PT work is archived, allowing analysis of both the process of this work and its outcomes.

Design

Two studies of the OMG are reported. In the first, 27 PTs' (2M, 25 F) online work with the OMG and class assignments were studied to describe the culture of their classroom. In the second, an intervention conducted with students from the same university in the same course during the following year, one half of the PTs (14: 14 F) served as controls and were approved by their professor as they were in Study 1, and one half of the PTs (14: 2M, 12 F) were scaffolded by trained mentors using a content-informed scaffolding rubric in which mathematics provided the basis of the exchange (Renninger, Ray, Luft, & Newton, 2006).

Results and Discussion

In Study 1, combined methods were employed to address the culture of the preservice mathematics classroom and its impact on what PTs might need from an online extension of the classroom. The problem-solving stance, or mathematical beliefs, of this group of PTs suggests that their prior experience of mathematics has led them to focus on accuracy (Bereiter & Scardamalia, 2003). They are, as a group, in need of support to develop their mathematical content knowledge (Hill, Rowen, & Ball, 2004). While working together on problem solving in the classroom provides the PTs with important and/or needed support for mathematics and problem solving, the professor comments that the OMG allows her to push the PTs further than she could if she were not using the OMG as part of the course. This feedback, coupled with findings indicating that (a) on exam problems the professor provides the PTs with the methods they should use to set up and solve the problems independently; and (b) the professor gives the PTs high grades when they follow through to do what she suggests, indicates that more consistent support for scaffolding in the online environment may help PTs to develop their understanding of and readiness to scaffold the elementary students' work with the FunPoW.

In Study 2, combined methods were employed to consider the impact of content-informed scaffolding on PTs' mathematical thinking and scaffolding of elementary students. Findings from this intervention indicate that target PTs experienced gains in mentoring and control PTs did not. Analysis of target PTs' scaffolding reveals that they learned to respond to two groups of students: those who had little idea of what a problem asked or those who had a full understanding of the problem. Their abilities to work with elementary students who had only a basic understanding of the FunPoW did not change. Given that in the OMG the PTs were provided with a number of possible solution strategies, this finding appears to reflect their own limited understanding of mathematics and ability to do the types of error analysis required. While the target PTs' work with FunPoWs from the beginning of the course to the end of the course suggests increases in mathematical thinking, they did not reach significance. Patterns of PT performance appear to be mediated by interest for mathematics and problem-solving stance (see Ray & Renninger, in preparation).

To summarize, answers to the questions guiding the two studies suggest that (a) PTs with weak mathematics skills are not very effective at assessing strengths and weaknesses of pupil submissions and using this information to scaffold. However, targeted mathematical scaffolding does support them to improve the quality of their scaffolding; (b) PTs' abilities to scaffold are constrained by their interest for mathematics and their stance toward problem solving; and (c) changes to three aspects of the OMP appear warranted: (1) the professor could make work with the OMG congruent with classroom practice, (2) the students could be assigned additional mentored work with the FunPoW prior to working with the OMG, and (3) online modules might be developed to accompany the OMG, which would provide support for PTs to develop their mathematics skills through work with specific problem content, error analysis, and live scaffolding. Importantly, the PTs and professors in both studies reported liking work with the OMG and recommended its use in subsequent classes. Thus, despite the challenges of its mathematical content, these data suggest that the OMG has good potential as a tool for comprehension monitoring. Considering that PTs who received mathematical scaffolding improved in their own scaffolding of mathematics, it seems possible that with appropriate modules in place, the OMP could become a powerful online comprehension tool for mathematics.

References

Bereiter C., & Scardamalia, M. (2003). Learning to work creatively with knowledge. In E. De Corte, L. Verschaffel, N. Entwistle, & J. van Merriënboer (Eds.), *Powerful learning environments: Unravelling basic components and dimensions (pp. 55-68).* New York: Pergamon

Hill, H. C., Rowan, B., & Ball, D. (2005). Effects of teachers' mathematical knowledge for teaching on student achievement. *American Educational Research Journal, 42*(2), 371- 406.

Nason, R., & Woodruff, E. (2004). Online collaborative learning in mathematics: Some necessary innovations. In T. Roberts (Ed.), *Online collaborative learning: Theory and practice (pp. 103-131).* London: Infosci.

Ray, L. S. & Renninger, K. A. (in preparation*). Preservice teachers' readiness to engage content-informed scaffolding for mathematics: Interest and mathematical beliefs as explanatory constructs.*

Renninger, K. A., Ray, L. S., Luft, I., & Newton, E. L. (2006). Coding online scaffolding of mathematical thinking. Special issue, *New Ideas in Psychology.*

Renninger, K. A. & Shumar, W. (2004). The centrality of culture and community to participant learning at and with the Math Forum. In S. Barab, J. Grey, & R. Kling (Eds.), *Designing for virtual communities in the service of learning (pp. 60-95).* New York, NY: Cambridge University Press.

Acknowledgements

We appreciate the assistance of Math Forum staff members Claire Meade and Annie Fetter and the participating PTs and their professors. Support for this study was provided by National Science Foundation Grant #9618223.

Justification of Socioscientific Claims as the Basis for Assessing Argumentation

Troy D. Sadler, University of Florida
2403 Norman Hall, PO Box 117048, Gainesville, FL 32611 tsadler@ufl.edu

Abstract: This investigation introduces a novel rubric for the assessment of argumentation quality relative to socioscientific issues and presents results from a field test of its application. Forty-five students participated in interviews designed to elicit socioscientific argumentation regarding genetic engineering issues. A five point rubric was developed to assess how well individuals justified the claims they advanced. Implications for the use of this tool for advancing research agendas in the learning sciences will be discussed.

Toulmin's (1958) philosophical exploration of argumentation has had profound impacts on the study and assessment of argumentation particularly with respect to science education. Toulmin's Argument Pattern (TAP) provides a framework for analyzing argument structure and specifies features such as claims, data, warrants, backings, and rebuttals. TAP has served as the primary analytic tool for many (probably most) studies which have sought to evaluate the quality of arguments offered by students in scientific and socioscientific contexts (e.g., Osborne, Erduran, & Simon, 2004; Sadler & Zeidler, 2005). Despite its frequent use, TAP presents a number of methodological limitations. Chief among the problems associated with TAP is the ambiguous nature of argument structures identified by TAP (Osborne, et al., 2004; Kelly, Druker & Chen, 1998). Distinguishing what counts as data, warrants, and backings can be particularly tricky leaving the reliability of TAP-based assessment schemes questionable. Some of the most recent advances in the application of TAP to science education (Osborne et al., 2004) have minimized the problems associated with the ambiguity of argument structures by collapsing the most problematic categories (i.e., data, warrants, and backings) and focusing heavily on the emergence of rebuttals. While this approach is certainly powerful for some research contexts, it presents its own methodological limitation in that it can only be applied to group discussions.

Research focused on group discourse is certainly important for the study of science education and argumentation; however, it typically positions a group, and not an individual as the unit of analysis. In some instances, particularly in the current era of scientifically-based research, it is necessary to gauge individual student aptitude, epistemic orientation, and progress. If argumentation is a key element to scientific literacy and educators need methods for documenting change in the scientific literacy of individual students, which they surely do given the calls for evidence-based research, then assessment schemes which reliably evaluate the quality of arguments offered by individual students is necessary. This study proposes such an assessment scheme and applies it in order to answer questions relative to factors which influence socioscientific argumentation.

Methods

The development of the assessment scheme was grounded in Kuhn's (1991) work on informal reasoning and argumentation, Osborne et al.'s (2004) modifications of TAP, and the author's previous work related to socioscientific argumentation (Sadler & Zeidler, 2005). Participants were engaged in interviews and asked to articulate positions in response to three genetic engineering issues (gene therapy for Huntington's disease, gene therapy to improve intelligence, and reproductive cloning). The discussion of each scenario was preceded by a short written description providing details and context. An interviewer provided additional verbal prompts to encourage participants to articulate a position and justification. Responses to each of the three scenarios were analyzed according to justification themes.

Forty-five interviews were conducted with individuals in both high school and college. Fifteen high school students participated along with 15 non-science major college students and 15 college students majoring in biology. An a priori framework, based on results of previous work, was used to establish the basis of the argumentation quality rubric, and inductive analyses of the data were employed in order to refine the rubric and clarify distinctions among levels within the rubric. Inter-rater reliability exceeded 90%.

Results

Table 1 presents the argumentation assessment rubric and interview excerpts representative of each category.

Table 1. Argumentation quality rubric

Score - Description	Excerpt
0 - No justification	*In response to the reproductive cloning scenario*: "Yes, I think so [reproductive cloning should be developed]."
1 - Justification with no grounds	*In response to the gene therapy for Huntington's Disease scenario*: "If they can stop someone from suffering, then sure."
2 - Justification with simple grounds	*In response to the reproductive cloning scenario*: I don't think it's right because if you're not able to have a child, it's not God's will. If God wants you to have a child, you should have a child, and you will have a child. But if it's not for you to have a child, I mean, I think you shouldn't tamper with it.
3 - Justification with elaborated grounds	*In response to the gene therapy for intelligence scenario*: "They will develop a dichotomy even more so than we see now with the rich and poor. Now we will have the smart vs. the stupid or those who can afford this procedure and those who cannot. And that will create all kinds of sociological problems. I think that is meddling too much."
4 - Justification with elaborated grounds and a counter-position	*In response to the gene therapy for Huntington's Disease scenario*: "I think that gene therapy, it should be actually used very sparingly because what it does is narrows the diversity—like everyone gets the good copy now so that is not necessarily good because then we do not have a backup for anything. But in cases like this, where the only cure would be replacing the actual gene, then it could be beneficial… If there are no other treatments for it, that would be the only way that I would support using gene therapy for something like that...

Conclusions & Educational Significance

If argumentation is to become a significant aspect of science education as advocated in progressive calls for the enhancement of science education, then researchers require tools for documenting the effectiveness of curricula and pedagogies. Likewise, teachers require tools for documenting individual student growth and success. The assessment scheme developed as a part of this study provides such a tool. It does not provide assessment of all aspects of argumentation (and given the complexity of argumentation a single strategy for doing so is likely impossible), but it does provide a tool for the evaluation of justifications offered in support of claims, which represents a fundamental aspect of argumentation. In this particular study, the rubric was applied to interview data, but it could also be used with data collected through classroom conversations, writing assignments, or technology enhanced argumentation opportunities.

References

Kelly, G. J., Drucker, S., & Chen, K. (1998). Students' reasoning about electricity: Combining performance assessment with argumentation analysis. *International Journal of Science Education, 20*, 849-871.

Kuhn, D. (1991). *The skills of argument*. Cambridge: Cambridge University Press.

Osborne, J., Erduran, S., & Simon, S. (2004). Enhancing the quality of argumentation in school science. *Journal of Research in Science Teaching, 41*, 994-1020.

Sadler, T. D., & Zeidler, D. L. (2005). The significance of content knowledge for informal reasoning regarding socioscientific issues. *Science Education, 89*, 71-93.

Toulmin, S. (1958). *The uses of argument*. Cambridge: Cambridge University Press.

Using Handheld PCs and Peer Instruction to Improve Science Teaching and Learning in Higher Education

Perry Samson, Stephanie D. Teasley, Ben van der Pluijm, Peter Knoop
University of Michigan, 1539 Space Research Bld., Ann Arbor, MI 48109-2143
Email: [samson, steasley, vdpluijm, knoop]@umich.edu

Abstract: Many of the core concepts in earth science systems are complex and counter-intuitive, but well illustrated through imagery and/or animation. We have developed a new tool, "ImageQuiz," that uses wireless technologies to present images and provide a question requiring a point response. In the study presented here, we use Peer Instruction techniques (Mazur, 1997) in a large geosciences class and deliver ImageQuizes via wireless PocketPC computers. We will discuss development, implementation and learning outcomes.

Introduction

Introductory science teaching at the under-graduate level typically relies on static textbooks and course packs with presentation of materials delivered as monologs in front of large, mostly passive audiences. For example, Wenzel (1999) observed that in large science classes, 92% of the time is spent on lectures, 4% on student questions, and 4% in silence. With the growing use of course management systems and pod-casting of lectures, students are left with little incentive to come to class, much less participate. Over the past decade, instructors in higher education have been experimenting with ways of making large lecture classes more interactive (e.g., Bligh, 2000). Increasingly instructors are harnessing developments in information and communications technology to transform classroom participation and learning in large classes. In particular, the flexibility, mobility and decreasing cost of handheld computers have made them a popular technology for introducing innovative pedagogical techniques inside the classroom and out (e.g., Roschelle et al., 2003; Davis, 2003).

Although the use of handheld devices in classrooms is diverse, in general they are employed to engage learners and to increase active participation in the classroom (Judson & Sawada, 2002). In the study presented here, we use Peer Instruction techniques as originally described by Mazur (1997) in one large geosciences class and extend this pedagogical technique through use of interactive spatial concept challenges utilizing wireless PocketPC computers. The technologies we employ (browser, PocketPC, wireless networks) are largely off-the shelf technologies and the Peer Instruction techniques are well documented as being successful in undergraduate science classes (Crouch & Mazur, 2001). However, the combination is not widely employed due to cost, perceived level of effort to implement, and a relatively modest volume of data documenting its value to student learning. In this paper we will discuss the development, implementation and preliminary assessment of cognitive outcomes from teaching in this IT-enhanced classroom, involving interactive image quizzes and data manipulation in class at a large research university in the Midwest.

Research Methods, Design, & Setting

Geosciences: Extreme Weather is a large introductory undergraduate course designed to provide an introduction to the physics of extreme weather events. Students examine solar eruptions, climate change, floods, monsoons, hurricanes, tornados, and other extreme weather events to illustrate the physical laws that produce these events. Students are expected to apply these principles to a series of homework assignments including hands-on weather forecasting and analysis of storm events. Students' grades are also based on three exams. The class size for the Fall 2005 term is 178 students who meet in lecture 3 times per week for 1 hour per session. The auditorium where this class is taught is outfitted with a video/data projector, wired Internet connection at the instructor's podium, wireless hub for Internet connectivity throughout the room, and 170 PocketPCs (made available through a Hewlett-Packard Foundation Higher Education Grant).

Many of the core concepts in earth science systems are complex and counter-intuitive, but the concepts being developed are often well illustrated through imagery and/or animation. We have developed a new tool entitled "ImageQuiz" that uses wireless technologies to communicate images to students along with providing a driving question that requires students to make a point response (see Figure 1). We have adapted the ConcepTests developed by Mazur (1997) to the specific geosciences course content. ConcepTests are presented in class, students work with a partner to determine a joint answer which they then indicate via the PocketPC. After 3-5 minutes, the instructor projects anonymized answers to the class, and students are then given 3 more minutes to discuss the results and change their answers if they so desire. The instructor then solicits discussion about why some answers have changed and explains or restates the accurate answer.

Figure 1. ImageQuiz with spatial ConcepTest.

By requiring students to login to use the PocketPCs we are collecting data logged by the ImageQuiz software to track their responses to the ConcepTests. Students in the class are presented the course material in three ways: 1) standard lecture with no ImageQuiz, 2) ImageQuiz employed during lecture with no peer instruction, and 3) ImageQuiz with group display and peer instruction. Specifically, we hypothesize that students will demonstrate better comprehension of concepts presented via the combination of interactive graphic display coupled with the peer instruction than those concepts introduced in standard lecture format or via ImageQuiz without peer instruction.

References

Bligh, D. (2000). *What's the Use of Lectures*? San Francisco, CA: Jossey-Bass.

Crouch, C. H. and E. Mazur (2001). Peer Instruction: Ten years of experience and results. *American Journal of Physics*, *69*, 970-977.

Davis, S. (2003). Observations in classrooms using a network of handheld devices. *Journal of Computer Assisted Learning*, *19*, 298-307.

Judson, E., & Sawada, D. (2002). Learning from the past and present: Electronic response systems in college lecture halls. *Journal of Computers in Mathematical and Science Teaching*, *21*, 167-181.

Mazur, E. (1997). *Peer Instruction: A Users' Manual*. Englewood Cliffs, NJ: Prentice Hall.

Roschelle, J., Vahey, P., Tatar, D., Kaput, J., & Hegeduc, S. (2003). Five key considerations for networking in a handheld-based mathematics classroom. In N. A. Pateman, B. J. Dougherty, & J. T. Zilliox (Eds.), *Proceedings of the 2003 Joint Meeting of PME and PMENA* (pp.71-78). Honolulu, Hawaii.

Wenzel, T. J. (1999). The lecture as a learning device. *Analytical Chemistry*, *71* (23), 817-819.

Modeling Modern Methods in High School Physics Classes

Hal Scheintaub, Governor Dummer Academy, Byfield, MA USA hscheintaub@gda.org

Abstract: Interactive computer models and simulations can extend traditional learning in high school biology classes (Scheintaub, 2004). Results of this study show that computer models can enhance high school physics learning, too. They do so by extending experiences beyond the limits imposed by text and lab. Computer models complement data gathering and analysis software to bring inquiry to the classroom. The author proposes that validation is critical to a model's effectiveness as a learning tool.

Introduction

Technology helps students perform experiments that are reliable enough to be an integral part of many inquiry-based high school physics courses. Students use Logger Pro software (Vernier) to collect meaningful data and Excel to analyze it. Students find mathematical relationships in their data and can make predictions based on those relationships. However, time and equipment restraints prohibit most experiments from being confirmed and most predictions from being tested. These constraints limit opportunities for students to design and conduct investigations. Consequently, students miss out on important parts of the scientific process. The author found that computer models could bring verification and student spawned experiments into high school physics classes. The computer models chosen (PhET, 2005, Molecular Workbench, 2005) generated data quickly. The models provided a fluid environment where trial and error was possible, and they were good enough to be used by students voluntarily. The models supported physics curricular goals and allowed for meaningful inquiry to happen in the classroom.

Design

In an introductory unit of two inquiry based physics courses, 28 students performed two physical experiments with springs (Scheintaub & Wilson, 2005). They established by experiment that the stretch of a spring was directly proportional to the mass hanging on it. Then students found that the period of a bouncing spring was not directly related to mass, but proportional to the square root of the mass attached. Appropriate textbook readings (Hewitt, 2002) and mathematical analysis accompanied the experiments. After doing and discussing the spring experiments, students were shown two interactive computer simulations of springs (PhET, 2005, Molecular Workbench, 2005). They established the validity of the computer models by duplicating the experiments that they had performed at the bench. They designed and ran experiments with their models. The spring experiments served several curricular goals. They revealed a role of mathematics in interpreting data. They helped set a tone of inquiry and investigation for the year, and they helped establish computers as an integral part of the course. The unit served as an introduction to a semester that would include the study of waves, sound and light. As a final activity, students considered the role of simulations, labs, text and lecture in their learning.

Results

Students cited the physical experiments as their favorite learning method (see Table 1). Computer models and class discussion were valued learning methods, too. The physical lab seemed most effective in specific content and general science learning, but computer models added an important new dimension. Loggerpro (Vernier) and Excel were used to collect and analyze data, but students reported that it was the computer models that taught them about the role of computers in experiments. Students used models to perform experiments of their own design that included investigations into the effect of friction on bounce and gravity on stretch. The latter experiment provided an opportunity to introduce the concept of force to the class. Five students said that they learned about the relationship between spring stiffness and period using models. Few of the student-designed experiments could have been performed physically in the school lab. Fifty percent of the students chose to use computer models to conduct an experiment that was a part of their unit test. Students cited comfort as the reason for their choice. The classes that used the computer models kept pace with classes that didn't. Classes took similar assessments, with no significant difference in grade distributions.

Discussion

This study shows how computer models can add extra dimensions to high school physics classes. In addition to supporting traditional concept learning, the models provided opportunities for inquiry. Students designed and conducted experiments not usually possible in school, and tested hypotheses. The combination of lab and computer model can be very powerful. The computer occupies a position of authority and influence in young people's lives; so when computer models give the same results that a student got in the lab on her own, she feels validated. The confidence generated by validation may stimulate learning. However, just as authority figures may have power by virtue of position, they have to earn respect by being relevant to the young person. So it is with the computer. Computer models in this unit achieve relevance by producing results that match the young person's real world experience. So the model validates experience and is validated by it; and once validated the student willingly learns from the model. The models cited here are only two of many that are available and will be used throughout the year. The author looks forward to reporting on student responses to other models in future communications.

Table 1. How & What Students Learned About Springs

What Students Learned *Spring Specifics* / **Learning Method →**	1	2	3	4	5	6	7	8	Totals
As mass increases, period increase nonlinearly	1	5	1	8	0	0	0	1	**16**
As mass increases, stretch increases	1	2	0	4	1	0	3	0	**11**
As stiffness increases, period decreases	1	0	0	0	0	0	3	2	**6**
distance vs. t graph is sine curve	2	1	1	3	0	0	1	0	**8**
Amp decreases, f remains constant	0	4	0	3	0	1	0	1	**9**
Springs are efficient systems	0	3	0	5	0	0	0	0	**8**
Springs have friction	1	0	0	1	0	0	1	0	**3**
Can use springs to find mass	0	0	0	2	1	0	1	0	**4**
Other comments and connections	1	4	1	6	1	3	1	3	**20**
General science (non-spring) learning									
role of computers in experiments	0	0	0	0	0	1	3	3	**7**
graphs and calculations	0	1	4	5	1	2	1	0	**14**
writing a lab report, do experiment	0	1	2	4	1	0	2	4	**11**
do a good experiment	0	0	0	3	0	0	0	3	**3**
how this class works	0	1	0	1	0	1	3	0	**3**
many variables are in an experiment	0	0	0	1	0	0	0	1	**2**
Totals	**7**	**23**	**9**	**43**	**5**	**8**	**15**	**12**	**122**

Learning Method **1**. text, **2**. class notes & discussion, **3**. doing homework **4**. performing experiment, **5**. writing up experiment, **6**. collaborating with classmates, **7**. PhET computer model, **8**. molecular workbench

References

Hewitt, Paul. (2002). Conceptual Physics The High School Physics Program. Prentice Hall. Needham, MA.

Molecular Workbench. 29 October 2005. <http://mw.concord.org/modeler/index.html>

Physics Education Technology. *Interactive Physics Simulations* 23 October 2005 http://www.colorado.edu/physics/phet/web-pages/index.html

Scheintaub, H., Klopfer, E., Yoon, S. (2004). *Complex Systems Modeling Supports and Extends Secondary School Science Learning*. Presented at National Association of Research in Science Teaching (NARST) 2004.

Scheintaub, H and Wilson, K. *Physics Folder*. 29 October 2005 http://www.gda.org

Vernier Loggerpro software version 2.2

Personalized Identity, Mentoring and Mathematical Conversation: The Math Forum's Online Mentoring Project

Wesley Shumar, Drexel University, Philadelphia, PA 19104, wes@drexel.edu

Abstract: Drawing on current thinking about identity, social group boundary and informational technology, the research presented in this poster discusses a unique online interactive project at the Math Forum called The Online Mentoring Project. The importance of this work for digital libraries will be highlighted.

The OMG

The Online Mentoring Project (OMP) at The Math Forum developed a curriculum structure called the Online Mentoring Guide (OMG) where pre-service teachers learn to think about math problems and the idea of mathematical thinking. They then learn to mentor by first mentoring each other followed by instruction on how The Math Forum thinks about mentoring. Finally, they have a "pre-field" experience mentoring K-12 students in The Math Forum's Problem of the Week (PoW) environment and reflect upon their mentoring experience.

Theory: Hybrid Social Worlds

The Internet has made possible the transformation of social space such that individuals can craft the spaces in which they operate and the times that are convenient for them to operate. This space/time transformation makes possible the re-imagination of the community that one operates within and the identity that one presents within that community (Shumar & Renninger, 2002). The transformation of social space brought about by brining the online world into communication with the f2f world is at the center of the vision of the OMP.

Learning and Identity Work

Digital libraries can be used by people to reorganize their social lives in new ways allowing them to "personalize" the communities to which they belong (Wellman, 2001). Further the transformation of the learning space that an interactive digital library allows makes it possible for teachers and students to rethink their identity as learners as part of the learning process (Cobb and Hodge, 2003). Central to the process of learning for students (perhaps as well as teachers) is a process of boundary crossing and identity work where one has to safely imagine oneself as a valuable member of a community of practice in order to collaboratively construct knowledge with an other (Anderson, 1991; Cobb and Hodge, 2003; Harlen and Doubler, 2004). In this way an individual's knowledge can grow rather than being channeled into a struggle to maintain an identity in the face of an uncaring system.

Method

Modeled after much design-based research project (Design-based Research Collective, 2003; Hoadley, 2002) the OMP collected survey data from pre-service teachers after they used the Online Mentoring Guide (OMG) the curriculum unit that linked pre-service teachers to the Math Forum's Problem of the Week (PoW) environment. Further, staff members of the OMP discussed in detail and regularly the experiences of the pre-service teachers with the university faculty who were supervising the teachers. The university faculty themselves took an "approver's version" of the OMG so that they would have direct experience with the guide their students used. They also approved the mentoring work of their students and so were directly involved in the mentoring experiences of their students. OMP staff met regularly taking the survey results from students who used the guide and interview data from the faculty to think about the potential impact of online curriculum units like the OMG on f2f courses in math education.

Discussion

For many pre-service teachers, especially elementary teachers, the OMG instills them with a sense of confidence around math and technology. Further they get an opportunity to think deeply and critically about mentoring, math and technology. Feedback from pre-service teachers suggests that online environments like the OMG not only can train students efficiently but it allows them an opportunity to connect with a different kind of community of practice, in this instance The Math Forum. Those kinds of connections, coupled with increased opportunities for communication, create the potential for students like the pre-service teachers to overcome their fear and resistance to learning and engage with others in new and productive kinds of ways. While the OMG helped students with their confidence in math and technology, evaluation has shown that problem solving skills and mathematical thinking has not improved much (Renninger et al., 2006). This is not surprising in that the goal of the OMG was originally just to provide training in mentoring. And yet it is clear that mentoring and content-knowledge cannot be separated. Future versions of the guide are being planned that would include new problem writing and problem solving components to further enhance the ability of the online world to positively impact f2f classes.

References

Anderson, B. (1991). *Imagined Communities: reflections on the origin and spread of nationalism.* London; New York: Verso.

Cobb, P. & Hodge, L. L. (2003). Students' Construction of Identities as Doers of Mathematics in the Context of Statistical Data Analysis. Talk presented as part of the session Identity, Equity and Mathematical Learning in the Context of Statistical Data. Chicago, IL. American Educational Research Association, April 23, 2003.

Design-Based Research Collective (2003). Design-based research: An emerging paradigm for educational inquiry. *Educational Researcher* 32(1)5-8.

Harlen, W. & Doubler, S. (2004). Can teachers learn through inquiry on-line? *International Journal of Science Education*, 26:1, 1- 21.

Hoadley, C. P. (2002). Creating context: Design-based research in creating and understanding CSCL. *Proceedings of Computer Support for Cooperative Learning (CSCL)* Boulder, CO.

Renninger, K. A. et al. (2006). A Comprehension Tool for Mathematics?: The Math Forum@Drexel's Online Mentoring Guide. Poster presentation at ICLS to be published in the *Conference Proceedings of ICLS 2006.*

Shumar, W. & Renninger, K. A. (2002). On Conceptualizing Community. In K. A. Renninger & W. Shumar (Eds.) *Building Virtual Communities: Learning and Change in Cyberspace.* NY: Cambridge University Press.

Wellman, B. (2001). Physical place and CyberPlace: The rise of personalized networking. *International Journal of Urban and Regional Research, 25.*

Acknowledgments

National Science Foundation funding to The Math Forum (grant #0127516) supported the work overviewed in this poster. Interpretation of these data does not necessarily represent the views of the National Science Foundation. Our thanks to the Math Forum at Drexel staff for their continued support on this project.

Facilitating Social Creativity through Collaborative Designing

Pirita Seitamaa-Hakkarainen, Savonlinna Department of Teacher Education, University of Joensuu, P.O. Box 86, Savonlinna, Finland, Email: Pirita.seitamaa-hakkarainen@joensuu.fi
Uotila, Minna, Faculty of Arts, University of Lapland, P.O. Box 122, SF-96101 Rovaniemi, Finland
Email: minna.uotila@ulapland.fi

Abstract. The present study introduces the "Facilitating Social Creativity through Collaborative Designing" project, an undertaking aimed at developing and testing Virtual Design Studios (VDS) in education and professional communities. VDS is a pedagogical approach supported by collaborative technologies, focused on engaging learners in the co-design of various artefacts. The present poster provides a synthesis of results concerning multiple design experiments regarding VDS at the elementary, higher educational and professional levels. The reviewed data generally support the usefulness and benefits of VDS, and indicate the areas where improvements are desirable.

Introduction

Virtual and networked working practices, which allow sharing of expertise and competencies, are becoming more and more common, both in workplaces and in education. The increased need to rely on information networks and virtual design studios (VDS) is likely to radically transform the work of designers and students. '*VDS*' refers to a computer-supported environment or www-based resource that allows communities separated by time and space to work with shared design objects (Maher et al., 2000). The purpose of the project "Facilitating Social Creativity through Collaborative Designing" was to develop pedagogical practices and models that promote collaborative designing in education and in the practices of professional design, and to gather data on their fruitfulness and efficacy, as well as participants' experiences in the design process in this new medium (Lahti et al., 2004). The project examined how social creativity can be integrated by means of probe collaboration models and tools supporting distributed work. More generally, the present investigators developed virtual design studios in education according to the following objectives; 1) to develop and implement authentic and meaningful design contexts in VDS, 2) facilitate creation of shared design ideas in design teams, 3) support participation of end users in VDS, 4) provide expert-support for the virtual design process, 5) create scaffolds for design thinking based on a progressive inquiry model, and 6) carry out empirical case studies at the elementary, higher educational and professional levels, to gather data on the effects and effectiveness of the VDS's and document their process.

Longitudinal studies at the elementary level

The first longitudinal school project at elementary level was organized in close collaboration between the class teacher and the researchers. The aim of the "Artifact project" (Seitamaa-Hakkarainen et al., 2004) was to create a collaborative knowledge-building culture in an elementary education setting and to develop knowledge-building practices by using a progressive-inquiry model. The aim of the second school project, the "Architecture project", was to continue to use the knowledge building practices in students' collaborative design process. In the second project the students participated in architects' professional working practices and engage in solving an authentic and challenging design task. In the school projects, both the material and the conceptual aspects of artifacts were productively involved. The parallel pursuit of these two aspects of artifacts was greatly facilitated by Knowledge Forum (KF), a computer-supported environment that helped to put students' ideas into the center of discussion (Scardamalia, 1999).

Design experiments at higher education

The first VDS experiment in higher education focused on examining how the progressive inquiry model of collaborative designing (see Seitamaa-Hakkarainen et al. 2001) bears fruit in these settings. Collaborative computer use, working to produce shared artefacts, characterizes advancement of designing in VDS (Seitamaa-Hakkarainen et al., in press). In addition, the researchers were interested in how members of design teams develop shared design ideas and organize their collaborative activity within VDS. The second VDS experiment focused on examining the role of participatory design in design education. The researchers looked at what roles users come to have in design process. In the third experiment, researchers looked for means of integrating support of domain experts as a part of

VDS. The aim was to analyze how the virtual design studio supports multi-professional design teams in order to achieve mutual understanding and transform design ideas into desired products.

Professional designing

In professional level collaborative design, we carried out studies through the "Intelligent Clothing Design Project", which was divided into three main phases: design, prototyping and evaluation of the concept. The project provided an opportunity to explore an authentic collaborative design process in which the end-users of the product also participated. In the concept-design phase, the objective was to examine how end-users and experts could participate in the concept-design process in VDS. The researchers were interested in what role the VDS would play in the communication with the design-team members and the kinds of collaborative processes taking place between the team members. Another goal was to use the VDS to experiment with ways of representing the concept so as to get feedback from team members. In the prototyping phase, the study examined how the VDS would facilitate the prototyping process and communication between members of the prototyping team, design team, and project personnel. In the concept evaluation phase, the intent was to inquire how the visual prototype and representation would succeed in taking the evaluation process forward and in how informative the visual prototype was in terms of the concept's functional, expressive and aesthetic properties. In addition, the research studied how usable the actual visual representation was, as seen from the end-users' and the researchers' points of view. We summarize the findings in the next section.

Summary of Results; Conclusions

The students and professionals involved in team-related activities during the processes of design undertake complex multifaceted activities. As design projects become more complex, relationships and roles become more varied. The extent and character of virtual design can be affected a number of variables, including the distance between members, the length of time the virtual team has functioned together, and the experience with technical skills of the team members. The research findings revealed that the mode of collaboration can vary from constant to intermittent collaboration. Further, the results showed that there are various ways to implement user-centered or participatory design in VDS. The design experiments provided evidence that it is important for the design process that students and participants construct a coherent design context and specify design constraints by structuring the process iteratively, together. The collaborative design process is not just designing the products, but also jointly designing the process itself. In all, the findings of the various design experiments provide a clearer understanding of the implications for working collaboratively in the VDS and evidence regarding desired outcomes. The collaborative virtual design process is different from traditional team-work. The differences between traditional team-work and virtual design team are encapsulated in collaboration between participants when creating a new artefact, creating sharable externalizations and organizing the process. Our evidence shows areas where further improvements are desirable. In further studies, we need to analyze participants' situational awareness, styles and strategies in order to improve virtual design. Further, we will need to deepen our understanding of how to motivate the end-users and experts to actively participate in the participatory design processes, and how to get end-users' and other experts' implicit knowledge into an explicit form using the VDS.

References

Lahti, H., Seitamaa-Hakkarainen, P. & Hakkarainen, K. (2004). Collaboration patterns in computer-supported collaborative designing. Design Studies, 25/4, 351-371.

Maher, M. L., Simoff, S. J. & Cicognani, A.: 2000, Understanding Virtual Design Studios, Springer-Verlag, London.

Scardamalia, M. (1999) Moving ideas to the center. In L. Harasim (Ed.), Wisdom & Wizardry: Celebrating the pioneers of online education (pp. 14-15).Vancouver, BC: Telelearning Inc.

Seitamaa-Hakkarainen, P., Engeström, R., Kangas, K., Bollström-Huttunen, M., & Hakkarainen, K (2004) The Artifact Project: Hybrid Knowledge Building in a Networked Learning Environment. A paper presented the Scandinavian Summer Cruise at the Baltic Sea, June 18-21, 2004.

Seitamaa-Hakkarainen, P, Lahti, H. & Hakkarainen, K. (2005, in press) Three Design Experiments for Computer Supported Collaborative Design. Art, Design and Communication in Higher Education.

Seitamaa-Hakkarainen, P., Raami, A., Muukkonen, H., & Hakkarainen, K. (2001). Computer-support for collaborative designing. International Journal of Technology and Design Education, 11, 181-202.

Learning Science by Participating in Design: A Case Where Multiple Design Subgoals Interfere with Systematic Progress

Eli M. Silk and Christian D. Schunn, University of Pittsburgh, Pittsburgh, PA
Email: esilk@pitt.edu, schunn@pitt.edu

Abstract: Two contrasting teams were analyzed qualitatively in a science unit in which students collaborate in teams to learn science concepts through a design project. The unit was focused on learning concepts of electricity by designing an electronic alarm system. The difference in the success of one of the teams to learn the science content can be attributed to their ability to focus systematic efforts on exploring one lower-level design goal at a time.

Introduction

There are an increasing number of science education researchers who investigate the use of classroom design projects as a method for learning science (Fortus, Dershimer, Krajcik, Marx, & Mamlok-Naaman, 2004; Puntambekar & Kolodner, 2005). We further elaborate on the conditions necessary for students to learn science through design by investigating an eighth grade science unit in which students learn about the nature of electricity by working in teams to design an electrical alarm system. The task is both open-ended, as each team chooses their own alarm to design based on a personal need from their everyday lives, and authentic, as electronics components and electricity concepts are, for the most part, only introduced when they are useful for solving particular design challenges. In general, we have observed that students who participate in this unit are more engaged, improve their design process skills, and learn more abstract knowledge of the physics of electricity than students who engage in a more traditional scripted inquiry approach (Mehalik, Doppelt, & Schunn, 2005). Despite these successes, some students who participate in the unit acquire considerably more knowledge of the science content than others. In order to come to a greater understanding of how all students may benefit from learning science through design, we have attempted to look in depth at two contrasting teams as they underwent their design process in this unit.

Theory

A considerable amount of work has been conducted recently in the context of making design projects more effective for student learning of science. Fortus et al. (2004) designed a curriculum in which students participate in multiple iterations of a design cycle, each focused on different content, in order to help students transfer. Puntambekar and Kolodner (2005) designed scaffolds to provide students with multiple opportunities to justify decisions in individual work and in whole class discussions. Baumgartner and Reiser (1998) articulated a set of teacher strategies important for helping students stay on task and managing the complexity of the design process.

In addition to focusing at these levels, students spend a considerable amount of time collaborating with their team members, so it is useful to take the team as a unit of analysis. A major task of individuals when working in teams is to negotiate shared conceptual structures through conversational interaction (Roschelle, 1992). In addition to the cognitive level, there are added social factors that determine the success of a collaborative team, such as the willingness to accept or discuss explanations versus ignoring or rejecting them (Barron, 2003). Although explanatory activities through conversation are necessary for team members to learn effectively, by themselves the explanations are not sufficient unless accompanied by data from crucial experiments required to support the explanation (Okada & Simon, 1997). In the case of design activities, the crucial experiments are manifested in the physical artifacts that embody the design. Our purpose for this research was to consider cognitive, social, and material level factors together by analyzing a contrasting case of collaborative design teams in detail.

Curriculum Context

All teams participating in the Alarm System unit maintain the high-level design goal of creating a working alarm system. Along the way to their high-level design goal, teams are forced to solve a variety of low-level design goals that are challenging. These lower-level design challenges include: getting an indicator component to work (i.e., a bulb to light or a buzzer to sound), getting a indicator component to be louder or brighter, getting a detector components to work (e.g., have a light detector affect the brightness of the bulb), incorporating an on/off switch that doesn't short circuit the batteries, limiting what is passed through a component so it doesn't get overheated or so it turns all the way off when the detector is activated.

Methods

The data was collected in the classroom of one teacher's four sections of eighth grade science. In each section, two student teams were randomly assigned to be videotaped for a total of eight teams. Each team was recorded with a dedicated camera that was positioned to record talk, gestures, and the physical circuit designs that were created. Each team consisted of three or four students. At the end of the unit, teams presented their final system to the class and took a post-test intended to measure their science concept knowledge. The final presentations were also videotaped, and the post-tests and student design portfolios were collected as well. We chose to focus on two teams at the extremes of the post-test performance for this analysis.

Results

Both teams were from the same eighth grade section. Team 1 included two males both of whom attended the school districts' gifted program, and one female who did not attend the gifted program. Team 2 included one male who attended the gifted program and three females, two of whom attended the gifted program. Team 1 had a mean score of 48% on the post-test, and Team 2 had a mean score of 75%. As a result, we are contrasting two groups of similar status as high-achievers according to district standards, but with stark contrast in terms of performance on the post-test for the unit. One major factor by which the two groups differed is in the amount of circuit designs that they created and tested. Team 1, the low-performing group averaged 13 circuit designs per day over the four-day period. Team 2, on the other hand, averaged over 35 circuit designs per day. Although clearly, Team 2 covered a considerably larger portion of the design space than Team 1, and therefore that factor alone may explain the difference in performance, there may also be some mediating factors involved.

The additional factor that distinguishes these two groups was the systematicity by which they explored lower-level design goals. Team 1 had a difficult time focusing on one lower-level design goal at a time, and therefore did not explore as many combinations of designs as was required to understand the underlying conceptual ideas. For instance, they had difficulty separating the design challenge of getting the bulb brighter with that of eliminating short circuits. Because of that, they never considered putting batteries in series and made claims that the bulb could not get any brighter. On the other hand, Team 2 was much more focused on one design challenge at a time. They solved the short circuit challenge first and only after all members of the team understood it, did they move on to the challenge of making the bulb as bright as possible. While pursuing one design challenge at a time, the team was able to consider thoroughly the majority of ideas suggested by the team members as possible solutions. They were also much less likely to stop their exploring and say that the design challenge was not possible with the given materials.

Discussion

Our findings suggest that there is an important influence of design goals on the systematicity by which teams collaborate to explore design challenges. Focusing efforts on one lower-level design goal at a time may be a mediating factor in allowing teams to consider a greater portion of the design space, and this lead to greater overall learning of the science concepts.

References

Barron, B. (2003). When smart groups fail. *The Journal of the Learning Sciences, 12*(3), 307–359.

Baumgartner, E., & Reiser, B. J. (1998). *Strategies for supporting student inquiry in design tasks.* Presented at the Annual Meeting of the American Educational Research Association, 1998, San Diego, California.

Fortus, D., Dershimer, R. C., Krajcik, J., Marx, R. W., & Mamlok-Naaman, R. (2004). Design-based science and student learning. *Journal of Research in Science Teaching, 41*(10), 1081–1110.

Mehalik, M. M., Doppelt, Y., & Schunn, C. D. (2005). *Addressing performance and equity of a design-based, systems approach for teaching science in eighth grade.* Paper presented at the annual meeting of the American Educational Research Association, 2005, Montreal, Canada.

Okada, T., & Simon, H. A. (1997). Collaborative discovery in a scientific domain. *Cognitive Science, 21*(2), 109–146.

Puntambekar, S., & Kolodner, J. L. (2005). Toward implementing distributed scaffolding: Helping students learn science from design. *Journal of Research in Science Teaching, 42*(2), 185–217.

Roschelle, J. (1992). Learning by collaborating: Covergent conceptual change. *The Journal of the Learning Sciences, 2*(3), 235–276.

Adaptive Simulations

Mark K. Singley, Tracee Vetting Wolf, Peter Fairweather, and Richard B. Lam, IBM Thomas J. Watson Research Center, Yorktown Heights, New York 10598
Email: {ksingley, tlwolf, pfairwea, rblam} @us.ibm.com

Abstract: We propose a new kind of learning environment called an adaptive simulation that more deeply explores and exploits the potential synergy between simulations and intelligent tutoring systems. In an adaptive simulation, the simulation environment is not fixed but rather can be modified by a tutoring agent for optimal pedagogical effect. Types of adaptations include manipulations of simulation time and state, changes in representation to facilitate explanations and/or task performance, and adjustments in simulation complexity by the addition and/or removal of components. Open research issues include how to perform these adaptations and when to employ them for optimal effect.

Simulations as Learning Environments: Unrealized Potential?

There is a long history of interest in simulations as learning environments, primarily because of their ability to support learning-by-doing in authentic, risk-free, immersive settings. Indeed, this interest only appears to be growing: One study by IDC projects that, whereas simulations comprised 8-10% of corporate learning content in 2004, that number will grow to 40% by 2008. Although widely regarded as having great promise, if deployed in isolation, simulations have a number of associated learning problems, primarily having to do with learner understanding and management of system complexity and the lack of built-in instructional support. To remedy these problems, simulations may be supplemented by an instructional component; sometimes this takes the form of an intelligent tutoring system. When present, the tutoring component typically has been used to provide performance support in the form of hints and corrective feedback on actions taken by the learner, as well as the progressive selection and sequencing of tasks based on estimates of learner proficiency. Performance support of this type and task sequencing both serve to keep the learner on track toward instructional goals, maximizing the productive use of time and minimizing confusion and frustration. Thus, to be truly effective, it seems simulations must know something about the learner and the task the learner is trying to accomplish (Fletcher, 1999).

However, even when an instructional component is present, it may have been added as an afterthought once the simulation itself had been built in isolation. This necessarily restricts the kinds of synergies that can be exploited between the two systems. In our work, we are striving for a much tighter linkage between the simulation and instructional components. Specifically, we are considering what value may result if the simulation is put under much more direct and masterful control of the tutor. We are developing a vision of "adaptive simulations" that we think may better realize the true promise of simulations as learning environments.

Radical Adaptation

As mentioned above, in the standard pairing of simulation and tutoring components, adaptation to the learner is achieved primarily through task monitoring and task selection by the tutor. However, the simulation environment itself is largely fixed. The only things that change are the tasks and the guided paths through them. However, we believe there are many other potentially more powerful kinds of adaptation that are possible, adaptations that involve more radical kinds of reconfiguration of the simulation environment by the tutor. Specifically, we are investigating three different broad categories of adaptation:

1. Tutorial Control of Simulation Time and State

The tutor should be able to arbitrarily set the simulation's time and state for its own pedagogical purposes. (This goes beyond the standard simulation tactic of time compression in order to achieve future states faster than real time). We are envisioning a system that can "rewind" the simulation to an earlier critical juncture and either step through what happened with the learner as a form of review or to give the learner another opportunity to practice with either the same simulation state first encountered or a similar one. Another potential use of this capability would be to provide episodic summaries of learner behavior to an interested third party such as a teacher, mentor, or fellow learner cast in the role of critic.

To do this effectively, we need to employ not only a good theory of task structure but also a good theory of reminding: If we take the learner back in time, what cues are required to re-establish context? How do we artfully re-tell what happened so that the main points are summarized and the appropriate inferences and reflections are fostered? We are striving for what might be termed "intelligent replay."

2. Tutorial Adjustment of Simulation View and/or Representation

In order to promote perceptions of authenticity as well as maximize the overlap between training and performance environments, simulations often strive for a high-fidelity representation of the system and/or setting being modeled. However, such realistic representations might not always be best for instructional purposes. In some circumstances, it may be beneficial to expose the hidden workings of a device or the internal state of a process. Additionally, it may be beneficial to strip away what might be considered the extraneous detail of a complex situation and focus on the truly important and meaningful elements. Such representations that expose hidden elements and remove extraneous details might be termed "schematic." The tutor should be able to change the outward view or representation of the simulation, moving along the realistic/schematic continuum to suit the current pedagogical goal.

Aside from swapping in more schematic representations of the simulation model, we are also exploring the use of scaffolding representations of learner tasks to provide transitional support during all phases of learner behavior. Here are some brief examples: **(a) Perceiving:** In complex situations where there are multiple information streams distributed throughout the environment whose monitoring and integration is critical to task performance, a useful simplification might be to reconfigure the interface so that these sources are placed together in a prominent position. **(b) Planning:** In order to support tutorial discourse about the learner's plans and goals, it might be useful to reify them as trees or networks in the interface. **(c) Acting:** Learner action can be scaffolded by activating only task-appropriate controls, and conveying this action space through highlighting, shading, or some other graphical technique.

3. Tutorial Selection of Simulation Components

Finally, aside from just changing the outward representation, the tutor should be able to change the underlying deep structure of the simulation as well. By adding and/or removing components, the tutor should be able to adjust simulation complexity and focus attention on current instructional goals. The challenge here is author the simulation in such a way as to enable this kind of decomposition and modular assembly on the fly. This is the focus of much current work on simulation in the learning objects community

All of these factors combine into what might be called a "scaffolding gradient," a multi-dimensional space of possibilities that can be navigated by the tutoring agent for optimal pedagogical effect. Just how, when, and where to navigate in this space is a subject of active research interest.

References

Fletcher, J.D. (1999). What have we learned about intelligent tutoring systems and what do we need to do next? *Proceedings of the NASA Workshop on Advanced Training Technologies and Learning Environments.*

Toward a General Student Model: Accounting for Individual Learner Differences across Multiple Learning Environments

Garrett W. Smith, Binghamton University, State University of New York, 10 Webster Ct., Binghamton, NY 13903
gsmith1@binghamton.edu

Abstract: A framework is presented for allowing computer-based learning environments to share student information. Such a framework would enable a learning environment to obtain previous data collected on a specific student in order to enhance the system's student model, and in turn become better able to assist the student in learning. The motivation for this framework, its technical implementation, and its potential benefits are discussed.

Introduction

Many different types of computer-based learning environments have become increasingly prevalent in recent years. As the pervasiveness of computer-based learning environments increases, progressively more students will have the opportunity to interact with such systems. In fact, as computer-based learning environments become more common, individual students may interact with a variety of learning environments over the course of their studies. However, the focus of student modeling research has remained on modeling the student within the context of a single learning environment. There have been a number of studies exhibiting the ability of Intelligent Tutoring Systems and similar systems to improve student learning through modeling the student's knowledge of the current domain (e.g., Koedinger et al., 1997). Other studies have successfully modeled various individual learner differences as they apply to the domain and system at hand (e.g., Arroyo, Beck, Schultz, & Woolf, 1999). Yet few studies have explored the possibility of learning environments sharing student information with each other in order to develop a more general student model: a model that accounts for individual learner differences that remain constant across many different learning domains and environments. There are a number of learner attributes that could be applied globally across multiple learning domains and environments, such as intelligence, cognitive abilities, learning style, personality traits, and prior knowledge. (Jonassen & Grabowski, 1993) Harnessing such information previously learned about a student could allow a learning environment to further customize the student's experience and thus potentially improve learning further. With this in mind, the goal of the current research is to develop a framework for modeling student attributes across learning environments, which will better support student learning.

Overview of the Framework

The General Student Model (GSM) framework consists of: a database, for the storage of student information and meta-data on the structure of the student information; a web service, to allow learning environments to dynamically retrieve and update student information; a programming interface, for the interaction between the GSM and individual learning environments; and a web interface, to allow researchers to specify the form of student data that will be stored. The specific form of the student data collected is governed by a set of custom-made XML (Extensible Markup Language) schemas, which specify the exact structure of the student model, as well as the allowed values of the various student attributes stored. Such schemas afford individual researchers and learning environment authors the ability to subscribe to existing schemas or to create their own. A graphical user interface for researchers to create and edit the schemas is also provided. This use of XML schemas permits the creation of complex custom models of learner attributes. Additionally, the use of a web service allows any authorized computer-based system with access to the internet to utilize student data, independent of operating system, platform, programming language, or type of computer-based learning environment.

In order to make use of the GSM, researchers and learning environment authors would first visit the GSM website, browse for relevant student attribute schemas, and select which schemas will be used by the learning environment. (Optionally, they could also create their own schemas, guided by the schema-creation interface.) Once the schemas to be employed are known, the individual learning environment would first consume the web service, extract any relevant information about the student, and revise its own student model. It would also have the ability to update the General Student Model with any additional student information discerned by the learning environment.

Discussion

A prototype of the GSM framework is operational in its current state, and is being tested on students learning two separate domains through two separate learning environments. The effect of using the framework to share information on the students' cognitive abilities between an Intelligent Tutoring System and an Educational Adaptive Hypermedia System is being studied. Though the learning environments being used to test the GSM prototype were constructed specifically for the purpose of testing the GSM framework, existing learning environments could be easily modified to utilize the framework. Those learning environments that are already collecting potentially beneficial student information could re-route the data to go through the GSM, allowing other learning environments access to the data. For those learning environments that do not currently make use of any such student information, utilizing the GSM would require modifications to the learning environment such that pedagogical decisions are influenced by the student data from the GSM.

As learning environments become increasingly ubiquitous, and more students begin to interact with a variety of learning environments, the GSM framework could be used to make the most of a vast amount of student data available. Realistically, for many potentially domain-general individual differences, collecting and utilizing the student data may prove ineffective. However, the General Student Model framework can be used as a test bed to distinguish between student attributes: those that can be successfully applied across different learning environments and those that are inseparable from the learning context.

References

Arroyo, I., Beck, J. E., Schultz, K., & Woolf, B. P. (1999). *Piagetian Psychology in Intelligent Tutoring Systems.* Paper presented at the Proceedings of the Ninth International Conference on Artificial Intelligence in Education.

Jonassen, D. H., & Grabowski, B. L. (1993). *Handbook of Individual Differences, Learning and Instruction.* Hillsdale, NJ: Lawrence Erlbaum Associates.

Koedinger, K. R., Anderson, J. R., Hadley, W. H., & Mark, M. A. (1997). Intelligent Tutoring Goes To School in the Big City. *International Journal of Artificial Intelligence in Education, 8*, 30-43.

Conflicts in Pedagogical and Technical Knowledge: Pre-service Teachers' Understanding and Misconception of Integrating Technology into PBL Lessons

Hyo-Jeong So, National Institute of Education, Nanyang Technological University
1 Nanyang Walk Singapore 637616, hjso@nie.edu.sg
Bosung Kim, University of Missouri, Columbia
303 Townsend Hall MO 65211, bkq22@mizzou.edu

Abstract: Fifty-one pre-service teachers' understandings and misconceptions of Information and Communications Technology (ICT) and Problem-based Learning (PBL) integration were examined in this study. Data from questionnaire and student projects were analyzed to identify the conceptual and practical difficulties integrating ICT tools into PBL lessons. While participants showed good theoretical understandings of PBL approaches, their lesson designs showed a mismatch between ICT tools and learning objectives, indicating conflicts in translating pedagogical knowledge into technology-integrated lessons.

Introduction

In order to prepare pre-service teachers to effectively integrate technology into their future classrooms, teacher development programs have implemented a variety of technology integration courses. However, one critical problem in various technology courses is that they have not adequately prepared future teachers to understand how to integrate pedagogical and technology knowledge (Moursund & Bielefeldt, 1999; Vannatta & Beyerbach, 2000). For instance, although stand-alone technology courses have exposed pre-service teachers to a variety of technology to some extent and have provided them with the opportunity to learn and practice technical skills, it has been criticized that exposing to a number of technical tools does not necessarily mean that pre-service teachers can learn an ability to design effective technology-integrated lessons. Conversely, focusing solely on pedagogical issues without teaching foundational technical skills can create frustrations in designing and delivering technology-integrated instruction (Mehlinger & Powers, 2002).

Indeed, there is a need to understand how teacher development programs should provide pre-services teachers with a balance between pedagogical and technical knowledge. To meet this need, it is important for learning sciences researchers to identify pre-service teachers' conceptual understandings and practical difficulties in integrating pedagogical and technical knowledge. The main purpose of this research, therefore, was to examine how pre-service teachers integrated their knowledge of information and communications technology (ICT) tools into the design of pedagogically-sound lessons for teaching high-order skills. The pedagogical knowledge, specifically examined in this study, was problem-based learning (PBL).

Methods

Data Collection and Analysis

Participants were 51 pre-service elementary teachers in Singapore. Thirty-nine students were females while 12 students were males. Their average age was 26.6 with approximately 7 months of contract-teaching experiences in schools. Participants took a twelve-week module on the ICT integration for teaching and learning. One of the assignments that pre-service teachers worked on was to designing a PBL lesson with the integration of ICT tools. Regarding previous exposure to PBL, 31 students indicated that they had learned PBL in other modules such as educational psychology and mathematics. A questionnaire with 5 demographic items and 5 open-ended items was developed to identify participants' understandings, misconceptions, and difficulties on the integration of ICT and PBL. Two coders identified types and frequencies of common themes emerged from student responses. In addition to self-reported data from the questionnaire, student projects on the ICT-based PBL lessons were analyzed to further understand how pre-service teachers applied their knowledge of PBL and ICT integration into designing lessons on various topics in elementary education.

Results

Overall, participants showed good theoretical understandings on PBL. Student teachers listed a) authentic problems (n=20), b) student-centered approach (n=17), c) teacher's role as a facilitator (n=16), and d) collaborative learning (n=13) as important characteristics of PBL. Next, the two areas that participants had the most difficulties with designing PBL lessons were a) generating problem statements (n=19) and b) integrating ICT tools and resources (n=18). Participants expressed that they were not sure about what components should constitute problem statements and how to make problems concise, interesting, and authentic. Additionally, a number of the participants reported that they had no or lack of experiences using ICT tools, and they had difficulties selecting appropriate tools and resources.

Results from the analysis of ICT-based PBL lessons revealed pre-service teachers' lack of understanding on two major areas: a) technology integration to better support students' PBL and b) teachers' role as a facilitator. First, student teachers tended to use technology as a mere delivery medium rather than an instructional tool supporting cognitive activities. For example, several pre-service teachers' PBL lessons simply consisted of a presentation of problem statements and a collection of websites. Secondly, lack of understanding on teachers' roles confused pre-service teachers about how much and what kinds of scaffolding strategies they needed to design ahead in their PBL lessons. For instance, while some of pre-service teachers pre-specified all of the learning activities with the belief that teachers needed to scaffold the entire learning process, some pre-service teachers provided little scaffolding since PBL lessons was meant to be independent and discovery learning where students had to find their own resources and answers.

Conclusions and Implications

An important question to ask based on data in this research is "why student teachers have difficulties translating their theoretical knowledge of PBL and ICT integration to designing technology-integrated lessons." Overall, the analysis of student teachers' projects showed that there was a mismatch between the use of ICT tools and the learning goals specified in their lessons. One possible explanation about this problem is related to the *complexity* of designing a lesson for teaching high-order thinking skills. Designing a PBL lesson is challenging to pre-service teachers who have little previous exposure to such student-centered and independent types of learning. When technology is added to this challenge, designing a lesson becomes even more complicated. Thus, many pre-service teachers ended up *adding* technology, instead of *integrating* it into their lessons.

This study has implications to the current practices in teacher training education. In order to resolve conflicts in pedagogical and technical knowledge, pre-service teachers should be *continuously* exposed to new and innovative teaching practices throughout their teacher training. Previous studies have shown that teachers' understanding and implementation of new teaching practices are affected by their epistemological beliefs and prior knowledge (Schraw & Olafson, 2002). Considering that most student teachers come to the teacher training programs with little previous exposure to student-centered and technology-integrated learning, teacher education should be structured in a way that allows pre-service teachers to change their limited thinking within exiting models of teaching and learning. Designing a series of integrated modules, providing student teachers with situated practice for formative feedback and epistemological reflection, and presenting various examples of technology integrated lessons with their impacts on student learning would be possible ways to help pre-service teachers achieve deeper connections between pedagogical and technical knowledge.

References

Mehlinger, H. D., & Powers, S. M. (2002). *Technology and teacher education: A guide for educators and policymakers.* Boston: Houghton Mifflin.

Moursund, D., & Bielefeldt, T. (1999). Will new teachers be prepared to teach in a digital age?: A national survey on information technology in teacher education. Milken family foundation. Retrieved June 14, 2003, from http://www.mff.org/pubs/ME154.pdf

Schraw, G., & Olafson, L. (2002). Teachers' epistemological worldviews and educational practices. *Issues in Education, 8*(2), 99-148.

Vannatta, R. A., & Beyerbach, B. (2000). Facilitating a constructivist vision of technology integration among education faculty and pre-service teachers. *Journal of Research on Computing in Education, 33*(2), 132-148.

Engineering girls gone wild: Developing an engineering identity in Digital Zoo

Gina Navoa Svarovsky, David Williamson Shaffer
University of Wisconsin, 1025 W. Johnson St., Madison, WI 53706
Email: mnsvarovsky@wisc.edu, dws@education.wisc.edu

Abstract: In the Digital Zoo *epistemic game*, middle school girls work as engineers to design virtual, ambulatory creatures. The activities of the game were based on an ethnographic study of an undergraduate engineering design course. As a result of gameplay, the girls demonstrated an increase in thinking of themselves as engineers. Moreover, both the girls and undergraduates linked their engineering identity development to meeting with – and getting feedback from – external clients and experts.

The "incredible shrinking pipeline" (Camp, 1997) of women engineers – the decreasing number of women graduating with bachelors degrees in engineering – is attributed in part to girls being unable to envision themselves as successful engineering professionals. Initiatives such as "Introduce a Girl to Engineering Day" and the "Engineering Girl!" website (www.engineergirl.org) provide young women with information about the profession, but do little in the way of engineering identity development. Here, we examine a different approach to helping girls see themselves as engineers. In the Digital Zoo *epistemic game* (Shaffer, in press), middle school girls work as engineers by engaging in activities modeled after an undergraduate engineering design course. In this poster, we analyze how gameplay based on the profession of engineering can foster the development of engineering identity in young women.

Theoretical Framework

Becoming an engineer means developing the *epistemic frame* (Shaffer, in press) of engineering – the particular combination of skills, knowledge, values, identity, and epistemology that characterizes the profession. Like most professionals, engineers develop this frame in a practicum: a structured learning environment in which new members of a profession work on authentic problems under the guidance of an experienced mentor. The theory of *epistemic games* suggests that a game which simulates the conditions of a professional practicum – such as an engineering design course – can help young players develop the epistemic frame of a profession. Designing such a game requires a detailed understanding of how the curriculum, tools, and interactions contribute to the development of the epistemic frame in the professional practicum.

In this study, we look at a key element of an epistemic frame, professional identity, and how it is cultivated both within an epistemic game and in the professional practicum on which it is based. Specifically, we investigate how undergraduates in an engineering design course and the players in Digital Zoo come to see themselves as engineers. We ask: 1) whether conducting an ethnographic study of an engineering practicum uncovers salient processes through which an engineering identity is developed; 2) whether creating and implementing an epistemic game for girls based on these results help them develop an engineering identity, and 3) whether the process of professional identity development for the students in the practicum and girls in the epistemic game is similar.

Methods

Ethnographic study

An ethnographic study was conducted on Biomedical Engineering (BME) 201, a design course at a large Midwestern state university. During the semester, sophomore engineering students work in teams on actual design problems from external clients. Data was collected in observational field notes, individual interviews with professors, and three focus groups. Data was analyzed within a grounded theory framework (Strauss & Corbin, 1998).

Epistemic game

The design of Digital Zoo was based on the ethnographic study of BME 201. In the game, students develop wire-frame prototypes of ambulatory characters for an upcoming animated film within a computational spring-mass modeling environment. At the end of each week, formal design reviews are held with external engineering experts who provide players with input and feedback on their designs. In the summer of 2005, seven middle school girls played Digital Zoo during a three-week summer program. Six of the players were students of color. Clinical pre- and post-interviews with the players were transcribed and analyzed within a grounded theory framework.

Results

BME 201 undergraduates developed an engineering identity

One emergent theme from the focus group data was the development of engineering identity throughout BME 201. Of the 12 focus group participants, 10 (83.3%) responded positively to the question "Do you feel like an engineer?", and 7 of 12 (58%) students linked their engineering identity to client interaction. In addition, there was a statistically significant correlation between student references to client interaction and receiving client feedback ($r = 0.85$, $p<0.01$). For example, in response to the "Do you feel like an engineer?" question, one student said:

> Yeah, I do, especially when talking to the client. Coming in [to their office] and asking them to see what to do is helpful. A lot of [engineering] comes down to communication with the client.

In other words, meeting with the external client and receiving feedback on their design work were essential to the process of engineering identity development for the undergraduates.

Digital Zoo players developed an engineering identity

The number of Digital Zoo players who indicated they had thought of themselves as engineers increased from pre- (2/7, 29%) to post-interview (7/7, 100%, $p<0.01$), with all players responding positively to the "Have you ever thought of yourself as an engineer?" question in the post-interview. Five players (71%) linked their engineering identity to external expert interactions. In addition, there was a statistically significant correlation between player references to expert interaction and receiving expert feedback ($r = 1.00$, $p<0.01$). For example, when asked whether she had ever thought of herself as an engineer in the post-interview, one student responded, "Yeah, during Digital Zoo." When asked when specifically she felt like an engineer, she replied:

> Like the [Friday] presentations and the presentation at the end. That was when I saw myself as an engineer…I liked presenting my things and showing everybody what I made… I learned that there were things I could change about [my designs] because they like they had certain things to say about it – like some things worked better than like another thing… so then I could like… make mine even better.

In other words, meeting with the external engineering experts and receiving feedback on their virtual creatures were essential to the process of engineering identity development for the Digital Zoo players.

Discussion

Both the undergraduates in BME 201 and the players in Digital Zoo developed an engineering identity, and interacting with clients or experts external to the learning environment contributed to that development. Moreover, the significantly high correlations between client/expert interaction and client/expert feedback suggest that it was not only the external interaction, but also the content of the interaction, that impacted both groups.

The close alignment between the engineering identity development experiences of the BME 201 undergraduates and the Digital Zoo players suggests that: 1) conducting an ethnography of an engineering design course is a useful way to uncover the salient activities and interactions that contribute to professional identity development, 2) designing and implementing an epistemic game based on this ethnographic study can help middle school girls develop and cultivate an engineering identity, and 3) the processes of identity development for epistemic game players and practicum students were, in fact, similar. Thus, by helping girls see themselves as engineers, epistemic games such as Digital Zoo are potentially powerful and transformative tools for addressing the lack of women in engineering.

References

Camp, T. (1997). The incredible shrinking pipeline. *Communications of the ACM,* 40(10), 103-110.

Strauss, A., & Corbin, J. (1998). *Basics of qualitative research* (second ed.). Thousand Oaks, CA: Sage Publications, Inc.

Shaffer, D. W. (in press). Epistemic games. *Computer Education.*

Formative Assessment: Reducing Math Phobia and Related Test Anxiety in a Geology Class for Non-Science Majors

Vanessa Svihla, The University of Texas at Austin, 1 University Station, Austin, TX, vsvihla@hotmail.com

Abstract: Math and test anxiety are common in science classes for non-science majors. Formative assessment was used to prepare such students for exams. This included weekly quizzes that were challenging, graded harshly, and completely correctable (corrected grade completely replaced original grade). By the midterm, 100% of the students mastered rate calculations, and when retested at the final, 80% of the students retained the ability to solve the rate calculations. Students also reported feeling less math phobic.

Math and Test Phobia

Students in science classes for non-science majors often excel in other academic areas but believe they are not able to do math or to do well on science tests, and this disabling math and test anxiety prevents students from learning. This recursive cycle serves to confirm what the students already believe about themselves: they are poor at math and science. Math and test anxiety can be characterized, regardless of the original source, as an inability or unwillingness to engage in risk-taking behavior (Williams, 1988). The main causes stem from poor preparation and negative feedback, and in some cases, teachers run the risk of spreading the "communicable disease of math anxiety" that they themselves are carriers of (Williams, 1988). An estimated two thirds (Jackson and Leffingwell, 1999) to 93% (Burns, 1998) of Americans have negative associations with math. Test anxiety may result from poor study skills, the setting of unrealistic goals, hostile test environments, and impromptu testing, such as pop-quizzes (Sogunro, 1998).

How can math and test anxiety be reduced?

Previous research has suggested both pedagogical and therapeutic techniques for reducing math and test anxiety. Pedagogical techniques include creating positive experiences to replace the negative ones that fostered the anxiety, and using informal and ongoing assessment (Steele and Arth, 1998) with "regular and constructive feedback" (Sogunro, 1998). Therapeutic techniques include confronting negative experiences, journaling, various types of counseling, and offering personal stories of success to offer students hope. We are cautioned that "changing negative beliefs is a slow process" (Dodd, 1992).

Formative Assessment

Formative assessment provides a space for students to practice intellectual risk-taking behavior. When feedback is provided, followed by time to revise thinking, learning is promoted because the assessment is not seen only as a measure of success/failure (Black and Wiliam, 1998). Because formative assessment helps to make the student thinking more visible, the teacher may respond to specific needs or discover that a topic may need to be retaught.

Methods and Interventions

Participants were University of Texas students with regular attendance (fewer than 5 absences) enrolled in spring 2003 sections of Earth, Wind, and Fire, a geology class for non-science majors (N=50). 66% of the students were female, though gender turned out not to be a significant predictor of math and test anxiety. Students are expected to master calculations of rate, area, and unit conversion as tools for understanding geology, but experience with this course in previous years suggested that rather than serving to elucidate, these math problems act as blocks. Participants were surveyed about math and test anxiety and the instructor discussed the purpose of formative assessment and math and test anxiety. Quizzes were given weekly and graded harshly without indication of where errors had been made. New topics were added weekly and troublesome topics were repeated. The approximate average quiz grade each week ranged from 40-60%. Students were then encouraged to correct the quizzes; the new grade completely replaced the original grade. Students reported using various methods to correct the quizzes: Instructor office hours, notes and book, groups, and a few even copied/cheated (However, this was not entirely a negative effect because to get full credit, work had to be shown. Therefore, a student who is copying an answer is effectively taking notes). Grades on quizzes and number of quizzes corrected by students were tested for correlations with the midterm and final exam grades.

Results

All participants mastered the math by the midterm exam, and most (80%) were still able to do the math on the final exam. Mastery of math in sections not using this method of formative assessment ranged from 40% to 70% on the midterm exam and 30% to 60% on the final exam. There is a significant positive correlation between number of quizzes a student corrected and midterm and final exam grade ($r = 0.346$, $n=50$, $p<0.01$), and there is also a significant positive correlation between average quiz grade and midterm and final exam grade ($r = 0.41$, $n=50$, $p<0.01$). There were no significant gender differences.

Additionally, students reported feeling less nervous about the exam, compared to how they felt about other exams science and math exams. Comments from students' course evaluations suggest that they understood the reasoning behind the quizzes: "I really like the policy of correcting quizzes and having them often." "She teaches exactly how school should be taught, less emphasis on grades (because she allowed corrections) and more on learning which is what class is all about anyway." Prior to the midterm, many students left questions completely unanswered when they were unsure, but after their success on the midterm, most of the students made some sort of attempt to answer all questions, even if they were unsure. This suggests that the quizzes opened up a space for students to engage in intellectual risk-taking behavior.

Conclusions and Implications

Students with math and test anxiety can be given successful experiences to replace past failures through formative assessment. A supportive environment enables students to understand the purpose of the quizzes: to instruct, not just to evaluate. By frankly discussing math anxiety, a safe environment was created for students to engage in intellectual risk-taking behavior. The quizzes helped to interrupt damaging practices common among math anxious students by making them aware that they are not the only ones who struggle and by showing them that they *can* do the math. This method also relieves test anxiety because students get opportunities to learn the instructors' assessment style, to receive feedback, and to assess what they still need to study.

References

Burns, M.(1998). *Math:Facing an American Phobia*. Sausalito, CA: Math Solutions Publications.

Dodd, A. (1992, Apr.) Insights from a Math Phobic. *Mathematics Teacher*. 85(4), 296-98.

Jackson, C., Leffingwell, R. (1999, Oct.) The Role of Instructors in Creating Math Anxiety in Students from Kindergarten through College. *Mathematics Teacher*. 92(7), 583-86.

Sogunro, O. (1998, Win.). Impact of Evaluation Anxiety on Adult Learning. *Journal of Research and Development in Education*. 31(2), 109-120.

Steele, D., Arth, A. (1998, Jan-Feb). Math Instruction and Assessment: Preventing Anxiety, Promoting Confidence. *Schools in the Middle*. 7(3), 44-48.

Williams, W. (1988 Feb.). Answers to Questions about Math Anxiety. *School Science and Mathematics*. 88(2), 95-104.

HelioRoom: Problem-solving in a whole class visual simulation

Mark Thompson and Tom Moher
Department of Computer Science, University of Illinois at Chicago, Chicago, IL 60607 USA
Email: mthomp2@uic.edu, moher@uic.edu

Abstract: HelioRoom simulates the orbital motion of the planets in the Solar system on a set of synchronized computer displays situated on the walls of the classroom, with planets "orbiting" around the periphery of the room. Third grade students used the application for a problem-solving activity requiring the collection of evidence in support of theories concerning the identity of planets whose size and surface characteristics were intentionally obscured.

Introduction

Classroom phenomenaria such as ant farms and moth hatcheries afford students access to phenomena whose rate of change requires observation and data collection ranging over extended courses of time, important skills in observational sciences such as astronomy and seismology. Phenomenaria of this kind have three important characteristics that arguably contribute to their value as learning artifacts, and that could inform the design of technology analogues. First, they are public, in that they are accessible to all members of the class. Second, they are persistent; phenomenaria are accessible continuously, during the whole school day. Finally, they involve the presentation of the phenomena over days and weeks instead of class periods. In this paper, we briefly describe an effort to construct a simulation of one phenomenon—the orbital motion of the planets in the Solar system—incorporating these three characteristics in our design, and our experience with its use in a third grade classroom to support an evidence-based learning activity.

HelioRoom

HelioRoom is a visual simulation of the orbital motion of the planets in the Solar system that explicitly attempts to adopt the public, persistent, and long term attributes of phenomenaria. In our implementation, a tablet computer is Velcroed to the middle of each of the four walls of a classroom. Adopting the pretense that the Sun is coincident with the center of the room, the tablet computers become synchronized viewports into the Solar system, with the planets revolving 360° around the periphery, temporarily entering a viewport, then leaving and becoming invisible for a while, then entering the next viewport, and so on. HelioRoom presents a greatly simplified model of the Solar system. The Solar system is reduced from ratio to ordinal scale; the order of the planets is maintained, but the distances among them are not proportional to their actual distances from the Sun. Orbital periods are reduced proportionately. Size and surface features are intentionally ignored; each planet is represented only as a uniform size sphere of a distinct color. The overall illusion is of colored discs traveling in a counter-clockwise fashion at different speeds, with some discs crossing in front of other discs as they overtake them (see Figure 1).

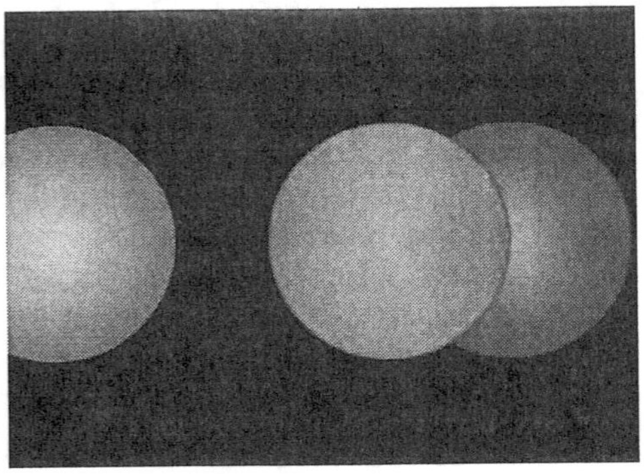

Figure 1. HelioRoom display.

Classroom Experience

HelioRoom was introduced to a third grade classroom of 25 children, with the cover story that our research lab had built the simulation, but now couldn't remember which color belonged to which planet. The students had just completed an introductory unit on the Solar system, focusing on the order and properties (e.g., size, orbital period) of the planets. Our goal was to leverage their nascent declarative astronomy knowledge in the performance of an ambitious evidence-based inquiry. The simulation ran continuously for nine class days (until the end of the school year). During that period, as students would make observations about the relative order of colored disks, they wrote their observations on index cards and posted them (and theories drawn from them) to a public "Idea Board" on the wall. Periodically, the students would come together as a whole class to propose theories about planet colors. As consensus was reached on the identity of a planet-color combination, it was written on the blackboard.

Not surprisingly, the task proved challenging for the third graders. As a group, after nine class days they had correctly identified six planets. The primary instructional design implication of the activity became evident after the first few group discussion sessions: the density and lack of organization of the observations on the Idea Wall made it extremely difficult for students to retrieve the evidence they needed to construct argument chains to support their theories. Rather than populating a data space with observations and then exploring the aggregate data set for a global solution, the students adopted an incremental "inside-out" strategy, first identifying (within seconds of the introduction of the activity) Mercury, and then building out planet by planet away from the Sun.

As individuals, students posted an average of 3.5 index cards (many with multiple observations or theories) and verbally presented an average of 3.3 theories over the course of the whole-class discussions. Some students "specialized" in certain planets; Pluto, for example, drew over 30% of references during class discussions and 20% of references on the index cards. Students supported written theories with evidence just over 50% of the time; support for theories was a procedural requirement during the group discussions. Interestingly, students favored the velocity evidence base over occlusion evidence by about a 2:1 ratio.

There was concern at the outset that the dynamism of the displays might raise problems of competing attention during other class activity. In practice, this proved not to be a problem, as the students quickly relegated the displays to the background of their attention as appropriate. The classroom teacher encouraged participation and devoted occasional class time for students to work on the task.

Conclusion

HelioRoom is an example of a broader class of applications that we call embedded phenomenon: simulations that map dynamic science phenomena to the physical space of classrooms, and allow students to act as scientists by using computers as simulated instruments for measuring or viewing those phenomena (Moher, et al., 2005). Inspired by the concepts of participatory simulations (Colella, 2000) and ambient devices (Wisneski, et al., 1998), embedded phenomena share important commonalities with other research-based classroom (Rogers, et al., 2002) and outdoor (Klopfer, Squire, & Jenkins, 2002) environments, including the use of distributed embedded technologies to represent simulation state to groups of learners. Embedded phenomena differ from these along the dimensions of persistence and duration; it is not used as a serial component of instruction, but rather runs concurrently and continuously as instruction proceeds. HelioRoom is currently undergoing a second classroom trial, augmented by a scaffolding application that provides a simple database where students can store and retrieve observation data.

References

Colella, V. (2000). Participatory Simulations: Building collaborative understanding through immersive dynamic modeling. *The Journal of Learning Sciences, 9(4)*, 471-500.

Klopfer, E., Squire, K., & Jenkins, H. (2002). Environmental Detectives: PDAs as a window into a virtual simulated world. *Proceedings Wireless and Mobile Technologies in Education 2002*, 95-98.

Moher, T., Hussain, S., Halter, T., & Kilb, D. (2005). RoomQuake: Embedding dynamic phenomena within the physical space of an elementary school classroom. *Extended Abstracts ACM Conference on Human Factors in Computing Systems 2005 (CHI 2005)*, 1665-1668.

Rogers, Y., Scaife, M., Harris, E., Phelps, T., Price, S., Smith, H., Muller, H., Randell, C., Moss, A., Taylor, I., Stanton, D., O'Malley, C., Corke, G. & Gabrielli, S. (2002). Things aren't what they seem to be: innovation through technology inspiration. *Proceedings Designing Interactive Systems 2002*, 373-377.

Wisneski, C., lshii, H., Dahley, A., Gorbet, M., Brave, S., Ullmer, B., & Yarin, P. (1998). Ambient displays: Turning architectural space into an interface between people and digital information. *Proceedings International Workshop on Cooperative Buildings 1998*, 22-32.

Professional Development that Considers Teachers' Attitudes Toward an Innovation

Jeannine E. Turner, ChanMin Kim, Florida State University, 307 Stone Building, Tallahassee, FL, 32306
turner@coe.fsu.edu, cmk04f@fsu.edu

Abstract. This study investigated the extent to which teachers' motivation and attitudes for professional development training facilitated their willingness to implement reform strategies. Teachers completed surveys prior to training and after receiving training. Analysis compared the responses of beginning teachers (new to the process) and advanced teachers (receiving advanced training). Advanced teachers showed that their instructional strategies and goals corresponded to the innovations at the start. At the end of the training, Beginning teachers gave positive ratings for the training and their emotions toward implementing the training.

Introduction

Researchers have suggested that potential adopters' attitudes toward an innovation should be considered for it's diffusion (e.g., Ellsworth, 2000). However, few studies have examined how to address this (Ertmer, Conklin, Lewandowski, Osika, Selo, & Wignall, 2003). This study investigated the extent to which a professional development training, one that regards teachers' attitudes and beliefs as being important elements to consider when designing professional development, may facilitate teachers' willingness to adopt instructional ideals and strategies of the innovation.

The professional development training in this study was Great Expectations (GE) in Oklahoma. As a whole-school reform model, primary objectives of the training is to instruct teachers on ways to increase students' knowledge, self-esteem, and social competencies while also focusing on instructional strategies that align with constructivist principles. For example, similar to research on exemplary teachers (e.g., Allington & Johnston, 2002), model GE teachers are exceptional classroom managers because they establish and explain routines/procedures and they emphasize student self-regulation. In a high-implementation GE classroom, disciplinary actions are rarely observed. Additionally, GE teachers use instructional strategies that emphasize cross-curricular, meaningful lessons in which cooperation and effort are emphasized. Also similar to exemplary teachers, GE teachers express high expectations for their students' learning and carefully monitor their students' understanding (Turner & Shapley, 2000). Perhaps most importantly, teachers' implementation of GE practices has been shown to positively and significantly affect students' achievement (Biscoe & Harris, 2005).

To accomplish these overall objectives, GE focuses on the transformation of teachers through. Evaluation results have shown that teachers who fully implement GE (Turner & Shapley, 2000) exhibit instructional and relational behaviors that have been described as "exemplary" in excellent teachers. By examining differences between teachers with and without experience of the GE training, this study investigated possible effects of the GE training, for example, addressing the question, "To what extent might model professional development training impact teachers' attitudes, motivation, and willingness to implement the training?"

Methodology

Participants were 158 teachers enrolled in a week-long GE summer institute. Of the participants, 97 were taking basic GE Methodology courses (beginning teachers), and 61 were taking advanced GE courses (advanced teachers). Prior to the beginning of the training, participants were asked to complete the following surveys: Incentives for Training (i.e., Self-Improvement, External Approval, Mandatory Pressure); Instructional Strategies (Mastery Approaches, Performance Approaches; from PALS, Midgely et al., 2000), and emotions for attending training (e.g., positive emotions and negative emotions). Following the training, participants completed an evaluation survey. The current analysis is part of a larger study that focuses on changes in teachers' attitudes and behaviors over time.

Results

First, there were significant differences between beginning teachers and advanced teachers with respect to their incentives for attending the training. Advanced teachers gave themselves higher ratings with respect to being motivated to attend the training by self-improvement (t=-2.389, p<.05), while beginning teachers gave themselves higher ratings for attending the training because of mandatory pressure (t=-2.389,

$p<.01$).Second, with regard to feelings about attending the GE training, advanced teachers rated themselves as feeling significantly more excited (t=-3.391, $p<.01$), enthusiastic (t=-3.155, $p<.01$), content (t=-3.492, $p<.01$), determined (t=-2.102, $p<.05$) and optimistic (t=-2.670, $p<.01$). Third, with regard to instructional strategies, advanced teachers gave themselves higher ratings with respect to using "mastery" instructional strategies (t=-2.252, $p<.05$). Lastly, with regard to planning instructional goals for their students, beginning teachers gave themselves higher ratings with respect to being motivated by mandatory, external curricular goals (t=5.518, $p<.01$), beginning teachers were more focused on covering the required curriculum, than on students' learning.

Once the training had been delivered, we were interested in understanding if the training had effected beginning teachers' emotions, such that they would be more likely and willing to implement the strategies taught in the training. Our results indicated that following the training, both groups of teachers increased positive emotions such as feeling excited ($p<.001$) and enthusiastic ($p<.001$). Interestingly, although the beginning teachers rated themselves significantly lower in these emotions at the beginning of the training, they had reached levels of these positive emotions almost at the same intensity levels as the advanced participants. For example, beginning teachers, on average, rated 3.99 for excitement at the beginning of the training; while advanced teachers had an average excitement rating of 4.37. At the end of the training, the beginning teachers increased their excitement to 4.50; while advanced teachers rated their excitement as 4.75.

In addition to teachers' emotions following the training, we investigated possible differences with respect to teachers' perceptions of the quality of the training. There were no significant differences between beginning teachers' and advanced teachers' ratings on items that assessed the extent to which (1) training objectives were clear, (2) instructors adequately addressed the objectives, (3) instructors were knowledgeable and Great Expectations, (4) participants had opportunities to obtain valuable feedback, and (5) participants had opportunities to learn from other participants. It is anticipated that beginning teachers' increase in positive emotions and perceptions of the training is—at the very least—a precursor for their willingness to implement the training. Further data collection and analysis is needed to understand the extent to which these feelings were translated into behavior changes in the classroom.

Discussion

The findings from this study indicated that the GE trainings, which acknowledged teachers' attitudes, experiences, and perceptions toward training, provided useful supports for teachers' willingness to implement this program. Although the findings do not necessarily explain reasons for the differences between beginning teachers and advanced teachers without in-depth research, they suggest that advanced teachers' previous exposure to GE trainings might have resulted in positive experiences on several aspects. Our data suggested that, prior to the training, advanced teachers valued the GE trainings and they were excited and optimistic about what they would learn. They had already understood and implemented the basic principles of GE, which were grounded in the beliefs that all students can learn and teachers need to learn methods that prepare them to be flexible and responsible for students' learning. Additionally, the data suggested that, although beginning teachers tended to indicate that (1) they were participating in the training for mostly external and mandatory reasons, and that they (2) entered the training with lower levels of positive emotions than advanced teachers, they were predominately supportive and feeling positive emotions after the training had concluded. It is anticipated that, with these positive emotions, teachers may be more willing to implement the strategies learned at the training. Future research will investigate the specific strategies of trainings to address teachers' attitudes.

References

Allington, D. L., & Johnston, P. H. (2002). *Reading to learn: Lessons from exemplary fourth-grade classrooms*. NY: Guilford Press.

Bisco, B. & Harris, B. (2005). *Great Expectations Evaluation 2003-04. Technical Report.*

Ellsworth, J. B. (2000). *Surviving change: A survey of educational change models. NY: ERIC Clearing house on Information and Technology.* New York, NY: ERIC.

Ertmer, P. A., Conklin, D., Lewandowski, J., Osika, E., Selo, M., & Wignall, E. (2003). Increasing preservice teachers' capacity for technology integration through the use of electronic models. *Teacher Education Quarterly, Winter.*

Midgley, C., Maehr, M. L., Hruda, L. Z., Anderman, E., Anderman, L., Freeman, K. E., et al. (2000). *Patterns of Adaptive Learning Strategies (PALS) Manual*: University of Michigan.

Turner, J., & Shapley, K. (2001). *An evaluation of the implementation of Great Expectations in six Oklahoma elementary schools.* Austin, TX: Southwest Educational Development Laboratory.

A Teacher-Friendly Interface To Assessment Data

Jody S. Underwood, Diego Zapata, & Waverely Hester, ETS, Princeton, NJ
{junderwood, dzapata, whester}@ets.org

Abstract: We present the results of research about teachers' use and understanding of assessment data, focusing on (a) questions they want answered, (b) their use of an instructional data management system, and (c) their reactions to a more teacher-friendly interface to the system that is designed to facilitate instruction.

A push toward data-driven decision making (3DM) is moving quickly into K-12 schools, largely as a result of requirements of the No Child Left Behind Act (e.g., Consortium for School Networking, 2003). In current accountability practices, districts and schools define performance objectives based on standards, then use data (e.g., results of student testing, portfolios collected during classroom work) to track progress throughout the year. Teachers team together to share strategies, goals, and student plans with principals and district administrators, as well as with students and their parents. There are a number of approaches to achieving 3DM goals, ranging from principals and school leaders guiding grade-level teacher planning sessions around printed score and performance reports to teachers using 3DM software themselves.

Unfortunately, it is not easy for many teachers to make effective use of student assessment data in their day-to-day teaching. Teachers might not have the time necessary to interpret data in instructionally meaningful ways. They might not be familiar enough with the software that could help them find and interpret data. Even if a teacher can obtain relevant test scores, many reports of standardized tests do not address the main questions teachers have about their students' performance, and these reports often do not present data in easily interpretable ways.

Various software packages have been developed to streamline and analyze student data (e.g., Wayman *et al*, 2004; eSchool News, 2005). Most of these systems are used to report on large-scale assessment data (e.g., state and district level), while some of these address the administration and use of data from small-scale tests, such as those that assess what students have learned this week (e.g., homework). All these data can help inform instructional decisions, yet teachers are not trained to collect and use the evidence of student learning (or lack thereof) obtained in these tests to their fullest.

Although data management tools facilitate access to student information, research on strategies and tools that help teachers interact with assessment information themselves is still needed. Wayman (2005) states that additional teacher support should be provided in the form of professional development, leadership for a supportive data climate, and collaboration among educators to learn about effective ways of using data. Integrated approaches consider a variety of tools, representations, and processes that can be used to support teachers' use of assessment information to solve a particular problem. Chen et al. (2005), for example, describe how teachers can use different aspects of the Quality School Portfolio web-based tool to identify, intervene, and monitor at-risk students.

Our research focuses on teacher use of 3DM software tools, in particular, on the tension between bottom-up and top-down approaches to data interaction. The bottom-up approach, typically used by 3DM software products, is designed around the data, rather than the user. Interfaces developed as a result of this approach are often complex. The top-down approach instead focuses on what information would be useful to teachers. We hypothesize that *instructional actions* are useful to teachers (e.g., What should I do on Monday?) and that providing a question-based interface to the assessment data linked to those actions would facilitate teachers' use of the system. These question-based queries should provide data that are more easily interpreted by teachers, facilitating their decisions about instructional actions. In our research, we analyzed focus group discussions of teachers talking about score reports and a particular 3DM system. We mapped instructional actions expressed by teachers to questions that would give them the information they would need in order to carry out those actions (see Table 1 for some examples).

Table 1. Examples of instructional actions mapped to supporting questions.

Action	Questions
Group students	What are my students' areas of weaknesses? How difficult was each test question my students had difficulty with?
Help individuals	Who just barely made it into a performance level? What in geometry does John Smith need help in?
Communicate with parents	How do all the schools in my town compare? How has John Smith's performance changed over time?
Understand the standards	What standards come under Number Sense or Geometry? What standard(s) is this question linked to?
Planning/ Validating	What standards under Number Sense did my students have trouble with? How did my limited English students do?

As stated above, our goal is to design a teacher-friendly question-based 3DM user interface design that meets teachers' needs. We will design and test this interface design through focus groups and interviews in the coming year. Other areas of focus of this research are to (1) present the assessment data in a form that is easily, or with some training, understandable by teachers, and (2) consider modes of facilitating communities of practice for teachers interested in using data to improve teaching and learning processes (i.e., ongoing professional development that includes the sharing of best practices and interesting cases).

In this session, we will present results of our focus group analysis, an in-progress 3DM interface design based on this analysis, and early teacher feedback on the systems. We will also discuss our sample score reports that demonstrate targeted presentation of useful information, leading to improved score report readability and improved use of assessments results.

References

Chen, E., Heritage, M., and Lee, J. (2005) Identifying and Monitoring Students' Learning Needs with Technology. Journal of Education for Students Placed at Risk, 10(3), 309-332

Consortium for School Networking (2003). *Vision to know and do: The power of data as a tool in educational decision making*. Retrieved February 4, 2005 from http://www.3d2know.org/publications.html

eSchool News Online (2005). *Assessment & Accountability: Technology will be key to schools' reform efforts*. eSchool News Special Report. Retrieved October 24, 2005 from http://www.eschoolnews.com/resources/reports/assessment/

Wayman, J.C. (2005) Involving Teachers in Data-Driven Decision Making: Using Computer Data System to Support Teacher Inquiry and Reflection. Journal of Education for Students Placed at Risk, 10(3), 295-308

Wayman, J.C., Stringfield, S., & Yakimowski, M. (2004). *Software enabling school improvement through analysis of student data* (Report No. 67). Baltimore: Johns Hopkins University, Center for Research on the Education of Students Placed at Risk. Retrieved July 26, 2005 from http://www.csos.jhu.edu/crespar/techReports/Report67.pdf.

Perspectives and problem solving in an algebra classroom

Carla van de Sande, University of Pittsburgh, LRDC, cav10@pitt.edu

Abstract: Perspective theory, an extension and generalization of schema theory, adapts the notion of perspective from psycholinguistics to capture the cognitive and interactional creativity in reasoning and problem solving. This poster applies perspective theory to two problem solving episodes of classroom mathematical discourse. The episodes illustrate the negotiation of differing perspectives, participants' commitment to perspective and demonstrate how perspectival constructions can be interactively achieved. Characteristics of task and positioning may encourage participation in exploratory perspectival construction.

In our analyses of classroom mathematical discourse, our research group has encountered many instances of cognitive and interactional creativity that cannot be understood by appealing to schema theory. In order to characterize these episodes of learning, we have identified a need for a generalization of schema theory that incorporates the concept of entities and relations but that also includes a point of view, or perspectival, construct. See Greeno & MacWhinney (these proceedings) for a discussion of perspective theory. In problem solving discussions, the participants are often involved in considering alternatives and engaging in effortful interactions in order to reach mutual understanding. These interactions can be characterized as instances of exploratory construction, in which at least one of the participants needs to discover and arrange a perspectival construction, rather than fitting entities into a prefabricated arrangement based on a schema.

In support of a perspective theory of understanding, this poster presents episodes from a progressive eighth grade algebra classroom. In one episode, students negotiate alternative perspectives on constructing (linear) functions to describe pattern configurations. The discussion reflects each participant's commitment to her own perspective and the role validity plays in the resolution of multiple perspectival views. In the second episode involving an algebraic word problem, the teacher and two students interactively construct a perspective that is different than the schema-based perspective that the teacher initially planned to develop. Both episodes provide evidence for the existence of perspectives in the context of problem solving and allow us to distinguish between perspectives that are schema-based and perspectives that are not schema-based but have schema-based components. In addition, both episodes provide an account of the way in which perspectival flow and shift result in conceptual schema alignment and the discourse surrounding constructive listening. We conclude that perspectival alignment is a critical component of mathematical learning that can occur within a single representational system.

Exploring Patterns

As a homework assignment, students completed two complementary worksheets entitled "Exploring Patterns" and "Graphing Functions." "Exploring Patterns" consisted of six pattern configurations of either toothpicks or tiles in which the first three 'steps' were depicted. Students were instructed to draw steps 4 and 5 for each configuration, answer how many elements would be in step 10, and describe how the pattern was changing or growing. Each pattern configuration corresponded to a function for which students were to construct a T-table for values 0 through 5, 10, 17, and 'n' and draw a corresponding graph. Students were organized in small groups during the homework check to compare and discuss their solutions. In the group of students (J, D, and G) we observed, the answer to the question of how the pattern is changing or growing revealed three differing perspectives, each setting up relations between the mathematical entities from a point of view. J focused on the mathematical relationship between step numbers and reasoned (incorrectly since the linear relationships had a constant term) that step 10 would have twice as many elements as step 5. J maintained this perspective throughout the discussion despite the presentation (and validation) of the other group members' perspectives. D focused on the relationship between step numbers and number of toothpicks, identifying a relationship that worked for each step/toothpick configuration (e.g. $2n + 1$, where n denotes step number). In contrast to these schema-based perspectives, G focused on the number of elements in step 1 and the relationship between successive steps, namely how many elements were added each time (e.g. $3 + (n - 1)*2$). G and D constructively listened to one another during the discussion and established that both of these perspectives were valid.

The Garden Lap Problem

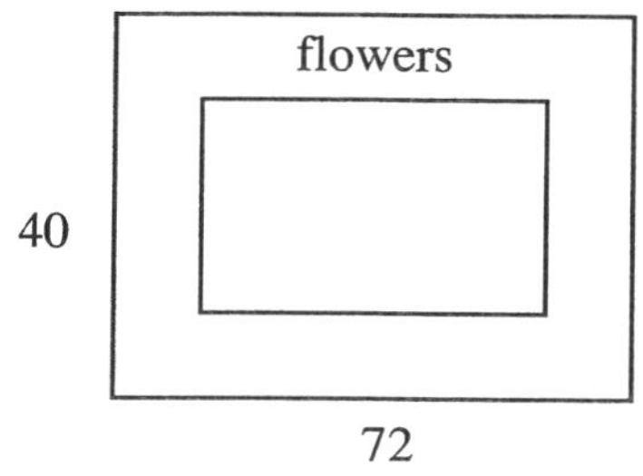

Sally's backyard is 40 feet wide by 72 feet long, and it is structured so that a central rectangle of grass is surrounded by an even border of flowers. The area of the border (flowers) is 5/12 of the area of the whole garden. If Sally wants to be sure to walk her dog for .25 mile, how many laps will she have to take around the grass?

Figure 1. The Garden lap problem

On the first day of the garden lap problem (see Figure 1) discussion, students calculated numerical values for the area of the whole garden (2880 ft^2), the border (1200 ft^2), and the central rectangle (1680 ft^2) and guessed values for the dimensions of the central rectangle that would satisfy the two solution constraints. On the second day of discussion, the goal of the class was to construct an algebraic solution to the problem. This was judged to be a difficult task for the students, and the teacher (T) attempted to communicate her perspective to the class. After reproducing the problem diagram with numerical area values on the board, T labeled the left and top border widths with question marks (?'s) and, surmising that she "gave it away" with this cue, asked the class "What would my variable be?" Note that assigning a variable, say w, for the border width would result in the quadratic equation (72 – 2w)(40 - 2w) = 1680, the solution of which could then be subtracted from the dimensions of the whole garden to produce the dimensions of the central rectangle, and subsequently the central rectangle perimeter needed to answer the question of the requisite number of laps. The students, however, did not respond to T's hinted suggestion of identifying a variable with the border width; they did not share the schema and, despite hints, were unable to 'view the problem' as T had with a focus on the border width. Instead, when the question of variable was again raised in conjunction with the question "What am I trying to figure out here?," one of the students (G) introduced an alternative perspective by drawing attention to "the two lengths of the inside square" and suggesting that these could be given labels, x and y. Because this was a different perspective than T had entertained and because G was only able to present disjoint pieces of the corresponding solution, arriving at mutual understanding required considerable effort and negotiation. It was at this juncture that T, G, and another student (H) embarked on an extended exploratory construction that included explaining entities (G: "So, if you do 40 minus x divided by 2, you'll get the two widths, I think."), questioning referents (T: "Can you point out where the 72 minus y is going to be that question mark?"), and suggesting relations (H: "I mean, you could make another equation, x times y equals 1680."). The result was a publicly available (via the white board) system of two equations in two unknowns [x times y = 1680 and (72-y)/2 = (40-x)/2], the solution of which would yield numerical values for the dimensions of the central rectangle, its perimeter, and consequently the requisite number of laps. Following this exploratory construction, T acknowledged to the class that "this is a completely different way than I looked at it" and instructed the class to finish solving the problem from this perspective.

Conclusions

We show how students exercise conceptual agency by presenting, constructing, and negotiating alternative perspectives in the classroom and how novel understanding resulted from conceptual alignment.

References

MacWhinney, B. (2005). The emergence of grammar from perspective taking. In D. Pecher & R. Zwann (Eds.), The Grounding of Cognition (pp. 198-223). Cambridge, England: Cambridge University Press.Brown, A. (1992) Design experiments: Theoretical and methodological challenges in creating complex interventions in classroom settings. *The Journal of Learning Sciences*, *2*(2), 141-178.

Acknowledgments

This research was supported by a grant from the Spencer Foundation.

3D Game Design with Programming Blocks in StarLogo TNG

Kevin Wang, Harvard Graduate School of Education, Technology in Education Program, Longfellow Hall Rm. 321, Appian Way, Cambridge, MA 02138, kevinkw@gmail.com
Corey McCaffrey, Daniel Wendel, Eric Klopfer, Massachusetts Institute of Technology Teacher Education Program, 77 Massachusetts Ave, Rm. 10-337, Cambridge, MA 02139
Email: coreymcc@mit.edu, djwendel@mit.edu, klopfer@mit.edu

Abstract: Research on the effectiveness of using a block programming language with a three-dimensional environment and game design as the basis for curriculum to teach children concepts in Computer Science. We observed a lower barrier to entry and faster learning in seventh to ninth graders exposed to the new curriculum using StarLogo TNG.

Background

In a recent speech to an audience of computer science faulty, Bill Gates lamented that despite all the leaps in technology, he wondered why there more people are not interested in CS as a career. "Are they making breakthroughs like speech recognition or AI? I'm dying to see these new games they're inventing" (Seattle Post, July 19, 2005). The Computing Research Association reported in May 2005 that interest in CS as a major dropped 60% between 2000 and 2004. Even more distressing is that only 0.5% of incoming female freshmen expressed an interest in a CS undergraduate degree, an all time low since the early 1970s when programming involved paper hole punches (Vegso 2005). StarLogo TNG is a 3D graphics-based programming environment that uses drag-and-drop programming blocks instead of the more traditional text-based approach. We hypothesize that lowering the entrance barrier, making the learning curve shallower, and producing more exciting end results will yield increased interest in CS in middle school and high school age students while improving their logical thinking and problem solving skills.

StarLogo TNG

While StarLogo TNG is designed upon the basic framework of Logo, there are two distinct improvements that separate it from its predecessor. The programming is now done with programming blocks instead of text commands (see Figure 1). The obvious advantage is that now the program has moved from the abstract to the visual. As many students were already familiar with using a computer by dragging and dropping objects, StarLogo TNG came very naturally to them. The programming blocks are arranged by color based on their function, and it enables students to associate similar programming blocks with each other. Since the programming blocks are puzzle piece shaped, only syntactically sensible blocks can fit into each other, which eliminates a whole host of bugs for the students. Seymour Papert found in *Mindstorms* that modular form representation of a process makes it easier to debug (Papert 1993), we took it one step further and have a visual representation of that modular form. In the past we have found that in StarLogo 2, text-based syntax errors seemed to be a significant barrier to Logo implementation by teachers. For example, the equals block has two cutouts that reminds the students that they need to compare a variable to a number, not just saying "= 17" and forgetting that the computer needs to be explicitly told what to compare 17 to. In addition, studies have shown that block programming lessens the intimidation factor of programming to girls and has a greater appeal than that of text-based languages (Begel 2004).

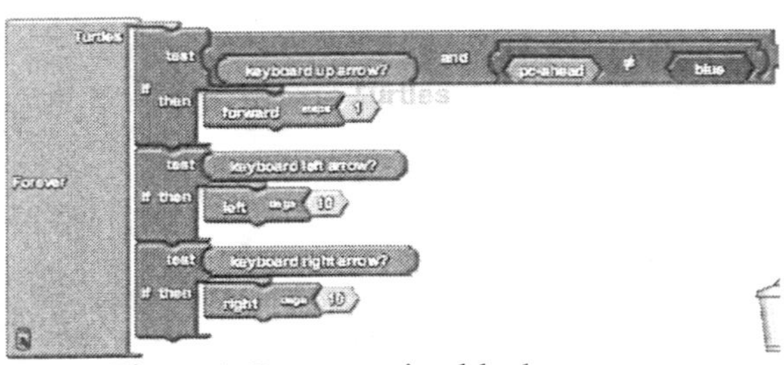

Figure 1. Programming blocks.

Figure 2. 3D maze.

Approach

Because of the significant differences between StarLogo TNG and previous versions of Logo, we decided that the math and physics approach to teaching the language was not the best use of its capabilities. The goals have changed from Papert's pioneering work with the Lincoln School in Brookline, MA, but much of the core ideas remain the same (Papert 1979). We still wanted the students to be comfortable with telling computer what they want it to do (Papert 1979). We also wanted the students to learn the Logo block programming language and be able to make interactive programs while learning informally about some basic concepts of CS. Due to the focus as a game design course, the concepts in programming were introduced as needed. Most of the effort was put towards the interactivity and the creation of simple playable games. Certain concepts in programming lend themselves more readily to games than others. For example, forever and repeat loops made much more sense than recursion, game character interactions dictated that students understood the concepts of object-orientated programming as different agent breeds and behaviors. The timeline for when CS concepts were determined by need, not by difficulty level or their traditional place within a CS textbook.

Process

As the pilot project to introduce StarLogo TNG, we assembled a group of eight students (grades 7 to 9 with diverse backgrounds) from a local secondary charter school and formed an after school class around them. The class met once a week for 90 minutes and attendance was not mandatory. We were not sure how quickly students would be able to grasp certain concepts in StarLogo TNG, so we initially based the pace of the class on a class that used traditional Logo from prior experience. We planned to be somewhat more instructionist in our teaching style first rather than spending sparse meeting time for constructionist moments, as there were a basic set of programming blocks that the students needed to understand before they can do with it what they want. After the first of two such meetings, the instruction was gradually cut back to less than one-third of the meeting time. After the third meeting, the teaching process became much more constructionist, and we became programming counselors more than teachers. The identification of a newly needed game element would lead to a new problem that they would need to solve. That, in turn, leads to an application of their current understanding combined with new information that is scaffolded for them to build new game elements upon. The idea of a 3D Pac-Man style maze led to the need of having a first person perspective and the appropriate controls (see Figure 2). The idea of a loop that continuously checks for input was then introduced. All of these ideas introduced to the students had a practical need in the game design. The feedback we received from the students is also affecting changes to our software; block arrangement and organization, as well as the upcoming debugging features have all benefited from student input.

Evaluation

What we found was that it took students much less time to get started and use StarLogo TNG than traditional Logo, thus lowering the entry point for the language. Because of the inherent nature of block programming, as soon as the concept is clear, programming usually yielded instant gratification that the kids enjoyed. The nature of the programming blocks prevented students from making errors that would usually frustrate them; it kept their interest level high without getting bogged down. The visual blocks provided a certain amount of implicit programming guidance that text does not offer. When bugs did happen, the students ended up debugging their programming logic rather than syntax. The textual abstraction of their idea was visually represented in StarLogo TNG, and they often pointed to and followed the programming blocks as they were debugging. Even though the meetings were weekly, the highly visual aspect of StarLogo TNG made it easy for students to recall blocks they learned in the previous weeks. They only needed to recognize the blocks as opposed to the commands plus the syntax. In a short span of 5 meetings, students were able to create an interactive maze that provided a first person view and score keeping. Object-oriented programming came naturally, and when we introduced the concept of different breeds of turtles with their own set of behavior, it was no different from the students learning the repeat loop. Making a new object did not involve a series of new syntax, just more blocks. We conclude that the advantages provided by block programming lowers the entry point for programming, and the built-in error prevention mechanisms give students a more structured programming environment than that of the traditional text entry model.

References

Begel, A., & Klopfer, E. (2004). StarLogo TNG: An Introduction to Game Development. *The Journal for E-Learning*. (in press).

Papert, S. (1979). Final Report of the Brookline Logo Project, MIT AI Lab Memo No. 545.

Papert, S. (1993). *Mindstorms*. Cambridge, MA. Perseus Books.

Vegso, J. (2005). Interest in CS as a Major Drops Among Incoming Freshmen. *Computing Research News*, Vol. 17 No. 3.

Learning by Tagging: Group knowledge formation in a self-organizing learning community

Jude Yew, School of Information, University of Michigan, jyew@umich.edu
Faison Gibson, Ross School of Business, University of Michigan, fpgibson@umich.edu
Stephanie Teasley, School of Information, University of Michigan, steasley@umich.edu

Abstract: This research explores the use of Social Tagging as a means by which group knowledge is formed within a learning community. A study of an undergraduate Business School class that utilizes Social Tagging is undertaken to analyze the patterns and evolution of use of tags in order to make a case for Social Tagging as a viable means to visualize and facilitate group knowledge formation.

Introduction*:*

Social Tagging describes the collaborative activity of marking shared online content with keywords, or tags, as a way to organize content for future navigation, filtering or search. It is proposed that Social Tagging systems employed within a learning community can both facilitate and provide evidence of knowledge formation within the group. Social Tagging facilitates the sensemaking efforts of the individual and the learning community through the collective act of associating keywords with documents/artifacts and by sharing those terms with the rest of the community. The use of Social Tagging systems also provide learning communities with a means to visualize and be made aware of the tags used by the group. By extension, this provides learners with an indication of the patterns of cognition taking place within the class on a particular topic. This study will analyze of the use of Social Tagging in an undergraduate Business School class. Analyzing the content of the students' contributions and correlating that with the frequencies and patterns in the use of certain tags, this study traces the evolution of this learning community's knowledge-formation. Such a study makes a case for Social Tagging as a viable means through which group knowledge can be tangibly visualized and formed.

Characteristics of learning community:

BIT 320, a Database and Information class being offered at a large Midwestern university, utilizes various technologies to create a shared online space in which group learning can occur. The class, dubbed the BIT 320 Remix by its instructor, is so named based on Lawrence Lessig's notion of a "remix culture" which describes a society that allows and encourages efforts to improve upon, change, integrate, or otherwise remix the work of copyright holders. (wikipedia, 2005). The class aims are to convey the latest principles in Business Databases and Information systems through a philosophy of "learning by doing". Participation in the class is mandated through the weekly submission of 5 blog posts and 10 bookmarks to the class "remix" site (see http://thecommunityengine.com/bit320/remix/) that aggregates all the students' contributions. Students maintain individual blog and social bookmarking accounts, and are encouraged to contribute their knowledge by sharing relevant links, questions, answers, and observations of the material being taught in the class. This open sharing of information is promoted to create a vibrant learning community where group knowledge is built collectively through the efforts of the individuals in the class.

Figure 1. Portion of the BIT320 tag cloud (10/30/05)

The formation of group knowledge is facilitated in the class through the use of Social Tagging systems. The goal of the instructor here is to create a system where students are able to make contributions so that they are aware of each other and are able to find pertinent information from the pool of contributions. Students in the class are encouraged to assign categories, or tags, when contributing their blog and URL submissions. Unlike more orthodox and controlled forms of classification, Social Tagging allows the users in the community to assign any keyword/category that they view as relevant. Various visualizations, such as the use of tag clouds (see Fig.1) helps members of the class to be made aware of the current and most frequently submitted topics/posts are by way of the tags. This paper argues that Social Tagging is a means by which new information submitted to the class is made sense of by the entire community. (Weick et al, 2005).

Social Tagging as evidence of group learning:

Tagging is essentially a process of mapping meaning and personal understanding to the essential characteristics of the entities that are being organized. The tags associated with a particular item are a representation of how a learner has activated related knowledge in his/her mind and associated it with the item. Social Tagging expands this notion to a community of learners where each tag associated with an item provides "immediate self and social feedback" (Sinha, 2005). Social tagging systems allow anyone in the community to freely attach keywords/tags to content. These tags are "socially translucent" (Erickson et al, 1999) meaning that they allow each student an awareness of both their individual tags as well as the tags and content that others contribute to the class. In other words, there are at once both personal and public aspects to collaborative tagging systems that make it easier for students to make individual contributions of one's understanding as well as to build on the knowledge that others have contributed. These are essential to the formation of a learning community and the group learning that takes place within them. This paper proposes that the tags being used in a learning community such as BIT 320 can be utilized to assess the scope and the content of the knowledge being formed by the class. Tag clouds, which aid visualization of what current tags are being used and what their frequency of use is. Thus, studying the evolution of the tag clouds of a learning community over time will provide one with an ideal representation of the evolution and change in group knowledge formation.

Methodology of the study: Tracing the evolution of the tag clouds

This study will attempt an analysis of the use of Social Tagging utilizing the following methods:

- ***Content analysis*** of the students' blog and bookmark contributions will be related to the tags. It is expected that there will be a variety terms that are being used by different members of the class for a particular content type/topic. Examining the range of vocabulary used for a particular topic will allow insight into the group knowledge being formed around particular topics.
- ***Analysis of relative frequencies and patterns*** in tag use will provide an indication of two contrasting effects: the popularity of certain topics, and the stabilization of certain tags used to categorize particular topics. Patterns in the use of tags will also reveal insights in to group cognition. For example, having a certain topic tagged differently by two distinct clusters of the class might indicate opposing viewpoints on a particular topic.
- ***Citation & Social Network Analysis*** will be used as a method to surface the interaction patterns of the students in the class. Such an analysis provides a picture of the community structure in the class through visualizations called sociograms. These visualizations help us to identify key "idea leaders" in the class who generate tags that are adopted by a large proportion of the students. As such, being able to picture who generates the ideas and who is likely to adopt them will allow insight into the dynamics of group knowledge formation for BIT 320.

References:

Erickson, T., Smith, D. N., Kellogg, W. A., Laff, M., & Brander, E. (1999). A sociotechnical approach to design: Social proxies, persistent conversations, and the design of Babble. In Proceedings of the ACM Conference on Human Factors in Computing Systems (CHI '99, Pittsburgh, PA, May), ACM Press, New York, NY. pp. 72-79.

Sinha, R. (2005). A cognitive analysis of tagging (or how the lower cost of tagging makes it popular). Rerieved October 5th, 2005, from http://www.rashmisinha.com/archives/05-09/tagging-cognitive.html

Weick, K., Sutcliffe, K. & Obstfield, D. (2005) Organizing and the Process of Sensemaking. *Organizational Science*, Vol. 16, No. 4, July – August 2005, pp. 409-421.

Remix Culture (2005, October 8). *Wikipedia: The Free Encyclopedia.* Retrieved October 10, 2005, from http://en.wikipedia.org/wiki/Remix_culture

A Multi-Level Assessment Strategy: (Dis)Continuity in Making Learning Visible Differently

Steven J. Zuiker and Daniel T. Hickey
Indiana University
szuiker@indiana.edu, dthickey@indiana.edu

Abstract: The range of assessment follows from theoretical assumptions that represent skills and concepts differently, and increasingly wrestle with representations of practices. A pragmatic strategy for coordinating and leveraging these differences may provide degrees of continuity across each, and scaffold both individual performance and collective participation in domain practices. This poster profiles a case study of (dis)continuity across one such pragmatic organization of assessment. Findings suggest methodological limits for illuminating discontinuity and a more tractable approach.

Theoretical assumptions determine the role of assessment for research on learning. However, theoretical divides across assessment may be usefully re-framed in order to understand the multidimensionality of learning and to shift focus to questions of what learning means rather than what learners know (cf. Delandshere, 2002). To this end, practical tensions underlying the competing demands of stakeholders and the conflicting functions of assessment call for larger degrees of cooperation and coordination. To this end, case studies of knowledge practices (Greeno, et al., 1998) may illuminate multiple meanings of learning across assessments, and usefully relate contemporary views of knowing and learning to conventional views of accountability (Hickey & Zuiker, 2003). They may also advance an increasingly coherent assessment framework for meeting the disparate needs of multiple stakeholders. This study considers one such case for a high school biology unit on genetics with three distinct assessments. A pragmatic strategy frames these assessments across three levels (Hickey, Zuiker, Taasoobshirazi, Schafer, & Michael, in press), in which family resemblance to broad categories of learning theory delineate each level. As a caveat, any representation yields some degree of meaning for any particular theory, but all theories value particular representations over others. With these attendant orientations in mind, multiple-choice items that probe associations resonate more with behavioral orientations (e.g., Skinner, 1954); performance assessments that characterize conceptual understandings align best with cognitive approaches; and scientific argumentation as a broad yet central scientific practice serves socio-cultural perspectives (e.g., Lemke, 1990). Notwithstanding the contention (and concession) that such boundaries inhere, these levels necessarily represent learning differently, shifting debates towards what learning genetics means across theoretical divides and for various stakeholders.

These multi-level assessments frame a 20-hour, technology-enhanced genetics curriculum in a high school life science course. Investigations across three thematic units feature the *GenScope* software tool, which models genetic organization from genes to populations. Each unit concludes with an individual assessment and small group discussion of the answers. Toulmin's (1958/2003) argumentation model structures both the assessment and collaboration, ideally supporting formulations of genetics knowledge practices to warrant and/or back claims (i.e., response to each question). In this way, group discussion constitutes a first, socio-cultural level of assessment. At the second level, a pre-post performance assessment orders 25 items in terms of a developmental model of expertise that scaffolds performance across increasingly complex problems and accurately and broadly assesses expertise (Kindfield, Hickey, & Yessis, 1999). The third level is a pre-post multiple-choice assessment that includes 13 items randomly selected from SAT II biology items related to genetics and a textbook's chapter test bank, which together represent a range of associations presented in the curriculum. These latter two assessments bear family resemblance to cognitive and behavioral assessment strategies respectively (see Hickey, Zuiker, et al., in press).

The teacher solicited eight groups across four participating classes to be videotaped during argumentation discussions. He based selection on good attendance, constituting a convenience sample. In order to consider the underlying theoretical organization of multi-level assessment, this case study concerns a dyad that consistently engaged in discussion and completed both pre-post measures. At the same time, the case focuses exclusively on a single, non-trivial knowledge practice - predicting pedigrees using charts. Pedigree prediction is a challenging aspect of introductory inheritance curricula because learners must reason backward from effect to cause, constructing patterns across generations to predict the genotypes that affected that pattern.

Multifaceted Rasch procedures scaled pre-post data on a t-scale (mean=50; s.d.=10). Scaling in this way generates a more accurate estimate of performance than simply summing correct responses. The overall mean gain (n=53) was 19.8 for the performance assessment and 10.6 for the multiple-choice assessment. Repeated measures ANOVA revealed significant improvements for each, $F(1, 52)= 158.73$, $p<0.001$ and $F(1, 52)= 27.95$, $p<0.001$. Both assessments frame compelling evidence of classroom-wide learning, and the individual gains of both students in the case study echo these; the first gained 27 and 22 and the second 14 and 7. At the same time, a comparison of pedigree prediction items revealed conflicting results for the pair. Four items on the performance assessment suggest that neither student learned about pedigree prediction while two items on the multiple-choice assessment suggest that they have. Analyses of argumentation discussions further amplify the (dis)continuity in what learning means.

Discourse analysis of the argumentation discussions focuses specifically on *epistemic stance* (Ochs, 1996). An epistemic stance is an utterance that addresses the certainty, reliability, and/or limitations of a proposition. These uses of language highlight the evidential systems reflected in knowledge practices and modern science in general. Transcripts from the initial curricular activity and two subsequent discussions demonstrate the pair's discursive interactions around pedigree prediction. During the initial curricular activity, neither student formulated an epistemic stance in relation to the questions, suggesting that neither engaged in the relevant knowledge practices. For example, while one of the two identifies a correct solution, he does not discuss his reasons or identify evidence in the pedigree chart. The subsequent argumentation discussion illustrates persistently narrow practice, seemingly unchanged in the short time between the curricular and assessment activities. However, both do begin to enlist evidence during this discussion, even positioning it strategically to persuade one another. For example, one student's account begins with "'cause remember…", and the other rejects an appeal, recasting the argument in his own terms - "but it's saying…". These phrases work to relate and to persuade, building a nascent, shared understanding of problems and illustrating the relational work involved in meaningful argumentation. The final argumentation discussion three days later did suggest differences in practice, albeit contrary to the evidence from the pedigree prediction-related items. That is, the formulations of the student who performed better in general but worse on pedigrees, in particular, ultimately suggested degrees of competent knowledge practice while the formulations of the student who performed better on pedigree prediction specifically suggested sustained misunderstandings. In general, this case study indicates that representations of one group's demonstrated practice and performance fail to cohere. Despite warranting claims with sound practice, the same student failed to perform well on a similar question in the performance assessment. By the same token, the other student never demonstrated competent practice during argumentation episodes, but answered the relevant multiple-choice items correctly.

The degrees of discontinuity across levels of assessment may be troubling, but also revealing of a question at the center of all assessment: what does learning mean through one or across many assessments? Continuity is desirable. Therefore debates about when multi-level strategies cohere and when they do not may prove useful in advancing such a question. Moreover, it does so with attention to the demands and functions of assessment for research and practice simultaneously, underscoring goals of the learning sciences. Future research may consider not only organizing assessment around innovative curricula but also within them, especially as technology increasingly affords such embeddedness.

References

Delandshere, G. (2002). Assessment as inquiry. *Teachers College Record, 104*(7), 1461-1484.

Greeno, J. G., & the Middle School Mathematics Through Application Project Group. (1998). The situativity of knowing, learning, and research. *American Psychologist, 53*(1), 5-26.

Hickey, D. T., & Zuiker, S. J. (2003). A new perspective for evaluation of innovative science environments. *Science Education, 87*(3), 539-563.

Hickey, D. T., Zuiker, S. J., Taasoobshirazi, G., Schafer, N. J., & Michael, M. A. (in press). Balancing formative and summative assessment to attain system validity. *Studies in Educational Evaluation*.

Kindfield, A. C. H., Hickey, D. T., & Yessis, L. M. (1999, March). *Assessing student understanding of genetics: The NewWorm assessment.* Paper presented at the Annual Meeting of NARST, Boston, MA.

Lemke, J. (1990). Talking science: Language, learning, and values. Norwood, NJ: Ablex.

Ochs, E. (1996). Linguistic resources for socializing humanity. In J. J. Gumperz & S. C. Levinson (Eds.), *Rethinking Linguistic Relativity* (pp. 407-437). Cambridge: Cambridge University Press.

Toulmin, S. E. (1958/2003). *The uses of argument* (Updated ed.). New York: Cambridge University Press.

Symposia

What's a Situation in Situated Cognition? – A Constructionist Critique of Authentic Inquiry

Dor Abrahamson (Organizer), Andrea A. diSessa, Graduate School of Education,
University of California–Berkeley, Berkeley, CA 94720-1670
dor@berkeley.edu, disessa@soe.berkeley.edu
Paulo Blikstein and Uri Wilensky, Center for Connected Learning and Computer-Based Modeling,
School of Education and Social Policy, Northwestern University, 2120 Campus Drive, Evanston, IL 60208-0001
paulo, uri@northwestern.edu
David H. Uttal, Meredith M. Amaya, and Loren M. Marulis, Department of Psychology,
2029 Sheridan Road, Evanston, IL, 60208-2710
duttal, m-amaya@northwestern.edu, lmarulis@ekit.com
Allan M. Collins (Discussant), Northwestern University, collins@bbn.com

Abstract: Four papers by learning scientists engaged either in design research or cognitive-developmental studies consider concreteness, context, content, pedagogy, and situativity and their implications for design that fosters opportunities for students to learn subject matter through experiencing authentic scientific/mathematical inquiry. The authors furnish both theoretical considerations and recent classroom- and laboratory-based empirical findings to question prior interpretations of students' capacity to model and abstract from situations, to generate examples, to transfer, and to make insightful connections. The papers jointly suggest that even simple objects may nevertheless undergird *emergent situativity* that provides sufficient context to which learners can bring diverse personal resources. Model-based design may be as intellectually honest, culturally respectful, cognitively generative, and scientifically/mathematically authentic as learning that draws more directly on students' out-of-school resources. The authenticity of 'authentic inquiry' may depend more on engagement and reasoning it enables than on specific content and a priori "good-science" practices it recruits.

Overview of Symposium Panel

Education researchers and psychologists involved in the design and study of student interaction with learning tools have demonstrated the potential roles of modeling—building models, interacting with models—as vehicles of meaningful teaching and learning of subject matter content (Lesh & Doerr, 2003; Verschaffel, Greer, & De Corte, 2000; Wilensky, 1999). At the same time, proponents of 'situated learning' have proposed that student learning is more engaging, meaningful, and democratic when students have opportunities to draw on real-world situations and especially situations they are personally immersed in, such as issues of their community (Freire, 1974; Ladson-Billings, 1995; Lave & Wenger, 1991; Greeno, 1998). It may appear, then, that practices of authentic inquiry would be best fostered through engagement in activities that are both model based and situated in students' real-world activities. Indeed, some designers have interpreted the combined calls for modeling-based and real-world-driven inquiry by creating activities that "go out to the streets" to collect data that is then analyzed both to practice scientific/mathematical skills and, in turn, to facilitate change back in the community. Whereas we recognize the potential of dialogical pedagogy to create richly contextualized learning activities that leverage students' out-of-school situatedness and agency, we submit that intramural situatedness, too, can achieve these goals. That is, a more nuanced interpretation of 'context,' which complexifies relationships between pedagogy and content, may enable designers to appreciate the potential of *emergent situativity* of scientific inquiry. Even Lego bricks or computer-screen pixels, a far cry from what some may call 'rich context,' enfold potential for an engaging, personally meaningful, and authentic exploration into content.

In this symposium, we will: (a) examine prevalent interpretations of the notion that 'situations' should be imported 'as is' from students' extramural activities; (b) suggest that modeling-and-simulation learning environments that include manipulable and/or programmable objects can elicit the necessary situatedness of learning activities; (c) propose that model-based learning activities can be designed to draw from both real-world situations and from "hard-boiled content"—we see modeling as living in the middle (see also Gobert & Buckley, 2000; Lehrer & Schauble, in press; Levy & Wilensky, 2004; Stieff & Wilensky, 2003; Wilensky & Reisman, in press). The epistemic game (Collins & Ferguson, 1993) of building and "running" models enables coordination between the world as we naively know it and the world as scientists and mathematicians know it (see also Schön, 1981).

The authors in this symposium build on empirical data to interpret the constructs 'situation,' 'context,' 'concrete,' and 'authentic' not according to superficial criteria of the materiality or familiarity of media, learning tools, and content, but as indexed by the phenomenology of students who are immersed in model-based learning environments and are recruiting cognitive resources that include personal context, imagination, and pretense skills. diSessa warns that too narrow an interpretation of cultural situatedness may preclude the potential generativity of intuitive, "abstractable," knowledge inherent in cultural practices. Abrahamson argues for the authenticity of mathematics-learning experiences grounded in immersive construction-and-simulation activities—given an interesting problem, liberty to explore, and judicious shepherding, a community of learners can build intellectual edifices from simple blocks. Blikstein and Wilensky present an innovative computer-based learning environment that integrates and juxtaposes within a single medium real-time experimentation in physical and simulated phenomena—this design challenges the dichotomies outdoors—indoors and real—model. Comparing this physics design to Abrahamson's mathematics design demonstrates what source materials each domain requires so as to construct valid models. Uttal, Amaya, and Marulis demonstrate that interaction factors and not materiality per se affect the likelihood that young learners will appropriate objects as representations. All the authors agree that the authenticity of designed inquiry is measured by the conceptual processes and appropriation of procedures that it promotes. From this perspective, any medium, technology, or activity—any context—where students learn content through solving difficult problems, for which staple algorithms are not provided, is authentic.

Abstracts of Panel Participants

Culturally Wide-Spread, Abstract Structures and Their Implications for Learning Mathematics and Science

Andrea A. diSessa

Education is full of exhortations that learning activities must be embedded in the everyday lives and contexts of students in order to be maximally effective. One of the most pointed and important versions of this idea is that the particulars of diverse cultural communities should be exploited as "funds of knowledge" (Moll, Amanti, Neff, & González, 1992) in making "abstract" school mathematics and science sensible to and appreciated by non-white, non-middle class students. So, common activities, such as crafts, art, and pastimes of non-mainstream cultures should be brought into school to motivate, situate, and support learning math and science with *culturally specific competence*.

While supporting the essence of this advice, the contention of this presentation is that conventional interpretations of it unnecessarily narrow the field of consideration for creating "authentic" and "culturally situated" learning activities. There are several moves that open up a much greater range of possibilities. The first is the recognition that cultural activities are deeply generative. Within any culture or community, new "games" and variations of old activities are easily taken on because they share a family resemblance with well-known particular ones. Thus, to be well-connected to a student's heritage, we need only exploit those family resemblances, not literal activity importation. The second move stems from a deeper view of the nature and generativity of cultural and intuitive knowledge. We will make the case that much of this kind of knowledge is—counter to what is probably the mainstream view—highly abstract in nature, and thus not bound in literal reproduction of culturally or individually specific experiences. The possibility of an abstract deep structure in cultural or individual experiences opens up the field of "authentic and situated" activities far beyond stereotyped or quickly recognizeable ones. Even more, "abstract deep structure" suggests the possibility of a much wider reservoir of "funds of knowledge," which are simply NOT culturally specific.

These largely theoretical arguments will be exemplified in a current project called "Patterns of Change and Control." In this project, we seek to understand the intuitive pools of knowledge lying behind children's abilities to comprehend and control many situations in the world—physical, social, and otherwise. The intuitive patterns we believe children know about are things like "balance," "threshold," "stability," "stickiness," "pumping," and so on. In a summer course aimed at eliciting and developing ideas like these, we feel we developed good preliminary evidence that many "naïve" student ideas are, in essence, highly abstract and travel easily across very great divides, such as between physical and social phenomena (diSessa, 2000; diSessa, in press). They are emphatically not "bound" to one or a few recognizable, particular activities. Example data includes the fluid ability of students to generate examples in highly diverse particular settings. Drug addiction, sumo wrestling, and the break-up of a dating pair are all seen easily as examples of one particular pattern (threshold). Furthermore, we see very little reason to expect much difference in these ideas across cultures, although examples students can give and explain likely are more culturally specific. Finally, we believe that certain simple mathematizations (in particular, writing computer programs to model such phenomena) are exceedingly natural and productive (rather than abstract and needing extensive coaching and scaffolding). This last claim, however, probably depends on cultural experiences that may not be as universal as those that support understanding patterns in their own terms.

By the time of ICLS, we will have further classroom data testing the abstract nature of students' knowledge of patterns and their ability to mathematize it, and we will have done at least one controlled, laboratory experiment aimed specifically at illuminating the level of abstractness in students' knowledge of "patterns of change and control."

"Because In the World, There Are More Blocks of This Type": The Real-Worldness of Immersive Combinatorial Analysis as a Grounding of Simulated Probability Experiments

Dor Abrahamson

Underlying any administration of mathematical concepts is a covert dissemination of values, norms, and beliefs pertaining to mathematical practice and learners' critical agency therein (Cobb, Gravemeijer, Yackel, McClain, & Whitenack, 1997). Specifically for mathematical inquiry, I ask, 'Which designs foster opportunities for students both to develop deep understanding of content and to experience effective practices?' My argument is that *the authenticity of 'authentic inquiry' depends more on the types of engagement and reasoning it enables than on the specific content or structures it recruits.* I support the argument with data from an implementation of a modeling-based design for probability.

In discussing school-based situational contexts, I examine pedagogies that apparently motivate the design of the learning environments where mathematical content is situated. However, the objective of this paper is *not* to evaluate pedagogies per se but to comment on designs that purport to implement these pedagogies. That is, mathematical and scientific meaning can emerge successfully both through Freirean design (e.g., Blikstein, 2002) and design for discursive classrooms (e.g., Cobb & Hodge, 2002). Yet whereas choices of pedagogy are more likely to be informed by educators' deep-rooted philosophical and ethical dispositions, by considerations of the resources and needs of target populations, and by political contexts, agendas, and motivations, choices of particular designs could be informed by the extent to which these designs are likely to implement the desired pedagogy. Specifically, I submit that students can potentially engage in deep mathematical discussion of personally-relevant matters even when and *because* students' agency plays out in arenas that are, at least initially, one step removed from "the thing itself"—namely, arenas such as model-based learning environments.

The roles of modeling as supports for deep understanding of mathematical content have been discussed widely (e.g., Lesh & Doerr, 2003; Verschaffel et al., 2000; Wilensky, 1995). A focus on building/interacting with models suggests a shift in the interpretation of 'context.' Extramural situations may initially trigger and frame the mathematical reasoning, yet the model, a medium more amenable for exploration, *gradually* constitutes the locus of active reflection, imagination, and conjecture. The model becomes a rich object onto its own that enables students to embody and pursue coherent structures through generating, examining, discerning, and articulating emergent patterns of relational regularity bearing beyond specific data sets. In sum, initially "neutral" materials are more generative than raw data in terms of: (a) eliciting a diversity of students' personal interpretations; (b) suggesting relations to other mathematical concepts; and (c) enhancing the prospects that students will correctly model situations in future encounters with suitable situational contexts. The modeling materials take on a mathematical life.

To support my position I will discuss findings from implementations of *ProbLab* (Abrahamson & Wilensky, 2002; see Figure 1, below) an experimental model-based unit designed for middle-school students studying probability and statistics. Specifically, I will argue that students who were immersed in collaboratively constructing a complicated combinatorial space of a stochastic device created a locally *real* world of *emergent situativity* that enabled productive processes of authentic mathematical inquiry. These students subsequently leveraged personal insights into the designed contexts so as to *concretize* (Wilensky, 1991) distributions of random outcomes that were generated by computer-based simulations of probability (compare, in Figure 1, the two right-most pictures). These findings suggest that authenticity of mathematical inquiry is indexed not so much by a priori extramural situativity per se as much as by any generative reasoning that the designed materials and activities afford. Also, students' general engagement around very simple tools suggests that any lack off motivation to study mathematics lies not necessarily in the "dullness" of mathematical objects but in activity design and facilitation.

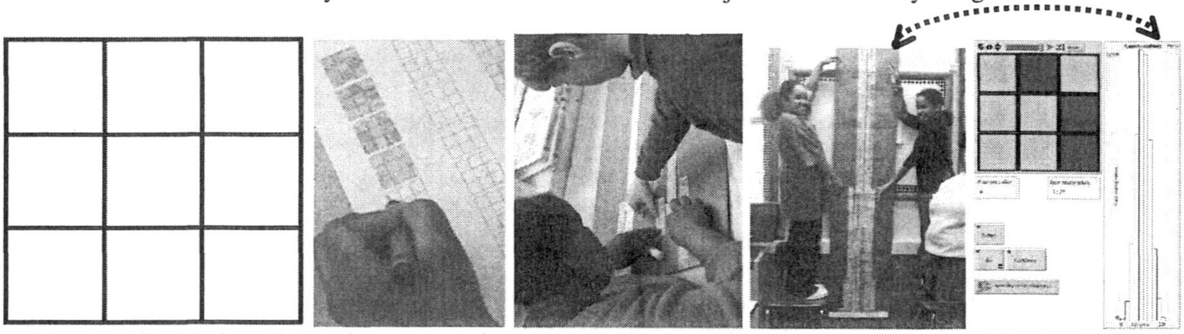

Figure 1. *ProbLab*: collaborative construction of the combinatorial space of the *9-Block*, a 3-by-3 grid, in which cells are either green or blue. Students construct a *combinations tower* and then compare it to simulated experiments.

Implications of this study are that real-world experiences can be created in model-based mathematics learning environments. Thus, modeling-based design could be instrumental in implementing *culturally-relevant pedagogy* (Ladson-Billings, 1995). For example, design for statistics education need not focus primarily on practices of assembling reliable data sets, e.g., through quasi-ethnographic charting of the community, as much as on conceptual processes of making sense of such data through constructing generative models that accommodate the data as a case study. The pragmatics of available resources, e.g., classroom time, may, too, bear on designers' decisions whether students should go out to the streets or whether the streets should be reconstructed in the classroom (see also von Glasersfeld, e.g., 1992).

Linking Real-World Sensing and Multi-Agent-Based Computer Models

Paulo Blikstein and Uri Wilensky

What do we obtain from "going out to the world" as a platform for learning? The multiple aspects of this experience have been explored by different schools of thought in education. John Dewey (1916) was one of the first to emphasize the importance of connecting school learning and real-world experiences. Critical pedagogy argued that departing from the learner's context and previous knowledge is crucial to foster de-facto emancipating and motivating learning (Freire, 1974). Constructionist educators (Papert, 1991) posited that building personally-meaningful public artifacts is central to promote sustainable and deep learner engagement. However, critics of such pedagogies would argue that the world might not afford the necessary information and opportunities for students to learn the 'official' school content: One cannot make sure that acid-base reactions, for instance, are out there situated in the world.

While concurring with claims about the relevance of the learner's context, background, and concrete experiences for education design, we acknowledge that the current tools for scientific exploration available for students limit the kind and complexity of their real-world investigations. Thus, we submit that the disconnect between what one can learn in a fully situated environment and the more traditional school content is due, perhaps, to the lack of appropriate tools to 'dissect' reality to the appropriate level of analysis. Even if, by definition, Physics, Chemistry, and Biology are 'out-there' in the world, most phenomena are invisible to human vision and time scale. Many patterns in nature are too long, too fast, too small, or too large for learners to extract and understand their underlying structures. Canonical examples are weather behavior, chemical reactions, housing and traffic pattern, particle physics, and population ecology. We need, thus, new technological tools which foreground and unveil the deep structures of such phenomena. In this paper, our focus will be *hybrid modeling*, a framework for scientific exploration and modeling which merges two types of educational technologies commonly used (separately) in schools. The first kind is robotics and electronic sensing (Martin, 1996; Resnick & Ocko, 1991), which makes possible a wide range of experimental activities in the real world. The second technology is multi-agent simulation, which enables learners to create models to understand complex social and natural phenomena departing from very simple behaviors embedded into elementary computational agents (Wilensky & Reisman, in press; Wilensky & Resnick, 1999).

This paper describes a research project that, by linking the two technologies, attempts to simultaneously broaden the possibilities of situated investigation and ground computer modeling with real-world validation. For that goal, we are developing software and hardware tools to bridge computer models and sensing in real time (see Figure 2, below). Typically, students build a computer model of a particular phenomenon, such as heat transfer, and a sensor-equipped physical device. These are connected by an analog-to-digital interface. Students are able to run their computer models in tandem with the physical apparatus, comparing the outcomes of both, and debugging their model until it matches the real-world data. We are currently building proof-of-concept systems for 'hybrid' explorations in heat transfer, gas laws, acid-based and oscillating reactions, and Materials Science. Our main goal, however, is to create a technological infrastructure to enable students to build their own systems.

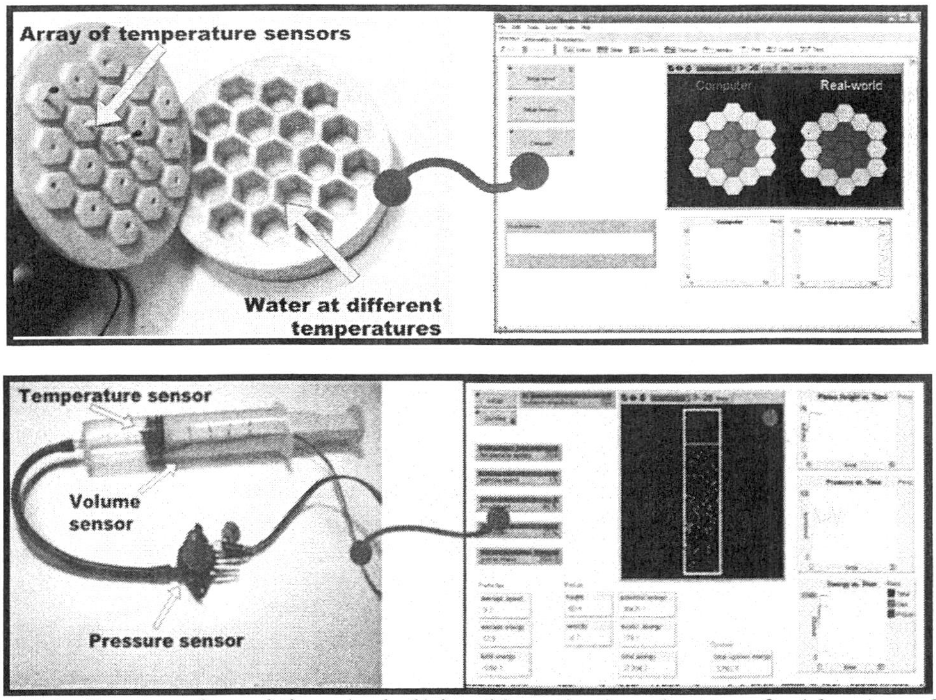

Figure 2. Two 'linked' systems for real-time physical/virtual investigations: heat transfer (above); gas laws (below).

We conducted a case study comparing the artifacts generated by undergraduate and graduate students in two distinct conditions. In the first condition, students created multi-agent-based models *with no* sensors. In the second situation, another group of students built hybrid models *with* sensors. All students built their models as an assignment in an 'Educational Design' class. Based on our analysis of their artifacts and interviews, we are identifying the learning benefits of hybrid, "trans-media," sensor-equipped models as well as determining to what extent this approach can effectively expand the possibilities of situated investigation (see also http://ccl.northwestern.edu/netlogolab).

When, How, and Why Do Concrete Objects Facilitate Young Children's Learning?

David H. Uttal, Meredith M. Amaya, & Loren M. Marulis

The assumption that young children's thinking is inherently concrete is a central tenet of many developmental and educational theories. Scholars such as Montessori (1917; Lillard, 2005) and Piaget (1970) have suggested that young children know the world primarily through physical interactions with it. Their mental representations thus are based on the way in which the information is experienced, rather than on symbolic, abstract representations of concepts. Although many researchers (Gelman, 2003; Simons & Keil, 1995) have challenged this notion, it continues to have great sway (Ball, 1992; Clements, 1997).

The idea that young children's thinking is based on their experiences with the environment has led to the development of concrete educational tools that are designed to be physically manipulated. For example, one can find letter or number magnets stuck to refrigerators in many American homes. In the classroom, teachers can use a variety of more formal systems, such as mathematics manipulatives, that are intended to capitalize on young children's concrete thinking.

Despite the enthusiasm for the use of concrete materials, relatively little controlled research has evaluated their effectiveness. The research that has been conducted has yielded mixed results. Consider, for example, research on the effectiveness of concrete mathematics manipulatives. On the one hand, several studies have demonstrated that the use of concrete manipulatives can facilitate children's understanding of mathematical concepts (Resnick & Omanson, 1987; Martin & Schwartz, 2005). Yet on the other hand, systematic reviews of research on the effectiveness of the use of manipulatives have not found a consistent advantage over other forms of instruction (Sowell, 1989; Uttal, Scudder, & DeLoache, 1997), and research has shown that children consistently fail to transfer what they learn from using manipulatives to written representations (Resnick & Omanson, 1987).

Our research examines the effectiveness of concrete objects in a variety of learning contexts. Our goal is to reveal, through systematic and controlled studies, the conditions under which concrete objects facilitate (or inhibit) learning. We will present the results of two sets of studies. The first focuses on 4-year-olds' learning of the symbolic properties of letters and numbers. We asked the children either to play with concrete (magnetic) letters or numbers or control stimuli (standard toys that involved games similar to those played with the letters or numbers). We then tested the children's use of the letters and numbers to represent quantities or objects. For example, the children were asked to use the magnetic numbers as well as a crayon to represent the number of "cookies" hidden in a container. Likewise, they were asked to use letter magnets and a crayon to represent the identity of a hidden toy animal.

We found that playing with the concrete objects does not facilitate learning. In fact, in some situations, it actually hurt performance. However, using the concrete objects in a symbolic way (to represent quantity or identity) does promote symbolic understanding. For example, using a magnetic letter to represent the identity of an object made it easier for the children to use a crayon to do something similar. These results suggest that concreteness per se may matter less than how or why the objects are used. We will also discuss additional lines of research that focus on the use of concrete manipulatives in the classroom. Taken together, our studies suggest that, as a Learning-Sciences community that frames design principles for learning with understanding, we may wish to reexamine what we mean by 'concrete.' For example, is concreteness an inherent property of learning material or a psychological relationship that the learner develops towards any material (see also Wilensky, 1991)?

References

Abrahamson, D., & Wilensky, U. (2002). *ProbLab*. The Center for Connected Learning and Computer-Based Modeling, Northwestern University, Evanston, IL. http://ccl.northwestern.edu/curriculum/ProbLab/

Ball, D. (1992). Magical hopes: Manipulatives and the reform of mathematics education. *American Educator, 16*(2), 14-18, 46-47.

Blikstein, P. (2002). *The Trojan Horse as a Trojan Horse: Impacting the ecology of the learning atmosphere.* Unpublished MSc. thesis, Cambridge: M.I.T.

Clements, D. H. (1997). (Mis?)constructing constructivism. *Teaching Children Mathematics, 4*, 198-200.

Cobb, P., & Hodge, L. (2002). Learning, identity, and statistical data analysis. Paper presented at the Sixth International Conference on Teaching Statistics (ICOTS6), Cape Town, South Africa.

Cobb, P., Gravemeijer, K., Yackel, E., McClain, K., & Whitenack, J. (1997). Mathematizing and symbolizing. In D. Kirshner & J. A. Whitson (Eds.), *Situated cognition: Social, semiotic and psychological perspectives* (pp. 151–233). Mahwah, NJ: Lawrence Erlbaum Associates.

Collins, A., & Ferguson, W. (1993). Epistemic forms and epistemic games: Structures and strategies to guide inquiry. *Educational Psychologist, 28*(1), 25-42.

Dewey, J. (1961). *Democracy and education.* New York: Macmillan. Originally published 1916.

diSessa, A. A. (2000). Does the mind know the difference between the physical and social worlds? In L. Nucci, G. Saxe, and E. Turiel (Eds.), *Culture, Development and Knowledge* (pp. 141-166). Mahwah, NJ: Lawrence Erlbaum Associates.

diSessa, A. A. (in press). Systemics of learning for a revised pedagogical agenda. In R. Lesh (ed.), *Foundations for the future in mathematics education.* Mahwah, NJ: LEA.

Freire, P. (1974). Pedagogy of the oppressed. New York: Seabury Press.

Gelman, S. A. (2003). *The essential child: Origins of essentialism in everyday thought.* New York, NY: Oxford University Press.

Gobert, J., & Buckley, B. (2000). Special issue editorial: Introduction to model-based teaching and learning. *International Journal of Science Education, 22(9),* 891-894.

Greeno, J. (1998). The situativity of knowing, learning, and research. *American Psychologist, 53*(1), 5-26.

Ladson-Billings, G. (1995). Toward a theory of culturally relevant pedagogy. *American Education Research Journal, 35*, 465 – 491.

Lave, J., & Wenger, E. (1991). *Situated learning: Legitimate peripheral participation.* New York: Cambridge University Press.

Lehrer, R., &, Schauble, L. (in press). *Cultivating model-based reasoning in science education.*

Lesh, R. & Doerr, H. M. (2003). *Beyond constructivism: A models and modeling perspective on mathematics problem-solving, learning, and teaching.* Mahwah, NJ: Lawrence Erlbaum Associates

Levy, S. T., & Wilensky, U. (2004, April). *Making sense of complexity: Patterns in forming causal connections between individual agent behaviors and aggregate group behaviors.* Paper presented at the annual meeting of the American Educational Research Association, San Diego, CA.

Lillard, A. S. (2005). *Montessori: The Science behind the Genius.* New York: Oxford University Press.

Martin, F. (1996). Ideal and Real Systems. In Y. Kafai & M. Resnick (Eds.), *Constructionism in Practice* (pp. 297-332). Mahwah, NJ: Lawrence Erlbaum Associates Inc.

Martin, T., & Schwartz, D.L. (2005). Physically distributed learning. *Cognitive Science, 29*(4), 587-625.

Moll, L. C., Amanti, C., Neff, D., & González, N. (1992). Funds of knowledge for teaching: Using a qualitative approach to connect homes and classrooms. *Theory into Practice, 31*(2), 132-141.

Montessori, J. (1917). *The advanced Montessori method.* New York: Frederick A. Stokes.

Papert, S. (1980). *Mindstorms*: Children, computers, and powerful ideas. NY: Basic Books.

Papert, S. (1991). Situating constructionism. In S. Papert & I. Harel (Eds.), *Constructionism.* NJ: Ablex.

Piaget, J. (1970). *Science of education and the psychology of the child.* New York: Orion Press.

Resnick, L. B., & Omanson, S. F. (1987). Learning to understand arithmetic. In R. Glaser (Ed.), *Advances in instructional psychology* (Vol. 3, pp. 41-96). Hillsdale, NJ: LEA.

Resnick, M., & Ocko, S. (1991). Lego/Logo: Learning through and about design. In S. Papert & I. Harel (Eds.), *Constructionism.* NJ: Ablex

Schön, D. (1981). *Intuitive thinking? A metaphor underlying some ideas of educational reform (Working Paper 8)*: Division for Study and Research, M.I.T.

Simons, D. J., & Keil, F. C. (1995). An abstract to concrete shift in the development of biological thought: The insides story. *Cognition, 56*, 129-163.

Sowell, E. J. (1989). Effects of manipulative materials in mathematics instruction. *Journal for Research in Mathematics Education, 20*, 498-505.

Stieff, M., & Wilensky, U. (2003). Connected Chemistry: Incorporating interactive simulations into the chemistry classroom. *Journal of Science Education & Technology, 12*(3). 285 – 302.

Uttal, D. H., Scudder, K.V., & DeLoache, J.S. (1997). Manipulatives as symbols. *Journal of Applied Developmental Psychology, 18*(1), 37-54.

Verschaffel, L., Greer, B., & De Corte, E. (2000). *Making sense of word problems.* Lisse, The Netherlands: Swets & Zeitlinger.

Wilensky, U. (1991). Abstract meditations on the concrete and concrete implications for mathematics education. In I. Harel & S. Papert (Eds.), *Constructionism* (pp. 193–204). Norwood, NJ: Ablex.

Wilensky, U. (1995). Paradox, programming and learning probability. *Journal of Mathematical Behavior, 14*(2), 231-280.

Wilensky, U. (1999). GasLab: An extensible modeling toolkit for exploring micro- and macro- views of gases. In N. Roberts, W. Feurzeig & B. Hunter (Eds.), *Computer Modeling and Simulation in Science Education.* Berlin: Springer Verlag.

Wilensky, U., & Reisman, K. (in press). Thinking like a wolf, a sheep or a firefly. *Cognition & Instruction.*

Wilensky, U. & Resnick, M. (1999). Thinking in levels: A dynamic systems approach to making sense of the world. *Journal of Science Education and Technology 8*(1), 3-19.

von Glasersfeld, E. (1992). Aspects of radical constructivism and its educational recommendations (Working Group #4). Paper presented at the Seventh International Congress on Mathematics Education (ICME7), Quebec. http://srri.nsm.umass.edu/vonGlasersfeld/onlinePapers/html/195.html

Clubs, Homes, and Online Communities as Contexts for Engaging Youth in Technology Fluency Building Activities

Brigid Barron, Stanford University, Barronbj@Stanford.edu
Yasmin B. Kafai, University of California, Los Angeles, Kafai@gseis.ucla.edu

Abstract: The goal of this session is to advance our understanding of the relationships between access to computing tools, learning opportunities, and the development of technological fluency. Understanding variability in the kinds of material and social resources that children have access to is crucial for a better understanding of how to create more equitable learning opportunities. Overview talks of three research programs and their theoretical frameworks will start this session. A poster session will follow that showcases nine empirical or design projects that have emerged from the research programs. In keeping with the conference theme, the overview presentations and empirical work highlight how learning to use technology in empowered ways can be nurtured within and across a broad range of contexts.

Overview

Adolescents typically use computers more frequently at home than they do at school (Kaiser Family Foundation, 2004; Pew, 2002). During this out of school time the social contexts of their use and the nature of the activities vary widely. Although playing games is a common activity, children and teens also use the computer to communicate with friends, do research for school, find information about hobbies, and to download and listen to music. Some teens also use their computing tools for activities that involve authoring such as multimedia story writing, robotics, programming, or web design. These creative activities are particularly likely to build aspects of what has been called technological fluency as they require some understanding of fundamental concepts and frequently a great deal of persistence and trouble shooting (NRC, 1999). Recent research suggest that opportunities to engage in fluency building activities out of school are not equally distributed. Children who have greater access at home to tools such as high speed Internet access, scanners, cameras, and printers are more likely to have engaged in fluency building activities (Barron, Shatz, & Martin, in preparation). However, the strong association between access to tools at home and experience can be moderated when learning opportunities are provided for elsewhere such as in after school clubs or community centers (Resnick, Rusk, & Cooke, 1998).

In this symposium we discuss three research programs that are designed to advance our theoretical understanding of how learning to use technology in empowered ways can be nurtured within and across a broad range of contexts. In addition, we hope to advance the conversation about how to empirically document learning that occurs out of school. We believe that understanding variability in the kinds of material and social resources that children have access to is crucial for a better understanding of how to create more equitable learning opportunities. The research that will be presented includes data from children who have high levels of interest, access at home to knowledge resources and tools, and opportunities to participate in out of school summer camps or online classes that are funded by their parents as well as children who have interest but little to no access at home and find resources through after school clubs or community centers that provide opportunities for fluency building activities. The session will begin with a 30 minute overview consisting of three papers that will summarize the research programs and theoretical frameworks that drive them. Next, audience members will have 45 minutes to visit the nine posters. For the final 15 minutes of the session the authors will gather and the audience will be invited to participate in an open discussion.

Overview Paper I. Mapping learning across contexts: The role of informal and school based contexts in the emergence of expertise and the development of interest

Brigid Barron

Understanding how learning to use technology is distributed among multiple settings and resources is an increasingly important goal. There are widespread concerns about inequities among children in whether they learn to use computers in ways that can promote their own development and about who becomes interested in pursuing advanced knowledge that would position them to work in technological design fields (AAUW, 2000; Attewell, 2001; Camp, 1997). Schools are being asked to cultivate technological fluency, digital literacy, and other 21st

century competencies (NRC, 1999). Yet, as with other subjects, schools differ widely in the kinds of learning resources they offer (Warschauer, 2000). A better understanding of how learning takes place across settings and of the possible synergies and barriers between learning contexts may help educators find ways to supplement school based learning. To make progress on understanding learning across the life spaces of home, school, community, work, and neighborhood we need frameworks and perspectives that help articulate questions that will advance theory and guide data collection.

In this paper a learning ecologies framework for studying the emergence of interest and the development of technological fluency is presented. A learning ecology is defined as the set of contexts, comprised of configurations of activities, material resources, and relationships found in physical or virtual spaces that provide opportunities for learning (Barron, 2004). A *learning ecologies perspective* foregrounds that 1) adolescents are simultaneously involved in many settings; 2) they are active in creating activity contexts for themselves within and across settings, and 3) that interest driven activities tend to be self-sustaining given adequate resources. In this overview paper conjectures about the development of interest and the dynamics of how a learning ecology can develop over time will be presented along with ideas for how we might collect data to test some of these ideas and inform the design of learning environments.

Poster 1. **Profiles of interest, access, and fluency building experience in Silicon Valley: When interest isn't enough.** Colin Schatz, Brigid Barron, and Sarah Walter, Stanford University

In order to better understand who gains access to fluency building experiences, survey and interview data was collected from an economically diverse group of middle school students attending one of two public schools in the Silicon Valley region. In this report we share analyses that examine the relationship between teens' experience with fluency building activities and a number of variables including access to tools at home, use of a various learning resources, and interest in learning about computing technology. Our results suggest that the children with the most experience typically have high levels of interest and access to tools at home but that students who have high interest without tools at home sometimes find ways to gain these experiences inside or outside of school. Results from cluster analysis further suggest a compelling set of three different profiles of students based on the variables of fluency, interest and home access to tools. Notably, students matching a profile of low fluency and limited home access to tools but high interest appear to exhibit a different general pattern of technology use (e.g., participating more frequently in entertainment activities than in communication or learning activities involving technology) compared to students matching a profile of high interest, access and fluency or to students matching a profile of high access, medium interest, and average fluency. Results from analysis of individual activities are also notable: Students matching the first profile, for instance, reported playing educational games and writing for fun substantially more often than average for the overall sample population; Moreover, they used "instant messaging" substantially less often than average, while instant messaging was an activity among the most frequent activities for students matching the other two profiles. Interview data help present more detailed profiles of the learning ecologies of students who vary in their experience/resource/interest profiles.

Poster 2. **Community-based computer clubhouses as contexts for bridging divides: Evidence for their central role in supporting the technological fluency of children without home access.** Caitlin Martin, Susie Wise, Brigid Barron, and Sarah Lewis, Stanford University

In order to look more deeply at the learning ecologies of youth who have found a way to develop technological fluency despite low home access, we conducted two years of ethnographic research in technology programs at after-school community centers in areas with low SES. We developed a set of case portraits of youth in this environment through weekly participant observation, surveys and interviews conducted with participants around their technology projects and experiences, and interviews with parents and staff. Our poster will discuss youth whose central source of fluency development is the community center, focusing on cases from two club contexts: a computer clubhouse space and a long-term web design program. Results suggest that youth are highly interested in the opportunities and that some are able to use the human and material resources at the community center to build fluency, but that there are few instances where this excitement and knowledge are nurtured by other contexts like school. We will frame the cases in the local community, drawing on survey and interview data collected from 160 students from a local middle school that was located 1.7 miles away from the community center that served as a focal context for our research.

Poster 3. **The role of online and face-to-face social networks in nurturing interest and experience.**
Rachel Fithian, Brigid Barron, Karin Chapin, and Lori Takeuchi, Stanford University

This poster presents findings from recent case studies of middle school children in Silicon Valley who exhibit high levels of technological fluency and engagement. A primary goal of conducting these case studies was to gain understanding of the learning ecologies that support these high-fluency children including their social networks and access to learning activities in an out of school. We share the stories of two children from this set of case studies and the role that online and "live" communities play in their learning and development. "Layla" is on her school's math team and participates in an online math forum. Layla's mathematical expertise is central to her identity, and her involvement in this forum led to her interest in learning about programming which she acted on by enrolling in a class at school. "Caleb" is experienced in the fields of computer science and technology; he started programming and tinkering at toddler age and has amassed an extensive resume of technological accomplishments. In interviews, Caleb presents himself as a contributing member of a "live" community of technology experts. While both children are members of learning communities, the motivations they express for membership, their pathways into participation, and the outcomes of involvement differ. We will discuss themes around the role of community including contribution to feelings of belonging and identity, and positioning in larger networks involving issues of power hierarchies and molding the future.

Overview paper II: Supporting Urban Youth in Developing Empowered Technology-User Identities by Bridging Home, School and Afterschool Contexts

Diana Joseph & Nichole Pinkard

Many middle-class children naturally and automatically acquire the technological fluency they need to successfully mediate school, home and community environments. In stark contrast, for the majority of children from low-income urban families, this experience is far from reality. Our project aims to level the playing field by scaffolding the development of empowered technology user identities in disadvantaged urban youth. Extensive research has highlighted the importance of identity as a determiner of goals and effort (cf. Eccles et al, 1983). Cultural factors play a key role in determining identities that operate in academic and work settings (cf van Knippenberg, 2000). Our work places this set of ideas at the center of the design of a program to foster technological fluency associated with identities that empower urban youth to work and play in new media domains.

Working in the middle school grades at an urban charter elementary school, we have begun to implement Digital Youth, a program that spans the worlds of school, home, and after-school activities. Our program immerses youth in frequent, substantial, meaningful, pleasurable technology learning opportunities in multiple ecological settings (Barron, 2004). Through this immersion, they develop technological fluency and take on identities as powerful users, creators, and teachers of technology. We believe that as young people begin to contribute technological expertise across their environments, they will develop the knowledge, dispositions, skills, and social connections to enter technology careers and degree programs.

The Digital Youth program serves approximately sixty middle-school students at an urban charter school serving African-American students. Each student has a laptop for their own use in and out of school. The school curriculum integrates the use of laptops, especially in milestone projects in the major academic content areas. After school, students participate in interest-based clubs. In addition, workshops highlight key skills needed in school and in clubs, including tool workshops (such as Excel Basics and FinalCut ProBasics) and skill workshops (Digital Storytelling, Teaching Technology Skills to Peers). Skilled participants offer tutorial office hours to other young people before and after school. We aim to provide summer internship opportunities for students who have earned an advanced credential. Because the laptop travels home with students, families have new opportunities to learn about technology, and to identify their children as technology experts. A centerpiece of the program is the credentialing system, which articulates skills that learners can demonstrate in order to earn specific quasi-professional titles, rights and responsibilities. Our presentations in this symposium highlight design and preliminary findings from the pilot year of the Digital Youth program.

Poster 1. **Three club designs to foster the development of empowered identities.** R. Benjamin Shapiro, Karla Thomas, Nick Jaffe & Todd Carter, University of Chicago

In an effort to create a sustainable model, the Digital Youth program makes use of club leaders and club models from a variety of sources. This poster highlights similarities, differences, and examples of student work, and preliminary design lessons found by looking across three club designs. These clubs are intended to draw students into new identities as technology users. Video Game Design Club is led by a graduate student with technical and learning environment design skills. The work involved in this club takes place mainly in the virtual space of Alice (http://www.alice.org/), with occasional use of platform gaming systems. The club is physically set in the school's science classroom, including substantial infrastructure designed to support purposes other than those of the club. Robotics Club is led by four professional engineers at a major firm. The club is centralized around a Lego robotics competition, and the attendant materials. This club works in a space used only after school. Digital Music is led by two musicians with extensive experience as club leaders and creators of digital music studios in schools. They have created an established and articulated learning environment designed and tested over several years. Their work takes place in a digital music studio with instruments, microphones, computers and other recording equipment, built into what once was a small office in the school. The space is designed so that, as in a professional studio, each physical object has a specific location and routines for its use. This poster describes the implications of club leader experience, curriculum design, physical materials, and space for identity development.

Poster 2. **Digital connectors: Using human resources to bridge between existing sociocultural identities and new empowered technology-user identities.** Nichole Pinkard and Tiffanie Jackson, University of Chicago

Researchers such as Gee (2003), Bryson et al. (2003) and Pinkard (2005) conjecture that many children, especially minority youth, lack access to digital savvy mentors whose presence and products could serve to engage other youth in acquiring new media literacies. Gender research (Bryson & de Castell, 1996; de Castell& Bryson,1997; Hawkins, 1985) has shown that the lack of female role models and female peers willing to engage in technical courses dramatically limits the number of women willing to pursue activities that require technological abilities. Barron (2004) suggests that youth new to programming are more likely to learn from a peer or parent in an informal context while a technically experienced youth was more likely to take courses and learn from books. In order to invite learners into taking on new identities, our design calls on adults with expert identities in technology fields, and adults with whom young participants in our program identify. Drawn from local colleges, universities and an arts education organization, club and workshop leaders create as well as social environments that reflect how technology user identities operate in the real world. At the same time, they interpersonal connections with students that we expect will allow them to guide these youth in moving toward taking on technology identities. In this poster, a club leader and the program manager present initial designs at the program and club levels, and describe participant responses.

Poster 3. **Credentials as an invitation to empowered technology-user identities.** Diana Joseph and Akili Lee, University of Chicago

Young people develop clear images of the learning stages required to accomplish goals connected to identities they care about (Nasir, 2002). We conjecture that most urban youth have limited exposure to adults in technology professions. The identities associated with these types of careers are likely to appear unattainable or undesirable. To help students get on the path for technology-based careers, we must first help them perceive how technological skills are related to desirable identities, how they are developed over time and how they enable lead to new and more interesting tasks. Similarly, we want students to understand how technologists interact with, educate, and problem solve with their peers, and push each other's thinking and creativity. In order to guide youth in learning new media literacies and adopting identities that highlight their growing knowledge, we are creating a system of credentials. These credentials, based in professional work identities, lay out requirements for demonstrations of skills and ethical practices. These demonstrations lead to related rights that serve the needs and capacities of the school and community. For example, a youth who demonstrates web design skills and ethics and thus earns the Webmaster credential might acquire the right to post pages on the school's website, and the responsibility to manage a section of that website. view the credential system as an important vehicle for helping youth understand the language and relationship between new media literacies, and how to move from one set of skills to the next. We conjecture that as youth complete certifications along a developmental pathway they will begin to internalize the language, skills, processes, affordances and constraints of new media literacies.

Overview Paper III: Beyond Point & Click: Creating Programming Technologies and Opportunities for Supporting Technology Fluency in Afterschool Programs

Yasmin Kafai

Many after-school programs have been installed to compensate for the lack of computer resources found in low-income communities. Congress appropriated over $991 million for after-school programs in 2005 for the 21st Century Community Learning Centers (CCLC) Program. These after-school programs not only include academic and extracurricular activities, but also technology education programs. There are currently more than 2,000 Community Technology Centers (CTCs) and related projects serving low-income and minority students nationwide. These include libraries, youth organizations, settlement houses, housing development centers, and stand-alone computing centers (Schwartz, 2003). Most of these after-school programs offer structured, directed instruction on basic computer operation, software application packages and basic internet use very much like the "point & click" vocational classes students encounter in their schools. Even those few offering a less structured environment, without pre-existing instructions or adult-led classes, focus on self-contained software packages, such as educational games and interactive storybooks. Hardly any program attempts to offer programming as part of their afternoon activities. Opportunities to learn about creative applications and programming in community technology settings are virtually absent.

Our presentations will focus on findings from two years of developing and implementing a new media-rich programming environment and activities in a Los Angeles community technology center (CTC) visited by a predominantly Latino/a and African-American youth ages 8-18. Unlike most schools, the guiding philosophy of our CTC had already cast a wider net around technology use and design by promoting access to technology fluency — in contrast to computer literacy — and by emphasizing personal expression as an essential catalyst for the learning and use of technology (NRC, 1999). The center, where children and youth are considered "members" (as opposed to students) of a learning community, encourages them to devise multi-media, multi-application activities that are founded upon their personal interests (Resnick, Rusk, & Cooke, 1998). Yet our initial observations at the site revealed that programming, unlike many other creative technologies, was not part of the members' activities.

Our framework which builds on Jeannie Oakes (1992) model examines the political, normative and technical dimensions that inform the introduction of technology fluency activities within the CTC. We address the "technical changes" such as the development of a new media-rich programming environment, approaches to mentoring, and new activities that are critical but not sufficient in introducing change. The *normative* dimensions address deep-seated beliefs about what kind of technology activities are appropriate for community members. Finally, the *political* dimensions focus on the cross-institutional relationships and alliances between the CTC and other organizations that are aimed at addressing the lack of technology fluency. These political changes are critical, in that they build necessary support for providing both the commitment and resources for the changes to occur, and to be sustained. Such analytical lenses are not often discussed within the learning sciences but they will help us understand the resistances and opportunities in changing activity structures and interaction processes.

Poster 1. **Designing Software to Foster Technological Fluency in Community-Based Learning Centers**. Mitchel Resnick, MIT

This poster will discuss the guiding principles underlying the design of a new programming environment, called Scratch, that is grounded in the practices and social dynamics of Computer Clubhouses, a network of after-school centers in low-income communities. Scratch adds programmability to the media-rich and network-based activities that have proven most popular among youth at Computer Clubhouses. With Scratch, kids can create new types of digital-arts projects, dynamically transforming images with Photoshop-like filters, mixing in sound clips and drum beats, and integrating inputs from real-world sensors. Scratch is designed to make computer programming more accessible and motivating, expanding the range of what Clubhouse members can design and create with computers, while also helping them learn important concepts and ways of thinking associated with computer programming.

Poster 2. **Creative Partnerships: New Approaches to Mentoring as Pathways towards Technology Fluency**. Yasmin B. Kafai, Kylie Peppler, Shiv Desai, and Grace Chiu, UCLA

This poster presents a recent intervention that introduced undergraduate mentors into programming and provided support for programming projects in CTCs. While community service learning (Vogelsang & Astin, 2000) is now considered an essential part of undergraduate education, it is seldom done with the intention of having undergraduates learn new skills — let alone advanced skills like programming — for the purposes of mentoring in a community technology center. Traditionally, one would expect to have computer science and not liberal arts majors mentoring young children in learning programming. However, we contend that inexperienced programmers are a valuable resource for members because the undergraduates are able to provide support and collaborate with members creating a more equitable partnership. We will present findings from an analysis of mentor/mentee interactions results from two undergraduate classes in the education minor that participated in this effort, highlighting their perceptions of mentoring and their relationship to technology before and after the intervention.

Poster 3. **Hook-ups: Integrated Physical and Virtual Design**. Amon D. Millner, MIT

This poster discusses a new initiative, called Hook-ups, that engages youth in multiple, integrated types of design activities. In working on Hook-ups projects, youth build physical input devices to control computer programs that they write themselves. The poster focuses on the relationships between three aspects of the Hook-ups building experience: collaboration, physical design, and virtual design. We present examples from diverse youth working on Hook-up projects at Computer Clubhouse after-school centers. Several cases are presented where learners work alone, in groups, and begin projects by planning or tinkering with physical or virtual objects. We also discuss design criteria for technical and social aspects of the Hook-ups project.

References

American Association of University Women (2000). *Tech-savvy: Educating girls in the new computer age.* Washington, DC: Educational Foundation of the American Association of University Women.

Attewell, P. (2001). *Children of the digital divide.* Paper presented at the annual meetings of the American Educational Research Association, New Orleans, USA.

Barron, B. (2004). Learning Ecologies for Technological Fluency: Gender and Experience Differences. *Journal of Educational Computing Research*, 31(1), 1-36.

Barron, B. (accepted for publication). Interest and self-sustained learning as catalysts of development: A learning ecologies perspective. To appear in *Human Development.*

Barron, B., Shatz, C. & Martin, C. (in preparation). Profiles of interest, access, and fluency building experience in Silicon Valley: When interest isn't enough. Manuscript in preparation.

Bryson, M., Petrina, S., de Castell, S., & Braundy, M. (2003)."Conditions for Success"?" Sex-disaggregated analysis of performance and participation indicators in technology-intensive courses in B.C. secondary schools. *Canadian Journal of Science, Mathematics and Technology*, 3, 185-195.

Bryson, M. & de Castell, S. (1996). Learning to make a difference: Gender, new technologies, and in/equity. *Mind, Culture and Activity*, 2(1), 3-21.

Camp, T. (1997). The incredible shrinking pipeline. *Communications of the ACM*, 40(10).

de Castell, S, & Bryson, M. (Eds.). (1997). Radical in<ter>ventions: Identity, politics, and difference/s in educational praxis. Albany, NY: SUNY Press.

Eccles, J. S., Adler, T. F., Futterman, R., Goff, S. B., Kaczala, C. M., Meece, J. L., et al. (1983). Expectancies, values, and academic behaviors. In J. T. Spence (Ed.), *Achievement and achievement motivation* (pp. 75-146). San Francisco: W. H. Freeman.

Gee, J. (2003). *What video games have to teach us about learning and literacy*. New York: Palgrave Macmillan.

Hawkins, J. (1985). Computers and girls: Rethinking the issues. *Sex Roles*, 13, 163–180.

Kaiser Family Foundation (2005). *Generation M: Media in the lives of 8-18 year olds.* Menlo Park, CA: Kaiser Family Foundation.

Nasir, N. (2002). Identity, Goals and Learning: Mathematics in Cultural Practice. *Mathematical Thinking and Learning*, 4(2 & 3), 213-247.

National Research Council (1999). *Being fluent with information technology.* A report of the Committee on Information Technology Literacy. Washington, DC: National Academy Press.

Oakes, J. (1992). Can tracking research inform practice? Technical, normative and political considerations. *Educational Researcher, 21*(4), 12-21.
Pew Reports. (2002). The digital disconnect: The widening gap between Internet-savvy students and their schools. Internet and American Life Project. Washington, DC. 4 August 2005. http://www.pewinternet.org/reports/toc.asp?Report=67.
Pinkard, N.(2005). How The Perceived Masculinity and/Or Femininity Of Software Applications Influences Students' Software Preferences In *Journal of Educational Computing Research*, 32, 57-78.
Resnick, M., Kafai, Y. B., & Maeda, J. (2003). *A Networked, Media-Rich Programming Environment to Enhance Technological Fluency at After-School Centers in Economically-Disadvantaged Communities*. Proposal (funded) to the National Science Foundation: Arlington, VA.
Resnick, M., Rusk, N., and Cooke, S. (1998). Computer Clubhouse: Technological fluency in the inner city. In D. Schon, B. Sanyal, and W. Mitchell (eds.), *High Technology and Low-Income Communities*. Cambridge: MIT Press.
Schwartz, W. (2003). After-school and community technology education programs for low-income families. New York: ERIC Clearinghouse on Urban Education. Retrieved on July 15th, 2005 at http://www.eric.ed.gov.
van Knippenberg, D. (2000). Work Motivation and Performance: A Social Identity Perspective. *Applied Psychology: An International Review*, 49(3), 357-371.
Vogelsang, L.J. & Astin, A. W. (2000). Comparing the effects of community service and service-learning. *Michigan Journal of Community Service Learning, 3*, 25-34.
Warschauer, M. (2000). Technology and school reform: A view from both sides of the track. *Educational Policy Analysis Archives*. 8(4).

Acknowledgements

Barron's research was supported by an NSF Early Career award (NSF REC – 0238524) and funds awarded through a Science of Learning Center grant from the National Science Foundation (NSF REC - 0354453), by an Iris Litt award, and by the International Collaborative Education Foundation. Kafai's research is conducted in collaboration with Mitchel Resnick's group at the MIT Media Lab and supported by a grant of the National Science Foundation (NSF-0325828). Joseph & Pinkard's work was supported by an NSF Early Career award granted to Pinkard (NSF-00333002) and by a grant from the John D. and Catherine T. MacArthur Foundation. The views expressed are those of the authors and do not necessarily represent the views of the supporting funding agencies or the host research institutions.

Understanding the cultural foundations of children's biological knowledge: Insights from everyday cognition research

Philip Bell, Leah A. Bricker, Tiffany R. Lee, Suzanne Reeve, Heather Toomey Zimmerman
Cognitive Studies in Education, University of Washington, Miller Hall Box 353600, Seattle, WA 98195
Email: {pbell, lbricker, tlee13, sreeve, htoomey}@u.washington.edu

Abstract: This session explores the cultural foundations of children's knowledge of the living world. Cognitive research on students' conceptual understandings has overly relied upon sequestered tasks and structured interviews; we argue that participant observation can provide insight into important particulars of everyday life to answer fundamental questions about the nature of children's learning of biology. These papers report on studies of the everyday cultural and social contexts in which children's informal ideas about the living world develop and are applied. The research employs a learner-centered focus and a cognitive ethnographic approach to explore children's knowledge as they utilize it in their homes, at school, and in an interactive science center. Research focuses on personally consequential biology topics including health, nutrition, and ecology. The papers report on the cultural experiences that shape children's biological knowledge and decision-making, similarities and differences between cultural groups, and implications for coordinating home and school experiences.

Introduction

In this session, we look at how interactions with images of nature across and within various social and discourse practices help constitute children's knowledge of the life sciences. Children are continually presented with images of nature and how it works through the foods they eat, books and advertisements they read, television shows they watch, and animals they keep as pets. School instruction can also provide extensive images of nature. This paper set explores the cultural foundations of children's knowledge of the living world based on their everyday experiences with images of biology, especially on topics of personal consequence like health, nutrition, and the local environment.

The *first symposium paper* looks at how the social practices of a community within and around one elementary school constitute images of and ideas about nutrition, health, and local environmental conditions for 4th and 5th grade children. Data come from student-teacher interactions around three in-school curriculum units, relevant in-school peer talk, and family activities involving health, food and nutrition. The *second paper* examines 4th and 5th grade students' argumentation practices to study how these students establish knowledge claims about biological topics through their talk and action. The *third paper* examines how K-6th grade children and their parents make sense of life science content in one science center, based on their shared experiences with scientific inquiry processes, with biology, and with each other. The analysis focuses on how families' knowledge is expressed through narrative, claims of expertise distributed among family members, and articulated gestures, some of which are taken to be embodied conceptual representations. *Professor Brian Reiser* (Northwestern University) will serve as the discussant for the symposium.

Nature of children's life sciences knowledge

Cognitive anthropologists and psychologists refer to people's non-scientific understandings of the natural world as *folk biology* or *naïve biology* (e.g., Hatano & Inagaki, 1999). Much has been written about various aspects of these understandings, including their developmental origins, conceptual structure, and the ages at which they are first acquired (e.g., Carey, 1985). Most of this work concerns folkbiological knowledge of children from ages 3-12, and most has been conducted in a cognitive psychological tradition, in which children's understandings are assessed on the basis of responses to structured interview questions and sequestered performance tasks. In contrast, the work we present here documents the knowledge and conceptual understandings of elementary-aged children in naturalistic settings and activities. We theoretically approach knowledge as being part of a conceptual ecology, where individuals' understandings are viewed as complex systems of diverse knowledge elements (diSessa, 2002). We elaborate this view by recognizing the social and material influences on such knowledge (Cole, 1996; Hutchins, 1995) and the distribution of intelligence that occurs in most natural settings (Pea, 1993). Accordingly, explanation or action is governed by a contextualized coordination of different knowledge elements, and the genesis of such knowledge derives from social, cognitive, and material experiences. This view contrasts significantly with more unitary cognitive architectures common in cognitive psychology that largely ignore social and cultural influences and posit that reasoning is contingent upon only a few kinds of knowledge. One of the challenges of a conceptual ecology perspective is trying to understand the developmental influences for a diverse constellation of knowledge elements. Our examinations of learning in situ allow for a more comprehensive accounting of the conceptual ecologies implicated in children's biology learning.

Methodological approach: Cognitive ethnography of everyday science learning

Little research in the cognitive literature has attempted to move beyond structured, sequestered tasks and interviews to directly understand the everyday cultural and social contexts in which children's informal ideas about the living world develop. We attempt to do this by linking observations of daily interactions to children's folk conceptions of biology and their understanding of classroom science instruction. Additionally, little work has looked at how children's social experiences with the same topics are linked across various settings—in order to understand the contributing influences of home, school, and community activities. As a result, many questions remain unanswered that are of vital importance to both formal and informal science instruction, such as: What role do home, community, and school situations play in young people's understandings of biology? Do children transfer their understanding of what is learned in school to what they do at home? How might children's knowledge differ as a function of socioeconomic status, ethnic background, or media and technology access? What role do institutions of informal learning, such as museums or interactive science centers, play in this process? The papers collected in this set have these questions as their focus.

These papers share a learner-centered focus and a cognitive ethnographic approach, deeply exploring children's knowledge about the living world as they express it in their homes, at school, and in an interactive science center. Researchers observed children in various social settings to understand the development of science-related discourse and social practices that are associated with an understanding of the life sciences. Data consist of field notes, ethnographic interviews, clinical interviews, video recordings of activities, and self-documented images taken by participants. All papers draw heavily upon transcribed sequences from audiotapes and video-recordings as evidence of specific findings.

Paper 1: The everyday cultural foundations of children's biological understanding in an urban high-poverty community by *Philip Bell, Leah A. Bricker, Tiffany R. Lee, Suzanne Reeve, & Heather Toomey Zimmerman, University of Washington*

Studies of human development and learning took an ethnographic turn over the past 15 years (Jessor, Colby, & Shweder, 1996). The aim of our research is to develop a theoretical framework that describes the cultural foundations of children's learning about biology across the activity systems of their lives. We focus our attention on biological topics that are highly relevant to upper elementary school children and their families, specifically personal health, nutrition, and local environmental conditions. In this analysis, we focus on how the social practices of a community within and around one elementary school constitute images of and ideas about health, nutrition, and local environment for fourth and fifth grade children.

The Everyday Expertise Theoretical Framework

Many theoretical frameworks have sought to account for cultural influences on development and learning (see Bransford et al, in press and Nasir, Rosenbery, Warren & Lee, in press for a discussion of a range of perspectives). In order to develop a more comprehensive accounting of science learning across cognitive, social, cultural, and affective dimensions, we are articulating a theoretical framework through everyday cognition research that recognizes and accounts for the profound influence of *culturally-patterned activity systems* on the development of children's *conceptual ecologies* as they participate in *peer and family ideocultures* (Fine, 1983) that are co-constituted through talk and activity. Situated activity systems are frequently dependent upon cultural resources, tools, and artifacts that broadly permeate society and are available uniquely at specific historical moments (cf. Swidler, 1986). Table 1 presents a high-level sketch of the Everyday Expertise Framework under development. The developmental processes frequently shape and co-constitute each other (e.g., epistemological knowledge shapes social interaction choices; resources of a cultural toolkit [e.g., specific technologies] shape possible situated activities; engagement in situated activity systems shapes knowledge).

Table 1: The Everyday Expertise Framework

Analytical Plane	*Conceptual Focus*	*Learning Phenomena*
individual	*Cognitive ecology:* conceptual & epistemological resources; interests, goals & motives	Range of knowledge and interests developed by individuals
social	*Situated activity systems:* Social and material actions performed within and across ideocultures	Social practices and interactional patterns used across settings; social network development and use
cultural	*Cultural toolkits:* Learning resources or tools available at a particular historical moment	Awareness and localized use of pervasive cultural products found in a society

We seek to document the cultural foundations of biological knowledge, including the variations that exist across segments of society. Some prior research on cultural learning processes essentialized findings to specific cultural groups or assigned learning traits to individuals from specific ethnicities. In contrast, we adopt the theoretical perspective that patterned everyday activities should be a primary unit of analysis, to allow for natural variance in labeled cultural groups and to allow individuals to develop idiosyncratic expertise based on routine experiences with particular activity systems (cf. Gutiérrez & Rogoff, 2003). Our cross-site ethnographic approach allows us to sample a broader range of children's activity systems related to their biology learning.

Research focus

Over a century ago, John Dewey (1900/1990) spoke about the need to connect formal education to everyday experiences. We still, however, know very little about the informal ideas students bring with them to the classroom, and which ideas learned in school they then incorporate into their everyday life. Researchers have argued that making such connections through the cultural dimensions of children's backgrounds will help promote social equity within urban educational systems (Barton, 2001). The research described in this paper contributes to bridging the gap between children's experiences in the home and community and their formal school instruction. We report on everyday cognition research conducted in specific cultural contexts, with a focus on how upper elementary school children develop an understanding of biology and the information used in health decision-making. This paper reports on the influence of the activities children engage in at home and in other non-school settings on their understanding of food, health, and nutrition and how that coordinates with what they are being asked to learn in school. Prior research on children's socialization has overemphasized children as 'adults in the making' (Kyratzis, 2004). However, peer micro-cultures serve important everyday functions for the children who constitute and maintain them, irrespective of the broader adult culture (Nespor, 1997).

In our study, we document the role of biological understanding within participants' peer and family micro-cultures (i.e., an emic perspective). We also analyze member knowledge from the perspective of imposed (etic) theoretical accounts. This dual emic-etic approach allows us to document how biological understanding serves children's own purposes as well as how it differs or fits with perspectives that derive from important social institutions (i.e., school and professional scientific communities).

Study design

Developmental research on informal biology has attempted to speak to the influence of everyday activities on understanding (e.g., Hatano & Inagaki, 1999), but an artifact of the typical research methodology—clinical interviewing and cognitive task performance—is that the research data can only speak indirectly to learning as it occurs in everyday settings. In contrast, we draw upon various ethnographic data sources to directly analyze family decisions and activities, peer interactions, and personal hobbies related to understanding biology. We employ participant observation in multiple settings (home, school, neighborhood), ethnographic interviewing, clinical interviewing, and self-documentation methods with elementary students from a high-poverty urban community in the Pacific Northwest—their families, peers, and classroom teachers. Participants attend an elementary school in a large city in the Pacific Northwest. Approximately 65% of the student body is Asian or Pacific Islander, 16% of the student body is Hispanic, 12% of the student body is African American, and 5% of the student body is Caucasian. Study participants were chosen to reflect this diversity in race/ethnic make-up, socioeconomic status, and the family's familiarity with science. Many of the children are from first-generation immigrant families, and during the

2004-2005 school year, 60% of the students qualified for free or reduced lunch. In this analysis, we focus on 4th and 5th grade students' student-teacher interactions around three relevant school curriculum units, relevant peer talk, and family activities involving health, food and nutrition.

Data analyses & findings

Given the everyday importance of biological literacy (as it relates to matters of personal health), we have documented the personal life repercussions for children's understanding of the living world. Within children's everyday learning experiences, we have also been documenting areas of alignment with academic pathways into science as well as areas where non-school activities may be at odds with such pathways. Our future goal is to help educators develop approaches and tools to connect home learning with school learning to minimize the gap between these two valuable educational settings. We discuss how everyday activities in some families and peer cultures have direct connections to academic science, yet show how the families and students may not consider these activities to be related to science. We report on these categories of findings and discuss specific educational implications.

Subsequent design experimentation research in the classrooms of these children will seek to engineer new innovations in science learning based on these cultural insights (Bell, 2004a). Cognitive research in education has strongly focused on orchestrating learning experiences in order to demonstrate specific learning gains before and after instruction. While important, much work remains to connect such cognitive measures to behavioral change in the myriad of everyday settings encountered by learners. This research is working toward establishing this bridge from engineered formal learning and sophisticated everyday cognition.

Paper 2: Children's everyday argumentation: Causal claim-making associated with everyday biological phenomena by *Leah Bricker & Philip Bell, University of Washington*

This paper focuses on future research directions for supporting scientific argumentation in science classrooms by arguing that we must take into account students' everyday argumentation practices. In keeping with the theme of this symposium, we specifically examine the causal claims children construct as explanations for biological phenomena encountered in their everyday lives. We focus—from both emic and etic perspectives—on the purposes of children's argumentation related to biological topics and issues, the linguistic skills (e.g., format tying, embodied argumentation) children use to craft arguments related to biological topics and issues, and how children use argumentation as a learning practice. We also examine the relationships between children's decision making and causal claim making practices.

Research purpose and theoretical framework

Argumentation is a central practice in science because it serves important epistemic functions (e.g., Bell, 2004b; Kelly and Bazerman, 2003). It is central to the development of scientific knowledge, and occurs within research groups and across scientific communities. In all cases, scientists use argumentation to critically examine each other's work by scrutinizing the links between specific evidence and the generalizations and claims that evidence purports to champion. Toulmin and colleagues (Toulmin, Rieke, Janik, 1984) discuss two types of scientific argumentation: regular and critical. *Regular scientific arguments* are the products of science — the phenomena under study and the scientific explanations generated to account for the workings of those phenomena or parts of them. An example of a regular scientific argument is that some human illnesses, such as the common cold, are caused by viruses. *Critical scientific arguments* are generated by scientists as a process of examining and analyzing regular scientific arguments for their plausibility, in light of the evidence used to support them. Examples of critical scientific arguments are found as part of the peer review process associated with scientific journal articles and as part of formal scientific conferences.

It is important to realize that scientists are not the only ones who routinely engage in argumentation. Argumentation is a well-established part of youth peer culture (Kyratzis, 2004). Young people are surrounded by argumentation in their everyday lives and are expert at producing and interpreting specific argument forms. For example, we know young people engage in argumentation in order to explore and hone their language capabilities (Goodwin & Goodwin, 1987) and to learn how to engage in theory building (Ochs, Taylor, Rudolph, and Smith, 1992). Young people's argumentation can also signify status within and allegiance to their peer culture (Corsaro, 2003). Knowing what argumentation knowledge and skill young people bring with them to their science classrooms based on everyday experiences is a critical piece absent from the work of most scholars, who advocate for structuring science education through an argumentation/explanation frame in order to make young people's science education experiences more representative of the discipline those experiences purport to model. For example, do children construct claims similar to regular scientific arguments? If so, do they employ practices similar to critical scientific arguments in order to evaluate their claims and those made by others? This paper reports on efforts to examine children's argumentation related to biological phenomena, with these research questions as a focus.

Methods and data sources

This study uses ethnographic methods. Research subjects are the children and families reported on in the first paper in this symposium. Focal participants were observed in the various contexts of their lives, including their school classrooms, homes, and recreational activity spaces. Data sources include: (1) field notes from observations of study participants in various contexts, (2) video recordings of study participants' argumentation practices in various contexts, (3) transcripts from both ethnographic and clinical interviews, and (4) photographs and written notes produced by participants, documenting what they labeled as argumentation in their everyday lives.

Findings and implications

Our findings support the claim that young people are indeed expert at producing and interpreting arguments across the various contexts of their lives, and they do make causal claims to explain some of the biological phenomena they encounter in their everyday lives. In some instances, children support their claims with evidence from their daily lives—evidence stemming from sources such as their experiences and people whom they deem to be authority figures (e.g., parents and teachers). Furthermore, it appears that children do use their argumentation practices to learn about biological topics and issues. For example, children construct arguments in order to clarify their understandings of biological issues such as nutrition, personal health, and the effects of pollutants on the environment. Instances of children making decisions, or weighing in on decisions being pondered by others, are documented, and links are established between decision making and argumentation practices.

We ultimately seek to use argumentation as an instructional platform for the learning of science. For this reason, we are currently documenting how everyday argumentation allows the participants to consider a broader repertoire of ideas, how it allows them to learn from the arguments of others, and how evidence is marshaled during the evaluation of arguments. In subsequent classroom-based research, we plan to use children's competencies with everyday argumentation to shape the design of instruction.

Paper 3: Understanding images of biology: Shared family experiences as sense-making processes in a science center by *Heather Toomey Zimmerman, Suzanne Reeve & Philip Bell, University of Washington*

Families across the United States seek out interactive science centers both as places of recreation and of education. These specialized museums provide opportunities for families to engage with science and with each other by various means. Our research project seeks to answer questions about the ways in which families understand and learn about scientific topics in their everyday lives, by studying in detail the interactions of families in one science center as they encounter and discuss various images of biology. We study how family members use their shared family resources and common experiences alongside the exhibit resources to make sense of life science content. The analysis focuses on how families' understandings of biology and of science are expressed through narratives, claims of expertise by various family members, questions posed, and articulated gestures, some of which are taken to be embodied conceptual representations.

Conceptual frame

We present our analysis from a study of fifteen experienced museum-going families as they interact with exhibits in one large science center in the Pacific Northwest. Our analysis has two goals. First, we examine the types of *learning processes* that families use to make sense of life sciences exhibit content. We focus on how families use shared experiences, family discourse styles, and narratives. Second, we look at the families' conversations for evidence of their *understanding of biology* through their theories, questions, and the evidence they use to explain their ideas. By looking at learning processes and interactions with images of biology, we hope to better understand the relationship between families' prior knowledge about the living world and what they learn through their science center visit. We employ the Everyday Expertise framework presented above to understand family learning in everyday situations.

Methodology

Research participants are families with at least one child between the ages of five and eleven years (kindergarten to 6th grade), who have sought out this science center not only for regular visits (as science center members) but also as a place of learning for their children in specialized programs. All families qualified for the study because they sent at least one elementary-aged child to a science center camp within the past year. For these reasons, we consider these families to be *practiced museum-goers*.

Cognitive ethnographic methods (e.g, Jessor, Colby, & Shweder, 1996) are used in the study in order to understand sense-making processes from the perspective of the family members. The data collection procedures entailed following families for one to two hours each at the science center, as they visited exhibits of their choice. Data come from pre- and post-visit interviews, video-taped observations of families during their museum visits, and fieldnotes. Content logs (Jordan & Henderson, 1995), which captured key moments of activity and discourse, were created from the videotapes to aid analysis. Two researchers used these logs and the video record to independently identify significant conversational episodes. They then created transcripts that described verbal and non-verbal interactions during the families' visits. The qualitative data analysis software Atlas.ti was used to develop emergent codes and for subsequent analysis from the field notes, transcripts, interview data, and content logs. Family conversations were analyzed with a discourse and interaction (Lemke, 1990) framework. In addition to emergent themes, the literature on learning in museums provided relevant codes for participants' discourse and actions (e.g., specific chapters in Leinhardt, G., Crowley, K. & Knutson, K., 2002).

Findings

Our findings show that family members use a variety of personal resources, such as narrative talk, humor, and connections to family experiences, as cognitive tools to make sense of the images of biology presented in the science center exhibits. Additionally, family members employ distributed expertise and complex individual conceptual ecologies in sense-making conversations. For example, in one ten-minute segment from a family's visit to a dinosaur exhibit, parents and children use a variety of ideas to understand both petrifaction of bone and dinosaur feeding, including references to popular culture and mythology, ideas about lava, foods the children eat, comparisons to other species, the etymology of word segments, humor in the form of word plays, and verbal reconstructions of a family vacation to a petrified forest. Our data also show that parental and child involvement in conversation is strongly influenced by their personal or professional involvement in the sciences. In a second family's visit to an insect display, the children's informal hobby of bug collecting shapes what the children know and do not know about insects and other arthropods. This interest also focuses the types of information the children and their mother seek out from the exhibit. In a third family, the parents' training and employment as biologists help them lead their young children through a genetics exhibit in ways that focus heavily on the life science content. A final finding is that, across cases, family members express their ideas about animals in a range of scientific and everyday (e.g., affective or aesthetic) ways. During one family's experience at a model tide pool, knowing about the life science content was not limited just to scientific understandings, but also encompassed emotive, aesthetic and tactile responses. Demonstrating knowledge through teaching others and through a performance were two key additional sense-making processes.

This interactional learning research contributes to the field by furthering what we know about how families understand science and education, how they learn science in museums, and how families interact with each other while working together on science activities. The results of the study will help us understand more about science learning in both formal and informal environments by looking for connections between family practices and formal science education practices in schools.

References

Barton, A.C. (2001). Science education in urban settings: Seeking new ways of praxis through critical ethnography. *Journal of Research in Science Teaching, 38*, 899-917.

Bell, P. (2004a). On the theoretical breadth of design-based research in education. *Educational Psychologist, 39*(4), 243-253.

Bell, P. (2004b). Promoting students' argument construction and collaborative debate in the science classroom. In M.C. Linn, E.A. Davis, and P. Bell (Eds.), *Internet environments for science education* (pp. 115-143). Mahwah, NJ: Erlbaum.

Bransford, J., Vye, N., Stevens, R. Kuhl, P. Schwartz, D. Bell, P., Meltzoff, A. Barron, B., Pea, R. Reeves,B., Roschelle, J. & Sabelli, N. (in press). Learning Theories and Education: Toward a Decade of Synergy In P.

Alexander & P. Winne (Eds.), *Handbook of Educational Psychology* (Second Edition). Mahwah, NJ: Erlbaum.
Bruner, J. (1987). *Actual minds, possible worlds*. Cambridge, MA: Harvard University Press.
Carey, S. (1985). *Conceptual change in childhood*. Cambridge, MA: Bradford/MIT Press.
Cole, M. (1996). *Cultural psychology: A once and future discipline*. Cambridge, MA: Belknap Press of Harvard University Press.
Corsaro, W.A. (2003). *We're friends right? Inside kids' culture*. Washington, DC: Joseph Henry Press.
Dewey, J. (1900/1990). *The school and society and the child and the curriculum*. Chicago, IL: University of Chicago Press.
diSessa, A. (2002). Why "conceptual ecology" is a good idea. In M. Limón & L. Mason (Eds.), *Reconsidering conceptual change: Issues in theory and practice* (pp. 29-60). Dortrecht: Kluwer.
Fine, G.A. (1983) *Shared fantasy: Role playing games as social worlds*. Chicago: University of Chicago Press.
Goodwin, M.H., & Goodwin, C. (1987). Children's arguing. In S.U. Phillips, S. Steele, & C. Tanz (Eds.), *Language, gender, and sex in comparative perspective* (pp. 200-248). Cambridge, UK: Cambridge University Press.
Gutiérrez, K., & Rogoff, B. (2003). Cultural ways of learning: Individual traits or repertoires of practice. *Educational Researcher, 22*(5), 19-25.
Hatano, G. & Inagaki, K. (1999). A developmental perspective on informal biology. In Medin, D.L. & Atran, S. (Eds.), *Folkbiology* (pp. 321-354). Cambridge, MA: MIT Press.
Hutchins, E. (1995). *Cognition in the wild*. Cambridge: MIT Press.
Jessor, R., Colby, A., & Shweder, R. A. (1996). *Ethnography and human development*. Chicago: The University of Chicago Press.
Jordan, B., & Henderson, A. (1995). Interaction analysis: Foundations and practice. *The Journal of the Learning Sciences, 4*(1), 39-103.
Kelly, G..J., & Bazerman, C. (2003). How students argue scientific claims: A rhetorical-semantic analysis. *Applied Linguistics, 24*(1), 28-55.
Kyratzis, A. (2004). Talk and interaction among children and the co-construction of peer groups and peer culture. *Annual Review of Anthropology, 33*, 625-649.
Leinhardt, G., Crowley, K. & Knutson, K (2002), *Learning conversations in museums* (pp. 259-304). Mahwah: Lawrence Erlbaum Associates.
Lemke, J. L. (1990). *Talking science: language, learning, and values*. Norwood, N.J.: Ablex Pub. Corp.
Nasir, N. S., Rosebury, A.S., & Lee, C.D. (2006, in press). Learning as a cultural process: Achieving equity through diversity. In K. Sawyer (Ed.), *Cambridge handbook of the learning sciences*. New York: Cambridge University Press.
Nespor, J. (1997). Intersections of kids, signs, and popular culture. *Tangled up in school: Politics, space, bodies and signs in the educational process* (pp. 162-195). Mahwah, NJ: Erlbaum.
Ochs, E., Taylor, C., Rudolph, D., & Smith, R. (1992). Storytelling as a theory-building activity. *Discourse Processes, 15*, 37-72.
Pea, R. D. (1997). Practices of distributed intelligence and designs for education. In Salomon, G., ed. *Distributed cognitions: Psychological and educational considerations*. Cambridge: Cambridge University Press.
Swidler, A. (1986). Culture in action: Symbols and strategies. *American Sociological Review, 51*(2), 273-286.
Toulmin, S., Rieke, R., & Janik, A. (1984). *An introduction to reasoning*, 2nd Edition. New York, NY: Macmillan Publishing Company.

Acknowledgments

This work has been conducted by members of the Everyday Science & Technology Group (http://everydaycognition.org/) as part of the Learning in Informal and Formal Environments (LIFE) Science of Learning Center (http://life-slc.org/). We gratefully acknowledge the intellectual influence of our LIFE colleagues and wish to thank the National Science Foundation for their support and for the opportunity (Award # 0354453). Of course, all opinions expressed are strictly our own.

Innovative Session: Early Childhood Robotics for Learning

Marina Bers, Chris Rogers, Laura Beals, Merredith Portsmore, Kevin Staszowski, Erin Cejka, Adam Carberry, and Brian Gravel, Tufts University, Medford, MA
Email: marina.bers@tufts.edu, chris.rogers@tufts.edu, laura.beals@tufts.edu, merredith.portsmore@tufts.edu, Kevin_joseph.staszowski@tufts.edu, erin.cejka@tufts.edu, adam.carberry@tufts.edu, brian.gravel@tufts.edu
Janice Anderson and Michael Barnett, Boston College, Newton, MA
Email: anderaab@bc.edu, barnetge@bc.edu

Abstract: Robotics is a powerful learning manipulative for young children (four through seven years) as it enables the early introduction of engineering and programming. This session begins with a theoretical introduction to the robotic technology of programmable LEGO® bricks and its relationship to developmentally appropriate practice. This will be followed by an interactive poster and demonstration session where participants can learn about and discuss different research projects using robotics in early childhood education, including: fostering interactions between parents and children; promoting problem-solving skills; engaging teachers with different teaching styles; innovative partnerships between pre-service teachers, in-service teachers, and engineers; innovative curriculum projects using this technology; and the use of robotics with special needs students. A table with LEGO bricks and computers with ROBOLAB™ software will be available so participants can explore the materials in a hands-on workshop environment. After the presentations, the session organizer will lead an open discussion.

Objectives of the Session

This session aims to introduce a research program that uses an educational technology that has a broad range of applications for early childhood in classrooms as well as in after-school settings and programs. The technology, programmable robotic LEGO bricks, is comprised of two parts: (1) physical robotic LEGO pieces, and (2) ROBOLAB programming software. The robotics pieces include traditional LEGO pieces, a microcomputer (called an RCX), motors, lamps, light sensors, touch sensors, wires, axles, and gears. ROBOLAB is a drag-and-drop graphical interface that has several levels of difficulty, so the user can tailor the functions that are available to their personal skills and developmental stage (Resnick, et al, 1996; Portsmore, 1999). Research methodologies used with this technology and research findings about this technology will be presented via the posters, and the open-ended discussion that concludes the session. The open-ended discussion will include implications for classroom practice, pre-service and in-service teacher education, home-school connections, curriculum development, integration of new technologies in the classroom, and new methods of data collection.

Session Format

For this interactive session, a set of posters highlighting research projects using robotics in early childhood will be provided along with demonstrations of the technology and videos of the technology being used. To open the session, however, the session organizer will give a short introduction to the technology and area of research (as summarized below), then there will be time for people to circulate the room—viewing the six posters (as described below) and asking questions—followed by an open discussion moderated by the session organizer. The LEGO brick materials and the ROBOLAB programming software will be available on a table so that participants in the session will have an opportunity to explore and gain a better understanding of the technology used in all of these research projects. Resources for additional learning will be provided at the end of the session.

Introduction: Early childhood and robotics

The use of technology as an educational tool is becoming widespread. The use of traditional manipulatives as a teaching aid is evident at the youngest ages—most early childhood settings have building bricks, Pattern Blocks, Cuisenaire Rods, etc. in order to allow students to build, design, experiment, and be creative (Brosterman, 1997). "Digital manipulatives" are now supplementing traditional hands-on materials, but they also afford students the opportunity to explore ideas and concepts beyond what traditional manipulatives can provide (Resnick, 1998).

The use of robotic manipulatives can serve as an ideal hands-on tool for children to learn about science, technology, engineering, and math (STEM) concepts. Children can explore traditionally abstract concepts such as gears, levers, joints, motors, and sensors in a concrete manner. While using robotic materials, children can learn STEM concepts—which are traditionally taught through boring and uninspired means—in a fun and creative way by engaging in their own design projects. This type of work with the robotic LEGO bricks is done in the sprit of "constructionism," which conceives the computer as a material to build and design with (Papert, 1980). Bers identified four pillars of educational experiences designed within a constructionist framework: (1) the potential of technological environments to help learners learn by doing, by actively inquiring, and by playing, (2) the importance of objects for supporting the development of concrete ways of thinking and learning about abstract phenomena, (3) the need for powerful ideas that span across different areas of the curriculum, and (4) the premium of self-reflection which engages learners in meta-cognition (Bers, Ponte, Juelich, Vera, & Schenker, 2002). These four pillars are consistent with developmentally-appropriate practice in early childhood settings (Bredekamp, 1997). The introduction to the session will present this theoretical work and implications for classroom practice, teacher education, home-school connection, curriculum development, integration of new technologies in the classroom, and research methods.

Poster 1: Fostering a Home-School Connection Through Robotics

New technologies are slowly making it into the early childhood classroom; however, many families expose their children to these technologies before they encounter them in the formal school setting. Thus many parents serve as the first teachers of technological literacy to their children. Or, as is more frequent, parents and children learn together new computational skills. What are the complexities hidden behind this learning process in which both adults and children are learning at the same time?

In response to these questions, Project Inter-Actions was designed (Bers, New, & Boudreau 2004). The study was developed to examine: (a) the interactions between children and parents as they both learn a new technology and as they work together to create personally meaningful projects; (b) the interactions between an abstract technology, such as a computer program, and a concrete technology, such as LEGO bricks; (c) the interactions between the technological ability of young children and the developmental appropriateness of technology for young children; and (d) the interactions between technology, art, and culture. This, study, called "Project Inter-Actions" was also developed with three major educational philosophies and concepts in mind: (a) the philosophy of constructionsim (Papert, 1993), (b) the concept of the zone of proximal development (Vygostky, 1978), and (c) the concept of peer learning environments (Blumenfeld, Marx, Soloway, & Krajcik, 1996).

For this study, 17 parent-child dyads and 20 first and second grade children were taught, during five weekend sessions, to use robotic programmable LEGO bricks to create their own meaningful final projects involving both programming and building components. The programmable LEGO kits are especially ideal as support for constructionism because students can explore abstract thoughts, ideas, and designs with concrete materials. Based on the four pillars of constructionism (Bers, et al., 2002), Project Inter-Actions workshops were designed to allow participants to learn with hands-on, fun activities with concrete materials, to explore powerful ideas, and to allow participants opportunities for self-reflection upon their projects.

In order to analyze Project Inter-Actions, four main data sources were used: (1) videotapes of the workshops, (2) "memos" that were written by every instructor at the end of each session, (3) photographs and descriptions of the final projects written by the participants and posted on the project website, and (4) pre- and post-questionnaires that were completed by all participants (and the parents of participants in the children-only sessions). Using these data sources, final projects were evaluated by the teachers/researchers by developing a scoring system which evaluated building and programming skills displayed by the projects.

A significant difference was found between building and programming aspects of final projects between the children-only projects and the parent-child projects (Beals & Bers, in press). This suggests that Vygotzky's zone of proximal development played an important role, but it is argued that the children in the parent-child groups did not learn as much as the children in the children-only groups, as the parents were too involved in their own learning and did not tailor their instruction to their children at a level appropriate for the children to understand. The findings from this study will shed light over different ways in which parents and children can spend time together learning something new—learning about a new technology is part of a larger picture of collaborative family learning, Children's fascination with new technologies provide a unique opportunity to engage families in learning together. However, just as teachers go through years of school to learn how to teach, the more opportunities parents have to learn with their children, the better their collaboration will become.

Poster 2: Exploring the impact of an engineering design curriculum on first grade students' problem solving strategies

This presentation describes a newly developed research project that focuses on exploring how engineering design activities impact students' problem-solving abilities. The presentation will identify the need for engineering education in early elementary education and explore the toolset that Tufts University's Center for Engineering Educational Outreach (CEEO) has selected for bringing engineering activities to young children. The methods of data collection that have been piloted in the research project will be described, preliminary conclusions will be presented, and issues and difficulties will be discussed.

While it is clear that successfully completing engineering projects requires problem-solving skills, it is not obvious whether students develop those problem-solving skills through their participation in open-ended design challenges. This presentation reports on a pilot study conducted with five first-grade classrooms in a suburban Boston school district (approximately 40 students) to implement 12 weeks of a curriculum entitled *Engineering by Design*. *Engineering by Design* is a sequence of activities that introduces mechanical concepts like structures, gears, and pulleys as well as engineering design ideas, such as constraints, testing, and redesign, to young children through open ended LEGO-based challenges. Projects range from constructing a chair for a stuffed animal to building a motorized snowplow. The goal of the activities is to increase students' exposure to engineering concepts and integrate key math and science concepts. In addition, *Engineering by Design* seeks to enhance their competence and confidence in problem solving. However, to date there are no developed assessment methods that aim to evaluate if the curriculum impacts students' problem solving.

Two of the classrooms serve as intervention classrooms by participating in *Engineering by Design* for the first few weeks of school while the remaining classrooms serve as the control (and will complete the activities later in the year). The pre- and post-testing is conducted during one-on-one interviews during which the student is asked to perform an engineering problem solving task (rescue a toy from an enclosure, retrieve keys from a box). These interviews are video-taped and coded for strategies used, number of attempts, response to success or failure, and persistence. In addition, the interactions in the intervention classroom are also video-taped and students' classroom work (journals, creations) is collected. Parents also complete a survey on their child's interests, experiences, and choices in play. Finally, teachers assess each student's competence with respect to grade level for major subject areas (reading, mathematics). Results from these assessments (which are only in their pilot stage) will be presented as well as the issues of reliability and validity that have arisen.

Poster 3: Simple Machines, Complex Style—Teaching Methodology in a ROBOLAB Environment

Even though ROBOLAB technology is being integrated into educational settings, teachers have received little training on how to effectively teach with this technology. The objective of this research project was to determine the instructional benefits and challenges associated with the interaction between teaching style and an early-childhood robotics curriculum. A group of first- and second-grade children participated in one of two week-long ROBOLAB workshops. The curriculum used in these workshop introduced children to the building and programming components of the LEGO robotic and ROBOLAB technologies and the concept of simple machines. One session of the workshop was taught with an emphasis on a child-centered, constructionist philosophy of teaching, while a teacher-directed, didactic philosophy was emphasized in the second session of the workshop. Otherwise, the curriculum covered the same materials and ideas in each workshop. Data presenting differences both within and between the two workshop groups will be presented as well as the innovative method for data collection.

Poster 4: Innovative Teaching Partnerships: Bringing engineering into elementary school classrooms through collaboration

Bringing robotics into elementary classrooms (PreK–4) places new demands on teachers regarding content knowledge, teaching style, pedagogical beliefs, and general classroom management. Engaging 25 young children in hands-on design challenges that interface with battery-powered microprocessors that can be programmed on a computer is a daunting challenge for any educator. This project describes innovative partnerships between engineering students and members of industry with pre-service and in-service teachers to provide these educators with the support and resources they need to engage in meaningful, open-ended projects.

STOMP and I-STOMP

STOMP (Student Teacher Outreach Mentorship Program) was developed at Tufts University to leverage the resources of engineering students to aid teachers in bringing engineering activities to their classrooms. STOMP uses the model of a two-way mentorship—where engineering students are helping teachers to learn about engineering content and the teachers are helping the engineering students learn about education and how to interact with young students. The outcome of this two-way mentorship is a teacher who is more knowledgeable and confident about using engineering activities in his or her classroom and an engineering student who is aware of the educational and societal issues in engineering and the need for early engineering education. The program does not seek to transform engineers into educators but to help them understand the issues in education so that as future leaders of industry and as voting citizens they can make informed decisions to support education. To date, the STOMP program has had over 60 engineering students supporting 40 K–12 teachers and an estimated 1800 K–12 students. The STOMP model is being used to create similar outreach programs at other universities and modified for use in high school as well.

Industrial STOMP (I-STOMP) works with engineering and technology companies to encourage, train, and support employee classroom volunteers. The employee volunteers—majority of whom are engineers—help teachers bring hands-on LEGO robotics activities that focus on developing math, science, technology, and engineering skills into the classroom. Currently, the program includes two major engineering companies with volunteers in central Texas elementary schools and British primary schools. In addition to supporting the teachers, the industry volunteers serve as mentors for the elementary students and bring real-world engineering experience into the classrooms.

Collaborative Classes: Pre-Service Elementary School Teachers and First Year Engineering Students

Pre-service elementary school teachers at Tufts, in one of their courses, focus on developing innovative curriculum in math and science and tackle the question of how to integrate new technologies in their classrooms. Typically, this course can be frustrating because the pre-service teachers need a great deal of support at the university and in the classroom environment. The instructor of the course generally has limited resources to help each student work on a meaningful project that allows them to grapple with the issues of math, science and technology. Meanwhile across campus, a class offered through the College of Engineering teaches first-year engineering students basic robotics and the engineering design process. Here the instructor grapples with providing the students with an authentic design process that allows them to create something for a "real" client.

A solution to both instructors' dilemmas is pairing pre-service teachers and first-year engineering students together to work on developing a robotic technology-based lesson. The pre-service teachers focus on the educational content and how to engage the students in a lesson while the engineering students focus on how to design and develop supporting technology. This collaboration gives each group purpose and expertise while allowing them opportunities to develop communication and project management skills. The result of these collaborations have ranged from robotic cars that move up and down the number line to a robotic "Simon Says" that allowed children to explore patterns and simple machines. This presentation will discuss results from this collaboration.

Poster 5: Innovative Curriculums and Tools: From ROBOTables to Underwater Robotics

As Lego robotic technology becomes more widespread in schools, educators are challenged to develop new and innovative curriculums to continue to engage students in learning. Three new tools and related curriculums are presented: (a) underwater robotics, (b) ROBOTable, and (c) stop-action moviemaking (SAM). These tools and curriculums are able to be scaled for use in early-childhood classrooms up to college-level courses.

Underwater Robotics

The CEEO is developing a curriculum for underwater robotics that will give hands-on experiences for elementary students to explore concepts such as buoyancy, propulsion, and water properties. Underwater robotic activities allow students to experiment with many types of materials to explore how boats and submarines work. This new curriculum is early in its developmental stages, but has gained much interest and attention from both teachers and students. A number of underwater activity possibilities giving early elementary students an opportunity to design and build submersible vehicles will be presented.

The ROBOTable

The ROBOTable is a frosted glass or Plexiglas tabletop that acts as a rear-projection screen. Through a mounted projector below the table, an extended computer screen is projected on to the table via a mirror below (see Figure 1). The table uses video conferencing capabilities, a camera to track objects and user interactions, and an Internet connection for sharing data with other ROBOTables. Through the table, users can see two-dimensional projections of remote robots while they navigate the tabletop with their own robot.

Figure 1. ROBOTable set-up.

Development of the ROBOTable is progressing in two areas. The first is to create a self-contained learning environment for training industry professionals, teachers, and volunteers for mentorship and outreach work in schools. The aim is to familiarize teachers with engineering and engineers with teaching by practicing with pre-designed activities from an online database. The second is to create a distance-learning tool for communication, collaboration, and real-time competition. Participants at different geographic locations can share an activity or compete in the same shared workspace. Both goals can be realized by producing an interactive learning environment that is enhanced by judiciously including new technologies such as augmented reality (AR) and tangible user interface (TUI) devices. Five example activities have been developed aimed at assisting the user in learning how to build with LEGO bricks and program in ROBOLAB.

Stop-Action-Movies (SAM)

SAM is stop action movie making software that gives students the chance to make simple animations as a way to explore and share ideas. By taking single-frame images and controlling the speed at which they are played back, we empower students to make scientifically and mathematically accurate predictions of phenomena prior to experimentation or design. With robotics, students can make (a) predictions of how a robot will behave under certain conditions, (b) kinematic predictions of specific robot actions, or (c) an animation demonstrating what their robots can do. The power comes in allowing students to control time and thus demonstrate things through animation that may be difficult with video. For younger students, simply using the concept of demonstrating understanding in animation format offers another mode of expression but also a window for the teacher, researchers, etc. into what the student understands. For example, say a student is asked to make a movie explaining the "reasons for the seasons." To effectively display this concept through an animation, the student must have a certain understanding of the content. With traditional written deliverables, students can copy what they have heard or read elsewhere. With an animation, the chance of them producing something simply from memory is quite rare. Thus the animation they produce will essentially be their personal understanding of the content at hand.

The actual process of making the animation also forces students to examine their beliefs on the subject. Building and watching the movie allows them to critique their own understanding—if something does not look "right" in the movie, they will either change their thought to match what they observed or change the movie to match their prior understanding. With robotics, SAM can be used as a method for younger students to communicate what their robot does. The relative ease-of-use in making single-frame animations makes this approachable for students of younger ages. In one school local to the CEEO, fourth-grade students animations explaining the phases of the moon to second graders. While there were some misconceptions in these animations, the students spent a longer time thinking more critically with the content than with the traditional written methods of reporting. This tool is an alternative media for students that provides a new dimension for sharing their knowledge with fellow students, teachers, parents, and others.

Poster 6: Using Activity Theory and Situated Cognition to Analyze and Describe Special Needs Students Understanding of Engineering Design Principles Through LEGO Robotics

This paper represents a pilot study of a LEGO Robotics Curriculum which is currently being used to teach the Engineering Design Principles that are presently tested on the Massachusetts Comprehensive Assessment System (MCAS) to a group of special needs students in grades one through five at the Chamberlain Elementary School (pseudonym) in Allston-Brighton, Massachusetts. The curriculum represents the current trend to move away from the traditionalist models of learning that are more didactic in their approach. Instead of conceptualizing knowledge and learning as being transmitted from the teachers to students, a social constructivist approach, with students emerging as active participants in their own learning experiences, has emerged.

Two special needs classes at Chamberlain Elementary were used in the study. Class A consisted of six students, all male, in a special needs class for grades one through three. Class B consisted of twelve students, eleven boys and one girl, in a fourth and fifth grade special needs class. These classes met with the science specialist once a week on Friday afternoons for fifty minutes.

This naturalistic inquiry study utilizes a mixed methodological approach with grounded interpretations (Guba & Lincoln, 1983). Quantitative surveys and drawings as well as qualitative ethnographic data was collected over a several month period of time through direct observation and field notes directed at specific groups participating in the activity. Activity theory was used as both the theoretical lens and tool of analysis in this study. The relation of the participant and the object as it was mediated by the components of the activity system were examined.

The preliminary data suggests that it is important to begin to look at the complexities of the dynamics of the LEGO robotic activity that exist. The dualities or tensions that arise may lead to outcomes which have not been anticipated as was seen in the Student / Classroom tensions and the Group A / Group B interaction tensions. These experiences will alter how future studies are situated. Additionally, it is important to harness tensions in order to analyze how they affect classroom culture and learning goals.

Additional Resources

Tufts University Center for Engineering Educational Outreach (CEEO): www.ceeo.tufts.edu

Developmental Technologies, Eliot-Pearson Department of Child Development, Tufts University: http://ase.tufts.edu/devtech/

Urban Sciences Research and Learning Group, Boston College: http://www2.bc.edu/%7Ebarnetge/urslg/urslhome.html

References

Beals, L., & Bers., M. (in press). Robotic technologies: When parents put their learning ahead of their child's. *Journal of Interactive Learning Research.*

Bers, M. U., Ponte, I., Juelich, K., Viera, A., & Schenker, J. (2002). Teachers as designers: Integrating robotics into early childhood education. *Information Technology in Childhood Education Annual, 2002*(1), 123–145.

Bers, M, New, B. & Boudreau, L (2004) "Teaching and learning when no one is expert: Children and parents explore technology" Journal of Early Childhood Research and Practice.

Bredekamp, S, Copple, C (1997) *Developmentally Appropriate Practice in Early Childhood Programs: Serving Children from Birth to Eight.* NAYEC Position Statement NAYEC, Washington, D.C.

Blumenfeld, P. C., Marx, R. W., Soloway, E., & Krajcik, J. (1996). Learning with peers: From small group collaboration to collaborative communities. *Educational Researcher, 25*(8), 37–40.

Brosterman, N. (1997). *Inventing Kindergarten*. New York: Harry N. Adams Inc.

Guba, E. G., & Lincoln, Y. S. (1983). Epistemological and methodological bases of naturalistic inquiry. In G. F. Madaus, M. S. Scriven, & D. L. Stufflebeam (Eds.), *Evaluation models: Viewpoints on educational and human services evaluation* (pp. 311–334). Boston: Kluwer-Nijhoff Publishing.

Papert, S. (1980). *MINDSTORMS: Children, Computers, and Powerful.* NY: Basic Books

Papert, S. (1993). *The children's machine: Rethinking school in the age of the computer.* New York, NY: Basic Books.

Piaget, J., & Inhelder, B. (1969). *The Psychology of the Child.* New York: Basic Books, Inc.

Portsmore, M. (Spring/Summer 1999). ROBOLAB: Inuitive robotic programming software to support life long learning. *APPLE Learning Technology Review,* 26–39.

Resnick, M., Bruckman, A., & Martin, F. (1996). "Pianos Not Stereos: Creating Computational Construction Kits". *Interactions*, vol. 3, no. 6, pp. 41-50.

Resnick, M. (1998). "Technologies for Lifelong Kindergarten. " *Educational Technology Research and Development*, vol. 46, no. 4.

Vygotsky, L. M. (1978). *Mind in society: The development of higher psychological processes.* Cambridge, MA: Harvard University Press.

Whither Education Research? Science Policy Implications of NSF Research Support

John C Cherniavsky, Janice Earle, Hari Narayanan, National Science Foundation, 4201 Wilson Blvd, Room 855, Arlington VA 2230
jchernia@nsf.gov, jearle@nsf.gov, nnarayan@nsf.gov
Roy Pea, Stanford University, Wallenberg Hall, Building 160, Stanford CA, roy.pea@stanford.edu
John Bransford, University of Washington, College of Education, 210 Miller Hall, Seattle WA, bransj@u.washington.edu
Marcia Linn, University of California Berkeley, 4611 Tolman, Berkeley CA 95720, mclinn@berkeley.edu

Abstract: This session addresses policy implications of NSF support for the learning sciences. The session is organized around recent activities of NSF in the support of the learning sciences. The first presentation will address the report Cyberinfrastructure for Education and Learning for the Future and how the Learning Science community can respond to the research challenges in this report. A second theme will be a retrospective look at the Interagency Education Research Initiative and the Centers for Learning and Teaching programs and their affect on practice. A third presentation addresses the appropriateness of the core individual researcher programs in learning science at NSF. The final presentation will review some of the newly funded Science of Learning Centers from the researchers' perspectives. Discussions within this innovative session will revolve around science policy issues of funding learning science research in a constrained environment and the affect of that funding on research and practice.

Introduction

This innovative session is planned to generate discussion on the affect of NSF support on research and practice in the learning sciences. Lead discussants familiar with the NSF programs, as researchers, will introduce four topics from the NSF learning science research portfolio spanning the range from individual research support to large centers. Moderated discussions will revolve around two issues:

- Has the research supported by NSF lead to either innovations in practice or to innovations in advancing learning science?
- What should the future support of Learning Sciences look like?

The session is organized around four themes: the CELF report (CRA, 2005) *Cyberinfrastructure for Education and Learning for the Future*; an assessment of two programs (the Interagency Education Research Initiative and the Centers for Learning and Teaching) that were intended to fund research that would affect practice; an assessment of the two main NSF programs supporting learning science research (the Advanced Learning Technologies program and the Research on Learning and Education program); an early assessment of the Science of Learning Centers.

Cyberinfrastructure for Education and Learning for the Future

The CELF report is the result of an NSF sponsored set of workshops whose purpose was to determine the role of education research in the context of cyberinfrastructure (Atkins, 2003). The workshops were sponsored by the Computing Research Association and the Society for Learning Sciences and were organized around four themes: *Modeling, Simulation and Gaming Technologies Applied to Education; Cognitive Implications of Virtual or Web-Enabled Environments; How Emerging Technology and Cyberinfrastructure Might Revolutionize the Role of Assessment in Learning; and The Interplay Between Communities of Practice and Cyberinfrastructure.* The report is organized around the themes of *Blending Formal and Informal Learning; Lifelong Learning Chronicles; Teaching Through Cyberinfrastructure; and Communities of Learners* with a final section on *Educational Policy and Cyberinfrastructure*. Numerous policy and research recommendations to the learning science community on how cyberinfrastructure will enable new research and raise new challenges to the learning science research community were presented.

A new Office of Cyberinfrastructure (OCI) has been established at NSF. The establishment of this Office gives opportunities to the Learning Science community to participate in cyberinfrastructure activities. The responsibilities of this office are described below (from the NSF Web Site):

- The Office of Cyberinfrastructure coordinates and supports the acquisition, development and provision of state-of-the-art cyberinfrastructure resources, tools and services essential to the conduct of 21st century science and engineering research and education.
- OCI supports cyberinfrastructure resources, tools and related services such as supercomputers, high-capacity mass-storage systems, system software suites and programming environments, scalable interactive visualization tools, productivity software libraries and tools, large-scale data repositories and digitized scientific data management systems, networks of various reach and granularity and an array of software tools and services that hide the complexities and heterogeneity of contemporary cyberinfrastructure while seeking to provide ubiquitous access and enhanced usability.
- OCI supports the preparation and training of current and future generations of researchers and educators to use cyberinfrastructure to further their research and education goals, while also supporting the scientific and engineering professionals who create and maintain these IT-based resources and systems and who provide essential customer services to the national science and engineering user community.

Interagency Education Research Initiative

The Interagency Education Research Initiative (IERI) is a three agency (NSF, NIH, and the Department of Education) program designed to fund projects that investigated education innovations at scale. The intent of the program was to develop a research capacity to investigate innovations, which were shown to work in small contexts, in large contexts (e.g. from classrooms to school districts; from districts to states; etc.). This program was unique within NSF as no other program had explicit research goals of both doing scale-up and studying the process of scale-up for research on learning in K-12. The program invested more than $150 million over its 6 years in this type of research. As part of the IERI program, the Data Resources and Development Center (DRDC) was established at NORC, a research center at the University of Chicago. This center has acted as a synthesis for the activities of the IERI grantees and it has compiled two books (forthcoming from Rowman and Littlefield Publishing) that have resulted from Program work. *Scale-up in Principle* suggests that education researchers would benefit from interactions from researchers in other fields (engineering or health, e.g.) and creates new frameworks for thinking about what it means to "scale up" in schools and districts. *Scale-up in Practice* draws on the work of the IERI investigators and describes how to design and conduct studies that provide compelling evidence of an intervention's impact in school settings and how to implement a specific intervention with fidelity once it as been tested. Below are two examples of IERI projects and some of their findings:

> *Modeling Across the Curriculum* (Paul Horwitz, Concord Consortium)
>
> This project is developing learning tools that enable students' to visualize and understand complex scientific phenomenon. The tools are easy to use, easy to incorporate into curriculum, and freely distributed. The simulations cover all of high school science ranging from biology to chemistry to physics. The study is in its fourth year and longitudinal results are just beginning to be reported. The simulations are being used in curricula affecting more than 200 high schools in high school science classes around the country.
>
> As an example, initial results using chemical reaction simulations within the *Connected Chemistry* curriculum show significant score gains for those students using the simulations as opposed to those students not using the simulations. These simulations are freely available on the web at *http://www.concord.org/downloads/*. Additional longitudinal studies are being conducted to further understand the properties of the simulations that contribute most to learning science.
>
> *An Evaluation of Teacher Training for Triarchic Instruction and Assessment* (Robert Sternberg, Yale University)
>
> This project directly addresses the training of teachers of science and mathematics to better enable their students to learn. Triarchic cognitive theory posits that individuals learn in three modalities, analytic

thinking, creative thinking, and practical thinking and that these modes of learning are present in all learners, but in different concentrations. Triachic instruction is instruction that builds upon each modality – for example in learning addition of whole numbers there would be a combination of analytic instruction (number tables and addition algorithms), creative (e.g. working with manipulatives) instruction, and practical (e.g. real world problem solving) instruction. The theory, validated in small studies, says that building upon all three modalities improves learning especially when instruction is tailored to each individuals preferred modalities.

The project studied a Triarchic instruction intervention for teachers (12 hours in the summer) to enable them to utilize the triarchic theory in their own lessons. The study had three interventions – triarchic, a memory based/analytic intervention, and a critical thinking intervention. Strong gains were made under all three interventions with the triarchic intervention having the best gains.

This study involved 196 teachers and 7702 students. It spanned four years, 9 states, 14 school districts, and 110 schools. The participating districts spanned the spectrum of social and economic status. The samples included primarily classrooms of fourth-graders, but also included third- and fifth- graders who were taught by teachers participating in the study with their fourth-graders.

The project results demonstrated how a theoretical model could be translated into educational practices with proven learning gains, inexpensively, that meet national and state standards in reading, science, and mathematics.

Centers for Learning and Teaching

The Centers for Learning and Teaching (CLT) program focuses on the advanced preparation of science, technology, engineering, and mathematics (STEM) educators, as well as the establishment of meaningful partnerships among education stakeholders, especially Ph.D.-granting institutions, school systems, and informal education performers. Its goals are to renew and diversify the cadre of leaders in STEM education; to increase the number of K-16 educators capable of delivering high-quality STEM instruction and assessment; and to conduct research into STEM education issues of national import (e.g., the nature of learning, teaching strategies, and reform policies and outcomes). The effect of these programs on practice are just now being assessed and both CLT and IERI have gathered a considerable amount of information about working with schools and about working at a larger scale. This session will take a retrospective look at how these programs affected practice and a discussion of the overall need for such programs.

Technology Enhanced Learning in Science (TELS). (Marcia Linn, UC Berkeley). TELS is a partnership that includes UC Berkeley, Arizona State, Penn State, Mills College, Technion, Concord Consortium, Norfolk State, and North Carolina State along with school district partners in Cambridge and Maynard (MA), Tempe (AZ), Mount Diablo and Berkeley (CA) and Durham (NC). TELS creates resources so that the field can investigate the impact of technology on science learning and instruction. The Center has created resources for teachers, defined a research agenda, and conducted investigations to advance the agenda. Resources produced to date include:

- Technologies. TELS merged WISE (UC Berkeley) and Pedagogica (Concord Consortium) to offer the research community a platform for design, development and delivery of inquiry science curricula that includes dynamic visualizations and models.
- Benchmark Assessments and Knowledge Integration Rubric. Working with teachers, TELS identified science topics that perplex students, align with standards, and could benefit from visualizations and models. Twelve topics were selected and for each topic TELS designed assessments that tapped the integrated understanding shown to lead to learning from prior research.
- Curriculum Projects. Inquiry activities were designed for each of the twelve topics using the TELS technologies.
- Design Principles Database. The database includes features from over 50 technology-enhanced innovations.
- Perspectives. To build on research in the field, each of the twelve partnerships reviewed the research on their topic and created a short perspective written for a general audience to identify the

challenges of learning the topic, the common intuitions students bring to sciences classes, and any relevant prior research along with promising directions for design.

- Collaborative Courses. Courses are jointly designed for postdoctoral scholars, fellows, and researchers. In 2004 the course was on Metacognition and Technology.
- Research Agenda. TELS participants have identified six research themes: science curriculum design, scientific modeling and visualization, knowledge integration assessment, professional and leadership development, science learning for diverse contexts and populations.

Center on Assessment and Evaluation of Student Learning (CAESL). (Steve Schneider, WestEd). CAESL is a collaboration with WestEd, Stanford, UC Berkeley, UCLA and the Lawrence Hall of Science. The partnership also includes several California school districts. CAESL focuses on improving science teaching and learning through the informed use of quality assessments. The Center also builds the knowledge base through creating a set of resources for practitioners, researchers, parents, and policymakers. The Center,

- Develops professional capacity for assessment and evaluation professionals through the development masters and doctoral programs.
- Provides professional development in assessment for practicing science teachers.
- Promotes in-depth assessment training for preservice teachers.
- Conducts research and development on formative assessment. And
- Makes outreach to parents, administrators, policymakers and the general public available through the production of online learning tools.

Most recently, WestEd (with CAESL partners) provided leadership for the development of the 2009 NAEP Science Assessment Framework.

After three years of program operation, an external evaluation conducted by Abt Associates, SRI, and Westat (2005) showed that the CLTs have involved sizable numbers of disciplinary faculty in the work and that more STEM faculty are becoming engaged in STEM education research. The graduate programs have engaged over 300 doctoral students to date, and 90% of those students indicate that participating in a collaborative center that includes multiple institutions has value over and above other single institution graduate programs. They cite increased opportunities to interact with faculty and students at other institutions, and faculty indicate that the CLT students are better prepared in multiple areas.

Research On Learning and Education and Advanced Learning Technologies

The main programs for individual researcher grant support are the Research on Learning and Education (ROLE) program and the new Advanced Learning Technologies (ALT) program. The ROLE program has typically funded projects at levels above the typical NSF research project under the rationale that NSF needed to build capacity for research in this area. It has been the main supporter of Learning Sciences Research at NSF. The ALT program is a joint Computer and Information Science and Engineering (CISE) directorate and Education and Human Resources (EHR) directorate program aimed at funding innovations in technology that show great promise for learning sciences. The size of ALT awards is substantially smaller than ROLE awards. This session will look both retrospectively on the affect of the ROLE program on learning sciences and prospectively as to how these programs can adapt to new funding realities – in particular given the program realignment as described in the FY 2007 budget.

As part of this realignment, a new division, the Division of Research on Learning in Formal and Informal Settings (DRL) has been proposed as part of the FY 2007 budget. This division incorporates much of the Division of Elementary, Secondary, and Informal Education and the Division of Research, Evaluation, and Communication. A new program, Research on Education and Evaluation in Science and Engineering (REESE), incorporates the ROLE, IERI, and evaluative research programs. Below are two examples of projects funded by ROLE and ALT:

Adaptive E-Learning for Middle-School Mathematics (Valerie Shute, Educational Testing Service)

With the goal of helping teachers provide individualized instruction to students with disabilities - and to do so in the same classroom as students without disabilities - NSF-funded researchers and educators have successfully demonstrated a computer-based learning system for mathematics that can accommodate both visually impaired and sighted students. The system uses text enlargement on normal displays for low vision students, a Talking Tactile Tablet for blind students, and normal displays for fully sighted students. In addition, the system develops a model for each student's understanding of mathematical concepts, and then uses those models to provide problem-solving advice to students regardless of their visual acuity. The student models have been validate in a pilot test of 50 students, and the system is now being tested with over 300 blind, visually impaired, and fully sighted students.

Developing Teacher's Mathematical Knowledge for Teaching (Heather Hill, University of Michigan)

Over the past decade, policymakers have funded a range of professional development efforts designed to improve elementary teachers' knowledge of the mathematics they teach. However, there has been little rigorous research investigating whether and when teachers develop mathematical knowledge from professional development, and if so, what features of professional development contribute to teacher learning. This project provides an example of how such research might be done. Its preliminary results could lead to profound changes in teacher professional development.

Using new measures of teachers' mathematical knowledge for teaching, and a pre-test/post-test design that compared the progress of teachers participating in California's Mathematics Professional Development Institutes (MPDIs) to those not participating, an assessment of whether and how teachers grew as a result of this experience was carried out. The analyses show that teachers participating in the MPDIs did improve their performance on these measures during the extended summer workshop portion of their experience. In the first year evaluation, teachers grew roughly half a standard deviation; in the second year evaluation, teachers grew roughly a third of a standard deviation. Teachers in the comparison group, by contrast, did no better on the post-test than on the pre-test. The analysis also suggests that program length (as measured in days in the summer workshop) and workshop focus on mathematical exploration, communication, analysis, and proof positively predicted teachers' learning. Lessons from this study are being published in the Journal of Research in Mathematics Education and in Educational Policy (forthcoming).

Science of Learning Centers

The final session will provide a brief overview of the four Science of Learning Centers funded by NSF in FY 2004. At least two of these centers have a focus directly related to ISLS researchers. The session will look prospectively at the promise of these centers, in particular in regard to broader participation of the ISLS community in them and how they fit in with existing learning science programs in EHR.

The moderated discussions after these sessions will focus on the balance between modalities of support; on new research opportunities afforded by cyberinfrastructure; on missed research opportunities; and on success stories from the learning sciences research community.

References

Atkins, D.E. (Ed.) (January 2003) *Revolutionizing Science and Engineering Through Cyberinfrastructure: A Report on the National Science Foundation Blue-Ribbon Advisory Panel on Cyberinfrastructure.* http://www.cise.nsf.gov/sci/reports/atkins.pdf.

CRA (November 2005) *Cyberinfrastructure for Education and Learning for the Future: A Vision and Research Agenda.* Computing Research Association, Washington, DC. http://www.cra.org/reports/cyberinfrastructure.pdf

Theorizing Games in/and Education

Richard Halverson, David Shaffer, Kurt Squire, Constance Steinkuehler
University of Wisconsin- Madison, 225 North Mills Street, Madison, Wisconsin
Email: halverson@education.wisc.edu, dws@education.wisc.edu; kdsquire@education.wisc.edu; e.steinkuehler@wisc.edu

Abstract: Games are a nascent topic for educational research, with an increasing numberof conferences (e.g. *Games, Learning, & Society*), print publications (e.g. *Games & Culture*), and even federal grants (e.g. *Quest Atlantis, RiverWorld, Whyville*) recently given to the study and design of gaming technologies in/for education. However, to date, games have been chronically under-theorized – a "technology in search of a paradigm" (Gredler, 1996). This symposium proposes new conceptualizations of games in relation to education. Our collective goal is to better articulate the nature of contemporary interactive technologies so as to forward educational theory; each paper addresses crucial aspects of games and gaming culture against a backdrop of research on learning, education, and society (c.f. Shaffer, Squire, Halverson, & Gee, 2005; Steinkuehler, in press). To do so, this unique symposium combines (a) ethnographies of naturally occurring game environments, (b) game-based learning programs based on findings of how learning occurs in such environments (c) a an empirical model based on *games for thought*, a type of professional practice simulation games, and (d) a research project using games and game technologies for social science theorizing. Together, these papers suggest new directions for the cognitive sciences pointing toward how to design learning systems for an information age networked society.

Games as a Highly Visible Medium for the Study of Distributed, Situated Cognition: Constance A. Steinkuehler

Early academic discussions in game-related fields about what games are and how they ought to be studied tend to fall back on a tired dichotomy drawn between *ludology* (the study of games as formal rule systems) and *narratology* (the study of games as texts), even when core scholars on both sides acknowledge that the debate is an unfortunate red herring (cf. Aarseth & Jenkins debate, 2005). Games are *designed experiences* (Squire, in press) and, as such, their study requires an understanding of the full range of human practices through which players actively inhabit those worlds of rules and texts and render them meaningful. Games are a "mangle" (Pickering 1995) of production and consumption – of human intentions (with designers and players in conversation with one another, Robison in press), material constraints and affordances, evolving sociocultural practices, and brute chance. While rules and stories partially constitute the designed object or little-g "game" at the center of a given individual's play experience with it, it is the emergent culture or big-G "Game" around them that renders them meaningful and consequential (Gee, 1999; Shaffer, 2005; Shaffer, et al. 2005; Squire, 2002, Steinkuehler, in press).

Such big-G Games provide a highly visible medium for the study of cognition as inter(action) in the social and material world. Accounts of thinking, learning, and understanding based solely on a symbolic processing model, which treats the mind as a wet-wired symbol processing system analogous to the computer (e.g. Anderson & Lebiere, 1998; Simon, 1989), cannot easily account for the range of everyday human activity or its meaning – how it is distributed across tools, representations, and other people; how it is situated in the material, social, spatial, and temporal context in which it occurs; how it ontologically changes who and what the person is (rather than just the epistemic contents in the head) (Packer & Goicoechea, 2000); or how it is tied to larger sociocultural (and political) "forms of life" (Wittgenstein, 1958) enacted out in the world. In order to construct such accounts, we must rethink cognition as a distributed and situated event.

Games are an extremely valuable context for the study of cognition within this paradigm. They provide a representational trace of both individual and collective activity and how it changes over time, enabling the researcher to unpack the bidirectional influence of self and society – how a given sociocultural context shapes and influences individual activity and meaning-making through socialization and enculturation (Nasir, 2005), and how the individual shapes and influences the culture in which she participates in return. As both designed object and emergent culture, g/Games (a) consist of over-lapping well-defined problems enveloped in ill-defined problems that render their solutions meaningful, (b)function as naturally occurring, self-sustaining, indigenous versions of the online learning communities produced by various groups in fields such as distance education and eLearning (with somewhat lackluster success), and (c) simultaneously function as both culture and cultural object – as microcosms for studying the emergence, maintenance, transformation, and even collapse of online affinity groups and as talkabout- able objects that function as tokens in public conversations of broader societal issues within contemporary offline society. In this paper, I will unpack each of these claims in the context of the massively multiplayer online games.

Designing Learning Environments for an Interactive Age: Kurt D. Squire

Interactive immersive entertainment or video games have emerged as a major entertainment medium and enculturation force for today's youth. Videogames epitomize a potentially destabilizing wave of technologies where students access information and social networks any time, anywhere. More importantly, videogame cultures have tacit assumptions about knowledge, learning, expertise, and formal institutions which may be at odds with school (Beck & Wade, 2004; Gee, 2003; Lankshear & Knobel 2003; Squire & Giovanetto, in press). As students confront more and more sophisticated digital worlds outside of school, a challenge becomes how will schools react: Do we present and expect students to pursue print-based literacies, ignoring the visual culture and computer mediated worlds they inhabit out of school? And, perhaps most importantly, what identities do we make available to students in school? Whereas our schools ask students to all learn at the same rates, in the same ways, at the same time, games make a variety of different paths to learning available.

This research paper describes findings from an ongoing design experiment iteratively building and researching an after-school learning environment around Civilization III and now IV. In this after school program, kids learn world history through playing and designing historical scenarios (Squire, Giovanetto, Devane, & Durga, in press). Building on ethnographies of online gaming "Universities," the program aims to move players from game "players" to "designers" of historical scenarios, a program in which students develop historical knowledge, historical modeling and reasoning skills, and new digital literacies around game development. This project seeks to develop an educational model for an interactive age (c.f. Lemke,) in which students are self-directed, draw on multi-modal discourses, and participate in socio-technical networks appropriate for the digital age through drawing on Crowley's (2002) notion of islands of expertise, coupled with Gee's (2004) notion of affinity spaces, and Jenkins (in press) notions of participatory media structure.

Specifically, this paper draws on data from a year long, ongoing after-school club with fourth sixth grade underachieving students (mostly of color) where they reciprocally play and develop historical modifications for the computer game Civilization III. It follows the trajectory of three students who entered the program as novice game players and reluctant producers of media, to skilled historical modelers. Drawing on roughly 100 hours of observations, videotaped interactions, and clinical interviews with students, it provides narrative case study accounts of how they develop new historical and technical literacies, deeper conceptual understandings of geographical history, and transformations in identity from consumers to producers of media. This process includes students' developing (a) an interest in the game history, (b) students seeking outside sources (including texts) to meet developing curiosities, (c) desires to create historical scenarios to communicate ideas and impress their colleagues, (d) a desire to interact with other developers over the Internet.

The study details specific historical understandings that evolved through participation in this program, such as systemic view of the geographical impact on the fate of civilizations, and explores the limitations of students' understandings, particularly as they develop in a non-linear context. Using prepost tests administered every 3 months, or after 20 hour intervals, it details growth in their historical vocabulary, understanding, and interest in history. The paper concludes with a tentative model for how such clubs might be developed and replicated at other sites, addressing key issues of scalability and sustainability in design research projects (Shaffer & Squire, in press).

Games as Social Systems Theory Testing: Games for Instructional Leadership: Richard Halverson

This paper explores how video game design can provide social science researchers with a powerful method for testing theory adequacy and interdependence, outlining our effort to bring the principles of game design and play into the world of school leadership in the form of the Instructional Leadership Game (ILG). We take theories of school improvement and school leadership as a subset of social science theories in order to investigate how videogames might test social science theory adequacy and reliability. We know that school leaders play a critical role in developing structures and communities for sustained learning across schools – without good leadership, the best research-proven educational innovations fail. The ILG provides a research-driven context for leaders to see the short- and long-term consequences of trying out new strategies, engaging in the politics of leadership, and practicing the micro-tasks of supervision, management and planning. In so doing, the ILG not only helps novice school leaders learn new practices but also provides a sandbox for experienced leaders to customize the game to their schools and engage in what-if experimentation. The paper provides a review of our efforts to build the ILG as an occasion to discuss the emerging role of videogames and social science research. The birth of cognitive science was marked by the new capacity of information technologies to simulate complex cognitive processes, such as chess playing and decision-making (Gardner, 1985). Such simulations enabled researchers to see complex interactions in simplified environments, which in turn informed the development of models in disciplines from weather to economics. Social science theories, however, have proven particularly difficult to test in domains representing complex practices, such as school leadership. Yet, recent advances in videogame design have opened new possibilities for including interactivity in complex systems models, thus enabling researchers to study how, for example, agency plays out within complex systems. Real-time strategy games such as *Rise of Nations* and *Civilization* immerse players in complex, research-based theories-of action through the development of rich, open-ended narrative environments that allow players to participate in complex systems and to learn from the consequences of their actions. Thus, videogames allow for two directions of theory testing: 1) game design allows for the articulation and specification of models for how theories play out in practice (see, for example, Burns, 2002 on the influence of Jared Diamond's (1997) *Guns, Germs and Steel* on the design of the *Civilization* games), and 2) game play allows individuals to experiment with complex theoretical models in order to understand, as it were, social theories from the inside.

The paper is structured into three parts. First, we review the ILG *game design* by describing how we operationalized key components of school improvement efforts, such as professional community, data-driven decision-making, high-stakes accountability and theories of day-to-day administrative practice into the underlying systems model of the ILG. We found that each component theory was radically underspecified and that we needed to engage in interviews and basic research in schools to understand how the theories would play out in practice. Assembling the model involved extensive user testing to insure that the designed process actually represented authentic practices. Second, we describe *game play* with a review of our user-testing process. We asked eight school leaders to interact with the game and reflect on a) what they learned, and b) how the game could be improved. Finally, we discuss the implications for video-game design as a tool for vetting existing school improvement theories and speculate on the next-generation of theory development that might result from game-modeled research.

Games for Thought: The Future of Education and How We Can Get There: David Shaffer

In this talk, I present the concept of *Games for Thought*, a view of games that moves our education system beyond traditional academic disciplines and classroom practices to a new model of learning through meaningful activity in virtual worlds as preparation for meaningful activity in a postindustrial, technology-rich society. I argue that practices in the world, such as the professions, have coherent epistemic frameworks (Shaffer, 2005, in press). So the ways in which professionals and members of other valued communities acquire their practices provide an alternative educational model: a model based on epistemic games – games that recreate the training and practice of professions and other socially-valued communities (Shaffer, 2004; Shaffer, et al., 2005).

To do this, I examine two epistemic games, using these games to illustrate an educational system of *Games for Thought* in which students learn to think as urban planners, architects, engineers, journalists, and other socially-valued practitioners not in order to train them for these pursuits in the traditional sense of vocational education but because learning to work as members of these communities of practice provides students with an opportunity to learn about the world in ways that are fundamentally grounded in meaningful activity and well aligned with core skills, knowledge, identities, values, and epistemologies for life in a postindustrial society.

Digital Zoo

In the epistemic role-playing game *Digital Zoo* (Svarovsky & Shaffer, in press), children cultivate their natural tendencies to explore, create, and design by working as professional biomechanical engineers who solve design problems in a realtime persistent world. By playing *Digital Zoo*, students develop scientific understanding by seeing, thinking, and acting as engineers.

Stage One: In-House Design.

Middle school students solve engineering design challenges on SodaConstructor, a Java-based spring-mass modeling simulation using rapid iterations of the Design-Build-Test cycle – the core practice of engineering design – to learn physics through epistemic gameplay.

Stage Two: Prototyping for External Clients.

Students level up to work as biomechanical engineers developing structural character prototypes on SodaConstructor for the next *Pixar* movie. They conduct prototype evaluations, interface with clients, and balance competing design objectives as they learn about engineering design, physics, and animation. In this paper, I present an overview of *Digital Zoo* and data from both stages of gameplay, focusing on how engaging in authentic iterations of the engineering Design-Build-Test cycle develops scientific knowledge and engineering values.

MyCity

Human beings are the architects and planners of cities, so good stewardship and good citizenship require an understanding of the relationship between the built and natural world. One way students can gain an awareness of a city's ecological relationships is through urban simulation: for example, in computer games such as *SimCity*, where players solve urban problems by managing a fictitious urban environment. But before there was *SimCity* there were real cities, and the real urban planners who organize their growth and development. The epistemic game *MyCity* (Beckett & Shaffer, in press) shows how a game based on the authentic practices of urban planning helps players think like urban planners about the complex relationships of urban ecology. In *MyCity*, high school students learn about urban ecology by working as urban planners, using an interactive planning model to redesign a popular downtown pedestrian mall. Studies of the *MyCity* game show that students begin to think like urban planners by inhabiting a virtual world in which they take up such roles.

Methods

Each of these epistemic games was pilot tested through 10 hours of game play by 10-15 students (middle school students for *Digital Zoo* and high school students for *MyCity*). Clinical interviews were conducted immediately before and after game play, including "content questions" and "game play" questions. Content questions were analyzed for changes between pre- and post-test. Game play questions were analyzed within a grounded theory framework which attempted to relate students' assessment of and experiences in the game to each other and to changes in content questions.

Results

In both games, students showed a statistically significant change in their knowledge of scientific concepts. Both games also showed that students developed ways of thinking characteristic of the profession they were role-playing. Finally, in both games there was a significant qualitative and quantitative relationship between changing understanding of science and development of professional ways of thinking and acting.

References

Aarseth, E. & Jenkins, H. (2005). *Aarseth-Jenkins debate on (computer) game studies*. Presented at the HUMlab, IT University of Copenhagen, January 18.

Anderson, J. R. & Lebiere, C. (1998). *The atomic components of thought*. Mahwah NJ: Erlbaum.

Beck, J. & Wade, (2004). *Got game: How the gamer generation is reshaping business forever*. Cambridge, MA: Harvard Business School Press.

Beckett, K. L., & Shaffer, D. W. (in press). Augmented by reality: The pedagogical praxis of urban planning as a pathway to ecological thinking. *Journal of Educational Computing Research*.

Burns, A. (2002) Civilization III: Digital game-based learning and macrohistory simulations. Australian Foresight Institute/Disinformation, Accessed July 31,2005 at http://www.disinfo.com/archive/images/linda/CivilizationIII.pdf

Crowley, K. & Jacobs, M. (2002). Islands of expertise and the development of family scientific literacy. In G. Leinhardt, K. Crowley, & K. Knutson (Eds.) *Learning conversations in museums*. Mahwah, NJ: Lawrence Erlbaum Associates.

Diamond, Jared (1997). *Guns, Germs, and Steel: The Fate of Human Societies*. New York: W.W. Norton & Co.

Games-to-Teach Team. (2003). Design principles of next-generation digital gaming for education. *Educational Technology, 43*(5), 17-33.

Gardner, H. (1985). *The mind's new science: A history of the cognitive revolution*. New York: Basic Books, Inc.

Gee, J. P. (1999). *An introduction to discourse analysis: Theory and method.* New York: Routledge.

Gee, J. P. (2003). *What video games have to teach us about learning and literacy*. New York: Palgrave/St. Martin's.

Gee, J.P. (2004). *Situated language and learning: A critique of traditional schooling.* NY: Routledge.

Gredler, M. E. (1996). Educational games and simulations: A technology in search of a (research) paradigm. In D. H. Jonassen (Ed.), *Handbook of research for educational communications and technology* (pp. 521-540). New York: Simon & Schuster Macmillan.

Jenkins, H. (in press). *Media convergence*. NY: NYU Press.

Klopfer, E. & Squire, K. (in press). Environmental Detectives: The development of an augmented reality platform for environmental simulations. *Educational Research Technology & Development.*

Lankshear, C. & Knobel, M. (2003). *New literacies*. London: Open University Press.

Lemke, J. (1998). Metamedia Literacy: Transforming meanings and media. In D. Reinking, L. Labbo, M. McKenna, & R. Kiefer (Eds.), *Handbook of literacy and technology: Transformations in a posttypographic world.* Hillsdale, NJ: Erlbaum. (pp.283-301).

Nasir, N. S. (2005). Individual cognitive structuring and the sociocultural context: Strategy shifts in the game of dominoes. *The Journal of the Learning Sciences, 14*(1), 5-34.

Packer, M. J. & Goicoechea, J. (2000). Sociocultural and constructivist theories of learning: Ontology, not just epistemology. *Educational Psychologist, 35*(4), 227-241.

Pickering, A. (1995). *The mangle of practice: Time, agency, and science*. Chicago: The University of Chicago Press.

Robison, A. J. (in press). Videogame designers as literacy pedagogues. In Y. Ming-tu (Ed.), *Reformation: The Teaching and Learning of English in Electronic Environments*. Taipei: Tamkang University Press.

Shaffer, D. W. (2004). Pedagogical praxis: The professions as models for post-industrial education. *Teachers College Record, 106*(7).

Shaffer, D. W. (2005). Epistemic Games. *Innovate, 1*(6), http://www.innovateonline.info/index.php?view=article&id=79.

Shaffer, D. W. (in press). Epistemic frames for epistemic games. *Computers & Education.*

Shaffer, D. W., Squire, K. A., Halverson, R., & Gee, J. P. (2005). Video games and the future of learning. *Phi Delta Kappan, 87(2),* 104-111. .

Simon, H. A. (1989). *Models of thought, Vol. 2*. New Haven CT: Yale University Press.

Squire, K.D. (2002). Rethinking the role of games in Education. *Game Studies, 2*(1).

Squire, K. D. (in press). *From content to context: Videogames as designed experiences*. To appear in *Educational Researcher*.

Squire, K. D. (2005). Educating the fighter. *On the Horizon, 13(2)* 75-88.

Squire, K. & Gionavetto, L. (in press). The Higher Education of gaming. *Elearning*.

Squire, K. D., Gionavetto, L., Devane, B. & Durga, S. (in press). Building a learning community for gaming production in an after school learning community. To appear in *Technology Trends*.

Steinkuehler, C. A. (in press). Massively multiplayer online videogames as participation in a Discourse. To appear in *Mind, Culture, and Activity*.

Svarovsky, G., & Shaffer, D. W. (in press). SodaConstructing knowledge through exploratoids. *Journal of Research in Science Teaching*.

Wittgenstein, L. (1958). *Philosophical Investigations.* Oxford: Basil Blackwell.

Making a difference with attention to content, technology, and scale: A session honoring the memory of Jim Kaput

Stephen Hegedus, University of Massachusetts, 128 Chase Road, Dartmouth MA 02747, shegedus@umassd.edu
Dick Lesh, Indiana University, School of Education, Bloomington IN 47405, ralesh@indiana.edu
Jeremy Roschelle, SRI International, 333 Ravenswood Ave, Menlo Park CA 94025, Jeremy.Roschelle@sri.com

Abstract: The theme of this year's ICLS, "making a difference," resonates with the life-work of our dear colleague, Jim Kaput, who unexpectedly passed away in summer 2005. Kaput's approach to making a difference was grounded in the Learning Sciences and distinctively attended to the nature of mathematical content, the role of technology, and the problematic of scale. In this symposium, we honor his memory by discussing the current projects of three investigators who continue to drive Kaput's vision forward. These projects address: (1) "foundations for the future" based in a deep reconceptualization of mathematical content (2) technology as representational and connectivity infrastructure that democratizes access to mathematics worth knowing and (3) scale as a challenging problematic essential to "making a difference."

Introduction

While learning scientists can present rich accounts of learning in complex contexts, convincing policy makers, teachers, and other researchers of the theoretical and practical value of our work is not a straightforward process. We must show impact at the local level while at the same time, work to have claims of more global significance. In other words, we must make clear that the learning sciences make a difference.
(from the ICLS 2006 web site)

We, like most of our colleagues, are learning scientists because we want to make a difference in the lives of learners. We find ourselves drawn together in departments, conferences, and projects because we see the scientific process as providing tools of inquiry that could unlock paths to richer, fuller learning of important mathematics and science for many more learners. The seductive allure of learning sciences lies in its potential to clarify foundational issues and inspire innovative approaches which could dramatically improve education. The shine wears off when we find that the path from insight to widespread betterment of education is anything but well-defined. "Getting to scale" is rare in education (Elmore, 1996). Too little of what learning scientists create survives the process of "fatal mutation" eloquently described by Ann Brown (Brown, 1991). Faced with this challenge, our field needs pathmakers--innovators with vision, practical wisdom, and the ability to persevere against the odds and encourage others to follow. Jim Kaput was such a person.

Kaput provided a vision of *how* the learning sciences could make a difference: by **democratizing access** to important mathematics (Kaput, 1994). Kaput saw a positive strand of development in human history in which more people could gain access to important conceptual tools (Kaput & Roschelle, 1998). Centuries ago, only a few scribes could write. Now we expect everyone to do it. The printing press commoditized books, but parallel developments in developing new genres, switching from Latin to the vernacular, standardizing printed language, and developing new pedagogical methods were required in order to democratize access to knowledge through reading. Similarly, in mathematics there was a time in which multiplication and division were very specialized skills, available only to those who could travel to particular universities. As late as 100 years ago, only 3% of students were expected to learn Algebra. Now 70% do, and we expect "Algebra for All." Today 3% of students are expected to learn Calculus. Given that we live in a time dominated by dynamism and change, Kaput felt confident that we would need to dramatically increase opportunities to learn this mathematics and we might not have a century to do it in. Hence the SimCalc project was born (J. Roschelle *et al.*, 2000).

The Learning Sciences provide deep and broad tools of inquiry. Because the tools are deep, they afford pushing foundational changes that could democratize access to mathematics worth knowing. But because they are broad, they could be applied to potentially every aspect of education. In some areas, this approach to inquiry is likely to be fruitful; in some areas it may not be. Hence, problem selection is critical. We need to understand *what* the Learning Science could contribute to democratizing access.

Kaput provided a clear vision of what the Learning Sciences could contribute: new **technological infrastructures** for representation and connectivity and **reconceptualization of subject matter** to open new opportunities to learn (Kaput, 1992, 2002). Kaput took a strong position that technology should be thought of as an infrastructural, not as particular applications and tools. Rather he saw new representations, particularly graphical and dynamic representations, as making concepts more accessible to students. He expected that these representations could be embodied in many media, devices, applications, and tools. He was interested in the new classes of representation made possible by technology (e.g. directly editable graphs of piecewise functions) and their relationship to learning. Likewise, in his last major project, Kaput saw within-classroom network connectivity as providing a new infrastructure – an infrastructure that created new structures and opportunities for classroom participation in doing and commenting on mathematics. In many presentations, Kaput used the phrase "new technology without new curriculum isn't worth the silicon its written in" to indicate his believe that reconceptualization of subject matter would be necessary to realize the learning benefits of new infrastructure. Kaput took responsibility for reconceptualizing a "mathematics of change and variation" strand from elementary school through the first year of university. He was experimented deeply, for instance, with the benefits of introducing piecewise functions much earlier in the curriculum, finding that they were intuitive to students and highlighted conceptually important contrasts in a way that students could more readily perceive.

Finally, Kaput embodied a proactive approach to the issue of **scale**. He understood scale to be a multi-dimensional problem, some of which was political, some commercial, and only a part scientific (J Roschelle *et al.*, in press). Hence, he worked with colleagues to influence standards. He engaged commercial companies to make his representations available. He built a network of researchers and research projects, so as to examine scaleability across settings. And he engaged in projects directly related to scaling up.

In this symposium, we invite presenters, discussants and the audience to engage in reflecting on Kaput's approach to making a difference: What are researchers doing now to carry forward Kaput's themes? Do these approaches make sense for a broader cross-section of the learning sciences? How could the community employ these themes to make a difference?

Symposium Agenda

We plan to open with a short introduction that recapitulates the text above, setting the context and agenda. Then we will invite three presenters, each of whom was working with Kaput on a major project when he died and is still carrying that project forward, to share the current state of their efforts to make a difference. We will then invite two discussants to each speak for a few minutes about the thematic content of the session, before opening the floor to the audience for commentary. Our discussants, Roy Pea (Stanford) and Corey Brady (Texas Instruments), will represent the Learning Sciences and commercial efforts to make a difference, respectively.

0:00 Welcome and Introduction
0:10 Presentation 1: Stephen Hegedus
0:25 Presentation 2: Dick Lesh
0:40 Presentation 3: Jeremy Roschelle
1:00 Discussants: Roy Pea and Corey Brady
1:15 Audience Participation
1:30 End

"Representational and Connectivity Infrastructure"

Stephen Hegedus, University of Massachusetts

Since the early 1990's, Kaput's vision to create dynamic visualization tools to allow students better access to core mathematics has evolved into a powerful suite of technologies with complementary curriculum materials that has had impact on students and teachers in middle and high schools, as well as undergraduate students in College Freshmen and Pre-service courses. Such work has not only made a difference on students and teachers though, but it has helped researchers and educational software developers understand new perspectives of the role of technology in 21st century mathematics education. His theoretical insights which draws deeply on the history and evolution of notation systems has led to new perspectives on software design for the purpose of enabling all students to explore multiple-linked representations of algebraic concepts, model real situations, develop problem-solving skills and discover core principles of Calculus, hitherto left for an elite population of students; ideas that help students understand the mathematics of change and variation.

Kaput's idea of a representational infrastructure has become an extremely useful model to describe dynamic vs static aspects of educational software that provides new ways for teaching and learning mathematics.

This model was deeply embedded and exemplified in his software SimCalc MathWorlds. Representational features include direct manipulation of graphically editable functions, and direct, hot links between graphically editable functions and their derivatives or integrals. Others include, connections between representations and simulations, the ability to import physical motion, and re-animate it, and the use of hybrid physical/cybernetic devices embodying dynamical systems. Since all such representational features are linked, they provide an infrastructure for a multitude of activities and learning opportunities.

Five years ago, we began to combine our software, which previously existed separately on hand-held devices and desktop computers, to work in parallel. It was not an easy task to allow functions created on an assembly language application to be reproduced in a Java environment. But it was not just about technological innovation, it was a new avenue to allow students working with our software on affordable graphing calculators to be aggregated via classroom networks into our desktop software in *mathematically meaningful ways*. We did this using various forms of connectivity but the prevalent one being Texas Instruments' Navigator system, a hub-spoke semi-wireless intranet, which can be self-configured for local, classroom based networking without an expensive network infrastructure (e.g. Internet). So now, classrooms could support connectivity without the need for a laboratory of computers with massive associated overheads and physical configurations that do not support, active, collaborative work. The SimCalc Connected Classroom was born, which allowed a distribution of cost and deliverables for maximal learning benefits; the cheapness, yet low resolution and power of many hand-held devices, with the expense but computational and representational power of desktop computers. This new system was not just about costs and affordances, but the genesis of new types of activity structures, that allowed students to contribute mathematical work all at once to a social workspace, via a teachers computer being projected on a whiteboard. There teachers can facilitate discussion to allow more students to investigate, analyze and discover mathematical relationships from observing and listening to how their work fitted into a broader set of students' work. For example, consider a class split into groups where each group has to control an actor's motion graphically or algebraically, who runs the same amount of time as a target actor (e.g. 2 ft/sec for 6 seconds; algebraically Y=2X), but you need to start at a position 3 times your group number ahead of such a target, but end the race in a tie with your target. This calls for each group to develop a different function, whose variation is in terms of slope and intercept in the algebraic form Y=MX+B, and which can be examined publicly when each group is aggregated. Such group work, calls all students to participate, not necessarily vocally, enhancing legitimate peripheral participation via mathematically enhanced communication infrastructures. It allows a student to project their self, their own identity, from a private workspace to a more collaborative social workspace. Jim believed this was a new type of mathematical learning and thinking and one that would prove to be a new educational landscape of the 21st century.

The present project that Jim and I directed has explored the impact of this representational and technological innovation on student participation and engagement as well as the impact on traditional forms of pedagogy, classroom interaction, and learning. We are deep in the midst of discovering new forms of interaction cycles that occur in Connected SimCalc classrooms, new types of questions that can be asked to help the majority of students in a classroom engage in mathematical analysis. We are also observing shifts in teaching beliefs about effective methods for instructing core mathematical ideas such as linearity, slope as rate and simultaneous equations. I shall present core activity structures that have evolved from recent work, participation structures that are evident in SimCalc connected classroom vs traditional environments, as well as data on impact on student learning and teaching practice from our collaborative analyses with our participants teachers.

"Foundations for the Future of Mathematics"

Richard Lesh, Indiana University

Any description of Jim Kaput's work should involve future-oriented themes. So, in this presentation, I'll describe a next project that we were laying the groundwork to undertake. It was intended to extend our joint vow, taken years ago, to focus on "democratizing access to powerful ideas." The next step, was to focus on what Jim referred to as "curriculum futures." And, a first step toward this project is a book that we just finished on Foundations for the Future in Mathematics Education (Lesh, Hamilton & Kaput, in press). In fields ranging from aeronautical engineering to agriculture, and from biotechnologies to business administration, future-oriented university programs increasingly emphasize the fact that, beyond school, the nature of problem solving activities has changed dramatically during the past twenty years. For example, powerful tools for computation, conceptualization, and communication have led to fundamental changes in the levels and types of mathematical understandings and abilities that are needed for success in such fields.

These observations raise the following questions:

- What is the nature of typical problem-solving situations where elementary-but-powerful mathematical constructs and conceptual systems are needed for success in a technology-based age of information?
- What kind of "mathematical thinking" is emphasized in these situations?
- What does it mean to "understand" the most important of these ideas and abilities?
- How do these competencies develop?
- What can be done to facilitate development?
- How can we document and assess the most important (deeper, higher-order, more powerful) achievements that are needed: (i) for informed citizenship, or (ii) for successful participation in the increasingly wide range of professions that are becoming heavy users of mathematics, science, and technology?

We believe that such questions should be investigated through research—not simply resolved through political processes (such as those that are used in the development of curriculum standards or tests). We also believe that researchers with broad and deep expertise in mathematics and science should play significant roles in such research and that input should be sought not just from creators of mathematics (i.e., "pure" mathematicians), but also heavy users of mathematics (e.g., "applied" mathematicians and scientists). This is because the questions listed above are about the changing nature of mathematics and situations where mathematics is used; they are not simply questions about the nature of students, human minds, human information processing capabilities, or human development.

Upon further reflection and research about the preceding issues, we gradually developed the opinion that, for most topics that we have tried to teach, the kind of mathematical understandings and abilities that are emphasized in mathematics textbooks and tests tend to represent only a shallow, narrow, and often non-central subset of those that are needed for success when the relevant ideas should be useful in "real life" situations. For example, in projects such as Purdue University's Gender Equity in Engineering Project, when students' abilities and achievements were assessed using tasks that were designed to be simulations of "real life" problem solving situations, the majority of understandings and abilities that emerged as being critical for success included were not among those emphasized in traditional textbooks or tests. Consequently, when we recognized the importance of a broader range of deeper understandings and abilities, a broader range of students naturally emerged as having extraordinary potential. Furthermore, many of these students came from populations that are highly under represented in fields that emphasize mathematics, science, and technology; and this was true precisely because their abilities were previously unrecognized. ... Such observations return us to the following fundamental question:

What kind of understandings and abilities should be emphasized to decrease mismatches between: (i) the narrow band of mathematical understandings and abilities that are emphasized in mathematics classrooms and tests, and (ii) those that are needed for success beyond school in the 21st century?

Many people assume that students simply need more practice with ideas and abilities that have been considered to be "basics" in the past. Others assume that old conceptions of "basics" should be replaced by completely new topics and ideas (such as those associated with complexity theory, discrete mathematics, systems theory, or computational modeling). Still others assume that new levels and type of understanding are needed for both old and new ideas. Examples include understandings that emphasize graphics-based or computation-based representational media.

"The Problematic of Scale"

Jeremy Roschelle, SRI International

In a 4-year "Interagency Educational Research Initiative" (IERI) project, we are conducting a series of experimental trials in which hundreds of teachers will use SimCalc curriculum and software across the state of Texas. This project has brought the team of Principal Investigators (which formerly included Kaput) face to face with scale as a research problematic which is quite different from business-as-usual in the Learning Sciences.

In this project, we consider SimCalc as an instance of a coupled representational technology and re-organized curriculum, which we support with teacher professional development in order to form a testable intervention. Because SimCalc was always conceived as a curricular strand and not a full-year mathematics curriculum, we are testing SimCalc via a replacement unit in 7th and 8th grade.

The primary research question we ask across studies is about variation at the teacher level. Most learning science design projects are subject to the "Boutique Critique;" that is, "sure the intervention works with your special teachers, but I don't believe it will work with my average teachers." To counter this, we have recruited a wide variety of teachers (over 100 for the 7th grade study, from 4 regions across

Texas and representing a diversity of backgrounds, settings, and pedagogical styles). In addition to seeing if SimCalc "works," we seek to model how variations in student achievement with SimCalc materials correlate with teacher variability

Many of the critiques of the lack of experimental designs in past educational research might give the impression that researchers avoided this path because they were incompetent, biased, or lazy. Kaput always held that this was not the case; rather, he felt that carrying out such research without a very careful team who carefully documented each step could only result in dubious knowledge. Our experience has born out this conviction.

A first problematic is the disjunction between how the innovators envision their intervention working at scale vs. what can actually be tested in today's schools. Kaput always envisioned technology as infrastructural – e.g. ubiquitiously available and often used. In contrast, in the real schools we are involving in Texas, teachers still have to take students to a computer lab. This is known to be an undesirable setting for using computers, but yet it's what we can actually study. There is a chicken-and-egg problem here, because middle school math teachers are unlikely to gain access to ubiquitous technology without evidence that it works and yet one can only approximate eventually effects if teachers and students are basically unfamiliar with the technology in their everyday classroom experience.

A second problematic occurs in the design of a control condition. When the intervention is a new technology and curriculum, it is impossible for teachers to be blind to condition. A good control condition must give teachers a positive experience and some expectation that they may perform well – teachers are unlikely to motivate their students to do well if they feel they are in the conditions that's not supposed to do well. Further, we did not want to "design" the control for fear that we would be accused of intentionally or un-intentionally crippling the control. Hence, we choose to have every teacher (in both groups) attend a first professional development, which was chosen because of its high reputation for quality across Texas; then only SimCalc teachers had additional professional development. This fails to balance for additional time-on-task of teachers in professional development and hence, if we get positive results, we won't be able to discern whether it was because of more professional development or the technology-and-replacement unit.

A third problematic has to do with conflicts between ideal teacher professional development and experimental difficulty of handling teacher clustering. It is common wisdom in teacher professional development that teachers should work together within a school site or at least work in teams or pairs. This becomes challenging when working in Texas middle schools, where many schools have only one math teacher! Further, if teachers collaborate effectively, a larger n is needed and instead of a two-level design (teacher, student) one needs a three-level design (school, teacher, student) which is incredibly expensive to execute.

Yet, despite these and other difficulties, we believe that research on scale can be a valuable adjunct to ordinary Learning Sciences research. On one hand, as Kaput insisted, there will be no single "definitive" experiment that establishes whether curriculum reorganization, representational infrastructure, or new classroom connectivity capabilities are "what works." On the other hand, research on scale can overcome important credibility problems. Today, there are no large-scale, systematic, rigorous studies that measure the effects of representational technology in middle school mathematics. Given the high-level of funding for this area over many years, this creates a credibility gap that we hope our study will address. Further, only through large-scale research can we address the "boutique critique" by showing a learning-sciences based intervention can work across a wide range of ordinary settings and teachers. Finally, we can learn something about how teacher variation mediates outcomes which could enable learning sciences researchers who are designing new innovations to be more methodical about doing design research in the settings and with the teachers whose circumstances tend to diminish outcomes.

Acknowledgements

This work was supported under National Science Foundation grants #0437861 and #0337710. Any opinions are those of the authors and not the funding agency.

References

Brown, A. (1991). Design experiments. Theoretical and methodological challenges in evaluating complex interventions in classroom settings. *Journal of the Learning Sciences.*

Elmore, R. F. (1996). Getting to scale with good educational practice. *Harvard Educational Review, 66*(1).

Kaput, J. (1992). Technology and mathematics education. In D. Grouws (Ed.), *A handbook of research on mathematics teaching and learning* (pp. 515-556). New York: Macmillan.

Kaput, J. (1994). Democratizing access to calculus: New routes using old roots. In A. Schoenfeld (Ed.), *Mathematical thinking and problem solving* (pp. 77-155). Hillsdale, NJ: Erlbaum.

Kaput, J. (2002). Implications of the shift from isolated, expensive technology to connected, inexpensive, diverse and ubiquitous technologies. In F. Hitt (Ed.), *Representations and mathematical visualization*. Mexico: Departmento de Matematica Educativa del Cinvestav - IPN.

Kaput, J., & Roschelle, J. (1998). The mathematics of change and variation from a millennial perspective: New content, new context. In C. Hoyles, C. Morgan & G. Woodhouse (Eds.), *Rethinking the mathematics curriculum*. London, UK: Falmer Press.

Roschelle, J., Kaput, J., & Stroup, W. (2000). Simcalc: Accelerating student engagement with the mathematics of change. In M. J. Jacobsen & R. B. Kozma (Eds.), *Learning the sciences of the 21st century: Research, design, and implementing advanced technology learning environments.* (pp. 47-75). Hillsdale, NJ: Erlbaum.

Roschelle, J., Tatar, D., & Kaput, J. (in press). Getting to scale with innovations that deeply restructure how students come to know mathematics. In A. E. kelley & R. Lesh (Eds.), *Foundations for the future: Reconceiving the goals in mathematics education in the 21st century.* Hillsdale, NJ: Erlbaum.

Analyzing collaborative learning: Multiple approaches to understanding processes and outcomes

Chair: Cindy E. Hmelo-Silver, Rutgers University, 10 Seminary Place, New Brunswick, NJ 08901-1183, USA, chmelo@rci.rutgers.edu

Abstract: It is important to consider collaborative processes from multiple perspectives because collaborative learning environments are complex, often requiring multiple methodological approaches to understand their different aspects (Hmelo-Silver, 2003). Collaborative learning is the subject of study in a wide variety of disciplines such as developmental psychology (e.g., socio-cognitive conflict), social psychology (person perception, motivation, group processes), sociology (status, power and authority), cognitive psychology (how learning occurs, learning outcomes) and sociocultural perspectives (cultural influence on interaction, mediation of learning). These different perspectives suggest that a variety of methodological tools are needed to understand collaborative interactions. Each of the papers in this symposium explores one or more methods for examining the quality of collaborative interactions. The discussion will focus on criteria for good analyses of collaborative work as well as strengths and limitations of various methods.

Collaborative learning environments are complex beasts, often requiring multiple methodological approaches to understanding interactions (Hmelo-Silver, 2003). Like Rummel & Spada, 2004, we argue that it is important to consider collaborative processes from multiple perspectives. Collaborative learning is the subject of study in a wide variety of disciplines such as developmental psychology (e.g., socio-cognitive conflict), social psychology (person perception, motivation, group processes), sociology (status, power and authority), cognitive psychology (how learning occurs, learning outcomes) and sociocultural perspectives (cultural influence on interaction, mediation of learning). These different perspectives suggest that a variety of methodological tools are needed to understand collaborative interactions. We consider methodological tools that examine the quality of processes and trajectories of interactions.

Two commonly used approaches for analyzing data are to classify individual learners' statements and to provide descriptive, qualitative analyses of transcripts. Researchers using the first approach have used a diverse range of approaches to classifying individual students' statements, ranging from classifying cognitive strategies (such as elaboration or explanation) used by individual students (Webb & Farivar, 2000) to classifying moves such as giving or receiving help. This general approach provides information about individuals' performance within groups but does not provide a picture of the overall structure or flow of the group discourse or how individuals contribute to this overall structure or flow. Researchers using the second, more descriptive approach have provided rich pictures of interactions, but this is not a method that is well suited for making systematic comparisons across different groups or discussions.

Each of the papers in this symposium explores one or more methods for examining the quality of collaborative interactions. Chinn discusses five different approaches to analyzing argumentative discourse, noting the strengths and limitations of each approach for generating both qualitative and quantitative understandings of discourse quality. O'Donnell examines how individual contributions during dialogue can be traced in terms of their influence on others. Hmelo-Silver, Chernobilsky, and Mastov discuss representations that can aid in the interpretation of complex collaborative learning environments. Erkens and Janssen discuss how the coding of dialogue acts can be made more tractable through reliable and valid automated coding mechanisms.

Brigid Barron will comment on the presentations. The discussions among panelists and the discussant will include a focus on criteria for good analyses of collaborative work. Examining the range of methods that we have collectively used to examine the quality of group interactions, we will discuss criteria that should be met by methodological tools that succeed at capturing the richness of group interaction and the limitations of the different approaches.

Assessing the Quality of Collaborative Argumentation

Clark A. Chinn, Rutgers University, 10 Seminary Place, New Brunswick, NJ 08901-1183, USA,
cchinn@rci.rutgers.edu

Introduction

One important type of collaborative discourse is argumentation. Many tasks designed to develop students' inquiry skills have engaged collaborative groups of students in argumentation (see Duschl & Osborne, 2002). Hence, it is important to develop effective methods of assessing the quality of argumentation in collaborative groups.

Criteria for developing measures of collaborative argumentation

Measures of argumentation should provide insights into both the quality of the *overall group* argumentation and the quality of *individual* contributions to the group. They should illuminate the *structure* of the discourse and the *content* of the discourse. And they should ideally provide both *qualitative* and *quantitative* windows into discourse quality.

Measuring features of argumentation

I discuss five methods that have been used to analyze collaborative argumentation. I discuss these methods in the context of a study with seventh graders who were discussing epidemiological studies they had read about.

Coding *speech acts* is a very common way of measuring aspects of many forms of discourse, including argumentative discourse (e.g., Resnick et al., 1993). When applied to argumentation, speech act analysis involves classifying statements into functional categories such as claims, supporting reasons, qualifiers, counterarguments, rebuttals, concessions, and so on. Speech act analysis of argumentation provides a one-dimensional picture of the distribution of speech acts in a group and in individuals. It does not provide insights into the structure or the content of discussions.

More *specific reasoning strategies* can also be coded. For instance, in the seventh graders' discussions, we code the use of particular reasoning strategies in the discussion such as weighing sample size, evaluating the adequacy of comparison groups, and examining whether measurements are biased. Unlike speech act analyses, analyses of specific reasoning strategies can distinguish between good reasons (e.g., arguing that a conclusion should be rejected because the methodology of a study is flawed) and poor reasons (e.g., arguing that West Nile disease is contagious on the basis of a single person's impressions).

The two measures discussed so far do not capture the structure of discourse. In contrast, an adaptation of Toulmin's (1958) well-known method of diagramming arguments allows researchers to represent argumentation as *argument networks* (see Chinn & Anderson, 1998). The figures below shows the structural outlines of a simple (left) and complex (right) argument network. Rectangles represent claims made. Reasons for claims are in ovals connected to claims by arrows. Reasons given to support or contradict other reasons create deeper layers within the network. Chinn, O'Donnell, and Jinks (2000) showed that students in groups of fifth graders who participated in scientific discussions learned more when argument networks were more complex than when argument networks were simpler.

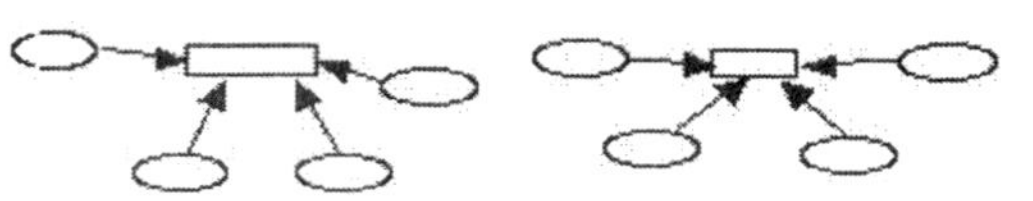

Figure 1. Prototypical simple argument network

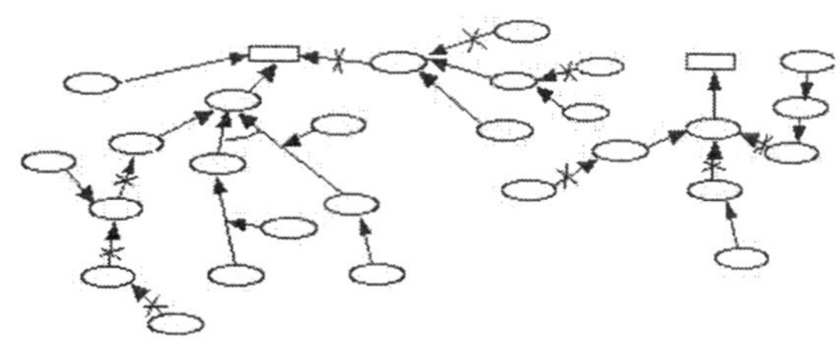

Figure 2. Prototypical complex argument network

Argument networks are like speech act analyses in that they show the presence of claims and supporting reasons, but they go further in that they capture the structure of the discussion. Argument networks can be used to generate quantitative measures of both the quality of the group discussion and the quality of each individual's contribution (Chinn & Anderson, 1998). Argument networks do not, however, provide any information about the content of the discussion. The complex argument network above could equally represent argumentation with strong reasons and evidence and argumentation marked by sophistry.

Analysis of *argument schemas* is a fourth approach that can be used to evaluate the quality of reasoning in argumentation. In this approach, learning to argue is viewed as learning a variety of argument schemas (Chinn, 2006). For example, reasoners who employ arguments about sample size can be viewed as having rich underlying schemas that specify when the sample size argument can be applied, when it is inapplicable, why the sample size argument is valid, how the needed sample size varies according to relevant variables such as the variability of the population, and so on. Reasoning schema analyses can be used to chart the development of particular argument forms used by individuals and groups. This method provides a rich understanding of students' understanding of the content of reasoning.

A fifth type of measure that could be applied to argumentation but has not yet been extensively applied is an analysis of the overall *argumentative stance* taken in the argumentation. In some argumentation, the predominant stance is one of *persuasion*; participants are trying to persuade each other that their view is correct. Other argumentation seems to take a *problem solving* approach, where reasons are advanced not primarily to persuade (though persuasion may occur) but to solve a problem jointly. Other possible stances exist, as well. It seems reasonable that the stance taken may powerfully influence the cognitive and affective outcomes of argumentation.

Summary

Although none of these measures taken singly provides a full picture of the quality of students' argumentation, careful choice of two or three measures together can provide a much more complete picture of collaborative argumentation. Researchers could improve research on argumentation by employing a broader range of measures.

Representations for Analyzing Tool-mediated Collaborative Learning

Cindy E. Hmelo-Silver, Ellina Chernobilsky, Olga Mastov, Rutgers University, 10 Seminary Place, New Brunswick, NJ 08901-1183, USA, chmelo@rci.rutgers.edu, ellinac@eden.rutgers.edu, omastov@eden.rutgers.edu

Introduction

Sociocultural theories 1) argue that learning is inherently social and situated and 2) emphasize the critical role of tools in mediating learning (Cole, 1996). This suggests a view of learning that is quite complex, There are a variety of approaches to examining collaborative learning discourse. Analyzing the complexity of such collaborations is often done using intricate multilevel coding schemes (e.g, Chinn & Anderson, 1998; Engle & Conant, 2002; Hmelo-Silver, 2003). Other researchers have used more qualitative approaches to studying collaboration, such as Roschelle's (1996) study of computer-mediated convergent collaborative conceptual change. The latter provides a detailed look at portions of a collaborative process, focusing on social and linguistic processes. Some of the former approaches blend reliable cognitive and social analyses over larger periods of time but lose the chronological detail and often, the relation between different kinds of utterances. Because we are interested in how the different aspects of discourse relate to each other, as well as to the tools being used in the collaborative learning process, a better understanding of how collaborations unfold and how tools are used is crucial. This requires going beyond the coding of individual speech acts. The use of Chronologically-ordered Representation for Tool-Related Activity (CORDTRA) is one way of achieving this understanding. This technique is a generalization of the CORDFU methodology developed by Luckin et al (2001). Luckin and colleagues used this approach to examine how alternative ways of structuring hypermedia affected collaborative discourse, allowing them to explore relations between the software's features and collaborative knowledge construction.

CORDTRA Diagrams

CORDTRA diagrams contain parallel timelines that allow a researcher to juxtapose a variety of codes to understand an activity system—for example, these might be discourse, gestural, or tool-related codes (see Figure 1 for an example from Hmelo-Silver et al., 2005). Initially, we used this technique to examine face-to-face collaboration in a problem-based learning (PBL) tutorial to understand how constructing a drawing mediated learning (Hmelo-Silver, 2003). The work was expanded to study online collaborative learning in the eSTEP system (Hmelo-Silver & Chernobilsky, 2004; Hmelo-Silver *et al.*, 2005). eSTEP is an integrated online PBL environment for preservice teachers (Derry, 2006), containing a learning sciences hypermedia, a library of videocases, and an online activity structure that gives students access to a suite of individual and collaborative tools. We hypothesize that student learning and transfer will be enhanced when they repetitively bring together the conceptual ideas of the learning sciences with perceptual ideas from the classroom video. To explore this, we contrasted two groups who had used eSTEP (Hmelo-Silver & Chernobilsky, 2004). The CORDTRA analysis demonstrated that the more effective group started with initial discussion and exploration of the hypermedia and looked at the video as needed throughout their work—offering new ideas as they explored the video and deepening them during independent research. The students collaboratively developed and refined their ideas using the hypermedia and video in cycles. The less effective group worked sequentially, using the video early in their process and the hypermedia later. They engaged in a lot of tool-related discussion until late in the activity and spent little time on their final group product. We have used this analysis to generate hypotheses about how these tools might effectively mediate collaborative learning. We have also used CORDTRA diagrams to study the development of one group over time as they eSTEP on three problems (Hmelo-Silver *et al.*, 2005). The CORDTRA diagrams allowed us to see how the activity patterns changed over time as students moved from parallel lurking to active participation.

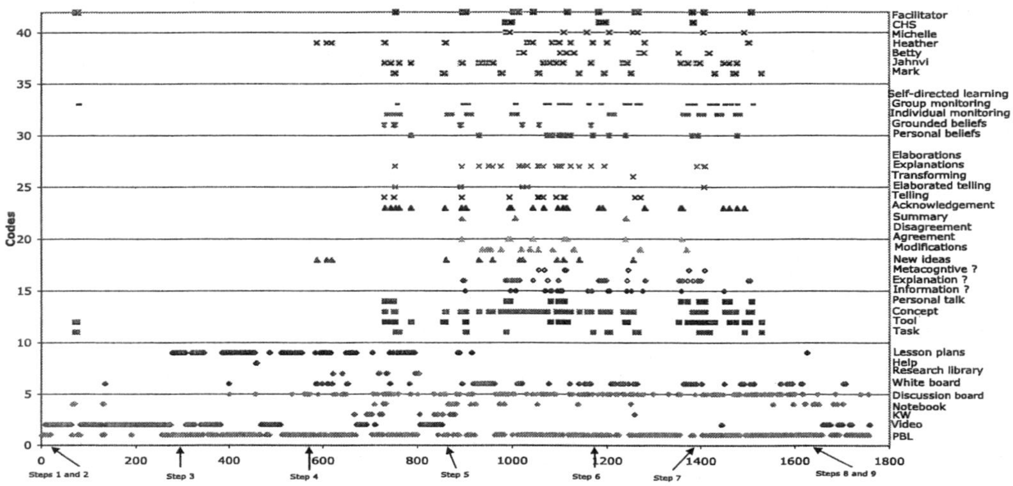

Figure 1. Example CORDTRA diagram

Understanding Patterns of Collaboration

We are expanding the use of CORDTRA as a means to examine patterns in many groups over time, determining how the nature of online discourse affects tool use and how the tools in turn affect the online discourse. CORDTRA analyses are an important addition to multilevel coding schemes, allowing researchers studying collaborative learning to go beyond coding and counting to seeing the larger patterns that emerge. This presentation will show examples of how CORDTRA diagrams can be used to illuminate tool-mediated collaborative learning.

A Perspective on Collaborative Learning informed by a Focus on Outcomes

Angela M. O'Donnell, Rutgers University, 10 Seminary Place, New Brunswick, NJ 08901-1183, USA, angelao@rci.rutgers.edu

Introduction

What should we expect peers to learn from opportunities to collaborate with others? Various implementations and analyses of collaboration learning reflect significant differences in underlying theory, methods, and outcomes. Depending on the group process that occurs within a collaborative group, the actual collaborative process of different groups engaging in the same task may be explained by appealing to differing theoretical perspectives. Analyses of groups from the perspectives of these varied theoretical perspectives may allow for the identification of dimensions of interaction that are necessary to allow for explanations of effective groups.

In the study described here, students in three-person groups were asked to read a case about the classroom difficulties experienced by a new teacher. They were asked to identify her problems and to develop a plan to help her solve the problems. No strategy was imposed on student groups. They were to come to consensus on their plan. All participants were provided with the actual case but groups of participants were provided with access to varied ancillary information. The purpose of doing so was to increase the information sources available in the group.

Method

Participants took part in two sessions, separated by a one-week interval. Students signed up in triads. The first set of questions (# 1-5) were intended to have students rehearse knowledge of the specifics of the case. Question 6 was the central question: "What should Maggie do about the class behavior? Develop a plan for what she should do." Participants were directed to come up with a joint plan. They could either make a single record of the agreed-upon plan or they could record this agreed-upon plan separately. During the second session, which took place a week later, participants were asked to recall the jointly constructed plan for what Maggie should do about the classroom behavior. They were reminded that they were to recall the *group's plan* and not their own. A total of 76 groups (n=228) participated.

Results

Transcripts of the discussions that resulted in the initial plan allow for the identification of contributors to decisions made that subsequently were recorded as part of the group plan. The individual recall protocols from the second session allow for the analysis of whose ideas were recalled. These data allow an examination of how influence is accomplished in a group. The plan created by each group was used as the basis for the analysis. Each idea in the plan was listed. The transcript of the session related to the development of the plan was examined to identify who had contributed ideas that were eventually included in the plan agreed upon by members of the group. Each idea recorded on the plan was credited to the student who introduced the idea on the tape. In addition, if another student picked up on this idea in the discussion (e.g., supported the idea, elaborated upon it), that student was also credited. Each students' recall was rated for the number of ideas recalled, the number of ideas in the recall that were not part of the group's plan, the number of ideas that the student recalled and had been contributed by that student in the transcript, and the number of ideas that they recalled that were contributed by others. Analyses of these data suggest that individuals tend to retrieve the ideas they personally contributed to a plan and are influenced rather infrequently by others. This pattern of influence may be best described by information processing theory. Not all group's interactions and influences can be described in this way, however. Further analyses of groups that did not conform to this interpretation are currently being conducted.

Discussion

The method used to look at "joint cognition" has promise. The recorded plan for groups represented what the group members believed to be their consensus about how Maggie (the first year teacher) should proceed. However, recall of the joint plan was often poor and a great many additions were often added. Group cohesion can be detected in the shared recalls of group members.

In many ways, the characterization of what constitutes "joint cognition" here is very mechanistic. There is little attention paid (thus far) to the quality of the plan. The purpose here is mainly descriptive and answers the question: "Do people include other people's ideas in their recall?" This work is beginning to address within this limited context what is learned in groups.

Automatic coding of communication in collaboration protocols

Gijsbert Erkens & Jeroen Janssen, Research Centre Learning in Interaction, Utrecht University, The Netherlands, G.Erkens@fss.uu.nl, J.J.H.M.Janssen@fss.uu.nl

Introduction

Initially, analyses of computer-supported collaboration focused on surface level characteristics of the communication, such as the number of messages sent (Strijbos, Martens, Prins, & Jochems, 2006). However, over the last 15 years the analysis of communication protocols is being used more and more to study collaboration processes (Rourke & Anderson, 2004). The development of a systematic and valid method that can be used to analyze communication protocols can be difficult. Furthermore, the process of analyzing a great number of protocols can be time consuming. Therefore, in order to speed up the process of coding communication protocols, an automated coding system was developed. This paper aims to describe the automatic coding procedure. Furthermore, it focuses on reliability, validity and limitations concerning the developed procedure.

Method and Results

The coding system developed identifies 'dialogue acts,' that is, the communicative function of each utterance typed by students during online collaboration and communication. Five main communicative functions are distinguished: *argumentative* (indicating a line of argumentation or reasoning), *responsive* (e.g., confirmations, denials, and answers), *informative* (transfer of information), *elicitative* (questions or proposals requiring a response), and *imperative* (commands). A total of 29 different dialogue acts are specified. For instance, an *imperative action (ImpAct)* indicates a commanding utterance with regard to a specific action to be taken.

To automatically code a protocol and identify which dialogue acts are used during collaboration, the *Multiple Episode Protocol Analysis* (MEPA) computer program is used (Erkens, 2003). This program can be used for the analysis and coding of collaborative discussions. Additionally, the program offers facilities for automatic coding. A production rule system was created that automatically categorizes utterances into dialogue acts. A set of *if-then* rules uses pattern matching to look for typical words or phrases, in this case for discourse markers. Discourse markers are characteristic words signaling the communicative function of a phrase in conversation in natural language (Schiffrin, 1987). For example, *why* at the beginning of an utterance usually indicates an *open question (EliQstOpn)*. The developed production rule system consists of a rule system for automatic segmentation of utterances in single messages (300 rules) and a rule system for dialogue act coding (1250 rules). This way, MEPA is able to code a protocol consisting of 1,000 utterances in less than a second.

Although automatic coding can dramatically speed up the coding process, several methodological issues concerning reliability and validity need to be addressed. One concern is the reliability of the automatic coding procedure. A previous study showed that reliability of the automatic coding procedure was high: two independent coders established that over 90% of the utterances were coded correctly (Erkens, Jaspers, Prangsma, & Kanselaar, 2005).

Examinations of group differences can be used to establish validity of the automatic coding procedure (Rourke & Anderson, 2004). Since previous research has shown that men and women behave differently during collaboration (Leaper & Smith, 2004): women use more affiliative speech (e.g., praise and responsiveness), whereas men use more assertive speech (e.g., negative speech and directives), it would be useful to examine these if differences are replicated using the automatic coding procedure. Indeed, in our sample female students used more responsive dialogue acts, whereas male students used more imperative dialogue acts. This result is a first step in validating the automatic coding procedure. Another way to establish validity of the automatic coding procedure may be through experimental intervention (Rourke & Anderson, 2004). In order to stimulate student participation and argumentative knowledge construction, a new tool was added to an existing CSCL-environment. Indeed, as expected students with access to this tool used more argumentative dialogue acts, compared to students without access to this tool. Thus, the results described above indicate that the automatic coding procedure does not only speed up the coding process, but also seems to yield reliable and valid results.

Conclusion

Preliminary results indicate favorable results concerning the validity and reliability of the automatic coding procedure. Additionally, the results of the automatic coding procedure will be compared to results obtained with a manual coding procedure. This manual coding focused on the collaborative activities students perform during collaboration in a CSCL-environment (Janssen, Erkens, Kanselaar, & Jaspers, in press). Results concerning this comparison of 'dialogue acts' and 'collaboration acts' will also be presented. Although results of the automatic coding procedure do not provide insight into the structure of online discussions (see also Chinn, this symposium), the procedure can be a starting point for more complex, sequential analyses. These sequential analyses can subsequently be used to capture the structure and quality of online discussion (e.g., Erkens, Janssen, Jaspers, & Kanselaar, 2006). Taken together, such an approach may constitute a valuable tool for researchers interested in analyzing collaborative discussions

References

Chinn, C. A. (2006). Learning to argue. In A. M. O'Donnell, C. Hmelo-Silver & G. Erkens (Eds.), *Collaborative learning, reasoning, and technology* (pp. 355-383). Mahwah, NJ: Erlbaum.

Chinn, C. A., & Anderson, R. C. (1998). The structure of discussions that promote reasoning. *Teachers College Record, 100*, 315-368.

Chinn, C. A., O'Donnell, A. M., & Jinks, T. S. (2000). The structure of discourse in collaborative learning. *Journal of Experimental Education, 69*, 77-97.

Cole, M. (1996). *Cultural psychology: A once and future discipline*. Cambridge MA: Harvard.

Derry, S. J. (2006). STEP as a case of theory-based web course design. In A. O'Donnell, C. E. Hmelo-Silver, & G. Erkens (Eds.), *Collaboration, Reasoning and Technology* (pp. 171-196). Mahwah, NJ: Erlbaum.

Duschl, R. A., & Osborne, J. (2002). Supporting and promoting argumentation discourse in science education. *Studies in Science Education, 38*, 39-72.

Engle, R., & Conant, F.. (2002). Guiding principles for fostering productive disciplinary engagement: Explaining an emergent argument in a community of learners classroom. *Cognition and Instruction, 20*, 399-484.

Erkens, G. (2003). *Multiple Episode Protocol Analysis (MEPA)*. Version 4.9. Retrieved October 24, 2005, from http://edugate.fss.uu.nl/mepa/

Erkens, G., Janssen, J., Jaspers, J., & Kanselaar, G. (2006). Visualizing participation to facilitate argumentation. Paper to be presented during the symposium "Argumentative Knowledge Construction in CSCL" at the 7th International Conference of the Learning Sciences.

Erkens, G., Jaspers, J., Prangsma, M., & Kanselaar, G. (2005). Coordination processes in computer supported collaborative writing. *Computers in Human Behavior, 21*(3), 463-486.

Hmelo-Silver, C. E. (2003). Analyzing collaborative knowledge construction: Multiple methods for integrated understanding. *Computers and Education, 41*, 397-420.

Hmelo-Silver, C. E., & Chernobilsky, E. (2004). Understanding collaborative activity systems: The relation of tools and discourse in mediating learning. In Y. Kafai, W. Sandoval, N. Enyedy, A. Nixon & F. Herrera (Eds.), *Proceedings of ICLS 2004* (pp. 254-261). Mahwah NJ: Erlbaum.

Hmelo-Silver, C. E., Chernobilsky, E., & Nagarajan, A. (2005). *Two sides of the coin: Multiple perspectives on collaborative knowledge construction in online problem-based learning.* Paper presented at the European Association for Research on Learning and Instruction, Nicosia, Cyprus.

Janssen, J., Erkens, G., Kanselaar, G., & Jaspers, J. (in press). Visualization of participation: Does it contribute to successful computer-supported collaborative learning? *Computers & Education.*

Leaper, C., & Smith, T. E. (2004). A meta-analytic review of gender variations in children's language use: Talkativeness, affiliative speech, and assertive speech. Developmental Psychology, 40(6), 993-1027.Luckin, R., Plowman, L., Laurillard, D., Stratfold, M., Taylor, J., & Corben, S. (2001). Narrative evolution: Learning from students' talk about species variation. *International Journal of Artificial Intelligence in Education, 12*, 100-123.

Luckin, R., Plowman, L., Laurillard, D., Stratfold, M., Taylor, J., & Corben, S. (2001). Narrative evolution: Learning from students' talk about species variation. *International Journal of Artificial Intelligence in Education, 12*, 100-123.

Resnick, L. B., Salmon, M., Zeitz, C. M., Wathen, S. H., & Holowchak, M. (1993). Reasoning in conversation. *Cognition and Instruction, 11*, 347-364.

Roschelle, J. (1996). Learning by collaborating: Convergent conceptual change. In T. D. Koschmann (Ed.), *CSCL: Theory and practice of an emerging paradigm* (pp. 209-248). Mahwah NJ: Erlbaum.

Rourke, L., & Anderson, T. (2004). Validity in quantitative content analysis. Educational Technology Research and Development, 52(1), 5-18.

Rummel, N. & Spada, H. (2004). Cracking the nut—but which nutcracker to use? Diversity in approaches to analyzing collaborative processes in technology-supported settings. In Y. B. Kafai, W. A. Sandoval, N. Enyedy, A. S. Nixon & F. Herrera (Eds.), *Proceedings of the Sixth International Conference of the Learning Sciences* (pp. 23). Mahwah NJ: Erlbaum.

Schiffrin, D. (1987). Discourse markers. Cambridge, MA: Cambridge University Press.

Strijbos, J.-W., Martens, R. L., Prins, F. J., & Jochems, W. M. G. (in press). Content analysis: What are they talking about? Computers and Education.

Toulmin, S. E. (1958). *The uses of argument*. Cambridge, England: Cambridge University Press.

Webb, N. M., & Farivar, S. (1999). Developing productive group interaction in middle-school mathematics. In A. M. O'Donnell & A. King (Eds.), *Cognitive perspectives on peer learning* (pp. 117-150). Mahwah NJ: Erlbaum.

Learning at the nanoscale: Research questions that the rapidly evolving interdisciplinarity of science poses for the learning sciences

Sherry His, The Exploratorium & NISE Network, 3601 Lyon Street, San Francisco, CA, 94123
Nora Sabelli, SRI International, 333 Ravenswood Ave, BN-316, Menlo Park CA 94025
Joseph Krajcik, University of Michigan and NCLT, 610 East University Avenue, Ann Arbor, Michigan, 48109
Robert Tinker, The Concord Consortium, 10 Concord Crossing, Suite 300, Concord, MA 01742
Kirsten Ellenbogen, Science Museum of Minnesota and NISE Network, 120 West Kellogg Boulevard, Saint Paul, MN 55102
NCLT and NISE Network researchers
Email: sherryh@exploratorium.edu, nora.sabelli@sri.com, krajcik@umich.edu bob@concord.org, kellenbogen@smm.org

Abstract: Recent interdisciplinary discoveries in the sciences and engineering at the nanoscale, specifically in our ability to manipulate, molecules at atomic scales, suggests a need for the education community to reconsider the ways in which disciplinary-based sciences and mathematics are being taught in schools, as well as how the public might engage with nanoscale phenomena. This session will discuss key learning questions and their importance in helping to advance both conceptual reasoning from the macro, micro, nano, and atomic levels, as well as their implications for curricular restructuring, public programming, and teacher professional development. The timeliness and broader importance of this research derives in part from two NSF-sponsored workshops on nanoscale education held in 2005, the National Nanotechnology Initiative, and two multi-institutional NSF awards: a National Center for Learning and Teaching and the Nanoscale Informal Science Education Network. This session will discuss research implications for the learning sciences and education community.

Background

The U.S. federal government has placed nanoscience and nanotechnology as one of its top R & D priorities because of its potential to revolutionize medicine, computing, materials science, energy production, and manufacturing. This investment has created the National Nanotechnology Initiative (NNI; NSTC/NSET, 2005) and the National Nanotechnology Infrastructure Network to support the development of research, programs, and tools to advance nanoscience and nanotechnology research and education (Roco and Bainbridge, 2002; Roco 2003) The impact of nanotechnology on manufacturing processes and everyday applications makes this investment important for education, and calls for cognitive and pedagogical research around issues of scale which run across all scientific disciplines.

To make these advances visible and comprehensible to all audiences, the National Science Foundation has made two substantial awards. One award targets public audiences through the establishment of a national infrastructure that links science museums and other informal science education organizations with nanoscale science and engineering research organizations, called the National Nanoscale Informal Science Education (NISE)[1] Network led by the Museum of Science Boston along with the Exploratorium and the Science Museum of Minnesota. NISE's goal is to foster public awareness, engagement, and understanding of nanoscale science, engineering, and technology. The second award, the Nanoscale Center for Learning and Teaching (NCLT)[2], with Northwestern University, Purdue, the University of Michigan, and a large number of institutional partners, is aimed at the college and pre-college science education communities.

In addition, two NSF-sponsored workshops were held recently to consider aspects of nanoscale education: one at SRI's Center for Technology and Learning (CTL) and other at the National Science Foundation. The CTL workshop at SRI International brought together a wide variety of participants including educational researchers and science educators (spanning high school, community college, and university levels), nanoscientists, science museum and informal learning specialists, and workforce development staff to consider the integration of concepts of the nanoscale with science education. In particular, the workshop identified core nanoscale concepts and discussed their representations, and considered needs and directions for research related to nanoscale education (Sabelli et al., 2005).

The primary goal of the NSF workshop was to bring together principal investigators of awards funded by the NSF Division of Elementary, Secondary, and Informal Education and the education coordinators of several nanoscience research centers, to facilitate both knowledge transfer among participants, and moves towards defining a coherent nanoscience education vision.

Introduction – A Climate for NSET Education

This ICLS session will explore the need for learning scientists to consider educational implications of the initiatives in nanoscale science, engineering, and technology (NSET). Researchers concurrently and collaboratively working on middle school science curricula, interactive modeling software, teacher professional development, exhibitions in museums, and public understanding of nanotechnology will share the multiple approaches and challenges in which learning at the nanoscale is being facilitated, implemented, and assessed across settings and audiences.

The nanoscale is unfamiliar to students and relatively inaccessible. Compared to everyday experience, different forces are important, friction is almost never encountered, everything is in thermal motion, and odd quantum effects are observed. To develop an understanding of this world, the learner needs to depend on indirect evidence, mental models, and computational environments. It could be argued that these concepts are too difficult to tackle until students reach an advanced undergraduate level and can handle sophisticated mathematics. It is, however, desirable for a much broader range of students to gain a general conceptual understanding of the area for various civic and economic reasons and because the complex, interdisciplinary nature of nanotechnology better reflects modern science than the usual disciplinary treatment. Furthermore, the science concepts that are important at nano scale provide deep linkages between disciplines. Taught at a conceptual level, they could make large parts of science more accessible and motivated. It is possible that student exploration of computational models can develop the needed concepts (Tinker, 2005a; 2005b).

A conceptual framework, responsive to the new interdisciplinary, system-oriented ways of doing and using science is needed if a *coherent* curriculum vision can be refined. While views of the curriculum have evolved (AAAS, 1989; AAAS, 2001), the underlying expectations and structure assume the current sequencing, and does not yet reflect the cumulative impact of the changes that have taken place in the field of science, engineering, and technology. Two possible frameworks derived from the technologically-driven methodological advances are catalysts for deep science curricula reform. They are (a) complexity: i.e. the systemic, self-inferential, multi-level nature (Waldron, 1992, Holland, 1998, Kaput et al., 1999) of the scientific issues that confront citizens in making sense of political discussions and reaching personal decisions (global change and risk assessment of genetically engineered foodstuffs for example), and (b) the scientific and technological advances that have enabled the study and manipulation of matter at the nanoscale, where chemistry, physics, biology overlap, and where engineering and design takes a more eminent role. Either complexity (see Sabelli, 2005) or nanotechnology can be used as a lens to analyze ways in which curriculum can addresses the evolution of science in support of science education goals.

In this session we will discuss the educational importance of looking at the nature of matter as a continuum that has been made clear by the practical applications of nanotechnology (see, for example, Roco, 2004). This approach shares a starting point with Lederman's "physics first" curriculum, which uses the interdisciplinary molecular basis of nature as its conceptual underpinning (Lederman, 2001). Our aim is to explore how learning sciences research can use the issues of learning at the nanoscale to help learners to develop a more coherent and integrated understanding of science and its methods, without adding nanoscience to an already impacted curriculum to benefit from the affordances of interdisciplinarity.

Emerging NSET education research question

The two events mentioned in the background section generated preliminary key research questions that need the help of the learning sciences to be addressed. In March 2005, SRI International convened a working meeting to discuss conceptual issues related to *integrating the science and technology of the nanoscale into science education* (Sabelli et al., 2005). In October 2005, NSF convened a workshop on K12 and Informal Nanoscale Science and Engineering Education gathering participants from different science and technology centers and education outreach projects to take stock in the progress so far in nanoscience education and outreach. A key goal of this NSF workshop was to promote synergies between researchers and practitioners working in the formal and informal learning areas, and move towards defining a coherent nanoscience education vision. The two workshops were complementary: nanoscience education and awareness (NSF) and integrating scale in science education (SRI CTL).

In both these meetings, key learning research questions and nanoscience key principles were identified by consensus and agreed upon as important to address. With the participation of the learning sciences community, these questions could be further investigated to convert principles into learning goals and to formalize a research agenda.[3] A workshop to start the process is being planned for early 2006.

The broad set of questions posed during the workshops are as follows:

- What are possible development trajectories for 5 – 12th grade students to learn major learning goals related to nanoscience (or interdisciplinarity and complexity)?
- How do people reason about scale? How do we get learners to understand crossing boundaries from macro, micro, nano, and atomic levels?
- Given that people cannot see nanoscale phenomena with the naked eye, what do learners extract from the various visualizations, representations and models we design for them?
- What is the role of physicality and experiential activities when dealing with nanoscale phenomena?
- What are the scaffolds, models, representations, and/or exhibit interactions that lead to educational progress? And how do they evolve/change with the learner over time?

Cognitive research questions relate to the importance of understanding not only each scale independently, but also the transition between scales of matter: When does an object stop being a collection of individual atoms or molecules and become a "material?" If the components are identical when there is a larger aggregate of particles, forming a bulk amount of the same substance, is it the same "material" or not? Is there a rule that aptly describes the transition area between a nanoscale object and a bulk object? These questions apply in physics as much as in chemistry and in biology. There is not a "nanoscience" as such, rather a science of matter at the nanoscale where the boundaries between disciplines becomes blurred. It is thus educationally exciting to explore how integrating scale into science school subjects can lead to a more coherent conceptual understanding of science. It is where the boundaries between disciplines blur that we can attempt an integrative pedagogy.

In addition to cognitive aspects, there are epistemological considerations about the nature and conception of 'small' and beliefs about what exists when the science phenomenon is invisible to the naked eye. For example, when adults, teens, and children were asked about the smallest thing as objects they could conceive, a majority across all ages said a piece of dirt or a grain of sand. (see Waldron et al., 2005) Can learners really reason mathematically or conceptually at 10^{-9} meter scales? Or does this even matter that this might not be comprehensible or teachable? Research into conceptual bridges of how to teach ideas that small quantitative changes lead to large qualitative differences, and that matter can be studied as individual particles, a group of particles or a large group of particles, might help lower barriers to understanding of why nanotechnology has become so important, and how it forces the interconnections among scientific disciplines. This, in turn, could help learners acquire a more coherent version of science and of scientific advances.

Prior and Related Research and Evaluation on NSET

Prior research has addressed some of these questions in the context of discipline-based classroom teaching such as chemistry or physics (Harrison and Treagust, 1996; DeWos and Verdonk, 1996; Johnstone, 1993) Some of these questions have been addressed by research into advanced learning tools to support visualization and haptic interactions by students to address learning morphologically accurate models of viruses (Jones et al., 2002). Other interventions have demonstrated the success of linking molecular representations with symbolic and macroscopic phenomena using multimedia-based instruction (Ardac and Akaygun, 2004). For example, the Concord Consortium has developed a molecular dynamics (MD) engine for education that uses classical mechanics to predict the motion of particles that act under forces that approximate the forces on atoms and molecules (Pallant and Tinker, 2004; Xie and Tinker, 2005). Using molecular dynamics software, students can interact with and build models of liquid crystals, self-assembly, and protein conformation. [4]

Because the field of nanoscience is still new to many, there are few if little documented prior studies of conceptions or misconceptions about nanotechnology among the public or learners in both the US and in Europe (Cobb and Macoubrie, 2004; Lee, Scheufele, and Lewenstein, in press). This presents an interesting opportunity for NSET learning sciences research and education in formal and informal settings.

In museums and science centers, several formative studies and evaluations have been conducted that studied visitors' ideas about atoms, molecules, and scale before visiting exhibitions; and public audience reactions to exhibitions that focus on nanoscale phenomena, nanoscience and nanotechnology (e.g., *NanoZone, Strange Matter, Marvelous Molecules* (Serrell and Associates, 2001) *It's a NanoWorld, Too Small to See.*)) These studies found that visitors have difficulty reasoning about things they can't see, don't differentiate between micro (10^{-6}) and nano (10^{-9}), and had difficulty ranking an atom, DNA, and cell by size (Stafford and Molinaro, 2005; Holladay, 2005; Waldron et al., Korn et al., 1999). Adults and children alike are challenged by interactions and phenomena at the nanoscale. Social sciences research has also been done on public perceptions of nanotechnology focusing upon people's assessment of potential benefits and risks associated with the field, preferences for learning about applications, and their limited awareness of nanotechnology issues (Flagg, in press). As more public forums, educational media, and new NSET exhibitions are developed, learning scientists have even more opportunities to study learning at the nanoscale with the learners of all ages in the general public, and to contribute research-informed design principles to foster designs for greater engagement with and understanding of nanoscale science, engineering, and technology in a more comprehensible and interdisciplinary way.

Conclusions

Nanoscale research challenges both the learning and science research communities to jointly explore new pedagogies needed and to create approaches to communicate why the work of nanoscale scientists and engineers has attained such visibility and how it might also engage the general public, not only nanotechnology specialists. Changes in observable properties with scale are not cognitively obvious, and the ability to manipulate matter at these small scales is creating a new paradigm in manufacturing. To inform the public about the advances in scientific research, and to capture the imagination of new generations of diverse communities of youth who may choose careers in science and engineering requires research that considers changes in science when these changes have become so fundamental to society. Addressing these challenges will hopefully lead to new thinking, techniques, and partnerships between learning scientists, educators, and scientists, just as the advancement of nanoscale science, engineering, and technology has led to new disciplines, technologies, and collaborations. The learning sciences community has both a body of empirical research and prior knowledge to contribute, as well as expertise to advance research on learning and teaching at the nanoscale. However, without focused collaboration and continued interactions across disciplinary boundaries and without learning scientists taking an active role and voice in these endeavors, another opportunity will be missed to make deep science educational progress.

Endnotes

(1) NISE URL: http://www.nisenet.org

(1) NCLT URL: http://www.nclt.us/
(1) The latest version of both reports will be available at the ICLS session.
(1) The force used in most Molecular Dynamics simulations from the Concord Consortium is derived from the Lennard-Jones potential. Through the tools, three objects and related forces can be added to the basic MD model that allows the system to illustrate some important nano-science concepts: Gay-Berne particles, Smart Surfaces, and water interactions. Using these, students can interact with and build models of liquid crystals, self assembly, and protein conformation.

References

American Association for the Advancement of Science. (2001). *Atlas of science literacy*. New York: Oxford University Press.

American Association for the Advancement of Science. (1989). *Science for all Americans*. Washington, DC, American Association for the Advancement of Science.

Ardac, D. & Akaygun, S. (2004). Effectiveness of Multimedia-Based institution that emphasizes molecular representations on students: Understanding of chemical change. *Journal of Research in Science Teaching* 41, 317-337

Bainbridge, W. S. (2002). Public attitudes toward nanotechnology. *Journal of Nanoparticle Research*, 4, 561-570.

Cobb, M. D., & Macoubrie, J. (2004). Public perceptions about nanotechnology: Risks, benefits and trust. *Journal of Nanoparticle Research, 6*, 395-405.

DeWos, W. & Verdonk, A. H. (1996). The particulate nature of matter in science education and in science. *Journal of Research on Science Teaching*. 33, 657-664

Flagg, B. (in press). Nanotechnology and the Public. *Informal Learning Review* for 2006 issue.

Johnstone, A. H. (1993) The development of chemistry teaching: a changing response to a changing demand. *Journal of Chemical Education*.70, 701-705

Harrison, A. J, & Treagust, D. F. (1996). Secondary students' models of atoms and molecules: implications for teaching chemistry. *Science education.* 80, 509-534

Holland, J. (1998). *Emergence: From Chaos to Order*, Addison-Wesley.

Jones, D. G. C. (1991). Teaching modern physics - Misconceptions of the photon that can damage understanding, *Physics Education*, *26* (2) 92-98.

Jones, M. G, Bokinsky, A., Andre, T., Kubasko1, D. , Negish, A., Taylor, R., & Superfine, R., (2002) NanoManipulator Applications in Education: The Impact of Haptic Experiences on Students' Attitudes and Concepts. *Proceedings of the IEEE Computer Science Haptics 2002 Symposium*, pp. 295-298. Orlando, Florida: IEEE Computer Society.

Kaput, J., Bar-Yam, Y., Jacobson, M., Jakobsson, E., Lemke, J., Wilensky, U. et al. (1999). Planning documents for a National Initiative on Complex Systems in K-16 Education. Retrieved August 2005, from http://necsi.org/events/cxedk16/cxedk16.html

Korn, R. & Associates (1999). *A front-end evaluation of Materials MicroWorld*. Prepared for the Materials Research Society.

Korn, R. & Associates (2004). *Strange Matter Summative Evaluation.* Prepared for the Materials Research Society.

Lederman, L. (2001) *Revolution in Science Education: Put Physics First!* Physics Today, September issue.

Lee, C., Scheufele, D., & Lewenstein, B. (in press) Public attitudes toward emerging technologies: Examining the interactive effects of cognitions and affect on public attitudes toward nanotechnology. *Science Communication.*

Macoubrie, J. (2005). *Informed public perceptions of nanotechnology and trust in government.* Project on emerging technologies at the Woodrow Wilson International Center for Scholars. Retrieved from http://www.wilsoncenter.org/index.cfm?fuseaction=events.event_summary&event_id=143410

NISE Network, The Nanoscale Informal Science Education Network. http://www.nisenet.org

NNI, National Nanotechnology Initiative, http://nano.gov. See also http://www.nano.gov/html/edu/home_edu.html

NNIN, National Nanotechnology Initiative Network, http://www.nnin.org/

Pallant, A., & Tinker, R. (2004). Reasoning with atomic-scale molecular dynamic models. *Journal of Science Education and Technology: 13* (1), 51-66.

Roco, M.C. (2003). Converging science and technology at the nanoscale: opportunities for education and training. *Nature Biotechnology, 21* (10) 1247.

Roco, M.C., (2004). Nanoscale Science and Engineering: Unifying and Transforming Tools. *American Institute of Chemical Enguneers Journal, 50* (5) 890.

Roco, M.C. & Bainbridge, W.S. (eds.) (2002). Converging Technologies for Improving Human Performance: Nanotechnology, Biotechnology, Information Technology and Cognitive Science. Retrieved from http://www.wtec.org/ConvergingTechnologies

Sabelli, N., Schank, P., Rosenquist, A., Stanford, T., Patton, C., Cormia, R., & Hurst, K. (2005). Report of the Workshop on Science and Technology Education at the Nanoscale. Menlo Park, CA: SRI International. Retrieved from http://nanosense.org/documents/reports/NanoWorkshopReportDraft.pdf

Sabelli, N. (in press). Complexity, Technology, Science and Education, *International Journal of the Learning Sciences.*

Serrell and Associates. (2001). *Marvelous Molecules: The Secret Life.* Summative Evaluation. Retrieved from www.informalscience.org/tools/summative.html

Stafford, C. L., Molinaro, M., & Nanozone Leader Team. (2005) Lessons learned from Nanozone. Retrieved from nanozone.org/museum.htm

Scheufele, D. A., & Lewenstein, B. (forthcoming). The public and nanotechnology: How citizens make sense of emerging technologies. *Journal of Nanoparticle Research.*

Schummer, J. (2005). Reading nano: The public interest in nanotechnology as reflected in purchase patterns of books. *Public Understanding of Science, 14* (2), 163-183.

Tinker, R. (2005a). *Molecular Dynamics in Education.* Berkeley, CA: The University of California, Berkeley.

Tinker, R. (2005b). *Nano-engineering with the Molecular Workbench*. Berkeley, CA: The University of California, Berkeley.

Waldrop, M (1992). *Complexity: The Emerging Science at the Edge of Chaos and Order*, Touchstone Press

Waldron, A., Spencer, D., & Batt, C. (forthcoming). Too Small to See: The Current State of Public Understanding of Nanotechnology. Nanobiotechnology Center. Cornell University

Xie, Q., & Tinker, R. (in press). Molecular dynamics simulation of chemical reactions for use in education. *Journal of Chemical Education.*

Complex Systems in Education: Conceptual Principles, Methodologies, and Implications for Research in the Learning Sciences

Michael J. Jacobson, Nanyang Technological University, Singapore, jacobson@nie.edu.sg
Uri Wilensky, Northwestern University, U.S.A., uri@northwestern.edu
Robert Goldstone, David Landy, Ji Son, Richard Lesh, Indiana University, U.S.A.
Email: rgoldsto@indiana.edu, dlandy@indiana.edu, jys@indiana.edu, ralesh@indian.edu
Cindy E. Hmelo-Silver, Rutgers Unviersity, U.S.A., chmelo@rci.rutgers.edu
Roger Azevedo, University of Maryland, U.S.A., razevedo@umd.edu

Abstract. The symposium has two main goals: First, it would allow the contributors to the recent JLS special issue on complex systems in education to provide an overview of the issues raised in their respective papers as well as to discuss updated research of relevance. Second, it is hoped that this symposium will provide a forum for discussing the potential implications of complex systems perspectives for research in the learning sciences, and more generally for educational research, curriculum development, and educational policy and reform initiatives.

Symposium Overview

The Journal of the Learning Sciences (JLS) has recently inaugurated a series of research strands on timely and developing issues (Kolodner, 2003). Each of these strands is to have an orienting paper and commentaries as part of a special issue that would help contextualize and perhaps guide subsequent research papers submitted to the strand over the next few years. One of the initially identified strands is *learning and school environments as complex systems,* for which a special issue has recently appeared in the JLS (Azevedo & Hmelo, 2006;; Goldstone, 2006; ; Jacobson & Wilensky, 2006; Lesh, 2006; Sabelli, 2006) {why this ref for the special issue? Shouldn't we ref all our papers in that issue?} that is the focus of this symposium.

As background to this session, there are four thematic perspectives that emerge from the papers. First, there is a growing body of research that is documenting how students at the pre-graduate school level can in fact learn dimensions of core knowledge that are being articulated by scientists who study complex physical and social systems. While this is an important general finding in itself, a second argument is that helping students learn complex systems principles may also address other long standing research issues and learning challenges, such as how best to help students learn knowledge in deep and meaningful ways, how to help students apply or use this knowledge in new and different contexts, and what are the boundaries of knowledge and conceptual difficulty that students at particular ages and developmental levels might be capable of learning. Third, concepts derived from a complex systems analytical perspective have the potential to provide a degree of conceptual coherence to the otherwise bewildering properties of diverse phenomena in the physical and social sciences. Thus it may be that infusing complex systems concepts into the curricular content of school subjects could form the basis of a new type of scientific literacy that also would have important implications for how curricula in the physical and social sciences are developed and sequenced across grade levels from elementary school to college. Fourth, there are concepts and methodologies being articulated by scientists in the physical and social sciences who are involved with advanced complex systems research that raise important issues of theoretical and methodological centrality in the learning sciences and in fields involved with research in education and educational policy.

Presentation Overviews

Complex Systems In Education: Importance, Implications, and Issues

Michael J. Jacobson, National Institute of Education, Nanyang Technological University

The multi-disciplinary study of complex systems in the physical and social sciences over the past quarter of a century has led to the articulation of important new conceptual perspectives and methodologies that are of value both to researchers in these fields as well as to professionals, policy makers, and citizens who must deal with challenging social and global problems in the 21st century. This presentation will: (a) argue for the importance of learning these ideas at the pre-college and college levels; (b) discuss the significant challenges inherent in learning complex systems knowledge from the standpoint of theory and research; (c) argue that the cognitive and socio-cultural factors related to learning complex systems knowledge are relevant and challenging areas for learning sciences research; and (d) consider ways that concepts and methodologies from the study of complex systems raise important issues of theoretical and methodological centrality in the fields related to the learning sciences. Also, this paper provides a background for issues that will be considered in other papers in this session.

Complex Systems and Reformulating Scientific Disciplines: Implications for Learning, Analysis af Social Systems, and Educational Policy

Uri Wilensky, Northwestern University

A complex systems perspective has enabled scientists to study a wide variety of systems in principled ways that had not previously been possible and, in turn, this has also lead to a deepening of our understanding of the connections between scientific disciplines. However, of perhaps even greater potential impact for student learning of new scientific views of complex systems is the ability to replace traditional algebraic or mathematical formalisms with computational representations. In particular, it is now possible to understand important aspects of how systems function and dynamically change in terms of many simple rules using technologies such as cellular automata and agent-based modeling instead of through the listing of differential equations. An important advantage of this approach is that it enables scientists and learners to conceptually and visually "see" the explicit connections between the micro level behaviors and the macro level phenomena. A complex systems perspective means that in helping our students to learn important knowledge in the physical and social sciences, we no longer have to be content with descriptions of only the aggregate level of phenomena (e.g., birds flocking, neighborhood segregation patterns), but instead can also explore mechanisms related to micro level interactions (the behavior of an individual bird or individual house-dweller). An important consequence of these developments is that the reformulation of scientific disciplines (also referred to as restructurations (Wilensky & Papert, 2005)) and the use of perspectives and methodologies from work on complex systems can enable students to study advanced content in the physical and social sciences at a deep level without requiring that they have an advanced knowledge of mathematics. A related consequence is that this will enable many more students to have access to this content. This paper will provide an overview of the research at the Northwestern Center for Connected Learning and Computer-Based Modeling (CCL) that has investigated learning in the context of restructurations in fields such as chemistry, evolutionary and population biology, materials science, and electrostatics. The CCL has authored restructurated curricula using agent-based models as the representational form (Wilensky, 1999; Blikstein & Wilensky, 2004; Levy, Kim & Wilensky, 2004; Sengupta & Wilensky, 2005; Wilensky & Reisman, 2006). This research has been investigating how students learn with these restructurated curricula and whether students can use similar sets of computational rules and algorithms in different domains of inquiry and, if so, whether such perspectives enable students to transfer ideas across very different disciplines. Other work to be discussed in this paper includes how complex systems modeling techniques may be used to look at educational and social systems, modeling these systems, and examining the implications for policy decisions.

Seeing Through Complex Systems

Robert L. Goldstone, David Landy, Ji Son, Indiana University

A complex systems perspective offers the promise of unifying increasingly fragmented scientific communities, and also facilitating transfer of knowledge across widely dissimilar domains, one of the greatest unsolved challenges for education. We will report on the results from a series of laboratory experiments exploring transfer of complex systems principles by undergraduate students. These experiments manipulate several design aspects of the computer simulations that are used to instantiate the principles: the graphical concreteness/idealization of the simulation elements, the specificity of the words describing elements, and the amount of contextualizing information or experience given to ground the simulations. Given these experiments and our experience using these simulations, we suggest that the most effective way to promote cross-domain transfer is to get learners to automatically see new situations using perceptual processes that have been adapted to previous situations, rather than relying on generalization from equations or abstract schemas.

Core Challenges in Understanding Complex Systems

Roger Azevedo, University of Maryland

Cindy E. Hmelo-Silver, Rutgers University

Understanding and reasoning about complex systems places a huge burden on our cognitive resources and often violates our intuitions (Feltovich, Coulson, & Spiro, 2001; Narayanan & Hegarty, 1998). Yet, education about complex phenomena often ignores the phenomena themselves and instead has learners focus on memorizing the names of the parts of the system (AAAS, n.d.). Thus, it is not surprising that most people understand complex systems as collections of parts with little understanding of how the system works (Hmelo-Silver & Pfeffer, 2004; Hmelo-Silver, Marathe, & Liu, 2004). There are some deep principles that underlie many complex systems, some of which Jacobson and Wilensky have discussed, such as structure-behavior-function and emergence (see Goldstone & Sakamoto, 2003 for others). What differentiates these complex systems from complicated systems is the heterogeneity of components and their multiple levels of organization. Supporting learning about complex systems are key research issues for the learning sciences, and we have identified several challenges that must be addressed to help students better understand complex systems. One of the major issues affecting students' ability to learn about complex systems is their cognitive, metacognitive, and self-regulatory processes. Students' ability to learn about complex systems and other challenging topics (Azevedo, in press; Quintana, Zhao, & Krajcik, in press) is somewhat dependent on being able to plan, sustain, and reflect on the complex mechanisms underlying learning about complex systems. There is a faulty assumption that students not only have these skills, but that they are motivated and can effectively make decisions regarding their learning (Azevedo, Cromley, & Seibert, 2004). We need to reconsider these assumptions and to examine their role in fostering students' learning about complex systems. There are developmental issues related to the use of cognitive, metacognitive, and motivational skills required to sustain learning in specific contexts (Azevedo, in press). Studying the use of metacognitive processes in understanding complex systems is critical to understanding how we can facilitate learning about complex systems, as learners engage in monitoring multiple activities during such learning—their emerging understanding and the aspects of their learning environment. Besides learning mechanisms, there are reasoning skills that must the deployed while learning about complex systems in technology-based environments such as simulations and modeling environments. Learners need knowledge about the nature of models, domain knowledge, general cognitive and metacognitive skills and scientific reasoning skills. Without such knowledge, it is difficult to learn about a complex system through simulation and modeling. This suggests that the field must strive for explanations of the roles these underlying mechanisms and scientific skills play in supporting learning about complex systems and what kinds of scaffolding are needed.

The learning sciences is at an early stage of understanding how people think about complex systems (e.g., Jacobson, 2001; Hmelo-Silver & Pfeffer, 2004) and how they learn about such systems (e.g., Azevedo, in press-b; Charles & D'Appolonia, 2003; Wilensky & Resnick, 1999). Our presentation will highlight a number of issues that the field must better understand if we are going to support students' learning about complex systems. Understanding these issues requires that learning scientists identify and carry out a broad research program with respect to how students and teachers learn about complex systems.

The Teaching and Learning of Complex Systems in Education: Paradigm Shifts Beyond Current Ways of Thinking

Richard Lesh, Indiana University

This presentation accepts the premise that it is important to understand how students might learn about complex systems. However, it is argued that current learning science theories are not necessarily *sufficient* to provide answers to most questions about the nature of the conceptual systems that students would need to develop in order to understand complex systems. In contrast, I believe that the most exciting point about learning science investigations of complex systems is precisely that such research is likely to require a variety of significant paradigm shifts beyond current ways of thinking. Furthermore, I believe that these paradigm shifts should have implications for learning and problem solving related to a wide range of constructs and situations where relationships to systemic understandings are far less obvious than in the case of complex systems. The paper will make four main points. First, investigations about what it means to "understand" complex systems are important in their own right because in the 21st century such systems are becoming increasingly important in the everyday lives of ordinary people. Second, investigations of such systems should have implications far beyond the topic of complex systems because "systemic understandings" that are highlighted in the context of complex systems also are involved in the development of many other types of concepts, skills, principles, beliefs, and attitudes, and problem solving processes that are not as obviously systemic in nature. Third, investigations of what it means to "understand" such systems should provide productive venues to advance learning science theories precisely because knowledge about such systems is not likely to be reducible to lists of simple closed form functions. Fourth, complexity theory introduces a wealth of language, models, metaphors, and tools that could provide very productive alternatives to traditional rule-based ways of thinking about the nature of knowledge, learning, and problem solving. We are at an exciting time in which a paradigmatic shift has been occurring in many fields with respect to complex systems. Learning scientists are uniquely positioned to understand the implications of this shift; especially as it relates to facilitating the learning of and about these complex systems as well as how complex systems principles can inform our understanding of how people learn.

Discussants

Nora Sabelli, SRI

Allan Collins, Northwestern University

References

AAAS. (n.d.). *AAAS project 2061 biology textbooks evaluation.* Retrieved November 19, 2003, from http://www.project2061.org/research/textbook/hsbio/about.htm

Azevedo, R. (2005). Using hypermedia as a metacognitive tool for enhancing student learning? The role of self-regulated learning. *Educational Psychologist, 40*(4), 199-209.

Azevedo, R., Cromley, J.G., & Seibert, D. (2004). Does adaptive scaffolding facilitate students' ability to regulate their learning with hypermedia? *Contemporary Educational Psychology, 29*, 344-370.

Blikstein, P. & Wilensky, U. (2004) MaterialSim: an agent-based simulation toolkit for Materials Science learning. *Proceedings of the International Conference on Engineering Education*. Gainesville, Florida.

Feltovich, P. J., Coulson, R. L., & Spiro, R. J. (2001). Learners' (mis)understanding of important and difficult concepts. In K. D. Forbus & P. J. Feltovich (Eds.), *Smart machines in education: The coming revolution in educational technology* (pp. 349-375). Menlo Park, CA: AAAI/MIT Press.

Goldstone, R. L., & Sakamoto, Y. (2003). The transfer of abstract principles governing complex adaptive systems. *Cognitive Psychology*, 414-466

Hmelo-Silver, C. E., Marathe, S., & Liu, L. (2004, June). *Understanding complex systems: An expert-novice comparison*. Paper presented at annual meeting of the American Psychological Association. Honolulu, HI.

Hmelo-Silver, C. E., & Pfeffer, M. G. (2004). Comparing expert and novice understanding of a complex system from the perspective of structures, behaviors, and functions. *Cognitive Science, 28*, 127-138.

Jacobson, M. J. (2001). Problem solving, cognition, and complex systems: Differences between experts and novices. *Complexity, 6*(2), 1-9.

Jacobson, M.J. & Wilensky, U. (2006). Complex systems in education: scientific and educational importance and research challenges for the learning sciences. *Journal of the Learning Sciences.*

Kolodner, J. L. (2003). From the editor. *The Journal of the Learning Sciences, 12*(1), 1-3.

Levy, S.T., Kim, H., & Wilensky, U. (2004). Connected Chemistry - A study of secondary students using agent-based models to learn Chemistry. In J. Gobert (Chair) and N. H. Sabelli (Discussant) *Modeling Across the Curriculum (MAC): Technology, Pedagogy, Assessment, & Research*. The annual meeting of the American Educational Research Association, San Diego, CA, April 12 - 16, 2004.

Narayanan, N. H., & Hegarty, M. (1998). On designing comprehensible interactive hypermedia manuals. International Journal of Human-Computer Studies, 48, 267-301.

Quintana, C., Zhang, X., & Krajcik, J. (in press). A framework for supporting metacognitive aspects of on-line inquiry through software-based scaffolding. *Educational Psychologist.*

Sabelli, N. (2006). Understanding complex systems strand: Complexity, technology, science, and education. *The Journal of the Learning Sciences, 15*(1), 5-9.

Sengupta, P. & Wilensky, U. (2005). N.I.E.L.S: An Emergent Multi-Agent Based Modeling Environment for learning Physics. Proceedings of AAMAS 2005 (ABSHL session), Utrecht, Netherlands.

Wilensky, U. (1999). GasLab—an Extensible Modeling Toolkit for Exploring Micro-and Macro-Views of Gases. In Roberts, N. Feurzeig, W. & Hunter, B. (Eds.) Computer Modeling and Simulation in Science Education. Berlin: Springer Verlag. pp. 151 – 178.
Wilensky, U. & Papert, S. (2005). Restructurations: Reformulations of Knowledge Disciplines through new representational forms. (Paper in preparation).
Wilensky, U., & Reisman, K. (2006). Thinking like a Wolf, a Sheep or a Firefly: Learning Biology through Constructing and Testing Computational Theories. Cognition & Instruction, 24(2), 171-209.
Wilensky, U., & Resnick, M. (1999). Thinking in levels: A dynamic systems approach to making sense of the world. *Journal of Science Education and Technology, 8*, 3-19.

"Theory in pieces" – the communal development of a theory

Orit Parnafes, Andrea diSessa, Joseph Wagner, Jose Mestre, Tom Thaden-Koch & Bruce Sherin
Organizer's address: Graduate School of Education, University of California, Berkeley, oritp@berkeley.edu

Abstract: This symposium aims to expose some of the social dynamics of theory development in the learning sciences by examining one particular case. It examines how individual studies contribute to theory development by using and extending an original theory of conceptual development, coordination class theory. We show how the diversity of contexts in which these ideas have been applied has contributed, not so much to validation, but to genuine expansion of meaning and power of the theory. This pattern emphasizes the essentially social nature of theory construction, and also a striking parallel between theory development in professional science and ideas about conceptual development in students that emphasize the role of multiple contexts. We discuss theoretical and methodological issues of communal development of a theory, such as theoretical power, fit, extension and generality.

Symposium Overview

This symposium discusses meta-theoretical questions relevant to the core issue of how theories are developed by a community of researchers. It attempts to expose some of the social dynamics of theory development in the learning sciences through the case of coordination class theory.

What is a coordination class theory? Briefly speaking, coordination classes provide a means for getting a certain class of information (e.g., force, velocity, energy etc.) from the world. The very idea of coordination classes is explicated in diSessa (2002):

> **The fundamental assumption behind the idea of coordination classes is that information is not transparently available in the world. Instead, we have to learn how to access different kinds. Indeed, in different circumstances, we may need to use very different means to determine the same kind of information.**

A well-formed coordination class guarantees that the same type of information would be inferred across different contexts and situations. A coordination class includes two parts: a perceptual part and an inferential part. The perceptual part includes the methods by which information is collected from the world by means of selecting attention to specific aspects. These are called "readout strategies." The inferential part includes the body of knowledge and reasoning strategies that determine the inferences from the readout information. This body of knowledge is called "causal net".

While diSessa originally sketched the foundations of the theory, several other researchers joined the enterprise of building a coherent theory that applies to a wide range of contexts. The theory originated in two sophisticated papers that lay the grounds for the theory in much detail and nuance (diSessa, 1991; diSessa, 1994). The widely cited paper by diSessa & Sherin (1998) followed, and attempted to outline the necessary and foundational theoretical constructs of coordination class theory through the examination of a single freshman physics student trying to make sense of the concept of force. The theory was picked by other researchers for its perceived power to generate insights in specific research contexts. The use of the theory in a diversity of contexts led to a genuine expansion of meaning and power.

Wagner's dissertation (Wagner, 2003) focused on extended case studies of several undergraduate students as they learned statistics and, in particular, "the law of the large numbers." This work applies coordination class theory in at least three new directions. First, the domain explored is mathematics, which is new for coordination class theory. Second, the larger theoretical framing of the work is the issue of knowledge transfer. Third, this was the first attempt to demonstrate processes of learning as viewed from a coordination class perspective. Prior studies that applied coordination classes only examined students' knowledge without necessarily observing real conceptual change. These new directions drove the elaboration and modification of some pieces of the theory.

Mestre, et al. (2004), based on Thaden-Koch's dissertation (Thaden-Koch, 2003), analyzed students' judgments of realism of animations of different trajectories among physics-naïve and physics-knowledgeable undergraduates. The study highlighted the important role that readout strategies play in this particular context. While in prior research applying coordination classes the role of the causal net was highlighted in the process of conceptual change, this research presents a specific context where the causal net interacts strongly with readout strategies, resulting in the inability of most of the physics-knowledgeable students to perform accurate readouts (i.e., an inability to detect anomalous motion that was detected by most of the physics-naïve students).

Parnafes' dissertation (Parnafes, 2005) used coordination class theory in the context of studying students' development understanding of harmonic oscillation through the use of computer-based representations. This research expands the theory to the use of representations. In addition, the idea of *coordination clusters*, mentioned briefly in diSessa & Wagner (2005), becomes a central construct in some of the cases explored and is further developed (Parnafes, in review).

Finally, Levrini (Levrini, 2005; Levrini, in preparation) implemented coordination class theory in the context of proper time in special relativity. The particular case highlights *span, alignment and concept projection* as keys for interpreting the process of conceptual change activated by students in transitioning from a Newtonian conception of time to a relativistic one.

Four of these attempts to develop and extend the theory are summarized below. Each presentation, in addition to delineating the context and the theory extension, also refers to the following issues of communal theory development:

Theoretical fit: Why was coordination class theory a good candidate as a theoretical framework for this case, and how is the theory mapped onto this particular case? Were there features in the data corpus that served as particularly strong indicators?

Theoretical power: In what ways was the idea of coordination class insightful for the analysis of this particular case? In other words, were there some important insights that wouldn't have been possible without coordination classes?

Theory extension: How did the particular case suggest modifications or elaborations on the framework?

Specificity and generality: What are the particular properties of the case that led to the particular extension of the theory? In what sense did this case serves as a prototype for general classes of cases or contexts?

Presentations

Coordination Classes: Theoretical and Meta-Theoretical Issues

Andrea A. diSessa, University of California, Berkeley, disessa@soe.berkeley.edu

This presentation aims to set a general frame for considering multiple lines of research—exemplified by the work of the other contributors to the symposium—inspired by the idea of coordination classes (CC). The presentation gives a sketch of the basic ideas of CC theory and suggests some meta-theoretical issues relevant to the core issue of how theories are developed by a community of people: Why do some theories "catch on" and why don't others? Is it appropriate to consider some theories as more generative than others (without any presumption of "correctness"), and how can generativity be judged or created in advance? Is there a tension between social and epistemic aspects of theory building, and, if so, how do researchers manage the tension?

Coordination Class Theory

Coordination class theory provides a rough model of a particular kind of concept (a coordination class) as a complex system. The model answers three primary questions: (1) What is the primary function of a concept (specifically, a CC)? (2) What are the performance characteristics that allow the concept effectively to perform its function? (3) Structurally, can we decompose the concept (CC system) into parts? Thus:

(1) The primary function of a coordination class is to allow one to *determine a particular class of information in many world circumstances.* (2) The main difficulty that must be overcome is the diversity of situations in which one needs to determine the relevant information. Information is never transparently available, and people need opportunistically to use whatever is easily "read out" of a given situation, and then creatively to infer the particular CC-characteristic information from that. However, all the diverse strategies must be coordinated (hence the name) in order to determine reliably the *same* information in *all* circumstances. (3) A first-cut in terms classifying parts of a CC is to distinguish perceptual-proximal strategies (more directly "seeing") from inferences that may be made on the basis of what is seen. The perceptual-proximal elements, which select and manage attention, are called *readout strategies.* The post-perceptual body of knowledge and reasoning strategies, which takes readouts and infers the required information, is called the *causal* or *inferential net.* In the talk, I will give examples and additional details of the model, including ideas of span, alignment, and concept projections

Meta-theoretical Properties of Coordination Classes

Below I name several more-or-less "designed" characteristics of coordination class theory that might have contributed to its apparent generativity and use by others.

1. The theory is inviting because of its explicitly tentative nature, allowing other researchers both to fill in and to adapt to their particular contexts. CC theory is self-consciously a rough sketch, and limitations have been as highlighted as defining aspects.
2. The theory makes progress by dividing off a subcontext from a complex, but perhaps intractably diverse terrain. CCs are only one type of concept, not all possible concepts. The theory is driven, in part, by the assumption of diversity in kinds of concepts, and it might draw some of its power from this "restricting of domain."
3. The theory went through a self-conscious phase of simplification—although, in its present form, it is still not, and was never intended to be, a "popularly accessible" idea. Simplification can be both sociologically and epistemologically powerful, although there may also be a tension—for example, over-simplifying to promote accessibility.
4. Coordination class theory is one of the few existing technical models of the internal structure of concepts as a complex system, and it allows both theoretical analysis (e.g., of typical difficulties) and empirical tracking of processes of concept use and development. Here, the value of the theory may not be in its details, but primarily in a new grain size of analysis.
5. The theory may be productive mainly for introducing a focus on an, until-now, neglected characteristic of concepts: their perceptual aspects.

Transferring a Theory to a New Context

Joseph F. Wagner, Xavier University, wagner@xavier.edu

In setting out to take a new look at the problem of "knowledge transfer" (Wagner, 2003), I had no expectation that diSessa's research would serve as the primary theoretical underpinning for my own. Early considerations of my data—extended teaching interviews with undergraduate statistics students wrestling with their understandings of the law of large numbers—led me to reconsider the way the problem of transfer has usually been considered. Traditionally, the problem has been framed liked this: *How is it that knowledge learned in one context can be applied to a different context?* I proposed in Wagner (2003) that a different question might be asked that just as readily articulated as the problem of transfer: *How is it that individuals come to see two different situations (contexts) as alike, in that they might be considered examples of the same (mathematical) principle?* This change of focus—from the state of the knowledge to be applied in a new context to the individual's ability to perceive a new situation as an instantiation of some concept—led me to diSessa's work on coordination class theory.

Reframing the question in this way made inseparable "knowledge of a concept" and "the ability to perceive a concept in particular situations." The coordination class components of *readout strategies* and the *causal net* together suggest that learning to recognize some concepts in the world involves learning very particular and context-sensitive means of attending to information relevant to that concept. In other words, the ability to perceive a concept as relevant to a particular situation is not due primarily, if at all, to the "abstract" nature of conceptual knowledge; rather, learning to recognize and see as relevant a concept in a situation depends on an individual having acquired appropriate readout strategies suited to that situation. In this interpretation, it is quite possible for a person to develop a meaningful understanding of some concept that is consistently useful in *some* situations but is not perceived as useful in other situations that may be relevant by normative standards. In our language, we would say that it is common for a learner to construct a *concept projection* for a particular concept that suffices in some situations, but not in others (diSessa & Wagner, 2005; Wagner, 2006). diSessa's theory predicts the very problem that knowledge transfer has always posed: Why is it that some people make good use of knowledge in some situations but not in others?

In Wagner (2003; 2006) I showed how diSessa's coordination ideas, situated within his larger knowledge-in-pieces epistemological framework, could be extended to offer some coherent and powerful insights to the long-standing problem of knowledge transfer. Data were drawn from microgenetic analyses of in-depth interviews carried out over several weeks with undergraduate students learning elementary concepts of probability and statistics. These analyses revealed that knowledge transfer may be rooted in the construction of cognitive structures significantly different from those traditionally assumed in the transfer literature. diSessa's insistence on the context-sensitivity of different forms of knowledge was supported by the data. Analyses suggested that the key to knowledge transfer is not found in the "abstractness" of knowledge that somehow *overlooks* contextual differences, but through the increasing complexity of conceptual structures that include context-sensitive readout and coordination strategies that *account for* contextual differences.

The process of my own research reflected the very theory of transfer that diSessa's and my ideas suggested. Coordination class theory was not simply "applied" to a new set of data in any abstract way. Rather, my ability to perceive it as useful within the specific context of my work emerged only as I learned to attend to particular aspects of my data that served as affordances for "seeing" aspects of diSessa's theory; as the theory itself suggested new ways of looking at my data; and as the occasional lack of fit between the two suggested ways in which the theory itself could be expanded.

Coordination clusters in oscillatory motion

Orit Parnafes, University of California, Berkeley, oritp@berkeley.edu

In the context of investigating how computer-based representations facilitate conceptual change in the domain of harmonic oscillation (Parnafes, 2005), the application of coordination class theory seemed to be an appropriate fit. First, coordination class theory enables one to look at the process of conceptual change at a fine-grained level, which matches the type of analysis that I do, aiming to describe mechanisms of developing understanding. Second, since coordination class theory refers to perceptual processes (in addition to conceptual processes), it was particularly suitable for analyzing processes of learning with external representations, and generated an opportunity to examine possible relations between representations and conceptual change.

More specifically, through observation of eight pairs of students interacting with both physical oscillators and a simulation of oscillatory motion, I examined how students differentiate the concepts of velocity and frequency in oscillatory motion, facilitated by the use of representations. The close examination of this processes led to the refinement of the idea of *coordination cluster*.

The idea of a coordination cluster was motivated and developed through the analysis of students' efforts to make sense of the term "fast" both with physical oscillators, and with a simulation of oscillation. Everyday talk usually refers to both velocity and frequency as "fast", and in many contexts this undifferentiated use is unproblematic. However, in a scientific context, the use of terms to denote certain concepts requires more precision in order to use those concepts properly in a wide range of contexts and relations and with a proper alignment. Moreover, in the context of oscillation, where the term "fast" denotes at least two different scientific concepts (velocity and frequency), precise differentiation becomes even more crucial. A proper differentiation between these two concepts requires that students develop a system that coordinates two coordination classes: velocity and frequency. This system is what we called a coordination cluster, which requires two-level coordination:

1. Coordinating information within one coordination class – students need to learn ways to get information from multiple situations about frequency (or about velocity, in the case of coordination class of velocity).

2. Coordinating information across coordination classes – students need to learn to differentiate the two concepts of velocity and frequency and to know when to use each concept and what the relations between those concepts are. Even if they have a coordination class of frequency, and they know how to get information about frequency, they still need to know that they are dealing with the concept of frequency and not with the concept of velocity.

The construct of coordination cluster seems to be particularly useful for cases of concept differentiation, or in cases where students use different concepts interchangeably. In these cases, the development of one coordination class is constructed with the simultaneous construction of other coordination classes in the cluster.

The application of coordination class theory on Students' Judgments about Animated Motion

Tom Thaden-Koch, University of Minnesota, ttkoch@physics.umn.edu
Jose Mestre, University of Illinois, mestre@uiuc.edu

We will discuss an application of coordination class theory to a situation in which students were asked to judge the realism of computer animations showing metal balls rolling on a pair of metal tracks. The animations were based on a variant of a common physics classroom demonstration, sometimes called "High Road/Low Road." Given different sets of animations, students were asked to identify the "most realistic" one from the set. When presented with animations of a single ball, most students focused on the presence or absence of realistic speed changes. Adding a second ball (moving in an adjacent track) to the animations drastically changed the strategies that many students used, to the extent that they identified as realistic a particular (unrealistic) motion with two balls that they had ruled out minutes before with one ball. This motion featured a ball speeding up as it rolled uphill, which the students found unrealistic in the one-ball context. When both balls were present, this same motion (with a ball speeding up while rolling uphill) showed one ball speeding ahead of the other before they reached the ends of their tracks together (a pattern that many students identified as a characteristic of realistic motion on these tracks).

We attempted a concrete (often phrase-by-phrase) mapping of student interview data onto the structures postulated for coordination classes. Students often repeated similar descriptions of similar motions, which allowed us to identify several common expectations of realistic motion, and some of the sources for those expectations; these we mapped onto the causal net. The same repeated descriptions of well-specified stimuli allowed us to make plausible inferences about the readout strategies students used in different circumstances.

Our analysis particularly highlights the effect that students' knowledge can have on the observations they make. The participants in the study were drawn from two different college courses. Students from an introductory physics course were especially prone to the problem of accepting anomalous motion as realistic, as described above. In contrast, students from an educational psychology class were virtually immune to the problem. Mapping interview data onto coordination class structures facilitates an explanation in terms of the knowledge that students brought to the task (causal net elements), and the sorts of observations (readout strategies) that they focused on based on that knowledge. In this explanation, the readout strategies evoked were strongly dependent on the knowledge that students brought to bear on the task, and on details of the context. The emphasis in other applications of coordination class theory attends mostly to the use of readout strategies to gather information, on which the causal net will operate. In our case, different causal net inferences led to very different ways of observing the world—that is, the causal net affected readout strategies.

Another feature of this application of coordination classes is that virtually no attempt was made to identify knowledge structures or concepts that could qualify as coordination classes. To the extent that it is useful, the case provides evidence that coordination, and the language of coordination classes, can be fruitful even in cases where "coordination classes" are of only peripheral interest. These issues are discussed in more detail in a recent article extending our prior work (Thaden-Koch, Dufresne & Mestre, under review).

Summary

Each presentation in the symposium demonstrates the application and extension of coordination class theory. As researchers who attempt to apply this theoretical construct on a corpus of data, one thing that we must do is to refine our ability to recognize that construct in our research context. A number of researchers seem to agree that coordination class is a powerful idea. However, it is not obvious that any two researchers would "see" the same coordination class in the same data, or even that they count the same thing as a coordination class. As part of community theory building, we need to refine the ways in which we "see" things in our data through the lens of the theory. In other words, we need to refine our coordination class of coordination class.

Discussant

Bruce Sherin, Northwestern University, bsherin@northwestern.edu

References

diSessa, A. A., & Wagner, J. F. (2005). What coordination has to say about transfer. In J. Mestre (Ed.), *Transfer of learning from a modern multi-disciplinary perspective* (pp. 121-154). Greenwich, CT: Information Age Publishing.

diSessa, A. A. (2002). Why "conceptual ecology" is a good idea. In M. Limon & L. Mason (Eds.), *Reconsidering conceptual change: Issues in theory and practice* (pp. 29–60). Dortrecht, Netherlands: Kluwer.

diSessa, A. A., & Sherin B. L. (1998). What changes in conceptual change? *International Journal of Science education, 20*(10), 1155–1191.

diSessa, A. A. (1994). Speculations on the foundations of knowledge and intelligence. In D. Tirosh (Ed.), *Implicit and Explicit Knowledge: An Educational Approach.* Norwood, NJ: Ablex, 1-54.

diSessa, A. A. (1991). Epistemological micromodels: The case of coordination and quantities. In J. Montanegro & A. Tryphon (Eds.), *Psychologie Genetique et sciences cognitives.* (Volume from the Eleventh Advanced Course.) Geneva: Archives Jean Piaget, 169-194.

Levrini, O. (in preparation). Proper time as coordination class.

Levrini, O. (2005). Proper time as coordination class. Unpublished research report, "Marco Polo" program, University of Bologna, Italy.

Mestre, J., Thaden-Koch, T., Dufresne, R. & Gerace, W. (2004). The dependence of knowledge deployment on context among physics novices. In E. Redish & M. Vicentini (Eds.), *Proceedings of the International School of Physics "Enrico Fermi", Course CLVI, Research on Physics Education.* Amsterdam: IOS Press, 367-408.

Parnafes, O. (in review). These are at the same skinniness level but they're not as high - Understanding the Physical World through Representations.

Parnafes, O. (2005). The development of conceptual understanding through the use of computer-based representations. *Unpublished doctoral dissertation*, University of California at Berkeley.

Thaden-Koch, T. (2003). A coordination class analysis of college students' judgments about animated motion. *Unpublished doctoral dissertation*, University of Nebraska.

Thaden-Koch, T., Dufresne, R. & Mestre, J. (under review). Coordination of knowledge in judging animated motion.

Wagner, J. F. (2006). Transfer in pieces. *Cognition and Instruction, 24*(1), 1-71.

Wagner, J. F. (2003). The construction of similarity: Context sensitivity and the transfer of mathematical knowledge. *Unpublished doctoral dissertation*, University of California, Berkeley.

Moving forward: The learning sciences and the future of education

R. Keith Sawyer, Washington University, St. Louis MO 63130, ksawyer@wustl.edu
Allan Collins, Northwestern University, Evanston IL 60208, a-collins@northwestern.edu
Jere Confrey, Washington University, St. Louis MO 63130, jconfrey@wustl.edu
Janet L. Kolodner, Georgia Institute of Technology, Atlanta GA 30332, janet.kolodner@cc.gatech.edu
Marlene Scardamalia, University of Toronto, Toronto, Canada M5S 1V6, mscardamalia@oise.utoronto.ca

Abstract. In Spring 2006, *The Cambridge Handbook of the Learning Sciences (CHLS)* was published. *CHLS* is the first introduction and handbook of the learning sciences, and combines breadth of coverage with definitive statements by leading scientists working in the learning sciences. As such, it is an important milestone for the field. In this interactive session, the handbook's four advisory board members and its editor, along with the session participants, will explore two sets of questions that were raised during the preparation of the *CHLS*, and which to some extent remain unresolved. The first is inward—how to define the learning sciences, and how it is intellectually structured. The second is outward—how the learning sciences might impact education in the years to come.

Learning sciences was born in 1991, when the first international conference was held, and the *Journal of the Learning Sciences* was first published. The National Research Council report *How People Learn* (Bransford, Brown, & Cocking, 2000) was the first overview of the new sciences of learning. That book provided an accessible introduction to the learning sciences for a broad audience. In Spring 2006, *The Cambridge Handbook of the Learning Sciences (CHLS)* was published. The *Cambridge Handbook of the Learning Sciences (CHLS)* picks up where the NRC report left off: *CHLS* shows how educators can use the learning sciences to design more effective learning environments—whether school classrooms, informal settings such as science centers or after-school clubs, on-line distance learning, or computer-based tutoring software. *CHLS* is the first introduction and handbook of the learning sciences, and combines breadth of coverage with definitive statements by leading scientists working in the learning sciences. As such, it is an important milestone for the field.

In this interactive session, the handbook's four advisory board members and its editor, along with the session participants, will explore two sets of questions that were raised during the preparation of the *CHLS*, and which to some extent remain unresolved. The first is inward—how to define the learning sciences, and how it is intellectually structured. The second is outward—how the learning sciences might impact education in the years to come.

Overview of the *Cambridge Handbook of the Learning Sciences*

The 34 chapters of the *CHLS* are organized into six parts.

The editor's Introduction and Conclusion explain why the learning sciences are important not only to education, but to our entire society. The major advanced nations and the entire global economy are rapidly changing. These two chapters draw on a large body of recent scholarship that describes the mismatch between the schools we have today and the demands of the knowledge age. Because the learning sciences are discovering how to teach the deep knowledge, skills, and attitudes required in the knowledge society, they are positioned to provide the blueprint for the schools of the future.

Part 1, Foundations, introduces the reader to many of the big ideas that have been most influential throughout the learning sciences. Part 1 contains chapters on interdisciplinarity, constructionism, cognitive apprenticeship, cognitive tutors, situativity, and knowledge building.

Part 2, Methodologies, describes the unique research approaches used by learning scientists to study and to design new learning environments. Experiments are an important research methodology, but they are typically not useful in designing and engineering classrooms, and learning scientists have developed a variety of new methodological tools. Part 2 contains chapters on learner-centered design, design studies, design-based research, guiding inquiry-based learning, analyzing collaborative discourse, and assessing for deep understanding.

Part 3, The Nature of Knowledge, presents new research on the kinds of deep knowledge that support expert activity. Learning scientists are not simply trying to help students memorize textbook facts better, because memorizing isolated facts and step-by-step procedures is not enough in today's knowledge society. Instead, learning scientists study how to help students understand underlying explanations and causes, and how to solve complex, real-world problems. Part 3 contains chapters on case-based reasoning, knowledge integration, conceptual change, spatial representations and imagery, and literacy.

Part 4, Making Knowledge Visible, shows how learning scientists are using these new discoveries about the nature of knowledge to design classroom activities that help students learn by making visible the deep knowledge they need to learn—often with sophisticated computer displays. Part 4 contains chapters on project-based learning, making authentic practices accessible to learners, developing curricular structures for inquiry science, model-based reasoning, and exploring mathematics through construction and collaboration.

Part 5, Learning Together, emphasizes the important role of collaboration in learning. A wide range of educational research has found that collaboration contributes to learning. Unlike an older generation of educational software, where each student worked in isolation at his or her own computer, the advent of the Internet and of wireless handheld devices supports students in learning collaborations, so that computers bring students together instead of pulling them apart. Part 5 contains chapters on computer-supported collaborative learning, wireless handheld devices, argumentation, and online communities.

Part 6, Learning Environments, tackles the real-world problems that face any educational reform—teacher professional development, equity for all students, and scaling up innovations throughout school districts and ultimately, throughout the country. Part 6 contains chapters on motivation and cognitive engagement, learning as a cultural process, transforming schools with technology-supported assessment, Internet use in schools, teacher learning research, and scaling up.

Two short essays follow the editor's Conclusion: an Afterword by Seymour Papert titled "After how comes what", and an Epilogue by Roger Schank titled "The fundamental issue in the learning sciences".

Session objectives

The objectives of the proposed ICLS session are to bring together the contributors to the *CHLS*, other scholars in the learning sciences community, and a broad audience of ICLS members who are interested in participating in a wide-ranging discussion about how the learning sciences defines itself at this point in its history, and how the learning sciences can and should contribute to improving education in the next decade.

The first questions focus inward, on the learning sciences itself. In preparing the handbook, difficult decisions had to made about which chapters to include. A second difficult issue was how to structure the handbook into its six parts, which essentially represent one version of the epistemology of the field—how it is divided up intellectually into research questions. The five session participants had many discussions about both which chapters to include, and how to structure the handbook. The particular representation of the learning sciences captured in the *CHLS* is one of many potential representations, and in this session its structure will provide a "tool to think with" about these unresolved questions. What defines a research project as being "learning sciences"? Breaking down boundaries is always appealing, but without boundaries, potentially all education research would count as learning sciences. And most members of the community feel that there's something unique and different about the learning sciences. So what defines the essence of learning sciences research? Second, what is the epistemology of the learning sciences—what are the major research topics that projects tend to cluster around? Although most of the research is on science and math learning, learning scientists generally believe that the key issues are not content-area specific—that the basic epistemological categories are cross-domain.

The second session topic will focus on outward issues. Who should be the target audience for our research? What is the appropriate scope of that audience—is it other researchers and new graduate students, or is our research ready for a broader audience? These questions about scope are really versions of a deeper question: What is the potential impact of the learning sciences on schooling? What is our vision for the future of education? How will the findings emerging from the learning sciences impact education in the future? This discussion will span across schools and also other learning environments, such as museums, libraries, apprenticeships, and on-line learning.

Instead of studying small incremental changes to today's schools, learning scientists ask a more profound question: are today's schools really the right schools for the knowledge society? Most learning sciences researchers are committed to improving schools, and they believe that school reform should involve working together with teachers, engaging in professional development, and integrating new software into classrooms. But learning sciences research might also lead to more radical alternatives that would make schools as we know them obsolete. Roger Schank and Seymour Papert have argued that computer technology is so radically transformative that schools as we know them will have to fade away before the full benefits are realized. Everything is subject to change: schools may not be physical locations where everyone goes, students may not be grouped by age or grade, students could learn anywhere at any time. As of 2005, twenty-two states had established on-line virtual schools; during the 2003-2004 school year, the Florida Virtual School became the state's 73rd school district, and now receives per-student funding from the state just like any other district (Borja, 2005).

The future of education

The chapters in *CHLS* each describe exciting new classroom environments, based on the latest science about how children learn. These classroom environments combine new curricular materials, new collaborative activities, support for teachers, and innovative educational software, often using the unique advantages of the Internet to extend learning beyond the walls of the school. *CHLS* is a true "handbook" in that readers can use it to design the learning environments of the future—environments that are based on learning sciences research, and that draw on the full potential of computer and Internet technology to improve our students' experiences. The learning sciences are supporting deep links between formal schooling and the many other learning institutions available to students—libraries, science centers and history museums, after school clubs, on-line activities that can be accessed from home, and even collaborations between students and working professionals.

Many of the cutting-edge classrooms described in *CHLS* make use of advanced computer technology—but not just for technology's sake. Learning scientists are well aware that computers have generally failed teachers and students; that they are, in Larry Cuban's famous words, "oversold and underused" (Cuban, 2001). Learning sciences researchers have discovered that computers only benefit learning when they take into account what we know about how children learn, and when they are designed to be closely integrated with teacher and student interactions in the classroom. Computer software is only one component of *CHLS*; various chapters propose new teaching strategies, alternative ways of bringing students together in collaborating groups, and new forms of curriculum that cross traditional grades and disciplines. Some chapters even propose radical new ways of thinking about schooling and learning. Many of these proposals are "outside the box" approaches that will change the way we think about learning and schooling.

In the next ten years, the task facing all knowledge societies will be to translate learning sciences research into educational practice. Perhaps the most solid finding to emerge from the learning sciences is that significant change can't be done by fiddling around at the edges of a system that was designed in the industrial age. Instead, the entire educational system will have to be replaced with new learning environments that are based on the learning sciences. Many tasks have to be accomplished:

Parents, politicians, and school boards must be convinced that change is necessary. The shift will require an initial investment in computers, software, and network infrastructure—perhaps even new buildings with as-yet-undetermined architectural designs—but once the shift is in place the annual costs will not necessarily be any more than current expenditures on textbooks and curricular materials.

Textbooks must be rewritten (or even reconceived as laptop-based software packages), to present knowledge in the developmentally appropriate sequence suggested by the learning sciences, and to present knowledge as a coherent, integrated whole, rather than as a disconnected series of decontextualized facts.

The shift to customized, just-in-time learning will result in a radical restructuring of the school day, and will make many features of today's schools obsolete: schools years will no longer be grouped by age, school days will no longer be organized into class periods, standardized tests will no longer be administered en masse to an auditorium of students, not everyone will graduate high school or start college at the same age. Many of the socially entrenched aspects of schools that are not directly related to education will have to change: organized sports, extracurricular activities, class parties used as rites of passage.

The relationship between the institution of school and the rest of society may need to change, as network technologies allow learners to interact with adult professionals outside the school walls, and as classroom activities become increasingly authentic and embedded in real-world practice.

Standardized tests must be rewritten to assess deep knowledge instead of surface knowledge, and to take into account the fact that due to customization, different learners might learn different subject matter.

Teacher education programs must change to prepare teachers for the schools of the future rather than the instructionist schools of the past.

We are at an exciting time in the learning sciences. The work began in the 1970s, in psychology, cognitive sciences, sociology, and other disciplinary traditions. In the 1980s and 1990s, researchers increasingly worked closely with educators and in schools. As these scholars continue to work together in a spirit of interdisciplinary collaboration, the end result will be an increasingly detailed understanding of how people learn. And once that understanding is available, the final step to transform schools must be taken by our whole society: parents and teachers, and the administrators and politicians who we entrust with our schools.

Significance

The proposed session will be significant because the release of this first handbook represents an important coming of age event for the learning sciences community. It is the first time that the core findings emerging from the learning sciences have been collected into a single volume. As such, it provides an opportunity for the field to reflect both inwardly and outwardly—both on the next steps for the learning sciences, and on how this research could impact education in the future. The interactive session format will provide a unique opportunity for the panelists to present their views on these issues. It will also provide an opportunity for handbook contributors and other members of the community to participate in an open discussion about the role of the learning sciences, and to work together to determine the best new directions for future research.

References

Bransford, J. D., Brown, A. L., & Cocking, R. R. (Eds.). (2000). *How people learn: Brain, mind, experience, and school*. Washington, DC: National Academy Press.

Borja, R. J. (2005, May 5). Cyber schools' status. *Education Week, 24*, 22-23.

Cuban, L. (2001). *Oversold and underused: Computers in the classroom*. Cambridge, MA: Harvard.

At home with mathematics: Meanings and uses among families

Reed Stevens, Veronique Mertl, Sheldon Levias & Laurie McCarthy (University of Washington, Miller Hall, Seattle, WA, 98195)
Email:reedstev@u.washington.edu,vmertl@u.washington.edu,sheldonlevias@comcast.net, lsmccarthy@earthlink.net
Shelley Goldman, Lee Martin, Roy Pea, Angela Booker and Kristen Pilner Blair (Stanford University, 485 Lasuen Mall, Palo Alto, CA, 94305)
Email:sgoldman@stanford.edu, lmmartin@stanford.edu, roypea@stanford.edu, booker@stanford.edu, kpilner@stanford.edu
Na'ilah Suad Nasir, Michael Heimlich, Grace Atukpawu, & Kathleen O'Connor (Stanford University, 485 Lasuen Mall, Palo Alto, CA, 94305)
Email: nasir@stanford.edu, heimlich@stanford.edu, gca@stanford.edu, koc@stanford.edu

Abstract: Everyday mathematics research has examined the activities of buyers (Lave, 1988) and sellers in markets (Nunes, Schliemann, & Carraher, 1993; Saxe, 1990); it has examined the practices of both high and lower status occupational work (e.g. Hall & Stevens, 1995; Scribner, 1985; Stevens & Hall, 1998), and it has examined the mathematics that is embedded in competitive play (Nasir, 2000) but the family as locus of mathematical activity is understudied. The three projects represented in this symposium focus on mathematical practices in the context of families. The first project takes an activity focus, examining mathematical practices in the context of a consequential context of family activity—money and its uses. The second project takes a topical focus, describing a wide range of practices in families that are seen as mathematical. The third paper focuses on a particular cultural group, attending to the meanings and uses of both informal and schooled mathematics in the family context. Together the papers provide a new perspective on qualities of mathematical practice outside of school and its actual, and potential, relations to school mathematics.

Money Matters: The Social and Material Organization of Consequential Financial Practices in Families

In the first project, we extend prior work that develops an approach through a series of ethnographic case studies of mathematical activity in and out of schools (Hall & Stevens, 1995; Stevens & Hall, 1998; Stevens, 1999; Stevens, 2000; Stevens, under review). It follows this prior line of research in focusing on how problems emerge in the context of daily activities and how they are resolved, often through quantitative practices not easily recognizable as "mathematics" (Stevens, 1999; Stevens, 2000; Stevens, under review). The activities that are our focus in this study—financial activities within families—were selected because these contexts of activity are recognizably *consequential* to the people we are studying. Activities that we documented range from routine bill-paying practices and monthly budgeting to major decisions including the selection of high-premium insurance policies, home buying, and saving for a child's college education.

This study builds upon prior everyday mathematics research for its theoretical framing but, by focusing on consequential contexts of quantitative practice, responds to perceived limitations in this line of work (see Palinscar, 1989) that suggest that by studying low-stakes problem-solving activities like supermarket best-buy choices (Lave, 1988) and weight-watchers measurements (delaRocha, 1986) we fail to see the full range of mathematical resources that people can and do use in everyday life. This was, of course, very much the theoretical point that studies like those by Lave were making—that mathematical practices in everyday contexts are fitted to endogenous criteria for success rather than an omni-relevant standard of mathematical problem solving dictated by disciplinary mathematics—but it leaves open the question of whether the mathematical practices in other more consequential everyday contexts would be appreciably different in response to different practical conditions. It also leaves open the question of whether more school-like forms and functions (Saxe, 1990) of mathematics will appear in these consequential situations of quantitative practice.

The study was conducted in the homes of eight families, each with a described intention to make a near-term consequential financial decision and with at least one resident high-school aged child. We purposively sampled for families with high-school aged children because we thought this would provide the most likely context among parents and children for informal teaching and learning around finances, since the young people are so close to legal adulthood and being "on their own." Families varied across socioeconomic levels, race, structure (single/two-parent households) and reported formal math abilities. Our data include videotaped observations of family financial activities over a 10-month period, documentation of resources and artifacts, two simulation tasks (cf. Scribner, 1985) and interviews with family members. In addition to seeking to understand the details of mathematical work in the context of family financial practices, the study also had the goal of exploring these financial practices as a context for informal, intergenerational learning between parents and children. The study was also intended to explore the resources that families, varying in SES, had and could access in solving the financial problems they posed for themselves or were posed for them by circumstance.

The first finding involves the ways the range of ways that informal learning was organized within financial practices among parents and children. One widely regarded model of informal learning is guided/intent participation (Rogoff, 2003). Though guided and intent participation differ as models and are understood to obtain under different practical and cultural conditions, both describes how young people are brought into practices thorough observation and guidance by knowledgeable others. These models of participation relate to broader notions of apprenticeship (Lave and Wenger, 1991) in which newcomers learn from oldtimers; though, typically this learning involves forms of participation that do not resemble those of Western schooling. In our study, we have found guided participation and apprenticeship-like conditions in our families, but we have also found other informal learning arrangements. The following are some of the different arrangements we have documented: in a couple cases young people are using their parents' practices reflexively as a resource for espousing alternative practices. They are in other words learning more from what they perceive as their parent's mistakes rather than being guided in their participation in shared practice as Rogoff describes. In other cases, guided participation and apprenticeship are not good descriptions, because parents deliberately occlude financial practices from children thus rendering them invisible; to use Hutchins' term, they are denied "horizons of observation" (1995) from which to occupy a position of peripheral participant (Lave & Wenger, 1991); in still other cases parents have opportunistically taken our study's presence in their lives as a pedagogical opportunity to teach their children about finances. For example, we provide $250 to families that they are asked to "invest" in some manner of their choosing, that we then document. In two higher SES families, this is considered a small enough sum that parents plan to have their children make the decision about the money's use as context for learning how to make good decisions with money. Taken together, we have a diversity of learning arrangements that challenge any single model of informal learning and in turn, we believe, the idea of singular models of learning. This study points us toward a view that learning may not be best understood in terms of any singular model or process—as typically pursued with psychology and cognitive science—but as something achieved by drawing from a repertoire of cultural practices for learning (e.g. proximal apprenticeship, coaching, intent participation, or direct instruction) that are fitted to current practical conditions and goals.

Our second finding involves the *resources* that family members *assemble* and *coordinate* to solve problems they encounter in these financial situations. Building upon an analysis of quantitative practice in a high status workplace environment (Stevens, 1999; under review), we are characterizing problems that are resolved through *routines* and those that are resolved with *innovations* (cf. Schwartz, Bransford, & Sears, in press). Innovations appear to be born of new and often urgent forms of trouble in family circumstances or from routines within which family members recognize "chronic snags" (delaRocha, 1986). Our key finding is that in comparison to the resources that are required for school mathematics problems, the assembled resources used to solve problems in these domestic situations are *radically heterogeneous*. An example of such a problem resolution, that we characterize as an innovation, was initiated by a bit of trouble in one of our low SES families. The family was suddenly faced with a problem, because the teenage son in the family wrecked his car. Rather than take the full pay out amount for the insurance, the single mother in the family collaborated with her son to take $400 less than the maximum payout while keeping the totaled car. The mother and son then decided to cannibalize the car for parts that the son would then sell through an online vendor or, in the case of aftermarket parts like an alarm and radio, reuse in his next car. They made this decision with the expectation of making or saving more than the $400 they gave up by keeping the totaled car rather than relinquishing it. These funds, along with the insurance money, would be put toward the purchase of a newer and more expensive car than the one he crashed. As we followed the course of this problem's resolution, we found that the family did indeed make a profit of $200 as well as recouping the cost of the alarm and car stereo. In addition however, there were a number of emergent learning opportunities that were presented and taken within the family. First, since the son did not know enough to disassemble the car, he took the opportunity to ask friends who had this knowledge to help him to do so, which they did. In so doing, he learned a great deal about the inner workings of a car and how to disassemble one. The mother reported learning a great deal about this as well. The cannibalization approach also provided the mother with a temporary pool of liquid funds to pay off some expensive debts, in effect using the insurance payout as interest free loan until her son has completed his work and was ready to buy the replacement car of his choice, a Stealth. The story has more elements but for purposes of our argument, this portion of this story involves at least the following heterogeneous resources that were innovatively assembled: knowledge of options available under an insurance policy, a network of friends and their manual skills, basic calculations, and a local online marketplace for the sale of used merchandise called Craig's List.

Both of our findings urge us toward for more complex models of learning and problem solving and, more generally, toward a rethinking of received goals in the cognate disciplines that directly inform the learning sciences—psychology and cognitive science—of singular models of phenomena like learning and problem solving. In turn, these findings pose interesting questions about and suggest design implications for the conduct of school mathematics education.

Problem Emergence, Problem Solving, and Mathematics in Family Life

The second project has investigated the diverse contexts and activities in which middle school age learners and their families engage in mathematical practices and problem solving. We describe the resources family members use for solving problems, characterize the structure of their mathematical activities, and analyze the social conditions and arrangements for family-based mathematics practices.

This draws its results from interviews and observations of 13 families who reside in the San Francisco Bay Area representing economic, racial and ethnic diversity. We used a semi-structured interview protocol organized around mathematically relevant contexts identified in prior studies, including: financial and time budgeting, hobbies and crafts, home repairs and home chores for kids, purchasing of larger items (such as phone plans, cars, homes, or major appliances), local and long-distance travel, family entertainment activities, and cooking (Goldman, 2005). This focus allowed interviews to center on activities that most families engage in, while allowing families to give us their particularized versions of how they accomplish each life task (including technology use and systems for representing mathematical relationships). The interview also included a simulation task in which families chose a cell phone plan to meet the family's needs.

Analysis of data is qualitative, and includes individual's descriptions, family discourse and interaction. Our approach is to understand how the problems arising in family-based, math-relevant settings generate new knowledge and make certain kinds of thinking and action adaptive. Data analyses show that mathematical problem solving in the family looks quite different than school-based problem solving. School-based math problems vary in their realism, but the particulars of school problems are most often vehicles for math content. In contrast, the mathematics involved in tackling problems in families generally remains subordinate to the problem itself, and as such, family math can easily remain invisible.

We have found that mathematical problem solving in the family, while less explicit than school math, is complex and varied, and while occasionally based in routines, commonly requires adaptive flexibility due to specifics of the situation. Unlike many school-based problems, math in family life does not come prepackaged with normative solution paths. When problems emerge or re-occur, family members must decide how to deal with them. These decisions involve consideration of, at a minimum, the availability of resources such as materials, money, space and time), historical approaches to the problem within the family, the distribution of expertise within the family, who is available to work on solutions (Pea 1993), the timetable at hand, and the potential risks and benefits at stake. The complex web of contingencies that is considered in even ordinary family problem solving contexts greatly exceeds what would be expected in most school settings. The mathematical content put to use in families is wide ranging as well, including fractions, decimals and percents; ratios and proportions (direct and indirect); measurement and conversion; probability and odds; basic geometry; charts and graphs; statistics (such as averages), and statistical comparisons. Problems may take several steps to solve and, most often, more than one type of math is brought to bear on the problem. Math in the context of family life is often co-occurring with solving compelling life issues, and it is the family issues to which people resonate. Problem solving in the family can approximate the ways adults problem solve problems with math in the workplace. Such work skills and practices include logical reasoning, categorization, approximation and estimation (Steen, 2004), which all appear frequently in family problem solving. While these skills are often identified with work, our research finds that people apply these mathematical skills in the contexts of family life.

We present examples from the data, discuss types of problems, their characteristics, and ways people define problems and accomplish solutions. We discuss implications of our research for understanding how learning at home provides unique opportunities and how those opportunities correspond to, or contradict learning in other settings.

Supporting Math Achievement at Home: Practices that Matter for the School Math Achievement of African-American Students

The third project explores the relation between home mathematics practices, sense of mathematical identity, and mathematics achievement among high and low- achieving African American students in math. This project speaks to a long history of disparities by race in mathematics achievement (such that African-American students routinely perform less well than other groups) are widely cited and pervasive (Oakes, 1990; Secada, 1995; Walker & McCoy, 1997). One approach to addressing such inequities is to better understand differences between more and less successful African American students. In this project, we take such an approach to understanding the kinds of home and out-of-school experiences that seem to support the math achievement of African American students. This is critical to understanding the role home practices might play in the math achievement of African American students, as we know very little about how African American students interact with mathematics in practices outside of school (Nasir, 2000), nor do we know much about how African American families may be supporting (or failing to support) the mathematics learning of their high school students.

In this project, we focus on differences in students' experiences with mathematics outside of school and in support for mathematics at home. Data are drawn from a study of African-American students' experiences with mathematics at school and at home. 12 high and 12 low achieving African-American students were interviewed about the type and extent of their experiences with informal mathematics at home and in out-of-school contexts, and about the type and availability of support for school mathematics at home, as well as about their sense of themselves as math learners during school and home math activities. The interview also included questions on students' sense of their identities and learning in the math classes, and their sense of themselves as African-American. The sample was half male and half female and all were 10th and 11th graders. Interviews ranged from one hour to one and a half hours.

Findings reveal several interesting differences in out-of-school mathematics practices and home math of high- and low-achieving African American students. These include differences in: 1) level of direct family support, 2) participation in activities that seem to mediate academic identity in general, and 3) differences in how students "see" the math in settings outside of school, and 4) differences in how students' view themselves as competent math students (including how students draw upon conceptions of "the kind of math person" other families members are).

Differences in the direct level of family support were not surprising. While all students reported that their families checked their report card grades and wanted them to do well in mathematics, the families of higher achieving students more often expected higher grades in mathematics (and in general). Further, higher achieving students were more likely to have family members who helped them with their math homework, and with selecting mathematics courses. Clearly, this direct support (and cultural capital around which courses to take) influenced students' math achievement in very straightforward ways.

Rather than directly affecting students' ability to engage in mathematics classes, participation in other out-of-school activities seemed to mediate students' academic identities more generally. Specifically, higher achieving students were more likely to participate in organized sports and church. Student reports suggest that both of these settings seem to offer students positive messages about their ability to be strong students, and they also seem to encourage continued and full participation in school and school activities.

The third difference we describe is that higher-achieving students were more likely to "see" mathematics in practices outside of school. This was interesting because low- and high- achieving students did *not* seem to differ in their participation in the types or numbers of settings outside of school where they engaged with mathematics. The difference, then, was in students' ability to see these activities as being mathematically-relevant. For instance, while almost all of the students mentioned shopping as an activity that they were involved with, lower-achieving students were less likely to see it as an activity that might involve math, while higher-achieving students tended to describe the way they used math in shopping activities. For instance, one higher-achieving student said, " So if I buy something that's like 80 dollars save 25% off, that means it's like 60 dollars."

Finally, higher-achieving students were more likely to see themselves as competent in math and were more likely to be comfortable with problems that they couldn't figure out—that is, facing a difficult problem did not trigger for them a sense that they were "not good" at math, as it did for lower-achieving students. Hence, they were more willing to persist in the face of difficult problems.

These differences between low- and high- achieving African American students in mathematics are an important start to initial efforts to describe the types of home and out-of-school practices that seem to be related to math achievement for African American students. The relative influence of direct factors like level of homework support and guidance with course selection, as well as more indirect factors like supporting engagement in school generally, and seeing oneself as a "math person" are interesting to consider, though further work will be needed to understand the nuances of how much, and how each of these kinds of influences may matter.

References

de la Rocha, O. (1986). *Problems of sense and problems of scale: An ethnographic study of arithmetic in everyday life.* Unpublished dissertation. University of California, Irvine.

Goldman, S. (2005). A new angle on families: Connecting the mathematics in daily life with school mathematics. In Bekerman, Z., Burbules, N., Silberman-Keller, D. & (Eds.), *Learning in Places: The Informal Education Reader*. Bern: Peter Lang Publishing Group.

Hall, Rogers, and Stevens, Reed. (1995). Making space: A Comparison of mathematical work in school and professional design practices. In S. L. Star (Ed.), *The Cultures of Computing*, (pp. 118-145). London: Basil Blackwell.

Hutchins, E. (1995). *Cognition in the Wild* (pp. 263-316). Cambridge: MIT Press.

Lave, Jean. (1988). *Cognition in practice: Mind, Mathematics and Culture in Everyday Life.* Cambridge, England: Cambridge University Press.

Nasir, N. (2000). Points Ain't Everything: Emergent Goals and Average and Percent Understandings in the Play of Basketball Among African-American Students. *Anthropology and Education Quarterly*, 31(3): 283-305.

Nunes, T., Schliemann, A. D., & Carraher, D. W. (1993). *Street mathematics and school mathematics.* New York, NY, US: Cambridge University Press.

Oakes, J. (1990). Opportunities, achievement, and choice: Women and minority students in science and mathematics. *Review of Research in Education*, 153-222.

Palincsar, A. (1989). Less charted waters. *Educational Researcher*: 18(2): 5-7.

Pea, R. D. (1993). Practices of distributed intelligence and designs for education. In G. Salomon (Ed.). *Distributed cognitions*. New York: Cambridge University Press, pp. 47-87.

Polya, George. (1971). How to Solve It; a new aspect of mathematical problem solving. Princeton, New Jersey: Princeton University Press.

Rogoff, B. (2003). *The cultural nature of human development*. New York: Oxford University Press.

Saxe, Geoffrey. (1990) *Culture and cognitive development: Studies in mathematical understanding*. Hillsdale, NJ: Lawrence Erlbaum Associates.

Schwartz, D., Bransford, J., & Sears, D. (in press). Efficiency and innovation in transfer. To appear in J. Mestre (Ed.), *Transfer of learning: Research and perspectives*. Greenwich, CT: Information Age Publishing.

Scribner, S. (1985). Knowledge at work. *Anthropology and Education Quarterly*, *16*(3), 199-206.

Scribner, S. (1986). Thinking in action: Some characteristics of practical thought. In R.J. Sternberg and R.K. Wagner (Eds.), *Practical intelligence: Nature and origins of competence in the everyday world* (pp. 13-30). New York: Cambridge University Press.

Secada, W.G. (1992). Race, ethnicity, social class, language, and achievement in mathematics. In D. A. Grouws (Ed.) *Handbook of research on mathematics teaching and learning* (pp. 623-660). New York: MacMillan.

Steen, Lynn. A. (2004). Back to the Future in Mathematics education. *Education Week*, April 7 V23n30 34,36. http://www.edweek.org/ew/ewstory.cfm?slug=30steen.h23.

Stevens, R. & Hall, R. (1998). Disciplined perception: Learning to see in technoscience. In M. Lampert & M. L. Blunk (Eds.), *Talking Mathematics in School: Studies of teaching and learning*. Cambridge, UK: Cambridge University Press.

Stevens, R. (1999). Disciplined perception: Comparing the development of embodied mathematical practices at work and in school. Doctoral dissertation, University of California, Berkeley.

Stevens, R. (2000). Who counts what as math: Emergent and assigned mathematical problems in a project-based classroom. In J. Boaler (Ed.), *Multiple perspectives on Mathematics Teaching and Learning*. New York: Elsivier.

Stevens, R. (under review). Distributed by design: The Social and material organization of mathematical practices in one high status workplace.

Walker, E., & McCoy, L. (1997). Students' voices: African-Americans and Mathematics. In NCTM, *Multicultural and gender equity in the mathematics classroom: The gift of diversity, 1997 yearbook*. Reston, VA: NCTM.

Acknowledgements

This work has been conducted by members of the Informal Learning Strand of the Learning in Informal and Formal Environments (LIFE) Science of Learning Center (http://life-slc.org/). We wish to thank the National Science Foundation for their support (Award # 0354453). All interpretations and claims presented are our own.

Argumentative Knowledge Construction in CSCL

Armin Weinberger, Knowledge Media Research Center, Konrad-Adenauer-Str. 40, 72072 Tübingen, Germany
Douglas Clark, College of Education, Payne 203F, Arizona State University, Tempe, AZ 85287-0911, USA
Gijsbert Erkens, Research Centre Learning in Interaction, Utrecht University, Heidelberglaan 1, 3584 CS Utrecht, NL
Victor Sampson, College of Education, Payne 203F, Arizona State University, Tempe, AZ 85287-0911, USA
Karsten Stegmann, Knowledge Media Research Center, Konrad-Adenauer-Str. 40, 72072 Tübingen, Germany
Jeroen Janssen, Research Centre Learning in Interaction, Utrecht University, Heidelberglaan 1, 3584 CS Utrecht, NL
Jos Jaspers, Research Centre Learning in Interaction, Utrecht University, Heidelberglaan 1, 3584 CS Utrecht, NL
Gellof Kanselaar, Research Centre Learning in Interaction, Utrecht University, Heidelberglaan 1, 3584 CS Utrecht, NL
Frank Fischer, Knowledge Media Research Center, Konrad-Adenauer-Str. 40, 72072 Tübingen, Germany
Email: a.weinberger@iwm-kmrc.de, Douglas.B.Clark@asu.edu, G.Erkens@fss.uu.nl, victor.sampson@asu.edu, k.stegmann@iwm-kmrc.de, j.j.h.m.janssen@fss.uu.nl, j.jaspers@fss.uu.nl, G.Kanselaar@fss.uu.nl, f.fischer@iwm-kmrc.de

Abstract: Knowing how to argue is a prerequisite to participation in scientific discourse. In argumentative knowledge construction, learners collaboratively construct and engage in arguments with the goal of learning to argue within a domain. Students have difficulties, however, constructing and evaluating arguments. Computer-supported collaborative learning (CSCL) attempts to address these difficulties by providing students with additional resources and tools to visualize and guide their argumentation. This symposium presents results from empirical studies on facilitating and analyzing argumentative knowledge construction in CSCL. These studies assess the structural and conceptual quality of learners' arguments; provide sequential analyses of how learners exchange arguments in discourse, and investigate the relationship between cognitive processes of learners and the construction of arguments in discourse.

Argumentative Knowledge Construction in CSCL

Current research suggests that *argumentative knowledge* is an important component of critical thinking and decision-making in everyday situations (Kuhn, 1991) and understanding and participating in scientific discourse (Driver, Newton, & Osborne, 2000; Sandoval & Millwood, 2005). The term argumentative knowledge refers to an understanding of how to examine and evaluate data and then construct arguments for and against a course of action or point of view. Students in secondary schools and universities, however, have difficulties constructing reasoned arguments and evaluating the arguments of others (Duschl & Osborne, 2002; Kuhn, 1991). This lack of argumentative knowledge has fuelled research on how to facilitate learners' construction of argumentative knowledge (Perkins, 1989; Kuhn, Shaw, & Felton, 1997).

In *argumentative knowledge construction* learners engage in argumentation in order to learn how to argue within a domain (Kuhn et al, 1997). But engaging students in argumentative knowledge construction raises a paradox: participating in argumentative discourse with the goal to learn how to argue within a domain may be the best way to develop students' argumentative knowledge, but students' understanding of how to construct and evaluate arguments may interfere with this process. To address this concern, a number of computer-supported collaborative learning (CSCL) environments have been designed to support students as they engage in argumentative knowledge construction.

Current research suggests that CSCL environments have a number of advantages over traditional forms of classroom instruction for facilitating the process of argumentative knowledge construction (Andriessen, Baker, & Suthers, 2003; Joiner & Jones, 2003; Kirschner, Buckingham Shum, & Carr; 2003; Marttunen & Laurinen, 2001; Weinberger & Fischer, 2006). First, CSCL encourages peer interaction, which has been successfully drawn upon to facilitate argumentative knowledge construction (Kuhn et al., 1997; Schwarz, Neuman, Gil, & Ilya, 2003). Second, in CSCL environments, asynchronous communication can be used as a way to encourage learners to construct and (re-)evaluate arguments by providing them with as much time as they require when generating comments or responding to the comments of others (Joiner & Jones, 2003; Pea, 1994). Third, CSCL environments can implement special tools and scaffolds to guide learners in effective argumentative knowledge construction. For example, Kirschner et al. (2003) developed a tool that enables learners to visualize single arguments and sequences of argumentation while Jermann and Dillenbourg (2003) developed tools that script and scaffold learners' interaction by assigning and prompting roles for the learners. Taken together, this body of research suggests that computer-supported collaborative learning environments can facilitate the development of argumentative knowledge.

Research Presented

Building upon this research, this symposium provides new insights into the teaching and learning of argumentation. The papers (a) discuss ways to provide students with additional resources and tools to visualize and guide their argumentation, (b) present results of empirical studies on different facets of facilitating and analyzing argumentative knowledge construction in CSCL, and (c) introduce new ways to assess the structural and conceptual quality of learners' arguments and their understanding of argumentation. Taken together, these studies emphasize that argumentation is more than a cognitive activity of coordinating data around claims; it is also a social practice of persuasion and collaborative knowledge construction.

Visualizing participation to facilitate argumentation

Gijsbert Erkens, Jeroen Janssen, Jos Jaspers, & Gellof Kanselaar
Research Centre Learning in Interaction, Utrecht University

Introduction and Theoretical Background

Participation and equality of participation are important prerequisites for effective and beneficial collaborative learning (Cohen, 1994; Weinberger & Fischer, 2006). Unfortunately, students do not always participate equally in argumentative discussions in CSCL environments (Lipponen, Rahikainen, Lallimo, & Hakkarainen, 2003). However, Michinov and Primois (2005) and Zumbach, Hillers, and Reimann (2004) suggest that providing a way for students to visualize levels of participation in a discussion can stimulate participation and thus facilitate argumentative knowledge construction. Providing a visualization of students' participation creates opportunities for social evaluation and constitutes a possible motivational incentive to increase group members' participation (Shepperd, 1993). Providing a visualization of participation also raises students' awareness of the constructive, communicative, and social processes taking place during argumentative discussion (Kreijns, 2004).

In order to investigate the degree to which visualization of participation stimulates group members' participation rates and facilitates argumentative knowledge construction, a new tool was added to an existing CSCL-environment (Virtual Collaborative Research Institute/VCRI, Jaspers, Broeken, & Erkens, 2004). This *Participation Tool* visualizes the contributions of each group member to the group's online communication (see Figure 1). Each student is represented by a sphere. The distance of a sphere to the group center indicates the number of messages sent by the student; whereas the size of the sphere indicates the average length of messages. The Participation Tool therefore visually clarifies the quantity and the homogeneity/heterogeneity of participation. An earlier study demonstrated that, compared to control group students, students with access to the Participation Tool (treatment group students) participated more actively during online collaboration (more and longer utterances) and engaged more deeply in the coordination of social activities (Janssen, Erkens, Kanselaar, & Jaspers, in press). These findings raise two new questions. (1) Is participation a sufficient condition for effective argumentative knowledge construction? (2) Does improving participation also improve the quality of argumentative knowledge construction?

Methods and Data Analysis

We conducted sequential analyses of the arguments group members constructed. In lag-sequential analysis (Bakeman & Gottman, 1997; Wampold, 1992), the transition patterns between the arguments in a discourse protocol can be statistically tested on different intervals (lags) between the events. The computer program *Multiple Episode Protocol Analysis* (MEPA), which was developed at Utrecht University, is used for sequential analysis and coding of argumentative discussions of collaborating students. The chat protocols of 52 treatment group students (17 groups) and 17 control group students (5 groups) were analyzed. These students (age 16-18) worked for eight lessons in groups of three or four students on an inquiry-based group task as part of their history curriculum. The communicative function of each chat utterance was coded into 'dialogue acts'. The dialogue acts were organized into 28 sub-categories within five main categories of communicative function: *argumentative* (indicating a line of argumentation or reasoning), *responsive* (answers to questions and proposals), *informative* (transfer of information), *elicitative* (questions or proposals requiring a response), and *imperative* (commands).

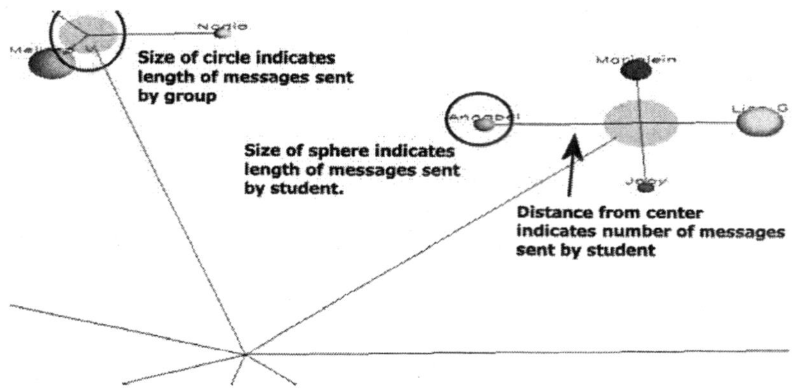

Figure 1. Screenshot of the Participation Tool

Results and Conclusions

The results of our analyses show that Participation Tool students engage in a higher number and frequency of argumentative dialogue acts. This increase is due to an increase in counter arguments and conditional arguments. Furthermore, results of sequential analyses indicate that treatment groups use different argumentation patterns compared to control groups. More specifically, treatment groups engage in longer sequences of argumentation. Finally, sequential analysis indicates that successful groups (those who write better reports) use different argumentation patterns than less successful groups. Not only does the Participation Tool help students construct arguments, it also helps students construct arguments in specific cycles with their group members. In conclusion, visualizing participation appears to facilitate argumentative knowledge construction by raising students' awareness the manner in which they are collaborating, thereby stimulating them to construct more arguments and engage in different argumentation patterns. In our future research, we will try to facilitate argumentative knowledge construction further by visualizing argumentative discourse of participants during online collaboration.

Scripting Online Discussions: Effects on Argumentative Discourse, Cognitive Processes, and Knowledge Acquisition

Armin Weinberger, Karsten Stegmann, & Frank Fischer
Knowledge Media Research Center (KMRC), Tübingen

Introduction and Theoretical Background

A central goal of university education is to develop students' ability to understand and participate in argumentative discourse within a specific field of study. In argumentative knowledge construction, learners are believed to expand their *argumentative* and *domain-specific knowledge* on a cognitive level by constructing arguments and counterarguments as they solve a complex problem case in their domain (Andriessen, et al., 2003; Marttunen & Laurinen, 2001; Weinberger & Fischer, 2006). Learners, however, often do not know how to engage in argumentative discussions (Kuhn, 1991).

Recently, *computer-supported collaboration scripts* were developed to facilitate processes of argumentative knowledge construction (Jermann & Dillenbourg, 2003). Based on O'Donnell's (1999) scripted cooperation approach, computer-supported collaboration scripts pre-structure roles and activities, e.g., by providing text prompts that guide learners to engage in specific interaction patterns (Baker & Lund, 1997; Nussbaum, Hartley, Sinatra, Reynolds, & Bendixen, 2002). We hypothesize that scripts for argumentative knowledge construction can guide learners as they construct arguments and in so doing, their argumentative knowledge can be improved on a cognitive level. Results so far show that scripts can facilitate specific discourse activities, such as epistemic activities that aim to construct knowledge, but this does not always contribute to the facilitation of knowledge acquisition (Mäkitalo, Weinberger, Häkkinen, Järvelä, & Fischer, 2005). Some scripts appear to hinder cognitive processes by oversimplifying the learning task (Reiser, 2002; Weinberger, Ertl, Fischer, & Mandl, 2005). However, little is known about the relationship between the construction of arguments in discourse and the cognitive activities of individual learners. If scripts facilitate the construction of arguments in discourse, do they also facilitate the cognitive elaboration of knowledge?

Methods and Data Analysis

We conducted two experimental studies with different foci of analysis in a CSCL environment with groups of three students enrolled in Educational Science. In the first study (n = 60), we analyzed the effects of a computer-supported collaboration script that aimed to support the construction of single arguments on the processes and outcomes of argumentative knowledge construction (see figure 3) based on the written online discussions of the learners with regard to the epistemic quality of arguments (i.e., the extent the arguments contributed to solving the learning task by applying specific theoretical concepts) and the formal argumentative quality of arguments (i.e., the extent the arguments included claims, warrants, data, and qualifiers). In the second study (n = 54) with the script for the construction of single arguments (vs. control) we also analyzed the cognitive processes of argumentative knowledge construction based on think-aloud protocols during the text-based collaboration, regarding the level and focus of elaboration, as well as their relation to the respective discourse activities.

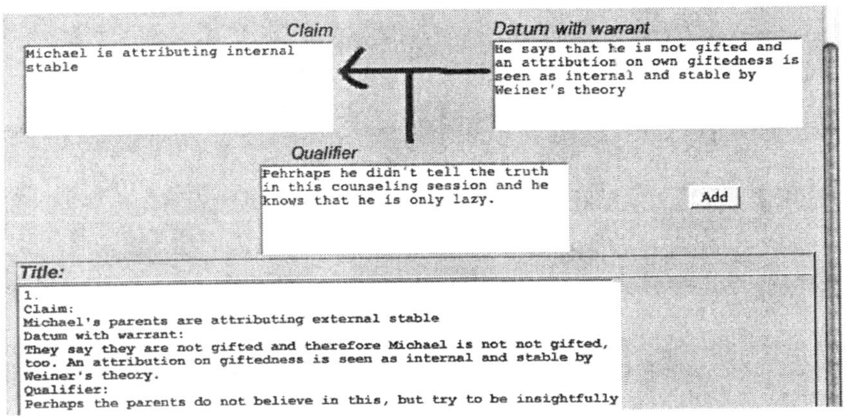

Figure 3: Input mask remodeled by a script for constructing single arguments

Results and Conclusions

Results of the first study show that computer-supported scripts can facilitate specific processes and outcomes of argumentative knowledge construction. Learners with scripts construct arguments of higher structural quality and acquire more argumentative knowledge than learners without scripts. Results of the second study show that constructing formally adequate arguments in discourse fosters cognitive processes and acquisition of argumentative knowledge. The acquisition of domain-specific knowledge, however, depends on the epistemic quality of arguments constructed in online discussions and the focus of elaboration. Learners' activities on a cognitive level are generally closely related to discourse activities as well as to individual knowledge acquisition. Learners who acquire more domain-specific knowledge than average spend more effort to cognitively elaborate single arguments rather than to construct many arguments with little cognitive elaboration.

Evaluating Argumentation in Science: New Assessment Tools

Douglas Clark & Victor Sampson
College of Education, Arizona State University

Introduction and Theoretical Background

Researchers have developed several different methods to investigate argumentative discourse. To date, most of these investigations have relied heavily on Toulmin's (1958) model of argument structure in one way or another (e.g., Erduran, Osborne & Simon, 2004). In these studies, emphasis is placed on the identification of the structural features of arguments (e.g., claims, data, warrants, backings, and rebuttals). Such approaches seek to identify the absence or presence of the components of argument and use this information to assess argumentation quality. These types of structural analyses of student arguments have contributed a great deal to our understanding of how students assimilate the desired practices of argumentation and provide a great deal of information about the form and type of reasoning that students use when they construct arguments based on their everyday experiences (Driver et al., 2000). However, they provide little information about (a) the types of argumentative knowledge and skill young people bring with them to their science classrooms, (b) how students ideas about the nature of science influence the ways they participate in argumentative discussions, and (c) how students' conceptual ideas about the subject matter change as a result of participation in dialogic argumentation.

The Instruments

Specifically, this study presents (a) an analytic scheme for assessing argumentative discourse in asynchronous online environments that extends beyond the structural analysis that has been the focus of much argumentation research, (b) *The Nature of Science as Argument Questionnaire* (NSAAQ) which evaluates students' epistemological commitments related to argumentation, and (c) an *Argumentation in Science Rating Task* (ASRT) which evaluates the criteria used by students for evaluating the quality of arguments and argumentative discourse.

An analytic scheme for assessing argumentative discourse in asynchronous online environments. Our scheme first scores the individual comments in terms of structural operation, grounds quality, and conceptual quality. Each comment is coded in the context of its parent comment. Structural operation is a categorical (nominal) code representing the comment's role or intended role in a co-constructed dialogic argument. Sample structural operation categories include: claim, rebuttal against grounds, organization of participation, and off-task comments. Grounds Quality is an ordinal code with four levels representing the quality of grounds included with a comment: no grounds (level 0), explanation only (level 1), explanation with evidence (level 2), and explanation that coordinates evidence (level 3). Conceptual Quality is an ordinal code with four levels representing the conceptual quality of the scientific subject matter including non-normative (level 0), transitional (level 1), normative (level 2), and nuanced (level 3) use of content. After coding the individual comments, the discussion is parsed into discourse episodes based on the second-order comments. This is a completely mechanical process based on responses to the initial seed claims. We then assign a structural quality code to each discourse episode based on the structural operation codes of the constituent comments. The structural quality code is an ordinal code with six levels measuring the opposition within the episode from a structural (not conceptual) perspective. These structural quality levels include non-oppositional episodes (level 0), argumentation with claims or counterclaims but no grounds or rebuttals (level 1), argumentation with claims or counterclaims and grounds but no rebuttals (level 2), argumentation with grounds and a single rebuttal (level 3), argumentation with multiple rebuttals (level 4), and argumentation with multiple rebuttals and at least one rebuttal against grounds (level 5).

The Nature of Science as Argument Questionnaire (NSAAQ). This instrument was developed in order to identify important aspects of an individual's epistemological beliefs related to the role argumentation plays in the generation and evaluation of scientific knowledge. We hypothesize that the difficulties students have engaging in scienitifc argumentation that are so well documented in the literature may be explained, in part, by exmining the epistemological commitments they have about the nature and limits of scientific knowledge. If students do not share the same epistemological committments that guide and constrain scientific argumentation within the scientific community, then it is unlikely that students will engage in scientific argumentation in a way that reflects the norms of the scientific community. The NSAAQ is designed to measure and characterize an individual's epistemological beliefs regarding: (a) the nature of scientific knowledge; (b) the methods used to generate scientific knowledge; (c) how scientific knowledge should be evaluated; and (d) whether or not science is a social and cultural practice. The NSAAQ consists of 26 *contrasting alternatives* items (see figure 4) divided into four subsclaes. The validity and reliability of the NSAAQ was examined using a methodological framework proposed by Gubba and Lincoln (1990) who suggest that a credible instrument must have strong construct and criterion validity in addition to being reliable.

Viewpoint A	A not B	A > B	A = B	B > A	B not A	Viewpoint B
Science is best described as a process of exploration and experiment.	1	2	3	4	5	Science is best described as a process of explanation and argument.

Figure 4. An example of a NSAAQ contrasting alternatives item

The Argumentation in Science Rating Task (ASRT). Scientists construct arguments by relating the evidence they have gathered to the conclusions they reach through the use of warrants and backings (Erduran, Simon, & Osborne, 2004). Scientists also challenge the acceptability or validity of the claims proposed by other scientists by challenging the evidence, warrants, and backings that were used to justify a given conclusion (Latour & Woolgar, 1986; Longino, 1990). Therefore, the ASRT was developed in order to assess the criteria used by students for evaluating the quality of arguments and the quality of challenges to arguments used during argumentative discourse. The ASRT consists of six items, three that focus on the quality of argument that can be used to justify a claim and three that focus on the quality of a challenge to an argument. For each item, individuals are asked to rank six arguments or six challenges to an argument in terms of quality. An example of an ASRT is shown in figure 5. The validity and reliability of the ASRT was examined using the same methodological framework that was used to develop and validate the NSAAQ.

Claim: Objects that are in the same room are the same temperature even though they feel different because...	**Your Ranking**
...when we measured the temperature of the table, it was $23.4^{\circ}C$, the metal chair leg was $23.1^{\circ}C$, and the computer keyboard was $23.6^{\circ}C$.	________
...good conductors feel different than poor conductors even though they are the same temperature.	________
...objects that are in the same environment gain or lose heat energy until everything is the same temperature. Our data form the lab proves that point: the mouse pad and plastic desk were both $23^{\circ}C$.	________
...objects will release and hold different amounts of heat energy depending on how good of an insulator or conductor it is.	________
...our textbook says that all objects in the same room will eventually reach the same temperature.	________
...we measured the temperature of the wooden table and the chair leg and they were both $23^{\circ}C$ even though the metal chair leg feels colder. If the metal chair leg was actually colder it would have been a lower temperature when we compared it to the temperature of the table.	________

Figure 5. An example of an ASRT item

Results and Conclusions

The inter-rater reliability of argumentative coding scheme, which is designed to provide a reliable method to parse, code, and analyze student argumentation in asynchronous online forums based on structure, grounds, and conceptual quality of individual comments, is 93% for structural operation, 94% for conceptual quality, and 95% for grounds quality. Taken together, these statistics indicate that the coding scheme is reliable despite its complexity. The construct validity of the NSAAQ and the ASRT has been established by assessing the content, face, translation, and discriment validity of the instruments. The criterion validity of the NSAAQ and ASRT was assessed by examining the convergent and concurrent validity of the instruments based on their psychometric properties. Hence, these instruments are likely to give data from which valid conclusions can be drawn. This means that the NSAAQ and the ASRT are likely to be useful tools for researchers who wish to measure the degree in which an individual's epistemological beliefs reflect those of the scientific community and the criteria used by students for evaluating the quality of arguments and argumentative discourse.

References

Andriessen, J., Baker, M., & Suthers, D. (Eds.). (2003). *Arguing to learn. Confronting cognitions in computer-supported collaborative learning environments*. Dordrecht: Kluwer.

Bakeman, R. & Gottman, J.M. (1997). *Observing interaction: An introduction to sequential analysis*. Second Edition. Cambridge: University Press.

Baker, M., & Lund, K. (1997). Promoting reflective interactions in a CSCL environment. *Journal of Computer Assisted Learning, 13*, 175-193.

Bell, P. (2004). Promoting disciplinary-sensitive argumentation across history and science in the elementary school classroom. In Y. B. Kafai, W. A. Sandoval, N. Enyedy, A. S. Nixon, & F. Herrera (Eds.), *Embracing Diversity in the Learning Sciences. Proceedings of the International Conference of the Learning Sciences*. Mahwah, NJ: Erlbaum.

Cohen, E. G. (1994). Restructuring the classroom: Conditions for productive small groups. *Review of Educational Research, 64*(1), 1-35.

Driver, R., Newton, P., & Osborne, J. (2000). Establishing the norms of scientific argumentation in classrooms. *Science Education, 84*(3), 287-313.

Duschl, R. A., & Osborne, J. (2002). Supporting and promoting argumentation discourse in science education. *Studies in Science Education, 38*, 39-72.

Erduran, S., Simon, S., & Osborne, J. (2004). TAPing into argumentation: Developments in the application of Toulmin's argument pattern for studying science discourse. *Science Education, 88*, 915-933.

Gubba, E. G., & Lincoln, Y. S. (1990). *Fourth generation evaluation.* Newbury Park, CA: Sage

Hewson, P. W. (1985). Epistemological commitments in the learning of science: Examples from dynamics. *European Journal of Science Education, 7*, 163-172.

Janssen, J., Erkens, G., Kanselaar, G., & Jaspers, J. (2005, in press). Visualization of participation: does it contribute to successful computer-supported collaborative learning? *Computers & Education.*

Jaspers, J., Broeken, M., & Erkens, G. (2004). *Virtual Collaborative Research Institute (VCRI)* (Version 2.0). Utrecht: Onderwijskunde Utrecht, ICO/ISOR.

Jermann, P., & Dillenbourg, P. (2003). Elaborating new arguments through a CSCL script. In P. Dillenbourg (Ed.), *Learning to argue* (Vol. 1, pp. 205-226). Dordrecht: Kluwer.

Joiner R., & Jones S. (2003). The effects of communication medium on argumentation and the development of critical thinking. *International Journal of Educational Research, 39*(8), 861-971

Kirschner, P., Buckingham Shum, S. J., & Carr, C. S. (Eds.). (2003). *Visualizing argumentation. Software tools for collaborative and educational sense making*. Dordrecht: Kluwer.

Kreijns, K. (2004). *Sociable CSCL environments: Social affordances, sociability, and social presence*. Unpublished PhD thesis, Open Universiteit, Heerlen, The Netherlands.

Kuhn, D. (1991). *The skills of argument*. Cambridge: University Press.

Kuhn, D., Shaw, V., & Felton, M. (1997). Effects of dyadic interaction on argumentative reasoning. *Cognition and Instruction, 15*(3), 287-315.

Lipponen, L., Rahikainen, M., Lallimo, J., & Hakkarainen, K. (2003). Patterns of participation and discourse in elementary students' computer-supported collaborative learning. *Learning and Instruction, 13*(5), 487-509.

Mäkitalo, K., Weinberger, A., Häkkinen, P., Järvelä, S., & Fischer, F. (2005). Epistemic cooperation scripts in online learning environments: Fostering learning by reducing uncertainty in discourse? *Computers in Human Behavior, 21*(4), 603-622.

Marttunen, M., & Laurinen, L. (2001). Learning of argumentation skills in networked and face-to-face environments. *Instructional Science*, 29, 127-153.

Michinov, N., & Primois, C. (2005). Improving productivity and creativity in online groups through social comparison process: New evidence for asynchronous electronic brainstorming. *Computers in Human Behavior, 21*(1), 11-28.

Nussbaum, E. M., Hartley, K., Sinatra, G. M., Reynolds, R. E., & Bendixen, L. D. (2002, April). *Enhancing the quality of on-line discussions*. Paper presented at the Annual meeting of the American Educational Research Association, New Orleans, LA.

O'Donnell, A. M. (1999). Structuring dyadic interaction through scripted cooperation. In A. M. O'Donnell & A. King (Eds.), *Cognitive perspectives on peer learning* (pp. 179-196). Mahwah, NJ: Erlbaum.

Osborne, J., Erduran, S., & Simon, S. (2004). Enhancing the quality of argumentation in science classrooms. *Journal of Research in Science Teaching, 41*(10), 994-1020.

Pea, R. D. (1994). Seeing what we build together: Distributed multimedia learning environments for transformative communications. Special Issue: Computer support for collaborative learning. *Journal of the Learning Sciences, 3*(3), 285-299.

Perkins, D. N. (1989) Reasoning as it is and as it could be: An empirical perspective, in D. M. Topping, D. C. Crowell, & V.N. Kobayashi (Eds.), *Thinking across Cultures: the third international conference on thinking* (175-194). Hillsdale, NJ: Erlbaum.

Perkins, D. N., & Simmons, P. E. (1988). Patterns of misunderstanding: An interactive model for science, math, and programming. *Review of Educational Research, 58*, 303-326.

Reiser, B. J. (2002). Why scaffolding should sometimes make tasks more difficult for learners. Paper presented at the CSCL Conference, Boulder, CO.

Sandoval, W. A., & Millwood, K. A. (2005). The quality of student's use of evidence in written scientific explanations. *Cognition and Instruction, 23*(1), 23-55.

Schwarz, B. B., Neuman, Y., Gil, J., & Ilya, M. (2003). Construction of collective and individual knowledge in argumentative activity. *The Journal of the Learning Sciences, 12*(2), 219-256.

Shepperd, J. A. (1993). Productivity loss in performance groups: A motivation analysis. *Psychological Bulletin, 113*(1), 67-81.

Toulmin, S. (1958). *The uses of argument*. Cambridge: University Press.

Wampold, B.E. (1992). The intensive examination of social interaction. In T.R. Kratochwill & J.R. Levin (Eds.) *Single-case research design and analysis: New directions for psychology and education* (p.93-133). Hillsdale, NJ: Erlbaum.

Weinberger, A., & Fischer, F. (2006). A framework to analyze argumentative knowledge construction in computer-supported collaborative learning. *Computers & Education, 46*, 71-95.

Weinberger, A., Ertl, B., Fischer, F., & Mandl, H. (2005). Epistemic and social scripts in computer-supported collaborative learning. *Instructional Science, 33*(1), 1-30.

Zumbach, J., Hillers, A., & Reimann, P. (2004). Distributed problem-based learning: The use of feedback mechanisms in online learning. In T. S. Roberts (Ed.), *Online collaborative learning: Theory and practice* (pp. 86-102). Hershey, PA: Idea Group.

Acknowledgements

The projects were partly funded by the Netherlands Organization for Scientific Research as part of the CRoCiCL project (nr. 411-02-121), the US National Science Foundation (NSF-CLT), and the Deutsche Forschungsgemeinschaft (DFG; FI 792/2-2).

Author Index